VLSI DESIGN TECHNIQUES FOR ANALOG AND DIGITAL CIRCUITS

McGraw-Hill Series in Electrical Engineering

Consulting Editor

Stephen W. Director, *Carnegie-Mellon University*

CIRCUITS AND SYSTEMS
COMMUNICATIONS AND SIGNAL PROCESSING
CONTROL THEORY
ELECTRONICS AND ELECTRONIC CIRCUITS
POWER AND ENERGY
ELECTROMAGNETICS
COMPUTER ENGINEERING
INTRODUCTORY
RADAR AND ANTENNAS
VLSI

Previous Consulting Editors

Ronald N. Bracewell, Colin Cherry, James F. Gibbons, Willis W. Harman, Hubert Heffner, Edward W. Herold, John G. Linvill, Simon Ramo, Ronald A. Rohrer, Anthony E. Siegman, Charles Susskind, Frederick E. Terman, John G. Truxal, Ernst Weber, and John R. Whinnery

VLSI

Consulting Editor

Stephen W. Director, *Carnegie-Mellon University*

Elliott: *Microlithography: Process Technology for IC Fabrication*
Geiger, Allen, and Strader: *VLSI Design Techniques for Analog and Digital Circuits*
Offen: *VLSI Image Processing*
Ruska: *Microelectronic Processing: An Introduction to the Manufacture of Integrated Circuits*
Seraphim: *Principles of Electronic Packaging*
Sze: *VLSI Technology*
Tsividis: *Operation and Modeling of the MOS Transistor*
Walsh: *Choosing and Using CMOS*

VLSI DESIGN TECHNIQUES FOR ANALOG AND DIGITAL CIRCUITS

Randall L. Geiger

Department of Electrical Engineering
Texas A&M University

Phillip E. Allen

Department of Electrical Engineering
Georgia Institute of Technology

Noel R. Strader

MCC
Austin, Texas

McGraw-Hill Publishing Company

New York   St. Louis   San Francisco   Auckland   Bogotá   Caracas
Hamburg   Lisbon   London   Madrid   Mexico   Milan
Montreal   New Delhi   Oklahoma City   Paris   San Juan
São Paulo   Singapore   Sydney   Tokyo   Toronto

VLSI DESIGN TECHNIQUES FOR ANALOG AND DIGITAL CIRCUITS
INTERNATIONAL EDITION 1990

Exclusive rights by McGraw-Hill Book Co. — Singapore, for manufacture and export. This book cannot be re-exported from the country to which it is consigned by McGraw-Hill.

234567890 FSP PMP 95432

This book was set in Times Roman by Publication Services, Inc.
The editors were Alar E. Elken and John M. Morriss.
The production supervisor was Janelle S. Travers.
The cover was designed by Robin Hessel.
Project supervision was done by Publication Services, Inc.

Library of Congress Cataloging-in-Publication Data

Geiger, Randall L.
  VLSI design techniques for analog and
  digital circuits.

  (McGraw-Hill series in electrical engineering)
  Includes index.
  1. Integrated circuits—Very large scale
integration-Design and construction. I. Allen, P. E.
(Phillip E.) II. Strader, Noel R. III. Title.
IV. Series.
TK7874,G43 1990   621.381 '73   88-37737
ISBN 0-07-023253-9

When ordering this title use ISBN 0-07-100728-8

Printed in Singapore

CONTENTS

Preface   xiii

1 Practical Considerations   1

1.0   Introduction   2
1.1   Size and Complexity of Integrated Circuits   4
1.2   The Microelectronics Field   10
1.3   IC Design Process   12
1.4   Economics   16
1.5   Yield   19
1.6   Trends in VLSI Design   28
      References   29
      Problems   29

2 Technology   32

2.0   Introduction   32
2.1   IC Production Process   32
      2.1.1   Processing Steps   33
      2.1.2   Packaging and Testing   41
2.2   Semiconductor Processes   42
      2.2.1   MOS Processes   46
              2.2.1a   NMOS Process   49
              2.2.1b   CMOS Process   55
              2.2.1c   Practical Process Considerations   59
      2.2.2   Bipolar Technology   64
      2.2.3   Hybrid Technology   68
2.3   Design Rules and Process Parameters   72
2.4   Layout Techniques and Practical Considerations   78
      References   85
      Problems   85

Appendixes   95

2A   Process Characterization of a Generic NMOS Process   95
2B   Process Characterization of a Generic CMOS Process   108

2C   Process Characterization of a Generic Bipolar Process   118
2D   Process Characterization of a Generic Thick Film Process   127
2E   Process Characterization of a Generic Thin Film Process   130

3   Device Modeling   132

3.0   Modeling   132
   3.0.1   dc Models   134
   3.0.2   Small Signal Models   134
   3.0.3   Use of Device Models in Circuit Analysis 139
3.1   MOS Models   143
   3.1.1   dc MOSFET Model   144
   3.1.2   Small Signal MOSFET Model   158
   3.1.3   High Frequency MOSFET Model   161
   3.1.4   Measurement of MOSFET Model Parameters   167
   3.1.5   Short Channel Devices   171
   3.1.6   Subthreshold Operation   174
   3.1.7   Operation in the Third Quadrant of the $I_D - V_{DS}$ Plane   177
   3.1.8   Modeling Noise Sources in MOSFETs   180
   3.1.9   Simple MOSFET Models for Digital Applications   185
3.2   Diode Models   187
   3.2.1   dc Diode Model   187
   3.2.2   Small Signal Diode Model   190
   3.2.3   High-Frequency Diode Model   190
3.3   Bipolar Models   191
   3.3.1   dc BJT Model   192
   3.3.2   Small Signal BJT Model   202
   3.3.3   High-Frequency BJT Model   205
   3.3.4   Measurement of BJT Model Parameters   208
3.4   Passive Component Models   210
   3.4.1   Monolithic Capacitors   211
   3.4.2   Monolithic Resistors   213
3.5   Summary   221
   References   221
   Problems   222

4   Circuit Simulation   237

4.0   Introduction   237
4.1   Circuit Simulation Using Spice   237
4.2   MOSFET Model   240
   4.2.1   Level 1 Large Signal Model   241
   4.2.2   Level 2 Large Signal Model   244
   4.5.3   High-Frequency Model   246
   4.2.4   Noise Model of the MOSFET   251
   4.2.5   Temperature Dependence of the MOSFET   251
4.3   Diode Model   252
   4.3.1   Large Signal Diode Current   253
   4.3.2   High-Frequency Diode Model   254
4.4   BJT Model   255
   4.4.1   Large Signal BJT Model   256
   4.4.2   High-Frequency BJT Model   261

4.4.3   BJT Noise Model   262
4.4.4   Temperature Dependence of the BJT   263
4.5   Summary   264
      References   264
      Problems   265

Appendixes   271

4A   Mosfet Parameter Definitions   271
4B   Diode Parameter Definitions   280
4C   BJT Parameter Definitions   282

5   Basic Integrated Circuit Building Blocks   287

5.0   Introduction   287
5.1   Switches   289
5.2   Active Resistors   302
5.3   Current Sources and Sinks   318
5.4   Current Mirrors/Amplifiers   333
5.5   Voltage and Current References   354
5.6   Summary   372
       References   372
       Problems   373
             Design Problems   376

6   Amplifiers   378

6.0   Introduction   378
6.1   Inverting Amplifiers   379
       6.1.1   General Concepts of Inverting Amplifiers   379
       6.1.2   MOS Inverting Amplifiers   389
       6.1.3   BJT Inverting Amplifiers   407
6.2   Improving the Performance of Inverting Amplifiers   414
       6.2.1   Current-Driven CMOS Cascode Amplifier   416
       6.2.2   Voltage-Driven CMOS Cascode Amplifier   418
       6.2.3   Improving the Gain of the CMOS Cascode Amplifier 419
       6.2.4   The BJT Cascode Amplifier   426
6.3   Differential Amplifiers   431
       6.3.1   CMOS Differential Amplifiers   432
       6.3.2   BJT Differential Amplifiers   444
       6.3.3   Frequency Response of Differential Amplifiers   449
       6.3.4   Noise Performance of Differential Amplifiers   452
6.4   Output Amplifiers   454
       6.4.1   Output Amplifiers without Feedback   455
       6.4.2   Output Amplifiers with Feedback   466
6.5   Operational Amplifiers   473
       6.5.1   Characterization of Op Amps   473
       6.5.2   The BJT Two-Stage Op Amp   481
       6.5.3   The CMOS Two-Stage Op Amp   485
       6.5.4   Cascode Op Amps   488
       6.5.5   Op Amps with an Output Stage   491
       6.5.6   Simulation and Measurement of Op Amps   494

6.6 Comparators 499
   6.6.1 Characterization of Comparators 499
   6.6.2 High-Gain Comparators 502
   6.6.3 Propagation Delay of Two-Stage Comparators 507
   6.6.4 Comparators Using Positive Feedback 511
   6.6.5 Autozeroing 514
6.7 Summary 518
   References 518
   Problems 519
      Design Problems 524

7 Digital Circuits 525

7.0 Introduction 525
7.1 Design Abstraction 526
7.2 Characteristics of Digital Circuits 528
   7.2.1 Logic Level Standards 528
   7.2.2 Inverter Pair Characteristics 530
   7.2.3 Logic Fan-out Characteristics 532
   7.2.4 Digital Logic Analysis 532
7.3 Single-Channel MOS Inverters 534
   7.3.1 Basic Inverter 534
   7.3.2 Inverter Device Sizing 537
   7.3.3 Enhancement-Load versus Depletion-Load Inverters 539
7.4 NMOS NOR and NAND Logic Circuits 540
   7.4.1 Basic NMOS NOR Logic Circuits 540
   7.4.2 Basic NMOS NAND Logic Circuits 542
   7.4.3 Multi-Input NAND and NOR Logic Circuits 543
7.5 Complementary MOS Inverters 544
   7.5.1 A Basic CMOS Inverter 546
   7.5.2 CMOS Inverter Logic Levels 546
   7.5.3 Inverter Device Sizing 548
7.6 CMOS Logic Gates 551
   7.6.1 CMOS NOR Logic Gate 551
   7.6.2 CMOS NAND Logic Gate 553
   7.6.3 Multi-Input CMOS Logic Gates 556
7.7 Transmission Gates 558
   7.7.1 NMOS Pass Transistor 559
   7.7.2 CMOS Transmission Gate 562
7.8 Signal Propagation Delays 564
   7.8.1 Ratio-Logic Model 565
   7.8.2 Process Characteristic Time Constant 570
   7.8.3 Inverter-Pair Delay 570
   7.8.4 Superbuffers 573
   7.8.5 NMOS NAND and NOR Delays 575
   7.8.6 Enhancement versus Depletion Loads 578
   7.8.7 CMOS Logic Delays 579
   7.8.8 Interconnection Characteristics 582
7.9 Capacitive Loading Considerations 584
   7.9.1 Capacitive Loading 584
   7.9.2 Logic Fan-out Delays 585

	7.9.3	Distributed Drivers	587
	7.9.4	Driving Off-Chip Loads	588
	7.9.5	Cascaded Drivers	590
7.10	Power Dissipation	593
	7.10.1	NMOS Power Dissipation	595
	7.10.2	CMOS Power Dissipation	597
7.11	Noise in Digital Logic Circuits	599
	7.11.1	Resistive Noise Coupling	599
	7.11.2	Capacitive Noise Coupling	601
	7.11.3	Definition of Noise Margins	602
	7.11.4	NMOS Noise Margins	603
	7.11.5	CMOS Noise Margins	605
7.12	Summary	607
	References	608
	Problems	608

8 Analog Systems   612

8.0	Introduction	612
8.1	Analog Signal Processing	612
8.2	Digital-to-Analog Converters	615
	8.2.1 Current-Scaling D/A Converters	623
	8.2.2 Voltage-Scaling D/A Converters	626
	8.2.3 Charge-Scaling D/A Converters	629
	8.2.4 D/A Converters Using Combinations of Scaling Approaches	633
	8.2.5 Serial D/A Converters	638
8.3	Analog-to-Digital Converters	642
	8.3.1 Serial A/D Converters	648
	8.3.2 Successive Approximation A/D Converters	651
	8.3.3 Parallel A/D Converters	659
	8.3.4 High-Performance A/D Converters	664
	8.3.5 Summary	671
8.4	Continuous-Time Filters	673
	8.4.1 Low-Pass Filters	674
	8.4.2 High-Pass Filters	685
	8.4.3 Bandpass Filters	688
8.5	Switched Capacitor Filters	692
	8.5.1 Resistor Realization	693
	8.5.2 Passive RLC Prototype Switched Capacitor Filters	703
	8.5.3 Z-Domain Synthesis Techniques	716
8.6	Analog Signal Processing Circuits	729
	8.6.1 Precision Breakpoint Circuits	729
	8.6.2 Modulators and Multipliers	735
	8.6.3 Oscillators	747
	8.6.4 Phase-Locked Loops	762
8.7	Summary	765
	References	770
	Problems	773

9 Structured Digital Circuits and Systems   778

| 9.0 | Introduction | 778 |
| 9.1 | Random Logic versus Structured Logic Forms | 779 |

9.2		Programmable Logic Arrays	783
	9.2.1	PLA Organization	784
	9.2.2	Automatic PLA Generation	790
	9.2.3	Folded PLAs	791
	9.2.4	Large PLAs	792
9.3		Structured Gate Layout	793
	9.3.1	Weinberger Arrays	794
	9.3.2	Gate Matrix Layout	796
9.4		Logic Gate Arrays	799
9.5		MOS Clocking Schemes	805
9.6		Dynamic MOS Storage Circuits	808
	9.6.1	Dynamic Charge Storage	808
	9.6.2	Simple Shift Register	811
	9.6.3	Other Shift Registers	814
9.7		Clocked CMOS Logic	815
	9.7.1	C^2MOS	815
	9.7.2	Precharge-Evaluate Logic	817
	9.7.3	Domino CMOS	819
9.8		Semiconductor Memories	821
	9.8.1	Memory Organization	822
9.9		Read-Only Memory	824
	9.9.1	Erasable Programmable Read-Only Memory	825
	9.9.2	Electrically Erasable Programmable Read-Only Memory	826
9.10		Static RAM Memories	827
9.11		Dynamic RAM Memory	835
9.12		Register Storage Circuits	839
	9.12.1	Quasi-Static Register Cells	840
	9.12.2	A Static Register Cell	842
9.13		PLA-Based Finite-State Machines	845
9.14		Microcoded Controllers	848
9.15		Microprocessor Design	853
	9.15.1	Data Path Description	856
	9.15.2	Barrel Shifter	857
	9.15.3	Arithmetic Logic Unit	858
	9.15.4	Microcoded Controller	860
9.16		Systolic Arrays	861
	9.16.1	Systolic Matrix Multiplication	861
	9.16.2	General Linear System Solver	862
	9.16.3	Bit-Serial Processing Elements	863
9.17		Summary	866
		References	866
		Problems	867

10 Design Automation and Verification

			872
10.0		Introduction	872
10.1		Integrated Circuit Layout	873
	10.1.1	Geometrical Specification Languages	875
	10.1.2	Layout Styles	878
10.2		Symbolic Circuit Representation	880
	10.2.1	Parameterized Layout Representation	880
	10.2.2	Parameterized Module Generation	883

	10.2.3	Graphical Symbolic Layout	884
	10.2.4	Logic Equation Symbology	885
10.3		Computer Check Plots	889
10.4		Design Rule Checks	894
	10.4.1	Geometrical Design Rules	894
	10.4.2	Computer Design Rule Checks	897
	10.4.3	Design Rule Checker Output	898
10.5		Circuit Extraction	901
	10.5.1	A Simple Circuit Extraction Algorithm	902
	10.5.2	Circuit Extractor Output	903
	10.5.3	Interface to Other Programs	908
10.6		Digital Circuit Simulation	908
10.7		Logic and Switch Simulation	909
	10.7.1	Logic-level Simulation	909
	10.7.2	Switch-level Simulation	913
	10.7.3	Hardware Logic Simulation	917
10.8		Timing Analysis	918
	10.8.1	Timing Analysis Methodology	918
	10.8.2	Timing Analysis Tools	919
10.9		Register-Transfer-Level Simulation	923
	10.9.1	Simple RTL	923
	10.9.2	ISPS Specification and Simulation	925
	10.9.3	RTL Simulation with LISP	926
10.10		Hardware Design Languages	929
	10.10.1	EDIF Design Description	930
	10.10.2	EDIF Net List View of Full Adder	931
	10.10.3	EDIF Mask Layout View of Full Adder	931
	10.10.4	VHDL Design Description	935
10.11		Algorithmic Layout Generation	938
	10.11.1	Bristle Blocks Silicon Compiler	938
	10.11.2	MacPitts Silicon Compiler	941
	10.11.3	Commercial Silicon Compilers	943
10.12		Summary	944
		References	945
		Problems	946
		Index	951

PREFACE

Growing technological requirements and the widespread acceptance of sophisticated electronic devices have created an unprecedented demand for large-scale, complex, integrated circuits. Meeting these demands has required technological advances in materials and processing equipment, significant increases in the number of individuals involved in integrated circuit design, and an increased emphasis on effectively utilizing the computer to aid in the design.

Advances in growing fields, such as Very Large Scale Integrated Circuits (VLSI), generally parallel "graduate level" academic and industrial research efforts. As a result, these concents quite naturally appear initially in university curricula at the graduate level. However, one must inevitably consider how to present this new material to a wider range of students with less sophsticated backgrounds. Integrated circuit design of LSI and VLSI systems is an area where both the required technical background and demand indicate that the material can and should be introduced at the undergraduate level. It is the purpose of this text to accomplish this objective.

The textbook has grown out of notes prepared for a one-semester senior level course that presents the fundamentals of integrated circuit design. This course has been offered every semester at Texas A&M University since the fall of 1981. Sufficient technical background for this text can be provided by an introductory level circuits course and an introductory digital logic course. Limited knowledge of material covered in an introductory electronics course is also assumed, but those sections requiring this knowledge can be either skipped or be augmented by the instructor without a major loss of continuity.

Each semester, students in the course participate in an integrated circuit design project using the multiproject chip (MPC) approach. Both NMOS and CMOS technologies have been used for the MPC, Process discussions closely parallel those available through the MOSIS program, thus facilitating participation in the MOSIS fabrication program by students who have MOSIS access. Past design projects have been intentionally limited in scope to keep the student's time commitments at a reasonable level. Past projects have included ring oscillators, PLAs, flip-flops, simple comparators and operational amplifiers, and 16-bit static RAMs. Although the availability of the processing capability helps provide an appreciation of all the details involved in the design of an integrated circuit, the material in this text is designed to be useful with or without access to foundry services.

The text includes a qualitative discussion of semiconductor processing in order to make the student cognizant of the processing steps required. Beyond this, a set of process parameters used in device modeling are assumed to serve as the interface between the process and the design engineers. The physical relationship between circuit design and actual silicon layout and area is strongly emphasized as is the anticipated performance of the circuit as affected by typical variations in the process parameters, temperature, and so on.

This book adopts the philosophy that the design engineer should be comfortable with either analog or digital circuitry and that the basic differences in the fundamental blocks are minimal. Integrated circuit design is presented as a systematic merging of a set of design rules, device models, and process parameters in a personnel- and area-efficient manner to develop a circuit that meets required electrical specifications. With this approach, the NMOS, CMOS, Bipolar, thick film, and thin film technologies are introduced in parallel. Each of these maintains a uniqueness through a specific set of design rules and device models. Advantages and tradeoffs in regard to area, performance, and processing costs among the technologies are considered. A typical set of design rules and a list of process parameters, sufficient for actual design, are given for each of the processes. These characteristics are used to maintain proper performance perspectives and to make that crucial link between circuit schematic and silicon layout. Since the size of components has been steadily decreasing, the design rules are given in terms of a variable, λ, whenever practical. Although design rules for the MOS and Bipolar processes scale quite well for typical 3, 5, and 8 micron processes, it is emphasized that the actual design rules and process parameters corresponding to the specific fabrication process employed should be adopted.

The ultimate goal of the circuit designer is not a clever circuit schematic or a computer simulation that predicts the circuit works as anticipated, but an efficiently designed physical piece of silicon that satisfies the original specifications. To this end, practical considerations are discussed including limitations of device models, parasitic and nonlinear effects, and clever component placement on the circuit layout, along with their effects on performance.

This book is directed to individuals with no previous integrated circuit design experience who need a working understanding of the subject. The text will also provide a broadened perspective for experienced designers. In addition to the university classroom, this text should find application in industrial training programs, as an interface for groups using or planning to use silicon foundries, and as a resource for the non-semiconductor-based industries that use electronic circuitry and must make the decision of when, if, and how to integrate their systems. It may also serve as a reference book on the subject of integrated circuit design.

Chapter 1 presents an overview of the field of integrated circuit design while focusing on past and present techniques, trends, and performance along with the technological challenges. A discussion of both yield and economics is included in this chapter.

Technology is discussed in Chapter 2. Processing steps are presented from a qualitative point of view, followed by detailed discussions of the NMOS, CMOS, and Bipolar processes along with the thick and thin film technologies. Design rules, layout techniques, and the role of the computer are discussed.

Models for the MOS and Bipolar transistors suitable for design are presented in Chapter 3, as are more sophisticated models necessary for computer simulation. The characteristics of various types of semiconductor passive components are also investigated.

Computer-aided circuit analysis is discussed in Chapter 4. Use of the widely available SPICE program for this purpose is investigated.

Chapter 5 is used to introduce basic analog building blocks.

Building blocks that are useful for constructing analog circuits are discussed in Chapter 6. Both MOS and Bipolar versions are developed in parallel because of the similarity of the circuit topologies.

A digital counterpart to Chapter 5 is presented in Chapter 7. This discussion originates with the inverter, followed by the generation of basic logic gates. Methods of driving large external loads while maintaining acceptable speed are investigated. The emphasis in Chapter 7 is on the MOS technologies because of their widespread acceptance for large digital systems.

In Chapter 8, the design of analog systems is considered. These systems employ some of the basic building blocks discussed in Chapters 5 and 6. Systems considered include A/D and D/A converters, continuous-time filters, switched-capacitor filters, oscillators, multipliers, and modulators.

Digital systems are discussed in Chapter 9. These include PLAs, gate arrays, static and dynamic memories, microprocessors, and systolic arrays.

Design automation is addressed in Chapter 10. The variety of design aids necessary for layout verification is discussed.

Much of the material in the book comes as an outgrowth of the design and testing of integrated circuits that have been included on past MPCs as well as the instruction that has been necessary to prepare students to participate in these designs. The fabrication of the MPCs by Texas Instruments, Inc., and the MOSIS Program is gratefully acknowledged.

McGraw-Hill and the authors would like to thank the following reviewers for their many helpful comments and suggestions: Jorge J. Santiago-Avilés; Steven Bibyk, Ohio State University; David J. Dumin, Clemson University; Yu Hen Hu, University of Wisconsin; David L. Landis, University of South Florida; H.C. Lin, University of Maryland; M.A. Littlejohn, North Carolina State University; R.A. Saleh, University of Illinois; S.M. Sze, AT&T Bell Laboratories; and Herbert Taub, City College of the City University of New York.

Randall L. Geiger
Phillip E. Allen
Noel R. Strader

VLSI DESIGN TECHNIQUES FOR ANALOG
AND DIGITAL CIRCUITS

CHAPTER
1

PRACTICAL CONSIDERATIONS

The field of VLSI design is a resource-intense engineering discipline. Project and product definitions are economically motivated, and competition on a worldwide basis is very keen. The market potential for innovative designs is very large, but the market window is often short due to both competition and changing consumer demands. Financial gain potential for both individuals and companies in this field is phenomenal, but the risks can also be very large. Some of the most advanced equipment and CAD resources available in any discipline are focused toward VLSI design and production; this focus makes the field very dynamic but also necessitates a continuing training and learning effort on the part of the design engineers to remain current and productive in this field.

It is our goal in this book to introduce basic electronic principles needed by the integrated circuit designer and to discuss engineering tradeoffs and practical considerations that are necessary for the student to make the transition from the classroom to industry as an integrated circuit designer. Although it is impossible to discuss all the practical aspects considered by experienced designers, it is our hope that through the discussions and comments presented in this book, the student will develop a sense of what types of practical questions must be addressed throughout the design process.

This chapter gives a brief historical overview, followed by a discussion of some of the terminology and jargon specific to the VLSI design field. (We have chosen to adopt the jargon used in the field because this is the language used by VLSI designers to communicate.) Size and complexity perspectives of VLSI circuits are discussed, and the basic types of processes used in IC and VLSI design are qualitatively summarized. The design process itself and the tools available to the designer are covered. Finally, a brief discussion of economics is presented to give the reader a basic appreciation of design costs and fabrication costs of integrated circuits. Included is a simple discussion of the relationship between yield and chip area, which often is the key factor in determining whether a design will be economically viable.

1.0   INTRODUCTION

Historically, several events trace the evolution of what is currently termed VLSI technology. In the early 1930s, theoretical developments by Lilienfeld[1] and Heil[2] discussed the predecessor to what is now commonly called the field effect transistor (FET). Technological challenges delayed the practical utilization of this device for nearly three decades. In 1947 and 1948, three researchers at Bell Laboratories—Brattin, Bardeen, and Schockley—introduced the bipolar junction transistor (BJT). This development marked the practical beginning of the microelectronics industry. For the next 15 years, large numbers of different BJTs were produced and applied in a wide range of instrumentation systems. The BJTs replaced vacuum tubes in many applications and provided the impetus for a host of new electronic systems.

In the summer of 1958 Jack Kilby, an engineer at Texas Instruments, invented the first integrated circuit. Early the following year Robert Noyce of Fairchild independently reported on a procedure that more closely resembles integrated circuits of today. The specific details of Kilby's circuit are inconsequential, but the impact of his approach has been phenomenal.[3,4] The work of Kilby and Noyce marked the beginning of what has become the field of VLSI design.

Germanium was widely used as a semiconductor in some of the early discrete devices. Silicon has been the dominant semiconductor material used for integrated circuit fabrication for the past two decades, and most experts agree that it will remain dominant for the next decade. Since over 25% of the earth's crust is made of silicon, a real silicon shortage is highly unlikely! Other materials, such as gallium arsenide, are gaining acceptance in niche markets, which may be quite profitable.

Improvements in technology—ranging from improvements in materials and photolithography to advancements in processing—have been propelled by the significant financial gains offered to groups that excel in this area. Many integrated circuits of today contain a very large number of transistors, over 1 million in some designs. Conventional methods for circuit design that involved iteration at the breadboard level proved impractical for designing integrated circuits. This is due to poor designer productivity and the high cost associated with fabricating ICs. Methods of efficiently handling large quantities of design data were needed. Models of transistors that accurately predict experimental performance were required. Methods were needed for increasing designer productivity and reducing the design cycle time as the size and complexity of circuits increased.

The tools available now to the IC designer are very powerful and dynamic. Most require the use of large computers or, more recently, powerful graphics-intense workstations. The continued investment in both hardware and software needed for current integrated circuit design is high but is also crucial to remaining competitive. As powerful and dynamic as these tools may be, the fierce competition in the marketplace has resulted in the evolution of user-friendly software with which the engineer can establish proficiency with a modest investment of time and effort. In the following chapters the tools needed to design VLSI circuits are investigated.

In spite of the sophistication and cost of both the hardware and software necessary to remain competitive in the field of VLSI design, most major contributions to this field are based upon relatively simple and basic innovations by the engineer. These innovations occur in circuit design, processing, and modeling as well as in the evolution of the CAD tools themselves. They are often made by young engineers. Because of the economic impact of innovations in the VLSI design field, advancement potential and rewards for talented and ambitious engineers are essentially unlimited. This potential exists for both young and old in institutions ranging from small start-up companies to the giants of the industry.

Integrated circuit fabrication requires the use of mechanical and optical equipment and materials capable of precisely maintaining close tolerances and small geometries. As with any high-technology field, a large amount of technical jargon has evolved, which must be mastered by anyone wishing to be conversant with those working in the area. The balance of this chapter is devoted to practical considerations and an introduction of terminology associated with the field of integrated circuit design.

An *integrated circuit (IC)* is a combination of interconnected circuit elements inseparably associated on or within a continuous substrate.

The *substrate* is the supporting material upon or within which an IC is fabricated or to which an IC is attached.

A *monolithic IC* is an IC whose elements are formed in place upon or within a semiconductor substrate with at least one of the elements formed within the substrate.

A *hybrid IC* consists of a combination of two or more IC types or an IC with some discrete elements.

A *wafer* (or *slice*) is the basic physical unit used in processing. It generally contains a large number of identical ICs. Typically, the wafer is circular; production wafers have a diameter of 4, 5, or 6 in.

The *chip* is one of the repeated ICs on a wafer. A typical production wafer may contain as few as 20 or 30 ICs or as many as several hundred or even several thousand, depending upon the complexity and size of the circuit being fabricated. The terms *die* and *bar* are used interchangeably for *chip* in some companies.

A *test plug*, or process control bar (PCB), or process control monitor (PCM), is a special chip that is repeated only a few times on each wafer. It is used to monitor the process parameters of the technology. After processing, the validity of the process is verified by measuring, at the wafer probe level, the characteristics of devices and/or circuits on the test plug. If the measurements of key parameters at the test plug level are not acceptable, the wafer is discarded.

A *test cell*, or *test lead*, is a special chip repeated only a few times on each wafer. It differs from the test plug in that the circuit designer includes this cell specifically to monitor the performance of elementary subcircuits or subcomponents.

Considerable effort has been expended toward using the entire wafer as a single IC, but this approach is challenged by defects in processing and the associated decline in yield and by the inherent delay in signals that must transverse the wafer. Those efforts are in the field termed wafer scale integration (WSI)[5–10].

1.1 SIZE AND COMPLEXITY OF INTEGRATED CIRCUITS

Integrated circuits are typically classified in terms of the number of devices or potential devices used in the design of the circuit and in terms of the feature size of the process. The device count is generally restricted to the number of active devices (either FETs or BJTs). As will be seen later, most integrated circuits contain large numbers of BJTs or FETs but contain few, if any, passive components. The classification of integrated circuits by device count is summarized in Table 1.1-1.

Classifications based upon feature size are also common. This classification is in terms of a typical minimum feature size (such as minimum gate length or minimum polysilicon width or minimum metal width) or in terms of the pitch (minimum of the sum of the minimum width of a feature and minimum spacing between similar features). The pitch is often nearly twice the minimum feature size. In the early to middle 1970s, the minimum feature size was typically 7 μ to 10 μ. In the late 1970s and early 1980s feature sizes to 5 μ were popular. In the mid-1980s, the minimum feature size had shrunk to under 2 μ, with some groups producing 1 μ and $1\frac{1}{4}$ μ circuits. The early 1990s should see practical submicron processes in production with feature sizes between 0.75 μ and 0.25 μ.

The impact of shrinking the feature size on silicon warrants discussion. For reference purposes, a sketch of a FET appears in Fig. 1.1-1. The FET is composed of a conductive gate region, which is separated from the surface of the substrate by a very thin insulating layer. Diffusions on either side of the gate form what are termed the drain and source regions. The minimum feature size of this

TABLE 1.1-1
Classification of integrated circuits by device count

Nomenclature	Active device count	Typical functions
SSI	1–100	Gates, op amps, many linear applications
MSI	100–1000	Registers, filters, etc.
LSI	1000–100,000	Microprocessors, A/D, etc.
VLSI	10^5–10^6	Memories, computers, signal processors

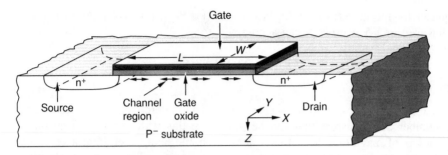

FIGURE 1.1-1
Simplified 3-dimensional view of a FET.

process is roughly the minimum allowable value for L and W. For example, in a 5 μ process the minimum permissible value of L and W would be 5 μ. The area required for the gate of the transistor in such a process would be 25 μ^2. Even though the lateral dimensions of the FET (x and y directions in Fig. 1.1-1) are small, the vertical dimensions are typically much smaller. For example, the thin insulating layer under the gate in a typical 5 μ process is about 1000 Å thick. The relative perspective of the lateral and vertical (z direction) dimensions is grossly underemphasized in Fig. 1.1-1. Because of the large differences in lateral and vertical dimensions of FETs, the lateral dimensions are generally expressed in microns (or occasionally mils) and the vertical dimensions in angstroms. It is very important that the designer have an appreciation for both lateral and vertical feature sizes in any process. Conversions from meters to angstroms as well as a comparison with English units are given in Table 1.1-2. In this table, and throughout this book, the term *micron* and the abbreviation μ, which corresponds to the industry-accepted jargon for the micrometer, will be used.

We are now in a position to develop a realistic perspective for the number of devices (transistors) that can be fabricated on a given piece of silicon. Assume initially that the area required for a single FET is essentially equal to the area

TABLE 1.1-2
Conversion of parameters used for device characterization in semiconductor industry

Unit	Symbol	Angstroms	Microns	Mils	Meters	Inches
				Conversion		
Angstrom	Å	—	$10^{-4}\ \mu$	3.94×10^{-6} mil	10^{-10} m	3.94×10^{-9} in
Micron	μ	10^4Å	—	0.0394 mil	10^{-6} m	3.94×10^{-5} in
Mil	mil	2.54×10^5 Å	$25.4\ \mu$	—	2.54×10^{-5} m	0.001 in
Meter	m	10^{10} Å	$10^6\ \mu$	3.9×10^4 mil	—	39 in
Inch	in	2.54×10^8 Å	$2.54 \times 10^4\ \mu$	10^3 mil	2.54×10^{-2} m	—

required for the gate (i.e., $W \cdot L$ in Fig. 1.1-1). With this assumption, a 4 inch wafer used in a 5 μ process can accommodate

$$N_{5\mu} = \frac{\pi(2 \text{ in})^2}{25\mu^2} \cdot \left(\frac{2.54 \times 10^4 \mu}{\text{in}}\right)^2 = 3.24 \times 10^8$$

transistors. Actually, due to spacing restrictions and interconnection requirements, the number of transistors that can be placed on this wafer will be from one to two orders of magnitude less. Regardless, it should be apparent that a very large number of transistors can be fabricated on such a wafer. The impact of shrinking the feature size can now be appreciated. If we could build transistors that were 0.5 $\mu \times 0.5 \mu$, the number of transistors that could be accommodated by the same 4 inch wafer in the 0.5 μ process becomes

$$N_{0.5\mu} = \frac{\pi(2 \text{ in})^2}{0.25\mu^2} \cdot \left(\frac{(2.54 \times 10^4 \mu)}{\text{in}}\right)^2 = 3.24 \times 10^{10}$$

subject to the same reduction for spacing and interconnections as in the 5 μ process. Nonetheless, the 100-fold increase in device count is very significant.

To obtain an appreciation for the significance of a 100-fold increase in device count, assume one piece of silicon was used to design a small computer system. The same piece of silicon could be used to build 100 identical computer systems if a 100-fold increase in device count were obtained. Correspondingly, with a fixed chip area, the high-density circuit could perform the work of 100 of the small computer systems. In addition, from an economics viewpoint, the cost of fabricating wafers has increased only modestly as the device geometries have decreased.

Beyond the increase in device count, two other major benefits are derived by shrinking device sizes. First, as the device sizes decrease, the speed of circuits increases approximately linearly with feature size reduction. In the previous "small computer" example, it can be observed that in addition to obtaining a significant increase in the number of "equivalent computers" with decreasing device sizes, each of the smaller computers will work much faster! The other major benefit relates to yield, size, and complexity. It will be seen later that the yield depends primarily upon the silicon area (more precisely, active silicon area) of a chip and is relatively independent of the number or size of transistors in this area. Correspondingly, decreasing feature size makes possible some useful designs, which were either physically too large or which had low yields in a large feature size process.

There are some limitations associated with shrinking the feature size. These include a deterioration in matching characteristics, increased cost of equipment required for processing the wafers, additional capability requirements for software design aids, and an increased impact of interconnection delays. Concerns about increased power dissipation density and processing complications associated with heat cycling limitations during fabrication also exist. It is generally agreed, however, that the benefits of shrinking the minimum feature size far outweigh the limitations, and a major worldwide research effort is ongoing to further shrink device sizes.

The number of devices that could potentially be placed on a wafer (calculated above) is strongly dependent upon the wafer size. Of more importance is the number of devices that can be placed on a chip, which represents a small portion of the area of a wafer as indicated in Fig. 1.1-2. From a practical viewpoint, the chip size seldom is (reference 1989) much in excess of 1 cm^2. The chip area of Texas Instruments' (TI) 1M DRAM is 0.54 cm^2. That of the Motorola 68020 microprocessor is 0.85 cm^2. Even in 1 cm^2, a large number of devices can be utilized. For example, in a 5 μ process, the 1 cm^2 chip can accommodate the gates of about 4 million 5 $\mu \times 5 \mu$ transistors. As mentioned previously, the realistic number of practical devices is from one to two orders of magnitude smaller. For example, the 68020 microprocessor has about 200,000 transistor sites and was designed in a 1.8 μ process. The TI 1M DRAM, designed in a 1 μ process, has 1,048,576 transistors and an equal number of capacitors in the basic memory array, along with about 52,000 transistors in the control circuit. The TI 16M DRAM, which should be in volume production in 1991, will have a die area of nearly 1 cm^2, will have 16,770,000 transistors and an equal number of capacitors in the basic array along with over 150,000 transistors in the control circuit, and will be fabricated in a 0.6 μ process.

An analogy between the features on an integrated circuit and the features on the map of a large city is often drawn to obtain a realistic appreciation of the complexity of existing integrated circuits. This is motivated, in part, by the observation that under a high-power microscope, a dense integrated circuit shows a resemblance to a street map of a city with the interconnections corresponding to the city streets. Assuming that the pitch of a process maps to one city block, that a city block is 200 meters on a side, and that the pitch equals twice the minimum feature size, it follows that the magnification factor is $10^8 : x$ where x

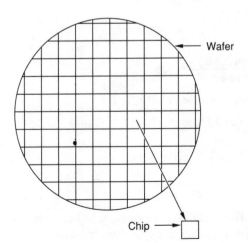

FIGURE 1.1-2
Sketch of a wafer showing repeated "chips." (See Plate 1 in the color insert of this book for a color photograph of a commercial wafer.)

is the minimum feature size of the process in microns. For the 10 μ processes of the early 1970s with a typical die 2.5 mm on a side, this magnification would map the die to a city about 14 miles on a side, which corresponds to a city about the size of Tulsa, Oklahoma. For a 5 μ process with a die 5 mm on a side, which was popular in the late 1970s, the map increases to that of a city nearly 60 miles on a side. This corresponds to a city the size of the greater Chicago metropolitan area. For the 1 μ processes of the late 1980s, with a 1 cm^2 die size, the mapping is to a city 600 miles on a side, which would correspond to a city that is 30% larger than the entire state of Texas. Finally, for the projected 0.25 μ processes with a die 2 cm on a side, this same mapping would be to a city nearly 5,000 miles on a side. This would correspond to a city with an area equal to nearly half the earth's land surface.

Many integrated circuits require a silicon area that is considerably less than the maximum practical chip size. Several advantages are offered by using smaller-sized die. First, since the cost of processing a wafer is essentially independent of the size of the die, a smaller chip size will result in fabrication of more chips per wafer and, thus, a reduction in the effective cost per chip. Second, the yield (percentage of chips that are good) decreases rapidly with increasing chip size; details of this are discussed in Sec. 1.5. In addition, since rectangular chips are fabricated on round wafers, the amount of wafer wasted around the periphery is reduced with smaller chips.

> **Example 1.1-1.** Assume an operational amplifier (op amp) requires an area 100 mil × 100 mil and a microprocessor requires an area 1 cm × 1 cm. (*a*) How many of each type of chip can be fabricated on a 5 inch wafer? (*b*) If the yield for the op amp is 98% and that for the microprocessor is 30%, compare the average number of good chips per wafer of each device that can be anticipated. (*c*) If the fabrication cost per wafer is $400, what is the effective cost per good chip for each device?
>
> **Solution.** (*a*) Neglecting the area loss on the periphery of the wafer, we calculate the number of op amps and microprocessors as
>
> $$n_{\text{opamp}} = \frac{\pi(2.5 \text{ in})^2}{(0.1 \text{ in})^2} = 1963$$
>
> $$n_{\mu\text{proc}} = \frac{\pi(2.5 \text{ in})^2}{(1 \text{ cm})^2} = 126$$
>
> (*b*) $$n_{\text{opamp,effective}} = (0.98)(1963) = 1923$$
>
> $$n_{\mu\text{proc,effective}} = (0.3)(126) = 37$$
>
> (*c*) $$C_{\text{opamp}} = \frac{\$400}{1923} = 20.8¢$$
>
> $$C_{\mu\text{proc}} = \$10.53$$

One naturally poses the question: How small will device sizes ultimately become? Although we will not quantitatively answer this question, we will address some of the major factors which place limits on decreasing device dimensions.

Up to now, limitations were imposed primarily by limitations in resolution of processing equipment. We are approaching the point, however, where the physics of the semiconductors themselves are starting to cause problems. Gate oxides (the insulating layer under the gate) below 100 Å thick are being investigated in conjunction with submicron research efforts. The density of silicon atoms in single crystal silicon is 5×10^{22} atoms/cm^3. This corresponds to an "average" atom spacing of 2.71 Å. The nearest-neighbor distance is 1.18 Å and the lattice constant is 5.43 Å. It should be apparent that the sub–100 Å gate oxide layers have dimensions approaching the dimensions of the atomic structure of the semiconductor crystalline structure itself. Silicon dioxide, which is typically used as the insulating layer, is even coarser than silicon. The silicon dioxide density is about 2.3×10^{22} molecules/cm^3, with an "average" molecular spacing of 3.52 Å. It should be apparent that irregularities in surfaces of the order of magnitude of a few molecules become significant in sub–100 Å oxide layers. Quantum mechanical tunneling occurs if oxide thicknesses become thinner than about 50 Å, thus placing a practical lower bound on oxide thicknesses.[11]

High electric field strengths, which may cause device failures, also are of concern. Voltages up to 5 V are regularly applied across the 1000 Å silicon dioxide insulating layers. This corresponds to electric fields of the order of magnitude of

$$E_{1000 \text{ Å}} = \frac{5 \text{ V}}{1000 \text{ Å}} = \frac{500 \text{ kV}}{\text{cm}}$$

This electric field is *very large* but still less than the breakdown field of silicon dioxide, which is in the 5–10 MV/cm range depending on how the oxide was grown. If, however, the same 5 V were applied to the 100 Å oxide layer, the electric field strength would be in the neighborhood of the breakdown field for the oxide. Furthermore, the irregularities in the very thin oxide layers can cause further significant local increases in field strength. The only option is to decrease the voltage applied to the oxide layer, but this is unattractive for two reasons. First, as the voltage across this oxide decreases, noise effects become more significant, thus increasing the chance of occasional errors in circuits using these devices. Second, existing systems have well-defined voltage levels, which a large number of manufacturers adhere to. Since parts made by various manufacturers are often interconnected to form complex systems, interfacing parts with nonstandard signal levels causes a significant increase in design complexity.

It is generally desirable to scale the vertical as well as the lateral dimensions when decreasing device sizes. The method under which this scaling occurs affects both the reliability and performance specifications of the process. Various scaling strategies are possible as the lateral dimensions of the MOSFETs decrease. In the *constant field scaling strategy*, the vertical dimensions typically decrease at the same rate as the lateral dimensions. To maintain a fixed electric field, the operating voltage also decreases at the same rate. The *constant voltage scaling strategy* is attractive because electrical compatibility with existing circuits is maintained. In a constant voltage scaling strategy that has been proposed, the vertical dimensions decrease quadratically relative to the lateral dimensions.[12]

Obviously tradeoffs among performance, yield, compatibility with existing technology, reliability, process complexity, device performance, and impact of parasitics must be made when selecting a scaling strategy.

1.2   THE MICROELECTRONICS FIELD

The microelectronics field is quite broad. Many different types of processes and approaches have found niches in the microelectronics market place. Figure 1.2-1 depicts the major processes that have received a reasonable degree of acceptance.

The first division in process types occurs between active and inert substrates. The high-volume integrated circuits typically utilize the active substrates. Some of the more demanding requirements as well as specialized and/or low-volume circuits use the inert substrates. The inert substrates are also used in most hybrid ICs. These latter circuits are often noted for requiring relatively modest investments in processing equipment, but the consumer cost of the hybrid ICs themselves is quite high.

Two types of processes that utilize inert substrates are particularly important. These are the thin and thick film processes. These processes are capable of producing good resistors with attractive temperature characteristics. This is difficult to achieve with the standard active substrate processes.

The active substrate is generally silicon or doped silicon although considerable research effort has been expended over the last decade in using gallium arsenide (GaAs). Two primary separate types of silicon processes have evolved. The bipolar process uses the BJT as the basic active device whereas the MOS processes use the metal oxide semiconductor field effect transistor, or MOSFET (sometimes termed IGFET for insulated gate FET), as the basic active device.

The bipolar process was the most popular through the 1960s and early 1970s. The bipolar process offers potential for operation at very high frequencies and offers some performance advantages such as large transconductances, which are of benefit in many linear applications. The power dissipation in bipolar integrated circuits is, however, often quite high, and the device density is not as high as that attainable with the MOS processes. The popular TTL logic family, ECL, and I^2L all fall under the bipolar label. Many linear ICs also are fabricated in the bipolar processes. Although the relative amount of research effort in the bipolar area is small compared to that focusing on the MOS processes, the production volume of bipolar ICs is still very large, and some new developments still use the bipolar process. There is, however, considerable development work ongoing in the design of smart bipolar power devices, which contain the control circuitry along with the power devices.

The MOS process is often divided into three categories: NMOS, PMOS, and CMOS. The basic devices in MOS processes are the p-channel and n-channel MOSFETs discussed in Chapter 2. The term PMOS refers to a MOS process that uses only p-channel FETs. The PMOS process was used in some of the earlier MOS designs, but is rarely used today primarily because the electrical characteristics of p-channel MOSFETs are not as attractive as those of n-channel MOSFETs. This is because the mobility (discussed in Chapter 3) of p-type material is considerably poorer than that of the n-type material. The term

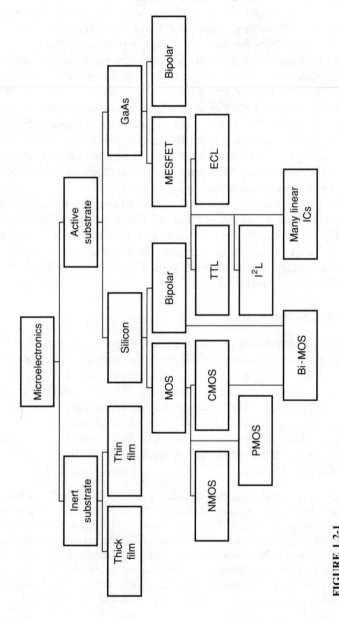

FIGURE 1.2-1
Types of major processes used in IC fabrication.

11

NMOS refers to a MOS process using only n-channel FETs. Excellent density and reasonable performance characterize the NMOS process. The term CMOS (complementary MOS) refers to a MOS process that simultaneously provides both n-channel and p-channel devices. The availability of both types of FETs offers the designer considerable additional flexibility over that attainable with either an NMOS or PMOS process. In digital applications, the availability of complementary devices offers potential for *very* low static power consumption. In analog applications, the circuit complexity can often be reduced in the CMOS process relative to what is attainable with either the NMOS or PMOS processes. The increased flexibility of CMOS is partially offset by increased fabrication costs and an increase in the silicon area required to implement basic digital functions. The tradeoffs generally favor the CMOS process over NMOS in most new designs. MOS processes are used for most VLSI scale circuits. Applications include memories, interfacing, microprocessors, basic logic functions, and a host of linear and mixed linear and digital applications.

Recently there has been a major effort toward combining both bipolar and MOS devices in a single process. This more complex and expensive process, termed Bi-MOS, is becoming cost-effective in a growing class of applications. Some processes also include thin film components with MOS and/or bipolar devices, but the expense associated with adding the thin film layer is justifiable only in specialized applications.

1.3 IC DESIGN PROCESS

It is generally the goal of the IC designer to design an integrated circuit that meets a given set of specifications while expending minimal labor and physical resources in a short time frame. Furthermore, the production yield should be high, the process simple, and the die area small. The conventional approach to circuit design often involves much iteration at the breadboard level. Because of the complexity of many VLSI designs and the cost of resources associated with IC design and fabrication, the conventional approach is totally unacceptable. A simple example is useful for obtaining an appreciation for the magnitude of the task facing the VLSI designer.

> **Example 1.3-1.** Assume that the productivity of a "conventional" discrete compo-
> nent circuit designer is measured in terms of the average number of transistors per
> day that the designer produces for a circuit and that the productivity is independent
> of the complexity of the circuit. If it is assumed that a two person-month effort is
> required to design a 20-transistor circuit following a conventional approach, how
> long will it take the same designer to design a circuit that has 500,000 transistors
> using the same design approach? How large will the circuit schematic be if it
> requires an average of 2 cm² of space for each transistor in the circuit?
>
> *Solution.* The productivity rate of the designer is 20 transistors/2 person-months =
> 10 transistors/person-month. Thus, the 500,000-transistor VLSI circuit would require
> 50,000 person-months, or about 4200 person-years. Note that 4200 person-years is
> equivalent to about 105 productive person-lifetimes! The schematic would occupy
> $(500,000)(2)$ cm² $= 10^6$ cm² of area. This is the area of a square 10 m on a side!

From Example 1.3-1, two things should be apparent. First, designer efficiency *must* be improved in the field of VLSI design. Second, much more efficient methods of handling large amounts of design data associated with schematic drafting, layout, and simulation are required.

At the outset, one might suspect that designer productivity will actually decrease with circuit complexity. Although this is typically the case for unstructured designs, most existing VLSI circuits are regularly structured and utilize a small number of basic circuits a large number of times. Powerful design aids, mostly in the form of powerful computer programs, are crucial for the successful design of VLSI circuits.

Two approaches to IC design are philosophically identifiable. In the first, called a *bottom-up approach*, the designer starts at the transistor or gate level and designs subcircuits of increasing complexity, which are then interconnected to realize the required functionality. In the second, termed the *top-down approach*, the designer repeatedly decomposes the system-level specifications into groups and subgroups of simpler tasks. The lowest-level tasks are ultimately implemented in silicon, either with standard circuits that have been previously designed and tested (often termed *standard cells*) or with low-level circuits designed to meet the required specifications. In the extreme case, the top-down approach results in a *silicon compiler*, discussed later, in which all blocks are automatically designed with a computer.

The top-down approach is used for some digital designs and often results in a significant increase in designer productivity. Considerable effort has been expended at following the top-down approach for analog design, but analog design requirements are sufficiently specialized that the top-down approach is currently practical only in certain classes of analog designs. It is often the case that both analog and digital system designs use varying combinations of top-down and bottom-up design concepts.

A block diagram of the conventional IC design process is shown in Fig. 1.3-1. The starting point is a set of design specifications. On complicated designs, a major effort is required to obtain a complete set of circuit and system specifications.

Preliminary designs are based upon simple models of devices or subcircuits. These are typically at the behavioral or logic level for digital circuits and at the component or device level for analog circuits. A preliminary computer simulation using more accurate models is used to verify the performance of the preliminary design. Good device and subcircuit models are crucial. A model is "good" if it accurately predicts experimental performance after fabrication and is sufficiently simple to avoid the requirement of excessive computer time during the simulation. Considerable time is often invested in the initial computer simulation and preliminary design loop.

Once the preliminary design is deemed acceptable, the actual layout takes place. The layout phase is often entered on subcircuits prior to the completion of the preliminary design phase. A good overall floorplan is obtained early in the design after a good estimate of the overall architecture and size of the subcircuits is obtained. The floorplan contains all major busing and cell (subcircuit) placement information as well as I/O pad designations.

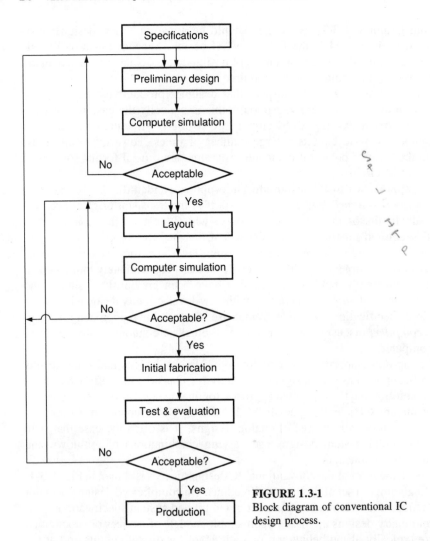

FIGURE 1.3-1
Block diagram of conventional IC design process.

Additional computer simulation is undertaken on subcircuits after layout and ultimately on the entire circuit. These simulations are crucial since parasitic effects associated with the layout play a significant role in both analog and digital circuits. In analog circuits the parasitics tend to degrade performance specifications whereas in digital circuits the parasitics generally cause additional unwanted delays or potentially disastrous race conditions. Software also exists at this level in the design for verifying that the layout violates no major design rules and that the circuit in the layout corresponds to the initial circuit schematic. The results of the computer simulation often necessitate changes in the layout or changes in the design itself if the effects of the parasitics cannot be resolved with changes in the layout.

Following an acceptable computer simulation of the entire circuit, the circuit is committed to fabrication. In evolving processes or complicated designs, subcircuits and/or test structures are often fabricated early in the design process to provide modeling information and/or verify functionality of subcircuits. The commitment of the design to fabrication is an expensive proposition.) Dollar costs for a single fabrication run of $20,000 to $40,000 are common, and delays of 1 to 4 months from submission of the design for fabrication to physical silicon for testing are typical. A *single* error in the circuit design, simulation, or layout generally makes the circuit either partially or totally nonfunctional. Based upon the experimental evaluation, either the circuit is released to production or the appropriate step of the design process is re-entered. Although first silicon is often not acceptable for production, the timeliness of the market window and the costs associated with fabrication make repeated iteration at the silicon level unacceptable. Improvements in design tools and methodologies are, however, producing a rapidly growing trend toward fully functional first silicon.

Significant resources have been invested on a worldwide basis at increasing the effectiveness of the computer-based design aids. A common goal is to automate repetitive and tedious tasks and minimize the amount of human interaction required in the design process. The rationale for this goal is twofold. First, it helps improve designer productivity, and second, it helps reduce errors that are often directly attributable to the designer. Additional information about the CAD tools available to the IC designer is provided throughout this text. Some of the tools and alternative approaches available to the designer deserve mention at this point.

Gate arrays and "seas of gates" are becoming quite popular for certain applications such as replacing large number of SSI chips with a single IC. Such arrays are integrated circuits containing a large number (several hundred) of digital gates or transistor cells, which can be used to implement complicated logic functions. These circuits are initially processed up to but not including the interconnection layers to form a versatile and generic building block. Computer programs that determine the interconnections necessary to implement customer-specific logic functions are widely available and are used to determine the required interconnections. One or more interconnection layers are then added to the generic array circuit, resulting in an economical, production-ready integrated circuit that can be fabricated in a few days. These mask programmable arrays are most practical in low- to medium-volume applications where custom design and production costs cannot be justified or in applications that require very quick turn-around. Silicon area is not, however, efficiently utilized in these arrays, making them less attractive for high-volume applications, in which silicon costs become a major factor in overall fabrication costs.

Some groups have been successful at automating the design process in restricted applications to the extent that the input to a computer program is the system specification and the output is a layout that should yield production-ready silicon. These programs are called silicon compilers, and they partially remove the conventional IC designer from the design cycle. The resulting simplification on the typical block diagram of Fig. 1.3-1 should be apparent. These programs support the premise that the circuits will be correct by construction, thus minimizing the need for verification by simulation. Although it might appear that silicon compilers will eventually make the IC designer obsolete, this is highly unlikely. These types of CAD tools will, rather, provide the experienced designer with additional capability for meeting more complicated and challenging design goals and provide basic silicon access to other design engineers.

1.4   ECONOMICS

Although the field of VLSI design is challenging from both engineering and scientific viewpoints, neither government nor industry is willing to support its evolution on these merits alone. Both research and developmental efforts are generally focused toward areas where investments can be recouped in the marketplace within a relatively short time. It is thus crucial that the designer be familiar with the economics of IC production.

Two questions naturally arise prior to developmental efforts on any VLSI circuit. First, does a sufficiently large market exist to justify development? Second, can a product be developed and produced so that a reasonable profit will be realized over the expected life of the product? We will not attempt to consider the first question in this text, but the second question is easier to address. On a product that is anticipated to have a relatively small total sales volume, the developmental costs will typically dominate. On a product with a large projected sales volume over the life of the product, the actual production costs dominate.

The developmental costs can be estimated once the amount of engineering effort required to bring a product into production is known. It should be pointed out that even for seemingly simple designs, the developmental costs may become quite large. For example, a design that requires a 12-month effort by an experienced designer may accrue a total project development cost of $350,000 to $450,000 or more even though the base salary of the designer may be only $40,000/year. The burden (multiplier on the base salary of the designer) is quite high because of various expenses: standard fringe benefits the employer generally provides, technician support, applications engineering, computer time charges, equipment amortization, documentation preparation, test procedure development, mask generation, pilot production, and so on. The burden factor varies considerably from project to project and from company to company. Detailed estimates of the specific costs will generally be made because of differing project requirements. Information about design costs within a company is highly proprietary. Nevertheless, it should be apparent that IC design is a very expensive proposition.

The production costs are somewhat easier to estimate. These can be grossly decomposed into the costs listed in Table 1.4-1; typical values are listed in Table 1.4-2. The wafer fabrication costs are dependent on the size of the wafer, the number of mask steps, and the type of processing done at each step. These costs are determined by labor costs, materials and maintenance costs, and amortization costs of the processing equipment. Correspondingly, the wafer probe and final test results are dependent on both type and complexity of the circuit itself. Because good testers are quite expensive ($500,000 to $1.5 million for good digital testers

TABLE 1.4-1
Major costs associated with wafer processing and fabrication

		Cost	
		Per wafer	Per die
Wafer fabrication			
Blank wafer	x_1	✓	
Wafer processing	x_2	✓	
Wafer probe	x_3	✓	
Wafer sawing	x_4	✓	
Die attach, bonding, and packaging	x_5	✓	
Packaging	x_6		✓
Final test	x_7		✓

TABLE 1.4-2
Typical processing and packaging costs for 12-mask, $3\ \mu$ CMOS process (1988) based upon volume production

	Processing costs	
	4" process	5" process
Wafer fabrication		
Blank wafer	$x_1 = \$10$	$x_1 = \$15$
Wafer processing	$x_2 = \$140$	$x_2 = \$150$
Wafer probe (per wafer)	$x_3 = \$25$	$x_3 = \$40$
Wafer sawing (per wafer)	$x_4 = \$3$	$x_4 = \$3$
Die attach and bonding (per wafer)	$x_5 = \$3$	$x_5 = \$5$
Packaging	x_6 (see below)	x_6 (see below)
Final test (per package)	$x_7 = 30¢/cm^2$	$x_7 = 30¢/cm^2$

Package costs†		
Plastic DIP	8 pin	$0.032
Plastic DIP	16 pin	0.048
Plastic DIP	24 pin	0.091
Plastic DIP	64 pin	0.70
Ceramic side brazed	16 pin	1.05
Ceramic side brazed	24 pin	1.50
Ceramic side brazed	64 pin	4.95
Ceramic CERDIP	16 pin	0.096
Ceramic CERDIP	24 pin	0.26
Ceramic CERDIP	40 pin	0.64
Ceramic pin grid array	68 pin	6.40
Ceramic pin grid array	84 pin	7.50
Ceramic pin grid array	132 pin	10.15
Ceramic pin grid array	224 pin	18.00

†Packaging cost estimates courtesy Dr. W.E. Loeb of W.E. Loeb and Associates.[13]

in 1989), these costs become significant if much time on the tester is required. The die attach and bonding costs shown in Table 1.4-1 are listed as a per-wafer cost. Some groups prefer to figure these as per-die costs instead.

The packaging costs depend on both the type and size of the package. As is shown in Table 1.4-2, low pin count plastic packages cost a few cents, whereas ceramic packages with a large number of pins could cost several dollars. Pin styles also differ. The standard dual inline packages (DIP) have recently been replaced, in some applications, with pin grid arrays and surface mount packages. The plastic surface mount small outline integrated circuit (SOIC) packages are a little less expensive than the DIP structures shown in Table 1.4-2, as are the plastic lead chip carriers (PLCC). For example, a 68-pin PLCC would cost about $0.30 compared to $0.70 for the 64-pin plastic DIP.

Since the processing equipment is quite expensive (a single line for processing standard CMOS 5 inch wafers in a 2 μ process may cost $30 million) and the labor costs to keep a line operational are quite high, the amortization costs are also dependent on the accounting procedures used by the individual companies. For example, during periods when the demand for semiconductors is high and the production facilities are running near capacity, the fabrication costs per wafer are reduced if the costs are based upon instantaneous amortization costs. Correspondingly, when the demand for semiconductors is soft, this method of accounting results in significant increases in the per-wafer fabrication costs, which may be somewhat misleading. These economy-dependent variances could be as much as 2:1 or more.

It may appear from the information presented in Table 1.4-2 that elimination of the wafer probe step could reduce system costs. In general, this is far from true, as indicated by Example 1.4-1.

Example 1.4-1. Compare the costs of producing an integrated circuit in a conventional 3 μ, 12-mask CMOS process with the options for processing, testing, and packaging as shown in Table 1.4-3. Assume the die size is 0.5 cm × 0.5 cm, the yield at wafer probe is 50%, the packaging yield (sawing, die attach, bonding, and packaging) is 90%, and that Table 1.4-2 gives realistic values for both fabrication and packaging costs. Approximate the number of potential dies by the wafer/die-area ratio, and assume that dies are discarded as soon as they are determined to be defective.

TABLE 1.4-3
Processing, testing, and packaging options for Example 1.4-1

Option	Wafer size	Wafer probe	Type of package
1	4 in	Yes	16-pin plastic
2	5 in	Yes	16-pin plastic
3	4 in	Yes	16-pin sidebrazed ceramic
4	4 in	No	16-pin plastic
5	4 in	No	16-pin sidebrazed ceramic

Solution. The number of potential dies for the 4 inch and 5 inch wafers are approximately

$$N_4 = \frac{\pi(2 \text{ in})^2}{(0.5 \text{ cm} \times 0.5 \text{ cm})} = 324$$

$$N_5 = \frac{\pi(2.5 \text{ in})^2}{(0.5 \text{ cm} \times 0.5 \text{ cm})} = 506$$

The actual number of potential dies is somewhat smaller since all potential dies around the perimeter of the wafer are incomplete and hence useless. These effects become more significant as the die size increases and as the wafer size decreases.

For options 1, 2, and 3, the production cost per good package becomes

$$C = \left[\left(\frac{x_1 + x_2 + x_3 + x_4 + x_5}{N} \right) \left(\frac{1}{\theta_{\text{probe}}} \right) + x_6 + x_7 \frac{A_W}{N} \right] \left[\frac{1}{\theta_{\text{package}}} \right] \tag{1.4-1}$$

where θ_{probe} and θ_{package} represent probe and package yields respectively, x_1–x_7 are as in Table 1.4-1, A_W is the wafer area, and N is the number of potential dies.

For options 4 and 5, the production cost per good package becomes

$$C = \left(\frac{x_1 + x_2 + x_4 + x_5}{N} + x_6 + x_7 \frac{A_W}{N} \right) \left(\frac{1}{\theta_{\text{probe}}} \right) \left(\frac{1}{\theta_{\text{package}}} \right) \tag{1.4-2}$$

Substituting from Table 1.4-2, we obtain the following costs for options 1–5 respectively, $C_1 = \$1.38$, $C_2 = \$1.07$, $C_3 = \$2.49$, $C_4 = \$1.34$, and $C_5 = \$3.57$.

This example clearly demonstrates several points. First, very significant differences in packaging costs exist. The ceramic packages are much more expensive than plastic. Ceramic packages do, however, provide better isolation from the ambient external environment and are necessary in some high-reliability applications. The importance of the wafer probe step for low-yield parts packaged in expensive packages should be apparent. This allows defective dies to be identified and culled prior to packaging, thus avoiding the expensive proposition of packaging defective dies. The wafer fabrication and packaging costs considered in the example are reasonably independent of circuit complexity. The fabrication yield, however, is strongly a function of die size; it decreases rapidly with increasing die size, as will be demonstrated later in this chapter. In this example, the value of the die itself constitutes a relatively small portion of the overall IC cost. This is typical for small dies. For large dies, the die value generally dominates because of the significant decrease in yield. The probe and final test costs were also relatively small in this example, but testing costs become very significant for larger complicated circuits.

1.5 YIELD

Generally, some of the dies on any wafer do not meet the performance specifications. The percentage of dies that do meet performance specifications is termed the *wafer yield*. In general, the yield decreases rapidly with increasing die area. Consequently, die area plays a major role in the economics of IC design, to the extent that estimates about the die area and yield are almost always considered when making decisions about whether IC development for specific needs will be economically justifiable. A basic understanding about the economic impact of yield is very important, and since some of the terminology needed to discuss yield is first introduced in Chapters 2 and 3, the reader may need to make an occasional forward reference to those chapters while reading this section.

Accurate IC yield prediction is difficult to obtain due to the variety of factors that impact yield. Yield is dependent on the specific type of circuit, the design methodology followed by the designer, the layout itself, and the physical fabrication process. The factors that affect yield include *dust* particles (by definition, any unwanted foreign objects in solid, liquid, or gaseous state), crystal defects, mask defects, alignment errors, breakage and human handling errors, and parameter drifts. The dust particles on wafers, which introduce local defects, are foreign particles that adversely affect either the photolithographic process or the subsequent processing steps. If large enough, these dust particles will cause problems such as failure of a transistor, breaks in an interconnection, or shorting of two adjacent devices, levels, or interconnections. These types of defects are generally assumed to be randomly distributed over the surface of the wafer and from wafer to wafer. Dust particles on a mask or reticle, if large enough, will also cause failures that are repeated every time that portion of the reticle or mask is used. These defects typically occur at the same geometrical position on all wafers in a lot.

Crystal defects are present in the wafer prior to fabrication and cause local circuit defects such as failure of transistors. Mask defects may be local or global, depending on the cause. Alignment errors will typically be limited to a single wafer. It is, however, often the case that all dies on the wafer will be defective if alignment errors occur.

Parameter drifts will cause transistors to have characteristics different from those desired. These parameter drifts are introduced during processing and are attributable to the inherent practical and physical limitations associated with processing steps such as photolithography, deposition, and diffusion. These changes may affect all wafers in a lot or may affect individual transistors on a wafer. The average values of key parameters at the lot level are closely monitored. Lots are rejected if these values lie outside a predefined acceptability region. On a single wafer, the parameters are considered to vary statistically from transistor to transistor. Statistical circuit parameter variations large enough to cause circuit failures are more common in analog circuits than in digital circuits. Failures due to parameter variations are termed *soft* faults, and those failures that cause complete transistor failure or interconnection errors are termed *hard* faults. Whereas a hard fault generally results in nonfunctionality of part or all of the circuit, circuits with soft faults may well be functional but fail to meet specifications. A single hard fault or soft fault will often cause rejection of a die. Most digital circuits are designed so that they are unaffected by all but the most serious parameter variations. Thus, failures in digital circuits generally result from hard faults. Both soft faults and hard faults are of concern in analog circuits.

Faults are bad for two reasons. First, since they cause failure of the die, they drive up the effective costs of a good die. Second, they are often difficult and expensive to detect. In fact, questions about whether some complicated circuits are even testable arise. It is now an accepted responsibility of the designers to address the testing problem at the design stage. ICs often contain additional circuitry, which is used in the testing of the circuit itself. The testing question is definitely not trivial for complicated designs, and it represents an active area of research. Related to this problem is the field of fault-tolerant technology, also an active area of research, in which circuits are designed so that they remain functional even if some faults do exist.

The probability of having one or more hard faults on any die associated with particulate material or crystal defects generally increases with both die area and circuit complexity. The reason for the increase with die area should be apparent; it is more likely that a die will contact some fixed defects on a wafer if the die area is increased. This is illustrated in simplified form in Fig. 1.5-1, where varying die sizes are considered with a fixed defect distribution. It should be apparent from this example that with 52 potential dies, 45 will be free of defects (Fig. 1.5-1b). With 12 potential dies (Fig. 1.5-1c), 7 will be free of defects, and with 4 potential dies none will be free of defects (Fig. 1.5-1d). In this example, yield decreases from 86% to 0% as the die size increases.

Although not accounted for in the previous example, the density of defects which will cause die failure also increases with die complexity. If a die is

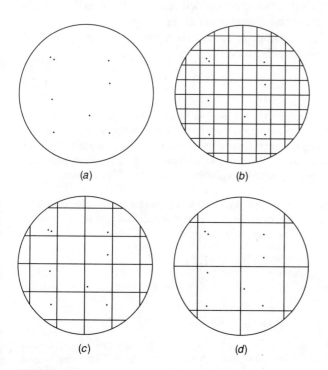

(a)   (b)

(c)   (d)

FIGURE 1.5-1
Effects of defects on yield: (a) Defect locations, (b) Small die size, (c) Larger die size, (d) Die size with zero yield.

not heavily utilized, some defects may occur in areas where no components or interconnections exist, so die failure will not result. Likewise, some types of defects are more likely to cause a fault if they occur where a transistor is located than where interconnections are made. It can be shown, however, that for a fixed circuit schematic overall yield decreases with increasing die size and increases if the devices are densely packed on the die. The reader is thus cautioned not to draw the conclusion that the yield can be improved by decreasing the density if more silicon area for a given circuit is used. In general, the decrease in failure density on a die with a loosely packed circuit will be more than offset by the total number of defects anticipated in the die with larger area.

Several models are used to predict yield associated with crystal- and particulate-related defects. A simple model based upon using the Poisson distribution to predict the probability of K defects in a die area, A, with an average defect density of D defects per unit area results in the expression for the probability that a given die of area A has zero defects:

$$P = e^{-AD} \tag{1.5-1}$$

The defect density, D, is typically in the range of 1 to $2/cm^2$.

Since many defects cause a failure only if the defect occurs in an active area, it may be preferable to use the active area and the corresponding average active area defect density in Eq. 1.5-1. Alternatively, even better results should be obtainable if the active and interconnection defects are considered separately. If A_A and A_I denote the active and interconnect areas, respectively, and D_A and D_I denote the average defect densities in those two regions, then the probability that a die is good can be obtained by modifying Eq. 1.5-1

$$P = e^{-(A_A D_A + A_I D_I)} \tag{1.5-2}$$

Example 1.5-1. If the average defect density is $1/cm^2$, what is the average cost per good die for a 4" wafer if the die size is $1\ cm^2$? $0.2\ cm^2$? What would be the price per good die if the average defect density increased to $2/cm^2$? Neglect die losses associated with the wafer edges. Assume the cost for the 4" wafer and processing is $200 and that Eq. 1.5-1 models the probability that a device is good.

Solution. The average cost per good die is $200/NP$ where P is the probability the die is good and N is the number of potential dies per wafer. The number of potential $1\ cm^2$ dies in a 4" wafer is (neglecting edge losses)

$$N_{1cm} = \frac{\pi \left[(2\ in)(2.5\ cm/in) \right]^2}{1\ cm^2} = 81$$

Likewise

$$N_{0.2cm} = 405$$

For a $1/cm^2$ defect density, it follows from Eq. 1.5-1 that the probability that the $1\ cm^2$ die is good is 36%, whereas the probability that the $0.2\ cm^2$ die is good is 82%. The corresponding cost per good $1\ cm^2$ die is thus $6.86. The cost per good $0.2\ cm^2$ die is 60¢. If the defect density were to increase to $2/cm^2$, the average cost per good 1 cm^2 die increases to \$18.24 and the 0.2 cm^2 die increases to 74¢. From this example it should be apparent that increasing either the defect density or die area significantly increases the average die cost once the product of A and D exceeds unity.

Example 1.5-2. If the average defect density is 1.5/cm^2, what is the yield if the die size is increased to that of an entire 4" wafer? On the average, how many such wafers must be fabricated to give one good die? If the cost of each wafer is \$200, what would be the average cost per good die? Use the simple model of Eq. 1.5-1 to predict yield.

Solution. From Eq. 1.5-1, the probability that the die is good is

$$P = e^{-\pi(2 \text{ in})^2(2.54 \text{ cm/in})^2(1.5)/\text{cm}^2}$$

$$P = 1.53 \times 10^{-53}$$

It thus requires, on the average, $1/P = 6.5 \times 10^{52}$ wafers to yield one good die. At a cost of \$200/wafer, the average cost per good die would be \$1.3 $\times 10^{55}$.

Two important observations can be made from the simplified calculations of the previous example. First, the effective cost of good large die is very high. Second, the concept of using the entire wafer as a single IC is totally impractical if the circuit is not tolerant of any faults. The concept of using the entire wafer as a single IC (termed wafer scale integration or WSI), is sufficiently attractive, however, that considerable effort has been devoted to research in this area. These circuits must, of course, provide for a mechanism of repair—either through inherent redundancy or some form of mechanical reconfiguration (e.g., laser trimming)—to be viable, since some defects will occur during processing.

For large devices the yield predicted by Eq. 1.5-1 is somewhat pessimistic. Two other models used are the Seeds model[14] and Murphy model[15], which are characterized respectively by the following expressions for the probability that a given die is good:

$$P = e^{-\sqrt{AD}} \tag{1.5-3}$$

$$P = \left(\frac{1 - e^{-AD}}{AD}\right)^2 \tag{1.5-4}$$

Additional information about yield prediction can be found in references 16–19.

Soft faults due to parameter drifts also affect yield in a statistical sense. The soft faults play a major role in yield of analog circuits. The effects of parameter drifts can best be appreciated by considering Fig. 1.5-2, in which the statistical distributions of the parameter X are shown. In Fig. 1.5-2a the statistical distribution of the average of the parameter over repeated processing runs is shown. X_{MAX} and X_{MIN} define a process window within which the average value of the parameter must reside. Both design and processing groups must agree on an acceptable process window. The cost of fabricating an IC increases with a decreasing process window and approaches infinity as the width of the process window converges to zero. It is often the case that X_{MAX} and X_{MIN} differ from

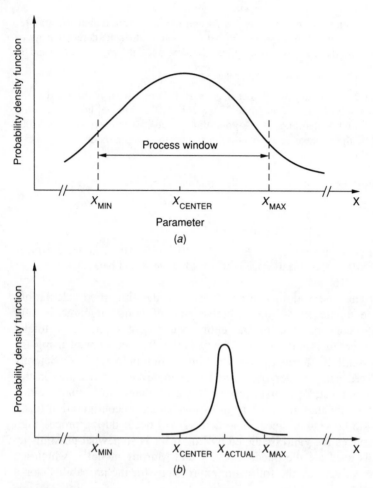

FIGURE 1.5-2
Statistical parameter spreads in a variable X: (a) Process window, (b) Wafer level variations.

X_{CENTER} by 10% to 50% for most of the major process parameters. More details about parameter spreads can be found in Chapter 2. Good designs will meet specifications over a wide process window. It often requires considerable effort on the part of the designer to produce designs that meet specifications over a wide process window. This is particularly true of analog designs.

Even at the wafer level, statistical variations in the parameter occur across the wafer. These variations are somewhat dependent on proximity of devices and, because of the way parameters are defined, the symmetry in layout. This variation, not including either device proximity or layout, is shown in Fig. 1.5-2b, where X_{ACTUAL} represents the average value of the parameter X on a given wafer. X_{ACTUAL} is thus considered a random variable relative to processing but a fixed parameter once processing is complete. The statistical variance at the wafer level is generally much smaller than the variance at the processing level.

For example, the capacitance density of oxide capacitors may have a processing variation (variance) of 10% of the mean whereas the wafer-level variation may be less than 0.1% of the mean. Two interesting observations can be made from the curves in Fig. 1.5-2. First, after fabrication the parameters are distributed around X_{ACTUAL} rather than the process center, X_{CENTER}. In fact, after processing the probability that a parameter is close to X_{CENTER} may be quite small. Second, it should be apparent that designs should meet specifications over *both* process window and wafer-level variations.

Most good digital designs are functionally tolerant to large process parameter variations of all key parameters and are quite insensitive to wafer-level variations. This insensitivity is inherent in most of the basic digital circuit structures. These variations, however, play a major role in the speed specifications of digital circuits, with faster circuits commanding a premium price in the marketplace.

The analog designer, on the other hand, must pay considerable attention to both process window and wafer-level variations. The process window variations are actually so large that many design approaches used in discrete component design are totally impractical in monolithic designs. For reasons that will become apparent in later chapters, the performance of many analog designs is strongly dependent on close matching of devices and device characteristics and relatively tolerant of nominal parameter variations within the process window. Consequently, the curve of Fig. 1.5-2b plays a key role in many analog designs.

Although the exact shape of the parameter distributions shown in Fig. 1.5-2 is of interest, that information is not widely distributed. Rather, a single parameter that in some sense characterizes the parameter distribution is more commonly available. For example, a comment about the threshold voltage, V_T, such as $V_T = 0.5$ V $\pm 20\%$ means that the value of V_T after processing will "usually" be within $\pm 20\%$ of 0.5 V. Actually, depending on the process acceptance criteria, the average value of V_T may be within this window for all accepted wafers. Correspondingly, a comment such as "V_T matching is to 5 mV" means that the wafer-level parameter variations such as those shown in Fig. 1.5-2b typically differ by less than 5 mV from the measured average value. Whereas the bounds on the process window may be fixed due to rejection of wafers that do not meet the acceptance criterion, the wafer-level variations are essentially not bounded. Unless stated differently, it will be assumed throughout this text that a wafer-level or process window distribution as specified above corresponds to a window within which *99.73% of the devices* will fall. This corresponds to a ± 3 standard deviation window if the random variable is normally distributed—an assumption that is often made.

Example 1.5-3. Assume the die of a circuit is 6 mm on a side with a defect density of 0.7/cm². Assume also that the die includes an analog section, which includes 100 transistors in which the characteristics must all be matched to within 0.5% of the die average value to meet specifications. Assume that the matching characteristics of the transistor are dominated by a single parameter that is normally distributed with a ± 3 standard deviation window, characterized by a variation from the die average of $\pm 0.5\%$.

(a) Using the Seeds model for defect density, determine the approximate yield if potential soft faults in the analog section are neglected.

(b) Estimate the yield if both hard and soft faults are considered.

(c) Repeat (b) if matching to 0.25% is required in the analog section.

Solution. (a) From (Eq. 1.5-3), the hard yield is the probability that a die is good, which is given by

$$P_H = e^{-\sqrt{AD}} = e^{-\sqrt{(6\text{mm})^2(7\times10^{-3})/\text{mm}^2}} = 60.5\%$$

(b) The probability that a die has no soft faults is equal to the probability that *all* 100 transistors meet the matching specifications. The probability that each transistor meets the matching requirements is $P = .9973$. Thus, the probability that all 100 transistors meet the specifications is

$$P_S = (.9973)^{100} = .763$$

The overall yield is thus the product of the hard and soft fault yield, which is

$$P = P_H P_S = 46\%$$

(c) For a matching to 0.25%, it follows from a standard investigation of the normal distribution that the probability that a given transistor meets the specifications is equal to the probability that the normal random variable is within ± 1.5 standard deviations of the mean. From a probability density table for the normal distribution, it follows that the probability that any one transistor meets the specifications is 0.8664. Thus, the probability that all 100 transistors meet specifications is

$$P_S = (0.8664)^{100} = 5.9 \times 10^{-7}$$

Thus, from part (a), the overall yield is

$$P = P_S P_H = 3.5 \times 10^{-6} = 3.5 \times 10^{-5}\%$$

Note that this modest increase in matching requirement from 0.5% to 0.25% results in a yield that is so small as to make such a design totally impractical.

The previous example demonstrates a very important point. If very much matching is required in analog circuit design, then the matching requirements must not be too severe if the yield is to be high enough to make the circuit economically feasible.

Since considerable variation from the process center occurs, as indicated in Fig. 1.5-2a, one naturally asks the question: What value should be used for the parameters at the design stage? Stated alternately, the problem is to find the design target, or the design center, for each parameter. The process center is widely used for the design center. It can, however, be shown that in some cases, the yield can be improved if something other than the process center is used for the design center. The field of design centering and yield optimization addresses these questions. Unless stated otherwise, it will be assumed throughout this book that the desired design center corresponds to the process center.

The reader should be cautioned to avoid the temptation of using experimental parameter centers obtained from measurements made on one or two wafer lots in lieu of the design center that has evolved with the process itself. It should be apparent from Fig. 1.5-2 that using experimentally measured parameters rather than the process center as design centers will statistically bias designs in a way that will often be accompanied by a decrease in yield.

Industry is keenly aware of the relationship among the specified process window (which dictates the design specification range), the actual wafer-level variations, and the corresponding yield. A *capability index*, which relates these variables for any process parameter, is defined by the expression[20]

$$C_p = \frac{\text{Design specification width}}{\text{Process width}} \qquad (1.5\text{-}5)$$

where the process width is generally defined to be ± 3 standard deviations (σ) about the mean. Assuming a normally distributed process around the mean in which the process width is characterized by the $\pm 3\sigma$ window, it follows that if the process window is centered in the design specification window, then the probability that a parameter of a device lies inside the design specification window is

$$P = \frac{1}{\sqrt{2\pi}} \int_{-3C_p}^{3C_p} e^{-(x^2/2)} dx \qquad (1.5\text{-}6)$$

This error function, erf (x), integral is readily obtainable from tables of the normal probability distribution, which appear in most elementary statistics texts. If C_p is small, the probability that a device parameter is actually within the process window is small; the yield will be poor and will deteriorate even more if the mean of a parameter for a wafer is not centered within the design specification window. Correspondingly, if C_p is large, the yield will be high and the process will be reasonably tolerant to small shifts in the wafer-level parameter center from the design specification center. Setting the design specification width so that $C_p = 2$ will result in reasonable yield in many applications, although this may place unrealistic performance demands on the designer for some design projects.

Example 1.5-4 clearly demonstrates the yield implications associated with properly establishing the capability index.

Example 1.5-4. If 1000 devices on a chip must have a specific parameter within the specified design process window, determine the soft yield if the process has been characterized by a capability index of (*a*) $C_p = 0.5$, (*b*) $C_p = 1.0$, (*c*) $C_p = 1.5$, and (*d*) $C_p = 2.0$.

Solution. With $C_p = 0.5$, it follows from Eq. 1.5-6 and a normal random variable table that $P = .8664$. Thus, the probability that all 1000 devices have a parameter within the design specification window is $P_{1000} = (.8664)^{1000} \approx 0$. If $C_p = 1.0$, $P = .9973$ and $P_{1000} = .067$, which represents about a 6.7% yield. If $C_p = 1.5$, $P = .999993$ and $P_{1000} \approx .993$. Finally, if $C_p = 2.0$, $P = .999999998$ and $P_{1000} \approx 1.0$, indicating essentially a 100% yield.

1.6   TRENDS IN VLSI DESIGN

Several trends in the production of VLSI circuits are readily identifiable. Some of these have already been discussed in this chapter. The most visible is the continual shrinking of the minimum geometrical feature size. Although this trend will continue, the rate at which the minimum feature size decreases is slowing. This slowing is partially attributable to inherent physical limitations in the photolithographic process and the rapidly increasing costs associated with very fine resolution processing equipment. Problems associated with power dissipation density, the effects of additional diffusion in small devices due to subsequent heat cycle steps during processing, and concerns about a practical alternative to the widely used standard local oxidation (LOCOS) processing step are all becoming significant in submicron processes. The size of the silicon atom and the silicon dioxide molecule will also be of increasing concern in submicron processes. These concerns about size place very real lower bounds on the conventional approach to integrated circuit design.

A trend in increasing speed in digital circuits is readily identifiable. Some research efforts with gallium arsenide (GaAs) suggest that this material may ultimately supplant silicon at very high frequencies. GaAs is attractive because of higher electron mobility and, in some applications, because of reduced sensitivity to radiation. Continual improvement in the performance of silicon circuits raises doubts, however, about when and if a transition to GaAs will occur. The increase in speed and increase in circuit complexity are direct results of the reduction in feature size.

A third trend is the increasing complexity of circuit function and device count on a die. This trend is crucial for the development of new markets for integrated circuits.

A fourth trend is toward increased designer productivity and an ever-growing dependence on the computer in the design process. Design methods that were standard a decade ago would be totally unworkable in many current design projects.

A fifth trend is the continual shift of where design, production, and markets are geographically located. A decade ago most major and innovative design efforts and a significant portion of the production were done in the United States and Western Europe, with more mature technologies being transferred to the Far East. Production was generally most profitable in countries where labor costs were low. An increasing shift in the design efforts to the more developed Far Eastern countries has occurred in recent years, with the mature production shifting more into the less-developed Far Eastern countries, where labor costs remain low. The marketplace is also shifting, with a large number of less-developed countries now experiencing the data processing and telecommunications revolution that swept the West a decade earlier. A trend of the design and production activities geographically following the marketplace is also observable.

A sixth trend is a growing coupling of a specific process and its processing equipment. As feature sizes shrink and processes become more complex, the process is becoming increasingly dependent on the performance of specific pieces of equipment.

Other trends include the use of more powerful CAD tools, which extends VLSI design to the realm of the systems designer, and increasing the complexity of processes by using silicon on insulator (SOI) or combining both MOS and bipolar technologies into a single process.

REFERENCES

1. J. E. Lilienfeld, U.S. Patent 1,745,175; 1930.
2. O. Heil, British Patent 439,457; 1935.
3. T. R. Reid, *The Chip*, Simon & Schuster, New York, 1985.
4. J. D. Ryder and D. G. Fink, "Engineers and Electrons", IEEE Press, New York, 1984.
5. I. Catt, "Wafer-Scale Integration," *Wireless World (GB)*, vol. 87, no. 1546, pp. 57–59, July 1981.
6. W. R. Moore, "Introducing Wafer-Scale Integration," *Silicon Design*, vol. 6, p. 9, January 1986.
7. R. Aubusson and I. Catt, "Wafer-Scale Integration—A Fault Tolerant Procedure," *IEEE J. Solid State Circuits*, vol. SC-13, no. 3, pp. 339–344, June 1978.
8. D. L. Peltzer, "Wafer-Scale Integration: The Limits of VLSI?" *VLSI Design*, vol. IV, no. 5, pp. 43–47, September 1983.
9. R. R. Johnson, "The Significance of Wafer-Scale Integration in Computer Design," presented at the *IEEE Int. Conf. on Computer Design: VLSI in Computers*, Port Chester, NY, pp. 101–105, October 1984.
10. IEEE, "Whatever Happened to Wafer-Scale Integration?," *IEEE Spectrum*, vol. 19, no. 6, p. 18, June 1982.
11. R. H. Dennard, E. H. Gaensslen, H. -N. Yu, V. L. Rideant, E. Bassous, and A. R. LeBlanc, "Design of Ion-Implanted MOSFETS with Very Small Physical Dimensions," *IEEE J. Solid State Circuits,* vol. SC-9, pp. 256–268, October 1974.
12. Eric Demoulin, "Fabrication Technology of MOS ICs for Telecommunications," *Design of MOS VLSI Circuits for Telecommunications*, ed. Y. Tsividis and P. Antognetti, Prentice-Hall, Englewood Cliffs, N.J. 1985, Chapter 1.
13. W. E. Loeb, "IC Packages, Costs, Trends and Forecasts," W. E. Loeb and Associates, Soquel, Calif., June 1987.
14. R. B. Seeds, "Yield and Cost Analysis of Bipolar LSI," IEEE Int. Electron Devices Meeting, Washington, D.C., p. 12, 1967.
15. B. T. Murphy, "Cost-Size Optima of Monolithic Integrated Circuits," *Proc. IEEE*, vol. 52, pp. 1537–1545, December 1964.
16. D. G. Ong, *Modern MOS Technology, Processes, Devices and Design*, McGraw-Hill, New York, 1984.
17. W. E. Ham, "Yield-Area Analysis: Part I—Diagnostic Tool for Fundamental Integrated Circuit Process Problems," *RCA Review*, vol. 39, pp. 231–249, June 1978.
18. T. Okabe, M. Nagata and S. Shimada, "Analysis on Yield of Integrated Circuits and a New Expression for Yield," *Electrical Engineering in Japan*, vol. 92, pp. 135–141, 1972.
19. C. H. Stapper, A. N. McLaren, and M. Dreckmann, "Yield Model for Productivity Optimization of VLSI Memory Chips with Redundancy and Partially Good Product," *IBM J. Res. Develop.*, vol. 24, pp. 398–409, 1980.
20. V. E. Kane, "Process Capability Indices," *Journal of Quality Technology,* vol. 18, pp. 44–51, January 1986.

PROBLEMS

Section 1.1

1.1. How many SiO_2 molecules will be required to form the insulating layer under the gate of a MOSFET that has a 3 μ × 3 μ gate area if the silicon dioxide thickness is 800 Å? Repeat if the gate is 0.5 μ × 0.5 μ with a 100 Å SiO_2 layer.

1.2. What is the average number of vertically stacked SiO_2 molecules in an 80 Å gate oxide layer?

Section 1.4

1.3. If the average resistance density (resistance/unit area) is $1.2\ \Omega/\mu^2$ and the capacitance density is $0.7\ fF/\mu^2 (1\ fF = 10^{-3}\ pf = 10^{-15}\ F)$ and if a 5 inch wafer costs $250 to produce, what is the cost (based upon area) of a 250 kΩ resistor? What is the cost of a 100 pF capacitor? How many $2\ \mu \times 2\ \mu$ transistors can be placed in the area required for the 250 kΩ resistor? For the 100 pF capacitor? What is the cost per transistor if spacing and interconnection area are neglected? What is the cost per transistor if spacing and interconnection increase the area per transistor by a factor of 10?

Section 1.5

1.4. If a 4 inch wafer costs $200 and the defect density is $D = 2/cm^2$, what is the maximum permissible die area that can be used if the effective die cost (cost per good die) must not exceed 45¢? Assume the Seeds model characterizes the yield of the process and neglect area losses associated with placing square dies on a round wafer.

1.5. If an 8-bit flash A/D converter has 2^8 comparators and all must have an offset voltage less than 40 mV ($-40\ mV < V_{offset} < 40\ mV$) for the device to operate properly, and if the offset voltage for the comparators in this process is 20 mV, what percentage of the dies will fail due to soft faults associated with the offset voltage? If the same approach is used to build a 10-bit converter, the offset voltage requirement is more stringent (10 mV). If the same process is used, what percentage of the dies will now fail due to soft faults associated with the process?

1.6. Derive an expression for and plot the effective die cost (cost per good die) versus die area if the defect density is $2/cm^2$ for both the simple model of Eq. 1.5-1 and Seeds model. Also obtain an expression for and plot the cost per unit area and the cost per good unit area versus die area for both models. Assume the wafer size is 4 inch and the wafer cost after processing is $200.

1.7. What is the average cost per good 24-pin plastic DIP package of a die that is 0.1 inch on a side if it is fabricated on a 5 inch wafer and the average defect density is $1.5/cm^2$? Assume that wafer probing is used to eliminate defective dies and that the packaging yield is 85%. Use the typical processing costs listed in Table 1.4-2 for your calculations.

1.8. Repeat Example 1.4-1 if the die size is decreased to 0.2 cm × 0.2 cm and the defect density is $1.5/cm^2$. Assume the yield model of Eq. 1.5-1 and a packaging yield of 95%.

1.9. Assume an integrated circuit has a die size of 0.8 cm × 0.8 cm, defect density of $2/cm^2$, a wafer size of 4 inch, a package requirement of 64 pins, and a packaging yield of 90%.
(a) Calculate the average cost per good package if wafer probing is used and parts are packaged in plastic DIP packages.
(b) Compare the results of part (a) with the average cost per good package if wafer probing is omitted and parts are packaged in ceramic side brazed packages.
Use the processing and packaging cost estimates of Table 1.4-2.

1.10. A 5 inch wafer is yielding 85% at wafer probe with a die size of 0.2 cm × 0.2 cm. Determine the defect density assuming the process is characterized by the Seeds model.

1.11. Assume an area overhead per die of 250,000 μ^2 to allow for interconnection of a die to the outside world. Assume that a minimum size transistor is 3 μ^2 and an additional 60 μ^2 is needed for spacing and internal interconnection for each transistor. Assume also that the die is fabricated on a 4 inch wafer and that production costs are characterized by the values given in Table 1.4-2.

   (*a*) Calculate and plot the average cost of fabrication per transistor on this die as the number of transistors on the die ranges between 1 and 100,000.

   (*b*) Calculate and plot the average cost per good transistor on good dies if the fatal defect density in the external interconnection area is 0.1/cm² and that in the area devoted to transistors (transistor, spacing, and interconnection) is 1.5/cm². Use the model of Eq. 1.5-2.

1.12. Determine the minimum acceptable capability index for characterizing a process if a soft yield of 95% must be maintained on a die that contains 2000 devices.

CHAPTER
2

TECHNOLOGY

2.0 INTRODUCTION

A good understanding of processing and fabrication technology on the part of the circuit designer is necessary to provide the flexibility needed to optimize integrated circuit designs. With this knowledge the actual layout can be considered during design and the appropriate parasitics can be included in the analysis. Innovative techniques that improve performance often involve circuits or geometries that are dependent on and applicable to a particular process. Knowledge of processing characteristics enables the designer to make yield calculations during design and consider tradeoffs between yield, performance and design simplicity.

In this chapter processing technology is discussed from a qualitative viewpoint. This is followed by a detailed discussion of typical NMOS, CMOS, bipolar, thick film, and thin film processes. Most processes in industry can be viewed as either a straightforward variant or extension of these processes. These processes are summarized in the appendices of this chapter. Included in the appendices are process scenarios, graphical process descriptions, design rules, process parameters, and some computer simulation model parameters. These appendices should provide a useful reference for material that is presented in later chapters of this book. This chapter is concluded with a discussion of practical layout considerations and comments about some CAD tools that have become an integral part of the IC design process.

2.1 IC PRODUCTION PROCESS

The major steps involved in producing integrated circuits are considered from a qualitative viewpoint in this section. These steps are used in the MOS and/or bipolar processes that will be discussed later in this chapter.

2.1.1 Processing Steps

CRYSTAL PREPARATION. The substrate of bipolar and MOS integrated circuits is generally a single crystal of silicon that is lightly doped with either n- or p-type impurities. The substrate serves both as the physical medium upon and within which the IC is built and as part of the electrical circuit itself. These crystals are sliced from large right-circular cylinders of crystalline silicon, which are carefully grown to lengths up to 2 m and which vary in diameter from 1 to several inches. The slices are typically 250 μ to 400 μ thick. From an electrical viewpoint much thinner slices would be acceptable; however, the thicker slices have been adopted because they are more practical to handle (less breakage) and are less likely to warp during processing. The size of the wafers has been increasing rapidly with time to allow for both large chips and a larger number of chips per wafer. As of 1989, many of the older processing lines were using 4 inch wafers, but the newer lines are typically using 5 and 6 inch wafers. The crystals are often cut so that the surface is oriented approximately in the ‹100› direction.

MASKING. IC masks are high-contrast (black on clear) photographic positives or negatives. They are used to selectively prevent light from striking a photosensitized wafer during the photolithographic process. The masks are typically made of glass covered with a thin film of opaque metal, although less costly and less durable emulsion masks are sometimes used. The masks are produced from a digitized description of the desired mask geometries. There are several different methods of generating the masks (called pattern generation) from the digitized circuit description. One method involves photographically reducing large copies of the desired patterns that have been generated with a computer-controlled drafting machine. This method was used widely in the past but has largely been replaced by the next two. A second uses a laser beam as a pattern generator in a raster-scan mode. Both of these methods generally also require a high-resolution step and repeat and/or reduction camera to make the final masks that will be used. The intermediate image that is created is called a reticle and is usually 5 or 10 times real size. A third method uses an electron beam (E-beam) to generate the actual patterns directly onto the final masks. This method produces the best quality masks and is used extensively for very small geometries, but it requires considerable time and expensive equipment.

PHOTOLITHOGRAPHIC PROCESS. Photoresist is a viscous liquid. It is applied in a thin, uniform layer (about 1 μ thick by spinning the wafer) to the entire surface of a wafer following cleaning. After application the photoresist is hardened by baking. The physical characteristics of the photoresist can be changed by exposure to light. The photoresist thus acts as a film emulsion and can be exposed by light through the transparent areas of a mask (either by contact printing or projection), by a projection of light through a reticle containing the same information (called direct step on wafer), or by an electron beam (E-beam) that scans the desired regions. Following exposure, the resist is developed to selectively remove the resist from unwanted areas. This step is often followed by another baking to further harden the remaining photoresist.

Both positive and negative photoresists are available.. With negative photoresist the unexposed areas are removed during development, and with positive resist the exposed areas are removed. Negative resists are noted for being quite unaffected by etchants used in processing, but finer resolution can typically be obtained with positive resists. Photoresists serve as protective layers to many etchants and oxidizing agents, and as a barrier to ion implants.

Proper mask alignment is essential to maintain device operation, characteristics, and yield. Alignment markings are generally included with the circuit information when the masks are made so that these marks will appear on the wafer during and after processing. A machine called a mask aligner is used to align and expose the wafers. Figure 2.1-1 shows typical alignment characteristics. The physical size and geometry of the masks used for fabrication is governed by the particular technique used by the mask aligner to expose the wafer. Mask aligners that use contact printing have multiple copies of the individual circuits at actual size (i.e., 1×) accurately patterned on the mask. These aligners have a large throughput and are relatively inexpensive. The large masks, however, have a very short lifetime (typically 3 to 10 exposures) because of damage incurred when the mask contacts the photoresist for exposure. This increases effective mask costs. The direct step on wafer aligners typically use a 5× mask (often called a reticle) as a negative. It typically will contain only a single copy of the circuit, though several copies may be used for small ICs. The image is optically reduced to 1× upon exposure. The wafer must be repeatedly moved to the next location after each exposure until the entire wafer is exposed. The lifetime of the mask is very long since no physical contact is made, but the throughput has been decreased considerably to allow for the successive wafer movements. The

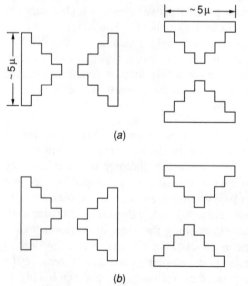

(a)

(b)

FIGURE 2.1-1
Alignment marks: (a) Mask marks, (b) Simulated positioning of alignment marks after fabrication.

equipment is also considerably more expensive because of the precision needed to maintain consistent and repeated uniform stepping of the wafer. Both types of aligners are widely used in industry.

One of the most practical and popular methods of exposure actually combines the mechanical economics of the 1× aligners and the mask life of the steppers. In this approach, a thin protective membrane, called a pelicle, is placed above the emulsion of 1× chrome masks for protection of the mask and long mask life. Although the membrane itself may get dirty or scratched, it is placed far enough away from the mask so as to remain out of focus and thus not project defects onto the wafer when columniated light is focused through the mask onto the wafer.

A fourth method of exposure actually uses no masks at all. Instead, a narrow electron beam (E-beam) is selectively focused on the wafer in a raster-scan manner in small regions, with wafer stepping to position successive portions of the wafer under the beam. The same digital database that is used to generate masks can be used to drive the E-beam system. This approach gives better resolution than any of the previously discussed methods but involves very expensive equipment and has a much smaller throughput. It is practical for only the most demanding applications.

DEPOSITION. Films of various materials must be applied to the wafer during processing for most existing semiconductor processes. Often these films are very thin (200 Å or less for some SiO_2 layers) but may be as thick as 20 μ for "thick film" circuits. Films that are deposited include insulators, resistive films, conductive films, dielectrics, n- and p-type semiconductor materials, and dopants that are subsequently forced deeper into the substrate. Deposition techniques include physical vapor deposition (evaporation and sputtering), chemical vapor deposition (CVD), and screen printing for the thick films. With the exception of the screen-printed films, the depositions are nonselective and are placed uniformly over the entire wafer.

Evaporation refers to evaporating the material that is to be deposited by controlling the temperature and pressure of the host material environment. A film is formed when the material condenses. A continuous evaporation–condensation process is established that allows for a controlled growth rate of the film.

Sputtering involves bombardment of the host material with high energy ions to dislodge molecules, which will reattach themselves to the surface of the wafer (as well as to other surfaces in the sputtering apparatus). Often two different host materials are simultaneously bombarded at different rates to establish the characteristics of the sputtered material. This dual host bombardment is termed cosputtering. With some materials, sputtering offers advantages over evaporation in host material integrity on the deposition surface.

Chemical vapor deposition (CVD) is achieved in two ways: (1) by causing a reaction of two gases near the substrate, a reaction occurs that creates solid molecules, which subsequently adhere to the substrate surface; or (2) by pyrolytic decomposition (a decomposition caused by heating) of a single gas, which also frees the desired molecules for reattachment.

ETCHING. Etching refers to selectively removing unwanted material from the surface of the substrate. Photoresist and masks are used to selectively pattern (expose) the surface of the substrate. Following this patterning, the physical characteristics of the surface are changed by etching. A single IC will generally undergo several different etches during processing. The chemicals used for etching are chosen to selectively react with unprotected areas on the wafer while not affecting the protected areas. A summary of the effects of some commonly used etchants on typical semiconductor materials is shown in Table 2.1-1.

There are two types of etches used in production: wet and dry. The *wet etches*, often called chemical etches, use liquid etching agents, which are applied to the substrate surface. Although they have received widespread application in the past, they etch horizontally as well as vertically into the surface of the substrate. This horizontal etching causes undercutting of the patterned areas. Unless the width of the nonetched regions is orders of magnitude greater than the thickness of the material being etched, the nonuniformity of the horizontal etching causes significant changes in desired device characteristics.

TABLE 2.1–1
Characteristics of commonly used fabrication materials

I. Materials used in IC fabrication		
Purpose	**Materials**	**Comments**
Silicon crystal substrates	$SiCl_4$	Silicon source for growth of single crystal silicon
	$SiHCl_4$	Silicon source for growth of single crystal silicon
	SiO_2 (Sand)	Silicon source for growth of single crystal silicon
Silicon layers (both single crystalline and polysilicon)	$SiCl_4$ and H_2	The hydrogen gas strips the Cl atoms to form solid silicon.
	SiH_4	Heat causes the release (pyrolysis) of H_2 gas.
	SiH_2Cl_2	Heat causes the release (pyrolysis) of HCl gas.
Oxides	O_2	Used to grow SiO_2 by thermal oxidation
	H_2O (Steam)	Used to grow SiO_2 by thermal oxidation
	SiH_4 and O_2	Used for CVD deposition of SiO_2 and to grow protective "glass" (SiO_2)
Nitride layers	Si_4 and NH_3	The ammonia causes the release of hydrogen gas and leaves Si_3N_4.
	$SiCl_4$ and NH_3	The ammonia causes the release of HCl and leaves Si_3N_4.
Etches, wet	HF	Hydrofluoric acid etches SiO_2 but not Si, Si_3N_4, or photoresist.
	HF and HNO_3	Etches Si

TABLE 2.1–1
(Continued)

Purpose	Materials	Comments
	H_3PO_4	Hot phosphoric acid etches Si_3N_4 but not SiO_2. Removes some types of photoresist.
Etches, dry	CHF_3	Etches SiO_2
	C_3F_8	Etches SiO_2
	SF_6	Etches silicon
	CF_4	Etches Si_3N_4
	CCl_4	Etches aluminum
Patterning	Photoresist	Used as barrier to ion implants. Also used to pattern SiO_2 since photoresist is not affected by HF, a common SiO_2 etchant.
	SiO_2	Acts as a barrier to some p- and n-type impurities
	Si_3N_4	Used as protective layer over silicon or SiO_2 to prevent thermal growth of SiO_2. Also serves as a barrier to low-energy ion implants although thin layers can be and are penetrated with higher-energy implants. Also serves as a diffusion barrier to impurities such as Ga, Al, Zn, and Na.

II. Sources of impurities

	Impurities	Source
n-type	Arsenic	As_2O_3, AsH_3
	Antimony	Sb_2O_3, Sb_2O_4
	Phosphorus	P_2O_5, $POCl_3$ (liquid), PH_3 (gas— implant or diffusion)
p-type	Gallium	
	Aluminum	
	Boron	BN (solid), BBr_3 (liquid), B_2O_3 (gas), BCl_3, (gas), B_2H_6 (gas), BF_3 (for implants)

III. Impurity migration in silicon

Impurity	Silicon	SiO_2
Arsenic†(n)	moderate	very slow
Antimony (n)	moderate	very slow
Phosphorus (n)	fast	slow
Gallium (p)	moderate	fast
Aluminum (p)	fast	fast
Boron (p)	fast	slow

†Arsenic is often preferred to the other n-type impurities because it gives more abrupt junction gradients, which yield better frequency response and improved current gain in bipolar transistors. Due to environmental concerns, however, the use of arsenic in the semiconductor industry is limited.

Dry etching, also termed ion etching, is directional and thus much less susceptible to the undesirable horizontal undercutting. Dry etching techniques include sputter etching, ion-beam etching, and plasma etching. Since no liquid chemicals are involved, a significant reduction of costs associated with disposal of spent chemicals is realized when dry etches are used. The etch rate for dry etches is generally lower than the wet etch rate. Dry etching is recognized as a practical alternative to wet etching and is widely used.

The characteristics of an ideal wet etch and an ideal directional etch are shown in Fig. 2.1-2. The nondirectional etch is termed an isotropic etch. The edge profile appears approximately circular, with radius r and center at point A. If the etch is stopped precisely when the underlying layer is exposed the radius r will be T, the thickness of the layer, and the undercut of the protective layer, X, will be also T. If the etch is not stopped precisely when the underlying layer is exposed, the radius will be T_1, which is greater than T, and both the effective opening and the undercut will thus be larger than desired.

An ideal directional etch is termed an anisotropic etch. Note that an anisotropic etch has a very abrupt edge, which causes problems for applying subsequent layers uniformly and reliably across this edge.

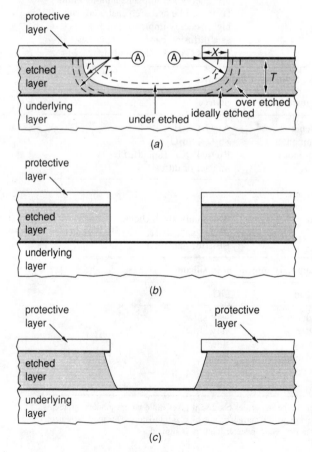

(a)

(b)

(c)

FIGURE 2.1-2
Characteristics of etches:
(*a*) Isotropic etch, (*b*) Anisotropic etch, (*c*) Preferential etch.

The term preferential etch characterizes an etch that prefers one direction but is less directional than an anisotropic etch. A preferential etch is depicted in Fig. 2.1-2c. The preferential etch may be preferable where subsequent layer coverage of an anisotropic etch is problematic.[1]

DIFFUSION. Diffusion, in the sense of an IC processing step, refers to the controlled forced migration of impurities into the substrate or adjacent material. The resultant impurity profile, which plays a major role in the performance of the integrated circuit, is affected by temperature and time as well as the temperature–time relationship during processing. Subsequent diffusions generally cause some additional migration of earlier diffusions. Actually, the diffusion process continues indefinitely, but at normal operating temperatures of the integrated circuit it takes tens of years or longer for the additional movement to become significant.

The method by which the impurities are introduced varies. A solid deposition layer or a gaseous layer above the surface can be used as the source of impurities. Impurities can also be accelerated to selectively bombard the substrate so that they actually become lodged inside the substrate very near the surface. This technique, termed *ion implantation*, offers very accurate control of impurity concentrations but causes significant crystal damage near the surface.

The purpose of a diffusion following deposition is to cause a migration of carriers into the substrate from either solid or gaseous surface layers. A diffusion step following ion implantation is used to mend or anneal bombardment–induced fractures in the single crystalline structure at the surface of the substrate as well as to cause additional impurity migration.

As in the etching process, the direction of impurity diffusion is difficult to control with accuracy. Impurities typically diffuse both vertically and laterally from the surface at comparable rates in a manner similar to that observed for the isotropic etch of Fig. 2.1-2a.

CONDUCTORS AND RESISTORS. Aluminum or other metals are often used as conductors for interconnection of components on an integrated circuit. These metals are typically deposited, patterned, and etched to leave interconnects where desired. The thickness of the popular aluminum films is typically about 6000–8000 Å but may be as much as 20,000 Å for linear (analog) single-level metal processes. Metal films are particularly useful for interconnects that must carry large currents, but traces must be wide enough to avoid the *metal migration*, or *electromigration* problem. Electromigration is the movement of atoms with current flow and can be likened to wind erosion of dirt. If significant metal migration occurs, the conductors become open, resulting in failure of an integrated circuit. Metal migration is insignificant provided the peak current density in the conductor is below a certain threshold. For aluminum, this threshold is around 1 mA/μ^2. This threshold is material dependent and ranges from 0.05 mA/μ^2 to 2 mA/μ^2 for other similar materials.

Nonmetallic films are widely used for conductors and interconnects when current flow is small. These materials are typically worse conductors than metals and thus cause a significant voltage drop when currents are large. These materials find limited applications as resistors.

Polysilicon is one of the most popular nonmetallic conductors. Polysilicon differs from single crystalline silicon, which is often used as a substrate material, only in that polysilicon is composed of a large number of nonaligned, randomly oriented, small silicon crystals. Although polysilicon is chemically identical to single crystal silicon, its electrical characteristics are much different. Polysilicon is a good conductor when heavily doped and a good resistor when lightly doped. Polysilicon is often used for gates of field effect transistors (MOSFETs) and as an electrode for capacitors. Polysilicon can be deposited over SiO_2. SiO_2 can also be readily grown on polysilicon and is often used to serve as a dielectric and isolate two polysilicon layers in processes where double polysilicon (*double poly*) layers are available. Polysilicon's characteristics are dependent on the size of the small crystals, often termed the grain size. It can be deposited on a variety of materials and the growth rate can be fairly fast. Polysilicon films are typically about 2000 Å thick and are often termed *poly*.

Silicides and/or refractory metals are often used on top of or in place of polysilicon for fabricating conductors. These materials are often much better conductors than polysilicon.

OXIDATION. Oxidation is the process whereby oxygen molecules from a gas above the substrate or surface material cause the growth of an oxide on the surface. Since the substrate or surface material is typically silicon, the oxidation process produces silicon dioxide. The speed at which the SiO_2 layer grows is a function of the doping concentration and the temperature of the substrate during oxidation. The SiO_2 layer serves as a very good insulator between the substrate or surface material and whatever is placed upon it. When the SiO_2 layer is grown on the substrate, a small amount of the Si in the substrate is consumed to provide for the Si molecules in the oxide. The growth of x microns of SiO_2 consumes approximately $0.47x$ microns of single crystal silicon.

As an alternative to oxidation, the SiO_2 layer can be applied by CVD. This technique is used extensively when the SiO_2 layer must cover something other than Si since no silicon molecules are available for oxidation. CVD can also be done at lower temperatures, which is advantageous if additional diffusion of previously deposited materials must be minimized. SiO_2 layers formed by oxidation are generally more uniform than those formed by a CVD process.

Other types of oxides are also used as insulating layers in fabricating ICs. Doped deposited oxides such as phosphosilicate glass (PSG) are often used as insulators on top of polysilicon. Some of these are doped to improve reflow characteristics during annealing. This doping helps reduce sharp boundaries (improve step coverage) introduced during etching of polysilicon.

Nitride (Si_3N_4) is also used as a dielectric between two levels of polysilicon in some processes. The dielectric constant of Si_3N_4 is about four times that of SiO_2. This offers potential for much higher capacitance densities for fixed dielectric thicknesses or much thinner dielectrics for a fixed capacitance density. A thin layer of SiO_2 is generally applied to the Si prior to the Si_3N_4 to minimize the mechanical stress associated with a direct Si interface to Si_3N_4. This stress is caused by a difference in the lattice characteristics of single-crystal silicon and the Si_3N_4 layer.

Although somewhat different chemically, polyimides are also used as insulating layers, most notably between two metal layers. Polyimides tend to smooth abrupt underlying irregularities, thus reducing the effects of sharp boundaries of underlying metal layers.[2]

EPITAXY. Epitaxial growth is generally a CVD. It warrants singling out, however, because of the extensive use of this process step in bipolar integrated circuitry and because epitaxial layers are ideally single crystalline extensions of the substrate. Epitaxial layers are grown slowly enough that the molecules added to the surface can align with the underlying crystalline structure of the substrate to form a crystalline epitaxial layer. A small amount of n- or p-type impurities is generally intentionally introduced into the epitaxial layer during the epitaxial growth to obtain a doped epitaxial layer.

Several excellent textbooks provide considerably more detail about semiconductor processing; the interested reader may consult References 3–6.

2.1.2 Packaging and Testing

After processing, the integrated circuits are tested and packaged. The first step in the testing process generally involves a process verification to make certain that the process parameters are within the tolerances acceptable for the product. To facilitate this verification, *test plugs* containing special test structures specially designed for this purpose are included on the wafer at several locations in place of the regular circuits themselves. Alternatively, to avoid sacrificing the potential production die sites that are devoted to test plugs, there is a growing trend to integrate the test patterns into the *scribe lines*, which are existing grid lines void of circuitry where cuts will be made to separate the dies. A wafer prober is used to make mechanical contact with the test plugs so that electrical measurements can be made. Assuming the process parameters are within tolerance, the individual dies are automatically probed and electrically tested. Defective dies are marked with ink and later discarded. After probing, the wafer is scribed (typically with a wafer saw) both horizontally and vertically between adjacent dies, and the dies are separated. Following separation the individual dies are *die attached*, or *die bonded*, to a carrier or to the IC package itself. Wire bonds are subsequently made from the pins of the package to the appropriate locations on the die. The bonding wires are typically of either gold or aluminum. The diameter of this wire is in the range of 1 mil. After the wire bonds are complete, the packages are formed or closed and a final electrical test (and burn in for some parts) is completed.

Packaging technology saw minimal advancements through the late 1970s and early 1980s. It is well recognized that existing packaging techniques are a major bottleneck in the evolution of IC technology. Considerable effort on a worldwide basis is focused on the packaging problem. Practical alternatives to the conventional packaging approach, described above, will likely evolve in the next few years.

2.2 SEMICONDUCTOR PROCESSES

There are currently three basic processes used for the fabrication of monolithic integrated circuits containing active devices. These are the NMOS, CMOS, and bipolar processes. The first two are both termed MOS (Metal Oxide Semiconductor) processes even though, as will be discussed later, the standard acronym is no longer completely descriptive. A fourth approach essentially combines bipolar and MOS technologies into a single but more involved process. The mixed bipolar–MOS process is called Bi–MOS. A fifth method for constructing ICs is termed the hybrid process. These processes are depicted in Fig. 1.2-1.

Generic processes similar to those used in industry will be discussed in this section. The generic NMOS and CMOS processes discussed are very similar to those available through MOSIS† and the same terminology and conventions that have been established by MOSIS will be followed when practical. Several excellent references provide additional information about the NMOS and CMOS processes available through MOSIS and about MOS processing in general.[1, 2, 7-11.] Additional information about these generic processes, such as design rules and process parameters, are discussed in Section 2.3. Details about a typical Bi–MOS process are not presented, but the basic approach should be apparent after studying the basic MOS and bipolar processes.

The NMOS (n-channel MOS) and CMOS (Complementary Metal Oxide Semiconductor) processes are quite similar in that both have the field effect transistor (FET or MOSFET) as the basic active device. In the NMOS process n-channel MOSFETs are available as the active devices whereas in the CMOS process both n-channel and p-channel devices are available. When compared to the NMOS, the CMOS process offers advantages in design simplicity at the expense of more processing steps. It is often the case that CMOS also offers improvements in power dissipation and performance and in some cases even size over NMOS. These tradeoffs must be considered when selecting the most economical process for a given application. Another MOS process, PMOS, is available but will not be singled out because it is essentially a dual of the NMOS process. In the PMOS process the basic active device is the p-channel MOSFET. Although the PMOS process was commonly used for some of the earlier MOS circuits, the NMOS process offers some advantages due to characteristics of

---

†The MOSIS (MOS Implementation System) program is sponsored by the U.S. Department of Defense Advanced Research Projects Agency (DARPA). Academic participation in this program has been supported by NSF since 1981. Authorized participants undertake designs in one of several MOS processes supported by the program and submit these designs to MOSIS for fabrication. Designs from a large number of different institutions are combined on a multiproject chip format to significantly reduce the fabrication costs below what would be experienced if designs were independently fabricated. MOSIS assumes responsibility for both mask generation and processing. Eight to ten weeks after the published closing date for a specific processing lot, the designer is scheduled to receive packaged parts and occasionally some unpackaged dies. Technical information about these parts is also included. Additional information about the MOSIS program can be obtained from USC Information Sciences Institute, 4676 Admiralty Way, Marina Del Rey, CA 90292-6695, (213) 822-1511.

semiconductor materials available (specifically, electron mobility is higher than hole mobility) and is more popular today.

The bipolar process is so named because the basic active device is the Bipolar Junction Transistor (BJT). Higher speeds are currently available with the bipolar process than for the NMOS and CMOS processes although significant improvements in the speed of the latter processes have been and continue to be made. Bipolar integrated circuits are noted for their considerable internal power dissipation compared to that of the NMOS and CMOS processes. For logic circuits the NMOS and CMOS circuits have a significantly higher component density than their bipolar counterparts.

The hybrid process combines thin and/or thick film passive components that are on one or more separate substrates with active devices from a separate substrate onto a common carrier. This makes hybrid ICs quite expensive. For applications that require precise and temperature-stable passive components, the hybrid process often offers a practical solution.

MATERIAL CHARACTERIZATION. Some terminology that is common to most semiconductor processes is best introduced at this point. Throughout this text the notation n^+ will denote a heavily doped n-type semiconductor region, and n^- will denote a lightly doped region. The designation n^+ or n^- will be assumed relative to the context in which this designation is made. No superscript will be included if the region is doped somewhere between n^+ and n^- or if it is not necessary to make the distinction in the given context. The same convention will be followed for p, p^+, and p^- designations.

The *resistivity* of a homogeneous material is a volumetric measure of resistive characteristics of the material. The resistivity is typically specified in terms of ohms-cm (Ω-cm). If a right rectangular solid of material of length L and cross sectional area A (see Fig. 2.2-1a) has a measured resistance of R between the two ends, then the resistivity of the material is given by

$$\rho = \frac{AR}{L} \tag{2.2-1}$$

where it is assumed that the contacts on the two ends cover the entire surface and are perfectly conducting.

The *sheet resistance* is a measure of the characteristics of a large, uniform sheet or film of material that is arbitrarily thin. The sheet resistance is specified in terms of *ohms per square* of surface area. If a rectangular sheet of material of length L and width W (see Fig. 2.2-1b) has a measured resistance R between the two opposite ends, then the sheet resistance of the material is given by

$$R_\square = R\frac{W}{L} \tag{2.2-2}$$

where it is assumed that the contacts on the two edges cover the entire edge and are perfectly conducting. It should be emphasized that both the resistivity and sheet resistance are characteristics of materials independent of particular values for A, L, W, and R in the previous equations.

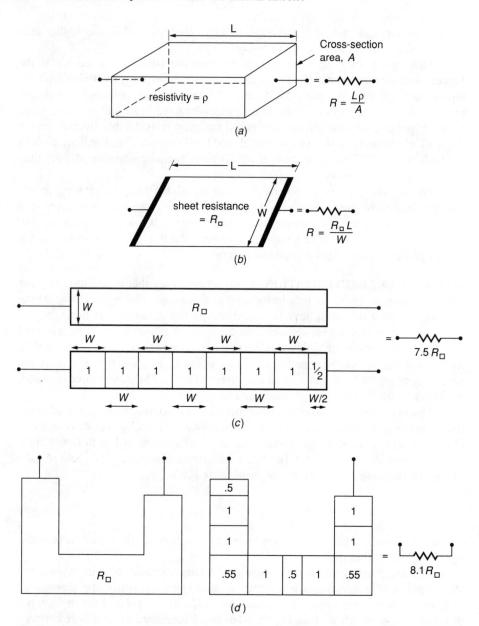

FIGURE 2.2-1
Resistive characteristics of bulk and sheet materials: (*a*) Resistivity, (*b*) Sheet resistance, (*c*)&(*d*) Graphical calculations from sheet resistance.

Example 2.2-1. Determine the length of a 100 kΩ rectangular resistor that is 25 μ wide and is to be constructed from a thin sheet of material with a sheet resistance of $R_\square = 100\Omega/\square$.

Solution. From Eq. 2.2-2,

$$L = \frac{WR}{R_\square} = (25\ \mu)\left(\frac{100\ \text{k}\Omega}{100\ \Omega}\right) = 2.5\ \text{cm}$$

Note the excessive length of the 100 kΩ resistor!

The sheet resistance of a thin layer of thickness z constructed from a material that has a resistivity ρ is given by

$$R_\square = \frac{\rho}{z} \qquad (2.2\text{-}3)$$

The resistance of thin rectangular regions of length L and width W on an integrated circuit can be readily obtained from the sheet resistance by counting the number of square blocks of length W that can be placed in the rectangular region. If N blocks can be placed adjacently in the region, then the resistance in terms of the sheet resistance, $R_\square$, is given by

$$R = NR_\square \qquad (2.2\text{-}4)$$

An example illustrating this technique is depicted in Fig. 2.2-1c.

Occasionally it is necessary to determine the resistance of nonrectangular regions such as that shown in Fig. 2.2-1d or the serpentined pattern of Problem 2.11. The problem of determining resistance of irregular regions is difficult, but for rectangular regions containing the right angles shown, the rule of thumb of adding 0.55 squares for each corner is often used.

Example 2.2-2. If $R_\square = 45\Omega/\square$, determine the value of the U-shaped resistor of Fig. 2.2-1d.

Solution. The U-shaped resistor is broken into squares of length W in the same figure. Counting squares and assigning 0.55 squares to each corner, we obtain a resistor of value 8.1 $R_\square = 364.5\ \Omega$.

It is often necessary to specify the temperature characteristics of resistors and capacitors. The Temperature Coefficient of Resistance (TCR) and Temperature Coefficient of Capacitance (TCC) are typically used for this purpose. These temperature coefficients, which are generally expressed in terms of ppm/°C, are defined by

$$\text{TC} = \left(\frac{1}{x}\right)\left(\frac{dx}{dT}\right)10^6\text{ppm/°C} \qquad (2.2\text{-}5)$$

where x is the temperature-dependent value of either the resistor or the capacitor.

If the temperature coefficient is independent of temperature, then the value of the component at a temperature T_2 can be obtained from its value at temperature T_1 by the expression

$$x(T_2) = x(T_1)e^{[\text{TC}(T_2-T_1)/10^6]} \qquad (2.2\text{-}6)$$

which is often closely approximated by

$$x(T_2) \simeq x(T_1)[1 + (T_2 - T_1)(\text{TC}/10^6)] \qquad (2.2\text{-}7)$$

If the TC is a function of temperature, then the previous expressions are good only in local neighborhoods of T_1. The value of TC, which can be either positive or negative, is determined by the material properties and is often quite small. The absolute values of TC are often less than 1000 ppm/°C. Unfortunately, since integrated circuits are often expected to operate over a relatively wide temperature range (0–70°C commercial or −55 to 125°C military) the effects of the TC can be significant.

> **Example 2.2-3.** Determine the percentage error introduced in calculating $x(T_2)$ from $x(T_1)$ by using the simpler linear equation (2.2-7) compared to (2.2-6) if $T_1 = 30°C$, $T_2 = 60°C$, and the temperature coefficient is constant and given by TC $= 1000$ ppm/°C.
>
> **Solution.** Using the exact expression we obtain
>
> $$x(60) = x(30)e^{(.03)} = x(30)(1.0304545)$$
>
> Using the approximate expression we obtain
>
> $$x(60) = x(30)[1 + (30)(.001)] = x(30)(1.030000)$$
>
> Thus, the error is about 0.044%.

Some resistors and capacitors, in addition to being temperature dependent, are also somewhat voltage dependent. This voltage dependence introduces non-linearities in circuits using these devices along with the corresponding harmonic distortion (THD) in many applications. The voltage dependence of resistors and capacitors is characterized by the voltage coefficient, defined by

$$\text{VC} = \left(\frac{1}{x}\right)\left(\frac{dx}{dV}\right)10^6 \text{ppm/V} \qquad (2.2\text{-}8)$$

where x is the voltage-dependent value of a resistor or capacitor. The voltage coefficient is analogous to the temperature coefficient, as can be seen by comparing Eqs. 2.2-5 and 2.2-8.

2.2.1 MOS Processes

A brief qualitative discussion of the principle of operation of the MOS transistor at dc and low frequency is now presented to provide insight into the MOS process itself. A detailed quantitative presentation about modeling these devices appears in Chapter 3.

OPERATION OF THE MOSFET. Consider the n-channel enhancement MOSFET shown in Fig. 2.2-2. In the cross-sectional views it can be seen that the gate (Metal

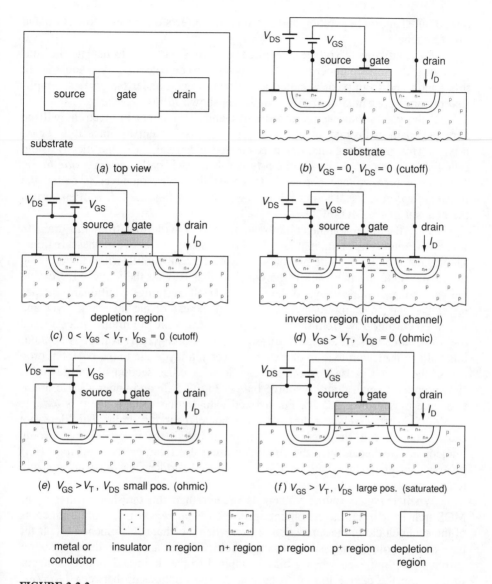

FIGURE 2.2-2
Operation of n-channel MOSFET (horizontal and vertical scale factors are different).

or conductor) is over the insulator (Oxide), which is in turn over the substrate (Semiconductor). The source of the acronym MOSFET should be apparent. If the substrate is tied to the source as shown in Fig. 2.2-2b, then with a zero gate–source voltage the n-type drain and source regions are isolated from each other by the p-type substrate, preventing any current flow from drain to source. A depletion region also forms between the n^+ drain and source regions and the lightly doped substrate, as depicted in Fig. 2.2-2b-f. The corresponding pn junction is reverse biased under normal operation and has minimal effects on current flow at dc and low frequencies.

If a positive gate voltage is applied, electrons will start to deplete the substrate near the surface under the gate. This tends to deplete the p-type substrate in this region and form what is called a depletion region under the gate. A simplified pictorial presentation of this situation is shown in Fig. 2.2-2c.

If the gate voltage is increased sufficiently, a number of electrons will be attracted to the substrate surface under the gate sufficient to make this region n-type. This n-type region, which is created electrically (by the electric field established by the gate bias) in the p-type substrate, is called an *inversion layer*. The gate–source voltage necessary to create the inversion layer is called the *threshold voltage*, V_T. The inversion layer, shown in Fig. 2.2-2d, is often termed the *channel* of the MOSFET.

Once the inversion layer is created, current will flow from the drain to source or source to drain if a small voltage is applied between these regions. The insulator under the gate prevents any gate current from flowing, thus forcing the current entering the drain to be equal to that leaving the source. Increasing the gate–source voltage beyond the threshold voltage brings additional electrons under the gate, causing an increase in the thickness of the inversion layer and increased current flow from the drain to source (or source to drain) under a fixed drain-to-source bias. If a large drain–source (or source–drain) voltage is applied, this voltage itself will tend to deplete the inversion layer due to the potential drop across the region caused by the current flow. A cross section of the device is shown under a small drain-to-source bias in Fig. 2.2-2e and under a large drain-to-source bias in Fig. 2.2-2f. For a fixed gate–source voltage, there is a value of V_{DS} that effectively pinches off the channel near the drain. This does not cause a decrease in drain current (I_D), for if it did, the inversion layer would immediately reappear since the channel current itself causes the pinching of the inversion layer. If the value of V_{DS} is increased further, the drain current will remain nearly constant.

When the gate–source voltage is greater than the threshold voltage, the MOS transistor is said to be operating in the *ohmic region* prior to the pinching of the channel and in the *saturation region* when the channel is pinched off. If the gate–source voltage is less than the threshold voltage, almost no drain or source current will flow even when a bias is applied to the drain and source contacts. In this case the device is said to be *cutoff*. The relationship between I_D, V_{DS}, and V_{GS} for a typical MOSFET, termed the output characteristics, is shown in Fig. 2.2-3, along with the ohmic and saturation regions of operation. The cutoff region is the $I_D = 0$ line in this figure. The gate current remains at $I_G = 0$ in all three regions of operation.

The value of the threshold voltage is determined by the concentration of the p-type impurities in the substrate. If some n-type impurities are added to the region under the gate near the surface of the substrate, the threshold voltage will decrease. If sufficient impurities are added, the region itself will become n-type and the threshold voltage will become negative. An n-channel device with

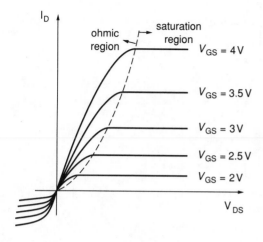

FIGURE 2.2-3
Typical output characteristics for an n-channel MOSFET.

a positive threshold voltage is termed an *enhancement MOSFET* and those with a negative threshold voltage are termed *depletion MOSFETs*. MOS devices formed in a p-substrate (or tub) and thus having n-type drain and source diffusions and an n-type channel are termed *n-channel transistors*. Those formed in an n-type substrate (or tub) with p-type drain and source diffusions and a p-type channel are termed *p-channel transistors*. In contrast to the convention introduced above for n-channel transistors, p-channel transistors with a negative threshold voltage are termed enhancement devices and those with a positive threshold voltage are termed depletion devices.

Commonly used symbols for enhancement and depletion n- and p-channel devices are shown in Fig. 2.2-4. Since the polarity of the substrate is often known for either the NMOS or PMOS processes, the simplified notation shown in Fig. 2.2-4, which does not maintain this information in the device symbol, has been widely adopted for both NMOS and PMOS devices.

2.2.1*a* NMOS Process

Although both NMOS and PMOS processes are currently available, the NMOS process has been used more extensively in recent years. The NMOS process is preferred because the characteristics of the n-channel MOSFET are preferable to those of the p-channel MOSFET. This is attributable to a higher mobility for electrons than for holes. The discussion that follows will be based upon the NMOS process. Modifications of this presentation to describe the PMOS process are straightforward and are thus left to the reader.

A discussion of a generic double-polysilicon, self-aligned silicon gate NMOS enhancement/depletion process follows. This can be considered as a typical standard process although processes that offer more as well as less flexibility are also standard. This process is similar to a widely used MOSIS NMOS process augmented by a second polysilicon layer. The same basic approach used

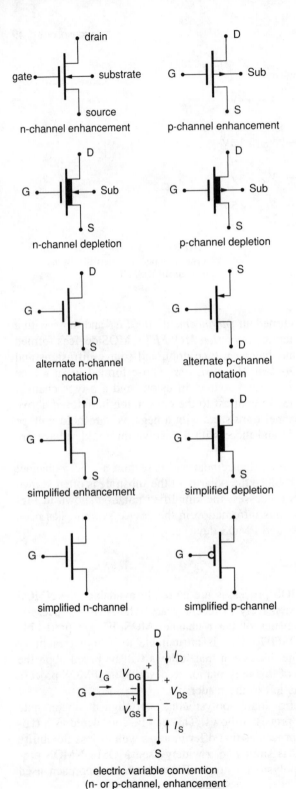

n-channel enhancement

p-channel enhancement

n-channel depletion

p-channel depletion

alternate n-channel
notation

alternate p-channel
notation

simplified enhancement

simplified depletion

simplified n-channel

simplified p-channel

electric variable convention
(n- or p-channel, enhancement
or depletion)

FIGURE 2.2-4
Symbols for MOS transistors.

here is used for other NMOS processes. The MOS transistors in this process are similar to those depicted in Fig. 2.2-2, with the exception that polysilicon (a good conductor) is used instead of metal for the gate. Field effect transistors with polysilicon gates are also called MOS transistors or MOSFETs even though the acronym MOS is no longer completely descriptive.

The devices that are available in this process are

1. n–channel enhancement MOSFETs.
2. n–channel depletion MOSFETs.
3. Capacitors.
4. Resistors.

The method of physically constructing each of these components in this process and interconnecting them to form the simple circuit shown in Fig. 2.2-5 will now be addressed. Both top views and cross-sectional views are presented in Fig. 2A.1 of Appendix 2A. Cross sections are along sections AA' and BB' of Fig. 2A.1a. A summary of the major process steps appears in Table 2A.1 of Appendix 2A. Additional information about this process relating to layout sizing rules, physical feature sizes, and electrical characterization parameters of the generic NMOS process can be found in Tables 2A.2–2A.5 of Appendix 2A. (Table 2A.3 appears in Plate 5 in the color plate insert.) The circuit designer must present the top view of each mask level for fabrication but must have a firm understanding of the cross-sectional view for effective design.

For the NMOS process, the starting point is a polished p-type silicon disc. The thickness of the disc is typically around 500 μ. A layer of SiO_2 in the neighborhood of 1000 Å thick is first added to the entire wafer using the oxidation process. On top of this a layer of Si_3N_4 (about 1500 Å thick) is applied by the

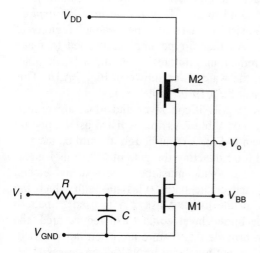

FIGURE 2.2-5
A simple NMOS circuit.

CVD process. Following the application of a layer of photoresist, Mask #1 is used to pattern the surface. Mask #1, which is often called the *moat*, or n^+ *diffusion* mask, defines in photoresist the drain, source, and channel regions of all transistors as well as any other regions where n^+ implants are desired. After exposure, development removes the photoresist layer in areas that are not to be moat (i.e., the *complement of the moat*, or the *antimoat*). A top (Mask #1 pattern) and cross-sectional view at this stage of what will be the two transistors appear in Fig. 2A.1*a*. The Si_3N_4 is then etched from the areas not protected by the photoresist. A high-energy implant of p-type impurities (typically boron) is then applied to the entire wafer. The remaining photoresist protects the moat regions from this implant. This heavy implant is used to raise the threshold voltage in the antimoat region (often called the *field*) and to provide electrical isolation between adjacent devices. After this field implant and a drive in diffusion, the remaining photoresist is stripped. A thick layer of SiO_2 (about 10,000 Å) is then thermally grown by the oxidation process over the wafer. This layer is formed in the field, but no oxidation can take place in the region protected by the Si_3N_4 because Si_3N_4 does not oxidize. The thick field oxide layer is termed a local oxidation layer and is often called *LOCOS*. The oxidation consumes some of the substrate silicon. The second cross section in Fig. 2A.1*a* shows the state of the wafer following growth of the field oxide. This corresponds to Step 10 in the process scenario of Table 2A.1. Following removal of the Si_3N_4, the thin layer of SiO_2 under the Si_3N_4 is stripped and another SiO_2 layer is grown.

With the moat now protected only by the very thin SiO_2 layer, a light n-type implant over the entire wafer can be applied (optional) to set the threshold voltage of the enhancement devices. This implant is light enough so that all p-type regions remain p-type. If used, the implant is applied to the entire wafer to avoid the need for an additional mask.

A heavier selective implant is required in regions that are to serve as the channels of depletion transistors. To achieve this, a second layer of photoresist is applied to the entire wafer, and the second mask, Mask #2 (termed the *implant* mask), is used to pattern the photoresist so that only the channel regions of depletion transistors are unprotected. Another n-type implant is used to make the exposed regions n-type with the remaining photoresist serving as an implant mask. After stripping the photoresist, the wafer is as shown in Fig. 2A.1*b*. This corresponds to the status of the wafer at Step 19 in Table 2A.1.

Direct contacts between the lower polysilicon layer and moat are termed buried contacts. In the process scenario of Table 2A.1 this is listed as an optional step and is not used in the layout shown in Fig. 2A.1 although it could be used, if available, to reduce the area required for contacting the gate of M2 to its source. To make a buried contact, the thin gate oxide must be patterned and etched to remove the insulating SiO_2 layer and create paths (vias) through which the following polysilicon layer can contact the moat. Mask #A is used to pattern the buried contact vias. Although the buried layer contact can reduce area, the additional processing costs needed to provide this feature are often not justified; hence the buried contact feature is often not available in NMOS processes.

After stripping of any thin oxides that may be present at this stage in the moat region, a uniform thin layer of SiO_2, often termed *gate oxide* (200 to 1000 Å thick), is grown on the surface of the wafer. Stripping and regrowing provide better control of the critical gate oxide thickness. A layer of polysilicon (termed POLY I), which is about 2000 Å thick, is then deposited on the surface of the entire wafer. This is covered with photoresist, patterned with Mask #3, and etched to remove unwanted POLY I. The POLY I layer is used as gates for both enhancement and depletion transistors, as a plate for capacitors, as a conductor, and for resistors. The formation of a capacitor, a resistor, and enhancement and depletion transistors can be seen in Fig. 2A.1*c*. This corresponds to Step 27 in the process scenario of Table 2A.1. Note that the POLY I layer is over gate oxide in cross section AA' and above field oxide in cross section BB'.

The remaining uncovered thin layers of SiO_2 are stripped and another thin layer (500–1000 Å) of SiO_2 is again grown over the entire surface. This serves as the dielectric for POLY I–POLY II capacitors, as an insulator for POLY I–POLY II crossovers, and as the gate oxide for transistors that use the POLY II layer as the gate. The thickness of this oxide layer is often ideally the same as that of the first gate oxide layer. By stripping the unexposed oxide and regrowing, a buildup in the depth of the oxide layers is prevented and more uniformity is attained. A second layer of polysilicon (termed POLY II) is then deposited, followed by photoresist and patterning with Mask #B. In the circuit shown in Fig. 2.2-5, the POLY II layer is used only for the upper plate of the capacitor, as shown in Fig. 2A.1*d* (Step B.9 of Table 2A.1). Note that it is slightly smaller than the underlying POLY I layer. This difference is standard practice when trying to accurately match capacitors to make one plate a little smaller than the other so that the smaller plate will effectively define the capacitor area independent of slight misalignments of the two plates. Additional practical considerations that further improve matching will be discussed later.

After stripping the thin SiO_2 layers, an n^+ diffusion is applied to the entire wafer. The field oxide and polysilicon layers serve as masks to the diffusion and prevent impurities from reaching the substrate in the protected areas. The n^+ diffusion creates the n-type drain and source regions of all transistors and makes any other unprotected moat areas n-type. The portion of the light depletion diffusion that is not protected by the polysilicon gates also becomes more heavily doped. Note that although no mask is used at this step, the n^+ diffusion mask, which was used as the first masking step, has essentially determined the n^+ diffusion regions fabricated at this step. The n^+ diffusion also penetrates into any exposed polysilicon layers, increasing the conductivity in these regions. The n^+ diffusion depth is about 5000 Å. It will be seen in the section discussing process parameters that the sheet resistance for POLY I and POLY II layers is about the same but that the sheet resistance of POLY I under POLY II is higher. This is due to the absence of the additional n^+ diffusion in the lower layer. Since the polysilicon gates serve as masks for the n^+ drain and source diffusions, the process is said to be *self-aligned*. In a self-aligned process, small misalignments of the gate (POLY I or POLY II) masks will not affect the gate geometry or dimensions, nor will they make the transistors nonfunctional.

Next, another insulating layer is deposited over the wafer surface. Doped deposited oxide, such as PSG, is often used for this purpose. This rather thick layer, $\sim$ 6000 Å, serves as an insulator between the uppermost polysilicon layer and the subsequent metal layer. The field oxide depth is further increased with this deposited oxide layer. The entire wafer is again covered with photoresist, and Mask #4 (actually the fifth or sixth mask if POLY II and/or buried contact options are available) is used to pattern *contact openings* for the purpose of obtaining electrical contact from the top with the desired components. After the photoresist is developed, an etch that attacks the insulating layer but does not affect polysilicon or silicon makes the required openings. This etch is stopped in the vertical direction only by polysilicon or the single-crystal silicon of the substrate. The wafer takes the form shown in Fig. 2A.1e (Step 34 of Table 2A.1).

Metal (typically aluminum) is then deposited over the entire wafer, followed by another layer of photoresist. This metal layer is typically about 7000 Å thick. This photoresist is patterned by Mask #5, followed by an etch to remove unwanted metal. The metalization is used to interconnect components and provide external access to the integrated circuit. A metalization that interconnects the four basic components to form the circuit shown in Fig. 2.2-5 is shown in Fig. 2A.1f (Step 40 of Table 2A.1).

Large, square metal areas, called *bonding pads*, are needed to allow for contact with the IC package. Small bonding wires will later be connected from these pads to the pins on the IC package. These pads are also patterned with the metalization mask but are not shown in Fig. 2A.1f because of the large amount of area required for bonding pads relative to that needed for the components in Fig. 2.2-5.

A bonding pad is shown in Fig. 2A.1g. Four of these would be needed to interface the circuit of Fig. 2.2-5 with the IC package. The V_{BB} contact comes from the bottom side of the substrate. The bonding pad size has remained relatively constant for a long period of time even though considerable reductions in feature size of geometries on the die itself have been experienced. This is because the methods of physically mounting the die in packages and interconnecting the bonding pads to the pins in the package have not changed much. With bonding wires typically about 1 mil in diameter, it is difficult to reduce bonding pad size significantly.

The entire surface is finally covered with a passivation layer (often called glass or p-glass) to provide long-term stability of the IC by minimizing atmospheric contamination. A layer about 10,000 Å thick is often used for passivation. Since this layer is also an electrical insulator, it is necessary to again pattern it and make openings above the metal pads to allow for attaching the bonding wires. The final mask, Mask #6, is used for this purpose and is shown in Fig. 2A.1g.

For the simple circuit of Fig. 2.2-5, the area required for the bonding pads dominates that needed for the circuit itself. For simple circuits this is generally the case but as the complexity of the circuit increases, the percentage of the total area required for bonding pads becomes quite small.

Giving the information for each mask separately, as was done in Fig. 2A.1, makes it difficult to perceive the entire circuit and determine layer to layer alignment. Sophisticated software packages termed layout editors are widely used, in which layers are color-coded and displayed simultaneously on high-resolution monitors. A single layout that simultaneously shows all mask information is shown in color in Plate 2. A color convention has been established for distinguishing separate layers. The color convention adopted in Plate 2 corresponds to that used in the MOSIS process and is discussed in more detail later in this chapter.

An interesting observation can be made from the layout of the MOS transistors of Fig. 2A.1. The MOS devices are totally geometrically symmetric with respect to drain and source and so must also be electrically symmetric. The designation of *drain* and *source* is thus arbitrary. In many applications a convention has evolved for convenience and consistency in device modeling in regard to drain and source designation. This convention will be discussed in Chapter 3. When appropriate, we will follow the established convention throughout this text.

In the process described, several alternative methods for constructing resistors and capacitors are available. For example, a region of moat with two contacts can be used as a resistor, and a capacitor can be made between POLY I and metal.

Processing step modifications such as omission of one polysilicon layer, omission of the depletion mask, substitution of metal gates for the polysilicon gates, and addition of another mask and implant to create enhancement transistors with two different threshold voltages are possible and common. Process procedure modifications such as using diffusions instead of implants; changing types of impurities; varying the thickness of oxide, polysilicon, or metal layers; including or excluding oxide stripping and regrowing steps; and changing types of photoresist are widespread and play major roles in yield, fabrication costs, and performance. The IC design engineer must be familiar with the process steps that will be used in fabrication when embarking on a new design.

For the process just described, it is the responsibility of the circuit designer to provide all information necessary to construct the seven masks shown in Fig. 2A.1. The size, shape, and spacing of the components are judiciously determined. The size and shape affect the performance of the circuit and are at the control of the circuit designer for optimizing performance, within constraints of minimum allowable size as determined by the capabilities of the process and maximum size as determined by economics. The spacing is also constrained by the capabilities of the process itself. The spacing and sizing specifications are obtainable from the design rules of the process, which are discussed later in this chapter. A process engineer will typically be responsible for providing design rules for a particular process.

2.2.1*b* CMOS Process

A discussion of a typical generic single-polysilicon silicon gate, p-well, n-substrate CMOS process follows. As in the NMOS case, variants in this process — such as a second metal layer, a second polysilicon layer, additional implants, oppositely doped substrate, or metal gates — are also well established. The devices available in the CMOS process under consideration are

1. n-channel MOSFETs.
2. p-channel MOSFETs.
3. Capacitors.
4. Resistors.
5. Diodes.
6. npn bipolar transistors.
7. pnp bipolar transistors.

The diodes and bipolar transistors are often considered parasitic components and are generally not extensively used as components in the circuit design itself. The process is tailored to maintain optimal characteristics in the n- and p-channel MOSFETs at the expense of poor characteristics for the bipolar transistors.

A method of physically constructing each of the first four components in the list will be considered. The approach followed here is similar to that followed for the NMOS process except that all mask details are included on the single layout of Fig. 2B.1 of Appendix 2B. A color version of this figure appears in Plate 3. Fewer details about oxide growth, photoresist application and patterning, and so on are provided since these steps are very similar to the corresponding steps for the NMOS process. Cross-sectional views along AA' and BB' in Fig. 2B.1a after each major step are shown in Fig. 2B.1. Interconnections follow the approach used in Section 2.2-1a for the NMOS process and are not discussed here. A summary of the major process steps appears in Table 2B.1. Additional information about this process relating to layout sizing rules, physical feature sizes, and electrical characterization parameters of the generic CMOS process can be found in Tables 2B.2–2B.5 of Appendix 2B. The process described here is very similar to the 3 μ CMOS/bulk process available through MOSIS.[7]

The starting point of this CMOS process is a polished n-type silicon disc. A layer of SiO_2 is first grown on the entire disc, followed by the application of a layer of photoresist. This photoresist is patterned with Mask #1 to provide openings for a p-tub (alternatively, p–well), which will serve as the substrate for the n-channel MOS devices. Either a deposition or implant is used to introduce the p-type impurities that form the tub. This diffusion is quite deep (about 30,000 Å). The remaining photoresist and SiO_2 are then stripped, a thin layer of SiO_2 regrown, and the entire surface covered with a layer of Si_3N_4.

Mask #2, termed the *moat mask* or the *active mask* by MOSIS, is used to pattern the Si_3N_4 layer. The Si_3N_4 layer is then etched away except above the regions that are to be the n^+ and p^+ diffusions or channel regions for the n-channel and p-channel MOSFETs. These diffusions will be added by subsequent processing steps to form drain and source regions for MOSFETs as well as to form guard rings. These protected regions are again termed moat. After the Si_3N_4 layer is opened, the remaining photoresist is stripped. Figure 2B.1b depicts the wafer after Step 15 of the process scenario of Table 2B.1.

An optional field threshold adjust step may be introduced at this point. This field threshold adjust would be used to raise the threshold voltage in the n-type substrate in regions that will not contain devices. This will provide increased isolation between the p-channel transistors. Although an additional mask is required for this field adjust (Mask #A1 of Table 2B.1), the mask would be the complement of the union of the p-well mask and the active mask, Masks #1 and #2. As such, this mask information would be generated automatically and need not be separately provided by the designer.

A thick layer of field oxide (typically 10,000 Å) is grown in the regions not protected by the remaining Si_3N_4 that was patterned with Mask #2. The Si_3N_4, along with the remaining SiO_2 that was under this layer, are then stripped. The wafer at this stage is as depicted in Fig. 2B.1c. This corresponds to Step 18 in the process scenario of Table 2B.1. Note that along cross section AA' several isolated areas are not protected by the field oxide. These areas will be used for fabricating transistors and guard rings. No breaks in the field oxide appear in the BB' cross section. This corresponds to the region where the resistor and capacitor will appear; these devices are fabricated on top of the field oxide.

Next, a thin, uniform layer of SiO_2 (200 to 1000 Å), called in this case gate oxide, is regrown. A layer of polysilicon (typically 2000 Å) is then deposited, covered with photoresist, and patterned with Mask #3. This polysilicon layer, termed POLY or POLY I, is used for the gates of all transistors, as a plate on capacitors, for resistors, and for interconnects. Following etching and stripping, the wafer takes the form shown in Fig. 2B.1d. This corresponds to Step 25 in the process scenario of Table 2B.1.

An optional second polysilicon layer, termed POLY II, could be included here, as provided in the process scenario. The second polysilicon layer is not depicted in Fig. 2B.1. This second polysilicon layer would be separated from the first by a thin (500 to 1000 Å) insulating layer of SiO_2. The main purpose of the second polysilicon layer would be for the formation of capacitors with POLY I and POLY II as electrodes, although this layer would also find some use in interconnects and crossovers if available. The capacitance density and electrical characteristics of the poly–poly capacitors are more attractive than those obtainable with other capacitors available in this process. An additional mask, termed the POLY II or *electrode mask*, is needed to pattern this polysilicon layer. The etch of both the POLY I and POLY II layers produces an abrupt, sharp edge, making reliable coverage of this edge with thin material difficult. Since the oxide between POLY I and POLY II is thin, crossing of a POLY I boundary with POLY II may result in either a break in the POLY II or a shorting of POLY I and POLY II. To circumvent these problems, the crossing of a POLY I boundary with POLY II is often not permitted.

At this stage the drain and source diffusions for both the n-channel and p-channel transistors are added. Although two different types of diffusions and hence two separate masks are required, the designer need specify only one of the two masks. In this process, only those areas not protected by field oxide are capable of accepting any diffusion impurities. This is termed the moat, or active, region. It is further provided in this process that any moat area that is not exposed to n-type impurities will be exposed to p-type impurities. Consequently, the designer selects those moat regions that are to become p-type with Mask #4, which is termed the p^+ select mask. The n^+ select mask (Mask #5), which is used to pattern those regions of moat that are to become n-type, is automatically generated from the complement of the p^+ select mask intersected with the moat (active) mask. p^+ select is used in the substrate to form p-channel transistors and interconnects and is used in the p-well to provide ohmic contact to the p-well as well as for guard rings.

Correspondingly, n^+ select is used in the p-well to form n-channel transistors and interconnects, and in the substrate to make top ohmic contacts as well as additional guard rings. Further comments about guard rings and their role in latch-up protection appear in Section 2.4. As was the case in the NMOS process, the polysilicon layer or layers are patterned prior to the p^+ and n^+ diffusions. The polysilicon that lies in the moat serves as a diffusion mask for these diffusions and provides self-alignment of the gate with the drain and source regions.

The n^+ and p^+ diffusions are much shallower than the p-well diffusion and are typically in the 5000 Å and 7000 Å ranges, respectively. Following the p^+ and n^+ diffusions, which occur prior to Step 36 in the process scenario, the cross-sectional profile is as shown in Fig. 2B.1e. The n-channel and p-channel transistors, along with the ohmic contacts and guard rings, are clearly visible at this stage. A thick insulating layer, which is a deposited oxide (often PSG), is then placed over the entire wafer. This insulating layer is about 6000 Å thick and serves as an insulator between the uppermost polysilicon layer and the subsequent metal layer. This causes a further thickening of the field oxide and is depicted above the dashed interface of the field oxide layer shown in Fig. 2B.1f.

Mask #6 is used to pattern contact openings. Areas unprotected by photoresist after patterning are etched away. This etch will consume insulating layers but is stopped by either polysilicon or the silicon substrate. This provides for metal contact of either a polysilicon layer or a p^+ or n^+ diffusion depending on which is the uppermost layer present.

After the contacts are opened, metal is applied uniformly to the wafer and patterned with Mask #7. This is termed the *metal mask* (or, if subsequent metal layers are to be added, the *metal 1 mask*). This corresponds to Step 48 in the process scenario and the cross section of Fig. 2B.1f.

An optional second metal can be added at this stage. This requires two additional mask steps, one for making contact with underlying metal 1 and the other for patterning the second metal layer. The mask used to pattern the contact openings, or vias, between the two metal layers is termed the *via mask*. Polyimide is often used as the insulating layer between the two metals because it offers advantages in step coverage over other commonly used insulating layers.

Following application of a passivation layer, often termed p-glass, the passivation is opened above the bonding pads to provide for electrical contact from the top with Mask #8. This is often termed the *glass mask*. The pad layout is similar to that discussed for the NMOS process and depicted in Fig. 2A.1g.

This completes the CMOS processing steps for the generic CMOS process scenario of Table 2B.1. The resistor, capacitor, n-channel MOSFET, and p-channel MOSFET should be apparent from Figs. 2B.1a and 2B.1f.

2.2.1c Practical Process Considerations

The equipment needed for the CMOS process is basically the same as is needed for the NMOS process previously described. With this equipment the minimum feature size for the CMOS process is comparable to that for the NMOS process. It should be noted that eight masks and considerably more processing steps than are required for the basic six-mask NMOS process are needed for this CMOS process. In addition, it will be seen later that considerably more area is required for the same number of devices in a CMOS process than in an NMOS process with the same feature size. The increase in size is due largely to the required size of the large p-tubs and the n- and p-type guard rings. These increases in area are, however, often offset by less complicated designs and/or the superior performance that is attainable with the CMOS process.

Several physical and processing-dependent material characteristics cause the physical MOSFET to differ from the ideal. The processing-dependent material characteristics will be considered first.

WIDTH AND LENGTH REDUCTION. A typical cross section of the n-channel MOSFET along EE' and FF' of Fig. 2B.1a is compared with the ideal in Fig. 2.2-6. These cross sections are intentionally not to scale so that they will better illustrate the actual characteristics.

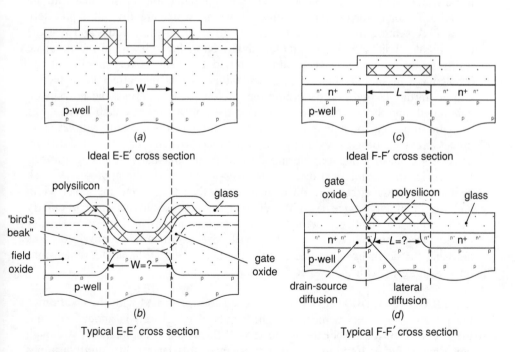

FIGURE 2.2-6
Width and length reduction in MOSFETS.

It will be seen later that the width and length of the MOSFET are key parameters at the control of the designer that play a major role in device performance. The width, W, is the width of the moat, or active, region as depicted in Fig. 2.2-6a, which corresponds to the EE' cross section of the MOSFET, and the length L is the distance between the drain and source diffusions, as indicated in the FF' cross section of Fig. 2.2-6c. It should be emphasized that the device dimensions are determined by the size of the *intersection* of the poly mask and the active mask and not by the dimensions of the poly pattern that forms the gate.

In the typical cross section of Fig. 2.2-6b, it can be seen that during the field oxide growth, encroachment into the active region effectively reduced the width of the transistor. This oxide encroachment is termed *bird's beaking* due to the distinctive shape of the encroachment. This is particularly troublesome because the width of the transistor is no longer precisely defined and because the exact amount of width reduction is not easily controllable. A second factor that affects the effective width is the accuracy with which the protective Si_3N_4 layer used to pattern the field oxide can be controlled. The effective width of this layer is affected by both the patterning of the photoresist and the problems associated with etching that were discussed in Section 2.1. In addition, since a thin SiO_2 layer (200–800 Å) is applied prior to the Si_3N_4 to minimize mechanical stress at the Si_3N_4 interface, the encroachment of the SiO_2 growth also limits accuracy.

Similar problems in controlling the length of the transistor exist, as indicated in Figs. 2.2-6c and d. The major source of length reduction is associated with the lateral diffusion of the drain and source diffusions, which are difficult to precisely control. Assuming the lateral and vertical diffusion rates are equal and that the diffusion depth is 5000 Å, the total length reduction due to lateral diffusion, since it diffuses in from both ends, would be around 1 μ. This is very significant and problematic in short channel transistors. Other factors that affect the effective length are the accuracy in patterning the photoresist that defines the polysilicon gate length and the accuracy in controlling the polysilicon gate etch itself.

In summary, both length and width reduction are inherent with existing processing technologies. Although they can be partially compensated for by considering these reductions during design or automatically adjusting (termed *size-adjust*) the geometrical database to over- or undersize the appropriate mask geometries, these effects are difficult to precisely control, and the exact width and length of the device are difficult to define. These effects are particularly troublesome for small geometries with device dimensions in the 1 μ or smaller range. Partial compensation with the mask size-adjust is often provided, thus allowing the designer to assume that the nominal value of the actual dimensions on silicon agree with those specified on the design.

LATERAL WELL DIFFUSION. Lateral diffusion associated with the creation of the p-well also deserves mention. The depth of the p-well is about 3 μ and, the lateral diffusion associated with the well formation is comparable. Although not a major factor limiting device performance, this lateral diffusion consumes considerable surface area and forces the designer to leave a large distance between isolated p-wells and between any p-well and p^+ diffusion in the substrate, thus increasing chip cost by increasing die area. One way to partially minimize the impact of the large amount of area associated with well boundaries is to group large numbers of n-channel transistors into a single p-well when the wells for these transistors are to be tied to the same potential. Tradeoffs between these area savings and the corresponding increase in interconnect area must be made.

LATCH-UP. The physics of layered doped silicon is also problematic. It is well known that a four-layer sandwich of doped material, npnp or pnpn, forms a Silicon Controlled Rectifier (SCR). Once an SCR is "fired" (switched to on conducting state), it continues to conduct until the gate signal is removed and current flow is interrupted. Several parasitic bipolar transistors and an SCR are identified on the cross section of Fig. 2.2-7 which is based on Fig. 2B.1f. Several diodes can also be identified. Although this CMOS process has not been optimized for obtaining good performance of these bipolar devices, there are limited practical applications of some of the diodes and bipolar transistors. The SCR, however, is very undesirable and if it is caused to fire, excessive current will usually flow, causing destructive failure of the integrated circuit. The firing of the SCR is termed *latch-up* in CMOS circuits. The CMOS designer must make certain that latch-up cannot occur in any design.

Latch-up problems are strongly layout dependent. A theoretical treatment of the latch-up problem is beyond the scope of this text, but a thorough understanding of this problem is not needed for successfully designing CMOS circuits provided the designer is familiar with layout techniques that circumvent the problem. Guard rings are widely used to prevent latch-up. Exact requirements for guard ring

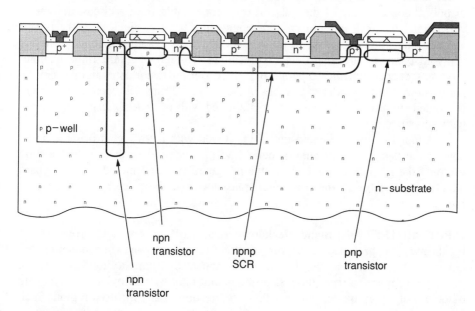

FIGURE 2.2-7
Parasitic transistors in a p-well CMOS process.

placement will be determined once a particular CMOS process is defined. In some processes, separate and additional n^+ and/or p^+ diffusions are included specifically for guard ring formation. This requires additional masks and additional processing steps. In the CMOS process discussed in this section, no additional masking or processing steps are required since the normal drain and source diffusions are also used to fabricate guard rings.

One way to obtain latch-up protection in the generic CMOS process of this section is to completely encircle every p-well with a p^+ guard ring. Such a guard ring is shown in Fig. 2B.1a around the periphery of the p-well. Metal contact is made as often as possible to this guard ring to further reduce resistance. The guard ring will then typically be connected via metallization to the lowest dc potential in the circuit—V_{SS} or ground, for example. Although not shown in Fig. 2B.1a, encircling the p-well with an n^+ guard ring provides additional protection and is also desirable. A partial n^+ guard ring separating the p-well from the p-channel substrate transistor can be seen in the same figure. As before, numerous metal contacts are made to this guard and it is subsequently tied to the highest potential in the circuit.

Breaks in a guard ring must be avoided since these breaks could provide a path for breakdown. Consider first the p^+ guard ring in the p-well. Breaks can occur one of two ways. The most obvious is to exclude a segment from either the moat mask or the p^+ select mask. The other way is to cross the guard ring *anywhere* with polysilicon in the process described in Table 2B.1. Such a crossing will cause a break because the polysilicon is patterned prior to the p^+ diffusion and serves as a mask to this diffusion. The break would thus occur under any polysilicon crossing of the intended guard ring. The exclusion of polysilicon crossing of the guard ring is undesirable from a circuit designer's viewpoint because it complicates interconnection between devices in the p-well and those outside the p-well; all interconnection crossings must be made of metal to avoid breaking the guard ring. Polysilicon crossing of guard rings in other process scenarios where a separate p^+ guard ring diffusion is available may be permissible. Correspondingly, breaks in the n^+ guard ring will occur if a segment is omitted from the active mask, if it is crossed with p^+ select, or if it is crossed with polysilicon.

Although complete enclosure of the p-well with the n^+ guard ring is desirable, some designers using the generic CMOS process described in this section use only the p^+ guard ring or have the p^+ guard ring and include the n^+ guard material only between the p-channel transistors and the p-well, as depicted in Fig. 2B.1a.

INPUT PROTECTION. Static breakdown is also of concern, and protection of inputs must be provided to prevent destructive breakdown when handling the devices. The major sources of concern are inputs that have a direct connection to a region separated from the rest of the circuit only by thin oxide, such as gate oxide or poly–poly oxide, with no direct connection to any diffused region. Such inputs would include the gates of any transistors or any connection to a floating polysilicon capacitor electrode. The breakdown is due to a destructive breakdown of this thin oxide due to electric fields that exceed the oxide breakdown voltage. As stated in Chapter 1, silicon dioxide will break down when electric fields are in the 5 MV/cm to 10 MV/cm range. With 1000 Å gate oxides, this would occur for voltage inputs in the 50 V to 100 V range. Although these are beyond the maximum allowable input voltages specified for a typical 3 μ CMOS process, these voltages are much less than the static voltages experienced when handling these chips. The problem is even worse for thinner gate oxides. Such breakdown is destructive and must be prevented. Input protection circuitry is used for this purpose. This input protection must not interfere with the normal operation of the circuit. A single simple protection circuit is typically developed and is used repeatedly by connecting it to each pad that requires protection.

One common protection scheme involves connecting the input pads through a small polysilicon resistor to a reverse-biased diode that nondestructively breaks down at voltages below the critical gate oxide breakdown voltage. The node that is to be protected then becomes an internal node coincident with the node corresponding to the interconnection between the protection resistor and the diode. The resistor is used to safely limit peak current flow in the protection diode. In the CMOS process described in this section, this diode would be constructed by putting an n^+ diffusion in a p-well with a p^+ select guard ring around the periphery of the well. This guard ring would be connected to the lowest potential in the circuit, typically ground or V_{SS}, and the n^+ diffusion would be connected to the pad that is to be protected through the polysilicon resistor. This protection circuit provides protection through the reverse breakdown voltage of the diode if the input is positive and through normal forward-biased diode conduction if the input is negative. For the NMOS process, single diode protection can be attained by connecting the critical node through a polysilicon resistor to an n^+ diffusion. No guard ring is available or required in an NMOS circuit.

An alternative that provides all protection through normal forward-biased diode conduction is obtained if a second diode of opposite polarity shunts the diode just described. This diode is constructed from a p^+ diffusion in the substrate, with the n-substrate connected to the highest potential in the circuit and the p^+ diffusion connected to the intersection node of the first diode and the polysilicon resistor. It is recommended that this p^+ diffusion be encircled by an n^+ guard ring, which also would be connected to the substrate. Under normal operation the diodes in the input circuitry do not conduct, so the input protection is ideally transparent to the user. Actually, the diodes do contribute to a small amount of leakage current. They also contribute to a small parasitic capacitance connected to an ac ground, which may be of limited concern in some applications.

Although the input protection schemes discussed could be used on any input or output pad, such circuitry is generally not required on pads that are already directly connected to a diffusion region, even if they are also connected to layers separated by thin oxide from other nodes in the circuit, because the diffused region itself forms part of the diode and thus provides inherent self-protection. Nevertheless, care should always be exercised when handling any MOS devices, even if good circuit-level protection has been included, to reduce the chance of destroying the integrated circuit by static breakdown.

2.2.2   Bipolar Process

The basic active devices in the bipolar process are the npn and pnp transistors. These names are descriptive since the devices are constructed with three layers of n- or p-type semiconductor material, with the middle layer different from the other two. These layers can be fabricated either laterally or vertically. A simplified pictorial description of these transistors, including the established symbols for the devices, appears in Fig. 2.2-8. Several excellent references discuss the basic operation of the BJT.[3,12–17] The modeling of the BJT is discussed in Chapter 3. As will be seen later, the characteristics of the collector and emitter regions as well as their geometries are intentionally different and as such the designation of the collector and emitter contacts is not arbitrary. The convention that has been established for designating the collector and emitter contacts will be discussed in Chapter 3.

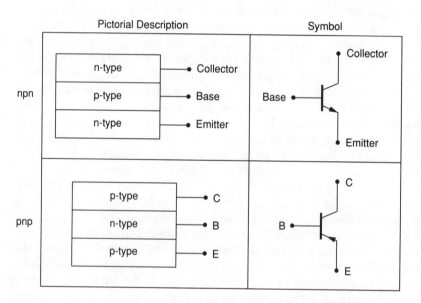

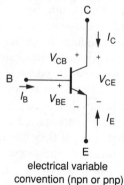

electrical variable
convention (npn or pnp)

FIGURE 2.2-8
Bipolar transistors.

The components available in the bipolar process are

1. npn bipolar transistors.
2. pnp bipolar transistors.
3. Resistors.
4. Capacitors.
5. Diodes.
6. Zener diodes.
7. Junction Field Effect Transistors (JFETs)—not available in all bipolar processes.

A familiarity with the process is crucial to utilizing this wide variety of components in the design of an integrated circuit. Unlike discrete component circuit design with these same devices, whose characteristics can be specified over a wide range and which can be connected in any manner, the basic characteristics of the devices available for bipolar integrated circuits are determined by the process and the range of practical values and parameters is severely limited. In addition, the methods of interconnection are strictly limited, the basic devices have characteristics that are quite temperature dependent, and the passive component values are typically somewhat dependent on the signal applied. In spite of these restrictions (to be discussed later), very clever analog and digital bipolar integrated circuits have evolved. The bipolar process is used for the popular TTL, ECL, and I^2L digital logic families as well as a host of linear integrated circuits, including the 741 operational amplifier, the 723 voltage regulator, and the 565 phase locked loop. Although minor variances in the processing steps are common, the major differences are in device sizes and impurity concentrations and profiles. The discussion of a typical seven-mask bipolar process follows. The major process steps are outlined in Table 2C.1 of Appendix 2C.

The construction of npn transistors, pnp transistors, resistors, and capacitors will be considered. The location of these components can be seen in the top view containing mask information shown in Fig. 2C.1*a* of Appendix 2C.

The starting point in this bipolar process is a clean, polished p-type silicon wafer. A layer of SiO_2 is first grown over the wafer. Following application of a layer of photoresist, Mask #1 is used to pattern the n^+ buried layer. The n^+ buried layer serves the purpose of decreasing collector resistance and minimizing the parasitic current flow from collector to substrate in npn transistors. It also helps decrease the base resistance in lateral pnp transistors. Either a deposition or implant, followed by a drive in diffusion, can be used to introduce the n-type impurities into the substrate through the openings provided by Mask #1. A layer of oxide, which grows during the diffusion, is then stripped. After the n^+ diffusion the wafer takes the form shown in Fig. 2C.1*b*.

An n-type epitaxial (crystalline) layer is then grown over the entire wafer. The thickness of this layer typically varies between 2 μ and 15 μ, with the thinner layers used for digital circuits and the thicker layers for analog circuits. This layer will be used for the collector region in npn transistors. The epitaxial layer is shown in Fig. 2C.1c. Note that some of the impurities in the buried layer have migrated (or *out-diffused*) into the epitaxial layer during its growth. A thick layer of SiO_2 (typically 5000 Å) is then grown over the entire surface.

Mask #2 is used to pattern the SiO_2 layer for the p^+ isolation diffusion. SiO_2 is etched from the areas not photographically protected by Mask #2 to allow for this drive in diffusion following a p^+ deposition. The p^+ isolation diffusion is used to electrically separate adjacent transistors. It is wide and deep since it must completely penetrate the epitaxial layer to provide the required isolation. The wafer at this stage is as shown in Fig. 2C.1d. Although the isolation diffusion is shown with vertical edges in the figure, lateral diffusion, typically comparable to the vertical diffusion, causes significant out-diffusion laterally under the oxide layer, thus making the top of the channel stop considerably wider than the bottom. Following this diffusion, another thick layer of SiO_2 is grown over the entire wafer.

An optional shallow, high-resistance p-diffusion could be added at this step. This is not depicted in Fig. 2C.1 but is listed as an option in Table 2C.1. This step would provide a mechanism for making practical diffused resistors in the 1 $k\Omega$ to 20 $k\Omega$ range. A typical sheet resistance of this region would be 1 $k\Omega/\square$ to 2 $k\Omega/\square$. Mask #A in Table 2C.1 is used to pattern these regions.

Mask #3 is used to pattern the SiO_2 layer and define the base regions for the npn transistors as well as the collector and emitter regions for lateral pnp devices. A p-type deposition and a subsequent drive in diffusion create these regions in the unprotected areas. This diffusion is much shallower than was the isolation diffusion and must not penetrate the epitaxial layer. The isolation mask openings provided by Mask #2 are typically reopened with Mask #3 to provide a few additional p-type impurities. The wafer at this stage is shown in Fig. 2C.1e.

Following growth of another layer of SiO_2, Mask #4 is used to pattern the emitter regions for the npn transistors. An n^+ deposition followed by a drive in diffusion creates the emitter regions. Openings are also made in the oxide above the collector to add small n^+ wells in the lightly doped collector region to provide for better electrical contact from the surface. The integrated circuit at this stage is as depicted in Fig. 2C.1f. The emitter diffusions must be shallow so as not to penetrate the relatively shallow p-type base regions already created. The amount and profile of the impurities in the n^+ emitter regions and the thickness of the p-type base region, which is now sandwiched between the n^+ emitter and the n-collector, strongly influence the gain of the transistor.

Mask #5 is used to pattern contact openings to allow for top contact of the circuit with the metallization. The entire circuit is then covered with a thin layer of metal. Mask #6 is used to pattern the metal, followed by the addition of a passivation layer. The completed cross-sectional view of the four components under consideration is shown in Fig. 2C.1g. Mask #7 patterns pad openings to allow for electrical contact to the bonding pads.

Two modifications of this process deserve mention. One involves adding a *deep collector* diffusion. This requires an additional masking step and is used to diffuse impurities under the area where the collector contacts are to be made. This step would occur either before or after the isolation diffusion and is used to extend n^+ impurities all the way from the surface to the buried layer. Since this is such a deep diffusion, an area penalty in the collector is experienced. The deep diffusion is used to reduce collector resistance in high-current applications. The second modification involves adding an additional p-diffusion in the p-channel stops. This also requires an additional mask step and is used to avoid surface inversion in high-voltage parts. With the exception of open collector circuits, this step is not common in basic logic parts.

The npn and pnp transistors in this process are depicted in Fig. 2.2-9. The npn transistor is called a vertical npn device since the emitter, base, and collector regions are stacked vertically. It can now be seen that the n^+ buried layer decreases the collector resistance that must be modeled in series with the collector.

The pnp transistor is called a lateral device since it is stacked laterally (horizontally). The base width cannot practically be made as narrow and the base area is not as accurately controllable as for the npn device. In addition, the emitter and collector regions must have the same impurity profile. The characteristics of the lateral transistors are generally considered poorer than those of the vertical devices. Other pnp transistors, not shown in Fig. 2C.1, can be constructed by using the p-type base diffusion as the emitter, the n-type epitaxial layer as the base, and the p-type substrate as the collector. These devices are called substrate transistors. The performance of these devices is also mediocre, and applications are restricted since all collectors of substrate transistors are common.

The capacitor that was constructed in Fig. 2C.1 may at the outset appear to be merely a diode. It would serve the purpose of a diode, even though the area is considerably more than may be required in most applications. When reverse biased, however, the depletion layer forms the dielectric, and the p and n regions on either side form the capacitor plates. Capacitors made like this, with total

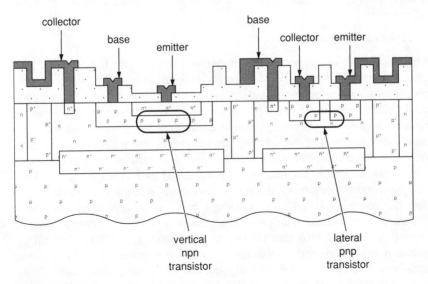

FIGURE 2.2-9
Vertical and lateral transistors in a bipolar process.

capacitances from the sub-picofarad to the 100 picofarad range, have proven practical. The capacitors are not without limitations, however. The requirement that the junction must always be reverse biased severely limits the interconnection flexibility of this device. The width of the depletion layer is voltage dependent, making the capacitance nonlinear. Temperature also affects the capacitance value. Finally, the base–emitter junction typically breaks down with a reverse bias of about 7 V, limiting the maximum voltage that can be applied to the capacitor. The base–collector junction can also be used as a capacitor. Its characteristics are very similar to the base-emitter capacitor with the exception that it offers an increased reverse breakdown at the expense of a lower capacitance density. Junction capacitors will be discussed in more detail in Chapter 3. An alternative to the junction capacitor would be a metal–oxide–semiconductor capacitor formed between the metal and the n^+ emitter diffusion. Although the characteristics of this capacitor would be better than those of the junction capacitors, an extra mask step is generally required to provide a means of selectively stripping the thick oxide above the emitter region so that a thin oxide can be regrown. The thin oxide is needed to get the capacitance density up to a practical level.

The resistor of Fig. 2C.1 is actually just a serpentined strip of the lightly doped p-type base diffusion. The underlying n-type epitaxial layer is generally contacted and taken to the highest potential in the circuit to prevent current flow into this region. Several other techniques for fabricating resistors in this process are available. They will be discussed in Chapter 3.

Although minimum feature sizes are comparable for the bipolar and MOS processes, standard bipolar processes require more area per device than do the NMOS processes. A major reason for this increased area is the deep and wide p^+ channel stops that are required for device isolation in standard bipolar processes. An alternative bipolar process using trench isolation[23] is available which offers a significant improvement in component density over the standard bipolar process.

2.2.3 Hybrid Technology

The hybrid approach to integrated circuit design involves attaching two or more integrated circuit dies (typically of different types), along with some discrete components in some cases, in a single package to form what is called a hybrid integrated circuit. It is often, and desirably, transparent to the consumer whether the circuit is monolithic or hybrid; in some cases, however, the hybrid packages are considerably larger. The hybrid integrated circuit is typically more costly than the monolithic structures. The extra cost and size of hybrid integrated circuits is offset, in some demanding applications, by improved performance capabilities.

Hybrid circuits containing discrete components occupy considerably less area than the conventional PC board/discrete component approach. They have played a major role in demanding analog signal processing applications such as high-resolution A/D and D/A converters and precision active filters. Tolerances, temperature dependence, and area-induced component value limits for resistors and capacitors in standard MOS and bipolar processes have limited the development of monolithic integrated circuits for precision continuous-time signal processing. Thick film and thin film passive components have reasonable tolerances, are easily trimmable, have acceptable temperature coefficients that can be tailored for tracking, and offer reasonable tradeoffs between area required and component values. These thick film and thin film networks are commonly used for the passive components in hybrid integrated circuits. A discussion of thick film and thin film processing technologies follows.

THICK FILM CIRCUITS. The thick film technology is relatively old, requires considerable area compared to monolithic circuits, can be used for relatively high-power applications, and can be applied at relatively high frequencies (up to 1 GHz) although it is typically limited to a few MHz. The increased area required by the thick film circuits is offset by the reduced cost in equipment and processing materials required for the thick film process, the latter being a small fraction of that required for either bipolar or MOS processes.

The components available in a thick film process are resistors and capacitors along with conducting interconnects. Layers of different material are successively screened onto an insulating substrate. These materials are used for resistors and conductors as well as for the dielectrics of capacitors.

The number of resistive layers varies but practical limitations generally restrict this to at most three. Typical thickness of these layers (called pastes or inks) is about 20 μ, but they may vary considerably by design. The actual thickness of these layers is not accurately controllable ($\pm$ 30%) due to limitations in the screening process itself.

The thick film process offers the most advantages for resistor fabrication. Although capacitors are often included, the electrical characteristics of thick film capacitors are not outstanding and the capacitance density is quite low. Discrete chip capacitors, which have much better characteristics than their thick film counterparts, are often bonded to thick film resistive networks in hybrid circuit applications.

The minimum conductor width in a typical thick film process is about 250 μ, and minimum resistor widths are about 1250 μ. It can be seen that these are orders of magnitude larger than the corresponding minimum feature sizes for the MOS and bipolar processes (1–5 μ).

Screening involves forcing the paste through small holes in a tightly stretched piece of fabric called a screen, typically constructed of stainless steel. The grid is quite regular. The spacing of the holes can be specified, but practical physical limitations relating to both the mechanical characteristics of the steel and the physical characteristics of the inks prevent the use of extremely fine meshes. Screens with a grid spacing·ranging from 100 to 300 filaments/inch are typical. This spacing restricts thick film resolution to somewhere around 500 μ. Where paste is not desired, holes in the screen are plugged by a mask. A squeegee is used to force the ink through the unrestricted areas. Following screening, each layer is fired to harden it.

Inks are available with sheet resistances that satisfy the equation

$$1 \ \Omega/\square < R_{\square} < 10 \ M\Omega/\square \tag{2.2-9}$$

for fired layers 20 μ thick. This large latitude in ink characteristics allows for a wide range of resistor values. Since only one type of ink can be used for each resistor layer, the tradeoffs between area and sheet resistance must be considered when specifying the ink sheet resistances. Even though adjusting the length is a convenient means of establishing resistor values, long thick film resistors are to be avoided because they develop "hot spots" and are difficult to trim. The "hot spots" are caused at regions where the resistive layer is a little thinner and/or narrower than surrounding regions. This causes an increased resistance in this small region, which under constant current causes increased local power dissipation. This power dissipation causes heating, which typically further increases the resistance and power dissipation. Heating causes deterioration of the film layer at these points. Deterioration in these regions can eventually result in device failure. Short, wide resistors are also to be avoided. The main problem with short, wide resistors is the inability to accurately specify the size of the resistor since the contacts will overlap with a considerable portion of the device. A reasonable rule of thumb for the allowable width (W) / length (L) ratio for a rectangular resistor is

$$\frac{1}{10} < \frac{W}{L} < 3 \tag{2.2-10}$$

Although the W/L ratio is constrained, the values for W and L remain to be specified within the design rules of the process. It is a good practice to make the resistors large if the area is available to minimize edge roughness effects, increase power dissipation capability, and make trimming easier.

Serpentined patterns such as shown in Problem 2.11 should also be avoided with thick film technology. This is due to the increased current density that will result from current crowding at the inner corners of serpentined structures.

A capacitor is constructed by screening a conductive layer, followed by a dielectric, followed by another conductor. The dielectric is generally applied in two coats to minimize pinholes, which would short the capacitor plates together. With the two layers of dielectric, the chances of a pinhole coincident with both layers are greatly reduced. Since a thick film capacitor is actually a parallel plate capacitor, the capacitance is given by

$$C = \epsilon_R \epsilon_0 \frac{A}{t} \tag{2.2-11}$$

where $\epsilon_0 = 8.854$ pF/m, A is the area of the capacitor plates, t is the dielectric thickness, and ϵ_R is the relative dielectric constant. Inks with relative dielectric constants from 10 to 1000 are available. The high dielectric constants offer a reasonable capacitance density at the expense of large and nonlinear temperature coefficients. The lower dielectric materials offer improved performance but are restricted to applications requiring small capacitors due to a low capacitance density. As in the MOS and bipolar processes, the upper plate of thick film capacitors is typically a little smaller than the lower to minimize capacitance changes caused by minor misalignments. The two conductive layers used for the capacitor plates also serve as interconnects. If crossovers of two conductors are required, the dielectric layer can be used as an insulator at the expense of creating a small parasitic capacitor at the crossover.

The screen geometries, along with a cross-sectional view of a typical thick film process, are depicted in Fig. 2D.1 of Appendix 2D. This process has two resistive screenings as well as two conductive layers and a dielectric for capacitor fabrication. The major process steps are listed in Table 2D.1. Process parameters and characteristics, along with design rules for a typical thick film process, are also given in Appendix 2D.

Thick film resistors can be trimmed with a laser or by abrasion. These trims, which can be very accurate, remove part of the thick film layer and thus increase the resistance. For this reason, resistors that are to be trimmed are typically targeted to be undersized in value by about 40% to guarantee trimmability in spite of process variations.

Thick film capacitors can also be trimmed by abrasively removing part of the upper plate (along with some dielectric). Since this decreases the capacitance, the thick film capacitors are typically targeted to be oversized by about 40%.

THIN FILM CIRCUITS. The components available in thin film processes are resistors and capacitors, although often only resistors are included due to both the specific applications which naturally benefit from thin film technology and the practical limitations of thin film capacitors. Thin film circuits are much smaller than thick film circuits. They are similar to thick film circuits in that successive layers are applied to an insulating substrate as contrasted to the MOS and bipolar processes, where some of the processing steps involve diffusions that actually penetrate the substrate. For conductors, thin film thicknesses are typically from 100 to 500 Å although thicknesses of several thousand angstroms are occasionally used if a high conductivity is needed. Film thicknesses from 100 to 2000 Å for resistors and film thicknesses in the 3000 Å region for dielectrics of capacitors are common. Note that these film thicknesses are comparable to the thicknesses of layers applied in the MOS and bipolar processes but are orders of magnitude thinner than the 20 μ (200,000 Å) typical of thick films. The sheet resistance range for thin film resistors is typically from 50 $\Omega/\square$ to 250 $\Omega/\square$, which is considerably less than is available in thick film processes. The thin film layers are applied by uniformly coating the entire wafer with the film. Then unwanted areas are selectively patterned and etched with a photolithographic process similar to that used in the MOS and bipolar cases.

The minimum feature sizes for the thin film components are comparable to those of the MOS and bipolar processes. The temperature characteristics and performance of thin film components are quite good with the exception of the dielectrics for capacitors, which are quite lossy. "Hot spots," which were a problem with thick film circuits for long resistors, are not a major problem with thin film resistors since the thin films are typically more uniform and since thin film applications generally require smaller current flow.

Thin film circuits are much more expensive to produce than their thick film counterparts because of the sophisticated equipment that is needed for both the photolithographic process and the film depositions and etching. They are used extensively in telecommunication circuits at low frequencies but also find applications at higher frequencies (up to 30 GHz) as well.

Thin film resistors can be accurately trimmed by a laser. Thin film capacitors are not well adapted to a continuous trim although binarily weighted capacitors connected with laser-fusible links are trimmable in quantized decrements.

Thin films can also be applied on top of monolithic structures, offering considerably more performance capability than is attainable with either the thin film or monolithic approaches themselves. Problems with film technology and the decreased yield per wafer associated with both increased die area and an increased number of processing steps have slowed the development of such processes.

The mask layouts, along with cross-sectional views of a typical thin film resistive process, are depicted in Fig. 2E.1 of Appendix 2E. This is a subtractive process because all film layers are added prior to any patterning, and it has a single resistive layer and a single conductive layer. The major process steps are listed in Table 2E.1 of the same appendix. Process parameters and design rules for a typical thin film process are also given in Appendix 2E.

2.3 DESIGN RULES AND PROCESS PARAMETERS

Design rules are generally well-documented specifications listing minimum widths of features (conductor, moat, resistor, etc.), minimum spacings allowable between adjacent features, overlap requirements, and other measurements that are compatible with a given process. Factors such as mask alignment, mask non-linearities, wafer warping, out-diffusion (lateral diffusion), oxide growth profile, lateral etch undercutting, and optical resolution and their relationships with performance and yield are considered when specifying the design rules for a process. It is not our intention in this text to rigorously investigate the technical details about how design rules are derived but rather to consider the design rules and process parameters as a set of constraints within which the circuit designer must work. This is justifiable because the basic format of the design rules and process parameters remains relatively fixed, with changes in the process contributing only to numerical perturbations of the design rules and process parameters. The design rules, the process parameters, and their relationship with device characteristics serve as an interface between the process engineers and the circuit designers. Both groups, along with representatives from marketing (since yield is affected by the design rules), have input into the evolution of these interfaces.

Although the minimum feature sizes, which ultimately determine the design rules, have been steadily decreasing with time to the benefit of yield and production costs, it is important that designers adhere to the design rules once a process has been selected for a particular project. Most large semiconductor houses have developed or purchased sophisticated computer software to verify that layouts violate no design rules. In the process of verifying design rules, it is often the case that layout errors are also detected since these errors will often violate a design rule. For large designs that involve thousands of transistors, it is crucial that these verifications be made since a single design rule violation or layout error will often be fatal (i.e., the circuit won't work). The importance of adhering to design rules and utilizing verification programs for simple as well as complicated designs cannot be overemphasized. If design rules are intentionally violated, the verification software cannot be fully utilized and perhaps not utilized at all.

Typical sets of design rules and process parameters for the NMOS, CMOS, bipolar, thick film, and thin film processes discussed in Sec. 2.2 are summarized in Appendices 2A–2E. Some of the parameters listed in those appendices have not been defined yet but will be discussed in Chapter 3. The $3\,\mu$ NMOS parameters and the $3\,\mu$ CMOS parameters are very similar to those provided by MOSIS for their $3\,\mu$ NMOS and $3\,\mu$ CMOS processes in 1988. We have attempted to maintain most of the notation established by MOSIS to aid students who will be doing designs in a MOSIS process.

A discussion of selected key design rules and process parameters for the CMOS process follows. Many of these comments apply either directly or with obvious modifications to the other processes. In the interest of conserving space, the interpretation of the parameters and design rules for the remaining processes will be left to the reader.

CMOS DESIGN RULES. The CMOS design rules are listed in Table 2B.2 of Appendix 2B. These rules are depicted graphically in Table 2B.3.

The design rules list guidelines (actually restrictions) about how each of the geometrical figures on each mask level align relative to each other and to other mask levels. Unless specifically stated to the contrary with the comment "exactly," all rules are minimum spacings between the corresponding geometrical figures. In general, the designer may exceed these minimum spacings to whatever degree is deemed appropriate. It should be emphasized, however, that from both cost and performance viewpoints, the die area should be as small as is practical. At this stage one might be tempted to conclude that a margin of safety, or improved reliability, could be obtained if a more conservative set of rules were established by the designer. With the exception of some matching considerations that will be discussed later in this book, few benefits are derived from following this strategy since an economically motivated margin of safety was considered when establishing the design rules. The rules were derived under the assumption that large circuits with many devices sized at the minimum allowable levels must have good performance and high yield.

In Table 2B.2, two sets of dimensions are specified. The first corresponds to those specified in a $3\,\mu$ CMOS process provided by MOSIS. The second set is in terms of the scaling parameter, λ, which characterizes the feature size of the process. The feature size (minimum poly width, active width, and metal width) is 2λ. This parameterization is used so that the design rules do not need to be rewritten as the feature size of the process shrinks. Substituting $\lambda = 1.5$ μ will give a process very similar to the $3\,\mu$ process characterized in the first column of this table. Although similar in intent, the scalable parameters listed in this table are not identical to those characterizing the MOSIS scalable CMOS process.

The mask geometries themselves may differ somewhat from the geometries specified for the corresponding geometrical feature by the designer. The exact geometries specified by the designer are termed *drawn* features. The change in feature sizes on a mask from those specified by the designer is termed *size adjust* and is undertaken in cooperation with those responsible for the processing. This allows for precompensation of effects, such as lateral etching or out-diffusion, that make the physical dimensions on silicon different from the mask dimensions. Size adjust is often used so that the "effective" dimension (the physical dimension realized after fabrication) is nominally equal to the drawn dimension. Specific comments about selected key rules follow.

p-well. The spacing (Rule 1.2) between two p-wells at different potential is very large. This allows for accommodation of the lateral diffusion. Since the p-well is very deep (3–4 μ), the lateral diffusion is also significant.

Via. The via level is used for interconnecting Metal 1 and Metal 2. The via design rules are very similar to those for the contact openings. Both involve making openings in thick oxide layers.

Pads. The dimensions for the metal bonding pads have not scaled with decreases in feature size of the processes. The size of the capillaries used for attaching bonding wires, which are several mils in diameter to accommodate the nominal 1 mil bonding wire, has not decreased significantly for a long while, thus necessitating both large bonding pads and large spacing. Smaller probe pads are often included on designs to facilitate diagnostic probing during the debugging stage.

Active. Size adjust, sometimes termed mask bias, is used to preadjust feature sizes on the active mask so that the targeted effective feature sizes are close to the drawn feature sizes. This allows for compensation of the field encroachment into the active region. Also, this size adjust thus compensates for the width reduction experienced during processing. Note that a large spacing between active and p-well is provided to accommodate for the lateral p-well diffusion.

Poly. The poly overlap rules are primarily to provide compensation for mask alignment errors between poly and active. Although the process is self-aligned, this self-alignment is achieved only for modest misalignment of devices. If, for example, the misalignment is so bad that the poly does not entirely cover the active region, then the subsequent n^+ or p^+ drain and source diffusions will create a conductive region between the drain and source that cannot be controlled by the gate. Design Rule 3.4 governs this concern. Size adjust is used on the POLY mask to do length adjustment for lateral diffusion.

   If a second poly layer is available, it may not cross a boundary of POLY I. The sharp edge of POLY I would make the step coverage of this edge with the thin oxide unreliable. The integrity of the POLY II over this step would also be in question. Nor is POLY II permitted for transistor gates although such devices would likely be functional. The main purpose of POLY II is as a second plate on poly–poly capacitors although some applications as an interconnect medium or as a resistor may exist.

p^+ select. The p^+ select rules are used primarily to allow for mask misalignments with the active mask and the poly mask.

Contact. The contact openings are specified exactly rather than minimally. Although it is often the case that a large contact between two regions is desirable to reduce contact resistance, a large single contact opening is not permitted; rather, numerous separate contacts must be used. Multiple individual contacts were used for contacting the p-well in Fig. 2B.1*a*. The reason for restricting the contact opening size and making all essentially the same can be best appreciated by considering what the contact-opening etch must accomplish. The contact openings must penetrate a thick (5000 to 7000 Å) layer of oxide. Thus, this step must consume much more oxide than is required during the thin oxide stripping steps. If a large contact opening were permitted, the central areas of these openings would be etched away before the oxide was completely removed for the smaller contact openings. As the etching continued in the small openings, any pinholes in the large open area could be further attacked by the etchant. Since the underlying poly layer thicknesses and diffusion depths are comparable in thickness to the layer that must be removed during contact openings, and since underlying thin oxides are *much* thinner, these pinholes could cause device failure. Although the probability of failure due to a single larger contact may be very low, the probability of a single failure that would render a circuit defective if a large number of these large openings were permitted may be unacceptably large. Even if the pinholes did not cause shorting, the reliability of such devices deteriorates with increased risks of premature device failures after the part is in use. For these reasons, contact openings on the gates of transistors (no contact to poly inside active) are usually not permitted either.

Contact openings to POLY II on top of POLY I are permitted. Although this type of contact is also plagued by the pinhole problem, the POLY II layer is generally used in analog applications as an upper plate of a capacitor. The total number of capacitors in these circuits is generally quite small compared to the number of transistors in a large digital circuit, thus minimizing (in the probabilistic sense) the failures due to the pinhole problem (see Problem 2.12).

Example 2.3-1. A thick film resistor layout strategy is shown in Fig. 2.3-1. Determine the minimum substrate size ($L \cdot H$) if the resistor is to have a nominal value of 325 kΩ and is to use the layout strategy of this figure. Use the design rules of Table 2D.2 ($\lambda = 250\ \mu$) and the process parameters of Table 2D.3.

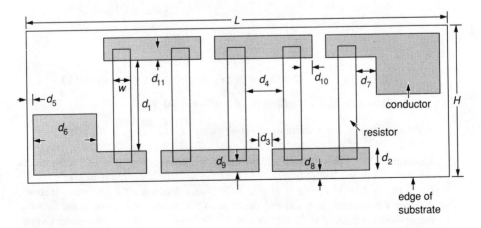

FIGURE 2.3-1
Layout for Example 2.3-1.

Solution. Since $R = 325$ kΩ and since the goal is to minimize area, the highest sheet resistance screening will be used for the resistors. From Table 2D.3, we obtain $R_\square = 10,000$ $\Omega/\square$. If the contact resistance and sheet resistance are neglected, we require n $= 325$ k$\Omega/R_\square = 32.5$ squares of resistive material. Since there are five equal width resistors in series, each of width W, the length of each (d_1) must equal $32.5W/5 = 6.5W$.

From Fig. 2.3-1, it follows that the length and height of the substrate are given, respectively, by

$$L = 2d_5 + 2d_6 + 2d_7 + 5W + 4d_4$$

$$H = 2d_8 + 2d_2 + d_1$$

From Table 2D.2, the following minimum sizes are obtained for each of the parameters d_2–d_{11} and W.

Parameter	Rule	Size
d_2	1.1	2λ
d_3	1.2	2λ
d_4	2.2	2λ
d_5, d_8	1.5	2λ
d_6	4.0	4λ
d_7	2.3	2λ
d_9	1.3a	λ
d_{10}	1.3b	λ
d_{11}	2.4	λ
d_1, W	2.1	5λ

It should be noted that even though these are minimum spacings, the layout itself may impose more stringent requirements to avoid layout violations. Specifically,

$$d_4 \geq d_3 + 2d_{10} = 4\lambda$$

$$d_2 \geq d_9 + d_{11} = 2\lambda$$

$$d_1 \geq 5\lambda$$

We thus obtain

$$L = (2)(2\lambda) + (2)(4\lambda) + 2(2\lambda) + (5)(5\lambda) + (4)(4\lambda) = 57\lambda$$

$$H = (2)(2\lambda) + (2)(2\lambda) + (6.5)(5\lambda) = 40.5\lambda$$

With $\lambda = 250$ μ, the minimum substrate size is 1.425 cm $\times$ 1.0125 cm.

Example 2.3-2. An n-channel and p-channel transistor designed in a CMOS process are depicted in the layout of Fig. 2.3-2. If the p-channel device is of size $L/W = 6$ and the n-channel device is of size $L/W = \frac{1}{2}$, determine the minimum distance between the edge of the p-tub and the edge of the p-moat, d, shown in the figure if the devices are packed as closely as possible following the layout placement shown. Assume the devices are designed in the CMOS process discussed in Sec. 2.2 with the design rules of Table 2B.2. Assume $\lambda = 0.75$ μ.

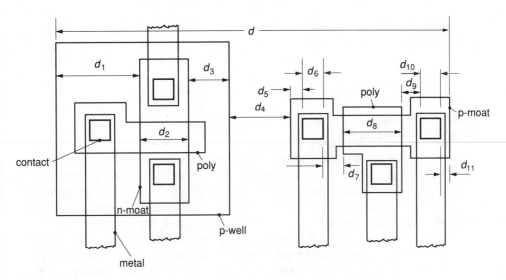

FIGURE 2.3-2
Layout for Example 2.3-2.

Solution. Since only the L/W ratios are specified, W will be chosen minimum size for the n-channel transistor and L will be chosen minimum size for the p-channel device.

The dimensions d_1–d_{11} must satisfy the design rules of Table 2B.2. The restriction on these dimensions as imposed by the design rules are as follows.

Dimension	Design rule	Minimum size
d_1, d_3	2.5	2λ
d_2, d_8	2.1, 3.1	2λ
d_4	2.3	6λ
d_5, d_{11}	5.8	λ
d_6, d_{10}	5.1	2λ
d_7, d_9	5.6	2λ

The layout itself introduces some additional constraints. From the L/W ratios specified, it can be concluded that $d_2 \geq 2L_{\min}$ and $d_8 \geq 6W_{\min}$. From design rules 2.1 and 3.1 of Table 2B.2, it can be concluded that $d_2 \geq 4\lambda$ and $d_8 \geq 12\lambda$. The layout itself also places constraints on d_1. Since the contact as well as the edges of the metal and poly on the left-hand side of the n-channel transistor are to remain inside the p-well (a somewhat arbitrary requirement) it can be argued by design rule 5.6 that the contact must be at least 2λ from the n-moat, and from design rule 5.1 that the contact width must be 2λ. From design rules 5.4 and 5.7, the poly and metal must overhang the contact by λ. Since there is no minimum spacing between the poly and p-tub, the left-hand edge of the poly in the tub can be coincident with the tub edge (although the guard ring may be broken). It thus follows that

$$d_1 \geq 5\lambda$$

But

$$d = \sum_{i=1}^{11} d_i$$

which from above becomes d $= 39\lambda = 29.25\ \mu$.

2.4   LAYOUT TECHNIQUES AND PRACTICAL CONSIDERATIONS

Once a circuit design is complete, it becomes necessary to provide an area-efficient layout of the circuit to generate the masks necessary for fabrication. Although at the outset it appears that the circuit designer's job is complete at this point and that the layout can be undertaken by a draftsman (as is commonly done with PC board versions of discrete component designs), this is far from the case in IC design. Some companies provide draftsmen for this purpose who interact closely with the designers, whereas other philosophies leave this task entirely to the design engineer. In either case, the design engineer is still involved at this stage because component sizing and spacing, as well as the parasitics associated with integrated circuit components, must typically be considered in the design itself since their effects are often significant. This is particularly important in designs including analog circuitry. Even the opening sentence of this paragraph is an oversimplification of the situation since the initial design itself will likely not be complete until the layout is finished—as was indicated in Fig. 1.3-1. Although the design engineer is typically not responsible for any steps in the fabrication process once the mask information has been delivered, he or she is generally still responsible for the project until the product is in production. For complicated circuits, first silicon (the physical integrated circuits produced by the initial design) will generally not be acceptable for marketing because of either the circuit's failure to meet some specifications or total circuit failure caused by (1) a design or layout error, (2) failure of the designer to adequately account for all relevant parasitics, or (3) unacceptably low yield due to failure to center the design parameters appropriately in the actual process window.

One of the first considerations in the layout is sizing the devices as well as the interconnections. For the long rectangular resistor shown in Fig. 2.4-1, the total resistance is obtained from the sheet resistance by the expression

$$R = (L/W)R_\square \tag{2.4-1}$$

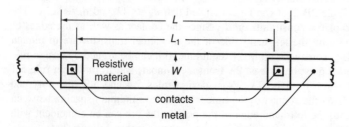

FIGURE 2.4-1
Resistor component sizing considerations.

provided that L is long enough so that the difference between L and L_1 is negligible (because $L - L_1$ is fixed by the design rules). Since the L/W ratio rather than either L or W determines the resistance, it may seem to make little difference what the values of L and W actually are, but this is often not the case. In addition to the difficulty in determining the effective length (L or L_1?) for short resistors, the edges will typically be somewhat rough due to unevenness in processing. This unevenness will cause variations in resistance. Making W and L larger reduces the relative effects of both the edge variations and the difference between L and L_1. In addition, the power-handling capability will be increased with larger devices. These improvements with larger devices are obtained at the expense of increased area, which will reduce the number of dies per wafer.

For MOSFETs, it will be shown in Chapter 3 that the length/width ratio, rather than the length and width themselves, plays one of the major roles in the device model. Again, increasing the area for a fixed length/width ratio will reduce the effects of unevenness in the edges, but this is obtained at the expense of increased area and increased gate capacitance.

As mentioned earlier, it is common practice when laying out capacitors to make one plate (typically the upper) a little smaller than the other so that the smaller plate effectively defines the plate area even if minor misalignments in the masks occur. This also makes the edge field effects easier to account for. Although the area of the smaller plate essentially determines the capacitance, the geometry of this plate itself remains to be determined. If the relationship between this capacitor value and others in the circuit is not of major importance, the shape of the capacitor will likely be selected to conform to available spaces around adjacent components, thus minimizing circuit area.

Many applications require that resistor or capacitor ratios be accurately determined. This is particularly common in analog signal-processing circuits. Ratio matching requirements of 1% to 0.1% or better are common. Although absolute component value tolerances better than 1% (or even 10%) are not currently feasible without trimming in any of the processes discussed in Sec. 2.2, the ratio accuracy specified above is attainable in some processes and is maintainable over a wide range of temperature. For resistor layouts both the individual L/W ratios, as well as the area and shape, become design parameters available to the circuit designer. The area of the resistors should be large enough to make the effects of edge roughness acceptably small, but they should be small enough to make the circuit economical and to avoid deviations caused by global variations in processing characteristics.

An example of realizing a resistor with a 3:1 ratio to R1 by three different techniques is shown in Fig. 2.4-2. Since conductors are quite good, R4 offers several distinct advantages over R2 and R3 for attaining this ratio. Comments about the different approaches follow.

1. The long resistor, R2, often cannot be conveniently placed on the circuit in an area-efficient manner. Furthermore, the question of exact length remains open and the fact that the number of contacts are not related by the 3:1 ratio limits the accuracy of R2/R1.

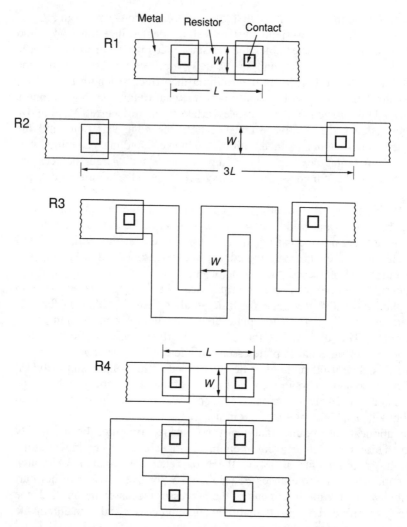

FIGURE 2.4-2
Resistor ratio-matching considerations.

2. The serpentine pattern used for R3 is quite common to keep overall aspect ratios practical. However, the difficulty in accurately accounting for the corners (using the .55 rule) and the differences in periphery length will generally make the R3/R1 ratio the least accurate of the schemes shown in the figure. The contact resistances are also not accounted for in the ratio with R1.

3. Even though the exact "length" is difficult to define, the three serpentined resistors in R4 are ideally identical to R1, so the ratio accuracy is maintained. This approach also accounts for any contact resistance associated with the contacts themselves as well as differences in temperature characteristics of the resistive and contact regions.

For realizing capacitor ratios, the area should be large enough to make the effects of edge roughness acceptably small. If the areas are too large, however, the circuits become impractical both because of the area requirements and because of the increased failure rate due to an increased likelihood of dielectric defects (one or more pinholes), which will short the capacitor plates together. Variations in dielectric thickness must also be considered if large areas are involved. In addition to maintaining the required ratio, the periphery lengths should also adhere to the ratio if possible. Fig. 2.4-3 shows three different methods of realizing a 3:1 capacitance ratio to C1. Several comments about these approaches follow.

1. C2 maintains the same geometry but the length of the perimeter differs somewhat. This will limit ratio accuracy due to variations in etching of the POLY

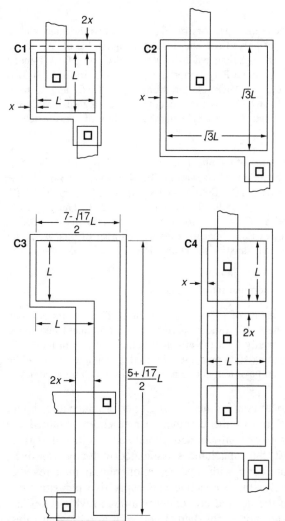

FIGURE 2.4-3
Capacitor ratio-matching considerations.

II edge. Furthermore, the ratio of the small capacitance from the conductor to the lower plate of C2 is 1:1 instead of 3:1.

2. C3 has a periphery that is three times that of C1, but the small capacitance from the conductor to the lower plate is still 1:1 with that of C1. The number of inside and outside corners in C1 and C3 does not ratio by 3:1, thus further limiting accuracy.

3. C4 has the same periphery as C1 as well as the same parasitics from the conductor to lower plates. This will give the best ratio of the three approaches. If the capacitor areas are large, even this approach will be affected by variations in dielectric thickness. Since the oxide layer is typically quite uniform locally, the ratio accuracy for large areas can be improved if each of the capacitors is further subdivided in an identical manner and the smaller capacitors for C1 and C4 are interleaved.

Example 2.4-1. Assume the four capacitors of Fig. 2.4-3 are fabricated with a dielectric between two layers of polysilicon and that the design value of L is 25 μ. Assuming the POLY I–POLY II capacitance density is 0.7 fF/μ^2, the POLY I–metal capacitance is .04 fF/μ^2, the nominal Poly I overlap of Poly II (x in Fig. 2.4-3) is 2 μ and all metal widths are 3 μ. Determine the ratios $C_2/C_1, C_3/C_1$ and C_4/C_1 if overetching of the upper plate (which was not accounted for during design) during etching was 0.5 μ, and calculate the effective number of bits of ratio-matching. accuracy in each case.

Solution. With $L = 25\,\mu$, the area of the upper plate of C1 is $A_{1p} = [25 - 2(0.5)]^2$ $\mu^2 = 576\,\mu^2$, and the area of the metal overlap of Poly I is $A_{1M} = (3\,\mu)(4\,\mu + 0.5\,\mu) = 13.5\,\mu^2$. Thus, $C_1 = (A_{1p})(0.7\ \text{fF}/\mu^2) + (A_{1M})(0.04\ \text{fF}/\mu^2) = 403.74$ fF. Likewise, $C_2 = 1252.878$ fF, $C_3 = 1208.98$ fF, and $C_4 = 1211.22$ fF. Thus, $C_2/C_1 = 3.103$, $C_3/C_1 = 2.9945$, and $C_4/C_1 = 3.0$. To determine the effective number of bits of resolution in each case, assume that the effective number of bits, n, is the maximum integer value of n that satisfies the expression

$$2^n < \frac{\text{nominal ratio}}{|\ \text{nominal ratio} - \text{actual ratio}\ |}$$

Thus, the effective number of bits of C_2/C_1 is 4, and of C_3/C_1 is 9. Based upon the model presented here, the C_4/C_1 ratio is perfect. Edge roughness and oxide thickness variations will practically limit the effective number of bits in the C_4/C_1 ratio to the 8–11 bit range with existing processes. From this example, it should be apparent that care in layout can have a major impact on ratio-matching accuracy.

Parasitics can cause significant deviations in circuit performance and should be minimized during layout. Some of the common parasitics encountered are (1) the resistances associated with polysilicon and doped semiconductor regions when used as conductors, and (2) the capacitances associated with any crossover, from any conductor to substrate, and with any depletion region in a reverse-biased pn junction. Unfortunately, these resistive and capacitive parasitics can be comparable in magnitude to the desired component values to which they are connected if good layout rules are not established. Even with good layout rules, the values of these parasitics may be significant. Clever design techniques and inclusion of the unavoidable parasitics in the analysis when possible, however, help overcome some of the parasitic limitations. The parasitics associated with a depletion region of a reverse-biased pn junction are particularly troublesome since they are voltage dependent and thus difficult to properly account for in analysis and design. Even if accounted for, the parasitic capacitances often cause unwanted *cross talk* between signal paths, and the nonlinear capacitors can cause nonlinear signal distortion that may be unacceptably large.

Cleverness in layout will also often save a considerable amount of area. Even though the concern for minimizing area is always present, it is especially important to minimize area in small digital blocks that will be repeated thousands of times in high-volume VLSI circuits. Three different techniques for connecting the gate to the drain of an enhancement MOSFET are depicted in Fig. 2.4-4. The layout of Fig. 2.4-4*a*, which uses a conventional metal interconnect, requires considerable area. The circuit of Fig. 2.4-4*b* is more area-efficient, but it is not allowed in many processes because of the concern of reduced yield associated with having pinholes, which cause device failure when gate contact is made in the channel. The connection of Fig. 2.4-4*c*, which is termed a *butting contact*, is the most area-efficient, although butting contacts are only available in some processes. Note that a single contact opening is used for the butting contact.

A doped semiconductor region, a second conductor, or a polysilicon strip can be used as a conductor or as a crossover, provided that an insulating layer exists between the devices. Crossovers are often required since jumper wires are totally impractical in integrated circuit design.

In the double-poly NMOS process described in Sec. 2.2, three-level conductor stacking (metal, POLY I, and POLY II) is possible although only a two-level crossover of Poly I and metal is permitted since Poly II cannot cross a Poly I boundary. Metal over a moat diffusion will also serve as a crossover. In the CMOS process previously described, poly–metal, metal–p-well, and metal–moat (either n^+ or p^+) overlaps can all serve as two-level crossovers. In the bipolar process described metal–n^+ or metal–p (base diffusion) overlaps make

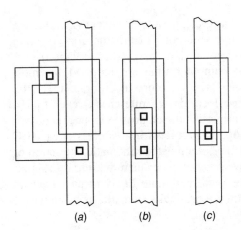

(a)   (b)   (c)

FIGURE 2.4-4
Poly-to-moat contacts: (*a*) Contact off of channel, (*b*) Contacts above channel, (*c*) Butting contacts.

practical two-level crossovers. A metal–epitaxial crossover is also possible, but the resistance associated with the epitaxial layer may be too high to make this practical in many applications.

Most design groups do the layout on an interactive graphics computer system, which serves as a workstation. As capability increases and price decreases, the trend is toward providing each design engineer with a dedicated workstation. Any or all mask levels can be displayed simultaneously, and rapid zooms and scrolls are generally available to provide both local and global information. Once the individual polygons or macros characterizing a mask feature are placed on the CRT, they are added to the geometrical database. After the layout in the CRT is in its final form, so is the database.

As an alternative to the engineer's part in layout, considerable research effort in the past 10 years has been devoted to automatic layout and routing programs. With this approach the computer will place the components and provide all appropriate interconnects (route) directly from the electrical description of the circuit. In addition to saving the layout time, layout errors can be eliminated with these programs. Programs that perform this task are available today and are quite useful for low-volume products requiring a fast turnaround where the area of the IC itself is not of major concern. Widespread use of automatic routing programs is particularly apparent with gate array products, although some of these programs get "stuck" in complicated regions and need human interaction to overcome these problems. Handpacked designs are generally denser than those obtainable with the automatic layout and routing programs. The challenges associated with the automatic layout and routing problem were recognized years ago from research on PC board layout.

Interactive layout and routing routines are also useful since the computer can rapidly do the drafting required in nonchallenging portions of the circuit, whereas the operator can often make better choices for placement or routing in tight situations. Although it may appear to the unwary that the development of such a program is straightforward, the challenge of such a program is attested to by the fact that many millions of dollars have been spent on the development of the routing and placement programs over the past decade, and research activity in this area is still intense.

Layout verification programs, such as Design Rule Checkers (DRCs), are useful for confirming that no design rule violations occur and for detecting some layout errors (since these errors often cause a design rule violation). For large circuits, considerable amounts of computer time are required for most sophisticated verification programs. Some layout editors incorporate the DRC algorithms into the layout program and do local design rule checks each time a feature is added to the database, thus ensuring that the database violates no design rule as it is created. One of the more popular programs in this class is MAGIC from the University of California at Berkeley. Automated schematic extraction or hand generation of a circuit schematic by someone other than the initial designer (who may be too familiar with the design and thus more likely to pass over an error again), followed by comparison with the original schematic, is often useful for detecting layout errors.

REFERENCES

1. N. Weste and K. Eshraghian, *Principles of CMOS VLSI Design: A Systems Perspective*, Addison-Wesley, Reading, MA, 1985.
2. W. S. Ruska, *Microelectronic Processing*, McGraw-Hill, New York, 1987.
3. A. B. Glaser and G. E. Subak–Sharpe, *Integrated Circuit Engineering*, Addison-Wesley, Reading, MA, 1977.
4. S. M. Sze, *Physics of Semiconductor Devices*, 2nd ed., Wiley, New York, 1981.
5. A. B. Grebene, *Bipolar and MOS Analog Integrated Circuit Design*, Wiley, New York, 1984.
6. S. K. Ghandi, *VLSI Fabrication Principles*, Wiley, New York, 1983.
7. "MOSIS User's Manual," USC Information Sciences Institute, Marina del Rey, CA.
8. A. Makherjee, *Introduction to NMOS & CMOS VLSI System Design*, Prentice-Hall, Englewood Cliffs, NJ, 1986.
9. D. A. Pucknell and K. Eshraghian, *Basic VLSI Design Principles and Applications*, Prentice-Hall, Sydney, Australia, 1985.
10. W. C. Till and J. T. Luxon, *Integrated Circuits: Materials, Devices, and Fabrication*, Prentice-Hall, Englewood Cliffs, NJ, 1982.
11. W. Maly, *Atlas of IC Technologies: An Introduction to VLSI Processes*, Benjamin/Cummings, Menlo Park, CA, 1987.
12. A. Sedra and K. Smith, *Microelectronic Circuits, 2nd ed.*, Holt, Rinehart, and Winston, New York, 1987.
13. P. Chirlian, *Analysis and Design of Integrated Electronic Circuits*, Harper and Row, New York, 1987.
14. D. Hodges and H. Jackson, "Analysis and Design of Digital Integrated Circuits," McGraw-Hill, New York, 1983.
15. J. Millman, *Microelectronics, Digital and Analog Circuits and Systems*, McGraw-Hill, New York, 1979.
16. P. Gray and R. Meyer, *Analysis and Design of Analog Integrated Circuits, 1st or 2nd ed.*, Wiley, New York, 1977 or 1984.
17. J. Millman and A. Grabel, *Microelectronics*, McGraw-Hill, New York, 1987.
18. E. A. Vittoz, "The Design of High–Performance Analog Circuits on Digital CMOS Chips," *IEEE J. Solid State Circuits*, Vol. SC-20, pp. 656–665, June 1985.
19. J. B. Shyu, G. C. Temes, and F. Krummenacher, "Random Error Effects in Matched MOS Capacitors and Current Sources," *IEEE J. Solid State Circuits*, Vol. SC-19, pp. 948–955, Dec. 1984.
20. J. L. McCreary and P. R. Gray, "All-MOS Charge Redistribution Analog-to-Digital Conversion Techniques—Part I," *IEEE J. Solid State Circuits*, Vol. SC-10, pp. 371–379, Dec. 1975.
21. Y. S. Lee, L. M. Terman, and L. G. Heller, "A 1 mV MOS Comparator," *IEEE J. Solid State Circuits*, Vol. SC-13, pp. 294–298, June 1978.
22. J. L. McCreary, "Matching Properties, and Voltage and Temperature Dependence of MOS Capacitors," *IEEE J. Solid State Circuits*, Vol. SC-16, pp. 608–616, Dec. 1981.
23. A. H. Shah, et al, "A 4-MBit DRAM with Trench-Transistor Cell," in *IEEE J. Solid State Circuits*, vol. SC-21 (1988), pp. 618–626.

PROBLEMS

Section 2.2

2.1. Sketch a cross-sectional view of the circuit of Fig. 2A.1 in Appendix 2A after fabrication is complete along section line CC′ of Fig. 2A.1a. Repeat with section line CC′, DD′, EE′, and FF′ of Fig. 2B.1a and CC′ of Fig. 2C.1a.

2.2. A POLY I resistor has a TCR of $0.1\%/°C$. What % change in R will be obtained if the temperature of the resistor changes from $0°$ to $100°C$?

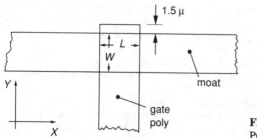

FIGURE P2.5
Problem 2.5.

2.3. What is the maximum permissible current in a minimum width metal trace (Metal I) in the CMOS process of Appendix B if metal migration is to be prevented?

2.4. Compare the incremental cost (cost of adding an additional device) of fabricating a 3 μ × 3 μ transistor, a 1 pF capacitor, and a 10 kΩ resistor designed in the process of Appendix 2B assuming the typical processing costs of Table 1.4-2.

2.5. If the poly gate on the device shown in Fig. P2.5, which ideally has $W = 2.5\ \mu$ and $L = 2.5\ \mu$, has a ±1.25 μ variation in either the X or Y direction due to registration limitations, what is the worst case W/L ratio due to improper registration?

2.6. It is desired to monolithically realize the first-order lowpass filter shown in Fig. P2.6 with a 3 db cutoff frequency of 1 kHz [i.e., $RC = 1/(2\pi 1000)$]. If the resistance density is $R_d = 1.6\ \Omega/\mu^2$ and the capacitance density is $C_d = 0.7\ fF/\mu^2$, determine the values of R and C for minimum area.

2.7. Assuming the typical processing costs of Table 1.4-2, calculate the cost per minimum size transistor (3 μ × 3 μ), cost per unit for a poly–poly capacitor ($/pF), and cost per unit resistance ($/$\Omega$) for a polysilicon resistor in the CMOS process of Appendix 2B if fabricated on 5 in. wafers.

2.8. A resistor is constructed as shown in Fig. P2.8. If $R_s = 45\ \Omega/\square$, determine the nominal value of this resistor.

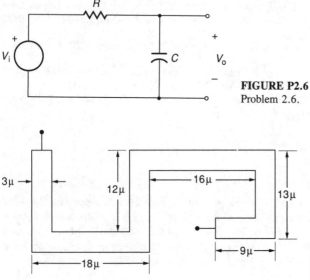

FIGURE P2.6
Problem 2.6.

FIGURE P2.8
Problem 2.8.

2.9. In discrete component design the relative "cost" of components is generally as shown in the following list (from lowest to highest). Make a comparable list for the four most common devices in a CMOS process.

Discrete   CMOS

1. Resistor   1.
2. Capacitor   2.
3. Transistor 3.
               4.

2.10. Etching is used in one process step to pattern polysilicon and in a later process step to make contact openings in SiO_2 to gain top contact to residual polysilicon. Why does the contact opening etch not consume the underlying polysilicon?

2.11. Assume that in Fig. P2.11 $W = 5 \ \mu, R_\square = 30 \ \Omega/\square$ for both poly layers and that the poly–poly capacitance density is 0.7 fF/μ^2.
(*a*) Determine the resistance between nodes A and B.
(*b*) Determine the capacitance between nodes A and C (node B floating).

2.12. Assume the probability of failure for making contacts over a gate of a transistor or on POLY I on top of POLY II is 0.01% because of pinhole problems. If only defects due to gate pinholes are considered, compare the yield of a 50,000-transistor digital circuit with contacts over the gate to a 20-capacitor analog circuit with contacts over the dielectric oxide.

Section 2.3

2.13. Using the design rules of Appendix 2A with $\lambda = 1.5 \ \mu$, lay out the circuit shown in Fig. P2.13. Your goal is to minimize effective area minimizing the cost function

$$f = A_1 + \frac{A_2}{10}$$

where A_1 is the area of an imaginary rectangle that encloses all the components

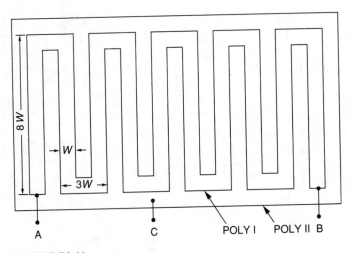

FIGURE P2.11
Problem 2.11.

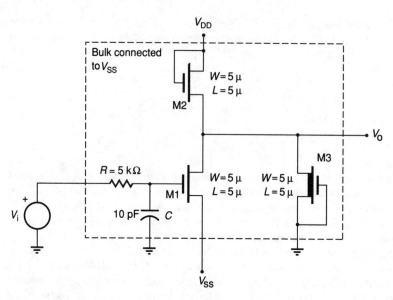

FIGURE P2.13
Problem 2.13.

inside the dashed box and A_2 is the area of a larger rectangle, which encloses the entire circuit (including bonding pads).

2.14. Repeat Problem 2.13 using the design rules of Appendix 2B with $\lambda = 1.5\ \mu$ in the layout of the circuit shown in Fig. P2.14. The substrate is to be connected to V_{DD} and the p-well to ground.

2.15. Repeat Problem 2.13 using the design rules of Appendix 2C with $\lambda = 2.5\ \mu$ in the layout of the circuit shown in Fig. P2.15.

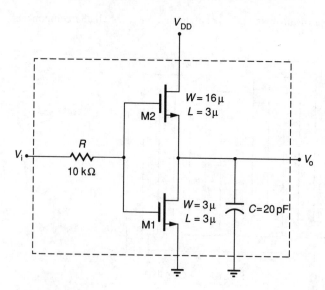

FIGURE P2.14
Problem 2.14.

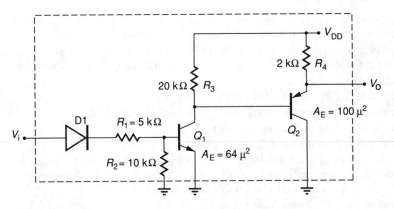

FIGURE P2.15
Problem 2.15.

Section 2.4

2.16. A first-order RC filter with a POLY I resistor and a poly–poly capacitor is shown in Fig. P2.16. What can be said about the following?

(a) The variation (3σ) of the 3 db cutoff frequency due to process parameter variations.

(b) The variation of the 3 db cutoff frequency due to temperature variations (assume TCR = 0.1%/°C and TCC = 200ppm/°C) over the temperature range 0°C to 70°C?

(c) The silicon area required for the circuit.

(d) The overall practicality of such a circuit.

Assume the circuit is to be fabricated in the CMOS process characterized by the design rules and process parameters of Appendix B. Be quantitative with your response.

2.17. Modify the layout of the circuit of Fig. 2.2-5, shown in Fig. 2A.1 of Appendix 2A, to use the buried contact instead of metal for connecting the gate of M2 to its source.

2.18. Design and lay out an input pad protection device using the two-diode protection circuit discussed in Sec. 2.2.1C. Use the design rules and process parameters of Appendix 2B.

2.19. The layout of a single-diode input protection scheme is shown in Fig. P2.19a.

(a) If this is modeled by the circuit in Fig. P2.19b, determine the approximate values of R and C. Assume the devices are fabricated in the 3 μ CMOS process characterized by the parameters in Table 2B.4.

(b) How does the size of the capacitor compare to that inherent in a normal bonding pad?

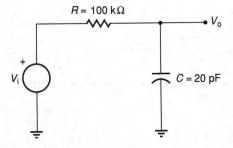

FIGURE P2.16
Problem 2.16.

(*c*) How does the size of the capacitor compare to the typical parasitic capacitance seen on a pin in a dual inline package which is approximately 1.5 pF?

2.20. A layout of a Schmitt trigger circuit that is to be fabricated in the CMOS process of Appendix 2B is shown in Plate 8 in the color plates. Obtain the circuit schematic, including device sizing.

2.21. Repeat Problem 2.20 for the latch circuit of Plate 9.

2.22. Repeat Problem 2.20 for the common source amplifier of Plate 10.

2.23. Repeat Problem 2.20 for the flip-flop of Plate 11.

2.24. Repeat Problem 2.20 for the differential amplifier of Plate 12.

2.25. A die photograph of a CMOS logic circuit fabricated in the CMOS process of Appendix 2B is shown in Plate 13. Obtain the circuit schematic, including device sizing. Assume the minimum metal width in the plate is 5 μ.

2.26. Repeat Problem 2.25 for the logic circuit of Plate 14.

2.27. Repeat Problem 2.25 for the current source circuit of Plate 15.

2.28. Lay out the following circuits using the design rules of Appendix 2B. Try to use good layout techniques and keep the die area to a minimum.
(*a*) Common source amplifier circuit of Fig. P2.28*a*.

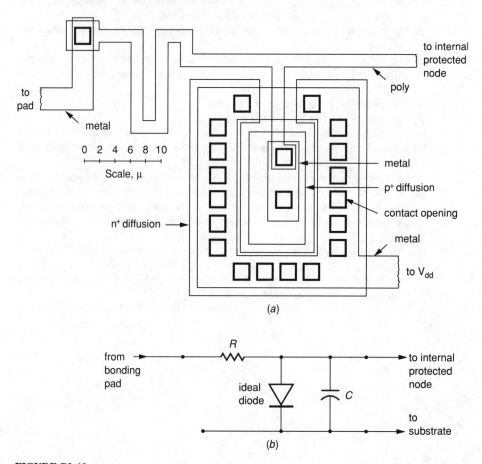

FIGURE P2.19
Single-diode input protection scheme: (*a*) Layout, (*b*) Circuit.

(b) Static RAM Cell of Fig. P2.28b.

(c) Current mirror of Fig. 5.4-12 on p. 349 (device sizes given on p. 348).

(d) Op amp of Fig. 6.5-15a on p. 480 with device sizes given in Table 6.5-12 on p. 487. Provide bonding pads for external connection of R_{BIAS} and assume C_c is a 2 Pf poly-poly capacitor (see Table 2.B.4).

(e) The CMOS Nand gate of Fig. 7.6-14 on p. 554 if all devices are equally sized with $W = L = 3\mu$.

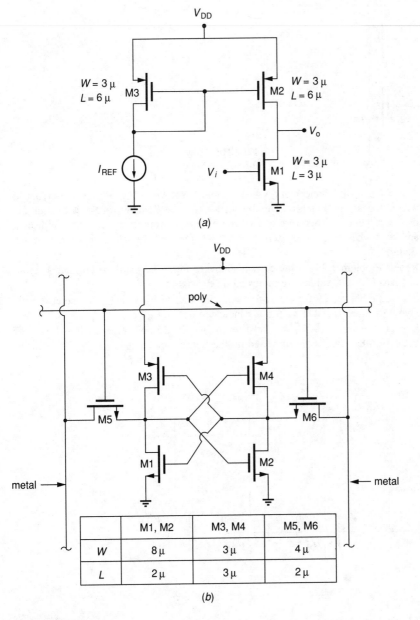

(a)

(b)

FIGURE P2.28
Problem 2.28: (a) Common source amplifier circuit, (b) Static RAM cell.

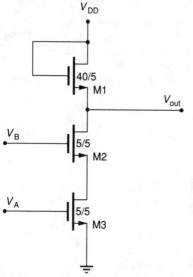

FIGURE P2.29
2-input NAND gate.

2.29. A two-input all enhancement NAND circuit is shown in Fig. P2.29, the layout of which appears in Plate 16. This layout was for the CMOS process of Section 2B of the Appendix. There are one or more layout errors in this layout. Find them and state what needs to be done to correct them. *W/L* values are indicated on the figure.

2.30. Repeat Problem 2.29 for the current source of Fig. P2.30 and the erroneous layout of Plate 17. *W/L* values are indicated on the figure.

2.31. Repeat Problem 2.29 for the differential amplifier of Fig. P2.31 and the erroneous layout of Plate 18. *W/L* values are indicated on the figure.

2.32. Repeat Problem 2.29 for the flip-flop of Fig. P2.32 and the erroneous layout of Plate 19. *W/L* values are indicated on the figure.

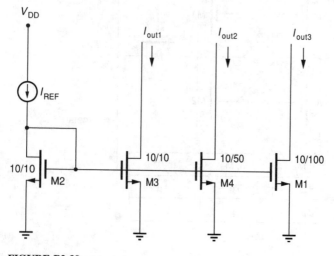

FIGURE P2.30
Current source.

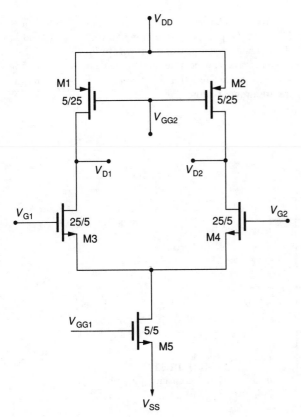

FIGURE P2.31
Differential amplifier.

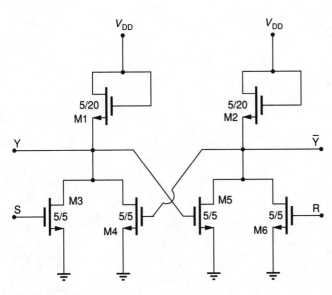

FIGURE P2.32
Flip-flop.

2.33. The NMOS process of Appendix 2A is termed *self-aligned*. Assume that the moat mask was misaligned by $0.75\ \mu$ in the positive x direction and perfectly aligned in the y direction relative to the rectangular coordinates shown (in Fig. P2.33). How much misalignment of the gate mask can be tolerated in each of the following directions if the transistors are to remain functional? Assume $\lambda = 1.5\ \mu$ and the features shown in the figure are drawn features.
(*a*) Positive x direction.
(*b*) Positive y direction.
(*c*) Negative x direction.
(*d*) Negative y direction.

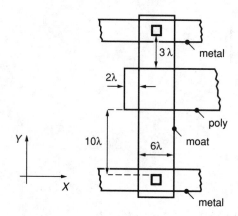

FIGURE P2.33
Mask information for problem 2.33.

APPENDIX 2A
PROCESS CHARACTERIZATION OF
A GENERIC NMOS PROCESS

TABLE 2A.1
Process scenario of major process steps in typical NMOS process[a]

1.	Clean wafer	
2.	GROW THIN OXIDE	
3.	Deposit Si_3N_4	
4.	Apply photoresist layer	
5.	PATTERN ANTIMOAT	(MASK #1)
6.	Develop photoresist	
7.	Etch Si_3N_4	
8.	FIELD IMPLANT	
9.	Strip photoresist	
10.	GROW FIELD OXIDE	
11.	Strip Si_3N_4	
12.	Strip thin oxide	
13.	GROW THIN OXIDE	
14.	Channel implant (optional)	
15.	Apply photoresist	
16.	PATTERN DEPLETION TRANSISTOR CHANNELS	(MASK #2)
17.	Develop photoresist	
18.	DEPLETION IMPLANT	
19.	Strip photoresist	
20.	Strip thin oxide	
21.	GROW THIN OXIDE	
	Optional buried contact steps	
	A.1 Apply photoresist	
	A.2 Pattern buried contact	(MASK #A)
	A.3 Develop photoresist	
	A.4 Etch SiO_2 (open via for buried contacts)	
	A.5 Strip photoresist	
22.	POLYSILICON DEPOSITION (POLY I)	
23.	Apply photoresist	
24.	PATTERN POLY I	(MASK #3)
25.	Develop photoresist	
26.	Etch POLY I	
27.	Strip photoresist	
	Optional second polysilicon layer	
	B.1 Strip thin oxide	
	B.2 GROW THIN OXIDE	
	B.3 POLYSILICON DEPOSITION (POLY II)	
	B.4 Apply photoresist	
	B.5 PATTERN POLY II	(MASK #B)
	B.6 Develop photoresist	
	B.7 ETCH POLY II	
	B.8 Strip photoresist	
	B.9 Strip thin oxide	

TABLE 2A.1
(Continued)

28.	CHANNEL DIFFUSION	
29.	Grow oxide	
30.	Apply photoresist	
31.	PATTERN CONTACT OPENINGS	(MASK #4)
32.	Develop photoresist	
33.	ETCH OXIDE	
34.	Strip photoresist	
35.	DEPOSIT METAL	
36.	Apply photoresist	
37.	PATTERN METAL	(MASK #5)
38.	Develop photoresist	
39.	ETCH METAL	
40.	Strip photoresist	
41.	APPLY PASSIVATION	
42.	Apply photoresist	
43.	PATTERN PAD OPENINGS	(MASK #6)
44.	Develop photoresist	
45.	Etch passivation	
46.	Strip photoresist	
47.	ASSEMBLE PACKAGE AND TEST	

[a] Major functional steps shown in capital letters

TABLE 2A.2
Design rules for a typical NMOS process
(See Table 2A.3 in color plates for graphical interpretation)

		Scalable dimension
1.	n^+ Diffusion (moat) (CIF[a] Green, Mask #1)[b]	
	1.1 Width	2λ
	1.2 Spacing	3λ
2.	Implant (CIF Yellow, Mask #2)	
	2.1 Overlap of depletion transistor channel	2λ
	2.2 Spacing to channel of enhancement transistor	1.5λ
3.	Buried contact (CIF Brown, Mask #A)	
	3.1 Spacing to transistor channel	2λ
	3.2 Buried contact overlap of diffusion	2λ
	3.3 Buried overlap of poly or field	λ
	3.4 Buried contact space to unrelated poly or diffusion	2λ

TABLE 2A.2
(Continued)

	Scalable dimension
4. POLY I (CIF Red, Mask #3)	
4.1 Width	2λ
4.2 Spacing	2λ
4.3 Spacing to diffusion	λ
4.4 Overlap of channel diffusion	2λ
4.5 Distance to n^+ diffusion source or drain edge	2λ
5. Contact (CIF Black, Mask #4)	
5.1 Size (exactly)	$2\lambda \times 2\lambda$
5.2 n^+ diffusion overlap of contact	λ
5.3 POLY I overlap of contact	λ
5.4 Contact-to-contact spacing	2λ
5.5 Contact-to-transistor channel spacing	2λ
5.6 Metal overlap of contact	λ
6. Metal (CIF Blue, Mask #5)	
6.1 Width	3λ
6.2 Spacing	3λ
6.3 Maximum current density	1 mA/μ width
6.4 Minimum bonding pad size	100 $\mu \times$ 100 μ
6.5 Minimum probe pad size	75 $\mu \times$ 75 μ
6.6 Minimum pad spacing	50 μ
6.7 Pad to circuitry	40 μ
7. Passivation (CIF Purple, Mask #6)	
7.1 Minimum bonding pad opening	90 $\mu \times$ 90 μ
7.2 Minimum probe pad opening	65 $\mu \times$ 65 μ
8. POLY II (CIF Purple, Mask #B)	
8.1 Width	2λ
8.2 Spacing	2λ
8.3 POLY I overlap of POLY II[c]	λ
8.4 Overlap of contact	2λ

[a] The Caltech Intermediate Format (CIF) is a format for the geometrical database used to describe the layout of an integrated circuit.

[b] Mask numbers are relative to the process scenario of Table 2A.1.

[c] POLY II may not cross a POLY I boundary. POLY I must always be under POLY II.

TABLE 2A.3
Graphical interpretation of NMOS design rules

(See color plate 5 in insert section)

TABLE 2A.4

Process parameters for a typical NMOS process[a]

Parameter	Typical	Tolerance[b]	Units
Square law model parameters			
V_{T0} (threshold voltage)			
Enhancement	0.8	± 0.15	V
Depletion	−3.0	± 0.5	V
K' (conduction factor)			
Enhancement	25	± 20%	$\mu A/V^2$
Depletion	25	± 20%	$\mu A/V^2$
γ (body effect)			
Enhancement	0.4	± 25%	$V^{1/2}$
Depletion	0.4	± 25%	$V^{1/2}$
λ (channel length modulation)	0.01	± 50%	V^{-1}
ϕ (surface potential)	0.6	± 0.1%	V
Process parameters			
μ (channel mobility)	700	±100	$cm^2/(V \cdot s)$
Doping			
Substrate (N_{SUB})	10	±1	$10^{15}/cm^3$
Enhancement n^+	5	±4	$10^{15}/cm^3$
Depletion n^+	1	±0.5	$10^{15}/cm^3$
Channel stop	150	±120	$10^{15}/cm^3$
Physical feature sizes			
T_{OX} (gate oxide thickness)	500	±100	Å
POLY I to POLY II oxide thickness	750	±100	Å
Total lateral diffusion, LD	0.5	±0.25	μ
Width reduction	0.5	±0.25	μ
X_j (n^+ diffusion depth)	0.5	±0.2	μ
Capacitances[c]			
C_{OX} (gate to channel)	0.7	±0.1	fF/μ^2
POLY I to substrate	0.055	±0.01	fF/μ^2
POLY II to substrate	0.06	±0.01	fF/μ^2
Metal to substrate	0.025	±0.005	fF/μ^2
POLY II to POLY I	0.5	±0.1	fF/μ^2
Metal to POLY II	0.05	±0.1	fF/μ^2
Metal to POLY I	0.04	±0.01	fF/μ^2
Metal to moat	0.07	±0.01	fF/μ^2
n^+ diffusion to substrate (bottom)	0.12	±0.03	fF/μ^2
n^+ diffusion to substrate (sidewall)	0.2	±0.1	fF/μ perimeter

TABLE 2A.4
(Continued)

Resistances			
Substrate (resistivity)	25	±20%	$\Omega \cdot cm$
Moat	10	±20%	$\Omega/\square$
POLY I (covered by POLY II)	60	±25%	$\Omega/\square$
POLY I (uncovered) and POLY II	25	±25%	$\Omega/\square$
Metal	0.03	±25%	$\Omega/\square$
Contact resistance (per minimum size contact)			
Metal-poly	0.3	±25%	Ω
Metal-n^+ diffusion	1.5	±25%	Ω

Breakdown voltages, leakage currents, migration currents and operating conditions		
Punchthrough voltages (gate oxide and POLY I-POLY II)	>7	V
Diffusion reverse breakdown voltage	>20	V
Metal-field threshold voltage	>10	V
Poly-field threshold voltage	>7	V
Maximum operating voltage	7	V
n^+ diffusion to substrate leakage current	0.1	fA/μ^2
Maximum metal current density	1.0	mA/μ width
Maximum device operating temperature	125	$^\circ C$
Minimum device operating temperature	−60	$^\circ C$

[a]Parameter values based upon a 3 μ (λ = 1.5μ) process. Most are the same as used for parameter targets for a 3 μ MOSIS process. Some parameters are not self consistent with others listed in the table and the interrelationships established in Chapters 3 and 4 (e.g., $K' \neq \mu C_{OX}$). This is due to the way parameters have been experimentally extracted from test circuits.
[b]The tolerance is in terms of the absolute value of the parameter relative to processing variations from run to run. Matching characteristics on a die are much better. For example, chip-level matching of V_{TO} is in the 1 to 20 mV range, and K' matching is in the 0.5% to 5% range.[18−22]
[c]Junction capacitances at zero bias.

TABLE 2A.5
SPICE MOSFET model parameters of a typical NMOS process (MOSIS)[a]

Parameter (Level 2 model)	Enhancement	Depletion	Units
VTO	1.14	−3.79	V
KP	37.3	32.8	$\mu A/V^2$
GAMMA	0.629	0.372	$V^{1/2}$
PHI	0.6	0.6	V
LAMBDA	3.1E−2	1.0E−6	V^{-1}
CGSO	1.60 E−4	1.60 E−4	fF/μ width
CGDO	1.60 E−4	1.60 E−4	fF/μ width
CGBO	1.70 E−4	1.70 E−4	fF/μ width
RSH	25.4	25.4	$\Omega/\square$
CJ	1.1E−4	1.1E−4	pF/μ^2
MJ	0.5	0.5	
CJSW	5.0 E−4	5.0 E−4	pF/μ perimeter
MJSW	0.33	0.33	
TOX	544	544	Å
NSUB	2.09E15	1.0E16	$1/cm^3$
NSS	0	0	$1/cm^2$
NFS	1.90E12	4.31E12	$1/cm^2$
TPG	1	1	
XJ	1.31	0.6	μ
LD	0.826	1.016	μ
UO	300	900	$cm^2/(V \cdot s)$
UCRIT	1.0E6	0.805E6	V/cm
UEXP	1.001E−3	1.001E−3	
VMAX	1.0E5	6.75E5	m/s
NEFF	1.001E−2	1.001E−2	
DELTA	1.16	2.80	

[a] The SPICE parameters were obtained by assuming them to be empirical parameters and then fitting measured device characteristics to the mathematical equations which comprise the model by using a numerical optimization algorithm. This approach gives good fit to the model but causes a deviation from the typical parameters of Table 2A.4 and results in parameter relationships which may not be self-consistent with some of the fundamental relationships developed in Chapters 3 and 4.

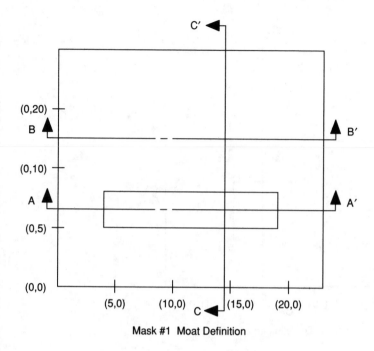

Mask #1 Moat Definition

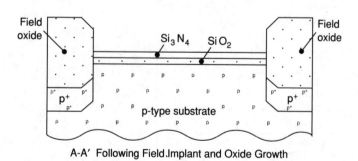

Photoresist layer

$Si_3 N_4$

SiO_2

p-type   Crystalline substrate

A-A′ Following Moat Patterning

Field oxide

Field oxide

$Si_3 N_4$ SiO_2

p^+

p^+

p-type substrate

A-A′ Following Field Implant and Oxide Growth

(a)

FIGURE 2A.1
Process description for the NMOS process.

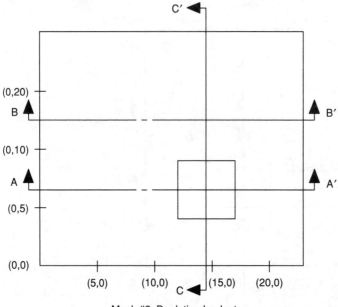

Mask #2 Depletion Implant

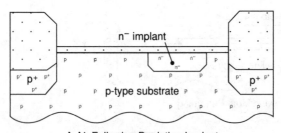

A-A′ Following Depletion Implant

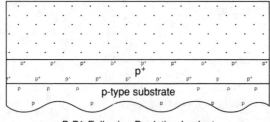

B-B′ Following Depletion Implant

(b)

FIGURE 2A.1
(Continued)

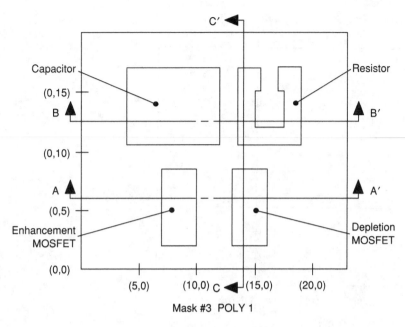

Mask #3 POLY 1

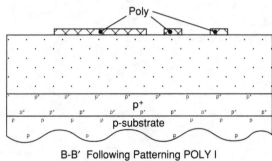

A-A' Following Patterning POLY I

B-B' Following Patterning POLY I

(c)

FIGURE 2A.1
(Continued)

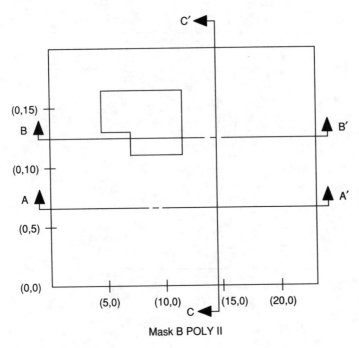

Mask B POLY II

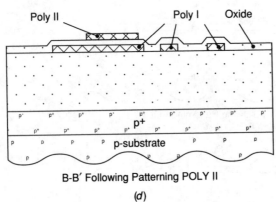

B-B′ Following Patterning POLY II

(*d*)

FIGURE 2A.1
(*Continued*)

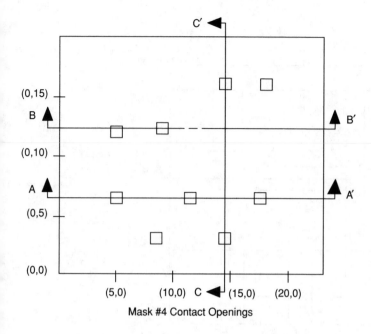

Mask #4 Contact Openings

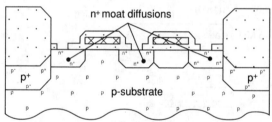

A-A′ Following Moat Diffusion and Contact Openings

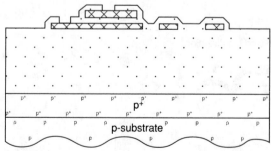

B-B′ Following Moat Diffusion and Contact Openings

(e)

FIGURE 2A.1
(Continued)

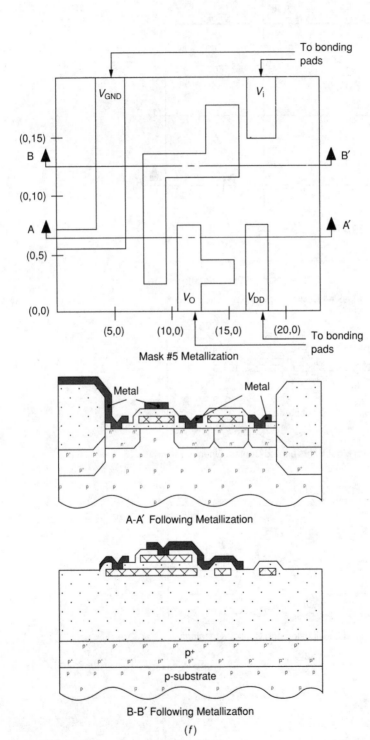

Mask #5 Metallization

A-A′ Following Metallization

B-B′ Following Metallization

(f)

FIGURE 2A.1
(Continued)

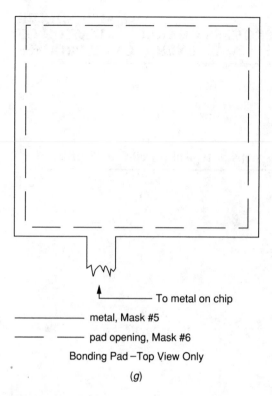

To metal on chip

——————— metal, Mask #5

—— —— —— pad opening, Mask #6

Bonding Pad – Top View Only

(*g*)

FIGURE 2A.1
(Continued)

APPENDIX 2B
PROCESS CHARACTERIZATION OF
A GENERIC CMOS PROCESS

TABLE 2B.1
Process scenario of major process steps in typical p-well CMOS process[a]

1.	Clean wafer	
2.	GROW THIN OXIDE	
3.	Apply photoresist	
4.	PATTERN P-WELL	(MASK #1)
5.	Develop photoresist	
6.	Deposit and diffuse p-type impurities	
7.	Strip photoresist	
8.	Strip thin oxide	
9.	Grow thin oxide	
10.	Apply layer of Si_3N_4	
11.	Apply photoresist	
12.	PATTERN Si_3N_4 (active area definition)	(MASK #2)
13.	Develop photoresist	
14.	Etch Si_3N_4	
15.	Strip photoresist	
	Optional field threshold voltage adjust	
	A.1 Apply photoresist	
	A.2 PATTERN ANTIMOAT IN SUBSTRATE	(MASK #A1)
	A.3 Develop photoresist	
	A.4 FIELD IMPLANT (n-type)	
	A.5 Strip photoresist	
16.	GROW FIELD OXIDE	
17.	Strip Si_3N_4	
18.	Strip thin oxide	
19.	GROW GATE OXIDE	
20.	POLYSILICON DEPOSITION (POLY I)	
21.	Apply photoresist	
22.	PATTERN POLYSILICON	(MASK #3)
23.	Develop photoresist	
24.	ETCH POLYSILICON	
25.	Strip photoresist	
	Optional steps for double polysilicon process	
	B.1 Strip thin oxide	
	B.2 GROW THIN OXIDE	
	B.3 POLYSILICON DEPOSITION (POLY II)	
	B.4 Apply photoresist	
	B.5 PATTERN POLYSILICON	(MASK #B1)
	B.6 Develop photoresist	
	B.7 ETCH POLYSILICON	
	B.8 Strip photoresist	
	B.9 Strip thin oxide	

TABLE 2B.1
(Continued)

26.	Apply photoresist	
27.	PATTERN P-CHANNEL DRAINS AND SOURCES AND P$^+$ GUARD RINGS (p-well ohmic contacts)	(MASK #4)
28.	Develop photoresist	
29.	p$^+$ IMPLANT	
30.	Strip photoresist	
31.	Apply photoresist	
32.	PATTERN N-CHANNEL DRAINS AND SOURCES AND N$^+$ GUARD RINGS (top ohmic contact to substrate)	(MASK #5)
33.	Develop photoresist	
34.	n$^+$ IMPLANT	
35.	Strip photoresist	
36.	Strip thin oxide	
37.	Grow oxide	
38.	Apply photoresist	
39.	PATTERN CONTACT OPENINGS	(MASK #6)
40.	Develop photoresist	
41.	Etch oxide	
42.	Strip photoresist	
43.	APPLY METAL	
44.	Apply photoresist	
45.	PATTERN METAL	(MASK #7)
46.	Develop photoresist	
47.	Etch metal	
48.	Strip photoresist	
	Optional steps for double metal process	
	C.1 Strip thin oxide	
	C.2 DEPOSIT INTERMETAL OXIDE	
	C.3 Apply photoresist	
	C.4 PATTERN VIAS	(MASK #C1)
	C.5 Develop photoresist	
	C.6 Etch oxide	
	C.7 Strip photoresist	
	C.8 APPLY METAL (Metal 2)	
	C.9 Apply photoresist	
	C.10 PATTERN METAL	(MASK #C2)
	C.11 Develop photoresist	
	C.12 Etch metal	
	C.13 Strip photoresist	
49.	APPLY PASSIVATION	
50.	Apply photoresist	
51.	PATTERN PAD OPENINGS	(MASK #8)
52.	Develop photoresist	
53.	Etch passivation	
54.	Strip photoresist	
55.	ASSEMBLE, PACKAGE AND TEST	

[a]Major functional steps shown in capital letters.

TABLE 2B.2
Design rules for a typical p-well CMOS process
(See Table 2B.3 in color plates for graphical interpretation)

		Dimensions	
		Microns	Scalable
1.	p-well (CIF Brown, Mask #1[a])		
	1.1 Width	5	4λ
	1.2 Spacing (different potential)	15	10λ
	1.3 Spacing (same potential)	9	6λ
2.	Active (CIF Green, Mask #2)		
	2.1 Width	4	2λ
	2.2 Spacing	4	2λ
	2.3 p^+ active in n-subs to p-well edge	8	6λ
	2.4 n^+ active in n-subs to p-well edge	7	5λ
	2.5 n^+ active in p-well to p-well edge	4	2λ
	2.6 p^+ active in p-well to p-well edge	1	λ
3.	Poly (POLY I) (CIF Red, Mask #3)		
	3.1 Width	3	2λ
	3.2 Spacing	3	2λ
	3.3 Field poly to active	2	λ
	3.4 Poly overlap of active	3	2λ
	3.5 Active overlap of poly	4	2λ
4.	p^+ select (CIF Orange, Mask #4)		
	4.1 Overlap of active	2	λ
	4.2 Space to n^+ active	2	λ
	4.3 Overlap of channel[b]	3.5	2λ
	4.4 Space to channel[b]	3.5	2λ
	4.5 Space to p^+ select	3	2λ
	4.6 Width	3	2λ
5.	Contact[c] (CIF Purple, Mask #6)		
	5.1 Square contact, exactly	3×3	$2\lambda \times 2\lambda$
	5.2 Rectangular contact, exactly	3×8	$2\lambda \times 6\lambda$
	5.3 Space to different contact	3	2λ
	5.4 Poly overlap of contact	2	λ
	5.5 Poly overlap in direction of metal 1	2.5	2λ
	5.6 Space to channel	3	2λ
	5.7 Metal 1 overlap of contact	2	λ
	5.8 Active overlap of contact	2	λ
	5.9 p^+ select overlap of contact	3	2λ
	5.10 Subs./well shorting contact, exactly	3×8	$2\lambda \times 6\lambda$
6.	Metal 1[d] (CIF Blue, Mask #7)		
	6.1 Width	3	2λ
	6.2 Spacing	4	3λ
	6.3 Maximum current density	0.8 mA/μ	0.8 mA/μ

TABLE 2B.2
(Continued)

		Dimensions	
		Microns	**Scalable**
7.	Via [e](CIF Purple Hatched, Mask #C1)		
	7.1 Size, exactly	3×3	$2\lambda \times 2\lambda$
	7.2 Separation	3	2λ
	7.3 Space to poly edge	4	2λ
	7.4 Space to contact	3	2λ
	7.5 Overlap by metal 1	2	λ
	7.6 Overlap by metal 2	2	λ
	7.7 Space to active edge	3	2λ
8.	Metal 2 (CIF Orange Hatched, Mask #C2)		
	8.1 Width	5	3λ
	8.2 Spacing	5	3λ
	8.3 Bonding pad size	100×100	$100\ \mu \times 100\ \mu$
	8.4 Probe pad size	75×75	$75\ \mu \times 75\ \mu$
	8.5 Bonding pad separation	50	$50\ \mu$
	8.6 Bonding to probe pad	30	$30\ \mu$
	8.7 Probe pad separation	30	$30\ \mu$
	8.8 Pad to circuitry	40	$40\ \mu$
	8.9 Maximum current density	$0.8\ \text{mA}/\mu$	$0.8\ \text{mA}/\mu$
9.	Passivation[f] (CIF Purple Dashed, Mask #8)		
	9.1 Bonding pad opening	90×90	$90\ \mu \times 90\ \mu$
	9.2 Probe pad opening	65×65	$65\ \mu \times 65\ \mu$
10.	Metal 2 crossing coincident metal 1 and poly[g]		
	10.1 Metal 1 to poly edge spacing when crossing metal 2	2	λ
	10.2 Rule domain	2	λ
11.	Electrode (POLY II)[h] (CIF Purple Hatched, Mask #A1)		
	11.1 Width	3	2λ
	11.2 Spacing	3	2λ
	11.3 POLY I overlap of POLY II	2	λ
	11.4 Space to contact	3	2λ

[a] Mask numbers are relative to the process scenario of Table 2B.1. CIF format discussed in footnote of Table 2A.2.

[b] Add 2.5 microns for a source/drain width of 3μ for worst-case mask misalignment.

[c] No contact to poly inside active.

[d] For single metal process, pads are made with metal 1 following design rules 8.3–8.8.

[e] Via must be on a flat surface; metal 1 must be under a via.

[f] There must be metal 2 under the pad openings in a double-metal process.

[g] Objective: Avoidance of too large a step for metal 2.

[h] POLY I must always be under POLY II.

TABLE 2B.3
Graphical interpretation of CMOS design rules.

(See color plate 6 in insert section)

TABLE 2B.4
Process parameters for a typical[a] p-well CMOS process

	Typical	Tolerance[b]	Units
Square law model parameters			
V_{T0} (threshold voltage)			
n-channel (V_{TN0})	0.75	± 0.25	V
p-channel (V_{TP0})	−0.75	± 0.25	V
K'(conduction factor)			
n-channel	24	± 6	$\mu A/V^2$
p-channel	8	± 1.5	$\mu A/V^2$
γ(body effect)			
n-channel	0.8	± 0.4	$V^{1/2}$
p-channel	0.4	± 0.2	$V^{1/2}$
λ(channel length modulation)			
n-channel	0.01	± 50%	V^{-1}
p-channel	0.02	± 50%	V^{-1}
ϕ(surface potential)			
n- and p-channel	0.6	± 0.1	V
Process parameters			
μ (channel mobility)			
n-channel	710		$cm^2/(V \cdot s)$
p-channel	230		$cm^2/(V \cdot s)$
Doping[c]			
n^+ active	5	±4	$10^{18}/cm^3$
p^+ active	5	±4	$10^{17}/cm^3$
p-well	5	±2	$10^{16}/cm^3$
n-substrate	1	±0.1	$10^{16}/cm^3$
Physical feature sizes			
T_{OX} (gate oxide thickness)	500	± 100	Å
Total lateral diffusion			
n-channel	0.45	± 0.15	μ
p-channel	0.6	± 0.3	μ
Diffusion depth			
n^+ diffusion	0.45	± 0.15	μ
p^+ diffusion	0.6	± 0.3	μ
p-well	3.0	± 30%	μ
Insulating layer separation			
POLY I to POLY II	800	± 100	Å
Metal 1 to Substrate	1.55	± 0.15	μ
Metal 1 to Diffusion	0.925	± 0.25	μ
POLY I to Substrate (POLY I on field oxide)	0.75	± 0.1	μ
Metal 1 to POLY I	0.87	± 0.7	μ
Metal 2 to Substrate	2.7	± 0.25	μ
Metal 2 to Metal I	1.2	± 0.1	μ
Metal 2 to POLY I	2.0	± 0.07	μ

TABLE 2B.4
(Continued)

	Typical	Tolerance[b]	Units
Capacitances[d]			
C_{OX} (gate oxide capacitance, n- and p-channel)	0.7	±0.1	fF/μ^2
POLY I to substrate, poly in field	0.045	±0.01	fF/μ^2
POLY II to substrate, poly in field	0.045	±0.01	fF/μ^2
Metal 1 to substrate, metal in field	0.025	±0.005	fF/μ^2
Metal 2 to substrate, metal in field	0.014	±0.002	fF/μ^2
POLY I to POLY II	0.44	±0.05	fF/μ^2
POLY I to Metal 1	0.04	±0.01	fF/μ^2
POLY I to Metal 2	0.039	±0.003	fF/μ^2
Metal 1 to Metal 2	0.035	±0.01	fF/μ^2
Metal 1 to diffusion	0.04	±0.01	fF/μ^2
Metal 2 to diffusion	0.02	±0.005	fF/μ^2
n^+ diffusion to p-well (junction, bottom)	0.33	±0.17	fF/μ^2
n^+ diffusion sidewall (junction, sidewall)	2.6	±0.6	fF/μ
p^+ diffusion to substrate (junction, bottom)	0.38	±0.12	fF/μ^2
p^+ diffusion sidewall (junction, sidewall)	3.5	±2.0	fF/μ
p-well to substrate (junction, bottom)	0.2	±0.1	fF/μ^2
p-well sidewall (junction, sidewall)	1.6	±1.0	fF/μ
Resistances			
Substrate	25	±20%	Ω-cm
p-well	5000	±2500	Ω/□
n^+ diffusion	35	±25	Ω/□
p^+ diffusion	80	±55	Ω/□
Metal	0.003	±25%	Ω/□
Poly	25	±25%	Ω/□
Metal 1–Metal 2 via (3 μ × 3 μ contact)	<0.1		Ω
Metal 1 contact to POLY I (3 μ × 3 μ contact)	<10		Ω
Metal 1 contact to n^+ or p^+ diffusion (3 μ × 3 μ contact)	<5		Ω
Breakdown voltages, leakage currents, migration currents and operating conditions			
Punchthrough voltages (Gate oxide, POLY I to POLY II)	>10		V
Diffusion reverse breakdown voltage	>10		V
p-well to substrate reverse breakdown voltage	>20		V
Metal 1 in field threshold voltage	>10		V
Metal 2 in field threshold voltage	>10		V
Poly-field threshold voltage	>10		V
Maximum operating voltage	7.0		V
n^+ diffusion to p-well leakage current	0.25		fA/μ^2
p^+ diffusion to substrate leakage current	0.25		fA/μ^2
p-well leakage current	0.25		fA/μ^2
Maximum metal current density	0.8		mA/μ width
Maximum device operating temperature	200		°C

[a] Parameters based upon a 3μ ($\lambda = 1.5\mu$) CMOS process.

[b] The tolerance is in terms of the absolute value of the parameter relative to processing variations from run to run. Matching characteristics on a die are much better. For example, chip-level matching of V_{T0} is in the 1 mV to 20 mV range, and K' matching is in the 0.5% to 5% range.[18–22]

[c] Impurity concentration varies with depth.

[d] Junction capacitances at zero bias.

TABLE 2B.5
SPICE MOSFET model parameters of a typical p-well CMOS process (MOSIS[a])

Parameter (Level 2 model)	n-channel	p-channel	Units
VTO	0.827	−0.895	V
KP	32.87	15.26	$\mu A/V^2$
GAMMA	1.36	0.879	$V^{1/2}$
PHI	0.6	0.6	V
LAMBDA	1.605E−2	4.709E−2	V^{-1}
CGSO	5.2E−4	4.0E−4	fF/μ width
CGDO	5.2E−4	4.0E−4	fF/μ width
RSH	25	95	$\Omega/\square$
CJ	3.2E−4	2.0E−4	fF/μ^2
MJ	0.5	0.5	
CJSW	9.0E−4	4.5E−4	fF/μ perimeter
MJSW	0.33	0.33	
TOX	500	500	Å
NSUB	1.0E16	1.12E14	$1/cm^3$
NSS	0	0	$1/cm^2$
NFS	1.235E12	8.79E11	$1/cm^2$
TPG	1	−1	
XJ	0.4	0.4	μ
LD	0.28	0.28	μ
UO	200	100	$cm^2/(V \cdot s)$
UCRIT	9.99E5	1.64E4	V/cm
UEXP	1.001E−3	0.1534	
VMAX	1.0E5	1.0E5	m/s
NEFF	1.001E−2	1.001E−2	
DELTA	1.2405	1.938	

[a] The SPICE parameters were obtained by assuming them to be empirical parameters and then fitting measured device characteristics to the mathematical equations which comprise the model by using a numerical optimization algorithm. This approach gives good fit to the model but causes a deviation from the typical parameters of Table 2A.4 and results in parameter relationships which may not be self-consistent with some of the fundamental relationships developed in Chapters 3 and 4.

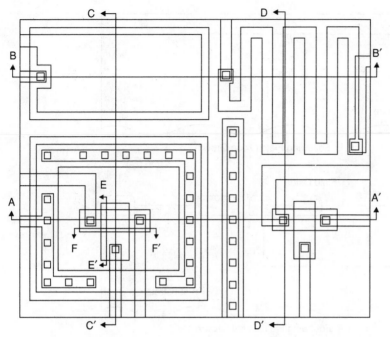

(*a*) Top View (color version appears in plate 3)

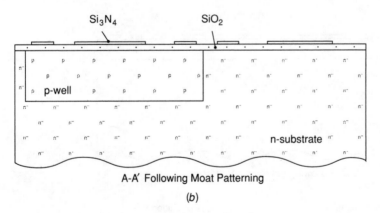

A-A′ Following Moat Patterning

(*b*)

FIGURE 2B.1
Process description for the CMOS process.

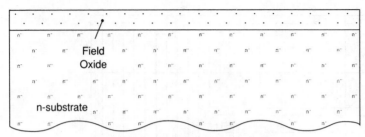

B-B Following Field Oxide Growth

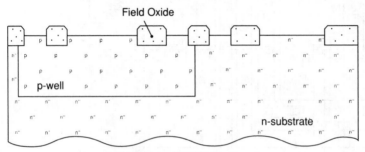

A-A′ Following Field Oxide Growth

(c)

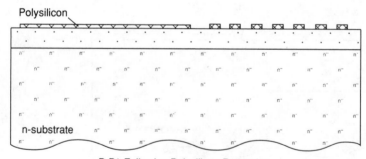

B-B′ Following Polysilicon Patterning

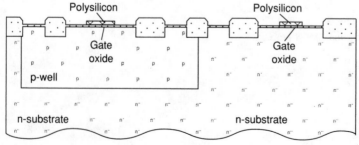

A-A′ Following Polysilicon Patterning

(d)

FIGURE 2B.1
(Continued)

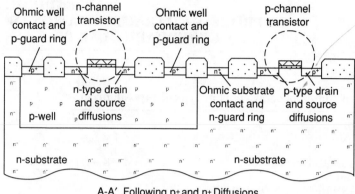

A-A′ Following p+ and n+ Diffusions

(e)

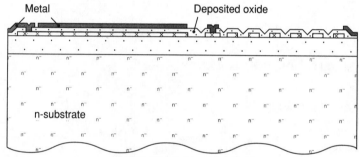

B-B′ Following Metal Patterning

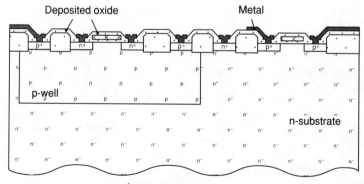

A-A′ Following Metal Patterning

(f)

FIGURE 2B.1
(Continued)

APPENDIX 2C
PROCESS CHARACTERIZATION OF
A GENERIC BIPOLAR PROCESS

TABLE 2C.1
Process scenario of major process steps in typical bipolar process[a]

1. Clean wafer (p-type)
2. GROW THIN OXIDE
3. Apply photoresist
4. PATTERN n$^+$ BURIED LAYER   (MASK #1)
5. Develop photoresist
6. DEPOSITION AND DIFFUSION OF n-BURIED LAYER
7. Strip photoresist
8. Strip oxide
9. GROW EPITAXIAL LAYER (n-type)
10. Grow oxide
11. Apply photoresist
12. PATTERN p$^+$ ISOLATION REGIONS   (MASK #2)
13. Develop photoresist
14. Etch oxide
15. DEPOSITION AND DIFFUSION OF p$^+$ ISOLATION
16. Strip photoresist
17. Grow oxide
    Optional high-resistance p-diffusion
    A.1 Apply photoresist
    A.2 PATTERN p-RESISTORS   (MASK #A)
    A.3 Develop photoresist
    A.4 Etch oxide
    A.5 DEPOSITION AND DIFFUSION OF p-RESISTORS
    A.6 Strip photoresist
    A.7 Grow oxide
18. Apply photoresist
19. PATTERN BASE REGIONS   (MASK #3)
20. Develop photoresist
21. Etch oxide
22. DEPOSITION AND DIFFUSION OF p-TYPE BASE
23. Strip photoresist
24. Grow oxide
25. Apply photoresist
26. PATTERN n-TYPE EMITTER REGIONS   (MASK #4)
27. Develop photoresist
28. Etch Oxide
29. n$^+$ DEPOSITION AND DIFFUSION
30. Strip photoresist
31. Grow oxide
32. Apply photoresist
33. PATTERN CONTACT OPENINGS   (MASK #5)
34. Develop photoresist
35. Etch oxide
36. Strip Photoresist
37. APPLY METAL
38. Apply photoresist
39. PATTERN METAL   (MASK #6)

TABLE 2C.1
(Continued)

40.	Develop photoresist
41.	ETCH METAL
42.	Strip photoresist
43.	APPLY PASSIVATION
44.	Apply photoresist
45.	PATTERN PAD OPENINGS (MASK #7)
46.	Develop photoresist
47.	Etch passivation
48.	Strip photoresist
49.	ASSEMBLE, PACKAGE, AND TEST

[a] Major functional steps shown in capital letters.

TABLE 2C.2
Design rules for a typical bipolar process ($\lambda = 2.5\ \mu$)
(See Table 2C.3 in color plates for graphical interpretation)

	Dimension
1. n^+ buried collector diffusion (Yellow, Mask #1)	
1.1 Width	3λ
1.2 Overlap of p-base diffusion (for vertical npn)	2λ
1.3 Overlap of n^+ emitter diffusion (for collector contact of vertical npn)	2λ
1.4 Overlap of p-base diffusion (for collector and emitter of lateral pnp)	2λ
1.5 Overlap of n^+ emitter diffusion (for base contact of lateral pnp)	2λ
2. Isolation diffusion (Orange, Mask #2)	
2.1 Width	4λ
2.2 Spacing	24λ
2.3 Distance to n^+ buried collector	14λ
3. p-base diffusion (Brown, Mask #3)	
3.1 Width	3λ
3.2 Spacing	5λ
3.3 Distance to isolation diffusion	14λ
3.4 Width (resistor)	3λ
3.5 Spacing (as resistor)	3λ
4. n^+ emitter diffusion (Green, Mask #4)	
4.1 Width	3λ
4.2 Spacing	3λ
4.3 p-base diffusion overlap of n^+ emitter diffusion (emitter in base)	2λ
4.4 Spacing to isolation diffusion (for collector contact)	12λ
4.5 Spacing to p-base diffusion (for base contact of lateral pnp)	6λ
4.6 Spacing to p-base diffusion (for collector contact of vertical npn)	6λ
5. Contact (Black, Mask #5)	
5.1 Size (exactly)	$4\lambda \times 4\lambda$
5.2 Spacing	2λ
5.3 Metal overlap of contact	λ
5.4 n^+ emitter diffusion overlap of contact	2λ
5.5 p-base diffusion overlap of contact	2λ
5.6 p-base to n^+ emitter	3λ
5.7 Spacing to isolation diffusion	4λ

TABLE 2C.2
(Continued)

	Dimension
6. Metalization (Blue, Mask #6)	
6.1 Width	2λ
6.2 Spacing	2λ
6.3 Bonding pad size	$100\ \mu \times 100\ \mu$
6.4 Probe pad size	$75\ \mu \times 75\ \mu$
6.5 Bonding pad separation	$50\ \mu$
6.6 Bonding to probe pad	$30\ \mu$
6.7 Probe pad separation	$30\ \mu$
6.8 Pad to circuitry	$40\ \mu$
6.9 Maximum current density	$0.8\ \text{mA}/\mu$ width
7. Passivation (Purple, Mask #7)	
7.1 Minimum bonding pad opening	$90\ \mu \times 90\ \mu$
7.2 Minimum probe pad opening	$65\ \mu \times 65\ \mu$

TABLE 2C.3
Graphical interpretation of bipolar design rules.

(See color plate 7 in insert section)

TABLE 2C.4
Process parameters for a typical bipolar process[a]

Parameter	Typical	Tolerance[b]	Units
Ebers-Moll model parameters			
β_F (forward β)			
npn—vertical	100	50 to 200	
pnp—lateral			
(at $I_C = 500\ \mu\text{A}$)	10	±20%	
(at $I_C = 200\ \mu\text{A}$)	6	±20%	
β_R (reverse β)			
npn—vertical	1.5	±0.5	
pnp—lateral			
(at $I_C = 500\ \mu\text{A}$)	5	±20%	
(at $I_C = 200\ \mu\text{A}$)	3	±20%	
V_{AF} (forward Early voltage)			
npn—vertical	100	±30%	V
pnp—lateral	150	±30%	V
V_{AR} (reverse Early voltage)			
npn—vertical	150	±30%	V
pnp—lateral	150	±30%	V
J_S (saturation current density)			
npn—vertical	2.6×10^{-7}	−50%to + 100%	pA/μ^2
pnp—lateral	1.3×10^{-5}	−50%to + 100%	pA/μ emitter perimeter

TABLE 2C.4
(Continued)

Parameter	Typical	Tolerance[b]	Units
Doping			
n$^+$ emitter	10^4	$\pm30\%$	10^{16}/cm^3
p-base			
Surface	10^5	$\pm20\%$	10^{16}/cm^3
Junction	1	$\pm20\%$	10^{16}/cm^3
Epitaxial layer	0.3	$\pm20\%$	10^{16}/cm^3
Substrate	0.08	$\pm25\%$	10^{16}/cm^3
Physical feature size			
Diffusion depth			
n+ emitter diffusion	1.3	$\pm5\%$	μ
p-base diffusion	2.6	$\pm5\%$	μ
p-resistive diffusion	0.3	$\pm5\%$	μ
n-epitaxial layer	10.4	$\pm5\%$	μ
n$^+$ buried collector diffusion			
Into epitaxial	3.9	$\pm5\%$	μ
Into substrate	7.8	$\pm5\%$	μ
Oxide thickness			
Metal to epitaxial	1.4	$\pm30\%$	μ
Metal to p-base	0.65	$\pm30\%$	μ
Metal to n$^+$ emitter	0.4	$\pm30\%$	μ
Capacitances			
Metal to epitaxial	0.022	$\pm30\%$	fF/μ^2
Metal to p-base diffusion	0.045	$\pm30\%$	fF/μ^2
Metal to n$^+$ emitter diffusion	0.078	$\pm30\%$	fF/μ^2
n$^+$ buried collector to substrate (junction, bottom)	0.062	$\pm30\%$	fF/μ^2
Epitaxial to substrate (junction, bottom)	0.062	$\pm30\%$	fF/μ^2
Epitaxial to substrate (junction, sidewall)	1.6	$\pm30\%$	fF/μ perimeter
Epitaxial to p-base diffusion (junction, bottom)	0.14	$\pm30\%$	fF/μ^2
Epitaxial to p-base diffusion (junction, sidewall)	7.9	$\pm30\%$	fF/μ perimeter
p-base diffusion to n$^+$ emitter diffusion (junction, bottom)	0.78	$\pm30\%$	fF/μ^2
p-base diffusion to n$^+$ emitter diffusion (junction, sidewall)	3.1	$\pm30\%$	fF/μ perimeter

TABLE 2C.4
(Continued)

Parameter	Typical	Tolerance[b]	Units
Resistance and resistivity			
Substrate resistivity	16	±25%	$\Omega \cdot cm$
n^+ buried collector diffusion	17	±35%	$\Omega / \square$
Epitaxial layer	1.6	±20%	$\Omega \cdot cm$
p-base diffusion	160	±20%	$\Omega / \square$
p-resistive diffusion (optional)	1500	±40%	$\Omega / \square$
n^+ emitter diffusion	4.5	±30%	$\Omega / \square$
Metal	0.003		$\Omega / \square$
Contacts $(3\mu \times 3\mu)$	<4		Ω
Metal-n^+ emitter (contact plus series resistance to BE junction)	<1		Ω
Metal-p-base[c] (contact plus series resistance)	70		Ω
Metal-Epitaxial[d] (contact plus series resistance to BC junction)	120		Ω
Breakdown voltages, leakage currents, migration currents, and operating conditions			
Reverse breakdown voltages			
n^+ emitter to p-base	6.9	±50 mV	V
p-base to epitaxial	70	±10	V
Epitaxial to substrate	>80		V
Maximum operating voltage	40		V
Substrate leakage current	0.16		fA/μ^2
Maximum metal current density	0.8		mA/μ width
Maximum device operating temperature (design)	125		$^\circ C$
Maximum device operating temperature (physical)	225		$^\circ C$

[a] Process parameters based on the process of Tables 2C.1 and 2C.2.

[b] The tolerance is in terms of the absolute value of the parameter relating to processing variation from run to run. Matching characteristics on a die are much better. For example, β_F matching for identical devices on the same die to ±5% and J_s matching to ±5% are achievable.

[c] The base series resistance is strongly dependent on layout. Value given is for double base contact.

[d] The collector series resistance is strongly layout-dependent. It is primarily dependent on the vertical distance between contact and buried layer and buried layer to base.

TABLE 2C.5
SPICE model parameters of typical bipolar process

Parameter[a,b,c]	Vertical npn	Lateral pnp	Units
IS[c]	0.1	0.78	fA
BF	80	225	
NF	1	1	
VAF	100	150	V
IKF	100	0.1	mA
ISE	0.11	0.15	fA
NE	1.44	1.28	
BR	1.5		
NR	1	1	
VAR[b]	19	38	V
ISC		1.5	fA
NC	1.44	1.28	
RB	70	250	Ω
RE	1	4	Ω
RC	120	130	Ω
CJE	0.62	0.48	pF
VTE	0.69	0.65	V
MJE	0.33	0.40	
TF	0.45	40	ns
CJC	1.9	0.48	pF
VJC	0.65	0.65	V
MJC	0.4	0.4	
XCJC	0.5	0	
TR	22.5	2000	ns
CJS[d]	1.30	0	pF
VJS	0.49	0	pF
MJS	0.38	0	

[a] Parameters are defined in Chapters 3 and 4.

[b] Some of these Gummel-Poon parameters differ considerably from those given in Table 2C.4. They have been obtained from curve fitting and should give good results with computer simulations. The parameters of Table 2C.4 should be used for hand analysis.

[c] Parameters that are strongly area-dependent are based upon an npn emitter area of 390 μ^2 and perimeter of 80 μ, a base area of 2200 μ^2 and perimeter of 200 μ, and a collector area of 10,500 μ^2 and perimeter of 425 μ. The lateral pnp has rectangular collectors and emitters spaced 10 μ apart with areas of 230 μ^2 and perimeters of 60 μ. The base area of the pnp is 7400 μ^2 and the base perimeter is 345 μ.

[d] CJS is set to zero for the lateral transistor because it is essentially nonexistent. The parasitic capacitance from base to substrate, which totals 1.0 pF for this device, must be added externally to the BJT.

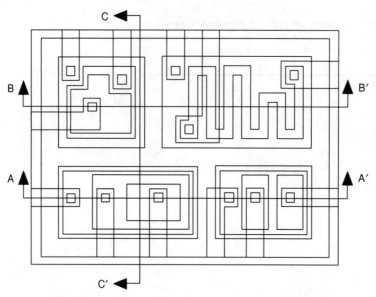

(a) Top View of Bipolar Die[a] (color version appears in Plate 4)

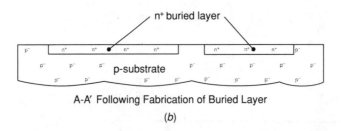

n+ buried layer

p-substrate

A-A′ Following Fabrication of Buried Layer

(b)

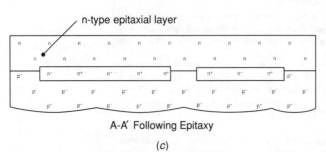

n-type epitaxial layer

A-A′ Following Epitaxy

(c)

FIGURE 2C.1

Process description for the bipolar process.

[a] The base-emitter junction which must be reversed biased forms the capacitor in the upper left. A p-base diffused resistor is in the upper right. The vertical npn transistor and lateral pnp appear in the lower left and lower right respectively.

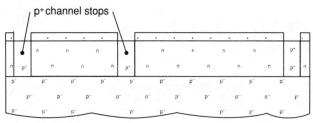

B-B′ Following Isolation Diffusion

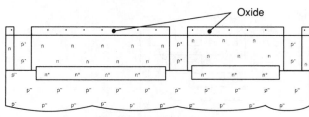

A-A′ Following Isolation Diffusion

(*d*)

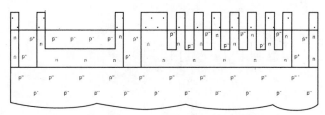

B-B′ Following p-type Base Diffusion

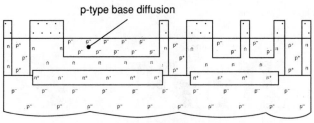

A-A′ Following p-type Base Diffusion

(*e*)

FIGURE 2C.1
(*Continued*)

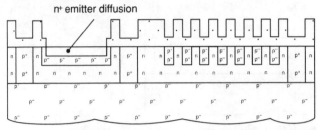

B-B′ Following n⁺ Emitter Diffusion

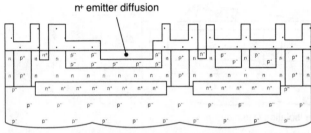

A-A′ Following n⁺Emitter Diffusion

(f)

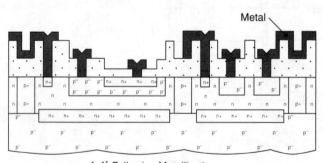

B-B′ Following Metallization

A-A′ Following Metallization

(g)

FIGURE 2C.1
(Continued)

APPENDIX 2D
PROCESS CHARACTERIZATION OF
A GENERIC THICK FILM PROCESS

TABLE 2D.1
Process scenario of major process steps in typical thick film process

1. Screen conductor material	(Screen 1)
2. Fire conductor material	
3. Screen resistive layer 1	(Screen 2)
4. Screen resistive layer 2	(Screen 3)
5. Screen resistive layer 3	(Screen 4)
6. Screen dielectric—first pass	(Screen 5)
7. Fire dielectric	
8. Screen dielectric—second pass	(Screen 6)
9. Fire dielectric	
10. Screen second conductor	(Screen 7)
11. Fire circuit	

TABLE 2D.2
Design rules for a typical thick film process

	Minimum dimension[a]
1. Conductor	
1.1 Width	2λ
1.2 Spacing	2λ
1.3 Metal larger than contacting resistor	
1.3a In direction of resistor	λ
1.3b Perpendicular to resistor	λ
1.4 Overlap of second contacting conductor	λ
1.5 Spacing to edge of substrate	2λ
2. Resistors	
2.1 Width or length	5λ
2.2 Spacing (same or different screenings)	2λ
2.3 Spacing to unconnected conductor	2λ
2.4 Overlap of conductor	λ
2.5 Spacing to resistor or conductor in trim region	
2.5a For laser trims	λ
2.5b For abrasive trims	4λ
2.6 Spacing to edge of substrate	2λ
3. Dielectric	
3.1 Dielectric larger than upper conductor (on top of lower conductor)	λ
4. Pad size	4λ

[a] λ is typically around 250 μ. Design rules depicted graphically in Fig. 2D.1.

TABLE 2D.3
Process parameters for a typical thick film process

Parameter	Typical	Tolerance	Units
Conductor sheet resistance (after firing)	0.5	±40%	$\Omega/\square$
First resistor sheet resistance (after firing)	100	±30%	$\Omega/\square$
Second resistor sheet resistance (after firing)	1000	±30%	$\Omega/\square$
Third resistor sheet resistance (after firing)	10,000	±30%	$\Omega/\square$
Screen mesh size	200		per inch
Thickness after firing (resistors and conductors)	20	±20%	μ
Dielectric thickness	40	±30%	μ
Capacitance density[a]	0.8	±40%	pF/cm^2
TCR$_1$	−150	±20%	ppm/°C
TCR$_2$	+50	±20%	ppm/°C
TCR$_3$	200	±20%	ppm/°C
TCC	10	±10%	ppm/°C
VCR (all resistors)	≤ 60		ppm/V

[a] The capacitance density is strongly a function of the characteristics of the material used for the dielectric.

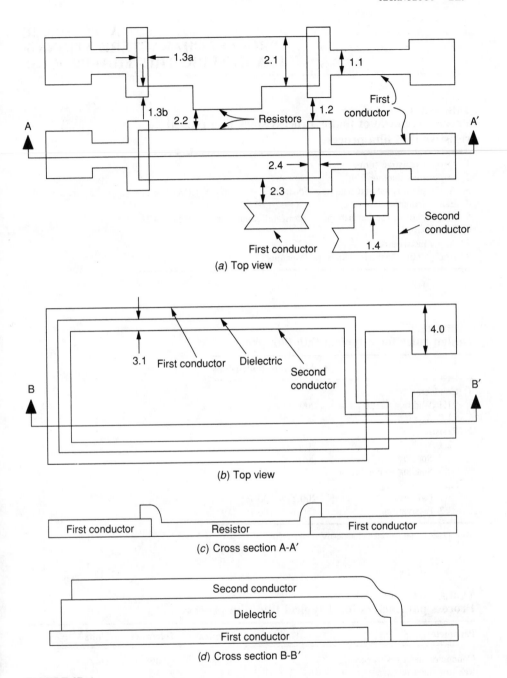

(a) Top view

(b) Top view

(c) Cross section A-A′

(d) Cross section B-B′

FIGURE 2D.1
Process description for the thick film process.

APPENDIX 2E
PROCESS CHARACTERIZATION OF
A GENERIC THIN FILM PROCESS

TABLE 2E.1
Process scenario of major process steps in a typical resistive thin film process

1. Deposit resistive film
2. Deposit conductive film
3. Apply photoresist and pattern conductor (Mask #1)
4. Etch conductor
5. Apply photoresist and pattern resistor (and conductor) (Mask #2)
6. Etch resistor
7. Apply passivation
8. Apply photoresist and pattern pad openings (Mask #3)

TABLE 2E.2
Design rules for a typical thin film process

	Minimum dimensions
1. Conductor	
1.1 Width	200 μ
1.2 Spacing	200 μ
2. Resistor	
2.1 Width	20 μ
2.2 Spacing	20 μ
2.3 Spacing to conductor	200 μ
3. Pads	
3.1 Pad size	200 $\mu \times$ 200 μ
3.2 Passivation	180 $\mu \times$ 180 μ

Note: Design rules depicted graphically in Fig. 2E.1.

TABLE 2E.3
Process parameters for a typical thin film process

Parameter	Typical	Tolerance	Units
Conductor sheet resistance	0.25	±20%	$\Omega/\square$
Resistor sheet resistance	100	±20%	$\Omega/\square$
Temperature coefficient of resistance	100		ppm/°C
Voltage coefficient of resistance	5		ppm/V/mm length
Resistor matching (untrimmed)	±5%		
Conductor film thickness	1000		Å
Resistor film thickness	1000		Å

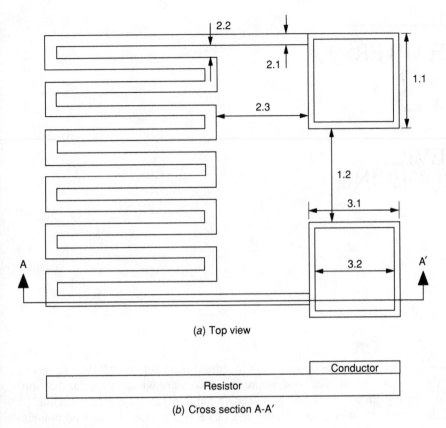

(a) Top view

(b) Cross section A-A'

FIGURE 2E.1
Process description for the thin film process.

CHAPTER
3

DEVICE MODELING

In this chapter device models are discussed. Models for the MOSFET, diode, and BJT are presented. The models presented here are widely used for developing design equations, hand analysis, and initial computer simulations. Both dc models, which are useful for biasing and large signal analysis, and ac models, which are useful for small signal sinusoidal steady state analysis, are discussed.

3.0 MODELING

The fundamental goal in device modeling is to obtain the functional relationship among the terminal electrical variables of the device that is to be modeled. These electrical characteristics depend upon a set of parameters including both geometric variables and variables dependent upon the device physics. In the models discussed, all variables that appear in the equations will be identified as either process or design parameters. The circuit designer has control of the design parameters and judiciously sets these parameters during design. The process parameters are characteristic of the semiconductor process itself and are not at the control of the circuit designer once the process has been specified. The circuit designer may, however, interact with the process engineer to help specify the process that will be used for a particular design.

For most physical electrical devices, at best only a good approximation to the actual relationship of the electrical variables can be obtained. Tradeoffs are often made between the quality of the approximation and its complexity. The required accuracy and the intended use of the model are factors the engineer considers when making these tradeoffs. A very simple model is generally necessary to provide insight for design and facilitate symbolic hand manipulations whereas a more accurate and correspondingly more sophisticated model is generally preferred for computer simulations of circuits employing these devices. Typically, the models are initially developed by analytically applying basic physical principles and then empirically modifying the resulting mathematical expressions to improve agreement between theoretical and experimental results. For the convenience of the circuit designer, it is often also required that the device models have electrical characteristics identical to those of relatively simple circuits composed of basic circuit components.

The starting point for modeling both the BJT and MOSFET discussed here will be a dc model. From this dc model, a linear small signal model and equivalent simplified ac and dc circuits will be derived. The models will then be expanded upon to provide better agreement between the theoretical and experimental results for use in computer simulation. This approach is summarized in Fig. 3.0-1.

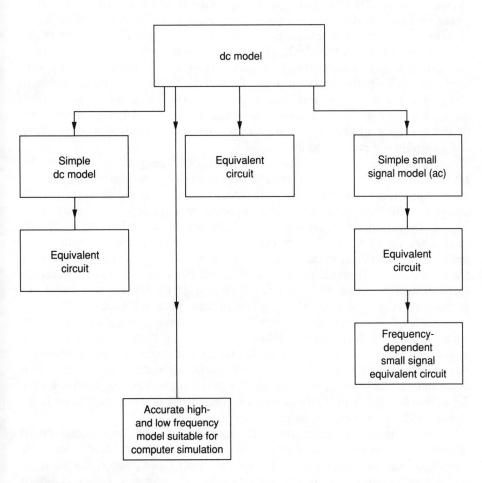

FIGURE 3.0-1
Approach to device modeling.

3.0.1 dc Models

The dc model of a device is a mathematical or numerical relationship that relates the actual terminal voltages and currents of the device at dc and low frequencies. The dc model should be valid over a large range of terminal voltages and currents. It is valid at frequencies where the difference between the actual and dc solution is deemed negligible for the problem under investigation.

For the MOSFET, diode, and bipolar transistor, the dc model is far from linear. This generally makes a dc analysis of circuits containing these devices somewhat tedious.

3.0.2 Small Signal Models

Most circuits perform the task for which they were intended only over a limited excitation range. This range is typically specified in terms of a maximum input signal excursion about some nominal point. Internal to the circuit, these input variations typically cause excursions around some nonzero dc operating point. Often these inputs are sinusoids of small amplitude compared to the supply voltages providing power to the circuit. An analysis of how these *small sinusoids* propagate through the circuit is termed small signal analysis or ac analysis. The points (nodal voltages and branch currents) about which the circuit operates are termed the *bias points* or quiescent points (*Q-points*). Although it might be desirable to have all Q-points at either zero volts or zero amps, it is not practical and generally not possible to do this.

For small signal applications circuits are often designed so that both the MOSFETs and BJTs behave as linear devices even though the devices themselves are actually very nonlinear. This is achieved by restricting signal excursions to a region sufficiently small to obtain approximately linear device behavior. It will be shown later that because of the high degree of nonlinearity in the dc models for the MOS and bipolar transistors, considerable simplification in the small signal analysis of circuits often results if the nonlinear large signal models for the transistors are replaced with small signal linear models that are valid for small excursions about the Q-point. These simpler models are also extremely useful for design purposes. The question of how small the signals must be to be considered *small signals* is often avoided by both authors and practicing engineers, thus raising concern about the validity of analyses based on these models. When addressing this problem, one must consider the circuit topology, device characteristics, and Q-point as well as the maximum tolerable distortion at the output. For some circuits the small signal analysis may be justifiable only for sinusoidal signals in the 10 mV range, whereas for others it may be good for signals in the 10 V range or larger.

To distinguish between small signal, quiescent, and large signal (total) values, the following convention will be adopted. An upper case variable, or when necessary an upper case variable with an upper case subscript or a numeral, will denote the instantaneous total variable value. A lower case variable (with or without a subscript) will denote a small signal value and an upper case variable with a lower case subscript will denote the quiescent value. The relationship between these variables is given by

$$V_C = v + V_c \qquad (3.0\text{-}1)$$

where for small signal analysis V_C is assumed to be periodic with period T and the quiescent value is defined by

$$V_c = \frac{1}{T} \int_0^T V_C(t)\, dt \qquad (3.0\text{-}2)$$

The small signal variable is thus the time-varying component of V_C. It is often the case that for small v, the quiescent value V_c is nearly independent of the amplitude of v. Unless specifically noted to the contrary, it will be assumed in this text that the quiescent value is independent of the amplitude of v. The relationship between $V_C, V_c,$ and v is depicted in Fig. 3.0-2 where V_P and V_1 are constants.

The electrical behavior of linear multiple terminal networks can typically be modeled in terms of one or more established sets of transfer function parameters, such as the h parameters, y parameters, or g parameters. It will be shown later in this chapter that the y parameter (admittance parameter) model of the linear

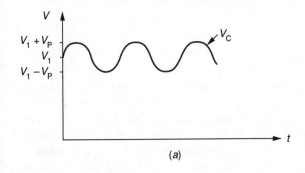

(a)

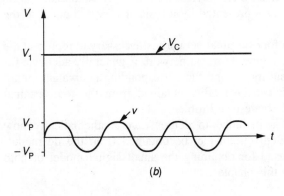

(b)

FIGURE 3.0-2
Relationship between total (V_C), small signal (v), and quiescent (V_c) values (a) total instantaneous value, (b) quiescent and small signal values.

small signal equivalent circuit of both the MOSFET and BJT exists. This model has been widely adopted for modeling these devices. The small signal linear model can usually be obtained very easily and systematically from the dc model of a device. A discussion of four-terminal and three-terminal small signal linear networks and how they can be derived from a nonlinear dc device model follows.

For the linear small signal four-terminal network shown in Fig. 3.0-3a, one terminal (terminal 4) is selected as a reference. With this reference and the assumption of linearity, it follows by definition that the y-parameters relate the terminal voltages and currents by the expressions

$$i_1 = y_{11}v_1 + y_{12}v_2 + y_{13}v_3$$
$$i_2 = y_{21}v_1 + y_{22}v_2 + y_{23}v_3 \tag{3.0-3}$$
$$i_3 = y_{31}v_1 + y_{32}v_2 + y_{33}v_3$$

where

$$y_{kj} = \left. \frac{i_k}{v_j} \right|_{v_m=0\,,\, m \in \{1,\, 2,\, 3\},\, m \neq j} \tag{3.0-4}$$

Since the small signal voltage and current variables are the time-varying part of the corresponding total terminal voltage and current variables in the parent network relative to the Q-point (see Fig. 3.0-3b), then it follows that the y–parameters can be obtained from the large signal variables and thus from the dc model by the expression

$$y_{kj} = \left. \frac{\partial I_k}{\partial V_j} \right|_{V_m = quiescent\ value,\ m \in \{1,\, 2,\, 3\}} \tag{3.0-5}$$

A small signal equivalent circuit of the multiport network is often found useful for circuit analysis and design. It is easy to verify that the circuit shown in Fig. 3.0-3c has the same i-v characteristics as the four-terminal network of Fig. 3.0-3a, which is characterized by Eqs. 3.0-3 and hence is electrically indistinguishable. In Fig. 3.0-3c and throughout this book, the same symbol is used to denote both resistance and conductance. It is assumed that from the context the reader will correctly distinguish these devices and that any conductor can be equivalently and interchangeably represented by a resistor of value equal to the reciprocal of that conductor.

It will be seen later that a four-terminal network is necessary to represent the small signal MOSFET whereas a three-terminal network is generally adequate for the BJT. The linear small signal model and the corresponding equivalent circuit for the three-terminal network can be readily obtained from the four-terminal network formulation discussed above (see Problem 3.1).

The following example is included to demonstrate mathematically how easily the small signal equivalent circuit can be obtained from the dc model. This same technique will be used for obtaining the small signal model of both the MOSFET and BJT later in this chapter.

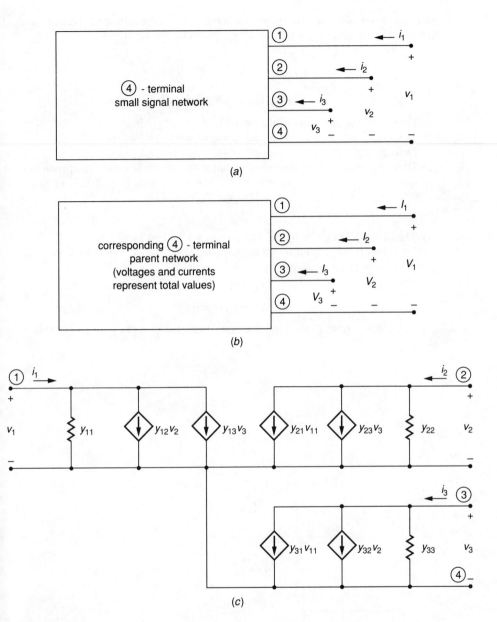

FIGURE 3.0-3
General four-terminal network: (*a*) Small signal, (*b*) Parent network, (*c*) Equivalent circuit for small signal network.

Example 3.0-1. For the network shown in Fig. 3.0-4, the mathematical relationship between the variables $V_1, V_2, I_1,$ and I_2 is given by the equations

$$V_1 = I_1 R_1$$

$$I_2 = \begin{cases} I_O e^{k_1 V_1} + V_2/R_2 & V_1 > 0 \\ k_2 V_1^2 + I_O + V_2/R_2 & V_1 < 0 \end{cases}$$

(a) Determine the dc model of the network.

(b) Determine the small signal model of the network for $V_1 > 0$.

(c) Determine the small signal model of the network for $V_1 < 0$.

(d) Draw the small signal equivalent circuit if the device is biased to operate at a quiescent value of $I_1 = 10$ mA and $V_2 = 4$ V. Assume $I_O = 5$ mA, $k_1 = 0.2$ V^{-1}, $k_2 = 3$ mA/V^2, $R_1 = 2$ kΩ, and $R_2 = 4$ kΩ.

Solution.

(a) The dc model is given by the expressions for V_1 and I_2.

(b) From Problem 3.1 it follows that the small signal voltage and current variables are related by

$$i_1 = y_{11} v_1 + y_{12} v_2$$

$$i_2 = y_{21} v_1 + y_{22} v_2 \tag{3.0-6}$$

For $V_1 > 0$, it follows from (3.0-6) and the expressions for V_1 and I_2 with $V_1 > 0$ that

$$y_{11} = \left. \frac{\partial I_1}{\partial V_1} \right|_{\substack{V_1 = V_{1Q} \\ V_2 = V_{2Q}}} = \frac{1}{R_1}$$

$$y_{12} = \left. \frac{\partial I_1}{\partial V_2} \right|_{\substack{V_1 = V_{1Q} \\ V_2 = V_{2Q}}} = 0$$

$$y_{21} = \left. \frac{\partial I_2}{\partial V_1} \right|_{\substack{V_1 = V_{1Q} \\ V_2 = V_{2Q}}} = k_1 I_O e^{k_1 V_1}$$

$$y_{22} = \left. \frac{\partial I_2}{\partial V_2} \right|_{\substack{V_1 = V_{1Q} \\ V_2 = V_{2Q}}} = \frac{1}{R_2}$$

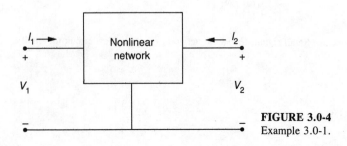

FIGURE 3.0-4
Example 3.0-1.

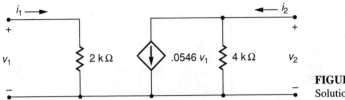

FIGURE 3.0-5
Solution of Example 3.0-1.

(c) From (3.0-6) and the expressions for V_1 and I_2, it follows that $y_{11} = 1/R_1, y_{12} = 0, y_{21} = 2k_2V_1$, and $y_{22} = 1/R_2$.

(d) Since $I_1 > 0$, it follows from the expression for I_2 that $V_1 > 0$ and hence from part (b) that $y_{11} = 1/(2\text{ k}\Omega), y_{12} = 0, y_{22} = 1/(4\text{ k}\Omega)$, and

$$y_{21} = (0.2\text{ V}^{-1})(5\text{ mA})e^{(0.2\text{ V}^{-1})(10\text{ mA})(2\text{ k}\Omega)} = 54.6\text{ mmho}$$

It thus follows from Problem 3.1 that the small signal equivalent circuit is as shown in Fig. 3.0-5.

3.0.3 Use of Device Models in Circuit Analysis

Electrical circuits typically are composed of one or more active devices, such as BJTs or MOSFETS, possibly along with some passive components, such as resistors or capacitors. The designer is generally interested in controlling the relationship between two or more electrical port variables. A typical two-port network is shown in Fig. 3.0-6 along with both the large signal and small signal port variables. The relationships of interest often include the large signal transfer characteristics, such as V_O versus V_I or V_I versus I_1, and the small signal transfer characteristics such as the voltage gain, $A_v = v_o/v_i$ or the input impedance, $Z_{in} = v_i/i_i$. These latter characteristics are often frequency dependent.

The analog IC designer is often simultaneously interested in both the small signal and large signal characteristics. The performance specifications the analog designer must meet are typically expressed in terms of the small signal characteristics, whereas knowledge of the large signal characteristics is necessary for biasing (setting the Q-point).

The dc transfer characteristics of a circuit are obtained by using the dc device models to characterize all devices in the network. A standard nodal analysis of the electrical network that includes the nonlinear device models is often made. It will be seen later that the dc analysis of even very simple circuits that contain BJTs or MOSFETs is often unwieldy. Relating to the unwieldy nature of the analysis of circuits containing nonlinear devices, two points deserve mention. First, most existing practical circuits are composed of very simple building blocks. The overall analysis can often be conveniently decomposed into the analysis of the individual blocks. This approach has evolved because most engineers cannot comprehend complicated nonlinear structures well enough to design structures that are not readily decomposable into simpler blocks. Second, to develop insight

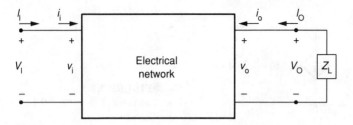

FIGURE 3.0-6
Typical electrical network structure.

into the dc performance of even simple networks, it is often necessary to make simplifying assumptions on the device models. Without these assumptions, the mathematical expressions relating the electrical parameters of interest are often so complicated that they obscure even the basic functionality of the circuit. The simplified dc analysis is, moreover, often sufficiently accurate to be useful for biasing purposes and can also provide useful insight into the small signal operation of a circuit.

The low-frequency small signal characteristics of a circuit are typically obtained in one of two ways. The first involves replacing all devices and elements with a linear small signal equivalent circuit in which the parameters in the small signal models are a function of the Q-point. (The small signal equivalents of all independent dc voltage sources are short circuits, and the small signal equivalents of all independent dc current sources are open circuits—see Problem 3.2.) The resulting circuit is linear and can be readily analyzed. The second method is based directly upon the dc transfer characteristics. If x_i and x_o are the small signal input and output variables of interest and X_I and X_O are the corresponding large signal variables, then these variables are related by the expression

$$\frac{x_o}{x_i} = \frac{\partial X_O}{\partial X_I}\bigg|_{\text{Q-point}} \tag{3.0-7}$$

where the partial derivative of the large signal variable is evaluated at the Q-point. Equation 3.0-7 is functionally similar to Eq. 3.0-5. The results obtained from a direct small signal analysis will be identical to those obtained by differentiation of the large signal variables provided that the small signal models of the devices are obtained from the same dc model used to obtain the dc transfer characteristics.

There are, however, some distinct advantages offered by obtaining the small signal transfer characteristics directly from a small signal analysis rather than from differentiation of the dc variables. First, since the small signal equivalent circuit is linear, the analysis of the small signal equivalent circuit is typically less involved than the dc analysis. Second, more accuracy is *practically* attainable with the direct small signal analysis. The direct small signal analysis is more accurate because simplifying assumptions are often necessary in the dc analysis to maintain mathematical tractability for obtaining X_O and these assumptions make the required derivative of (3.0-7) less accurate. Only a modest increase in complexity results if the more exact small signal device models are employed in the small signal analysis.

Finally, the frequency response of a network is expressed in terms of the small signal electrical parameters. The small signal equivalent network used for obtaining the frequency response is obtained by adding identifiable parasitic capacitors and devices to the small signal equivalent circuit and the small signal device models, respectively. Addition of the capacitors does not affect linearity, so the modelling is straightforward. No practical alternatives exist for obtaining the frequency response directly from the large signal transfer characteristics.

Example 3.0-2. Assume a two-port device is characterized by the equations

$$I_1 = 0$$

$$I_2 = hV_1^2(1 + \lambda V_2) \text{ for } V_1 > 0 \text{ and } V_2 > 0$$

This device is used in the circuit of Fig. 3.0-7.

(a) Obtain the small signal model of the two-port device for $V_1 > 0$ and $V_2 > 0$.

(b) Obtain the dc transfer characteristics of the circuit in the figure relating V_O to V_I if $V_{CC} = 5$ V, $h = 0.04$ mA/V^2, $\lambda = 0.1$ V^{-1} and $R_L = 4$ kΩ.

(c) Obtain parametrically the dc large signal transfer characteristics if the model is simplified by assuming $\lambda = 0$.

(d) Obtain v_o/v_i from the simplified dc large signal transfer characteristics of part (c) if the circuit is biased to operate at $V_I = 5$ V. Assume $V_{CC} = 5$ V, $\lambda = 0.1$ V^{-1}, and $h = 0.04$ mA/V^2.

(e) Obtain v_o/v_i from the small signal analysis if the circuit is biased to operate at a Q-point of $V_I = 5$ V.

(f) If the device has an internal parasitic capacitance from node ② to node ④, determine the frequency response of the circuit of Fig. 3.0-7.

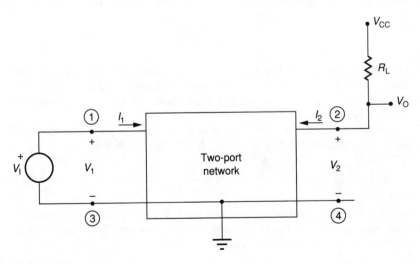

FIGURE 3.0-7
Circuit for Example 3.0-2.

Solution.

(a) From Eq. 3.0-5,

$$y_{21} = \left.\frac{\partial I_2}{\partial V_1}\right|_{Q\text{-pt}} = \left.2hV_I(1 + \lambda V_O)\right|_{Q\text{-pt}}$$

$$y_{22} = \left.\frac{\partial I_2}{\partial V_2}\right|_{Q\text{-pt}} = \left.\lambda h V_I^2\right|_{Q\text{-pt}}$$

$$y_{12} = y_{11} = 0$$

We thus obtain the equivalent circuit of Fig. 3.0-8a.

(b) From the expression for I_2 and KVL (Kirchoff's Voltage Law) at the output, $V_O = V_{CC} - I_2 R_L$, we obtain $V_O = V_{CC} - 0.16\, V_I^2(1 + \lambda V_O)$. A plot of the dc transfer characteristic appears in Fig. 3.0-8b. Note that this expression is nonlinear.

(c) If $\lambda = 0$, it follows from part (b) that $V_O = V_{CC} - (4 \text{ k}\Omega)hV_I^2$. Note that the simplifying assumption $\lambda = 0$ significantly simplifies the input-output relationship.

(d)

$$A_v = \frac{v_o}{v_i} = \left.\frac{\partial V_O}{\partial V_I}\right|_{V_I=5\text{ V}} = \left.-2(4\text{ k}\Omega)hV_I\right|_{V_I=5\text{ V}}$$

If $V_I = 5\ V$, then

$$A_v = \left.\frac{\partial V_O}{\partial V_I}\right|_{V_I=5\text{ V}} = -1.6$$

(e) The small signal equivalent circuit is shown in Fig. 3.0-8c. Hence

$$\frac{v_o}{v_i} = \frac{-y_{21}}{y_{22} + g_L}$$

From part (b), if $V_I = 5$ V, then $V_O = 0.714$ V. Therefore from (a) $y_{21} = 0.429$ and $y_{22} = 0.1$. Since $g_L = 1/R_L = 0.25$ mmho, it follows that $v_o/v_i = -1.23$. Note that this more exact gain differs appreciably from that obtained by assuming $\lambda = 0$ in part (d).

(f) If a parasitic capacitor is added from node ② to node ④, we obtain the small signal equivalent circuit of Fig. 3.0-8d. It follows directly that

$$\frac{v_o}{v_i} = \frac{-y_{21}}{y_{22} + g_L + sC}$$

where s is the standard normalized frequency variable ($s = j\,\omega$). The circuit thus behaves as a first-order lowpass network (see the Bode plot of Fig. 3.0-8e) with a 3 dB cutoff frequency of

$$f_{3\text{ dB}} = \frac{y_{22} + g_L}{2\pi C}$$

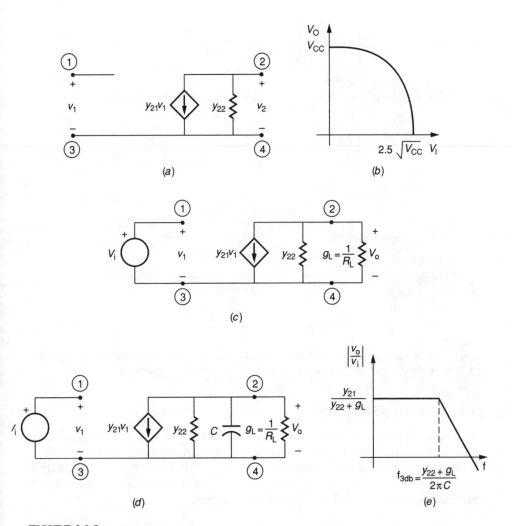

FIGURE 3.0-8

Solution of Example 3.0-2: (a) Small signal device model, (b) Large signal transfer characteristics, (c) Small signal equivalent circuit, (d) Small signal equivalent circuit including parasitic capacitor, (e) Magnitude of frequency response.

3.1 MOS MODELS

The n-channel and p-channel enhancement MOSFET devices along with the convention for the electrical variables established in Chapter 2 are shown in Fig. 3.1-1 along with a top view of the typical geometrical layout. The same electrical conventions and geometric gate definitions are followed for depletion devices.

The following model development will be restricted to the n-channel transistor. The p-channel development is identical with the exception of sign changes in some of the equations. Results only for the p-channel devices will be presented following the n-channel discussions.

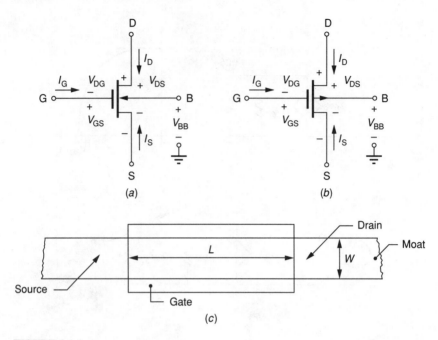

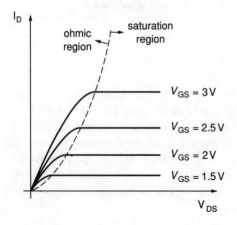

FIGURE 3.1-1
Convention for electrical variables of MOS transistors: (*a*) n-channel, (*b*) p-channel, (*c*) Top view of device geometry. Not shown is V_{BS}, the voltage from bulk (B) to source (S).

3.1.1   dc MOSFET Model

The experimentally obtained $I_D - V_{DS}$ characteristics as a function of V_{GS} for a typical MOSFET were shown in Fig. 2.2-3, and are repeated in Fig. 3.1-2. It is desired to obtain a mathematical model of the MOSFET that will accurately predict the experimental characteristics over a wide range of geometrical and process parameters as well as operating conditions.

FIGURE 3.1-2
Typical output characteristics for n-channel MOSFET.

The starting point will be the dc model introduced by Sah[1] in 1964, which is given by

$$I_D = \begin{cases} \dfrac{K'W}{L}\left[(V_{GS} - V_T) - \dfrac{V_{DS}}{2}\right]V_{DS} & V_{GS} > V_T \\[2ex] 0 \end{cases} \qquad (3.1\text{-}1)$$

$$I_G = 0 \qquad\qquad\qquad\qquad V_{GS} < V_T \qquad (3.1\text{-}2)$$

which was derived for small values (both positive and negative) of V_{DS}. Small values of V_{DS} correspond to the ohmic region of operation discussed in Chapter 2. In this equation, L = channel length, W = channel width, K' = transconductance parameter, and V_T = threshold voltage. L and W are design parameters and are depicted in Fig. 3.1-1c. Note that these refer to the *dimensions of the channel* (intersection of gate and moat). K' and V_T are process parameters and will be discussed later. Although both W and L are at the designer's control, only their ratio appears in the device model. The W/L ratio is the only geometrical design parameter available to the design engineer that affects the performance of MOS transistors. Assuming the parameters K' and V_T are constant, it can be shown (see Problem 3.4) from Eq. 3.1-1 that the device is electrically symmetric with respect to drain and source. The choice of which end of the channel to designate as source and drain is thus arbitrary. This electrical symmetry was anticipated because of the geometrical symmetry of the MOSFET as shown in Fig. 3.1-1c. It will be shown later that V_T is somewhat voltage dependent. The models discussed in this text that include the voltage dependence of V_T are not electrically symmetrical. Electrical symmetry is sacrificed in these models to reduce both model and computational complexity. A convention for the designation of the drain and source regions with the asymmetric model will be discussed later.

A plot of I_D versus V_{DS} for a MOSFET as given by Eq. 3.1-1 is shown in Fig. 3.1-3 for several values of V_{GS}. The portions of the curves that have negative derivatives are dashed because Sah's model is good only when the derivatives are positive. The region where (3.1-1) is valid is termed the *ohmic, linear,* or *active* region. The point where the partial derivative of I_D with respect to V_{DS} is zero is easily found (see Problem 3.5) from (3.1-1) to be

$$V_{DS} = V_{GS} - V_T \qquad (3.1\text{-}3)$$

This value of V_{DS} causes the channel to pinch off, as mentioned in the qualitative discussion of MOSFET operation in Section 2.2.1. For $V_{DS} > V_{GS} - V_T$, the current remains practically constant (independent of V_{DS}) at the value obtained when the channel first pinched off. This value can thus be obtained by evaluating (3.1-1) at $V_{DS} = V_{GS} - V_T$ to obtain

$$I_D = \frac{K'W}{2L}(V_{GS} - V_T)^2 \qquad (3.1\text{-}4)$$

which is good for $V_{DS} > V_{GS} - V_T$ and $V_{GS} > V_T$. The region of operation where (3.1-4) is valid is termed the *saturation region*. It should be noted from

(3.1-4) that I_D is independent of V_{DS}. The reader should be cautioned that the term *saturation region* for a MOSFET does not correspond to the saturation region for a BJT, as will be seen in Sec. 3.3.

For reasons that will become apparent later, the MOSFET is operated in the saturation region in most linear applications. It follows from (3.1-4) that when operating in the saturation region, the MOSFET is inherently a transconductance-type device with the input a voltage, V_{GS}, and the output a current, I_D.

The segment of the curve in the third quadrant of Fig. 3.1-3 where $V_{DS} < V_{BS}$ is also dashed. Equation 3.1-1 is no longer valid for $V_{DS} < V_{BS} - 0.5$ V because the drain substrate interface, which is actually a pn junction, becomes forward biased, causing considerable bulk current to flow. No additional details about the device model for values of $V_{DS} < V_{BS} - 0.5$ V will be given here because the devices are seldom operated in this mode. The MOSFET model based upon (3.1-1) and (3.1-4) is termed Sah's model. This is the simplest model that will be discussed here. In many situations, this model is quite tractable for hand calculations and adequate for the analytical portions of the design.

It can be shown both theoretically and experimentally that the drain current in the saturation region increases slightly in approximately a linear manner with V_{DS}. This is physically due to a slight shortening of the channel as V_{DS} is increased in the saturation region. Defining λ to be the coefficient that represents the linear dependence of I_D on V_{DS}, a more accurate expression for the drain current in the saturation region is given by

$$I_D = \frac{K'W}{2L}(V_{GS} - V_T)^2(1 + \lambda V_{DS}) \qquad V_{DS} > V_{GS} - V_T,\ V_{GS} > V_T \quad (3.1-5)$$

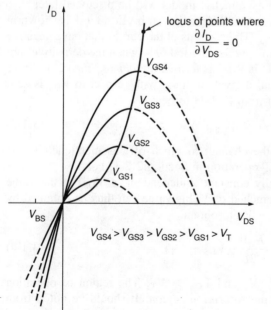

FIGURE 3.1-3
I_D–V_{DS} characteristics of MOSFET as predicted by Sah's equation.

The parameter λ (termed the channel length modulation), in Eq. 3.1-5 should not be confused with the unrelated parameter λ (discussed in Chapter 2) that was used to characterize the minimum feature size of a process. The coefficient λ is quite small for long devices but increases considerably for very short transistors. The effects of λ on MOSFET performance will be discussed later. The MOSFET model defined by (3.1-1) and (3.1-5), which differs from the model of Sah only through the parameter λ, is termed the Shichman-Hodges model[2]. Some authors also multiply the drain current in the ohmic region by the parameter $(1 + \lambda V_{DS})$. We have not done so because there is no physical justification to do so, since the model becomes more complicated in the ohmic region, and since λV_{DS} is so small in the ohmic region that it has little effect on I_D. By not making such a modification, however, we are creating a slight discontinuity in our device model at $V_{DS} = V_{GS} - V_T$ (see Problem 3.10). This discontinuity could cause problems in computer simulations, which require continuity of the functions as well as of the derivatives, but should not cause much of a problem for hand calculations since the device is seldom operated at the saturation–ohmic transition region. The discontinuity due to λ effects is depicted in Fig. 3.1-4. Note that all projections from the saturation region into Quadrant 2 intersect the V_{DS} axis at $-1/\lambda$. It should be emphasized that the discontinuity in the model has been introduced only for reducing model complexity and that models used in computer simulators, such as the program SPICE which will be discussed in Chapter 4, are invariably continuous at this transition.

The threshold voltage, V_T, is somewhat dependent upon the bulk–source voltage. This dependence can be anticipated since the bulk–channel voltage will affect the carriers in the depletion region under the gate, which in turn affect the voltage that must be applied to the gate to form the inversion layer. This dependence can be approximated by

$$V_T = V_{T0} + \gamma \left(\sqrt{\phi - V_{BS}} - \sqrt{\phi} \right) \tag{3.1-6}$$

where V_{BS} is the bulk–source voltage and V_{T0}, γ, and ϕ are process parameters:

$$V_{T0} = \text{threshold voltage for } V_{BS} = 0$$

$$\gamma = \text{bulk threshold parameter}$$

$$\phi = \text{strong inversion surface potential}$$

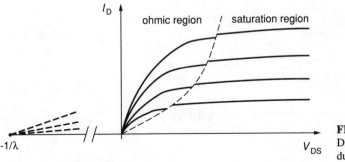

FIGURE 3.1-4
Discontinuity in model due to λ effects.

At this point it appears that the design engineer can control V_T with V_{BS} and thus have a second means (in addition to the W/L ratio) of controlling the characteristics of the MOS transistor. This V_{BS} dependence, which typically is controlled through the bulk voltage, V_{BB}, actually offers very little additional flexibility to the designer for two reasons. First, the threshold voltage is only weakly dependent upon V_{BS}. Second, since the bulks of all transistors are common in an NMOS process, the bulk voltage for the entire IC is established at a single value. Tailoring the characteristics of individual transistors is therefore impossible. For CMOS it is conceptually possible to have individual control of those MOSFETS formed in the tubs (wells) by independently controlling the tub voltages. For practical considerations, however, all tubs of the same type (p or n) are often tied together and connected to a common voltage, thus removing this potential flexibility in controlling individual device characteristics although individual tub potentials are established in some analog circuits. A typical plot of V_T versus V_{BS} appears in Fig. 3.1-5. Note that the change in V_T can be quite significant for large V_{BS}. The effect becomes even worse with larger γ.

Note also that V_T as modeled by (3.1-6) is not symmetric with respect to drain and source. This causes the expression for I_D to be asymmetric with respect to drain and source. This is somewhat disturbing because of the geometrical symmetry of the MOSFET. Models of the MOSFET that maintain the electrical symmetry are available[3], but the increased complexity makes them unsuitable for most hand manipulations. The approximation for V_T given in (3.1-6) gives reasonably close agreement between theoretical and experimental results while still maintaining an acceptable degree of mathematical tractability in hand calculations. The convention usually followed in making the drain and source designations is to label these regions so that $V_{DS} > 0$. With this convention, the drain and source designations may not remain fixed in some analyses.

For n-channel transistors the devices are termed enhancement if $V_{T0} > 0$ and depletion if $V_{T0} < 0$. p-channel MOSFETs are enhancement mode devices if $V_{T0} < 0$ and depletion type if $V_{T0} > 0$.

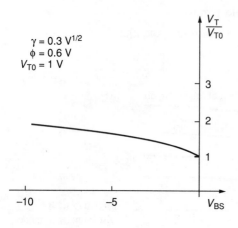

$\gamma = 0.3\ V^{1/2}$
$\phi = 0.6\ V$
$V_{T0} = 1\ V$

FIGURE 3.1-5
Effects of V_{BS} on threshold voltage.

The transconductance parameter, K', can be expressed in terms of other physical process parameters by

$$K' = \mu C_{\text{ox}} \tag{3.1-7}$$

where C_{ox} = capacitance density (capacitance per unit area) of the gate-channel capacitor, and μ = channel mobility.

A summary of the MOSFET model for both n-channel and p-channel devices that is adequate for most dc hand calculations appears in Table 3.1-1. For the purpose of subsequent calculations, process parameters for typical $3\,\mu$ NMOS and CMOS processes such as those described in Section 2.2.1 using the design rules of Tables 2A.2 and 2B.2 are given in Table 3.1-2. This simplified parameter set is compatible with the more detailed descriptions of Tables 2A.4 and 2B.4.

TABLE 3.1-1
Low-frequency MOSFET model

n-channel MOSFET

| $I_G = 0$ | | (1) |

$$I_D = \begin{cases} 0 & V_{\text{GS}} < V_{\text{T}} \text{ (cutoff)}, \ V_{\text{DS}} \geq 0 \quad (2) \\[2mm] \dfrac{K'W}{L}\left(V_{\text{GS}} - V_{\text{T}} - \dfrac{V_{\text{DS}}}{2}\right) V_{\text{DS}} & V_{\text{GS}} > V_{\text{T}}, \ 0 < V_{\text{DS}} < V_{\text{GS}} - V_{\text{T}} \text{ (ohmic)} \quad (3) \\[2mm] \dfrac{K'W}{2L}(V_{\text{GS}} - V_{\text{T}})^2 (1 + \lambda V_{\text{DS}}) & V_{\text{GS}} > V_{\text{T}}, \ V_{\text{DS}} > V_{\text{GS}} - V_{\text{T}} \text{ (saturation)} \quad (4) \end{cases}$$

where $\quad V_{\text{T}} = V_{\text{T0}} + \gamma(\sqrt{\phi - V_{\text{BS}}} - \sqrt{\phi})$ (5)

p-channel MOSFET

| $I_G = 0$ | | (6) |

$$I_D = \begin{cases} 0 & V_{\text{GS}} > V_{\text{T}} \text{ (cutoff)}, \ V_{\text{DS}} \leq 0 \quad (7) \\[2mm] -\dfrac{K'W}{L}\left(V_{\text{GS}} - V_{\text{T}} - \dfrac{V_{\text{DS}}}{2}\right) V_{\text{DS}} & V_{\text{GS}} < V_{\text{T}}, \ 0 > V_{\text{DS}} > V_{\text{GS}} - V_{\text{T}} \text{ (ohmic)} \quad (8) \\[2mm] -\dfrac{K'W}{2L}(V_{\text{GS}} - V_{\text{T}})^2 (1 - \lambda V_{\text{DS}}) & V_{\text{GS}} < V_{\text{T}}, \ V_{\text{DS}} < V_{\text{GS}} - V_{\text{T}} \text{ (saturation)} \quad (9) \end{cases}$$

where $\quad V_{\text{T}} = V_{\text{T0}} - \gamma(\sqrt{\phi + V_{\text{BS}}} - \sqrt{\phi})$ (10)

Design parameters: W = channel width
                        L = channel length

Process parameters: K' = transconductance parameter
                        V_{T0} = threshold voltage for $V_{\text{BS}} = 0$
                        γ = bulk threshold parameter
                        ϕ = strong inversion surface potential
                        λ = channel length modulation parameter

K', γ, ϕ, and λ are positive for both n-channel and p-channel transistors. n-channel transistors are termed enhancement if $V_{\text{T0}} > 0$ and depletion if $V_{\text{T0}} < 0$. p-channel transistors are termed enhancement if $V_{\text{T0}} < 0$ and depletion if $V_{\text{T0}} > 0$.

TABLE 3.1-2
Typical process parameters for 3 μ NMOS and CMOS processes

Parameter	n-channel	p-channel	units
K'	24	8	$\mu\,A/V^2$
V_{T0E}	0.75	−0.75	V
V_{T0D}	−3	3	V
$\gamma_{(CMOS)}$	0.8	0.4	$V^{1/2}$
$\gamma_{(NMOS)}$	0.4		$V^{1/2}$
ϕ	0.6	0.6	V
λ	0.01	0.02	V^{-1}
θ (for short channels)	0.2	0.2	V^{-1}

Plots of I_D versus V_{DS} for Sah's model and the Shichman-Hodges model are compared in Fig. 3.1-6. In this plot, the Shichman-Hodges model includes the $(1 + \lambda V_{DS})$ multiplier in the ohmic region to maintain continuity at the transition.

Many algorithms exist for extracting model parameters from experimental data. Since the models do not perfectly match the physical devices, the various parameter extraction schemes will not yield identical parameter values. A parameter extraction scheme that gives reasonably good correlation between experimental and theoretical results in the neighborhood of the intended operating point should be adopted (see Problem 3.6).

The operating regions of the MOSFET in the I_D–V_{DS} plane are shown in Fig. 3.1-7. The near linear relationship between V_{DS} and I_D can be seen in the ohmic (linear) region. The dependence of I_D on V_{GS}, and essential independence from V_{DS}, should be apparent in the saturation region.

Equivalent circuits for the dc operation of the MOSFET are shown in Fig. 3.1-8. The first circuit is valid for small V_{DS} in the ohmic region. The model that corresponds to this circuit can be obtained from the expression for I_D in the ohmic

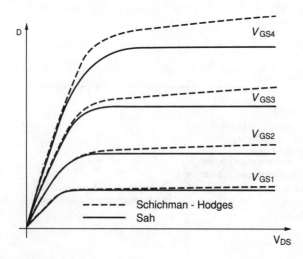

FIGURE 3.1-6
Comparison of Sah's model and the Shichman-Hodges model.

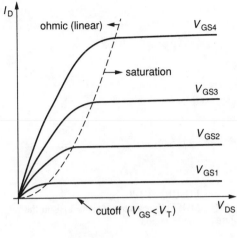

ohmic (linear)

saturation

V_{GS4}

V_{GS3}

V_{GS2}

V_{GS1}

cutoff ($V_{GS} < V_T$)

$V_T < V_{GS1} < V_{GS2} < V_{GS3} < V_{GS4}$

FIGURE 3.1-7
Regions of operation of MOSFET in I_D–V_{DS} plane.

region (Eq. 3.1-1) by assuming $V_{DS}/2$ is negligible compared to $(V_{GS} - V_T)$. With this assumption a linear relationship between I_D and V_{DS} ensues and results in an equivalent FET resistance of

$$R_{FET} \simeq \frac{L}{W\,K\,'(V_{GS} - V_T)} \qquad (3.1\text{-}8)$$

As V_{DS} increases towards $(V_{GS} - V_T)$, it follows from (3.1-1) that the relationship between I_D and V_{DS} becomes nonlinear. For many applications the nonlinear

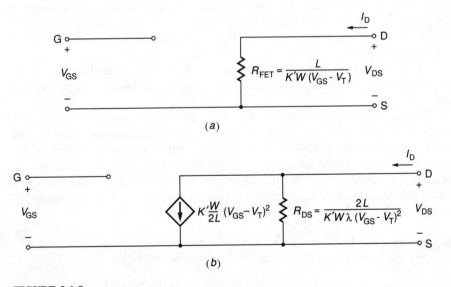

FIGURE 3.1-8
Equivalent circuits of MOSFET for dc operation: (*a*) Ohmic region (small V_{DS}), (*b*) Saturation region.

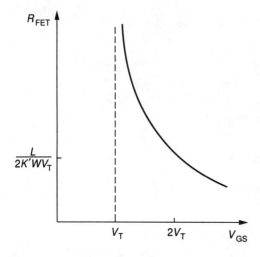

FIGURE 3.1-9
MOSFET resistance versus V_{GS} in the ohmic region.

effects, which generally cause harmonic distortion, are small provided $V_{DS} < (V_{GS} - V_T)/3$. The MOSFET is often used in the ohmic region as a Voltage Variable Resistor (VVR) by using V_{GS} as the controlling voltage. A plot of R_{FET} versus V_{GS} obtained from Eq. 3.1-8 is depicted in Fig. 3.1-9. Note that a very large adjustment range is possible but that R_{FET} is very sensitive to small changes in V_{GS} for values of V_{GS} close to V_T. In addition to the high sensitivity for V_{GS} close to V_T, two other concerns practically preclude utilizing this device as a very high impedance resistor in this region. First, the model we introduced in Table 3.1-1, which was used to derive (3.1-8), is not very accurate for small $(V_{GS} - V_T)$. A more accurate model in this region based upon what is called weak inversion operation is discussed in a later section. Second, the assumption that $| V_{DS} | < V_{GS} - V_T$ forces the allowable signal swing across the resistor to approach 0 as V_{GS} approaches V_T. This practically limits where this "large" resistor can be used.

At this point, it is assumed that the VVR is used in applications where $I_D > 0$. Extension to bidirectional currents can be made. Details can be found in Sec. 3.1.7.

The equivalent circuit of Fig. 3.1-8b is valid in the saturation region. This can be verified by observing that the voltage and current characteristics of the circuit agree with the MOSFET model in the saturation region defined by Eq. 3.1-5. The effects of the resistor R_{DS} in this equivalent circuit are negligible in most dc applications. This dc equivalent circuit, which is useful for biasing, is highly nonlinear and should not be confused with the small signal equivalent circuit, which will be discussed in the following section.

Example 3.1-1. Using the typical NMOS process parameters of Table 3.1-2,
(*a*) Determine the output voltage for the circuit shown in Fig. 3.1-10 if $R = 15$ kΩ.
(*b*) Determine the maximum value of R allowable to keep M1 operating in the saturation region.

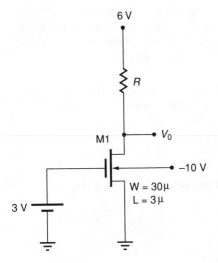

FIGURE 3.1-10
Example 3.1-1.

Solution.

(a) Initially the region of operation of M1 must be determined. To make this determination, it is necessary to obtain V_T. From (3.1-6) it follows that

$$V_T = 0.75 \text{ V} + 0.4 \text{ V}^{1/2}(\sqrt{0.6 \text{ V} - (10 \text{ V})} - \sqrt{0.6 \text{ V}}) = 1.74 \text{ V}$$

Note that this differs considerably from $V_{T0} = 0.75$ V! Since $V_{GS} = 3$ V, it can be concluded that M1 is in either the ohmic or saturation region. At this point, it is expedient to assume a state for M1, solve for V_O, and then either verify the assumption is valid or conclude that the device is operating in the alternate state.

With this approach, assume M1 is in the saturation region. Then, neglecting λ effects,

$$I_{D1} = K' \frac{W}{2L} (V_{GS} - V_T)^2$$

$$= 24 \ \mu\text{A/V}^2 \left(\frac{30 \ \mu}{3 \ \mu}\right)\left(\frac{1}{2}\right)(3 \text{ V} - 1.74 \text{ V})^2$$

$$= 190.5 \ \mu\text{A}$$

Thus

$$V_O = 6 \text{ V} - I_{D1}R = 3.14 \text{ V}$$

It remains to verify the region of operation. Since $V_{DS} = V_O$, it follows that $V_{DS} > V_{GS} - V_T$. Thus, the initial assumption on the region of operation was valid and the value of $V_O = 3.14$ V is correct.

(b) The maximum value of R (R_{MAX}) for saturation region operation will be that value which makes $V_{DS} = V_{GS} - V_T$. Hence,

$$6 \text{ V} - (190.5 \ \mu\text{A})R_{MAX} = (3 \text{ V} - 1.74 \text{ V})$$

and thus

$$R_{MAX} = 24.9 \text{ k}\Omega.$$

Example 3.1-2. Determine the size of M2 in Fig. 3.1-11 with minimum area so that $V_O = 3$ V. Assume M1 is minimum size. Use the NMOS process discussed in Sec. 2.2-1 along with the design rules of Appendix 2A (with a feature size $\lambda = 1.5 \, \mu$) and the process parameters of Table 3.1-2. Neglect λ effects.

Solution. M1 will be considered first. Since $V_{BS} = 0$, it follows that $V_{T1} = V_{T0} = 0.75$ V. The region of operation for M1 must be determined. Since $V_{GS1} = 2$ V $> V_{T1}$, it can be concluded that M1 is not cutoff. Checking

$$\frac{V_{DS1}}{(V_{GS1} - V_{T1})} = \frac{3}{(2 - 0.75)} = 2.4 > 1$$

it can be concluded that M1 is operating in the saturation region. Thus,

$$I_{D1} = \frac{K'W_1}{2L_1}(V_{GS1} - V_{T1})^2$$

Considering now M2, $V_{BS2} = -3$ V (since $V_{BS1} = 0$ and $V_{S2} = V_O$). From Table 3.2-1, the nominal threshold voltage of M2, V_{T20}, is $V_{T0D} = -3$ V. Therefore,

$$V_{T2} = V_{T20} + \gamma \left[\sqrt{\phi - V_{BS}} - \sqrt{\phi} \right] = -2.55 \text{ V}$$

To check the region of operation of M2, observe that $V_{GS2} = 0 > V_{T2}$, so M2 is in either the active or saturation region. Checking

$$\frac{V_{DS2}}{V_{GS2} - V_{T2}} = \frac{5}{[0 - (-2.55)]} = 1.96 > 1$$

Thus, it can be concluded that M2 is also operating in the saturation region. Hence

$$I_{D2} = \frac{K'W_2}{2L_2}(V_{GS2} - V_{T2})^2 = \frac{K'W_2}{2L_2}V_{T2}^2$$

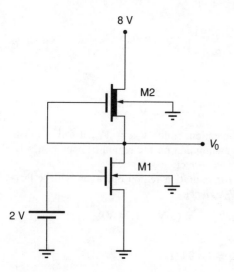

FIGURE 3.1-11
Example 3.1-2.

Since $I_{D1} = I_{D2}$, it follows from equating currents that

$$\frac{W_2/L_2}{W_1/L_1} = \left(\frac{V_{GS1} - V_{T1}}{V_{T2}}\right)^2 = 0.24$$

To minimize the area of M2, it is necessary to minimize the product of W_2 and L_2 while still satisfying the design rules of the process. From the design rules of Table 2A.2 with $\lambda = 1.5 \mu$, it follows that $W_{min} = 3 \mu$ and $L_{min} = 3 \mu$. Since M1 is minimum size, $W_1/L_1 = 1$. If one were to pick $L_2 = L_{min}$, then solving the previous equation for W_2 yields $W_2 = 0.72 \mu$, which violates the minimum width of the moat as specified in the design rules. Picking $W_2 = W_{min} = 3 \mu$, we obtain $L_2 = 12.5 \mu$, which is acceptable within the existing design rules.

Example 3.1-3. A p-well CMOS inverter is shown in Fig. 3.1-12. Assuming the typical process parameters of Table 3.1-2 were used for the process, that the substrate is connected to ground, and that the value of V_{DD} is 6 V, obtain an expression for and plot V_O versus V_I for $0 \text{ V} \le V_I \le 6 \text{ V}$.

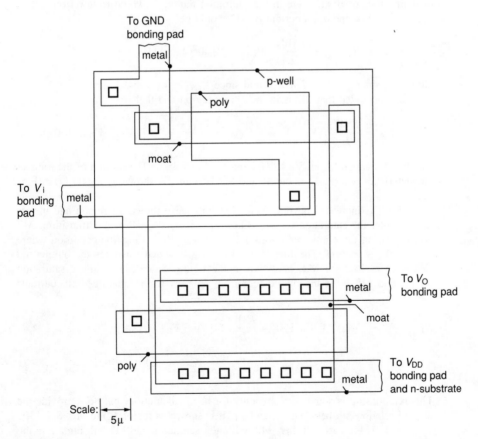

FIGURE 3.1-12
Example 3.1-3—CMOS inverter.

Solution. Initially one must obtain the circuit schematic along with device sizing information from Fig. 3.1-12. The equivalent circuit is shown in Fig. 3.1-13a along with the component sizing information obtained from the layout.

The threshold voltages of both M1 and M2 are needed to determine the regions of operation of the devices as well as for the analysis. Since the bulk of M2 is tied to the source of M2 and since the p-well (which also serves as the bulk for M1) is connected to the ground, it follows that $V_{BS} = 0$ for both M1 and M2. The threshold voltages for M1 and M2 are thus given respectively by V_{TON} and V_{TOP}, which can be obtained, along with the remaining process parameters, from Table 3.1-2. The balance of the analysis presented here is parameterized to make it more general; quantitative results follow directly by substituting the numerical parameters into the symbolic expressions.

The regions of operation for M1 and M2 must be obtained. Since V_I varies from 0 to 6 V, it can be readily concluded that both M1 and M2 will operate in at least two different operating regions in this circuit.

Consider first the case where $V_I < V_{TON}$. It follows that M1 is cutoff and thus from (2) of Table 3.1-1 that $I_{D1} = 0$. Since $V_{GS2} = V_I - V_{DD} < V_{TOP}$ for the parameter values listed in Table 3.1-2, it follows that M2 is in either the saturation or ohmic region. If M2 were in the saturation region, it would follow from (9) of Table 3.1-1 that the drain current of M2 would be

$$I_{D2} = -\frac{(K_2'W_2)}{2L_2}(V_{GS2} - V_{TOP})^2(1 - \lambda[V_O - V_{DD}])$$

However, since $I_{D2} = -I_{D1} = 0$ and since $V_{GS2} \neq V_{TOP}$ and $V_O \neq 1/\lambda + V_{DD}$, it must be concluded that M2 is in the ohmic region and that

$$I_{D2} = \frac{K'W_2}{L_2}\left([V_I - V_{DD} - V_{TOP}] - \frac{[V_O - V_{DD}]}{2}\right)(V_O - V_{DD}) = 0$$

which will happen for all $V_I < V_{TON}$ only if $V_O = V_{DD}$. The portion of the transfer characteristics where M1 is cutoff and M2 is ohmic is shown as region ① in Fig. 3.1-13b.

If V_I is increased beyond V_{TON}, M1 will leave the cutoff region and immediately enter the saturation region. Since V_{DS2} is very small at this transition, M2 will remain in the ohmic region until V_O drops to $V_I - V_{TOP}$ (the condition where $V_{DS2} = V_{GS2} - V_{T2}$). The line $V_O = V_I - V_{TOP}$, which separates the ohmic and saturation regions for M2, is shown in the figure. Since M1 is in the saturation region and M2 is in the ohmic region, it follows from equating drain currents that

$$K_1'\frac{W_1}{2L_1}(V_I - V_{TON})^2(1 + \lambda V_O) = \frac{K_2'W_2}{L_2}\left\{\left([V_I - V_{DD} - V_{TOP}]\right.\right.$$
$$\left.\left. - \frac{[V_O - V_{DD}]}{2}\right)(V_O - V_{DD})\right\}$$

This relationship is somewhat unwieldy for hand calculations but does provide the desired relationship between V_O and V_I. It is shown as region ② in Fig. 3.1-13b.

If V_I is increased further, M2 will enter saturation and M1 will remain in the saturation region provided $V_{DS1} > V_{GS1} - V_{T1}$ (i.e., provided $V_O \geq V_I - V_{TON}$). A plot of $V_O = V_I - V_{TON}$ is also shown on Fig. 3.1-13b. With both M1 and M2

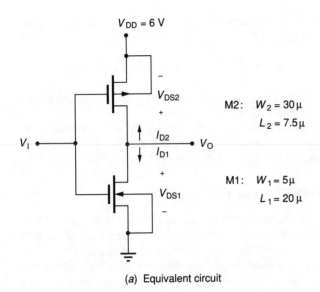

M2: $W_2 = 30\,\mu$
$L_2 = 7.5\,\mu$

M1: $W_1 = 5\,\mu$
$L_1 = 20\,\mu$

(a) Equivalent circuit

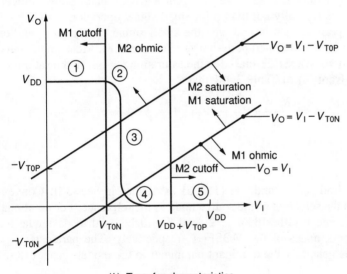

(b) Transfer characteristics

FIGURE 3.1-13
Solution of Example 3.1-3.

in saturation it follows by equating drain currents that V_O and V_I are related by the expression

$$K_1'\frac{W_1}{2L_1}(V_I - V_{TON})^2(1 + \lambda V_O) = K_2'\frac{W_2}{2L_2}(V_I - V_{DD} - V_{TOP})^2[1 + \lambda(V_O - V_{DD})]$$

This relationship between V_O and V_I is shown as region ③ in Fig. 3.1-13b.

Increasing V_I further causes a further decrease in V_O, forcing M1 into the ohmic region and driving M2 deeper into saturation. In this region, which is depicted as region ④ in Fig. 3.1-13b, and which is valid until M2 enters cutoff, the relationship between V_O and V_I is given by

$$\frac{K_1' W_1}{L_1}\left[(V_I - V_{\text{TON}}) - \frac{V_O}{2}\right]V_O = K_2'\frac{W_2}{2L_2}(V_I - V_{\text{DD}} - V_{\text{TOP}})^2[1 + \lambda(V_O - V_{\text{DD}})]$$

For $V_I > V_{\text{DD}} + V_{\text{TOP}}$, M2 is in cutoff, forcing I_{D2} and, correspondingly, V_O to 0. This is shown as region ⑤ in Fig. 3.1-13b.

It should be noted that if the value of V_{DD} were sufficiently reduced or the values of V_{TON} or V_{TOP} were changed by a large enough amount, some of the five regions of operation indicated in Fig. 3.1-13b would not occur (see Problem 3.7).

3.1.2 Small Signal MOSFET Model

The small signal model of the MOS transistor will now be obtained. From Sec. 3.0.2 it can be concluded that the small signal model can be obtained directly from the dc model summarized in Table 3.1-1. Since there are three regions of operation identified in the dc model, there are different small signal models for the MOSFET corresponding to each of these regions. In the cutoff region the drain current is essentially zero, resulting in a trivial small signal model. Since the MOSFET is typically not biased for small signal operation in the ohmic region because of performance limitations, the small signal model for operation in this region will not be developed here (but see Problem 3.8). Most small signal applications employ the MOSFET biased in the saturation region. In the saturation region, it follows from (4) of Table 3.1-1 that

$$I_D = \frac{K'W}{2L}(V_{\text{GS}} - V_T)^2(1 + \lambda V_{\text{DS}})$$

and

$$I_G = I_B = 0$$

(3.1-9)

It remains to find y_{kj}, k, and $j \in \{1, 2, 3\}$ as defined in Sec. 3.0. Convention has resulted in the selection of the source node as the reference. For notational convenience, g, d, and b rather than 1, 2, and 3 will be used to designate the gate, drain, and bulk nodes of the MOSFET, respectively. The parameter y_{dg}, often termed g_m, is generally the dominant parameter in the model. From (3.0-5) and (3.1-9),

$$y_{\text{dg}} = g_m = \left.\frac{\partial I_D}{\partial V_{\text{GS}}}\right|_{\substack{V_{\text{DS}}=V_{\text{DSQ}}\\V_{\text{BS}}=V_{\text{BSQ}}\\V_{\text{GS}}=V_{\text{GSQ}}}} = \left.\frac{K'W}{L}(V_{\text{GS}} - V_T)(1 + \lambda V_{\text{DS}})\right|_{\substack{V_{\text{DS}}=V_{\text{DSQ}}\\V_{\text{BS}}=V_{\text{BSQ}}\\V_{\text{GS}}=V_{\text{GSQ}}}}$$

(3.1-10)

Upon relating $V_{\text{GS}} - V_T$ to the quiescent drain current and noting that the λ effects are typically negligible in this model, it follows that

$$g_m \simeq \sqrt{\frac{2K'W}{L}}\sqrt{|I_{\text{DQ}}|}$$

(3.1-11)

TABLE 3.1-3
Nonzero small signal model parameters for MOSFET

$$g_m = \sqrt{\frac{2K'W}{L}} \sqrt{|I_{DQ}|}$$

$$g_{mb} = \eta g_m$$

$$g_{ds} \simeq \lambda |I_{DQ}| \qquad\qquad (r_{ds} = 1/g_{ds})$$

where $\quad \eta = \dfrac{\gamma}{2\sqrt{\phi - V_{BSQ}}}$

The other parameters can readily be obtained (see Problem 3.18) from Eqs. 3.1-9 and 3.0-5. The nonzero parameters are summarized in Table 3.1-3, and the small signal model equivalent circuit appears in Fig. 3.1-14. It should be noted that if $v_{bs} \neq 0$, any ac signals that appear on the bulk will also modulate the drain current. Although g_{mb} is typically considerably less than g_m, it will be seen in later chapters that g_{mb} is one of the major factors that limits the performance of many circuits. Since the current $g_m v_{gs}$ typically dominates the drain current, it should be apparent that the small signal MOSFET is inherently a good transconductance amplifier. Its performance directly as a current amplifier, voltage amplifier, or transresistance amplifier would be quite poor.

Example 3.1-4. For the circuit of Fig. 3.1-15, obtain
(a) The quiescent output voltage.
(b) The small signal steady state output voltage.
(c) The total output voltage.
Use the NMOS process parameters of Table 3.1-2.

Solution.
(a) Following an approach similar to that of Example 3.1-1, it can be concluded that the MOSFET is operating in the saturation region with $V_T = 1.085$ V. The quiescent drain current is approximately (by neglecting λ effects) $I_{DQ} \simeq 44.0\ \mu$A. The quiescent output voltage is 3.60 V. If λ effects are included, one obtains $I_{DQ} = 46.79\ \mu$A and $V_{OQ} = 3.321$ V.

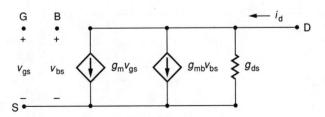

FIGURE 3.1-14
Small signal model equivalent circuit for MOSFET.

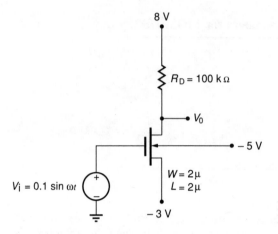

FIGURE 3.1-15
Example 3.1-4.

(b) The small signal equivalent circuit shown in Fig. 3.1-16 can be readily obtained from Fig. 3.1-14 and Fig. 3.1-15. From Table 3.1-3 it follows that

$$g_m = \sqrt{2\frac{K'W}{L}} \sqrt{|I_{DQ}|} = 4.60 \times 10^{-5} \text{ mho}$$

$$g_{ds} = 4.68 \times 10^{-7} \text{ mho}$$

$$g_{mb} = 5.71 \times 10^{-6} \text{ mho}$$

Since $v_{bs} = 0$, the small signal voltage gain is $-g_m/g_{ds} = -4.39$, and hence the small signal output voltage is

$$v_o(t) = -.439 \sin \omega t$$

(c) The total output voltage is the sum of the small signal and quiescent values, which is simply

$$V_o(t) = 3.32 \text{ V} - .439 \sin \omega t$$

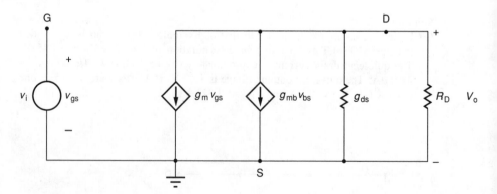

FIGURE 3.1-16
Solution of Example 3.1-4.

3.1.3 High Frequency MOSFET Model

At high frequencies both the dc and small signal models of the MOSFET introduced in the previous sections are generally considered inadequate. These limitations are to a large extent attributable to the unavoidable parasitic capacitances inherent in existing MOS structures. These parasitic capacitances can be
divided into two groups. The first group is composed of those parasitic capacitors formed by sandwiching an insulating dielectric of fixed geometric dimensions between two conductive regions. The capacitance of these types of devices
remains essentially constant for local changes in the voltage applied to the plates
of the capacitor. Assuming the area of the normally projected intersection of the
capacitor plates is A and that the distance between the plates is constant with
thickness d, then this capacitance is given by the expression

$$C = \varepsilon \frac{A}{d} \tag{3.1-12}$$

where ε is the permittivity of the dielectric material separating the plates. Often
it is more convenient to combine ε/d into a single parameter, C_d, called the
capacitance density. Following this convention,

$$C = C_d A \tag{3.1-13}$$

C_d is thus a process parameter and A is a design parameter.

The second group is composed of the capacitors formed by the separation
of charge associated with a pn junction. The depletion region associated with the
semiconductor junction serves as the dielectric. These junction capacitors are
quite voltage dependent. They are typically expressed in terms of the process
parameter C_{j0}, which denotes the junction capacitance density at zero volts bias.
The capacitance of these devices can be approximated by

$$C = \frac{C_{j0} A}{(1 - V_F/\phi_B)^n} \tag{3.1-14}$$

where A is the junction area, V_F is the dc forward bias voltage of the pn junction,
ϕ_B is the barrier potential (alternately, built-in potential), and n is a constant
depending upon the type of junction. This expression is reasonably good for
$-\infty < V_F < \phi_B/2$. These junctions are seldom operated under forward bias in
MOS integrated circuits and thus V_F is normally negative. The model for $V_F >
\phi_B/2$ is, however, discussed in Sections 3.2.3 and 3.3.3.

The relationship between the process parameter ϕ_B and process-controllable
parameters can be found in Chapter 4. ϕ_B is typically in the 0.7 V range and
will be assumed to be 0.7 V unless otherwise specified. The constant n is used
to denote the type of junction. For step-graded and linearly graded junctions, n
assumes the values 1/2 and 1/3, respectively. A plot of the junction capacitance
density versus the forward bias voltage is shown in Fig. 3.1-17.

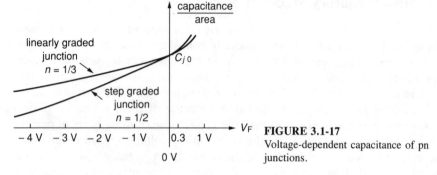

FIGURE 3.1-17
Voltage-dependent capacitance of pn junctions.

The parasitic capacitors that dominate the high-frequency behavior of MOS transistors are shown in Fig. 3.1-18. The capacitors C_{BD1}, C_{BC1}, and C_{BS1} are all voltage-dependent junction capacitors. The remaining capacitors are parallel plate capacitors governed by (3.1-13). Some of the parasitic capacitors are actually distributed devices. In addition, some of the capacitor values are operating region dependent. To simplify analysis, a model of the MOSFET in each of the three operating regions containing only lumped nodal capacitors will be presented. Comments about each of the parasitic capacitors follow.

C_{ox} represents the capacitance density of the gate/oxide/channel capacitor. The capacitance density appeared earlier in the expression for K' (Eq. 3.1-7). If $\varepsilon_{\mathrm{SiO_2}}$ is the relative permittivity of the silicon dioxide dielectric, which is assumed to be of thickness t_{ox}, then

$$C_{\mathrm{ox}} = \frac{\varepsilon_0 \varepsilon_{\mathrm{SiO_2}}}{t_{\mathrm{ox}}} \tag{3.1-15}$$

where ε_0 is the permittivity of free space.

C_{GDO} and C_{GSO} are the gate–drain and gate–source overlap capacitors, respectively. Their existence can be attributed to the unwanted diffusion under the gate of some of the impurities used to create the drain–source regions. In addition to contributing to the parasitic capacitance, this diffusion causes a small

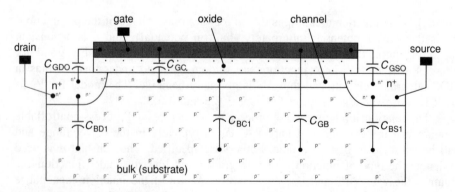

FIGURE 3.1-18
Parasitic capacitors in MOS transistors, shown for n-channel device.

decrease in the effective length of the transistors. If L_D represents the distance of the lateral moat diffusion under the gate, then both of these parasitic capacitors are nearly rectangular with length W and width L_D, resulting in a capacitance of

$$C_{GDO} = C_{GSO} = C_{ox}WL_D \qquad (3.1\text{-}16)$$

C_{GC} represents the gate-to-channel capacitance. In the cutoff region the channel is not formed, so $C_{GC} = 0$. In the ohmic region the channel is quite uniform, extending from drain to source under the entire gate region. In this region, the total gate-to-channel capacitance is given by

$$C_{GC} = C_{ox}WL \qquad (3.1\text{-}17)$$

Actually, the length of the channel obtained by subtracting $2L_D$ from the "drawn length" L would be more accurate, but this additional notational complexity is often not justified for hand analysis. Since the channel is a distributed rather than a lumped circuit element connecting the source to drain, and since no node corresponding to the channel appears in the MOSFET model, it is typically assumed that half of C_{GC} appears directly from gate to source and the other half appears from gate to drain to simplify calculations when the device is operating in the ohmic region. In the saturation region, the majority of the channel area acts as an ohmic extension of the source region. Typically $\frac{2}{3}C_{ox}WL$ is modeled as a lumped element between gate and source, and the remaining $\frac{1}{3}C_{ox}WL$ is neglected.

C_{GB} represents the gate–bulk capacitance. Far in the cutoff region (i.e., no depletion region in the channel), the inversion layer (alternately channel) does not exist, so the bulk region extends to the bottom side of the gate oxide layer and $C_{GB} = C_{ox}WL$. C_{GB} becomes voltage dependent and decreases with bias when operating in cutoff with a depletion region present in the channel. In both the saturation and ohmic regions, the existence of the inversion layer makes C_{GB} essentially zero. A small gate–bulk capacitance associated with gate material overlapping the bulk with the thick field oxide as a dielectric does exist. This is highly layout dependent and will be associated with layout parasitics; it is therefore not included in the model of Fig. 3.1-18.

C_{BC1} is the bulk-to-channel junction capacitance. In the cutoff region, the inversion layer does not exist, causing C_{BC1} to vanish. In both the ohmic and saturation regions, a junction capacitance, from the bulk to channel exists, with value approximated by (3.1-14). To maintain lumped element modeling, the $\frac{1}{2}{:}\frac{1}{2}$ and $\frac{2}{3}{:}0$ rules used previously for C_{GC} are often used in the ohmic and saturation regions, respectively, to distribute this parasitic capacitance between the drain and source.

C_{BS1} and C_{BD1} are the capacitances of the bulk/source and bulk/drain junctions. These are often approximated with (3.1-14) using the source and drain areas and the process parameter C_{BM0}, which represents the zero bias bulk–moat capacitance density.

Other parasitic capacitors are often included in computer simulations but will not be considered in this section. All junction capacitances have, to this point, been assumed to be determined by the lateral junction area. For short channel transistors (less than 3–5 μ in length) the lateral capacitance associated with the edge of the junctions becomes significant. These are descriptively termed *sidewall capacitances*. Another significant source of parasitic capacitance that typically plagues both small and large devices is the capacitance associated with the layout-dependent interconnections. Additional details about parasitic capacitors in MOS devices can be found in Chapter 4.

The lumped parasitic capacitors considered in Fig. 3.1-18 are shown in Fig. 3.1-19a. Note that the distributed capacitors C_{GC} and C_{BCl} have been lumped and split between the drain and source nodes. The values for these capacitors in the three regions of operation discussed above are listed in Fig. 3.1-19b.

Conspicuously absent from the model of Fig. 3.1-19a is a parasitic capacitance between the drain and source. It can, however, be seen from Fig. 3.1-18 that no physical mechanism exists to create such a capacitor.

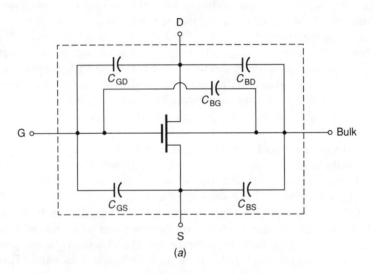

(a)

	Region		
	Cutoff	Ohmic	Saturation
C_{GD}	$C_{OX}WL_D$	$C_{OX}WL_D + \frac{1}{2}WLC_{OX}$	$C_{OX}WL_D$
C_{GS}	$C_{OX}WL_D$	$C_{OX}WL_D + \frac{1}{2}WLC_{OX}$	$C_{OX}WL_D + \frac{2}{3}WLC_{OX}$
C_{BG}	$C_{OX}WL$	0	0
C_{BD}	C_{BD1}	$C_{BD1} + \dfrac{C_{BC1}}{2}$	C_{BD1}
C_{BS}	C_{BS1}	$C_{BS1} + \dfrac{C_{BC1}}{2}$	$C_{BS1} + \frac{2}{3}C_{BC1}$

(b)

FIGURE 3.1-19

Parasitic capacitors: *(a)* Lumped model, *(b)* values, *(c)* Small signal equivalent circuit.

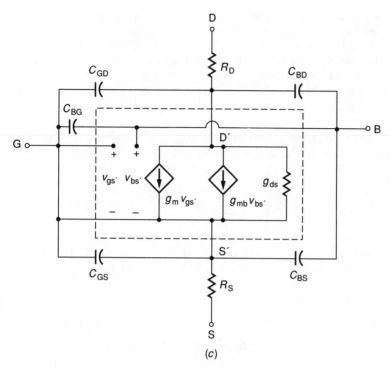

FIGURE 3.1-19
(*continued*)

The small signal equivalent circuit of the MOSFET including the capacitive parasitics is shown in Fig. 3.1-19c. The resistors R_D and R_S have been included to account for the ohmic resistance in the drain and source regions from the physical drain and source connections to the actual drain (D') and source of the device. For large physical drain and source areas, these resistors become quite large. Techniques discussed in Chapter 2 can be used to determine these values from the sheet resistance and physical dimensions of the drain and source regions. For minimum size drain and source regions, these resistances will be in the 50 Ω range.

The careful reader may be concerned that the rather qualitative approach to modeling the parasitic capacitances associated with the MOSFET may seriously limit use of this model to *accurately* predict high-frequency MOSFET performance. Although the concern is well-founded, because of the inability to accurately control the parasitic capacitances during processing and because of the operating region and voltage dependence of these capacitances, practical designs *must not* have important specifications directly dependent upon these parasitic capacitances. The designer thus designs "away from" these capacitances and consequently a crude model of these parasitics is usually sufficient for the designer to verify that these parasitics will not significantly impact the key performance specifications in a design.

Example 3.1-5. Calculate all of the parasitic capacitors included in Fig. 3.1-19a for M1 in the circuit of Fig. 3.1-20. Use the CMOS process parameters of Table 2B.4 in Chapter 2. Assume the areas of the sources of both M1 and M2 are equal to 100 μ^2 and that the drain areas of M1 and M2 are each 60 μ^2. Neglect junction sidewall capacitances. (Note that this circuit has a large voltage gain at the Q-point established, and thus the Q-point is highly sensitive to changes in either bias voltages or device sizes.)

Solution. The region of operation for M1 must initially be determined along with the operating point. Assume initially that M1 and M2 are both operating in saturation. With this assumption, it follows upon equating drain currents that

$$\frac{K'_N W_1}{2L_1}(V_I - V_{TN})^2(1 + \lambda_N V_O) = K'_P\frac{W_2}{2L_2}(V_I - V_{DD} - V_{TP})^2(1 - \lambda_P[V_O - V_{DD}])$$

Inserting the given excitation voltages, dimensions, and process parameters from Table 2B.4 into this equation, it follows that $V_O = 5$ V. It is readily verified that the assumption initially made that both transistors are operating in the saturation region is valid.

From Table 2B.4 and (3.1-16) it follows that

$$C_{\text{ox}} = 0.7 \text{ fF}/\mu^2$$

$$C_{\text{GDO}} = (0.7 \text{ fF}/\mu^2)(0.45 \mu)W_1 = 1.58 \text{ fF}$$

$$C_{\text{GSO}} = (0.7 \text{ fF}/\mu^2)(0.45 \mu)W_1 = 1.58 \text{ fF}$$

$$C_{\text{BD}} = (0.33 \text{ fF}/\mu^2)(60 \mu^2) = 19.8 \text{ fF}$$

$$C_{\text{BS}} = (0.33 \text{ fF}/\mu^2)(100 \mu^2) = 33 \text{ fF}$$

$$C_{\text{BC}} = (0.33 \text{ fF}/\mu^2)(5 \mu)(10 \mu) = 16.5 \text{ fF}$$

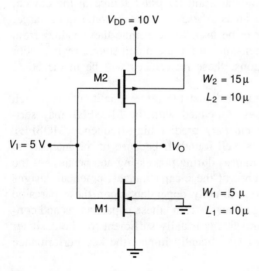

$V_{DD} = 10$ V

M2

$W_2 = 15\mu$
$L_2 = 10\mu$

$V_I = 5$ V

V_O

$W_1 = 5 \mu$
$L_1 = 10\mu$

M1

FIGURE 3.1-20
Example 3.1-5.

Thus from the third column of Fig. 3.1-19b,

$$C_{GD} = 1.58 \text{ fF}$$

$$C_{GS} = 24.9 \text{ fF}$$

$$C_{BG} = 0$$

$$C_{BD} = 19.8 \text{ fF}$$

$$C_{BS} = 44.0 \text{ fF}$$

Note the small size of these parasitic capacitors relative to those associated with discrete electronic circuitry. Although they are small, it will be seen later that the effects of these parasitics are significant at high frequencies.

3.1.4 Measurement of MOSFET Model Parameters

Typical values of process parameters are generally available at the start of a design. Knowledge of the process parameters themselves, as well as of statistical and/or worst case information, is necessary during the design stage so that tradeoffs between performance, complexity, and yield can be considered by the designer. Experimentally measured process parameters also serve as an interface between the fabrication and design groups. A check to verify that the process parameters fall within previously agreed-upon bounds is typically made after fabrication and prior to extensive circuit testing by the designers. These measurements are made over a large enough number of dies to establish confidence in the measurements.

Automated device characterization equipment is readily available for measuring many of the parameters that are used to characterize devices. In the absence of this equipment, some of the more important parameters can be measured with reasonable accuracy using standard laboratory instruments. Techniques for measuring the parameters K', V_{T0}, γ, and λ that appear in the model of the MOSFET previously introduced are discussed in this section. Since models are not perfect, it is advisable to measure model parameters in the same regions where the device will be operated and near the intended operating point if possible. The following discussion assumes that the reader is familiar with the basic operation of an operational amplifier. For those lacking background in this area, most electronics texts have a brief, self-contained section discussing operational amplifiers (e.g., References 4 and 5).

Measurement of λ. Consider the expression for the drain current of the MOSFET in the saturation region as given in Table 3.1-1:

$$I_D = \frac{K'W}{2L}(V_{GS} - V_T)^2(1 + \lambda V_{DS}) \qquad \text{for} \quad V_{DS} > V_{GS} - V_T, V_{GS} > V_T$$

$$(3.1\text{-}18)$$

This equation is plotted in Fig. 3.1-21 for different values of $(V_{GS} - V_T)$ with constant V_{BS}. Projection of these curves into quadrant 2 shows that all curves

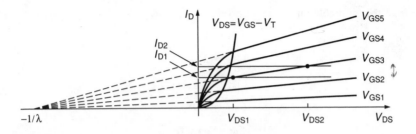

FIGURE 3.1-21
Measurement of λ.

intersect the V_{DS} axis at $V_{DS} = -1/\lambda$. The parameter λ can thus be determined by fixing V_{GS} and V_{BS}, thus fixing $(V_{GS} - V_T)$, and determining the $-V_{DS}$ axis intercept of I_D versus V_{DS}. If I_{D1} and I_{D2} are the currents corresponding to two distinct values of V_{DS}, V_{DS1}, and V_{DS2} (see Fig. 3.1-21), then it readily follows that

$$\lambda = \frac{I_{D2} - I_{D1}}{I_{D1}V_{DS2} - I_{D2}V_{DS1}} \tag{3.1-19}$$

The circuit of Fig. 3.1-22 with S1 in position 1 is useful for measuring λ. V_{GS} and V_{BS} are fixed so that $V_{GS} > V_T$. The operational amplifier (op amp) is used to establish the relationship $V_O = -I_D R$ while maintaining a source voltage of nearly 0 V. If V_{DS1} and V_{DS2} are the two distinct values of V_{DS} required in

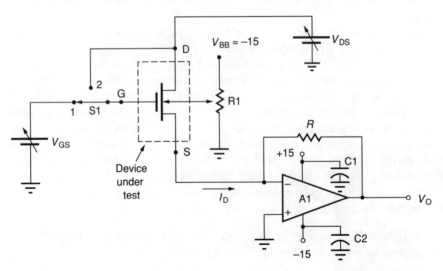

A 356 op amp is a reasonable choice for A1. C1 and C2, which may be needed for stability, should be as close to the supply terminals of the op amp as possible to prevent oscillation. A value of 1μF is reasonable for these capacitors.

FIGURE 3.1-22
Circuit for measuring MOSFET parameters. V_{GS}, V_{DS}, and V_{BB} should be of opposite polarity when measuring p-channel parameters.

(3.1-19) and V_{O1} and V_{O2} respectively are the output voltages of the op amp for these inputs, it follows that

$$\lambda = \frac{V_{O2} - V_{O1}}{[V_{O1}V_{DS2} - V_{O2}V_{DS1}]} \tag{3.1-20}$$

Measurement of V_T and V_{T0}. With V_{BS} and V_{DS} fixed, the values of I_D (I_{D1} and I_{D2}) corresponding to two distinct values of V_{GS} (V_{GS1} and V_{GS2}) can be measured. If the device is operating in saturation for both values of V_{GS}, a routine calculation shows

$$V_T = \frac{V_{GS2}(I_{D1}/I_{D2})^{1/2} - V_{GS1}}{(I_{D1}/I_{D2})^{1/2} - 1} \tag{3.1-21}$$

If V_{BS} is set to 0 V, it follows by definition that the expression in (3.1-21) yields V_{T0}. The circuit of Fig. 3.1-22 with S1 in position 1 can again be used to measure V_T.

Measurement of K'. Once λ and V_T have been measured, it follows from (3.1-18) that K' can be determined from a measurement of I_D for fixed values of V_{GS} and V_{DS} from the expression

$$K' = \frac{2LI_D}{W(V_{GS} - V_T)^2(1 + \lambda V_{DS})} \tag{3.1-22}$$

The circuit of Fig. 3.1-22 is again useful for this measurement.

Another scheme is often used for measuring K' and V_T. Since λV_{DS} is typically much less than 1, it follows from (3.1-18) that

$$I_D \simeq \frac{K'W}{2L}(V_{GS} - V_T)^2 \qquad \text{for} \quad V_{GS} > V_T, V_{DS} > V_{GS} - V_T$$

To guarantee operation in the saturation region for enhancement devices, it is convenient to tie the gate to the drain by setting switch S1 to position 2 and for depletion devices to establish a large dc bias on V_{DS} with S1 in position 1, yielding

$$I_D = \frac{K'W}{2L}(V_{GS} - V_T)^2 \qquad V_{GS} > V_T \tag{3.1-23}$$

A typical plot of $\sqrt{I_D}$ versus V_{GS} is shown in Fig. 3.1-23 for both enhancement and depletion MOSFETs for several different values of V_{BS}. In all cases the slopes of the straight lines are $[(K'W)/(2L)]^{1/2}$, enabling a ready determination of K'. Note the bending of the curves for low values of V_{GS}. This bending is due to subthreshold currents and is not included in the models discussed up to this point. A discussion of subthreshold operation appears in Section 3.1.6. The drain current must be large enough so that the slope is not affected by the subthreshold effects when measuring V_T. The horizontal axis intercept of the projection of the straight lines is the threshold voltage. The intercept corresponding to $V_{BS} = 0$ is V_{T0}. The circuit of Fig. 3.1-22 is useful for measuring V_T and K' following this approach.

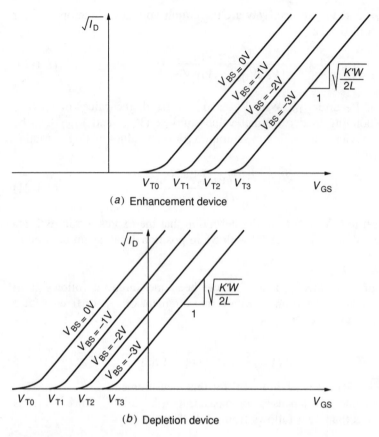

FIGURE 3.1-23
Alternate method of measuring K' and V_T: (a) Enhancement device, (b) Depletion device.

Measurement of γ. From Table 3.1-1 recall that

$$V_T = V_{T0} + \gamma\left(\sqrt{\phi - V_{BS}} - \sqrt{\phi}\right) \tag{3.1-24}$$

Since methods of measuring both V_T and V_{T0} have been presented, both γ and ϕ can be determined by obtaining values of V_T from two distinct nonzero values of V_{BS}. Details about obtaining these parameters from either of these two distinct values or by applying some minimum mean squared error approximation from several measured values is left to the reader.

For large values of V_{BS}, the threshold voltage is only weakly dependent upon ϕ. In that case, using a typical value of ϕ, ϕ_{typ}, a good approximation to γ can be obtained with a single large value of V_{BS} from the expression

$$\gamma \simeq \frac{V_T - V_{T0}}{\sqrt{\phi_{\text{typ}} - V_{BS}} - \sqrt{\phi_{\text{typ}}}} \tag{3.1-25}$$

Information about the parasitic capacitance parameters is often required for accurate time domain analysis of MOS circuits. The parasitic capacitors discussed in the previous section are quite small for minimum-sized MOSFETs (well under 1 pF). Some were also seen to be voltage dependent. Due primarily to their small size, it is nearly impossible to measure directly these capacitances with any acceptable degree of accuracy using standard laboratory equipment. Special test circuits are often included on an IC for the purpose of obtaining information about the parasitic capacitances. These test circuits may contain either geometrically large devices so that the total parasitic capacitance is large enough to measure easily or they may contain more complicated circuit structures (such as ring oscillators) from which these parasitics can be calculated indirectly from measurements of other characteristics of the circuits.

Other measurement considerations. The methods presented above provide simple measurement of some of the key parameters of a MOSFET. Questions about such problems as accuracy and Q-point were avoided. Regardless of what measurement technique is used, it is advisable to measure these parameters as close to the intended device operating point (Q-point) as possible because model inaccuracies can cause significant global variations in these parameters whereas local variations are usually quite small. Also, measurements at several data points in the neighborhood of the Q-point, followed by data smoothing or curve fitting, usually give better results than single-point or two-point measurements. This is easily achieved if computer-controlled measurement equipment is available. The extension of these measurement methods to smoothing or curve fitting is straightforward and is left to the reader.

Finally, the question of how accurately one has measured these parameters and how much accuracy is needed naturally arises. Unfortunately, the functional form of the model presented here is not perfect, and thus the parameters, along with the functional form of the model, only approximate the device performance. Because of this imperfect fit, it is inherent that different measurement algorithms will give slightly different values for these parameters. This problem is analogous to the problem of trying to fit a second-order polynomial to data points obtained from a third-order polynomial. Nevertheless, the model for the MOSFET is quite good, and the measured parameters are useful for predicting device performance. In applications where matching or ratio matching of parameters is particularly important, the same parameter measurement algorithms should be employed for each to avoid introducing systematic errors.

3.1.5   Short Channel Devices

Downward trends in device scaling have caused minimum MOSFET device lengths to decrease from the 10 μ range of the mid-1970s to the 1 μ range of the mid-1980s. Device lengths in the 0.5 μ range or below are projected by the early 1990s. The models that we discussed earlier in this chapter are quite good for channel lengths longer than 5 μ. The models gradually deteriorate for shorter channel lengths. Transistors with channel lengths less than 3 to 5 μ are termed short channel devices. With short channel devices the ratio between lateral and vertical dimensions is reduced. Geometrically, the channel region changes from a rather uniform, thin right-rectangular region to a much more irregular structure. The effects of the transition region from the drain and source diffusions to the channel become significant, causing need for increased complexity in the device model.

Short channel transistors offer some significant advantages over larger transistors but also have serious limitations. The major advantages are the reduced area requirements and improvements in speed that are attainable with circuits employing short channel transistors. The improvements in speed are mostly attributable to the reduced input capacitance associated with the smaller devices. The major limitation is a deterioration in the output impedance characteristics. Good matching of short channel transistor characteristics is also more difficult to achieve.

The typical output characteristics of a short channel transistor are compared with that of a longer channel device in Fig. 3.1-24. A simple empirical model of the MOSFET which is essentially an extension of the long channel model summarized in Table 3.1-1 is given by the following equations:

$$I_G = 0 \tag{3.1-26}$$

$$I_D = \begin{cases} 0 \quad V_{GS} < V_T \text{ (cutoff)} \\[2mm] \dfrac{K'W_{eff}}{L_{eff}}\left(V_{GS} - V_T - \dfrac{V_{DS}}{2}\right)V_{DS}\left[1 + \lambda\left(\dfrac{1 + \theta L_{eff}}{\theta L_{eff}}\right)V_{DS}\right] \\[2mm] \qquad\qquad V_{GS} > V_T,\ 0 < V_{DS} < V_{GS} - V_T \text{ (ohmic)} \quad (3.1\text{-}27) \\[2mm] \dfrac{K'W_{eff}}{2L_{eff}}(V_{GS} - V_T)^2\left[1 + \lambda\left(\dfrac{1 + \theta L_{eff}}{\theta L_{eff}}\right)V_{DS}\right] \\[2mm] \qquad\qquad V_{GS} > V_T,\ V_{DS} > V_{GS} - V_T \text{ (saturation)} \quad (3.1\text{-}28) \end{cases}$$

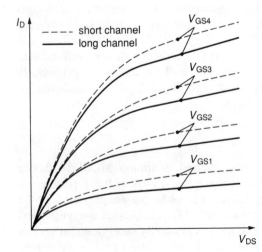

FIGURE 3.1-24
Short channel effects on MOSFET performance. Solid curves for 5 μ device, dashed curves for 1 μ device.

The parameter θ has units $(\text{length})^{-1}$. A typical value of θ may be 0.2 μ^{-1}. The parameters W_{eff} and L_{eff} denote the effective channel width and length respectively. These are given by

$$W_{\text{eff}} = W - W_{\text{R}} \qquad (3.1\text{-}29)$$

$$L_{\text{eff}} = L - 2L_{\text{D}} - L_{\text{R}} \qquad (3.1\text{-}30)$$

where W and L are the drawn width and length, W_{R} and L_{R} are constants representing width and length reduction due to processing, and L_{D} is the lateral diffusion of the source or drain under the gate. W_{eff} and L_{eff} could also be used to model W and L in the model of the long channel MOSFET presented earlier and are, in fact, included in most good models used for simulation. The use of W_{eff} and L_{eff} for hand analysis of large structures is not so important since the difference between these values and the drawn width and length is relatively small. For short channel devices, however, the relative effects of the width and length reduction and the lateral diffusions become more pronounced. Short channel effects should be considered for channel lengths less than 5 μ. This model is still usable in hand calculations. It should be noted that a size adjust of the appropriate mask is often done so that the effective length and/or width ideally agrees with the drawn length and/or width. The designer should be aware of what size adjusts, if any, will be used at mask generation.

More accurate models of the short channel effects are available.[6-7,19] These models are much more involved and not amenable to hand calculations but do give reasonable results when used for computer simulations. The model in Reference 7 is incorporated into the popular circuit simulator, SPICE. For the reasons discussed below, a simple model such as that of (3.1-27) and (3.1-28) is often adequate for hand analysis of circuits utilizing short channel transistors.

Were it not for the additional notational complexity, the model presented in Table 3.1-1 could be replaced with the short channel model introduced in this section. Note, in particular, that for large L the short channel model is essentially equivalent to that for the longer transistors. It can be concluded that the short channel model can be appropriately used for short as well as long device sizes if desired. The empirical short channel model parameter θ was included in Table 3.1-2.

We close this section by comments about where short channel devices are used. Short channel devices are widely used in digital logic, where a net improvement in speed and reduction in circuit area are readily achievable in spite of the performance limitations of the short channel MOSFET. In analog applications, where good matching characteristics and high output impedance are often critical, short channel transistors find fewer applications in spite of the improved frequency response. When analog circuits are built in processes where short channel lengths are available, most devices will be somewhat larger than minimum size; some performance benefits in terms of device matching will, however, be derived in these processes because of the more stringent lithography requirements that must be maintained in the small feature size processes.

3.1.6 Subthreshold Operation

In the dc model of the MOSFET introduced in Sec. 3.1.1, the drain current for positive V_{DS} was assumed to be zero for $V_{GS} < V_T$ and nonzero for $V_{GS} > V_T$ as indicated by Eq. 3.1-1. In physical devices such an abrupt transition is not anticipated and does not occur experimentally. The drain current is, however, much smaller for $V_{GS} < V_T$ than for $V_{GS} > V_T$ and hence in most applications the assumption that $I_D = 0$ for $V_{GS} < V_T$ is justifiable.

Applications do exist, however, where it is crucial that current levels be extremely small. These include, but are not limited to, biomedical applications such as pacemakers and other implantable devices that must operate for several years with small nonrechargeable batteries. Useful circuits with extremely low supply currents in which $V_{GS} < V_T$ find applications in such situations. If $V_{GS} > V_T$, the devices are said to be operating in strong inversion. If $V_{GS} < V_T$, the devices are said to be operating in weak inversion, or equivalently, in the subthreshold region. At room temperature, the transition between strong inversion and weak inversion actually occurs around $V_{GS} \simeq V_T + 100$ mV. The expression

$$V_{GS} = V_T + 2nV_t \qquad (3.1-31)$$

where n is a constant between 1 and 2, can be used to predict the transition at other temperatures.[8] The term V_t is equal to kT/q where k is Boltzmann's constant ($k = 1.387 \times 10^{-23}$ V · C/°K), T is the device temperature in degrees Kelvin, and q is the charge of an electron ($q = 1.6 \times 10^{-19}$ C). At room temperature, $V_t = 26$ mV.

A plot of I_D versus V_{GS} for the MOSFET with $V_{DS} = V_{GS}$ is shown in Fig. 3.1-25 for a wide range of V_{GS} values. As can be seen from this figure, the current in weak inversion is much smaller than the current in strong inversion, as previously stated. The behavior is, however, well characterized far into weak inversion and varies exponentially rather than quadratically with V_{GS}. The potential for extremely low power dissipation should be apparent.

Example 3.1-6.

(a) Compare the power dissipation required for a single device operating with $V_{GS} = 3V_T$ driven from a 5 V source to the power dissipation required for the same device operating from a 1 V supply biased at $V_{GS} = 0.85V_T$. Assume the device has characteristics as shown in Fig. 3.1-25.

(b) If ideal batteries with a total stored energy of 1 watt-hr are used to power the two devices, what is the battery life of each?

Solution.

(a) From Fig. 3.1-25a, it follows that with $V_{GS} = 3V_T$, $I_{D1} \simeq 150$ μA, and from Fig. 3.1-25b, with $V_{GS} = 0.85V_T$, $I_{D2} \simeq 1$ nA. The power dissipation ratio is thus $(5I_{D1})/(I_{D2}) = 7.5 \times 10^5$.

(b) The battery life with the 5 V system would be

$$T = 1 \text{ watt-hr}/(150 \text{ μA·5 V}) = 1333 \text{ hr} \simeq 8 \text{ weeks}$$

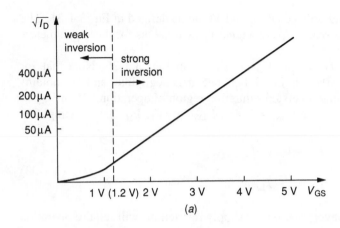

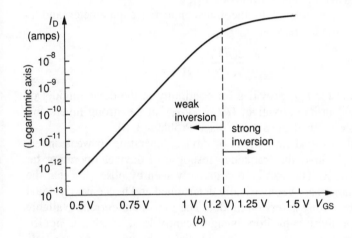

FIGURE 3.1-25
Typical I_D-V_{DS} characteristics for MOSFET operating in weak inversion: (a) Quadratic vertical axis, (b) Logarithmic vertical axis ($V_T = 1\ V$, $V_{DS} = V_{GS}$).

and the battery life with the 1 V system would be

$$T = 1\ \text{watt-hr}/[(1\ \text{nA}) \cdot 1\ \text{V}] \simeq 10^9\ \text{hr} \simeq 114,000\ \text{years}$$

It should be apparent that the subthreshold system may be practical whereas the strong inversion system would be impractical in many applications.

A dc model for the MOSFET operating in weak inversion is needed for both design and simulation. The following model is useful in weak inversion.[9]

$$\left. \begin{aligned} I_G &= 0 \\ I_D &= \frac{W}{L} I_{DO} e^{-V_{BS}[(1/(nV_t)) - (1/V_t)]} (1 - e^{-V_{DS}/V_t}) e^{(V_{GS} - V_T)/(nV_t)} \end{aligned} \right\} \tag{3.1-32}$$

where V_T is the threshold voltage and n and V_t are as defined in Eq. 3.1-31. The constants I_{DO} and n are process parameters. Typical values for these parameters are $I_{DO} \simeq 20$ nA and $n = 2$.

A typical plot of I_D versus V_{DS} is shown in Fig. 3.1-26. Note that for $V_{DS} > 3V_t$, the term e^{-V_{DS}/V_t} in Eq. 3.1-32 becomes negligible, and one obtains the equivalent of the strong inversion saturation region of operation. Often $V_{BS} = 0$. Under the assumption that $V_{BS} = 0$ and $V_{DS} > 3V_t$, Eq. 3.1-32 simplifies considerably, to

$$\left. \begin{array}{l} I_G = 0 \\[2mm] I_D \simeq \dfrac{W}{L} I_{DO} e^{(V_{GS} - V_T)/(n V_t)} \end{array} \right\} \tag{3.1-33}$$

It is often the case, however, that power supply restrictions will require operation of subthreshold devices with smaller values of V_{DS}.

The parameter I_{DO} is related to the transconductance parameter and is approximately given by the expression

$$I_{DO} \simeq \frac{K'2(n V_t)^2}{e^2}$$

This approximation for I_{DO} provides for continuity in the device model of (3.1-33) and (3.1-4) and in its derivative, $(\partial I_D / \partial V_{GS})$, at the strong inversion–weak inversion interface defined in (3.1-31)—see Problem 3.30.

There are several practical limitations of devices operating in weak inversion that deserve noting. First, the frequency response of devices operating far into weak inversion is poor. This can be qualitatively seen by observing that the parasitic device capacitances are geometrically determined and hence nearly equal to those discussed in the strong inversion model. The maximum current available to charge and discharge these capacitors is significantly less, causing a significant deterioration of frequency response. Second, the drain and source substrate currents associated with the reverse-biased moat–substrate junction are not necessarily negligible compared to subthreshold drain currents. Third, the linearity

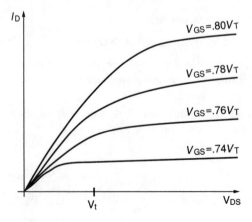

FIGURE 3.1-26
Typical I_D–V_{DS} characteristics for MOSFET operating in subthreshold.

is quite poor for $V_{DS} < 3V_t$, making linear designs more challenging. Fourth, the deterioration of matching characteristics of MOS transistors with decreasing drain currents further complicates linear design.

Because of these practical limitations, it is often desirable to operate near the transition region between strong inversion and weak inversion, where some of the benefits of reduced power associated with weak inversion can be derived but where these other limitations are not too problematic. Whereas diffusion current dominates weak inversion operation and drift current dominates strong inversion operation, both mechanisms interact in the transition region and thus complicate the modeling problem. A discussion of the modeling problem in this region is beyond the scope of this text and continues to receive attention in the technical literature. Even weak inversion models used in simulation programs such as SPICE have major limitations. Nevertheless, some designers do design useful circuits that operate in this transition region.

3.1.7   Operation in the Third Quadrant of the I_D–V_{DS} Plane

Although MOS devices are typically operated with $I_D > 0$ and $V_{DS} > 0$, (Quadrant 1 in Fig. 3.1-7), there are applications where the device is biased to operate in Quadrant 3 of the I_D–V_{DS} plane for some inputs. For notational convenience, a MOS transistor without drain and source designations is shown in Fig. 3.1-27, along with plots of I_1 versus V_{12} for different values of V_{32} and fixed V_B. The normal convention for nodal designations if the device were operating in Quadrant 1 would be ① → drain, ② → source, and ③ → gate. For operation in Quadrant 3, the drain and source designations would be reversed, based upon the device models discussed earlier in this chapter.

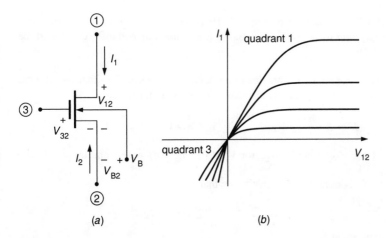

(a)   (b)

FIGURE 3.1-27
Operation of the MOSFET in the third quadrant: (a) Terminal convention, (b) I–V characteristics.

It should be apparent that the I–V characteristics do not display symmetry from Quadrant 1 to Quadrant 3. The asymmetry becomes more pronounced with decreasing reverse bulk bias. It should also be apparent that, based upon the device model introduced earlier in this chapter, the drain–source designations are not arbitrary.

To obtain a qualitative appreciation for how the device behaves in Quadrant 3, assume that $0 < V_{32} < V_T$ and that subthreshold currents are negligible. By the previous model, we are tempted to conclude that the device is cutoff since "$V_{GS} < V_T$" and hence conclude that $I_1 = 0$. If, however, the voltage at terminal ① in Fig. 3.1-27 were made negative relative to terminal ③ and if V_{13} is less than $-V_T$, it can be argued that the gate–channel voltage near terminal ① is greater than V_T, causing the formation of an inversion layer which would, in turn, cause a positive current I_2 to flow. This is what happens in an actual MOSFET. This biasing strategy is consistent with that discussed earlier in this chapter, provided the nodal designations ① → source, ② → drain, and ③ → gate are made.

For consistency with the model summarized in Table 3.1-1, the MOS device will be modeled in Quadrant 3 by using the model of Table 3.1-1 with the agreement that the designations *source* and *drain* will be made so that $V_{DS} > 0$. This means that in some applications, the drain and source designations change during normal operation of the device.

As an alternative to allowing the drain and source designations to change so that $V_{DS} \geq 0$ at all times, the designations can be arbitrarily fixed and the device model in Quadrant 3 can be defined to be equal to that which would be attained were the designations changed. Following this approach, the equivalent fixed drain–source designation model (for the n-channel transistor) summarized in Table 3.1-4 is obtained. The parameter λ has been included in the ohmic region expressions in this model to maintain continuity in the device characteristics. The regions of operation in the V_{DS}–V_{GS} plane are depicted in Fig. 3.1-28 for a fixed bulk bias.

Example 3.1-7. The device of Fig. 3.1-29 is to be used as an active grounded resistor. Verify that the I–V characteristics are continuous and differentiable at the origin ($V = 0$).

Solution. Since for small V, this depletion device is operating in either the forward ohmic or reverse ohmic regions, it follows from Table 3.1-4 that

$$I = K' \frac{W}{L} \left(-V_{Ti} - \frac{V}{2} \right) V (1 + \alpha_i \lambda V) \qquad i = 1, 2$$

where $i = 1$ for $V > 0$ and $i = 2$ for $V < 0$, where $\alpha_1 = +1$ and $\alpha_2 = -1$, and where $V_{DS} = V$.

To verify continuity, we must show that

$$\lim_{V \to 0^+} I = \lim_{V \to 0^-} I$$

From the expression for I,

$$\lim_{V \to 0^+} I = 0 = \lim_{V \to 0^-} I.$$

TABLE 3.1-4
Low-frequency fixed-terminal MOSFET model in four quadrants.

$$I_D = \begin{cases} 0 & \begin{array}{l} V_{GS} < V_{T1} \\ V_{DS} > V_{GS} - V_{T2} \end{array} & \text{cutoff} \\[2ex] \dfrac{K'W}{2L}(V_{GS} - V_{T1})^2(1 + \lambda V_{DS}) & \begin{array}{l} V_{GS} > V_{T1} \\ V_{DS} > V_{GS} - V_{T1} \end{array} & \begin{array}{l}\text{forward} \\ \text{saturation}\end{array} \\[2ex] \dfrac{K'W}{L}\left(V_{GS} - V_{T1} - \dfrac{V_{DS}}{2}\right)V_{DS}(1 + \lambda V_{DS}) & \begin{array}{l} 0 < V_{DS} < V_{GS} - V_{T1} \\ V_{GS} > V_{T1} \end{array} & \begin{array}{l}\text{forward} \\ \text{ohmic}\end{array} \\[2ex] \dfrac{K'W}{L}\left(V_{GS} - V_{T2} - \dfrac{V_{DS}}{2}\right)V_{DS}(1 - \lambda V_{DS}) & \begin{array}{l} V_{GS} > V_{T2} \\ V_{DS} < 0 \end{array} & \begin{array}{l}\text{reverse} \\ \text{ohmic}\end{array} \\[2ex] -\dfrac{K'W}{2L}(V_{GS} - V_{DS} - V_{T2})^2(1 - \lambda V_{DS}) & \begin{array}{l} V_{GS} < V_{T2} \\ V_{DS} < V_{GS} - V_{T2} \end{array} & \begin{array}{l}\text{reverse} \\ \text{saturation}\end{array} \end{cases}$$

$$V_{T\circ}{}^a = V_{T0} + \gamma\left(\sqrt{\phi - V_{BB}} - \sqrt{\phi}\right)$$

$$V_{T1} = V_{T0} + \gamma\left(\sqrt{\phi - V_{BS}} - \sqrt{\phi}\right)$$

$$V_{T2} = V_{T0} + \gamma\left(\sqrt{\phi - V_{BS} + V_{DS}} - \sqrt{\phi}\right)$$

[a] $V_{T\circ}$ characterizes the V_{DS} transition in Fig. 3.1-28.

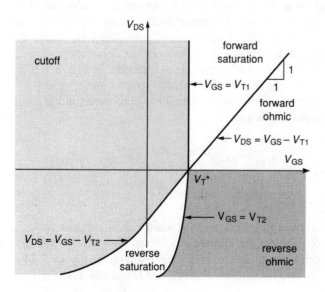

$$V_{T^*} = V_{T0} + \gamma\left(\sqrt{\phi - V_{BB}} - \sqrt{\phi}\right)$$
$$V_{T1} = V_{T0} + \gamma\left(\sqrt{\phi - V_{BS}} - \sqrt{\phi}\right)$$
$$V_{T2} = V_{T0} + \gamma\left(\sqrt{\phi - V_{BS} + V_{DS}} - \sqrt{\phi}\right)$$

FIGURE 3.1-28
Model extension regions of operation of MOSFET (fixed V_{BS}).

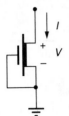

FIGURE 3.1-29
Grounded simulated resistor of Example 3.1-7.

To verify differentiability, we must show

$$\lim_{V \to 0^+} \frac{\partial I}{\partial V} = \lim_{V \to 0^-} \frac{\partial I}{\partial V}$$

From the expression for I, it follows that

$$\frac{\partial I}{\partial V} = -\frac{K'W}{2L}\left[V^2\left(3 + 2\frac{\partial V_{Ti}}{\partial V}\right)(\alpha_i \lambda) + V\left(2 + 4\alpha_i \lambda V_{Ti} + \frac{2\partial V_{Ti}}{\partial V}\right) + 2V_{Ti}\right]\Bigg|_{V_{DS}=0\,V}$$

and hence that

$$\lim_{V \to 0} \frac{\partial I}{\partial V} = -\frac{K'W}{L}V_{Ti}\Bigg|_{V_{DS}=0\,V} \qquad V = \frac{K'W}{L}\left(V_{T0} + \gamma\left[\sqrt{\phi - V_{BB}} - \sqrt{\phi}\right]\right)$$

for $i = 1,2$. The model is therefore differentiable at the origin.

3.1.8 Modeling Noise Sources in MOSFETs

Two mechanisms are the primary contributors to the presence of noise in MOSFETs. One is thermal noise associated with the carriers in the channel. The second is flicker noise associated with the trapping and releasing of electrons in the Si–SiO$_2$ interface region. These noise sources contribute to the total drain current and can thus be modeled as a current source between the drain and source in either the large signal or small signal device model, as indicated in Fig. 3.1-30a, where this current source combines the effects of both types of noise.

The thermal noise current is white noise, which has zero mean and is most easily characterized by its spectral density:

$$S_{IW} = \begin{cases} \dfrac{4kT}{R_{FET}} & \text{ohmic region} \\[2ex] \dfrac{8kT g_m}{3} & \text{saturation} \end{cases} \tag{3.1-34}$$

where T is temperature in degrees Kelvin, k is Boltzmann's constant ($k = 1.381 \times 10^{-23}$ J/°K), R_{FET} is the equivalent FET resistance given by (3.1-8), and g_m is the small signal transconductance at the operating point given by (3.1-11). At room temperature ($T = 300°$K), the coefficient $8kT/3$ equals 1.1×10^{-20} V · A · sec.

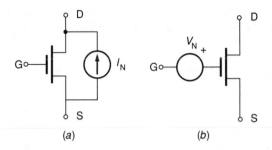

FIGURE 3.1-30
Model of noise sources in the MOSFET:
(a) Current source in output, (b) Input-
referred voltage source for small signal
operation in the saturation region.

It can be seen that the units of S_{IW} are $A^2 \cdot$ sec. The RMS noise current will be obtained from the spectral density later in this section. Both current and voltage spectral densities are used to characterize noise, and these are often termed the *power spectral densities*. Although it may appear from the saturation region expression in (3.1-34) that the small signal MOSFET model plays a role in characterizing the noise of the MOSFET in the saturation region due to the presence of g_m, this may be somewhat misleading. It can be shown that the expression for the thermal noise contains a $\sqrt{V_{GS} - V_T}$ term, which also appears in the small signal g_m expression of (3.1-11), thus motivating the use of the g_m term in the noise current Eq. 3.1-34. Actually, the thermal noise current is just that associated with the channel source resistance of the MOSFET when operating in the saturation region (see Problems 3.22 and 3.23). Thus, in the ohmic regions, the thermal noise current is identical to that of a resistor of value R_{FET}, and in the saturation region it is equal to that in a resistor of value $3/(2g_m)$.

The flicker noise current in both the saturation and ohmic regions is characterized by the spectral density

$$S_{If} = \frac{2K_f K' I_{DQ}}{C_{ox} L^2 f} \tag{3.1-35}$$

where K_f is the flicker noise coefficient, I_{DQ} is the quiescent current, f is frequency, and K', C_{ox}, and L are the MOSFET model parameters introduced in Sec. 3.1.1. K_f is typically[10] about 3×10^{-24} $V^2 \cdot F$. The flicker noise is often termed $1/f$ noise because of the $1/f$ dependence in (3.1-35).

The white noise and $1/f$ noise sources are statistically uncorrelated, and hence the spectral current density of the noise current source, I_N in Fig. 3.1-30a, can be obtained by adding S_{IW} and S_{If} to obtain

$$S_N = S_{IW} + S_{If} \tag{3.1-36}$$

It is well known that the RMS noise current source in the frequency band $[f_1, f_2]$ can be obtained from the spectral density and is given by

$$I_{NB} = \sqrt{\int_{f_1}^{f_2} S_N \, df} \tag{3.1-37}$$

It should be pointed out that if we define the RMS white noise and flicker noise currents by the square root of the integrals of the spectral densities

$$I_{\text{WB}} = \sqrt{\int_{f_1}^{f_2} S_{\text{IW}}\, df} \qquad (3.1\text{-}38)$$

and

$$I_{\text{FB}} = \sqrt{\int_{f_1}^{f_2} S_{\text{If}}\, df} \qquad (3.1\text{-}39)$$

then these currents add in the RMS sense by the equation

$$I_{\text{NB}} = \sqrt{I_{\text{WB}}^2 + I_{\text{FB}}^2} \qquad (3.1\text{-}40)$$

The current I_{NB} is the contribution to I_{N} in Fig. 3.1-30 in the frequency band $[f_1, f_2]$.

The relationship between small signal voltages and/or currents in a circuit and the total output noise voltage or current is often of interest because it characterizes the impact noise has on the performance of a circuit. Two commonly used indicators of this relationship are the signal-to-noise ratio (SNR) and the dynamic range. Since the noise signal amplitudes are usually sufficiently small to be considered small signals, the small signal model of the MOSFET is often used to analyze the noise performance of circuits. This analysis is usually much simpler than a noise analysis based on the large signal models of the MOSFETs.

It can be readily shown that if the MOSFET in Fig. 3.1-30a is replaced by its small signal model, then an *equivalent* small signal model that characterizes the noise performance can be obtained by replacing the noise current source from drain to source with a noise voltage source in series with the gate, as denoted by V_{N} in Fig. 3.1-30b. This is termed an *input-referred* noise source. The spectral density of the input-referred noise voltage source relates to the noise spectral density of the noise current source by the expression

$$S_{\text{VN}} = \frac{S_{\text{IN}}}{g_{\text{m}}^2} \qquad (3.1\text{-}41)$$

Correspondingly, the input-referred noise voltage source relates to the noise current source by the expression

$$V_{\text{N}} = \frac{I_{\text{N}}}{g_{\text{m}}} \qquad (3.1\text{-}42)$$

where g_{m} is the small signal transconductance gain of the MOSFET. In the common case where the MOSFET is operating in the saturation region, the parameter g_{m} is given by (3.1-11). The input-referred model is useful for simplifying the analysis of some circuits.

Two points about the input-referred noise model of Fig. 3.1-30b deserve mention. First, the reader must keep in mind that this is *merely* a small signal equivalent circuit characterization. The mechanisms that contribute to noise are inherently associated with the drain current. Second, whereas the noise model of Fig. 3.1-30a was valid for either a large signal or small signal model of the MOSFET, the input-referred model of Fig. 3.1-30b was developed under the assumption of small signal operation of the MOSFET. The equivalence of the circuit in Fig. 3.1-30b as characterized by (3.1-42) is not valid for large signal MOSFET operation.

Example 3.1-8. A simple transconductance amplifier is shown in Fig. 3.1-31.

(a) Calculate the output noise current spectral density, the input-referred voltage spectral density and the RMS output thermal noise current, the RMS output flicker noise current, the output RMS noise current, and the input-referred RMS noise voltage in the flat frequency band from 100 Hz to 1 MHz if the small signal input, v_i, is zero. Assume $W = 5$ μ, $L = 5$ μ, $V_{gg} = 2$ V, $K_f = 3 \times 10^{-24}$, $V^2 \cdot F$. Use the typical CMOS parameters of Table 2B.4 in Appendix 2B.

(b) Repeat for $W = 200$ μ, $L = 5$ μ, and $V_{gg} = 1.25$ V.

Solution.

(a) Observe that the MOSFET is operating in the saturation region since $V_{DS} = V_{DD} > V_{GS} - V_T$. From (3.1-34) and (3.1-35), both g_m and I_{DQ} are needed.

$$I_{DQ} = \frac{K'W}{2L}(V_{GSQ} - V_T)^2 = 18.75 \ \mu\text{A}$$

$$g_m = \sqrt{\frac{2K'W}{L}} \sqrt{I_{DQ}} = 30.0 \ \mu\text{A/V}$$

Thus, from (3.1-34), (3.1-35), and (3.1-36),

$$S_{IW} = 3.3 \times 10^{-25} \ \text{A}^2 \cdot \text{sec}$$

$$S_{If} = \frac{1.54 \times 10^{-19}}{f} \ \text{A}^2 \cdot \text{sec}$$

$$S_N = 3.3 \times 10^{-25} + \frac{1.54 \times 10^{-19}}{f} \ \text{A}^2 \cdot \text{sec}$$

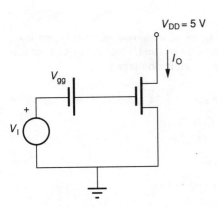

FIGURE 3.1-31
Example 3.1-8.

From (3.1-38), (3.1-39), and (3.1-40),

$$I_{WB} = \sqrt{\int_{10^2}^{10^6} S_{IW} \, df} = 0.489 \text{ nA (RMS)}$$

$$I_{FB} = \sqrt{\int_{10^2}^{10^6} S_{If} \, df} = 1.190 \text{ nA (RMS)}$$

$$I_{NB} = \sqrt{I_{WB}^2 + I_{FB}^2} = 1.29 \text{ nA (RMS)}$$

and from (3.1-42)

$$V_N = \frac{I_N}{g_m} = 43 \ \mu\text{V (RMS)}$$

(b) Repeating with the new device sizes,

$$I_{DQ} = 120 \ \mu\text{A}$$

$$g_m = 48 \text{ mA/V}$$

$$S_{IW} = 5.28 \times 10^{-24} \text{ A}^2 \cdot \sec$$

$$S_{If} = (9.87 \times 10^{-19}/f) \text{ A}^2 \cdot \sec$$

$$I_{WB} = 2.29 \text{ nA (RMS)}$$

$$I_{FB} = 3.01 \text{ nA (RMS)}$$

$$I_{NB} = 3.78 \text{ nA (RMS)}$$

$$V_N = 7.88 \ \mu\text{V (RMS)}$$

Note that in the previous example the $1/f$ noise is strongly dominant in the first part whereas the relative contributions are comparable in the second part. Device sizes and bias current affect both the noise current and the relative significance of the two types of noise. At higher frequencies the thermal noise effects dominate whereas the flicker noise, because of its $1/f$ type spectral density, dominates at lower frequencies.

Example 3.1-9. Obtain an expression in terms of the quiescent excess gate bias, $V_{GS} - V_T$, that shows where the spectral density of the $1/f$ noise crosses over that of the thermal noise. Assume operation in the saturation region.

Solution. Equating spectral densities from Eqs. 3.1-34 and 3.1-35, we obtain

$$\frac{8kT g_m}{3} = \frac{K_f 2K' I_{DQ}}{f C_{ox} L^2}$$

From (3.1-4) and (3.1-11), this simplifies to

$$f = \frac{3}{8} \frac{K' K_f}{kT C_{ox}} \left(\frac{V_{GS} - V_T}{L^2} \right)$$

Using typical values of these parameters from Table 2B.4, we obtain

$$f \approx \left(9.5 \, \frac{\mu^2}{V}\right)\left(\frac{V_{GS} - V_T}{L^2}\right) \text{ MHz}$$

From Example 3.1-9 it can be observed that the relative impact of the flicker noise and thermal noise are strongly dependent on the quiescent operating point and the device size.

3.1.9 Simple MOSFET Models for Digital Applications

Many digital applications involve large numbers of gates and transistors, which make hand analysis using the device models, presented in Sec. 3.1.1 and summarized in Table 3.1-1, totally impractical. A very simple model that makes hand analysis tractable is needed for these applications. Such a model will, of necessity, not provide highly accurate results. We are willing to accept the tradeoffs between model accuracy and simplicity in these applications. Models that are widely used for this purpose are shown in Fig. 3.1-32.

In the circuit of Fig. 3.1-32a, the switch S1 is open if $V_{GS} < V_H/2$ and closed if $V_{GS} > V_H/2$ where V_H is the logical *high* voltage in the digital logic family and where the logical *low* voltage is assumed to be near zero. The values of C_μ and R are given by

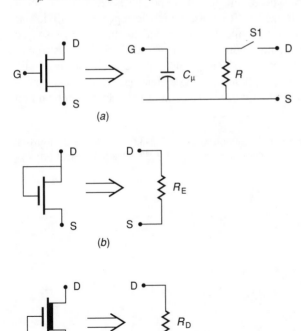

(a)

(b)

(c)

FIGURE 3.1-32
Models for the MOSFET used for simple analysis of digital circuits: (*a*) Three-terminal MOSFET, (*b*) Two-terminal enhancement, (*c*) Two-terminal depletion.

$$C_\mu = C_{ox} W L \tag{3.1-43}$$

$$R = \frac{L}{K'W (V_H - V_T)} \tag{3.1-44}$$

where V_T is the threshold voltage of the MOSFET. The two-terminal enhancement and depletion configurations of Figs. 3.1-32b and c are characterized by

$$R_E \doteq \frac{L}{K'W (V_H - V_{TE})} \tag{3.1-45}$$

$$R_D = \frac{L}{K'W \, | V_{TD} |} \tag{3.1-46}$$

where V_{TE} and V_{TD} denote the threshold voltages of the enhancement and depletion transistors.

The model of Fig. 3.1-32a is motivated by the observation that in most digital circuits, the inputs to the logic gates are typically inputs to the gates of transistors, which swing between the high and low logic levels. From the results presented in Section 3.1.3, it follows that the gate input port is capacitive with a value near $C_{ox} W L$ throughout most of the input signal swing. When the input is low, the output port looks nearly like an open circuit; and when the gate of the MOSFET is driven to V_H, which is typically much larger than V_T, the output voltage is sufficiently low through most of the high to low transition to force operation in the ohmic region. The ohmic region impedance which is modeled by R in Fig. 3.1-32 is characterized by (3.1-8), which is repeated in (3.1-44). In applications where the gate is permanently connected to the drain or source as shown in Fig. 3.1-32b and c, the approximation of (3.1-8) is less justifiable but still widely used (see Problem 3.17). These models are used for simple dc and timing analysis in Chapter 7 with modest modifications of the resistances given in (3.1-45) and (3.1-46) to obtain closer agreement between theoretical and experimental results.

Example 3.1-10. Using the simple models of Fig. 3.1-32, obtain the dc transfer characteristics, V_O versus V_I, for the circuit of Fig. 3.1-33. Use the typical process parameters of Table 3.1-2.

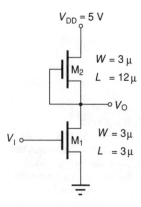

$V_{DD} = 5$ V

$W = 3\,\mu$
$L = 12\,\mu$
M2

V_O

V_I
M1
$W = 3\,\mu$
$L = 3\,\mu$

FIGURE 3.1-33
Simple digital inverter.

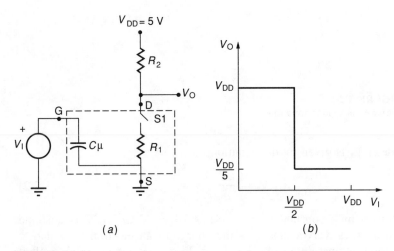

(a)   (b)

FIGURE 3.1-34
Solution of Example 3.1-10: (a) Equivalent circuit, (b) Plotting of results.

Solution. It follows from the models of Fig. 3.1-32 that the equivalent circuit can be drawn as shown in Fig. 3.1-34a. Assuming the logic high, V_H, is 5 V, it follows from Table 3.1-2 and Eqs. 3.1-44 and 3.1-45 that $R_2 = 39.2$ kΩ and $R_1 = 9.8$ kΩ. For $V_I < V_{DD}/2$, switch S1 is open, so $V_O = V_{DD} = 5$ V. For $V_I > V_{DD}/2$, the switch S1 is closed and the resistive voltage divider yields an output of $V_O = V_{DD}/5 = 1$ V. These idealized results are plotted in Fig. 3.1-34b.

3.2   DIODE MODELS

The pn junction diode with the convention used here for the electrical variables is shown in Fig. 3.2-1. The junction diode is characterized by a region of n-type material adjacent to a region of p-type material. A depletion region is formed at the interface. With a sufficiently large forward bias, considerable current will flow, but very little current flows under reverse bias. Such a device, which passes current in one direction and blocks it in the opposite direction, has many practical applications.

3.2.1   dc Diode Model

The diode depicted in Fig. 3.2-1 is characterized at low frequencies by the equation

$$I = I_S\left(e^{\frac{v}{nV_t}} - 1\right)$$ (3.2-1)

where the parameters I_S, n, and V_t characterize the device. The parameters in the equation are designated by

$$I_S = \text{saturation current}$$

$$n = \text{emission coefficient}$$

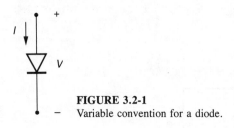

FIGURE 3.2-1
Variable convention for a diode.

and the parameter V_t is given by the equation

$$V_t = \frac{kT}{q} \tag{3.2-2}$$

where k is Boltzmann's constant ($k = 1.381 \times 10^{-23}$ V·C/°K), T is absolute temperature in degrees Kelvin, and q is the charge of an electron ($q = 1.6 \times 10^{-19}$ C). At room temperature (300 °K), $V_t = 26$ mV. Equation 3.2-1 is often called the "diode equation."

The emission coefficient takes on a value of about 1 for silicon. The saturation current can be expressed as

$$I_S = J_S A \tag{3.2-3}$$

where J_S is a process parameter equal to the saturation current density and A is the cross-sectional area of the junction.

The I–V characteristics of a typical diode are shown in Fig. 3.2-2. The current scale for $I < 0$ is considerably smaller than that for $I > 0$ to allow for plotting of the entire diode characteristics, in a meaningful manner, on one set of axes.

The breakdown that occurs for a large reverse bias is not predicted by the diode equation. In discrete diodes this may be quite large (often -100 V or higher). Since the knee is typically very sharp, the breakdown can be gainfully used in voltage-reference applications. Diodes that are intentionally designed to operate in breakdown are called zener diodes. The breakdown voltage for zener diodes is intentionally reduced. Discrete zener diodes with breakdown voltage specifications from the low volt range to over 20 V are readily available.

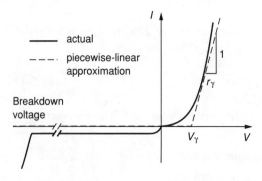

FIGURE 3.2-2
I–V characteristics of a diode.

In IC applications, diodes are often parasitic devices formed in the process of making other devices, as can be seen from the descriptions of the typical CMOS and bipolar processes in Chapter 2. As such, the process is tailored to optimize performance of the MOSFET (in a MOS process) or the BJT (in a bipolar process) rather than the diode. The reverse breakdown voltage of the base-emitter junction in a bipolar process is typically in the 7 V range, making this diode a useful parasitic zener diode. The reverse breakdowns of the parasitic diodes in the MOS processes and for the base-collector junction in a bipolar process are typically much larger. The latter junctions are seldom operated intentionally in the breakdown region.

The diode equation simplifies considerably for $V >> nV_t$. Under forward biases greater than 0.25 V, essentially no accuracy is lost in modeling the diode by

$$I = I_S e^{\frac{V}{nV_t}} \tag{3.2-4}$$

Likewise, for $V < -0.25 \, V$, the diode is accurately modeled by

$$I = -I_S \tag{3.2-5}$$

The piecewise-linear model indicated by the dashed curves in Fig. 3.2-2 is often used for biasing and/or large signal applications. The piecewise-linear model is mathematically characterized by the equations

$$\left. \begin{array}{ll} V = I r_\gamma + V_\gamma & \text{for } I > 0 \\ I = 0 & \text{for } V < V_\gamma \end{array} \right\} \tag{3.2-6}$$

where r_γ is the *on* resistance of the diode and V_γ is the diode cut-in voltage.

The equivalent circuit corresponding to this piecewise-linear model is shown in Fig. 3.2-3. The value of r_γ is obtained by measuring the slope of the $I-V$ characteristics near the desired point of operation. V_γ is the V-axis intercept of the corresponding tangent line; r_γ is typically in the tens of ohms range while $V_\gamma \simeq 0.7$ V. An ideal diode is one in which $r_\gamma = 0$ and $V_\gamma = 0$. In many applications, little accuracy is lost by assuming $r_\gamma = 0$.

Example 3.2-1. Assume $I_S = 10^{-14}$A, T = 300°K, and $n = 1$.
(a) Show that $V \simeq 0.7$ V for diode currents in the 1 mA to 100 mA range.
(b) Determine V_γ and r_γ at $I = 1$ mA and $I = 100$ mA.

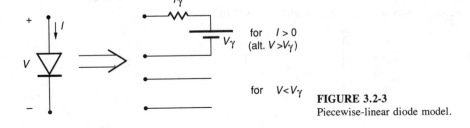

FIGURE 3.2-3
Piecewise-linear diode model.

Solution.

(*a*) Referring to the variable convention of Fig. 3.2-1, assume that $V > 0.25$ V (this must be later verified). It thus follows from Eq. 3.2-4 that

$$V = n V_t \ln\left(\frac{I}{I_s}\right)$$

At about room temperature, we thus have for 1 mA $\le I \le$ 100 mA

$$0.658 \text{ V} \le V \le 0.778 \text{ V}$$

The initial assumption that $V > 0.25$ V is verified and the conclusion that $V_\gamma \simeq 0.7$ V follows.

(*b*) From part (*a*), it suffices to consider the model of (3.2-4) at $I = 1$ mA and $I = 100$ mA. Upon differentiation of (3.2-4) we obtain

$$r_\gamma = \frac{n V_t}{I} \tag{3.2-7}$$

which at 1 mA and 100 mA becomes 26 Ω and 0.26 Ω respectively. The corresponding V_γs are given by

$$V_\gamma = V - I r_\gamma$$

where V and I are the coordinates of the operating point. It follows from part (*a*) and the values obtained for r_γ that V_γ is 0.632 V for $I = 1$ mA and V_γ is 0.752 V for $I = 100$ mA. In practical applications, V_γ is often approximated by 0.7 V, independent of I.

3.2.2 Small Signal Diode Model

The diode is seldom used in low-frequency small signal applications and, as such, a small signal model need not be developed. Since the small signal model of the diode is, however, very simple, it will be mentioned in passing. For reverse bias, the low-frequency small signal model is an open circuit. Under forward bias, it is modeled by a single resistor of value determined by (3.2-7), evaluated at the dc operating point. The diode is occasionally used in high-frequency small signal applications as a capacitor. When used as a capacitor, the diode is often termed a vari-cap or a varactor diode. These diode capacitances are strongly dependent upon the quiescent voltage. A discussion of the high-frequency diode model follows.

3.2.3 High-Frequency Diode Model

At high frequencies, the capacitance formed by the depletion region in the pn junction becomes significant. This capacitance is modeled by a capacitor connected between the terminals of the diode of value

$$C = \begin{cases} \dfrac{C_{j0} A}{\left(1 - \dfrac{V}{\phi_B}\right)^n} & V < \dfrac{\phi_B}{2} \tag{3.2-8} \\[4ex] 2^n C_{j0} A \left[\dfrac{2n V}{\phi_B} + (1 - n)\right] & V > \dfrac{\phi_B}{2} \tag{3.2-9} \end{cases}$$

where the parameters C_{j0}, A, ϕ_B, and n are as defined for the parasitic junction capacitances of the MOSFET in Section 3.1.3. Note that for $V < \phi_B/2$, this parasitic capacitance agrees with that of the MOSFET given by (3.1-14). It can be readily shown (see Problem 3.31) that the value for $V > \phi_B/2$ is the continuous and differentiable linear extension of the reverse-bias value across the boundary defined by $V = \phi_B/2$.

3.3 BIPOLAR MODELS

The npn and pnp bipolar transistors and the convention for the electrical variables established in Chapter 2 are shown in Fig. 3.3-1, along with a top view of a typical geometrical layout of a bipolar transistor. The following model development will

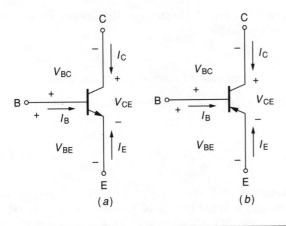

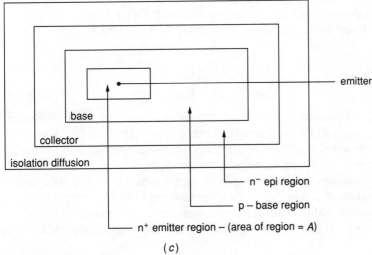

FIGURE 3.3-1
Convention for electrical variables of BJT transistors: (*a*) npn, (*b*) pnp, (*c*) Top view of vertical npn transistor geometry.

be restricted to the npn transistor. The pnp development is identical with the exception of sign changes in some of the equations. Results only for the pnp devices will be presented following the npn discussion.

3.3.1 dc BJT Model

The starting point will be the dc model introduced by Ebers and Moll in 1954[11]. In this model the relationship between the terminal variables is given by

$$I_C = I_S(e^{(V_{BE}/V_t)} - 1) - \frac{I_S}{\alpha_R}(e^{(V_{BC}/V_t)} - 1) \tag{3.3-1}$$

$$I_E = \frac{-I_S}{\alpha_F}(e^{(V_{BE}/V_t)} - 1) + I_S(e^{(V_{BC}/V_t)} - 1) \tag{3.3-2}$$

where the four parameters I_S, α_R, α_F, and V_t characterize the device. The parameters in these equations are designated by

I_S = transport saturation current

α_R = large signal reverse current gain of common base configuration

α_F = large signal forward current gain of common base configuration

and

$$V_t = \frac{kT}{q} \tag{3.3-3}$$

where k is Boltzmann's constant (k $= 1.381 \times 10^{-23}$ V· C/°K), T is absolute temperature in degrees Kelvin, and q is the charge of an electron ($q = 1.602 \times 10^{-19}$ C). At room temperature (300 °K), $V_t \simeq 26$ mV. This is the same V_t that appeared in the diode model and the subthreshold MOSFET model.

The two Ebers-Moll equations along with KVL and KCL applied to the transistor itself

$$I_B = -I_C - I_E \tag{3.3-4}$$

$$V_{CE} = V_{BE} - V_{BC} \tag{3.3-5}$$

provide four independent equations relating the six terminal variables, $I_C, I_B, I_E, V_{CE}, V_{BC},$ and V_{BE}. The BJT is characterized by these four equations.

It should be noted that there is complete functional symmetry in the device model with respect to the collector and emitter terminals. This is comforting since the npn transistor can be thought of as a sandwich of a p-type region between two n-channel layers. Since the shape and impurity concentrations of the collector and emitter differ, however, one would not expect these terminals to be interchangeable. The lack of geometrical symmetry causes large differences in α_F and α_R.

The parameters α_F and α_R are determined by impurity concentrations and junction depths, and as such are process parameters. The parameter V_t is a function of two physical constants and temperature and thus cannot be considered a design parameter. The parameter V_t should not be confused with the threshold voltage for a MOSFET, which uses the symbol V_T. Because of the temperature dependence, V_t can be considered an environmental parameter. The transport saturation current can be expressed as

$$I_S = J_S A \tag{3.3-6}$$

where A is the area of the emitter and J_S, the transport saturation current density, is a process parameter. The parameter J_S can be further expressed as

$$J_S = q \overline{D}_n n_i^2 / Q_B \tag{3.3-7}$$

where $\overline{D}_n$ is the average effective electron diffusion constant, n_i is the intrinsic carrier concentration in silicon ($n_i = 1.45 \times 10^{10}$ atoms/cm^3 at 300 °K), and Q_B is the number of doping atoms in the base per unit area.

From the model presented, it can be seen that the emitter area, A, is the only design parameter available to the design engineer for the vertical bipolar transistor. The shape of the emitter, the size and shape of the base, and the size and shape of the collector have no effect on the dc model of the BJT just introduced.

Typical values of $\overline{D}_n$ and Q_B are 13 cm^2/sec and 7.25×10^{12} atoms/cm^2, respectively. α_R is typically between 0.3 and 0.8. α_F is generally close to unity, falling in the range of 0.9 to 0.999. Typical values for the bipolar parameters that will be used in examples in this text are given in Table 3.3-1.

Labeling of the emitter and collector terminals is arbitrary at this point. Convention has been established, however, for making this distinction. The typical values for α_R and α_F given in the previous paragraph follow this convention. Specifically, the emitter and collector designations are established so that $\alpha_F > \alpha_R$.

An equivalent circuit for the bipolar transistor based upon the Ebers-Moll model is sometimes useful. The circuit of Fig. 3.3-2 serves as such an equivalent circuit where the currents in the two diodes satisfy the standard diode equations

$$I_F = \frac{I_S}{\alpha_F} (e^{(V_{BE}/V_t)} - 1) \tag{3.3-8}$$

$$I_R = \frac{I_S}{\alpha_R} (e^{(V_{BC}/V_t)} - 1) \tag{3.3-9}$$

TABLE 3.3-1
Typical process parameters for vertical npn transistor in bipolar technology

J_S	$= 6 \times 10^{-10}$	μA/mil^2
α_F	$= 0.99$	($\beta_F = 100$)
α_R	$= 0.3$	($\beta_R = 0.43$)
V_{AF}	$= 200$ V	
V_{AR}	$= 200$ V	

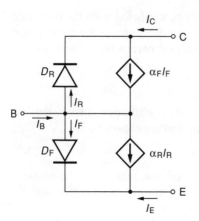

FIGURE 3.3-2
Equivalent circuit of BJT based upon Ebers-Moll model.

Several different regions of operation for the BJT are readily identifiable. Those that are of the most interest are depicted in the $V_{BC}-V_{BE}$ plane shown in Fig. 3.3-3. The forward active, reverse active, and saturation regions are defined by the dashed curves. The cutoff region is defined to be the third quadrant of the $V_{BC}-V_{BE}$ plane. No particular designation is made of the lightly shaded region. Most applications involve operation in one of the four well-defined regions, with possible excursions through the lightly shaded region in digital circuits during switching transitions. For power dissipation reasons, operation in the reverse and forward active regions is generally restricted further to the hatched regions and in the saturation region to the heavily shaded region (see Problem 3.40). It will be shown that major simplifications in the Ebers-Moll equations are possible in all except the lightly shaded region of Fig. 3.3-3. These simplifications are crucial for hand analysis because of the unwieldiness of the Ebers-Moll Eqs. 3.3-1 and 3.3-2 in even relatively simple problems (see Problem 3.38). Simplified models for the forward and reverse active, saturation, and cutoff regions will now be discussed.

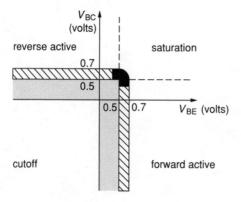

FIGURE 3.3-3
Regions of operation of npn silicon bipolar transistor.

FORWARD AND REVERSE ACTIVE REGIONS OF OPERATION. The BJT is typically operated in the forward active region in most linear applications. If $V_{BE} > 0.5$ V and $V_{BC} < 0.3$ V, then it can be shown that (3.3-1) and (3.3-2) simplify to

$$I_C = I_S e^{(V_{BE}/V_t)} \tag{3.3-10}$$

$$I_E = -\frac{I_S}{\alpha_F} e^{(V_{BE}/V_t)} \tag{3.3-11}$$

Note that " $=$ " was used rather than " $\simeq$ " in these equations. A simple calculation (see Problem 3.39) will show that the terms dropped in obtaining (3.3-10) and (3.3-11) are several orders of magnitude smaller than the terms that were retained!

It is often more convenient to use I_B and I_C rather than I_C and I_E as the dependent variables when modeling the BJT. Defining β_F by

$$\beta_F = \frac{\alpha_F}{1 - \alpha_F} \tag{3.3-12}$$

it follows from (3.3-10) and (3.3-11) that I_C and I_B can be written as

$$I_C = I_S e^{(V_{BE}/V_t)} \tag{3.3-13}$$

$$I_B = \frac{I_S}{\beta_F} e^{(V_{BE}/V_t)} \tag{3.3-14}$$

Note that in the forward active region the BJT acts as a good current amplifier from the base to the collector with the gain relationship

$$I_C = \beta_F I_B \tag{3.3-15}$$

This should be contrasted to the MOSFET, which is inherently a good transconductance amplifier.

Similarly, if β_R is defined as

$$\beta_R = \frac{\alpha_R}{1 - \alpha_R} \tag{3.3-16}$$

then the Ebers-Moll equations in the reverse active region ($V_{BC} > 0.5$ V, $V_{BE} < 0.3$ V) simplify to

$$I_E = I_S e^{(V_{BC}/V_t)} \tag{3.3-17}$$

$$I_B = \frac{I_S}{\beta_R} e^{(V_{BC}/V_t)} \tag{3.3-18}$$

As before, it follows that the base-to-emitter current gain in the reverse active region is given by

$$I_E = \beta_R I_B \tag{3.3-19}$$

Actually, it can be shown both theoretically and experimentally that the collector current of the BJT in the forward active region increases slightly in approximately a linear manner with V_{CE}. Defining V_{AF} to be the coefficient that represents the linear dependence on V_{CE}, the following improvement on (3.3-13) can be made:

$$I_C \simeq I_S e^{(V_{BE}/V_t)} \left(1 + \frac{V_{CE}}{V_{AF}} \right) \tag{3.3-20}$$

Correspondingly, this type of linear dependence in the reverse active region can be characterized by the parameter V_{AR}, resulting in the following improvement on (3.3-17):

$$I_E \simeq I_S e^{(V_{BC}/V_t)} \left(1 - \frac{V_{CE}}{V_{AR}} \right) \tag{3.3-21}$$

The parameters V_{AF} and V_{AR} are process parameters and are referred to as the forward and reverse Early voltages, respectively. V_{AF} and V_{AR} for the BJT serve the same role as the parameter λ (actually $1/\lambda$) in the MOSFET, as can be seen by comparing Eqs. 3.3-20 and 3.1-5.

Many IC applications require base currents in the 0.1 μA to 1 mA range. It is shown in Example 3.3-1 that in the forward active region the base–emitter voltage is typically in the 0.5 V to 0.75 V range. For hand manipulations it is often sufficient to obtain the base–emitter voltage to within 0.1 V ($V_{BE} = 0.6$ V is often used) in this region.

Example 3.3-1. Show that at around room temperature the base–emitter voltage is between 0.5 V and 0.75 V for base currents in the 0.1 μA to 1 mA range for transistors with 1 mil^2 emitter areas and reverse-biased base–collector junctions. Use the process parameters of Table 3.3-1.

Solution. From Eqs. 3.3-6 and 3.3-14 it follows that

$$I_B \simeq \frac{A J_S}{\beta_F} e^{(V_{BE}/V_t)}$$

With $A = 1$ mil^2 and $J_S = 6 \times 10^{-10}$ μA/mil^2, we can write

$$0.1 \ \mu A \leq 6 \times 10^{-10} e^{(V_{BE}/.026 \ V)} \leq 1 \ mA$$

It thus follows that

$$0.5 \ V < V_{BE} < 0.75 \ V \tag{3.3-22}$$

It can be shown that even with substantial changes in temperature, J_S, or A, the changes in V_{BE} for the current range considered in this example are modest.

An even simpler model is often used for characterizing the BJT in the forward and reverse active regions. As indicated in Example 3.3-1, the base–emitter voltage is about 0.6 V in the forward active region for a wide range of base currents. The model

$$V_{BE} = 0.6 \ V \tag{3.3-23}$$

$$I_C = \beta_F I_B \tag{3.3-24}$$

is often adequate for biasing applications and operating point calculations when the device is operating in the forward active region. In the reverse active region the simplified model becomes

$$V_{BC} = 0.6 \text{ V} \qquad (3.3\text{-}25)$$

$$I_E = \beta_R I_B \qquad (3.3\text{-}26)$$

The reader should be cautioned, however, not to attempt to use the value of V_{BE} or V_{BC} as given by (3.3-23) or (3.3-25) directly in the Ebers-Moll equations to obtain I_C or I_B. Small errors in these junction voltages will result in large errors in the currents because of the exponential relationship of the model.

SATURATION REGION. It will be seen later that most (although not all) digital applications involve switching the BJT between the saturation and cutoff regions. When the device is operating in the saturation region with large positive base and collector currents, it is operating near the forward active region. The base–emitter voltage will be near 0.7 V and the base–collector voltage near 0.5 V. The device can thus be modeled by two voltage sources, $V_{BE} = 0.7$ V and $V_{CE} = 0.2$ V, when operating in this region. This collector–emitter voltage in saturation is often termed V_{CESAT}. When the device is operating in saturation with a large positive base current and a large negative collector current, the device is operating near the reverse active region. The base–collector voltage will be near 0.7 V and the base–emitter voltage near 0.5 V. In this case the device will be modeled by two voltage sources, $V_{BC} = 0.7$ V and $V_{CE} = -0.2$ V. This simple modeling approach for the saturation region will be adequate for most hand manipulations. The reader again must be cautioned that these are approximate junction voltage values and thus cannot be used to obtain I_C and I_E in the Ebers-Moll equations since small changes or errors in V_{BC} and V_{BE} cause large changes in the corresponding currents. When the collector and base currents must be accurately determined for devices operating in the saturation region, they are often obtained from equations describing the network itself (KVL or KCL) rather than directly from the Ebers-Moll equations. This situation is illustrated in the following example.

Example 3.3-2. Determine good approximations ($\pm$ 5% accuracy is close enough) for the base current, collector current, V_{BE}, and V_{CE} for the circuit of Fig. 3.3-4

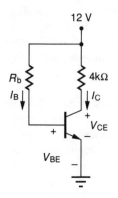

FIGURE 3.3-4
Example 3.3-2.

if (a) $R_b = 500$ kΩ, (b) $R_b = 100$ kΩ. Also obtain an accurate expression for V_{BE}.
Assume the transistor has an emitter area of 4 mil^2, $\beta_F = 100$, $\beta_R = 0.2$, $J_S = 6 \times 10^{-10}$ μA/mil^2, and $T = 300$ °K.

Solution. Assume initially that I_B is in the 0.1 μA to 1 mA range. From Example 3.3-1 it can be concluded that $V_{BE} \simeq 0.6$ V and consequently the current through R_b, which is also the base current, can be approximated by $I_b \simeq (11.4$ V$)$ $/R_b$.

(a) With $R_b = 500$ kΩ, it follows that $I_B \simeq 0.0228$ mA, which satisfies the criterion established in Example 3.3-1 on I_B and thus justifies the initial assumption $V_{BE} \simeq 0.6$ V. If it is now assumed (a fact that must later be verified) that the device is operating in the forward active region, it follows from (3.3-15) that $I_C \simeq 2.28$ mA. With $I_C \simeq 2.28$ mA it follows that $V_{CE} = 12 - (4$ k$\Omega)$ $(2.28$ mA$)$ $= 2.88$ V. With V_{BE} in the 0.6 V range, it thus can be concluded that $V_{BC} < 0$, thus verifying the initial assumption of operation in the forward active region. It remains to accurately determine V_{BE}. Since I_C is now approximately known, it follows from (3.3-13) with $V_t = 26$ mV that

$$V_{BE} = (.026 \text{ V})\ln(I_C/I_S)$$

$$= (.026 \text{ V})\ln[2.28 \text{ mA}/(6 \times 10^{-10} \cdot 4 \ \mu\text{A})] = 0.717 \text{ V}$$

(b) With $R_b = 100$ kΩ, it follows that $I_B \simeq (11.4$ V$)/(100$ k$\Omega) = 0.114$ mA. If we were to assume, as in part (a), that the transistor were operating in the forward active region, we would conclude that $I_C = 11.4$ mA. Consequently, $V_{CE} = -33.6$ V, yielding a value for V_{BC} of 34.2 V, which is in strong violation of the assumption $V_{BC} < 0.3$ V that was necessary to obtain (3.3-15). It can thus be concluded that the collector current is too large for operation in the forward active region and thus the device is operating in saturation near the forward active region. From the above modeling in the saturation region it can be concluded that

$$V_{BE} \simeq 0.7 \text{ V}$$

$$I_B \simeq \frac{12 \text{ V} - 0.7 \text{ V}}{100 \text{ k}\Omega} = 0.113 \text{ mA}$$

$$V_{CE} \simeq 0.2 \text{ V}$$

$$I_C \simeq \frac{12 \text{ V} - 0.2 \text{ V}}{4 \text{ k}\Omega} = 2.95 \text{ mA}$$

CUTOFF. When the BJT is operating in cutoff, the collector and base currents are very small compared to those which typically flow in the active and saturation regions. In many applications it is adequate to model the device with $I_C = 0$ and $I_B = 0$ when operating in the cutoff region. The relative magnitude of the currents in the BJT when operating in cutoff to those when operating in the forward active region are shown in Example 3.3-3.

BJT MODEL SUMMARY. A summary of the simplified dc model for the BJT in the four major regions of operation—forward active, reverse active, saturation, and cutoff—appears in Table 3.3-2. This simplified model should be adequate for most hand calculations except in the seldom used transition region (between cutoff and forward or reverse active) indicated by the lightly shaded region in

TABLE 3.3-2
Simplified dc model for bipolar transistors

npn

$$I_C = J_S A e^{(V_{BE}/V_t)}[1 + (V_{CE}/V_{AF})] \tag{1}$$

$$I_B = \frac{J_S}{\beta_F} A e^{(V_{BE}/V_t)} \tag{2}$$

Forward active $\left(\begin{array}{c} V_{BE} > 0.5 \text{ V} \\ V_{BC} < 0.3 \text{ V} \end{array} \right)$

$$I_E = J_S A e^{(V_{BC}/V_t)}[1 - (V_{CE}/V_{AR})] \tag{3}$$

$$I_B = \frac{J_S}{\beta_R} A e^{(V_{BC}/V_t)} \tag{4}$$

Reverse active $\left(\begin{array}{c} V_{BC} > 0.5 \text{ V} \\ V_{BE} < 0.3 \text{ V} \end{array} \right)$

$$I_B = I_C = 0 \tag{5}$$ Cutoff $(V_{CE} < 0, V_{BC} < 0)$

$$V_{BE} = 0.7 \text{ V}, \quad V_{CE} = 0.2 \text{ V} \tag{6}$$ Forward saturated

$$V_{BC} = 0.7 \text{ V}, \quad V_{CE} = -0.2 \text{ V} \tag{7}$$ Reverse saturated

pnp

$$I_C = -J_S A e^{-(V_{BE}/V_t)}[1 - (V_{CE}/V_{AF})] \tag{8}$$

$$I_B = -\frac{J_S A}{\beta_F} e^{-(V_{BE}/V_t)} \tag{9}$$

Forward active $\left(\begin{array}{c} V_{BE} < -0.5 \text{ V} \\ V_{BC} > -0.3 \text{ V} \end{array} \right)$

$$I_E = -J_S A e^{-(V_{BC}/V_t)}[1 + (V_{CE}/V_{AR})] \tag{10}$$

$$I_B = -\frac{J_S A}{\beta_R} e^{-(V_{BC}/V_t)} \tag{11}$$

Reverse active $\left(\begin{array}{c} V_{BC} < -0.5 \text{ V} \\ V_{BE} > -0.3 \text{ V} \end{array} \right)$

$$I_B = I_C = 0 \tag{12}$$ Cutoff $(V_{CE} > 0, V_{BC} > 0)$

$$V_{BE} = -0.7 \text{ V}, \quad V_{CE} = -0.2 \text{ V} \tag{13}$$ Forward saturated

$$V_{BC} = -0.7 \text{ V}, \quad V_{CE} = +0.2 \text{ V} \tag{14}$$ Reverse saturated

Design parameters: A
Process parameters: $J_S, \beta_F, \beta_R, V_{AR}, V_{AF}$
Environmental parameter: V_t
All design, process, and environmental parameters are positive for both npn and pnp transistors.

Fig. 3.3-3. For operation in this transition region, the more complicated Ebers-Moll equations 3.3-1 and 3.3-2 are needed.

For biasing or operating point calculations, an even simpler model is often adequate. This model is summarized in Table 3.3-3. An equivalent circuit appears in Fig. 3.3-5. This model can be used in place of the model of Table 3.3-2 to reduce computational complexity with minimal loss of accuracy in most biasing applications. This simplified model is generally justified if the base current can be reasonably accurately determined from the circuit in which the BJT is embedded (as in Example 3.3-2) rather than from the exponential relationship between I_B and V_{BE} (as in Problem 3.38b).

Early voltage effects can be readily included in the Ebers-Moll equations 3.3-1 and 3.3-2 by multiplying I_C by $(1 + V_{CE}/V_{AF})$ for $V_{CE} > 0$ or multiplying I_E by $(1 - V_{CE}/V_{AR})$ for $V_{CE} < 0$. Since the BJT is inherently a good current amplifier, it is common to look at the collector current versus V_{CE} for different

TABLE 3.3-3

Simplified model of BJT used for biasing and operating point calculations

Region	npn		pnp	
Forward active	$I_C = \beta_F I_B$	(1)	$I_C = \beta_F I_B$	(11)
	$V_{BE} = 0.6$ V	(2)	$V_{BE} = -0.6$ V	(12)
Reverse active	$I_E = \beta_R I_B$	(3)	$I_E = \beta_R I_B$	(13)
	$V_{BC} = 0.6$ V	(4)	$V_{BC} = -0.6$ V	(14)
Forward saturated	$V_{BE} = 0.7$ V	(5)	$V_{BE} = -0.7$ V	(15)
	$V_{CE} = 0.2$ V	(6)	$V_{CE} = -0.2$ V	(16)
Reverse saturated	$V_{BC} = 0.7$ V	(7)	$V_{BC} = -0.7$ V	(17)
	$V_{CE} = -0.2$ V	(8)	$V_{CE} = 0.2$ V	(18)
Cutoff	$I_C = 0$	(9)	$I_C = 0$	(19)
	$I_B = 0$	(10)	$I_B = 0$	(20)

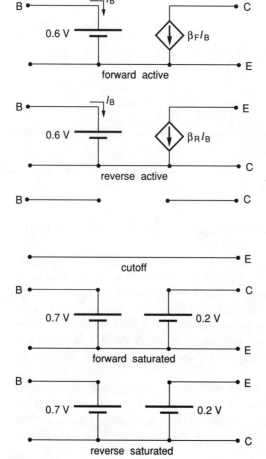

FIGURE 3.3-5
Equivalent circuits of npn BJT for biasing and operating point calculations.

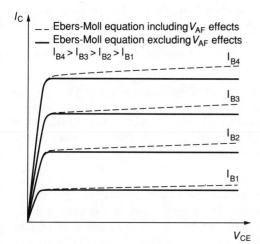

FIGURE 3.3-6
Typical output characteristics of npn BJT based upon Ebers-Moll model.

values of the base current, I_B. Such a plot describes what are termed the *output characteristics*. A plot of the output characteristics for a typical BJT is shown in Fig. 3.3-6 for operation in Quadrant 1 of the I_C–V_{CE} plane. The same basic relationship (except curves are spaced closer together) is obtained in Quadrant 3. Results are shown with and without Early voltage effects. The regions of operation of the BJT in the I_C–V_{CE} plane are shown in Fig. 3.3-7. Comparison of the nomenclature used to define the regions of operation of the BJT in Fig. 3.3-7 to that used to identify the corresponding regions for the MOSFET of Fig. 3.1-7 shows that the term *saturation* is used to define *nonanalogous* regions for the BJT and MOSFET. As mentioned when the terminology for the operating regions of the MOSFET was discussed, the reader should be aware of this nomenclature to avoid possible confusion.

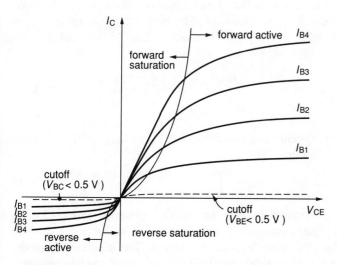

FIGURE 3.3-7
Regions of operation for BJT in I_C–V_{CE} plane.

Example 3.3-3. Compare, using the Ebers-Moll model, the collector and base currents in the forward active region to those in cutoff for a transistor with 1 mil^2 emitter area if $V_{BE} = 0.66$ V, $V_{BC} = -10$ V in the forward active region, and $V_{BE} = -0.3$ V, $V_{BC} = -10$ V in the cutoff region. Use the typical process parameters of Table 3.3-1.

Solution. From (3.3-1) and (3.3-2), I_C and I_B in cutoff are 1.4×10^{-9} μA and 1.406×10^{-9} μA respectively. In the forward active region, it follows from the same equations that $I_C = 63.4$ μA and $I_B = 0.641$ μA. The relative "smallness" of the device currents in the cutoff region should be apparent from these calculations.

3.3.2 Small Signal BJT Model

The small signal model of the bipolar transistor will now be obtained. From Sec. 3.0.2 it can be concluded that the small signal model can be obtained directly from the dc model introduced in the last section. Since there are four regions of operation that have been previously identified in the dc model, there is a different small signal model of the BJT corresponding to each of these regions. The BJT is biased to operate in the forward active region for most small signal applications. The small signal model developed here will be restricted to this region of operation. In the forward active region the collector and base currents can be obtained from

$$I_C = J_S A e^{(V_{BE}/V_t)}\left(1 + \frac{V_{CE}}{V_{AF}}\right) \tag{3.3-27}$$

$$I_B = \frac{J_S A}{\beta_F} e^{(V_{BE}/V_t)} \tag{3.3-28}$$

Since the BJT is modeled as a three-terminal device, it remains to find y_{11}, y_{12}, y_{21}, and y_{22}, as defined in Sec. 3.0 to obtain the small signal BJT model. Convention has resulted in the selection of the emitter node as the reference. For notational convenience b and c rather than 1 and 2 will be used to denote the base and collector nodes of the BJT, respectively. The parameter y_{cb}, often termed g_m, is generally the dominant parameter in the model. From (3.0-5) and (3.3-27) it follows that

$$y_{cb} = g_m = \frac{\partial I_C}{\partial V_{BE}}\bigg|_{\substack{V_{CE}=V_{CEQ} \\ V_{BE}=V_{BEQ}}} = \frac{J_S A}{V_t} e^{(V_{BEQ}/V_t)}\left(1 + \frac{V_{CEQ}}{V_{AF}}\right) \tag{3.3-29}$$

Evaluating (3.3-29) at the Q-point and observing that $V_{CEQ}/V_{AF} \ll 1$, it follows from (3.3-27) and (3.3-29) that

$$g_m = \frac{I_{CQ}}{V_t} \tag{3.3-30}$$

The balance of the y parameters can be readily obtained from (3.0-5), (3.3-27), and (3.3-28). These parameters are summarized in Table 3.3-4. Also listed in this table is the equivalent h parameter model. The h parameter model has been included since it is also widely used. The small signal model equivalent circuits appear in Fig. 3.3-8.

TABLE 3.3-4
Small signal model parameters for the BJT

y Parameters	h Parameters
$y_{cb} = g_m = \dfrac{I_{CQ}}{V_t}$	$h_{fe} = \beta_F$
$y_{be} = g_\pi = \dfrac{g_m}{\beta_F}$	$h_{ie} = \dfrac{\beta_F V_t}{I_{CQ}}$
$y_{bc} = 0$	$h_{re} = 0$
$y_{cc} = g_o = \dfrac{g_m V_t}{V_{AF}} = \dfrac{I_{CQ}}{V_{AF}}$	$h_{oe} = \dfrac{I_{CQ}}{V_{AF}}$

Fundamental parameter relationships

$$r_\pi = 1/g_\pi = h_{ie}$$

$$r_o = 1/g_o = 1/h_{oe}$$

$$\beta_F = g_m r_\pi$$

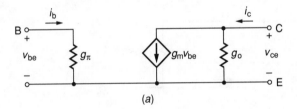

(a)

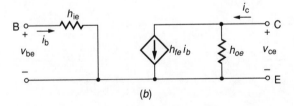

(b)

FIGURE 3.3-8
Small signal model of bipolar transistor: (a) y parameter model (Note: $r_\pi = 1/g_\pi$, $r_o = 1/g_o$ and $\beta_F = g_m r_\pi$), (b) h parameter model.

Example 3.3-4. For the circuit shown in Fig. 3.3-9, determine (a) the quiescent output voltage, (b) the small signal steady state output voltage, and (c) the total output voltage. Use the typical process parameters of Table 3.3-1 to characterize the BJT.

Solution
(a) To obtain the Q-point it suffices to use the equivalent circuits of Fig. 3.3-5. If it is assumed that the BJT is operating in the forward active region, the circuit of Fig. 3.3-10a is obtained. From Ohm's law, it follows that

$$I_{BQ} = (12 \text{ V} - 0.6 \text{ V})/(600 \text{ k}\Omega) = 19 \text{ }\mu\text{A}$$

so that

$$I_{CQ} = \beta_F I_{BQ} = 1.9 \text{ mA}$$

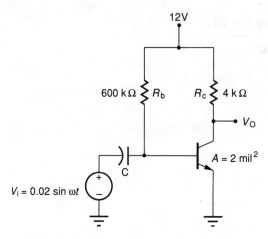

FIGURE 3.3-9
Example 3.3-4.

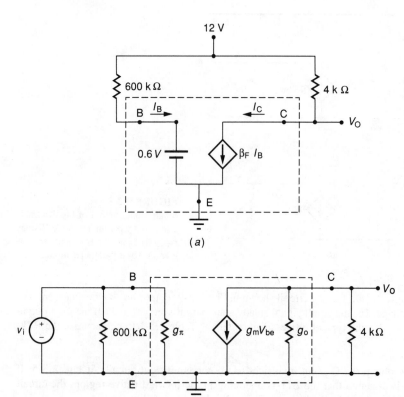

(*a*)

(*b*)

FIGURE 3.3-10
Solution of Example 3.3-4: (*a*) Equivalent circuit for biasing, (*b*) Small signal equivalent circuit.

Hence the quiescent output voltage, V_{OQ}, is given by $V_{OQ} = 12\ \text{V} - I_{CQ}R_c = 4.4$ V. With $V_O = 4.4$ V it follows that the assumption of operation in the forward active region is valid.

(b) Assuming C is large enough to act as a short circuit for ac signals, it follows from the model of Fig. 3.3-8 that the circuit can be drawn as in Fig. 3.3-10b. From Table 3.3-4 it follows that the small signal transistor g parameters at room temperature ($V_t = 26$ mV) are

$$g_m = 73.1\ \text{mmho}$$

$$g_\pi = 0.731\ \text{mmho}$$

$$g_o = 9.5\ \mu\text{mho}$$

From Ohm's law

$$v_o = (-g_m v_i)\left(\frac{1}{g_o + 1/(4\text{k}\Omega)}\right)$$

$$v_o/v_i = -282$$

The small signal steady state output voltage thus becomes

$$v_o(t) = 5.64 \sin \omega t$$

(c) The total output voltage is the sum of the quiescent and small signal steady state values; hence

$$V_O(t) = 4.4\ \text{V} - (5.64 \sin \omega t)\ \text{V}$$

The minus sign appears in the sum to maintain the correct phase relationship between V_O and I_I in this example.

3.3.3 High-Frequency BJT Model

At high frequencies both the dc and small signal models of the BJT introduced in the previous sections are generally considered inadequate. These limitations are primarily attributable to the unavoidable parasitic capacitances inherent in existing bipolar integrated circuits.

These capacitances are of two types. The first type is composed of pn junction capacitances. These capacitances, which are voltage dependent, can be modeled as in the MOSFET and diode cases by (3.1-14) and (3.2-8) provided the junction is not forward biased by any more than $\phi_B/2$ or about 0.35 V. Since the BJT is typically operated with at least one junction forward biased, it is necessary to model the parasitic junction capacitances under forward bias.

For forward biases greater than $\phi_B/2$, it follows from (3.2-9) that the charge storage capacitance can be approximated by[12]

$$C_j = 2^n C_{j0} A\left[2n\frac{V_F}{\phi_B} + (1 - n)\right] \tag{3.3-31}$$

where V_F is the forward bias on the junction. This linear approximation is a continuous extension of (3.1-14) across $V_F = \phi_B/2$ that also agrees in slope at the transition point (see Problem 3.31). The model of the BJT junction capacitances is identical to that of the pn junction diode given in (3.2-8) and (3.2-9).

The cross sections of a vertical npn and a lateral pnp transistor are shown in Fig. 3.3-11. The parasitic junction capacitors for all junctions are identified. Note that the vertical structure has parasitic base–collector, base–emitter, and collector–substrate capacitances, whereas the lateral structure has base–emitter, base–collector, and base–substrate parasitics.

The second type of capacitance is due to majority carrier charge accumulation in the base region, which occurs under forward bias near the emitter junction and introduces a second parasitic between the base and emitter. This capacitance, which is also voltage dependent, can be modeled by

$$C_{\text{AC}} = \frac{t_f I_{\text{CQ}}}{kT} = t_f g_m \qquad (3.3\text{-}32)$$

where t_f is the forward base transit time and I_{CQ} is the quiescent collector current. The process parameter t_f is related to the base width, W_B, and the electron diffusion constant, D_n, by the expression

$$t_f = \frac{W_B^2}{2D_n} \qquad (3.3\text{-}33)$$

The capacitance C_{AC} is added to the base–emitter junction capacitance to obtain the total base–emitter parasitic capacitance. Typical values of t_f range from 0.1 to 1 ns for vertical npn transistors and from 20 to 40 ns for lateral pnp transistors.[13] The parasitic capacitors for both the vertical and lateral BJT are summarized in Table 3.3-5.

A high-frequency small signal equivalent circuit for the BJT is shown in Fig. 3.3-12. In addition to the parasitic capacitors discussed above, four resistive parasitics are shown. These resistive parasitics are present at all frequencies. The resistance R_C, R_E, and R_B represent the ohmic resistance between the metal contact and the junctions in the transistor. Layouts that minimize the distance between the contacts and junctions minimize these resistors. Note that a "primed"

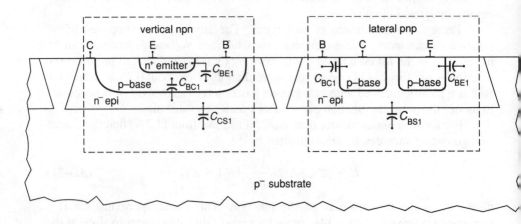

FIGURE 3.3-11
Parasitic junction capacitors in vertical npn and lateral pnp transistors.

TABLE 3.3-5
Parasitic capacitance for the BJT

| | Alternate notation | Transistor type | |
		Lateral	Vertical
C_{BE}	C_π	$C_{BE1} + C_{AC}$	$C_{BE1} + C_{AC}$
C_{BC}	C_μ	C_{BC1}	C_{BC1}
C_{BS}		C_{BS1}	0
C_{CS}		0	C_{CS1}

notation has been used to denote the E, B, and C terminals of the effective BJT. The distinction between the "primed" terminals and the actual terminals is necessary since the series ohmic resistances in the emitter, base, and collector leads were neglected when the model of the BJT was derived.

R_E is in the 1 Ω range and is essentially voltage independent. This low value is due to the shallow depth and high doping density of the emitter region. Although the value is small, the reader must be cautioned that even small resistors in the emitter circuit can significantly affect circuit performance (see Problem 3.44). The resistors R_C and R_B are typically in the 100 Ω range. They are both somewhat voltage dependent.

The resistor r_μ, which appears from the base to collector, is large in value and can be approximated by[13]

$$r_\mu \simeq 10\beta_F/g_o \qquad (3.3\text{-}34)$$

In many applications r_μ can be ignored.

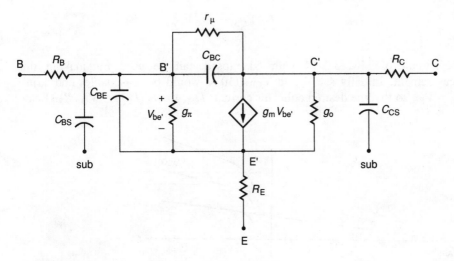

FIGURE 3.3-12
High-frequency small signal equivalent circuit of BJT.

3.3.4 Measurement of BJT Model Parameters

As stated in Section 3.1.4, experimentally measured process parameters are of considerable use to the circuit designer. As in the MOS case, automated measurement equipment is available for bipolar process characterization. In the absence of such equipment, several of the more important BJT device parameters can be measured with reasonable accuracy in the laboratory using standard laboratory equipment. Techniques for measuring J_S, β_F, β_R, V_{AF}, and V_{AR} will be discussed in this section.

From Table 3.3-2, the expressions for the collector and base currents of the npn transistor in the forward active region are

$$I_C = J_S A e^{(V_{BE}/V_t)} \left(1 + \frac{V_{CE}}{V_{AF}} \right) \tag{3.3-35}$$

and

$$I_B = \frac{J_S}{\beta_F} A \exp\left(\frac{V_{BE}}{V_t} \right) \tag{3.3-36}$$

These expressions will serve as a guide for measuring J_S, β_F, and V_{AF}. Measurements of the parameters should be made with I_C close to the intended operating point if possible.

Measurement of V_{AF}. Equation 3.3-35 (extended by Eq. 3.3-1 for small V_{CE}) is plotted in Fig. 3.3-13 for several different values of V_{BE}. Note that all extended curves intersect the V_{CE} axis at $V_{CE} = -V_{AF}$. The parameter V_{AF} can thus be determined by fixing V_{BE} and measuring the V_{CE} axis intercept. If I_{C1} and I_{C2} are the collector currents corresponding to the two different collector–emitter voltages V_{CE1} and V_{CE2} respectively, as depicted in Fig. 3.3-13, then

$$V_{AF} = \frac{I_{C2} V_{CE1} - I_{C1} V_{CE2}}{I_{C1} - I_{C2}} \tag{3.3-37}$$

The circuit of Fig. 3.3-14 with S1 closed can be used for making this measurement. Initially set V_{CE} at V_{CE2} (10 V would be reasonable) and adjust $V_1 = V_{BE}$ so that the desired collector current, I_{C2}, flows ($I_C = -V_O/R$). Leav-

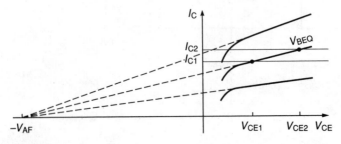

FIGURE 3.3-13
Projection of I–V characteristics of BJT into second quadrant.

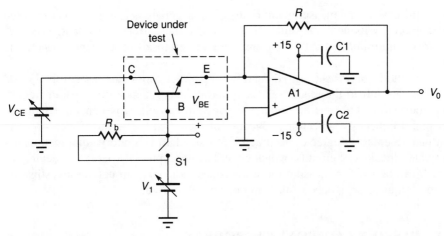

A 356 op amp is a reasonable choice for A1. C1 and C2, which may be needed for stability, should be as close as possible to the supply terminals of the op amp to prevent oscillation. A value of 1μF for these capacitors is reasonable. Note: Care should be taken to avoid ever making $V_1 > V_{CE}$ with S1 closed, as this will permanently damage the transistor since no mechanism is provided to limit current flow when the base-collector junction is forward biased.

FIGURE 3.3-14
Circuit for measuring bipolar transistor parameters.

ing V_{BE} fixed ($V_{BE} = V_{BEQ}$), reduce V_{CE} (2 V would be reasonable) to V_{CE1} and measure the current I_{C1}. V_{AF} now follows from (3.3-37). Reasonably wide separation between V_{CE1} and V_{CE2} should be maintained to reduce the sensitivity to the measured voltages and currents.

Measurement of J_S. The previous circuit with S1 closed can be used for measuring $I_S = J_S A$. By measuring the temperature in °K, V_t can be calculated from Eq. 3.3-3. If I_{C2} and V_{CE2} are the initial collector current and collector–emitter voltage used in the measurement of V_{AF}, then it follows from (3.3-35) that it remains to accurately measure $V_{BE} = V_1$ to obtain I_S from the expression

$$I_S = \frac{I_{C2}\exp(-V_{BE}/V_t)}{1 + V_{CE2}/V_{AF}} \qquad (3.3\text{-}38)$$

Once I_S is obtained, J_S can be determined by dividing by the emitter area, A.

For measuring J_S little accuracy would be lost by either neglecting V_{AF} or using a typical value of V_{AF} in (3.3-38). Accurate measurement of V_{BE} is, however, required.

Measurement of β_F. The circuit of Fig. 3.3-14 with S1 open can be used to measure β_F. Adjust V_1 to obtain the desired collector current, $I_C = -V_O/R$, and adjust V_{CE} to obtain the desired collector–emitter voltage. Measure $I_B = (V_1 - V_{BE})/R_b$. From (3.3-34) and (3.3-35) it thus follows that

$$\beta_F = \frac{I_C/I_B}{1 + V_{CE}/V_{AF}} \qquad (3.3\text{-}39)$$

As in the case of the measurement of J_S, little accuracy is lost if V_{AF} is neglected or replaced by its nominal value. Since β_F is quite current dependent, it is *particularly important* that it be measured at a value close to the intended operating point.

Methods of measuring β_R and V_{AR} parallel those discussed for β_F and V_{AF} and are left to the reader, as are modifications for measuring parameters of pnp transistors. Information about the parasitic capacitors is generally required for high-frequency applications. Because of their small size, direct measurement with an acceptable degree of accuracy using standard laboratory equipment is not possible. Special test circuits, which either have exceptionally large test devices or which can be used to measure these parasitics indirectly through an investigation of the frequency response of the circuit, are often used.

3.4   PASSIVE COMPONENT MODELS

Discrete passive components are quite easy to model. Resistors and capacitors can generally be modeled by ideal resistors and capacitors respectively. The major limitations are manufacturing tolerances and temperature deviations—both of which can be reduced to acceptable levels in most applications through judicious component selection/specification.

Monolithic resistors and capacitors are far from ideal. They are typically both temperature and voltage dependent. The practical range of values is seriously limited by area constraints. Large resistor or capacitor values are impractical. Process deviations preclude accurate control of absolute component values. Parasitic effects are often quite significant. Relative accuracy (ratioing) between passive components is, however, often quite good.

The following figures of merit are used to characterize passive components.

Resistors

1. Sheet resistance
2. Resistance density
3. Temperature coefficient of resistance
4. Voltage coefficient of resistance
5. Absolute accuracy
6. Relative (ratio) accuracy

Capacitors

1. Capacitance density
2. Temperature coefficient of capacitance
3. Voltage coefficient of capacitance
4. Absolute accuracy
5. Relative (ratio) accuracy

The sheet resistance, temperature coefficients, and voltage coefficients were discussed in Chapter 2. The resistance density is generally a function of the process parameters and layout design rules. The capacitance density is a process parameter. The absolute accuracy is a measure of how accurately the actual resistor and capacitor values can be controlled during processing.

The relative (ratio) accuracy is a measure of how closely two resistors or capacitors can be matched. The ratio accuracy is affected by component placement on a die, device geometry, the physical size of the components, and the nominal relative values of the components themselves.

The parasitic effects were not listed above in the figures of merit primarily because of the difficulty in obtaining a single figure with which to meaningfully quantify the parasitic effects. Nevertheless, parasitic effects include contact resistance and distributed capacitances for resistors. Contact resistance, overlap stray capacitances, and edge capacitances are considered as parasitic effects for capacitors.

3.4.1 Monolithic Capacitors

Any structure in which a voltage-induced separation of charge occurs can serve as a capacitor. Some of the structures used for capacitors, along with their characteristics[14] are shown in Table 3.4-1. In a MOS process, the most common capacitors are formed by sandwiching a thin oxide layer between two conductive polysilicon layers. These capacitors are nearly independent of applied voltage and can be modeled as ideal capacitors. The major limitation is the large parasitic capacitor that is always formed between the lower plate and the substrate. This parasitic limits how these capacitors can be used although clever design techniques, such as stray-insensitive SC filters,[15-16] often evolve to minimize these effects.

When the luxury of the double polysilicon layers is not present in MOS processes, metal–poly, metal–diffusion (lower plate formed by a diffused region in the substrate), or poly–diffusion capacitors with an SiO_2 dielectric are used. These capacitors typically have a lower capacitance density and/or increased voltage dependence and/or a less conductive lower plate than the double poly capacitors.

In the bipolar process, the most desirable common capacitors are metal–diffusion capacitors with an SiO_2 dielectric. The heavily doped emitter diffusion is used for the lower diffusion plate. The characteristics are quite good, but an additional mask step is required for forming the dielectric region. Alternatives include the voltage-dependent junction capacitances formed by either the B–C or B–E junction. These capacitors are modeled by (3.1-14) and (3.3-31). The B–E junction offers reasonable capacitance density at the expense of a limited reverse breakdown voltage (typically 5 to 7 V). The B–C junction reverse breakdown voltage is quite high (typically in the 30 V range), but the capacitance density is quite low. All junction capacitors are limited by requirements that the junctions remain reverse biased (actually, not forward biased by more than a few tenths of a volt).

TABLE 3.4-1
Characteristics of monolithic capacitors

Capacitor type	Process	Dielectric	Absolute accuracy	Ratio accuracy	Voltage characteristic	Temperature	Comments
Poly-Poly	MOS	SiO_2	±20%	±0.06%	−5 ppm/V	25 ppm/°C	Most popular MOS, best characteristic
Poly–Diffusion	MOS	SiO_2	±10%	±0.06%	−20 ppm/V	25 ppm/°C	Lower plate potential often fixed
Metal–Diffusion (with thin oxide)	MOS/Bipolar	SiO_2	±10%	±0.06%	−20 ppm/V	25 ppm/°C	Most desirable bipolar
Moat–Substrate	MOS	Si					Voltage dependent
Base–Collector	Bipolar	Si					Must be reverse biased, low density
Base–Emitter	Bipolar	Si					Must be reverse biased
Conductor–Conductor	Thin film	Varies					Good characteristics
Screened	Thick film	Varies					Chip capacitors often preferred

3.4.2 Monolithic Resistors

Considerably more options exist for monolithic resistors. Some monolithic resistors are passive devices and others contain active devices. Major tradeoffs must be made between linearity, area, biasing complexity, and temperature characteristics in monolithic resistors. Table 3.4-2 lists the characteristics of some of the structures that are used for resistors.

In standard MOS processes, the most ideal resistors are merely strips of polysilicon. Diffusion strips are also used for resistors but exhibit an undesirable nonlinear relationship between voltage and current. Ion implants offer some advantages over depositions for the introduction of impurities to control absolute resistance values in diffused resistors. Thin film resistors with excellent characteristics are added in some specialized processes. For each of these types of resistors, a serpentine pattern is often used to improve packing density. The major limitations of these resistors are the low resistance densities, which limit the total resistance to quite small values; the high deviations in resistance due to process variations; and large temperature coefficients.

In bipolar processes epitaxial strips or diffusion strips are commonly used for resistors. These devices are quite linear. The base diffusion is often used because of its reasonably high sheet resistance. A base-diffused resistor is shown in Fig. 3.4-1a. To prevent forward biasing of the "base–collector" junction, a contact is needed to the epitaxial layer. This will be typically connected to the most positive power supply voltage used for the circuit.

It can be argued that the resistance of the base-diffused resistor could be increased if the depth of the p-base diffusion could be decreased. The depth of this diffusion, however, is generally determined to optimize performance of the BJTs themselves. An alternative is to place an n^+ emitter diffusion in the p base region. This masking step already exists and will result in a significant increase of the sheet resistance of the underlying p diffusion. Such a device, which is termed a *pinch* resistor, is shown in Fig. 3.4-1b. Contact must be made to both the n^+ emitter diffusion and the n^- epitaxial region. These regions are typically both connected to the most positive power supply voltage used for the circuit. Although the resistance increases significantly due to this pinching, the variance in emitter and base diffusion depths due to process variations makes the tolerances of pinch resistors quite wide. They also exhibit an increased voltage dependent nonlinearity and are limited in voltage range to circumvent breakdown of the reverse-biased base–emitter junction. Other types of pinch resistors (e.g., epitaxial pinch) can also be made.

Several *active resistors* are shown in Fig. 3.4-2. These active resistors often offer considerable reductions in area requirements compared to passive resistors at the expense of increased nonlinearity and/or reduced signal swing and/or complicated biasing requirements. A more detailed discussion of the active resistor structures appears in Chapter 5.

The circuit of Fig 3.4-2a is merely a MOSFET biased to operate in the ohmic region. From (3) of Table 3.1-1, the relationship between I_D and V_{GS} is

$$I_D = \frac{K'W}{L}\left(V_{GS} - V_T - \frac{V_{DS}}{2}\right)V_{DS} \tag{3.4-1}$$

TABLE 3.4-2
Characteristics of MOS Resistors

Device	Characterizing equation	Ideal resistance†
Poly Strip	$V = I R_\square \dfrac{L}{W}$	$R = R_\square \dfrac{L}{W}$
Diffusion	$V = I R_\square \dfrac{L}{W}$	$R = R_\square \dfrac{L}{W}$
MOSFET (Ohmic region, Fig. 3.4-2a)	$I = \dfrac{K'W}{L}[(V_{GS} - V_T) - \dfrac{V}{2}]V$	$R = \dfrac{L}{K'W(V_{GS} - V_T)}$
MOSFET (Saturated region, Fig. 3.4-2b)	$I = \dfrac{K'W}{2L}(V_{GS} - V_T)^2(1 + \lambda V)$	$R_{SS} = \dfrac{2L}{\lambda K'W(V_{GS} - V_T)^2}$
MOS depletion (Fig. 3.4-2c)	$I = \begin{cases} \dfrac{K'W}{L}(-V_T)V & V < -V_T \\[2mm] \dfrac{K'W}{2L}V_T^2(1 + \lambda V) & V > V_T \end{cases}$	$R = \dfrac{L}{K'W\,\lvert V_T \rvert}$ $R_{SS} = \dfrac{2L}{K'W V_T^2 \lambda}$
MOS Enhancement (Fig. 3.4-2d)	$I = \dfrac{K'W}{2L}(V - V_T)^2(1 + \lambda V)$	$R_{SS} = \dfrac{L}{K'W(V_Q - V_T)}$
Linearity Compensated[18] (Fig. 3.4-2e)	$I = \begin{cases} \dfrac{2K'W}{L}(-V_T)V & V < -V_T \\[2mm] \dfrac{K'W}{L}V_T^2(1 + \lambda V) & V > -V_T \end{cases}$	$R = \dfrac{L}{2K'W\,\lvert V_T \rvert}$ $R_{SS} = \dfrac{L}{K'W V_T^2 \lambda}$
Bootstrapped Budak[17] (Fig. 3.4-2f)	$I = \dfrac{K'W}{L}(V_C - V_T - V\dfrac{[\theta + 1]}{2})(1 - \theta)V$ $V < V_C - V_T$	$R = \dfrac{L}{K'W(1 - \theta)}$

If $V_{DS} << (V_{GS} - V_T)$, then, as seen in Eq. 3.4-1, the relationship between I_D and V_{DS} is linear (assuming V_{GS} is independent of V_{DS}), resulting in an equivalent resistance of

$$R_{eq} \simeq \frac{L}{K'W(V_{GS} - V_T)} \tag{3.4-2}$$

This approximation is quite good for $V_{DS} < 0.5(V_{GS} - V_T)$. A model that includes the nonlinearity is

$$R_{eq} \simeq \frac{L}{K'W[(V_{GS} - V_T) - V_{DS}/2]} \tag{3.4-3}$$

The resistance density (resistance per unit area) of the MOS resistor will now be calculated. Assume d_1 is the minimum moat width, d_2 the minimum

Resistance density‡	Temperature characteristic	Absolute accuracy	Relative accuracy	Comments
$\dfrac{R_\square}{d_4(d_s + d_4)}$	1500 ppm/°C	±30%	±2%	Linear, low resistance density
$\dfrac{R_\square}{d_3(d_s + d_4)}$	1500 ppm/°C	±35%	±2%	Somewhat voltage dependent
$\dfrac{1}{K'(V_{GS} - V_T)d_1(d_1 + 2d_2 + d_3)}$				To minimize distortion, $V < (V_{GS} - V_T)/2$
$\dfrac{1}{\lambda\dfrac{K'}{2}(V_{GS} - V_T)^2 d_1(d_1 + 2d_2 + d_3)}$				Small signal impedance only, high impedance values
$\dfrac{1}{K'\mid V_T\mid d_1(d_1 + 2d_2 + d_3)}$				Popular load device
$\dfrac{1}{\lambda\dfrac{K'}{2}V_T^2 d_1(d_1 + 2d_2 + d_3)}$				Quite nonlinear
$\dfrac{1}{K'(V_Q - V_T)d_1(d_1 + 2d_2 + d_3)}$				Quite nonlinear, good resistance density
$\dfrac{1}{2K'\mid V_T\mid d_1(d_1 + 2d_2 + d_3)}$				Major improvement in density
$\dfrac{1}{\lambda K'V_T^2 d_1(d_1 + 2d_2 + d_3)}$				
Depends upon how θV is realized				Good linearity potential

†R denotes large signal impedance; R_{SS} denotes small signal impedance only.
‡Assuming a minimum size layout, see Fig. 3.4-3 d_1, d_2, d_3, and d_4 as defined in Sec. 3.4.2.

required overlap of poly over moat, and d_3 the minimum poly–poly spacing as defined by the design rules of the process. If a large serpentine MOS device is constructed with minimum moat width and with separate polysilicon strips for each diffusion strip in the serpentine and if the incremental area required by the corners is neglected, then the diagram of Fig. 3.4-3 can be used to calculate the resistance density of this device. The section of length h has a resistance of

$$R = \frac{h}{K'd_1(V_{GS} - V_T)} \tag{3.4-4}$$

and an area of

$$A = h(d_3 + d_1 + 2d_2) \tag{3.4-5}$$

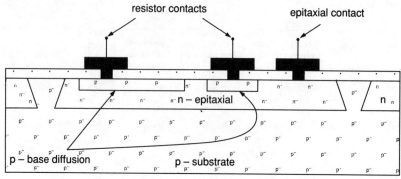

Cross-sectional view along AA´

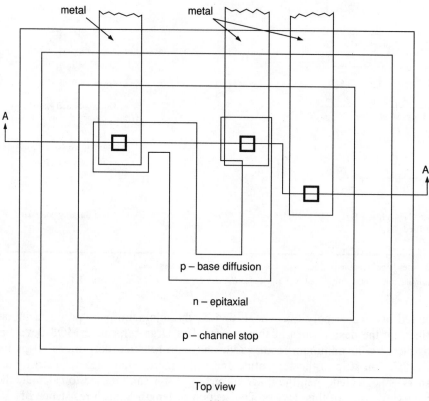

Top view

(a)

FIGURE 3.4-1
Monolithic resistors: (a) Base diffused, (b) Base-pinch.

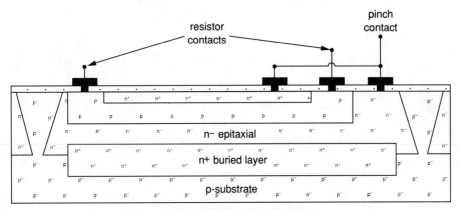

Cross-sectional view along BB′

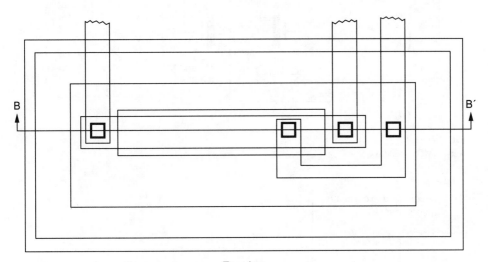

Top view

(b)

FIGURE 3.4-1
(*continued*)

so a resistance density of

$$R_d = \frac{1}{K'(V_{GS} - V_T)(d_1 + 2d_2 + d_3)d_1}$$ (3.4-6)

Although making V_{GS} close to V_T can make R_d very high, it is generally impractical due to process variations to directly make $V_{GS} - V_T < 1$ V. Some improvements in resistance density can be realized if the polysilicon strips are merged into one large rectangular region. In this case, the minimum diffusion spacings will determine how close the serpentined strips can be placed. If the MOSFET is a depletion device, it is particularly convenient to make $V_{GS} = 0$ as shown in Fig. 3.4-2c, thus eliminating the need for a voltage source.

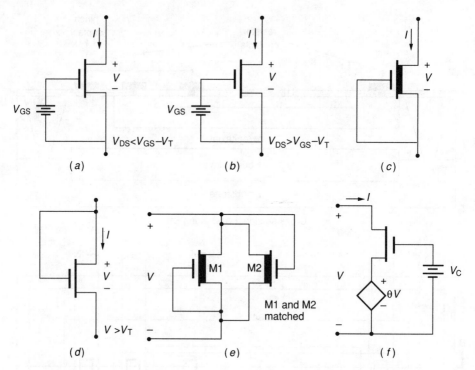

FIGURE 3.4-2
Active MOS resistors.

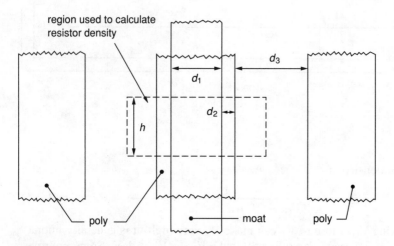

FIGURE 3.4-3
Calculation of resistance density of MOS resistor in ohmic region.

Example 3.4-1. Compare the area required to make a 1 MΩ resistor using a minimum size POLY I string with that using a MOS depletion resistor operating in the saturation region with $V_{GS} = 0$. Use the design rules and process parameters of the NMOS process discussed in Appendix 2A of Chapter 2. Assume the POLY I is uncovered and the feature size of the process is 3 μ (i.e., $\lambda = 1.5\ \mu$).

Solution. The resistance density of the POLY I string can be readily obtained (see Problem 3.55) and is given by

$$R_{dp} = \frac{R_\square}{d_4(d_3 + d_4)} \tag{3.4-7}$$

where d_3 is the minimum poly spacing, d_4 is the minimum poly width, and $R_\square$ is the sheet resistance of POLY I. From Tables 2A.2 and 2A.4 of Appendix A of Chapter 2, $d_3 = 3\ \mu, d_4 = 3\ \mu$, and $R_\square = 25\ \Omega/\square$. Substituting into (3.4-7), it follows that $R_{dp} = 1.39\ \Omega/\mu^2$.

If the MOSFET shown in Fig. 3.4-2c is biased to operate in the saturation region, then, from (4) of Table 3.1-1, the drain current is given by

$$I_D = \frac{K'W}{2L}(V_{GS} - V_T)^2(1 + \lambda V_{DS})$$

The small signal impedance can be obtained by differentiation (assuming V_{GS} and V_{BS} constant) with respect to V_{DS} to obtain

$$R_{ss} = \frac{2L}{[\lambda K'W(V_{GS} - V_T)^2]} \tag{3.4-8}$$

Defining d_1–d_3 as in Fig. 3.4-3, it follows that the resistance density for a large serpentined structure is

$$R_{ds} = \frac{2}{[\lambda K'd_1(V_{GS} - V_T)^2(d_1 + 2d_2 + d_3)]} \tag{3.4-9}$$

From Tables 2A.2 and 2A.4 of Chapter 2, $\lambda = 0.01\ V^{-1}$, $K' = 25\ \mu A/V^2$, $V_T = -3\ V$, $d_1 = 3\ \mu$, $d_2 = 3\ \mu$, and $d_3 = 3\ \mu$. Substituting into (3.4-9) and setting $V_{GS} = 0$, we obtain $R_{ds} = 74\ k\Omega/\mu^2$. It follows that the area ratio is the ratio of the resistance densities; that is, the ratio of R_{dp} to R_{ds}, which is about 67,000 to 1. The area required to make the 1 MΩ poly resistor is about $9 \times 10^5\ \mu^2$, whereas the active resistor requires an area of around 13 μ^2.

Note that for reasonable values of $V_{GS} - V_T$, the λ in the denominator of (3.4-9) makes the resistance density of the MOS resistor in the saturation region considerably higher than the resistance density of the same device biased to operate in the ohmic region. Small signal resistances in the 1 MΩ range become practical with the MOS resistor biased to operate in the saturation region.

Several other MOS active resistors are shown in Fig. 3.4-2. Those of Fig. 3.4-2c and d have proven the most popular in NMOS applications due to their simplicity. The structures of Fig. 3.4-2e and f offer improvements in linearity at the expense of increased area and/or complexity. The characteristics of these active loads are summarized in Table 3.4-2.

A popular bipolar active resistor is shown in Fig. 3.4-4. The equivalent resistance and resistance density will now be calculated.

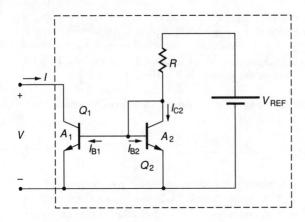

FIGURE 3.4-4
Active bipolar resistor.

Assuming Q_2 is operating in the active region and that β_F is large enough so that $(I_{B1} + I_{B2}) << I_{C2}$, it follows from (2) of Table 3.3-3 that

$$I_{C2} \simeq (V_{REF} - 0.6\,\text{V})/R \tag{3.4-10}$$

and from (1) of Table 3.3-2 (neglecting V_{AF}, which is justifiable since $V_{CE2} \simeq 0.6\,\text{V} << V_{AF}$),

$$I_{C2} \simeq J_S A_2 \exp\left(\frac{V_{BE2}}{V_t}\right) \tag{3.4-11}$$

Equating the two expressions for I_{C2}, it follows that

$$\exp\left(\frac{V_{BE2}}{V_t}\right) \simeq \frac{V_{REF} - 0.6\,\text{V}}{R J_S A_2} \tag{3.4-12}$$

Again, from (1) of Table 3.3-2, it follows that

$$I = J_S A_1\left(1 + \frac{V}{V_{AF}}\right)\exp\left(\frac{V_{BE1}}{V_t}\right) \tag{3.4-13}$$

Since $V_{BE1} = V_{BE2}$ it follows from (3.4-12) and (3.4-13) that

$$I = \frac{A_1\left(1 + \dfrac{V}{V_{AF}}\right)(V_{REF} - 0.6\,\text{V})}{A_2 R} \tag{3.4-14}$$

The small signal impedance follows from differentiation with respect to V and is given by

$$R_{eq} = \frac{V_{AF} A_2 R}{A_1(V_{REF} - 0.6\,\text{V})} \tag{3.4-15}$$

It can be shown that for large R, the area of R dominates that of Q_1 and Q_2; hence the resistance density is approximately m times that of R where

$$m = \left(\frac{V_{AF}}{V_{REF}}\right)\left(\frac{A_2}{A_1}\right) \tag{3.4-16}$$

It can be seen that this active resistor can easily result in an area savings of from 10 to 1000 over that required for the resistor R. The high output impedance of the circuit of Fig. 3.4-4 will be exploited in the discussion of current mirrors in Chapter 5.

Both active and passive resistors are used in IC designs. When area required for passive resistors becomes excessive, the designer should consider the active resistor alternative but must bear in mind that the active resistors are typically nonlinear and often require special biasing considerations.

3.5 SUMMARY

In this chapter, models for MOSFETs, diodes, BJTs, and passive components have been developed. Included are large signal dc models, small signal models, and high-frequency models of varying degrees of complexity. Small signal models were obtained by differentiation of the large signal dc models, and high-frequency models were obtained by identifying the relevant parasitic capacitances inherent in the processes in which the devices were fabricated. This multiple-model approach allows the user to select the simplest model acceptable for a given application. The most notable differences between the MOSFET and the BJT are (1) square law contrasted to exponential dc transfer characteristics, and (2) different input impedances, characterized by a nearly infinite input impedance for the MOSFET contrasted to a small input impedance for the BJT. The models developed here will be used for analysis and design throughout later chapters and will be expanded for use in computer simulations in Chapter 4.

REFERENCES

1. C. T. Sah, "Characteristics of the Metal-Oxide-Semiconductor Transistor," *IEEE Trans. Electron. Devices*, vol. ED-11, pp. 324–345, July 1964.
2. H. Shichman and D. A. Hodges, "Modeling and Simulation of Insulated-Gate Field-Effect Transistor Switching Circuits," *IEEE J. Solid State Circuits*, vol. SC-3, pp. 285–289, Sept. 1968.
3. R. Muller and T. Kamins, *Device Electronics for Integrated Circuits*, Wiley, New York, 1977, Chapter 7.
4. J. Millman and C. Halkias, *Integrated Electronics: Analog and Digital Circuits and Systems*, McGraw-Hill, New York, 1972.
5. A. Sedra and K. Smith, *Microelectronic Circuits*, Holt, Rinehart & Winston, New York, 1982.
6. C. Duvurry, "A Guide to Short Channel Effects in MOSFETS," *TI Engineering Journal*, Texas Instruments Inc., pp. 52–56, July–August 1984.
7. A. Vladimirescu and S. Liu, "The Simulation of MOS Integrated Circuits Using SPICE2," Memorandum No. UCB/ERL M80/7, Electronics Research Laboratory, University of California, Berkeley, Feb. 1980.
8. L. Stotts, "Introduction to Implantable Biomedical IC Design," *IEEE Circuits and Devices Magazine*, pp. 12–18 January 1989.
9. Y. Tsividis and P. Antognetti, eds., *Design of MOS VLSI Circuits for Telecommunications*, Prentice-Hall, Englewood Cliffs, New Jersey, 1985, Chapter 4.
10. P. Gray, D. Hodges, and R. Brodersen, eds., *Analog MOS Integrated Circuits*, IEEE Press, New York, 1980, p. 31.
11. J. J. Ebers and J. L. Moll, "Large Signal Behavior of the Junction Transistor," *Proc. IRE*, Vol. 42, pp. 1761–1772, Dec. 1954.

12. I. Getreu, *Modeling the Bipolar Transistor*, Tektronix Inc., Beaverton, Oregon, 1976.
13. P. Gray and R. Meyer, *Analysis and Design of Analog Integrated Circuits*, Wiley, New York, 1977.
14. P. E. Allen and D. R. Holberg, *CMOS Analog Circuit Design*, Holt, Rinehart & Winston, New York, 1987.
15. R. Gregorian and G. C. Temes, *Analog MOS Integrated Circuits for Signal Processing*, Wiley, New York, 1986.
16. P. E. Allen and E. Sánchez-Sinencio, *Switched Capacitor Circuits*, Van Nostrand Reinhold, New York, 1984.
17. K. Nay and A. Budak, "A Voltage-Controlled Resistance with Wide Dynamic Range and Low Distortion," *IEEE Trans. on Circuits and Systems*, vol. CAS-30, pp. 770–772, October 1983.
18. K. Peterson and R. L. Geiger, "CMOS OTA Structures with Improved Linearity," *Proc. 27th Midwest Symposium on Circuits and Systems*, Morgantown, WV, pp. 63–66, June 1984.
19. B. J. Sheu, D. L. Scharfetter, and P. K. Ko, "SPICE2 Implementation of BSIM", UCB/ERL M85/42, Engineering Research Laboratory, University of California, Berkeley, May 1985.

PROBLEMS

Section 3.0

3.1. A linear three-terminal network can be characterized in terms of the y-parameters by the equations

$$i_1 = y_{11}v_1 + y_{12}v_2$$

$$i_2 = y_{21}v_1 + y_{22}v_2$$

Obtain the corresponding small signal equivalent circuit.

3.2. Show that the small signal Thevenin equivalent circuits of both of the circuits in Fig. P3.2 are resistors of value R using the definitions of Section 3.0-3.

3.3. Develop a small signal model for a device characterized by the following equations:

$$I_1 = 5(V_1 - 4)$$
$$I_2 = -25(V_1 - 2)^3\left(1 + \frac{V_2}{5}\right)$$

Section 3.1

3.4. Verify that if a MOSFET is modeled by Eq. (3.1-1), the designation of "source" and "drain" is arbitrary (i.e., the same I–V characteristics are obtained if the node initially labeled "drain" is called the "source" and the node initially labeled "source" is called the "drain").

3.5. Derive an expression for the MOSFET for the locus of points in the I_D–V_{DS} plane where

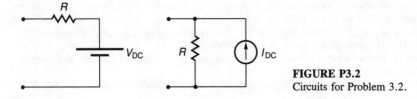

FIGURE P3.2
Circuits for Problem 3.2.

$$\frac{\partial I_D}{\partial V_{DS}} = 0$$

Assume the device is modeled by Eq. 3.1-1.

3.6. Assume a MOS device is to be modeled in the saturation region by the equation

$$I_D = \frac{K'W}{2L}(V_{GS} - V_T)^2 \qquad (P1)$$

but that the device is actually characterized by the equation

$$I_D = \frac{K'W}{2L}(V_{GS} - V_T)^2\left(1 + \frac{V_{DS}}{20}\right) \qquad (P2)$$

where V_T is assumed constant in both equations. Also assume that the unknown parameters K' and V_T are to be experimentally obtained from (P1) by measuring I_D at $V_{GS} = 2.0$ V and again at $V_{GS} = 2.2$ V with $V_{DS} = 2$ V and then solving simultaneously the two versions of (P1) to obtain the two unknowns. Further assume that $W = 5$ μ, $L = 15$ μ, and the measured values of I_D are 6.336 μA and 8.624 μA at 2.0 and 2.2 V respectively.

(a) What values will be obtained for the parameters K' and V_T?

(b) What percentage error between experimental and theoretical results will be obtained in using Eq. P1 and the parameters obtained in (a) to predict I_D if the device is to operate at $V_{GS} = 2.1$ V and $V_{DS} = 2.5$ V?

(c) What percentage error between experimental and theoretical results will be obtained in using Eq. P1 and the parameters obtained in (a) to predict I_D if the device is to operate at $V_{GS} = 6$ V and $V_{DS} = 15$ V?

(d) How can correlation between theoretical and experimental results be improved?

3.7. The transfer characteristics for the CMOS inverter shown in Fig. P3.7 are plotted parametrically in Fig. 3.1-13b for the case that $V_{DD} > V_{TON} - V_{TOP}$. Plot parametrically the transfer characteristics of this circuit if $V_{DD} < V_{TON} - V_{TOP}$ and identify the mode of operation of each transistor in each region.

3.8. The small signal model of the MOSFET is used most often for the analysis of MOS circuits in which the transistors are operating in the saturation region.

(a) Derive the small signal low frequency model for the MOS transistor operating in the ohmic region with Q-point I_{DQ}, V_{GSQ}, V_{DSQ}, and V_{BSQ}.

(b) What does this reduce to if $V_{DSQ} = 0$ V?

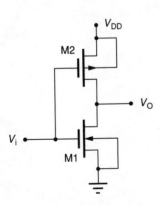

FIGURE P3.7
Circuit for Problem 3.7.

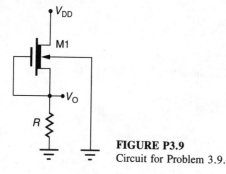

FIGURE P3.9
Circuit for Problem 3.9.

3.9. One easy way to include λ and γ effects in the calculation of V_O for the circuit shown in Fig. P3.9 is to set up an iteration defined for $N = 1$ by

$$V_{T1} = V_{T0}$$

$$I_{D1} = \frac{K'W}{2L}(V_{T1})^2$$

$$V_{O1} = I_{D1}R$$

and for $N > 1$,

$$V_{TN} = V_{T0} + \gamma\left(\sqrt{\phi + V_{O,N-1}} - \sqrt{\phi}\right)$$

$$I_{DN} = \frac{K'W}{2L}(V_{TN})^2[1 + \lambda(V_{DD} - V_{O,N-1})]$$

$$V_{ON} = I_{DN}R$$

How many iterations are required for I_{DN} to converge to within 0.01% of its actual value if M1 is fabricated in the NMOS process of Table 3.1-2 and if $W = 3\,\mu$, $L = 12\,\mu$, $R = 20\,\text{k}\Omega$, and $V_{DD} = 6$ V?

3.10. Obtain an expression for and plot the maximum deviation over the ohmic region, in percentage, from the current as predicted by (3.1-1) from that obtained if (3.1-1) is multiplied by $(1 + \lambda V_{DS})$ to maintain continuity at the ohmic region–saturation region interface.

3.11. Assume the MOSFET in Fig. P3.11 is characterized by the CMOS model parameters of Table 3.1-2.

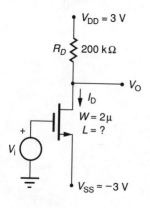

FIGURE P3.11
MOSFET for Problem 3.11.

(a) Determine L so that $A_V = v_o/v_i = -25$. What is the Q-point (V_{OQ}, I_{DQ}) with this value of L?

(b) Determine L so that $V_{OQ} = OV$. What is $A_V = v_o/v_i$ with this value of L?

3.12. Obtain the dc model for the devices shown in Fig. P3.12. Make a qualitative comparison of the performance of these structures.

3.13. The output characteristics for a MOSFET with $V_{BS} = 0$ are shown in Fig. P3.13.

(a) Determine as many parameters as possible from the set

$$\{K', V_{T0}, \gamma, \lambda, W, L, K'W/L, \phi, C_{ox}\}$$

(b) If the device is biased to operate at the point Q, determine as many parameters as possible of the set $\{g_m, g_{ds}, g_{mb}\}$.

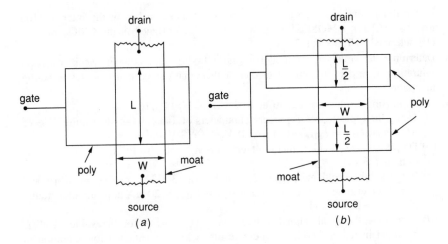

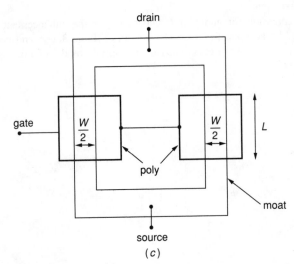

FIGURE P3.12
Devices for Problem 3.12.

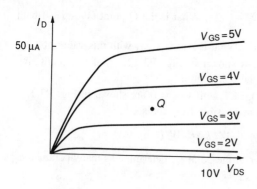

FIGURE P3.13
Graph for Problem 3.13.

3.14. Plot g_m, g_{ds}, and g_{mb} versus I_{DQ} on the same axis for I_{DQ} in the interval [100 nA, 10 mA] for a MOSFET with $W = L = 5\ \mu$ designed in the CMOS process characterized in Table 3.1-2.

3.15. Determine the small signal model of the MOSFET operating in weak inversion saturation. Compare this model to that of the same device if it operates in strong inversion.

3.16. A simple single transistor amplifier is shown in Fig. P3.16.

(a) Using the typical CMOS process parameters of Table 3.1-2, determine W/L of M so that $I_{DQ} = I_{BIAS} = 20\ \mu$A, if $V_{SS} = -2$ V and $V_i = 0$ V.

(b) Determine the small signal voltage gain $A_V = v_o/v_i$ for the value of W/L obtained in (a).

(c) If the subthreshold parameters I_{DO} and n of (3.1-32) are $I_{DO} = 20$ nA and $n = 2$, determine W/L of M so that $I_{DQ} = I_{BIAS} = 20\ \mu$A at room temperature if $V_{SS} = -0.1$ V and $V_i = 0$ V.

(d) Determine the small signal voltage gain $A_V = v_o/v_i$ for the value of W/L obtained in (c) and compare these results with that obtained for operation in strong inversion.

3.17. Obtain an expression for and plot I versus V for the enhancement load circuit of Fig. P3.17 based upon the MOSFET model of Table 3.1-1, and compare these transfer characteristics with those used for the simple model of Eq. 3.1-45.

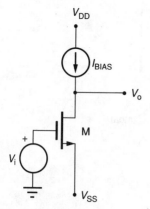

FIGURE P3.16
Problem 3.16.

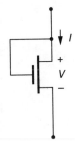

FIGURE P3.17
Circuit for Problem 3.17.

3.18. Derive the small signal model for the MOSFET operating in the saturation region from the dc model of the MOSFET given by Eq. 3.1-5. Verify that these results are equivalent to those given in Table 3.1-3.

3.19. If $I_B = 50\ \mu A$, then M1 in Fig. P3.19 is operating in strong inversion for $V_i = 0$. If I_B remains constant, how much must the W/L ratio of M1 be increased to force M1 into subthreshold? Assume $I_{DO} = 20$ nA, $n = 2$, $K' = 24\ \mu A/V^2$, and $V_T = 0.75$ V.

3.20. Consider a single MOS transistor. If $V_{BS} = 0$ and $V_{DS} > 3V_t$, determine the value of V_{GS} at the intersection of the strong inversion drain saturation current of (4) in Table 3.1-1 with the weak inversion current. How does this relate to the transition region of Eq. 3.1-31? Assume $I_{DO} = 20$ nA, $n = 2$ in Eq. 3.1-32, $K' = 24\ \mu A/V^2$, and $\lambda = 0$.

3.21. Obtain the output voltage for the circuit layout of Color Plate 10 if $V_{DD} = 5$ V and $V_I = 2$ V. Assume the devices were fabricated in the NMOS process summarized in Appendix 2A.

3.22. In the saturation region of operation, most of the channel region is characterized by an inversion layer, which is an extension of the source as depicted in Fig. 2.2-2f. This represents a series impedance in the source. Assuming the voltage drop is sufficiently small that Eq. 3.1-8 applies, calculate the series source–channel impedance, R_{sc}. *Note*: Due to a tapering of the channel near the drain, the source–channel impedance is actually about 50% larger than that predicted by (3.1-8).

3.23. If γ and λ effects are neglected, a MOSFET of width W and length L is equivalent to the series connection of the two devices as shown in Fig. P3.23 where ϵ is any real number which satisfies the expression $0 < \epsilon \le L$.

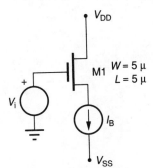

FIGURE P3.19
Circuit for Problem 3.19.

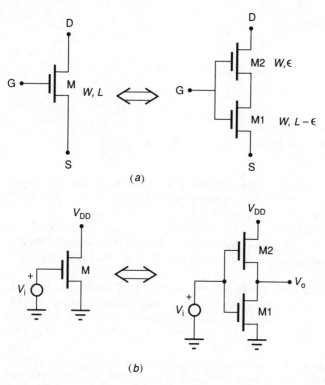

FIGURE P3.23
Circuits for Problem 3.23.

(a) If the MOSFET M is operating in the saturation region, show that in the equivalent circuit of Fig. P3.23a, M1 is operating in the ohmic region and M2 in the saturation region.

(b) If the equivalent MOSFET is connected as shown if Fig. P3.23b and M is operating in the saturation region, derive an expression for V_o in terms of V_i.

(c) Calculate the equivalent impedance of M1 in Fig. P3.23b assuming V_i is sufficiently small that (3.1-8) applies.

3.24. For the circuit of Fig. P3.24,

(a) Calculate parametrically the output thermal noise current in the frequency band $10 \text{ kHz} \leq f \leq 200 \text{ kHz}$ and the output flicker noise current in the same

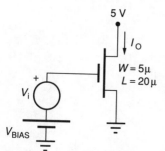

FIGURE P3.24
Circuit for Problem 3.24.

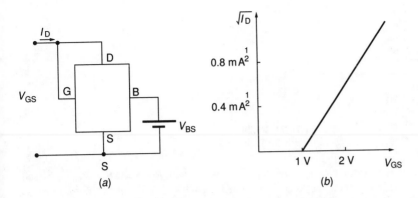

FIGURE P3.25
Circuit and graph for Problem 3.25.

band if $K_f = 3 \times 10^{-24}$ V^2·F at the dc operating point determined by $V_i = 0$.

(b) Calculate parametrically the equivalent input referred offset voltage.

(c) Calculate the signal to noise ratio of the output current if $V_{BIAS} = 2$ V and $V_i = 0.25 \sin 10^5 t$ over the frequency band given in (a). Neglect λ and γ effects and assume the remaining process parameters given in Appendix 2B.

3.25. A plot of V_{GS} versus $\sqrt{I_D}$ for an NMOS transistor is shown in Fig. P3.25. It has $\mu C_{ox} = 60$ μA/V^2, $V_{BS} = 0$, and the remainder of the characterization parameters as indicated in the NMOS design rules discussed in Chapter 2.

(a) Is the device a depletion or enhancement transistor?

(b) What mode of operation is the device in?

(c) What is W/L?

(d) What is the threshold voltage?

(e) What will the horizontal axis intercept if V_{BS} is changed to -9 V?

3.26. The pn junction between an n$^+$ moat diffusion and substrate is used to form a capacitor. Determine the value of this capacitor with a reverse bias of 6 V if the area of the n$^+$ moat diffusion is 16 mil^2. Assume the process parameters of the NMOS process of Appendix 2A.

3.27. Compare the minimum area required to build a first-order lowpass filter with a 3 db cutoff frequency of 2 kHz using the two techniques shown in Fig. P3.27a and b

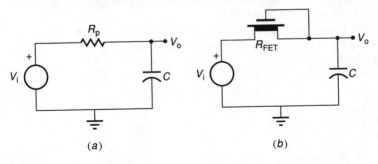

FIGURE P3.27
Circuits for Problem 3.27.

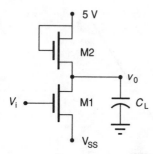

FIGURE P3.28
Circuit for Problem 3.28.

respectively. Assume R_p is made of a poly resistor with $R_\square = 30\ \Omega/\square$. R_{FET} is biased to operate in the ohmic region ($K' = 15\,\mu\text{A/V}^2$, $V_{T0} = -3.5\text{V}$, $\gamma = 0$, $\phi = 0$, $\lambda = 0$), the capacitance density is $0.2\ \text{pF/mil}^2$, and both R_p and R_{FET} are serpentined with minimum feature width of $5\ \mu$, minimum feature spacing of $5\ \mu$, and a gate–moat overlap of $2.5\ \mu$. Derive all equations needed.

3.28. The voltage V_{SS} can be used to establish the quiescent drain currents with $V_i = 0$. Obtain an expression for the 3 db bandwidth of the circuit in Fig. P3.28 in terms of I_{DQ} and the model parameters of M1 and M2. Neglect all parasitic capacitors in M1 and M2.

3.29. Determine the small signal equivalent circuit for the circuit shown in Fig. P3.29.

3.30. Assume a MOSFET is characterized in strong and weak inversion by Eqs. (3.1-4) and (3.1-33) respectively.

(a) Show that if the transconductance gain is to be continuous at the strong inversion–weak inversion interface, then the transition must occur at $V_{GS} = V_T - 2nV_t$.

(b) Show that if I_D is to be continuous at the transition determined in (a), then I_{DO} and K' must be related by the equation

$$I_{DO} = \frac{K'2(nV_t)^2}{e^2}$$

Section 3.2

3.31. Show that the forward-biased pn junction capacitance model of Eq. 3.2-9 is a continuous and differentiable extension of the reverse-bias model of Eq. 3.2-8 at the transition $V = \phi_B/2$.

3.32. Assume a depletion region capacitor is characterized by $C_{ox} = 250\ \text{fF/mil}^2$, $\phi = 0.6\text{V}$, $n = 1/2$, and $A = 6\ \text{mil}^2$. Determine the bias voltage required to reduce the capacitance to half of what it is at 0 V bias.

3.33. Accurately determine I in Fig. P3.33. Assume the diode is characterized by the BE diffusion of the bipolar process of Appendix 2C with a junction area of $500\ \mu^2$. Assume operation at $T = 30°\ \text{C}$.

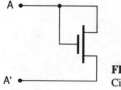

FIGURE P3.29
Circuit for Problem 3.29.

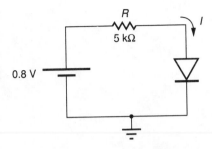

FIGURE P3.33
Circuit for Problem 3.33.

3.34. Assume the vertical npn base–collector junction of the process of Appendix 2C is to be used as a varactor diode.

(a) Determine the area of the base needed to generate a capacitance of 50 pF with a reverse bias of 3 V.

(b) Plot the capacitance of this diode versus reverse bias for $-5 \leq V_{BC} \leq 0$.

(c) Repeat part (a) if the BE junction is used instead of the BC junction in the same process.

3.35. A diode can be fabricated in the bipolar process of Appendix 2C in several ways. Give all ways that the diode can be fabricated and compare the performance characteristics from both dc and ac viewpoints. Include in your discussion a characterization of all relevant parasitics.

3.36. A "diode-connected transistor" is shown in Fig. P3.36a. Compare the performance of this to that of the BE and BC diodes (Figs. P3.36b and c) in the bipolar process of Appendix 2C.

3.37. The circuit shown in Fig. P3.37 is proposed as a rectifier. Compare the dc performance of this to that of the pn junction and that of the diode-connected transistor of Problem 3.36. How does the performance of this circuit as a rectifier change with W and L?

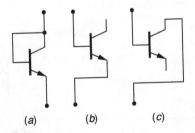

(a)   (b)   (c)

FIGURE P3.36
Diodes for Problem 3.36.

$W = 2\mu$
$L = 2\mu$

FIGURE P3.37
Circuit for Problem 3.37.

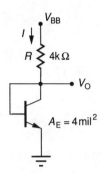

FIGURE P3.38
Circuit for Problem 3.38.

Section 3.3

3.38. Using Fig. P3.38, obtain V_O to within $\pm 1\%$ if (a) $V_{BB} = 12$ V and (b) $V_{BB} = 0.9$ V. Assume the BJT is characterized by the parameters of Table 3.3-1 and modeled by the Ebers-Moll Eqs. 3.3-1 and 3.3-2.

3.39. Determine the maximum error, in percentage, that results from using (3.3-10) and (3.3-11) instead of the more complicated Ebers-Moll equations of (3.3-1) and (3.3-2) in the region $V_{BE} > 0.5$ V, $V_{BC} < 0.3$ V. Assume the BJT is at room temperature and characterized by the parameters of Table 3.3-1.

3.40. Calculate the power that would be dissipated in a BJT if $A_E = 4$ mil^2 and the device is operating with (a) $V_{BE} = 0.6$ V and $V_{BC} = -5$ V, and (b) $V_{BE} = 1.6$ V and $V_{BC} = -5$ V. Assume the BJT is characterized by the process parameters of Table 3.3-1.

3.41. Plot the transconductance gain, g_m, versus bias current (collector or drain) for a MOSFET with $W = L = 10$ μ and a BJT with $A_E = 100$ μ^2. Use the typical process parameters of Tables 3.1-2 and 3.3-1.

3.42. Rewrite the Ebers-Moll equations of (3.3-1) and (3.3-2) using V_{BE} and V_{CE} as the independent variables in terms of the parameters I_S, β_F, β_R, and V_T.

3.43. At high frequencies, a small signal gate current flows into the gate of the MOSFET. Compare the unity small signal–short circuit current gain frequency (of $A_I = i_o/i_i$)

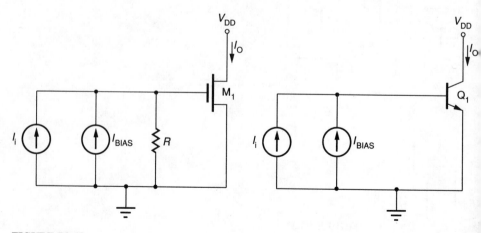

FIGURE P3.43
Circuit for Problem 3.43.

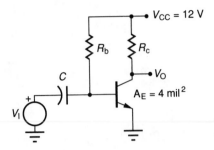

FIGURE P3.44
Circuit for Problem 3.44.

for the MOSFET to that of the BJT (see Fig. P3.43). Assume both devices are in their high-gain operating region, are of minimum size, are biased at $I_{OQ} = 200\,\mu\text{A}$, and are characterized by the process of Tables 2A and 2C of the Appendices of Chapter 2. Assume R is large.

3.44. (a) For the circuit shown in Fig. P3.44, bias the circuit (determine R_b) so that $V_{OQ} = 2$ V when $R_c = 500\,\Omega$. Determine the small signal voltage gain $A_v = v_o/v_i$ if it is assumed C is large. Use the typical process parameters of Table 3.3-1.

(b) Repeat part (a) if the parasitic emitter resistance is $R_E = 2\,\Omega$. Compare the results with those obtained in (a).

(c) Repeat parts (a) and (b) if $R_C = 10\,\text{k}\Omega$ and $V_{OQ} = 6$ V and compare with the results obtained in parts (a) and (b).

3.45. Assume the BJT of Fig. P3.45 is biased with R_b so that Q1 operates in the forward active region. What will be the tolerance in the value of V_{BE} due to processing? What will be the wafer-level tolerance in the value of V_{BE} due to wafer-level parameter variations? Assume the BJT process in which Q1 is fabricated is characterized by Table 2C.4 of Appendix 2C and that wafer-level variations (matching) are characterized by footnote 1 of that table.

3.46. The depletion region capacitance of the BE junction of an npn transistor with a rectangular emitter that is 0.3 mil × 6 mil is 0.63 pF at zero volts reverse bias. A circular transistor of the same test bar has the same emitter area. What is the depletion region capacitance of this device for a 6 V reverse bias at room temperature if the built-in potential, ϕ_B, is 0.70 V?

3.47. For the transistor shown in Fig. P3.47, $I_s = 2 \times 10^{-15}$ A and the emitter area is 1.5 mil². With $V = 1$ V, the current I is 52 μA, and with $V = 21$ V, I is 56 μA.
(a) Determine V_{AF}.
(b) Determine β_F.
(c) Determine V_{BE} at room temperature (300 °K).

3.48. If we plot ln I_C (vertical) versus V_{BE} (horizontal) for a bipolar transistor operating

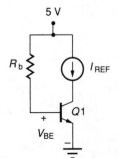

FIGURE P3.45
Circuit for Problem 3.45.

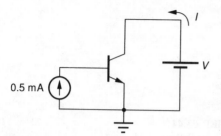

FIGURE P3.47
Transistor for Problem 3.47.

in the forward-active region, how can the area of the emitter be determined from the plot? What can be determined from the slope? Neglect Early voltage effects.

3.49. For the circuit shown in Fig. P3.49, assume the collector current is 10 mA, the emitter is a square with sides of 1 mil, the base is a square with sides of 3 mil, and the collector area is defined by a square with sides of 6 mil. For the following, assume that no changes are made in the circuit schematic.

(*a*) What will be the collector current if the sides of the base are increased to 4 mil?
(*b*) What will be the collector current if the emitter sides are decreased to 0.5 mil?
(*c*) What will be the collector current if the collector sides are increased to 7 mil?

3.50. A plot of $\ln I_{BE}$ versus V_{BE} for a BJT transistor, with emitter area 4 mil^2, and a base area of 10 mil^2, operating in the forward active region is shown by the solid line in Fig. P3.50. Determine as many of the following model parameters as possible: J_S, T, V_T, β_F, β_R, α_F.

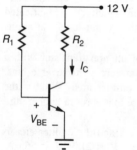

FIGURE P3.49
Circuit for Problem 3.49.

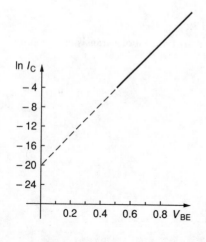

FIGURE P3.50
Graph for Problem 3.50.

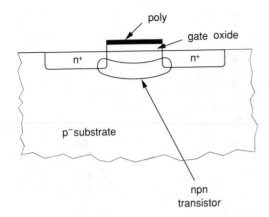

npn
transistor

FIGURE P3.51
NMOS structure for Problem 3.51.

3.51. The NMOS structure shown in Fig. P3.51 is proposed as an npn transistor to be used with n-channel MOSFET devices. Give two good reasons why this device may not be practical.

3.52. Assume the two circuits shown in Fig. P3.52 are biased (with V_{B1} and V_{B2} respectively) so that $V_{OQ} = 5$ V. Compare the small signal voltage gains of the two circuits.

3.53. Calculate the value of C_{JE} and C_{JC} for the npn vertical transistor characterized by the process of Table 2C.4 in Appendix 2C. Assume the emitter is square with dimensions $20\,\mu \times 20\,\mu$, the base is square with sides of $50\,\mu$, and the collector is square with sides of $100\,\mu$. Compare these results to the values listed in Table 2C.5.

3.54. Calculate the value of C_{JE}, C_{JC}, and the base–substrate capacitance for a lateral pnp transistor with $30\,\mu \times 30\,\mu$ square collector and emitter areas separated by a distance of $15\,\mu$ if they lie symmetrically inside an isolated square epitaxial region that is $10\,\mu$ on a side. Assume the process parameters of Table 2C.4 of the Appendix 2C.

3.55. From the equivalent circuit of Fig. 3.3-8, rigorously define the h parameters and derive an expression for the h parameters in the small-signal BJT model (a) in terms of the y parameters g_m, g_π, and g_o, and (b) in terms of the operating point and parameters used in the Ebers-Moll model.

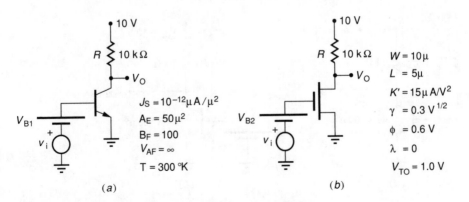

(a) (b)

FIGURE P3.52
Circuits for Problem 3.52.

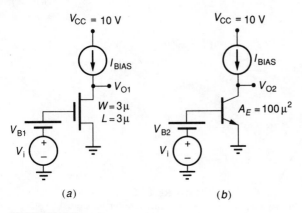

(a) (b)

FIGURE P3.56
Amplifiers for Problem 3.56.

3.56. Plot the small signal voltage gains, v_{O1}/v_i and v_{O2}/v_i, versus bias current for the two amplifiers shown in Fig. P3.56. Assume that V_{B1} and V_{B2} are adjusted so that $V_{O1Q} = V_{O2Q} = 5$ V. Use the typical process parameters of Tables 3.1-2 and 3.3-1.

3.57. Two different schemes for biasing the BJT are shown in Fig. P3.57. Assume the BJT is characterized by the process parameters of Table 3.3-1.

(a) Determine the value of R_B and V_B necessary to bias the outputs at 5 V.

(b) Determine the change in V_{O1} and V_{O2} that will be expected for each circuit if V_{CC} varies around 10 V by ± 0.1 V.

(c) Determine the change in V_{O2} that will be expected if V_B varies about the value obtained in part (a) by ± 0.1 V.

(d) What can be said about the sensitivity of the quiescent output voltage to the biasing voltages V_{CC} and V_B for the two circuits?

Section 3.4

3.58. If the sheet resistance of polysilicon is $R_\square$, the minimum poly width is d_4, and the minimum poly spacing is d_3, determine the resistance density of a large, minimum-feature-size, serpentined poly resistor in terms of d_3, d_4, and $R_\square$. Neglect any area associated with corners and contacts.

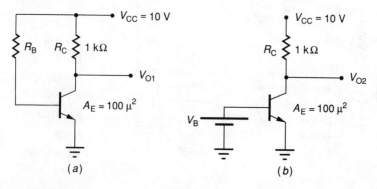

(a) (b)

FIGURE P3.57
Circuits for Problem 3.57.

CHAPTER
4

CIRCUIT SIMULATION

4.0 INTRODUCTION

Computer simulation of a circuit entails using a computer to predict, or simulate, the performance of a circuit or system. The circuit which is simulated may include anywhere from a few components to several hundred thousand. Many different types of computer programs are used for simulations of integrated circuits, depending on the type of analysis required and the size of circuit involved.

The major emphasis in this chapter is on the use of the SPICE simulation program for circuit simulation, and, in particular, on a discussion of the active device models used in SPICE and the interrelationship between these models and the device models discussed in Chapter 3. The simulation program SPICE was selected because of its long-term acceptance and use, as well as its widespread availability to both industrial and academic groups. The reader should have access to and be familiar with the SPICE User's Guide[1] and the basic use of SPICE.

In the design of state-of-the-art integrated circuits; circuit simulations comprise only a small portion of the overall use of the computer. The discussion of a circuit simulation program is included in this chapter because of the challenging nature of circuit simulation. Many students and even practicing engineers experience more problems with circuit simulation than with most of the other sophisticated CAD tools used for VLSI design. These problems largely result from unfamiliarity with the capabilities, limitations, and uses of the simulators.

4.1 CIRCUIT SIMULATION USING SPICE

The circuit simulation program called SPICE is the result of a continuing effort, which has spanned nearly 20 years, by a large group of individuals at the University of California at Berkeley. It was initially written in FORTRAN; later versions in that language are nearly 18,000 lines long. A C–Language version of SPICE was practically introduced in 1987, and now both the FORTRAN and C versions are widely used. SPICE has been adapted to a large number of different hardware configurations and is used in both industry and academia. Although there are several competing programs, some of which may offer advantages in some respects, none are as universally accepted as SPICE.

SPICE utilizes a modified nodal analysis approach. It can be used for nonlinear-dc, nonlinear-transient, and linear-ac analysis problems. It also includes modules for more specialized analysis such as noise analysis, temperature analysis, etc. The inputs can be constant or time varying. For the nonlinear-dc and nonlinear-transient analyses, the program includes the nonlinear effects of all devices specified by the user. For the ac analysis, the dc operating point is internally determined. From the dc operating point, the small signal equivalent circuit of each device is obtained. The resulting linear network is analyzed using the appropriate matrix manipulations. The small signal analysis *includes no nonlinear effects* of the devices.

A block diagram showing the fundamental operation of SPICE appears in Fig. 4.1-1. The subroutine READIN reads the SPICE input file. ERRCHK verifies that the input syntax is correct. Temperature effects are handled in SPICE by repeating the entire analysis for each temperature. The subroutines DCTRAN, DCOP and ACAN perform the bulk of the manipulations. DCTRAN and DCOP are used for dc transfer characteristics, dc operating point calculations, and transient analysis. ACAN performs the small signal ac analysis.

Documentation about the program SPICE is required for utilizing the program. At a minimum, the IC designer needs the following two documents available from Berkeley to effectively use SPICE for MOS IC design.

1. "SPICE User's Guide"[1]

2. "The Simulation of MOS Integrated Circuits Using SPICE"[2]

These publications, along with other relevant documentation[3–12,22,23] are listed in the references. The SPICE source code[6] contains good comments and serves as the ultimate reference document on the program.

One of the strong points of SPICE is its inclusion of respectable models for the basic active devices, specifically, the diode, BJT, JFET, and MOSFET. The user can create generic models for the active devices that correspond to, and are consistent with, the process parameters and design rules of the process used for a specific design. This model library may actually contain numerous generic device models for a given process, each of which contains as little or as much information as needed for the desired emphasis in the simulation. The designer can then use geometric parameters and specific model name references to specify the complete model for each active device in the circuit being analyzed.

To run SPICE[1], the user must first create a file, sometimes referred to as a SPICE deck, which contains a complete description of the circuit (including device models) along with a description of the excitation and the type of analysis desired. This file is accessed when the SPICE program runs.

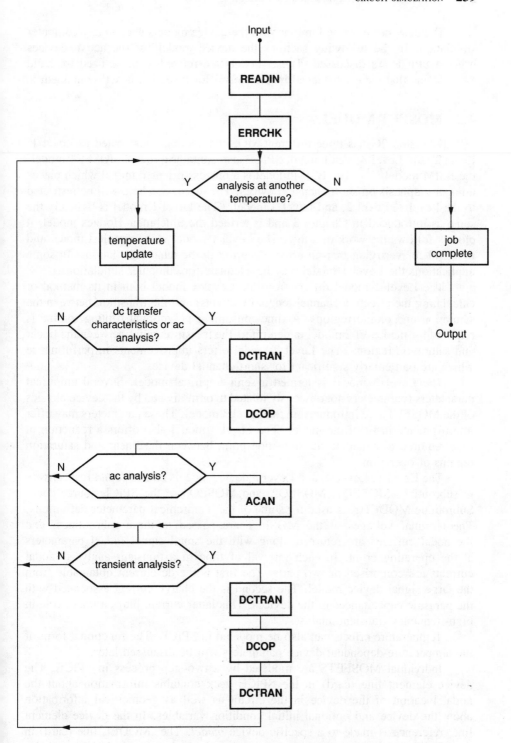

FIGURE 4.1-1
Simplified SPICE functional flowchart (boldface mnemonics indicate names of major subroutines).

The designer must be familiar with the device models used in any computer simulation. In the following sections the device models of the active devices used in SPICE are discussed. These models are related to those used for hand calculations that were introduced in Chapter 3. Each section is self-contained.

4.2 MOSFET MODEL

SPICE Version 2G has three different MOSFET models, designated as Level 1, Level 2, and Level 3. Version 3 of SPICE also contains a fourth MOSFET model, the BSIM model[7−12]. The BSIM model is a process-oriented model which places a major emphasis on short channel devices. The discussion here will be restricted to the Level 1, Level 2, and Level 3 models. The Level 1 model is basically the same as introduced in Chapter 3 and is termed the Shichman–Hodges model; it closely follows the work of Sah[13]. The Level 1 model is the simplest model and is useful for verifying that no errors occurred in the hand calculations. In some applications the Level 1 model may be adequate for computer simulations.

The Level 2 model differs from the Level 1 model both in its method of calculating the effective channel length (λ effects) and the transition between the saturation and ohmic regions. A time-consuming polynomial rooting routine is required for the Level 2 model to determine the transition point between the linear and saturation regions. The Level 2 model offers improvements in performance which are particularly significant for short channel devices.

The Level 3 model is termed a semi-empirical model. Several empirical parameters (parameters not obviously related to or motivated by the device physics of the MOSFET) are introduced in the Level 3 model. These parameters may offer improvements in fit of the model. The Level 3 model also offers a reduction in time required to calculate the transition point between the linear and saturation regions of operation.

The Level 1, Level 2, and Level 3 device models can be found respectively in subroutines MOSEQ1, MOSEQ2, and MOSEQ3 of the SPICE source code. Subroutine MODCHK is used for some of the hierarchical parameter definitions. The terminal voltages of the MOSFET are passed to these subroutines, and the nodal currents are returned along with the small signal model parameters at the operating point. In each interval of time in a transient analysis, nodal currents are comprised of two parts. The first is the dc current obtainable from the large signal device model. The second is the charge current associated with the parasitic capacitances in the devices. This latter current plays a major role in high-frequency transient analyses.

Temperature effects can also be modeled in SPICE. The functional form of the temperature-dependent device parameters will be discussed later.

Individual MOSFETS are modeled by a two-step process in SPICE. The device element line (card) in the SPICE deck contains information about the nodal location of the device in the circuit as well as geometrical information about the device and optional initial condition variables. In the device element line, reference is made to a specific device *model*. The .MODEL line (card) in the SPICE deck contains generic information about the electrical characteristics of devices formed in a process based upon the characterizing process parameters. Each device has a separate device element line. Typically, many devices will reference a single .MODEL line.

A simplified flowchart of MOSEQ1, MOSEQ2 and MOSEQ3 is shown in Figure 4.2-1. The large signal currents in Quadrant 1 of the $I_D - V_{DS}$ plane are calculated from the expression:

$$I_G = I_B = 0 \tag{4.2-1}$$

$$I_D = \begin{cases} I_{CUTOFF} & V_{GS} < V_{TH} & & \text{(4.2-2)} \\ I_{OHMIC} & V_{GS} > V_{TH} & V_{DS} < V_{DSAT} & \text{(4.2-3)} \\ I_{SAT} & V_{GS} > V_{TH} & V_{DS} > V_{DSAT} & \text{(4.2-4)} \end{cases}$$

where it is assumed that the drain and source are designated so that $V_{DS} \geq 0$. The parameter V_{TH} denotes the threshold voltage which was denoted by V_T in Chapter 3. V_{DSAT} is a parameter that characterizes the transition between the ohmic and saturation regions. Operation in Quadrant 3 of the $I_D - V_{DS}$ plane is characterized by the same equations, where the drain and source designations are internally made so that $V_{DS} \geq 0$.

The small signal parameters are calculated from the derivatives of I_D with respect to V_{GS}, V_{DS}, and V_{BS} as explained in Sec. 3.1. In what follows, the expressions used for I_D for the Level 1 and Level 2 models are given along with a description of each of the parameters that appear in the model; the default values used in SPICE are given if the parameter is not specified. The parameters are summarized in Appendix 4A.

Some parameters in the model may be specified in more than one way. For example, the transconductance parameter K', introduced in Sec. 3.1, may be entered directly or calculated from the expression $K' = \mu_0 C_{ox}$. A hierarchical convention has been adopted in SPICE to avoid ambiguity. If a parameter is specified, that value will be used. If a parameter is not specified but can be calculated from other parameters that are specified (or have a nonzero default value), the calculated value will be used. If a parameter is not specified and at least one of the other parameters which can be used to calculate it is not specified and defaults to zero, the default value of the original parameter is adopted. A summary of the Level 1 and Level 2 large signal models follows. The parameters used in these models are defined in the Appendices of this chapter.

4.2.1 Level 1 Large Signal Model

$$I_{CUTOFF} = 0 \tag{4.2-5}$$

$$I_{OHMIC} = K' \frac{W}{L_{eff}} \left([V_{GS} - V_{TH}] - \frac{V_{DS}}{2} \right) V_{DS} \tag{4.2-6}$$

$$I_{SAT} = \frac{K'}{2} \frac{W}{L_{eff}} (V_{GS} - V_{TH})^2 \tag{4.2-7}$$

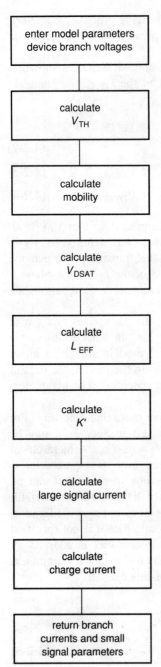

FIGURE 4.2-1
Simplified Flowchart of SPICE Subroutines MOSEQ1, MOSEQ2, and MOSEQ3.

where V_{DSAT} is given by

$$V_{DSAT} = V_{GS} - V_{TH} \qquad (4.2\text{-}8)$$

and the regions of operation are as defined in Eqs. 4.2-1 – 4.2-4.

The parameters V_{TH} and L_{eff} represent the threshold voltage and effective length of the device, respectively, and are given by

$$V_{TH} = V_{T0} + \gamma \left[\sqrt{\phi - V_{BS}} - \sqrt{\phi} \right] \qquad (4.2\text{-}9)$$

and

$$L_{eff} = \frac{L_{adj}}{1 + \lambda V_{DS}} \qquad (4.2\text{-}10)$$

where V_{T0} is the zero bias threshold voltage, γ is the bulk threshold parameter, ϕ is the surface potential, and λ is the channel length modulation parameter. λ is a SPICE input parameter. V_{T0}, γ, and ϕ can either be entered directly or be internally calculated, as discussed later. The parameter K', if not entered, can be calculated from the expression

$$K' = \mu_o C_{ox} \qquad (4.2\text{-}11)$$

where μ_o is the nominal channel mobility (if μ_o is not entered, the default value will be used) and C_{ox} is the gate oxide capacitance density which can be calculated from the gate oxide thickness, T_{ox}, by the expression

$$C_{ox} = \epsilon_{ox}/T_{ox} \qquad (4.2\text{-}12)$$

where ϵ_{ox} is the dielectric constant of SiO_2. The parameter L_{adj} represents the adjusted length which is the drawn length reduced by the lateral diffusion on the drain and source, LD.

$$L_{adj} = L - 2 \times LD \qquad (4.2\text{-}13)$$

The parameters in V_{TH}, if not input, are calculated from

$$\gamma = \frac{\sqrt{2q\epsilon_{si}N_{SUB}}}{C_{ox}} \qquad (4.2\text{-}14)$$

$$\phi = \frac{2kT}{q} \ln \left(\frac{N_{SUB}}{n_i} \right) \qquad (4.2\text{-}15)$$

and

$$V_{T0} = V_{FB} + \gamma\sqrt{\phi} + \phi \qquad (4.2\text{-}16)$$

where ϵ_{si} is the dielectric constant of silicon, N_{SUB} is the substrate doping, q is the charge of an electron, and n_i is the intrinsic carrier concentration of silicon. N_{SUB} is a SPICE input parameter and n_i and ϵ_{si} are physical constants defined in Appendix 4A. The flatband voltage, V_{FB}, is given by

$$V_{FB} = \phi_{ms} - \frac{qN_{ss}}{C_{ox}} \qquad (4.2\text{-}17)$$

where the input parameter, N_{ss}, is the effective surface state density and ϕ_{ms} is the semiconductor work function difference. ϕ_{ms} is calculated internally from

$$\phi_{ms} = W_{FN} - \frac{\phi}{2} \qquad (4.2\text{-}18)$$

where the parameter W_{FN} is an internal function of physical constants characteristic of the materials involved, TPG (which specifies the types of materials used to construct the device), and temperature.

4.2.2 Level 2 Large Signal Model†

$$I_{CUTOFF} = \begin{cases} 0 & NFS = 0 \\ I_{weak\ inversion} & NFS \neq 0 \end{cases} \qquad (4.2\text{-}19)$$

$$I_{OHMIC} = \frac{K_2' W}{L_{eff}} \left[\left(V_{GS} - V^*_{TH} - \eta \frac{V_{DS}}{2} \right) V_{DS} \right] + I_{BSO} \qquad (4.2\text{-}20)$$

$$I_{SAT} = \frac{K_2' W}{2L_{eff}} \left[(V_{GS} - V^*_{TH})^2 (2 - \eta) \right] + I_{BSS} \qquad (4.2\text{-}21)$$

where the cutoff transition region is determined by

$$V_{TH} = V_{T0} + \gamma \left[\sqrt{\phi - V_{BS}} - \sqrt{\phi} \right] -$$

$$\gamma \alpha \sqrt{\phi - V_{BS}} + (\phi - V_{BS}) \frac{\pi}{4} \frac{\epsilon_{si}}{C_{ox} L_{adj}} (DELTA) \qquad (4.2\text{-}22)$$

The parameter L_{adj} is defined by (4.2-13). The parameters DELTA and α will be discussed later.

The parameter V_{MAX} is used to characterize the saturation/ohmic transition region as specified in (4.2-3) and (4.2-4); it denotes the maximum drift velocity of carriers in the channel. If the parameter V_{MAX} is not input, the saturation/ohmic transition region is determined by

$$V_{DSAT} = \frac{(V_{GS} - V^*_{TH})}{\eta} + \frac{1}{2} \left[\frac{\gamma_s}{\eta} \right]^2 \cdot$$

$$\left\{ 1 - \left[1 + 4 \left(\frac{\gamma}{\eta} (1 - \alpha) \right)^{-2} \left(\frac{V_{GS} - V^*_{TH}}{\eta} + \phi - V_{BS} \right) \right]^{\frac{1}{2}} \right\} \qquad (4.2\text{-}23)$$

If V_{MAX} is input, V_{DSAT} is obtained from solution of a complicated fourth-order polynomial. V_{MAX} essentially reduces the value of V_{DSAT} and hence the saturation current in a manner more consistent with experimental measurements. If

---

†See SPICE source code for the SPICE Model of the MOSFET in weak inversion. The accuracy of the weak inversion MOSFET Models has been questioned by some individuals. [14–15]

V_{MAX} is input, computational time for calculating V_{DSAT} does increase. Additional details about V_{MAX} can be found in the paper by Vladimerescu and Liu.[2]

The parameters η, V^*_{TH}, I_{BSO} and I_{BSS} are given by the following equations:

$$\eta = 1 + \frac{\pi}{4} \frac{\epsilon_{\text{si}}}{C_{\text{ox}} L_{\text{adj}}} (\text{DELTA}) \tag{4.2-24}$$

$$V^*_{\text{TH}} = V_{\text{T0}} - \gamma\sqrt{\phi} + (\phi - V_{\text{BS}}) \frac{\pi}{4} \frac{\epsilon_{\text{si}}}{C_{\text{ox}} L_{\text{adj}}} (\text{DELTA}) \tag{4.2-25}$$

$$I_{\text{BSO}} = -\frac{2}{3} \frac{K'_2 W}{L_{\text{eff}}} \frac{\gamma_s}{\eta} \left[(\phi + V_{\text{DS}} - V_{\text{BS}})^{\frac{3}{2}} - (\phi - V_{\text{BS}})^{\frac{3}{2}} \right] \tag{4.2-26}$$

$$I_{\text{BSS}} = \frac{K'_2 W}{L_{\text{eff}}} \left[\left[(V_{\text{GS}} - V^*_{\text{TH}})(1 - \eta) - \frac{\eta}{2}(V_{\text{DSAT}} - (V_{\text{GS}} - V^*_{\text{TH}})) \right] \right.$$

$$\left. (V_{\text{DSAT}} - (V_{\text{GS}} - V^*_{\text{TH}})) - \frac{2}{3} \frac{\gamma_s}{\eta} \left[(V_{\text{DSAT}} - V_{\text{BS}} + \phi)^{\frac{3}{2}} - (\phi - V_{\text{BS}})^{\frac{3}{2}} \right] \right] \tag{4.2-27}$$

The parameter K'_2 is obtained from the expression

$$K'_2 = K' \frac{\mu_s}{\mu_o} \tag{4.2-28}$$

where μ_s is the effective surface mobility. If not input, K' is determined from (4.2-11). The parameter DELTA is a SPICE input parameter and is used to characterize width reduction (see Problem 4.17) where the effective width, W_{eff}, is given by $W_{\text{eff}} = W(2 - \eta)$.

The parameters V_{T0}, L_{adj}, and ϕ are determined as for the Level 1 model. The parameter γ_s is given by

$$\gamma_s = \gamma(1 - \alpha) \tag{4.2-29}$$

The parameter α is given by:

$$\alpha = \frac{1}{2} \frac{\text{XJ}}{L_{\text{adj}}} \left[\sqrt{1 + \frac{2W_{\text{S}}}{\text{XJ}}} + \sqrt{1 + \frac{2W_{\text{D}}}{\text{XJ}}} - 2 \right] \tag{4.2-30}$$

where

$$W_{\text{S}} = X_{\text{D}} \sqrt{\phi - V_{\text{BS}}} \tag{4.2-31}$$

$$W_{\text{D}} = X_{\text{D}} \sqrt{\phi - V_{\text{BS}} + V_{\text{DS}}} \tag{4.2-32}$$

and where XJ is a SPICE input parameter representing the metallurgical junction depth.

The parameter L_{eff} is defined by the expression

$$L_{\text{eff}} = L_{\text{adj}}(1 - \lambda V_{\text{DS}}) \tag{4.2-33}$$

If not specified as an input parameter, λ is calculated from the expression

$$\lambda = \frac{X_D}{L_{adj} V_{DS}} \left[\sqrt{\left(\frac{X_D V_{MAX}}{2\mu_s} \right)^2 + (V_{DS} - V_{DSAT})} - \frac{X_D V_{MAX}}{2\mu_s} \right] \quad (4.2\text{-}34)$$

The parameter X_D is given by the expression

$$X_D = \sqrt{\frac{2\epsilon_{si}}{qN_{SUB}}} \quad (4.2\text{-}35)$$

The effective surface mobility, μ_s, is given by

$$\mu_s = \begin{cases} \mu_o \left[\dfrac{\text{UCRIT} \cdot \epsilon_{si}}{C_{ox}(V_{GS} - V_{TH})} \right]^{\text{UEXP}} & \text{for Level 2} \\[4mm] \mu_o \left[\dfrac{\text{UCRIT} \cdot \epsilon_{si}}{C_{ox}(V_{GS} - V_{TH} - \text{UTRA} \cdot V_{DS})} \right]^{\text{UEXP}} & \text{for Level 3} \end{cases}$$

$$(4.2\text{-}36)$$

The parameters UCRIT, UTRA and UEXP are SPICE input parameters used to characterize mobility degradation.

4.2.3 High-Frequency MOSFET Model

The high-frequency MOSFET model is obtained from the dc model by adding the identifiable parasitic capacitances to the dc model previously discussed. Parasitic device capacitors in SPICE are essentially modeled as in Section 3.1.3 of Chapter 3. Those capacitors that are voltage independent are modeled by

$$C = \frac{\epsilon A}{t} \quad (4.2\text{-}37)$$

where ϵ is the dielectric constant (permittivity), A is the area of the intersection of the two plates and t is the dielectric thickness. The voltage independent capacitors are comprised of those that are operation-region dependent and those that are not.

The operation-region independent capacitors are comprised of those overlap capacitors that appear on the periphery of the MOSFET. A top view of these parasitic capacitors appears in Fig. 4.2-2. All are essentially rectangular in shape.

The effective area of the overlap component of the gate–source capacitance is $W \cdot LD$ where W is the channel width and LD is the lateral diffusion of the source. From (4.2-37) the gate–source overlap capacitor, C_{GSOL}, can be expressed as

$$C_{GSOL} = \frac{\epsilon \, LD \cdot W}{t} \quad (4.2\text{-}38)$$

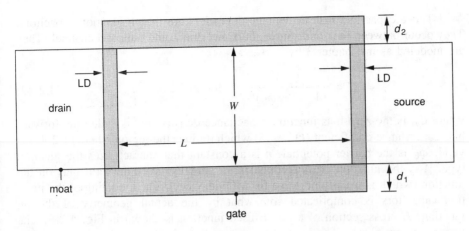

FIGURE 4.2-2
Top view of operation-region independent, or overlap (shaded) capacitors, in MOS transistors.

or

$$C_{GSOL} = C_{GSO}W \qquad (4.2\text{-}39)$$

where $C_{GSO} = \epsilon LD/t$ represents the overlap capacitance per unit width of the gate. C_{GSO} serves as an input parameter in SPICE to model the overlap capacitance. Since the dielectric thickness is the same as the gate oxide thickness, this parasitic has an area capacitance density of C_{ox}. If C_{GSO} is not entered in SPICE, C_{GSOL} is calculated from

$$C_{GSOL} = (C_{ox})(LD)W \qquad (4.2\text{-}40)$$

where C_{ox} is calculated via either the entered or defaulted value of the gate oxide thickness, T_{ox}. The gate-drain overlap capacitance is modeled in the same manner.

From Fig. 4.2-2, it follows that the gate–bulk overlap capacitance is linearly proportional to L and dependent upon d_1 and d_2. The dielectric thickness, however, is not constant for this parasitic. The dielectric thickness of the gate–bulk overlap is essentially equal to the gate oxide thickness on the sides adjacent to the channel and equal to the height of the field oxide on the sides farthest from the channel. Although it cannot be modeled by (4.2-37), it is voltage independent. Since it is proportional to L, it is modeled by

$$C_{GBOL} = C_{GBO}L \qquad (4.2\text{-}41)$$

where C_{GBO} represents the total gate–bulk capacitance per unit length of the device. C_{GBO} serves as an input parameter in SPICE to characterize the gate–bulk overlap. Since field oxide thickness is not considered in the MOSFET model, and since d_1 and d_2 are layout dependent, the C_{GB0} parameter must be entered if the effects of gate–bulk overlap are to be included in the model. It is common practice to assume that $d_1 = d_2 = d$ where d is the minimum overlap of the poly over the moat. With this assumption, any bulk-substrate capacitance associated with a larger gate polysilicon region is accounted for by adding an additional parasitic capacitance to the circuit schematic from gate to substrate.

Those capacitors that are voltage dependent are the pn junction capacitors. They occur between bulk and source, bulk and drain, and bulk and channel. They are modeled as in Chapter 3 by

$$C = \frac{C_{j0}A}{(1 - V_F/\phi_B)^n} \quad \text{for } V_F < FC \cdot \phi_B \quad (4.2\text{-}42)$$

where C_{j0} is the zero-bias junction capacitance density. FC is called the forward bias capacitance coefficient (FC $\simeq$ .5) which defines the region where (4.2-42) is valid, ϕ_B is the barrier potential, n is a constant that characterizes the junction type, A is the junction cross-sectional area, and V_F is the forward bias on the junction (which is usually negative for MOS devices). The modeling of the junction capacitors is complicated somewhat by the actual geometry of the pn junction. A cross section of a pn diffused junction is shown in Fig. 4.2-3. The junction is not planar. The impurity concentrations in the p and n type materials at the bottom of the junctions are different than the concentrations along the sidewalls causing the grading coefficient, n, to vary as a function of position. Although the sidewall capacitances become negligible for large structures, they may actually dominate for small or narrow junctions. The total junction capacitance associated with the "reverse biased" (actually for $V_F < FC \cdot \phi_B$) junction of either the source or drain is thus

$$C_{RB,\,TOTAL} = \frac{CJ \cdot A}{[1 - (V_F/\phi_B)]^{MJ}} + \frac{CJSW \cdot P}{[1 - (V_F/\phi_B)]^{MJSW}} \quad (4.2\text{-}43)$$

where CJ is the zero-bias bottom capacitance area density, CJSW is the zero-bias sidewall capacitance per unit length of the perimeter, MJ is the bottom junction

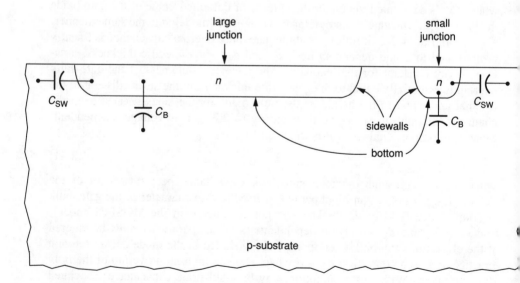

FIGURE 4.2-3
Cross section of diffused region showing parasitic junction capacitors.

grading coefficient, FC is the forward bias coefficient (which defines the region where (4.2–43) remains valid), and MJSW is the sidewall grading coefficient. A is the junction bottom area and P is the junction sidewall perimeter. The parameters FC, CJ, CJSW, MJ, MJSW and ϕ_B can be entered in SPICE on the .MODEL card (line). The parameters A and P for the drain and source junctions must be entered on the device card (line). If not input, CJ is calculated internally from N_{SUB} (if input), under the assumption of a step graded junction, from the expression

$$\text{CJ} = \sqrt{\frac{\epsilon_{si} q N_{SUB}}{2\phi_B}} \qquad (4.2\text{-}44)$$

As an alternative to specifying the drain and source geometries and the junction capacitance density, the user can specify the overriding parameters C_{BD} and C_{BS} which represent the total zero-bias bottom capacitance of the bulk-drain and bulk-source junctions, respectively. These are then used in place of $\text{CJ} \cdot A$ in (4.2–43).

Under forward bias ($V_F > \text{FC} \cdot \phi_B$), the total junction capacitances are modeled by

$$C_{FB,\,TOTAL} = \frac{\text{CJ} \cdot A}{(1-\text{FC})^{(1+\text{MJ})}} \left[1 - \text{FC}(1 + \text{MJ}) + \frac{V_{BS}}{\phi_B}\text{MJ} \right]$$

$$+ \frac{\text{CJSW} \cdot P}{(1-\text{FC})^{(1+\text{MJSW})}} \left[1 - \text{FC}(1 + \text{MJSW}) + \frac{V_{BS}}{\phi_B}\text{MJSW} \right] \quad (4.2\text{-}46)$$

This approximation represents a linear continuation of the reverse-bias capacitance which agrees functionally and in the first derivative at the transition point, $V_F = \text{FC} \cdot \phi_B$ (see Problem 3.31 of Chapter 3).

Finally, the operation-region dependent capacitances associated with the channel region itself must be considered. These are essentially distributed capacitances; as such they are more difficult to model. Furthermore, to ease calculations these parasitics are subsequently lumped internally and added to the operation-region independent components of the gate–source, gate–drain, gate–bulk, source–bulk, and drain–bulk capacitors discussed previously. Depending on the operating region, some of the channel capacitances are voltage independent and are modeled by (4.2-37), while others are actually junction capacitances modeled by (4.2-42). The user need not enter any additional parameters; the parasitic channel capacitances are calculated internally from the parameters that characterize the operation-region independent capacitors discussed above. The user is, however, at the mercy of the approximations employed in SPICE to model the channel capacitances. Some industrial groups are not satisfied with the channel capacitance modeling in SPICE and have made modifications which they believe offer some improvements. The exact formulation of the channel capacitances is quite involved and beyond the scope of this text. Details can be found in references 16 and 17, as well as in the SPICE source code itself [6]. The total parasitic capacitances (fixed plus voltage dependent) associated with the lumped approximation used in SPICE are basically as indicated in Fig. 4.2-4.

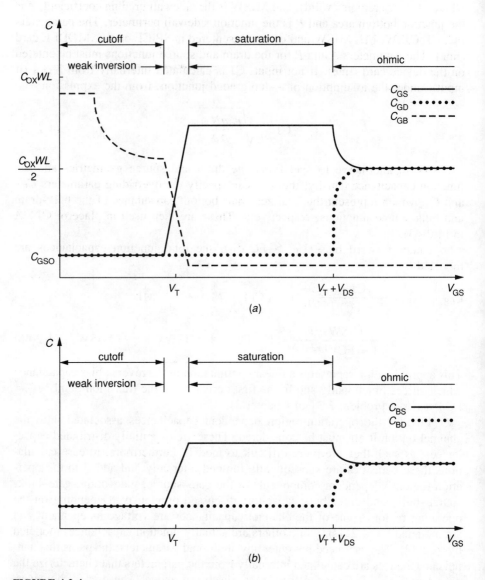

FIGURE 4.2-4
Lumped parasitic capacitances for MOSFET as a function of operating point: (*a*) Associated with gate charge, (*b*) Associated with bulk charge.

4.2.4 Noise Model of the MOSFET

There are four noise-current generators modeled in the MOSFET device model in SPICE.[18] Two of these represent thermal noise associated with the parasitic series resistances in the drain and source. These are modeled by spectral densities of

$$S_{\text{IRD}} = \frac{4kT}{\text{RD}} \tag{4.2-47}$$

and

$$S_{\text{IRS}} = \frac{4kT}{\text{RS}} \tag{4.2-48}$$

respectively, where k is Boltzmann's constant, T is the temperature in °K, and RD and RS represent the drain and source parasitic resistances.

The other two noise-current generators are modeled as current sources from drain to source. One represents white shot noise and the other flicker ($1/f$) noise. These are characterized in the saturation region by spectral densities of[1]

$$S_{\text{W}} = \frac{8kT g_{\text{m}}}{3} \tag{4.2-49}$$

and

$$S_f = \frac{(K_{\text{F}})I_{\text{DQ}}^{A_{\text{F}}}}{f C_{\text{ox}} W L_{\text{eff}}} \tag{4.2-50}$$

where K_{F} and A_{F} are user enterable parameters, g_{m} is the small signal transconductance gain at the Q-point, I_{DQ} is the quiescent drain current, L_{eff} is the effective channel length and f is frequency in Hz. All noise sources are assumed to be uncorrelated. S_{W} and S_f add to obtain the overall noise spectral density as discussed in Sec. 3.1.8.

4.2.5 Temperature Dependence of the MOSFET

Several of the parameters that characterize the MOSFET are temperature dependent. Specifically, SPICE models the temperature dependence of the parameters K', V_{T0}, μ_{o}, ϕ, ϕ_{B}, I_{S}, J_{S}, C_{BD}, C_{BS}, CJ, CJSW, K_{F} and A_{F}. The basic equations used to characterize the temperature dependence in most situations are given below. See Reference 9 and subroutine TMPUPD of the SPICE source code for additional details.

$$K'(T) = \left(\frac{T}{T_1}\right)^{\frac{3}{2}} K'(T_1) \tag{4.2-51}$$

$$\mu_{\text{o}}(T) = \left(\frac{T}{T_1}\right)^{\frac{3}{2}} \mu_{\text{o}}(T_1) \tag{4.2-52}$$

$$I_S(T) = I_S(T_1)e^{\left[\frac{EG(T)}{V_t(T)} - \frac{EG(T_1)}{V_t(T_1)}\right]} \tag{4.2-53}$$

$$J_S(T) = J_S(T_1)e^{\left[\frac{EG(T)}{V_t(T)} - \frac{EG(T_1)}{V_t(T_1)}\right]} \tag{4.2-54}$$

$$\phi(T) = \phi(T_1) \cdot (T/T_1) + \phi_{BF}(T) \tag{4.2-55}$$

$$\phi_B(T) = \phi_B(T_1) \cdot (T/T_1) + \phi_{BF}(T) \tag{4.2-56}$$

$$C_{BD}(T) = C_{BD}(T_1) \cdot [1 + \theta_C(T)] \tag{4.2-57}$$

$$C_{BS}(T) = C_{BS}(T_1) \cdot [1 + \theta_C(T)] \tag{4.2-58}$$

$$CJ(T) = CJ(T_1) \cdot [1 + \theta_C(T)] \tag{4.2-59}$$

$$CJSW(T) = CJSW(T_1) \cdot [1 + \theta_C(T)] \tag{4.2-60}$$

$$K_F(T) = K_F(T_1) \cdot [\phi_B(T)/\phi_B(T_1)] \tag{4.2-61}$$

$$A_F(T) = A_F(T_1) \cdot [\phi_B(T)/\phi_B(T_1)] \tag{4.2-62}$$

where T_1 is any reference temperature in °K , $V_t = kT/q$, and the parameters EG, ϕ_{BF}, and θ_C are defined respectively by the equations

$$EG(T) = [1.16 - (.000702T^2)/(T + 1108)]\text{volts} \tag{4.2-63}$$

$$\phi_{BF}(T) = -3V_t \ln (T/T_1) - EG(T) + (EG(T_1)) \cdot (T/T_1) \tag{4.2-64}$$

and

$$\theta_C(T) = MJ \cdot \{0.0004(T - T_1) + 1 - [\phi_B(T)/\phi_B(T_1)]\} \tag{4.2-65}$$

4.3 DIODE MODEL

Individual diodes are modeled by a two-step process in SPICE.[1,3,5] The device element line (card) contains information about the nodal location of the device in the circuit as well as geometrical information (relative junction cross-sectional area) and optional initial condition variables useful in transient analyses. In the device element line, reference is made to a specific device model. The .MODEL line (card) contains generic information about the electrical characteristics of devices formed in the process based upon the characterizing process parameters. Each diode has a separate device element line. Typically many devices will reference a single .MODEL line. Most of the diode modeling information can be found in subroutines DIODE and MODCHK in the SPICE source code. As is the case for all device models in SPICE, the small signal parameters which characterize the small signal operation of the diode are calculated from the appropriate derivatives. A philosophy distinctly different from that used for characterizing MOS processes has been adopted for characterizing the process used to fabricate diodes. This difference lies in that the characteristics of a specific "reference diode" are specified in the .MODEL line. The size of the reference diode is conceptually arbitrary although it is advised to select a reference that is geometrically similar in size and shape to those devices that will be modeled. In the device element line (card) the *relative area* of the reference diode used to characterize the model is specified.

The diode is modeled as the series combination of a resistor, r_s, and a non-ideal diode, D2, shunted by a parasitic capacitor C_D, as indicated in Fig. 4.3-1. The resistor, r_s, accounts for both the series resistance of the diode as well as high-level injection effects.[3,19] It is assumed to be an ideal resistor. In this section, emphasis will be placed upon the model of the series diode, D2, of Fig. 4.3-1b. As indicated in Fig. 4.3-1b, the current of diode D2 is modeled as the sum of a dc (large signal) current, denoted by I_{DC}, and a current that flows through a parasitic shunting capacitance associated with the pn junction. The large signal current and parasitic capacitance current will be considered separately in the following sections.

4.3.1 Large Signal Diode Current

The large signal diode current, I_{DC} in Fig. 4.3-1b, is modeled by that given in the standard diode equation

$$I_{DC} = I_S A_n (e^{V_D/(nV_t)} - 1) \tag{4.3-1}$$

where, as discussed in Chapter 3,

$$V_t = \frac{kT}{q} \tag{4.3-2}$$

$$I_S = \text{saturation current}$$

and

$$n = \text{emission coefficient.}$$

The parameter A_n represents the *normalized* cross-sectional area of the junction. It is a dimensionless parameter that is entered on the device element line; it represents the ratio of the cross-sectional area of the device on the device element

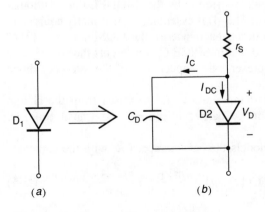

FIGURE 4.3-1
Diode model in SPICE: (*a*) Physical two-terminal device, (*b*) Equivalent circuit.

(*a*)   (*b*)

line to the reference model which is characterized on the .MODEL line. If not specified, SPICE adopts a default value of $A_n = 1$. The reverse breakdown voltage, BV, is not of major concern in VLSI design since BV generally exceeds the maximum voltages which will be permitted in VLSI circuits.

4.3.2 High-Frequency Diode Model

At high frequencies the parasitic junction capacitance of the diode plays a major role in the performance of the diode. The junction capacitance also affects the transient response. In the following the capacitance is defined by the expression

$$C_D = \frac{dQ}{dV_D} \tag{4.3-3}$$

C_D thus represents the small signal parasitic capacitance. In general, C_D is strongly a function of the instantaneous dc operating point of the diode. Although the model for C_D will be given here, the charge Q is regularly used internally in SPICE for transient analysis.

As discussed in Chapter 3 and Section 4.2, the characterization of a junction capacitor under reverse bias is different from the characterization under forward bias. Under reverse bias (actually for $V_D < \text{FC} \cdot \phi_B$), the capacitance is modeled by the equation

$$C_D = \frac{C_{jo}A_n}{[1 - (V_D/\phi_B)]^m} + \frac{\tau I_S A_n}{n V_t} e^{V_D/(n V_t)} \tag{4.3-4}$$

where I_S, A_n, n, and V_t are as previously defined, and the remaining parameters are defined by

$$
\begin{aligned}
C_{jo} &= \text{zero-bias junction capacitance} \\
\phi_B &= \text{capacitance barrier potential} \\
m &= \text{grading coefficient} \\
\tau &= \text{transit time} \\
\text{FC} &= \text{coefficient for forward/reverse bias transition}
\end{aligned}
$$

As was the case for I_S, it should be noted that C_{jo} is the zero-bias junction capacitance of the specific area device referred to by the .MODEL line. Although the first term on the right-hand side of (4.3-4) is essentially functionally equivalent to that used in the model of the junction capacitance for the MOSFET, (4.2-42) of Section 4.2, it should be emphasized that in SPICE C_{jo} represents the capacitance density in (4.2-42), whereas C_{jo} represents the capacitance of the reference diode itself in (4.3-4).

The second term on the right-hand side of (4.3-4) arises from the charge stored in the junction due to minority carrier injection. The transit time, τ, characterizes this capacitance.

For $V_D > \text{FC} \cdot \phi_B$, SPICE models the capacitance, C_D, with the equation

$$C_D = \frac{C_{jo}A_n}{(1 - \text{FC})^{(1+m)}} \left(1 - \text{FC}[1 + m] + \frac{m V_D}{\phi_B} \right) + \frac{\tau I_S A_n}{n V_t} e^{V_D/(n V_t)} \tag{4.3-5}$$

The first term on the right-hand side of (4.3-5) represents a continuous and differentiable linear extension of the first term on the right-hand side of (4.3-4) across the boundary $V_D = FC \cdot \phi_B$. The second terms on the right-hand side, of Eqs. 4.3-4 and 4.3-5 are identical.

4.4 BJT MODEL

The SPICE model of the BJT is based upon a modified Gummel–Poon model. [20,21] Simulations based upon the simpler Gummel–Poon model discussed in Chapter 3 can also be readily made by setting the appropriate Ebers–Moll parameters to zero as will be discussed later in this section. Use of the Ebers–Moll model in the early stages of a simulation may be useful for verifying theoretical hand calculations.

The bipolar junction transistor is modeled by two input lines (cards) in SPICE. The device line (card) is used for indicating the nodal connections of the BJT in a circuit. It is also used to reference a specific model, by name, which contains process information. An optional normalized parameter on the device line, A_n, is used to indicate the ratio of the area of the emitter to the emitter area of the device of the referenced model. An optional initial condition parameter can also be included on the device line if desired.

The second input line (card) that is used to model the BJT is the .MODEL line. SPICE version 2G.6 provides for user entry of up to 40 parameters on the .MODEL line for characterizing the device. As was the case with the diode, a user-selected reference transistor is used to characterize the bipolar process. The BJT model information is contained primarily in subroutines MODCHK and BJT in the SPICE source code. MODCHK does preprocessing of some of the input parameters (e.g., the reciprocals of some parameters are actually used as variables in the source code rather than the parameters themselves). The model itself basically appears in subroutine BJT.

As is the case for the other semiconductor models in SPICE, the BJT model is characterized by four types of input parameters. These are 1) large signal or dc parameters, 2) charge storage or capacitance parameters, 3) noise parameters, and 4) temperature characterization parameters.

The small signal low-frequency model used in SPICE is obtained from a symbolic differentiation of the large signal current equations evaluated at the dc operation point. As is the case for all small signal analyses in SPICE, the small signal model of the BJT is linear and thus the small signal simulation gives no distortion information. (Distortion information at a specific frequency can be obtained from a much more time consuming transient response with a sinusoidal excitation of fixed frequency and amplitude.) To obtain reliable distortion information, it is crucial that the transient analysis interval is long enough to guarantee essentially steady state operation.

A series resistance is modeled in series with each lead of the BJT as indicated in Fig. 4.4-1. These resistances are input parameters in SPICE. In the model discussion that follows, all formulation is relative to transistor T2 (denoted by nodes C, B, and E) in this figure; specifically, V_{BE} and V_{CE} represent the base–emitter and collector–emitter voltages of T2 rather than the actual base–emitter and collector–emitter voltages of the device (denoted by nodes C_A, B_A, and E_A)

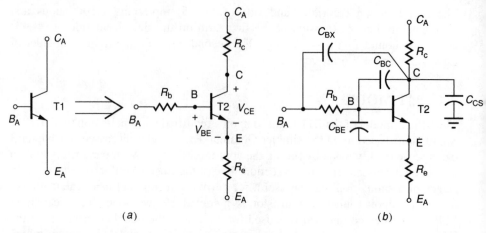

FIGURE 4.4-1
Modeling of the BJT in SPICE: (*a*) dc modeling, (*b*) High-frequency modeling.

which is to be modeled, T1. In the model that follows, junction breakdown voltages will not be discussed in detail since, with the exception of the reverse base-emitter breakdown, voltage levels in bipolar integrated circuits are usually considerably below the breakdown voltages of the BJT.

4.4.1 Large Signal BJT Model

The collector current and base current are characterized by the equations

$$I_C = \frac{I_S A_n}{Q_B}(e^{V_{BE}/(NF \cdot V_t)} - 1) - I_S A_n\left(\frac{1}{Q_B} + \frac{1}{BR}\right)(e^{V_{BC}/(NR \cdot V_t)} - 1)$$
$$- I_{SC} A_n(e^{V_{BC}/(NC \cdot V_t)} - 1) \quad (4.4\text{-}1)$$

$$I_B = \frac{I_S A_n}{BF}(e^{V_{BE}/(NF \cdot V_t)} - 1) + \frac{I_S A_n}{BR}(e^{V_{BC}/(NR \cdot V_t)} - 1) + I_{SE} A_n(e^{V_{BE}/(NE \cdot V_t)} - 1)$$
$$+ I_{SC} A_n(e^{V_{BC}/(NC \cdot V_t)} - 1) \quad (4.4\text{-}2)$$

where $V_t = kT/q$
A_n = normalized emitter area ratio
I_S = saturation current
I_{SE} = B-E leakage saturation current
I_{SC} = B-C leakage saturation current
NF = forward current emission coefficient
NR = reverse current emission coefficient
NE = B-E leakage current emission coefficient
NC = B-C leakage current emission coefficient
BF = ideal maximum forward β
BR = ideal maximum reverse β

and

$$Q_B = \left[\frac{1}{1 - (V_{BC}/V_{AF}) - (V_{BE}/V_{AR})} \right] \cdot$$

$$\left[\frac{1 + \sqrt{1 + 4[(I_S/I_{KF})(e^{V_{BE}/(NF \cdot V_t)} - 1) + (I_S/I_{KR})(e^{V_{BC}/(NR \cdot V_t)} - 1)]}}{2} \right] \tag{4.4-3}$$

The parameters in (4.4-3) are defined as

$$
\begin{aligned}
V_{AF} &= \text{Forward Early Voltage} \\
V_{AR} &= \text{Reverse Early Voltage} \\
I_{KF} &= \text{Corner for forward current gain roll-off} \\
I_{KR} &= \text{Corner for reverse current gain roll-off}
\end{aligned}
$$

This completes the large signal model of the BJT. A discussion of the characterizing parameters in the BJT model follows. In addition to providing insight into how these parameters impact performance of the BJT, this discussion should provide a mechanism for obtaining SPICE parameters from measured device data.

Although it may appear that all dependence of I_C and I_B on V_{BE} and V_{BC} is exponential, it can be seen from (4.4-3) that Q_B is a complicated function of V_{BC} and V_{BE}. If I_{KF} and I_{KR} are neglected (i.e., $I_{KF} = I_{KR} = \infty$), then Q_B reduces to

$$Q_B = \left(1 - \frac{V_{BC}}{V_{AF}} - \frac{V_{BE}}{V_{AR}} \right)^{-1} \tag{4.4-4}$$

so that the $\frac{1}{Q_B}$ term in (4.4-1) becomes

$$Q_B^{-1} = 1 - \frac{V_{BC}}{V_{AF}} - \frac{V_{BE}}{V_{AR}} = 1 + \frac{V_{CE}}{V_{AF}} - V_{BE}\left(\frac{1}{V_{AF}} + \frac{1}{V_{AR}} \right) \tag{4.4-5}$$

which is approximately equal to the multiplying factor used to model Early Voltage effects in the extended Ebers-Moll model of Chapter 3. Even if I_{KF} and I_{KR} effects are included, Q_B can be approximated by (4.4-4) until V_{BE} or V_{BC} becomes quite large, since I_{KF} is typically about ten orders of magnitude larger than I_S. For large V_{BE} or V_{BC}, however, I_C varies essentially linearly with $e^{V_{BE}/2NF \cdot V_t}$ or $e^{V_{BC}/2NR \cdot V_t}$.

Considerable insight into how the parameters affect device performance can be obtained by plotting I_C and I_B versus one device branch voltage, V_{BE} or V_{BC}, with the other branch voltage set to zero. For brevity, only the $V_{BC} = 0$ case will be considered here. The analysis for the $V_{BE} = 0$ case is essentially a mirror image of the $V_{BC} = 0$ analysis.

Under the assumption that $V_{BC} = 0$, (4.4-1), (4.4-2) and (4.4-3) simplify to

$$I_C = \frac{I_S A_n}{Q_B} (e^{V_{BE}/(NF \cdot V_t)} - 1) \tag{4.4-6}$$

$$I_B = \frac{I_S A_n}{BF}\left(e^{V_{BE}/(NF \cdot V_t)} - 1\right) + I_{SE}A_n\left(e^{V_{BE}/(NE \cdot V_t)} - 1\right) \tag{4.4-7}$$

$$Q_B = \left[\frac{1}{1 - (V_{BE}/V_{AR})}\right]\left[\frac{1 + \sqrt{1 + 4(I_S/I_{KF})\left(e^{V_{BE}/(NF \cdot V_t)} - 1\right)}}{2}\right]$$

$$\tag{4.4-8}$$

A plot of I_C and I_B versus V_{BE} for $V_{BE} < 0$ is shown in Fig. 4.4-2. The parameter A_n, which denotes the relative emitter area, is obtained from geometrical information. The projection of the linear portion of the I_C curve intercepts the I axis at $-I_S A_n$. The slope of the linear portion of the I_C curve can subsequently be used to determine V_{AR}. The vertical axis intercept of the projection of the linear portion of the I_B curve can be used to determine I_{SE} since I_{SE} is typically about four orders of magnitude larger than I_S/BF. Although the $V_{BE} < 0$ curves can be used to determine I_S, I_{SE} and V_{AR}, they are most useful for the V_{AR} determination. The parameters I_S and I_{SE} are typically determined from the $V_{BE} > 0$ plots.

A plot of I_C and I_B versus V_{BE} for $V_{BE} > 0$ is shown in Fig. 4.4-3 on a graph with a logarithmic scale for the vertical axis. Also shown are four straight lines which essentially represent asymptotic behavior of the BJT over a fairly wide range of V_{BE} values. The equations of these asymptotic lines are easily derived from (4.4-6)–(4.4-8). Several of the dc parameters that characterize the BJT can be readily determined from the curves shown in Fig. 4.4–3. A sequence of calculations follows for determining some of the dc parameters after V_{AR} has been determined from Fig. 4.4-2.

First, I_S and I_{SE} can be determined from the y-intercepts of Line 3 and Line 2, respectively. With I_S known, BF can be determined from the y-intercept of Line 4. I_{KF} can be determined from either the vertical axis intercept of Line 1 or the y-coordinate of the intersection of Lines 1 and 3. NF can be obtained

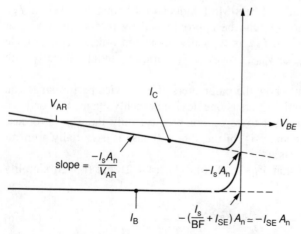

FIGURE 4.4-2
Plot of collector and base current vs. V_{BE} for $V_{BC} = 0$, $V_{BE} < 0$.

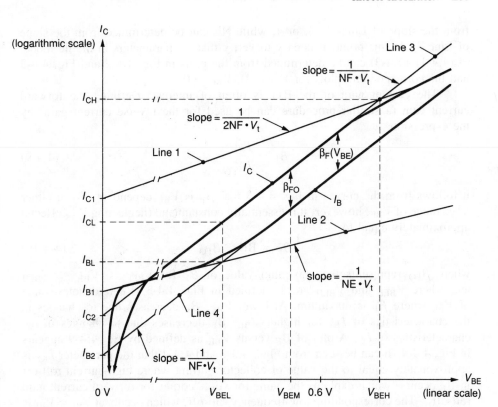

FIGURE 4.4-3

Plot of collector current and base current vs. V_{BE} for $V_{BC} = 0$, $V_{BE} > 0$ (logarithmic scale on vertical axis).

from the slope of Lines 1, 3, or 4, while NE can be determined from the slope of Line 2. At this point, it is easy to verify that *all* parameters in the dc model of (4.4-1)–(4.4-3) can be determined from the plots in Fig. 4.4-2 and Fig. 4.4-3 and the corresponding plots for $V_{BE} = 0$, $V_{BC} > 0$.

The current gain of the BJT is often of interest. Defining the forward current gain (a similar procedure can be used for the reverse current gain) by the expression

$$\beta_F = \frac{I_C}{I_B}\bigg|_{V_{BC}=0} \tag{4.4-9}$$

it follows from the curves in Fig. 4.4-3 that β_F is V_{BE} dependent. For a rather large range of V_{BE}, however, it is essentially constant and (neglecting V_{AR} effects) approximately equal to

$$\beta_F = \mathrm{BF} \simeq \beta_{FO} \tag{4.4-10}$$

where β_{FO} represents the maximum value of β_F for $V_{BEL} < V_{BE} < V_{BEH}$ and where V_{BEL} and V_{BEH} are as defined in Fig. 4.4-3. V_{BEM} denotes value of V_{BE} where β_F is maximum. At lower V_{BE}, β_F decreases due to changes in the characteristics of I_B; for higher V_{BE}, β_F decreases due to changes in the characteristics of I_C. A plot of β_F versus V_{BE} as defined by Eq. 4.4-9 appears in Fig. 4.4-4. It can be seen from Figs. 4.4-3 and 4.4-4 that the parameter I_{KF} is approximately equal to the value of collector current where high-current roll-off in β_F occurs, which explains the name for I_{KF}, "corner for forward current gain roll-off." The corresponding low-frequency roll-off, which occurs at $V_{BE} = V_{BEL}$, is not characterized by a single parameter but is strongly dependent upon the B–E leakage saturation current, I_{SE}.

This section concludes with a discussion of how the SPICE model parameters can be specified to do simulations based upon the simplified Ebers–Moll model of Chapter 3, characterized by Eqs. 3.3-1 and 3.3-2.

It follows from Eqs. 4.4-1–4.4-3 that if $I_{SE} = I_{SC} = 0$, $I_{KF} = I_{KR} = \infty$, $V_{AF} = V_{AR} = \infty$ and $\mathrm{NF} = \mathrm{NR} = 1$, the model will agree with this Ebers–Moll model. Since these variable assignments are the default values, the user only needs to specify IS, BF, and BR to use the simplified dc Ebers–Moll model.

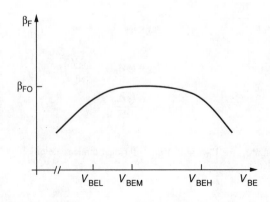

FIGURE 4.4-4
Forward current gain of BJT vs. $V_{BE}(V_{BC} = 0)$.

4.4.2 High-Frequency BJT Model

The high-frequency model of the BJT used in SPICE is obtained by adding three parasitic capacitors to the transistor T2 in Fig. 4.4-1 and one capacitor, CBX, between the base of T1 (node B_A) and the collector of T2 (node C). The parasitic capacitors are, in general, voltage dependent. The capacitor values used in SPICE are defined by the derivative

$$C = \frac{dQ}{dV} \tag{4.4-11}$$

where Q is the charge on the capacitor and V is the corresponding port voltage. Seventeen parameters are used to characterize the four parasitic capacitors in SPICE.

The parasitic capacitors are, in general, modeled by the parallel combination (sum) of a depletion region capacitor and a capacitor which occurs due to charge accumulation in the depletion region. The depletion region capacitor is voltage dependent and is modeled by Eqs. 3.2-8 and 3.2-9 of Chapter 3. The capacitor attributed to the charge accumulation is current dependent. Finally, under forward bias the model for the parasitic capacitors has a different parametric form, than under reverse bias. The voltage where transition must be made from the reverse bias parametric capacitance model to the forward bias parametric model is termed the transition voltage. A summary of the parasitic capacitors used in SPICE 2G.6 is shown in Table 4.4-1.

The depletion region reverse-biased junction capacitors are defined by the expressions

$$C_{BEDR} = A_n C_{JE} \left(1 - \frac{V_{BE}}{\phi_B} \right)^{-M_{JE}} \tag{4.4-12}$$

$$C_{BCDR} = \theta A_n C_{JC} \left(1 - \frac{V_{BC}}{\phi_C} \right)^{-M_{JC}} \tag{4.4-13}$$

$$C_{CSDR} = A_n C_{JS} \left(1 - \frac{V_{CS}}{\phi_S} \right)^{-M_{JS}} \tag{4.4-14}$$

$$C_{XSDR} = (1 - \theta) A_n C_{JC} \left(1 - \frac{V_{B^*C}}{\phi_C} \right)^{-M_{JC}} \tag{4.4-15}$$

where $M_{JE}, M_{JS}, M_{JC}, C_{JE}, C_{JS}$ and C_{JC} are input parameters. ϕ_B, ϕ_S, ϕ_C, and θ are also SPICE input parameters, denoted by PB, PS, PC and XCJC, respectively. The parameter θ represents the percentage of the B–C capacitance which is to be associated with the internal base node (base of T2 in Fig. 4.4-1). V_{B^*C} is the voltage from the base of T1 to the collector of T2 in Fig. 4.4-1.

The transition voltages $V_{BET}, V_{BCT}, V_{CST}$ and V_{XST} are FC $\cdot \phi_B$, FC $\cdot \phi_C$, 0 V, and FC $\cdot \phi_C$ respectively where FC is a SPICE input parameter used to characterize the transition.

The forward biased depletion junction capacitors $C_{BEDF}, C_{BCDF}, C_{CSDF}$, and C_{XSDF} are the continuous and differentiable linear extensions of Eqs. 4.4-12–

TABLE 4.4-1
Parasitic capacitors in BJT model

	Operating region				
	Reverse bias			Forward bias	
	Depletion junction	Accumulation charge	Transition voltage	Depletion junction	Accumulation charge
C_{BE}	C_{BEDR}	C_{BEAR}	V_{BET}	C_{BEDF}	C_{BEAF}
C_{BC}	C_{BCDR}	C_{BCAR}	V_{BCT}	C_{BCDF}	C_{BCAF}
C_{CS}	C_{CSDR}	$C_{CSAR} = 0$	$V_{CST} = 0$ V	C_{CSDF}	$C_{CSAF} = 0$
C_{XS}	C_{XSDR}	$C_{XSAR} = 0$	V_{XST}	C_{XSDF}	$C_{XSAF} = 0$

4.4-15, respectively, at the transition voltage. These capacitances are functionally of the form of the corresponding extension used for characterizing the diode capacitance under forward bias as given by (3.2-9).

The accumulated charge capacitors C_{CSAR}, C_{CSAF}, C_{XSAR}, and C_{XSAF} are all zero. The forward and reverse bias accumulation charge capacitors are assumed equal (i.e., $C_{BEAR} = C_{BEDF}$ and $C_{BCAR} = C_{BCDF}$). It remains to characterize C_{BEAR} and C_{BCAR}. The functional form of these capacitors is given in (3.1-29) of Chapter 3. Unfortunately, the transit time is affected by the operating conditions (V_{BE} and V_{BC}) of the BJT. The parameters TF, XTF, VTF, ITF, PTF, and TR are used to characterize the transit times. The expression for the effective transit times is quite unwieldly, so it will not be given here. The interested reader should examine subroutine BJT (especially the expressions for CAPBE and CAPBC) in the SPICE source code for details.[6]

4.4.3 BJT Noise Model

Five noise sources are used to model the noise characteristics of the BJT. Thermal resistance noise sources are characterized by current sources with a spectral density of

$$S_{NR} = \frac{4kT}{R_x} \qquad \text{for } x \in \{b, e, c\} \tag{4.4-16}$$

These are modeled in parallel with the three resistors R_b, R_e, and R_c of Fig. 4.4-1. Parameters in this equation are defined in Appendix 4C. Shot and flicker noise are modeled by two current sources, the first with a spectral density of

$$S_{NB} = 2qI_{CQ} \tag{4.4-17}$$

is connected from the base to the emitter of T2 in Fig. 4.4-1. The second current source has a spectral density of

$$S_{NC} = 2qI_{BQ} + \frac{K_F I_{BQ}^{AF}}{f} \tag{4.4-18}$$

and is connected from the collector to the emitter of T2 in the same figure. The parameters q, k, and T have been defined previously and are included in Appendix 4C. K_F and AF are SPICE input parameters and f is frequency in Hz. I_{BQ} and I_{CQ} represent the quiescent values of I_B and I_C, respectively. All noise sources in the BJT are assumed to be uncorrelated.

4.4.4 Temperature Dependence of the BJT

Several of the parameters that characterize the BJT are temperature dependent. SPICE models the temperature dependence of the saturation currents (I_S, I_{SE}, and I_{SC}), betas (BF and BR), the junction capacitance parameters (C_{JE}, C_{JC}, C_{JS}, ϕ_B, ϕ_C and ϕ_S), and the noise coefficients K_F and A_F. The saturation currents at a temperature T are characterized by the equations

$$I_S(T) = I_S(T_1)\left(\frac{T}{T_1}\right)^{XTI} \exp\left[\left(\frac{T}{T_1} - 1\right)\frac{EG(T) \cdot q}{kT}\right] \tag{4.4-19}$$

$$I_{SE}(T) = I_{SE}(T_1)\left(\frac{T}{T_1}\right)^{[(XTI/NE)-XTB]} \exp\left[\left(\frac{T}{T_1} - 1\right)\left(\frac{EG(T) \cdot q}{NE \cdot kT}\right)\right] \tag{4.4-20}$$

$$I_{SC}(T) = I_{SC}(T_1)\left(\frac{T}{T_1}\right)^{[(XTI/NC)-XTB]} \exp\left[\left(\frac{T}{T_1} - 1\right)\left(\frac{EG(T) \cdot q}{NC \cdot kT}\right)\right] \tag{4.4-21}$$

where T_1 is any reference temperature, EG(T) is given in Eq. (4.2-63) and the remaining parameters are SPICE input parameters.

The parameters BF and BR are given by the expressions

$$BF(T) = BF(T_1)\left(\frac{T}{T_1}\right)^{XTB} \tag{4.4-22}$$

$$BR(T) = BR(T_1)\left(\frac{T}{T_1}\right)^{XTB} \tag{4.4-23}$$

The temperature dependence of C_{JC}, C_{JE}, C_{JS}, ϕ_B, ϕ_C, and ϕ_S is given for $Y \in \{C, E, S\}$ by

$$C_{JY}(T) = C_{JY}(T_1) \cdot [1 + \theta_Y(T)] \tag{4.4-24}$$

where

$$\theta_Y(T) = MJY \cdot \{0.0004(T - T_1) + 1 - [\phi_Y(T)/\phi_Y(T_1)]\} \tag{4.4-25}$$

and

$$\phi_Y(T) = \phi_Y(T_1) \cdot (T/T_1) + \phi_{BF}(T) \tag{4.4-26}$$

and where $\phi_{BF}(T)$ is given by Eq. (4.2-64).

The temperature dependence of K_F and A_F is modeled by (4.2-61) and (4.2-62) where $\phi_B(T)$ is replaced with $\phi_E(T)$. Additional details can be found in subroutine TMPUPD of the SPICE source code.

4.5 SUMMARY

Models for the MOSFET, diode, and BJT which are used in the program SPICE have been presented. The similarity between these more detailed models and the simpler models discussed in Chapter 3 should be apparent. Although these models have been presented in the context of SPICE, they should be viewed, in their own right, as a more complete analytical characterization of the three basic devices, which form the nucleus of most integrated circuits. Many parts of these models were not developed specifically for SPICE but rather evolved over the years in the technical literature as researchers attempted to understand the fundamental operation of the basic devices. In many demanding situations, the designers should find the relevant analytical model equations presented in this chapter directly useful for design, insight, and optimization.

The authors have repeatedly observed confusion and uncertainty by both students and practicing engineers about the validity of simulations. This is often attributable to either lack of knowledge of the model used in their simulator or lack of understanding of how specific model parameters impact performance. A firm understanding of the models used in a simulator is essential for utilization of these powerful tools. The glossaries and tables which appear in the appendices of this chapter should prove to be a useful reference for SPICE users.

REFERENCES

1. A. Vladimirescu, K. Ahang, A. R. Newton, D. O. Pederson, and A. Sangiovanni-Vincentelli, "SPICE Version 2G User's Guide," Dept. of Electrical Engineering and Computer Sciences, University of California, Berkeley, CA, 1981.
2. A. Vladimirescu and S. Liu, "The Simulation of MOS Integrated Circuits Using SPICE 2," UCB/ERL M80/7, University of California, Berkeley, Engineering Research Laboratory, Feb. 1980 (Revised Oct. 1980).
3. L. W. Nagel, "SPICE 2: A Computer Program to Simulate Semiconductor Circuits," UBC/ERL M520, University of California, Berkeley, Engineering Research Laboratory, May 1975.
4. S. Liu, "A Unified CAD Model for MOSFETS," UCB/ERL M 81/31, University of California, Berkeley, Engineering Research Laboratory, May 1981.
5. G. D. Anderson, "Evaluation and Optimization of MOS Device Drain Conductance Modeling in the SPICE Level 2 Model," UCB/ERL M84/3, University of California, Berkeley, Engineering Research Laboratory, Jan. 1984.
6. SPICE Source Code, Version 2G.6, Electronics Research Laboratory, University of California, Berkeley, March 1983.
7. B. J. Sheu, D. L. Scharfetter, and P. K. Ko, "SPICE 2 Implementation of BSIM," UCB/ERL M85/42, University of California, Berkeley, Engineering Research Laboratory, May 1985.
8. W. Christopher, "SPICE 3A7 User's Manual," Dept. of Electrical Engineering and Computer Sciences, University of California, Berkeley, 1986.
9. T. Quarles, A. R. Newton, D. O. Pederson, and A. Sangiovanni–Vincentelli, "SPICE 3A7 User's Manual," Dept. of Electrical Engineering and Computer Sciences, University of California, Berkeley, 1986.

10. P. M. Lee, "BSIM—Substrate Current Modeling," UCB/ERL M86/49 University of California, Berkeley, Engineering Research Laboratory, June, 1986.
11. J. Pierret, "A MOS Parameter Extraction Program for the BSIM Model," UCB/ERL M84/99, University of California, Berkeley, Engineering Research Laboratory, November 1984.
12. M.–C. Jeng, B. J. Sheu, and P. K. Ko, "BSIM Parameter Extraction—Algorithms and User's Guide," UCB/ERL M85/79, University of California, Berkeley, Engineering Research Laboratory, October 1985.
13. C. T. Sah, "Characteristics of the Metal–Oxide–Semiconductor Transistor," *IEEE Trans. Electron Devices, vol. ED–11, pp. 324–345, July 1964.*
14. P. Antonetti, D. D. Cariglia, and E. Profumo, "CAD Model for Threshold and Subthreshold Conduction in MOSFETs," *IEEE J. Solid State Circuits,* vol. SC–17, pp. 454–458, June 1982.
15. T. Grotjon and B. Hoefflinger, "A Parametric Short–Channel MOS Transistor Model for Subthreshold and Strong Inversion Current," *IEEE J. Solid State Circuits,* vol. SC–19, pp. 100–112, Feb. 1984.
16. P. Yang, B. Epler, and P. K. Chatterjee, "An Investigation of Charge Conservation Problem for MOSFET Circuit Simulation," *IEEE J. Solid State Circuits,* vol. SC–18, pp. 128–133, Feb. 1983.
17. D. E. Ward and R. W. Dutton, "A Charge–Oriented Model for MOS Transient Capacitances," *IEEE J. Solid State Circuits,* vol. SC–13, pp. 703–708, October 1978.
18. "PSPICE Documentation," Micro Sim Corporation, Laguna Hills, CA, 1986.
19. R. N. Hall, "Power Rectifiers and Transistors," *Proc. IRE,* vol. 40, pp. 1512–1519, Nov. 1952.
20. H. K. Gummel and H. C. Poon, "An Integral Charge Control Model of Bipolar Transistors," *Bell Syst. Tech. Journal,* vol. 49, pp. 827–852, May 1970.
21. I. Getreu, "Modeling the Bipolar Transistor," Tektronix Inc., Beaverton, Oregon, 1976.
22. P. W. Tuinenga, "*SPICE: A Guide to Circuit Simulation and Analysis Using PSPICE,*" Prentice-Hall, Englewood Cliffs, NJ, 1988.
23. P. Antognetti and Massobrio, "*Semiconductor Device Modeling with SPICE,*" McGraw-Hill, New York, 1988.

PROBLEMS

4.1. Assume the transistor in Figure P4.1 is fabricated in the CMOS process characterized in Appendix 2B.

(a) Determine V_{SS} so that $V_{OQ} = 1$ V (when $V_i = 0$). Use the Level 1 SPICE MOSFET model.

(b) Compare the small signal voltage gain using the Level 1 and Level 2 models with V_{SS} as determined in (a).

(c) Compare the small signal 3 dB bandwidth using the Level 1 and Level 2 models at the same Q-point as used in (a) and (b).

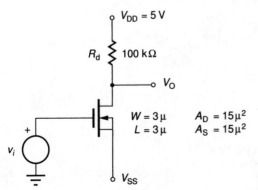

$W = 3\,\mu$ $A_D = 15\,\mu^2$
$L = 3\,\mu$ $A_S = 15\,\mu^2$

FIGURE P4.1
Problem 4.1.

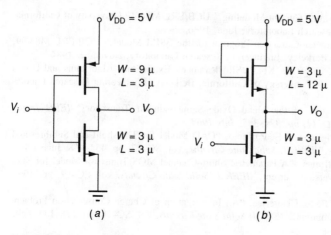

FIGURE P4.2
Problem 4.2.

4.2. (*a*) Use SPICE to obtain the dc transfer characteristics for the two circuits shown in Fig. P4.2, using first the Level 1 model and then the Level 2 model. Assume the transistors are characterized by the CMOS process of Appendix 2B.

(*b*) Obtain the low frequency small signal voltage gain for both circuits and plot as the quiescent input voltage is varied between 0 V and 5 V.

(*c*) If these circuits are loaded by a 50 fF capacitor, determine the response to a 5 V pulse input that lasts 100 μsec.

(*d*) If these circuits are biased at $V_{OQ} = 2.5$ V, determine the small signal 3 dB bandwidth of the voltage gain $A_v = v_o/v_i$.

4.3. Compare the dc transfer characteristics (I_D vs. V_{DS} as a function of V_{GS}) for a MOSFET using the Level 1 and Level 2 SPICE models. Use the SPICE process model parameters of Appendix 2B.

4.4. Compare the small signal output conductance when λ is an input parameter in the Level 2 model to that obtained if λ is calculated by Eq. 4.2-34. Assume the process parameters of the CMOS process discussed in the Appendices of Chapter 2 when making this comparison.

4.5. Plot I_D vs. V_{GS} for .3 V $< V_{GS} <$ 5 V for the circuit in Fig. P4.5 using a logarithmic I_D axis. Use the process of Appendix 2B and include any subthreshold currents.

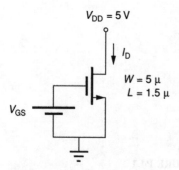

FIGURE P4.5
Problem 4.5.

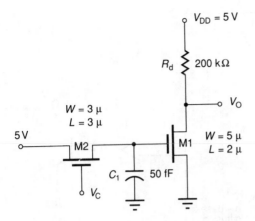

FIGURE P4.6
Problem 4.6.

4.6. In Fig. P4.6, at time $t = 0$ the control voltage V_C is taken from 5 V to 0 V and maintained at 0 V.
  (a) If M2 serves as an ideal switch (short between drain and source when $V_C = 5$ V and open when $V_C = 0$ V), what is $V_O(t)$?
  (b) Leakage current through the drain or source diffusion of M2 will discharge C. Use the process of Appendix 2B to find how M2 should be laid out to minimize the output voltage droop.
  (c) Plot $V_O(t)$ if the source diffusion of M2 contacting the gate of M1 is $3 \mu \times 12 \mu$.
4.7. Practically determine and illustrate the effect of the mobility degradation parameters UCRIT, ULTRA, and UEXP on the I_D–V_{DS} characteristics of the MOSFET.
4.8. Plot $C_{GS}, C_{GD}, C_{BD}, C_{BS}$, and C_{BG} in the following two cases for the MOSFET shown in Fig. P4.8.
  (a) vs. V_{GS} for $0 \leq V_{GS} \leq 5$ V if $V_{DS} = 5$ V and $V_{BS} = -5$ V.
  (b) vs. V_{GS} for $0 \leq V_{GS} \leq 5$ V if $V_{DS} = 5$ V and $V_{BS} = 0$.
4.9. Plot C_{BE}, C_{BC}, and C_{CS} vs. I_B for 1 nA $\leq I_B \leq 100$ μA for the BJT shown in Fig. P4.9. Assume $V_{CE} = 5$ V.

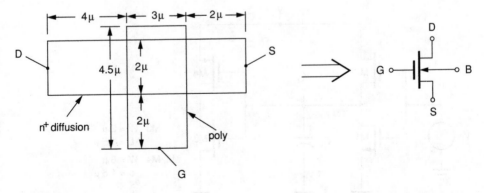

FIGURE P4.8
Problem 4.8.

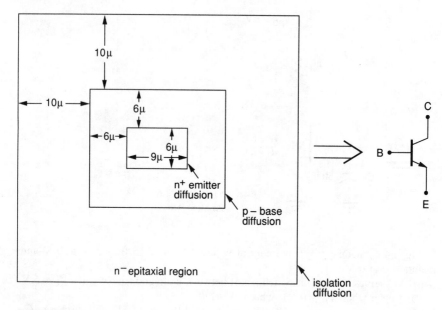

FIGURE P4.9
Problem 4.9.

4.10. A CMOS digital inverter loaded by an identical device is shown in Fig. P4.10. Assume the device is fabricated in the CMOS process of Appendix 2B.

  (a) If a pulse of height 5 V is applied to the input (V_i) at $t = 0$, what is the minimum pulse width that can be applied if V_{O1} must swing down to at least 0.5 V? Assume $C_L = 0$.

  (b) How does the minimum pulse width change if 40 identical inverters load the node V_{O1}? Assume $C_L = 0$.

  (c) If the digital inverter is loaded by only a 2pF load, how does the response time of this circuit compare to that obtained in (a)?

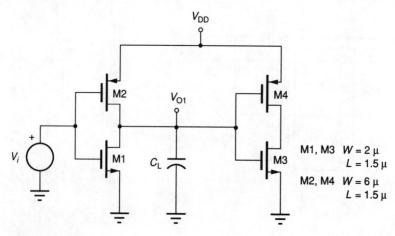

FIGURE P4.10
Problem 4.10.

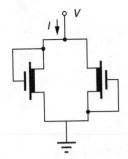

FIGURE P4.11
Problem 4.11.

4.11. Plot I vs. V for the circuit shown in Fig. P4.11 for $-3V \leq V \leq 3$ V. Assume M1 and M2 matched with $W = 3 \mu$ and $L = 30 \mu$. Use the NMOS process parameters of Appendix 2A.

4.12. If I_{BIAS} in Fig. P4.12 is set to 100 μA and V_{B1} and V_{B2} are adjusted so that $V_{O1Q} = V_{O2Q} = 5$ V, obtain from SPICE the small signal voltage gain and the 3 dB bandwidth of each circuit for a small signal excitation. Use the SPICE process model parameters of Appendices 2B and 2C and include realistic parasitics for M1 and Q1.

4.13. Assume that V_{B1} and V_{B2} in Problem 4.12 are fixed at the value needed to make $V_{O1Q} = V_{O2Q} = 5$ V at room temperature (30°C). What will happen to the Q-point, voltage gain and 3 dB bandwidth for the two circuits of Fig. P4.12 if the temperature is increased to 200°C? Decreased to −50°C?

4.14. The circuit shown in Fig. P4.14 has been proposed as a linear temperature transducer (output voltage linearly proportional to temperature). Plot V_O vs. temperature for $-50°C \leq T \leq 200°C$, and comment on the suitability of this device as a temperature transducer. Use the model parameters of Appendix 2C in your simulations. Assume $I_{REF} = 1 \mu A$.

4.15. Examine the MOSFET shown in Fig. P4.15.
(a) Adjust V_{BB} so that $V_{OQ} = 3$ V.

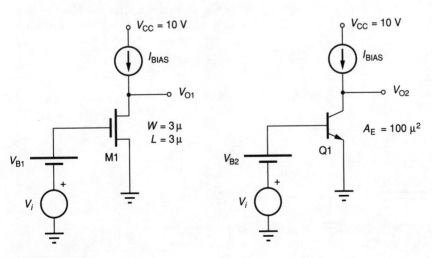

FIGURE P4.12
Problem 4.12.

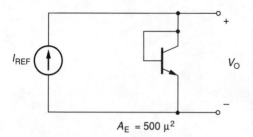

$A_E = 500 \ \mu^2$

FIGURE P4.14
Problem 4.14.

(b) Determine V_m so that the peak to peak output swing is about 2 V around the Q-point established in (a).

(c) If the time varying output voltage is 2 V p–p, determine the signal to noise ratio of the output voltage in the frequency band [100 Hz, 20 KHz]. Use the MOS process of Appendix 2B and typical noise parameters.

(d) Repeat parts (a), (b) and (c) if the MOSFET is replaced with a BJT with an emitter area of 500 μ^2 that is characterized by the process of Appendix 2C and compare with the results obtained for the MOSFET.

4.16. Use SPICE and the process description of Appendix 2C to find the following quantities in the circuit of Fig. P4.16.

(a) Determine the quiescent output voltage and the small signal model parameters of Q_1 at the Q-point.

(b) Determine the small signal voltage gain using the ac analysis in SPICE.

(c) Determine the steady state output voltage using a transient analysis if the input $v_i(t)$ is defined by

$$v_i(t) = \begin{cases} 0 & t < 0 \\ .005 \sin 1000t & t \geq 0 \end{cases}$$

(d) In calculating a steady state response due to a sinusoidal excitation with SPICE, how does the effort and computation time required for a transient analysis compare to that required for a small signal ac analysis?

4.17. (a) From Eqs. 4.2-21 and 4.2-24, obtain an expression for the effective width reduction, $WR = W - W_{eff}$, where $W_{eff} = W (2 - \eta)$ in terms of the parameter

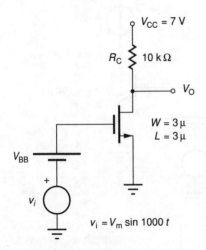

$v_i = V_m \sin 1000 \, t$

FIGURE P4.15
Problem 4.15.

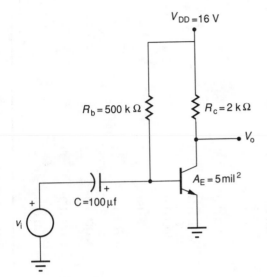

$V_{DD} = 16$ V

$R_b = 500$ k Ω

$R_c = 2$ k Ω

V_o

$A_E = 5$ mil^2

$C = 100\,\mu$f

v_i

FIGURE P4.16
Problem 4.16.

DELTA when the MOSFET is operating in the saturation region.
(b) For drawn widths of $W = 5\ \mu$, $2\ \mu$, and $1\ \mu$ plot the effective length, L_{eff}, of a MOSFET as the drawn length is reduced from $10\ \mu$ to $0.5\ \mu$. Assume the SPICE model parameters of Appendix 2B remain valid as the drawn length is varied.
(c) Using the same model, plot the effective device width as the drawn width is varied between $10\ \mu$ and $0.5\ \mu$ for drawn lengths of $L = 5\ \mu$, $2\ \mu$, and $1\ \mu$.

APPENDIX 4A
MOSFET PARAMETER DEFINITIONS

A brief alphabetical listing of the major parameters used in the MOS device models follows. Those parameters that serve specifically as SPICE input parameters are summarized in Table 4A. For more details about these parameters, the reader is referred to the SPICE User's Guide[1] or the SPICE source code[6].

AD represents the area of the drain diffusion. This serves as a SPICE input parameter which is entered on the device element card.

AF denotes the flicker noise exponent. This, along with the parameter KF, is used to characterize a noise current source that goes from drain to source in the MOSFET model. The RMS noise current density is given by

$$I_N = \sqrt{\frac{8kTg_m}{3} + \frac{KF \cdot I_{dq}^{AF}}{fC_{OX}L^2}} \qquad (4A\text{-}1)$$

where g_m is the saturation region transconductance gain at the operating point and I_{dq} is the quiescent drain current. The first term under the radical represents

TABLE 4A
SPICE input parameter summary for MOSFET

Parameter	Symbol	Name	Default if non-zero	How entered directly†	Levels valid	Characterizing eqs. if not entered	
						Level 1	Level 2
LEVEL		Model level (1,2, or 3)	1	.MOD (1)	all		
VTO	V_{TO}	Zero-bias threshold voltage		.MOD (2)	all	4.2-16	4.2-16
KP	K'	Transconductance parameter	$2 \times 10^{-5} A/V^2$	.MOD (3)	all	4.2-11	4.2-11
GAMMA	γ	Bulk threshold parameter		.MOD (4)	all	4.2-14	4.2-14
PHI	ϕ	Surface potential	.6 V	.MOD (5)	all	4.2-15	4.2-15
LAMBDA	λ	Channel-length modulation		.MOD (6)	2	4.2-34	4.2-34
RD		Drain ohmic resistance		.MOD (7)	all		
RS		Source ohmic resistance		.MOD (8)	all		
CBD	C_{BD}	Zero-bias bulk–drain junction capacitance		.MOD (9)	all		
CBS	C_{BS}	Zero-bias bulk–source junction capacitance		.MOD (10)	all		
IS		Bulk junction saturation current	10^{-14} A	.MOD (11)	all		
PB	ϕ_B	Bulk junction potential	.5 V	.MOD (12)	all		
CGSO	C_{GSO}	Gate–source overlap capacitance per meter of channel width of source		.MOD (13)	all		
CGDO	C_{GDO}	Gate–drain overlap capacitance per meter of channel width of drain		.MOD (14)	all		
CGBO	C_{GBO}	Gate–bulk overlap capacitance per meter of channel length		.MOD (15)	all		
RSH		Sheet resistance of drain & source diffusions		.MOD (16)	all		
CJ		Zero-bias bulk junction bottom capacitance area density		.MOD (17)	all		
MJ		Bulk junction bottom grading coefficient	.5	.MOD (18)	all		

TABLE 4A
(Continued)

Parameter	Symbol	Name	Default if non-zero	How entered directly†	Levels valid	Characterizing eqs. if not entered	
						Level 1	Level 2
CJSW		Zero-bias bulk junction sidewall capacitance per meter of junction perimeter		.MOD (19)	all		
MJSW		Bulk junction sidewall grading coefficient		.MOD (20)	all		
JS		Bulk junction saturation current area density		.MOD (21)	all		
TOX	T_{OX}	Gate oxide thickness	10^{-7} m	.MOD (22)	2,3		
NSUB	N_{SUB}	Substrate doping		.MOD (23)	all		
NSS	N_{SS}	Surface state density		.MOD (24)	all		
NFS		Fast surface state density		.MOD (25)	all		
TPG		Type of gate material	1	.MOD (26)	all		
XJ		Metallurgical junction depth		.MOD (27)	all		
LD	L_D	Lateral diffusion		.MOD (28)	all		
UO	μ_O	Nominal surface mobility	600 cm^2/V · A	.MOD (29)	all		
UCRIT		Critical field for mobility degradation	10^4	.MOD (30)	2		
UEXP		Critical field exponent in mobility degradation		.MOD (31)	2		
UTRA		Mobility transverse field coefficient		.MOD (32)	2		
VMAX	V_{MAX}	Maximum carrier drift velocity		.MOD (33)	all		
NEFF	N_{EFF}	Total channel charge	1.0	.MOD (34)	2		
XQC		Thin-oxide capacitance model flag and coefficient of channel charge	1.0	.MOD (35)	all		
KF	K_F	Flicker noise coefficient		.MOD (36)	all		
AF	A_F	Flicker noise exponent	1.0	.MOD (37)	all		
FC		Coefficient for forward-bias depletion capacitance	0.5	.MOD (38)	all		

TABLE 4A
(Continued)

Parameter	Symbol	Name	Default if non-zero	How entered directly†	Levels valid	Characterizing eqs. if not entered	
						Level 1	Level 2
DELTA		Width effect on threshold voltage		.MOD (39)	2,3		
THETA		Mobility degradation		.MOD (40)	3		
ETA		Static feedback		.MOD (41)	3		
KAPPA		Saturation field factor	0.2	.MOD (42)	3		
L		Drawn channel length		DE	all		
W		Drawn channel width		DE	all		
AD		Drain area		DE	all		
AS		Source area		DE	all		
PD		Drain perimeter		DE	all		
PS		Source perimeter		DE	all		
NRD		Drain sheet resistance		DE	all		
NRS		Source sheet resistance		DE	all		

†.MOD (x) denotes the entry is via the .MODEL card (line) at the xth parameter location in Reference 1. DE notes entry from the device element card (line). Since the input parser in SPICE looks for each parameter by name, the ordering as denoted by the parameter x is arbitrary but was included for convenient reference to Reference 1.

shot noise and the second term $1/f$ noise. The corresponding spectral densities appear in Eqs. 4.2-49 and 4.2-50.

α is used to correct γ for short channel effects. It is not an input parameter to SPICE and is defined by (4.2-30); it provides linear correction of γ as indicated in (4.2-29).

AS represents the area of the source diffusion. This serves as a SPICE input parameter which is entered on the device element card.

β is not used as a SPICE input parameter, but it is often used to reduce notational complexity in the dc MOSFET model. It is defined by the expression

$$\beta = \frac{\mu_0 C_{\text{OX}} W}{L} \tag{4A-2}$$

CBD and **CBS** (C_{BD} and C_{BS}) are SPICE input parameters which represent the zero-bias diffusion bottom capacitance of the bulk–drain and bulk–source junction capacitors, respectively. If not input, C_{BD} and C_{BS} are calculated from CJ, AD, and AS by the expressions

$$C_{\text{BD}} = \text{CJ} \cdot \text{AD}$$

$$C_{\text{BS}} = \text{CJ} \cdot \text{AS} \tag{4A-3}$$

CGBO, CGDO, and **CGSO** ($C_{\text{GBO}}, C_{\text{GDO}}$, and C_{GSO}) are SPICE input parameters that represent the *linear* capacitance density of the gate–bulk, gate–drain and gate–source overlap capacitors respectively. They are expressed in terms of capacitance per unit length. These capacitors are discussed in more detail in Sec. 4.2.3.

CJ is the SPICE input parameter which represents the zero-bias junction bottom capacitance density of the moat–bulk diffusions. It is expressed in terms of capacitance per unit area of the junction. The zero-bias junction bottom capacitance of the drain–bulk and source–bulk junctions can be obtained internally in SPICE from CJ by multiplying CJ by AD and AS, respectively. The total junction capacitances are then calculated from Eq. 4.2-43 for junctions under reverse bias and from Eq. 4.2-46 for junctions under forward bias. If not input, CJ is calculated internally from Eq. 4.2-44.

CJSW is the SPICE input parameter which represents the zero-bias sidewall capacitance density of the moat–bulk diffusions. It is expressed in terms of capacitance per unit length of the junction permitter. The zero-bias junction sidewall capacitances of the drain–bulk and source–bulk junctions are obtained internally in SPICE from CJSW by multiplying by PD and PS, respectively. The total junction capacitances are then obtained from Eq. 4.2-43 for junctions under reverse bias and from Eq. 4.2-46 for junctions under forward bias. If CJSW is not entered, the sidewall capacitances are assumed to be zero.

C_{ox} represents the capacitance density of the gate–channel junction. It is expressed in terms of capacitance per unit area. Although not input directly in SPICE, it is calculated internally from the expression

$$C_{\text{ox}} = \frac{\epsilon_{\text{ox}}}{T_{\text{ox}}} \tag{4A-4}$$

where ϵ_{ox} is the dielectric constant (more precisely, the real permittivity) of the gate oxide and T_{ox} is the gate oxide thickness. C_{ox} is a key parameter in the MOS device models. It appears in the defining expression of several major parameters including K' (4.2-11), γ (4.2-14), V_{TO} (4.2-16), V_{FB} (4.2-17) and V_{TH}.

DELTA is a SPICE input parameter that characterizes the effective width reduction in the Level 2 and Level 3 models. It appears in the expression for η given in (4.2-24). With DELTA equal to its ideal value of 0, η assumes the ideal value of 1. DELTA also appears in the expressions for V_{TH} and V_{TH}^{*} as given in (4.2-22) and (4.2-25), respectively.

ϵ_0 is the permittivity of free space. It is a physical constant equal to 8.86 $\times$ 10^{-14} F/cm.

ϵ_{ox} is the dielectric constant (more precisely, the real permittivity) of SiO_2. It is a physical constant and is equal to $3.9\epsilon_0$.

ϵ_{si} is the dielectric constant (more precisely, the real permittivity) of Si. It is a physical constant and is equal to $11.7\epsilon_0$.

ETA is a SPICE input parameter termed the static feedback effect parameter. It is an empirical constant and is used only in the Level 3 model. It should not be confused with the parameter η listed below.

η is not a SPICE input parameter; it is used to characterize width reduction in the Level 2 and Level 3 models. It is primarily dependent upon the SPICE input parameter DELTA as can be seen from (4.2-24). This should not be confused with the SPICE input parameter ETA discussed above.

FC is the SPICE input parameter which denotes the forward bias co-efficient in the parasitic junction capacitance model. The junction is assumed "reverse biased" for a forward bias less than FC $\cdot$ ϕ_B, and its capacitance is characterized by (4.2-43). For a forward bias greater than FC $\cdot$ ϕ_B, the junction is assumed "forward biased" and the junction capacitance is characterized by (4.2-46).

GAMMA (γ) is a SPICE input parameter called the bulk threshold. It plays a major role in the expression for the threshold voltage (Eqs. 4.2-9 and 4.2-16 for the Level 1 model, and 4.2-25 and 4.2-16 for the Level 2 model). If not input, it is calculated internally from N_{SUB} and T_{ox} by Eq. 4.2-14.

γ_s The parameter γ effectively decreases for short channel devices. The parameter $\gamma_s = \gamma(1 - \alpha)$, as defined by (4.2-29), is used in place of γ in the drain current expressions for the Level 2 and Level 3 models.

IS (I_S) is the bulk junction saturation current; it is a SPICE input parameter. The current flowing through the bulk junction is characterized by the standard diode equation

$$I = I_S\left(e^{\frac{V_{FB}}{V_t}} - 1\right) \tag{4A-5}$$

where V_{FB} represents the forward bias on the junction. This parameter is of particular concern in such circuits as the basic DRAM cell where the charge loss on switched storage capacitors is primarily due to current flow into the bulk through the reverse biased moat junction formed between either the drain or source diffusion of the switch and the bulk. Either IS or JS can be used to characterize the bulk junction current characteristics.

JS (J_S) is a SPICE input parameter that denotes the bulk junction current density; it is expressed in terms of current per unit area of junction area. If the parameter IS is not input, it is calculated from JS by multiplying JS by the junction area.

k is Boltzmann's constant. It is a physical constant equal to 1.381×10^{-23} J/°K.

K_2' is the transconductance parameter that appears in the expression for the drain current in the Level 2 model as indicated by (4.2-20) and (4.2-21). It differs from K' in that the effective mobility, μ_s, is used in place of μ_o in the defining equation (4.2-28).

KF is a SPICE input parameter called the flicker noise coefficient. It appears in the expression for the noise current as indicated by (4.2-47).

KP (K') is a key SPICE input parameter termed the transconductance parameter. It appears in the expression for the drain current of the Level 1 model as indicated in (4.2-6) and (4.2-7). If not input, K' is calculated from the mobility and C_{ox} by (4.2-11).

KAPPA is the saturation field factor. This SPICE input parameter is an empirical constant used only in the Level 3 model.

L denotes the drawn length of the MOS transistor. It is entered on the device element card. The out diffusion of the drain and source regions geometrically reduces the length of the device by twice the lateral diffusion, LD, to the adjusted geometrical length, L_{adj}.

L_{adj} is the adjusted geometrical length and is internally calculated by the expression

$$L_{adj} = L - 2LD \qquad (4A-6)$$

L_{eff} is the effective device length. In addition to the geometrical length reduction, additional reductions in the effective length occur due to the applied drain–source voltage. The expression for L_{eff} is given by (4.2-10) for the Level 1 model and by (4.2-33) and (4.2-34) for the Level 2 model.

LD is the SPICE input parameter denoting the lateral (out) diffusion of the drain and source regions under the gate. Since the out diffusion on the source side is generally equal to that on the drain side of the gate, the geometrical length is effectively reduced by 2LD as indicated by (4.2-52).

LEVEL indicates which model is to be used for analysis. If not entered on the MODEL card, Level 1 is assumed.

LAMBDA (λ) is a SPICE input parameter called the channel-length modulation parameter. It arises from the V_{DS} dependence of the effective channel length. The output conductance of the small signal model is also proportional to $1/\lambda$. If this parameter is forced by specifying it on the .MODEL input card, the robustness of the Level 2 model is seriously restricted. Specifically, λ as determined by (4.2-34) is not used in the calculation of L_{eff} by (4.2-33) if λ is an input parameter. If not input, the parameter defaults to 0 in the Level 1 model or is calculated from (4.2-35) in the Level 2 MOSFET model.

MJ and **MJSW** are SPICE input parameters for the bulk junction bottom grading coefficient and the bulk junction sidewall grading coefficient, respectively. They appear only in equations (4.2-43) and (4.2-46), which characterize the parasitic bulk–moat junction capacitances.

NEFF (N_{eff}) is an input parameter for the total channel charge coefficient. It is used only in the Level 2 model and only when V_{MAX} is specified. In this case, N_{eff} serves as an empirical constant that modifies (4.2-32) to read

$$XD = \sqrt{\frac{2\epsilon_{si}}{qN_{eff}N_{SUB}}} \tag{4A-7}$$

NFS is a SPICE input parameter called the effective fast surface state density. It is used only in the Level 2 and Level 3 models. NFS has two purposes. First, it serves as a flag to determine whether SPICE will assume the current in cutoff to be zero or $I_{weak\ inversion}$ as indicated in (4.2-19). Its second purpose is to characterize $I_{weak\ inversion}$ as shown in References 1 and 6.

n_i is the intrinsic carrier concentration of silicon and is equal to 1.45×10^{10} cm^{-3} at room temperature.

NRD and **NRS** are the number of squares of moat in the drain and source respectively. They can be entered on the device element card. If RD and RS are entered, these parameters are ignored. If RD and RS are not entered, the drain and source resistances are calculated from the expressions

$$RD = RSH \cdot NRD$$

$$RS = RSH \cdot NRS \tag{4A-8}$$

respectively, provided the sheet resistance of the moat, RSH, has been entered on the .MODEL card.

NSUB (N_{SUB}) is a SPICE input parameter indicating the substrate doping. It plays a key role in calculations of parameters used to define the threshold voltage.

NSS (N_{SS}) is a SPICE input parameter called the effective surface charge density. Although it can be used to define the flatband voltage (4.2-17), which subsequently determines V_{TO}, it is usually better to enter V_{TO} directly.

PB (ϕ_B) is a SPICE input parameter called the bulk junction potential (alternately, built-in potential). ϕ_B is used to characterize the bulk junction capacitors as indicated in (4.2-43) and (4.2-46).

PHI (ϕ) is a SPICE input parameter called the surface potential. If not input, this parameter is calculated from (4.2-15) provided N_{SUB} is input.

ϕ_{MS} is the metal-semiconductor work function difference. It is calculated internally in SPICE from (4.2-18) and is used to define the flatband voltage.

PS and **PD** can be entered on the device element card. They represent the perimeter of the source and drain, respectively. They are used for calculating the sidewall capacitance of the drain and source regions as indicated in (4.2-43) and (4.2-46).

q is the charge of an electron. It is a physical constant equal to 1.602×10^{-19} coulomb.

RD and **RS** are SPICE input parameters representing the series drain and source resistances, respectively. If not input, they are calculated from (4A-8), provided that the sheet resistance of the moat, RSH, is specified.

RSH is a SPICE input parameter representing the sheet resistance of the moat. To allow for geometrical device variations, it is often more convenient to specify RSH, NRD, and NRS, and then let SPICE calculate RD and RS from (4A-8), rather than to enter RD and RS directly.

T is a SPICE input parameter indicating the operating temperature of the circuit.

THETA is a SPICE input parameter. It is an empirical parameter used only in the Level 3 model.

TPG is a SPICE input parameter indicating the type of gate. It is a flag that assumes a value of $+1$ for poly gates with the same flavor (both n or both p doping) as the substrate, -1 for poly gates with the flavor opposite to that of the substrate, and 0 for aluminum gates.

TOX (T_{OX}) is the thickness of the gate oxide. It is a SPICE input parameter used to determine the key parameter C_{OX}.

UO (μ_o) is the surface mobility of the channel. It is a SPICE input parameter used to calculate K' (or K'_2) if T_{OX} is entered and K' is not entered.

μ_s represents the degraded surface mobility. It is an internal parameter and used only in the Level 2 model. SPICE uses the parameters UCRIT, UTRA, and UEXP to characterize μ_s as indicated by (4.2-36); the μ_s is used to define the transconductance parameter for the Level 2 model, K'_2, as shown in (4.2-28).

UCRIT, UEXP, and **UTRA** are SPICE input parameters used to characterize the degraded surface mobility, μ_s, as indicated by (4.2-36).

V_{FB} is the flatband voltage. It is an internal SPICE parameter characterized by (4.2-17).

VMAX (V_{MAX}) is the maximum drift velocity of carriers in the channel. It is a SPICE input parameter which partially defines the transition region between ohmic and saturation in the Level 2 model. See Reference 2 for a more complete discussion of V_{MAX}. It is ignored in the Level 1 model.

V_t is an internal parameter calculated from the expression

$$V_t = \frac{kT}{q} \tag{4A-9}$$

where k is Boltzmann's constant, T is temperature in °K, and q is the charge of an electron. It is used for calculating the bulk–moat reverse saturation current as indicated by (4A-5) and the drain current when operating in weak inversion. V_t should not be confused with V_T, the notation used for threshold voltage in Chapter 3.

VTO (V_{T0}) is a SPICE input parameter. It is the zero-bias ($V_{BS} = 0$) threshold voltage. If not input, it is calculated from (4.2-16).

V_T (See V_{TH} definition.)

V_{TH} is the threshold voltage of the device. It is used to characterize the cutoff transition region. It is an internal parameter determined by (4.2-9) for the Level 1 model and (4.2-25) for the Level 2 model. In Chapter 3, the variable V_T was used to denote the threshold voltage. V_T should not be confused with $V_t = kT/q$.

V^*_{TH} is nearly equal to V_{TH} in the Level 2 model. It is an internal parameter used to characterize the drain currents as indicated by (4.2-20) and (4.2-21). V^*_{TH} is determined from (4.2-25). V_{BIN} is used for V^*_{TH} in the SPICE source code and some of the other SPICE documentation.

W denotes the drawn width of the MOS transistor. It is entered on the device element card.

W_S and **W_D** are defined in equations (4.2-31) and (4.2-32), respectively.

XJ is the metallurgical junction depth. It is a SPICE input parameter which is used to characterize the effective bulk threshold parameter, γ_s, as indicated by (4.2-30).

XQC is a SPICE input parameter used to denote the percent of channel charge that is associated with the drain. It is used in the approximation which converts distributed channel charge to lumped drain and source charge when the device is operating in the saturation region. The reader is referred to Reference 2 and the SPICE source code[6] for additional details.

APPENDIX 4B
DIODE PARAMETER DEFINITIONS

A brief alphabetical listing of the major parameters used in the DIODE device models follows. Those parameters that serve specifically as SPICE input parameters are summarized in Table 4B. For more details about these parameters, the reader is referred to Reference 1 or to the SPICE source code[6].

AF (A_F) denotes the flicker noise exponent. This, along with the parameter KF, is used to characterize the flicker noise in the diode. A noise current source in shunt with diode D2 in Fig. 4.3-1 is used to characterize the shot and flicker noise in the diode. This RMS current source is modeled by the density equation

$$I_{N1} = \sqrt{2qI + \frac{KF \cdot I^{AF}}{f}} \tag{4B-1}$$

where I is the diode current, f is the frequency in Hz, and q is the charge of an electron. The noise model of the diode in SPICE is completed by adding a second noise current source, which represents thermal noise in R_s, in shunt with the series resistor R_s in Fig. 4.3-1. The density of this RMS current is given by

TABLE 4B
SPICE input parameter summary for diode

Parameter	Symbol	Name	Default if non-zero	How entered†
IS		Saturation current	10^{-14}A	.MOD (1)
RS	r_s	Ohmic resistance		.MOD (2)
N	n	Emission coefficient	1	.MOD (3)
TT	τ	Transit time		.MOD (4)
CJO	C_{jo}	Zero-bias junction capacitance		.MOD (5)
VJ	ϕ_B	Junction potential	1 V	.MOD (6)
M	m	Junction grading coefficient	0.5	.MOD (7)
EG		Activation energy	1.11 V	.MOD (8)
XTI		Saturation current temp.exp.	3.0	.MOD (9)
KF	K_F	Flicker noise coefficient		.MOD (10)
AF	A_F	Flicker noise exponent	1	.MOD (11)
FC		Coefficient for forward-reverse bias transition	0.5	.MOD (12)
BV		Reverse breakdown voltage	∞	.MOD (13)
IBV		Current at breakdown voltage	1 mA	.MOD (14)
AREA	A_n	Normalized junction area	1	DE

÷.MOD (x) denotes the entry is via the .MODEL card (line) at the xth parameter location in Reference 1, DE notes entry from the device element card (line). Since the input parser in SPICE looks for each parameter by name. the ordering as denoted by the parameter x is arbitrary but was included for convenient reference to Reference 1.

$$I_{N2} = \sqrt{\frac{4kT}{R_s}} \qquad (4B\text{-}2)$$

where k is Boltzmann's constant and T is temperature in degrees Kelvin.

AREA (A_n) denotes the ratio of the cross-sectional area of the pn junction on the device input line to the cross-sectional area of the device modeled in the referenced .MODEL line. A_n is thus a normalized area and is dimensionless.

BV is the reverse breakdown voltage of the diode.

CJO (C_{jo}) is the junction capacitance at zero bias on the pn junction of the device modeled on the .MODEL line. Note that this differs from the closely related parameter CJ, which was used to model the junction capacitance in the MOSFET; CJO represents the capacitance while CJ represents the capacitance density.

EG denotes the activation energy. It is used along with the parameter XTI to characterize the temperature dependence of the saturation current[3]. The temperature dependence of IS is characterized by the expression

$$\text{IS}(T) = \text{IS}(T_1) \cdot \left(\frac{T}{T_1}\right)^{\text{XTI}} \exp\left[\left(\frac{q(\text{EG})}{kT}\right)\left(\frac{T}{T_1} - 1\right)\right] \qquad (4B\text{-}3)$$

where T is temperature in degrees Kelvin, T_1 is any reference temperature, $\text{IS}(T_1)$ is the saturation current at T_1, k is Boltzmann's constant, and q is the charge of an electron.

FC is the forward bias coefficient in the parasitic junction capacitance model which characterizes the transition voltage between the "reverse bias" and "forward bias" capacitance models. The junction is assumed "reverse biased" for a forward bias less than FC · ϕ_B.

IBV is the current in the diode at breakdown. It represents the nearly constant current that flows in the diode prior to breakdown. There is a fixed relationship between IBV, BV, and IS. If this relationship is not established with the specified parameters, SPICE adjusts either IBV or BV to attain the required relationship. See subroutines MODCHK and DIODE in the SPICE source code for details.

IS (I_S) denotes the saturation current in a diode. This SPICE input parameter is a key parameter in the diode equation.

k is Boltzmann's constant. It is a physical constant equal to 1.381×10^{-23} J/°K.

KF is called the flicker noise coefficient. It is used, along with AF, to characterize the flicker noise in the diode as indicated by equation (4B-1).

M (*m*) is called the junction grading coefficient. It characterizes, along with ϕ_B and C_{jo}, the junction capacitance as indicated by (4.3-4).

N (*n*) is the emission coefficient that appears in the diode equation (4.3-1). It is typically near unity.

RS denotes the series resistance in the diode. It is assumed to be an ideal resistor in SPICE.

TT (τ) is called the transient time. It is used to characterize the effects of stored change in the junction due to minority carrier injection as indicated by (4.3-4) and (4.3-5).

VJ (ϕ_B) is called the junction potential. It characterizes, along with C_{jo} and *m*, the junction capacitance as indicated by (4.3-4). The FC · ϕ_B product also determines the transition between "reverse bias" and "forward bias" on the junction.

XTI denotes the saturation current temperature exponent. It is used along with EG to characterize the temperature dependence of IS as indicated by (4B-3).

APPENDIX 4C
BJT PARAMETER DEFINITIONS

A brief alphabetical listing of the major parameters used in the BJT device models follows. Those parameters that serve specifically as SPICE input parameters are summarized in Table 4C. For more details about these parameters, the reader is referred to Reference 1 or to the SPICE source code[6].

TABLE 4C
SPICE input parameter summary for the BJT

Parameter	Symbol	Name	Default if non-zero	How entered directly†
IS	I_S	Transport saturation current	1.0E-16 A	.MOD (1)
BF		Ideal maximum forward beta	100	.MOD (2)
NF		Forward current emission coefficient	1	.MOD (3)
VAF	V_{AF}	Forward Early voltage	∞	.MOD (4)
IKF	I_{KF}	Forward beta high-current roll-off	∞	.MOD (5)
ISE	I_{SE}	B-E leakage saturation current		.MOD (6)
NE		B-E leakage emission coefficient	1.5	.MOD (7)
BR		Ideal maximum reverse beta	1	.MOD (8)
NR		Reverse current emission coefficient	1	.MOD (9)
VAR	V_{AR}	Reverse Early voltage	∞	.MOD (10)
IKR	I_{KR}	Reverse beta high-current roll-off	∞	.MOD (11)
ISC	I_{SC}	B-C leakage saturation current		.MOD (12)
NC		B-C leakage emission coefficient	2	.MOD (13)
RB	R_B	Zero bias base resistance		.MOD (14)
IRB		Current where base resistance falls halfway to its minimum value	∞	.MOD (15)
RBM		Minumum base resistance at high currents	RB	.MOD (16)
RE		Emitter resistance		.MOD (17)
RC		Collector resistance		.MOD (18)
CJE	C_{JE}	Zero-bias B–E depletion region capacitance		.MOD (19)
VJE	ϕ_B	B–E built–in potential	.75	.MOD (20)
MJE	M_{JE}	B–E junction exponential factor	.33	.MOD (21)
TF		Ideal forward transit time		.MOD (22)
XTF		Coefficient for bias dependence of TF		.MOD (22)
VTF		Voltage describing B–C voltage dependence of TF	∞	.MOD (23)
ITF		High-current effect on TF		.MOD (24)
PTF		Excess phase at $f = \frac{1}{2\pi \cdot TF}$		.MOD (25)
CJC	C_{JC}	Zero-bias B-C depletion region capacitance		.MOD (26)
VJC	ϕ_C	B–C built–in potential	.75	.MOD (27)
MJC	M_{JC}	B–C junction exponential factor	.33	.MOD (28)
XCJC	θ	Fraction of B–C depletion capacitance connected to internal base node	1	.MOD (29)
TR		Ideal reverse transit time		.MOD (30)
CJS	C_{JS}	Zero-bias collector–substrate capacitance		.MOD (31)
VJS	ϕ_S	Substrate junction built–in potential	.75	.MOD (32)
MJS	M_{JS}	Substrate junction exponential factor		.MOD (33)
XTB		Temperature exponent for BF and BR		.MOD (34)
EG		Activation energy for temperature dependence of IS	1.11ev	.MOD (35)
XTI		Saturation current temperature exponent	3	.MOD (36)
KF	K_F	Flicker noise coefficient		.MOD (37)
AF	A_F	Flicker noise exponent	1	.MOD (39)
FC		Forward bias capacitor transition coefficient	0.5	.MOD (40)
AREA	A_n	Emitter area ratio	1	DE

†.MOD (x) denotes the entry is via the .MODEL card (line) at the xth parameter location in Reference 1. DE notes entry from the device element card (line). Since the input parser in SPICE looks for each parameter by name, the ordering as denoted by the parameter x is arbitrary but was included for convenient reference to Reference 1.

AF denotes the flicker noise exponent. This input parameter, along with the parameter KF, is used to characterize the flicker noise in the C–E noise source as indicated by (4.4-18).

AREA (A_n) denotes the ratio of the emitter area of the BJT on the device input line to the emitter area of the BJT modeled in the referenced .MODEL line. A_n is thus a normalized area and is dimensionless.

BF is the ideal maximum forward beta. It is one of the key input parameters used to characterize the BJT and is approximately equal to the current gain from the base to collector. It appears in the characterizing equation (4.4-2) and in Fig. 4.4-3.

β_F is by definition the ratio of the total collector current to the total base current under forward BE bias as indicated by (4.4-9); it is not a SPICE input parameter. It is shown pictorially in Fig. 4.4-3. β_F is operating point dependent but nearly equal to BF for midrange V_{BE} values.

BR is the ideal maximum reverse beta. This SPICE input parameter is most useful for characterizing the BJT in the reverse active region. It appears in the characterizing equation (4.4-1) and the plot corresponding to that of Fig. 4.4-3 obtained by forward biasing the BC junction and reverse biasing the BE junction.

β_R is by definition the ratio of the total emitter current to the total base current under forward BC bias evaluated at the Q-point; it is not a SPICE input parameter. It is the reverse active equivalent of β_F.

C2 and **C4** are parameters which were used to denote ISE and ISC in some earlier versions of SPICE. They are still used for this purpose in some SPICE documentation.

CJC, CJE, and **CJS (C_{JC}, C_{JE},** and C_{JS})** are the zero-bias depletion region capacitances of the base–collector, base–emitter and collector–substrate junctions. They are useful for characterizing the parasitic capacitances in vertical transistors. These SPICE input parameters appear in (4.4-12)–(4.4-15).

EG denotes the activation energy. It is used along with the parameter XTI to characterize the temperature dependence of the saturation current.[3] The temperature dependence of IS is characterized by the expression

$$\text{IS}(T) = \text{IS}(T_1) \cdot \left(\frac{T}{T_1}\right)^{\text{XTI}} \exp\left[\left(\frac{q\text{EG}}{kT}\right)\left(\frac{T}{T_1} - 1\right)\right] \tag{4C-1}$$

where T is temperature in degrees Kelvin, T_1 is any reference temperature, $\text{IS}(T_1)$ is the saturation current at T_1, k is Boltzmann's constant, and q is the charge of an electron.

FC is the SPICE input parameter which denotes the forward bias coefficient in the parasitic junction capacitance (B–C, B–E, and C–S). All junction capacitors are assumed "reverse biased" and characterized by (4.4-12)–(4.4-15) for a forward bias less than or equal to FC $\cdot$ ϕ_X, for $X \in \{B, C, S\}$. For a forward bias greater than FC $\cdot$ ϕ_X the junction capacitors are assumed "forward biased" and are characterized by the continuous and differentiable linear extension of the reverse-bias region at the transition voltage.

IKR is the corner for the reverse beta high-current roll-off. This SPICE input parameter is a dual of the parameter IKF for the reverse active mode of operation.

IKF is the corner for the forward beta high-current roll-off. This SPICE input parameter appears in (4.4-3) and Fig. 4.4-3.

IRB is the current where the base resistance falls half way to its minimum value. The base resistance is assumed to be current dependent and is characterized by the three parameters RB, IRB, and RBM.

IS is the transport saturation current of the BJT. This SPICE input parameter is a key parameter in the dc model as indicated by (4.4-1) and (4.4-2).

ISC and **ISE** (I_{SE} and I_{SC}) represent the B–C and B–E leakage saturation currents. They appear in the dc model as indicated by (4.4-1) and (4.4-2).

ITF is a SPICE input parameter which characterizes the forward transit time at high current levels. The reader should consult the SPICE source code in subroutine BJT for details.

k is Boltzmann's constant. It is a physical constant equal to $1.381 \times 10^{-23} \text{J}/^\circ\text{K}$.

KF is the flicker noise coefficient used to characterize noise in the collector–emitter noise source as indicated by (4.4-18).

MJC, MJE and **MJS** (M_{JC}, M_{JE} and M_{JS}) are the junction grading coefficients of the B–C, B–E, and C–S junctions, respectively. These SPICE input parameters appear as exponents in the voltage dependent depletion junction capacitances as indicated by (4.4-12)–(4.4-15).

NC, NE, NF, and **NR** are leakage emission coefficients and appear in the exponents of the dc characterizing equations, (4.4-1) and (4.4-2).

ϕ_C, ϕ_B, and ϕ_S (See VJC, VJE, and VJS.)

PTF is the excess phase at $f = \text{TF}/(2\pi)$ and is used to characterize the actual transit time. It is used in determining the accumulated charge on parasitic capacitors. The interested reader should refer to subroutine BJT in the SPICE source code for the specific formulation.

q is the charge of an electron. It is a physical constant equal to 1.602×10^{-19} coulomb.

RB is the zero-bias base resistance. The actual zero-bias base resistance used in SPICE, R_b of Fig. 4.4–1, is a function of RB, RBM, and IRB. If IRB is not specified, R_b is calculated from the expression

$$ R_b = \frac{RB}{A_n Q_B} + \frac{RBM}{A_n}\left(1 - \frac{1}{Q_B}\right) \tag{4C-2} $$

where Q_B is as defined in (4.4-8). If IRB is specified, the expression for R_b is quite unwieldy. For details, see subroutine BJT of the SPICE source code.

RBM is the minimum base resistance at high currents. The parameters RB, RBM, and IRB are used to characterize the base resistance.

RC and **RE** are the collector and emitter series resistances respectively. SPICE obtains the actual collector and emitter resistances by dividing these parameters by the area normalization factor, A_n.

θ (See XCJC.)

T is temperature in degrees Kelvin.

TF and **TR** are the forward and reverse transit times. These are key parameters in determining the accumulated charge parasitic capacitors. The reader should consult subroutine BJT in the SPICE source code for details.

VAF and **VAR** (V_{AF} and V_{AR}) are the forward and reverse Early voltages, respectively. These SPICE input parameters contribute considerably to the non-infinite output impedance at the collector of the BJT. The effects of the Early voltages on the dc I-V characteristics of the BJT are apparent from (4.4-1)–(4.4-3).

VJC, VJE, and **VJS** (ϕ_C, ϕ_B, ϕ_S) represent the built-in potential of the C–B, E–B, and C–S junctions. They are used to characterize the depletion region capacitances as indicated in (4.4-12)–(4.4-15).

V_t is an internal parameter calculated from the expression

$$V_t = \frac{kT}{q} \tag{4C-3}$$

The parameters k, T, and q have been previously defined.

VTF is a SPICE input parameter characterizing the B-C voltage dependence of the forward transit time. The interested reader should consult subroutine BJT in the SPICE source code for details.

XCJC is the fraction of the B–C depletion capacitance that is to be assigned to the internal base node. This SPICE input parameter appears as the parameter θ in equations (4.4-13) and (4.4-15).

XTB is the temperature exponent for both the forward and reverse beta as indicated by (4.4-22) and (4.4-23). XTB is a SPICE input parameter.

XTF is a SPICE input parameter which characterizes the bias dependence of TF. The reader should check subroutine BJT in the SPICE source code for details.

XTI denotes the saturation current temperature exponent. It is used along with EG to characterize the temperature dependence of IS as indicated by (4.4-19). XTI is a SPICE input parameter.

CHAPTER 5

BASIC INTEGRATED CIRCUIT BUILDING BLOCKS

5.0 INTRODUCTION

This chapter introduces various integrated circuit building blocks, which form the first step in integrated circuit design. Figures 5.0-1 and 5.0-2 illustrate the circuit diagrams of a BJT op amp and a CMOS op amp. Although such circuits will not be covered until Chapter 6, they are useful in illustrating how the various building blocks are combined to form more complex circuits. There are two important observations to make concerning these two figures. The first is that circuit design is remarkably similar for different technologies. The architecture of both op amps is identical although the performance may not be identical. This fact will permit circuit design ideas developed in one technology to be applicable to a new technology. The second observation is that some components in each op amp perform more than one function. For example, Q3 (M3) serves as an active resistor load but also serves as part of a current mirror. This characteristic of circuits makes it difficult to distinguish the function of a component in a circuit.

In this chapter, some of the building blocks of Figs. 5.0-1 and 5.0-2 will be discussed. These blocks include switches (not shown on Figs. 5.0-1 or 5.0-2), active resistors, current sinks and sources, current mirrors, and voltage and current references. These blocks, along with passive resistors and capacitors, will form the lowest level of the design hierarchy. The next level of hierarchy takes the blocks of this chapter and implements more complex circuits such as amplifiers or comparators. Chapters 6 and 7 address analog and digital circuits, respectively, implemented from the building blocks of this chapter. Chapters 8 and 9 address

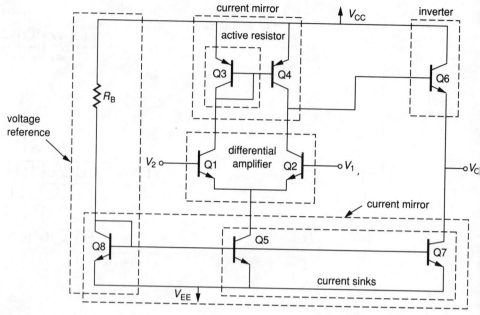

FIGURE 5.0-1
BJT op amp illustrating the various components.

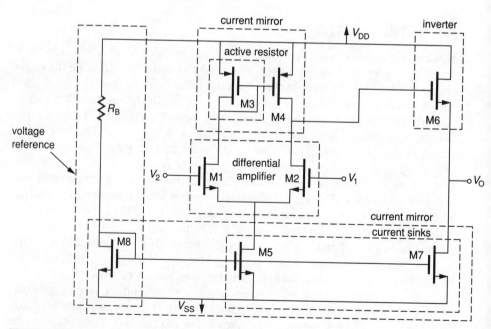

FIGURE 5.0-2
CMOS op amp illustrating the various components.

TABLE 5.0-1
Design hierarchy of Chapters 5 through 9

Design hierarchy	Analog design	Digital design
Systems	Chapter 8	Chapter 9
Basic circuits	Chapter 6	Chapter 7
Building blocks	Chapter 5	—

the use of these analog and digital circuits to perform analog and digital signal processing functions, respectively. The hierarchical relationships of this material are illustrated in Table 5.0-1.

Throughout this chapter, several key concepts are introduced. These concepts include both techniques and principles. How to use both positive and negative feedback in order to improve some aspect of the performance of the building blocks will be shown. The important principle of matched devices that is key to integrated circuit design will be presented and illustrated. Techniques such as how to make a mismatch analysis or how to attain the zero sensitivity of a circuit to some parameter will be described. These principles and techniques should be understood by the reader since they are invariant and applicable regardless of the technology. The summary will include a review of these important principles and techniques.

5.1 SWITCHES

Although the switch is not one of the components illustrated in Fig. 5.0-1 or Fig. 5.0-2, it will be considered first because of its simplicity and importance. The switch finds many applications in integrated circuit design. In analog circuits, the switch is used to implement such useful functions as the switched simulation of a resistor in Sec. 5.2. The switch is also useful for multiplexing, modulation, autozeroing and a number of other applications. The switch is used as a transmission gate in digital circuits and adds a dimension of flexibility not found in standard logic circuits. The objective of this section is to study the characteristics of switches that are compatible with integrated circuits.

Figure 5.1-1a illustrates a model of the ideal voltage-controlled switch. Terminals Ⓐ and Ⓑ represent the switch terminals, and terminal Ⓒ is the controlling terminal. Ideally, the voltage at V_C has two states. In one state, the switch is open (off) and in the other state the switch is closed (on). In the on state, the ideal switch presents a short circuit between terminals Ⓐ and Ⓑ. In the off state, the ideal switch presents an open circuit between terminals Ⓐ and Ⓑ.

Unfortunately, practical switch implementations only approximate the model given in Fig. 5.1-1a. Figure 5.1-1b is a model of the switch that includes some of the more important nonideal characteristics. R_{ON} is a resistance that represents the small but finite resistance between terminals Ⓐ and Ⓑ when the switch is on. R_{OFF} represents the large but not infinite resistance between terminals Ⓐ and Ⓑ when the switch is off. In many applications it will be desirable to have R_{ON} as small as possible and R_{OFF} as large as possible.

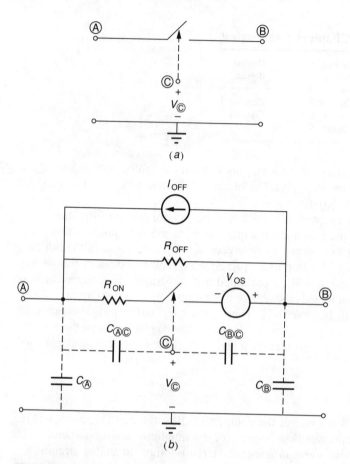

FIGURE 5.1-1
Models of the switch: (*a*) Ideal, (*b*) Nonideal.

Another practical characteristic of the switch is given by V_{OS} and I_{OFF} shown in Fig. 5.1-1*b*. The voltage that exists between terminals Ⓐ and Ⓑ when the switch is on but the current through it is zero is approximately the offset voltage and is modeled by an independent voltage source of V_{OS}. Similarly, the current that flows between terminals Ⓐ and Ⓑ when the switch is off but the voltage across the switch terminals is zero is approximately the offset current and is modeled by an independent current source of I_{OFF}. The polarities of the offset current and voltage are not known and have arbitrarily been assigned in Fig. 5.1-1*b*.

Figure 5.1-1*b* also shows some of the parasitic capacitances that exist between the various switch terminals and to ground. C_{AC} and C_{BC} will be particularly important when considering the influence of the controlling voltage on the switch performance. There are many other nonideal characteristics of the switch such as linearity, commutation time, noise, etc. that are not modeled by Fig. 5.1-1*b*.

The graphical characterization of a switch shown in Fig. 5.1-2 is useful in determining how well the switch can be implemented by a bipolar or MOS

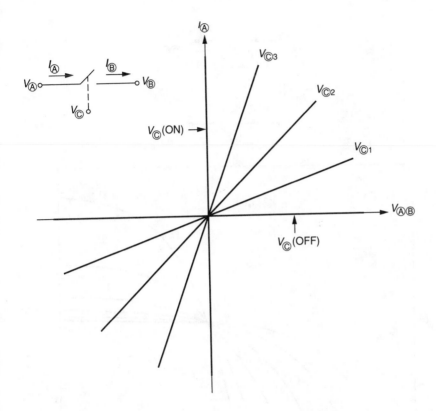

FIGURE 5.1-2
Graphical characteristics of a controlled switch.

transistor. $V_{\circledA\circledB} = V_{\circledA} - V_{\circledB}$ is the voltage across the switch, and $I_{\circledA}$ is the current into the terminal $\circledA$ and $I_{\circledB}$ the current out of terminal $\circledB$ of the switch. When $V_{\circledC} = V_{\circledC}(ON)$, ideally $V_{\circledA\circledB} = 0$ and $I_{\circledA}(I_{\circledB})$ can have any value. In the on state, the ideal switch is a short circuit. When $V_{\circledC} = V_{\circledC}(OFF)$, $I_{\circledA} = I_{\circledB} = 0$ and $V_{\circledA\circledB}$ can have any value and is identical to an open circuit. $V_{\circledC1}$, $V_{\circledC2}$, and $V_{\circledC3}$ are values of $V_{\circledC}$ that cause the switch to be between its on and off states. Normally $V_{\circledC}(OFF) < V_{\circledC1} < V_{\circledC2} < V_{\circledC3} < V_{\circledC}(ON)$.

Now consider the bipolar transistor as an implementation of the switch as shown in Fig. 5.1-3a, where $V_{\circledA\circledB} = V_{CE}$, $I_{\circledA} = I_C$, and $V_{\circledC} = V_B$. The right-hand side of these equalities refers to the transistor, whereas the left-hand side refers to the switch in Fig. 5.1-1 or 5.1-2. Typical BJT characteristics are shown in Fig. 5.1-3b with $V_{\circledB} = 0(V_E = 0)$. Several shortcomings of the BJT switch realization are immediately apparent in Fig. 5.1-3b. The first is that the origin of the characteristics for $I_{\circledA} = 0$ is not zero. Thus V_{OS} of Fig. 5.1-1 is approximately 16 mV. The second is the nonlinearity of the various curves for a constant $V_{\circledC}$. This would severely limit the dynamic range of the switch. Lastly, the switch characteristics are not symmetrical in the first and third quadrants. Another problem, which is not apparent from Fig. 5.1-3b, is that the BJT requires

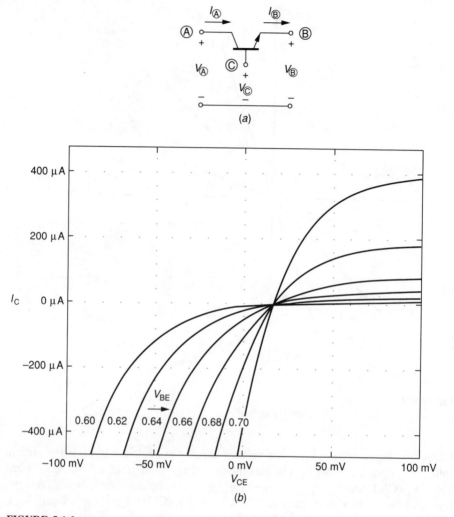

FIGURE 5.1-3

(*a*) Bipolar transistor as a switch, (*b*) Graphical characteristics of *a* where $V_{\text{Ⓐ}\text{Ⓑ}} = V_{\text{CE}}$, $I_{\text{Ⓐ}} = I_{\text{C}}$, and $V_{\text{Ⓒ}} = V_{\text{B}}$. Note that $V_{\text{E}} = 0$.

a small current flowing in the controlling terminal, causing the current flowing in terminal A to be different from that flowing out of terminal B.

Figure 5.1-4*b* shows the graphical characteristics of the MOS transistor of Fig. 5.1-4*a*, where $V_{\text{Ⓐ}\text{Ⓑ}} = V_{\text{DS}}$, $I_{\text{Ⓐ}} = I_{\text{D}}$, and $V_{\text{Ⓒ}} = V_{\text{G}}$. Again, the right-hand side of these inequalities refers to the MOS transistor while the left-hand side refers to the switch in Fig. 5.1-1 or 5.1-2. Comparison of Figs. 5.1-2, 5.1-3*b*, and 5.1-4*b* strongly suggests that the MOS transistor is a much better switch realization.

Figure 5.1-5 shows a MOS transistor that will be used as a switch. It will be important to consider the influence of the bulk voltage on the switch operation. The performance of this realization can be determined by comparing

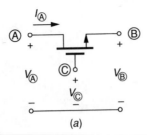

(a)

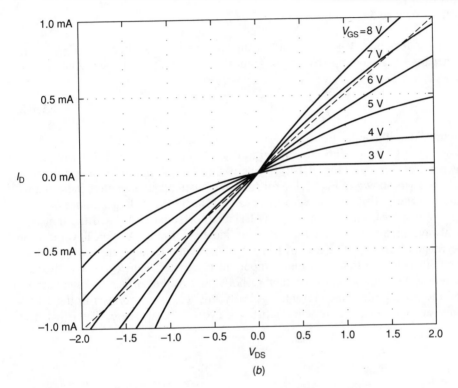

(b)

FIGURE 5.1-4
(a) MOS transistor as a switch, (b) Graphical characteristics of a where $V_{\text{Ⓐ}\text{Ⓑ}} = V_{\text{DS}}$, $I_{\text{Ⓐ}} = I_{\text{D}}$, and $V_{\text{C}} = V_{\text{G}}$. Note that $V_{\text{S}} = 0$.

Fig. 5.1-1b with the large signal model for the MOS transistor. We see that terminals Ⓐ or Ⓑ can either be the drain or source of the MOS transistor. The on resistance is seen to consist of the series combination of R_{D}, R_{S}, and whatever channel resistance exists. An expression for the on channel resistance can be found as follows. In the on state of the switch, the voltage across the switch should be small, and V_{GS} should be large. Therefore, the MOS device is assumed to be in the ohmic region. Furthermore, let us assume that the channel length modulation effects can be ignored. From Sec. 3.1, the drain current is given by

$$I_{\text{D}} = \frac{K'W}{2L}[2(V_{\text{GS}} - V_{\text{T}})V_{\text{DS}} - V_{\text{DS}}^2] \tag{5.1-1}$$

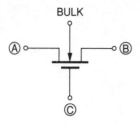

FIGURE 5.1-5
MOS transistor used as a switch.

if V_{DS} is less than $V_{GS} - V_T$ but greater than zero. (V_{GS} becomes V_{GD} if V_{DS} is negative.) Assuming that there is no offset voltage, the large signal channel resistance when $V_{GS} > V_T$ is

$$R_{ON} = \frac{1}{\partial I_D / \partial V_{DS}} = \frac{1}{(K'W/L)(V_{GS} - V_T - V_{DS})} \qquad (5.1-2)$$

Figure 5.1-6 illustrates Eq. 5.1-2 for very small values of V_{DS}. When $V_{GS} < V_T$ and $V_{DS} = 0$, R_{ON} is infinite. For large V_{DS}, the curves of Fig. 5.1-6 will start to decrease in slope (see Fig. 3.1-2) for increasing V_{DS}. A plot of R_{ON} as a function of V_{GS}/V_T is shown in Fig. 5.1-7 for small V_{DS} using the parameters indicated for various values of W/L. A lower value of R_{ON} is achieved for larger values of W/L.

When the switch is off, V_{GS} is less than or equal to V_T and the transistor is always in the cutoff region. R_{OFF} is ideally infinite. A typical value is in the range of $10^{12}\ \Omega$. Because of this large value, the leakage current from drain and source to substrate is a more important parameter than R_{OFF}. This leakage current is a combination of the subthreshold current, the surface leakage current, and the package leakage current. Typically this leakage current is in the 10 pA range at room temperature and doubles for every 10°C increase. The resistances

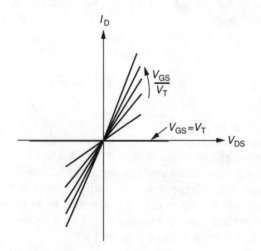

FIGURE 5.1-6
Illustration of the on state of a switch. V_{GS}/V_T is increasing in equal increments.

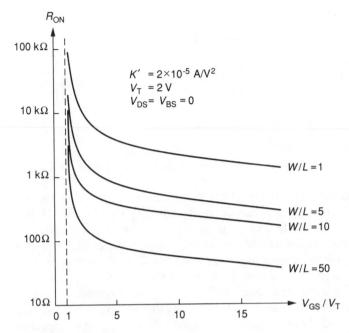

FIGURE 5.1-7
Illustration of the R_{ON} characteristics of an MOS transistor with W/L as a parameter.

representing this leakage current are called $R_{Ⓐ}$ and $R_{Ⓑ}$ and are connected from Ⓐ and Ⓑ to ground in Fig. 5.1-1 and are on the order of 10^{10} Ω. Unfortunately, $R_{Ⓐ}$ and $R_{Ⓑ}$ prevent the designer from achieving R_{OFF} of 10^{12} Ω.

The offset voltage of the MOS device is zero and does not influence the switch performance. The capacitors C_A, C_B, C_{AC}, and C_{BC} of Fig. 5.1-1b correspond directly to the capacitors C_{BD}, C_{BS}, C_{GD}, and C_{GS} of the MOS transistor of Fig. 5.1-4a. The maximum commutation rate of the MOS switch is determined primarily by the capacitors of Fig. 5.1-1b and the external resistances. Commutation rates for CMOS switches of 20 MHz are typical depending upon the load capacitance.

One important aspect of the switch is the range of voltages on the switch terminals compared to the control voltage. In the n-channel MOS transistor we see that the gate voltage must be considerably larger than either the drain or source voltage to insure that the MOS transistor is on. Typically the bulk is taken to the most negative potential for the n-channel MOS switch. The problem can be illustrated as follows. Suppose that the on voltage of the gate is the positive power supply V_{DD}. With the bulk connected to ground this should keep the MOS switch on until the signal on the switch terminals (which should be approximately identical at the source and drain) approaches $V_{DD} - V_T$. As the signal approaches $V_{DD} - V_T$, the switch begins to turn off. This often introduces an undesired nonlinear distortion in the transmission of analog signals. Typical voltages used for an n-channel MOS switch are shown in Fig. 5.1-8, where the switch is connected between two circuits and the power supplies are ±5 V.

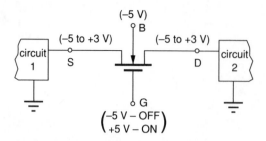

FIGURE 5.1-8
Application of an n-channel MOS transistor as a switch with typical terminal voltages indicated.

To illustrate the influence of the switches on the circuit, consider the use of a switch to charge an integrated capacitor, as shown in Fig. 5.1-9. M1 is a MOS transistor used as a switch, and ϕ_1 is called the clock. The on resistance of the switches can become important during the charge transfer phase of this circuit. For example, when ϕ_1 goes high, M1 connects C_1 to the voltage source V_{in}. The equivalent circuit at this time is shown in Fig. 5.1-10. It is seen that C_1 will charge to V_{in} with the time constant of $R_{ON}C_1$. For successful operation $R_{ON}C_1 << T$, where T is the time ϕ_1 is high. The value of R_{ON} is not constant during the charging of C_1 because the value of V_{GS} decreases as the capacitor charges. The assumption that R_{ON} is constant avoids the solution of nonlinear differential equations necessary for the exact solution.

The maximum acceptable value of R_{ON} will determine required values for W and L of M1. Typical values of C_1 are less than 20 pF because the area required to implement larger capacitors would be too large to be practical. If the time ϕ_1 is high is $T = 10 \ \mu s$ and $C_1 = 20$ pF, then R_{ON} must be less than 0.5 MΩ. Since small capacitors are used, switches with a large R_{ON} can still perform satisfactorily. As a result, the MOS devices used for switching typically use minimum geometries. For a clock of 10 V, the MOS device of Fig. 5.1-7 with $W = L$ and $V_{in} = 5$ V gives R_{ON} of approximately 6 kΩ, which is sufficiently small to transfer the charge in the desired time. The minimum size switches will also help to reduce parasitic capacitances.

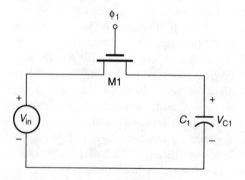

FIGURE 5.1-9
An application of a MOS switch.

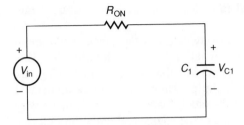

FIGURE 5.1-10
Model for the on state of the switch in Fig. 5.1-9.

The off state of the switch has little influence upon the performance of the circuit in Fig. 5.1-9 except for the leakage current. Figure 5.1-11 shows two cases where the leakage current can create serious problems. Figure 5.1-11a is a sample-and-hold circuit. If C_H is not large enough, then in the hold mode, where the MOS switch is off, the leakage current can charge or discharge C_H by a significant amount. Figure 5.1-11b shows an integrator. The leakage current can cause the circuit to integrate in a continuous mode, which can lead to large values of dc offset unless there is an external feedback path from V_{OUT} back to the inverting input of the operational amplifier. This feedback must contain resistors and may go through other dc circuits before returning to the input. If the

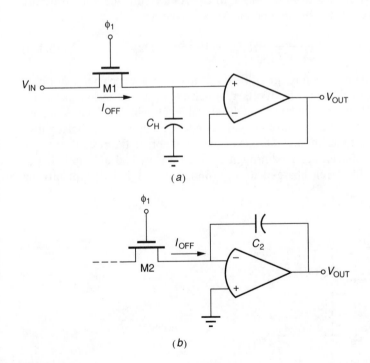

FIGURE 5.1-11
Examples of the influence of I_{OFF}: (a) Sample-and-hold circuit, (b) Integrator. Switch is off in both cases.

gate voltage of an MOS switch is equal to or less than the lowest source/drain potential, I_{OFF} is negligible.

One of the most serious limitations of switches is the clock feedthrough that can occur between the switch control signal and the switch terminals. This coupling occurs through the parasitic capacitors of the switch, namely C_{AC} and C_{BC} of Fig. 5.1-1b. Figure 5.1-12 shows the parasitic capacitances associated with the MOS switch of Fig. 5.1-9. Since the clock (gate) signal must make very large transitions, this signal can easily couple to the source and drain through C_{GS} or C_{GD}, respectively. The effects of clock feedthrough can be observed in Fig. 5.1-13 by following the sequence of events occurring when ϕ_1 is high. Assume that C_{GS} and C_{GD} are 2 fF, $C_1 = 1$ pF, $V_{in} = 5$ V and V_{C1}, is initially zero. The clock waveform is shown in Fig. 5.1-13 and has finite rise and fall times for purposes of explanation. Following the convention that the lowest potential determines the source of an MOS transistor, the source will be the side connected to the capacitor. During the time t_0 to t_1 the switch is off and the clock feeds through C_{GD} and C_{GS}. The feedthrough via C_{GD} has no effect because of the voltage source V_{in}. However, the feedthrough via C_{GS} will change the voltage across C_1. Assuming the switch turns on at t_1 and connects C_1 to V_{in}, any further feedthrough has no effect, again because the voltage source V_{in} is connected to C_1. The problem occurs when the switch turns off. From t_3 to t_4 the switch is still on so that any feedthrough is unimportant. However, from t_4 to t_5 the switch is off, and feedthrough occurs from the clock to C_1. As a result, the voltage across V_{C1} is decreased below V_{in} by an amount ΔV_{C1}, given as

$$\Delta V_{C1} = (\frac{C_{GS}}{C_1 + C_{GS}})(V_{in} + V_T) \approx 0.002V_{in} \qquad (5.1\text{-}3)$$

If V_{in} is 5 V, then a feedthrough of -10 mV to C_1 occurs during the ϕ_1 phase period. This feedthrough results in an offset, which can be a very serious problem. Furthermore, the offset is dependent upon the signal level, which will cause a non-linear offset. In general, the feedthrough will be dependent upon the switch configuration, the size of the switch, and the size of the capacitors in the circuit.

The situation concerning feedthrough is often not as bad as implied. For example, once C_1 has been charged to V_{in} (minus ΔV_{C1}) it will typically be

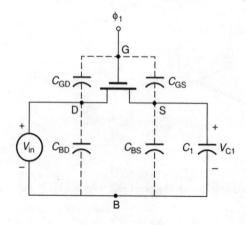

FIGURE 5.1-12
Illustration of the parasitics associated with the switch of Fig. 5.1-9.

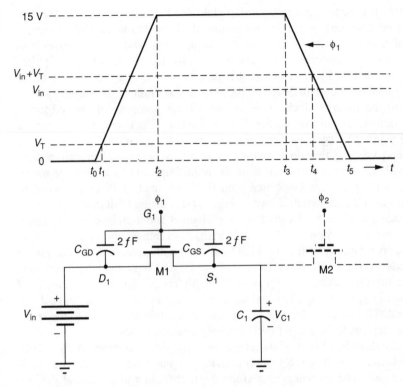

FIGURE 5.1-13
Illustration of switch feedthrough and the ϕ_1 waveform.

connected by some other switch (M2 in Fig. 5.1-13) to some other circuit. As M2 turns from off to on, there will be a positive feedthrough from ϕ_2 on to C_1 via the parasitic capacitance of M2. If the source of M2 is the terminal connected to C_1, then the net feedthrough should approximately cancel if M1 and M2 are identical. The problem is that the potential of the right-hand side of M2 is usually ground, making that side the drain and causing the positive feedthrough to be

$$\Delta V_{C1}(\text{due to M2}) = (\frac{C_{GD}}{C_{GD} + C_1})V_T \qquad (5.1\text{-}4)$$

which is less than that of Eq. 5.1-3 if $V_{in} \neq 0$.

It is possible to partially cancel some of the feedthrough effects using the technique illustrated in Fig. 5.1-14. Here a dummy MOS transistor, MD, with source and drain both attached to the signal line and the gate attached to the

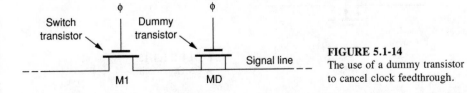

FIGURE 5.1-14
The use of a dummy transistor to cancel clock feedthrough.

inverse clock, is used to apply an opposing clock feedthrough due to M1. The area of MD can be designed to provide minimum clock feedthrough. Unfortunately, this method never completely removes the feedthrough, and in some cases may worsen it. Also, it is necessary to generate an inverted clock, which is applied to the dummy switch. In some cases, the dummy switch is a transistor with the gate attached to the source of M1, and the source and drain of the dummy switch connected to the inverse clock. This avoids charge pumping of the substrate, which can defeat the purpose of the dummy switch. Clock feedthrough can be reduced by using the largest circuit capacitors possible, using minimum geometry switches, and keeping the clock swings as small as possible. Typically, these solutions will create problems in other areas, requiring a compromise to be made.

Some of the problems associated with single-channel MOS switches can be avoided with the CMOS switch shown in Fig. 5.1-15. Using CMOS technology, a switch is usually constructed by paralleling p-channel and n-channel enhancement transistors; therefore, when ϕ is low ($\overline{\phi}$ is high) both transistors are off, creating an effective open circuit. When ϕ is high ($\overline{\phi}$ is low) both transistors are on, giving a low-impedance state. The on resistance of the CMOS switch can be lower than 1 kΩ while the off leakage current is in the 1 pA range. The bulk potentials of the p-channel (V_{BP}) and the n-channel devices (V_{BN}) are taken to the highest and lowest potentials, respectively. It is also possible to apply the clocks to the bulks of the MOS devices to improve their switching characteristics.

The CMOS switch has two advantages over the single-channel MOS switch. The first advantage is that the dynamic analog signal range in the on state is greatly increased. The second is that since the n-channel and p-channel devices are in parallel and require opposing clock signals, the feedthrough due to the clock will be diminished through cancellation.

The increased signal amplitude of the analog signal can be seen to be a direct result of using complementary devices. When one of the transistors is being turned off because of a large analog signal on the drain and source, this large analog signal will be causing the other transistor to be fully on. As a consequence, both transistors of Fig. 5.1-15 are on for analog signal amplitudes less than the clock

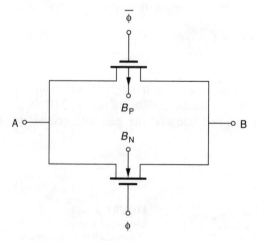

FIGURE 5.1-15
A CMOS switch.

magnitude, and at least one of the transistors is on for analog signal amplitudes equal to the magnitude of the clock signal.

The feedthrough cancellation of the CMOS switch in Fig. 5.1-15 is not complete for two reasons. One is that the feedthrough capacitances of the n-channel device are not necessarily equal to the feedthrough capacitances of the p-channel device. The second reason is that the turn-on delay of each type of transistor is not equal, and so the channel conductances do not necessarily track each other during turn-on and turn-off.

CMOS switches are generally used in place of single-channel switches when the technology permits. Although the CMOS switches have larger parasitics than single-channel switches, these parasitics can be minimized through the use of circuit techniques that will be illustrated in Chapter 8. The clock circuitry for CMOS switches is more complex because of the requirement for a complementary clock. The configuration of Fig. 5.1-15 is often called a transmission gate.

One must be careful in using switches where the power supply voltages are small. If $|V_{DD} - V_{SS}|$ is less than 5 V, it will become necessary to use a CMOS technology with twin wells so that the bulk potentials can be switched as shown in Fig. 5.1-16 in order to achieve low values of on resistance. It is

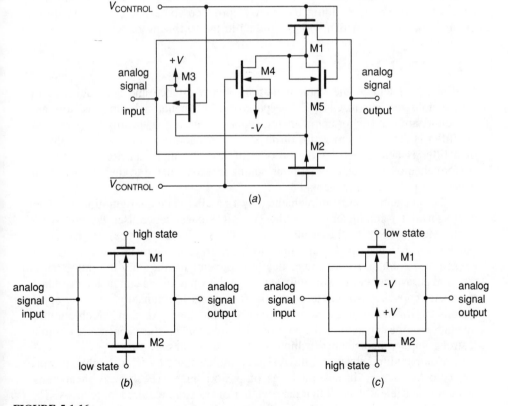

(a)

(b)

(c)

FIGURE 5.1-16
A twin-well CMOS switch with control circuitry: (a) Circuit, (b) On state, (c) Off state.

assumed that V_{CONTROL} and $\overline{V_{\text{CONTROL}}}$ are generated from the clock waveform. When V_{CONTROL} is high, the transmission gate is on. The equivalent circuit in this condition is shown in Fig. 5.1-16b. Here we see that the n-channel gate is taken to the high state and the p-channel gate is in the low state. Also the substrates have been connected together by means of the switches M3, M4, and M5. M3 and M4 are off while M5 is on. This helps to keep the switch on resistance from being a function of the analog signal potential. When V_{CONTROL} is low, the transmission gate is off and has the equivalent circuit shown in Fig. 5.1-16c. The bulks of the n- and p-channel device terminals have been taken to $-V$ and $+V$, respectively, since M3 and M4 are on and M5 is off. This insures that the off state will be maintained since V_{BS} is strongly reverse-biased and causes a large V_T.

If $| V_{\text{DD}} - V_{\text{SS}} |$ is less than 4 V, switches can only be used if a clock signal of 5 V or higher can be obtained. One can either apply external clocks or use a voltage doubler to provide an on-chip voltage which is higher than $| V_{\text{DD}} - V_{\text{SS}} |$.

In this section we have seen that the MOS transistor makes a good switch realization for integrated circuits. They require small area, dissipate very little power, and provide reasonable values of R_{ON} and R_{OFF} for most applications. This section has also illustrated the importance of the terminal voltages on the behavior of the MOS transistor. The incorporation of a good realization of a switch into the basic building blocks will produce some interesting and useful circuits and systems which will be studied in the following material.

5.2   ACTIVE RESISTORS

In Chapters 2 and 3, the implementation of a resistance and a capacitance by IC technologies was discussed. The passive components including resistors and capacitors are very important in analog signal processing. Typically the gain of an amplifier is determined by ratios of resistors or capacitors while the time constant of a filter is determined by the product of resistors and capacitors. Thus, the performance of many analog systems can be directly related to their resistive and capacitive passive components.

The capacitor can be implemented as a parallel plate configuration of a conductor-insulator-conductor sandwich. The MOS capacitance uses the thin oxide of the MOS process as the insulator while the conductors (plates) can be metal, polysilicon, or a heavily doped semiconductor. The conductor-insulator-conductor capacitor was found to be a near ideal component, having only the problems of size and parasitics. For reasonable area usage the value of the conductor-insulator-conductor capacitor is limited to the 10–20 pF range. Fortunately, in many applications the influence of the parasitics can be eliminated. Another possible implementation of the capacitor is the pn junction capacitance. This capacitance exhibits a strong voltage dependence, which limits its usefulness.

Compared to capacitors, the resistors implemented by IC technologies were found to be lacking in several areas of performance. The typical sheet resistance was sufficiently small that large values of resistors required large areas. The higher value of resistance attained with pinched resistors suffered nonlinearity. In addition, the tolerance of the resistors, their temperature coefficient, and their voltage coefficient were all poorer than those of the capacitor. Of course, modifications to the standard IC technology can result in better resistor implementation. However, the objective of this section is to investigate ways of emulating a resistor without having the inherent disadvantages using standard IC technologies.

We shall discuss two ways of implementing resistors that have found use in integrated circuit design. The first method is to use active devices, such as those introduced in Sec. 3.4, and the second method is to use switched capacitors. The first method has the advantage of minimizing the area required for resistors, and the second has the advantage of a resistor whose accuracy is dependent upon the frequency of a clock and a capacitor. It will be shown that the *RC* time constant accuracy of circuits using a switched capacitor resistor simulation is equivalent to the relative accuracy of the capacitor, which is quite good.

There are two distinct applications of resistors that are important. These applications are dc resistors and ac resistors. The dc resistor is typically used to provide a dc voltage drop given a dc current. The ac resistor provides an ac voltage drop given an ac current. Figure 5.2-1 illustrates the difference, although in many cases the resistor is used simultaneously as both an ac and dc resistor. As a dc resistor, Fig. 5.2-1 shows that a dc voltage drop of V_Q is produced for a dc current of I_Q. As an ac resistor, Fig. 5.2-1 shows that an ac voltage of ΔV_Q is produced for an ac current of ΔI_Q. The use of an active element to implement a dc resistor will be considered first.

Ignoring the substrate terminal for the moment, the MOS and BJT transistors are three-terminal devices. Through proper connection of these three terminals,

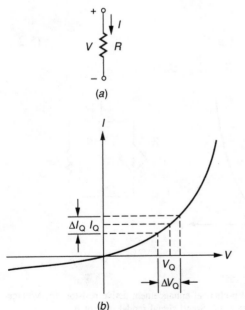

(a)

(b)

FIGURE 5.2-1
The distinction between a dc and an ac resistor. (a) Resistor, (b) I-V characteristics.

the active device becomes a two-terminal resistor called an *active resistor*. The active resistor can be used in place of a polysilicon or diffused resistor to produce a dc voltage drop and/or provide a small signal resistance that is linear over a small range. There are many cases where the area required to obtain a small signal resistance is more important than the linearity. A small MOS or BJT device can simulate a resistor in much less area than is required with an equivalent polysilicon or diffused resistor.

The active resistor can be implemented by simply connecting the gate of an n- or p-channel enhancement MOS device to the drain, as shown in Fig. 5.2-2a and b. For the n-channel device, the source should be placed at the most negative power supply voltage, V_{SS}, if possible, to eliminate the bulk effect. The source of the p-channel device should be taken to the most positive voltage for the same reason. Since V_{GS} is now equal to V_{DS}, the transconductance curve (I_D vs. V_{GS}) of the MOS transistor shown in Fig. 5.2-2c characterizes the large signal behavior of the active resistor. This curve is valid for both the n- and p-channel enhancement transistors for the polarities shown. It is seen that the resistance is not linear, which was anticipated. In many circumstances, the signal swing is very small, and in these cases the active resistor works very well. Since the connection of the gate to the drain guarantees operation in the saturation region for $V > V_T$, the *I–V* characteristics can be written as

$$I = I_D = \frac{K'W}{2L}\left[(V_{GS} - V_T)^2\right] \tag{5.2-1}$$

or

$$V = V_{GS} = V_{DS} = V_T + \left(\frac{2I_D L}{K'W}\right)^{1/2} \tag{5.2-2}$$

where

$$K' = \mu_o C_{ox} \tag{5.2-3}$$

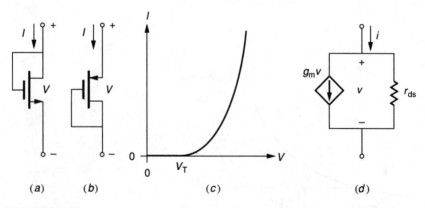

FIGURE 5.2-2
(*a*) n-channel enhancement active resistor, (*b*) p-channel enhancement active resistor, (*c*) Voltage–current characteristics of the MOS active resistor, (*d*) Small signal model of *a* or *b*.

If either V or I is defined, then the other variable can be found by using Eq. 5.2-1 or Eq. 5.2-2.

Connecting the gate to the drain means that V_{DS} controls I_D, and therefore the channel transconductance becomes a channel conductance. The small signal conductance can be found by differentiating Eq. 5.2-1 with respect to V, resulting in

$$g = \frac{\partial I}{\partial V} \cong \left(\frac{2I\,K'W}{L}\right)^{1/2} = \frac{K'W}{L}(V - V_T) \qquad (5.2\text{-}4)$$

Another method of finding the small signal conductance is to use the small signal model of the MOS transistor of Fig. 3.1-14. The small signal model of the active resistor valid for either the n- or the p-channel active resistor is shown in Fig. 5.2-2d where $r_{ds} = 1/g_{ds}$. Assuming $v_{bs} = 0$, it is easily seen that the small signal conductance of these circuits is

$$g = \frac{1 + g_m r_{ds}}{r_{ds}} \cong g_m \qquad (5.2\text{-}5)$$

where $g_m r_{ds}$ is greater than unity. The influence of an ac bulk voltage can be incorporated into Eq. 5.2-5 using the same model (see Prob. 5.8). In either case, we note how the value of g depends upon the dc values of V and I (refer back to Table 3.1-3 in Chapter 3 for the dependence of g_m and r_{ds} upon V and I).

The bipolar junction transistor can be used to form an active resistor in the same manner as for the MOS transistor. The circuit of Fig. 5.2-3 is topologically identical to the MOS circuit of Fig. 5.2-2. When operating in the forward active region, it follows from Eq. 3.3-10 that the I–V characteristics of the BJT active resistor can be expressed as

$$I \cong I_S \exp\left(V / V_t\right) \qquad (5.2\text{-}6)$$

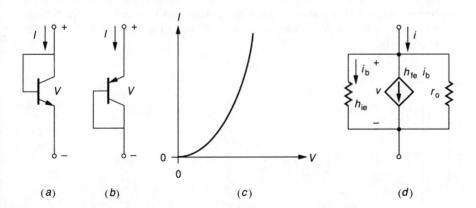

(a) (b) (c) (d)

FIGURE 5.2-3
(a) npn BJT active resistor, (b) pnp BJT active resistor, (c) Voltage-current characteristics of the BJT active resistor, (d) Small signal model for the BJT active resistor.

or

$$V = V_t \ln \left[\frac{I}{I_s} \right] \tag{5.2-7}$$

where

I_S = reverse saturation current of the emitter base junction
$V_t = (kT)/q = 0.026$ V at room temperature

The small signal conductance of the BJT active resistor can be found by differentiating Eq. 5.2-6 with respect to V ($= V_{BE}$) to get

$$g = \frac{\partial I}{\partial V} = \frac{|I|}{V_t} \tag{5.2-8}$$

The small signal model of Fig. 5.2-3d, derived from Fig. 3.3-8, can also be used to more accurately calculate the small signal conductance and gives

$$g = h_{oe} + \frac{1 + h_{fe}}{h_{ie}} \tag{5.2-9}$$

These small signal model parameters have been defined in Table 3.3-4 of Chapter 3. The dependence of g upon the dc values of the BJT active resistor are indicated by Table 3.3-4.

Active resistors can be used to produce a dc voltage or to provide a small signal resistance. An example illustrating the application of the active resistor to provide a dc voltage follows.

Example 5.2-1. Voltage division using active resistors. Figure 5.2-4 shows the use of an n-channel MOS active resistor and a p-channel MOS active resistor to provide a dc voltage, V_{out}. Find a W/L ratio for M1 and M2 that give V_{out} of 1 V if $V_{DD} = 5$ V, $V_{SS} = -5$ V and $I = 50$ μA. Assume that $V_{TN} = +0.75$ V, $V_{TP} = -0.75$ V, $K'_N = 2.4 \times 10^{-5}$ A/V^2 and $K'_P = 0.8 \times 10^{-5}$ A/V^2.

Solutions. Both bulks are connected to their respective sources so that the body effect has no influence. Also since $V_{DG} = 0$, both transistors are saturated. Since the currents through both transistors must be the same and V_{DS1} and V_{DS2} are defined, we can solve for the W/L ratios of M1 and M2 using Eq. 5.2-1 as 0.15 and 1.18, respectively.

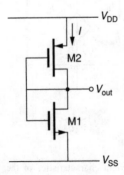

FIGURE 5.2-4
Use of active resistors to achieve voltage division.

BJT active resistors can be used to divide voltages in the same manner as illustrated in the example; however, the voltages across the BJT are limited to less than 1 V.

The use of active resistors to develop large dc voltages requires large currents or W/L ratios that are much less than unity. This can be circumvented by cascading devices as shown in Fig. 5.2-5. The voltages V_1, V_2 and V_3 are given by Eq. 5.2-2, where I is from a known current source. If the voltages are specified, then the W/L ratio of each device can be determined from Eq. 5.2-2 if the bulk–source voltage is taken into consideration. If the W/L ratios are given, then the voltages V_1 through V_3 can be calculated starting with V_1. Using more than one device to drop the voltage will result in W/L ratios closer to unity and smaller dc currents.

> **Example 5.2-2. Replacement of one active resistor by two.** An n-channel MOS active resistor is used to produce a dc voltage drop of 5 V from a 25 μA current. Assuming that the bulk–source effects can be neglected, (a) find the W/L ratio of a single active resistor, and (b) find the W/L ratio of two identical n-channel active resistors in series replacing the single active resistor of (a). Assume that the MOS parameters of Example 5.2-1 are valid in this example. Compare the gate area required for both cases.

> **Solution.** For case (a) we get $W/L = 1/8.7$. If we assume that W has a unit length, then the gate area required is 8.7 square units. For case (b) we find that the W/L of one of the transistors is $1/1.47$. If $W = 1$, then $L = 1.47$ with a gate area of 1.47, two identical active resistors would require 2.94 square units. A savings in gate area of almost 3 to 1 results in case (b) compared to case (a). The source and drain area would reduce this ratio.

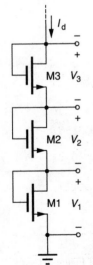

FIGURE 5.2-5
Use of cascaded devices to create large voltage drops.

The second application of a resistor is to provide an ac voltage (or current) for a given ac current (or voltage). In this presentation, the dc current will be zero. For a zero dc current, the active resistors of Figs. 5.2-2 and 5.2-3 are not satisfactory because the value of resistance approaches infinity. The switches of Figs. 5.1-3 and 5.1-4 make a much better realization of an ac resistor with the MOS switch being nearly linear and having no dc offset. By controlling the value of voltage between the gate and source, one can get a linear ac resistance for values ΔV up to 1 V.

> **Example 5.2-3. A MOS switch as an ac resistor.** Assume that the circuit of Fig. 5.1-4a is to be used to implement an ac resistor of 2000 Ω and that the device parameters are $V_T = 0.75$ V, $K'_N = 24 \,\mu\text{A/V}^2$, $\gamma_N = 0.8 \,\text{V}^{1/2}$, $\lambda = 0.01 \,\text{V}^{-1}$, and $\phi = 0.6$ V. If $W = 50 \,\mu$, $L = 10 \,\mu$, $V_{DS} = 0$, and $V_{BS} = -5$ V, find the value of V_{GS} ($= V_C$).
>
> **Solution.** The threshold voltage due to $V_{BS} = -5$ V is 2.023 V. Equating 2000 Ω to Eq. 5.1-2 of Sec. 5.1 gives a value of $V_{GS} = 6.19$ V. The dotted line in Fig. 5.1-4b corresponds to a resistance of 2000 Ω. Figure 5.1-4b shows that the 2000 Ω resistor is closely approximated by this value of V_{GS}.

The linearity of the ac resistor in the example is limited for negative values of V_{DS} by the effects of V_{BS} and for positive values of V_{DS} by V_{DS} itself. The bulk influences the linearity by causing V_T to change. The drain–source voltage influences the linearity by leaving the ohmic region and entering the saturation region. Techniques for eliminating both of these effects will now be considered.

Figure 5.2-6 shows how to eliminate the influence of V_{DS} upon the ac resistor realization.[1] The principle employed is to use two identical devices biased

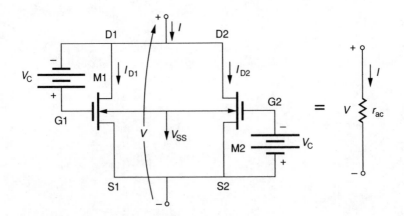

FIGURE 5.2-6
Configuration to eliminate the effects of V_{DS} in the ac resistor implementation of Figure 5.1-4a.

so that the influences of V_{DS} cancel. Using Eq. 3 of Table 3.1-1 to obtain expressions for I_{D1} and I_{D2} gives

$$
\begin{aligned}
I_{D1} &= K_N' \left(\frac{W_1}{L_1} \right) \left[(V_{GS1} - V_{T1}) V_{DS1} - \frac{V_{DS1}^2}{2} \right] \\
&= K_N' \left(\frac{W_1}{L_1} \right) \left[(V_{DS1} + V_C - V_{T1}) V_{DS1} - \frac{V_{DS1}^2}{2} \right] \qquad (5.2\text{-}10) \\
&= K_N' \left(\frac{W_1}{L_1} \right) \left[\frac{V_{DS1}^2}{2} + (V_C - V_{T1}) V_{DS1} \right]
\end{aligned}
$$

and

$$
\begin{aligned}
I_{D2} &= K_N' \left(\frac{W_2}{L_2} \right) \left[(V_{GS2} - V_{T2}) V_{DS2} - \frac{V_{DS2}^2}{2} \right] \\
&\qquad\qquad\qquad\qquad\qquad\qquad\qquad\qquad (5.2\text{-}11) \\
&= K_N' \left(\frac{W_2}{L_2} \right) \left[(V_C - V_{T2}) V_{DS2} - \frac{V_{DS2}^2}{2} \right]
\end{aligned}
$$

Noting that $V_{DS1} = V_{DS2} = V$ and assuming matched transistors allows the current I to be expressed as

$$
I = I_{D1} + I_{D2} = \frac{2K_N' W}{L} (V_C - V_T) V_{DS} \qquad (5.2\text{-}12)
$$

Thus the value of ac resistance found by differentiating Eq. 5.2-12 with respect to I is

$$
r_{ac} = \frac{\partial V_{DS}}{\partial I} = \frac{1}{2K_N'(W/L)(V_C - V_T)} \qquad (5.2\text{-}13)
$$

In the development of Eq. 5.2-13, it has been assumed that the transistors remain in the ohmic region or that V_{DS} is less than $V_{GS} - V_T$. This assumption places the following constraint on the value of V for Eq. 5.2-13 to be valid.

$$
V < (V_C - V_T) \qquad (5.2\text{-}14)
$$

Therefore, a larger value of V_C will lead to a larger range of V. While the linearity range has been increased, the dependence upon V_{BS} through V_T is still present and must be eliminated to achieve a wide linearity range.

In many applications, resistors are used differentially in pairs. In these cases it is possible to achieve an increase in linearity and to eventually even cancel the bulk effects. A method of canceling the effects of V_{DS} will be discussed first. Figure 5.2-7a shows a pair of ac resistors used in a differential configuration.[2] Note that a differential signal (V_1) is applied to the left-hand side of the resistors

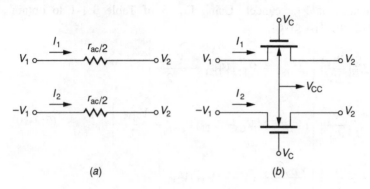

FIGURE 5.2-7
(a) Differential ac resistor configuration, (b) Single-MOS implementation of a.

while the right-hand side is at the same potential (although not physically connected). Again Eq. 3 of Table 3.1-1 can be used to write

$$I_1 = \frac{K_N'W}{L}\left[(V_C - V_2 - V_T)(V_1 - V_2) - \frac{1}{2}(V_1 - V_2)^2\right] \qquad (5.2\text{-}15)$$

and

$$-I_2 = \frac{K_N'W}{L}\left[(V_C + V_1 - V_T)(V_2 + V_1) - \frac{1}{2}(V_2 + V_1)^2\right] \qquad (5.2\text{-}16)$$

Adding Eqs. 5.2-15 and 5.2-16 gives

$$I_1 - I_2 = \frac{K_N'W}{L}(V_C - V_T)2V_1 \qquad (5.2\text{-}17)$$

Defining r_{ac} as

$$r_{ac} = \frac{2V_1}{I_1 - I_2} \qquad (5.2\text{-}18)$$

gives

$$r_{ac} = \frac{1}{(K_N'W/L)(V_C - V_T)} \qquad (5.2\text{-}19)$$

Therefore, Fig. 5.2-7a simulates a resistor r_{ac} which is independent of V_1 or V_2 as long as

$$|V_1 - V_2| = V < V_C - V_T \qquad (5.2\text{-}20)$$

Figures 5.2-8a and b show the I–V characteristics of the resistors of Figs. 5.2-6 and 5.2-7b using n-channel transistors having $W = 50\ \mu$, $L = 10\ \mu$ and model parameters of $V_T = 0.75$ V, $K_N' = 24\ \mu\text{A/V}^2$, $\gamma_N = 0.8\ \text{V}^{1/2}$, $\lambda_N = 0.01\ \text{V}^{-1}$, and $\phi_N = 0.6$ V. The characteristics of Fig. 5.2-8a and b are almost identical and considerably more linear than Fig. 5.1-4b. For large values of V_C, the linearity range increases, as predicted by Eq. 5.2-20.

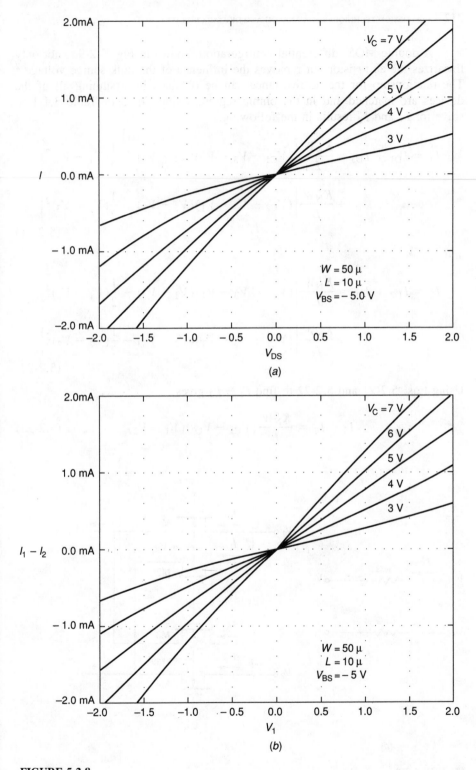

FIGURE 5.2-8
I–V characteristics of: (*a*) Parallel MOS resistor, (*b*) A single-MOS differential resistor. (Note that the actual voltage across Fig. 5.2-7 is $2V_1$.)

A double-MOS, differential configuration, shown in Fig. 5.2-9a, not only linearizes the ac resistor but removes the influence of the bulk-source voltage.[2] The relationship for the ac resistance can be obtained by assuming all of the devices are matched and in the ohmic region. Using Eq. 3 of Table 3.1-1 to solve for I_1 and I_2 results in the following.

$$I_1 = I_{D1} + I_{D3} = \frac{K_N'W}{L}\left[(V_{C1} - V_3 - V_T)(V_1 - V_3) - \frac{1}{2}(V_1 - V_3)^2\right]$$

$$+ \frac{K_N'W}{L}\left[(V_{C2} - V_3 - V_T)(V_2 - V_3) - \frac{1}{2}(V_2 - V_3)^2\right]$$

$$(5.2\text{-}21)$$

and

$$I_2 = I_{D2} + I_{D4} = \frac{K_N'W}{L}\left[(V_{C2} - V_3 - V_T)(V_1 - V_3) - \frac{1}{2}(V_1 - V_3)^2\right]$$

$$+ \frac{K_N'W}{L}\left[(V_{C1} - V_3 - V_T)(V_2 - V_3) - \frac{1}{2}(V_2 - V_3)^2\right]$$

$$(5.2\text{-}22)$$

Using Eqs. 5.2-21 and 5.2-22 to find $I_1 - I_2$ gives

$$I_1 - I_2 = \frac{K_N'W}{L}(V_{C1} - V_{C2})(V_1 - V_2) \qquad (5.2\text{-}23)$$

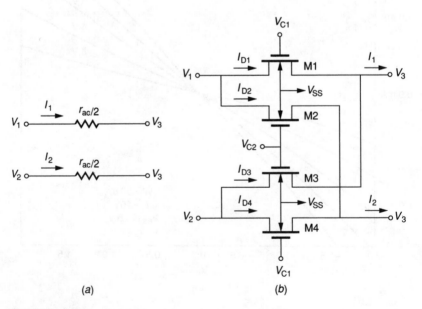

(a)   (b)

FIGURE 5.2-9

(a) Differential ac resistor configuration, (b) Double-MOS implementation of a.

r_{ac} can be found as

$$r_{ac} = \frac{V_1 - V_2}{I_1 - I_2} = \frac{1}{(K_N'W/L)(V_{C1} - V_{C2})} \qquad (5.2\text{-}24)$$

Because all devices have been assumed to be in the ohmic region, Eq. 5.2-24 only holds when

$$V_1, V_2 \leq \min[V_{C1} - V_T, V_{C2} - V_T] \qquad (5.2\text{-}25)$$

Figure 5.2-10 is a simulation of Fig. 5.2-9b when $V_{C1} = 7$ V, $V_3 = 0$, $V_{BS} = -5$ V and using the same device parameters as have been used for Figs. 5.1-4 and 5.2-7. It is of interest to compare the ac resistor realizations of Figs. 5.1-4, 5.2-6, 5.2-7b and 5.2-9b. Of all the realizations, the double-MOSFET differential resistor of Fig. 5.2-9b is superior in linearity. However, the double-MOSFET differential resistor is really a transresistance in that the voltages and currents are at different terminals. This restricts the double-MOSFET differential resistance to transresistance applications that are found in differential-in, differential-out op amps. The parallel MOS resistor of Fig. 5.2-6 and the single-MOSFET differential resistor of Fig. 5.2-7b are true resistor realizations that have approximately the same linearity. However, the parallel MOS resistor is a true floating resistor realization while the single MOSFET differential resistor must have a differential signal with reference

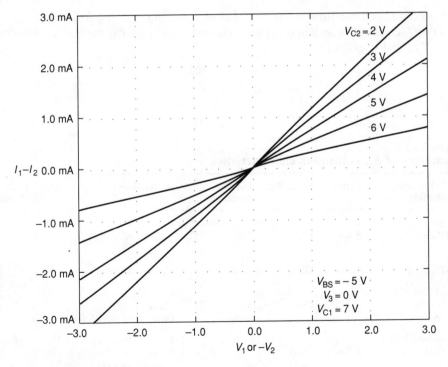

FIGURE 5.2-10
I–V characteristics of a double-MOS differential resistor.

to V_2 of Fig. 5.2-7b. The performances of the ac resistor realizations that have been presented are summarized in Table 5.2-1.

A second approach to realizing ac resistors uses switches and capacitors. This approach is *discrete-time* and is often called the *switched capacitor* (SC) realization. If the clock rate is high enough, combinations of switches and capacitors can implement a resistor that is dependent only on the clock frequency and the capacitor. Four combinations of switches and capacitors will be considered.

The first approach to resistor simulation is called the parallel switched capacitor realization and is shown in Fig. 5.2-11a. It will be shown that under certain conditions, namely those found in a sampled data system, that the switched capacitor of Fig. 5.2-11a is an approximate realization of the resistor of Fig. 5.2-11b. Figure 5.2-11c shows the clock waveforms that control the opening and closing of the switches in Fig. 5.2-11a. Let us assume that V_1 and V_2 are two independent dc voltage sources. This assumption represents no loss of generality since the conditions for a sampled data system state that the "signals," V_1 and V_2, are sampled at a rate that is sufficiently high that any change in V_1 or V_2 during a sampling period can be ignored.

Under steady state conditions, we can express the charge flow in the direction of I_1 over a time period from t_0 to $t_0 + T$ as

$$q_1(t_0 + T) = \int_{t_0}^{t_0 + T} I_1(t)\,dt \qquad (5.2\text{-}26)$$

However, this charge flow in the direction of I_1 during the time period from t_0 to $t_0 + T$ can be broken into two parts. The first part is the charge flowing from t_0 to $T/2$ and is given as

$$q_1\left(t_0 + \frac{T}{2}\right) = C\left[V_1\left(t_0 + \frac{T}{2}\right) - V_2(t_0)\right] \approx C(V_1 - V_2) \qquad (5.2\text{-}27)$$

TABLE 5.2-1
Summary of R_{ac} realization characteristics

AC resistance realization	Figure	Linearity	How controlled	Restrictions
Single MOSFET	5.1-4	Poor	Gate voltage W/L	$V_{BULK} < \min(V_S, V_D)$
Parallel MOSFET	5.2-6	Good	V_C W/L	$V < V_C - V_T$ $V_{BULK} < \min(V_S, V_D)$
Single-MOSFET differential resistor	5.2-7a	Good	V_C W/L	$\|V_1 - V_2\| < V_C - V_T$ $V_{BULK} < -V_1$ Differential around V_2
Double-MOSFET differential resistor	5.2-9a	Good	$(V_{C1} - V_{C2})$ W/L	$V_1, V_2 < \min(V_{C1} - V_T, V_{C2} - V_T)$ $V_{BULK} < \min(V_1, V_2)$ Transresistance only

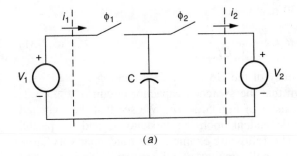

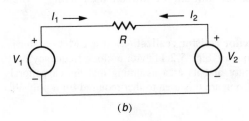

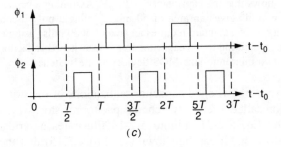

FIGURE 5.2-11
(a) Parallel switched capacitor resistor realization, (b) A continuous resistor, (c) Clock waveforms for the switches of a.

The second part is the charge flowing from $T/2$ to T and is given as

$$q_1(t_0 + T) - q_1\left(t_0 + \frac{T}{2}\right) = 0$$

Therefore, Eq. 5.2-26 can be written as,

$$q_1(t_0 + T) = C(V_1 - V_2) = \int_{t_0}^{t_0+T} I_1(t)dt \qquad (5.2\text{-}28)$$

Dividing both sides of Eq. 5.2-28 by T results in

$$\frac{C(V_1 - V_2)}{T} = \frac{1}{T}\int_{t_0}^{t_0+T} I_1(t) = I_1(\text{aver}) \qquad (5.2\text{-}29)$$

Now let us find the average current, $I_1(\text{aver})$, flowing into the left-hand side of the continuous resistor of Fig. 5.2-11b. This value is given as

$$I_1(\text{aver}) = I_1 = \frac{V_1 - V_2}{R} \qquad (5.2\text{-}30)$$

Equating Eqs. 5.2-29 and 5.2-30 results in

$$R = \frac{T}{C} = \frac{1}{Cf_{clock}}$$ (5.2-31)

where $f_{clock} = 1/T$ is the frequency of the clock signals ϕ_1 and ϕ_2.

Therefore, we have shown that the switched capacitor circuit of Fig. 5.2-11*a* simulates the continuous resistor of Fig. 5.2-11*b*. We see that the switched capacitor resistor realization is dependent upon the capacitor C and the period or the frequency of the clock. The following example illustrates that very large resistors can be realized with a small amount of silicon area using switched capacitors.

Example 5.2-4. Switched capacitor resistor realization. If a 1 MΩ resistor is to be realized using the SC technique of Fig. 5.2-11 with a clock frequency of 100 kHz find the value of the capacitor and its area assuming that the capacitor is a polysilicon-to-polysilicon type. Compare this area to that required for a polysilicon resistor of the same value.

Solution. Equation 5.2-31 shows that the capacitance is 10 pF. Assuming a capacitance per unit area of 0.2 pF/mil^2 gives an area of 50 mils^2. Using a polysilicon resistor with a sheet resistivity of 25 Ω/square requires an area of 3600 mils^2 using a minimum width of 0.3 mils. In addition to the capacitor area, the switched capacitor resistor realization requires two minimum-size MOS devices as the switches.

There are several other types of switched capacitor realizations of resistors. Figure 5.2-12 shows a realization called a series switched capacitor resistor, which results in a resistance given by Eq. 5.2-31. Figure 5.2-13 illustrates a series-parallel switched capacitor realization. It can be shown (see Prob. 5.15) that the equivalent resistance of the series-parallel switched capacitor resistor realization is

$$R = \frac{T}{C_1 + C_2} = \frac{1}{(C_1 + C_2)f_{clock}}$$ (5.2-32)

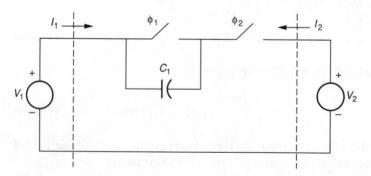

FIGURE 5.2-12
Series switched capacitor realization of a continuous resistor.

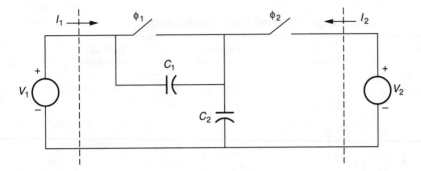

FIGURE 5.2-13
Series-parallel switched capacitor realization of a continuous resistance.

Figure 5.2-14 shows a switched capacitor resistor realization called the bilinear realization. The equivalent resistance of the bilinear switched capacitor resistance realization is (see Prob. 5.16)

$$R = \frac{T}{4C} = \frac{1}{4Cf_{clock}} \qquad (5.2\text{-}33)$$

Table 5.2-2 summarizes the four switched capacitor resistor realizations discussed here.

This section has focused on the realization of dc and ac resistors using methods compatible with the standard IC technologies. It is discovered the MOS technology offers many more opportunities in this area. The reader will see all of these resistor realizations used along with other components in the following material. The most important concepts presented are the methods by which the dependence of drain current on the drain–source and bulk–source voltages can be reduced and the method by which resistors can be simulated by switches

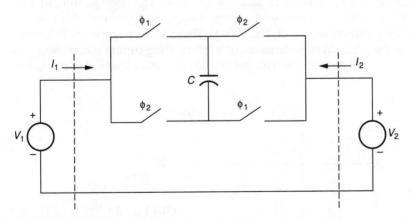

FIGURE 5.2-14
Bilinear switched capacitor realization of a continuous resistance.

TABLE 5.2-2
Summary of switched capacitor resistance realizations

SC resistor realization	Figure	Equivalent resistance	Type of resistance
Parallel	5.2-11a	T/C	Transresistance
Series	5.2-12	T/C	Resistance or transresistance
Series-parallel	5.2-13	$\dfrac{T}{C_1 + C_2}$	Transresistance
Bilinear	5.2-14	$\dfrac{T}{4C}$	Transresistance or resistance

and capacitors. Because the resistors realized by switched capacitor circuits are inversely proportional to capacitance, the effective RC time constants become proportional to capacitor ratios. The result is that time constants can be accurately realized using capacitors and switched capacitor resistor realizations.

5.3 CURRENT SOURCES AND SINKS

In this section we consider the realization of current sinks and sources that use standard bipolar or MOS devices. An ideal *current source* is a two-terminal element whose current is constant for any voltage across the source. The voltage across a current source depends upon the external circuitry. Figures 5.3-1a and b give the schematic symbol and the *I–V* characteristics of a current source whose value is I_o. Most current source applications require one of their terminals to be common with the most positive or the most negative dc voltage in the circuit. This leads to the two possible configurations illustrated in Fig. 5.3-2. V_P and V_N are the most positive and most negative dc voltages, respectively. The configuration of Fig. 5.3-2a will be referred to as a *current sink*. The configuration of Fig. 5.3-2b will be called a *current source* even though we have used this notation for the general current source of Fig. 5.3-1. These two categories will become important in the practical considerations of implementing current sources/sinks. A third category is the *floating current source*, where neither terminal is connected to V_P or V_N.

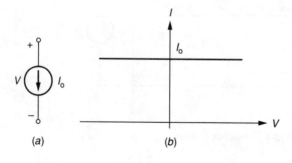

(a)   *(b)*

FIGURE 5.3-1
(*a*) Schematic symbol for a current source, (*b*) *I–V* characteristics of an ideal current source.

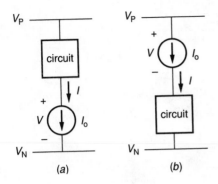

FIGURE 5.3-2
(a) A current sink, (b) A current source.

In most current source/sink realizations, the ideal curve of Fig. 5.3-1b is only approximated over a limited range of the voltage V. Also the current is rarely bidirectional. The resulting $I-V$ characteristics of a practical current source/sink realization are shown in Fig. 5.3-3. It is seen that there is a minimum voltage, V_{MIN}, below which the current source/sink will not be a good approximation to I_o. Further, it is seen that even in the region where the current source/sink is a reasonably good approximation to I_o, the actual source/sink deviates by a resistance R_o, which represents the parallel resistance of the current source/sink and ideally is infinite. Thus, the two major aspects by which a current source/sink is characterized are V_{MIN} and R_o.

Figure 5.3-4a shows a BJT realization of a current sink. V_{BB} is a battery used to bias Q1. It follows that for $V > V_{CE}$ (sat) the current value is given by the following relation.

$$I_o = I_S \exp\left(\frac{V_{BB}}{V_t}\right) \tag{5.3-1}$$

V_{CE} (sat) is the collector-emitter voltage where Q1 enters the forward saturation region.

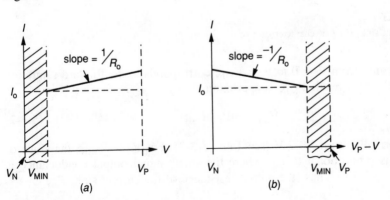

FIGURE 5.3-3
Practical $I-V$ characteristics for: (a) A current sink, (b) A current source.

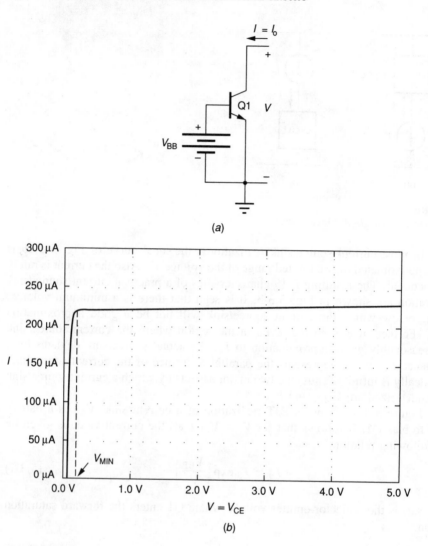

FIGURE 5.3-4
(*a*) BJT current sink, (*b*) *I–V* characteristics of *a*.

The region from $V = 0$ to $V = V_{MIN}$ corresponds to the forward saturation region of Q1. As a result V_{MIN} is approximated by

$$V_{MIN} \approx V_{CE}\,(\text{sat}) \tag{5.3-2}$$

which is normally around 0.2 V (see Table 3.3-2). For $V > V_{MIN}$, the slope of the current is proportional to g_o, where the small signal output conductance is given in Table 3.3-4. Thus, the output resistance of the current sink, R_o, is

$$R_o \approx \frac{1}{g_o} = \frac{V_{AF}}{I_o} \tag{5.3-3}$$

Equations 5.3-1 through 5.3-3 also hold for the current source as characterized by Fig. 5.3-3b.

Figure 5.3-4b shows the I–V characteristics of the circuit of Fig. 5.3-4a with $V_{BE} = 0.7$ V, $I_S = 0.4$ fA, $\beta_F = 100$, and $V_{AF} = 200$ V. With these values V_{MIN} should be approximately 0.2 V, $I_o = 219$ μA, and $R_o = 913$ kΩ for $V_t = 25.9$ mV. A SPICE simulation for the circuit of Fig. 5.3-4b gives $V_{MIN} = 0.2$ V, $I_o = 220$ μA, and $R_o = 889$ kΩ.

Figure 5.3-5a shows a MOS realization of a current sink. From Eq. 3.1-5, if $\lambda = 0$, the value of I_o is given as

$$I_o = \frac{K_N' W}{2L}(V_{GG} - V_T)^2 \tag{5.3-4}$$

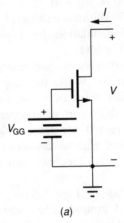

(a)

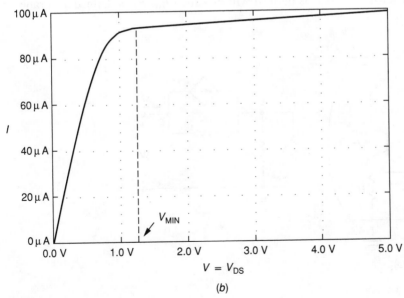

(b)

FIGURE 5.3-5
(a) MOS current sink, (b) I–V characteristics of a.

The value of V_{MIN} is equal to $V_{DS}(sat)$ and is given in Eq. 3.1-3 as

$$V_{MIN} = V_{GG} - V_T \tag{5.3-5}$$

The output resistance of the current sink for $V > V_{MIN}$ is equal to $1/g_{ds}$ of the small signal model parameters of the MOS (see Table 3.1-3) and is

$$R_o = \frac{1}{g_{ds}} = \frac{1}{\lambda |I_o|} \tag{5.3-6}$$

Equations 5.3-4 through 5.3-6 also hold for the MOS current source using the characterization of Fig. 5.3-3b.

Figure 5.3-5b shows the $I-V$ characteristics of the circuit of Fig. 5.3-5a with $V_{GG} = 2.0$ V, $W = 50\ \mu$, $L = 10\ \mu$, $V_T = 0.75$ V, $K'_N = 24\ \mu$ A/V^2, $\gamma_N = 0.8$ V$^{1/2}$, $\lambda = 0.01$ V^{-1} and $\phi = 0.6$ V. With these values, $V_{MIN} = 1.25$ V, $I_o = 94 \mu$A, and $R_o = 1.064$ MΩ. A SPICE simulation for Fig. 5.3-5b gives $V_{MIN} = 1.2$ V, $I_o = 97\ \mu$A, and $R_o = 1.079$ MΩ.

The BJT and MOS current source/sinks are reasonable approximations of the ideal for limited values of voltage. While the output resistance of both are similar, the BJT has a much smaller value of V_{MIN}. In many cases, the output resistance of the simple BJT or MOS current source/sinks is not sufficiently large. Of course, R_o can be increased by decreasing I_o but other methods exist which allow R_o to be increased without decreasing I_o. Two methods will be investigated. The first uses negative feedback and the second uses positive feedback.

Consider the BJT current sink of Fig. 5.3-6a, which has a resistor R connected between the emitter and ground. The output resistance seen at the terminals across which V is defined will be called R_o. R_o is defined as a ratio of

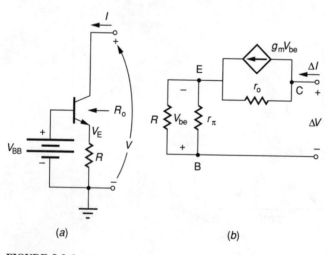

(a) (b)

FIGURE 5.3-6
(a) Increasing the output resistance of the BJT current source/sink by negative feedback, (b) Small signal model of a.

ΔV over ΔI. Assume that an increase in ΔV causes an increase in ΔI. However, the ΔI increase causes a ΔV_E increase resulting in a ΔV_{BE} decrease. The ΔV_{BE} decrease will cause a decrease in I opposing the assumed increase in ΔI. The feedback is negative series, which will cause the value of R_o to be larger than R_o with $R = 0$ by approximately the value of the feedback loop gain.

The dc current I_0 can be found by iteratively solving the voltage loop equation consisting of V_{BB}, V_{BE}, and the drop across R. The small signal model of the circuit of Fig. 5.3-6a (see Fig. 3.3-8) is shown in Fig. 5.3-6b. ΔV and ΔI are the small signal values of V and I, respectively. Analysis of this circuit gives

$$R_o = \frac{\Delta V}{\Delta I} = r_o[1 + (g_m + g_o)(r_\pi \| R)] \qquad (5.3\text{-}7)$$

If $R = 0$, Eq. 5.3-7 reduces to r_o. The magnitude of the feedback loop gain is given by the second term in the brackets. As R becomes large, Eq. 5.3-7 approaches $r_o(1 + \beta_F)$, which means that the output resistance of the circuit of Fig. 5.3-6a with $R = 0$ can be increased by a factor of up to $1 + \beta_F$ for large values of R.

Figure 5.3-7a shows this principle applied to the MOS current sink. I_o can be found from the large signal model and letting $V_S = I_oR$. In the MOS case, the value of V_{BS} is not zero, so the small signal model is that shown in Fig. 5.3-7b. The output resistance of the circuit of Fig. 5.3-7b is

$$R_o = \frac{\Delta V}{\Delta I} = r_{ds}[1 + (g_m + g_{mb} + g_{ds})R] \approx r_{ds}(1 + g_mR) \qquad (5.3\text{-}8)$$

where $g_m > g_{mb} > g_{ds}$. In the MOS case, the magnitude of the feedback loop gain is g_mR and continues to increase as R increases which helps to compensate for the fact that the g_m in Eq. 5.3-8 is typically less than the g_m in Eq. 5.3-7.

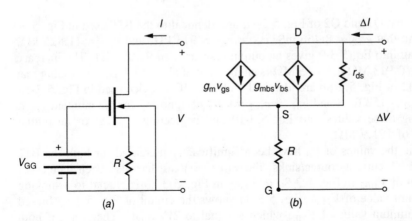

FIGURE 5.3-7
(a) Increasing the output resistance of the MOS current sink by negative feedback, (b) Small signal model of a.

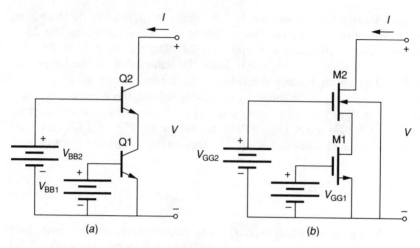

FIGURE 5.3-8
Practical implementation of: (a) Fig. 5.3-6a, (b) Fig. 5.3–7a.

An implementation of the circuits of Figs. 5.3-6a and 5.3-7a is shown in the circuits of Figs. 5.3-8a and 5.3-8b, respectively. The output current is the same as given in Eqs. 5.3-1 and 5.3-4. The output resistance of the circuit of Fig. 5.3-8a can be found by replacing R in Eq. 5.3-7 by the output resistance of Q1, r_o to give

$$R_o = r_{o2}[1 + (g_{m2} + g_{o2})(r_{\pi2} \| r_{o1})] \qquad (5.3\text{-}9)$$

Similarly, Eq. 5.3-8 can be used to find the output resistance of the circuit of Fig. 5.3-8b resulting in

$$R_o = r_{ds2}[1 + (g_{m2} + g_{mb2} + g_{ds2})r_{ds1}] \qquad (5.3\text{-}10)$$

Assuming that Q1 and Q2 of Fig. 5.3-8a are identical to the BJT used in Fig. 5.3-4b, we find that $g_{m2} = 8.456$ mS, $r_{o1} = r_{o2} = 913$ kΩ, and $r_{\pi2} = 11.826$ kΩ. Substituting into Eq. 5.3-9 gives an output resistance of 91.05 MΩ. The increase of R_o from 0.913 MΩ to 91.05 MΩ is an increase of almost $1 + \beta_F$. Assuming that M1 and M2 of Fig. 5.3-8b are identical with the MOS device used in Fig. 5.3-5a gives a $g_{m2} = 152.6\,\mu$S and $g_{ds1} = g_{ds2} = 0.97\,\mu$S ignoring for the moment g_{mb2}. Substituting these values into Eq. 5.3-10 and neglecting g_{mb2} gives an output resistance of 171.9 MΩ.

While the values of R_o have been significantly increased for both the BJT and MOSFET current source/sinks, the value of V_{MIN} has also been increased. The design of V_{BB2} in Fig. 5.3-8a or V_{GG2} in Fig. 5.3-8b is crucial to achieving the minimum value of V_{MIN}. Fig. 5.3-9a shows the circuit of Fig. 5.3-8a biased for the minimum value of V_{MIN} which is equal to $2V_{CE}(\text{sat})$. Therefore, if both transistors are identical, then $V_{BE1} = V_{BE2}$ will give the same current assuming large β_F. Thus V_{BB2} should be designed to equal

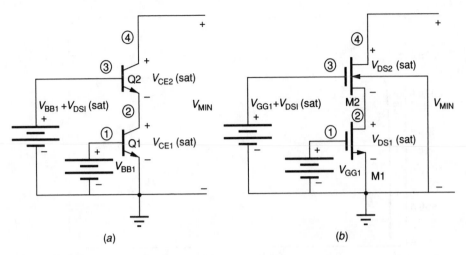

FIGURE 5.3-9
Minimum V_{MIN} design of: (a) Fig. 5.3-8a, (b) Fig. 5.3-8b.

$$V_{BB2} = V_{CE1}(sat) + V_{BB1} \qquad (5.3\text{-}11)$$

to achieve the minimum value of V_{MIN}. A similar consideration holds for the MOSFETs of Fig. 5.3-8b, which are redrawn in Fig. 5.3-9b. In this analysis we must include the effects of the bulk–source voltage on M2. To have the same current in both M2 and M1 implies that the following relationship must be true

$$V_{GS1} - V_{T1} = V_{GS2} - V_{T2} \qquad (5.3\text{-}12)$$

Therefore V_{GG2} of Fig. 5.3-8b is

$$V_{GG2} = V_{DS1}(sat) + V_{GS2} = V_{DS1}(sat) + V_{GG1} - V_{T1} + V_{T2} \qquad (5.3\text{-}13)$$

With this value of V_{GG2} the minimum value of V_{MIN} will be $2(V_{GG1} - V_{T1})$.

Figures 5.3-10a and b are the results of SPICE simulation of the circuits of Figs. 5.3-9a and b using the same model parameters as for the previous simulation and with $V_{BB2} = 0.4$ V and $V_{GG2} = (1.25 + 2.0 - 0.75 + 1.218) = 3.718$ V. It is seen that V_{MIN} for the BJT current sink of Fig. 5.3-9a is approximately 0.4 V. The output resistance is too large to be determined with any accuracy from the plots of Fig. 5.3-10a and b. Figure 5.3-10b shows that V_{MIN} for the MOS current sink of Fig. 5.3-9b is about 1.8 V. The advantage of BJTs over MOSFETs with regard to signal swing is very apparent in the circuits studied above.

The second method of increasing the value of R_o of a simple current source/sink uses positive feedback. Figure 5.3-11a shows the concept of this technique. I_o and R_o represent the current source or sink of Figs. 5.3-4a or 5.3-5a. The amplifier A of Fig. 5.3-11a is an ideal voltage-controlled, voltage source controlled by V. The battery V_o is used to permit a dc voltage drop across the

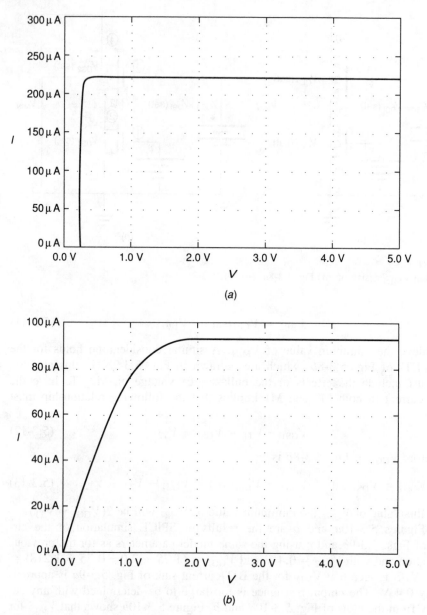

FIGURE 5.3-10
Simulation of: (a) Fig. 5.3-9a (b) Fig. 5.3-9b.

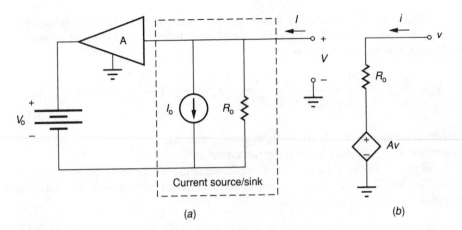

FIGURE 5.3-11

(a) Concept of using positive feedback to increase R_o, (b) ac model of a.

current sink/source. Figure 5.3-11b shows the ac model of the circuit of Fig. 5.3-11a. The output resistance can easily be found as

$$R_{out} = \frac{v}{i} = \frac{R_o}{1 - A} \qquad (5.3\text{-}14)$$

If A is slightly less than unity then $(1 - A)^{-1}$ is a large number causing R_{out} to be much greater than R_o. This technique is called *bootstrapping* and has many uses.

   While this technique works better with depletion devices (e.g., can make V_o in Fig. 5.3-11a with a depletion device), we shall first show how to apply bootstrapping to BJT and enhancement MOS transistors. Figure 5.3-12a shows how the current source of Fig. 5.3-4a can be bootstrapped by Q2. Because the ac voltage gain from the base of Q2 to the emitter of Q2 is always less than one, then the ac voltage at the emitter of Q1 follows the ac voltage at the collector of Q1. Consequently, there is very little ac change in voltage from the collector to emitter of Q1 thus boosting the output resistance value. The resistor R is necessary to allow the emitter of Q1 to follow its collector. Note that as the voltage V changes that all of this change is across R, and the current necessary to create this voltage comes from Q2. I_o is approximately equal to I_1.

   The value of V_{EE2} can be zero without influencing the circuit because Q1 is in the forward active region when $V_{CE1} = V_{BE2}$. Unfortunately, the resistance R keeps the bootstrapped current sink from having a low V_{MIN}. As V_{CE1} approaches V_{CE1} (sat), Q2 turns off. The voltage across R will be $I_1 R = IR$ until Q1 goes into saturation. As a result

$$V_{MIN} = V_{CE}(\text{sat}) + I_o R \qquad (5.3\text{-}15)$$

If R is small and V_{EE2} negative ($V_{CE1}(\text{sat}) - V_{BE2}$), a very low value of V_{MIN} with high R_o could be achieved.

Figure 5.3-12b gives the small signal model of Fig. 5.3-12a where the $g_{m2}v_{be2}$ has been simplified by source reduction. From this model the ac output resistance can be calculated as

$$R_o = \frac{v}{i} = \frac{r_{\pi2} \parallel r_{o1} + 1/g_{m2} \parallel R}{1 - g_{m2}R/(1 + g_{m2}R)} = \left[r_{\pi2} \parallel r_{o1} + \frac{1}{g_{m2}} \parallel R \right][1 + g_{m2}R]$$
$$(5.3\text{-}16)$$

Unfortunately, $r_{\pi2}$ tends to work against obtaining large values of ac output resistance using the BJT bootstrapped current sink.

Figure 5.3-13a shows a MOS implementation of the bootstrapped current sink. The MOS version does not suffer the $r_{\pi2}$ effects of the BJT version. The minimum value of V_{MIN} is given as

$$V_{MIN} = V_{DS1}(\text{sat.}) + I R \qquad (5.3\text{-}17)$$

and is achievable only when $V_{SS2} < V_{DS1}(\text{sat.}) - V_{T2}$. The bulk-source influence in M1 and M2 must also be considered in the design of Fig. 5.3-13a. The small signal model of the MOS bootstrapped current sink in Fig. 5.3-13b can be used to find the output resistance given as

$$R_o = \frac{v}{i} = \left[\frac{r_{ds1} + 1/g_m \parallel R}{1 - g_{m2}R/(1 + g_{m2}R)} \right] = \left(r_{ds1} + \frac{1}{g_{m2}} \parallel R \right)(1 + g_{m2}R) \quad (5.3\text{-}18)$$

It can be seen that the value of R_o of Fig. 5.3-5a can be increased by approximately $(1 + g_{m2}R)$.

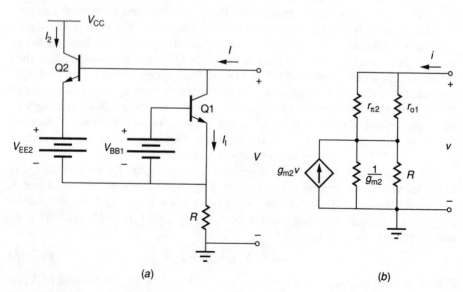

(a)   (b)

FIGURE 5.3-12
(a) BJT bootstrapped current sink, (b) ac model of a.

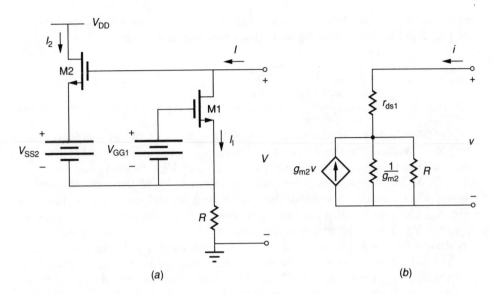

(a)   (b)

FIGURE 5.3-13
(a) MOS bootstrapped current sink, (b) ac model of a.

For depletion devices the dc polarity of V_{DS} and V_{GS} can be opposite. Examples are the depletion-mode MOSFET, the JFET, and the GaAs MESFET. Let us consider the n-channel depletion MOSFET as an example. Figure 5.3-14a shows that a depletion MOSFET current sink can be obtained by simply connecting the gate to the source. The $I-V$ characteristics are shown in Fig. 5.3-14b, where V_T is the pinch-off voltage and I_o is the drain-source current with $V_{GS} = 0$. The bootstrapping principle can be applied to the depletion MOSFET very conveniently, as shown in Fig. 5.3-15a. In this circuit, M2 bootstraps the channel resistance r_{ds1} of M1, causing the output resistance

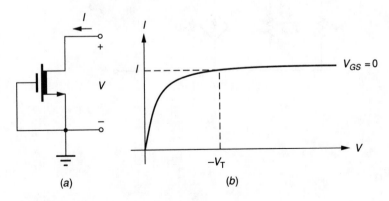

(a)   (b)

FIGURE 5.3-14
(a) n-channel, JFET current sink, (b) $I-V$ characteristics of a.

of this current source to be increased. Fig. 5.3-15b gives the small signal model of Fig. 5.3-15a. The small signal output resistance is given as

$$R_o = \frac{v}{i} = \frac{r_{ds1} + (1/g_{m2}) \| r_{ds2}}{1 - (g_{m2}r_{ds2})/(1 + g_{m2}r_{ds2})} = \left(r_{ds1} + \frac{1}{g_{m2}} \| r_{ds2} \right)(1 + g_{m2}r_{ds2})$$

$$(5.3\text{-}19)$$

Unfortunately, the minimum value of V_{MIN} is not small and is at least equal to $|V_T|$. Without the flexibility of bias voltages, the geometries of M1 and M2 will have to be adjusted to account for the fact that $V_{GS1} \neq V_{GS2}$.

A MOS current source/sink that outperforms any of the previous current source/sinks considered so far in the area of high R_o and low V_{MIN} is shown in Fig. 5.3-16a[3] and is called a *regulated cascode current sink*. The output current is given by Eq. 5.3-4. The ac output resistance of M1 can be increased by stabilizing its drain-source voltage. In the regulated cascode current sink, the gate voltage of M2, which is the same as the drain–source voltage of M1, is regulated by a feedback loop consisting of M2 and M4 as an amplifier and M3 as a voltage follower. If all transistors operate in saturation and if the bulk effects are ignored, the ac output resistance can be found as

$$R_o \simeq r_{ds1} \left(\frac{g_{m2}g_{m3}}{g_{ds3}(g_{ds2} + g_4)} \right)$$

$$(5.3\text{-}20)$$

where g_4 is the output conductance of the I_4 current source. It is seen that the output resistance is higher than any MOS circuit considered so far. If $I_4 = 2$ μA, and $I = 94$ μA; then $g_1 = 0.02$ μS, $g_{d2} = 0.02$ μS, $g_{m2} = 21.9$ μS, r_{ds1}

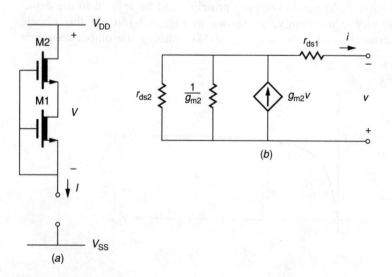

FIGURE 5.3-15
(*a*) Bootstrapped JFET current source, (*b*) Small signal model of *a*.

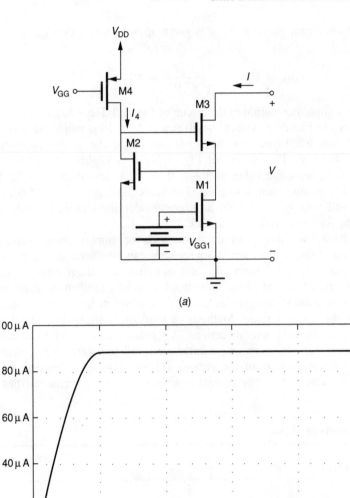

FIGURE 5.3-16
(a) Regulated cascode current sink, (b) Simulation results of Fig. 5.3-16a.

$= 1.064$ MΩ, $g_{m3} = 150.2$ μS, and $g_{ds3} = 0.94$ μS. Thus, the calculated value of R_o is 93.08 GΩ!

The circuit of Fig. 5.3-16a even works with a somewhat reduced R_o performance when the drain–source voltage across M3 is lowered to the point where it starts to operate in the ohmic region. The gate voltage of M3 may be driven by the feedback loop almost up to V_{DD}, causing the V_{DS} drop across M3 to stay small. Thus, the minimum value of V_{MIN} is given approximately by V_{GS2} and is written as

$$V_{MIN} = V_{GS2} = \sqrt{\frac{2I_1 L_2}{K'_N W_2}} + V_{T2} \qquad (5.3-21)$$

Figure 5.3-16*b* is a simulated output of the circuit of Fig. 5.3-16*a* when $I_1 = 2$ μA and all transistors are identical with $W = 50$ μ and $L = 10$ μ using the model parameters previously employed. For the conditions stated above, the minimum value of V_{MIN} is 0.93 V. The current of Fig. 5.3-16*b* is slightly less than the anticipated 94 μA because the value of V_{GS2}, 0.93 V, is less than the 1.25 V required to keep M1 in saturation. Using Eq. 3 of Table 3.1-1 gives $I_o = 87.6 \mu$A, which matches well with Fig. 5.3-16*b*. Similar considerations could be used to develop a high-performance BJT current-sink.

In this section, we have examined methods of implementing current source/sinks. It was seen that a current source/sink can be characterized by its current, small signal output resistance, R_o, and its minimum voltage drop, V_{MIN}. It was shown how negative and positive feedback could be used to increase the value of R_o. Because these techniques increased V_{MIN} it was necessary to consider how to minimize this characteristic. Methods of implementing the bias supplies will be considered in the next several sections. A regulated cascode MOS current sink was introduced that had superior performance to all previous MOS current sink realizations. A comparison of the various current sinks considered in this section is given in Table 5.3-1. The current sources have similar characteristics.

TABLE 5.3-1
Comparison of current sinks

Current sink	Figure	R_O	Minimum V_{MIN}
Simple BJT	5.3-4*a*	$\dfrac{V_{AF}}{I_o}$	$V_{CE}(\text{sat})$
Simple MOS	5.3-5*a*	$r_o = \dfrac{1}{\lambda I_o}$	$V_{GG1} - V_T$
Cascade BJT	5.3-9*a*	$r_{o2}[1 + g_{m2}(r_{\pi2} \,\|\, r_{o1})]$	$2V_{CE}(\text{sat})$
Cascade MOS	5.3-9*b*	$r_{ds2}[1 + (g_{m2} + g_{mbs2})r_{ds1}]$	$2(V_{GG1} - V_{T1})$
Bootstrapped BJT	5.3-12*a*	$\left[(r_{\pi2} \,\|\, r_{o1}) + \left(\dfrac{1}{g_{m2}} \,\middle\|\, R\right)\right](1 + g_{m2R})$	$V_{CE}(\text{sat}) + I_o R$
Bootstrapped MOS	5.3-13*a*	$\left(r_{ds1} + \dfrac{1}{g_{ms}} \,\middle\|\, R\right)(1 + g_{m2}R)$	$V_{DS}(\text{sat}) + I_o R$
Regulated cascoded	5.3-16*a*	$r_{ds1}\left(\dfrac{g_{m2}g_{m3}}{g_{ds3}(g_{ds2} + g_4)}\right)$	$\sqrt{\dfrac{2I_1 L_2}{K'_N W_2}} + V_{T4}$

5.4 CURRENT MIRRORS/AMPLIFIERS

In the previous section we considered the subject of current sources and sinks where the objective was to implement the ideal $I-V$ characteristics of Fig. 5.3-1b. A dc voltage source was used to bias the implementation of the current sources or sinks. This section considers similar circuits, with the exception that the current source or sink is biased by a dc current rather than a dc voltage.

The circuits of this section are distinct from those of the last in that they use the principle of matched devices. This section will begin by applying the principle of matched devices to bipolar and then to MOSFET circuits resulting in current mirrors/amplifiers. It will also be shown how to analyze so-called matched circuits when they are not matched. Because the matching principle is much like looking into a mirror, the circuits of this section are called *current mirrors*. The term *current amplifier* is also used for current mirrors when an input current change creates an output current change.

One of the advantages of integrated circuits over discrete components is the ability to practically match components without trimming. This matching feature is used in this section to provide a very versatile and useful block called the current mirror. Before considering the current mirror, let us introduce the principles of matched devices. Consider initially two npn bipolar junction transistors. If the Early voltage effects are neglected, it follows from Eq. 3.3-13 that the large signal collector currents in the active region with the base-emitter junction forward-biased and the base-collector junction reverse-biased are given as

$$I_{C1} = I_{S1} \exp\left(\frac{V_{BE1}}{V_t}\right) = I_{S1} \exp\left(\frac{q V_{BE1}}{kT}\right) \qquad (5.4\text{-}1)$$

and

$$I_{C2} = I_{S2} \exp\left(\frac{V_{BE2}}{V_t}\right) = I_{S2} \exp\left(\frac{q V_{BE2}}{kT}\right) \qquad (5.4\text{-}2)$$

where from Eq. 3.3-6 and Eq. 3.3-7 of Chapter 3,

$$I_{Si} = \frac{q n_i^2 \overline{D_n} A_i}{Q_{Bi}(V_{CBi})} , \ i = 1, 2 \qquad (5.4\text{-}3)$$

The parameters of Eq. 5.4-3 have been defined in Chapter 3. Solving for V_{BE1} and V_{BE2} gives

$$V_{BE1} = V_t \ln\left(\frac{I_{C1}}{I_{S1}}\right) \qquad (5.4\text{-}4)$$

and

$$V_{BE2} = V_t \ln\left(\frac{I_{C2}}{I_{S2}}\right) \qquad (5.4\text{-}5)$$

Now if the base and emitter of Q1 are connected to the base and emitter of Q2 and a source of base current exists, then the following relationship between I_{C1} and I_{C2} results.

$$\frac{I_{C1}}{I_{C2}} = \frac{I_{S1}}{I_{S2}} = \frac{qn_i^2 \overline{D_n} A_1}{Q_{B1}(V_{CB1})} \times \frac{Q_{B2}(V_{CB2})}{qn_i^2 \overline{D_n} A_2} = \frac{A_1 Q_{B2}(V_{CB2})}{A_2 Q_{B1}(V_{CB1})} \tag{5.4-6}$$

If the transistors are matched and if $V_{CB1} = V_{CB2}$, $A_1 = A_2$ and $Q_{B1} = Q_{B2}$, then $I_{C1} = I_{C2}$, which illustrates the principle of matched devices. This principle is very important and will be used both in biasing and small signal design of integrated circuits.

The application of the matching principle to implement a simple bipolar current sink is shown in Fig. 5.4-1. In this circuit, the base and the collector of Q1 are physically connected together for two reasons. The first is to provide a source of base current for both Q1 and Q2. The second is to keep V_{CE1} small so that R_1 essentially defines the current I_{IN}. The reader can note that V_{CC}, R_1 and the base-collector connected transistor Q1 actually implement V_{BB} of the current sink of Fig. 5.3-4a.

The above results will now be used to calculate the ratio of I_{C2} to I_{IN}. Initially, the emitter areas of Q1 and Q2 will be assumed to be equal and the Early voltage will be neglected so that differences in V_{CB1} and V_{CB2} can be ignored. If the bases of Q1 and Q2 and the emitters of Q1 and Q2 are physically connected together, then the matching principle gives

$$I_{C2} = I_{C1} \tag{5.4-7}$$

However,

$$I_{C1} = I_{IN} - I_{B1} - I_{B2} \tag{5.4-8}$$

and

$$I_{IN} = \frac{V_{CC} - V_{BE1}}{R_1} \tag{5.4-9}$$

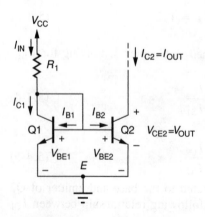

FIGURE 5.4-1
A simple bipolar current mirror.

Using the relationship, $I_C = \beta_F I_B$ and assuming $I_{B1} = I_{B2} = I_B$ and $B_{F1} = B_{F2} = B_F$, gives

$$I_{C2} = \frac{I_{IN}}{1 + (2/\beta_F)} = \frac{V_{CC} - V_{BE1}}{R_1[1 + (2/\beta_F)]} \qquad (5.4\text{-}10)$$

It should be noted that as β_F approaches infinity, I_{C2} approaches I_{IN}.

In the considerations above, the Early voltage was neglected which turns out to be a poor assumption in some applications. If the Early voltage, V_{AF} is included in the large signal expressions for the collector current, Equations 5.4-1 and 5.4-2 are modified as

$$I_C = I_S\left(1 + \frac{V_{CE}}{V_{AF}}\right) \exp\left(\frac{V_{BE}}{V_t}\right) \qquad (5.4\text{-}11)$$

Using the matched transistor principle, we can solve for the ratio of I_{C2} to I_{C1} as

$$\frac{I_{C2}}{I_{C1}} = \frac{I_{S2}[1 + (V_{CE2}/V_{AF})]}{I_{S1}[1 + (V_{CE1}/V_{AF})]} = \frac{1 + (V_{CE2}/V_{AF})}{1 + (V_{CE1}/V_{AF})} = \frac{1 + (V_{CE2}/V_{AF})}{1 + (V_{BE1}/V_{AF})} \qquad (5.4\text{-}12)$$

Note that even though the transistors are matched, I_{C2} is not necessarily equal to I_{C1}. As an example, assume that $V_{CE2} = 10$ V, $V_{BE1} = 0.6$ V and $V_{AF} = 100$ V. The ratio of I_{C2} to I_{C1} is 1.093. It should be apparent that the Early voltage effects cannot be neglected in some practical applications. Although a 9% error is somewhat discouraging, alternative configurations will be developed which significantly reduce this error in matched devices.

Before developing the configurations which eliminate the Early voltage effects, let us consider what happens if the transistors are not exactly matched. Assume that A, Q_B and $\alpha_F(= \beta_F/(1 + \beta_F))$ are not matched and are given by

$$A_1 = A + (\Delta A/2) \qquad (5.4\text{-}13)$$

$$A_2 = A - (\Delta A/2) \qquad (5.4\text{-}14)$$

$$Q_{B1} = Q_B + (\Delta Q_B/2) \qquad (5.4\text{-}15)$$

$$Q_{B2} = Q_B - (\Delta Q_B/2) \qquad (5.4\text{-}16)$$

$$\alpha_{F1} = \alpha_F + (\Delta\alpha_F/2) \qquad (5.4\text{-}17)$$

and

$$\alpha_{F2} = \alpha_F - (\Delta\alpha_F/2) \qquad (5.4\text{-}18)$$

where A, Q_B and α_F are the nominal values and corresponding parameters ΔA, ΔQ_B and $\Delta\alpha_F$ are the differences between the two values. I_{C1} may be expressed from Eq. 5.4-8 and Eq. 3.3-12 as

$$I_{C1} = \alpha_{F1}I_{IN} - \frac{\alpha_{F1}}{\beta_{F2}}I_{C2} \qquad (5.4\text{-}19)$$

Substituting Eq. 5.4-19 into Eq. 5.4-6 with $V_{CB1} = V_{CB2}$ results in

$$I_{C2} = \frac{(A_2 Q_{B1}/A_1 Q_{B2})\alpha_{F1}}{1 + (\alpha_{F1}A_2 Q_{B1}/\beta_{F2}A_1 Q_{B2})}I_{IN} \approx \left(\frac{A_2 Q_{B1}}{A_1 Q_{B2}}\right)\alpha_{F1}\alpha_{F2}I_{IN} \qquad (5.4\text{-}20)$$

where it has been assumed that

$$\frac{\alpha_{F1} A_2 Q_{B1}}{A_1 Q_{B2}} \approx 1 \tag{5.4-21}$$

Substituting Eqs. 5.4-13 through 5.4-18 into Eq. 5.4-20 results in

$$I_{C2} = I_{IN} \left[\frac{(1 - \Delta A/2A)(1 + \Delta Q_B/2Q_B)(1 + \Delta \alpha_F/2\alpha_F)(1 - \Delta \alpha_F/2\alpha_F)}{(1 + \Delta A/2A)(1 - \Delta Q_B/2Q_B)} \right] \tag{5.4-22}$$

which can be approximated for small ΔA, ΔQ_B and $\Delta \alpha_F$ by,

$$I_{C2} \cong I_{IN} \left[1 - \frac{\Delta A}{A} + \frac{\Delta Q_B}{Q_B} + \frac{\Delta \alpha_F}{\alpha_F} \right] \tag{5.4-23}$$

It can be shown that

$$\frac{\Delta I_S}{I_S} \cong \frac{\Delta A}{A} - \frac{\Delta Q_B}{A_B} \tag{5.4-24}$$

so that Eq. 5.4-23 can be written as

$$I_{C2} \cong I_{IN} \left[1 - \frac{\Delta I_S}{I_S} + \frac{\Delta \alpha_F}{\alpha_F} \right] \tag{5.4-25}$$

If a 5% mismatch for I_S and a 10% mismatch for β_F (which is a 0.1% mismatch in α_F for $\beta_F = 100$) is assumed, then Eq. 5.4-25 shows that the variation for the ratio of I_{C2} to I_{IN} is 0.949 to 1.051, or about $\pm 5\%$.

The simulated performance of the simple BJT current mirror is shown in Fig. 5.4-2. The transistors have been assumed to be equal and have the model parameters of $\beta_F = 200$, $\beta_R = 0.43$, $I_S = 0.4$ fA, $V_{AF} = 200$ V and $V_{AR} = 20$ V. An ideal current mirror would have horizontal curves whose value of $I_{C2}(I_{OUT})$ would be exactly equal to $I_{C1}(I_{IN})$ independent of V_{OUT}. As in the previous section, a measure of the "horizontalness" of the curves is given by the small signal resistance or conductance looking back into Q2 from the collector to ground. We shall designate this resistance or conductance as r_{out} or g_{out}. In the circuit of Fig. 5.4-1, r_{out} is simply r_{o2} which was derived in Chapter 3 as

$$r_{out} = r_{o2} = \frac{V_{AF}}{I_{C2}} \tag{5.4-26}$$

The small signal output resistance of the current mirror will be important in determining its performance.

When β_F is not large it can cause current ratio errors which may total a few percent, as indicated in Eq. 5.4-10. Since β_F is not accurately controlled at processing, the β_F effects are unacceptably large in some applications. Figure 5.4-3 shows a configuration which reduces the effect of β_F upon the current ratio of Q1 and Q2. Transistor Q3 requires less current by a factor of β_F from I_{IN} in order to provide the base currents for Q1 and Q2. Neglecting mismatch effects and Early voltage effects, it can be shown that

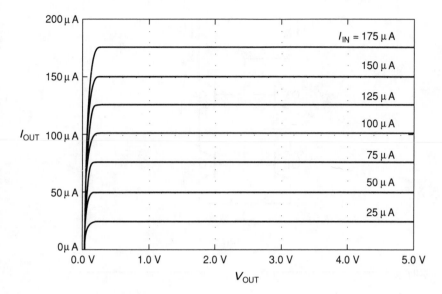

FIGURE 5.4-2
I–V characteristics of the simple bipolar current mirror of Fig. 5.4-1.

$$I_{C2} = \frac{I_{IN}}{1 + 2/[\beta_F(1 + \beta_F)]} \qquad (5.4\text{-}27)$$

Comparing Eqs. 5.4-10 and 5.4-27 shows that the transistor Q3 has reduced the β_F effects by about a factor of β_F, which is quite significant. It is also observed that two base-emitter drops rather than the single drop in Eq. 5.4-9 are subtracted from V_{CC} to find the voltage drop across R_1 which determines I_{IN}. This implies that for small values of V_{CC}, I_{IN} will be less well defined in the circuit of Fig. 5.4-3 than it was in the circuit of Fig. 5.4-1.

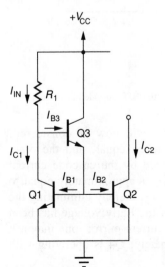

FIGURE 5.4-3
A circuit reducing the influence of β_F on the current mirror of Fig. 5.4-1.

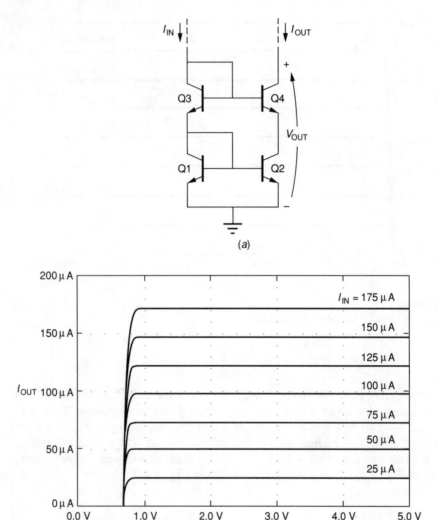

FIGURE 5.4-4
(a) Bipolar cascode current mirror, (b) Simulated performance of the BJT cascode current mirror.

Two methods of reducing Early voltage effects will now be considered. One is to constrain V_{CE1} and V_{CE2} of Fig. 5.4-1 to be equal, and the other uses negative feedback. The first method is illustrated by the cascode current mirror shown in Fig. 5.4-4a. Since the value of V_{BE3} is approximately equal to V_{BE4}, then V_{CE1} (V_{BE1}) is approximately equal to V_{CE2}, thereby eliminating the Early effect from Eq. 5.4-12. Although the effect of the Early voltage has been eliminated on the ratio of I_{C2} to I_{C1} of the cascode current mirror, one may ask about the effect of the Early voltage on Q4. Fortunately, Q4 is operating with

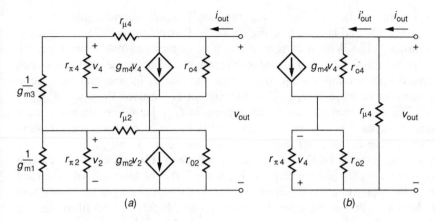

FIGURE 5.4-5
(*a*) Small signal model of Fig. 5.4-4*a*, (*b*) Simplified small signal model of *a*.

the base terminal at ac ground, which reduces the effect of the Early voltage by about a factor of β_F. The $I-V$ characteristics of the cascode current mirror are shown in Fig. 5.4-4*b*. The improvement of the cascode current mirror over the simple current mirror can be quantified by comparing the ac output impedances of the two circuits. The small signal model for the cascode current mirror is shown in Fig. 5.4-5*a*, where the frequency-independent, hybrid-pi model of Fig. 3.3-12 and the assumption that $(1/g_{m1})$ and $(1/g_{m3})$ are much less than $r_{\pi 2}$ or $r_{\pi 4}$ have been used. A simplified form of this model is shown in Fig. 5.4-5*b*. The small signal output resistance can be found by noting that

$$i'_{out} = g_{m4}v_4 + (v_{out} + v_4)/r_{o4} \qquad (5.4\text{-}28)$$

and

$$v_4 = -i_{out}(r_{\pi 4} \parallel r_{o2}) = -i_{out}\frac{r_{o2}}{1 + g_{m4}r_{o2}/\beta_{F4}} \qquad (5.4\text{-}29)$$

Substituting Eq. 5.4-29 into 5.4-28 gives

$$\frac{v_{out}}{i'_{out}} = r_{o4}\left[1 + \frac{r_{o2}(1 + g_{m4}r_{o4})}{r_{o4}[1 + (g_{m4}r_{o2}/\beta_{F4})]}\right] \qquad (5.4\text{-}30)$$

Finally, the small signal output resistance is found by combining the resistance represented by Eq. 5.4-30 and $r_{\mu 4}$ in parallel to give

$$r_{out} = \frac{v_{out}}{i_{out}} = r_{\mu 4} \parallel r_{o4}\left[1 + \frac{r_{o2}(1 + g_{m4}r_{o4})}{r_{o4}[1 + (g_{m4}r_{o2}/\beta_{F4})]}\right] \cong \beta_{F4}r_{o4} \qquad (5.4\text{-}31)$$

We see that the cascode current mirror does indeed have a small signal resistance, which is approximately β_F times the small signal resistance of the simple current mirror.

The emitter areas of Q1 and Q2 should be as large as possible for best matching. All other transistors can have minimum area.

A second method of increasing the small signal output resistance uses negative feedback and is shown in Fig. 5.4-6a. This circuit is called the Wilson current mirror.[4] The Wilson current mirror uses negative current-shunt feedback to stabilize the ratio of I_{C3} to I_{IN} and to increase r_{out}. The operation of the circuit is explained by assuming that I_{IN} is constant and that an incremental increase in V_{CE3} causes an increase in I_{C3}. This increase in I_{C3} causes V_{BE3} and V_{BE1} to increase. The V_{BE1} increase causes an increase in I_{C1}. However, since I_{IN} stays constant, an increase in I_{C1} means a decrease in I_{B3}, which causes a decrease in I_{C3} counteracting the original increase in I_{C3} caused by a change in V_{CE3}. The feedback loop consists of Q3 (as a voltage follower), Q1 and Q2 (as a current mirror), and Q1-R_1 (as an inverting voltage amplifier). The loop gain of the circuit is seen to be approximately $\beta_F/2$, so that the small signal output resistance will be comparable to that of the cascode current mirror. Figure 5.4-6b illustrates the I–V characteristics of the Wilson current mirror of Fig. 5.4-6a. It can be shown that

$$I_{OUT} = I_{IN}\left[1 - \frac{2}{\beta_F^2 + \beta_F + 2}\right] \tag{5.4-32}$$

r_{out} can be calculated from the small signal equivalent circuit of Fig. 5.4-6a shown in Fig. 5.4-7. The value of R_{eq} defined in Fig. 5.4–7 can be found to be

$$R_{eq} = \frac{v_1}{i} = \frac{r_{\pi 3} + R'}{1 + g_{m1}R'} \cong \frac{R'}{1 + g_{m1}R'} \cong \frac{1}{g_{m1}} \tag{5.4-33}$$

Using Eq. 5.4-33 allows us to express r_{out} as (see Prob. 5.27).

$$r_{out} = \frac{v_{out}}{i_{out}} = r_{o3}\left[1 + \frac{g_{m1}\beta_{F3}}{g_{m1} + g_{m2}}\right] + \frac{1}{g_{m1} + g_{m2}} \cong \frac{r_{o3}\beta_{F3}}{2} \tag{5.4-34}$$

It is apparent from Eq. 5.4-34 that r_{out} has been improved over the simple current mirror of Fig. 5.4-1 by a factor of $\beta_o/2$. The small signal output resistance of current mirrors can be further increased by the use of special techniques.[5]

In many cases, the mirrored currents are designed not to be equal. This can be accomplished by making the base-emitter junction areas of the two mirror transistors unequal. They should be made as large as possible for best matching ratio accuracy. In Eq. 5.4-6, it can be seen that the ratio of the current in Q1 to that of Q2 is proportional to the ratio of the areas of the respective base-emitter junctions. This relationship can be expressed as

$$I_{C2} \cong \frac{A_2}{A_1}I_{C1} \tag{5.4-35}$$

If the ratio of the currents is much different from unity, this approach can use significant area and will become less accurate due to the decrease in relative accuracy of large area ratios.

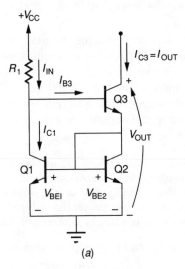

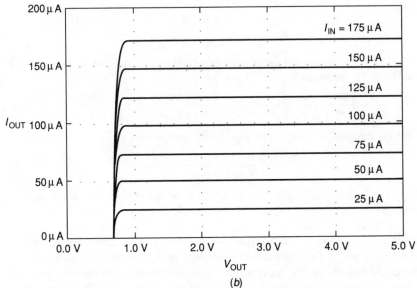

FIGURE 5.4-6
(a) Wilson BJT current mirror, (b) Simulated performance of the Wilson BJT current mirror of a.

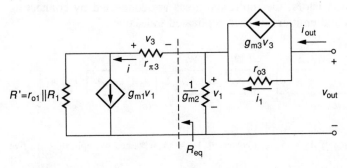

FIGURE 5.4-7
Small signal model for the Wilson current mirror of Fig. 5.4-6a.

The decrease in accuracy can be minimized using a principle called *replication*. Simply put, the replication principle states that an improvement in relative accuracy between two different sized areas occurs when the larger area is equal to an integer multiple of the smaller area. For example, suppose that $A_2 = mA_1$ where m is an integer. Improved relative accuracy is achieved when A_2 consists of m separate areas of A_1 connected appropriately. An example illustrates the replication principle.

Example 5.4-1. Assume that Q1 and Q2 of Fig. 5.4-1 are being used to create a simple mirror having $I_{C2} = 5I_{C1}$. Assume further that A_1 is a rectangular area of W_1 times L_1, as shown in Fig. 5.4-8a. Q2 will have two different shapes. The first is shown in Fig. 5.4-8b and the second in Fig. 5.4-8c. Let $L_1 = L_2 = L$ and $W_1 = W$. Compare the ratio matching accuracy of the two layout approaches.

Solution. Assume resolution of any edge is given as

$$W_1 = W \pm \Delta W$$

$$W_2 = 5W \pm \Delta W$$

$$L_1 = L_2 = L \pm \Delta L$$

where ΔW and ΔL are the uncertainty of W and L. The ratio of A_2 to A_1 of Fig. 5.4-8b can be expressed as

$$\frac{A_2}{A_1} = \frac{(5W \pm \Delta W)(L \pm \Delta L)}{(W \pm \Delta W)(L \pm \Delta L)} = \frac{5 \pm (\Delta W/W)}{1 \pm (\Delta W/W)} \cong 5 \pm 4\frac{\Delta W}{W} \qquad (5.4\text{-}36)$$

Similarly the ratio of A_2 to A_1 of Fig. 5.4-8c is expressed as

$$\frac{A_2}{A_1} = \frac{5(W \pm \Delta W)(L \pm \Delta L)}{(W \pm \Delta W)(L \pm \Delta L)} = 5 \qquad (5.4\text{-}37)$$

The advantage of the replication principle is shown by the increased relative accuracy.

If the ratio of areas is not equal to an integer, the replication principle can still be used. If in Example 5.4-1 the value of I_{C2} were $5.5I_{C1}$, the larger transistor could consist of the replication of A_1 five times plus an area equal to $0.5A_1$. The designer has the option of making the $0.5A_1$ area the same shape as the A_1 area or choosing some other shape. The resulting ratio, while not as accurate as the integer case, will be more accurate than simply ratioing areas. If the areas represent transistors, the replicated areas are connected by connecting the collectors, bases and emitters of each replicated transistor.

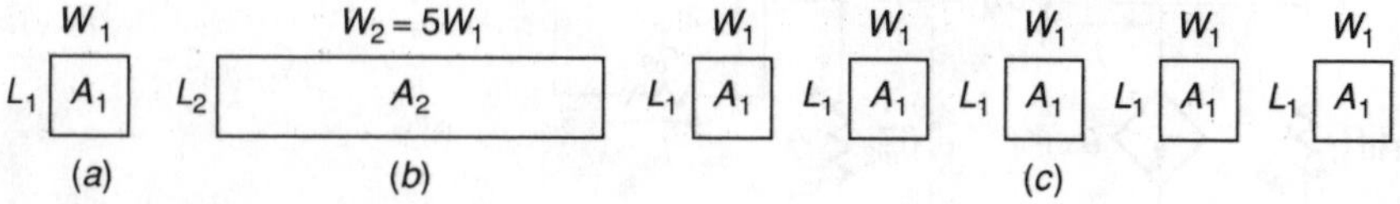

FIGURE 5.4-8
(a) Unit area A_1, (b) Area of $A_2 = 5A_1$, (c) Area of $A_2 = 5A_1$ obtained by replicating A_1 five times.

The large area ratio caused by unequal mirror currents can be avoided by using a resistor in series with the emitter of the lower current transistor, as shown in Fig. 5.4-9. This current mirror is called the Widlar current mirror[6] and can have large current differences with identical base-emitter areas. Note that the effect of R_2 will be to increase r_{out}. If Q1 and Q2 are matched and β_F is large, then the voltage drops around the base-emitter circuits can be written as

$$V_{BE1} - V_{BE2} = I_{C2}R_2 \qquad (5.4\text{-}38)$$

If the V_{AF} effects are neglected, it follows from Eq. 5.4-11 that

$$V_t \ln\left(\frac{I_{IN}}{I_{C2}}\right) = I_{C2}R_2 \qquad (5.4\text{-}39)$$

There are two cases in which Eq. 5.4-39 is used. The first is when I_{C2} and I_{IN} are known and R_2 is to be found. R_2 may be expressed as

$$R_2 = \frac{V_t}{I_{C2}} \ln\left(\frac{I_{IN}}{I_{C2}}\right) \qquad (5.4\text{-}40)$$

For example, if $V_{CC} = 5$ V, $R_1 = 4.3\,\text{k}\Omega$ and $I_{C2} = 10\,\mu\text{A}$, then we find that $I_{C1} = (5 - 0.7)/4.3\,\text{k}\Omega = 1$ mA and $R_2 = 11.97\,\text{k}\Omega$ We note that the ratio of I_{C1} to I_{C2} is 100 in this example. The second case, which uses Eq. 5.4-40, occurs when R_2 and I_{IN} are known. In this case, an iterative solution is required for I_{C2}. The effect of R_2 on r_{out} is to increase it. It can be shown (see Prob. 5.28) that r_{out} of the Widlar current mirror is given as

$$r_{out} = r_{\pi 2} \,\|\, R_2 + r_{o2}\big[1 + g_{m2}r_{\pi 2}\,\|\, R_2\big] \cong r_{o2}(1 + g_{m2}R_2) \qquad (5.4\text{-}41)$$

To obtain good ratio accuracies, Q1 and Q2 should have large emitter areas.

Because the output of the current mirrors is a current sink, it is important to have a small value of V_{MIN}, which was defined in the previous section. The same considerations for V_{MIN} and r_{out} apply to current mirrors. Unfortunately, the conditions of $V_{CE1} = V_{CE2}$ in order to eliminate the Early effects may not be

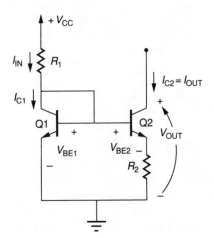

FIGURE 5.4-9
Widlar BJT current mirror.

compatible with the conditions for minimum V_{MIN}. For example, to obtain the minimum value of V_{MIN} in Fig. 5.4-4a requires that the dc voltage at the base of Q4 be equal to V_{CE2} (sat) $+ V_{BE4}$ (see Eq. 5.3-11). However, the voltage at the base of Q4 in Fig. 5.4-4a is equal to $2V_{BE2}$ assuming that all transistors are identical. A similar conflict between minimum V_{MIN} and large r_{out} exists for the Wilson current mirror of Fig. 5.4-6a. In this circuit, the minimum value of V_{MIN} is $V_{BE2} + V_{CE3}$(sat).

If one is willing to give up the constraint that V_{CE1} equals V_{CE2}, then it may be possible to achieve a minimum V_{MIN} design. Figure 5.4-10 shows one possible approach for the cascode current mirror of Fig. 5.4-4a. It has been assumed that Q1 through Q4 are identical transistors each having a base-emitter drop of V_{BE2}. It can be seen that if $V_{BE6} = V_{BE2} - V_{CE2}$(sat), that $V_{CE2} = V_{CE2}$(sat). V_{BE6} can be smaller than V_{BE2} by either decreasing the current of Q6 with respect to the current in Q1 through Q4 or by making the emitter area of Q6 much smaller than that of Q1 through Q4, or both. This can be seen by considering two different transistors designated as QA and QB. The difference in V_{BE} voltages can be expressed using Eqs. 5.4-4 and 5.4-5 as

$$\Delta V_{BE} = V_{BEA} - V_{BEB} = V_t \ln\left(\frac{I_{CA} I_{SB}}{I_{CB} I_{SA}}\right) \qquad (5.4\text{-}42)$$

Unfortunately, if ΔV_{BE} is much larger than V_t, the value of $(I_{CA}I_{SB})/(I_{CB}I_{SA})$ becomes too large to implement. For example, if the area of Q5 and Q6 of Fig.

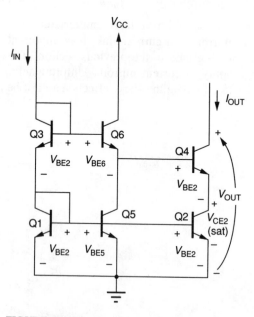

FIGURE 5.4-10
Reduction of V_{MIN} of the BJT cascode current mirror of Fig. 5.4-4a.

5.4-10 is 50 times less than the area of Q1 through Q4, then ΔV_{BE} of Eq. 5.4-42 would be approximately 200 mV at room temperature. However, any component whose area is 50 times different than another has several disadvantages. These disadvantages include a large area requirement and poor matching between devices. The principle behind the Widlar current mirror could be employed to reduce the current in Q5 and Q6 by placing a resistor in series with the emitter of Q5. The current ratio required to obtain a ΔV_{BE} of 200 mV is approximately 2500. This ratio results in a value of $R_2 = 507 \text{ k}\Omega$ at room temperature with $I_{C1} = 1 \text{ mA}$.

The BJT current mirrors that have been presented can be characterized from the viewpoint of accuracy, output resistance, and V_{MIN}. Table 5.4-1 summarizes the performance of the BJT current mirrors considered where $I_{C2} \approx I_{C1}$. Additional considerations include the proper sizes to achieve the desired matching accuracy.

The same principles developed in this section for current mirrors using the BJT device also hold true for the MOS device. In many cases, the MOS current mirrors are simpler in concept because no base current is required. On the other hand, the bulk effects create limitations not found in BJT mirrors. The matching principle applied to MOS devices can be developed from the simple current mirror of Fig. 5.4-11a. Note that for $V_{DS1} \geq V_{T1}$, M1 will always be in saturation since $V_{DG1} = 0$. Assuming that V_{DS2} is greater than $V_{GS1} - V_{T1}$ allows the use of the saturation model for both devices. Solving for $V_{GS1} - V_{T1}$ and $V_{GS2} - V_{T2}$ from Eq. 4 of Table 3.1-1 gives

$$V_{GS1} - V_{T1} = \left[\frac{2L_1 I_{D1}}{K'_{N1} W_1 (1 + \lambda_1 V_{DS1})} \right]^{1/2} \tag{5.4-43}$$

and

$$V_{GS2} - V_{T2} = \left[\frac{2L_2 I_{D2}}{K'_{N2} W_2 (1 + \lambda_2 V_{DS2})} \right]^{1/2} \tag{5.4-44}$$

TABLE 5.4-1
Comparison of BJT current mirror performance

BJT current mirror	Accuracy $(I_{C2} = I_{C1})$	r_{out}	V_{MIN}
Simple Fig. 5.4-1	Poor	$r_o = V_{AF}/I_o$	$V_{CE}(\text{sat})$
Cascode Fig. 5.4-4	Excellent	$r_o \beta_F$	$V_{BE} + V_{CE}(\text{sat})$
Wilson Fig. 5.4-6	Good	$\dfrac{r_o \beta_F}{2}$	$V_{BE} + V_{CE}(\text{sat})$
Modified cascode Fig. 5.4-10	Good	$r_o \beta_F$	$2V_{CE}(\text{sat})$

Since the bulk-source voltages of M1 and M2 are identical, then V_{T1} and V_{T2} are identical and the following expression results.

$$\frac{I_{OUT}}{I_{IN}} = \frac{I_{D2}}{I_{D1}} = \frac{K'_{N1} W_1 L_2 (1 + \lambda_2 V_{DS2})}{K'_{N2} W_2 L_1 (1 + \lambda_1 V_{DS1})} \tag{5.4-45}$$

It can be seen that the channel modulation effect, λ, has the same influence on the MOS current mirror that the Early voltage had on the BJT current mirror. Because transistor Ws and Ls are found in Eq. 5.4-45, the geometry of the MOS devices can be used to determine the gain of the current mirror. Figure 5.4-11b gives the simulated I–V characteristics using equal values of $W = 50 \, \mu$ and $L = 10 \, \mu$ and the model parameters of $V_T = 0.75$ V, $K'_N = 24 \, \mu A/V^2$, $\gamma_N = 0.8 \, V^{-1/2}$, $\lambda_N = 0.01 \, V^{-1}$, and $\phi = 0.6$ V. These characteristics indicate

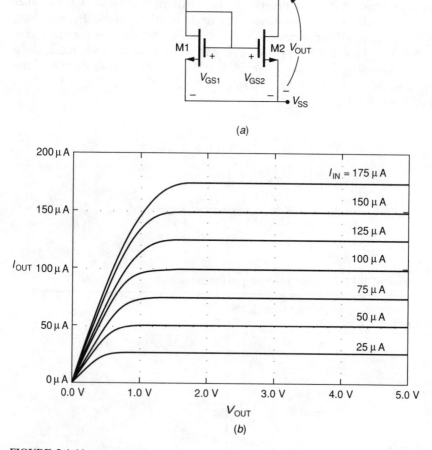

(a)

(b)

FIGURE 5.4-11
(a) Simple MOS current mirror, (b) Simulated performance of a.

that the channel modulation effect causes an increase in the slope of these curves preventing ideal current sink performance. A measure of the slope of these curves is given by the small signal output resistance and in this case is

$$r_{out} = \frac{v_{out}}{i_{out}} = r_{ds2} = \frac{1}{\lambda I_{D2}} = \frac{1}{\lambda I_{OUT}} \tag{5.4-46}$$

This corresponds to an output resistance of 1 MΩ when $I_{OUT} = 100$ μA. The value of V_{MIN} for the circuit of Fig. 5.4-11a which occurs when M2 transitions from the saturation to the active region can be shown to be 1.2 V when $I_{IN} = 100$ μA.

The matching accuracy of Eq. 5.4-45 can be determined in the same manner as was done for the BJT current mirror. The ratio of I_{D2} to I_{D1} (I_{OUT} to I_{IN}) can be expressed in general as

$$\frac{I_{D2}}{I_{D1}} = \frac{K'_{N2}(V_{GS2} - V_{T2})^2(1 + \lambda_2 V_{DS2})}{K'_{N1}(V_{GS1} - V_{T1})^2(1 + \lambda_1 V_{DS1})} \tag{5.4-47}$$

where it has been assumed that $W_2/L_2 = W_1/L_1$. In this discussion, the W/L ratios are assumed to be ideally matched. Using the following definitions

$$K'_{N1} = K'_N + (\Delta K'_N/2) \tag{5.4-48}$$

$$K'_{N2} = K'_N - (\Delta K'_N/2) \tag{5.4-49}$$

$$V_{T1} = V_T + (\Delta V_T/2) \tag{5.4-50}$$

$$V_{T2} = V_T - (\Delta V_T/2) \tag{5.4-51}$$

$$\lambda_1 = \lambda + (\Delta\lambda/2) \tag{5.4-52}$$

and

$$\lambda_2 = \lambda - (\Delta\lambda/2) \tag{5.4-53}$$

Eq. 5.4-47 may be expressed as

$$\frac{I_{D2}}{I_{D1}} = \frac{[K'_N - (\Delta K'_N/2)][V_{GS} - V_T + (\Delta V_T/2)]^2[1 + \lambda V_{DS} - (\Delta\lambda V_{DS}/2)]}{[K'_N + (\Delta K'_N/2)][V_{GS} - V_T - (\Delta V_T/2)]^2[1 + \lambda V_{DS} + (\Delta\lambda V_{DS}/2)]} \tag{5.4-54}$$

or as

$$\frac{I_{D2}}{I_{D1}} = \frac{(1 - \Delta K'_N/K'_N)[1 + \Delta V_T/2(V_{GS} - V_T)]^2(1 + \lambda V_{DS} - \Delta\lambda V_{DS}/2)}{(1 + \Delta K'_N/K'_N)[1 - \Delta V_T/2(V_{GS} - V_T)]^2(1 + \lambda V_{DS} + \Delta\lambda V_{DS}/2)} \tag{5.4-55}$$

Assuming that the differences in Eqs. 5.4-48 through 5.4-53 are small and that λV_{DS} is less than unity allows the simplification of Eq. 5.4-55 to

$$\frac{I_{D2}}{I_{D1}} \cong \left(1 - \frac{\Delta K'_N}{K'_N}\right)\left(1 + \frac{\Delta V_T}{V_{GS} - V_T}\right)^2(1 - \Delta\lambda V_{DS}) \tag{5.4-56}$$

or

$$\frac{I_{D2}}{I_{D1}} \cong 1 - \left(\frac{\Delta K'_N}{K'_N}\right) + \left(\frac{2}{(V_{GS}/V_T) - 1}\right)\left(\frac{\Delta V_T}{V_T}\right) - (\lambda V_{DS})\left(\frac{\Delta \lambda}{\lambda}\right) \qquad (5.4\text{-}57)$$

An example will illustrate these results

Example 5.4-1. Matching accuracy of a simple MOS mirror. Two MOS devices are used to implement the current mirror of Fig. 5.4-11a. Suppose that at $I_{IN} = 100 \ \mu A$, the various voltages were observed: $V_{GS1} = V_{GS2} = 3.6$ V and $V_{DS2} = 3.6$ V. Assume that the nominal parameters are $K'_N = 24 \ \mu A/V^2$, $V_T = 0.75$ V and $\lambda_N = 0.01 V^{-1}$. Furthermore, assume that the worst-case deviation about these values is $\pm 5\%$. Evaluate the deviation of the ratio of I_{D2}/I_{D1} from unity if $(W_1/L_1) = (W_2/L_2)$.

Solution. Substituting into Eq. 5.4-57 gives

$$\frac{I_{D2}}{I_{D1}} = 1 - (\pm 0.05) + (0.2598)(\pm 0.05) - (0.036)(\pm 0.05)$$

$$= 1 \pm 0.039$$

Under these conditions, the analysis of matching accuracy shows that a deviation of $\pm 4\%$ can occur. The value of this deviation will depend upon the operating conditions. In this example, V_{DS1} was chosen to be equal to V_{DS2} in order to eliminate the error due to λ.

A current mirror with higher output resistance than that obtained from the simple MOS mirror is shown in Fig. 5.4-12a. M3 and M4 keep the values of V_{DS1} and V_{DS2} nearly equal, effectively removing the influence of the channel modulation effect. M4 increases the output resistance of the mirror using the principle demonstrated in Fig. 5.3-7a to increase the output resistance of a simple MOS current sink. Figure 5.4-12a is called an MOS cascode current mirror and is topologically identical to the BJT cascode current mirror of Fig. 5.4-4a. If the mismatch effects are neglected, the current gain of the MOS cascode current mirror is given as

$$\frac{I_{OUT}}{I_{IN}} = \frac{(W_2/L_2)}{(W_1/L_1)} \qquad (5.4\text{-}58)$$

Figure 5.4-12b shows the I–V characteristics of the circuit of Fig. 5.4-12a when all Ws are 50 μ, all Ls are 10 μ, $V_T = 0.75$ V, $K'_N = 24 \ \mu A/V^2$, $\gamma_N = 0.8 \ V^{1/2}$, $\lambda_N = 0.01 \ V^{-1}$, and $\phi = 0.6$ V. These characteristics show that the output resistance of the MOS cascode mirror is significantly greater than the simple MOS mirror and that the accuracy is good.

The improvement in the slope reduction can be quantified by finding the small signal output resistance of the circuit of Fig. 5.4-12a. The output resistance of the MOS cascode current mirror is calculated using the small signal model of Fig. 5.4-13. First solve for v_{out}, which can be written as

$$v_{out} = v_4 + v_2 = r_{ds4}[i_{out} + g_{mb4}v_2 - g_{m4}(v_3 + v_1 - v_2)] + v_2 \qquad (5.4\text{-}59)$$

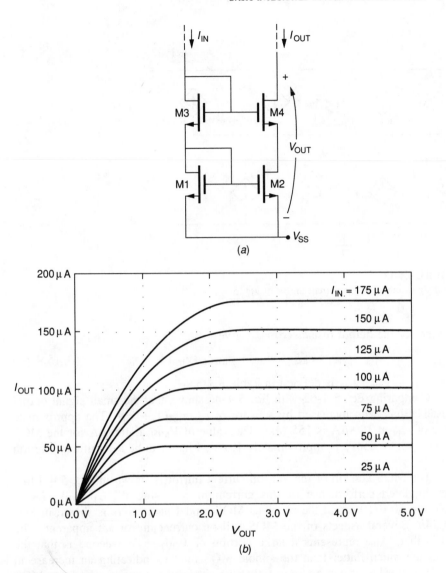

FIGURE 5.4-12
(a) MOS cascode current mirror, (b) Simulated performance of a.

Also,

$$v_2 = r_{ds2}(i_{out} - g_{m2}v_1) \tag{5.4-60}$$

Since $i_{in} = 0$ under small signal conditions, then v_1 and v_3 are also zero. Therefore, substitution of Eq. 5.4-60 into Eq. 5.4-59 results in,

$$v_{out} = i_{out}[r_{ds2} + r_{ds4} + r_{ds2}r_{ds4}(g_{m4} + g_{mb4})] \tag{5.4-61}$$

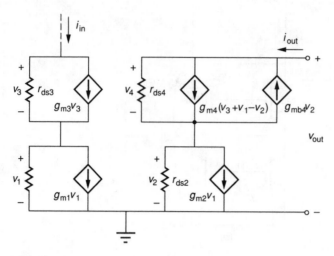

FIGURE 5.4-13
Small signal model of the current mirror of Fig. 5.4-12a.

Solving for the output resistance, r_{out}, gives

$$r_{\text{out}} = r_{\text{ds2}} + r_{\text{ds4}} + r_{\text{ds2}}r_{\text{ds4}}g_{\text{m4}}(1 + \eta_4) \qquad (5.4\text{-}62)$$

where $\eta_4 = g_{\text{mb4}}/g_{\text{m4}}$ is defined in Table 3.1-3.

Comparing Eq. 5.4-62 with Eq. 5.4-46 shows that the small signal output resistance has been increased by a factor of $r_{\text{ds4}}g_{\text{m4}}(1 + \eta_4)$. The approximate value of r_{out} at 100 μA is 155 MΩ. The value of V_{MIN} at 100 μA for the MOS cascode mirror above is approximately 1.6 V, which can be a significant portion of V_{OUT}.

The MOS version of the Wilson current mirror is shown in Fig. 5.4-14a. The simulated performance of this current mirror using $W_1/L_1 = W_2/L_2 = W_3/L_3 = 50$ $\mu/10$ μ and the previous MOS model parameters is shown in Fig. 5.4-14b. Several aspects of the MOS Wilson current mirror are apparent. The first is that V_{MIN} represents a large portion of V_{OUT}. The second is that the curves are much flatter than the simple MOS mirror, indicating an increase in r_{out}. And thirdly, it can be shown that the linearity (or accuracy) of the MOS Wilson current mirror is not good for high current levels. This nonlinearity is due to the difference in V_{DS1} and V_{DS2} for larger currents. Since V_{DS2} is less than V_{DS1}, Eq. 5.4-45 shows that the channel modulation effects will cause I_{D2} to be less than I_{D1} if M1 and M2 are matched. This problem can be alleviated if a fourth, drain-gate-connected device is connected in series with M1 between the drain of M1 and the gate of M3.

The output resistance of the MOS Wilson current mirror will quantify the slope reduction compared with the simple MOS mirror. It can be shown that the small signal output resistance of the Wilson current mirror is given as (see Prob. 5.31)

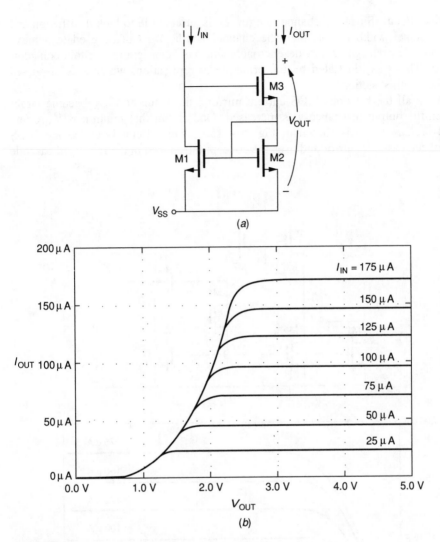

FIGURE 5.4-14

(*a*) MOS Wilson current mirror, (*b*) Simulated performance of *a*.

$$r_{\text{out}} = r_{\text{ds}3} + r_{\text{ds}2} \frac{1 + r_{\text{ds}3}g_{\text{m}3}(1 + \eta_3) + g_{\text{m}1}r_{\text{ds}1}g_{\text{m}3}r_{\text{ds}3}}{1 + g_{\text{m}2}r_{\text{ds}2}} \qquad (5.4\text{-}63)$$

The output resistance of Fig. 5.4-14*a* is found to be comparable with the MOS cascode mirror of Fig. 5.4-12*a*. Unfortunately, both of these current mirrors require at least $2V_T$ across the input before they behave as described above.

The Widlar current mirror can also be implemented by MOS transistors and will be left as a problem (see Prob. 5.32). A practical consideration in matching the devices that are mirroring the current is to keep the channel lengths of both devices equal. Since the channel length, L, is susceptible to lateral diffusion and the channel width is not, then the channel width, W, can be used to achieve nonunity current gains. Oxide encroachment has been ignored in this consideration. This was illustrated by the principle of replication, which was discussed earlier in this section.

In all the previous MOS current mirrors, the value of V_{MIN} became larger when the output resistance was increased. One circuit that minimizes V_{MIN} and still increases r_{out} is shown in Fig. 5.4-15a. This circuit is called the MOS regulated cascode mirror and uses the concept introduced in the regulated cascode

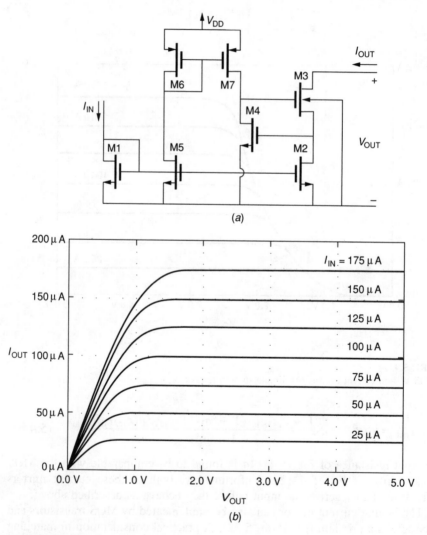

(a)

(b)

FIGURE 5.4-15
(a) MOS regulated cascode current mirror, (b) Simulated performance of a.

current sink of Fig. 5.3-16. The regulated cascode consists of M2, M3, and M4. M1 and M2 form a simple current mirror; however, because of M4, the value of V_{DS2} will not be much different than V_{DS1}, giving good accuracy. M5, M6, and M7 are used to provide a bias current for M4, which tracks the output current. If I_{D4} did not track I_{OUT} (I_{D3}), then the value of V_{GS2} would not be large enough at large values of I_{OUT} to keep M2 in saturation. If M2 is not in saturation, then the ratio of I_{D2} to I_{D1} will be smaller than what is expected. Figure 5.4-15b shows the simulated results for the regulated cascode current mirror of Fig. 5.4-15a when $W_1/L_1 = W_2/L_2 = W_3/L_3 = W_4/L_4 = W_5/L_5 = W_6/L_6 = 50 \mu/10 \mu$, $W_7/L_7 = 75 \mu/10 \mu$, and using the model parameters as before, with the addition of $K_P' = 8 \mu A/V^2$, $V_{TP} = -0.75$ V, $\gamma_P = 0.4 V^{-1/2}$, $\lambda_P = 0.02 V^{-1}$, and $\phi = 0.6$ V. It is seen that V_{MIN} is almost identical to that of the simple MOS mirror of Fig. 5.4-11b. In addition, the output resistance is given by Eq. 5.3-20 and is much higher than any of the other MOS mirrors presented so far. Clearly, Fig. 5.4-15a is a superior MOS current mirror realization in many respects. If the ratio of I_{D5} to I_{D2} is decreased below the 0.5 of Fig. 5.4-15b, the value of V_{MIN} decreases, but the ratio of I_{OUT} to I_{IN} becomes nonlinear as the currents increase.

Table 5.4-2 summarizes the performance of the MOS current mirrors having unity gain from the viewpoint of accuracy (linearity), output resistance, and V_{MIN}. Additional considerations include the size of devices. More ratio accuracy will be obtained for larger size devices. All of the current mirrors presented in this section used npn BJTs or n-channel MOSFETs. Opposite-type current mirrors can be implemented using pnp BJTs or p-channel MOSFETs. The circuits perform in an identical manner. The parametric expressions for the small signal resistances are identical in either case.

The important principles developed and used in this section include the matching principle, the replication principle, and the method by which mismatches between similar devices can be calculated. These principles will be employed where appropriate in the material that follows. The circuits developed in this section will be very useful in designing more complex analog circuits. They will find use in dc biasing and as high-resistance ac loads.

TABLE 5.4-2
Comparison of MOS current mirror performance

MOS current mirror	Accuracy ($I_{D2} = I_{D1}$)	r_{out}	V_{MIN}
Simple Fig. 5.4-11a	Poor	$r_o = \dfrac{1}{\lambda I_{out}}$	$V_{DS}(sat)$
Cascode Fig. 5.4-12a	Good	$g_m r_o^2$	$2V_{DS}(sat)$
Wilson Fig. 5.4-14a	Good	$\dfrac{g_m r_o^2}{2}$	$V_{GS} + V_{DS}(sat)$
Regulated cascode Fig. 5.4-15a	Good	$g_m^2 r_o^3$	$V_{DS}(sat)$

5.5   VOLTAGE AND CURRENT REFERENCES

In Sec. 5.3, current sinks/sources were presented. These circuits can be used to create a voltage by applying the current to a resistor. Such circuits represent one method of achieving a dc voltage or current. However, many applications require a dc voltage or current that is more stable than the circuits of Sec. 5.3. Circuits that yield a precise dc voltage or current independent of external influences are called *voltage references* or *current references*. The primary external influences of concern are power supply and temperature variations. The objective of this section will be to demonstrate the principles of voltage and current references that minimize their dependence on power supply and temperature.

In order to characterize the dependence of a reference on power supply and temperature, the concepts of sensitivity and fractional temperature coefficient are introduced. Assume that the reference is a voltage designated as V_{REF}. The sensitivity of V_{REF} to changes in a power supply V_{XX} is given as

$$S_{V_{XX}}^{V_{REF}} = \lim_{\Delta V_{XX} \to 0} \frac{\Delta V_{REF}/V_{REF}}{\Delta V_{XX}/V_{XX}} = \frac{V_{XX}}{V_{REF}} \left(\frac{\partial V_{REF}}{\partial V_{XX}} \right) \tag{5.5-1}$$

Eq. 5.5-1 emphasizes how the sensitivity can be calculated. However, once the sensitivity is known, it can be applied using the following form.

$$\frac{\Delta V_{REF}}{V_{REF}} \simeq \left(S_{V_{XX}}^{V_{REF}} \right) \left(\frac{\Delta V_{XX}}{V_{XX}} \right) \tag{5.5-2}$$

Eq. 5.5-2 can be interpreted as follows: if the sensitivity of V_{REF} with respect to V_{XX} is unity then a 10% change in V_{XX} will cause a 10% change in V_{REF}. Obviously, if V_{REF} is to be independent of V_{XX}, then the sensitivity of V_{REF} with respect to V_{XX} should approach zero. Sensitivities less than 1/100 are practical values for a monolithic voltage reference. The above formulation is valid for current references by simply replacing V_{REF} by I_{REF}.

While the sensitivity measure given in Eq. 5.5-1 with V_{XX} replaced with the temperature (i.e. $S_T^{V_{REF}}$) could be used as a measure of the dependence of the reference on temperature, it is customary to use the concept of fractional temperature coefficient introduced in Eq. 2.2-5 of Chapter 2. The fractional temperature coefficient (TC$_F$) of V_{REF} is defined as

$$TC_F(V_{REF}) = \frac{1}{V_{REF}} \frac{\partial V_{REF}}{\partial T} = \frac{1}{T} S_T^{V_{REF}} \tag{5.5-3}$$

where the relationship between the fractional temperature coefficient of V_{REF} and the sensitivity of V_{REF} to temperature (T) is also illustrated. The units of TC$_F$ are expressed in terms of parts per million per °C, or ppm/°C. Assuming that a sensitivity of V_{REF} with respect to temperature equal to 1/100 is indicative of a good voltage reference, then at room temperature $(T = 300°K)$ the fractional temperature coefficient is $(1/300) \times (1/100) \times 1,000,000 = 33.3$ ppm/°C. References with a TC$_F$ of less than 50 ppm/°C are considered to be stable with respect to temperature.

Figure 5.5-1 shows three simple voltage references which will be more useful for illustrating the analysis techniques than for implementing a good voltage reference. Figure 5.5-1a is simply a voltage divider providing a dc voltage between V_{XX} and ground. The value of dc voltage is

$$V_{REF} = V_{XX}\left(\frac{R_2}{R_1 + R_2}\right) \tag{5.5-4}$$

The sensitivity of V_{REF} with respect to V_{XX} is found to be

$$S_{V_{XX}}^{V_{REF}} = \frac{V_{XX}}{V_{REF}} \frac{\partial V_{REF}}{\partial V_{XX}} = 1 \tag{5.5-5}$$

The fractional temperature coefficient of this simple voltage reference is found after some algebraic manipulation to be

$$TC_F(V_{REF}) = \frac{1}{V_{REF}} \frac{\partial V_{REF}}{\partial T} = \left(\frac{R_1}{R_2} \frac{V_{REF}}{V_{XX}}\right)\left(\frac{\partial R_2}{R_2 \partial T} - \frac{\partial R_1}{R_1 \partial T}\right)$$

$$= \left(\frac{R_1}{R_2} \frac{V_{REF}}{V_{XX}}\right)[TC_F(R_2) - TC_F(R_1)] \tag{5.5-6}$$

where the resistors are assumed to be temperature-dependent and V_{XX} is temperature-independent. Equation 5.5-6 illustrates a very important property of temperature dependence. Note that if the fractional temperature coefficients of R_2, $TC_F(R_2)$, and of R_1, $TC_F(R_1)$, are equal then $TC_F(V_{REF})$ is zero. Thus, if both R_1 and R_2 are made from identical means, i.e., diffusion, polysilicon, etc., then temperature independence will be achieved. This result will hold true for ratios of similar components. It is easy to illustrate the principle from Eqs. 5.5-4 and

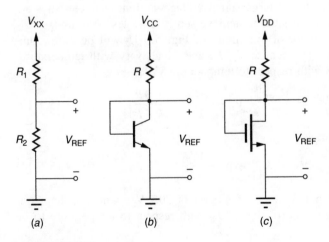

(a)   (b)   (c)

FIGURE 5.5-1
Simple voltage references: (a) Passive voltage divider, (b) BJT voltage reference and (c) MOS voltage reference.

5.5-6. If $TC_F(R_2)$ is equal to $TC_F(R_1)$, then the percentage changes are approximately equal. Suppose that $R_2 = 2\,\Omega$ and $R_1 = 1\,\Omega$. The value of V_{REF} is $V_{XX}/3$. If the temperature changes so that the resistors experience a 10% increase, they become $R_2' = 2.2\,\Omega$ and $R_1' = 1.1\,\Omega$. Substituting these values into Eq. 5.5-4 still gives V_{REF} of $V_{XX}/3$.

Figure 5.5-1*b* illustrates how a voltage reference can be achieved from a BJT and a resistor. The reference voltage can be found using the relationship for the collector current as a function of base–emitter voltage (Eq. 3.3-13 of Sec. 3.3). The result is

$$V_{REF} = V_t \ln \left(\frac{V_{CC} - V_{REF}}{RI_S} \right) \tag{5.5-7}$$

where V_t and I_S are parameters of the BJT defined in Chapter 3. Because V_{REF} is also inside the argument of the natural logarithm, an iterative solution is necessary to obtain V_{REF}. If V_{CC} is much greater than V_{REF}, then Eq. 5.5-7 simplifies to

$$V_{REF} \approx V_t \ln \left(\frac{V_{CC}}{RI_S} \right) \tag{5.5-8}$$

The sensitivity of V_{REF} with respect to V_{CC} can be found by differentiating either Eq. 5.5-7 or 5.5-8 and substituting into Eq. 5.5-1. Assuming that $V_{CC} \gg V_{REF}$ (see Prob. 5.34 when this is not true), the sensitivity of the circuit of Fig. 5.5-1*b* is

$$S_{V_{CC}}^{V_{REF}} \cong \frac{1}{\ln (V_{CC}/RI_S)} \tag{5.5-9}$$

If $V_{CC} = 5$ V, $R = 43\,\text{k}\Omega$ and $I_S = 0.4$ fA, the sensitivity of V_{REF} with respect to V_{CC} is 0.0379. If V_{CC} changes by 10%, V_{REF} will change by only 0.379%. Thus, a second principle emerges concerning low-sensitivity references. If two or more components which have different large signal voltage–current characteristics are used to divide voltage, it is possible to achieve sensitivities less than unity.

The temperature behavior of the circuit of Fig. 5.5-1*b* will be more complex than that of Fig. 5.5-1*a* because V_t, R, and I_S all vary with temperature. Differentiating Eq. 5.5-8 with respect to temperature yields

$$\frac{\partial V_{REF}}{\partial T} = \frac{V_{REF}}{T} - V_t \left(\frac{1}{I_S} \frac{\partial I_S}{\partial T} + \frac{1}{R} \frac{\partial R}{\partial T} \right) \tag{5.5-10}$$

Assuming that I_S is given as

$$I_S = KT^3 \exp \left(\frac{-V_{GO}}{V_t} \right) \tag{5.5-11}$$

where V_{GO} is the band gap voltage of silicon (1.205 V), which is temperature independent, allows the derivative of I_S with respect to temperature to be expressed as

$$\frac{\partial I_S}{\partial T} = \frac{3I_S}{T} + \frac{I_S}{T} \frac{V_{GO}}{V_t} \tag{5.5-12}$$

Substituting Eq. 5.5-12 into Eq. 5.5-10 and dividing by V_{REF} gives

$$TC_F(V_{REF}) = \frac{V_{REF} - 3V_t - V_{GO}}{V_{REF}T} - \frac{V_t}{V_{REF}}\left(\frac{1}{R}\frac{\partial R}{\partial T}\right) \qquad (5.5\text{-}13)$$

If $V_{REF} = 0.7$ V and the TC_F of R is 1500 ppm/°C, the $TC_F(V_{REF})$ of Fig. 5.5-1b at room temperature (300°K) is

$$TC_F(V_{REF}) = -2776 \text{ ppm/°C} - 56 \text{ ppm/°C} = -2832 \text{ ppm/°C} \qquad (5.5\text{-}14)$$

It is seen that this voltage reference has a large temperature coefficient for a voltage reference.

Figure 5.5-1c shows how MOS technology can be used to implement a voltage reference similar to the simple BJT voltage reference of Fig. 5.5-1b. Since the drain and gate are physically connected, the device is in saturation for $V_{GS} \geq V_T$ and V_{REF} can be expressed as

$$V_{REF} = V_T + \sqrt{\frac{2(V_{DD} - V_{REF})}{RK_N'(W/L)}} \qquad (5.5\text{-}15)$$

As before, an iterative method is used to solve for V_{REF}. If $V_{DD} = 10$ V, $V_T = 0.75$ V, $K_N' = 24 \ \mu\text{A/V}^2$, $W/L = 10$, and $R = 100 \ \text{k}\Omega$, then iterative methods give a V_{REF} of 1.972 V. If V_{DD} is greater than V_{REF}, then

$$V_{REF} \approx V_T + \sqrt{\frac{2V_{DD}}{RK_N'(W/L)}} \qquad (5.5\text{-}16)$$

Using Eq. 5.5-16 with these parameters and values gives $V_{REF} = 2.085$. The sensitivity of the circuit of Fig. 5.5-1c with respect to V_{DD} can be found for the case where $V_{DD} >> V_{REF}$ as

$$S_{V_{DD}}^{V_{REF}} = \frac{0.5}{1 + V_T\sqrt{RK_N'W/2V_{DD}L}} \qquad (5.5\text{-}17)$$

Using the above parameters and values gives a sensitivity of V_{REF} with respect to V_{DD} of 0.274. The sensitivity of the circuit of Fig. 5.5-1c is larger than the circuit of Fig. 5.5-1b because the power supply in the BJT case is in the argument of the logarithm, while in the MOS case it is within the argument of the square root. Since the logarithm is a weaker function than the square root, the sensitivity of the BJT voltage reference is smaller than the MOS voltage reference.

In order to analyze the temperature dependence, the temperature dependence of the MOS transistor must be characterized. The primary temperature-dependent parameters of MOS device are K' (mobility) and V_T. Their temperature dependence will be modeled as

$$K_N' = K_{NO}'\left(\frac{T}{T_O}\right)^{1.5} \qquad (5.5\text{-}18)$$

and

$$V_T = V_{TO} - \alpha(T - T_O) \qquad (5.5\text{-}19)$$

where K'_{NO} and V_{TO} are the values of K'_N and V_T at T_O and α is approximately 2.3 mV/°C. Assuming R, K'_N, and V_T are temperature-dependent and differentiating Eqs. 5.5-16, 5.5-18, and 5.5-19 gives

$$\frac{\partial V_{REF}}{\partial T} = \frac{\partial V_T}{\partial T} - \frac{1}{2}\sqrt{\frac{2V_{DD}}{K'_N R(W/L)}}\left(\frac{1}{R}\frac{\partial R}{\partial T}\right) - \frac{1}{2}\sqrt{\frac{2V_{DD}}{K'_N R(W/L)}}\frac{1}{K'_N}\frac{\partial K'_N}{\partial T}$$

$$\tag{5.5-20}$$

$$\frac{\partial K'_N}{\partial T} = -\frac{1.5}{T}K'_N \tag{5.5-21}$$

and

$$\frac{\partial V_T}{\partial T} = -\alpha \tag{5.5-22}$$

Substituting Eqs. 5.5-21 and 5.5-22 into Eq. 5.5-20 and dividing by V_{REF} gives

$$TC_F(V_{REF}) = \frac{-1}{V_{REF}}\left[\alpha + \frac{1}{2}\sqrt{\frac{2V_{DD}}{K'_N R(W/L)}}\left(\frac{1}{R}\frac{\partial R}{\partial T} - \frac{1.5}{T}\right)\right] \tag{5.5-23}$$

Using the values above with $V_{REF} = 2.085$ V and assuming that $TC_F(R) = 1500$ ppm/°C, the fractional temperature coefficient becomes

$$TC_F(V_{REF}) = \frac{-1}{2.085}[0.0023 - 0.0016] = -336 \text{ ppm/°C} \tag{5.5-24}$$

While the $TC_F(V_{REF})$ of Fig. 5.5-1c is almost 10 times less than that of Fig. 5.5-1b, this is due to the selection of the resistor and the particular manner in which the temperature-dependent variables combine to give the overall temperature dependence.

The simple voltage references of Fig. 5.5-1 illustrate the methods by which more complex references can be characterized. The value of V_{REF} of Figs. 5.5-1b and 5.5-1c can be increased by cascading active devices or by the method illustrated in Fig. 5.5-2. It can be shown that the reference voltages of Fig. 5.5-2a and b are equal to $(1 + R_2/R_1)$ times the values given in Eqs. 5.5-8 and 5.5-16, respectively.

Current references are also of interest in this section. Figure 5.3-4a and Fig. 5.3-5a show examples of simple current references. However, one important aspect of these two current references is the implementation of V_{BB} and V_{GG}. In most cases V_{BB} and V_{GG} are implemented using the circuits of Figs. 5.5-1b and c, respectively. The result is shown in Fig. 5.5-3a and b and is in fact the simple current mirrors of Sec. 5.4, where I_{IN} is defined by the voltage across R. Using the relationships of the last section and assuming ideal current mirrors gives

$$I_{REF} = \frac{V_{CC} - V_{BE}}{R} \tag{5.5-25}$$

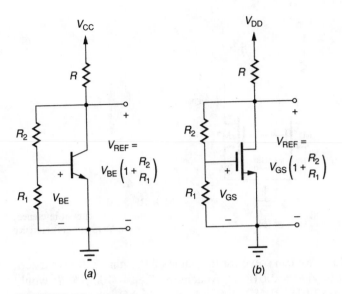

FIGURE 5.5-2
A method of increasing the value of V_{REF} for (a) Fig. 5.5-1b, (b) Fig. 5.5-1c.

and

$$I_{REF} = \frac{V_{DD} - V_{GS}}{R} \tag{5.5-26}$$

for Figs. 5.5-3a and 5.5-3b. It is obvious that the sensitivity of I_{REF} with respect to power supply is unity for both references if $V_{CC} \gg V_{BE}$ or $V_{DD} \gg V_{GS}$. The temperature coefficient of I_{REF} for Fig. 5.5-3a can be found by differentiating Eq. 5.5-25 with respect to temperature and dividing by I_{REF}. The result is

$$TC_F(I_{REF}) = \frac{-1}{I_{REF}}\left[\frac{\partial V_{BE}}{R \partial T} + I_{REF}\left(\frac{1}{R}\frac{\partial R}{\partial T}\right)\right] \tag{5.5-27}$$

Using the previous results for $\partial V_{BE}/\partial T$ yields

$$TC_F(I_{REF}) \approx \frac{1}{I_{REF}}\left[\frac{V_{GO} + 3V_t - V_{BE}}{RT}\right] - \left(\frac{1}{R}\frac{\partial R}{\partial T}\right) \tag{5.5-28}$$

where it is assumed that V_t is much less than $V_{CC} - V_{BE}$. If $I_{REF} = 100\ \mu A$, then $V_{BE} = 0.682$ V for $I_S = 0.4$ fA. If $R = 43$ k$\Omega(V_{CC} = 5$ V), $TC_F(R) = 1500$ ppm/°C and $T = 300$ K, then $TC_F(I_{REF})$ is equal to

$$TC_F(I_{REF}) = 466\ \text{ppm/°C} - 1500\ \text{ppm/°C} = -1034\ \text{ppm/°C} \tag{5.5-29}$$

The current reference above has an additional term with an opposite sign in the expression for $TC_F(I_{REF})$, which suggests the possibility of achieving a zero value of $TC_F(I_{REF})$. Setting Eq. 5.5-28 to zero results in

$$I_{REF}R = V_{CC} - V_{BE} = \frac{V_{GO} + 3V_t - V_{BE}}{T(1/R)(\partial R/\partial T)} \tag{5.5-30}$$

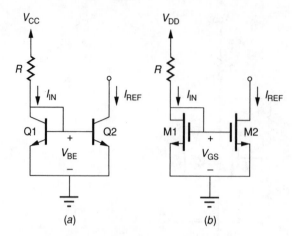

FIGURE 5.5-3
(a) A simple BJT current reference,
(b) A simple MOS current reference.

(a)   (b)

Using the previous values, we can solve for the value of V_{CC} that will give a zero $TC_F(I_{REF})$. The result is $V_{CC} = 2.018$ V. To achieve $I_{REF} = 100\ \mu A$, R would have to be decreased to $(2.018 - 0.682)/100\ \mu A = 13.36$ kΩ, which would not change the zero value of $TC_F(I_{REF})$.

The fractional temperature coefficient of the MOS current reference of Fig. 5.5-3b is found by differentiating Eq. 5.5-26 with respect to temperature and dividing by I_{REF} to get the following

$$TC_F(I_{REF}) = \frac{-1}{I_{REF}}\left[\frac{\partial V_{GS}}{R\partial T} + \frac{I_{REF}}{R}\frac{\partial R}{\partial T}\right] \qquad (5.5\text{-}31)$$

Using the results of Eqs. 5.5-20 through 5.5-23 in Eq. 5.5-31 gives

$$TC_F(I_{REF}) = \frac{1}{I_{REF}}\left[\frac{\alpha}{R} + \frac{1}{R}\sqrt{\frac{V_{DD}}{2K_N'R(W/L)}}\left(\frac{1}{R}\frac{\partial R}{\partial T} - \frac{3}{4T}\right)\right] - \left(\frac{1}{R}\frac{\partial R}{\partial T}\right) \qquad (5.5\text{-}32)$$

Assuming that $I_{REF} = 100\ \mu A$, $K'_N = 24\ \mu A/V^2$, $V_{TN} = 0.75$ V, and $W/L = 10$ gives $V_{GS} = 1.663$ V. If $V_{DD} = 10$ V, then $R = 83.37$ kΩ. Finally if $\alpha = 2/3$ mV/°C and $TC_F(R) = 1500$ ppm/°C, the TC_F of the circuit of Fig. 5.5-3b is

$$TC_F(I_{REF}) = 216\ \text{ppm/°C} - 1500\ \text{ppm/°C} = -1284\ \text{ppm/°C} \qquad (5.5\text{-}33)$$

Again, zero TC_F is possible. Setting Eq. 5.5-32 to zero and solving for $I_{REF}R$ gives

$$I_{REF}R = V_{DD} - V_{GS} = \frac{\alpha + \sqrt{(V_{DD}L)/(2K_N'RW)}[(1/R)(\partial R/\partial T) - (3/4T)]}{(1/R)(\partial R/\partial T)} \qquad (5.5\text{-}34)$$

Using the above values in Eq. 5.5-34 gives a $V_{DD} = 2.863$ V for a zero $TC_F(I_{REF})$. This lower supply voltage causes R to become 28.63 kΩ. The above analysis is only approximate since in calculating the temperature change of V_{GS}, Eq. 5.5-16 rather than Eq. 5.5-15 was used. The chapter problems deal with the exact case.

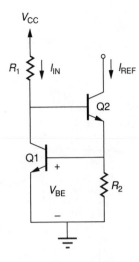

FIGURE 5.5-4
A method of obtaining a supply independent source by using V_{BE} to define the current.

So far, the references considered are not representative of stable voltage or current references. The remainder of the references presented will attempt to minimize the power supply dependence, the temperature dependence, or both. To achieve a reduction of the dependence of the current on the supply voltage, a technique of using the V_{BE} drop of a forward-biased pn junction is used. Such a circuit is shown in Fig. 5.5-4. Neglecting the base current, it follows from Eq. 3.3-10 that the reference current is expressed as

$$I_{REF} = \frac{V_{BE1}}{R_2} = \frac{V_t}{R_2} \ln\left(\frac{I_{IN}}{I_{S1}}\right) \tag{5.5-35}$$

It can be shown that

$$S_{V_{CC}}^{I_{REF}} \approx \frac{V_t}{I_{REF}R_2} \tag{5.5-36}$$

If $I_{IN} = 1$ mA, $I_{REF} = 100$ μA, and $I_{S1} = 0.4$fA, then from Eq. (5.5-35) $R_2 = 7.42$ kΩ. Therefore, the sensitivity of I_{REF} to V_{CC} is 0.035. Because the temperature performance of this current reference is not necessarily good and because the behavior is similar to that of Fig. 5.5-3a, it will not be pursued in further detail.

Another approach which uses the concept of generating the current from V_{BE} is shown in the bootstrap biasing circuit of Fig. 5.5-5a. The operating point of this circuit can be found by noting that if Q4 and Q5 are matched and if diode D1 is cutoff then these two devices form a simple unity gain current mirror. Neglecting base currents we obtain

$$I_{C1} = I_{C2} \tag{5.5-37}$$

and

$$V_{BE1} = V_t \ln (I_{C1}/I_{S1}) = I_{C2}R_1 \tag{5.5-38}$$

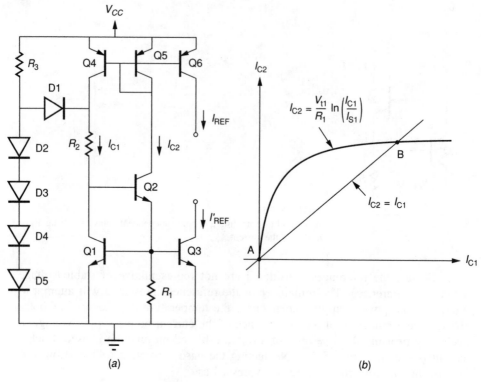

FIGURE 5.5-5
(*a*) A bootstrapped current source/sink, (*b*) Two possible operating points.

A closed form explicit expression for I_{C2} obtained by simultaneously solving Eqs. 5.5-37 and 5.5-38 in terms of basic functions does not exist. Plotting both Eqs. 5.5-37 and 5.5-38 on a curve of I_{C2} versus I_{C1} results in the curve of Fig. 5.5-5*b*. There are two operating points possible, designated as A and B. The operating point at A is undesirable since the value of $I_{C2}(I_{REF})$ is zero. Operation at the desired operating point, B, is determined by the start–up circuit consisting of R_3 and the five diodes. When V_{CC} is applied to the circuit, current flows through D_1 and R_2, forcing the circuit to the operating point at B. The value of $I_{C1}R_2$ is designed so that when the circuit is operating at B, D_1 is biased off disconnecting the start up circuit from the bootstrap current source/sink. Once the bootstrap current source/sink is operating at point B, the value of I_{REF} which is related to I_{C2} by the current mirror, Q5–Q6, should be independent of V_{CC}. I'_{REF} illustrates how a current sinking reference can be achieved.

The bootstrap current source can also be implemented in MOS technology as shown in Fig. 5.5-6*a*. The two equations corresponding to Eq. 5.5-37 and Eq. 5.5-38 are

$$I_{D1} = I_{D2} \tag{5.5-39}$$

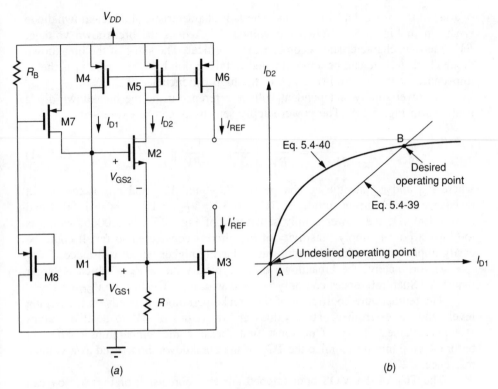

FIGURE 5.5-6
(a) A CMOS bootstrapped current source/sink, (b) Illustration of the two possible operating points.

and

$$I_{D2} = (V_{T1}/R) + \left[(2I_{D1}L_1/K'_N W_1)^{1/2}/R \right] \qquad (5.5\text{-}40)$$

Plotting Eq. 5.5-39 and Eq. 5.5-40 results in the curves shown in Fig. 5.5-6b where again two operating points are possible. R_B, M7, and M8 are used to start up the circuit, causing it to operate at point B. The values of V_{GS2} and V_{GS1} are designed so that M7 will be cutoff if the bootstrap current source/sink is operating at point B.

Both the BJT and MOS bootstrapped current sources represent good references for independence of power supply. However, second-order effects must be taken into account to achieve a minimum dependence. These second-order effects include the errors in current mirrors (see Sec. 5.4). Without including the second-order effects such as current mirror matching, the lower limit of power supply sensitivity is about 0.01 with these circuits.

In most silicon technologies it is possible to obtain a breakdown diode from a pn junction that is heavily doped on one side of the junction. In a bipolar process, a breakdown diode can be obtained by reverse biasing the base–emitter junction. In a CMOS process, a low voltage breakdown diode results from the overlap of the p^+ and n^+ diffusions. The $I-V$ characteristic of a breakdown diode is shown in Fig. 5.5-7. When the voltage V exceeds the breakdown voltage, BV, the $I-V$ characteristic becomes nearly vertical. The slope of the breakdown diode characteristic can be approximated in this region by $1/r_z$ where r_z is the ac impedance of the breakdown diode in the high-conductance region.

A power supply–independent voltage reference using the breakdown diode is shown in Fig. 5.5-8. The power supply sensitivity can be expressed as

$$S_{V_{CC}}^{V_{REF}} = \frac{V_{CC}}{V_{REF}} \frac{\partial V_{REF}}{\partial V_{CC}} = \left(\frac{V_{CC}}{BV}\right)\left(\frac{v_{ref}}{v_{cc}}\right) = \left(\frac{V_{CC}}{BV}\right)\left(\frac{r_z}{r_z + r_{out}}\right) \qquad (5.5\text{-}41)$$

where v_{ref} and v_{cc} are the ac changes of V_{REF} and V_{CC} and r_{out} is the output resistance of the current source. If $BV = 6.5$ V, $V_{CC} = 10$ V, $r_z = 1000\ \Omega$ and $r_{out} = 100$ kΩ, the power supply sensitivity of Fig. 5.5-8 is 0.0065, which is the lowest power supply sensitivity of the circuits considered so far. It could be easily improved by using a current mirror having higher output resistance.

Unfortunately, the breakdown diode typically has a V_{REF} which is larger than 5 V. Such references can only be used with higher values of V_{DD} or V_{CC}.

The temperature coefficient of the breakdown diode depends on the doping levels and varies from negative values at low values of BV to positive values at higher values of BV. One must first measure the temperature coefficient before attempting to minimize the TC_F of the breakdown diode used as a voltage reference.

The TC_F of the MOS bootstrapped current source/sink of Fig. 5.5-6a can be found as

$$TC_F = \left|\frac{1}{V_{T1} + (I_{D1}L_1/K_N'W_1)^{1/2}}\right| \frac{\partial V_{T1}}{\partial T} - \frac{\partial R}{R\partial T} = \frac{1}{V_{GS1}} \frac{\partial V_{T1}}{\partial T} - \frac{\partial R}{R\partial T}$$

$$(5.5\text{-}42)$$

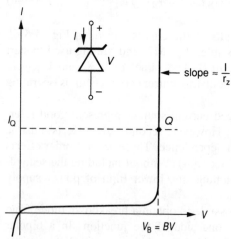

FIGURE 5.5-7
Current–voltage characteristics of a breakdown diode.

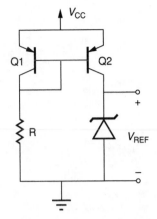

FIGURE 5.5-8
Power supply–independent voltage reference using the breakdown diode.

where we have assumed that I_{D1} and K_N' are independent of temperature. If I_{D2} has been designed such that $V_{GS1} = 1.5$ V and the value of the temperature coefficient of V_T is -0.18 mV/°C and the fractional temperature coefficient of R is $+1500$ ppm/°C (polysilicon), then the TC_F of the MOS bootstrapped current/sink is

$$TC_F = -110 \text{ ppm/°C} - 1500 \text{ ppm/°C} = -1610 \text{ ppm/°C}$$

It is interesting to note in this and previous references that R is the major contributor to temperature variation.

One approach to reducing the TC_F of current references is to try to use the opposite temperature coefficients of breakdown diodes and pn junction diodes (diode connected transistors) to cancel the dependence of the source upon temperature. Figure 5.5-9 shows a voltage reference that has the possibility of achieving this objective. It is assumed that I_o is sufficiently well-defined so that $V_B = BV$ can be assumed to be independent of V_{CC}. The reference voltage can be expressed as

$$V_{REF} = \left(\frac{R_2}{R_1 + R_2}\right) V_B - 2V_{BE}\left(\frac{R_2}{R_1 + R_2}\right) + V_{BE}\left(\frac{R_1}{R_1 + R_2}\right) \qquad (5.5\text{-}43)$$

assuming all V_{BE} are equal and all diodes are matched.

If Eq. 5.5-43 is differentiated with respect to T and set equal to zero, we get

$$-\frac{\partial V_B / \partial T}{\partial V_{BE} / \partial T} = \frac{R_1}{R_2} - 2 \qquad (5.5\text{-}44)$$

But if the temperature dependence of the breakdown diode is $+3$ mV/°C, then

$$\frac{\partial V_B / \partial T}{\partial V_{BE} / \partial T} \cong \frac{+3 \text{ mV/°C}}{-2 \text{ mV/°C}} \qquad (5.5\text{-}45)$$

Therefore, the ratio of R_1/R_2 for zero temperature dependence is 3.5. The value of V_{REF} under this constraint is $(2/9)V_B$ or approximately 1.4 V. The voltage reference of Fig. 5.5-9 should also be relatively independent of V_{CC}.

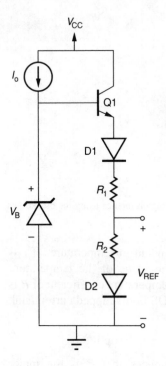

FIGURE 5.5-9
Use of cancellation between pn diode and breakdown diode temperature coefficients to obtain a temperature independent voltage reference.

One of the more popular and successful approaches to achieving a voltage reference, which is independent of both supply and temperature, is the *bandgap voltage reference*. The concept behind the bandgap voltage reference is illustrated in Fig. 5.5-10. A voltage V_{BE} is generated from a pn junction diode having a temperature coefficient of -2 mV/°C at room temperature. Also a voltage

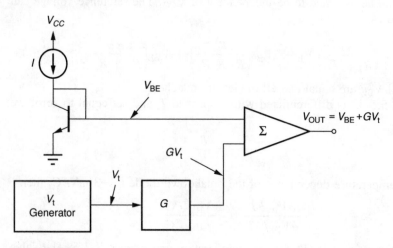

FIGURE 5.5-10
General concepts of a bandgap voltage reference.

$V_t (V_t = kT/q)$ is generated that has a temperature coefficient of $+0.085$ mV/°C at room temperature. If the V_t voltage is multiplied by a constant G and summed with the V_{BE} voltage, then the output voltage is given as

$$V_{REF} = V_{BE} + GV_t \tag{5.5-46}$$

On a first order basis, the value of G would be that which gives a zero value of temperature coefficient for V_{REF}. This value of G corresponds to 23.5 and produces a reference voltage of 1.26 V assuming V_{BE} is 0.65 V. A more detailed analysis is necessary to design the bandgap voltage reference so that zero temperature coefficient is achieved over a wide range of temperatures.[7]

A BJT version of the bandgap voltage reference is shown in Fig. 5.5-11. This voltage reference is called the Widlar bandgap reference.[8] As V_{CC} is increased from zero, Q1 and Q2 conduct when V_{BE1} is approximately 0.7 V. Since R_2 is greater than R_1, Q2 saturates. Further increase of V_1 (due to increasing V_{CC} during turn on) causes Q2 to come out of saturation due to R_3. The circuit stabilizes at $V_{BE3} = V_{BE}$ (on). Q1, Q2, and R_3 form a Widlar current mirror, as was discussed in Sec. 5.4. The current I_2 can be expressed as

$$I_2 = \frac{V_t}{R_3} \ln\left(\frac{I_1}{I_2}\right) \tag{5.5-47}$$

Equation 5.5-47 shows that the voltage V_t in Fig. 5.5-10 is generated by the difference between two base–emitter drops. The reference voltage of Fig. 5.5-11 can be given as

$$V_{REF} = V_{BE3} + \left(\frac{R_2}{R_3}\right) V_t \ln\left(\frac{I_1}{I_2}\right) \tag{5.5-48}$$

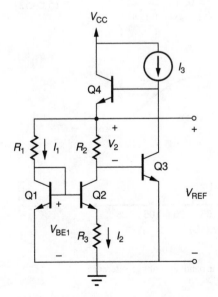

FIGURE 5.5-11
Widlar bandgap voltage reference.

Comparing (5.5-48) with (5.5-46) shows that

$$G = \left(\frac{R_2}{R_3}\right) \ln\left(\frac{I_1}{I_2}\right) \tag{5.5-49}$$

If we assume that $I_1/I_2 = 10$, then at room temperature we must have $R_2/R_3 = 10.2$ to obtain a zero temperature coefficient. Selecting $I_1 = 1$ mA gives $I_2 = 0.1$ mA and R_3 is found from Eq. 5.5-47 as 60 Ω. Thus, R_2 is 610 Ω. If we assume that $V_{BE3} = 0.65$ V, then V_{REF} is equal to 1.26 V. Figure 5.5-12 shows that the bandgap reference possesses zero temperature coefficient only around a nominal temperature. Another problem with this circuit is the dependence of I_3 on the supply voltage. Better implementations of the bandgap reference are discussed below.

An improved bandgap voltage reference can be developed using an op amp, as shown in Fig. 5.5-13a and b. The advantage of the op amp is to remove the dependence of the currents upon the power supply. The method by which this is done is to force the relationship

$$I_1 R_1 = I_2 R_2 \tag{5.5-50}$$

and to replace I_1/I_2 in the argument of the logarithm by R_2/R_1 which is independent of supply voltage. The performance of both the circuits is identical and can be described as follows. The current I_2 is found by writing a voltage loop equation around V_{BE1}, V_{BE2} and R_3, resulting in

$$I_2 = \frac{1}{R_3} V_T \ln\left(\frac{R_2 I_{S2}}{R_1 I_{S1}}\right) \tag{5.5-51}$$

The reference voltage can be expressed as

$$V_{REF} = V_{BE1} + I_2 R_2 = V_{BE1} + \frac{R_2}{R_3} V_t \ln\left(\frac{R_2 I_{S2}}{R_1 I_{S1}}\right) \tag{5.5-52}$$

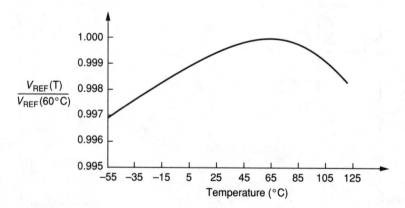

FIGURE 5.5-12
Illustration of the temperature dependence of the Widlar bandgap voltage reference.

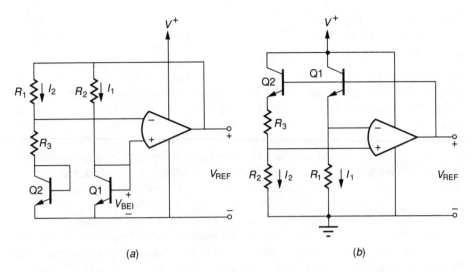

FIGURE 5.5-13
(*a*) A bandgap voltage reference using an op amp, (*b*) An alternate form of (*a*).

which is of the same form as the expression in Eq. 5.5-46. The areas of the emitters of transistors Q1 and Q2 are used to scale the argument of the logarithm. For example, if $A_{E2} = 10A_{E1}$, then $I_{S2} = 10I_{S1}$ and for zero temperature coefficient we find that $R_2/R_3 = 10.2$ if $R_2/R_1 = 1$.

The bandgap voltage reference of Fig. 5.5-10 can be implemented by either bipolar or CMOS technology. Q1 and Q2 would be the substrate transistors, which are available in CMOS technology. For p-well CMOS using an n^- substrate, the BJT is an npn substrate transistor and would be compatible with Fig. 5.5-13*b*. For an n-well CMOS technology using a p^- substrate, the circuit of Fig. 5.5-13*a* can be used if Q1 and Q2 are replaced by pnp transistors.

Exact cancellation of the dependence of V_{REF} upon temperature will not be possible because of component tolerances and second-order effects such as the nonlinearity of the dependence of V_{BE} on temperature[9] which has been neglected. Problem 5.41 shows that the influence of the op amp offset voltage is multiplied by $(1 + R_2/R_1)$ and can become a significant source of error and temperature dependence. Offset effects may be reduced by using multiple pn junctions or by offset canceling techniques.

Q1 and Q2 of Fig. 5.5-13 can be replaced by MOS devices operating in the weak inversion region if the current levels are small. Such voltage references use very little power. In the weak inversion region, the I–V characteristics of the MOS transistor are exponential and can be used to generate V_t. An equation describing the MOS transistor in weak inversion is given as (see (Eq. 3.1-32)[10]

$$I_D = \frac{W}{L} I_{DO} e^{-V_{BS}[(1/nV_t)-(1/V_t)]}(1 - e^{-V_{DS}/V_t})\, e^{(V_{GS}-V_T)/nV_t} \tag{5.5-53}$$

where $V_t = kT/q$
$n =$ slope factor
$I_{DO} =$ characteristic current

Eq. 5.5-53 only holds for the weak inversion region where $V_{DS} > 3V_t$. It is found[11] that n is controllable but has a strong temperature dependence. I_{DO} is difficult to control and also has a strong temperature dependence. A voltage reference using the above concepts was proposed by Tsividis and Ulmer[12]. While the reference voltage of this circuit was independent of I_{DO}, it was dependent upon n, which prevented satisfactory reduction of the temperature coefficient. A CMOS bandgap voltage reference which eliminated the dependence on n is shown in Fig. 5.5-14. The current mirrors M1–M3 and M2–M4 form a closed loop with an initial loop gain greater than unity. Therefore, the current in both branches increases until equilibrium is achieved when the loop gain is reduced to one by the voltage V_{R1} across R_1. If we assume that M1 through M4 operate in the weak inversion region and that V_{DD} is high enough to ensure saturation of M1 and M4, then V_{R1} can be expressed as follows where $S = W/L$

$$V_{R1} = V_t \ln\left(\frac{S_1 S_4}{S_2 S_3}\right) \tag{5.5-54}$$

Note that V_{R1} depends only on the thermal voltage and the ratio of the geometry of the devices and is independent of n. I_{R1} and I_E are related as

$$\frac{I_{R1}}{I_E} = \frac{S_3}{S_6} \tag{5.5-55}$$

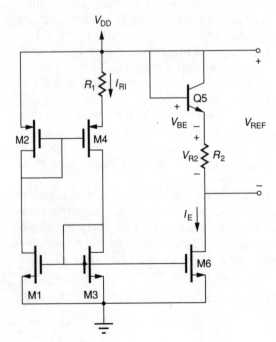

FIGURE 5.5-14
A CMOS bandgap voltage reference operating in weak inversion with no dependence on the process parameter n.

Solving for I_E gives

$$I_E = \left(\frac{S_6}{S_3}\right)\frac{V_t}{R_1}\ln\left(\frac{S_4 S_1}{S_2 S_3}\right) \qquad (5.5\text{-}56)$$

V_{REF} is given as

$$V_{REF} = V_{BE} + I_E R_2 = V_{BE} + \left(\frac{R_2}{R_1}\right)\left(\frac{S_6}{S_3}\right)V_t\ln\left(\frac{S_1 S_4}{S_2 S_3}\right) \qquad (5.5\text{-}57)$$

An expression for V_{BE} which emphasizes its temperature dependence is given by[13]

$$V_{BE}(T) = V_{GO}(1 - \frac{T}{T_o}) + V_{BEO}(\frac{T}{T_o}) + \frac{mkT}{q}\ln\left(\frac{T_o}{T}\right) \qquad (5.5\text{-}58)$$

where V_{GO} = the extrapolated bandgap voltage of silicon
   V_{BEO} = V_{BE} of a diode connected transistor at $T = T_o$
   m = constant dependent on the diode fabrication and temperature characteristics

It can be shown that the condition for $dV_{REF}/dT = 0$ is given by

$$\left(\frac{R_2 S_6}{R_1 S_3}\right)\ln\left(\frac{S_1 S_4}{S_2 S_3}\right) = \frac{q(V_{GO} - V_{BEO})}{kT} + m \qquad (5.5\text{-}59)$$

This results in a reference voltage of

$$V_{REF} = V_{GO} + \frac{mkT}{q} \qquad (5.5\text{-}60)$$

In order to ensure proper operation of the voltage reference described, the following precautions must be taken. First, the devices must be in weak inversion even at the highest temperature of operation. Secondly, leakage currents particularly in the n-channel devices must be minimized to prevent these currents from becoming a major source of error at higher temperature. Lastly, the output resistance of the devices must be large enough to ensure proper operation of the devices as current mirrors. This can be accomplished by using long devices or by use of the various current mirrors presented earlier.

This section has introduced the techniques and methods used to design voltage and current references that minimize their dependence on power supply and/or temperature. There are other characteristics of references which are important but are beyond the scope of the treatment given in this section. One of these is the noise introduced by the reference. Noise can be reduced by minimizing the number of devices and using small values of resistance. If MOS devices are used, p-channel MOS devices generally have less noise and the noise is reduced if the area of the device is increased.

Another area that was not covered was the creation of a voltage reference from a current reference and vise versa. At least one resistor will be present in this conversion process and cause the TC_F to be different. These conversions are best accomplished by using an op amp as a current-to-voltage or voltage-to-current converter.

5.6 SUMMARY

Five categories of building blocks have been presented in this chapter. These categories include switches, active resistors, current sources and sinks, current mirrors/amplifiers, and voltage and current references. Figures 5.0-1 and 5.0-2 show how these basic building blocks can be used to design or build more complex circuits. This chapter has paved the way to combine these building blocks with others to be discussed in the next chapter to form analog circuits.

The material discussed in this chapter has provided the opportunity to describe and illustrate many important principles and concepts that can be used in other applications. The section on active resistors illustrated methods by which the drain current dependence on the drain–source and the bulk–source voltage can be minimized. The use of switches and capacitors to implement a resistor was presented. Both positive and negative feedback were used to increase the small signal output resistance of current sources and sinks. Negative series feedback was used to increase the resistance while positive feedback was used for bootstrapping a resistor, increasing its effective resistance. The principles of replication and analyzing mismatched devices were demonstrated in the section describing current mirrors/amplifiers.

Finally, the last section introduced techniques which reduced the influence of temperature and power supply variation on the value of a voltage or current reference. It was shown how the temperature dependence can be reduced to zero in some cases.

REFERENCES

1. M. Banu and Y. Tsividis: "Floating Voltage–Controlled Resistors in CMOS Technology," *Electronic Letters*, vol. 18, no. 15, pp. 678–679, July 1982.
2. M. Banu and Y. Tsividis: "Fully Integrated Active RC Filters in MOS Technology," *IEEE J. of Solid–State Circuits*, vol. SC–18, no. 6, pp. 644–651, December 1983.
3. E. Sackinger and W. Guggenbuhl: "A Versatile Building Block: The CMOS Differential Difference Amplifier," *IEEE J. of Solid–State Circuits*, vol. SC–22, no. 2, pp. 287–294, April 1987.
4. G. R. Wilson: "A Monolithic Junction FET–NPN Operational Amplifiers," *IEEE J. of Solid–State Circuits*, vol. SC–3, no. 4, pp. 341–349, December 1968.
5. R. C. Jaeger: "A High Output Resistance Current Source," *IEEE J. of Solid–State Circuits*, vol. SC–9, no. 4, pp. 192–194, August 1974.
6. R. J. Widlar: "Some Circuit Design Techniques for Linear Integrated Circuits," *IEEE Transactions on Circuit Theory*, vol. CT–12, no. 4, pp. 586–590, December 1965.
7. P. R. Gray and R. G. Meyer: *Analysis and Design of Analog Integrated Circuits*, John Wiley & Sons, New York, pp. 254–258, 1977.
8. R. J. Widlar: "New Developments in IC Voltage Regulators," *IEEE J. of Solid–State Circuits*, vol. SC–6, no. 1, pp. 2–7, February 1977.
9. G. C. M. Meijer, P. C. Schmale, and K. van Zalinge: "A New Curvature–Corrected Bandgap Reference," *IEEE J. of Solid–State Circuits*, vol. SC–17, no. 6, pp. 1139–1143, December 1982.
10. E. Vittoz and J. Fellrath: "CMOS Analog Integrated Circuits Based on Weak Inversion Operation," *IEEE J. of Solid–State Circuits*, vol. SC–12, no. 3, pp. 224–231, June 1977.
11. G. Tzanateas, C. Salama and Y. Tsividis: "A CMOS Bandgap Voltage Reference," *IEEE J. of Solid–State Circuits*, vol. SC–12, no. 3, pp. 655–657, June 1979.
12. Y. P. Tsividis and R. W. Ulmer: "CMOS Reference Voltage Source," *ISSCC Digest of Technical Papers*, pp. 49–59, February 1978.
13. J. S. Brugler: "Silicon Transistor Biasing for Linear Collector Current Temperature Dependence," *IEEE J. of Solid–State Circuits*, vol. SC–2, no. 2, pp. 57-58, June 1967.

PROBLEMS

Section 5.1

5.1. What causes the nonsymmetry between the first and third quadrants in Fig. 5.1-4 for the MOS switch?

5.2. Assume a switch is made from a MOS transistor with equal W and L. If the CMOS parameters in Table 3.1-2 are applicable to this transistor, what are the highest and lowest values of voltages that can exist on the source/drain when the bulk is at -5 V and the gate at 5 V and still keep the switch on and working properly? Define the switch as on when the switch large signal resistance is 20 kΩ or less.

5.3. Calculate R_{ON} for the transistor of Fig. 5.1-5 when $V_{GS} = 5V_T$ and $W = L$ for $V_{BS} = 0$ V, $V_{DS} \approx 0$, and for $V_{BS} = 5$ V. Assume that $\gamma = 0.8$ V$^{-0.5}$ and $\phi = 0.6$ V.

5.4. Find R_{ON} of an n-channel MOS switch if $V_D \approx V_S = 2$ V, $V_B = 0$ V and $V_G = 5$ V if $W = L$ and the n-channel parameters of Table 3.1-2 are applicable.

5.5. Calculate the voltage feedthrough from the clock of Fig. 5.1-13a to C_1 of Fig. 5.1-13b (a) if C_1 is 5 pF and (b) if C_1 is 1 pF and $C_{GD} = C_{GS} = 50$ fF.

5.6. Use the SPICE computer simulation program to plot the on resistance of the circuit of Fig. 5.1-15 if $W/L = 10$ for all transistors. Assume that $V_{DD} = 5$ V and that $\bar{\phi}$ is 0 V and ϕ is 5 V. Use the parameters of Table 3.1-2 and obtain a plot of R_{ON} as a function of the voltage at the switch terminals to ground from 0 to 5 V. Note that because the switch is on, that the terminal voltages should be approximately equal.

Section 5.2

5.7. Evaluate the ac and dc resistance of the circuit of Fig. 5.2-2a when $V = 2V_T$ using the model parameters of Table 3.1-2. Repeat for the circuit of Fig. 5.2-2b. Assume that the source and bulk are connected together.

5.8. Use the small signal model of Fig. 5.2-2d to rederive Eq. 5.2-5 and include the bulk effect assuming that V_{BS} is positive.

5.9. Evaluate the ac and dc resistance of the circuit of Fig. 5.2-3a when $V = 0.6$ V using the model parameters of $I_s = 0.4$ fA and $\beta_F = 100$ at room temperature.

5.10. Repeat Ex. 5.2-1 if V_{out} is to be -1 V.

5.11. Repeat Ex. 5.2-2 if the bulk–source voltages are not neglected using the bulk threshold parameter of Table 3.1-2.

5.12. If W/L of M1 and M2 of Fig. 5.2-6 is 5, find the value of V_C necessary to realize an ac resistance of 2000 Ω using the model parameters of Table 3.1-2. Compare your results with that of Fig. 5.2-8a.

5.13. If the difference between V_{C1} and V_{C2} can vary from 1 to 5 V and W/L can vary from 1 to 10, what range of ac resistance can the double-MOS resistor implementation of Fig. 5.2-9 realize?

5.14. Use the double-MOS ac resistor configuration of Fig. 5.2-9 to implement the voltage amplifier shown in Fig. P5.14. The op amp is an ideal, differential-in, differential-out op amp. Assume that $V_{C1} = 5$ V and $V_{C2} = 4$ V. Use the parameters of Table 3.1-2.

5.15. Use the approach illustrated in the text for the parallel switched capacitor of Fig. 5.2-11 to show that the equivalent resistance of the series–parallel switched capacitor resistor realization of Fig. 5.2-13 is given by Eq. 5.2-32.

5.16. Use the approach illustrated in the text for the parallel switched capacitor of Fig. 5.2-11 to show that the equivalent resistance of the bilinear switched capacitor resistor realization of Fig. 5.2-14 is given by Eq. 5.2-33.

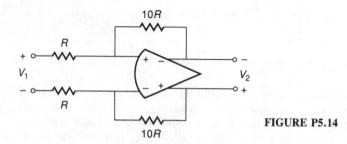

FIGURE P5.14

5.17. Figure P5.17 shows an inverting integrator. If R_1 is replaced by the series switched capacitor realization of Fig. 5.2-12, find an approximation expression for the transfer function, $V_2(s)/V_1(s)$. What is the accuracy of the integration constant $(1/R, C_2)$ in terms of the accuracy of the capacitors and the clock frequency?

Section 5.3

5.18. Assume that the model parameters of the npn transistor of Fig. 5.3-4a are $I_S = 0.4$ fA and $V_{AF} = 200$ V. Find the value of V_{BB} which will give a current sink of 500 μA. Using the values of Table 3.2-2, V_{MIN} and the value of the ac output resistance.

5.19. Use the model parameters of Table 3.1-2 for the MOS current sink of Fig. 5.3-5a to find V_{GG}, V_{MIN}, and R_o if the current is to be 500 μA.

5.20. Verify Eq. 5.3-8 for the MOS current sink of Fig. 5.3-7.

5.21. Verify Eqs. 5.3-15 and 5.3-16 for the bootstrapped current sink of Fig. 5.3-12.

5.22. Verify Eq. 5.3-19 for the output resistance of Fig. 5.3-15a.

5.23. Discuss a BJT realization of the regulated cascode MOS current sink of Fig. 5.3-16a. Give a schematic of a possible realization and find the output resistance and the minimum voltage drop across the current sink.

5.24. Verify Eq. 5.3-20 for the output resistance of Fig. 5.3-16a.

Section 5.4

5.25. Consider the circuit of Fig. 5.4-1 as a current amplifier. The input current will consist of a dc and an ac current. If the dc input current is 1 mA, find the ac input resistance, the ac output resistance, and the ac current gain (i_{out}/i_{in}) if $I_S = 0.4$ fA, $\beta_F = 100$, and $V_{AF} = 200$ V.

5.26. Find the ac input resistance of the circuit of Fig. 5.4-3 looking from R_1 toward the base of Q3 and collector of Q1. Compare this input resistance to that of the circuit of Fig. 5.4-1.

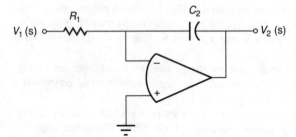

FIGURE P5.17

5.27. Verify Eqs. 5.4-33 and 5.4-34 of the BJT Wilson current mirror in Fig. 5.4-6.

5.28. Verify the ac output resistance of the BJT Widlar current mirror given in Eq. 5.4-41.

5.29. Assume that the output current is 0.5 mA for the BJT current mirrors listed in Table 5.4-1. Assume that the npn BJT parameters are $I_S = 0.4$ fA, $\beta_F = 100$, $V_{AF} = 200$ V, $V_{BE}(\text{sat}) = 0.7$ V and $V_{CE}(\text{sat}) = 0.2$ V. Find the value of r_{out} and V_{MIN} for each of the mirrors of Table 5.4-1.

5.30. Consider the circuit of Fig. 5.4-11a as a current amplifier. The input current will consist of a dc and an ac current. If the dc input current is 0.1 mA, find the ac input resistance, the ac output resistance, and the ac current gain (i_{out}/i_{in}) using the model parameters of Table 3.1-2 and assuming that both W/L values are equal.

5.31. Verify the ac output resistance of the MOS Wilson current mirror given in Eq. 5.4-63.

5.32. Develop a MOS realization of the BJT Widlar current mirror and find an expression for the output resistance and minimum voltage drop across the output of the mirror.

5.33. Assume that the output current is 0.2 mA for the MOS current mirrors listed in Table 5.4-2. Using the model parameters of Table 3.1-2 and assuming all W/L values are equal, find the value of r_{out} and V_{MIN} for each of the mirrors of Table 5.4-2.

Section 5.5

5.34. Redevelop Eq. 5.5-9 for the sensitivity of Fig. 5.5-1b when V_{CC} is not much greater than V_{REF}.

5.35. Use two collector–base connected BJTs in series in place of the single collector–base connected BJT in the circuit of Fig. 5.5-1b and find an expression for the sensitivity of V_{REF} with respect to V_{CC}.

5.36. If $V_{DD} = 10$ V, $W/L = 5$, and $R = 50$ kΩ, find the value of V_{REF} of the cirucit of Fig. 5.5-1c. Use the model parameters of Table 3.1-2. Assume that the TC$_F$ of R is $+1000$ ppm/°C and find the TC$_F$ of V_{REF}.

5.37. Assume for the circuit of Fig. 5.5-2a that $V_{CC} = 10$ V, $R_2 = 2R_1 = 2$ MΩ, $R = 100$ kΩ, and $I_S = 0.4$ fA. Assume also that $I_{R2} << I_C$ and find V_{REF}.

5.38. Repeat the development leading to Eq. 5.5-34 which gives the conditions for a zero TC$_F$ using Eq. 5.5-15 rather than Eq. 5.5-16. Evaluate the value of V_{DD} for the conditions given in the text.

5.39. Assume that the voltage V_{GS} in Fig. P5.39 is independent of temperature. Develop an expression that will give the value of V_{GS} necessary to achieve a drain current,

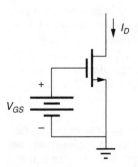

FIGURE P5.39

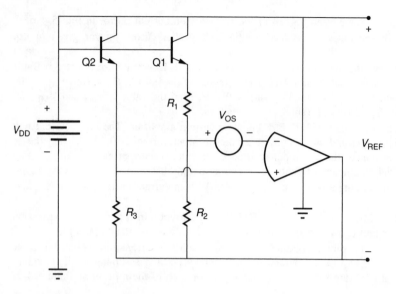

FIGURE P5.40

I_D, which will have zero temperature dependence. Assume that the temperature dependence of the MOS transistor is given by Eqs. 5.5-18 and 5.5-19. Find the value of V_{GS} and I_D which gives zero temperature dependence at (a) $T = 27°C$ and (b) $T = 200°C$.

5.40. For the bandgap voltage reference of Fig. P5.40, assume that the emitter area of Q1 is 10 times that of Q2, $V_{BE2} = 0.7$ V, $R_2 = R_3$, and $V_t = 0.026$ V. Find the value of R_2/R_1 necessary to give zero temperature coefficient at room temperature. For this problem assume $V_{OS} = 0$.

5.41. Develop an expression for V_{REF} for Fig. P5.40 if V_{OS} is not zero. Assume that R_2/R_1 is 10 and use the conditions of the previous problem to find V_{REF} if V_{OS} is 10 mV.

Design Problems

5.42. Design a switch using MOS technology which when closed will allow an uncharged 10 pF capacitor to be connected to a 5 V dc voltage source. The capacitor should reach 4.95 V within 10 ns. What is the value of the clock voltage which will meet this specification? Assume that the MOS technology to be used is defined by Table 3.1-2. Minimize the switch area in order to minimize the clock feedthrough.

5.43. Design a voltage divider which will provide 1 V dc from a 5 V dc voltage source. The temperature coefficient of the 1 V dc should not be larger than that of the 5 V dc voltage source. The sensitivity of the 1 V dc to changes in the 5 V dc supply should be less than 0.05. Keep the power dissipation of this voltage divider to less than 0.1 mW.

5.44. Design a current source having a value of 100 μA, output resistance of greater than 1 MΩ, and a minimum voltage of at most 1 V. Assume that ± 5 V power supplies are available. The design should be complete in the sense that when an external resistor is connected to it (the other end of the resistor is at -5 V) that 100 μA flows.

5.45. Use the current mirror concept to design a differential, current input amplifier which will provide an output current which is proportional to the difference between two input currents. Choose the gain control as 10 so that the expression

$$I_{out} = 10(I_1 - I_2)$$

is realized. The input resistances of this amplifier should be less than 1 kΩ and the output resistance should be greater than 1 MΩ. Assume that ± 5 V power supplies are available.

5.46. Design a bandgap voltage reference using the form of Fig. 5.5-13a or 5.5-13b. Use this bandgap voltage reference to design a dc current reference which doesn't deteriorate the temperature characteristics of the bandgap voltage. Assume that ± 5 V power supplies are available.

CHAPTER
6

AMPLIFIERS

6.0 INTRODUCTION

This chapter uses the building blocks of the last chapter to develop basic analog circuits and amplifiers. This material represents the middle step in the analog design hierarchy of Table 5.0-1. The primary focus of this chapter is the development of integrated circuit amplifiers using the building blocks of the last chapter. The concepts illustrated in Figs. 5.0-1 and 5.0-2 will be implemented in the following material.

The circuits included in this chapter are the inverting amplifier, the improved inverting amplifier, the differential amplifier, the output amplifier, the operational amplifier, and the comparator. The inverting amplifier, sometimes called an inverter, is one of the primary gain stages of analog amplifiers. The performance of the inverting amplifier can be improved as discussed in Sec. 6.2 by the use of additional devices. These additional devices typically appear in the cascode configuration, and are often termed *cascode amplifiers*. The improvements are not only in the area of performance, but also in the area of more degrees of design freedom.

Next in importance to the inverting amplifier is the differential amplifier. It is very useful as an input stage and is highly compatible with integrated circuit technology. The next one-stage amplifier to be considered is the output amplifier. This amplifier is necessary to interface the output of an amplifier to a low-resistance or low-capacitance load. Normally, amplifiers are incapable of driving a low-resistance/high-capacitance load. The output amplifier is difficult to design since it requires large, linear output swings across low resistive loads.

These amplifiers can be combined in the manner suggested by Figs. 5.0-1 and 5.0-2 to result in an operational amplifier. The operational amplifier is often considered the most useful circuit in analog integrated circuit design. It represents a good example in implementing circuit functions independent of its own performance characteristics using negative feedback. The last circuit presented in this chapter is the comparator. It is a circuit used to detect voltage thresholds and finds use in many analog and digital functions.

378

The emphasis of this chapter varies as the material progresses. The focus of the sections on inverting and differential amplifiers is on the small signal performance. This includes the ac gain, input and output resistances, bandwidth, and noise. These amplifiers are typically used as input or interstage amplifiers and do not have large signal swing requirements. The focus shifts to large signal considerations for output amplifiers. Here the key performance aspects include large signal swing, linearity, efficiency, and low output impedance. In operational amplifiers, the emphasis includes both small signal and large signal considerations. For the comparator, the focus is primarily on the large signal transient performance.

6.1 INVERTING AMPLIFIERS

One of the most useful amplifiers is the inverting amplifier, also called the inverter. As its name implies, the inverter produces an output that is inverted with respect to the input. If the input signal is changing in a positive (negative) manner, then the output will be changing in a negative (positive) manner. The inverter is widely used in both analog and digital circuits. In digital circuits, the inverter accomplishes the Boolean operation of negation or inversion. In analog circuits, the inverter is used to achieve amplification. Topologically, the simple analog and digital inverters are often identical. The use of the inverter in digital circuits will be described in more detail in Chapter 7. This section will examine the use of the inverter in analog circuits.

Coverage of the inverter naturally follows the material presented in the last chapter. Descriptions of the various forms of the inverter will use concepts from each section of Chapter 5, particularly the sections on active resistors and current sources/sinks. This section will be divided into three parts. The first part will present the general concepts of the inverter, independent of the technology used to implement it. The second part will examine inverters that use MOS technology. The last part will examine inverters using BJT technology.

The inverting amplifiers discussed in this section will be restricted to small signal, linear applications. Consequently, the emphasis will be on the fundamental concepts, the various inverter architectures, the small signal performance, and the noise performance. Large signal considerations, such as power dissipation, signal swing, nonlinearity and efficiency, will be emphasized in the section dealing with output amplifiers.

6.1.1 General Concepts of Inverting Amplifiers

The objective of the inverting amplifier used in analog circuits is to provide an inverting, small signal voltage gain greater than 1. One can appreciate the advantage of the inverting amplifier over a noninverting amplifier by noting that two cascaded inverters can implement a noninverting amplifier, but a noninverting amplifier cannot implement an inverting amplifier. Although inverting amplifiers are not restricted to voltage input and output variables, this form of the inverter will be considered here.

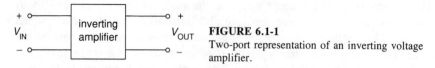

FIGURE 6.1-1

Two-port representation of an inverting voltage amplifier.

Figure 6.1-1 shows a two-port representation of the inverting voltage amplifier. The inverter can be characterized by the transfer characteristics defining the dependence of V_{OUT} on V_{IN}, the input resistance (R_{IN}), and the output resistance (R_{OUT}). In this section the characterization of the inverter is from the small signal viewpoint. Thus, an inverting voltage amplifier would be characterized by the small signal voltage gain, $v_{out}/v_{in} = A_v$, the small signal input resistance, r_{in}, and the small signal output resistance, r_{out}. It is necessary that the value of A_v should be negative and greater than unity. It is desirable but not necessary to have r_{in} large and r_{out} small.

The small signal performance of the inverter can be further characterized in the frequency or time domain. In the frequency domain, $A_v(\omega)$ of the ideal inverter should have a magnitude, A_{v0}, independent of frequency and a phase shift of $\pm 180°$. At some frequency, the magnitude of $A_v(\omega)$ of the practical inverter will decrease. The frequency at which the magnitude of $A_v(\omega)$ is equal to $A_{v0}/\sqrt{2}$ is called the -3 dB frequency ($\omega_{-3\ dB}$). Although inverters built from discrete components may have a finite lower -3 dB frequency (due to coupling capacitors), the gain of integrated circuit inverters is A_{v0} for all frequencies sufficiently below ω_{-3dB}. Thus the bandwidth of the inverter is equal to ω_{-3dB}. It is important that the inverter have sufficient bandwidth for its given application.

The small signal frequency response can alternately be characterized by the small signal time domain response. For the case just discussed, the inverter acts as a low-pass amplifier with a cutoff frequency of ω_{-3dB}. The pulse response of a first-order system would be characterized by a 10% to 90% rise time given approximately as $2.2/\omega_{-3dB}$. Another important aspect of the small signal performance of the inverter is noise. In many cases, the inverter is used as an input stage for a more complex amplifier. In order to reduce the noise of the complex amplifier, it is important to reduce the noise of the input stage.

In its most simple form, the inverting amplifier can be represented by two blocks. One of the blocks is a voltage-controlled current source, and the other is a load. It is important to recognize two types of voltage-controlled current sources. The distinction will be based on Fig. 5.3-2, which defined a current sink and a current source. In this case, the currents are controlled by the voltage at a third terminal. We shall define the blocks in Fig. 6.1-2 to schematically represent a voltage-controlled current sink and a voltage-controlled current source. V_P and V_N are defined as the most positive and negative dc voltages, respectively. The notation G will be used to designate a voltage-controlled current sink/source. The voltage-controlled current sinks/sources of Fig. 6.1-2 are three-terminal devices. The terminals are designated I for input, O for output, and X for the terminal common with V_N or V_P. The voltage between terminals I and X (X and I) controls the current at terminal O for Fig. 6.1-2a (Fig. 6.1-2b). In general, I_O for Fig. 6.1-2a can be expressed as

$$I_O = g_{sink}(V_{IX}, V_{OX}) \tag{6.1-1}$$

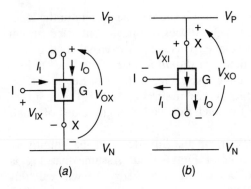

FIGURE 6.1-2
Schematic representations for (*a*) A voltage-controlled current sink and (*b*) A voltage-controlled current source.

and for Fig. 6.1-2*b* as

$$I_O = g_{\text{source}}(V_{XI}, V_{XO}) \tag{6.1-2}$$

The nonlinear functions in Eqs. 6.1-1 and 6.1-2 depend on the technology used to implement the controlled source/sink.

The voltage-controlled sources/sinks are combined with the two-terminal loads to implement the three basic types of inverter architectures shown in Fig. 6.1-3. Figure 6.1-3*a* illustrates an inverter using a voltage-controlled current sink and a load connected between O and V_P. This inverter is called a *sinking inverter* because it sinks the current through the load. Figure 6.1-3*b* uses a voltage-controlled current source and a load connected between O and V_N. This type

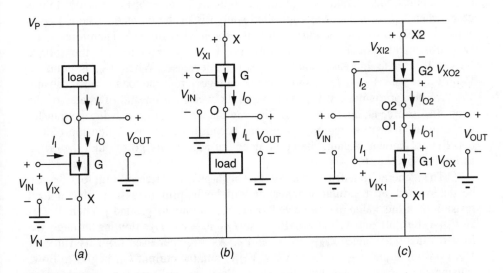

FIGURE 6.1-3
Generic representations of inverter architectures: (*a*) Sinking inverter, (*b*) Sourcing inverter, (*c*) Push-pull inverter.

of inverter is called a *sourcing inverter* because it sources the current in the load. The third architecture is shown in Fig. 6.1-3c. It uses a voltage-controlled current sink and a voltage-controlled current source. There is no external load in this architecture. This type of inverter is called a *push-pull inverter*. The loads in Fig. 6.1-3 can be any of the two-terminal active resistor realizations of Sec. 5.2 (Fig. 5.2-2, 5.2-3, or 5.2-6) or the dc current sources or sinks of Sec. 5.3. The use of dc current sources or sinks to realize the load will lead to high values of small signal voltage gain, A_v.

The large signal transfer behavior of the inverter can be intuitively developed. Consider the sinking inverter of Fig. 6.1-3a. Assume that V_{IN} is taken to V_N. With V_{IX} equal to zero, I_O will also be zero. We will call this the *off* state of the controlled sink. Because we are assuming that no external current flows, then I_L is also zero. When no current flows through the load, the voltage across it will be zero or close to zero. Therefore, V_{OUT} is approximately V_P. This corresponds to the upper left-hand corner of the plot of Fig. 6.1-4a. To simplify the analysis, we shall assume that the controlled sink turns on when $V_{IX} = V_{TH}$ ($V_{IN} = V_{TH} + V_N$). At this point the current I_O will start to flow. Because $I_O = I_L$, the voltage across the load starts to increase, causing V_{OUT} to decrease. As V_{IN} continues to increase, the voltage drop across the load approaches $V_P - V_N$, which implies that V_{OUT} approaches V_N. Under this condition, the controlled sink reaches a state where the current can no longer increase and the voltage V_{OX} is approximately zero. We will call this the *on* state of the controlled sink. The region between the off and on states will be called the *transition region*. The transfer curve in Fig. 6.1-4a is arbitrary because we have not used the actual relationships expressed by Eq. 6.1-1 for the controlled sink. It should be noted that the curve does not necessarily go through the origin, as implied in Fig. 6.1-4a.

Identical considerations hold for the sourcing inverter of Fig. 6.1-3b. In this case, when V_{IN} is at V_N, the controlled source is in the on state, where V_{XO} is approximately zero and the current through the load is limited. Therefore, V_{OUT} is approximately equal to V_P. At some point as V_{IN} is increased, the voltage V_{XO} will start to increase, causing V_{OUT} to decrease. When V_{XI} is equal to V_{TH} ($V_{IN} = V_P - V_{TH}$), I_O is zero and the voltage across the load is zero, causing V_{OUT} to be approximately V_N. The region between the on and off states of the controlled source is, again, the transition region. As with Fig. 6.1-4a, the transfer curve in the transition region is arbitrary because the exact relationship of Eq. 6.1-2 is not known. Again, the curve does not necessarily go through the origin as implied by Fig. 6.1-4b.

The general transfer curve for the push-pull inverter of Fig. 6.1-3c can be determined in a similar manner. It will be helpful to assume that a load resistor of large value is connected from the output to ground. When V_{IN} is at V_N, G1 is off and G2 is on. Because I_{O1} is zero, I_{O2} flowing through the load resistor will cause V_{OUT} to be at V_P. As V_{IN} increases from its value of V_N, V_{IX1} will equal V_{TH1} ($V_{IN} = V_N + V_{TH1}$) and the current I_{O1} begins to flow, causing the current in the load resistor to decrease and resulting in a decrease in V_{OUT}. At some point in the further increase of V_{IN}, $I_{O2} = I_{O1}$ and V_{OUT} is

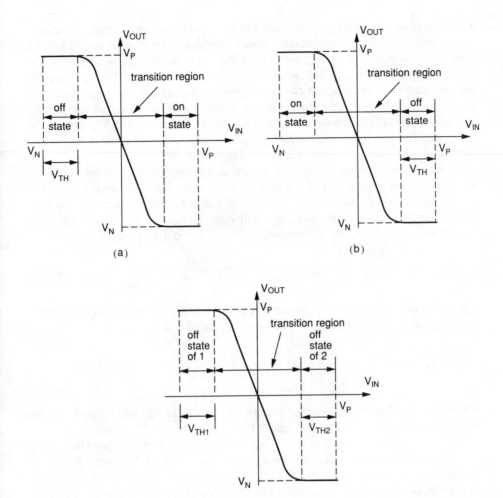

FIGURE 6.1-4
Typical voltage transfer functions for the inverters of Fig. 6.1-3: (*a*) Sinking inverter, (*b*) Sourcing inverter, (*c*) Push-pull inverter.

zero. Further increasing V_{IN} causes $I_{O1} > I_{O2}$, and V_{OUT} becomes negative and approaches V_N. When $V_{XI2} = V_{TH2}(V_{IN} = V_P - V_{TH2})$, G2 turns off and V_{OUT} is at V_N. The external load resistance used for this analysis turns out to be the output resistances associated with the controlled current sinks/sources. V_{OUT} is not necessarily zero at $V_{IN} = 0$ as implied by Fig. 6.1-4c.

The small signal voltage gain of the inverter can be related to the voltage transfer characteristics of Fig. 6.1-4 by the following definition.

$$A_v = \frac{v_{out}}{v_{in}} = \frac{\partial V_{OUT}}{\partial V_{IN}}\bigg|_{Q\text{-point}} \tag{6.1-3}$$

where the Q-point refers to a given value of the input or output voltage. Therefore, we see that the slope of the voltage transfer function of the inverter determines its gain. Obviously, the desired Q-point for a high-gain inverting amplifier is in the transition regions of Fig. 6.1-4, where the slope is the steepest. This will simplify our considerations because we can ignore the regions of operation outside of the transition region. This represents a major distinction between digital and analog circuits. In digital applications, the inverter will be operated from one extreme to the other. The two quiescent operating states of digital circuits will be in the flat portions of the voltage transfer curves of Fig. 6.1-4.

When the inverting amplifier is biased at a Q-point in the transition region, the next step is to linearize the circuit. This is done by expanding Eqs. 6.1-1 and 6.1-2 about a Q-point. While the formal mathematical characterization uses a multivariable series expansion, we shall approximate the result with only the first-order terms. Consider the approximation of Eq. 6.1-1, given as

$$I_O = g_{\text{sink}}(V_{IX}, V_{OX}) \approx I_o + \left.\frac{\partial I_O}{\partial V_{IX}}\right|_Q \Delta V_{IX} + \left.\frac{\partial I_O}{\partial V_{OX}}\right|_Q \Delta V_{OX} \quad (6.1\text{-}4)$$

where Q indicates operation at the dc bias point. Noting that the ac output current, i_o, is defined as $I_O - I_o$ allows us to express Eq. 6.1-4 as

$$i_o = I_O - I_o = \left.\frac{\partial I_O}{\partial V_{IX}}\right|_Q \Delta V_{IX} + \left.\frac{\partial I_O}{\partial V_{OX}}\right|_Q \Delta V_{OX} \approx g_m v_{ix} + g_o v_{ox}$$

$$(6.1\text{-}5)$$

where the signal swings are small enough so that the ac voltages v_{ix} and v_{ox} can be closely approximated by ΔV_{IX} and ΔV_{OX}, respectively. The notations g_m and g followed by other subscripts are used to relate the current dependence on a voltage at different terminals and voltage at the same terminals, respectively. g_m is called *transconductance* and g is called *conductance*. In a similar manner, the ac current of the voltage-controlled current source of Eq. 6.1-2 can be expressed as

$$i_o \approx g_m v_{xi} + g_o v_{xo} \quad (6.1\text{-}6)$$

In some of the practical voltage-controlled current sinks/sources, there may be an input current caused by the controlling voltage. This leads to two more expressions necessary to characterize the voltage-controlled current sink/source in addition to Eqs. 6.1-1 and 6.1-2. These general expressions are

$$I_I = g'_{\text{sink}}(V_{IX}) \quad (6.1\text{-}7)$$

and

$$I_I = g'_{\text{source}}(V_{XI}) \quad (6.1\text{-}8)$$

Repeating the considerations of Eqs. 6.1-1 and 6.1-2 for Eqs. 6.1-7 and 6.1-8 results in the following relationship for the voltage-controlled current sink:

$$i_i \approx g_i v_{ix} \quad (6.1\text{-}9)$$

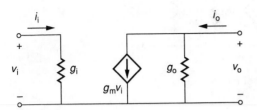

FIGURE 6.1-5
Small signal model for a voltage-controlled current sink/source.

and for the voltage-controlled current source:

$$i_i \approx g_i v_{xi} \tag{6.1-10}$$

g_i is called the input conductance and denotes the change of the input current due to a change in the input voltage.

Both Eqs. 6.1-5 and 6.1-9 or 6.1-6 and 6.1-10 can be modeled schematically as illustrated in Fig. 6.1-5. The small signal model for the voltage-controlled current sink and voltage-controlled current source are identical because small ac changes are insensitive to dc polarities. An ac model for the inverters of Fig. 6.1-3a and b can thus be obtained by adding the resistance (r_1) or a conductance (g_1) in parallel with the output of the circuit of Fig. 6.1-5, resulting in the complete model shown in Fig. 6.1-6. The value r_1 was typically designated as r_o for the loads discussed in Chapter 5. Alternately, r_1 could be derived by a development similar to that used in obtaining Eqs. 6.1-7 through 6.1-10.

The small signal ac performance of the sinking and sourcing inverters can be easily analyzed from the circuit of Fig. 6.1-6. It can be seen that the ac gain, the input resistance, and the output resistance are as follows.

$$A_v = \frac{v_{out}}{v_{in}} = \frac{-g_m}{g_o + g_1} = -g_m r_{out} \tag{6.1-11}$$

$$r_{in} = r_i = \frac{1}{g_i} \tag{6.1-12}$$

and

$$r_{out} = \frac{r_o r_1}{r_o + r_1} = \frac{1}{g_o + g_1} \tag{6.1-13}$$

The small signal model for the push-pull inverter is obtained by connecting two of the models in Fig. 6.1-5 in parallel, resulting in the model of Fig. 6.1-7.

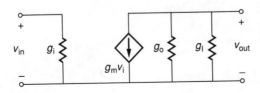

FIGURE 6.1-6
Small signal model for the inverters of Fig. 6.1-3a and b.

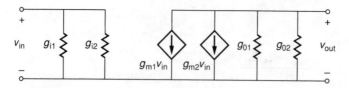

FIGURE 6.1-7
Small signal model for the push-pull inverter of Fig. 6.1-3c.

In this case, the ac gain, the input resistance, and the output resistance are given as follows.

$$A_v = \frac{v_{out}}{v_{in}} = \frac{-(g_{m1} + g_{m2})}{g_{o1} + g_{o2}} = -(g_{m1} + g_{m2})r_{out} \qquad (6.1\text{-}14)$$

$$r_{in} = \frac{r_{i1}r_{i2}}{r_{i1} + r_{i2}} = \frac{1}{g_{i1} + g_{i2}} \qquad (6.1\text{-}15)$$

and

$$r_{out} = \frac{r_{o1}r_{o2}}{r_{o1} + r_{o2}} = \frac{1}{g_{o1} + g_{o2}} \qquad (6.1\text{-}16)$$

Except for the sum of the transconductances in the numerator of A_v and the paralleling of the input resistances, the ac model for the push-pull inverter is similar to the ac model for the sinking and sourcing inverters.

In order to consider the frequency response, it is necessary to introduce parasitic capacitances into the ac models of Figs. 6.1-6 and 6.1-7. As was discussed in Chapter 3, parasitic capacitances are always present in any device and are due to actual capacitance or to the finite time required for carriers to move from one point to another. Figure 6.1-8 shows a model that is suitable for the ac frequency analysis of all three inverter architectures. r_1 is equal to r_{in}, r_2 is equal to r_{out}, and g_m is equal to g_{m1} or g_{m2} for the sinking or sourcing inverters and to $g_{m1} + g_{m2}$ for the push-pull inverter. C_1 and C_2 represent all parasitic capacitors associated with the input and output nodes, respectively. C_3 represents all capacitors connected between the input and output. Depending upon

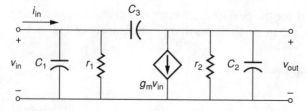

FIGURE 6.1-8
Small signal model including capacitances for the three inverter architectures of Fig. 6.1-3.

the technology used to implement the inverters, these capacitors could have values ranging from 5 fF to 5 pF.

We will consider the frequency response of Fig. 6.1-8 for two cases. The first is when the input source is a voltage, v_{in}, and the second is when the input source is a current, i_{in}. If the input source is a voltage, then the currents can be summed at the output node to give

$$V_{out}(s)(g_2 + sC_2) + sC_3[V_{out}(s) - V_{in}(s)] + g_m V_{in}(s) = 0$$

$$(6.1\text{-}17)$$

In Eq. 6.1-17, s is the complex frequency variable. Solving for the complex frequency transfer function $V_{out}(s)/V_{in}(s)$ gives

$$A_v(s) = \frac{-g_m[1 - s(C_3/g_m)]}{g_2\{1 + s[(C_2 + C_3)/g_2]\}} = A_{v0}\frac{(1 - s/z_1)}{(1 + s/p_1)} \qquad (6.1\text{-}18)$$

where the midband gain, A_{v0}, the zero, z_1, and the pole, p_1, are given as

$$A_{v0} = \frac{-g_m}{g_2} \qquad (6.1\text{-}19)$$

$$z_1 = \frac{g_m}{C_3} \qquad (6.1\text{-}20)$$

and

$$p_1 = \frac{-g_2}{C_2 + C_3} \qquad (6.1\text{-}21)$$

It is seen that the voltage-driven inverter has a first-order transfer function with a midband voltage gain corresponding to the ac voltage gains of Eq. 6.1-11 or 6.1-14, a zero in the right-half complex frequency plane, and a pole in the left-half complex frequency plane. Generally, the value of g_m is much greater than g_2 so that the zero has little influence upon the frequency response. In this case, the ω_{-3dB} frequency would be given as

$$\omega_{-3dB} = \frac{g_2}{C_2 + C_3} \qquad (6.1\text{-}22)$$

In some technologies, the value of g_m may not be sufficiently greater than g_2 so that the zero must be considered. The influence of the right-half plane zero has two important effects. The most obvious effect is to boost the magnitude of the frequency response. The less obvious effect is to cause a phase *lag* similar to a pole. If negative feedback is placed around such an inverter, it will have very poor stability characteristics. A typical frequency response for a voltage-driven inverter is shown in Fig. 6.1-9.

If the inverter of Fig. 6.1-8 is current-driven, then an equation in addition to Eq. 6.1-17 is required. This equation is found by summing currents at the input node and is given as

$$I_{in} = -(g_1 + sC_1)V_{in}(s) + sC_3[V_{in}(s) - V_{out}(s)] \qquad (6.1\text{-}23).$$

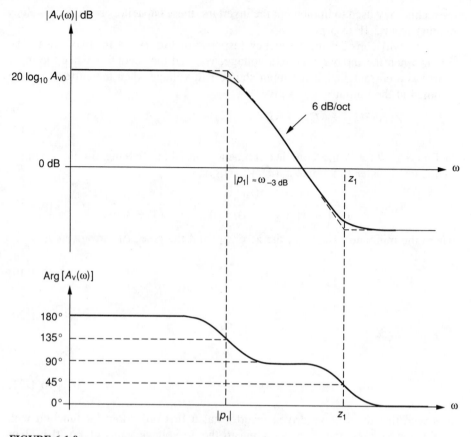

FIGURE 6.1-9
Typical frequency response for a voltage-driven inverter.

Simultaneously solving Eqs. 6.1-17 and 6.1-23 for the transfer function $V_{out}(s)/I_{in}(s)$ results in the following.

$$\frac{V_{out}(s)}{I_{in}(s)} =$$

$$\frac{-g_m[1 - s(C_3/g_m)]}{g_1 g_2 + s[g_1(C_2 + C_3) + g_2(C_1 + C_3) + g_m C_3] + s^2(C_1 C_2 + C_1 C_3 + C_2 C_3)}$$

(6.1-24)

Equation 6.1-24 can be rewritten as

$$\frac{V_{out}(s)}{I_{in}(s)} = \left(\frac{-g_m}{g_1 g_2}\right) [1 - s(C_3/g_m)] \bigg/ \{1 + s[(C_2 + C_3)/g_2 + (C_1 + C_3)/g_1$$

$$+ (g_m C_3)/(g_1 g_2)] + s^2(C_1 C_2 + C_1 C_3 + C_2 C_3)/(g_1 g_2)\}$$

(6.1-25)

The frequency response of the current-driven inverter is seen to have two poles, p_1 and p_2. In most inverters, the magnitude of one of the poles is much less than the magnitude of the other; in other words, $|p_2| \ll |p_1|$. In this case, we are able to find the pole locations in terms of the model parameters by the following method. Assume that the denominator of Eq. 6.1-25, $D(s)$, can be written as

$$D(s) = \left(1 - \frac{s}{p_1}\right)\left(1 - \frac{s}{p_2}\right) = 1 - s\left(\frac{1}{p_1} + \frac{1}{p_2}\right) + \frac{s^2}{p_1 p_2} \approx 1 - \frac{s}{p_1} + \frac{s^2}{p_1 p_2}$$

(6.1-26)

where $|p_1| \gg |p_2|$. Equating the denominator of Eq. 6.1-25 to Eq. 6.1-26 results in the approximate pole locations expressed as

$$p_1 = -\left(\frac{C_2 + C_3}{g_1} + \frac{C_1 + C_3}{g_2} + \frac{g_m C_3}{g_1 g_2}\right)^{-1} \approx -\frac{g_1 g_2}{g_m C_3}$$

(6.1-27)

and

$$p_2 = \frac{-g_m C_3}{C_1 C_2 + C_1 C_3 + C_2 C_3}$$

(6.1-28)

Assuming that C_1, C_2, and C_3 are all about the same value and that g_m is much greater than g_1 or g_2 leads to the conclusion that ω_{-3dB} is approximately given by

$$\omega_{-3dB} \approx \frac{g_1 g_2}{g_m C_3}$$

(6.1-29)

Comparing Eqs. 6.1-22 and 6.1-29 shows that the bandwidth of the current driven inverter is approximately A_{v0} ($= g_m/g_2$) less than that of the voltage-driven inverter. The reason for the decrease in bandwidth is the influence of the gain of the amplifier on the capacitor C_3. Because this capacitor is connected between the input and output, it has the voltage gain of the inverter across it. When viewed from the input, this makes the C_3 capacitor look $1 + A_{v0}$ larger than it really is. This effect is called the *Miller effect*. When the input is current-driven, the large Miller capacitance can create a dominant pole at the input as just shown. Figure 6.1-10 shows the typical frequency response for a current-driven inverter.

The last small signal characteristic we will examine is noise. Unfortunately, the noise models are sufficiently technology-dependent that it is more suitable to introduce the noise analysis after the technology has been selected.

In this subsection the inverter has been introduced from a generic viewpoint. The various types of inverter architectures were discussed and analyzed from both a large signal and a small signal viewpoint. In the following subsections, we will apply these ideas to inverters using MOS and BJT technologies.

6.1.2 MOS INVERTING AMPLIFIERS

The general concepts of inverting amplifiers will now be applied to MOS technology. The possible MOS implementations of the sinking inverter architecture of Fig. 6.1-3a are shown in Fig. 6.1-11. Each of the lower blocks is a realization of the voltage-controlled current sink using an n-channel transistor. Each of the upper blocks represents a realization of the load connected between

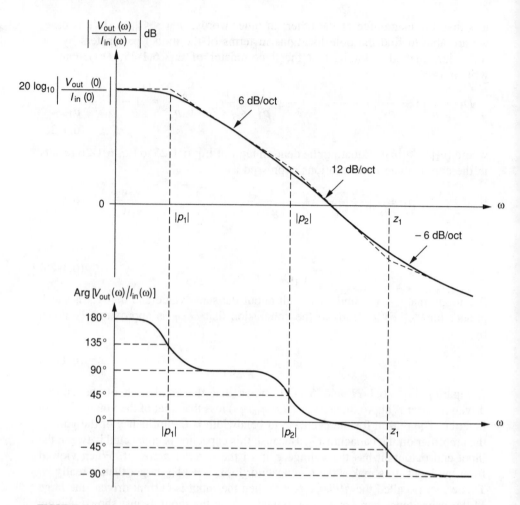

FIGURE 6.1-10
Typical frequency response for a current-driven inverter.

the output of the voltage-controlled current sink and V_{DD}. A CMOS technology having a depletion transistor capability is able to implement all of the inverters of Fig. 6.1-11. If the CMOS technology does not have a depletion transistor capability, then only the inverters of Fig. 6.1-11a, b, and c can be realized. An NMOS technology with a depletion transistor capability can realize the inverters of Fig. 6.1-11c or d. An NMOS technology that does not have a depletion transistor capability can realize only the inverter of Fig. 6.1-11c.

The voltage transfer function of the MOS inverters of Fig. 6.1-11 can be found using the approach demonstrated in Fig. 6.1-4. When V_{IN} of Fig. 6.1-11a is at V_{SS}, the drain current in M1 is zero. Because M2 has its drain and gate connected, it is always in the saturation region. Therefore, Eq. 9 of Table 3.1-1 shows that for zero current, the value of $V_{GS2}(V_{DS2})$ is equal to V_{T2}. Therefore, the value of V_{OUT} is $V_{DD} - V_{T2}$ until V_{IN} increases from V_{SS} to V_{T1}, where M1 turns on. At this point the output voltage starts to drop as in Fig. 6.1-4a.

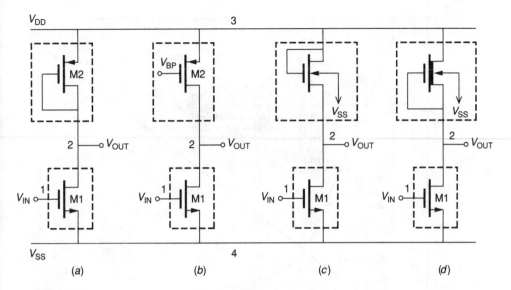

FIGURE 6.1-11
Possible realizations of the sinking inverter for Fig. 6.1-3a: (a) Active p-channel load, (b) Current source load, (c) Active n-channel load, (d) Depletion n-channel load. All potentials are with respect to ground.

Unlike the ciruit of Fig. 6.1-4a, however, the output voltage of Fig. 6.1-11a never reaches V_{SS}.

As the current in M1 and M2 increases because V_{IN} is approaching V_{DD}, the voltage across M1 only increases by the square root of the current. Figure 6.1-12 shows the resulting voltage transfer curve for the inverter of Fig. 6.1-11a when $W_1 = 15 \, \mu, L_1 = 10 \, \mu, W_2 = 5 \, \mu, L_2 = 10 \, \mu, V_{DD} = -V_{SS} = 5$ V, for a CMOS technology corresponding to the parameters in Table 3.1-2. The SPICE input file necessary to generate this plot is included in the figure.

It is of interest to identify in Fig. 6.1-12 the regions where M1 is off, ohmic, and saturated. M1 is off when $V_{IN} < V_{SS} + V_{T1} = -4.25$ V. M1 is saturated when

$$V_{DS1} > V_{GS1} - V_{T1} \Rightarrow V_{OUT} - V_{SS} > V_{IN} - V_{SS} - V_{T1} \Rightarrow V_{OUT} > V_{IN} - V_{T1}$$
(6.1-30)

The various regions of M1 are shown in Fig. 6.1-12. This information is important because now we know that the transition region corresponds (for the most part) to M1 operating in the saturation region. The large signal equation that governs the operation of both devices in the transition region is from Eq. 3.1-4

$$I_D \approx \frac{K'W}{2L}(V_{GS} - V_T)^2$$
(6.1-31)

where we have neglected the channel modulation effect (λ). Equating I_{D1} to I_{D2} results in the following relationship.

$$\frac{K_1'W_1}{2L_1}(V_{IN} - V_{SS} - V_{T1})^2 = \frac{K_2'W_2}{2L_2}(V_{DD} - V_{OUT} - V_{T2})^2 \quad (6.1-32)$$

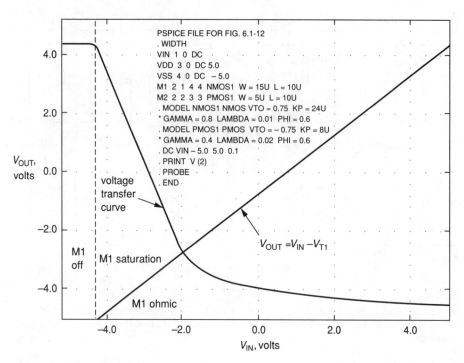

FIGURE 6.1-12
VTC of sinking inverter with active load.

If the inverter of Fig. 6.1-11a is biased in the transition region, then Eq. 6.1-3 can be used to find the small signal ac voltage gain. Applying Eq. 6.1-3 to Eq. 6.1-32 results in

$$A_v = \frac{v_{out}}{v_{in}} = \frac{\partial V_{OUT}}{\partial V_{IN}}\bigg|_Q = -\left(\frac{K_1' W_1 L_2}{K_2' L_1 W_2}\right)^{0.5} \quad (6.1\text{-}33)$$

We can also use the small signal model of Fig. 6.1-6 to calculate A_v. From Chapter 3, we know that $g_i = 0$, $g_m = g_{m1}$, $g_o = g_{ds1}$, and $g_1 = g_{m2} + g_{ds2} \approx g_{m2}$. Eq. 6.1-11 and Eq. 3.1-11 give the small signal voltage gain as

$$A_v = \frac{v_{out}}{v_{in}} = \frac{-g_{m1}}{g_{ds1} + g_{m2} + g_{ds2}} \approx -\frac{g_{m1}}{g_{m2}} = -\left[\frac{K_1'(W_1/L_1)}{K_2'(W_2/L_2)}\right]^{0.5} \quad (6.1\text{-}34)$$

The two approaches to finding A_v are seen to agree as expected. Using the small signal model, we can find the input and output resistances as

$$r_{in} = \infty \quad (6.1\text{-}35)$$

and

$$r_{out} = \frac{1}{g_{ds2} + g_{m2}} \approx \frac{1}{g_{m2}} \quad (6.1\text{-}36)$$

The frequency response of the inverter of Fig. 6.1-11a can be found by inserting the transistor capacitors used in Ex. 3.1-5 into the circuit of Fig. 6.1-11a and comparing the result with Fig. 6.1-8. C_1, C_2, and C_3 of the circuit of Fig. 6.1-8 become

$$C_1 = C_{GS1} + C_{GB1} \qquad (6.1\text{-}37)$$

$$C_2 = C_{BD1} + C_{GS2} + C_{BD2} + C_{GB2} \qquad (6.1\text{-}38)$$

and

$$C_3 = C_{GD1} \qquad (6.1\text{-}39)$$

Therefore, the upper -3 dB frequency for the voltage-driven inverter of Fig. 6.1-11a is found from Eq. 6.1-22 as

$$\omega_{\text{-3dB}} = \frac{g_{m2} + g_{ds1} + g_{ds1}}{C_{BD1} + C_{GS2} + C_{BD2} + C_{GD1} + C_{GB2}} \qquad (6.1\text{-}40)$$

The noise of an inverter is also one of the small signal performance characteristics of interest when inverters are used as small signal amplifiers. Noise is a phenomenon caused by small fluctuations of the analog signal within the components themselves. Noise results from the fact that electrical current is not continuous but the result of quantized behavior and is associated with fundamental processes in a semiconductor component. Common types of noise for semiconductor devices are thermal and $1/f$ noise.

Regardless of the type of noise, the model always can be characterized by an independent voltage or current source. In general, noise is expressed in terms of its mean-square value $[V(\text{rms})^2]$. Noise spectral density is the noise mean-square value per Hertz of bandwidth $[V(\text{rms})^2/\text{Hz}]$. The model for noise in an MOS device can be modeled as an independent voltage in series with the gate as shown in Fig. 3.1-30b. Figure 6.1-13 shows the noise models added to the active-load sinking inverter of Fig. 6.1-11a. $\overline{V}_{n1}^2$ and $\overline{V}_{n2}^2$ are the mean-square

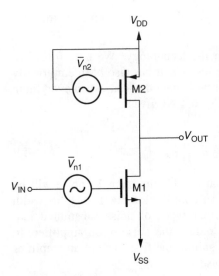

FIGURE 6.1-13
Noise model of Fig. 6.1-11a.

noise voltages of M1 and M2 modeled at the input (gate) of each device. Since $\overline{V}_{n1}$ and $\overline{V}_{n2}$ are uncorrelated, the output mean-square noise voltage can be calculated using superposition. The part of the output due to $\overline{V}_{n1}^2$ is

$$\overline{V}_{o1}^2 = \left(\frac{g_{m1}}{g_{m2}}\right)^2 \overline{V}_{n1}^2 \tag{6.1-41}$$

The part of the output due to $\overline{V}_{n2}^2$ is

$$\overline{V}_{o2}^2 = \overline{V}_{n2}^2 \tag{6.1-42}$$

It should be noted that all gains between the input and output are positive and squared. Also, the value of output due to $\overline{V}_{n2}^2$ is equal to $\overline{V}_{n2}^2$ because the gate voltage of M2 is constant ($\overline{V}_{n2}^2$ only changes the drain voltage). Summing Eqs. 6.1-41 and 6.1-42 gives the total output mean-square noise voltage.

It is customary to reflect the output mean-square noise voltage to the input of the amplifier. This input referred noise voltage obtained by dividing the output noise voltage by the voltage gain is called the equivalent, input-referred, mean-square noise voltage of the amplifier and is given as

$$\overline{V}_{eq}^2 = \overline{V}_{n1}^2 + \left(\frac{g_{m2}}{g_{m1}}\right)^2 \overline{V}_{n2}^2 \tag{6.1-43}$$

$\overline{V}_{eq}$ is a frequency independent noise because we used the midband or frequency independent voltage gain. Equation 6.1-43 represents the equivalent input mean-square noise voltage of Fig. 6.1-11a. When the designer knows the form of the noise mean-square voltages, then Eq. 6.1-43 can be used to minimize the noise. For example, the $1/f$ noise of a MOSFET was given in Eq. 3.1-35 and can be expressed in terms of noise-voltage spectral density in a 1 Hz band as

$$S_{VN} = \frac{S_{IN}}{g_m^2} = \frac{B}{fWL}(V^2/Hz) \tag{6.1-44}$$

where B is a constant that is dependent on the technology. We note from Eq. 6.1-44 that the larger-area devices will have less $1/f$. It has also been empirically observed that B is less for p-channel than for n-channel devices, when everything else is equal. Substituting Eq. 6.1-44 into Eq. 6.1-43 gives

$$S_{eq(1/f)} = \left(\frac{B_N}{fW_1L_1}\right)\left[1 + \left(\frac{K_P'B_P}{K_N'B_N}\right)\left(\frac{L_1}{L_2}\right)^2\right](V^2/Hz) \tag{6.1-45}$$

If the length of M1 is much smaller than that of M2, the input $1/f$ noise will be dominated by that of M1. To minimize the $1/f$ contribution due to M1, its width must be increased as much as possible. Other types of noise substituted into Eq. 6.1-43 will provide other guidelines to reduce the noise of an amplifier. In general, the designer should try to make the gain of the first stage of an amplifier as large as possible to reduce the overall noise.

An example follows to illustrate the small signal performance of the active-load sinking inverter of Fig. 6.1-11a.

Example 6.1-1. AC performance of inverter of Fig. 6.1-11a. Determine the small signal performance of the inverter of Fig. 6.1-11a using the model parameters of Table 3.1-2, assuming that $W_1/L_1 = 15 \, \mu/10 \, \mu$ and $W_2/L_2 = 5 \, \mu/10 \, \mu$ and $V_{DD} = -V_{SS} = 5$ V. The drain and source area (periphery) of M1 and M2 are $150\mu^2(50\mu)$ and $50\mu^2(30\mu)$, respectively. Assume that V_{out} is biased at 0 V. Also assume that the noise is white noise given in Eq. 3.1-34 and find the equivalent input-noise-voltage spectral density.

Solution. We begin the solution by finding the dc current in M1 and M2, calculating the value of V_{G1}, and determining the region of operation for M1. In these calculations we will ignore the influence of the channel modulation (λ). The dc quiescent current can be found from the voltage drop across M2 and is

$$I = \frac{K_P' W_2}{2L_2}(V_{DD} - V_{out} - V_{T2})^2 = \frac{8(5)}{2(10)}(5 - 0.75)^2 \, \mu A = 36 \, \mu A$$

Assume that M1 is saturated. The value of V_{gs1} that gives 36 μA is found as

$$V_{gs1} = V_{T1} + \left(\frac{2I L_1}{K_N' W_1}\right)^{0.5} = 0.75 + \left[\frac{(2)(36)(10)}{(24)(15)}\right]^{0.5} = 0.75 + 1.41 = 2.17 \text{ V}$$

Thus, M1 is in fact saturated and $V_{out} = 0$ V corresponds to $V_{in} = -2.83$ V, as seen in Fig. 6.1-12.

Next, we calculate the small signal parameters for M1 and M2. Using the formulas of Table 3.1-3 gives $g_{m1} = 50.91\mu S$, $g_{ds1} = 0.36\mu S$, $g_{m2} = 16.97\mu S$, and $g_{ds2} = 0.72\mu S$.
Equation 6.1-11 gives

$$A_v = \frac{-50.91}{16.97 + 0.36 + 0.72} = -2.82$$

Equation 6.1-13 gives

$$r_{out} = \frac{1}{(16.97 + 0.36 + 0.72)\mu S} = 55.4 \text{ k}\Omega$$

The capacitors of Eq. 6.1-40 are found using the formulas of Fig. 3.1-19b and the capacitances of Table 2B.4. In this example, we shall include the sidewall capacitances and will assume that the Value of n in Eq. 3.1-14 is 0.5 for both the bottom and sidewall junction capacitances. The capacitors of Eq. 6.1-40 are

$$C_{BD1} = (0.33)(150)[1 + (5/.6)]^{-0.5} + (0.9)(50)[1 + (5/.6)]^{-0.5} =$$
$$16.20\text{fF} + 14.73\text{fF} = 30.93\text{fF}$$

$$C_{GS2} = (0.7)(5)(0.6) + (0.67)(50)(0.7) = 2.1\text{fF} + 23.33\text{fF} = 25.43\text{fF}$$

$$C_{BD2} = (0.38)(50)[1 + (5/.6)]^{-0.5} + (1)(30)[1 + (5/.6)]^{-0.5} =$$
$$6.22\text{fF} + 9.82\text{fF} = 16.04\text{fF}$$

$$C_{GD1} = (0.7)(15)(0.45) = 4.73\text{fF}$$

$$C_{GB2} = 0$$

Substituting the above values in Eq. 6.1-40 results in

$$\omega_{-3dB} = \frac{18.05\mu S}{30.93\text{fF} + 25.43\text{fF} + 16.04\text{fF} + 4.73\text{fF}} = 234\text{Mrps} = 37.2\text{MHz}$$

Dividing the spectral noise density of Eq. 3.1-34 by g_m^2 gives for M1

$$S_{VWN} = 2.17 \times 10^{-16} V^2/Hz$$

and for M2

$$S_{VWP} = 6.51 \times 10^{-16} V^2/Hz$$

The equivalent input-noise-voltage spectral density can be found from Eq. 6.1-43 by replacing each mean-square noise voltage by its noise voltage spectral density and is

$$S_{eq} = S_{VWN} + \left(\frac{g_{m2}}{g_{m1}}\right)^2 S_{VWP} = 2.2 \times 10^{-16} + \left(\frac{16.97}{50.91}\right)^2 6.5 \times 10^{-16}$$

$$= 2.89 \times 10^{-16} V^2/Hz$$

The equivalent input-noise-voltage spectral density is equal to 17.0 nV/$\sqrt{Hz}$.

The performance of the inverter of this example is seen to have a low gain, a moderate output resistance (for MOS devices), a large bandwidth, and an input-referred noise that depends on the noise of the MOS devices. The performance of the active-load sinking inverter can be altered by changing the bias current or the W and L values of M1 and M2.

The voltage inverter of Fig. 6.1-11c will have characteristics similar to Fig. 6.1-11a with one exception. Because M2 is n-channel, it will experience bulk effects causing V_{T2} to increase as V_{OUT} increases. Consequently, the output high value of Fig. 6.1-11c will be less than that of Fig. 6.1-11a. In addition, the back-gate (bulk) transconductance (g_{mb2}) will cause the resistance of the load to be slightly less, resulting in less ac gain. If Fig. 6.1-11c is used in Example 6.1-1 with the same W/L values and current for M1 and M2, the ac gain is -1.56, the ac output resistance is 30.7 kΩ, the bandwidth is 42.8 MHz, and the equivalent input noise voltage spectral density is 17.3 nV/$\sqrt{Hz}$.

The ac voltage gains of the inverters of Fig. 6.1-11a and c are low because the resistance of the load device is low. The inverter of Fig. 6.1-11b uses a current source as its load and achieves a much higher gain. Figure 6.1-14 shows the voltage transfer curve of the current-source-load sinking inverter of Fig. 6.1-11b when V_{BP} is 2 V. When V_{IN} is at V_{SS}, M1 is off and the voltage across M2 is zero, causing V_{OUT} to be at V_{DD}. At some point when V_{IN} increases, M1 will begin to turn on, causing a current to flow in the inverter. This current flow causes a drop across M2 causing the output voltage to fall. As V_{IN} is increased past this point, all of $V_{DD} - V_{SS}$ is dropped across M2, causing M1 to be in the ohmic region with little voltage across it. In this condition, V_{OUT} is approximately V_{SS}.

The regions of operation can be found as before using the transition relationship between the ohmic and saturation regions. M2 is saturated when

$$V_{SD} > V_{SG} + |V_{T2}| \Rightarrow V_{DD} - V_{OUT} > V_{DD} - V_{BP} - |V_{T2}| \Rightarrow$$

$$V_{OUT} < V_{BP} - |V_{T2}| \quad (6.1\text{-}46)$$

The state of M1 is identified by Eq. 6.1-30. The various regions of operation of M1 and M2 are identified in Fig. 6.1-14. Again, we see that the desired ac operating region occurs in the transition region, where both M1 and M2 are

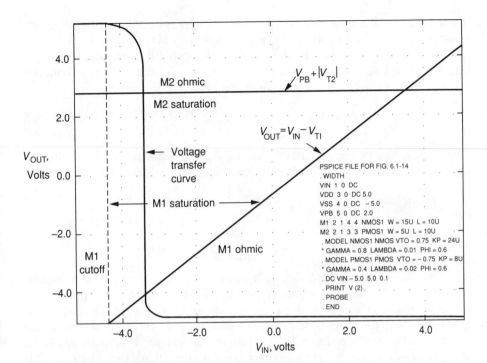

FIGURE 6.1-14
VTC of sinking inverter with current source load.

saturated. In the following discussion, we will assume that the inverter of Fig. 6.1-11b is biased with both M1 and M2 in the saturation region.

The operating point of the inverter of Fig. 6.1-11b can be found using the previous approach. This time, however, the channel modulation effects should be included in order to relate the drain-source voltage to the drain current. The relationship for M1 and M2 is given as

$$I_D = \frac{K'W}{2L}(V_{GS} - V_T)^2(1 + \lambda V_{DS}) \tag{6.1-47}$$

Equating I_{D1} to I_{D2} results in the following relationship for the inverter of Fig. 6.1-11b.

$$\frac{K'_N W_1}{2L_1}(V_{IN} - V_{SS} - V_{T1})^2[1 + \lambda_N(V_{OUT} - V_{SS})] =$$

$$\frac{K'_P W_2}{2L_2}(V_{DD} - V_{BP} - V_{T2})^2[1 + \lambda_P(V_{DD} - V_{OUT})] \tag{6.1-48}$$

Differentiating Eq. 6.1-48 with respect to V_{IN} results in the slope of the voltage transfer curve in the transition region. Applying Eq. 6.1-3 to Eq. 6.1-48 results in

$$A_v = \frac{v_{out}}{v_{in}} = \frac{\partial V_{OUT}}{\partial V_{IN}}\bigg|_Q \approx -\frac{[2K'_N(W_1/L_1)I]^{0.5}}{\lambda_N I + \lambda_P I} = -\frac{[2K'_N(W_1/L_1)]^{0.5}}{(\lambda_N + \lambda_P)(I)^{0.5}} \tag{6.1-49}$$

where the channel modulation effect of Eq. 6.1-47 has been ignored after differentiation and I is the dc current flowing through both M1 and M2.

We can also use the small signal model of Fig. 6.1-6 to calculate A_v. From Chapter 3, we know that $g_i = 0$, $g_m = g_{m1}$, $g_o = g_{ds1}$, and $g_1 = g_{ds2}$. Equation 6.1-11 and Table 3.1-3 give the small signal voltage gain as

$$A_v = \frac{v_{out}}{v_{in}} = \frac{-g_{m1}}{g_{ds1} + g_{ds2}} = -\frac{[2K'_N(W_1/L_1)]^{0.5}}{(\lambda_N + \lambda_P)(I)^{0.5}} \tag{6.1-50}$$

As expected, the two approaches to finding A_v give identical results. Using the small signal model, we can find the input and output resistances as

$$r_{in} = \infty \tag{6.1-51}$$

and

$$r_{out} = \frac{1}{g_{ds1} + g_{ds2}} \tag{6.1-52}$$

The current-source-load sinking inverter of Fig. 6.1-11b has a very unusual property. It is observed that in Eqs. 6.1-49 and 6.1-50 the dc current appears only in the denominator as the argument of the square root. This means that the ac gain is inversely proportional to the square root of the dc bias current. The reason for this can be seen from Table 3.1-3. The transconductance is proportional to the square root of the current, and the conductance is proportional to the current. This property of increasing ac gain as the dc current is reduced does not hold for the previous MOS inverters. When the dc current is reduced to subthreshold levels (~0.1 μA), the transconductance also becomes proportional to the dc current, and the ac gain is no longer dependent on the dc current.

The frequency response of the circuit of Fig. 6.1-11b can be found by inserting the transistor capacitors of Example 3.1-5 into the circuit of Fig. 6.1-11b and comparing the result with Fig. 6.1-8. C_1, C_2, and C_3 of Fig. 6.1-8 become

$$C_1 = C_{GS1} + C_{GB1} \tag{6.1-53}$$

$$C_2 = C_{BD1} + C_{GD2} + C_{BD2} \tag{6.1-54}$$

and

$$C_3 = C_{GD1} \tag{6.1-55}$$

Therefore, the upper -3 dB frequency for the voltage-driven inverter of Fig. 6.1-11b is found from Eq. 6.1-22 as

$$\omega_{-3dB} \approx \frac{g_{ds1} + g_{ds2}}{C_{BD1} + C_{GD2} + C_{BD2} + C_{GD1}} \tag{6.1-56}$$

The noise performance of the current-source-load sinking inverter of Fig. 6.1-11b can be investigated in a similar manner as before. It will be left until the problems to show that the noise performance expressed in Eq. 6.1-43 is also valid for the current-source-load sinking inverter. An example follows to illustrate the stated relationships for Fig. 6.1-11b.

Example 6.1-2. AC performance of the inverter of Fig. 6.1-11b. Determine the small signal performance of the inverter of Fig. 6.1-11b using the model parameters of Table 3.1-2 assuming that $W_1/L_1 = 15\ \mu/10\ \mu$, $W_2/L_2 = 5\ \mu/10\ \mu$, $V_{BP} = 2$ V, and $V_{DD} = -V_{SS} = 5$ V. The drain and source area (periphery) of M1 and M2 are $150\mu^2$ (50μ) and $50\mu^2$ (30μ), respectively. Follow the approach of Ex. 6.1-1 to calculate the capacitances. Assume that V_{out} is biased at 0 V. Also assume that the noise is white noise given in Eq. 3.1-34 and find the equivalent input-noise-voltage spectral density.

Solution. We begin by finding the dc current in M1 and M2, calculating the value of V_{G1}, and determining the region of operation for M1. From the given dc voltage, we know that M2 is saturated. The dc current can be found from the voltage drop across M2 and is

$$I = \frac{K_P' W_2}{2L_2}(V_{DD} - V_{BP} - |V_{T2}|)^2[1 + \lambda_P(V_{DD} - V_{out})] =$$

$$\frac{8(5)}{2(10)}(3 - 0.75)^2(1 + 0.1)\ \mu A = 11.14\ \mu A$$

Assume that M1 is saturated. The value of V_{GS1} that gives $11.14\ \mu A$ is found from the following equation ignoring channel modulation effects on M1.

$$V_{gs1} = V_{T1} + \left(\frac{2I L_1}{K_N' W_1}\right)^{0.5} = 0.75 + \left[\frac{(2)(11.14)(10)}{(24)(15)}\right]^{0.5} = 0.75 + 0.79 = 1.54\ V$$

Thus, M1 is in fact saturated and $V_{out} = 0$ V corresponds to $V_{in} = -3.46$ V, as seen in Fig. 6.1-14.

Next, we calculate the small signal parameters for M1 and M2. Using the formulas of Table 3.1-3 gives $g_{m1} = 28.32\mu S$, $g_{ds1} = 0.11\mu S$, $g_{m2} = 9.44\mu S$, and $g_{ds2} = 0.22\mu S$.
Equation 6.1-11 gives

$$A_v = \frac{-28.32}{0.11 + 0.22} = -84.74$$

Equation 6.1-13 gives

$$r_{out} = \frac{1}{(0.11 + 0.22)\mu S} = 2.99\ M\Omega$$

The capacitors of Eq. 6.1-56 are found using the formulas of Fig. 3.1-19b and the capacitances of Table 28.4. The value of n in Equation 3.1-14 will be 0.5 for both the bottom and sidewall junction capacitances. The capacitances of Eq. 6.1-56 are

$$C_{BD1} = (0.33)(150)[1 + (5/.6)]^{-0.5} + (0.9)(50)[1 + (5/.6)]^{-0.5} = 30.93\text{fF}$$

$$C_{GD2} = (0.7)(0.6)(5) = 2.1\text{fF}$$

$$C_{BD2} = (0.38)(50)[1 + (5/.6)]^{-0.5} + (1)(30)[1 + (5/.6)]^{-0.5} = 16.04\text{fF}$$

$$C_{GD1} = (0.7)(0.45)(15) = 4.73\text{fF}$$

Substituting the above values in Eq. 6.1-56 gives

$$\omega_{-3dB} = \frac{0.33\ \mu S}{30.93\ \text{fF} + 2.1\ \text{fF} + 16.04\ \text{fF} + 4.73\ \text{fF}} = 6.13\ \text{Mrps}$$

$$= 0.976\ \text{MHz}$$

Dividing the spectral noise density of Eq. 3.1-34 by g_m^2 gives for M1

$$S_{VWN} = 3.90 \times 10^{-16} V^2/Hz$$

and for M2

$$S_{VWP} = 11.70 \times 10^{-16} V^2/Hz$$

The equivalent input-noise-voltage spectral density can be found from Eq. 6.1-43 by replacing each mean-square noise voltage by its noise spectral density and is

$$S_{eq} = S_{VWN} + \left(\frac{g_{m2}}{g_{m1}}\right)^2 S_{VWP} =$$

$$3.90 \times 10^{-16} + \left(\frac{9.44}{28.32}\right)^2 11.70 \times 10^{-16} = 5.20 \times 10^{-16} V^2/Hz$$

The equivalent input-noise-voltage spectral density is equal to 22.8 nV/$\sqrt{Hz}$.

The performance of the inverter of this example is seen to have a high gain, a high output resistance, a moderate bandwidth, and a noise primarily determined by that of the MOS devices rather than the inverter configuration. As before, the performance can be altered by changing the bias current or the W and L values of M1 and M2.

There is one important difference in the potential noise performance of this inverter compared with the previous ones. Assume that the inverter is used in the first stage of an amplifier. Even though the equivalent input noise levels of the inverters are approximately equal, the inverter of Fig. 6.1-11b would be a much better choice for lower noise performance because its gain can be higher, causing the noise of the following stages to have less effect on the overall noise of the amplifier.

The remaining sinking inverter of Fig. 6.1-11 is the depletion-load sinking inverter (Fig. 6.1-11d). This inverter requires the technology that offers the ability to make n-channel transistors with a negative threshold voltage. If the gate and source of a depletion transistor are connected, a well-defined drain current will flow if $V_{DS} > 0$. Unfortunately, the depletion n-channel transistor of Fig. 6.1-11d is susceptible to bulk effects because its source is not at V_{SS}. This causes the load resistance to be approximately g_{mb2}, which is an improvement over the active-load sinking inverter of Fig. 6.1-11a but not as high as the current-source-load sinking inverter. If the inverter of Fig. 6.1-11d is used in Example 6.1-1 with the same W/L values for M1 and M2, the ac gain is -15.89, the ac output resistance is 312 kΩ, the bandwidth is 6.83 MHz, and the equivalent input-referred noise-voltage spectral density is 17.3 n$V / \sqrt{Hz}$.

The preceding MOS inverter realizations all correspond to the sinking inverter architecture of Fig. 6.1-3a. MOS realizations of the sourcing inverter architecture of Fig. 6.1-3b can be found by simply taking the inverse of the realizations of Fig. 6.1-11. The *inverse* here means to interchange V_{DD} and V_{SS} and to interchange each p-channel and n-channel transistor. In the sourcing inverter architecture, all of the voltage-controlled current sources are p-channel devices. As a result, for the same W and L values and dc currents, the sinking inverters will have a larger gain than the sourcing inverters because K'_N is greater than K'_P. The analysis of the sourcing inverters is left to the reader.

The remaining architecture of Fig. 6.1-3 that will be considered is the push-pull inverter of Fig. 6.1-3c. This inverter has only the CMOS realization shown in Fig. 6.1-15a. The voltage transfer curve can be found using the reasoning behind Fig. 6.1-4c. Figure 6.1-16 shows the resulting voltage transfer curve for the push-pull CMOS inverter when $W_1 = 5\ \mu$, $L_1 = 10\ \mu$, $W_2 = 15\ \mu$, $L_2 = 10\ \mu$, and $V_{DD} = -V_{SS} = 5$ V, using a CMOS technology corresponding to the parameters in Table 3.1-2. The SPICE input file necessary to generate this plot is included in the figure. Note that the W and L values have been changed in Fig. 6.1-16 so that the transition region is centered about $V_{IN} = 0$ V. The transition region of the push-pull CMOS inverter is much easier to design with respect to V_{IN} than any of the other inverters. The approach used in the design of the push-pull inverter of Fig. 6.1-16 is called *equal resistance*. If the product of K' and (W/L) are equal for both the n-channel and p-channel devices, then the design will have equal resistance or equal sinking and sourcing capability when V_{IN} is midway between the power supplies. An alternate approach is called *equal area* and uses equal values of W and L for both devices.

The regions of operation are identified in Fig. 6.1-16 using the previous methods. In the following analysis we will assume that both transistors are in the saturation mode, which corresponds to the steepest part of the transition region. Note that the current flowing through M1 and M2 is also plotted in Fig. 6.1-16. The scaling for the current is 20 μA = 1 V. It is seen that the current is highest in the transition region, reaching a peak value of approximately 115 μA.

The operating point of the inverter of Fig. 6.1-15a is difficult to calculate because both transistor drain currents are dependent on V_{IN}. The best way to

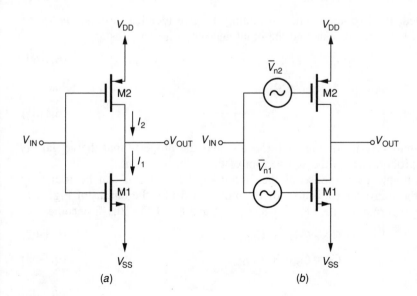

FIGURE 6.1-15
(a) Push-pull inverter, (b) Noise model of Fig. 6.1-15a.

design the operating point would be to use some form of negative dc feedback. For our consideration, we will assume the bias point has been established in the transition region, where both transistors are operating in saturation. Equating I_{D1} to I_{D2} results in the following relationship for Fig. 6.1-15a.

$$\frac{K_N' W_1}{2L_1}(V_{IN} - V_{SS} - V_{T1})^2[1 + \lambda_N(V_{OUT} - V_{SS})] =$$

$$\frac{K_P' W_2}{2L_2}(V_{DD} - V_{IN} - V_{T2})^2[1 + \lambda_P(V_{DD} - V_{OUT})] \quad (6.1\text{-}57)$$

Differentiating Eq. 6.1-57 with respect to V_{IN} results in the slope of the voltage transfer curve in the transition region. Applying Eq. 6.1-3 to Eq. 6.1-57 results in

$$A_v = \frac{v_{out}}{v_{in}} = \left.\frac{\partial V_{OUT}}{\partial V_{IN}}\right|_Q \approx -\frac{[2K_N'(W_1/L_1)I]^{0.5} + [2K_P'(W_2/L_2)I]^{0.5}}{\lambda_N I + \lambda_P I}$$

$$= -\frac{[2K_N'(W_1/L_1)]^{0.5} + [2K_P'(W_2/L_2)]^{0.5}}{(\lambda_N + \lambda_P)(I)^{0.5}} \quad (6.1\text{-}58)$$

where channel modulation effects in Eq. 6.1-57 have been ignored after differentiation, and I is the dc current flowing through both M1 and M2.

The small signal model of the circuit of Fig. 6.1-6 can also be used to calculate A_v. From Chapter 3, we know that $g_i = 0$, $g_m = g_{m1} + g_{m2}$, and $g_o = g_{ds1} + g_{ds2}$. Equation 6.1-11 gives the small signal voltage gain as

$$A_v = \frac{v_{out}}{v_{in}} = \frac{-(g_{m1} + g_{m2})}{g_{ds1} + g_{ds2}} = -\frac{[2K_N'(W_1/L_1)]^{0.5} + [2K_P'(W_2/L_2)]^{0.5}}{(\lambda_N + \lambda_P)(I)^{0.5}}$$

$$(6.1\text{-}59)$$

As expected, the two approaches to finding A_v give identical results. Using the small signal model, we can find the input and output resistances as

$$r_{in} = \infty \quad (6.1\text{-}60)$$

and

$$r_{out} = \frac{1}{g_{ds1} + g_{ds2}} \quad (6.1\text{-}61)$$

The push-pull inverter of Fig. 6.1-15a also has the property that the ac gain is inversely proportional to the square root of the dc bias current.

The frequency response of the circuit of Fig. 6.1-15a can be found by inserting the transistor capacitors of Example 3.1-5 into the circuit of Fig. 6.1-15a and comparing it with Fig. 6.1-8. C_1, C_2, and C_3 of Fig. 6.1-8 become

$$C_1 = C_{GS1} + C_{GB1} + C_{GS2} + C_{GB2} \quad (6.1\text{-}62)$$

$$C_2 = C_{BD1} + C_{BD2} \quad (6.1\text{-}63)$$

and

$$C_3 = C_{GD1} + C_{GD2} \quad (6.1\text{-}64)$$

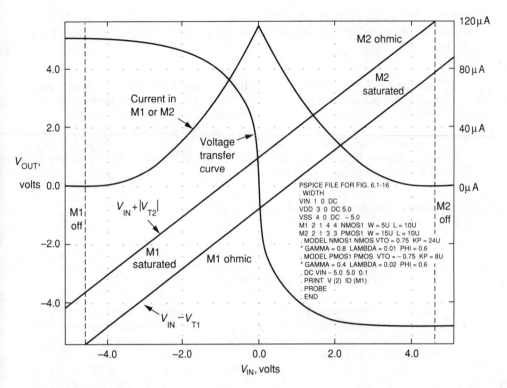

FIGURE 6.1-16
VTC of the push-pull CMOS inverter.

Therefore, the upper -3 dB frequency for the voltage-driven inverter of Fig. 6.1-15a is found from Eq. 6.1-22 as

$$\omega_{-3\text{dB}} \approx \frac{g_{\text{ds1}} + g_{\text{ds2}}}{C_{\text{BD1}} + C_{\text{BD2}} + C_{\text{GD1}} + C_{\text{GD2}}} \tag{6.1-65}$$

The noise of the push-pull inverter of Fig. 6.1-15a is modeled in Fig. 6.1-15b, where an input-noise-voltage spectral density source has been used to model the noise of each device. The noise spectral density at the output is

$$S_o = g_{\text{m1}}^2 (r_{\text{out}})^2 S_{\text{VN1}} + g_{\text{m2}}^2 (r_{\text{out}})^2 S_{\text{VN2}} \tag{6.1-66}$$

where r_{out} is given by Eq. 6.1-61. Dividing Eq. 6.1-66 by the square of the gain given in Eqs. 6.1-58 or 6.1-59 gives

$$S_{\text{eq.}} = \left[\frac{g_{\text{m1}}}{g_{\text{m1}} + g_{\text{m2}}} \right]^2 S_{\text{VN1}} + \left[\frac{g_{\text{m2}}}{g_{\text{m1}} + g_{\text{m2}}} \right]^2 S_{\text{VN2}} \tag{6.1-67}$$

If the transconductances are balanced ($g_{\text{m1}} = g_{\text{m2}}$), then the noise contribution of each device is 50% of the total if $S_{\text{VN1}} = S_{\text{VN2}}$. The total noise contribution can be reduced only by reducing the noise contributed by each device. An example follows to illustrate these relationships for the CMOS push-pull inverter of Fig. 6.1-15a.

Example 6.1-3. AC performance of the inverter of Fig. 6.1-15. Determine the small signal performance of the inverter of Fig. 6.1-15 using the model parameters of Table 3.1-2 assuming that $W_1/L_1 = 5\ \mu/10\ \mu$, $W_2/L_2 = 15\ \mu/10\ \mu$, and $V_{DD} = -V_{SS} = 5$ V. The drain and source area (periphery) of M1 and M2 are 150 μ^2 (50 μ) and 50 μ^2 (30 μ), respectively. Assume that V_{out} is biased at 0 V. Also assume that the noise in each transistor is white noise given in Eq. 3.1-34 and find the equivalent input-noise-voltage spectral density.

Solution. The dc current in M1 and M2 can be written as

$$I_1 = \frac{K'_N W_1}{2L_1}(V_{IN} - V_{SS} - V_{T1})^2[1 + \lambda_N(V_{out} - V_{SS})]$$

$$I_2 = \frac{K'_P W_2}{2L_2}(V_{DD} - V_{IN} - |V_{T2}|)^2[1 + \lambda_P(V_{DD} - V_{out})]$$

Setting $I_1 = I_2$ and solving simultaneously (by iteration), we obtain $V_{IN} = 0.05$ V and $I_1 = I_2 = 116.4\mu$A. The value of V_{IN} when $V_{OUT} = 0$ is called the *systematic offset voltage*. This offset voltage should be distinguished from that due to mismatches in device model parameters.

Next we calculate the small signal parameters for M1 and M2. Using the formulas of Table 3.1-3 gives $g_{m1} = 52.88\ \mu$S, $g_{ds1} = 1.17\ \mu$S, $g_{m2} = 52.88\ \mu$S, and $g_{ds2} = 2.33\ \mu$S.

Equation 6.1-11 gives

$$A_v = \frac{-(52.88 + 52.88)}{1.17 + 2.33} = -30.3$$

Equation 6.1-13 gives

$$r_{out} = \frac{1}{(1.17 + 2.33)\mu S} = 285.7\ \text{k}\Omega$$

The capacitors of Eq. 6.1-65 are found using the formulas of Fig. 3.1-19b and the capacitances of Table 2B.4. The value of n in Eq. 3.1-14 will be 0.5 for both the bottom and sidewall junction capacitances. The capacitances of Eq. 6.1-65 are

$$C_{BD1} = (0.33)(150)[1 + (5/.6)]^{-0.5} + (0.9)(50)[1 + (5/.6)]^{-0.5} = 30.93\ \text{fF}$$

$$C_{BD2} = (0.38)(50)[1 + (5/.6)]^{-0.5} + (1)(30)[1 + (5/.6)]^{-0.5} = 16.04\ \text{fF}$$

$$C_{GD1} = (0.7)(0.45)(15) = 4.73\ \text{fF}$$

$$C_{GD2} = (0.7)(0.6)(5) = 2.10\ \text{fF}$$

Substituting the above values in Eq. 6.1-56 gives

$$\omega_{-3dB} = \frac{3.50\ \mu S}{30.93\ \text{fF} + 16.04\ \text{fF} + 2.10\ \text{fF} + 4.73\ \text{fF}} = 65.06\ \text{Mrps or } 10.35\ \text{MHz}$$

Because $S_{VWN} = S_{VWP} = S_{VW}$, equation 6.1-67 gives

$$S_{eq} = (0.25 + 0.25)S_{VW} = 1.045 \times 10^{-16} V^2/Hz$$

The equivalent input-noise-voltage spectral density is equal to 10.2 nV/$\sqrt{Hz}$

To compare the performance of the inverter of Example 6.1-3 with that of the previous inverters, it is necessary to have the same currents. Multiplying A_v of Ex. 6.1-3 by the square root of 116.4/11.14 gives a voltage gain of -98. With equal W/L values and dc current, the push-pull inverter will have the largest voltage gain. The push-pull inverter can both sink and source output current proportional to the input voltage, which is very useful in output amplifier applications.

The MOS inverters presented in this section represent the more useful realizations of the voltage inverter. The realizations include inverters with active loads, current sink/source loads, depletion transistor loads, and push-pull inverters. A physical layout for the inverters of Fig. 6.1-11b, c, and d and Fig. 6.1-15a is shown in Fig. 6.1-17. The technology for this layout is a p-well CMOS technology having the capability of depletion n-channel devices. The ac performance of the inverters discussed in the section is summarized in Table 6.1-1.

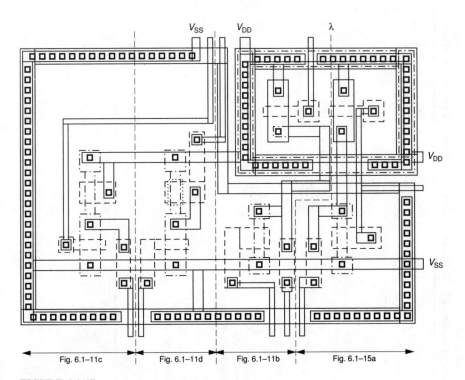

FIGURE 6.1-17
Physical layout of Fig. 6.1-11b, c, d and Fig. 6.1-15a.

TABLE 6.1-1
Comparison of the small signal performance of MOS inverters

Inverter	Figure	AC voltage gain	AC output resistance	Bandwidth ($C_{GB} = 0$)	Equivalent, input-referred, mean-square noise voltage
p-channel active load sinking inverter	6.1-11a	$\dfrac{-g_{m1}}{g_{m2}}$	$\dfrac{1}{g_{m2}}$	$\dfrac{g_{m2}+g_{mb2}}{C_{BD1}+C_{GD1}+C_{GS2}+C_{BD2}}$	$\overline{v}_{n1}^2\left(\dfrac{g_{m1}}{g_{m2}}\right)^2+\overline{v}_{n2}^2$
n-channel active load sinking inverter	6.1-11c	$\dfrac{-g_{m1}}{g_{m2}+g_{mb2}}$	$\dfrac{1}{g_{m2}+g_{mb2}}$	$\dfrac{g_{m2}+g_{mb2}}{C_{BD1}+C_{GD1}+C_{GS2}+C_{BD2}}$	$\overline{v}_{n1}^2\left(\dfrac{g_{m1}}{g_{m2}}\right)^2+\overline{v}_{n2}^2$
Current source load sinking inverter	6.1-11b	$\dfrac{-g_{m1}}{g_{ds1}+g_{ds2}}$	$\dfrac{1}{g_{ds1}+g_{ds2}}$	$\dfrac{g_{ds1}+g_{ds2}}{C_{BD1}+C_{GD1}+C_{GD2}+C_{BD2}}$	$\overline{v}_{n1}^2\left(\dfrac{g_{m1}}{g_{m2}}\right)^2+\overline{v}_{n2}^2$
n-channel depletion load sinking inverter	6.1-11d	$\sim\dfrac{-g_{m1}}{g_{mb2}}$	$\dfrac{1}{g_{mb2}+g_{ds1}+g_{ds2}}$	$\dfrac{g_{mb1}+g_{ds1}+g_{ds2}}{C_{BD1}+C_{GD1}+C_{GD2}+C_{BD2}}$	$\overline{v}_{n1}^2\left(\dfrac{g_{m1}}{g_{m2}}\right)^2+\overline{v}_{n2}^2$
Push-pull inverter	6.1-15a	$\dfrac{-(g_{m1}+g_{m2})}{g_{ds1}+g_{ds2}}$	$\dfrac{1}{g_{ds1}+g_{ds2}}$	$\dfrac{g_{ds2}+g_{ds2}}{C_{BD1}+C_{GD1}+C_{GD2}+C_{BD2}}$	$\left(\dfrac{\overline{v}_{n1}^2\,g_{m1}}{g_{m1}+g_{m2}}\right)^2+\left(\dfrac{\overline{v}_{n2}^2\,g_{m2}}{g_{m1}+g_{m2}}\right)^2$

6.1.3 BJT Inverting Amplifiers

The general concepts of inverting amplifiers can also be applied to BJT technology. However, the differences between BJT and MOS transistors reduces the number of practical BJT inverter realizations to one. This conclusion can be understood by examining the BJT active loads of Fig. 5.2-3. The voltage drop across the BJT active load is found to be limited to approximately 0.8 V in the forward-biased direction. The limitation is due to the exponential characteristic of the BJT and the fact that large forward-bias voltages will create extremely large currents. The result is that, unlike MOS active loads with their square law characteristic, BJT active loads are constrained to voltages less than 0.8 V. If a BJT active load is used in the generic inverter configuration of Fig. 6.1-3a and b, the output voltage would be limited to approximately 0.8 V below V_P or above V_N, respectively. The same reasoning applies to the push-pull inverter architecture of Fig. 6.1-3c. Therefore, the only practical inverter configurations for BJT technology are shown in Fig. 6.1-3a and b where the load is implemented by a current source or current sink, respectively.

Figure 6.1-18 shows the two possible configurations of the BJT inverting amplifier. The voltage transfer curve of the circuit of Fig. 6.1-18a can be found using the approach demonstrated in the circuit of Fig. 6.1-4 for the MOS inverting amplifiers. When V_{IN} is at V_{EE}, Q1 is off and no current is flowing in the inverter. Q2 is biased so that if current can flow, it will be determined by the difference between V_{CC} and V_{BB2} and the transistor characteristics of Q2. When V_{IN} is about 0.5 V above V_{EE}, Q1 begins to turn on and current starts to flow in the inverter. At the same time, the output voltage starts to make the transition from V_{CC} to V_{EE}. As V_{IN} approaches 0.6 to 0.7 V above V_{EE}, Q1 saturates and the output voltage is at V_{EE}. In the transition region, it follows from Eq. 3.3-20 that the current flowing in the inverter is given as

$$I_{C2} = I_{s2} \exp\left(\frac{V_{CC} - V_{BB2}}{V_t}\right)\left(1 + \frac{V_{CC} - V_{OUT}}{V_{AFP}}\right) \qquad (6.1\text{-}68)$$

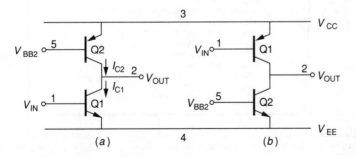

FIGURE 6.1-18
Practical BJT implementations of: (a) Sinking inverter, (b) Sourcing inverter.

Figure 6.1-19 shows the simulation of the circuit of Fig. 6.1-18a when $V_{CC} = -V_{EE} = 5$ V, $V_{BB2} = 4.25$ V, and the transistors have the parameters of Table 6.1-2. In the simulation both the pnp and npn transistors have an emitter area of 500 μ^2 and $V_t = 0.0259$ V. The current in the inverter is also shown in Fig. 6.1-19. Using the model parameters of Table 6.1-2 and assuming that V_{out} is -5 V gives $I_{c1} = 1.67$ mA, which is close to the 1.61 mA indicated in Fig. 6.1-19.

It should be noted that the transition region is very narrow and the slope is large, indicating a large small signal gain. The small signal voltage gain in the transition region can be found by equating the current in Q1 to the current in Q2, resulting in

$$I_{s1} \exp\left(\frac{V_{IN} - V_{EE}}{V_t}\right)\left(1 + \frac{V_{OUT} - V_{EE}}{V_{AFN}}\right) =$$

$$I_{s2} \exp\left(\frac{V_{CC} - V_{BB2}}{V_t}\right)\left(1 + \frac{V_{CC} - V_{OUT}}{V_{AFP}}\right) \quad (6.1\text{-}69)$$

Differentiating Eq. 6.1-69 with respect to V_{IN} and using Eq. 6.1-3 gives the small signal voltage gain as

$$A_v = \left.\frac{\partial V_{OUT}}{\partial V_{IN}}\right|_Q = \frac{-(1/V_t)}{(1/V_{AFN}) + (1/V_{AFP})} \quad (6.1\text{-}70)$$

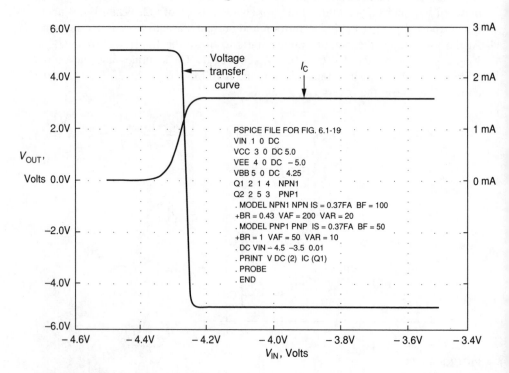

FIGURE 6.1-19
Voltage transfer curve of Fig. 6.1-18a.

TABLE 6.1-2
Typical BJT model parameters

Parameter	NPN	PNP	Units
J_s	6×10^{-16}	6×10^{-16}	A/mil^2
	9.3×10^{-19}	9.3×10^{-19}	A/μ^2
I_s (Emitter area = 500 μ^2)	0.37	0.37	fA
β_F	100	50	A/A
β_R	0.43	1	A/A
V_{AF}	200	50	Volts
V_{AR}	20	10	Volts
τ_f	0.4	20	ns
C_{je0}	0.5	0.5	pF
C_{jc0}	0.5	0.5	pf
ϕ	0.55	0.55	Volts

$V_t = 0.0259$ V at room temperature (300$°K$)

Equation 6.1-70 shows that the voltage gain of the BJT inverter in Fig. 6.1-18 is large and is independent of bias current. Using the parameters of Table 6.1-2 gives a small signal voltage gain of -1544. The large gain is typical of BJT inverters using current sink/source loads.

The small signal model of the circuit of Fig. 6.1-18 is shown in Fig. 6.1-20. The small signal model parameters shown are related to the large signal model parameters in Table 3.2-4. The ac voltage gain can easily be shown to be

$$A_v = \frac{v_{out}}{v_{in}} = \frac{-g_{m1}}{g_{o1} + g_{o2}} = \frac{-(I_{C1}/V_t)}{(I_{C1}/V_{AFN}) + (I_{C2}/V_{AFP})} = \frac{-(1/V_t)}{(1/V_{AFN}) + (1/V_{AFP})} \tag{6.1-71}$$

which is identical to Eq. 6.1-70 and where $I_{C1} = I_{C2} = I_{CQ}$. The principle that the gain can be calculated from the large signal or small signal model is again verified. In the case of the BJT inverter, the small signal input resistance is not infinity and is found as

$$r_{in} = r_{\pi 1} \tag{6.1-72}$$

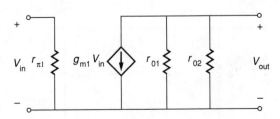

FIGURE 6.1-20
Small signal, midband model for Fig. 6.1-18 a or b.

The output resistance of Fig. 6.1-18 is

$$r_{\text{out}} = \frac{1}{g_{o1} + g_{o2}} = \frac{1}{I_{\text{CQ}}[(1/V_{\text{AFN}}) + (1/V_{\text{AFP}})]} \tag{6.1-73}$$

The frequency response of the voltage-driven BJT inverter can be found by inserting the parasitic capacitances of the BJT inverter in the small signal model of Fig. 6.1-8. Assume that Q1 is a vertical NPN and that Q2 is a lateral PNP. Fig. 3.3-11, Fig. 3.3-12, and Table 3.3-5 result in Fig. 6.1-21 where $C_{\text{BE}} + C_{\text{AC}} = C_{\pi}$ and $C_{\text{CB}} = C_{\mu}$. Therefore, the capacitances of Fig. 6.1-8 become

$$C_1 = C_{\text{BE1}} = C_{\pi 1} \tag{6.1-74}$$

$$C_2 = C_{\text{CB2}} + C_{\text{CS1}} = C_{\mu 2} + C_{\text{CS1}} \tag{6.1-75}$$

and

$$C_3 = C_{\text{CB1}} = C_{\mu 1} \tag{6.1-76}$$

The upper -3 dB frequency is given by Eq. 6.1-22 as

$$\omega_{\text{-3dB}} = \frac{g_{o1} + g_{o2}}{C_{\mu 2} + C_{\mu 1} + C_{\text{CS1}}} \tag{6.1-77}$$

The upper -3 dB frequency for a current-driven inverter is given by Eq. 6.1-29 as

$$\omega_{\text{-3dB}} \cong \frac{g_{\pi 1}(g_{o1} + g_{o2})}{g_{m1} C_{\mu 1}} \tag{6.1-78}$$

In many cases, the output of the inverter sees a load capacitance which must be incorporated into C_2 of Eq. 6.1-75.

The noise performance of the BJT inverter can be found in a similar manner as for the MOS inverters. Figure 6.1-22 shows a model suitable for calculating the noise. The noise sources will be assumed to be noise-voltage spectral density sources. The form of these sources is determined by the type of noise the designer is interested in analyzing. The noise spectral density of the output of Fig. 6.1-18 is found by superimposing the influence of S_{VN1} and S_{VN2} to get

$$S_{\text{OUT}} = S_{\text{VN1}} A_v^2 + S_{\text{VN1}} A_v^2 \left(\frac{S_{\text{VN2}}}{S_{\text{VN1}}} \right) \tag{6.1-79}$$

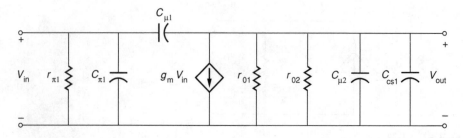

FIGURE 6.1-21
Small signal, high-frequency model for Fig. 6.1-18 a or b.

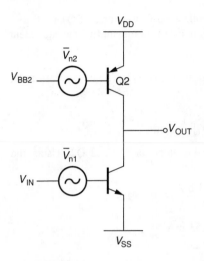

FIGURE 6.1-22
Model for noise calculations of Fig. 6.1-18a.

The equivalent noise-voltage spectral density at the input of the BJT can be found by dividing Eq. 6.1-79 by A_v^2. The result is

$$S_{eq} = S_{VN1}\left[1 + \left(\frac{g_{m2}}{g_{m1}}\right)^2\left(\frac{S_{VN2}}{S_{VN1}}\right)\right] \tag{6.1-80}$$

It is seen that the BJT inverter noise performance is the same form as that of the MOS inverter given by Eq. 6.1-43. When the form of the noise-voltage spectral density of the BJT is known, then Eq. 6.1-80 can be used to predict the noise performance. The current noise spectral densities of the BJT are given as

$$S_{IC} = 2qI_C \ (V^2/Hz) \tag{6.1-81}$$

and

$$S_{IB} = \left[2qI_B + \frac{K_F I_B^{AF}}{f}\right] \ (V^2/Hz) \tag{6.1-82}$$

where I_C and I_B are dc currents of the transistor, K_F is the $1/f$ noise constant, and AF is an exponent. Eq. 6.1-81 is the shot noise at the collector and Eq. 6.1-82 consists of both shot and 1/f noise at the base. These noise spectral densities are assumed to be uncorrelated.

The BJT inverters of Fig. 6.1-18 are identical in their small signal performance. An example follows to illustrate the small signal performance of the BJT inverter of Fig. 6.1-18.

Example 6.1-4. AC performance of the BJT inverter of Fig. 6.1-18a. Find the small signal performance of the BJT inverter of Fig. 6.1-18a using the model parameters of Table 6.1-2. Assume $V_{BB2} = 4.25$ V, $V_t = 25.9$ mV, $V_{CC} = -V_{EE} = 5V$, and that the inverter is biased so that V_{out} is at 0 V. Assume that the emitter areas of both transistors are 500 μ^2 and the collector-substrate area of Q1 is 50 $\mu \times$ 100 μ. If the shot noise spectral density of Eq. 6.1-81 is dominant find the equivalent input-noise-voltage spectral density.

Solution. We begin by finding the dc current in Q1 and Q2. The dc current can be found from Eq. 6.1-68;

$$I_{C2} = (0.37\text{fA}) \left[\exp\left(\frac{0.75}{0.0259}\right) \right] \left(1 + \frac{5}{50}\right) = 1.53 \text{ mA}$$

Next we calculate the small signal parameters for Q1 and Q2. Using the formulas of Table 3.3-4 gives

$$g_{m1} = \frac{I_{C1}}{V_t} = \frac{1.53 \text{ mA}}{0.0259} = 0.059 \text{ S}$$

$$g_{o1} = \frac{I_{C1}}{V_{AFN}} = \frac{1.53 \text{ mA}}{200} = 7.67 \text{ }\mu\text{S}$$

and

$$g_{o2} = \frac{I_{C2}}{V_{AFP}} = \frac{1.53 \text{ mA}}{50} = 30.7 \text{ }\mu\text{S}$$

Equations 6.1-70 and 6.1-71 give

$$A_v = \frac{-0.059 \times 10^6}{7.67 + 30.7} = -1544$$

Equation 6.1-72 gives

$$r_{in} = r_{\pi 1} = \frac{\beta_F}{g_{m1}} = \frac{100}{0.059\text{S}} = 1.695 \text{ }\Omega$$

Equation 6.1-73 gives

$$r_{out} = \frac{10^6}{7.67 + 30.7} = 26.06 \text{ k}\Omega$$

Next we must calculate the value of capacitances that determine the frequency behavior. Assuming V_{IN} is approximately 0.7 V gives $V_{CB1} = 4.3$ V. From Eq. 3.1-19 with $n = 0.5$, we find that $C_{CB1} = 0.168$ pF. Similarly, for Q2 we have $V_{CB2} = 4.25$ V, giving $C_{CB2} = 0.169$ pF. It is customary to estimate C_{BE1} of Table 3.3-5 as $2C_{je0}$, or 1 pF. With τ_f from Table 6.1-2 equal to 0.4 ns, Eq. 3.3-32 gives C_{AF1} as 23.6 pF. Table 2C.4 gives the zero-bias collector-substrate capacitance of 0.79 pF. Since the collector-substrate has a back bias of 5 V, $C_{CS1} = 0.335$ pF. Thus,

$$C_{\mu 1} = C_{CB1} = 0.168 \text{ pF}$$

$$C_{\pi 1} = C_{BE1} + C_{AF1} = 24.6 \text{ pF}$$

$$C_{CS1} = 0.335 \text{ pF}$$

and

$$C_{\mu 2} = C_{CB2} = 0.169 \text{ pF}$$

Equation 6.1-77 for the voltage driven inverter gives

$$\omega_{-3dB} = \frac{7.67 \text{ }\mu\text{S} + 30.7 \text{ }\mu\text{S}}{0.168 \text{ pF} + 0.169 \text{ pF} + 0.335 \text{ pF}} = 57.1 \text{ Mrps or } 9.09 \text{ MHz}$$

Equation 6.1-78 for the current driven inverter gives

$$\omega_{\text{-3dB}} = \frac{g_{\pi 1}(g_{o1} + g_{o2})}{g_{m1}C_{\mu 1}} = \frac{590 \ \mu S(7.67 + 30.7) \ \mu S}{0.059(0.168 \ \text{pF})} = 2.28 \ \text{Mrps} = 363 \ \text{kHz}$$

From Eq. 6.1-81, the collector shot-noise spectral density is

$$S_{IC} = 4.9 \times 10^{-22} \ A^2/\text{Hz}$$

Dividing by g_m^2 gives the equivalent noise voltage spectral density at the base for both transistors as

$$S_{VB} = 4.9 \times 10^{-22}/0.059 = 1.405 \times 10^{-19} \ V^2/\text{Hz}$$

Eq. 6.1-80 gives the equivalent input noise voltage spectral density as $0.53 \ \text{nV}/\sqrt{\text{Hz}}$.

The small signal analysis and design of inverting amplifiers has been addressed in Section 6.1. It was shown that these amplifiers consist of a voltage-controlled current sink/source and a load. In the case of the CMOS push-pull inverting amplifier, the load was also a voltage-controlled current source. It was seen that the voltage transfer curves of inverting amplifiers have three distinct operating regions. These regions are where the input is low and the output is high, where the input is high and the output low, and a region between these two called the transition region. Because the ac gain is proportional to the slope of the voltage transfer curve, the high gain inverting amplifier should be biased in the region with the steepest slope, which is the transition region. It was shown that in the transition region, the transistors are all operating in their normal regions of operation: the saturation region for the MOSFET and the forward-active region for the BJT. Therefore, the small signal model for the normal-region operation was used to predict the performance of the inverters considered in this section. The performance variables include the small signal voltage gain, the input resistance, the output resistance, the -3 dB bandwidth, and noise.

The inverter or inverting amplifier is a basic gain block and should be well understood before the following sections are studied. An example follows on how the designer approaches the implementation of an amplifier using an inverting amplifier. This example will show some of the tradeoffs that can be made based on the considerations presented in this section. It will also show some of the limitations of the inverter and why we must consider other types of amplifiers.

Example 6.1-5. Assume that you are to design an inverting amplifier with gain equal to or greater than -100, using power supplies of ± 2.5 V, having a power dissipation less than 1 mW, and using a dc value for both input and output voltages of 0 V. Select among the inverting amplifiers presented in this section. Assume that Tables 3.1-2 and 6.1-2 represent the model parameters of the MOS or BJT, respectively.

Solution. The first consideration is selection of one of the inverter architectures that have been discussed. From the specifications we note that the dc voltage across the voltage-controlled current sink/source will be 2.5 V. This is too much voltage to put across the base-emitter of a BJT, so we are restricted to MOS implementations.

Although only one of the MOS inverters was shown to have zero input dc voltage (the inverter of Fig. 6.1-15a), all could be biased with the input and output at 0 V if the W/L ratios were designed correctly. Thus, since the gain is large and we have no other specifications to suggest otherwise, let us select the CMOS push-pull inverter of Fig. 6.1-15a because it has the largest gain for similar dc current.

The dc current through the inverter will be selected to meet the power supply specification. It is seen that for power supplies of ±2.5 V, any current less than 200 μA will give a power dissipation less than 1 mW. Let us arbitrarily choose a dc current of 100 μA. The next step is to find the W_1/L_1 ratio that will give this current for a gate-source voltage of 2.5 V. Using the large signal equation in the saturation region, we get

$$\frac{W_1}{L_1} = \frac{2I_d}{K_N'(V_{gs1} - V_{TN})^2(1 + \lambda_N V_{ds1})} = \frac{2(100)}{(24)(1.75)^2(1.05)} = 2.59 \approx \frac{5}{2}$$

Solving for W_2/L_2 using the same approach gives

$$\frac{W_2}{L_2} = \frac{2I_d}{K_P'(V_{sg2} - |V_{TP}|)^2(1 + \lambda_P V_{sd2})} = \frac{2(100)}{(8)(1.75)^2(1.1)} = 7.42 \approx \frac{15}{2}$$

Putting these values into Eq. 6.1-59 gives a small signal voltage gain of −73.

Unfortunately, we now face the type of problem that a designer will encounter many times. The design meets two of the three specifications. If we are restricted to inverting amplifiers, what can be done to meet *all* of the specifications? One might be tempted to lower the current since it was shown that the ac gain was inversely proportional to the square of the dc current. However, this relationship only holds when everything else, such as W/L values, remains constant. If we attempt this approach, the requirement that $V_{GS1} = 2.5$ V will cause the W/L values to change, resulting in the same gain as before. If the preceding formulas for W/L are substituted into Eq. 6.1-59, it will be seen that V_{GS} must be changed to produce the correct gain. Unfortunately, this implies changing the power supplies, which is probably beyond the control of the designer. None of the other MOS configurations will meet all three specifications for the same reason that the push-pull CMOS inverter fails. One must turn to other architectures or change the specifications. This example will be reconsidered in the next section.

6.2 IMPROVING THE PERFORMANCE OF INVERTING AMPLIFIERS (CASCODE AMPLIFIERS)

A very useful amplifier called the inverting amplifier was introduced in Section 6.1. The inverting amplifier is intended to invert and amplify small signals. The objective of this section is to take a closer look at the performance of inverting amplifiers. By doing so, we will see areas where the small signal performance can be improved or design constraints eliminated. Some of the topics not addressed in the last section include controlling or designing the frequency response, achieving higher gain, and decoupling the ac and dc design constraints. These topics seriously limit the performance of the inverters of the previous section. For example, if the inverter is current-driven, the bandwidth is severely reduced from the bandwidth of the voltage-driven inverter. In many of the MOS inverters, an ac gain larger than -100 would be difficult to achieve. Example 6.1-5 illustrated the problems that develop between ac and dc specifications. In that example, we saw that it was impossible to satisfy all the design requirements simultaneously.

Let us first examine how the designer can control the frequency response of an inverting amplifier. Assume that the source can be represented by a Thevenin or Norton form having a source resistance of R_s. If the voltage amplifier of Fig. 6.1-8 is voltage-driven, then $R_s = 0$ and the -3 dB bandwidth is given from Eq. 6.1-22 as

$$\omega_{-3dB}(R_s = 0) = \frac{g_2}{C_2 + C_3} \tag{6.2-1}$$

where R_s is the resistance of the input source. If R_s is large, then the amplifier is current-driven. If this amplifier is current-driven, we have shown in Eqs. 6.1-27 and 6.1-28 that the poles are widely spaced and the -3 dB bandwidth is from Eq. 6.1-29

$$\omega_{-3dB}(R_s \neq 0) \approx \frac{g_1 g_2}{g_m C_3} \tag{6.2-2}$$

Since g_m is typically much greater than g_1, the bandwidth of the current-driven inverter is less than the voltage-driven inverter. A useful heuristic viewpoint of the current-driven inverter is shown in Fig. 6.2-1 for the inverting amplifier of the circuit of Fig. 6.1-11b. In many circuits, the poles can be closely approximated by the reciprocal product of the resistance and capacitance to ground at a node. In this circuit there are two poles. p_1 is associated with the input and p_2 with the output of the inverter. Typically, R_s is the output of another inverter and is approximately equal to the r_o of a MOSFET. The resistances associated with each pole are approximately the same in most cases. However, because of the Miller effect, the C_{gd1} capacitance is reflected in parallel with the gate and source of M1, causing p_1 normally to be much less than p_2. The objective of the following discussion is to show how to obtain current-driven inverters that have bandwidths approximately equal to those of voltage-driven inverters.

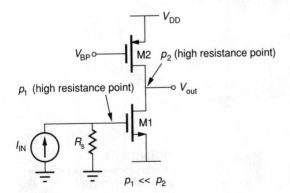

FIGURE 6.2-1
Current-driven CMOS inverter.

6.2.1   Current-Driven CMOS Cascode Amplifier

Consider Fig. 6.2-2, where the voltage-controlled current sink of Fig. 6.1-3a has been implemented by the architecture of Fig. 5.3-8b rather than the architecture of Fig. 5.3-5a. As in Sec. 6.1, the input is at the gate of M1. The gates of M2 and M3 are biased by the dc voltages V_{BP} and V_{BN}, respectively. M3 is called the *cascode transistor* and has a very important influence on the frequency performance. Figure 6.2-3a shows the small signal model for Fig. 6.2-2. Note that since the source of M3 is not on V_{SS}, bulk effects must be included. The small signal model can be redrawn as illustrated in Fig. 6.2-3b. An important observation is the influence of M3 on the resistance seen by the drain of M1. This resistance has been reduced from a level of $1/g_{ds}$ in the circuit of Fig. 6.1-11b to a level of less than $1/g'_{m3}$ (g'_{m3} refers to the sum of g_{m3} and g_{mb3}). The midband, small signal voltage gain from V_1 to V_2 is approximately $-g_{m1}/g'_{m3}$. Considerable mathematical manipulations can be avoided in finding the poles of the circuit of Fig. 6.2-2 if we assume that r_{ds3} is approximately infinity. This results in the approximate circuit shown in Fig. 6.2-3c, where the notation of Fig. 6.1-8 has been used for the left-hand part of the circuit. In this case, we can use Eqs. 6.1-27 and 6.1-28 to find the poles of the left-hand part of the circuit. Using the equivalent expressions given in Fig. 6.2-3c gives the poles of Fig. 6.2-2 as

$$p_1(\text{cascode}) = -\left[\frac{C_2 + C_3}{g_2} + \frac{C_1 + C_3}{g_1} + \frac{g_{m1}C_3}{g_1 g_2}\right]^{-1} \approx$$

$$\frac{-g_1}{C_1 + C_3[1 + (g_{m1}/g'_{m3})]} \qquad (6.2\text{-}3)$$

$$p_2(\text{cascode}) \approx \frac{-g'_{m3}[C_1 + C_3 + C_3(g_{m1}/g'_{m3})]}{C_1 C_2 + C_1 C_3 + C_2 C_3} \qquad (6.2\text{-}4)$$

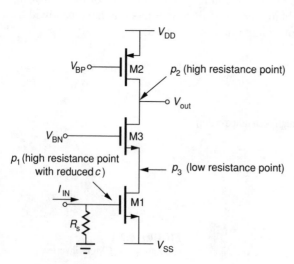

FIGURE 6.2-2
Current-driven cascode inverting amplifier ($V_{BS2} = 0$).

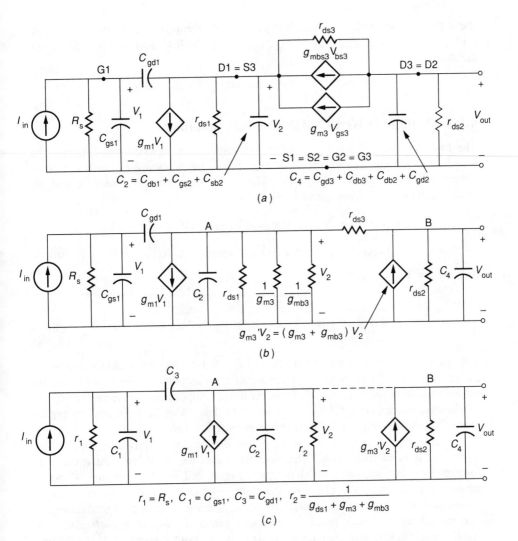

FIGURE 6.2-3
(a) Small signal model of Fig. 6.2-2, (b) Equivalent model of (a), (c) Model if r_{ds3} is assumed infinite.

The output pole associated with C_4 is

$$p_3(\text{cascode}) \approx \frac{-g_{o2}}{C_4} \qquad (6.2\text{-}5)$$

Comparing Eqs. 6.2-3 and 6.2-4 with Eqs. 6.1-27 and 6.1-28 shows that the influence of the cascode transistor (M3) is to bring the input pole back to the value it would have if C_3 were zero ($-g_1/C_1$ as seen from Fig. 6.2-3c). The higher inverter pole corresponding to Eq. 6.1-28 and now given by Eq. 6.2-4, has not been influenced very much by the cascode transistor. Looking at these results and assuming that all capacitors have approximately the same value within a factor of 5, that $g_{m1} \approx g'_{m3}$, and that R_s is less than or equal to r_o, we see that

$$| p_1(\text{cascode}) | \approx | p_3(\text{cascode}) | < | p_2(\text{cascode}) | \qquad (6.2\text{-}6)$$

6.2.2   Voltage-Driven CMOS Cascode Amplifier

The low-frequency voltage gain of the voltage-driven cascode amplifier can be found from the equivalent circuit of Fig. 6.2-3, by replacing I_{in} with a voltage source and noting that $V_{\text{in}} \approx V_1$. The nodal equations at nodes A and B, disregarding the capacitors, can be found as

$$(g_{ds1} + g_{ds3} + g_{m3} + g_{mbs3}) V_2 - g_{ds3} V_{\text{out}} = -g_{m1} V_1 \qquad (6.2\text{-}7)$$

$$-(g_{ds3} + g_{m3} + g_{mbs3}) V_2 + (g_{ds2} + g_{ds3}) V_{\text{out}} = 0 \qquad (6.2\text{-}8)$$

Solving for V_{out}/V_1 gives

$$\frac{V_{\text{out}}}{V_1} = \frac{V_{\text{out}}}{V_{\text{in}}} = \frac{g_{m1}(g_{m3} + g_{mbs3} + g_{ds3})}{g_{ds1}g_{ds2} + g_{ds1}g_{ds3} + g_{ds2}g_{ds3} + g_{ds2}(g_{m3} + g_{mbs3})} \approx -\frac{g_{m1}}{g_{ds2}}$$
$$(6.2\text{-}9)$$

This gain should be compared with that of Eq. 6.1-50 for the current-source-load sinking inverter of Fig. 6.1-11b. Because of the cascode influence of M3 on the output resistance of M1, $g_{ds1}(r_{ds1})$ is no longer important. Thus, under similar conditions, the cascode CMOS inverter should have an ac gain approximately twice that of the simple CMOS inverter of Fig. 6.1-11b.

Generally, with the addition of active devices, the equivalent input noise increases. It is of interest to determine the influence of M3 on the noise performance of the cascode CMOS inverter. Figure 6.2-4a shows a model appropriate for calculating the noise of the voltage-driven cascode CMOS inverter. Superposition is used to find the contribution of each noise source to the output. The contribution of $\overline{V}_{n3}$ requires particular attention. Figure 6.2-4b gives the small signal model that can be used to find the contribution of $\overline{V}_{n3}$. Writing nodal equations gives

$$(g_{ds1} + g_{ds3} + g_{m3} + g_{mb3}) V_{s3} - g_{ds3} V_{\text{out}} = g_{m3} \overline{V}_{n3} \qquad (6.2\text{-}10a)$$

$$-(g_{ds3} + g_{m3} + g_{mb3}) V_{s3} + (g_{ds2} + g_{ds3}) V_{\text{out}} = -\overline{V}_{n3} \qquad (6.2\text{-}10b)$$

Solving for $\overline{V}_{\text{out}}/\overline{V}_{n3}$ gives

$$\frac{\overline{V}_{\text{out}}}{\overline{V}_{n3}} = \frac{-g_{ds1}g_{m3}}{g_{ds1}g_{ds2} + g_{ds1}g_{ds3} + g_{ds2}g_{ds3} + g_{ds2}(g_{m3} + g_{mb3})} \cong$$

$$\frac{-g_{ds1}g_{m3}}{g_{ds2}(g_{m3} + g_{mb3})} \qquad (6.2\text{-}11)$$

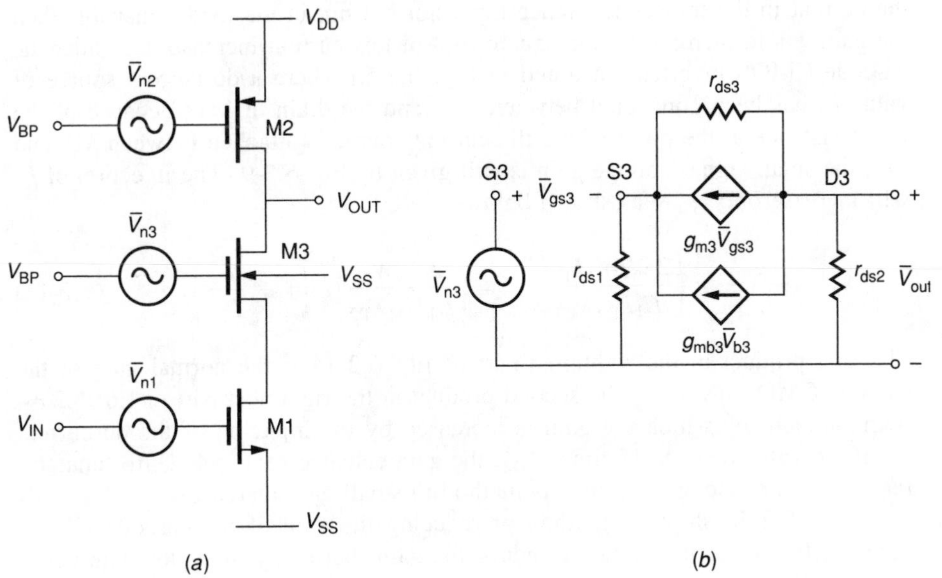

FIGURE 6.2-4
(a) Model for calculating the noise performance of the cascode CMOS inverter, (b) Model for calculating the noise of M3.

We note that under most normal circumstances, the gain of Eq. 6.2-11 will be less than unity. The reason for this is the large resistance (r_{ds1}) from the source to ground of M3. The total output-noise-voltage spectral density can be found as

$$S_{out} \approx \left(\frac{g_{m1}}{g_{ds2}}\right)^2 S_{VN1} + \left(\frac{g_{m2}}{g_{ds2}}\right)^2 S_{VN2} + S_{VN3} \qquad (6.2\text{-}12)$$

The equivalent input-noise-voltage spectral density is found by dividing Eq. 6.2-12 by the square of the small signal, frequency independent voltage gain $(g_{m1}/g_{ds2})^2$ to get

$$S_{eq.} = S_{VN1} + \left(\frac{g_{m2}}{g_{m1}}\right)^2 S_{VN2} + \left(\frac{g_{ds2}}{g_{m1}}\right)^2 S_{VN3} \approx S_{VN1} + \left(\frac{g_{m2}}{g_{m1}}\right)^2 S_{VN2} \qquad (6.2\text{-}13)$$

It is of interest to note that for all practical purposes, the addition of the cascode transistor, M3, does not influence the noise performance.

6.2.3 Improving the Gain of the CMOS Cascode Amplifier

The second performance limitation that was found particularly in the MOS inverting amplifiers of Fig. 6.1-11 was a small voltage gain. The ac voltage gain of the inverting amplifier was found to be g_m times the output resistance of the amplifier. One can increase g_m or r_{out} to increase the gain. If one could increase the current in the transconductance transistor but not in the load transistor, then the gain would increase by the square root of this current increase. Consider the cascode CMOS inverter illustrated in Fig. 6.2-5a where a dc current source of value I_o has been connected between V_{DD} and the drain of M1. Because of the low resistance at the point where the current source is attached between M1 and M3, the small signal voltage gain is still given by Eq. 6.2-9. The injection of I_o will increase only g_{m1}, as shown below.

$$A_v \approx \frac{-g_{m1}}{g_{ds2}} = \left(\frac{2K_N'W_1 I_{D1}}{L_1 I_{D2}\lambda_{P2}}\right)^{0.5} = \left(\frac{2K_N'W_1}{L_1 I_{D2}\lambda_{P2}}\right)^{0.5}\left(1 + \frac{I_o}{I_{D2}}\right)^{0.5} \qquad (6.2\text{-}14)$$

The first product in the rightmost part of Eq. 6.2-14 is the normal gain of the cascode CMOS inverter. The second product in the rightmost part of Eq. 6.2-14 is the amount by which the gain is increased by the injection of the dc current I_o. If the value of I_o is 15 times I_{D2}, the gain enhancement is 4. Unfortunately, the square root factor restricts this method to small gain increases.

Fig. 6.2-5b shows a method of reducing the gain of the cascode CMOS inverter. It may seem strange to reduce the gain, but many times the gain needs to be reduced. In this case, Eq. 6.2-14 is written as

$$A_v \approx \frac{g_{m1}}{g_{ds2}} = \left[\frac{2K_N'W_1 I_{D1}}{L_1 I_{D2}\lambda_{P2}}\right]^{0.5} = \left[\frac{2K_N'W_1}{L_1 I_{D2}\lambda_{P2}}\right]^{0.5}\left[1 - \frac{I_o}{I_{D2}}\right]^{0.5} \qquad (6.2\text{-}15)$$

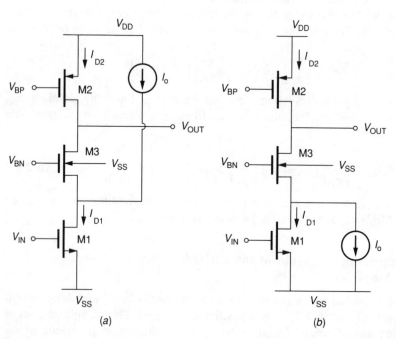

FIGURE 6.2-5
Modification of the ac gain by changing g_{m1}: (a) Gain enhancement, (b) Gain reduction.

We note that I_o cannot be larger than I_{D2}. The dc current control methods proposed in Fig. 6.2-5 for adjusting the dc gain of the CMOS inverter work primarily because of the low resistance seen at the source of M3.

The addition of a fourth transistor to achieve the cascode CMOS inverter of Fig. 6.2-6 is probably the best method of significantly increasing the ac gain of the CMOS current-source-load inverter. The effect of M4 is to cascode the current source M2 and to boost its output resistance seen by M1 and M3 by roughly a factor of $g_{m4}r_{ds4}$. This causes the output resistance of the inverter to increase the gain. An easy way to calculate the ac gain is to take advantage of previous work. The output resistance of the circuit of Fig. 6.2-6 can be calculated using the result of Eq. 5.3-10. This resistance is the parallel combination of two cascoded current sinks/sources and is expressed as

$$r_{out} = \frac{1}{(g_{ds1}g_{ds3})/(g_{ds1} + g_{ds3} + g_{m3} + g_{mb3}) + (g_{ds2}g_{ds4})/(g_{ds2} + g_{ds4} + g_{m4} + g_{mb4})}$$

$$\approx \frac{1}{(g_{ds1}g_{ds3}/g_{m3}) + (g_{ds2}g_{ds4}/g_{m4})} \qquad (6.2\text{-}16)$$

Multiplying r_{out} by $-g_{m1}$ gives the ac small signal voltage gain of the circuit of Fig. 6.2-6 as

$$A_v \approx \frac{-g_{m1}g_{m3}g_{m4}}{g_{ds1}g_{m4}g_{ds3} + g_{ds2}g_{m3}g_{ds4}} \qquad (6.2\text{-}17)$$

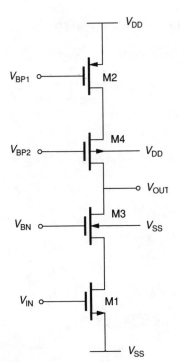

FIGURE 6.2-6
Fully cascoded current-sinking inverter.

It can be seen by comparing Eq. 6.1-50 with Eq. 6.2-17 that the ac voltage gain of the current-source-load inverter has been increased by a factor of approximately $g_m r_o/2$ assuming $g_{m3} \approx g_{m4}$ in Eq. 6.2-17. An example will illustrate some of the preceding concepts.

Example 6.2-1. Improving the performance of a CMOS inverting amplifier. Repeat Example 6.1-2 for the circuit of Fig. 6.2-6 with the following changes. Let all W/L ratios be $10 \ \mu/10 \ \mu$ and let $V_{BP1} = 3$ V, $V_{BP2} = 1$ V, and $V_{BN} = -1$ V. Assume that the values of capacitances still hold, although the widths of the transistors have changed.

Solution. The current can be found from knowing the voltages across M2. Ignore the drain voltage for the moment. The current is

$$I_{d2} \approx \frac{8}{2}(2 - 0.75)^2 = 6.25 \ \mu A$$

Ignoring the bulk effects on M4 and equating drain currents, it follows that $V_{GS4} = V_{GS2}$. Therefore, the source of M4 or drain of M2 is at 3 V. Using the fact that $V_{sd2} = 2$ V allows the recalculation of I_{d2} including the channel modulation as

$$I_{d2} = 6.25 \ \mu A[1 + (0.02)(2)] = 6.625 \ \mu A$$

Assuming that $V_{sb4} \approx 2$ V gives V_{T4}:

$$V_{T4} \approx 0.75 + 0.4[(2.6) - 0.6]^{0.5} = 1.085 \ V$$

This value of V_{T4} gives $V_{gs4} = 2.372$ V or $V_{sd2} \approx 1.628$ V. We could iterate toward a closer solution, but these results are sufficient. Assuming that the dc value of the output is at 0 V, both M2 and M4 are in saturation.

The dc value of V_{IN} can be found assuming $I_{d1} = 6.625 \ \mu A$, to get

$$V_{gs1} = 0.75 + \left[\frac{2(6.625)}{24}\right]^{0.5} = 1.493 \ V$$

Therefore, the quiescent value of V_{in} is -3.507 V. Ignoring the bulk effect on M3 gives $V_{gs3} = V_{gs1} = 1.493$ V so that $V_{d1} = V_{s3} \approx -2.493$ V. Using this value to calculate the threshold voltage of M3 including bulk effects gives

$$V_{T3} \approx 0.75 + 0.8(3.093 - 0.6)^{0.5} = 1.537 \ V$$

This value of V_{T3} gives $V_{gs3} = 2.280$ V. Subtracting this value from -1 V gives $V_{d1} = -3.280$ V or $V_{ds1} = 1.720$ V. We see that both M1 and M3 are also in saturation. As above, we could continue to iterate, but these values are sufficient for this example.

The small signal parameters are found from Table 3.1-3 as

$$g_{m1} = g_{m3} = [2(24)(6.626)]^{0.5} \ \mu S = 17.83 \ \mu S$$

$$g_{ds1} = g_{ds3} = 0.0663 \ \mu S$$

$$g_{mb3} = \frac{0.8(17.83 \ \mu S)}{2(1.720 + 0.6)^{0.5}} = 4.683 \ \mu S$$

$$g_{m2} = g_{m4} = [2(8)(6.626)]^{0.5} \ \mu S = 10.3 \ \mu S$$

$$g_{ds2} = g_{ds4} = 0.1325 \ \mu S$$

and

$$g_{mb4} = \frac{0.4(10.3\ \mu S)}{2(1.628 + 0.6)^{0.5}} = 1.380\ \mu S$$

Putting these values in Eq. 6.2-15 yields an output resistance of 601 MΩ. Multiplying by $-g_{m1}$ gives an ac voltage gain of $-10,716$. This gain has been increased over that of Example 6.1-2 for two reasons. The first is the addition of M3 and M4, and the second is the fact that the current is approximately one-half that of the previous example.

Assuming that the dominant pole is the one associated with the output, the -3 dB bandwidth can be found as

$$\omega_{-3dB} = \frac{1}{601\ M\Omega(C_{GD3} + C_{DB3} + C_{GD4} + C_{DB4})} =$$

$$\frac{1}{601\ M\Omega(4.73 + 30.93 + 2.1 + 16.04)pF} = 30.93\ \text{rps or } 4.92\,\text{KHz}$$

This extremely low bandwidth is a consequence of the high output resistance. The noise-voltage spectral density of the inverter in Fig. 6.2-6 can be found as

$$S_{eq.} \approx \left(100\ nV/\sqrt{Hz}\right)[1 + (10.31/17.83)2]^{0.5} = 115.5\ nV/\sqrt{Hz}$$

The noise performance is seen to be essentially identical to that of the CMOS inverting amplifier of Example 6.1-2.

One of the purposes of this section is to expand the degrees of design freedom for the inverting voltage amplifier. Example 6.1-5 of the preceding section depicted a case where not all of the design specifications could be met. It is appropriate to reconsider this example to show how the ideas of this section permit the specifications of Example 6.1-5 to be satisfied. The following example gives the details.

Example 6.2-2. The objective of this example is to show how to meet all of the specifications of Example 6.1-5 using the information introduced in this section. Recall that the design was to achieve a small signal voltage gain greater than -100 using ± 2.5 V power supplies and a dissipation less than 1 mW. The amplifier is also to be designed so that the dc value of input and output is 0 V.

Solutions. It was seen in Example 6.1-5 that MOS devices had to be used in order to allow a 2.5 V drop on the input device between the gate (base) and source (emitter). Unfortunately, the dc voltages defined the W/L ratios, resulting in a voltage gain of -73.

We will again choose MOS devices for the same reason. If we insert cascode devices in the design of Example 6.1-5, two problems will result. The first is that very little output voltage swing is possible if all transistors are to be kept in saturation. The second is that the gain will be much larger than -100. A better compromise is shown in Fig. 6.2-7a. A single n-channel transistor serves as the voltage-controlled current sink (M1) which is the input device and a cascoded current source (M2 and M3) is the load. It is important for the reader to understand the motivation for this choice. If we assume the same dc current level as in Example

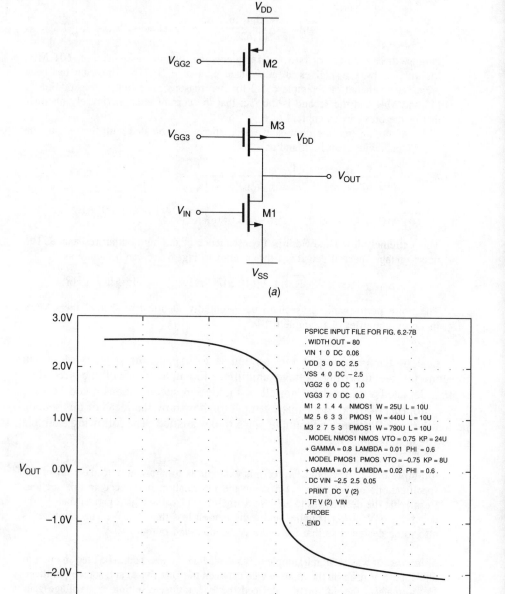

FIGURE 6.2-7
(*a*) Circuit for Example 6.2-2, (*b*) Simulation results.

6.1-5, then an inverter such as that of Fig. 6.1-11b would have a gain of $-g_{m1}/(g_{ds1} + g_{ds2})$, which for 100 μA of bias current gives

$$A_v \approx \frac{-g_{m1}}{g_{ds1} + g_{ds2}} = \frac{-109.5 \ \mu S}{1 \ \mu S + 2 \ \mu S} = -36.5$$

Because we are not using the push-pull configuration, the gain is one-half of -73. Next, we note that if we can use a cascode (M3) in the load, then the effective g_{ds2} in this expression becomes much less than g_{ds1}. Thus, the ac gain will be approximately -109.5, which exceeds the -100 gain specification. Note that this would not have worked if the input device (M1) were p-channel and the load devices (M2 and M3) were n-channel. Because the gate voltage of M2 is under our control (not required to be 0 V), we can carefully design the dc voltages associated with M2 and M3 to provide as much signal swing as possible and still keep these devices in saturation.

Although we are not yet really concerned with signal swing, let us attempt to bias M2 and M3 to achieve a good result. We begin by picking the voltage across the source-drain of M2 as 1 V. The gate voltage is selected to keep M2 in saturation using the following relationship.

$$V_{SD2} > V_{SG2} - |V_{TP}| \rightarrow V_{SG2} < V_{SD2} + |V_{TP}| = 1.75 \text{ V}$$

If we pick V_{GG2} as 1 V, V_{sg2} is 1.5 V, which satisfies the constraint. Assuming the dc current is 100 μA gives W_2/L_2 as

$$\frac{W_2}{L_2} = \frac{2I_D}{K_P'(V_{sg2} - |V_{TP}|)^2(1 + \lambda_P V_{ds2})} = \frac{2(100)}{8(0.75)^2(1.02)} = 43.6 \approx \frac{44}{1}$$

The large value of W/L is due to the choices of dc voltages.

With $V_{bs3} = -2.5$ V, we calculate $|V_{T3}|$ as 1.144 V due to bulk effects. For M3 to remain in saturation, $V_{SG3} < V_{SD3} + |V_{T3}|$ or $V_{DG3} < |V_{T3}|$. Therefore, selecting $V_{GG3} = 0$ V gives a maximum positive output voltage of $|V_{T3}|$ or 1.144 V. This could be increased by increasing V_{GG3}, however with $V_{GG3} = 0$ V no additional bias supply is required. The negative swing can be found by noting that

$$V_{DS1} > V_{GS1} - V_{TN} = 1.75 \text{ V}$$

Therefore, the negative swing is limited to 0.75 V. The value of W_3/L_3 is found from

$$\frac{W_3}{L_3} = \frac{2I_D}{K_P'(V_{sg3} - |V_{T3}|)^2(1 + \lambda_P V_{DS3})} = \frac{2(100)}{8(1.50 - 0.946)^2(1.03)} = 79.11 \approx \frac{79}{1}$$

Again, this large value of W/L is due to the small dc voltage drop associated with M3. If $V_{GG3} > 0$ V, then W_3/L_3 would be even larger, but the positive signal swing would be increased. Since the output signal swing was not a specification, we will leave the design as it is. With the given values, the ac resistance of M2 and M3 seen by M1 is approximately 89 MΩ. The ac gain turns out to be approximately -108, which meets the specification of Example 6.1-5. Figure 6.2-7b shows the simulation results of this example. The simulation output file shows that the ac gain is -112.5 and the power dissipation is 0.5 mW. The positive output voltage swing is higher than anticipated because the gain is not influenced significantly when M3 is in the triode region. The value of the output is not 0 V when $V_{in} = 0$ V because the gain is too high and the W/L values have not been precisely chosen. It is not worthwhile to go back and make this adjustment because the values of the model parameters are not that well known. The best approach is to get as close as possible (as illustrated) and assume that external negative feedback will be used to achieve the desired voltage levels.

6.2.4 The BJT Cascode Amplifier

The principles of increasing the performance of MOS inverting amplifiers covered in this section can also be applied to BJT inverting amplifiers. In the case of the BJT, it is not so important to increase the gain. Therefore, we will focus on the control of the frequency performance of the BJT inverting amplifier. Figure 6.2-8 shows the use of a cascode BJT (Q3) to reduce the Miller effect of the capacitance $C_{\mu 1}$ of Q1 when the amplifier is driven by a high-resistance source (current driver). The circuit of Fig. 6.2-9a shows the small signal model of Fig. 6.2-8. We assume initially that the input to the circuit is a current source I_{in}. Figure 6.2-9b shows the circuit after rearranging the $g_{m3}V_2$ transconductance source. If we assume that r_{o3} can be ignored, then Fig. 6.2-9c results. This simplified small signal model allows us to take advantage of the previous results. The previous development for the MOS version can be used for the BJT. The equations equivalent to Eqs. 6.2-3 through 6.2-5 for the BJT are

$$p_1(\text{cascode}) = -\left[\frac{C_2 + C_3}{g_2} + \frac{C_1 + C_3}{g_1} + \frac{g_{m1}C_3}{g_1 g_2}\right]^{-1} \approx$$

$$\frac{-g_1}{C_1 + C_3[1 + (g_{m1}/g'_{m3})]} = \frac{-g_{\pi 1}}{C_{\pi 1} + C_{\mu 1}[1 + (g_{m1}/g_{m3})]} \quad (6.2\text{-}18)$$

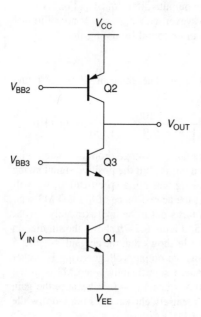

FIGURE 6.2-8
BJT cascoded inverting amplifier.

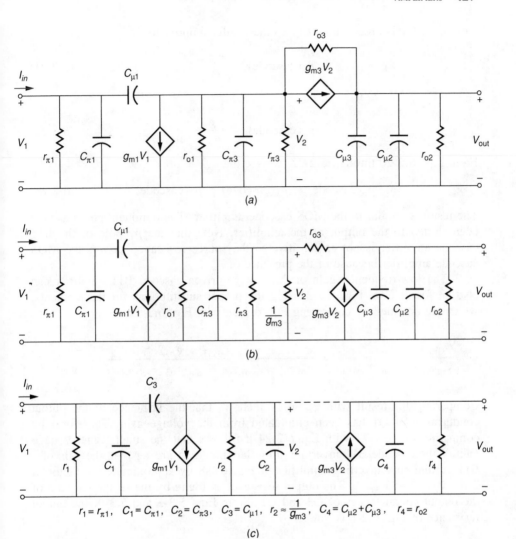

FIGURE 6.2-9

(a) Small signal model for Fig. 6.1-8, (b) Equivalent model, (c) Simplified model.

$$p_2(\text{cascode}) \approx \frac{-g_{m3}[C_1 + C_3 + C_3(g_{m1}/g_{m3})]}{C_1C_2 + C_1C_3 + C_2C_3} =$$

$$\frac{-g_{m3}[C_{\pi 1} + C_{\mu 1} + C_{\mu 1}(g_{m1}/g_{m3})]}{C_{\pi 1}C_{\pi 3} + C_{\pi 1}C_{\mu 1} + C_{\pi 3}C_{\mu 1}} \quad (6.2\text{-}19)$$

The output pole associated with C_4 is

$$p_3(\text{cascode}) \approx \frac{-g_4}{C_4} = \frac{-g_{o2}}{C_{\mu 2} + C_{\mu 3}} \quad (6.2\text{-}20)$$

Normally, C_π is greater than C_μ, so the results simplify to

$$p_1(\text{cascode}) \approx \frac{-g_{\pi 1}}{C_{\pi 1}} \tag{6.2-21}$$

and

$$p_2(\text{cascode}) \approx \frac{-g_{m3}}{C_{\pi 3}} \tag{6.3-22}$$

From Eqs. 6.2-20 through 6.2-22, we see that

$$p_3(\text{cascode}) < p_1(\text{cascode}) < p_2(\text{cascode}) \tag{6.2-23}$$

The result is similar to the MOS cascode amplifier. The dominant pole has now been shifted to the output of the amplifier. Note that the p_1 pole of the BJT cascode amplifier is not as sensitive to the source resistance as was the MOS cascode amplifier because of the presence of $r_{\pi 1}$.

The low-frequency gain of the voltage-driven cascode BJT amplifier can also be found from Fig. 6.2-3 using the proper substitutions for the elements, which are obtained by comparing Fig. 6.2-3a with Fig. 6.2-9a:

$$\frac{V_{\text{out}(o)}}{V_{\text{in}(o)}} = \frac{v_{\text{out}}}{v_{\text{in}}} = \frac{v_{\text{out}}}{v_1} = \frac{-g_{m1}(g_{m3} + g_{o3})}{g_{o1}g_{o2} + g_{o1}g_{o3} + g_{o2}g_{o3} + g_{o2}g_{m3}} \approx \frac{-g_{m1}}{g_{o2}}$$
$$\tag{6.2-24}$$

Comparing this result with Eq. 6.1-71 shows that the influence of the output conductance of Q1 has been eliminated from the voltage gain. Therefore, by comparing Eq. 6.1-71 with Eq. 6.2-24 it follows that the small signal voltage gain of the cascode BJT inverting amplifier should be greater than the gain of a BJT current sink inverting amplifier of Fig. 6.1-8 by approximately a factor of 2 if $|V_{\text{AFN}}| \approx |V_{\text{AFP}}|$. The output resistance is found by the reciprocal sum of the output conductances of Q3 and Q1. From Eqs. 5.3-3 and 5.3-9, the output resistance of Fig. 6.2-8 is

$$r_{\text{out}} = r_{o2} \| r_{o3}[1 + (g_{m3} + g_{o3})(r_{\pi 3} \| r_{o1})] \approx r_{o2} = \frac{I_1}{V_{\text{AFP}}}$$
$$\tag{6.2-25}$$

Comparing Fig. 6.2-9c with Fig. 6.2-3c and assuming that the dominant pole is equal to $p_3(\text{cascode})$, then Eq. 6.2-5 gives the -3 dB bandwidth as

$$\omega_{\text{-3dB}} \approx \frac{g_4}{C_4} = \frac{g_{o2}}{C_{\mu 2} + C_{\mu 3}} \tag{6.2-26}$$

Any capacitance at the output of the BJT cascode inverting amplifier must be added to C_4 in Eq. 6.2-26. The noise performance of the BJT cascode inverting amplifier is characterized by the previous analysis for the CMOS cascode inverter amplifier. It can be shown that Eqs. 6.2-12 and 6.2-13 also hold for the BJT cascode inverting amplifier of Fig. 6.2-8.

Example 6.2-3. Repeat Example 6.1-4 for the BJT cascode inverting amplifier of Fig. 6.2-8. Assume that V_{BB3} is -2 V.

Solutions. Using the results of Example 6.1-4, the current in all transistors is seen to be approximately 1.53 mA. Using the values calculated in Example 6.1-4 gives the small signal voltage gain as

$$A_v \approx \frac{-g_{m1}}{g_{o2}} = -\frac{0.059 \text{ S}}{30.7} \mu\text{S} = -1928$$

The gain is not increased much due to the fact that g_{o2} is approximately four times g_{o1}. The input resistance is still 1659 Ω and the output resistance is 13 M$\Omega \| 32.57$ k$\Omega = 32.49$ kΩ. The three poles of the current-driven amplifier are given from Eq. 6.2-20:

$$p_3(\text{cascode}) = 91.06 \text{ Mrps or } 14.5 \text{ MHz}$$

from Eq. 6.2-21:

$$p_1(\text{cascode}) \approx 23.98 \text{ Mrps} = 3.817 \text{ MHz}$$

and from Eq. 6.2-22:

$$p_2(\text{cascode}) \approx 2398 \text{ Mrps} = 381 \text{ MHz}$$

We see that the inequalities of Eq. 6.2-23 are not satisfied in this case. The low output resistance and the high value of C_π compared with C_μ has caused $p_1(\text{cascode})$ to determine the bandwidth. If we assume a 10 pF load at the output, then $p_3(\text{cascode})$ becomes 2.977 Mrps or 0.474 MHz and $p_3(\text{cascode})$ determines the bandwidth. If the poles are closely grouped, then an approximation to the -3 dB bandwidth is given as

$$\omega_{-3dB} \approx [p_1^2 + p_2^2 + p_3^2]^{1/2}$$

It can be seen that the noise is the same as for Example 6.1-4 if we make the assumption that the contribution of Q3 is negligible. One of the largest differences between this example and Example 6.1-4 is that the -3dB bandwidth of the current-driven cascode is approximately 10 times larger.

One of the reasons for introducing the cascode transistors was to enable a boosting or reduction in gain by current injection or removal from the circuit of Fig. 6.2-8. Because of the high gain available from BJT amplifiers, these techniques are less important and will not be considered. We will complete this section by considering the tremendous gain that can be achieved from the fully cascoded current-sinking inverter of Fig. 6.2-10. This inverter has an output resistance given as

$$r_{\text{out}} = \{r_{o3}[1 + (g_{m3} + g_{o3})(r_{\pi3} \| r_{o1})]\} \| \{r_{o4}[1 + (g_{m4} + g_{o4})(r_{\pi4} \| r_{o2})]\}$$

$$\approx r_{o3}(1 + \beta_{FN}) \| r_{o4}(1 + \beta_{FP}) = \frac{1}{I_{C3}/[V_{AFN}(1 + \beta_{FN})] + I_{C4}/[V_{AFP}(1 + \beta_{FP})]}$$

$$(6.2\text{-}27)$$

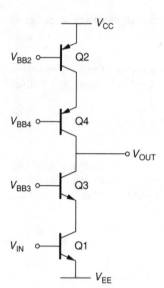

FIGURE 6.2-10
Fully cascoded BJT push-pull inverting amplifier.

The small signal voltage gain of the circuit of Fig. 6.2-10 is given as

$$A_v = -g_{m1}r_{out} = \frac{-I_{C1}/V_t}{I_{C3}/[V_{AFN}(1 + \beta_{BN})] + I_{C4}/[V_{AFP}(1 + \beta_{FP})]}$$

(6.2-28)

Normally $I_{C1} = I_{C3} = I_{C4}$ so Eq. 6.2-28 can be written as

$$A_v = -g_{m1}r_{out} = \frac{-1/V_t}{1/[V_{AFN}(1 + \beta_{FN})] + 1/[V_{AFP}(1 + \beta_{FP})]}$$

(6.2-29)

Note that the small signal gain of Eq. 6.2-29 is dependent only on the parameters of the BJT models and therefore is the maximum achievable gain given the BJT model parameters. If we assume the values given in Table 6.1-2, the voltage gain of the circuit of Fig. 6.2-10 is −87,420. The reason the gain is so large is that the output resistance is equal to 2.264 MΩ if the dc currents are 1 mA. This high output resistance also causes a low bandwidth. If $C_{\mu 3} = C_{\mu 4} = 0.2$ pF, the −3 dB bandwidth is 1.104 Mrps or 175 kHz if the output resistance is 2.264 MΩ. Typically, the capacitance at the output is more on the order of 10 pF (an oscilloscope probe is typically 14 pF). This causes the −3 dB bandwidth to be 6.81 kHz.

It has been shown how the use of additional devices can improve the small signal performance of the inverting amplifiers covered in Sec. 6.1. The bandwidth is extended in the case of the current-driven inverter. In addition, the gain is increased by two means. The first is the injection of dc current into the transistor acting as a voltage-controlled current sink (or source), and the second is the use of the cascode configuration to increase the ac output resistance.

The additional devices also give an extra degree of design freedom. The techniques presented in this section will be useful in improving or modifying the performance of more complex amplifiers containing inverting amplifiers.

6.3 DIFFERENTIAL AMPLIFIERS

The differential amplifier has become a very useful circuit because of its compatibility with integrated circuit technology, in addition to its ability to amplify differential signals. Any two signals can be decomposed into a *difference-mode* signal, V_D, and a *common-mode* signal, V_C. This is illustrated by the following relations, where V_1 and V_2 are two arbitrary input signals.

$$V_1 = \frac{V_D}{2} + V_C \qquad (6.3\text{-}1)$$

$$V_2 = -\frac{V_D}{2} + V_C \qquad (6.3\text{-}2)$$

It is easy to see that V_D and V_C are defined as

$$V_D = V_1 - V_2 \qquad (6.3\text{-}3)$$

and

$$V_C = \frac{V_1 + V_2}{2} \qquad (6.3\text{-}4)$$

The objective of the differential amplifier is to amplify only the difference between two input signals, regardless of the level of the common-mode signal.

The differential amplifier is characterized by its differential-mode gain and its common-mode gain. The ratio of the differential-mode gain to the common-mode gain is called the *common-mode rejection ratio (CMRR)*. Ideally, the CMRR should be as large as possible. This normally means that the common-mode gain should be as small as possible. Another characteristic of the differential amplifier is the *input common-mode signal range*, which specifies the range of common-mode values over which the differential amplifier continues to sense and amplify the differential-mode signal. Yet another characteristic that affects the performance of the differential amplifier is offset. When the input differential voltage or the input differential current is zero the output of the differential amplifier may not be zero. *Input offset voltage*, V_{OS}, is the magnitude of a voltage source connected between the inputs of a differential amplifier that would make the output equal to zero. Typically, the common-mode input voltage is also given, since the input offset voltage or current may be dependent on its value. V_{OS} should be treated as a random variable. The *input offset current*, I_{OS}, is the difference between two current sources applied to the inputs of the differential amplifier that is required to make the output equal to zero. I_{OS} should also be treated as a random variable. Both V_{OS} and I_{OS} are dependent on temperature in most differential amplifiers.

6.3.1 CMOS Differential Amplifiers

Figure 6.3-1 shows the circuit of a general MOS differential amplifier. The blocks labeled *active load* can consist of any of the circuits previously discussed that will replace resistances. The key aspect of the differential amplifier is the input source-coupled pair, M1 and M2.

We will first examine the large signal characteristics of the circuit of Fig. 6.3-1. Assume that M1 and M2 are in saturation. Neglecting channel modulation and assuming $V_{T1} = V_{T2}$, it follows that the pertinent relationship describing the large signal behavior is given as

$$V_{ID} = V_{G1} - V_{G2} = V_{GS1} - V_{GS2} = \left[\frac{2I_{D1}}{\beta_1}\right]^{1/2} - \left[\frac{2I_{D2}}{\beta_2}\right]^{1/2} \qquad (6.3\text{-}5)$$

and

$$I_{SS} = I_{D1} + I_{D2} \qquad (6.3\text{-}6)$$

where $\beta = K'(W/L)$. Assuming that $\beta_1 = \beta_2 = \beta$, substituting Eq. 6.3-6 into Eq. 6.3-5 and forming a quadratic allows the solution for I_{D1} and I_{D2} as

$$I_{D1} = \frac{I_{SS}}{2} + \frac{I_{SS}}{2}\left[\frac{\beta V_{ID}^2}{I_{SS}} - \frac{\beta^2 V_{ID}^4}{4I_{SS}^2}\right]^{1/2} \qquad (6.3\text{-}7)$$

and

$$I_{D2} = \frac{I_{SS}}{2} - \frac{I_{SS}}{2}\left[\frac{\beta V_{ID}^2}{I_{SS}} - \frac{\beta^2 V_{ID}^4}{4I_{SS}^2}\right]^{1/2} \qquad (6.3\text{-}8)$$

These relationships are valid only for

$$|V_{ID}| \leq \left[\frac{2I_{SS}}{\beta}\right]^{1/2} \qquad (6.3\text{-}9)$$

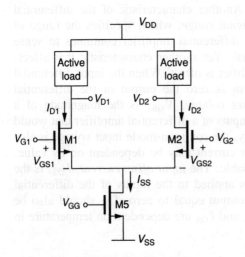

FIGURE 6.3-1

A general MOS differential amplifier configuration. $V_{BS1} = V_{BS2} = 0$.

and for M1 and M2 in saturation. Figure 6.3-2 shows a plot of the normalized drain current of M1 versus the normalized differential input voltage. The large signal voltage transfer characteristics of the differential amplifier can be found by using the results of Eqs. 6.3-7 and 6.3-8 along with the voltage-current characteristics of the active-load devices.

It is of interest to find the regions where M1 and M2 are in saturation. These regions can be found by using the definition in Eq. 6.3-3, rewritten as

$$V_{ID} = V_{G1} - V_{G2} \tag{6.3-10}$$

If we assume symmetry and no common mode excitation, then

$$V_{G1} = \frac{V_{ID}}{2} \tag{6.3-11}$$

and

$$V_{G2} = -\frac{V_{ID}}{2} \tag{6.3-12}$$

Therefore, M1 is in saturation if

$$V_{D1} \geq V_{G1} - V_{TN} = \frac{V_{ID}}{2} - V_{TN} \tag{6.3-13}$$

and M2 is in saturation if

$$V_{D2} \geq -\frac{V_{ID}}{2} - V_{TN} \tag{6.3-14}$$

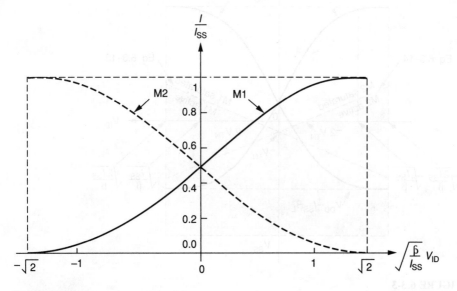

FIGURE 6.3-2
Large signal transconductance characteristic of the MOS differential amplifier.

One way to illustrate these constraints is to plot V_{D1} or V_{D2} as a function of V_{ID}. Assume that the loads of the circuit of Fig. 6.3-1 are resistors of value R_L. Figure 6.3-3 shows a plot of V_{D1} and V_{D2} for an arbitrary value of R_L. Equations 6.3-13 and 6.3-14 are plotted in Fig. 6.3-3 to show the regions where M1 and M2 are saturated. It is seen that the value of R_L will determine how much of the transfer characteristic is in the saturated region. For example, if $I_{SS}R_L \approx V_{DD}$, most of the transfer characteristic of M1 and M2 will be in the saturation region.

It is of interest to find an expression for the large signal transconductance of Fig. 6.3-1. Differentiating Eq. 6.3-7 with respect to V_{ID} and setting the quiescent value of V_{ID} equal to zero gives the differential transconductance of Fig. 6.3-1 as

$$g_m = \left.\frac{\partial I_{D1}}{\partial V_{ID}}\right|_{V_{ID}=0} = \left(\frac{\beta_1 I_{SS}}{4}\right)^{1/2} = \left(\frac{K'I_{SS}W_1}{4L_1}\right)^{1/2} = \left(\frac{K'I_{D1}W_1}{2L_1}\right)^{1/2} \quad (6.3\text{-}15)$$

Comparing this result with the expression for g_m of a single transistor (see Table 3.1-3) shows that a difference of 2 exists. The reason for this difference is that only half of the input voltage is applied to M1 or M2 of Fig. 6.3-1, resulting in half the output current. Correspondingly, the transconductance of Eq. 6.3-15 is called the *differential-in, single-ended output transconductance*. The *differential-out transconductance* (g_{md}), can be found by defining a differential output current I_{OD} as

$$I_{OD} = I_{D1} - I_{D2} \quad (6.3\text{-}16)$$

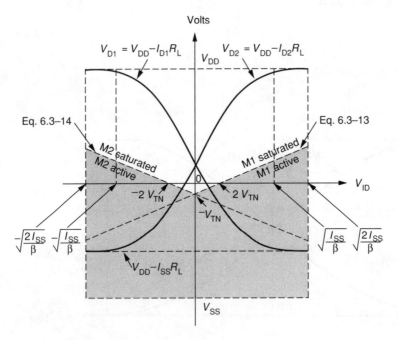

FIGURE 6.3-3
Voltage transfer characteristics of the differential amplifier.

g_{md} can be written as

$$g_{md} = \frac{\partial I_{OD}}{\partial V_{ID}}\bigg|_{V_{ID}=0} = (\beta_1 I_{SS})^{1/2} = \left(\frac{K'I_{SS}W_1}{L_1}\right)^{1/2} = \left(\frac{2K'I_{D1}W_1}{L_1}\right)^{1/2} \quad (6.3\text{-}17)$$

This transconductance is exactly equal to the transconductance of the common-source transistor if I_D is half of I_{SS}. The presence of I_{SS} in Eqs. 6.3-15 and 6.3-16 illustrates once more the important property that the dc performance is controlled by the dc variables.

The output voltage of the differential amplifier depends on how the active loads of Fig. 6.3-1 are implemented. Assume for the moment that the active loads are replaced by the n-channel enhancement active resistor of Fig. 5.2-2a, resulting in the circuit of Fig. 6.3-4a. The single-ended output voltages V_{D1} and V_{D2} are given as

$$V_{D1} = V_{DD} - V_{T3} - \left(\frac{2I_{D1}}{\beta_3}\right)^{1/2} \quad (6.3\text{-}18)$$

and

$$V_{D2} = V_{DD} - V_{T4} - \left(\frac{2I_{D2}}{\beta_4}\right)^{1/2} \quad (6.3\text{-}19)$$

where M3 and M4 are saturated. Equations 6.3-7 and 6.3-8 could be substituted into Eqs. 6.3-18 and 6.3-19 to achieve expressions for the drain voltages of M1 and M2 as a function of V_{ID}. These expressions, however, are complex and will be reserved for the problems. Instead, the large signal, differential to single-ended voltage gain will be evaluated at $V_{ID} = 0$ V. Differentiating Eq. 6.3-18 with respect to V_{ID} and multiplying by Eq. 6.3-17 gives

$$A_{vds} = \left(\frac{\partial V_{D1}}{\partial I_{D1}}\right)\left(\frac{\partial I_{D1}}{\partial V_{ID}}\right)\bigg|_{V_{ID}=0} = -\left(\frac{1}{\beta_3 I_{SS}}\right)^{1/2}\left(\frac{\beta_1 I_{SS}}{4}\right)^{1/2} = -\frac{1}{2}\left(\frac{\beta_1}{\beta_3}\right)^{1/2}$$

$$(6.3\text{-}20)$$

This gain should be half that of the MOS inverter in Fig. 6.1-11c since only half of the input is applied to M1. Comparing Eq. 6.3-20 with Eq. 6.1-34 shows that this relationship holds if the bulk effects, which have been neglected here, are ignored. The differential-in to differential-out voltage gain, A_{vdd}, is equal to the voltage difference between the drains of M1 and M2 divided by V_{ID}. This gain is twice A_{vds} and thus equal to that of an inverter with an enhancement active-load resistor (see Eq. 6.1-33 or 6.1-34).

The ac small signal model of the circuit of Fig. 6.3-4a is shown in Fig. 6.3-5a. It has been assumed under differential mode excitation that half of v_{id} is applied to the input of each transistor according to the relationship

$$v_{gs1} = -v_{gs2} = \frac{v_{id}}{2} \quad (6.3\text{-}21)$$

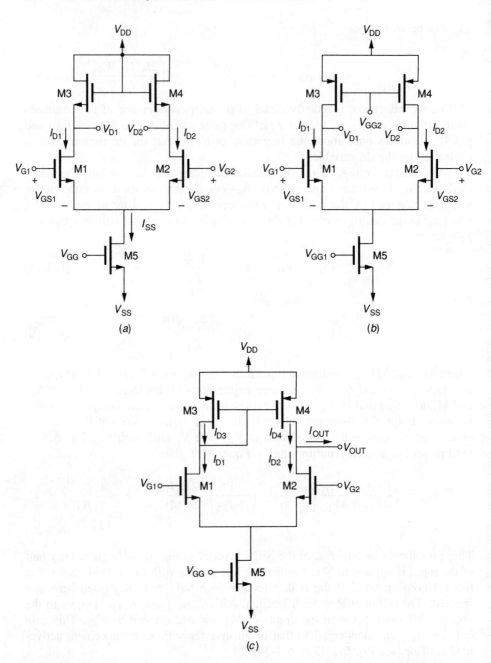

FIGURE 6.3-4
MOS differential amplifiers: (*a*) Enhancement active loads, (*b*) Current source loads, (*c*) Current mirror load.

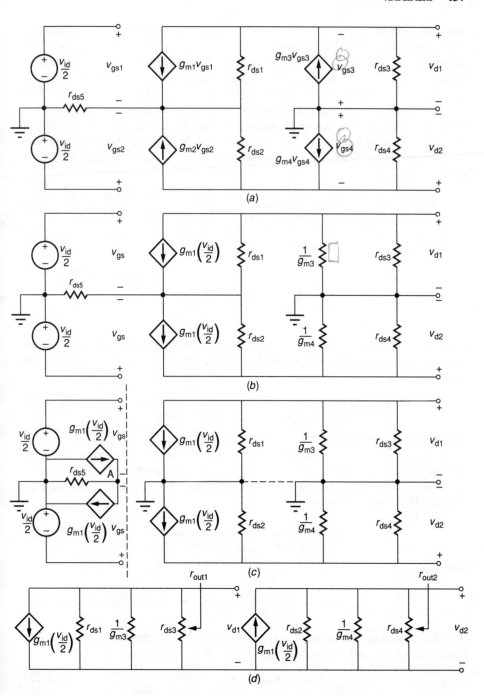

FIGURE 6.3-5
(a) Small signal model for differential amplifier of Fig. 6.3-4a, (b) Use of symmetry to simplify the input circuit, (c) Simplification by rerouting the controlled sources $g_{m1}v_{id}/2$, (d) Final small signal model.

Figure 6.3-5a is simplified in Fig. 6.3-5b, where symmetry between M1 and M2 has been assumed, which implies $g_{m1} = g_{m2}$ and $v_{gs1} = -v_{gs2} = v_{gs}$. Also the controlled sources, $g_{m3}v_{gs3}$ and $g_{m4}v_{gs4}$, have been replaced with their equivalent resistances of $1/g_{m3}$ and $1/g_{m4}$, respectively. If the current contributions of r_{ds1} and r_{ds2} to the sources of M1 and M2 and the drain of M5 can be ignored, then the controlled sources, $g_{m1}v_{id}/2$, can be rerouted in the model of Fig. 6.3-5c to show that point A is in fact an ac ground. Therefore, all the model to the left of the vertical dotted line can be ignored. The final form of the small signal model is shown in Fig. 6.3-5d. The calculations for v_{d1} and v_{d2} are independent of each other and are given as

$$A_{v1} = \frac{v_{d1}}{v_{id}} = \frac{-g_{m1}}{2(g_{m3} + g_{ds1} + g_{ds3})} \approx \frac{-g_{m1}}{2g_{m3}} = \frac{-1}{2}\left[\frac{K_N'(W_1/L_1)}{K_P'(W_3/L_3)}\right]^{1/2}$$

$$(6.3\text{-}22)$$

and

$$A_{v2} = \frac{v_{d2}}{v_{id}} = \frac{g_{m1}}{2(g_{m4} + g_{ds2} + g_{ds4})} \approx \frac{g_{m1}}{2g_{m4}} = \frac{1}{2}\left[\frac{K_N'(W_1/L_1)}{K_P'(W_4/L_4)}\right]^{1/2}$$

$$(6.3\text{-}23)$$

Comparing Eq. 6.3-22 or 6.3-23 with Eq. 6.3-20 shows that the small signal analysis agrees with the large signal analysis. The differential voltage gain is given as

$$A_{vdd} = \frac{v_{od}}{v_{id}} = \frac{v_{d1} - v_{d2}}{v_{id}} = -\frac{g_{m1}}{2g_{m3}} - \frac{g_{m1}}{2g_{m4}} = -\frac{g_{m1}}{g_{m3}} \qquad (6.3\text{-}24)$$

if M3 and M4 are also matched so that $g_{m3} = g_{m4}$.

The dc differential input resistance, r_{id}, is that resistance seen by the input voltage source, v_{id}. In this case, r_{id} is infinite. The single-ended output resistance comprises those resistances seen looking back into the output terminals of Fig. 6.3-5d. These resistances are

$$r_{out1} = \frac{1}{g_{m3} + g_{ds1} + g_{ds3}} \approx \frac{1}{g_{m3}} \qquad (6.3\text{-}25)$$

and

$$r_{out2} = \frac{1}{g_{m4} + g_{ds2} + g_{ds4}} \approx \frac{1}{g_{m4}} \qquad (6.3\text{-}26)$$

The differential output resistance, r_{od}, is equal to the ac resistance seen between the drains of M1 and M2 and can be written as

$$r_{od} = r_{out1} + r_{out2} \approx \frac{1}{g_{m3}} + \frac{1}{g_{m4}} \approx \frac{2}{g_{m3}} \qquad (6.3\text{-}27)$$

It is assumed in the above calculations that all the transistors of the differential amplifier are operating in the saturation region. We shall shortly examine the voltage ranges at the input and output over which this condition holds.

The voltage gain of the differential amplifier considered in Fig. 6.3-4a can be increased using current sources as loads. This differential amplifier is shown in Fig. 6.3-4b. The previous small signal analysis holds if we let $g_{m3} = g_{m4} = 0$. The small signal performance is summarized as

$$A_{vds1} = A_{v1} = \frac{v_{d1}}{v_{id}} = \frac{-g_{m1}}{2(g_{ds1} + g_{ds3})} \tag{6.3-28}$$

$$A_{vds2} = A_{v2} = \frac{v_{d2}}{v_{id}} = \frac{g_{m1}}{2(g_{ds2} + g_{ds4})} \tag{6.3-29}$$

$$A_{vdd} = \frac{v_{od}}{v_{id}} = \frac{-g_{m1}}{g_{ds1} + g_{ds3}} = \frac{-g_{m2}}{g_{ds2} + g_{ds4}} \tag{6.3-30}$$

$$r_{out1} = \frac{1}{g_{ds1} + g_{ds3}} \tag{6.3-31}$$

$$r_{out2} = \frac{1}{g_{ds2} + g_{ds4}} \tag{6.3-32}$$

and

$$r_{od} \cong \frac{2}{g_{ds1} + g_{ds3}} \tag{6.3-33}$$

It is seen that this differential amplifier has a performance that is identical to the current-source-load sinking inverter of Fig. 6.1-11b.

Another configuration of the load for a differential amplifier is shown in Fig. 6.3-4c. This method uses a current mirror to form the load devices. The advantage of this configuration is that the differential output signal is converted to a single-ended output signal with no extra components required. In this circuit, the output voltage or current is taken from the drains of M2 and M4. The operation of this circuit is as follows. If a differential voltage, V_{ID}, is applied between the gates as defined in Eq. 6.3-21, then half is applied to the gate-source of M1 and half to the gate-source of M2. The result is to increase I_{D1} and decrease I_{D2} by equal increments, ΔI. The ΔI increase I_{D1} is mirrored through M3-M4 as an increase in I_{D4} of ΔI. As a consequence of the ΔI increase in I_{D4} and the ΔI decrease in I_{D2}, the output must sink a current of $2\Delta I$. Therefore, the transconductance of the circuit of Fig. 6.3-4c, I_{out}/V_{id}, is equal to that of a single transistor. This differential amplifier is a very useful circuit and will be used further in analog integrated circuit design.

The small signal analysis of the circuit of Fig. 6.3-4c requires a modification of the model of Fig. 6.3-5. The model suitable for small signal analysis of the circuit of Fig. 6.3-4c is shown in Fig. 6.3-6. The small signal, differential-in, differential-out voltage gain (A_{vdd}) is

$$\frac{v_{out}}{v_{id}} = A_{vdd} = \frac{1}{2}\left(g_{m1} + \frac{g_{m1}g_{m4}}{g_{ds1} + g_{m3} + g_{ds3}}\right)\left(\frac{1}{g_{ds2} + g_{ds4}}\right) \tag{6.3-34}$$

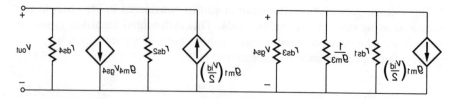

FIGURE 6.3-6
Small signal model for Fig. 6.3-4c.

If we assume that M3 and M4 are matched, then $g_{m3} = g_{m4}$, and since g_{m3} is much larger than either g_{ds1} or g_{ds3}, Eq. 6.3-34 can be simplified to

$$A_{vdd} \simeq \frac{g_{m1}}{g_{ds2} + g_{ds4}}$$

(6.3-35)

Substituting for the small signal parameters of Eq. 6.3-35 with the relationships specified in Table 3.1-3 gives

$$A_{vdd} = \frac{2(K'I_{SS}W_1/L_1)^{1/2}}{(\lambda_2 + \lambda_4)I_{SS}} = \frac{2}{(\lambda_2 + \lambda_4)}\left(\frac{K'W_1}{I_{SS}L_1}\right)^{1/2}$$

(6.3-36)

Again we note the dependence of the small signal performance on $I_{SS}^{-1/2}$ similar to that of the inverter. Assuming that $W_1/L_1 = 1$ and that $I_{SS} = 10$ μA, the small signal, differential-in, differential-out voltage gain of the circuit of Fig. 6.3-4c is 103. The differential-in, single-ended out voltage gain is equal to half the value of Eq. 6.3-36, although in the case of Fig. 6.3-4c this voltage is not available as it would be for the differential amplifiers of Fig. 6.3-4a and b. The small signal output resistance is found from Fig. 6.3-6 as

$$r_{out} = \frac{1}{g_{ds2} + g_{ds4}} = \frac{2}{(\lambda_2 + \lambda_4)I_{SS}} \simeq \frac{1}{\lambda I_{SS}}$$

(6.3-37)

Of course, the small signal, low-frequency input resistance of the MOSFET differential amplifier is infinity.

Another important characteristic of the MOS differential amplifier is the input common-mode voltage range, defined earlier. For our purposes, we will assume that the input common-mode range is defined by the input voltage range over which both M1 and M2 remain in saturation. Let us consider the input common-mode voltage range of Fig. 6.3-4c. Assume that $V_{G1} = V_{G2}$ and that M1 is on the threshold of saturation when $V_{DG1} = V_{T1}$. We may write V_{DG1} as

$$V_{DG1} = V_{DD} - V_{SD3} - V_{G1} = V_{DD} - V_{SG3} - V_{G1}$$

(6.3-38)

or

$$V_{DG1} = V_{DD} - \left(\frac{2I_{D3}}{\beta_3}\right)^{1/2} - |V_{TO3}| - V_{G1}$$

(6.3-39)

where V_{TO3} implies that M3 is unaffected by the bulk potential. If V_{DG1} is set equal to $-V_{T1}$, then we can solve for the maximum input voltage, $V_{G1}(\max)$, as

$$V_{G1}(\max) = V_{DD} - \left(\frac{I_{SS}}{\beta_3}\right)^{1/2} - |V_{TO3}| + V_{T1} \qquad (6.3\text{-}40)$$

As V_{GG} approaches V_{SS}, M1 will be in the saturation region and close to cutoff. Therefore, it makes more sense to relate $V_{G1}(\min)$ to V_{GG} when M5 is no longer in saturation. Solving for the drain-gate voltage of M5 gives

$$V_{DG5} = V_{G1} - V_{GS1} - V_{GG} \qquad (6.3\text{-}41)$$

Set $V_{DG5} = -V_{TO5}$ to get

$$V_{G1}(\min) \cong V_{GG} + \left(\frac{2I_{SS}}{\beta_1}\right)^{\frac{1}{2}} + V_{TO1} - V_{TO5} \qquad (6.3\text{-}42)$$

The large signal swing limitations of the output are also of interest. In this case, the swing limitations will be based on keeping both M2 and M4 in saturation. When V_{G1} is taken above V_{G2}, the output voltage, V_{OUT}, increases. The drain-gate voltage of M4 is given as

$$V_{DG4} = V_{DD} - V_{SD3} - V_{OUT} = V_{DD} - V_{SG3} - V_{OUT} \qquad (6.3\text{-}43)$$

M4 is at the edge of saturation when $V_{DG4} = -|V_{TO4}|$. Using this relationship and the value for V_{SD3} used in Eqs. 6.3-38 and 6.3-39 gives the maximum output voltage as

$$V_{OUT}(\max) = V_{DD} - \left(\frac{I_{SS}}{\beta_3}\right)^{1/2} - |V_{TO3}| + |V_{TO4}| \cong V_{DD} - \left(\frac{2I_{SS}}{\beta_3}\right)^{1/2}$$
$$(6.3\text{-}44)$$

The minimum output voltage is found by determining when M2 is at the edge of saturation. The minimum output voltage for Fig. 6.3-4c is

$$V_{OUT}(\min) = V_{G2} - V_{T2} \qquad (6.3\text{-}45)$$

Figure 6.3-7a shows a differential amplifier similar to Fig. 6.3-4c. The simulated voltage transfer characteristic corresponding to the W/L values given in the schematic is shown in Fig. 6.3-7b. The influence of V_{G2} upon V_{OUT} (min) is illustrated in this figure. The input and output signal limits of the differential amplifiers in Fig. 6.3-4a and b can be found in a similar manner.

The small signal common-mode gain of the differential amplifier can be found by connecting both inputs together and applying a single-ended input voltage. The small signal model for the differential amplifier of Fig. 6.3-4b is shown in Fig. 6.3-8a. If we assume that M1 and M2 are matched, then the model simplifies to that shown in Fig. 6.3-8b. To find the common-mode gain, we wish to solve for v_{d2} in terms of v_c. If the current contribution through r_{ds1} and r_{ds2} can be neglected, then the voltage across r_{ds5} can be written as

$$v_s \approx 2g_{m1}r_{ds5}v_c \qquad (6.3\text{-}46)$$

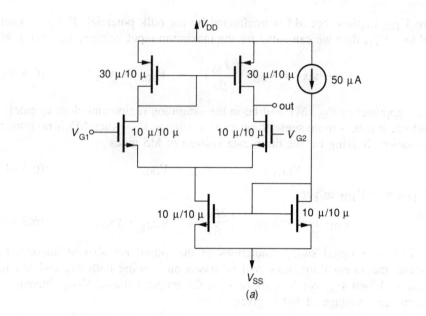

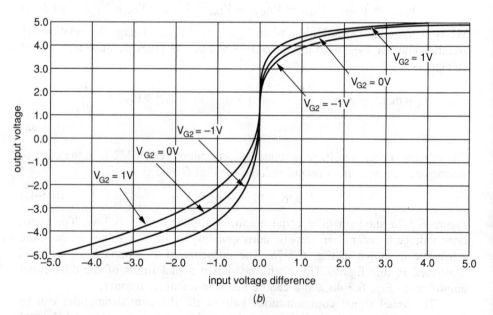

FIGURE 6.3-7

(a) n-channel input differential amplifier, (b) Simulation of voltage transfer curve for $V_{G2} = -1, 0$, and 1 V ($V_{DD} = 5$ V, $V_{SS} = -5$ V, $K_N' = 2K_P' = 28$ μA/V, $V_T = \pm 0.7$ V, and $\lambda_N = \lambda_P = 0.01$ V^{-1}).

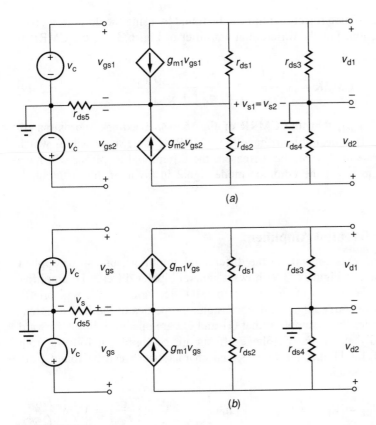

FIGURE 6.3-8
(a) Small signal model of Fig. 6.3-4b for common mode operation, (b) Simplified version of (a).

Using the relationship that $v_{gs} = v_g - v_s$, we may write

$$v_{gs} = \frac{1}{1 + 2g_{m1}r_{ds5}} v_c \qquad (6.3\text{-}47)$$

The voltage, v_{d2}, can be found by the superposition of the two sources, v_{gs}. The problem is considerably simplified if we ignore r_{ds1} and r_{ds2}. Therefore, the voltage gain, v_{d2}/v_c, can be expressed as

$$\frac{v_{d2}}{v_c} = A_{vc} \simeq \frac{-g_{m1}r_{ds3}}{1 + 2g_{m1}r_{ds5}} \qquad (6.3\text{-}48)$$

The common-mode voltage gain of the circuit of Fig. 6.3-4a can be found in a similar manner. However, the preceding method does not work for the differential amplifier of Fig. 6.3-4c because there is no point at which the single-ended output is available. In practice, Fig. 6.3-4c will exhibit a nonzero common-mode gain because of the fact that M1 and M2, and M3 and M4 are not perfectly matched. The mismatch effect for the differential amplifiers of Fig. 6.3-4a and Fig. 6.3-4b may dominate the actual common-mode gain.

The common-mode rejection ratio can be found by using the definition given earlier in this section. For the differential amplifier of Fig. 6.3-4b, the CMRR is found to be

$$\text{CMRR} = \frac{|A_{v\text{ds}}|}{|A_{vc}|} = \frac{g_{\text{ds}3}(1 + 2g_{m1}r_{\text{ds}5})}{g_{\text{ds}2} + g_{\text{ds}4}} \tag{6.3-49}$$

If $g_{\text{ds}2} \simeq g_{\text{ds}3} \simeq g_{\text{ds}4}$, then the CMRR of Fig. 6.3-4b becomes approximately equal to $g_{m1}r_{\text{ds}5}$. It is desirable to have the CMRR as large as possible, which suggests that if $r_{\text{ds}5}$ or g_{m1} can be increased, the differential amplifier will have a greater ability to reject the common-mode signal in favor of the differential-mode signal.

6.3.2 BJT Differential Amplifiers

The preceding concepts concerning the differential amplifier can also be applied to bipolar technology. Figure 6.3-9 shows a general bipolar differential amplifier configuration similar to that of Fig. 6.3-1 for MOS technology. We will briefly illustrate some of the large signal and small signal properties of the BJT differential amplifier. Under the assumption that Q1 and Q2 are operating in the forward active region and that the Early voltage effects are negligible, it follows from Eqs. 3.3-10 and 3.3-11 that the large signal characteristics can be found from the following relationships:

$$V_{\text{ID}} = V_{B1} - V_{B2} = V_{BE1} - V_{BE2} = V_t \ln\left(\frac{I_{C1}}{I_{S1}}\right) - V_t \ln\left(\frac{I_{C2}}{I_{S2}}\right) = V_t \ln\left(\frac{I_{C1}}{I_{C2}}\right)$$
$$\tag{6.3-50}$$

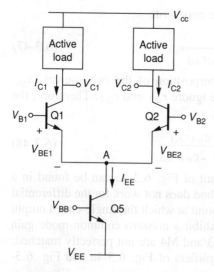

FIGURE 6.3-9
A general configuration for a BJT differential amplifier.

$$I_{EE} = \frac{I_{C1}}{\alpha_F} + \frac{I_{C2}}{\alpha_F} \tag{6.3-51}$$

where we have assumed that Q1 and Q2 are matched ($I_{S1} = I_{S2}$ and $\alpha_{F1} = \alpha_{F2} = \alpha_F$), and $V_t = kT/q$. Solving for I_{C1} and I_{C2} results in the following.

$$I_{C1} = \frac{\alpha_F I_{EE}}{1 + \exp(-V_{ID}/V_t)} \tag{6.3-52}$$

$$I_{C2} = \frac{\alpha_F I_{EE}}{1 + \exp(V_{ID}/V_t)} \tag{6.3-53}$$

From these two equations, it follows as in the MOS case that I_{C1} and I_{C2} are independent of the common mode excitation and the characteristics of the active load. Figure 6.3-10 shows a plot of the normalized collector current of Q1 and Q2 as a function of V_{ID}/V_t. The range of linear operation is seen to be limited to $|V_{ID}| \leq 2V_t$, or approximately ± 50 mV at room temperature.

Differentiating Eq. 6.3-52 gives the differential-in, single-ended transconductance as

$$g_m = -\frac{\alpha_F I_{EE}}{2V_t}\left[\frac{1}{1 + \cosh(V_{ID}/V_t)}\right] \tag{6.3-54}$$

If V_{ID} is set to zero, we obtain

$$g_m(V_{ID} = 0) = \frac{-\alpha_F I_{EE}}{4V_t} \tag{6.3-55}$$

The differential-in, differential-out transconductance (g_{md}) is found by multiplying the expressions given in Eqs. 6.3-54 and 6.3-55 by 2.

The large signal limits for the input and output of the BJT differential amplifier are found in a similar manner as for the MOS differential amplifier. The

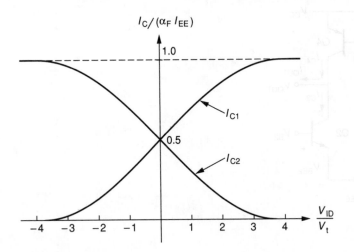

FIGURE 6.3-10
Large signal transconductance characteristics of the BJT differential amplifier.

objective again is to keep the BJT devices in the forward active region of operation, that is, the BE junction forward-biased and the BC junction reverse-biased.

Figure 6.3-11 shows the BJT differential amplifier that is topologically identical to the MOS differential amplifier of Fig. 6.3-4c. Assume that $V_{B1} = V_{B2}$. The highest value of V_{B1} is equal to

$$V_{B1}(\text{max}) \simeq V_{CC} - V_{BE3} - V_{CE2}(\text{sat}) + V_{BE2} = V_{CC} - 0.2 \text{ V} \qquad (6.3\text{-}56)$$

This relationship was developed under the conditions where Q1 is saturated. The lowest value of V_{B1} is given by

$$V_{B1}(\text{min}) \simeq V_{BE1} + V_{CE5}(\text{sat}) + V_{EE} = V_{EE} + 0.8 \text{ V} \qquad (6.3\text{-}57)$$

The output voltage of the circuit of Fig. 6.3-11 is limited to the range between

$$V_O(\text{max}) \simeq V_{CC} - V_{CE4}(\text{sat}) = V_{CC} - 0.2 \text{ V} \qquad (6.3\text{-}58)$$

and

$$V_O(\text{min}) \simeq V_{B2} - 0.5 \text{ V} \qquad (6.3\text{-}59)$$

where V_{B2} is the dc potential connected to the base of Q2.

Figure 6.3-12a shows a model suitable for small signal differential input excitation of the circuit of Fig. 6.3-11 neglecting r_μ and the frequency-dependent parameters of the model. If Q1 and Q2 are matched, we can assume that $r_{\pi 1} = r_{\pi 2} = r_\pi$, $g_{m1} = g_{m2}$, and $v_{be1} = -v_{be2}$. Neglecting the contribution of current through r_{o1} and r_{o2} into their common node allows the simplification of the small signal model to that shown in Fig. 6.3-12b. Since there is no ac current flowing through r_{o5}, it may be neglected. Also, we have replaced the current source, $g_{m3}v_{be3}$, by a resistor of $1/g_{m3}$ since v_{be3} is the voltage across this source. The final simplified small signal model for the BJT differential amplifier shown in Fig. 6.3-11 is given in Fig. 6.3-12c. The differential-out, differential-in voltage gain is

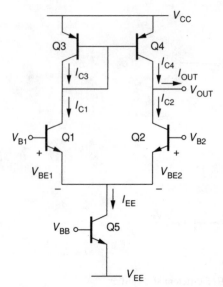

FIGURE 6.3-11
Practical version of the BJT differential amplifier.

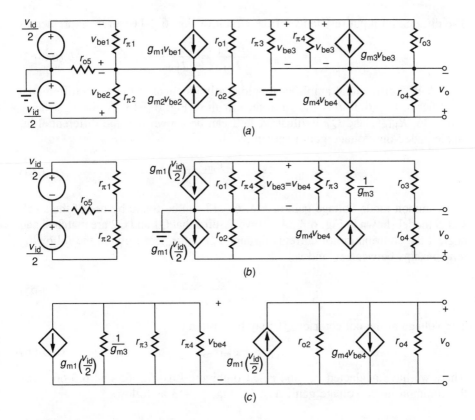

FIGURE 6.3-12
Small signal model for the BJT differential amplifier of Fig. 6.3-11: (a) Complete small signal model, (b) Simplification of (a), (c) Final small signal model.

$$\frac{v_o}{v_{id}} = A_{vdd} = \frac{1}{2}\left[g_{m1} + \frac{g_{m1}g_{m4}}{g_{m3} + g_{\pi 3} + g_{\pi 4}}\right]\left[\frac{1}{g_{o2} + g_{o4}}\right] \qquad (6.3\text{-}60)$$

If we assume that Q3 and Q4 are matched, then $g_{m3} = g_{m4}$, and since g_{m3} is larger than $g_{\pi 3}$ or $g_{\pi 4}$, Eq. 6.3-60 can be simplified to

$$A_{vdd} \simeq \frac{g_{m1}}{g_{o2} + g_{o4}} = \frac{1}{(V_t/V_{AFN}) + (V_t/V_{AFP})} \qquad (6.3\text{-}61)$$

where V_{AN} and V_{AP} are the Early voltages defined for the npn and pnp bipolar junction transistors. The small signal, differential-in, differential-out voltage gain of Fig. 6.3-11 is seen to be equal in magnitude to the BJT inverter of Sec. 6.1 (see Eq. 6.1-71). The small signal output resistance of the circuit of Fig. 6.3-11 is found as

$$r_{out} = \frac{1}{g_{o2} + g_{o4}} = \frac{1}{(I_{C2}/V_{AFN}) + (I_{C4}/V_{AFP})} = \frac{2V_{AFN}V_{AFP}}{I_{EE}(V_{AFN} + V_{AFP})} \qquad (6.3\text{-}62)$$

The differential input resistance of the circuit of Fig. 6.3-11 can be expressed as

$$r_{id} = 2r_{\pi 1} = \frac{\beta_F V_t}{I_{C1}} = \frac{2\beta_F V_t}{I_{EE}} \tag{6.3-63}$$

A BJT differential amplifier topologically identical to the MOS differential amplifier of Fig. 6.3-4b is shown in the circuit of Fig. 6.3-13. A biasing scheme using Q6, R_{BIAS}, and Q7 is illustrated. It can be shown that the differential-in, single-ended-out voltage gain is given by

$$A_{vds} = \frac{v_{c1}}{v_{id}} = \frac{-g_{m1} r_{o1} r_{o3}}{r_{o1} + r_{o3}} \tag{6.3-64}$$

The common-mode voltage gain of Fig. 6.3-13 can be found by use of the small signal model shown in Fig. 6.3-14a. If we assume that Q1 and Q2 are matched and neglect the contribution of currents through r_{o1} and r_{o2}, we obtain the following relationships between v_c and v_{be}.

$$v_{be} = \frac{v_c}{1 + 2(g_{m1} + g_{\pi 1})r_{o5}} \tag{6.3-65}$$

The voltage at the collector of Q1 may be written as

$$v_{c1} \cong -g_{m1} r_{o3} \tag{6.3-66}$$

where we have neglected r_{o1} and r_{o2}. Combining Eqs. 6.3-65 and 6.3-66 gives the common-mode voltage gain, A_{vc}, for Fig. 6.3-13 as follows.

$$A_{vc} = \frac{-g_{m1} r_{o3}}{1 + 2(g_{m1} + g_{\pi 1})r_{o5}} \cong \frac{-g_{m1} r_{o3}}{1 + 2g_{m1} r_{o5}} \tag{6.3-67}$$

The common-mode gain for the BJT differential amplifier of Fig. 6.3-11 is theoretically zero because the only output node is differential, similar to Fig. 6.3-4c. Mismatch effects will the common-mode gain to be nonzero.

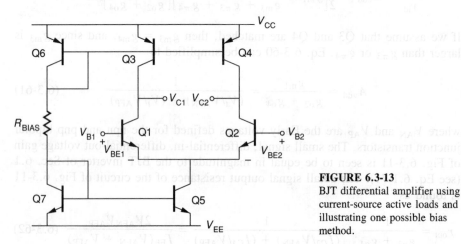

FIGURE 6.3-13
BJT differential amplifier using current-source active loads and illustrating one possible bias method.

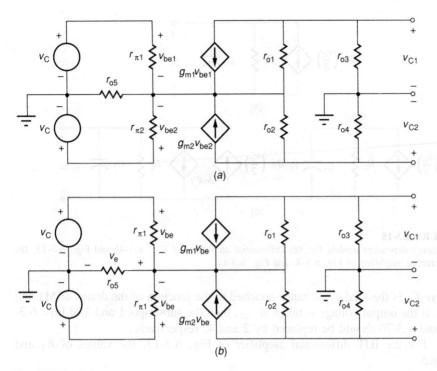

FIGURE 6.3-14
(a) Small signal model of Fig. 6.3-13 for common-mode operation, (b) Simplified version of (a).

The low-frequency CMRR for Fig. 6.3-13 can be found from Eqs. 6.3-64 and 6.3-67 and is expressed as

$$\text{CMRR} = \frac{|A_{vds}|}{|A_{vc}|} \simeq \frac{r_{o1}(1 + g_{m1}r_{o5})}{2(r_{o1} + r_{o3})} \simeq \frac{1 + g_{m1}r_{o5}}{4} \tag{6.3-68}$$

It is seen that as g_{m1} or r_{o5} increases, the CMRR will increase. The CMRR can be increased using a current sink with an output resistance greater than r_{o5}.

6.3.3 Frequency Response of Differential Amplifiers

The next subject of this section will be the frequency response of the differential amplifier. Figure 6.3-15a shows a frequency-dependent model of the differential-mode operation of either the MOS or BJT differential amplifier shown in Fig. 6.3-4b or 6.3-13, respectively. This model is suitable for finding v_{d1}/v_{id} or v_{d2}/v_{id}. For the MOS differential amplifier of Fig. 6.3-4b, R_1 is given in terms of Fig. 6.3-4b as

$$R_1 = r_{ds1} \| r_{ds3} \tag{6.3-69}$$

and C_1 is given by

$$C_1 = C_{gd1} + C_{gd3} + C_{db1} + C_{db3} + C_L \tag{6.3-70}$$

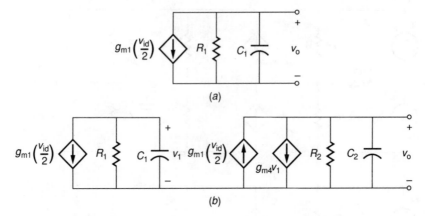

FIGURE 6.3-15
Frequency-dependent models for: (a) Differential amplifiers of Fig. 6.3-4b and Fig. 6.3-13, (b) Differential amplifiers of Fig. 6.3-4c and Fig. 6.3-11.

where C_L is the load capacitance attached to the junction of the drains of M1 and M3. If the output voltage is taken at v_{d2}, then the subscripts 1 and 3 of Eqs. 6.3-69 and 6.3-70 should be replaced by 2 and 4, respectively.

For the BJT differential amplifier of Fig. 6.3-13, the values of R_1 and C_1 are

$$R_1 = r_{o1} \| r_{o3} \tag{6.3-71}$$

and

$$C_1 = C_{\mu 1} + C_{CS1} + C_{CS3} + C_{\mu 3} + C_L \tag{6.3-72}$$

The same comment regarding subscript interchange holds for the BJT differential amplifier of Fig. 6.3-13.

The differential-mode frequency response of the circuit of Fig. 6.3-15a can be written as

$$A_{vds}(s) = \frac{A_{vds}(0)\omega_1}{s + \omega_1} = \frac{A_{vds0}\omega_1}{s + \omega_1} \tag{6.3-73}$$

where

$$A_{vds0} = -g_{m1}R_1 \tag{6.3-74}$$

and

$$\omega_1 = \frac{1}{R_1 C_1} \tag{6.3-75}$$

For a MOS differential amplifier with $I_{SS} = 100\ \mu A$, $\lambda = 0.01\ V^{-1}$, $C_{db} = 100$ fFg, $C_{gs} = 0.2$ pF, $C_{gd} = 50$ pF, and $C_L = 0.5$ pF, we find that $R_1 = 1\ M\Omega$ and $C_1 = 0.8$ pF. The -3 dB frequency of this MOS differential amplifier is 199 kHz. If $I_{EE} = 100\ \mu A$, $V_{AFN} = 100$ V, $V_{AFP} = 50$ V, $C_\mu = 1$ pF, $C_{CS} = 1$ pF, and $C_L = 5$ pF, then R_1 and C_1 are 0.667 MΩ and 9 pF, respectively. This gives a -3 dB frequency of 26.5 kHz for the BJT differential amplifier.

The differential-mode frequency response of the MOS differential amplifier of Fig. 6.3-4c and the BJT differential amplifier of Fig. 6.3-11 can be found from the small signal model given in Fig. 6.3-15b. For the MOS version, R_1, R_2, C_1, and C_2 can be written as

$$R_1 = \frac{1}{g_{m3}}||r_{ds1}||r_{ds3} \simeq \frac{1}{g_{m3}} \qquad (6.3\text{-}76)$$

$$R_2 = r_{ds2}||r_{ds4} \qquad (6.3\text{-}77)$$

$$C_1 = C_{gd1} + C_{gs3} + C_{gs4} + C_{bd1} + C_{b23} \qquad (6.3\text{-}78)$$

and

$$C_2 = C_{gd2} + C_{gd4} + C_{bd2} + C_{bd4} + C_L \qquad (6.3\text{-}79)$$

For the BJT differential amplifier, R_1, R_2, C_1, and C_2 are

$$R_1 = \frac{1}{g_{m3}}||r_{o3}||r_{\pi3}||r_{\pi4}||r_{o1} \simeq \frac{1}{g_{m3}} \qquad (6.3\text{-}80)$$

$$R_2 = r_{o2}||r_{o4} \qquad (6.3\text{-}81)$$

$$C_1 = C_{\mu1} + C_{CS1} + C_{\pi3} + C_{\pi4} + C_{CS3} \qquad (6.3\text{-}82)$$

and

$$C_2 = C_{\mu2} + C_{CS2} + C_{\mu4} + C_{CS4} + C_L \qquad (6.3\text{-}83)$$

The frequency response for Fig. 6.3-15b can be written as

$$A_{vds}(s) = \frac{v_o}{v_{id}} = \frac{-g_{m1}R_2\omega_2}{2(s + \omega_2)}\left[1 + \frac{g_{m4}R_1\omega_1}{s + \omega_1}\right] =$$

$$\frac{-g_{m1}R_2\omega_2[s + \omega_1(1 + g_{m4}R_1)]}{2(s + \omega_1)(s + \omega_2)} = \frac{A_{vds0}[(s/\omega_1') + 1]}{[(s/\omega_1 + 1)][(s/\omega_2) + 1]} \qquad (6.3\text{-}84)$$

where

$$A_{vds0} = -0.5g_{m1}R_2(1 + g_{m4}R_1) \qquad (6.3\text{-}85)$$

$$\omega_1 = \frac{1}{R_1C_1} \qquad (6.3\text{-}86)$$

$$\omega_1' = (1 + g_{m4}R_1)\omega_1 \qquad (6.3\text{-}87)$$

and

$$\omega_2 = \frac{1}{R_2C_2} \qquad (6.3\text{-}88)$$

It is of interest to note that the configuration of Fig. 6.3-15b introduces an extra pole-zero pair. The zero is in the left-hand plane and is equal to $(1 + g_{m4}R_1)$ times the pole. Since R_1 is approximately equal to the value of $1/g_{m3}$, the value of the zero is approximately twice that of the pole (called a *doublet*). In most cases, the effect of ω_1 and ω_2' approximately cancel each other out. Assume that $K_N' = 2K_P' = 25 \ \mu\text{A/V}^2$, all W/L ratios are unity $C_{gs} = 100$ fF, and $I_{SS} = 100 \ \mu\text{A}$. The MOS parameters used earlier permit the calculation of R_1, R_2, C_1, and C_2 as 19.6 kΩ, 1 MΩ, 0.35 pF, and 0.8 pF, respectively. This leads to a low-frequency gain magnitude of 100 and a -3 dB frequency of 199 kHz. If the current gain of the BJTs is $\beta_F = 100$, $C_\pi = 5$ pF, and $I_{EE} = 100 \ \mu\text{A}$, using the previous parameters permits the calculation of R_1, R_2, C_1, and C_2 for the BJT differential amplifier as 490 Ω, 0.67 MΩ, 13 pF, and 9 pF, respectively. This gives a low-frequency gain magnitude of 1340 and a -3 dB frequency of 26.4 kHz.

6.3.4   Noise Performance of Differential Amplifiers

The last consideration of this section deals with the noise performance of the differential amplifier. Because of the similarity in small signal performance between the differential amplifier and the inverting amplifier, we expect the noise performance to be similar. Let us consider the noise analysis of Fig. 6.3-4c and Fig. 6.3-11. The noise models for each of these circuits are shown in Fig. 6.3-16. The noise of I_{SS} and I_{EE} is neglected because they are common-mode inputs and have a much smaller influence on the output noise. A dc battery, V_{out}, has been connected to the output through which an output-noise-current spectral density flows. It can be shown for both amplifiers that

$$\overline{I}_{on}^2 = g_{m1}^2 \overline{V}_{n1}^2 + g_{m2}^2 \overline{V}_{n2}^2 + g_{m3}^2 \overline{V}_{n3}^2 + g_{m4}^2 \overline{V}_{n4}^2 \qquad (6.3\text{-}89)$$

This result is developed by using superposition techniques. The equivalent input-noise-voltage spectral density can be found by dividing Eq. 6.3-89 by g_{m1}^2 to get

$$S_{eq} = S_{VN1} + S_{VN2} + \left(\frac{g_{m3}}{g_{m1}}\right)^2 (S_{VN3} + S_{VN4}) \qquad (6.3\text{-}90)$$

where $g_{m1} = g_{m2}$ and $g_{m3} = g_{m4}$ has been assumed. Assuming that $S_{VN1} = S_{VN2}$ and $S_{VN3} = S_{VN4}$ gives

$$S_{eq} = 2S_{VN1}\left[1 + \left(\frac{g_{m3}}{g_{m1}}\right)^2 \left(\frac{S_{VN3}}{S_{VN1}}\right)\right] \qquad (6.3\text{-}91)$$

Although the type of noise has not been identified, in general the noise will be reduced if $g_{m3} \leq g_{m1}$.

The differential amplifier is a very useful building block which will be used in analog circuits that follow. The differential amplifier is an excellent choice as an input stage for several reasons. It allows the application of difference signals and rejects the common mode signals. This means that an unwanted singal

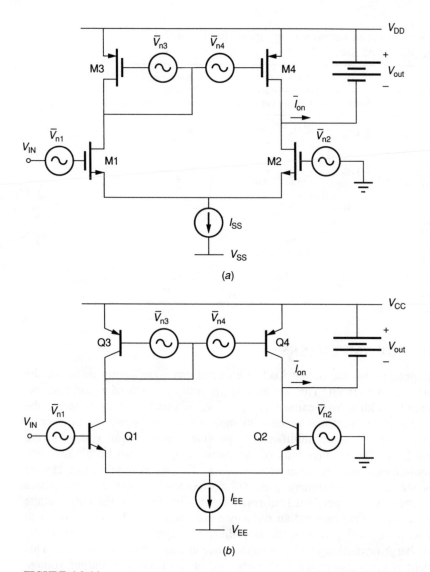

FIGURE 6.3-16
(a) Noise model for the CMOS differential amplifier of Fig. 6.3-4c. (b) Noise model for the BJT differential amplifier of Fig. 6.3-11.

present at both inputs will be rejected. The large input common-mode range allows the ac performance to be independent of the dc input voltage. A third advantage is that larger output signal swings can be obtained differentially. This is important as the trend to reduce power supplies makes it difficult to have sufficient dynamic range. Table 6.3-1 summarizes the performance of the differential amplifiers presented in this section.

TABLE 6.3-1
Comparison of small signal voltage gains for the differential amplifiers of Sec. 6.3

Differential amplifier	Figure	Differential-in, single-ended-out voltage gain, A_{vds}	Differential-in, differential-out voltage gain, A_{vdd}
MOS active load	6.3-4a	$\dfrac{g_{m1}}{2g_{m3}}$	$\dfrac{g_{m1}}{g_{m3}}$
MOS current source load	6.3-4b	$\dfrac{g_{m1}}{2(g_{ds2} + g_{ds4})}$	$\dfrac{g_{m1}}{g_{ds2} + g_{ds4}}$
MOS current mirror load	6.3-4c	$\dfrac{g_{m1}}{g_{ds2} + g_{ds4}}$	—
BJT current mirror load	6.3-11	$\dfrac{g_{m1}}{g_{o2} + g_{o4}}$	—
BJT current source load	6.3-13	$\dfrac{g_{m1}}{2(g_{o1} + g_{o3})}$	$\dfrac{g_{m1}}{g_{o1} + g_{o3}}$

6.4 OUTPUT AMPLIFIERS

In many applications, the output load of a circuit can significantly influence the performance of the circuit. The output load generally consists of a load resistor, R_L, in parallel with a load capacitor, C_L. If R_L is small or if C_L is large, the previous amplifiers may not be able to meet the output signal requirements. The objective of an output amplifier is to provide a large output voltage swing across the load. The requirements of the output amplifier can be divided into static requirements and dynamic requirements. The static requirement can be stated as the ability to maintain a dc voltage somewhere between the power supply limits across a specified load resistor. This implies that the output stage should have a low Thevenin output resistance and should be efficient in order to avoid large power dissipation in the amplifier. The dynamic requirement is the ability to charge or discharge a large capacitance at a specified voltage rate. This requirement is often associated with slew rate or the maximum output voltage rate of an analog circuit. The dynamic requirement does not require a low output resistance but does demand high currents to achieve the desired slew rate.

There are two distinct approaches to implementing output stages. These approaches depend on whether or not feedback is used. We will first consider the approach that does not use feedback. The first nonfeedback output amplifier type consists of the inverting amplifiers of Sec. 6.1. We will examine the large signal performance of these amplifiers to determine their suitability as output amplifiers. Figures 6.1-11a, 6.1-11b, 6.1-11c, and 6.1-18a represent the inverting amplifiers we will consider. In Sec. 6.1 we analyzed the small signal performance. Since the output amplifier is likely to have large output voltage swings, let us first consider the limitations of the output stage.

6.4.1 Output Amplifiers without Feedback

A conservative approach to characterize the output signal swings of MOS amplifiers is to assume that all devices must be in saturation. This constrains the operation to the transition region of the voltage transfer function of the amplifier. Figures 6.1-12 and 6.1-14 show that the resulting output range is not as large as that which could be achieved if some of the devices are allowed to operate in the active or ohmic region.

Consider the output swing limits of Fig. 6.1-11a. We assume that V_{IN} can have values between V_{DD} and V_{SS}. (This aggressive assumption partially compensates for the conservative approach of assuming all devices are saturated.) When $V_{IN} = V_{SS}$, M1 is off and the maximum output voltage is

$$V_{OUT}(\text{max}) \approx V_{DD} - | V_{TP} | \qquad (6.4\text{-}1)$$

When $V_{IN} = V_{DD}$, M1 is on and in fact is in the ohmic region because V_{DS1} will be small. The current in M2 which is in the saturation region is

$$I_{D2} = \frac{\beta_2}{2}(V_{SG2} - | V_{TP} |)^2 = \frac{\beta_2}{2}(V_{DD} - V_{OUT} - | V_{TP} |)^2 =$$

$$\frac{\beta_2}{2}(V_{OUT} - V_{DD} + | V_{TP} |)^2 \quad (6.4\text{-}2)$$

The current in M1 is

$$I_{D1} = \beta_1 \left[(V_{GS1} - V_{TN})V_{DS1} - \frac{V_{DS1}^2}{2} \right]$$

$$= \beta_1 \left[(V_{DD} - V_{SS} - V_{TN})(V_{OUT} - V_{SS}) - \frac{(V_{OUT} - V_{SS})^2}{2} \right] \qquad (6.4\text{-}3)$$

Equating Eq. 6.4-2 to Eq. 6.4-3 and solving for V_{OUT} gives

$$V_{OUT}(\text{min}) = V_{DD} - V_T - \frac{V_{DD} - V_{SS} - V_T}{\sqrt{1 + (\beta_2/\beta_1)}} \qquad (6.4\text{-}4)$$

where it has been assumed that $V_T = V_{TN} = | V_{TP} |$. Using the model parameters and voltages specified in Fig. 6.1-12 the above equations give a $V_{OUT}(\text{max})$ of 4.25 V and a $V_{OUT}(\text{min})$ of −4.52 V. If we used the saturation constraint, the lower voltage limit would be higher (approximately −2.8 V).

The MOS inverting amplifier of Fig. 6.1-11c has approximately the same large signal behavior, with one exception. Because the source of M2 is not connected to the bulk, V_{T2} will be larger than normal, causing the maximum value of V_{OUT} to be less, as seen from Eq. 6.4-1.

The MOS inverting amplifier of Fig. 6.1-11b has a higher ac gain than the previous two amplifiers. It can be seen that when $V_{IN} = V_{SS}$, M1 is off and V_{OUT} is at V_{DD}. Therefore,

$$V_{OUT}(\text{max}) \approx V_{DD} \qquad (6.4\text{-}5)$$

Using the approach outlined by Eqs. 6.4-2 and 6.4-3 we can show that

$$V_{OUT}(\min) = (V_{DD} - V_{SS} - V_{TN}) \cdot$$

$$\left[1 - \sqrt{1 - \left(\frac{\beta_2}{\beta_1}\right)\left(\frac{V_{DD} - V_{GG2} - |V_{TP}|}{V_{DD} - V_{SS} - V_{TN}}\right)^2} \right] + V_{SS} \quad (6.4\text{-}6)$$

if $V_{IN} = V_{DD}$. Evaluating these limits under the conditions given in Fig. 6.1-14, we get $V_{OUT}(\max) \approx 5$ V and $V_{OUT}(\min) \approx -4.97$ V, which agree with the results of Fig. 6.1-14.

The maximum output swing of the BJT inverting amplifier of Fig. 6.1-18a can be found in a similar manner. When $V_{IN} = V_{EE}$, Q1 is off and V_{OUT} is at V_{CC}. Therefore,

$$V_{OUT}(\max) \approx V_{CC} \quad (6.4\text{-}7)$$

When V_{IN} is increased so that Q1 becomes saturated, then V_{OUT} is equal to

$$V_{OUT}(\min) \approx V_{SS} + V_{CE1}(\text{sat}) \approx V_{SS} + 0.2 \text{ V} \quad (6.4\text{-}8)$$

It is seen that the BJT inverting amplifiers generally have a larger output swing than the MOS inverting amplifiers.

The previous considerations emphasized the ability to have large output voltage swings. However, no load was considered, so the results just given are appropriate for large resistance loads. Of perhaps more importance is the signal swing for small values of load resistance. Unfortunately, this is difficult to analyze. Instead, let us examine the ability to source or sink current when the output swings are small. Once again we consider the inverting amplifiers. Figures 6.4-1a and b show MOS and BJT amplifiers using a current-source load sometimes called a "pull-up". It will be assumed that current flows in both output devices during the entire swing of the output voltage. This is called Class

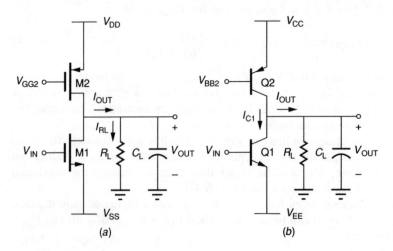

(a)   (b)

FIGURE 6.4-1
Class A output amplifiers: (a) Common-source configuration, (b) Common-emitter configuration.

A operation. Let us first consider the static performance (the ability to source and sink currents at a dc output voltage for which the output devices are both in saturation or forward active region).

The maximum source current, I_{OUT}^+, that can be obtained from the circuit of Fig. 6.4-1a occurs when M1 is off and M2 is saturated, is given as

$$I_{OUT}^+ = \frac{K_P' W_2}{2L_2}[V_{DD} - V_{GG2} - |V_{T2}|]^2 \qquad (6.4\text{-}9)$$

It is important to note that as long as M2 is saturated this current always flows in M2 regardless of the value of V_{IN}. The maximum sinking current, I_{OUT}^-, for Fig. 6.4-1a occurs when M1 is saturated and $V_{IN} = V_{DD}$ and is given as

$$I_{OUT}^- = \frac{K_N' W_1}{2L_1}(V_{DD} - V_{SS} - V_{T1})^2 - I_{OUT}^+ \qquad (6.4\text{-}10)$$

It should be observed that I_{OUT}^- must also include I_{OUT}^+ because of the Class A nature of the biasing. Fortunately, the current-sinking capability of M1 can easily exceed I_{OUT}^+ because the gate-source voltage of M1 can be very large.

If V_{OUT} approaches V_{SS}, then M1 will pass from the saturation to the ohmic region where $V_{DS1} < V_{GS1} - V_{T1}$. If a load resistance R_L is connected to the output, V_{DS1} is small, and $V_{IN} = V_{DD}$, then Eq. 6.4-10 for the ohmic region becomes

$$I_{D1} \approx \frac{K_N' W_1}{L_1}(V_{DD} - V_{SS} - V_{T1})(-I_{OUT}^- R_L - V_{SS}) \qquad (6.4\text{-}11)$$

Since I_{D1} is the sum of I_{OUT}^+ and I_{OUT}^-, we can solve for I_{OUT}^- as

$$I_{OUT}^- \approx \frac{-K_N'(W_1/L_1)(V_{DD} - V_{SS} - V_{T1})V_{SS} - I_{OUT}^+}{1 + K_N'(W_1/L_1)(V_{DD} - V_{SS} - V_{T1})R_L} \qquad (6.4\text{-}12)$$

When V_{OUT} approaches V_{DD}, I_{OUT}^+ will become dependent on R_L and have a smaller value than that of Eq. 6.4-9. Figure 6.4-2 shows a plot of the output voltage of the circuit of Fig. 6.1-11b as a function of the input for a 1 kΩ load resistor. Note that the W/L values have been increased to provide more current sinking and sourcing capability. Using the parameter values given in Fig. 6.4-2, I_{OUT}^+ is 202 μA and I_{OUT}^- is 2.53 mA. When multiplied by 1 kΩ, these currents give the maximum output voltages. It is seen that the sinking current is approximately 10 times the sourcing current. The sourcing current could be increased by decreasing the gate voltage on M2 or increasing W_2/L_2. In either case, the bias current that flows would increase, causing the power dissipation in the inverter to increase. It should be noted that the load resistance of 1 kΩ has caused the inverter voltage gain to be less than unity.

The small signal output resistance of the inverting voltage amplifier is a measure of how the ac gain will be influenced by the presence of a small load resistance. For example, consider the MOS inverter of Fig. 6.1-11b with the parameters given in Fig. 6.4-2, where $R_L = 1$ kΩ. Using Eq. 6.1-50, we find that at $V_{OUT} = 0$ V the ac voltage gain should be -36.3, assuming that R_L is

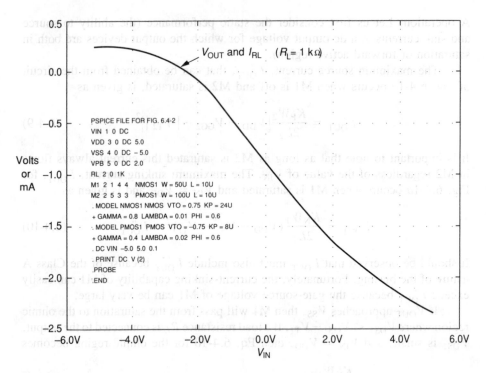

FIGURE 6.4-2
Simulation of Fig. 6.4-1a.

infinite. The output resistance under these conditions is found from Eq. 6.1-52 as $r_{out} = 165$ kΩ. When loaded with R_L, the new ac gain is given as

$$A_v' = A_v\left(\frac{R_L}{R_L + r_{out}}\right) \tag{6.4-13}$$

where A_v is the ac voltage gain for $R_L = \infty$ and A_v' is the gain for a finite R_L. In this case, A_v' is equal to $-36.3(1/166) = -0.22$. This value compares favorably with the simulated result of Fig. 6.4-2 at $V_{OUT} = 0$ V. Consequently, another desirable characteristic of an output amplifier is to have a small value of r_{out} so that the small signal voltage gain predicted by Eq. 6.4-13 is not reduced.

The maximum source/sink output currents and the ac output resistance characterize the static performance of the output amplifier. These two measures are related by the quiescent bias current (I_{BIAS}) of the amplifier. For example, suppose we want to sustain $+4$ V across a 10 kΩ load resistance. This would require an I_{BIAS} of at least 400 μA (assuming M1 is off). With a 400 μA bias current, the small signal output resistance is 125 kΩ if λ is 0.01 V^{-1}. Because of the large, small signal output resistance, the output of the common-source configuration is best modelled by a controlled current source in parallel with the 125kΩ output resistance.

Under dynamic conditions, the output sinking/sourcing current needed to charge or discharge C_L may be greater than that required to maintain a given dc voltage across R_L. It is assumed in the following analysis that the output voltage is in the range where both output transistors are in saturation. The current required to charge a capacitor C_L at a rate of dV_{OUT}/dt is given by

$$|I_{OUT}| = C_L\left[\frac{dV_{OUT}}{dt}\right] \tag{6.4-14}$$

If the desired rate of rise is 10 V/μs and C_L is 50 pF, then the bias current must be at least 500 μA. This consideration is valid for $V_{OUT} \approx 0$. As the output voltage deviates from 0 V, the current available for charging C_L is reduced by the current necessary to sustain a nonzero value of V_{OUT} across R_L.

Similar conditions hold for the BJT Class A inverting voltage amplifier of Fig. 6.4-1b. The maximum sourcing current is determined by Q2 and is given as

$$I_{OUT}^+ = I_{S2}\exp\left[\frac{V_{CC} - V_{BB2}}{V_t}\right] \tag{6.4-15}$$

There is an important distinction between this relationship and the similar one for the MOS amplifier in Eq. 6.4-9. That difference is that V_{BB2} must be able to sink from the base of Q2 a current of I_{OUT}^+/β_{F2}. Typically, Q2 is part of a current mirror so that I_{OUT}^+ is defined by the input current to the mirror. The maximum sinking current can be determined as V_{IN} is increased. As V_{BE1} is increased, the sinking current becomes very large. A more appropriate measure of the sinking current would be to examine more closely the circuit that is driving the amplifier of Fig. 6.4-1b. In general, any driver can be characterized by an equivalent voltage source, V_S, and series resistance, R_S. The maximum sinking current can be expressed as

$$I_{OUT}^- = \left[\frac{V_S(\text{max}) - V_{EE} - V_{BE1}}{R_S}\right]\beta_{F1} - I_{OUT}^+ \tag{6.4-16}$$

where $V_S(\text{max})$ is the maximum positive swing of V_S and $V_{BE1} \approx 0.7$ V. Assuming $V_S(\text{max}) \approx -2$ V and $R_S = 10$ kΩ for the conditions of Fig. 6.1-18a and Fig. 6.1-19, we get $I_{OUT}^+ \approx 1.39$ mA and $I_{OUT}^- = 21.6$ mA. For a 1 kΩ load resistance, the output voltage swing would be from $+1.39$ V to -5 V. Figure 6.4-3 shows a simulation of the circuit of Fig. 6.4-1b using the same parameters as for Fig. 6.1-19, except that a load resistance of 1 kΩ has been added. We note that the current in Q1 increases from 0 to 6.6 mA, which is sufficient to overcome I_{OUT}^+ and to sink 5 mA through $R_L = 1$ kΩ. We also note that the ac gain has been greatly reduced. The output sinking/sourcing analysis of Fig. 6.4-1b is similar to that of Fig. 6.4-1a and will not be repeated here.

The small signal output resistance can be used to predict the reduction of gain using Eq. 6.4-13. For example, the gain for $R_L = \infty$ and output resistance for the circuit of Fig. 6.4-1b were calculated in Example 6.1-4 for $V_{OUT} = 0$ V as -1544 and 26 kΩ, respectively. Using Eq. 6.4-13 we predict the new ac gain (at $V_{OUT} = 0$ V) as -57. This compares very well with the slope of Fig. 6.4-3 at $V_{OUT} = 0$.

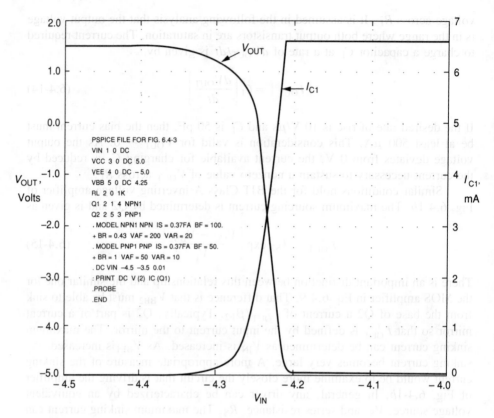

```
PSPICE FILE FOR FIG. 6.4-3
VIN 1 0 DC
VCC 3 0 DC 5.0
VEE 4 0 DC -5.0
VBB 5 0 DC 4.25
RL 2 0 1K
Q1 2 1 4 NPN1
Q2 2 5 3 PNP1
. MODEL NPN1 NPN IS = 0.37FA BF = 100.
+ BR = 0.43 VAF = 200 VAR = 20
. MODEL PNP1 PNP IS = 0.37FA BF = 50.
+ BR = 1 VAF = 50 VAR = 10
. DC VIN -4.5 -3.5 0.01
. PRINT DC V (2) IC (Q1)
.PROBE
.END
```

FIGURE 6.4-3
Simulation of Fig. 6.4-1b.

One of the disadvantages of the Class A inverting amplifiers of Fig. 6.4-1 is that considerable quiescent power is dissipated. It is well known that the maximum efficiency of the Class A amplifier is 25% for a sinusoidal signal. This means that under best conditions, for every milliwatt of ac power applied to R_L, 3 mW are dissipated in the transistors. For example, consider the two amplifiers of Fig. 6.4-1 with 1 kΩ load resistances. With the output signal at 0 V, the amplifier of Fig. 6.4-1a dissipates 2 mW and that of Fig. 6.4-1b dissipates 13.9 mW. The maximum symmetrical output voltage signal swing is 0.2 V (peak-to-peak) and 1.39 V (peak-to-peak) for Fig. 6.4-1a and b, respectively. Unfortunately, we have had to take the smaller of the positive or negative signal swing to avoid distortion. Assuming a sinusoidal output, the maximum power delivered to R_L is 0.04 mW and 1.93 mW, respectively. Correspondingly, the best sinusoidal efficiencies of the circuit of Fig. 6.4-1a and b are 2% and 13.9%, respectively. It is clear that the bias currents should be increased to reach the maximum output voltage signal swings if one wishes to approach more closely the maximum possible efficiency of 25%.

One advantage of the Class A amplifier is low distortion. This is a result of operating both MOS transistors in the saturation region or operating both BJT transistors in the normal active region over most of the output voltage swing.

A second method of implementing an output amplifier without feedback is the common-source or common-emitter, Class B or Class AB amplifiers. The circuits of Fig. 6.4-4a and b show MOS and BJT implementations, respectively. V_B is a floating battery used to establish the proper bias of the devices. The sinking/sourcing output current capability of such amplifiers is very large and is limited primarily by the power dissipation capability of the devices. If the transistors are biased so that no drain or collector current flows when V_{IN} is zero, the stage is termed Class B. When V_{IN} is positive, the lower device is on and the upper device is off. When V_{IN} is negative, the lower device is off and the upper device is on. The maximum possible efficiency of the Class B amplifier for a sinusoidal output signal is 78.5%, where the efficiency is defined as the ratio of the signal power dissipated in R_L to the power provided from the power supplies for sinusoidal input.

The primary advantage of the implementations of Fig. 6.4-4 is that the maximum sourcing/sinking current is not limited by the bias current. This allows output amplifiers to have I_{OUT}^- limitations similar to the I_{OUT}^+ levels of the Class A output amplifiers. Figure 6.4-5 shows the simulated output swing capability for the circuit of Fig. 6.4-4a with $V_B = 0$, $W_1/L_1 = 50 \ \mu/10 \ \mu$, $W_2/L_2 = 150 \ \mu/10 \ \mu$, and $R_L = 1 \ k\Omega$. This circuit has a maximum sink/source current limit given by Eq. 6.4-12 of 2.53 mA, resulting in a ± 2.53 V output signal swing. These calculations agree well with the simulation results of Fig. 6.4-5. The drain

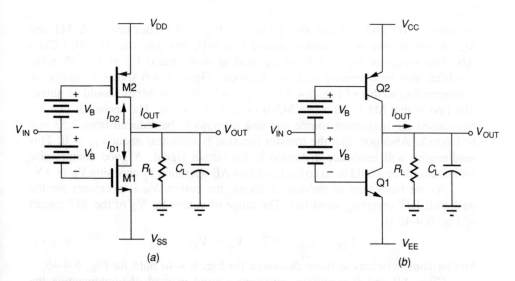

FIGURE 6.4-4

Class B and AB output amplifiers: (a) MOS common-source configuration, (b) BJT common-emitter configuration.

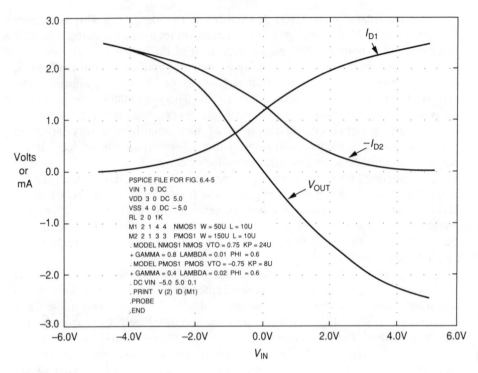

FIGURE 6.4-5
Simulation of Fig. 6.4-4a with $V_B = 0$ V.

currents in M1 and M2 are also plotted in Fig. 6.4-5. Because both M1 and M2 are conducting in the region around $V_{IN} \approx 0$, this amplifier is called Class AB. The results of Fig. 6.4-5 can be used to show that if $V_B \approx 4$ V, then the amplifier will be operating in Class B mode. Figure 6.4-6 shows a simulation corresponding to that of Fig. 6.4-5 for $V_B = 4$ V. Several things should be noted. The first is that M1 is off when M2 is on and vice versa. The second is that V_B has caused the maximum source and sink currents to be reduced from 2.53 mA to 1.6 mA. Also note that the transfer function is nonlinear about $V_{IN} = 0$. This nonlinearity will introduce distortion in the output signal. A good compromise for this amplifier would be to go back to Class AB operation by choosing $V_B \approx 3$ V.

As we have seen in previous sections, the battery V_B is necessary for the push-pull BJT inverting amplifier. The range of values for V_B of the BJT circuit of Fig. 6.4-4b is

$$V_{CC} - V_{IN} - 0.7 < V_B < V_{CC} - V_{IN} \qquad (6.4\text{-}17)$$

Similar considerations to those discussed for Fig. 6.4-4a hold for Fig. 6.4-4b.

Class AB and B amplifiers represent a good method of implementing the output amplifier having the ability to provide ± 3 V across 1 kΩ with ± 5 V power supplies. Consider now the sizing of M1 and M2 in the circuit of Fig. 6.4-4a. We can use Eq. 6.4-11 with $I_{D1} = I_{OUT}^-$ to calculate W_1/L_1. Let us assume

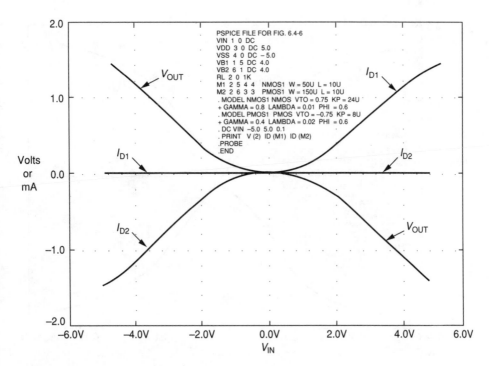

```
PSPICE FILE FOR FIG. 6.4-6
VIN 1 0 DC
VDD 3 0 DC 5.0
VSS 4 0 DC -5.0
VB1 1 5 DC 4.0
VB2 6 1 DC 4.0
RL 2 0 1K
M1 2 5 4 4  NMOS1 W = 50U L = 10U
M2 2 6 3 3  PMOS1 W = 150U L = 10U
. MODEL NMOS1 NMOS VTO = 0.75 KP = 24U
+ GAMMA = 0.8 LAMBDA = 0.01 PHI = 0.6
. MODEL PMOS1 PMOS VTO = -0.75 KP = 8U
+ GAMMA = 0.4 LAMBDA = 0.02 PHI = 0.6
. DC VIN -5.0 5.0 0.1
. PRINT V (2) ID (M1) ID (M2)
.PROBE
.END
```

FIGURE 6.4-6
Simulation of Fig. 6.4-4a with $V_B = 4$ V.

that $I^-_{OUT} = 4$ mA to anticipate the reduction in $I^-_{OUT}(I^+_{OUT})$ that will occur when V_B is non-zero. The results give $W_1/L_1 = 180$ $\mu/10$ μ. In order to balance the ability of the amplifier to source and sink current, $W_2/L_2 = (K_N/K_P)(W_1/L_1)$, or $W_2/L_2 = 540$ $\mu/10$ μ. From the results shown in Figs. 6.4-5 and 6.4-6, we will choose $V_B = 3$ V. Figure 6.4-7 gives the simulated results. While this design can provide an output swing of ± 3 V across 1 kΩ, it experiences distortion above ± 2.2 V. This distortion is caused by the fact that the transistor sourcing or sinking the current is entering the ohmic region, and the current increase is linearly related to the gate voltage rather than to the square of the voltage. This can be clearly seen by the current results in Fig. 6.4-7. Consider the positive output voltage swing. The current is being sourced by M2, and at about $V_{IN} = 2$ V, which corresponds to $V_{OUT} = 2.2$ V, the rate of current increase in M2 falls off. This circuit is more suitable for ± 2 V output swings. To achieve a linear ± 3 V output voltage swing, we would have to increase the power supply to ± 6 V. It should also be noted that the voltage gain turned out to be approximately -1. Since it is not necessary for the output amplifier to have a large gain, this is not a problem; however, the voltage gain, $-g_{m1}R_L(= -g_{m2}R_L)$, depends on the value of R_L and may be less than unity.

Although the small signal output resistance of the Class B amplifier is high, it represents a good solution to the output amplifier, except for the implementation

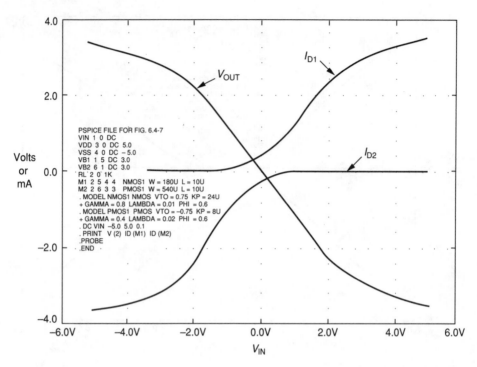

The figure contains the following PSPICE listing:

```
PSPICE FILE FOR FIG. 6.4-7
VIN 1 0 DC
VDD 3 0 DC 5.0
VSS 4 0 DC -5.0
VB1 1 5 DC 3.0
VB2 6 1 DC 3.0
RL 2 0 1K
M1 2 5 4 4 NMOS1 W = 180U L = 10U
M2 2 6 3 3 PMOS1 W = 540U L = 10U
.MODEL NMOS1 NMOS VTO = 0.75 KP = 24U
+ GAMMA = 0.8 LAMBDA = 0.01 PHI = 0.6
.MODEL PMOS1 PMOS VTO = -0.75 KP = 8U
+ GAMMA = 0.4 LAMBDA = 0.02 PHI = 0.6
.DC VIN -5.0 5.0 0.1
.PRINT V (2) ID (M1) ID (M2)
.PROBE
.END
```

FIGURE 6.4-7
Simulation of Fig. 6.4-4*a* with V_B = 3 V.

of the floating battery, V_B. Figure 6.4-8 shows how the cross-coupling of four devices can allow the design of Class AB or B operation. The operation (Class AB or B) is determined by the voltages V_{GG4} and V_{GG5} (V_{BB4} and V_{BB5}), which are used to establish the bias current in the output devices M1 and M2 (Q1 and Q2). When the input voltage is taken positive, the current in M8 (Q8) increases and the current in M7 (Q7) decreases. If the operation is Class B, then M7 (Q7) turns off. As the current in M8 (Q8) increases, it is mirrored as an increasing current in M1 (Q1), which provides the sinking capability for the output current. When V_{IN} is decreased, M2 (Q2) can source output current. The output signal swing is limited to within a V_T value of V_{DD} or V_{SS} (V_{BE} of V_{CC} or V_{EE}).

The frequency response of the inverting amplifiers is generally determined by the load resistance and the shunt capacitance at the output including the load capacitance. Since $R_L (= 1/G_L)$ is typically much less than r_{out} and C_L is typically much larger than the capacitances at the output node of the amplifier, the bandwidth is given as

$$\omega_{-3dB} = \frac{g_{out} + G_L}{C_{out} + C_L} \approx \frac{1}{R_L C_L} \qquad (6.4\text{-}18)$$

which is primarily a function of the loading. If C_L = 100 pF and R_L = 1 kΩ, then the −3 dB bandwidth is 10 Mrps or 1.59 MHz.

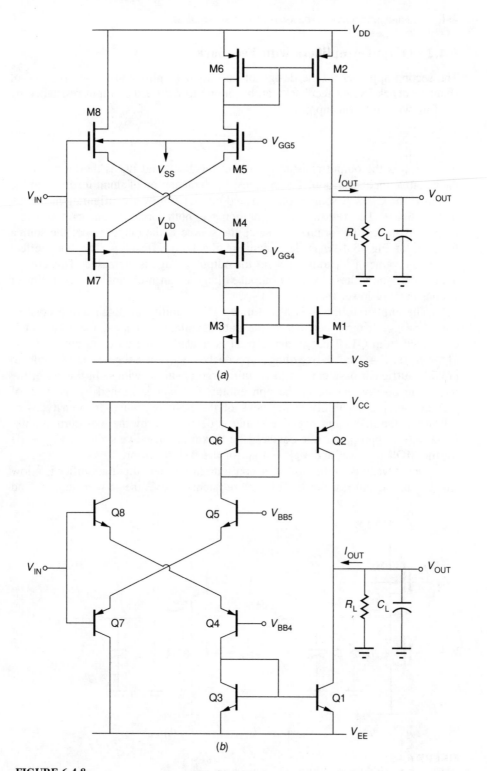

FIGURE 6.4-8
Class B or AB output amplifiers showing implementation of the floating battery for (a) Fig 6.4-4a and (b) Fig. 6.4-4b.

465

6.4.2   Output Amplifiers with Feedback

The second approach to the design of an output amplifier uses the principle of shunt feedback. Shunt feedback can be shown to reduce the output resistance by the following relationship

$$r'_{\text{out}} = \frac{r_{\text{out}}}{1 + \text{LG}} \tag{6.4-19}$$

where r_{out} is the output resistance without feedback and LG is the loop gain of the negative feedback loop. The simplest implementation of shunt feedback at the output is the Class A source follower and emitter follower configurations shown in Fig. 6.4-9. The follower configuration has both large current gain and low output resistance. Unfortunately, since the source is the output node, the source follower of Fig. 6.4-9a is dependent on the body effect, γ. The body effect causes the value of V_T to increase as the output voltage is increased. This creates a situation where the maximum output voltage of an n-channel source follower is considerably lower than $V_{\text{DD}} - V_{\text{TO}}$.

The emitter follower is also limited in its ability to obtain large positive output swing. It turns out that as the output voltage increases, more current is demanded from Q1. This emitter current is related to the base current by $I_E = (1 + \beta_F)I_B$. As the base voltage approaches V_{CC}, it becomes impossible to provide sufficient base current to sustain large positive swings. In this case, the maximum positive swing of the npn emitter follower is limited by the lack of current-sourcing capability at the peak of the positive swing. In both types of followers, the maximum negative swing is determined by the bias current sink. Usually, for appropriate size devices, the maximum negative swing is $V_{\text{SS}} + V_T$ for the MOS follower and $V_{\text{EE}} + V_{\text{BE}}$ for the BJT follower.

One advantage of the follower configuration as an output amplifier is a low small signal output resistance. This low resistance causes the ac voltage gain (and

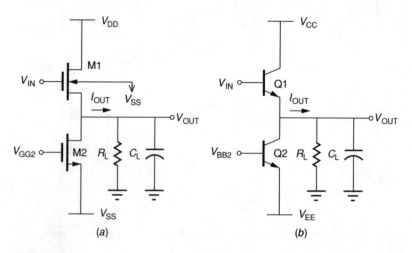

FIGURE 6.4-9
(a) Class A source follower, (b) Class A emitter follower.

frequency response) to be less dependent on R_L. The small signal model for the circuit of Fig. 6.4-9a is shown in Fig. 6.4-10. Figure 6.4-11 shows the small signal model for the emitter follower of Fig. 6.4-9b. Both of these circuits can be analyzed using Fig. 6.4-12 along with the appropriate values for the resistances and capacitances. For the source follower, we have

$$C_1 = C_{gd1} \qquad\qquad (6.4\text{-}20a)$$

$$R_2 = \infty \qquad\qquad (6.4\text{-}20b)$$

$$C_2 = C_{gs1} \qquad\qquad (6.4\text{-}20c)$$

$$R_3 = \left[g_{m1} + g_{mb1} + g_{ds1} + g_{ds2} + G_L \right]^{-1} \approx \left[g_{m1} + G_L \right]^{-1} \quad (6.4\text{-}20d)$$

and

$$C_3 \simeq C_L \qquad\qquad (6.4\text{-}20e)$$

For the emitter follower, we have

$$C_1 = C_{\mu 1} \qquad\qquad (6.4\text{-}21a)$$

$$R_2 = r_{\pi 1} \qquad\qquad (6.4\text{-}21b)$$

$$C_2 = C_{\pi 1} \qquad\qquad (6.4\text{-}21c)$$

$$R_3 = \left[g_{m1} + g_{o1} + g_{o2} + G_L \right]^{-1} \approx \left[g_{m1} + G_L \right]^{-1} \quad (6.4\text{-}21d)$$

and

$$C_3 \simeq C_L \qquad\qquad (6.4\text{-}21e)$$

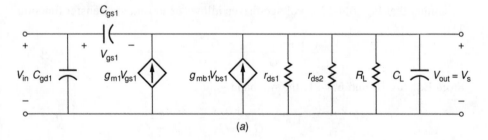

(a)

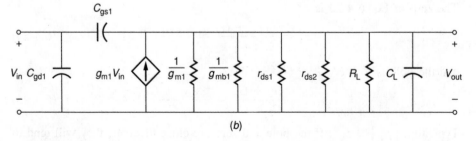

(b)

FIGURE 6.4-10
(a) Small signal model of Fig. 6.4-9a, (b) Simplified equivalent of (a).

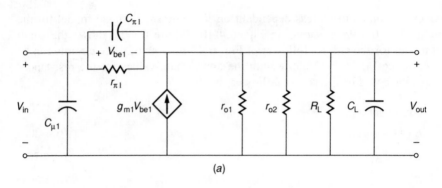

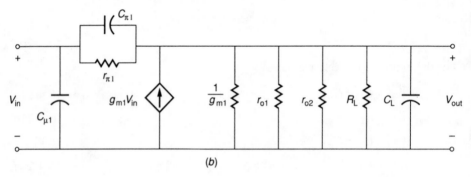

FIGURE 6.4-11

(a) Small signal model of Fig. 6.4-9b, (b) Simplified equivalent of (a).

Assuming that Fig. 6.4-12 is voltage-driven allows us to find the transfer function as

$$\frac{V_{out}(s)}{V_{in}(s)} = \frac{g_m + G_2 + sC_2}{G_2 + G_3 + s(C_L + C_2)} \tag{6.4-22}$$

From Eq. 6A-20 and 6.4-21, the midband gain is

$$\frac{V_{out}}{V_{in}} = A_{v0} = \frac{g_m + G_2}{G_2 + G_3} \approx \frac{g_{m1}}{g_{m1} + G_L} \tag{6.4-23}$$

The zero of Eq. 6.4-22 is

$$z_1 = -\frac{g_m + G_2}{C_2} \approx -\frac{g_{m1}}{C_2} \tag{6.4-24}$$

and the pole is

$$p_1 = -\frac{G_2 + G_3}{C_2 + C_L} \approx -\frac{g_{m1} + G_L}{C_L} \tag{6.4-25}$$

Typically, $|p_1| < |z_1|$. If the pole and zero are close together, they will tend to cancel each other.

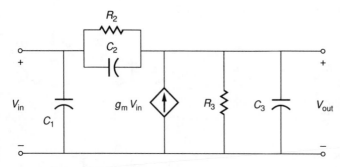

FIGURE 6.4-12
Generic small signal follower model.

The output resistance of the follower not including R_L is found from Fig. 6.4-12 as

$$r'_{out} = (G_2 + G_3)^{-1} = (G_2 + g_{m1})^{-1} \approx \frac{1}{g_{m1}} \qquad (6.4\text{-}26)$$

For the MOS follower, this resistance is expressed as

$$r'_{out} \approx \left(\frac{L_1}{2K'_N W_1 I_{D1}} \right)^{1/2} \qquad (6.4\text{-}27)$$

and for the BJT follower, the output resistance is

$$r'_{out} \approx \frac{V_t}{I_{C1}} \qquad (6.4\text{-}28)$$

If the bias current in both followers of Fig. 6.4-9 is 100 μA, and if $W_1 = 10L_1$ and $K'_N = 25$ μA/V^2, then the output resistance of the MOS follower is 4.47 kΩ and that of the BJT follower is 250 Ω.

The performance of the BJT follower is ideally independent of the emitter areas. Considerations of power dissipation and matching suggest large emitter areas whereas capacitive loading and high frequency response suggest small emitter areas.

The Class A shunt feedback follower configuration has the further disadvantage of an asymmetric current sinking and sourcing capability. For the followers of Fig. 6.4-9, the maximum current sourcing capability is limited primarily by the driver. For the MOS follower, the gate voltage of M1 must be sufficiently larger than the output voltage in order for M1 to source the required current. For the BJT follower, the current sourcing is directly related to the amount of base current the driver can provide. The sinking capability is equal to the bias current. As a consequence, the sourcing and sinking capabilities are usually different. The maximum efficiency of either follower configuration of Fig. 6.4-9 is 25%.

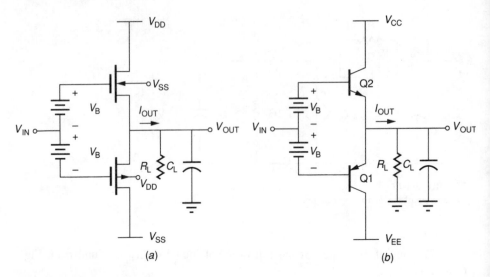

FIGURE 6.4-13
(a) Class B source follower, (b) Class B emitter follower.

In summary, the Class A follower has very low output resistance, poor signal swing, and low efficiency. The efficiency of the Class A follower can be improved by the Class B followers shown in Fig. 6.4-13. This configuration is also called the Class B push-pull amplifier. The maximum possible efficiency is 78.5%. Also, the maximum sourcing and sinking capabilities are likely to be of the same magnitude, although this depends on the driver. The signal swings at both the positive and negative limits will suffer from the increasing V_T for the MOS Class B follower and from the inability to provide sufficient base currents for the BJT Class B follower.

Figure 6.4-14 shows how the floating batteries, V_B, can be implemented for the Class B followers. In this case, the input is applied at the gate of M3 (base of Q3) instead of to the sources of M4 and M5 (bases of Q4 and Q5) and will require some form of level shifting. The bias current in M4 and M5 (Q4 and Q5) determines whether the circuit is Class B or Class AB. It is generally preferable to bias the output devices in Class AB in order to minimize the crossover distortion that occurs in the push-pull, follower type amplifier when the output current switches from one device to the other. Unfortunately, it is never possible to eliminate this distortion, and it is usually necessary to use external negative feedback to reduce the nonlinear distortion to an acceptable level. Figure 6.4-14 illustrates some of the problems in obtaining a large output signal swing for the Class B follower circuit. For example, the maximum output voltage of the circuit of Fig. 6.4-14a is approximately $V_{GG6} - V_{TO6} - V_{T2}$. This limit will usually be several volts below V_{DD}. The negative swing is a little better since M3 can take the gate of M1 to V_{SS}. Thus, the negative signal swing is approximately $V_{SS} + V_{T1}$. Unfortunately, V_{T1} will be larger than V_{TO1} because of the body effect.

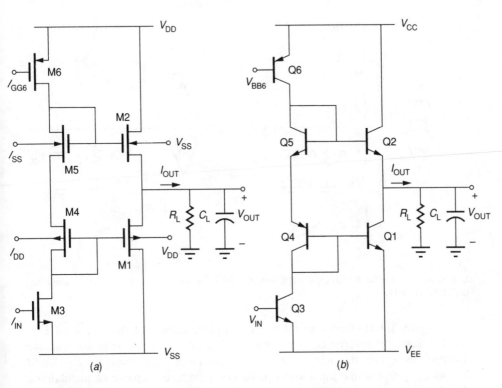

FIGURE 6.4-14
Implementation of: (a) Fig. 6.4-13a, and (b) Fig. 6.4-13b, including the implementation of V_B.

At this point we have a situation that often occurs in analog circuit design. The right principles have been identified, but the implementation is still not practical. None of the preceding output amplifiers have contained all of the desirable features of (1) large output signal swings, (2) low output resistance, (3) high efficiency, and (4) low nonlinear distortion. In addition, high frequency performance is also desirable. A practical solution to our problem is shown in Fig. 6.4-15, where we have taken the best candidate and concentrated on improving its negative characteristics. The Class B/Class AB common source (emitter) amplifiers in Fig. 6.4-4 offer good swing characteristics, high efficiency, and low nonlinear distortion. Their primary disadvantage is a high output impedance. Combining the shunt feedback principle with the common-source or common-emitter Class B or Class AB amplifier results in an output stage that meets all specifications even though it has been complicated by additional circuitry.

The output resistance of Fig. 6.4-4 will be reduced approximately by the value of loop gain as given in Eq. 6.4-19. The loop gain of the circuit of Fig. 6.4-15 will be that of the inverter plus the error amplifier. We note that the error amplifier could be implemented by the differential amplifiers of the preceding section. The error amplifiers are designed to turn on M1 or M2 (Q1 or Q2) in a manner that minimizes crossover distortion but maximizes efficiency.

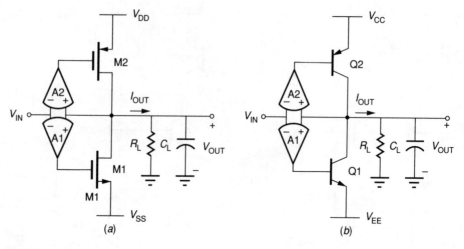

FIGURE 6.4-15
Use of negative feedback with error amplifiers A1 and A2 to obtain an improved output amplifier:
(*a*) MOS, (*b*) BJT.

Figure 6.4-16 shows an interesting implementation of the circuit of Fig. 6.4-15. Since the inverter can have reasonable gain, it is possible to use resistive feedback to replace the more complex error amplifier. The resistance R_2 should be twice R_1 so that the input signal does not have to be capable of maintaining the output signal swing. The resistors do not have to be carefully matched and could be polysilicon, diffusion, n- or p-well, or even transistors in the case of the MOS version. Assuming that $R_2 = 2R_1$, the loop gain would be

$$\text{LG} \simeq \frac{g_m R_L}{3} \tag{6.4-29}$$

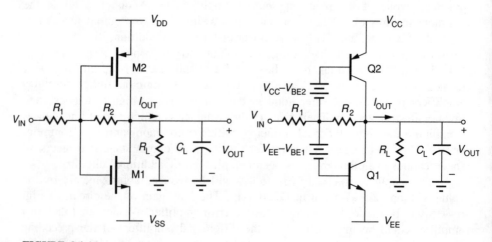

FIGURE 6.4-16
A possible implementation of Fig. 6.4-15.

where g_m is the transconductance of M1 or M2 (Q1 or Q2). Thus, the output resistance of the circuit of Fig. 6.4-16 is expressed as

$$r'_{out} \simeq \frac{r_{out}}{1 + (g_m R_L / 3)} \tag{6.4-30}$$

where r_{out} is the resistance of the output amplifier with the loop open.

The frequency response of output amplifiers should be large in order not to cause stability problems in the circuit driving the output amplifier. In general, the frequency response of the output amplifier is determined by its input resistance and capacitance. This implies that the input devices of the output amplifier should be as small as possible for high frequency response.

The design of an output amplifier capable of serving as a buffer between an integrated circuit amplifier and a load consisting of a small resistance and/or large capacitance has been considered in this section. Although not all approaches have been examined, the material discussed gives the principles and allows the reader to appreciate the problems involved. The performance of the various output amplifiers presented in this section is compared in Table 6.4-1. The comparison is made on a qualitative basis because of the complexity involved in the analysis of output amplifiers. In many cases, the performance of the output amplifier determines the performance of the overall circuit and will require much more attention than has been allocated in this section. All of the circuits presented have been used in actual integrated circuits and will be used in various circuits in the next section.

6.5 OPERATIONAL AMPLIFIERS

One of the most important circuits in analog circuit design is the operational amplifier (op amp). Its primary use is to provide sufficient gain to define and implement analog signal processing functions through the use of negative feedback. Such analog signal processing functions include amplification, integration, and summation. In this section we will consider the characteristics and architectures of general op amps. This will be followed by a "first-cut" design of two-stage BJT and CMOS op amps. Architectures capable of driving large load capacitance and small load resistance are presented and discussed. Finally, a brief consideration of simulation and testing of op amps will be given.

6.5.1 Characterization of Op Amps

An op amp has a differential input capability and is represented by the symbol shown in Fig. 6.5-1. The differential input voltages are V_1 and V_2, and the single-ended output voltage is V_O. The op amp ideally has infinite differential input resistance, R_{id}, infinite differential-mode voltage gain, A_v, and a zero output resistance, R_{out}. Although we have assumed the op amp is a voltage-controlled voltage-source, it can be implemented by any of the four types of controlled sources.

TABLE 6.4-1
Performance comparison of output amplifiers

Output amplifier	Figure	I_{OUT}^+	I_{OUT}^-	r_{OUT}	Efficiency	Linearity	Maximum voltage swing
Class A MOS inverter	6.4-1a	I_{BIAS}	$>> I_{BIAS}$	High	<25%	Good	Fair
Class A BJT inverter	6.4-1b	I_{BIAS}	$>> I_{BIAS}$	Medium	<25%	Good	Good
Class AB MOS inverter	6.4-4a	High for large W/L	High for large W/L	High	<50%	Fair	Fair
Class AB BJT inverter	6.4-4b	High if base current is large	High if base current is large	Medium	<50%	Fair	Good
Class B MOS inverter	6.4-4a	High for large W/L	High for large W/L	High	<75%	Poor	Fair
Class B BJT inverter	6.4-4b	High if base current is large	High if base current is large	Medium	<75%	Poor	Good
Class A MOS source follower	6.4-9a	High for large W/L	I_{BIAS}	Low	<25%	Poor	Poor (+) Good (−)
Class A BJT emitter follower	6.4-9b	High if base current is large	I_{BIAS}	Low	<25%	Poor	Poor (+) Good (−)
Class B MOS source follower	6.4-13a	High for large W/L	High for large W/L	Low	<75%	Poor	Poor
Class B BJT emitter follower	6.4-13b	High if base current is large	High if base current is large	Low	<75%	Poor	Poor
Class AB inverter with negative feedback	6.4-15	High if base current or W/L is large	High if base current or W/L is large	Low	<75%	Good	Good

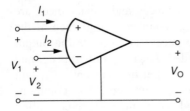

FIGURE 6.5-1
Symbol for the op amp.

In most cases, we can assume that the differential voltage gain, A_v, approaches infinity. If this assumption is valid, then the input terminals of the op amp realize a null port if the output, V_O, is connected back to the input (often through resistors or one or more op amp circuits) to achieve negative feedback. A *null port* is a two-terminal network whose voltage and current are simultaneously equal to zero. Thus, in Fig. 6.5-1, a null port is characterized by

$$| V_1 - V_2 | = 0 \qquad (6.5\text{-}1)$$

and

$$| I_1 | = | I_2 | = 0 \qquad (6.5\text{-}2)$$

These two relationships make it very easy to analyze the most common of op amp circuits when the differential gain is assumed to approach infinity and the output of an op amp is returned to the minus input to achieve negative feedback.

Unfortunately, the op amp only approaches the ideal op amp just described. Some of the nonideal op amp characteristics are illustrated in Fig. 6.5-2. This model will be used to define the various characteristics of the op amp. The finite differential input impedance is modeled by R_{id} and C_{id}. The output resistance

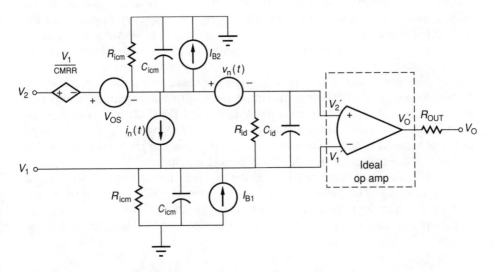

FIGURE 6.5-2
A model for a nonideal op amp showing some of the nonideal characteristics.

is modeled by R_{out}. The common-mode input resistances and capacitances are given by the resistances R_{icm} and capacitances C_{icm} connected from each of the inputs to ground. V_{OS} is the input offset voltage necessary to make the output voltage zero if both inputs of the op amp are grounded. I_{OS} (not shown) is defined as the magnitude of the difference between the two input bias currents, I_{B1} and I_{B2} necessary to make the output voltage of the op amp zero. The common-mode rejection ratio (CMRR) is approximately modeled by the voltage-controlled voltage source indicated as $V_1/CMRR$. The two sources designated as $\overline{V}_n$ and $\overline{I}_n$ are used to model the op amp noise and are called the noise voltage and noise current, in units of mean square volts and mean square amperes, respectively. Although these noise sources are weakly correlated, they are normally assumed to be uncorrelated.

Not all of the nonideal characteristics of the op amp are illustrated in Fig. 6.5-2. The output voltage of the op amp of Fig. 6.5-1 can be expressed as

$$V_o(s) = A_d(s)[V_1(s) - V_2(s)] + A_c(s)\left[\frac{V_1(s) + V_2(s)}{2}\right] \quad (6.5\text{-}3)$$

where the first term on the right is the differential portion of $V_o(s)$ and the second term is the common-mode portion of $V_o(s)$. The differential frequency response of the op amp is given as $A_d(s)$, and the common-mode frequency response is given as $A_c(s)$. A typical differential frequency response for an op amp is

$$A_d(s) = \frac{A_{od}\omega_1\omega_2\omega_3\ldots}{(s + \omega_1)(s + \omega_2)(s + \omega_3)\,\cdots} \quad (6.5\text{-}4)$$

where $\omega_1, \omega_2, \omega_3, \ldots$ are the poles of the operational amplifier. While the operational amplifier may have zeros, they will be ignored for the present. A_{od} (or simply A_o, where the use is understood) is the low-frequency gain of the op amp. Figure 6.5-3 shows the magnitude of a typical frequency response for the differential-mode gain, $A_d(j\omega)$ where $s = j\omega$. In this case, we see that ω_1 is much smaller than the rest of the poles, causing ω_1 to be the dominant influence in the frequency response. The objective of most compensation schemes which will be considered later is to achieve a single dominant pole so that the frequency response consists of just the -6 dB/octave slope until the magnitude of $A_d(j\omega)$ is less than 0 dB. The intersection of $|A_d(j\omega)|$ and the 0 dB axis is designated as the *unity-gain bandwidth* (GB) of the op amp. The *phase margin* is defined as the phase shift of the op amp at $\omega = GB$. A phase margin greater than 45° is desirable for negative resistive feedback around the op amp.

Other nonideal characteristics of the op amp not defined in Fig. 6.5-2 deserve mention. The *power supply rejection ratio* (PSRR) is defined as the ratio of the open loop gain of the op amp to the change in the output voltage of the op amp caused by the change in the power supply. Thus, the PSRR for V_{DD} is

$$PSRR(V_{DD}) = \frac{A_d}{(\Delta V_O/\Delta V_{DD})} = \frac{\Delta V_{DD}A_d}{\Delta V_O} \quad (6.5\text{-}5)$$

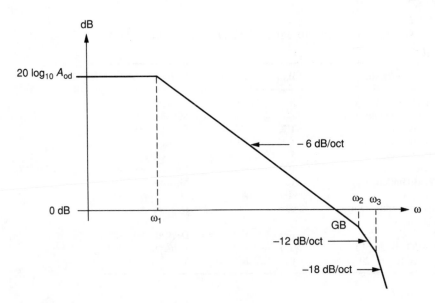

FIGURE 6.5-3
Typical frequency response of the magnitude of $A_d(j\omega)$ for an op amp.

An ideal op amp would have an infinite PSRR. The *common-mode input voltage range* is the voltage range over which the input common-mode signal can vary. Typically, this range is several volts less than the higher power supply voltage and several volts greater than the lower power supply voltage. The op amp has several other characteristics corresponding to those we have already considered for output amplifiers. These include the *maximum output sourcing* or *sinking current*, the *maximum output signal swing*, and the *slew rate*. Another characteristic of importance is the *settling time* defined as the amount of time the op amp requires in a given negative feedback configuration to respond to an input step and to settle to within a given percentage of the final value of the output step response.

The steps in designing an op amp depend on the desired values of these parameters. In this study we shall restrict ourselves to general purpose op amps that are implemented as part of an integrated circuit. Typical target specifications are shown in Table 6.5-1 for BJT and CMOS op amps. From these specifications we may propose several architectures.

The first possible op amp architecture is shown in Fig. 6.5-4*a* for the BJT op amp. This architecture is called the two-stage op amp. We observe that it consists of a differential amplifier similar to that of Fig. 6.3-11 cascaded with an inverter similar to that of Fig. 6.1-18*b*. The source of bias voltage for the differential amplifier current sink is also the source of bias voltage for the inverter's current-sink load. Two stages are often necessary because the differential amplifier generally has a voltage gain less then 60dB. The output resistance of the inverting amplifier is large and will not be capable of driving a low value of R_L. If the output resistance must be lower, then an output amplifier must be used, creating a third stage in the architecture.

TABLE 6.5-1
Typical specifications for integrated circuit BJT and CMOS op amps

Op amp specification	BJT	CMOS	Units
Differential gain, A_d	80	60	Decibels
Unity gain bandwidth, GB	1	1	Megahertz
Output resistance, r_{out}	1 K	100 K	Ohms
Input differential resistance, r_{id}	1 M	10^{12}	Ohms
Input offset voltage, V_{OS}	5	10	Millivolts
Input offset current, I_{OS}	100	-0	Nanoamperes
Power consumption, P_{DD}	10	5	Milliwatts
PSRR	80	80	Decibels
Phase margin (unity gain) (C_L = 20 pF)	60	60	Degrees
CMRR	100	100	Decibels
Slew rate (C_L = 20 pF)	± 1	± 1	Volts/microsecond
Settling time (C_L = 20 pF)	1	1	Microseconds

The two-stage architecture has the disadvantage of having two high-impedance nodes, which are indicated by A and B in Fig. 6.5-4a. This implies that two poles will be dominant, which will deteriorate the phase margin of the op amp. In order to resolve this situation, a Miller capacitance (C_c) is introduced between points A and B. The feedback path through C_c around the inverter causes these poles to split; it makes the pole at A dominant and for an appropriate value of C_c drives the pole at B out to or beyond GB. While this creates a single dominant pole, any large load capacitor will drive the pole at B back toward the origin, causing a poor phase margin.

The susceptibility of the Miller compensation scheme to capacitive loading has influenced the development of a second op amp architecture shown in Fig. 6.5-4b. This type of architecture is called the cascode configuration. A modification of this architecture, called the folded cascode configuration, is shown in Fig. 6.5-4c. In each of these cascode configurations, there is only one high-impedance node, which is at the output. The reason is that the input resistance of the cascode stage is very low ($1/g_m$), as was seen in Sec. 6.2. Since the gain of the cascode is approximately equal to that of the inverter, this is a very clever way of eliminating the high-impedance point at A of Fig. 6.5-4a. Compensation of the cascode op amp is accomplished by a capacitor from the output to ground. This has the attractive feature that as C_L increases, the compensation increases, keeping the op amp stable for large values of load capacitance.

Figure 6.5-5 shows the equivalent architectures for the CMOS op amp. The need for a second stage for the CMOS op amp is more obvious since the gain of a CMOS stage is typically less than that of an equivalent BJT stage. Although many other architectures for op amps exist, these represent the basic structures. They will aid in the designer's understanding of new or different architectures.

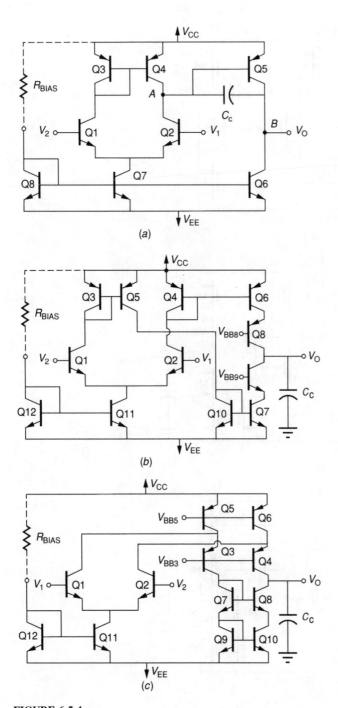

FIGURE 6.5-4
(a) Two-stage BJT op amp, (b) Cascode BJT op amp, (c) Folded cascode BJT op amp.

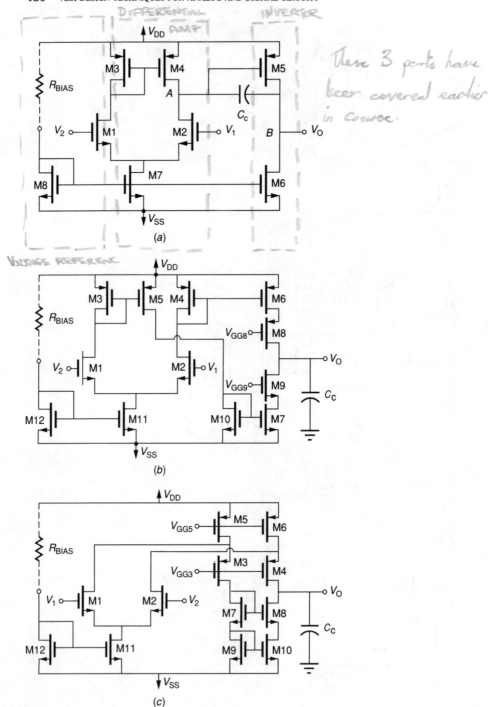

FIGURE 6.5-5
(a) CMOS two-stage op amp, (b) CMOS cascode BJT op amp, (c) CMOS folded cascode op amp.

6.5.2 The BJT Two-Stage Op Amp

The design of the two-stage BJT op amp will be considered first because it is the simplest.[1] Because the performance of the op amp is based on the small signal model, Fig. 6.5-6a shows the small signal model of the op amp of Fig. 6.5-4a. The first-stage model was developed in Fig. 6.3-15, where definitions of R_1, R_2, C_1, and C_2 are still valid, with the exception that $r_{\pi 5}$ is added in parallel to R_2, causing that resistance to be significantly decreased. The second stage in this model is simply that of an inverter. R_3 and C_3 are given as

$$R_3 = r_{o5} \parallel r_{o6} \tag{6.5-6}$$

and

$$C_3 = C_{\mu 5} + C_{\mu 6} + C_{CS5} + C_{CS6} + C_L \tag{6.5-7}$$

In order to simplify our considerations, assume that ω_1 and ω_1' of Eq. 6.3-84 approximately cancel and that $g_{m3} \simeq g_{m4}$. The resulting small signal, differential-input model for the two-stage BJT op amp is shown in Fig. 6.5-6b where $v_{id} = v_i - v_2$. The parameters of this model are defined as

$$g_{mI} = g_{m1} = g_{m2} \tag{6.5-8}$$

$$R_I = R_2 = r_{o2} \parallel r_{o4} \parallel r_{\pi 5} \tag{6.5-9}$$

$$C_I = C_2 = C_{\mu 2} + C_{\mu 4} + C_{\pi 5} + C_{CS2} + C_{CS4} \tag{6.5-10}$$

$$g_{mII} = g_{m5} \tag{6.5-11}$$

$$R_{II} = R_3 = r_{o5} \parallel r_{o6} \tag{6.5-12}$$

and

$$C_{II} = C_3 = C_{\mu 5} + C_{\mu 6} + C_{CS5} + C_{CS6} + C_L \tag{6.5-13}$$

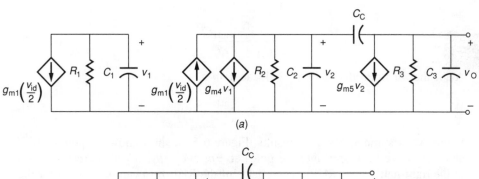

(a)

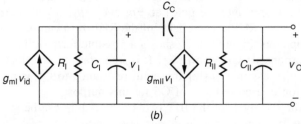

(b)

FIGURE 6.5-6
(a) Small signal model of Fig. 6.5-4a or Fig. 6.5-5a, (b) Simplified model of (a).

C_c is the compensation capacitance and is not included in C_I or C_{II}.

Analysis of the circuit of Fig. 6.5-6b illustrates how the Miller capacitor, C_c, splits the poles and accomplishes the dominant pole compensation. If C_c is zero, then the transfer function $V_O(s)/V_{ID}(s)$ is given as

$$\frac{V_O(s)}{V_{ID}(s)} = \frac{g_{mI}R_I g_{mII}R_{II}\omega_I'\omega_{II}'}{(s + \omega_I')(s + \omega_{II}')} = \frac{A_o\omega_I'\omega_{II}'}{(s + \omega_I')(s + \omega_{II}')} \tag{6.5-14}$$

where

$$\omega_I' = -p_I' = \frac{1}{R_I C_I} \tag{6.5-15}$$

and

$$\omega_{II}' = -p_{II}' = \frac{1}{R_{II}C_{II}} \tag{6.5-16}$$

p_I' and p_{II}' are the pole locations of Fig. 6.5-4a when C_c is zero.

When C_c is not zero, then the transfer function of Eq. 6.5-14 becomes

$$V_O(s)/V_{ID}(s) = A_o\big[1 - (sC_c/g_{mII})\big]\Big/\Big\{1 + s\big[R_I(C_I + C_{II}) + R_{II}(C_{II} + C_c) + $$

$$g_{mII}R_IR_{II}C_c\big] + s^2R_IR_{II}\big[C_IC_{II} + C_c(C_I + C_{II})\big]\Big\} \tag{6.5-17}$$

Applying Eq. 6.1-26 to Eq. 6.5-17 gives

$$p_I \simeq \frac{-1}{g_{mII}R_IR_{II}C_c} \tag{6.5-18}$$

and

$$p_{II} \simeq \frac{-g_{mII}C_c}{C_IC_{II} + C_{II}C_c + C_IC_c} \tag{6.5-19}$$

Also, the zero introduced by C_c is located at

$$z = \frac{g_{mII}}{C_c} \tag{6.5-20}$$

Figure 6.5-7 summarizes these results. Figure 6.5-7a shows how the poles at $-p_I'$ and $-p_{II}'$ have been split into the poles at $-p_I$ and $-p_{II}$. C_c also creates a zero in the right-half plane (RHP). The effects of the RHP zero can be ignored for the BJT two-stage op amp. Figure 6.5-7b shows a possible form of the magnitude of the frequency response if $GB < p_{II} < z$. It is important to note that the BJT op amp will have $|p_{II}'|$ less than $|p_I'|$ if the input resistance to Q5 is not increased. Often a Darlington is used in place of Q5 for this purpose.

The preceding analysis of the BJT two-stage op amp can be summarized as follows. The low-frequency open-loop gain is given as

$$A_o = g_{mI}g_{mII}R_IR_{II} \tag{6.5-21}$$

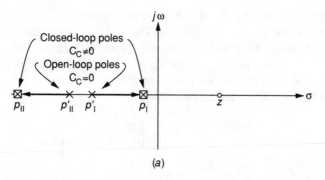

(a)

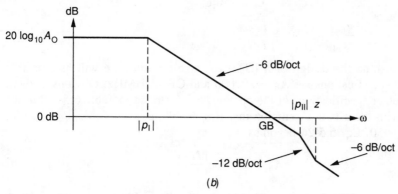

(b)

FIGURE 6.5-7
(a) Open- and closed-loop roots of Fig. 6.5-6b, (b) Closed-loop magnitude response of Fig. 6.5-6b.

The dominant pole is given by

$$| p_I | \simeq \frac{1}{g_{mII} R_I R_{II} C_c} \qquad (6.5\text{-}22)$$

The unity-gain bandwidth, GB, is found by the product of Eqs. 6.5-21 and 6.5-22 and is

$$GB = \frac{g_{mI}}{C_c} \qquad (6.5\text{-}23)$$

These three relationships form the basis of the two-stage op amp design along with two other constraints, which are developed below. For good phase margin, it is desirable to have $z > | p_{II} |$ and $| p_{II} | > GB$. From these two constraints, we get

$$g_{mII} > g_{mI} \qquad (6.5\text{-}24)$$

and

$$C_{II} < \frac{g_{mII}}{g_{mI}} C_c \qquad (6.5\text{-}25)$$

The design approach for the BJT two-stage op amp will be to establish the bias currents in the first and second stages of Fig. 6.5-4a to meet the specification for A_o and maintain the constraints of Eqs. 6.5-24 and 6.5-25. C_c will be chosen to meet the specification for GB. Replacing the small signal model parameters in terms of dc currents and device characteristics results in the following key equations which give a reasonable phase margin.

$$A_o \simeq \frac{g_{\mathrm{mI}} g_{\mathrm{mII}} r_{\pi 5}}{g_{o5} + g_{o6}} = \frac{\beta_{F5}/V_t}{1/V_{\mathrm{AN}} + 1/V_{\mathrm{AP}}}\left(\frac{I_{C1}}{I_{C5}}\right) \qquad (6.5\text{-}26)$$

$$GB = \frac{g_{\mathrm{mI}}}{C_c} = \frac{g_{\mathrm{mI}}}{C_c} = \frac{I_{C1}}{V_t C_c} \qquad (6.5\text{-}27)$$

$$\frac{g_{\mathrm{mII}}}{g_{\mathrm{mI}}} = \frac{g_{m5}}{g_{\mathrm{mI}}} = \frac{I_{C5}}{I_{C1}} \qquad (6.5\text{-}28)$$

To illustrate the design of a BJT two-stage op amp, we will assume that the desired specifications are $A_o \geq 10,000$ and GB $\simeq$ 1 MHz. Obviously, there are many other specifications of the op amp, as illustrated in Table 6.5-1, but we will start with these two. Assuming that $\beta_{FN} \simeq 200, \beta_{FP} \simeq 50, V_{AFN} \simeq 100$ V, and $V_{AFP} \simeq 50$, Eq. 6.5-26 becomes

$$A_o = 66,700\left(\frac{I_{C1}}{I_{C5}}\right) \qquad (6.5\text{-}29)$$

Choosing $I_{C5} = 5I_{C1}$ gives $A_o = 13,340$. Picking $C_c = 30$ pF gives $I_{C1} \simeq 5$ μA from Eq. 6.5-27. Thus, $I_{C5} \simeq 25$ μA. From these currents we can calculate the differential input resistance as $r_{\mathrm{id}} \simeq 2r_{\pi 1} = 2$ MΩ and the output resistance as $r_{\mathrm{out}} = 1.334$ MΩ. The slew rate is determined by how fast C_c can be charged and discharged. This is given by the expression

$$\text{Slew rate} = \text{SR} = \frac{I}{C_c} \qquad (6.5\text{-}30)$$

where I is the smaller of $2I_{C1}$ or I_{C5}. In this example, the slew rate of the op amp is $2I_{C1}/C_c = 0.33$ V/μs. It is seen that the design of the BJT two-stage op amp is simple but constrained in its ability to simultaneously satisfy many op amp specifications. The performance is satisfactory for most applications, with the possible exception of the high output resistance. The choices that were made in this design example can be varied to achieve different values of specifications.

Up to this point, the design of the BJT two-stage op amp has not depended on the geometries of the individual devices. In other words, while Q1 and Q2 should be matched and Q3, Q4, and Q5 should be matched, there is no geometric relationship between them. The sizes of Q6, Q7, and Q8 determine the currents. Generally, a resistor is connected from the collector of Q8 to V_{CC} to establish I_{C8}. This current will be dependent on power supply variations, leading to a poor PSRR. To improve the PSRR, the current for I_{C8} must be provided by one of the current sources of Sec. 5.3. When I_{C8} is defined, the ratio of the emitter areas of Q6, Q7, and Q8 can be used to define I_{C7} ($=I_{C1}/2$) and I_{C6} ($=I_{C5}$). It is important to keep each BJT operating in the forward active region for the best performance and largest signal swings. The sizing of the emitter areas depends on the application. Devices in the input (Q1 and Q2) and in all current mirrors should be as large as possible for matching without degrading the frequency response. The remaining device areas should be as small as possible if power dissipation is not a concern.

After an initial design has been obtained by the method illustrated, the next step is to use a simulator such as SPICE that permits the designer to consider second-order effects and examine the influence of parameter and process variation. This step is important since it gives the designer a good understanding of the performance of the op amp and of how to make tradeoffs using the computer to achieve the final design specifications.

6.5.3 The CMOS Two-Stage Op Amp

Let us consider next the design of the two-stage CMOS op amp shown in Fig. 6.5-5a. Since the small signal model of Fig. 6.5-6 holds for the CMOS case, Eqs. 6.5-21 through 6.5-25 are also valid. The values of $R_I, R_{II}, C_I,$ and C_{II} for the CMOS case are given as

$$R_I = r_{ds2} \| r_{ds4} \tag{6.5-31}$$

$$R_{II} = r_{ds5} \| r_{ds6} \tag{6.5-32}$$

$$C_I = C_{gd2} + C_{gd4} + C_{gs5} + C_{db2} + C_{db4} \tag{6.5-33}$$

and

$$C_{II} = C_{gd6} + C_{db5} + C_{db6} + C_L \tag{6.5-34}$$

The key equations pertaining to the CMOS two-stage op amp design are given as

$$A_o = g_{mI}g_{mII}R_IR_{II} = \frac{g_{m1}g_{m5}}{(g_{ds2} + g_{ds4})(g_{ds5} + g_{ds6})}$$

$$= \left[\left(\frac{1}{\lambda_2 + \lambda_4}\right)\left(\frac{2K_N'W_1}{I_{D1}L_1}\right)^{1/2}\right]\left[\left(\frac{1}{\lambda_5 + \lambda_6}\right)\left(\frac{2K_P'W_5}{I_{D5}L_5}\right)^{1/2}\right]$$

$$\simeq \frac{1}{2\lambda^2}\left(\frac{K_N'K_P'W_1W_5}{I_{D1}I_{D5}L_1L_5}\right)^{1/2} \tag{6.5-35}$$

$$GB = \frac{g_{mI}}{C_c} = \frac{g_{m1}}{C_c} = \frac{1}{C_c}\left(\frac{2K_N'W_1I_{D1}}{L_1}\right)^{1/2} \tag{6.5-36}$$

and

$$\frac{g_{mII}}{g_{mI}} = \frac{g_{m5}}{g_{m1}} = \left[\frac{K_N'I_{D1}(W_1/L_1)}{K_P'I_{D5}(W_5/L_5)}\right] \tag{6.5-37}$$

Comparing Eqs. 6.5-35 through 6.5-37 with Eqs. 6.5-26 through 6.5-28 reveals a very important difference between BJT and CMOS integrated circuits. This difference is that the performance of the CMOS op amp is dependent on the geometry of the devices, whereas the BJT op amp is independent of the geometry of its transistors. While this creates additional complexity in the expressions, the designer has much more freedom to meet the specifications of the design.

The additional degrees of freedom allow the designer to impose constraints that will ensure that all MOS devices operate in saturation over wide process variations. In Sec. 5.4, we showed how the ratio of the W/L values of two MOS devices connected gate-to-gate and source-to-source could control the ratio of the drain currents. This principle is employed in the circuit of Fig. 6.5-5a to ensure that M4 operates in saturation. All other devices either operate in saturation by their connection or by external potentials applied to the inputs or outputs. For matching and symmetry, we must choose $W_1/L_1 = W_2/L_2$ and $W_3/L_3 = W_4/L_4$. If we force V_{GS3} to be equal to V_{GS5} by the following relationship

$$\frac{W_3}{L_3} = \frac{W_5}{L_5}\left(\frac{I_3}{I_5}\right) \tag{6.5-38}$$

then since $I_5 = I_6$, $I_3 = I_4$, and $W_3/L_3 = W_4/L_4$, we may express Eq. 6.5-38 as

$$\frac{W_4}{L_4} = \frac{W_5}{L_5}\left(\frac{I_4}{I_6}\right) \tag{6.5-39}$$

However, because $I_4 = 0.5I_7$ and $I_7/I_8 = (W_7/L_7)/(W_8/L_8)$, the condition for M4 to remain in saturation becomes

$$\frac{W_4}{L_4} = \frac{(W_5/L_5)}{2}\left(\frac{W_7/L_7}{W_6/L_6}\right) = \frac{(W_5/L_5)}{2}\left(\frac{I_7}{I_6}\right) \tag{6.5-40}$$

To illustrate the design of a two-stage CMOS op amp such as that given in Fig. 6.5-5a, assume that the desired specifications are $A_o \geq 50{,}000$, GB $= 1$ MHz, and the slew rate is 2 V/μs. Assume that the device parameters are $K'_N = 2K'_P = 25$ μA/V^2, $\lambda = 0.01$ V^{-1} and $C_c = 5$ pF. From the slew rate specification and C_c, we see that $I_{D1} = 5$ μA. We will pick I_{D5} equal to 50 μA to make the zero due to Miller compensation larger than the second pole. Solving for W_1/L_1 in Eq. 6.5-36 gives $W_1/L_1 \simeq 4.0$. Since M1 and M2 are matched, W_2/L_2 is also 4.0. In Eq. 6.5-35 we may solve for W_5/L_5 to get 4.5. Since the ratio of current in M6 and M7 is I_{D5} to $2I_{D1}$, we may solve for W_4/L_4 from Eq. 6.5-40 as being 10 times less than W_5/L_5, or 0.45. Finally, one can solve for the value of W_8/L_8 necessary to establish a reasonable current in M8 and solve for W_6/L_6 and W_7/L_7 using the current ratios. The small signal input resistance, R_{id}, of the CMOS op amp is infinity because of the infinite gate resistance. The output resistance is equal to the parallel combination of r_{ds5} and r_{ds6} and is 1 MΩ for this example.

At this point, the circuit designer typically sets the smaller value of W or L equal to perhaps twice the smallest allowable value and solves for the remaining dimension. For a minimum L or W of 5 μ, Table 6.5-2 gives a set of possible

TABLE 6.5-2
**A set of first-cut W and L values for the design of a CMOS
two-stage op amp such as that shown in Fig. 6.6-5a**

	M1	M2	M3	M4	M5	M6	M7	M8
W (μ)	40	40	10	10	45	10	10	10
L (μ)	10	10	22	22	10	10	50	10

W and L values for the op amp of Fig. 6.5-5a if the current in M8 is 50 μA when $W_8/L_8 = 1$. At this point, the designer would turn to a simulator to refine and optimize the design.

Unfortunately, the transconductance of the MOS device is not as large as for the BJT, which causes a problem due to the zero of Eq. 6.5-20. Using the values of the preceding example, we find that the zero is located at 2.39 MHz (the RHP zero for the BJT two-stage op amp was at 10.6 MHz). This RHP zero will destroy the phase margin of the CMOS two-stage amplifier. Figure 6.5-8 shows a clever way to eliminate this zero and to make the two-stage CMOS op amp of Fig. 6.5-5a practical. It can be shown that the new zero location is given by

$$z' = \frac{1}{C_c\left[(1/g_{mII}) - R_z\right]} \tag{6.5-41}$$

With the nulling resistor, the designer can conceptually move the RHP zero to infinity; in fact, the zero can be moved into the left-hand plane and used for lead compensation. R_z is typically implemented by an n-channel and p-channel transistor in parallel with the gates taken to the appropriate power supply. For our example of the two-stage CMOS op amp, g_{m5} was 75 μS; therefore, a value of $R_z = 13.33$ kΩ would move the RHP zero to infinity and retrieve the good stability properties. The same nulling resistor technique can be applied to the two-stage BJT op amp if necessary.

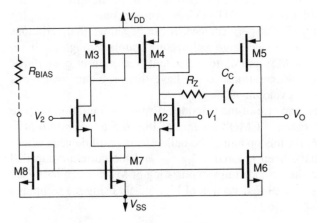

FIGURE 6.5-8
Nulling method to remove the effects of the RHP zero due to low device transconductance.

6.5.4   Cascode Op Amps

If the load to an op amp is primarily capacitive, it is not necessary to use a low resistance output stage to achieve satisfactory performance because large output currents are only required under dynamic conditions. The difficulty with a capacitive load for the two-stage op amp is that it destroys the Miller compensation and eventually causes the op amp to become unstable if C_L is too large or the closed-loop gain of the op amp approaches unity. In this case, the cascode architectures shown in Fig. 6.5-4 and Fig. 6.5-5 are very useful. Consider the BJT cascode op amp of Fig. 6.5-4b. The current from the collector of Q1 is mirrored into the collector current of Q7 while the collector current of Q2 is mirrored into the collector current of Q6. These currents are applied to the common-base configuration of Q8 and Q9. Q6 and Q8 and Q7 and Q9 are cascode amplifiers, as will be recognized from Sec. 6.2. The differential currents are combined at the collectors of Q8 and Q9, resulting in a single-ended output voltage, V_O. The important feature of the circuit of Fig. 6.5-4b is that the high-impedance point at A in Fig. 6.5-4a is no longer present. Since the output resistance is very high, the compensation can be accomplished by a capacitor connected from the output to ground. This means that a large load capacitance, C_L, will simply provide more compensation, keeping the op amp circuit stable. The low-frequency gain of the BJT cascode op amp is similar to that of the two-stage BJT op amp because the gain of the cascode stage is approximately equal to the gain of the inverter stage.

The BJT folded cascode op amp of Fig. 6.5-4c uses the same principle as the BJT cascode op amp to eliminate the high-impedance point at A, thus achieving a configuration with the high-impedance point at the output of the op amp. In this architecture, Q1-Q3 and Q2-Q4 form the cascode pairs. It is necessary to use a cascode current mirror (Q7 through Q10) to maintain the high output resistance of this configuration. The folded cascode is useful in acheiving a wide common-mode input voltage range.

In many cases, the two-stage BJT op amp is satisfactory for driving moderate values of C_L because of the higher values of g_m for a BJT. The higher value of g_m pushes the RHP zero away from the origin and keeps C_L from having a strong influence on the stability of the op amp. However, the CMOS cascode configurations of Fig. 6.5-5b and c are often used because of the low g_m of the MOS devices compared with that of the BJT devices. Another reason for using the cascode architecture is due to PSRR performance. It can be shown that variations in the upper power supply for the two-stage architecture couple through the base-emitter of Q5 (gate-source of M5) and C_c to the output, resulting in poor PSRR performance. The cascode configurations do not have this problem, which was another motivation for their development.

To understand the performance of the cascode op amp configuration in more detail, consider the folded cascode CMOS op amp of Fig. 6.5-5c. Figure 6.5-9a shows a small signal model for this op amp. The bulk effects of all devices whose source is not on ground have been ignored. r'_{in}, r'_{out} and the current-controlled current source, i, represent the cascode mirror consisting of M7 through M10 (see Sec. 5.4). Figure 6.5-9b is a simplified version of Fig. 6.5-9a using the technique

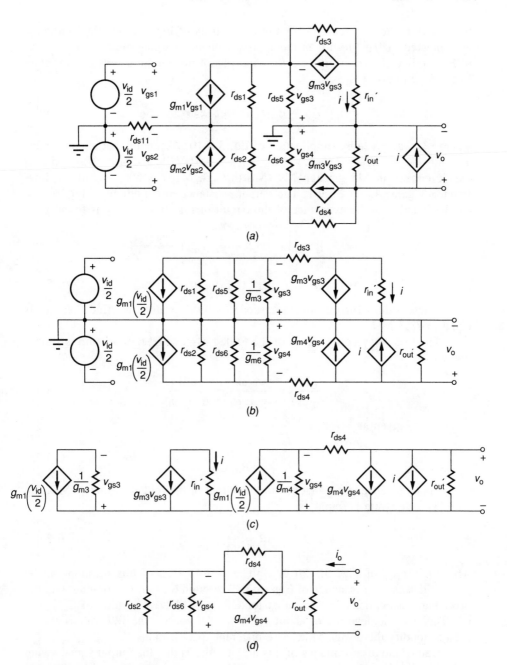

FIGURE 6.5-9
(a) Small signal model of the CMOS folded cascode op amp, (b) Simplification of (a), (c) Approximate model of (b), (d) Model for calculating the output resistance.

illustrated in Sec. 6.3 for the differential amplifier of Fig. 6.3-4c. Neglecting r_{ds} as compared to $1/g_m$ results in the approximate small signal model of the circuit of Fig. 6.5-5c shown in Fig. 6.5-9c. Analysis of this circuit shows that the low-frequency voltage gain is

$$\frac{v_o}{v_{id}} = A_o \simeq g_{m1}r'_{out} \simeq g_{m1}g_{m8}r_{ds8}r_{ds10} \tag{6.5-42}$$

where r'_{out} was given by simplication of Eq. 5.3-10. Assuming that all W/L ratios are unity, $K'_N = 2K'_P = 25$ $\mu A/V^2$, $\lambda_N = \lambda_P = 0.01$ V^{-1}, and $I_{D1} = I_{D2} = 5$ μA, the dc current in M5 through M9 (M6 through M10) is 50 μA and the low-frequency gain, A_o, is 22,361. The output resistance of the circuit of Fig. 6.5-5c can be found with the assistance of the circuit of Fig. 6.5-9d. r_{out} is found as

$$r_{out} = r'_{out} \parallel r_{ds4}\left[1 + (1 + g_{m4}r_{ds4})\frac{r_{ds2}r_{ds4}}{r_{ds2} + r_{ds4}}\right]$$

$$\simeq (g_{m8}r_{ds8}r_{ds10}) \parallel \left[(g_{m4}r_{ds4})(r_{ds2} \parallel r_{ds4})\right] \tag{6.5-43}$$

Using these values for the folded cascode CMOS op amp, we find that r_{out} is equal to 78.3 MΩ.

The frequency performance of the folded cascode CMOS op amp is simply given as

$$\frac{V_O(s)}{V_{ID}(s)} \simeq \frac{A_o\omega_I}{s + \omega_I} = \frac{GB}{s + \omega_I} \tag{6.5-44}$$

where ω_I is given as

$$\omega_I = \frac{1}{R_{out}C_L} \tag{6.5-45}$$

C_L is the total capacitance attached to the output of the folded cascode CMOS op amp. The slew rate is found as

$$SR = \frac{I}{C_L} \tag{6.5-46}$$

where I is I_{D11} of Fig. 6.5-5b or c. The performance of this op amp can be evaluated with the assistance of Eqs. 6.5-42 through 6.5-46. Continuing with the preceding assumptions, we find that for GB = 5 MHz, the value of C_L is 9.1 pF. This gives a slew rate of about 1.1 V/μs. Of course, the W/L values can be used to modify the design to achieve different specifications.

One of the disadvantages of this architecture is that the output signal swing is limited by the cascode configuration. This swing limitation can be alleviated using the technique described for cascode current mirrors (see Fig. 5.4-10). A practical implementation of the folded cascode CMOS op amp is shown in Fig. 6.5-10.[2] With ±5 V power supplies, the op amp has an output swing of ±4.1 V. It has a low-frequency gain of 5000, a GB of approximately 5 MHz, and a PSRR in the range of 60–70 dB. The input offset voltage, V_{OS}, is ±6 mV. In the basic

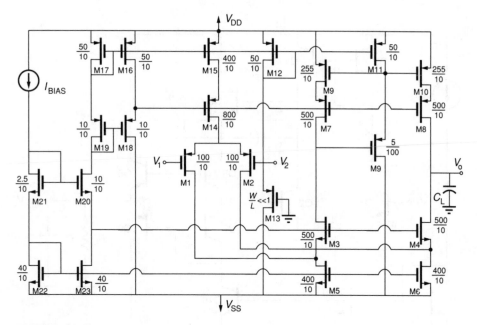

FIGURE 6.5-10
Folded cascode CMOS op amp design. *W/L* values are in microns.

folded cascode architecture of Fig. 6.5-5*c*, the operating region of all devices can be defined by external voltages so that ratio constraints are not necessary. In choosing the *W/L* values, one of the primary considerations is to increase the signal swings. The *W/L* values of the circuit of Fig. 6.5-10 correspond to $K'_N = 23.6$ μA/V^2, $K'_P = 5.84$ μA/V^2, $V_{TN} = 0.79$ V, $V_{TP} = -0.52$ V, $\gamma_N = 0.526$ V$^{1/2}$, $\gamma_P = 0.67$ V$^{1/2}$, $\lambda_N = 0.0207$ V^{-1}, and $\lambda_P = 0.0121$ V^{-1}.

6.5.5 Op Amps with an Output Stage

None of the op amps considered so far are capable of driving low values of load resistance. If the application requires a low output resistance, then the two-stage op amp can be followed with an output amplifier by use of the concepts of Sec. 6.4. Figure 6.5-11 shows the combination of the BJT two-stage op amp of Fig. 6.5-4*a* with the output stage of Fig. 6.4-14*b* to obtain an op amp with the ability to drive a low value of R_L. Q6 and Q7 are used to determine the operating current in the push-pull output transistors, Q8 and Q9. One of the difficulties in adding an output stage is to decide whether or not to include the output stage within the Miller compensation. The two choices are indicated in Fig. 6.5-11 by C_{c1} and C_{c2}. C_{c2} is less desirable because the pole due to the output stage will be large and close to GB, resulting in three poles inside the compensation loop. The Miller compensation method does not work well in this situation because complex conjugate poles can be created. The ability of the output stage to drive

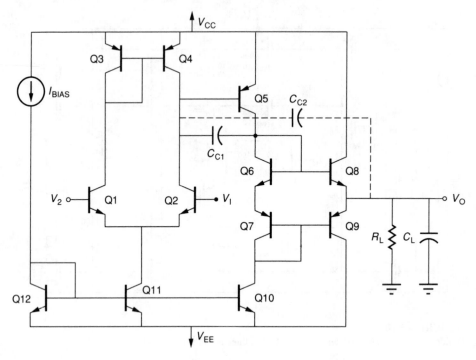

FIGURE 6.5-11
BJT two-stage op amp with a push-pull output stage.

a load resistance has been discussed in the preceding section. Further information can be found in the references.[3-7]

Figure 6.5-12a shows a two-stage CMOS op amp with an output stage similar to that of Fig. 6.4-14a. The compensation capacitor does not include the output stage and uses a nulling resistor, R_z, to achieve good stability properties. The ability to sink or source current is determined by the second stage of the op amp (M5). The bias current in the output devices (M8 and M9) should be chosen to reduce the crossover distortion and keep the quiescent dissipation low. Also, the bias current in the output devices will determine the small signal value of output resistance. The output swing of this op amp will be limited due to the body effects, causing V_T to increase as the positive or negative rail is approached by the output voltage.

Figure 6.5-12b shows use of the substrate BJT to create an output stage. This technique will provide low small signal output resistance because of the large value of g_m for the BJT. Unfortunately, the BJT suffers from the inability to source current for large positive output swings. Because the output devices are of a different type and in a different configuration (emitter follower and common source), the sourcing and sinking currents will be difficult to match. In addition, this configuration will create appreciable distortion.

A better solution to the output stage problem for the CMOS op amp is to couple the circuits of Fig. 6.4-15a and Fig. 6.5-10 resulting in the

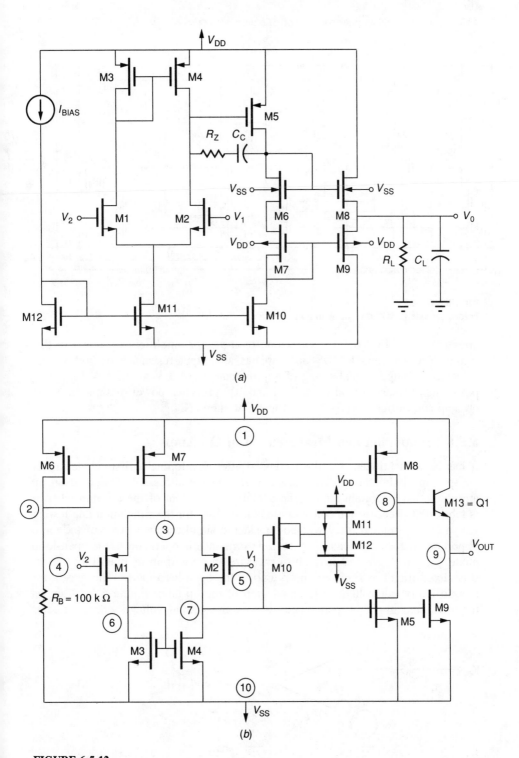

FIGURE 6.5-12
(a) CMOS two-stage op amp with a push-pull output stage, (b) CMOS two-stage op amp with a substrate BJT used in the output stage.

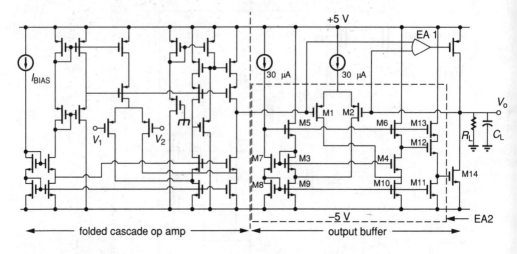

FIGURE 6.5-13
Folded cascode CMOS op amp with output buffer.

arrangement of Fig. 6.5-13. Only one of the error amplifiers is shown in this figure. The resulting CMOS op amp has an output resistance of 300 Ω and achieves an output signal swing of approximately -4.3 V to $+3.5$ V for ± 5 V power supplies and a load of 2000 Ω and 100 pF. Total power dissipation of the op amp and buffer stage is 5 mW for ± 5 V supplies.

6.5.6 Simulation and Measurement of Op Amps

It has been mentioned that the next step after developing a first-cut design of an op amp is simulation. This is a key step in the successful design of an op amp. Another important step is the actual measurement of the op amp when it is fabricated. Because the considerations necessary for the simulation and testing are so closely related, they will be considered simultaneously. One of the more important characterizations of op amp performance is operation in the open-loop mode. However, as it is difficult to measure an op amp in its open-loop mode, it is also difficult to simulate an op amp in the open-loop mode. The reason for this difficulty is the high differential gain of the op amp. Figure 6.5-14 shows how this step might be performed. V_{off} is an external voltage whose value is

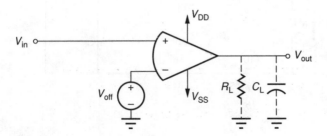

FIGURE 6.5-14
Open-loop mode with offset compensation.

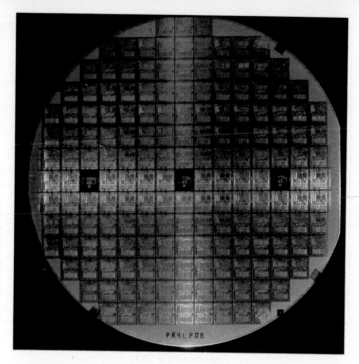

PLATE ONE Wafer photo — Motorola 68000 Family Microprocessor
(Photo courtesy of Motorola, Inc.)

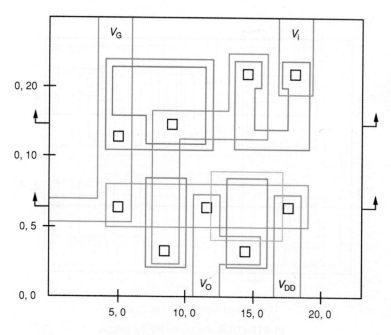

PLATE TWO Layout for NMOS process

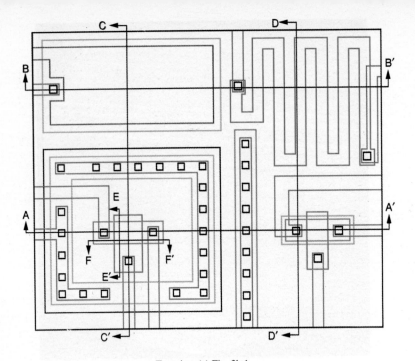

Top view (a) Fig. 2b.1a

PLATE THREE   Layout for CMOS process

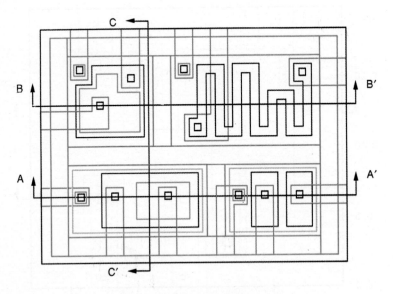

Top view of Bipolar Die (Fig. 2c.1a)

PLATE FOUR   Layout for Bipolar process

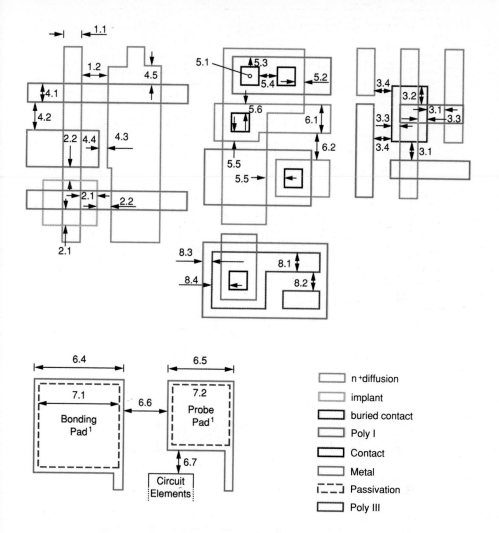

PLATE FIVE   Table 2A.3 Graphical interpretation of NMOS design rules of Table 2A.2
[1] Scale for pads is much smaller than scale for other features depicted in this figure.

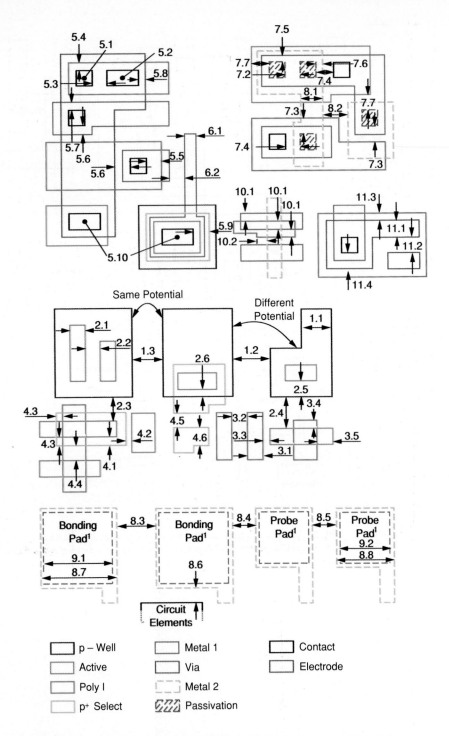

PLATE SIX Table 2B.3 Graphical interpretation of CMOS design rules of Table 2B.2

[1] Scale for pads is much smaller than scale for other features depicted in this figure.

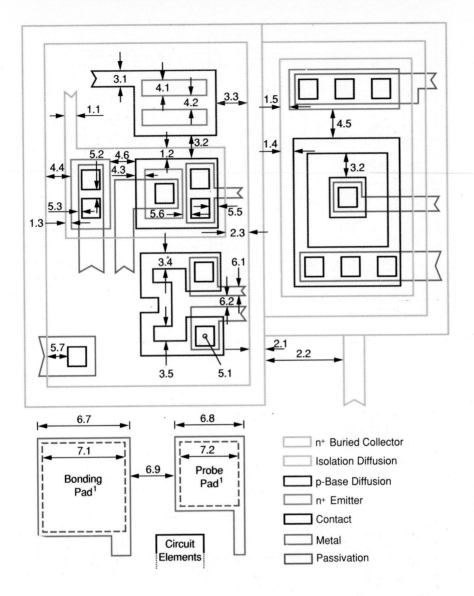

PLATE SEVEN Table 2C.3 graphical interpretation of Bipolar design rules of Table 2C.2
[1] Scale for pads is much smaller than scale for other features depicted in this figure.

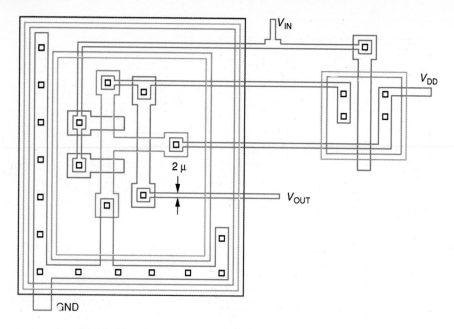

PLATE EIGHT   Layout of Schmitt Trigger circuit (see Problem 2.20)

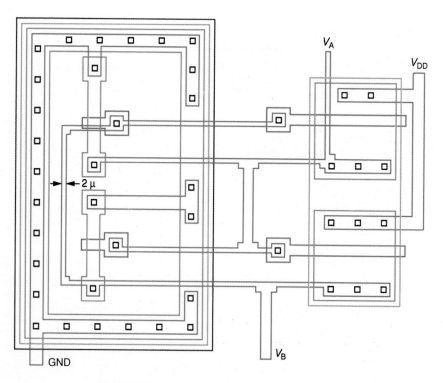

PLATE NINE   Layout of latch circuit (see Problem 2.23)

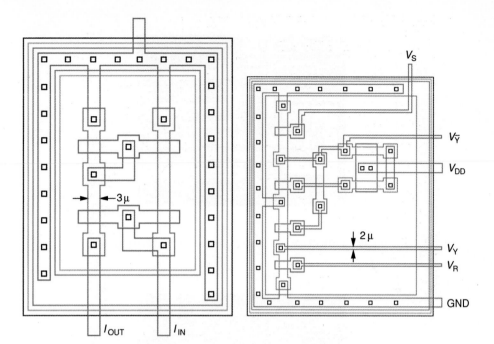

PLATE TEN Layout of common source amplifer (see Problem 2.22)

PLATE ELEVEN Layout of flip flop (see Problem 2.23)

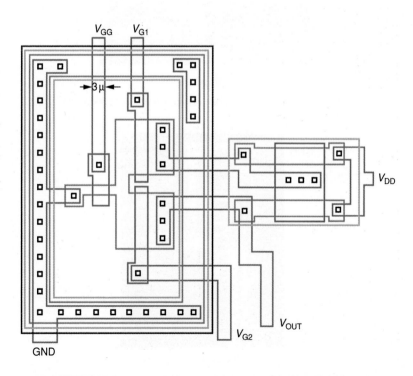

PLATE TWELVE Layout of differential amplifier with error (see Problem 2.31)

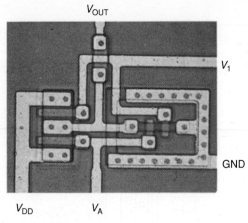

PLATE THIRTEEN Die photo of logic circuit (see Problem 2.26)

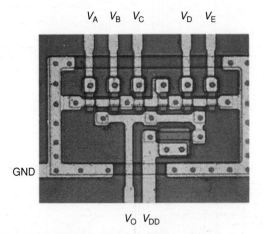

PLATE FOURTEEN Die photo of logic circuit (see Problem 2.26)

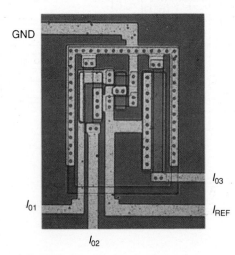

PLATE FIFTEEN Die photo of current source (see Problem 2.27)

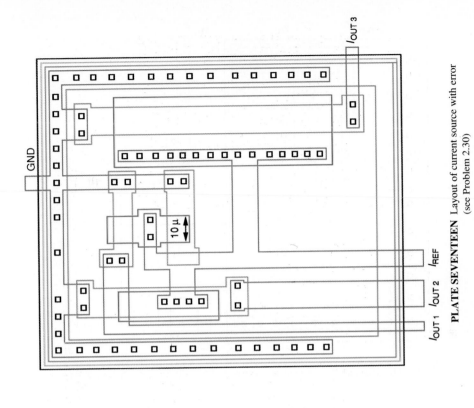

GND

10 μ

$I_{OUT\,3}$

$I_{OUT\,1}$ $I_{OUT\,2}$ I_{REF}

PLATE SEVENTEEN Layout of current source with error
(see Problem 2.30)

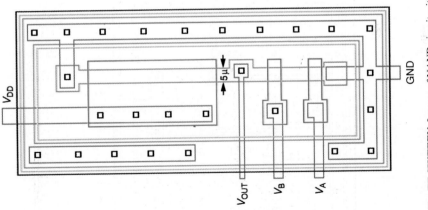

V_{DD}

5 μ

GND

V_{OUT}

V_B

V_A

PLATE SIXTEEN Layout of NAND circuit with
error (see Problem 2.29)

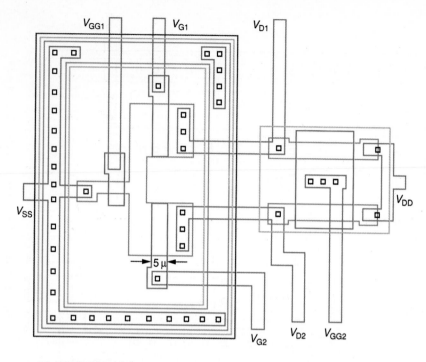

PLATE EIGHTEEN Layout of differential amplifier with error (see Problem 2.31)

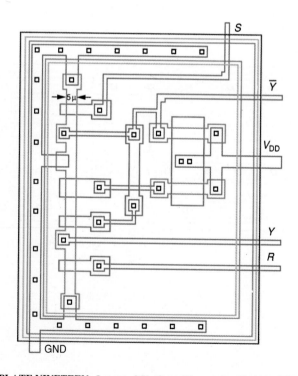

PLATE NINETEEN Layout of flip-flop with error (see Problem 2.32)

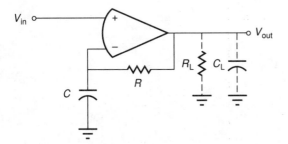

FIGURE 6.5-15
A method of measuring open-loop characteristics with dc bias stability.

adjusted to keep the dc value of V_{OUT} between the power supply limits. Without V_{off}, the op amp output will be at the positive or negative power supply for either the measurement or simulation case. The resolution necessary to find the correct value of V_{off} usually escapes the novice designer. It is necessary to find V_{off} to the accuracy of the magnitude of the power supply voltage divided by the low-frequency differential gain (typically in the range of millivolts).

The approach proposed in Fig. 6.5-14 to measure the open-loop gain is only practical for simulation. A better method of measuring the open-loop gain is shown in the circuit of Fig. 6.5-15. In this configuration, it is necessary to select the reciprocal RC time constant to be about 10 to 100 times less than the anticipated dominant pole of the op amp. Under these conditions, the op amp has total dc feedback, which stabilizes the bias. The dc value of V_{OUT} will be exactly the dc value of V_{IN}. The true open-loop frequency response characteristics will not be observed until the frequency is approximately 10 times $1/RC$. Above this frequency, the ratio of V_{OUT} to V_{IN} is essentially the open-loop gain of the op amp. This method works well for both simulation and measurement.

Simulation or measurement of the open-loop configuration of the op amp will characterize the open-loop transfer curve, the open-loop output swing limits, the phase margin, the dominant pole, the unity-gain bandwidth, and other open-loop characteristics. The designer should connect the anticipated loading at the output in order to get meaningful results. In some cases where the open-loop gain is not too large, it can be measured by applying v_{in} in Fig. 6.5-16 and measuring v_{out} and v_i. In this configuration, one must be careful that R is large enough not to cause a dc current load on the output of the op amp.

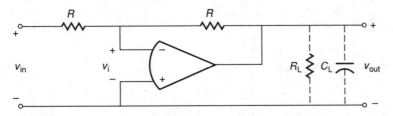

FIGURE 6.5-16
Configuration for simulating the open-loop frequency response for moderate-gain op amps.

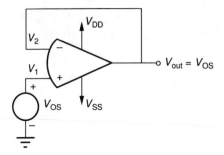

FIGURE 6.5-17
Configuration for measuring the input offset voltage.

The dc input offset voltage, V_{OS}, can be measured using the circuit of Fig. 6.5-17. If the dc input offset voltage is too small, it can be amplified by the use of a resistor divider in the negative feedback path. Figure 6.5-17 is also a good configuration for measuring or simulating the input common-mode range. Figure 6.5-18 shows the anticipated unity-gain transfer characteristic of the op amp in Fig. 6.5-17, illustrating the input common-mode range.

The common-mode gain is most easily simulated using the circuit of Fig. 6.5-19. It is seen that if V_{off} fails to keep the op amp in the linear region, this measuring configuration will fail. An alternate method of measuring the common-mode gain is given in Fig. 6.5-20. This circuit can be used to measure the CMRR, which will also give the common-mode gain. The method involves a sequence of two steps. The first step is to set V_{HH} to $V_{HH} + 1$ V, V_{LL} to $V_{LL} + 1$ V, and V_{out} to 1 V by applying -1 V to the input designated as $-V_{out}$. This is equivalent to applying a common-mode input signal of 1 V to the amplifier with the nominal supply values. The value at V_{OFF} is measured and designated as V_{OFF1}. Next, V_{HH} is set to $V_{HH} - 1$ V, V_{LL} to $V_{LL} - 1$ V, and V_{out} to -1 V

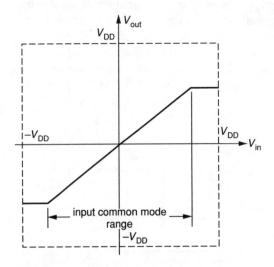

FIGURE 6.5-18
Unity-gain transfer function of the op amp.

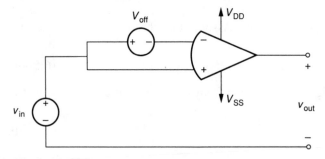

FIGURE 6.5-19
Configuration for simulating the common-mode gain.

by applying $+1$ V to the input designated as $-V_{out}$. V_{OFF} is measured and designated as V_{OFF2}. The CMRR can be found by

$$\text{CMRR} = \frac{2000}{|V_{OFF1} - V_{OFF2}|} \qquad (6.5\text{-}47)$$

This measurement is a spot measurement and must be modified to obtain the frequency response of the CMRR. The modification involves placing small sinusoidal signals of the proper phase in series with the power supplies.

The configuration of Figure 6.5-20 can also be used to measure the PSRR. First, set V_{HH} to $V_{HH} + 1$ V and V_{out} to 0 V by grounding $-V_{out}$. In this case, V_i is the input offset voltage for $V_{HH} + 1$ V. Measure V_{OFF} under these conditions, and designate it as V_{OFF3}. Next, set V_{HH} to $V_{HH} - 1$ V and V_{out} to 0 V, and measure V_{OFF}, designated as V_{OFF4}. The PSRR of the V_{HH} supply is given as

$$\text{PSRR of } V_{HH} = \frac{2000}{|V_{OFF3} - V_{OFF4}|} \qquad (6.5\text{-}48)$$

For the PSRR of V_{LL}, change V_{LL} and keep V_{HH} constant while V_{out} is at 0 V.

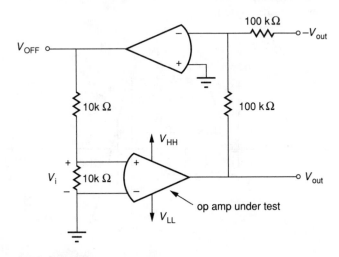

FIGURE 6.5-20
Circuit used to measure CMRR and PSRR.

The circuit of figure 6.5-17 can also be used to measure the PSRR of the positive or negative power supply. Assume that the output voltage can be expressed as

$$V_{\text{out}} = A_{\text{vd}}(V_1 - V_2) + A_{\text{dd}}V_{\text{dd}} \tag{6.5-49}$$

where A_{dd} is the small signal voltage gain from V_{dd} to V_{out}. It can be shown that

$$V_{\text{out}} = \frac{A_{\text{dd}}V_{\text{dd}}}{1 + A_{\text{vd}}} \simeq \frac{A_{\text{dd}}}{A_{\text{vd}}}V_{\text{dd}} = \frac{V_{\text{dd}}}{\text{PSRR}} \tag{6.5-50}$$

if $A_{\text{vd}} > 1$. Therefore, applying an ac signal V_{dd} in series with V_{DD} of Fig. 6.5-17 and measuring (or simulating) V_{out} will give the value of 1/PSRR.

The last configuration we will consider is for the large signal transient response. Figure 6.5-21a shows a configuration suitable for measuring the transient response of the op amp. Figure 6.5-21b shows a typical transient response. Both the positive and negative slew rates and the positive and negative settling times can be obtained from this configuration.

Other configurations not considered here include tests for noise, tolerances, process parameter variations, temperature, etc. The primary objective of any configuration is to keep the op amp in the desired region of operation and to maximize the accuracy of the measurement/simulation data.

The design of BJT and CMOS op amps has been introduced in this section. The basic two-stage architectures were introduced. The first-cut design of BJT and CMOS two-stage op amps was illustrated. This step should be followed by an extensive simulation of the design and the optimization of its performance. The CMOS two-stage op amp is unable to drive large capacitive loads, which led to the introduction of the cascode architectures. An example of a first-cut design for a CMOS folded cascode op amp was presented. This was followed by the addition of an output stage to permit the op amp to drive low resistive loads. Finally, the configuration and techniques useful in simulating and measuring the performance of op amps has been discussed.

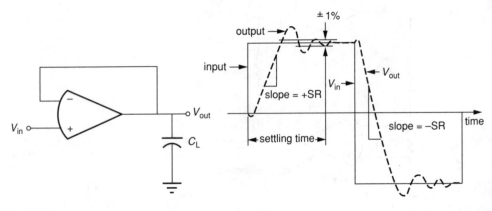

FIGURE 6.5-21
Measurement/simulation of slew rate and settling time.

The reader should be cautioned that the material presented was selected to give an appreciation for, and an introduction to, the subject of integrated circuit op amp design. The design of an actual op amp may deviate from the simplified examples considered in this section. If the reader is faced with the task of designing an op amp for a sophisticated application, this material is a good starting place. It should be followed by a careful reading of the technical literature — in particular, pertinent articles in the *IEEE Journal of Solid State Circuits* and some of the references cited in this section.

6.6 COMPARATORS

In many signal processing applications, the ability to compare two signals and identify which is larger is very important. A *comparator* is a circuit that compares one analog signal with another. The output of the comparator depends on which input signal is larger. Figure 6.6-1 shows the symbol for a comparator. We note that it has two inputs and one output.

6.6.1 Characterization of Comparators

The ideal operation of the comparator is illustrated by Fig. 6.6-2. In Fig. 6.6-2a, a noninverting comparator is shown. This characteristic can be described as

$$V_{\text{OUT}} = \begin{cases} V_{\text{OH}} & V_{\text{P}} \geq V_{\text{N}} \\ V_{\text{OL}} & V_{\text{P}} < V_{\text{N}} \end{cases} \qquad (6.6\text{-}1)$$

where V_{OH} is the upper limit and V_{OL} is the lower limit of the output voltage of the comparator. The comparator of Fig. 6.6-2a is called *noninverting* because the output goes from the low state to the high state when the voltage V_{P} becomes larger than V_{N}. Figure 6.6-2b shows an inverting comparator. This type of comparator can be described as

$$V_{\text{OUT}} = \begin{cases} V_{\text{OL}} & V_{\text{P}} \geq V_{\text{N}} \\ V_{\text{OH}} & V_{\text{P}} < V_{\text{N}} \end{cases} \qquad (6.6\text{-}2)$$

where the output goes from the high state to the low state when the voltage V_{P} becomes larger than V_{N}.

The comparator characteristics of Fig. 6.6-2 are ideal in the sense that they require the comparator to have infinite gain during the output transition. Figure

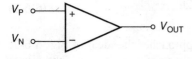

FIGURE 6.6-1
Circuit symbol for a comparator.

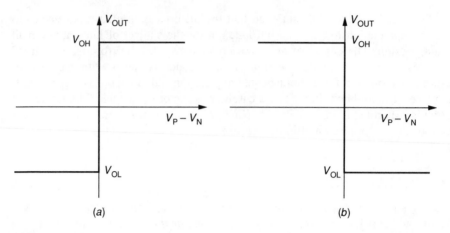

FIGURE 6.6-2
Ideal voltage transfer characteristics of: (*a*) A noninverting comparator, (*b*) An inverting comparator.

6.6-3 shows the transfer characteristics for comparators that do not have infinite gain. The noninverting comparator is described by

$$V_{OUT} = \begin{cases} V_{OH} & (V_P - V_N) > V_{IH} \\ A_v(V_P - V_N) & V_{IL} \leq (V_P - V_N) \leq V_{IH} \\ V_{OL} & (V_P - V_N) < V_{IL} \end{cases} \qquad (6.6\text{-}3)$$

where V_{IL} and V_{IH} represent the values of $(V_P - V_N)$ at which the output is at V_{OL} and V_{OH}, respectively, as $|V_P - V_N|$ is increased from zero. The inverting comparator is shown in Fig. 6.6-3*b* and is described as

$$V_{OUT} = \begin{cases} V_{OL} & (V_P - V_N) > V_{IH} \\ -A_v(V_P - V_N) & V_{IL} \leq (V_P - V_N) \leq V_{IH} \\ V_{OH} & (V_P - V_N) < V_{IL} \end{cases} \qquad (6.6\text{-}4)$$

The performance of a comparator can be characterized by its (1) resolving capability or threshold sensing, (2) input offset voltage, (3) speed or propagation delay time, and (4) input common-mode range. The *resolving capability* of a comparator is defined in terms of Fig. 6.6-3 as $V_{IH} - V_{IL}$. It is easy to see that the resolving capability of a comparator is related to its gain. Assuming that V_{OH} and V_{OL} are fixed by power supply limits, the resolving capability, ΔV, can be expressed as

$$\Delta V = \frac{V_{OH} - V_{OL}}{A_v} \qquad (6.6\text{-}5)$$

As A_v becomes large, the resolving capability approaches the ideal of Fig. 6.6-2. The input offset voltage, V_{OS}, is the value of voltage applied between the inputs

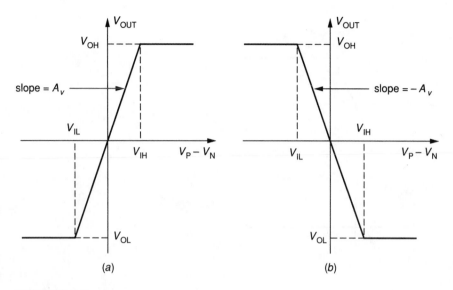

FIGURE 6.6-3
Practical voltage transfer characteristics of: (a) A noninverting
comparator, (b) An inverting comparator.

to make V_{OUT} equal to zero when V_P and V_N are connected together (i.e., the
comparator V_{OS} is the same as the op amp V_{OS}). Figure 6.6-4 shows the effect of
V_{OS} on the transfer characteristics of the noninverting comparator of Fig. 6.6-3a.

The *propagation time* of the comparator is a measure of how quickly the
output changes states after the input threshold has been reached. Figure 6.6-5
shows the time domain response of a noninverting comparator. The propagation

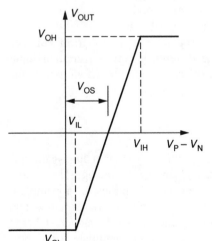

FIGURE 6.6-4
Practical noninverting voltage transfer characteristic
with input offset voltage illustrated.

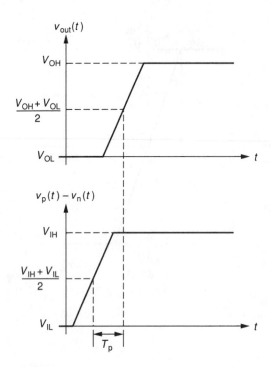

FIGURE 6.6-5
Time response for the practical noninverting comparator.

time, T_p, is the time between when $(V_P - V_N)$ is equal to zero, typically $0.5(V_{IH} + V_{IL})$, and when V_{OUT} is equal to $0.5(V_{OH} + V_{OL})$. This parameter is very important since it determines how many comparisons the comparator can make per unit of time. The propagation delay generally varies as a function of the slope, the amplitude of the input, and its common mode value. A larger input or a steeper slope will generally result in a smaller delay time.

The input common-mode range of the comparator is the range of voltages over which the inputs continue to sense the difference between applied input voltages. The resolving capability and input offset voltage are a function of the common-mode input voltage.

6.6.2 High-Gain Comparators

A comparator can be implemented by three methods: use of a high-gain differential amplifier, use of positive feedback, and charge balancing. The charge balancing comparator uses switches and a clock and functions as a comparator only at discrete periods of time. We will discuss only the first method and show how positive feedback can be used to enhance its performance. Charge balancing comparators are discussed elsewhere.[8,9] A good candidate for a comparator is the differential amplifier presented in Sec. 6.3. The key attribute of the differential amplifier is its ability to amplify the difference between the inverting and noninverting inputs over a wide common-mode range. As a result, the threshold point, or trip point, can be made independent of process and supply variations to a first order. The transfer curve describing the differential amplifier has been presented in Sec. 6.3. For the CMOS differential amplifier of Fig. 6.3-4c, the input common-mode range is given by Eqs. 6.3-40 and 6.3-44. The gain of this differential amplifier is given by Eq. 6.3-36 and was calculated as 103 if $K_N' = 24$ $\mu A/V^2$, $W_1/L_1 = 1$, $\lambda_N = \lambda_P = 0.01$, and $I_{SS} = 10$ μA. If it is assumed that the difference between V_{OH} and V_{OL} is 5 V, then the resolving capability is about 32 mV. If W_1/L_1 is increased to 10, the resolving capability is 10 mV. The BJT differential amplifier of Fig. 6.3-11 is a good implementation of a comparator. Because of the larger gain, the resolving capability is better than that of the CMOS differential amplifier of Fig. 6.3-4c. Assuming $V_{AN} = 100$ V, $V_{AP} = 50$ V, and $V_{OH} - V_{OL} = 5$ V, then the BJT differential amplifier has a gain of 1333 which gives a resolving capability of 3.75 mV.

The input offset voltage of the differential amplifier is due to the mismatches in the devices. Mismatches of this type are unavoidable and result from imperfections in the process. Offsets can be minimized by using a common-centroid geometry layout. Figure 6.6-6 illustrates a common-centroid geometry for a CMOS differential amplifier. It is also desirable to keep the number of bends and corners in the layout to a minimum for the two devices that must match. Typical offsets in the differential amplifier range from 5 to 15 mV for CMOS and from 3 to 10 mV for bipolar. The input offset voltage can be reduced by using large areas for the devices and by keeping the gate-source voltages small.

The propagation time of the differential amplifier used as a comparator is due to the pole at the output. Using Fig. 6.3-15b and ignoring the doublet gives a step response of

$$v_0(t) = V_0\left[1 - \exp\left(\frac{-t}{\tau_2}\right)\right]$$ (6.6-6)

where τ_2 is equal to R_2C_2 of Fig. 6.3-15b and V_0 is the final value of the output. The time at which $v_0(t)$ is 50% of V_0 is equal to $0.69\tau_2$. Assuming that the rise time of the input step is zero gives the propagation delay of the differential amplifier comparator as

$$T_p \approx 0.69\tau_2 = 0.69R_2C_2$$ (6.6-7)

Using the values $R_2 = 1$ MΩ and $C_2 = 0.7$ pF for the CMOS differential amplifier comparator gives a propagation delay of 0.43 μs. Using values of $R_2 = 0.67$ MΩ and $C_2 = 7$ pF for the BJT differential amplifier comparator gives a propagation delay time of 3.23 μs. The load capacitance seen by the differential amplifier comparator will greatly influence the propagation delay time. It will be seen that the propagation delay time may be determined by the large signal response (slew rate) rather than the linear step response.

The gain of most CMOS differential amplifier comparators is too small to give satisfactory resolving capability. In order to increase the gain, we turn to the

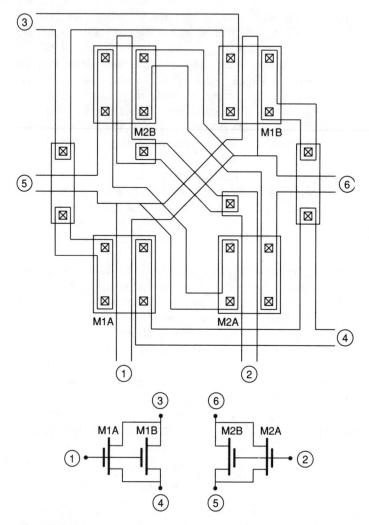

FIGURE 6.6-6
Cross-coupled transistor pair having a common-centroid geometry.

two-stage op amp as a possible architecture for a CMOS comparator. Consider the two-stage CMOS comparator shown in Fig. 6.6-7. It will be assumed that the bulk-source voltages of M1 and M2 are zero (i.e., M1 and M2 are in a floating p-well). This circuit should be designed so that all devices are in saturation. This can be achieved if M1 and M2 are matched and if M3 and M4 are matched and if $V_{SG3} = V_{SG4} = V_{SG5}$. Using these guidelines, we can establish design rules for transistor sizes in this circuit. In order to keep the circuit balanced, M1 and M2, and M3 and M4 must be matched. If the input is balanced, then when V_P and V_N are equal, the current flowing in M7 is split equally through M1 and M2. As a result, we have the following relationships.

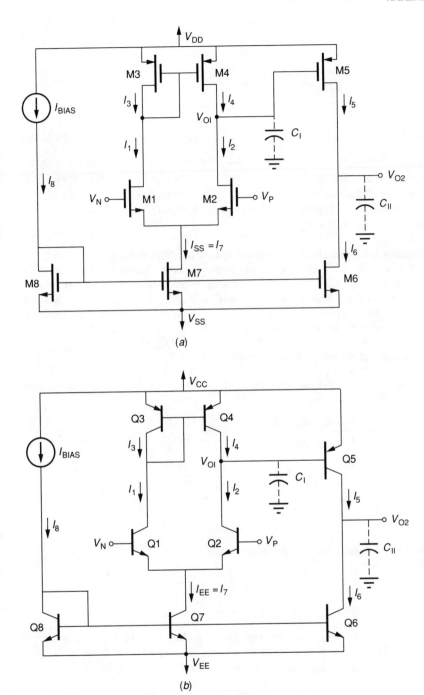

FIGURE 6.6-7
Two-stage comparators. (a) CMOS, (b) BJT.

$$\frac{W_1}{L_1} = \frac{W_2}{L_2} \qquad (6.6\text{-}8)$$

$$\frac{W_3}{L_3} = \frac{W_4}{L_4} \qquad (6.6\text{-}9)$$

and

$$I_1 = I_2 = 0.5I_7 = I_{SS} \qquad (6.6\text{-}10)$$

These relationships together with Eq. 6.5-40 completely describe the constraints necessary to achieve the desired balance conditions. Unfortunately, there will always be current mismatches in the current mirrors, which will lead to systematic offset (as opposed to a statistical device mismatch offset). This systematic offset is investigated in the following example.

Example 6.6-1. Calculation of systematic offset. The two-stage comparator of Fig. 6.6-7a with the following device sizes has been designed using Eqs. 6.6-8–6.6-10 and Eq. 6.5-40: $W_1/L_1 = W_2/L_2 = 20\ \mu/10\ \mu$, $W_3/L_3 = W_4/L_4 = 20\ \mu/10\ \mu$, $W_5/L_5 = 40\ \mu/10\ \mu$, $W_6/L_6 = 10\ \mu/10\ \mu$, $W_7/L_7 = 10\ \mu/10\ \mu$. Assume that $V_{DD} = 10$ V, $V_{SS} = 0$ V, $V_{DS7} = 3$ V, and $V_{DS3} = V_{DS4} = 2$ V. The pertinent process parameters are $K'_N = 24.75\ \mu\text{A/V}^2$, $K'_P = 10.13\ \mu\text{A/V}^2$, $|V_{TO}| = 1$ V, $\gamma_N = \gamma_P = 0.5\ \text{V}^{1/2}$, $\lambda_N = 0.015\ \text{V}^{-1}$, and $\lambda_P = 0.02\ \text{V}^{-1}$. Find the systematic offset voltage at the input of the comparator.

Solution. Assuming the bias current in M7 is 20 μA gives the following current ratios (see Sec. 5.4).

$$\frac{I_6}{I_7} = \left(\frac{1 + \lambda_N V_{DS6}}{1 + \lambda_N V_{DS4}}\right)\left(\frac{W_6/L_6}{W_7/L_7}\right) = \left[\frac{1 + (0.015)(5)}{1 + (0.015)(2)}\right](1) = 1.029$$

$$\frac{I_5}{I_4} = \left(\frac{1 + \lambda_P V_{DS5}}{1 + \lambda_P V_{DS4}}\right)\left(\frac{W_5/L_5}{W_4/L_4}\right) = \left[\frac{1 + (0.020)(5)}{1 + (0.020)(2)}\right](2) = 2.115$$

and

$$I_7 = 2I_4$$

Thus, the currents I_6 and I_5 can be expressed as

$$I_6 = (1.029)(2)I_4 = 2.058I_4$$

and

$$I_5 = 2.115I_4$$

Since I_5 is greater than I_6, then the current in M5 must be reduced. Next we determine by how much V_{GS5} must be reduced in order to make I_5 equal I_6. The method for accomplishing this is expressed by the following relationship.

$$\Delta V_{GS6} = \left[\frac{2L_5}{K_5 W_5}\right]^{1/2}\left[(I_6)^{1/2} - (I_5)^{1/2}\right] = -14.1 \text{ mV}$$

It can be shown that the voltage gain of the differential amplifier is 81.32. Dividing this value into ΔV_{GS6} gives the systematic offset at the input of the comparator as $|V_{OS}| = 0.174$ mV.

The two-stage BJT op amp is also suitable for use as a comparator. In many cases, the higher gain of the BJT differential amplifier comparator makes it unnecessary to turn to the two-stage architecture. We can note that if the two-stage comparator only switches from V_{OH} to V_{OL} or from V_{OL} to V_{OH}, that compensation is not necessary.

The performance of the input common-mode range of the two-stage BJT and CMOS comparators is identical to that of the BJT and CMOS differential amplifiers of Sec. 6.3. For the CMOS two-stage comparator, a procedure for designing the input stage for a specific common-mode input range is to size M3 to meet the maximum input requirement and design the sizes of M1 and M2 to meet the minimum input requirement. The input common-mode range limits for the CMOS differential amplifier were given in Eqs. 6.3-40 and 6.3-42. These limits, according to the device numbering in Fig. 6.6-7, are

$$V_{G1}(\text{max}) = V_{DD} - \left[\frac{I_7}{\beta_3}\right]^{1/2} - \mid V_{TO3} \mid -V_{T1} \qquad (6.6\text{-}11)$$

where $\beta_3 - K'_P(W_3/L_3)$ and

$$V_{G1}(\text{min}) \simeq V_{TO7} + V_{TO1} + V_{G7} \qquad (6.6\text{-}12)$$

However, since V_{G7} is not known, it is more convenient to express Eq. 6.6-12 as

$$V_{G1}(\text{min}) \simeq V_{SS} + V_{DS7} + \left[\frac{I_7}{\beta_1}\right]^{1/2} + V_{T1} \qquad (6.6\text{-}13)$$

where $\beta_1 = K'_N(W_1/L_1)$. An example will be given to illustrate the design of the input stage for a specified input common-mode range.

Example 6.6-2. Designing for a specified input common-mode range. Using the circuit of Fig. 6.6-7a, size the transistors M1 through M4 for an input common-mode range of 1.5 to 9 V with $V_{DD} = 10$ V and $V_{SS} = 0$ V.

Solution. Assume the same device parameters as used in Example 6.6-1, except that the magnitude of the p-channel and n-channel threshold voltages vary from 0.4 to 1.0 V, $I_7 = 20\ \mu\text{A}$, and $V_{DS}(\text{sat}) = 0.1$ V. Using Eq. 6.6-13 with $V_{G1}(\text{min}) = 1.5$ V, $V_{DS7} = 0.1$ V and $V_{T1} = 1$ V (worst case), we get $\beta_1 = 125\ \mu\text{A/V}^2$, which gives $W_1/L_1 = W_2/L_2 = 5.05$. Using Eq. 6.6-11 with $V_{G1}(\text{max}) = 9$ V and worst-case threshold voltages gives $\beta_3 = 125\ \mu\text{A/V}^2$, which gives $W_3/L_3 = W_4/L_4 = 12.34$.

6.6.3 Propagation Delay of Two-Stage Comparators

In completing the design of the two-stage CMOS comparator, the gain of the comparator will be achieved by the geometry and dc current of M5. The remaining characteristic to be examined is the propagation delay of the two-stage comparator. Since the comparator is made up of two stages, the total delay is determined by adding the propagation delays of each stage together. Figure 6.6-7 shows the

CMOS and BJT two-stage comparators and the two parasitic capacitors that will be the primary source of the propagation delay. These capacitors are the same ones used in Fig. 6.5-6b. C_c was not included in Fig. 6.5-6a because the comparators are not usually compensated since they do not normally operate in the linear range. Compensation is only necessary when negative feedback is applied around the comparator. The analysis for the propagation delay of the two-stage comparator is based on the waveforms illustrated in Fig. 6.6-8. The delay for the first stage is the time required for V_{OI} to go from its quiescent state (V_{OHI} or V_{OLI}) to the trip point (V_{TRP2}) of the second stage. The delay for the second stage is the time required for V_{OII} to go from its quiescent state (V_{OHII} or V_{OLII}) to the trip point of the load circuit, which will be assumed to be $0.5(V_{OHII} + V_{OLII})$.

We will consider the propagation delay time for both the BJT and CMOS two-stage comparators simultaneously. It is seen that the propagation delay time for a rising output (T_p^+) will be different from the propagation delay time for a falling output (T_p^-). As a result, we will define the propagation delay time of a comparator (T_p) as the average of T_p^+ and T_p^-. First, let us assume that the output of the comparator is falling and develop an expression for T_p^-. It will be assumed that the difference between V_P and V_N is large enough that M2 (Q2) is off and all of I_7 goes through M1 (Q1). Therefore, the current available to

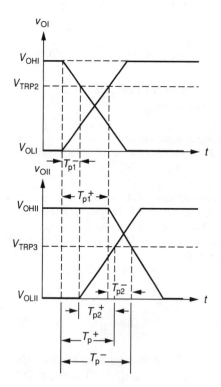

FIGURE 6.6-8
The slewing waveforms at the output of each stage of the two-stage comparator.

charge C_I from V_{OLI} to V_{OHI} is I_7. Thus, the rising propagation delay for the first stage (T_{p1}^+) is

$$T_{p1}^+ = C_I \frac{V_{TRP2} - V_{OLI}}{I_7} \qquad (6.6\text{-}14)$$

Similarly, the propagation delay time for the falling output of the second stage is

$$T_{p2}^- = C_{II} \frac{V_{OHII} - V_{OLII}}{2I_5} \qquad (6.6\text{-}15)$$

Adding Eqs. 6.6-14 and 6.6-15 together results in

$$T_p^- = C_I \frac{V_{TRP2} - V_{OLI}}{I_7} + C_{II} \frac{V_{OHII} - V_{OLII}}{2I_5} \qquad (6.6\text{-}16)$$

The trip point at the input of stage 2 for the BJT is approximately $V_t \ln (I_{BIAS}/I_s)$. I_{BIAS} is the bias current in the second stage, Q6. The trip point for the CMOS output stage is found by equating the currents in M5 and M6, assuming both devices are saturated. The result is

$$\frac{\beta_5}{2}[V_{GS5} - V_{T5}]^2 = I_6 = I_5 \qquad (6.6\text{-}17)$$

where $\beta_5 = K'_P(W_S/L_S)$ which gives a trip point of

$$V_{TRP2} = V_{DD} - V_{GS5} = V_{DD} - V_{T5} - \left[\frac{2I_5}{\beta_5}\right]^{1/2} \qquad (6.6\text{-}18)$$

The propagation delay time for a positive-going output is similar, except that the current source charging C_{II} is not limited by the dc value of I_5. The falling propagation delay time for the input stage is given as

$$T_{p1}^- = C_I \frac{V_{OHI} - V_{TRP2}}{I_7} \qquad (6.6\text{-}19)$$

The rising propagation delay time is given by

$$T_{p2}^+ = C_{II} \frac{V_{OHII} - V_{OLII}}{2I_5(\text{max})} \qquad (6.6\text{-}20)$$

where $I_5(\text{max})$ is the current M5 or Q5 can source to C_{II} when the gate or base is taken low. In order to find $I_5(\text{max})$, one must know the value of V_{GS5}. Obviously, the value of V_{GS5} will be somewhere between V_{TRP2} and V_{OLI}. Let us approximate V_{GS5} as halfway between V_{OHI} and V_{OLI}. This gives $I_5(\text{max})$ for the CMOS comparator as

$$I_5(\text{max}) \simeq \frac{\beta_5}{2}\left[\frac{V_{OHI} - V_{OLI}}{2} - V_{T5}\right]^2 \qquad (6.6\text{-}21)$$

For the BJT comparator, $I_5(\text{max})$ is

$$I_5(\text{max}) \simeq \beta_F 5 I_7 \qquad (6.6\text{-}22)$$

With this interpretation of $I_5(\text{max})$, the rising propagation delay time of the two-stage comparator is

$$T_p^+ = C_I \frac{V_{OHI} - V_{TRP2}}{I_7} + C_{II} \frac{V_{OHII} - V_{OLII}}{2I_5(\text{max})} \tag{6.6-23}$$

An example will illustrate the use of these relationships.

Example 6.6-3. Calculation of the propagation delay time for the two-stage comparator. Calculate the propagation time for the CMOS and BJT two-stage comparators of Fig. 6.6-7. Let $V_{DD} = -V_{SS} = 5$ V, $V_{OLI} = -3$ V, $V_{OHI} = 4$ V, $V_{OHII} = 4$ V, and $V_{OLII} = -4$ V. Using the values $C_{gs} = 0.2$ pF, $C_{ds} = 0.1$ pF, and $C_L = 0.5$ pF and assuming the model values of $K_P' = 12.5$ μA/V^2 and $W_5/L_5 = 4.5$. Let $V_{CC} = -V_{EE} = 5$ V, $V_{OHI} = -V_{OLI} = 4.7$ V and $V_{OHII} = -V_{OLII} = 4.5$ V. Furthermore, let us assume that $\beta_{F5} = 100$, $I_{s5} = 0.01$ pA, $C_\mu = 0.2$ pF, $C_\pi = 2$ pF, $C_{CS} = 0.4$ pF, and $C_L = 3$ pF.

Solution. Let us first consider the CMOS two-stage comparator. From Eqs. 6.6-18 and 6.6-21, the values of $V_{TRP2} = 2.67$ V and $I_5(\text{max}) = 112.5$ μA. From Eqs. 6.6-14 and 6.6-15, we obtain the values $T_{p1}^+ = 0.227$ μs and $T_{p2}^- = 0.056$ μs. Using Eq. 6.6-16 gives the falling propagation delay time as $T_p^- = 0.283$ μs. From Eqs. 6.6-19 and 6.6-20, we get $T_{p1}^- = 0.0132$ μs and $T_{p2}^+ = 0.0249$ μs. This gives a rising propagation delay time of 0.038 μs. The average propagation delay time is $T_p = 0.161$ μs. It is seen that the fastest transition of the CMOS comparator is for a rising output.

Next let us consider the BJT two-stage comparator. V_{TRP2} is equal to $V_{CC} - V_t \ln (I_5/I_{s5})$, which is 4.482 V. $I_5(\text{max})$ is equal to 1 mA from Eq. 6.6-22. From Eqs. 6.5-10 and 6.5-13 we find that $C_I = 3$ pF and $C_{II} = 3.8$ pF. Assuming $I_5 = 200$ μA and $I_7 = 40$ μA in Eqs. 6.6-14 through 6.6-16 gives $T_{p1}^+ = 0.69$ μs, $T_{p2}^- = 0.086$ μs, and $T_p^- = 0.775$ μs. Equations 6.6-19, 6.6-20, and 6.6-23 give $T_{p1}^- = 0.0164$ μs, $T_{p2}^+ = 0.0043$ μs, and $T_p^+ = 0.021$ μs. The average propagation delay time of the BJT two-stage comparator is found as $T_p = 0.398$ μs.

We note two things of interest about the two-stage comparator. First, as illustrated in Example 6.6-3, the propagation delay time for a falling output is different from the propagation delay time for a rising output. The reason is due to the value of V_{TRP2}. In both cases, V_{TRP2} is very close to the value of V_{OHI}, which minimizes the delay of the first stage. In addition, the ability to source more output current than sinking current at the output of the second stage reduces the delay time of the second stage. Therefore, two methods that will reduce the propagation delay time of a two-stage comparator are increasing the current sinking/sourcing capability and reducing the signal swings. Of course, smaller values of C_I and C_{II} will reduce the propagation delay times.

Another form of comparator is the *clamped comparator*, shown in Fig. 6.6-9. This comparator architecture attempts to reduce the propagation delay time by keeping the output swing of the first stage clamped. Closer examination of Fig. 6.6-9 shows that only the drains (collectors) of the output devices M5 and M6 (Q5 and Q6) have a large difference between V_{OH} and V_{OL}. Consequently, the propagation delay for the first stage is greatly reduced. While this comparator

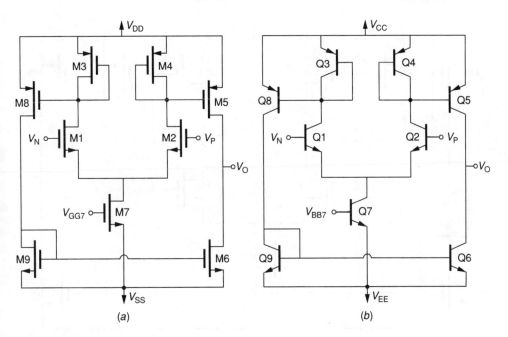

FIGURE 6.6-9
Two-stage clamped comparators: (*a*) CMOS, (*b*) BJT.

architecture reduces the propagation delay time, the overall comparator gain is reduced. Since the effective load devices of the input differential amplifier are smaller, the gain is significantly reduced. In fact, the voltage gain of the first stage will be approximately equal to the ratio of the transconductances of M1 (Q1) and M3 (Q3).

The use of weak positive feedback to overcome the low gain of the clamped comparator can result in satisfactory gain and minimized propagation delay time. One possible implementation is shown in Fig. 6.6-10, where M10 and M11 (Q10 and Q11) have introduced positive feedback paths between the outputs of the differential amplifier. The amount of positive feedback must be less than unity so that the stage still acts like a linear stage as a result of overall negative feedback provided by the source (emitter) connections of the input transistors M1 and M2 (Q1 and Q2).

6.6.4 Comparators Using Positive Feedback

The second approach to implementing comparators uses strong positive feedback or regenerative techniques. This approach is similar to that used in sense amplifiers for memories. Figure 6.6-11 shows a flip-flop with storage capacitors to ground at each output. The circuit works as follows. Assume that the strobe is low, so that M5 (Q5) is off. The flip-flop, consisting of M1 through M4 (Q1 through Q4), is deactivated since no current can flow through any of the devices. This mode

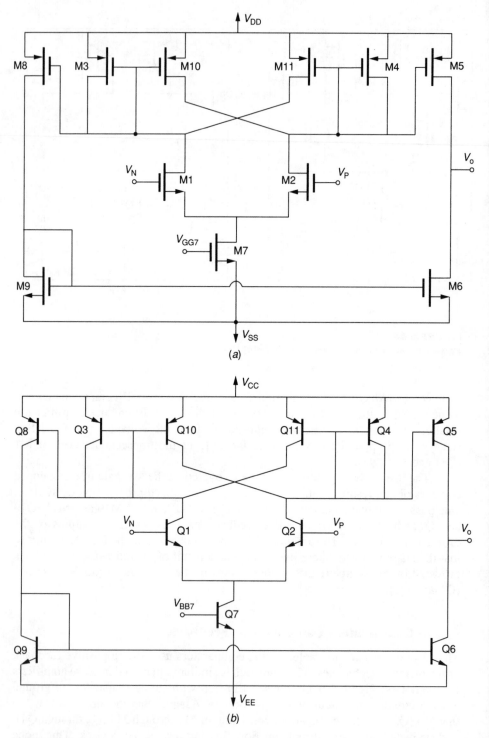

FIGURE 6.6-10
Two-stage, cross-coupled clamped comparator: (a) CMOS, (b) BJT.

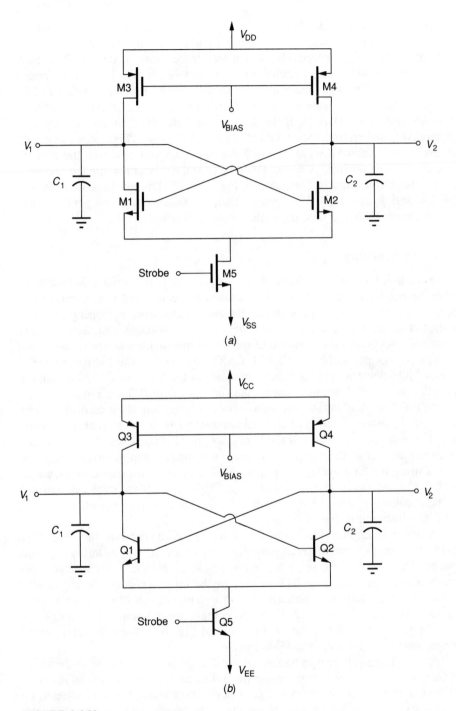

FIGURE 6.6-11
Strobed flip-flop: (a) CMOS, (b) BJT.

is called the *memory mode,* because the capacitors C_1 and C_2 will "remember" the states of V_1 and V_2. During this time, C_1 and C_2 can also be changed to new values of V_1 and V_2, respectively. When the strobe turns on the flip-flop, then it will go to the state corresponding to the values of V_1 and V_2. For example, if V_1 is greater than V_2, then when the strobe (clock) pulse is applied to M5 (Q5), the voltage at the gate (base) of M2 (Q2) will be higher than the voltage at the gate (base) of M1 (Q1). If the devices are matched, then the flip-flop will regeneratively switch to the state with V_1 high and V_2 low. This circuit can detect differences in V_1 and V_2 within 5 to 10 mV depending on how well the devices in the circuit are matched. A circuit showing how the clocks are applied and how the outputs are buffered is illustrated in Fig. 6.6-12. During the sample mode, ϕ_1 is low and ϕ_2 is high. If V_2 is greater than V_1, then the logic output Q is true. If V_1 is greater than V_2, then the logic output $\overline{Q}$ is true.

6.6.5 Autozeroing

One of the more serious problems of all comparators is the input offset voltage. Clever design techniques and careful layout can reduce but not eliminate the effects of offset. In most applications, the comparator does not operate continuously but rather makes a comparison between two voltages and then is reset. During the reset phase, it is possible to apply a technique called *autozeroing.* This technique works particularly well with CMOS because of the high input resistance of MOS devices. This is rather fortunate, as the offset of CMOS circuits is typically a factor of 2 or more worse than for equivalent BJT circuits.

Figure 6.6-13 illustrates an input offset voltage canceling algorithm. The comparator is shown in terms of an ideal comparator with an external offset voltage in Fig. 6.6-13*a*. A polarity is arbitrarily assigned for purposes of convenience. It is also assumed that the comparator works on a nonoverlapping two-phase clock cycle. During the first cycle, designated ϕ_1, the offset is measured as shown in Fig. 6.6-13*b* and stored in a capacitor, C_{AZ}. During the second cycle, designated ϕ_2, the capacitor is connected in such a manner as to cancel the effects of the offset, as illustrated in Fig. 6.6-13*c*.

A practical implementation of an autozeroed comparator is shown in Fig. 6.6-14. During ϕ_1, the offset is sampled and stored in C_{AZ}. During ϕ_2, the capacitor C_{AZ} is connected in such a manner as to cancel the offset voltage. The comparator can be CMOS or BJT as long as the input resistance is sufficiently large so that C_{AZ} does not discharge during ϕ_2. Figure 6.6-15*a* shows the configuration modified for the case where the comparator is noninverting and V_N is zero. Figure 6.6-15*b* shows the modification of Fig. 6.6-14 for the case where the comparator is inverting and V_P is zero.

Although the autozero technique seems like the perfect solution to the offset problem, it does not completely remove the influence of offset for several reasons. The first is that when the MOS switches open and close, charge is injected or removed by the large clock swings on the gates of the switches. Second, the capacitor C_{AZ} will lose some of its charge during the ϕ_2 phase. Third, if the offset is completely canceled for a given common-mode value of V_P and V_N

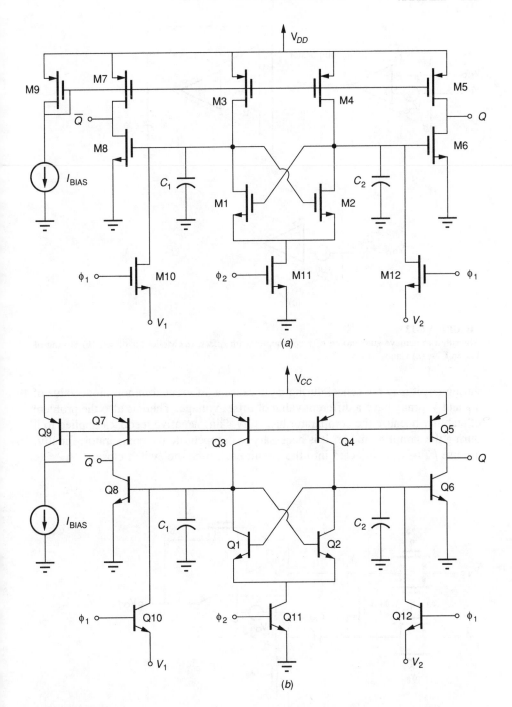

FIGURE 6.6-12
Sense amplifier used as a comparator: (*a*) CMOS, (*b*) BJT.

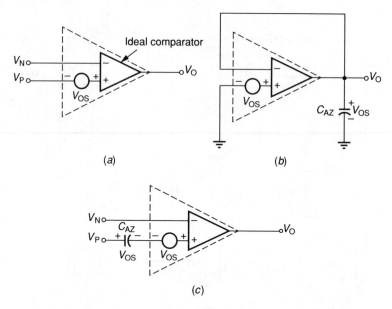

(a)

(b)

(c)

FIGURE 6.6-13
Algorithm to achieve autozeroing of a comparator with offset: (a) Model for offset, (b) Storing of V_{OS} in C_{AZ}, (c) Cancellation of V_{OS}.

during ϕ_1, it may not cancel during ϕ_2 because a different common-mode value of V_P and V_N may have a different value of offset voltage. There is also the problem of stability because the comparator has unity gain, negative feedback applied to it during the sampling mode. It is necessary to compensate the comparator. Finally, a noise kT/C_{AZ} is injected into the circuit each time the switch closes.

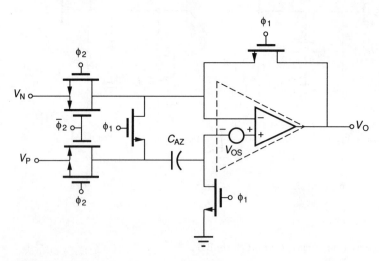

FIGURE 6.6-14
Practical implementation of an autozeroed comparator.

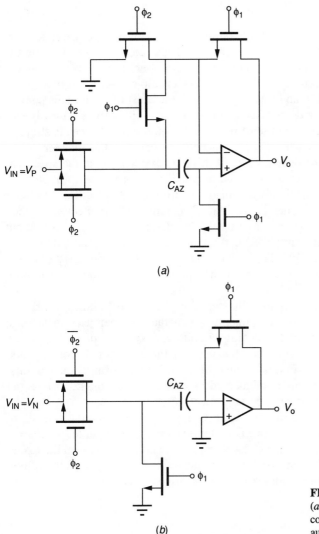

(a)

(b)

FIGURE 6.6-15
(a) Noninverting autozeroed comparator, (b) Inverting autozeroed comparator.

The design principles of voltage comparators and various architectures that can be employed have been presented in this section. The important parameters of the comparator are its resolving capability, its input offset voltage, its propagation delay time, and its common-mode input range. The performance of the various circuits was related to these parameters. Except for the considerations of propagation delay time, the comparator requirements were found to be similar to those of the op amp. The comparators in this section represent simple but practical designs. This section represents the starting point in the design of more complex comparators. It should allow the designer the ability to select the design most suitable for the specification. The next step is a thorough simulation of the comparator using a simulator.

6.7 SUMMARY

Basic circuits that form the high-level building blocks of analog integrated circuit design have been presented in this chapter. These circuit blocks include the inverter, the differential amplifier, the output amplifier, the op amp, and the comparator. Design procedures, principles, and examples were given for each type of circuit for both BJT and CMOS technologies. Most of the circuits considered used n-channel or npn devices as the input devices. This choice typically will lead to better performance. The use of p-channel or pnp input devices is straightforward and exactly follows the design concepts presented in this chapter.

It was shown that the design cycle of these blocks starts with the specifications of the circuit performance. Next, an architecture is proposed to implement the circuit. This architecture is always made up from building blocks or circuit blocks with which the designer is familiar. The proposed architecture is then analyzed (typically by hand) and modified by the designer, leading to a first-cut design. This design is then simulated with much more accuracy and detail using a circuit simulator such as SPICE2. The simulation is a very important part of the design cycle and is where the designer can explore process parameter variation and second-order effects.

The circuits presented in this chapter along with the building blocks of Chapter 5 form the blocks or components which the designer uses to achieve a circuit realization. Most of the analog circuits and systems presented in the remainder of this text are simply combinations of these blocks or components. In fact, some of the circuits in this chapter are combinations of previous circuits. For example, the op amp was implemented as a combination of the differential amplifier and the inverter or cascode amplifier.

The material presented in this chapter represents the simplest level of design because of limited space. In many applications, these simple circuits are sufficient. The basic design sequence has been illustrated and has given the reader an appreciation for the design process. This material should be a good starting point in the design of more complex analog integrated circuits.

REFERENCES

1. J. E. Solomon: "The Monolithic Op Amp: A Tutorial Study," *IEEE J. of Solid-State Circuits*, vol. SC-9, no. 6, pp. 314–332, December 1974.
2. B. K. Ahuja, W. M. Baxter, and P. R. Gray: "A Programmable CMOS Dual Channel Interface Processor," *IEEE Inter. Solid State Circuits Conf.*, pp. 232–233, 1984.
3. P. R. Gray and R. G. Meyer: *Analysis and Design of Analog Integrated Circuits*, 2nd ed., John Wiley & Sons, New York, 1984.
4. P. R. Gray and R. G. Meyer: "Recent Advances in Monolithic Operational Amplifier Design," *IEEE Trans. Circuits and Systems*, vol. CAS-21, pp. 317–327, May 1974.
5. P. R. Gray: "Basic MOS Operational Amplifier Design—An Overview," in *Analog MOS Integrated Circuits*, IEEE Press/John Wiley & Sons, New York, pp. 28–49, 1980.
6. P. E. Allen and D. R. Holberg: *CMOS Analog Circuit Design*, Holt, Rinehart & Winston, New York, 1987.
7. R. Gregorian and G. C. Temes: *Analog MOS Integrated Circuits*, John Wiley & Sons, New York, 1987.

8. Y. S. Lee, L. M. Terman, and L. G. Heller: "A 1mV MOS Comparator," *IEEE J. of Solid State Circuits*, vol. SC-16 no. 2, pp. 109–113, April 1981.
9. P. E. Allen and E. Sánchez–Sinencio: *Switched Capacitor Circuits*, Van Nostrand Reinhold Co., New York, 1984.

PROBLEMS

Section 6.1

6.1 Assume that Eq. 6.1-1, which corresponds to the circuit of Fig. 6.1-3a, is given as

$$I_O = V_{IX}^2 + \frac{V_{OX}}{100}$$

and that

$$I_L = \frac{V_P - V_{OUT}}{100}$$

Solve for the small signal voltage gain when $V_{IN} = V_{OUT} = 0$ V.

6.2 Use the relationships given in Prob. 6.1 and develop a linear small signal model similar to that of Fig. 6.1-6. Assuming $V_{IN} = V_{OUT} = 0$ V, find the small signal voltage gain.

6.3 Assume that $r_1 = 1$ MΩ, $r_2 = 100$ kΩ, $C_1 = 1$ pF, $C_2 = 1$ pF, and $g_m = 0.001$ S. Find the root (poles and zero) locations if $C_3 = 0$ and $C_3 = 1$ pF for the circuit of Fig. 6.1-8.

6.4 Repeat Example 6.1-1 if $W_1/L_1 = 100 \ \mu/10 \ \mu$ and $W_2/L_2 = 5 \ \mu/10 \ \mu$.

6.5 Repeat Example 6.1-2 if $W_1/L_1 = W_2/L_2 = 10 \ \mu/10 \ \mu$.

6.6 Repeat Example 6.1-2 for the inverter of Fig. P6.6. Assume the active area extends 10 μ beyond the polysilicon.

6.7 Figure P6.7 shows several MOS inverters. Assume that $K_N = 2K_P$, that $\lambda_N = \lambda_P$, and that the dc bias current through each inverter is equal. Qualitatively select, without using extensive calculations, which inverter(s) has (a) the largest ac small signal gain, (b) the lowest ac small signal gain, (c) the highest ac output resistance, and (d) the lowest ac output resistance. Assume all devices are in saturation.

6.8 Repeat Example 6.1-4 for $V_{BB2} = 4.3$ V.

6.9 Repeat Example 6.1-4 for the BJT inverter of Fig. 6.1-18b.

6.10 Figure 6.1-18 shows two BJT inverters. If $V_{AFN} = 2V_{AFP}$ and $\beta_{FN} = 2\beta_{FP}$, which inverter has (a) the highest ac voltage gain, (b) the smallest ac voltage gain, (c) the

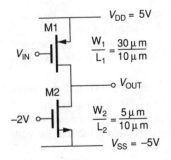

FIGURE P6.6

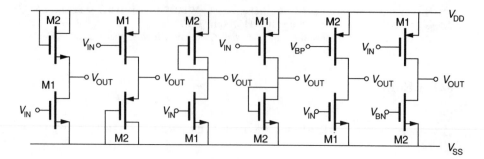

FIGURE P6.7

highest ac output resistance, and (d) the lowest ac output resistance. Assume that the bias currents are equal.

Section 6.2

6.11 Find the ac voltage gain and the output resistance for the circuit of Fig. 6.2-2 if the bias current is 100 μA, $W_1/L_1 = 100\ \mu/10\ \mu$, $W_2/L_2 = 100\ \mu/10\ \mu$, and $W_3/L_3 = 10\ \mu/10\ \mu$. Use the model parameters of Table 3.1-2 and assume all devices are saturated.

6.12 Repeat Example 6.2-1 with all W/L values equal to $20\ \mu/20\ \mu$.

6.13 Find the small signal voltage gain and output resistance for the circuit of Fig. 6.2-8 if $I_C = 1$ mA.

6.14 Repeat Prob. 6.13 for the circuit of Fig. 6.2-10.

Section 6.3

6.15 If the active loads of the circuit of Fig. 6.3-1 were replaced by identical drain–gate-connected enhancement n-channel transistors, sketch the large signal voltages, V_{D1} and V_{D2}, as a function of the differential input voltage V_{ID} if K_N' is 20 μA/V^2, $W_1/L_1 = W_2/L_2 = 10\ \mu/10\ \mu$, $W_3/L_3 = W_4/L_4 = 10\ \mu/40\ \mu$ (M3 and M4 are the drain–gate-connected active loads), and $I_{SS} = 50\ \mu$A. Assume $V_{DD} = 10$ V. Ignore the bulk effects of M3 and M4 in this problem.

6.16 Substitute Eq. 6.3-7 into Eq. 6.3-18 and develop an expression for V_{D1} as a function of V_{ID} as a function of $(\beta_1/I_{SS})^{1/2}V_{ID}$. Evaluate the large signal, differential to single-ended voltage gain at $V_{id} = 0$ V of Fig. 6.3-4a and compare with Eq. 6.3-20.

6.17 Develop expressions for the maximum and minimum input voltages, V_{G1}(max) and V_{G1}(min), for the differential amplifier of Fig. 6.3-4a assuming $V_{G1} = V_{G2}$. Develop expressions for the maximum and minimum output voltages, V_{D2}(max) and V_{D2}(min). Assume that these limits are found by keeping the appropriate devices in the saturation region.

6.18 Verify the small signal voltage gain, A_{vds} (Eqs. 6.3-20 and 6.3-28), and the output resistance, r_{out} (Eqs. 6.3-25 and 6.3-31) for the circuit of Fig. 6.3-4a and b.

6.19 Interchange the p-channel and n-channel devices in Fig. 6.3-4c. Assume that $W_1/L_1 = W_2/L_2$ and $I_5 = 10\ \mu$A. Using the parameters of Table 3.1-2 find the voltage gain, A_{vdd}, and output resistance, r_{out}.

6.20 Replace the current sink of Fig. 6.3-12b with the current mirror of Fig. 5.4-12a. I_{IN} is to be generated by connecting an arbitrary resistor to V_{DD}, and I_{OUT} is to be used as I_5. Develop an expression for the CMRR and compare with Eq. 6.3-49.

6.21 Assume that two equal resistors designated as R_E are placed between the emitters of Q1 and Q2 at point A in Fig. 6.3-9. Construct a plot similar to that of Fig. 6.3-10 of the normalized value of I_{C1} as a function of V_{ID}. Express the differential-in, single-ended-out transconductance for this case, g'_m, in terms of the transconductance, g_m, given by Eq. 6.3-55.

6.22 Find the small signal, differential-in, differential-out voltage gain, input differential resistance, and output resistance for the circuit of Fig. 6.3-11 if Q1 and Q2 are matched, Q3 and Q4 are matched, $I_{EE} = 100$ μA, $\beta_F = 100$, $V_{AFN} = 100$ V, and $V_{AFP} = 50$ V. Assume room temperature. Repeat for $I_{SS} = 10$ μA.

6.23 Verify the small signal expressions for A_{vds}, and A_{vc} and derive an expression for r_{out} and r_{id} of the circuit of Fig. 6.3-13.

6.24 Assume that $\lambda = 0.01$ V, $C_{gs} = 0.2$ pF, $C_{gd} = 0.1$ pF, and $C_L = 0.5$ pF for the MOS differential amplifier of Fig. 6.3-4b. Find the -3 dB frequency in Hertz and the low-frequency gain (A_{vds0}) if (a) $I_5 = 10$ μA and (b) $I_5 = 1$ mA.

6.25 Assume that $\beta_{FN} = 100$, $\beta_{FP} = 50$, $V_{AN} = 100$ V, $V_{AP} = 50$ V, $C_\mu = 1$ pF, $C_\pi = 2$ pF, $C_{CS} = 1$ pF, and $C_L = 5$ pF for the BJT differential amplifier of Fig. 6.3-11. Find the -3 dB frequency in Hertz and the low-frequency gain (A_{vds0}) if (a) $I_{EE} = 10$ μA and (b) $I_{EE} = 1$ mA.

6.26 Assume that the MOS differential amplifier of Fig. 6.3-4c has the parameters $K'_N = 2K'_P = 25$ $\mu A/V^2$, $\lambda = 0.01$ V, $W_1/L_1 = W_2/L_2 = 10$, $W_3/L_3 = W_4/L_4 = 1$, $C_{gs} = 0.2$ pF, $C_{gd} = 0.1$ pF, and $I_{SS} = 100$ μA. Find A_{vds0}, ω_1, ω'_1, and ω_2 defined in Eq. 6.3-84. Find the -3 dB frequency in Hertz for A_{vds}.

6.27 Assume that the BJT differential amplifier of Fig. 6.3-11 has the parameters of $\beta_F = 100$, $V_{AN} = 100$ V, $V_{AP} = 50$ V, $C_\pi = 5$ pF, $C_\mu = 1$ pF, and $I_{EE} = 100$ μA. Find A_{vds0}, ω_1, ω'_1, and ω_2 defined in Eq. 6.3-84. Find the -3 dB frequency in Hertz for A_{vds}.

Section 6.4

6.28 If the specifications of an output amplifier include the ability to output a voltage of ± 5 V and a slew rate of 10 V/μs, what is the maximum required output current if (a) $R_L = 10$ kΩ and $C_L = 50$ pF, (b) $R_L = 5$ kΩ and $C_L = 50$ pF, and (c) $R_L = 10$ kΩ and $C_L = 100$ pF?

6.29 If the dc bias current in a Class A amplifier is 400 μA and the power supplies are ± 5 V, find the signal power dissipated in a 10 kΩ load resistance for the maximum output sinusoidal signal. Calculate the power given by the power supplies and divide this value into the signal power to calculate the maximum efficiency of the Class A amplifier.

6.30 Use the small signal models for the MOS and BJT transistors to develop the expression given in Eqs. 6.4-24 and 6.4-25 for the circuit of Fig. 6.4-9a and b.

6.31 If the n-channel transistors in Fig. 6.4-9a have $K'_N = 25$ μA/V^2, $V_{TO} = 1$ V, $V_{GG2} = -3V_g$, $V_{DD} = -V_{SS} = 5$ V, $\gamma = 0.5$ V$^{1/2}$, $\phi_N = 0.6$ V , $W_1/L_1 = 10$, and $W_2/L_2 = 40$, find the maximum peak-to-peak output voltage swing if R_L is 10 kΩ, assuming that the gate of M1 can be driven to within 1 V of the $+5$ V power supply. What are the maximum positive and negative slew rates when the output voltage is passing through zero for a load capacitor of 50 pF (assuming that V_{IN} can be driven to $+4$ V)?

6.32 Show how the MOS differential amplifier of Fig. 6.3-4c can be used to implement the error amplifiers of Fig. 6.4-15a. Note that the implementation of one of the error amplifiers will require opposite-type devices. If all W/L ratios are 1 and each transistor has a bias current of 50 μA, calculate the loop gain and the small signal output resistance of the circuit of Fig. 6.1-15a if $K'_N = 2K'_P = 25$ μA/V^2.

Section 6.5

6.33 Assume that V_1 of Fig. 6.5-1 is zero and that a resistor R_1 is connected between a voltage source, V_{IN}, and V_2, and a resistor R_2 is connected from the output, V_O, back to the negative input of the op amp. Use the null port concept to find V_O/V_{IN}.

6.34 Repeat Prob. 6.33 if the resistor R_1 is connected from the negative input to the op amp to ground, and the voltage source, V_{IN}, is connected to the positive input of the op amp. R_2 is still connected between V_O and the negative input to the op amp.

6.35 Analyze the circuit of Fig. 6.5-6b and verify the expression given in Eq. 6.5-17. Use the techniques illustrated to derive the root locations as given in Eqs. 6.5-18, 6.5-19, and 6.5-20.

6.36 Determine the ratios of the emitter areas of Q6 to Q8 and Q7 to Q8 of Fig. 6.5-4a if I_{C1} is 5 μA and I_{C5} is 25 μA, and the 100 kΩ resistors are connected from the collector of Q8 to $V_{CC} = 5$ V and $V_{EE} = -5$ V.

6.37 For the two-stage BJT op amp, let $A_o = 100{,}000$, $R_{id} = 1$ MΩ, and $C_c = 20$ pF. Find I_{C1}, I_{C5}, GB (in MHz), and SR. Assume that the BJT parameters are $\beta_N = 200, \beta_P = 50, V_{AN} = 100$ V, and $V_{AP} = 50$ V. Give the ratios of the emitter area of Q6 to Q8 and Q7 to Q8, and determine the value of resistance to be connected from the collector of Q8 to V_{CC} if $V_{CC} = -V_{EE} = 5$ V.

6.38 Repeat Prob. 6.37 if each npn and pnp transistor is replaced with a pnp and a npn transistor, respectively.

6.39 On a log-log scale with the vertical axis running from 10^{-3} to 10^3 and the horizontal axis running from 1 μA to 100 μA, plot the low-frequency gain (A_o), the unity-gain bandwidth (GB), the power dissipation (P_d), the slew rate (SR), the output resistance (r_{out}), the magnitude of the dominant pole (p_1), and the magnitude of the RHP zero (z) normalized to their values at a bias current ($I_B = I_{DB}$) of 1 μA as a function of I_B for values of I_B from 1 μA to 100 μA for the CMOS two-stage op amp of Fig. 6.5-5a. Assume the op amp uses a Miller compensation capacitor, C_c, with no R_z.

6.40 If $W_1/L_1 = W_2/L_2 = 10\ \mu/10\ \mu$, complete the design of the two-stage CMOS op amp of Fig. 6.5-5a (i.e., find $W_3, L_3, W_4, L_4, W_5, L_5, C_c$, and R_z). Assume a minimum transistor dimension of 10 μ and use the smallest devices possible. The dc current is 100 μA in M7 and 200 μA in M8. The op amp is to have a low-frequency gain of 5000 and a unity-gain bandwidth of 1 MHz. In addition, all devices should be in saturation under normal operating conditions, and the effects of the RHP zero should be canceled. The pertinent model parameters are $K_N' = 2K_P' = 10\ \mu$A/V^2, $V_{TN} = -V_{TP} = 1$ V, and $\lambda_N = \lambda_P = 0.01$ V^{-1}. Estimate how much load capacitance, C_L, this amplifier should be able to drive without suffering a significant change in the phase margin. What is the slew rate of this op amp?

6.41 Find all currents in the circuit of Fig. P6.41, A_o, GB, SR, r_{out}, power dissipation (P_d), the dominant pole location (p_1), and the value of R_z required to cancel out the effects of the RHP zero. Assume $V_{DD} = -V_{SS} = 5$ V and $C_L = 10$ pF. The device parameters for this problem are $V_{TN} = -V_{TP} = 1$ V, $K_N' = 2K_P' = 24\ \mu$A/V^2, and $\lambda_N = \lambda_P = 0.01$ V^{-1}. Assume that $W_9/L_9 = 2W_{10}/L_{10}$, and find the value of the ratios that will implement R_z.

6.42 Design a folded cascode CMOS op amp that meets the following specifications: $A_o = 50{,}000$, GB $= 5$ MHz, and SR $= \pm 1$ V/μs for a load capacitance of 20 pF. Assume the device parameters of $K_N' = 2K_P' = 25\ \mu$A/V^2, $V_{TN} = -V_{TP} = 1$ V, $\lambda_N = \lambda_P = 0.01$ V^{-1}, all $V_{SB} = O$ V, and give the values of the W/L ratio and the dc currents for each device. What is the power dissipation of your design if the power supplies are ± 5 V?

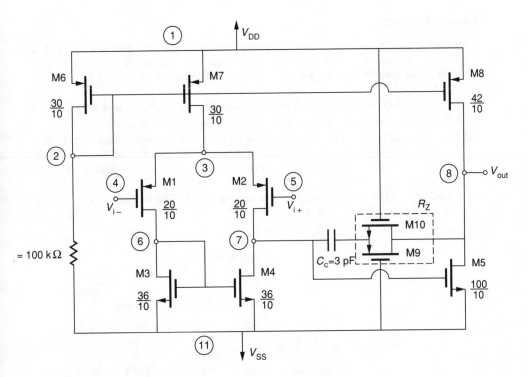

FIGURE P6.41

6.43 Use SPICE to obtain the open-loop magnitude and phase response of the two-stage CMOS op amp of Fig. 6.5-5a with a 20 pF load capacitance using the W and L values of Table 6.5-2. What is the phase margin of this op amp?

6.44 Propose and justify a method of measuring the open loop output resistance of an op amp.

Section 6.6

6.45 If $C_{\text{II}} = 0.7$ pF and $I_{SS} = 10$ μA, find the time required for the CMOS differential comparator of Fig. 6.6-7a to slew 5 V. If $C_{\text{II}} = 7$ pF and $I_{EE} = 20$ μA, find the time required for the BJT differential comparator of Fig. 6.6-7b to slew 5 V. Assume $I_6 = 10I_7$ and $C_{\text{I}} = 0$.

6.46 Repeat Example 6.6-1 for the calculation of the systematic offset for the BJT two-stage comparator. Use the device numbering scheme of Fig. 6.6-7. Also, assume that $V_{CC} = 10$ V, $V_{EE} = 0$ V, $V_{CE7} = 3$ V, and $V_{CE3} = V_{CE4} = 2$ V. The values of V_{AFN} and V_{AFP} are 100 V and 50 V, respectively, and the bias current in Q7 is 20 μA.

6.47 If $C_{gd} = 0.2$ pF, $C_{gs} = 0.3$ pF, and $C_L = 1$ pF, find the propagation delay times T_p^+, T_p^-, and T_p for the two-stage CMOS comparator of Example 6.6-3.

6.48 If $C_\mu = 1$ pF, $C_\pi = 5$ pF, and $C_L = 5$ pF, find the following propagation delay times T_p^+, T_p^-, and T_p for the two-stage BJT comparator of Example 6.6-3 if $I_7 = 40$ μA and $I_5 = 100$ μA.

Design Problems

6.49 Design a voltage-driven, inverting voltage amplifier that will provide a gain of at least -10 and a -3 dB frequency of at least 100 kHz when driving a load of 50 pF in parallel with 50 kΩ. Use the device parameters of Table 3.1-2 or Table 6.1-1.

6.50 Design a BJT inverter that will meet the specifications of Example 6.1-5.

6.51 Repeat Example 6.2-2 using a MOS current-sourcing cascode inverter.

6.52 Design a BJT differential amplifier with a differential to single-ended voltage gain of at least 100 and a common-mode voltage gain of at most 0.1. The differential input resistance should be greater than 100 kΩ. Use the parameters of Table 6.1-1.

6.53 Design a CMOS op amp using the topology of Fig. 6.5-5a that meets the following specifications:

$$A_v > 4000$$

$$V_{DD} = +5 \text{ V}$$

$$V_{SS} = -5 \text{ V}$$

$$GB \geq 1 \text{ MHz} \ (C_2 = 20 \text{ pF})$$

$$SR > 2 \text{ V}/\mu s \ (C_2 = 20 \text{ pF})$$

$$\text{Input common-mode range} \geq \pm 3 \text{ V}$$

$$\text{Output voltage swing} \geq \pm 4 \text{ V}(R_L = 200 \text{ k}\Omega)$$

$$P_{diss} < 10 \text{ mW}$$

Use the parameters of Table 3.1-2, and let all drawn channel lengths be 10 μ.

6.54 Design a BJT op amp that will meet the specifications of Prob. 6.6. Use the parameters of Table 6.1-1.

CHAPTER 7

BASIC DIGITAL BUILDING BLOCKS

7.0 INTRODUCTION

Digital microelectronic circuits dominate the applications of integrated circuits in terms of both sales volume and number of device types. Applications include subcomponents for computer systems and accessories, electronic games, hand-held calculators, digital instrumentation, and the ubiquitous microprocessor. Each of these applications uses circuits that are similar to those previously studied except that they are designed to operate with two-valued, or binary, inputs and outputs. Because these circuits require only two disjoint output voltage ranges to function correctly, practical circuits exist that can function reliably over wide ranges of voltages, currents, temperatures, and process characteristics. A relatively small number of basic digital circuits are used as building blocks. These building blocks are often interconnected to form complex circuits that perform tasks such as those just listed. Following an overview of the digital design process, these basic digital building blocks will be analyzed in this chapter.

MOS digital logic rather than bipolar digital logic is considered in the analysis presented here. The subject of small-scale circuits built from bipolar technology is adequately covered in many references. Most VLSI digital circuits are constructed using MOS technology. Exceptions are I^{2}L, GaAs, and bipolar gate arrays. These are limited applications compared to MOS VLSI circuits.

In digital circuits it is customary to drop the notations for a bulk connection on MOS transistors and to ignore the bulk effect on threshold voltages for simple logic analysis. When more accurate analysis is required, circuit simulators that include bulk effects are used. As a transition from the notation of previous chapters (see Fig. 2.2-4), the arrows on the source terminals that indicate n- or p-channel polarity will be dropped for digital circuits. Instead, a bubble on the gate of a transistor indicates a p-channel transistor. The plain enhancement transistor symbol will be used for n-channel transistors, and the filled drain-to-source bar will continue to indicate depletion transistors.

7.1   DESIGN ABSTRACTION

One powerful resource for digital integrated circuit design is the capability to use several levels of abstraction for a complete design. These design levels, as shown in Fig. 7.1-1, can include functional blocks, register transfer descriptions, logic diagrams, circuit schematics, and geometrical circuit layout.

The functional block level is usually described by a block diagram showing the major subcomponents of a design. For a computer, these blocks might include processor, memory, input/output, and special functions such as memory cache or A/D interfaces. These blocks are usually described textually rather than with a formal language, although this is changing.[1] The functional block level is the highest description level from which a designer works.

The next highest level, the register transfer level (RTL), consists of programlike statements describing the movement or processing of data between storage elements. One such language, the Instruction Set Processor Specification language,[2] has been used to describe many recent computers and other digital systems. The RTL level allows a formal definition of the operation of a digital processor system. Figure 7.1-1b shows a sequence of register transfer operations for a processor that adds the contents of two registers and stores the result in a third register.

The logic diagram is widely used to define the internal operation of blocks described at higher levels. A logic diagram contains well-defined logic functions such as NAND gates and latches, whose digital operation can be accurately described via Boolean logic.[3] For some styles of design, for example, gate array circuits, this is the lowest level of description required from a designer.

The circuit schematic is used to describe integrated circuits at the electrical level as in Fig. 7.1-1d. Circuit schematics may be provided for each logic block or may be used to describe portions of the circuit not directly describable by logic blocks—for example, MOS selector circuits or charge storage elements. The circuit level is characterized by discrete electronic components and their corresponding equations of operation. Within classical digital design, this level of detail is used infrequently. Because of the nature of MOS circuits, mixed descriptions are common, with classical logic functions described via logic symbols, and other functions—such as selectors—described by circuit schematics.

The geometrical layout level, depicted in Fig. 7.1-1e, most closely describes the physical realization of circuits and gates symbolized at the higher levels. Designer knowledge of this level is desirable because, to a large extent, the geometrical characteristics of circuit layout determine the performance and size of digital integrated circuits.

This chapter provides detailed information about several different types of logic circuits and their characteristics. In a later chapter we show that these simple

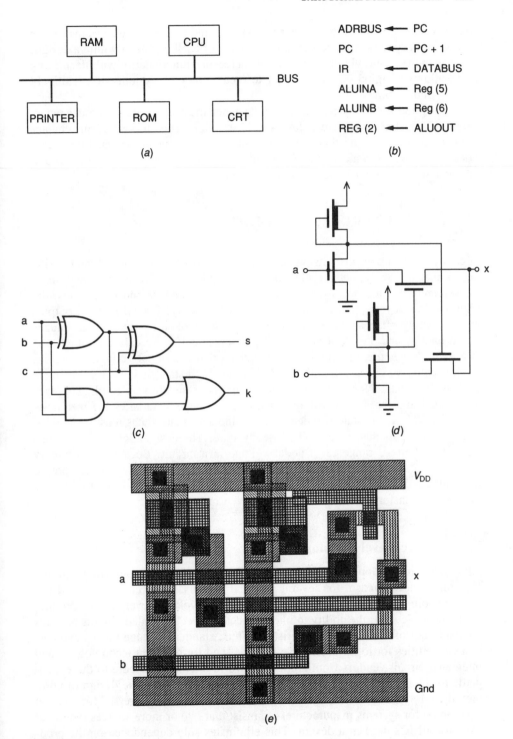

FIGURE 7.1-1
Levels of abstraction: (a) Functional blocks, (b) Register transfer level, (c) Logic diagram, (d) Circuit schematic, (e) Geometrical layout.

circuits can be composed into larger subsystems and that these subsystems can be used without specific attention to minute details of each transistor within a design. The capability to provide a hierarchy of increasing functionality with decreasing detail allows a digital circuit designer to create complex systems in a relatively short period of time.

For good digital system design, a designer must be aware of the characteristics and constraints of several levels of abstraction. The purpose of this chapter is to introduce concepts that are important for designing individual logic functions at the logic, circuit, and layout levels. A familiarity with the definitions and interaction of classical logic gates is assumed.

7.2 CHARACTERISTICS OF DIGITAL CIRCUITS

Digital circuits are almost always operated in a two-level, or binary, mode. This means that at steady state, each input and output is in one of two conditions. These conditions (or *states*) are often referred to as the true and false states, the high and low levels, or the 1 and 0 states, respectively. Because circuit outputs are generally voltages, these two states are characterized by two voltage ranges based on V_{IH} and V_{IL}, where $V_{IH} > V_{IL}$. V_{IH} and V_{IL} are called the high and low *logic thresholds*, respectively. It is agreed that if a nodal voltage V satisfies the inequality $V > V_{IH}$, then this node is in the high state; if $V < V_{IL}$, the node is in the low state. Nominally, the extreme limits of the allowable voltage ranges are ground and the supply voltage. If a nodal voltage V satisfies the inequality $V_{IL} < V < V_{IH}$, the state is indeterminate. Indeterminate states must be avoided in digital systems that have reached steady state. The designation of a state thus refers to a voltage range for a nodal voltage in a circuit. Because we are only interested in states, the exact value of the voltage within a range should not be of major concern. A procedure to determine values for V_{IL} and V_{IH} based on the dc voltage transfer characteristic will be given in Sec. 7.11.

7.2.1 Logic Level Standards

Although it might appear that the designer has total control in selecting V_{IH} and V_{IL}, this is not the case, for several practical reasons. First, each integrated circuit technology can generate certain high and low voltage levels more naturally than others. Second, the ability to interconnect distinct integrated circuits requires compatibility of electrical characteristics. Thus, standard voltage ranges and current capabilities for logic states have been defined for different technologies, and integrated circuit vendors from around the world attempt to adhere to these standards for their products. This standardization makes possible the design of complex digital systems that include ICs from different manufacturers. Moreover, it is common for systems manufacturers to insist that two or more sources (vendors) exist for all ICs used in a design. This eliminates sole dependence on the product of a single manufacturer. This *second-source* requirement provides additional incentive for integrated circuit manufacturers to adhere to standards.

TABLE 7.2-1
Logic voltage specifications

Family	V_{CC}	V_{IL}	V_{IH}
TTL	5.0	0.8	2.0
ALSTTL[1]	5.0	0.8	2.0
ECL	−5.2	−1.5	−1.1
HCMOS[2]	4.5	0.9	3.2
MOS		No standard	
I[2]L		No standard	

[1] Advanced Low-Power Schottky TTL
[2] High-speed CMOS

The recognized interface voltage levels for several different logic families are shown in Table 7.2-1.[4,5] Note that standard logic specifications are not provided for MOS and I[2]L. Some technologies do not have standard logic voltage specifications because they are used only within large-scale integrated circuits. These large-scale circuits contain input and output interface circuitry to adhere to some widely accepted standard for small-scale logic, usually the TTL logic standard. Although adherence to standards is essential at the input and output terminals of most integrated circuits, such standards are not usually applied internally. Thus, interface circuitry is normally required at all inputs and outputs of an integrated circuit to maintain compatibility with other circuits.

The standard electrical interface characteristics of a logic family are determined essentially by the characteristics of the basic inverter. The symbol for the inverter along with its truth table are shown in Fig. 7.2-1. To investigate the characteristics of a logic family, consider the cascade of inverters shown in Fig. 7.2-2. Assume that all inverters are identical and that the voltage transfer characteristic of an inverter, loaded by a following stage, is as shown in Fig. 7.2-3. Assume the input of the first inverter of Fig. 7.2-2 is at a voltage level V_{i1}, where V_{i1} is in the range that characterizes a high level. The output of the first inverter, V_{o1}, serves as the input to the second stage and is designated as V_{i2} in Fig. 7.2-2. Because of the transfer characteristic of Fig. 7.2-3, $V_{o1} = V_{i2}$ will be in the range that characterizes a low level. Continuing in this manner, one obtains the sequence of input voltages, V_{ik}, where V_{ik} is the input voltage to the kth inverter stage. By repeated application of the inversions of Fig. 7.2-3, it is found that the sequence of high-level voltages, $V_{i1}, V_{i3}, \ldots$, is decreasing and converging to a limit, whereas the sequence of low-level voltages $V_{i2}, V_{i4}, \ldots$, is also converging, typically to a different limit, but in an increasing manner. The limits of these sequences, specifically, V_L and V_H, are termed *equilibrium values*.

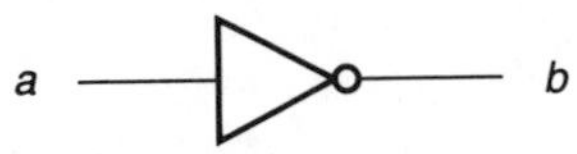

a	b
0	1
1	0

a ———▷o——— b

(a) (b)

FIGURE 7.2-1
Basic inverter: (a) Symbol, (b) Truth table.

V_{i1} $V_{o1} = V_{i2}$ V_{o3} V_{ik} $V_{ok} = V_{i(k+1)}$

$V_{o2} = V_{i3}$

FIGURE 7.2-2
Inverter cascade.

If an inverter with the transfer characteristic of Fig. 7.2-3 is to be useful in a logic family, the low-level sequence must remain in the voltage range that characterizes one of the logic states, and the high-level sequence must remain in the voltage range that characterizes the second logic state. It should be apparent from this example that the shape of the inverter transfer characteristic completely determines the typical logic levels, V_L and V_H, of a logic family. Instead of specifying high and low voltage levels a priori and checking to see if these levels are satisfied for a given inverter, we can ask the related questions: If an inverter has a given transfer characteristic, can this inverter be used as the basis for a viable family of logic? If so, what are the high and low logic voltage levels? These questions are easily answered. We look for the answers by analyzing a pair of cascaded inverters in the next section.

7.2.2 Inverter-Pair Characteristics

First, we examine a pair of inverters in the inverter cascade of Fig. 7.2-2 in greater detail. Assume that the cascade is long enough so that at stage k, the circuit is at equilibrium; that is, $V_{ik} = V_{i(k+2)}$. An *inverter pair*, shown in Fig. 7.2-4a, can be thought of as the kth and $(k+1)$th inverters in the cascade. The transfer characteristic for the inverter pair is shown in Fig. 7.2-4b where V_i and V_o are the input and output voltages, respectively. The slope of the transfer characteristic

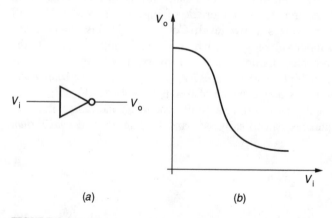

(a) (b)

FIGURE 7.2-3
(a) Inverter, (b) Voltage transfer characteristic.

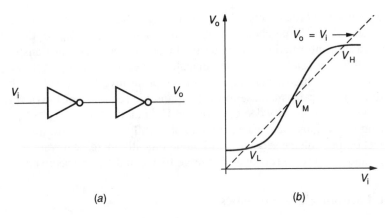

FIGURE 7.2-4
(*a*) Inverter pair, (*b*) Voltage transfer characteristic.

represents the voltage gain of the inverter pair. Note that for an input voltage of zero, the gain is less than one. As the input voltage increases, the gain increases to a value greater than one and then decreases to a value less than one as the input voltage reaches its maximum value. A logic family with an inverter-pair voltage transfer curve that exhibits a gain greater than unity for some region is called a *restoring* logic family. As a counter example, simple diode logic is a *nonrestoring* logic family. Restoring logic is so named because logic signals that are degraded in some way can be restored by the gain of subsequent logic. All widely used electronic logic circuits are of the restoring type.

The inverter-pair characteristic of Fig. 7.2-4*b* can be used to better understand the voltages representing the high and low logic states for a logic family. Note that the input and output voltages of an inverter pair must be equal for equilibrium voltages to exist in the inverter cascade of Fig. 7.2-2. Thus, the equilibrium voltages can be obtained by intersecting the straight line $V_o = V_i$ with the inverter-pair transfer characteristic of Fig. 7.2-4. Note that there are three points of intersection. The extreme intersection points are the high and low equilibrium values, designated by V_H and V_L, respectively. (V_H and V_L should not be confused with the logic threshold voltages V_{IH} and V_{IL} introduced at the beginning of this section.) The equilibrium voltages V_H and V_L represent stable values, as the voltage gain about these points is less than unity. Thus, any small input voltage perturbation about these equilibrium points will be diminished by the inverter pair. The middle intersection point in Fig. 7.2-4*b*, called the *switching threshold voltage* and denoted by V_M, represents an unstable value. Any small input voltage perturbation about V_M will be amplified by the (usually) large voltage gain about this point.

From the preceding analysis, it is apparent that two stable voltage ranges exist for an inverter pair when its characteristic exhibits less than unity gain in two regions. Yet the voltage transfer characteristic should exhibit greater than unity gain to restore degraded signals. Thus, an inverter forms the basis of a viable two-level logic family provided that its inverter-pair transfer characteristic crosses the unity gain line at exactly three points: V_L, V_M, and V_H. The high and low logic thresholds, V_{IH} and V_{IL}, will be chosen so that $V_H > V_{IH} > V_M > V_{IL} > V_L$.

Additional useful information can be derived from the inverter-pair transfer characteristic. If this characteristic is monotonically increasing and $V_L < V_i < V_H$, then the sequence of high-level output voltages of an inverter cascade with V_i as input will monotonically increase toward V_H and the sequence of low-level output voltages will monotonically decrease toward V_L. For $V_i < V_L$ or $V_i > V_H$, the high-level output voltage sequence will monotonically decrease toward V_H and the low-level output voltage sequence will monotonically increase toward V_L. Thus, the high- and low-level sequences converge to V_H and V_L, respectively.

7.2.3   Logic Fan-out Characteristics

The preceding analysis for a cascade of inverters was performed with the assumption that each inverter was loaded by a single, identical inverter to obtain the inverter-pair transfer characteristic. If an inverter output must be capable of driving more than a single load, as shown in Fig. 7.2-5a, then the analysis must be performed again to establish high and low logic levels. Assume each inverter output drives k identical inverter inputs. A new inverter-pair transfer characteristic curve can be obtained as in Fig. 7.2-5b to show the effects of this loading. Note that increasing the loading on each stage decreases the high-level equilibrium point and increases the low-level equilibrium point, thereby changing the desired voltages for logic levels. However, for MOS logic, the static loading caused by driving multiple loads is so small as to be imperceptible in a transfer characteristic curve such as that of Fig. 7.2-5b. Whether a given inverter structure with a specified loading is satisfactory for a logic family depends on the inverter-pair transfer characteristic with loading. The number of identical inverter loads to which a circuit is connected is defined as the *fan-out* of that circuit. The second inverter of Fig. 7.2-5a has a fan-out of k. Usually logic level voltage specifications for a logic family are defined for a specific maximum fan-out.

Inverter-pair dc transfer characteristics of some practical logic families are essentially unaffected by fan-out. Specifically, the inputs to logic functions fabricated with MOS technology are oxide-insulated gates of transistors that draw negligible quiescent input currents. Hence, dc characteristics of MOS logic functions are unaffected by fan-out to other MOS logic inputs. However, it will be shown later that the load capacitance attributed to a large fan-out seriously degrades the switching speed of MOS logic.

7.2.4   Digital Logic Analysis

Because the nodal voltages within a digital circuit can assume one of two distinct ranges, such circuits can be analyzed mathematically with Boolean algebra. This systematic way of characterizing digital systems is widely used by digital designers. It is assumed that readers of this book are familiar with the use of Boolean algebra to characterize digital systems. Relevant background information can be found in many references.[3,6]

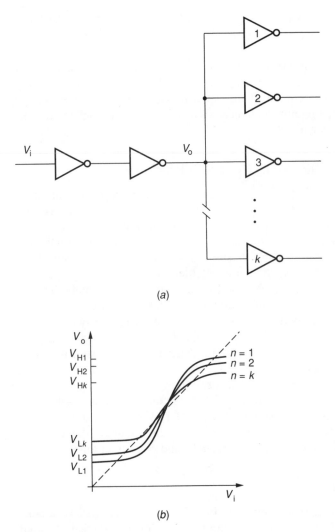

(a)

(b)

FIGURE 7.2-5
Logic fan-out characteristics (*a*) Inverter with fan-out of *k*, (*b*) Inverter pair transfer characteristics
with fan-out *n*.

Basic logic building blocks are often combined to realize complex logic functions. The most primitive set of logic functions consists of the AND, OR, and INVERT functions. This set is complete in the sense that any combinational logic function can be realized using only these three functions. However, the simplest electronic circuits used to realize logic functions always provide signal inversion (even diode logic circuits require signal amplification, and thus inversion, to restore voltage levels). Thus, basic electronic circuits provide the NOR rather than the OR and the NAND rather than the AND function. The NAND and the NOR functions are each individually complete in the sense defined previously. Either the NAND or the NOR logic circuit is the preferred structure in a given technology, causing one of these logically complete functions to be the basic building block for a logic family. This will be described more fully in Sec. 7.4 and Sec. 7.6.

The basic logic circuits are typically termed *logic gates* or simply *gates* because of their ability to control or *gate* logic signal flow. (This term should not be confused with the gate terminal of the MOS transistor.) The characteristics and structure of integrated circuit implementations of these basic logic gates will be studied in the remainder of this chapter.

7.3 SINGLE-CHANNEL MOS INVERTERS

Single-channel MOS technology has been widely used to create large-scale integrated circuits. Early MOS digital circuits used PMOS technology because the natural gate threshold voltage of a p-channel transistor was more suitable for logic applications than was the gate threshold voltage of the n-channel transistor. With the advent of processing techniques such as ion implantation to control the threshold voltage, NMOS became the dominant single-channel technology. Most early microprocessors, including the Motorola 6800 and 6809, the Intel 8080 and 8086, and the Zilog Z80, were manufactured with NMOS processes.

NMOS technology is preferred over PMOS technology primarily because of the greater switching speed achievable with n-channel transistors. MOS transistors are majority carrier devices; thus, the current for an n-channel transistor is carried by electrons whereas that for a p-channel transistor is carried by holes. A silicon semiconductor has an electron mobility that is two to three times its hole mobility. This advantage in charge mobility allows NMOS circuits to operate faster than comparable PMOS circuits. Because the analysis of PMOS and NMOS logic is identical except for a reversal of voltage signs, the predominant device type, NMOS, is used for explanation of single-channel logic circuits in this text.

7.3.1 Basic Inverter

Two basic n-channel inverters are shown in Fig. 7.3-1. Each consists of a pull-down transistor, denoted by M1, and a pullup transistor or load device, denoted by M2. A device connected so as to pull the output voltage to the lower supply voltage—usually 0 V—is called a *pulldown* device; a device connected so as to pull the output voltage to the upper supply voltage—usually V_{DD}—is called a *pullup* device. The circuit of Fig. 7.3-1a is termed a *depletion-load* inverter because the pullup device, M2, is a depletion transistor. The circuit of Fig. 7.3-1b with an enhancement transistor M2 is termed an *enhancement-load* inverter. Note that these inverters are topologically identical to the analog inverters of Fig. 6.1-11c and d.

A typical plot of the transfer characteristic for each of these inverters is shown in Fig. 7.3-2, along with the inverter-pair transfer characteristics for devices sized according to the relationship $(W_1L_2)/(L_1W_2) = 4$, where the subscript 1 refers to M1 and the subscript 2 refers to M2. Figure 7.3-2b shows that the enhancement-load inverter is incapable of pulling the output any higher

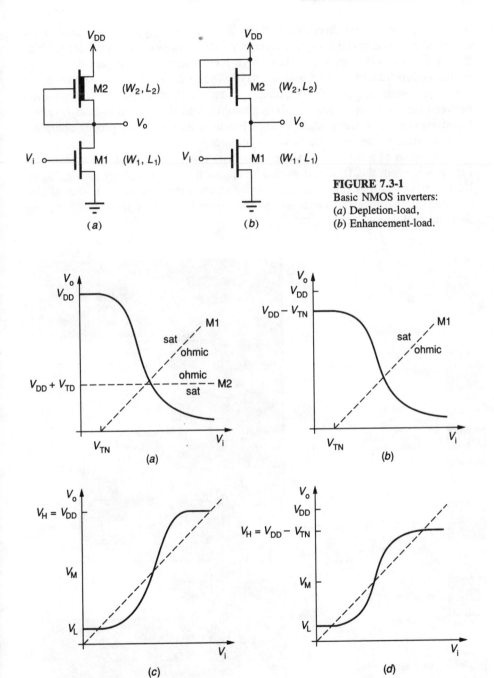

FIGURE 7.3-1
Basic NMOS inverters:
(*a*) Depletion-load,
(*b*) Enhancement-load.

FIGURE 7.3-2
Transfer characteristics of NMOS inverters: (*a*) Depletion-load inverter, (*b*) Enhancement-load inverter, (*c*) Depletion-load inverter pair, (*d*) Enhancement-load inverter pair.

than one enhancement threshold voltage V_{TN} below V_{DD} when the input is at a low level, whereas the output voltage of the depletion-load inverter of Fig. 7.3-2a can be pulled to V_{DD}. These high-level output voltages are determined by the pullup transistor types and are nearly independent of device sizing. From the inverter-pair transfer characteristics, it can be seen that a better separation between high and low logic levels is possible with the depletion-load inverter. Good separation between logic voltage levels is important for proper operation of an inverter in the presence of noise voltages.

A layout of a depletion-load inverter with $(W_1 L_2)/(L_1 W_2) = 4$ is shown in Fig. 7.3-3. From this figure, it should be apparent that the area for the depletion-load transistor is four times as large as that of the input transistor. It should also be observed that inverter layout area is dominated by interconnection and spacing area rather than gate area.

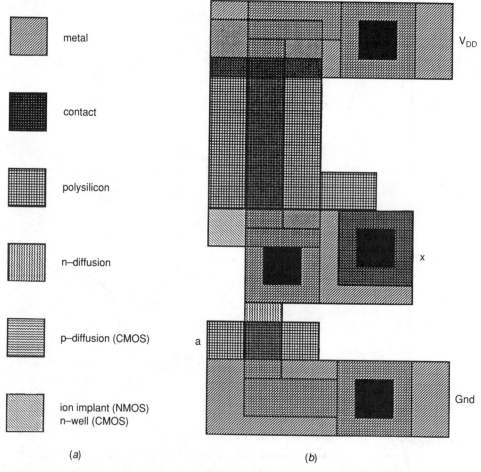

FIGURE 7.3-3
Depletion-load NMOS inverter. (a) Legend, (b) Layout with input a and output x.

7.3.2 Inverter Device Sizing

The question of how the two transistors forming an inverter should be practically sized naturally arises. Note that for the inverter circuits of Fig. 7.3-1, the highest voltage is determined by the pullup type rather than the pullup size. For example, the depletion-mode pullup acts as a resistor whose I-V characteristic has zero offset voltage from the origin. This causes the output voltage to be pulled to V_{DD} when the enhancement pulldown is off, irrespective of the relative sizes of the transistors. Because transistor sizing has minimal effect on V_H, relative sizing can be advantageously used to put V_M and V_L at acceptable levels.

Consider the depletion-load inverter of Fig. 7.3-1a. Because $V_H = V_{DD}$, it would be desirable to have the switching voltage V_M near $V_{DD}/2$ and V_L near 0 V. Observe from the voltage transfer characteristic (Fig. 7.3-2a) that M1 and M2 are typically in or near saturation for V_o near $V_{DD}/2$ using reasonable device sizes and process parameters. Hence, assuming that M1 and M2 are saturated, neglecting λ effects and assuming that $V_o = V_i = V_{DD}/2$, it follows from Eq. 3.1-4, upon equating drain currents, that

$$K'\frac{W_1}{L_1}\frac{[(V_{DD}/2) - V_{TN}]^2}{2} = K'\frac{W_2}{L_2}\frac{(V_{TD})^2}{2} \tag{7.3-1}$$

where V_{TN} and V_{TD} are the threshold voltages of the enhancement and depletion devices, respectively. Solving for the relationship between the design parameters, we obtain the expression

$$\frac{W_1 L_2}{L_1 W_2} = \left[\frac{V_{TD}}{(V_{DD}/2) - V_{TN}}\right]^2 \tag{7.3-2}$$

Defining the geometric device sizing parameter k by

$$k = \frac{W_1 L_2}{L_1 W_2} \tag{7.3-3}$$

it follows that although the designer has control of the four parameters W_1, W_2, L_1, and L_2, only a single degree of freedom as determined by the parameter k is actually available for controlling V_M. In a typical 5 V digital NMOS process with a desired voltage of 2.5 V for V_M, V_{TD} is set near -3 V and V_{TN} is set near 1 V. Solving Eq. 7.3-2 for the device size ratio gives

$$k = \frac{W_1 L_2}{L_1 W_2} = \left(\frac{-3}{2.5 - 1}\right)^2 = 4 \tag{7.3-4}$$

This inverter size ratio is important for digital logic circuits and is often termed the *4 : 1 inverter sizing rule.*

With the 4 : 1 size ratio and typical threshold voltages, it is easy to verify the initial assumption that M1 and M2 are at or near saturation when $V_o = V_i = V_{DD}/2$. For positive V_{TN}, the pulldown transistor is saturated for any $V_o = V_i$. For the pullup transistor with $V_{GS} = 0$, saturation occurs when $V_{DD} - V_o > -V_{TD}$. This condition is not satisfied for our example with $V_{DD} = 5$ V, $V_{TD} = -3$ V, and

$V_o = 2.5$ V; however, the shape of the I–V characteristic of Fig. 7.8-11 for the depletion-load device shows that the current is nearly constant for voltages near the saturation value. Because V_{DS} for the pullup transistor is within 0.5 V of the saturation value, the assumption of saturation current is reasonable.

Having used the device sizing ratio k to set V_M to $V_{DD}/2$, it is necessary to verify that V_L is near 0 V. To obtain V_L, assume that the inverter input is at V_H, causing $V_o = V_L$. Assume that M1 is in the ohmic region and M2 is saturated (Fig. 7.3-2a). Using Eq. 3.1-1 for the ohmic operating region of M1, again neglecting λ effects and equating drain currents, we obtain the expression

$$K' \frac{W_2}{L_2} \frac{(V_{TD})^2}{2} = K' \frac{W_1}{L_1} \left(V_i - V_{TN} - \frac{V_o}{2} \right) V_o \qquad (7.3\text{-}5)$$

Substituting $V_o = V_L$ and $V_i = V_H = V_{DD}$, it follows from Eq. 7.3-5 with the approximation

$$\left(V_{DD} - V_{TN} - \frac{V_L}{2} \right) \approx (V_{DD} - V_{TN}) \qquad (7.3\text{-}6)$$

that

$$V_L \approx \frac{W_2 L_1}{L_2 W_1} \frac{V_{TD}^2}{2(V_{DD} - V_{TN})} = \frac{1}{k} \frac{V_{TD}^2}{2(V_{DD} - V_{TN})} \qquad (7.3\text{-}7)$$

Using the parameters specified earlier and our typical device sizing strategy, it follows that

$$V_L \approx \left(\frac{1}{4} \right) \frac{9}{2(5-1)} = \frac{9}{32} \text{ V} \qquad (7.3\text{-}8)$$

The assumptions that M1 is ohmic and M2 is saturated are readily verified.

From the previous analysis, we can examine the operation of inverter logic more closely. Consider the flat segment of the transfer characteristic of Fig. 7.3-2a corresponding to $V_i < V_{TN}$. For this range of input voltages, the output voltage of a depletion-mode inverter will be at V_{DD}. If the output voltage $V_o = V_{DD}$ is used as the input voltage to a subsequent inverter, its output voltage will be less than V_{TN}, as shown by Eq. 7.3-8. In fact, for depletion-load inverters sized according to the 4 : 1 rule and with normal threshold voltages, any stable interconnection of inverters will have all logic voltages at either V_L or V_H for valid logic inputs.

The previous analysis showed that the 4 : 1 sizing rule gives attractive high and low logic levels that are approximately equidistant from V_M for an inverter. Because no dc loading is experienced when an inverter output drives many inverter inputs within MOS technology, these logic levels are maintained even in the presence of high fan-out. For this reason, the 4 : 1 sizing rule is widely followed in digital logic systems using depletion-load devices.

From a practical viewpoint, it is desirable to minimize area associated with layout. The 4 : 1 sizing ratio specifies only pullup/pulldown ratios and not the width and length of each transistor. Each process technology file specifies design rules for the minimum width and length of a transistor. Often M1 will be a minimum-size transistor and M2 will have a minimum width resulting in a length for M2 given by

$$L_2 = \frac{4L_1 W_2}{W_1} \tag{7.3-9}$$

An alternate construction for an inverter, still satisfying the minimum length and width rules but using less area, can be found (see Prob. 7.12). Subsequently, it will be shown that power and speed considerations may override the minimum area requirement in the determination of the appropriate device sizes.

Throughout the remainder of this book, performance comparisons will be made between a *reference inverter* and other logic circuits. It will be assumed that in any logic family, the sizing of a basic or reference inverter has been specified. The reference inverter used for NMOS will be a depletion-mode inverter formed from a minimum-size enhancement transistor and a minimum-width depletion-mode transistor with length given by Eq. 7.3-9. Although the following discussions are based on this reference inverter, equivalent results may be obtained for reference inverters of other sizes.

It might be instructive to question what improvements, if any, could be obtained by working with a sizing strategy other than 4 : 1. For smaller values of the device sizing parameter k, a modest reduction in area would be attained at the expense of a significant increase in V_L as given by Eq. 7.3-7. This reduces the separation between V_H and V_L, causing the inverter to be more susceptible to noise voltages. Larger values for k offer slight improvements in the signal swing, $V_H - V_L$, at the expense of increases in silicon area. More importantly, it will be shown later that larger k values seriously degrade the switching speed of an inverter.

Finally, it is worth emphasizing that threshold voltages are easily set through process changes. Thus, threshold voltages are chosen specifically to enhance the size and speed characteristics of logic devices. The values $V_{TN} = 1$ V, $V_{TD} = -3$ V and $V_{DD} = 5$ V used in deriving the 4:1 sizing rule are typical for processes used in building digital integrated circuits because they offer reasonable signal swings with practical silicon area requirements.

7.3.3 Enhancement-Load versus Depletion-Load Inverters

Following an analysis similar to the one used for the depletion-load inverter, a sizing rule can be derived for the enhancement-load inverter of Fig. 7.3-1b. This analysis would show that the same 4 : 1 sizing rule offers reasonable tradeoffs between signal swing and switching speed. The 4 : 1 sizing rule is thus widely used for single-channel logic circuits.

A comparison of depletion-load and enhancement-load inverters is in order. From a size viewpoint, the silicon area requirements of both types of inverters are nearly the same. From a signal-swing viewpoint, the depletion-load inverter is preferred because the output voltage of the enhancement-load inverter cannot be pulled higher than $V_{DD} - V_{TN}$. From a processing viewpoint, an extra process step is required for the depletion implant, raising the cost of depletion-mode logic relative to enhancement-mode logic. In terms of switching speed, the depletion-mode inverter is considerably faster than an enhancement-mode inverter in going from a low output voltage to a high output voltage. The reason for this variation is the large difference in equivalent resistances for the two transistors. (Fig. 7.8-11 shows this graphically).

For modern single-channel circuits, the advantages of the depletion-mode inverter far outweigh the cost disadvantage. As a result, enhancement-mode inverters are used only in specialized applications.

Single-channel MOS inverters were analyzed in this section. The inverter device sizing ratio was defined and a ratio of $k = 4$ was found to set the logic threshold near $V_{DD}/2$. Corresponding values of $V_H = V_{DD}$ and $V_L < V_{TN}$ were found with this ratio. A reference inverter was defined as the basis for analyzing a logic family. Depletion-load inverters were found to be preferable to enhancement-load inverters for most applications.

7.4 NMOS NOR AND NAND LOGIC CIRCUITS

In this section NMOS logic gates will be analyzed as extensions of the reference inverter of the previous section. Simple NOR, NAND, and multi-input gates will be considered.

7.4.1 Basic NMOS NOR Logic Circuits

The positive logic NOR function, in which the output is low if any of the inputs are high, is easily realized with NMOS circuits by a parallel connection of two or more pulldown transistors in place of the single pulldown transistor of the inverter circuits of Fig. 7.3-1. Figure 7.4-1 shows a circuit that realizes the positive logic NOR function along with the corresponding logic truth table. Also shown are the Boolean logic equation and the distinctive-shape logic symbol.

The operation of the depletion-load NOR gate will now be considered from a qualitative viewpoint. The analysis of the enhancement-load NOR gate is similar and is left to the reader. If inputs a and b of this circuit are both at a voltage near 0 V, neither of the two parallel pulldown transistors will conduct, and the pullup transistor will pull the circuit output to a voltage near V_{DD}. If either the a or the b input is connected to a voltage near V_{DD}, the corresponding pulldown transistor will conduct, causing the output to be pulled near 0 V irrespective of the other parallel pulldown transistor. Of course, if both inputs are connected to voltages near V_{DD}, then both pulldown transistors conduct, pulling the output to a voltage near 0 V as well.

The device sizing problem for the NOR gate must be addressed. It will be assumed that the device sizing of the NOR gate is done so that for normal input conditions, the high and low logic voltages at the output will be at least as high and low, respectively, as those established for the reference inverter. Thus, a

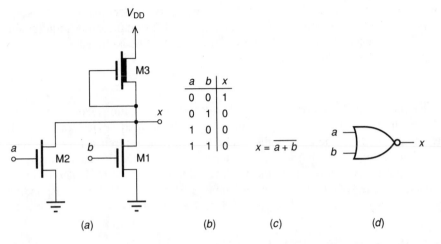

FIGURE 7.4-1
NMOS NOR gate with depletion pullup transistor: (a) Circuit, (b) Truth table, (c) Boolean equation, (d) Distinctive-shape symbol.

NOR gate will not cause a deterioration in logic signal levels. The same strategy is generally used to size all logic blocks in a family of logic.

By symmetry, it can be assumed that the pulldown transistors of Fig. 7.4-1, M1 and M2, are the same size. From the corresponding truth table, it is clear that there are only four possible logic conditions for the inputs. These will now be exhaustively considered. If both inputs are low, M1 and M2 are off, causing the output to go to V_{DD} irrespective of any device sizing. If the input to M1 is low and the input to M2 is high, M1 is off and hence allows no current to flow into its drain terminal. This makes the remainder of the NOR gate look like the reference inverter of Fig. 7.3-1a with M2 playing the role of the pulldown transistor and M3 the role of the load transistor. To maintain a low voltage level at least as low as that for the reference inverter, M2 and M3 must satisfy the $4:1$ sizing rule. This results in the requirement

$$\frac{L_3 W_2}{W_3 L_2} \geq 4 \tag{7.4-1}$$

Likewise, if the input to M1 is high and the input to M2 is low, we obtain the requirement

$$\frac{L_3 W_1}{W_3 L_1} \geq 4 \tag{7.4-2}$$

These requirements are equivalent since it was assumed that M1 and M2 are the same size. Finally, if the inputs to both M1 and M2 are high, the M1–M2 combination behaves as a single transistor of width $2W_1$ and length L_1. To maintain the low voltage level, the combination must satisfy the expression

$$\frac{L_3 2W_1}{W_3 L_1} \geq 4 \tag{7.4-3}$$

From Eq. 7.3-7 we can determine that a sizing ratio greater than $4:1$ causes a lower V_L. The requirements of Eqs. 7.4-1 and 7.4-2 dominate the requirement of Eq. 7.4-3, resulting in the following sizing rule for the NOR gate:

$$\frac{L_3 W_2}{W_3 L_2} = \frac{L_3 W_1}{W_3 L_1} = 4 \tag{7.4-4}$$

If each pulldown transistor for a NOR gate is of minimum size, as was the pulldown transistor for the reference inverter, then the load device for the NOR gate should be the same size as the load device for the reference inverter. With this sizing strategy, it is obvious that when both inputs to a NOR gate are high, the output is pulled even lower than the V_L level obtained for the reference inverter. In general, if the sizing rule for the reference inverter is $k:1$, the corresponding sizing rule for the N-input NOR gate of Sec. 7.4.3 is also $k:1$.

7.4.2   Basic NMOS NAND Logic Circuits

Figure 7.4-2 shows a circuit that realizes the positive NAND logic function along with its logic truth table, Boolean logic equation, and distinctive-shape logic symbol. For the NAND logic function, the pulldown transistors M1 and M2 are arranged in series rather than in parallel, as was the case for the NOR circuit. The operation of the depletion-load NAND gate will now be considered qualitatively. If either (or both) input a or b is near 0 V, the pulldown transistor corresponding to that input will not conduct. If either pulldown transistor does not conduct, the series path to ground is broken, and the pullup transistor M3 pulls the output

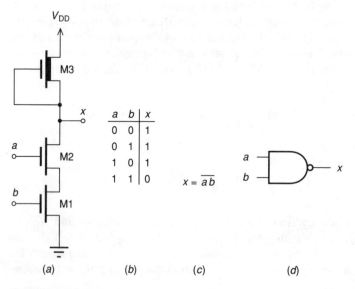

FIGURE 7.4-2
NMOS NAND gate with depletion pullup transistor: (*a*) Circuit, (*b*) Truth table, (*c*) Boolean equation, (*d*) Distinctive-shape symbol.

voltage near to V_{DD}. If both inputs a and b are set to V_{DD}, then both pulldown transistors conduct, pulling the output to a low voltage. This relationship between inputs a and b and output x realizes the NAND logic function.

Device sizing for the NAND gate must be addressed. Once again, it is assumed that the device sizing of the NAND gate is done so that for normal input conditions, the high and low logic voltages at the output will be at least as high and low, respectively, as those established for the reference inverter. With this choice, a NAND gate will not cause a deterioration in logic voltage levels.

The constraint that determines the sizing for the NOR gate corresponds to the weakest pulldown path that will force the output to the low state. For the NAND gate, the *only* pulldown path requires high input levels for both inputs a and b. This condition will determine the sizing for the NAND gate. From a quantitative viewpoint, if M1 and M2 are the same size and both inputs are high, the M1–M2 combination acts as a single transistor of length $2L_1$ and width W_1. To maintain the required output voltage for a low logic level, the 4 : 1 sizing rule can be applied. For the two-input NAND gate this results in

$$\frac{L_3 W_1}{W_3 2L_1} = 4 \tag{7.4-5}$$

or

$$\frac{L_3 W_1}{W_3 L_1} = \frac{L_3 W_2}{W_3 L_2} = 8 \tag{7.4-6}$$

as the sizing rule. In general, if the sizing rule for the reference inverter is $k : 1$, the corresponding sizing rule for the N-input NAND gate of Sec. 7.4.3 is $Nk : 1$.

Two approaches can be followed to achieve the 8:1 ratio for two-input NAND gates. In one approach, the two pulldown transistors are minimum-area devices ($L_1 = W_1 = L_2 = W_2 = $ minimum dimension), requiring the depletion pullup transistor to have the ratio $L_3/W_3 = 8$. In an alternate approach, the load device is sized like the depletion load for the reference inverter, and the two pulldown transistors are sized equally, with $W_1/L_1 = W_2/L_2 = 2$. The first approach is preferred because it provides minimum capacitive loading on preceding logic stages. It can be shown that the total transistor gate area requirement is slightly different for the two sizing strategies (see Prob. 7.14). Also note that, in either case, the minimum total gate area required for the NAND function is larger than that required for the NOR function.

7.4.3 Multi-Input NAND and NOR Logic Circuits

For simplicity, two-input gates were analyzed in the preceding section. Multi-input logic functions, with three or more inputs to a gate, are also widely used. An N-input NOR gate is easily formed by adding $N - 2$ enhancement transistors in parallel with the M1 and M2 transistors of Fig. 7.4-1. An N-input depletion-load NOR gate is shown in Fig. 7.4-3. Multi-input NOR gates that follow the same $k : 1$ sizing rule given for the two-input NOR gate have the same V_L and V_H values as the reference inverter with a sizing ratio of k.

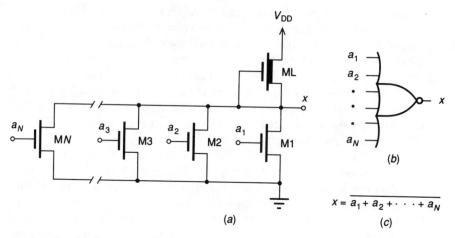

FIGURE 7.4-3
Multi-input NOR gate: (*a*) Circuit, (*b*) Distinctive-shape symbol, (*c*) Boolean equation.

Multi-input NAND gates are formed by adding enhancement transistors in series with the M1 and M2 pulldown transistors shown in Fig. 7.4-2. An N-input NAND gate requires the addition of $N - 2$ transistors in series, as shown in Fig. 7.4-4. Unfortunately, the ratio of the size of the load device to that of the pulldown devices increases with the number of inputs to maintain a good low logic voltage. This sizing ratio becomes Nk :1. An increase in this size ratio increases area and decreases switching speed. As a consequence, single-channel NAND gates with more than two or three inputs are seldom used. Rather, an equivalent multi-input NAND circuit is formed from the appropriate interconnection of inverters and multi-input NOR gates (see Prob. 7.17).

NAND and NOR logic gates are realizable directly as simple modifications to the reference inverter and are more widely used than AND or OR logic gates. When the AND or OR functions are required, they are realized by cascading a basic inverter after a NAND or a NOR gate, respectively.

The structure and sizing of two-input NOR and NAND gates in the NMOS technology were presented in this section. The analysis was generalized to N-input NAND and NOR gates.

7.5 COMPLEMENTARY MOS INVERTERS

The first MOS-based technology to be widely applied at the small-scale integration level was complementary MOS, or CMOS. However, because of the relative simplicity of processing and layout for single-channel MOS circuits, PMOS and then NMOS technologies were the first to achieve widespread use in large-scale integrated circuits. The few early large-scale CMOS circuits were reserved for applications that required the low power dissipation, stable temperature characteristics, or high noise immunity achievable with a CMOS process. Although such characteristics are desirable for all applications of integrated circuit technology, CMOS integrated circuits had disadvantages that limited their use in early VLSI designs.

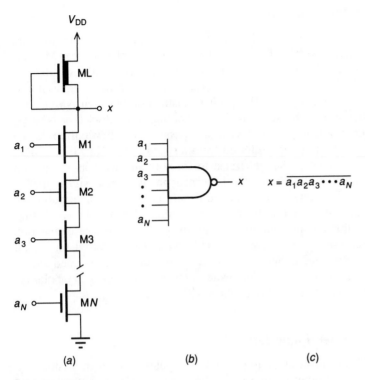

FIGURE 7.4-4
Multi-input NAND gate: (*a*) Circuit, (*b*) Distinctive-shape symbol, (*c*) Boolean equation.

The CMOS fabrication process is more complicated than NMOS fabrication, requiring additional steps to complete the processing of a wafer. Addition of p-channel transistors to a p-substrate process requires creation of an n-well area for the p-channel transistors. This reduces the achievable circuit density compared to an NMOS process. Similarly, a p-well area is required to add n-channel transistors to an n-substrate process. Also, traditional CMOS logic circuits require additional transistors compared to their NMOS counterparts. These disadvantages translate to increased fabrication costs with lower integrated circuit yield for CMOS.

Recent advances in fabrication methods for CMOS technology and in circuit design techniques for CMOS digital circuits have made CMOS more practical for large-scale applications. Also, the need to provide multiple-threshold n-channel devices for speed and power purposes has complicated the standard NMOS process. These factors have changed the relative merits of NMOS versus CMOS technologies for large-scale digital circuit design. Most integrated circuit manufacturers now use CMOS for new designs. For example, both the Intel 80386 and the Motorola 68030 microprocessors are fabricated with CMOS processes. Also, many integrated circuit manufacturers offer CMOS gate array circuits to provide large-scale integration of digital systems functions. In this section, basic CMOS inverter circuits are discussed.

7.5.1 A Basic CMOS Inverter

A CMOS inverter is similar to an NMOS inverter in that two transistors are required. In the CMOS inverter of Fig. 7.5-1a, the p-channel transistor M2 acts as a pullup device, and the n-channel transistor M1 acts as a pulldown device. In fact, for some CMOS processes (n-well process), the pulldown transistor is identical to its NMOS counterpart. The primary distinction between NMOS and CMOS inverters lies in the characteristics of the pullup transistors. For NMOS, either a passive enhancement pullup device or a passive depletion pullup device is used, with the depletion pullup preferred from a speed standpoint. In a CMOS process, an actively driven p-channel transistor is normally used as the pullup device. This p-channel pullup transistor is turned on by a gate signal that is opposite in polarity to the gate signal required to turn on the n-channel pulldown transistor. The digital symbol for the p-channel pullup device, shown in Fig. 7.5-1b, emphasizes this complementary polarity by showing the gate connection with a bubble to represent signal inversion. This symbol is preferred for digital CMOS circuits. As explained in Sec. 7.0, source designations are assumed understood with this notation. The use of opposite-polarity (complementary-polarity) transistors for load devices characterizes the CMOS inverter.

7.5.2 CMOS Inverter Logic Levels

Note that in the CMOS inverter of Fig. 7.5-1, the gates of both transistors are connected to the inverter input, unlike the comparable NMOS inverter circuit of Fig. 7.3-1. This circuit functions as an inverter because of the opposite transfer characteristics of the n-channel pulldown transistor and the p-channel pullup transistor. The threshold voltages, V_{TP} and V_{TN}, are established so that a voltage $V_i > V_{DD} + V_{TP} = V_{DD} - |V_{TP}|$ on the common gate node causes the n-channel device to conduct while it causes the p-channel device to turn off. (To reduce the potential for error, the notation $(-|V_{TP}|)$ will replace (V_{TP}) to ensure that

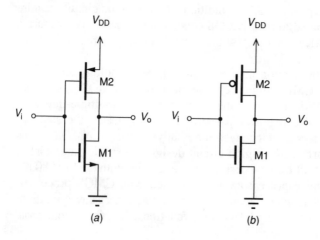

FIGURE 7.5-1
CMOS inverter circuit: (a) n-channel and p-channel designation, (b) Preferred notation for digital circuits.

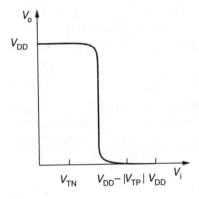

FIGURE 7.5-2
Voltage transfer characteristic for CMOS inverter.

a negative value is used in calculations with V_{TP}.) This results in an active pulldown capability at the output of the circuit. Because the pullup device is off, the pulldown transistor does not have to compete to establish a low-voltage condition on the output. At steady state, the output voltage will reach $V_o = 0$ V. On the other hand, a voltage $V_i < V_{TN}$ on the common gate node causes the n-channel device to turn off while it causes the p-channel device to conduct. This condition provides an active pullup transistor without competition from a pulldown device, allowing the inverter output to be pulled high. At steady state, $V_o = V_{DD}$ for this condition. Figure 7.5-2 shows a typical voltage transfer characteristic for a CMOS inverter.

For valid logic input voltages, note that when one transistor of a CMOS inverter is conducting, the complementary transistor is off. This condition is especially important for two reasons. First, it virtually eliminates static power dissipation in CMOS logic circuits because no current can flow from the voltage supply to ground through the inverter in steady state. Second, it allows a maximum logic voltage swing equal to the supply voltage V_{DD}.

Consider the steady state effect of a logic high voltage on the cascade of CMOS inverter stages of Fig. 7.5-3. Assume that a logic high voltage $V_{i1} > V_{DD} - |V_{TP}|$ is provided at the input to the first inverter. The output of this inverter will reach $V_{o1} = 0$ V because the pullup transistor is off for this input condition. Thus, the input to the second inverter is $V_{i2} = V_{o1} = 0$ V. This gives the condition $V_{i2} < V_{TN}$, causing the n-channel pulldown device of the

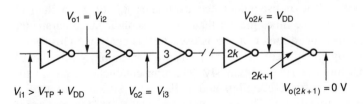

FIGURE 7.5-3
CMOS inverter cascade.

second inverter to be off. The output is then pulled to $V_{o2} = V_{DD}$ by the p-channel transistor. An extension of this analysis to the kth inverter pair shows that $V_{TN} > V_L = 0$ V and $V_{DD} - |V_{TP}| < V_H = V_{DD}$. This provides an ideal voltage swing of

$$V_H - V_L = V_{DD} - 0 \text{ V} = V_{DD} \qquad (7.5\text{-}1)$$

The best possible voltage swing for a single-polarity inverter output is equal to the difference between the upper and lower supply voltages to the inverter—in this case, V_{DD} and 0 V. It should be obvious that an analysis starting with a logic low voltage of $V_{i1} < V_{TN}$ for the CMOS inverter cascade will yield the same values for V_H and V_L.

7.5.3 Inverter Device Sizing

Device sizing for a CMOS inverter will now be considered. The ability of either transistor in a CMOS inverter to act as a low-resistance device with the complementary transistor turned off allows the design of ratioless inverters. A *ratioless* logic device is one in which, from a logic-level viewpoint, the steady state output voltage levels are independent of the ratio of the pullup and pulldown transistor sizes. This is in contrast to the single-channel inverters of Sec. 7.3, which are known as *ratio* logic devices because the pullup/pulldown size ratio k determines one of the equilibrium voltages V_L. The independence of logic voltage levels and transistor sizes allows other considerations to determine the relative sizes of the pullup and pulldown transistors in a CMOS inverter.

The primary effect of the sizes of the pullup and pulldown transistors is on the equivalent resistance of the transistors in the conducting state. Thus, sizing can be used to provide approximately equal capability to source or sink load current; this equality is termed *symmetric output drive*. In contrast, NMOS inverters provide asymmetric output drive because of the difference in pullup and pulldown resistance needed to achieve useful logic levels. The symmetric drive capability of CMOS allows comparable transition times for output voltages irrespective of the direction of the transition.

It is interesting to determine the relative sizes of n-channel and p-channel transistors required to achieve symmetric output drive for a CMOS inverter. An n-channel transistor for either an NMOS or an n-well CMOS process can be fabricated with similar characteristics. The minimum channel lengths and widths of transistors in both processes are set primarily by the resolution of the fabrication process. The transconductance parameter K'_N of an n-channel transistor is about two or three times greater than the transconductance parameter K'_P of a p-channel transistor; a factor of 2.5 is used in this analysis. This factor is caused primarily by the difference in majority carrier mobility for the p- and n-channel transistors described previously. The transconductance parameter difference influences the effective pullup and pulldown resistances of the p-channel and n-channel transistors. The equivalent resistances for the n-channel transistor R_N and for the p-channel transistor R_P are directly proportional to L and inversely proportional to K' and W as indicated by equations

$$R_N \propto \frac{L_N}{W_N K_N'} \qquad (7.5\text{-}2)$$

and

$$R_P \propto \frac{L_P}{W_P K_P'} \qquad (7.5\text{-}3)$$

Simple models for the n-channel and p-channel transistors composed of an ideal switch and the effective pullup and pulldown resistances are shown in Fig. 7.5-4 (also see Sec. 3.1-9). The switch is open or closed corresponding to the gate-to-source voltage that turns the transistor off or on, respectively. This simple model is useful for predicting current drive capability and approximating propagation delays in digital applications. Because the proportionality constants for Eqs. 7.5-2 and 7.5-3 are comparable, it follows that

$$R_N \approx \left(\frac{L_N}{W_N K_N'} \right) \left(\frac{W_P K_P'}{L_P} \right) R_P \qquad (7.5\text{-}4)$$

For symmetric output drive, it is required that $R_N = R_P$. If $K_N' = 2.5 K_P'$, then according to Eq. 7.5-4, the devices must be sized with

$$\frac{L_N W_P}{W_N L_P} = \frac{K_N'}{K_P'} = 2.5 \qquad (7.5\text{-}5)$$

With this sizing, the n-channel and p-channel transistors have symmetric $I\text{–}V$ characteristics. The layout for a CMOS inverter with these characteristics is given in Fig. 7.5-5. Note that the p-channel transistor width is 2.5 times the width of the n-channel transistor. In practice, symmetric drive capability is often sacrificed by the use of minimum-size transistors to reduce layout area.

In this section a basic CMOS inverter was analyzed. It was found that the output logic voltage levels of $V_L = 0$ V and $V_H = V_{DD}$ were ideal. Because the CMOS inverter is a ratioless logic circuit, device geometries can be used to obtain symmetric output drive.

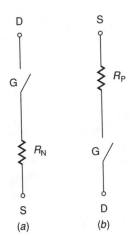

FIGURE 7.5-4
Simple transistor models for digital applications: (*a*) n-channel, (*b*) p-channel.

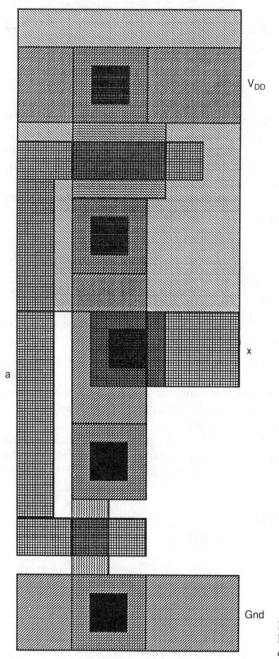

V_{DD}

x

a

Gnd

FIGURE 7.5-5
Layout for CMOS inverter with input
a and output *x*.

7.6 CMOS LOGIC GATES

Classical CMOS logic gates are described in this section. As their characteristics are developed, a comparison with the corresponding NMOS logic gates will be given. Two-input NOR and NAND logic gates are used to develop the unique characteristics of CMOS logic. A discussion of multi-input CMOS gates will conclude the section.

7.6.1 CMOS NOR Logic Gate

Once the reference inverter circuit for a particular logic family is defined, the design of circuits to implement other logic functions can be based on that inverter circuit. Figure 7.6-1 shows the circuit schematic for a CMOS two-input positive logic NOR gate based on the CMOS inverter of Fig. 7.5-1. This circuit is obviously different from the NMOS NOR logic circuit of Fig. 7.4-1 because four transistors are required to implement the logic function rather than three. The two pulldown transistors, M1 and M2, are in parallel as they were for the corresponding NMOS logic gate. However, two pullup transistors, M3 and M4, are required in a series connection to complete the CMOS NOR circuit. The layout of a two-input CMOS NOR gate with all minimum-size transistors is shown in Fig. 7.6-2. From this figure, it can be observed that greater silicon area is required compared to an equivalent layout of the NMOS NOR gate of Fig. 7.4-1 given a common basic process resolution. The slight decrease in pullup transistor area for the CMOS gate—the longer depletion pullup of NMOS is unnecessary—is more than offset by the additional circuit connections, the second pullup transistor, and the n-well isolation required for the CMOS pullup transistors.

The operation of the CMOS NOR gate of Fig. 7.6-1 can be explained as follows. When both inputs a and b are below V_{TN}, the parallel n-channel pulldown transistors are off and the series p-channel pullup transistors conduct. This condition provides an active pullup through the series transistors for the output of the CMOS gate. There is no competition from the pulldown transistors.

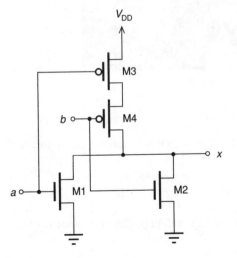

FIGURE 7.6-1
Two-input CMOS NOR gate.

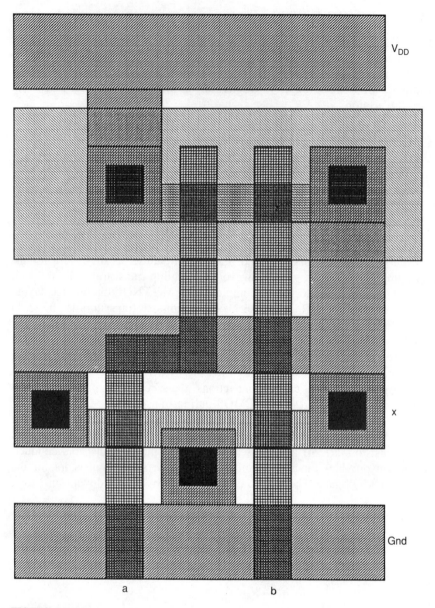

FIGURE 7.6-2
CMOS NOR gate layout with inputs a and b and output x.

Using the resistive model of Sec. 7.5 for the p-channel transistors, it follows that

$$R_{\text{UP}} = R_{\text{P3}} + R_{\text{P4}} \propto \frac{2L_{\text{P}}}{W_{\text{P}}K'_{\text{P}}} \qquad (7.6\text{-}1)$$

Thus, for equally sized pullup transistors, the equivalent pullup resistance is twice that of either pullup alone.

If input a is connected to a voltage greater than $V_{DD} - |V_{TP}|$, p-channel pullup transistor M3 is off and n-channel pulldown transistor M1 conducts. Now the series path to V_{DD} is broken, and the output node is pulled to 0 V by transistor M1. This gives a pulldown resistance

$$R_{N1} \propto \frac{L_1}{W_1 K_N'} \qquad (7.6\text{-}2)$$

A corresponding analysis for input b high, which turns M4 off, shows that the output node is pulled to 0 V by transistor M2. Now the pulldown resistance is

$$R_{N2} \propto \frac{L_2}{W_2 K_N'} \qquad (7.6\text{-}3)$$

If both inputs a and b are above $V_{DD} - |V_{TP}|$, then both transistors M3 and M4 are off and transistors M1 and M2 both conduct. This parallel connection results in a pulldown resistance that is equal to the parallel combination of R_{N1} and R_{N2}, thus ensuring that the output node is pulled to 0 V. Because the output is pulled low if input a or b or both are high, this circuit realizes the NOR logic function.

For the CMOS NOR gate, as for the CMOS inverter, the steady state output voltage is set by a ratioless connection of conducting transistors. Thus, the dc logic voltages are ideal; that is, the output voltage is pulled to either V_{DD} or 0 V. Because dc logic levels are not affected by the relative sizes of the pullup and pulldown transistors, these transistors can be sized to obtain the desired output drive characteristics, as was done previously for the CMOS inverter. Because of the presence of two inputs (and four logic input conditions) for the NOR gate, it is not possible to maintain symmetric output drive capabilities for all input conditions. A common approach is to size the devices so that the worst-case drive capability is as good as that of the reference inverter. If this strategy is adopted, then M3 and M4 can each be sized for half the effective pullup resistance of the reference inverter. If M1 and M2 are both of minimum size, then M3 and M4 would both have $W/L = 5$ to maintain this worst-case drive capability. In practice, minimum-size transistors are often used for both pullups and pulldowns to conserve area, resulting in asymmetric output drive.

A simple resistive model of the two-input NOR gate based on the device model of Fig. 7.5-4 is shown in Fig. 7.6-3. If all devices are of minimum size, then the pullup resistance is $2R_P = 5R_N$ for $K_N' = 2.5K_P'$. The pulldown resistance is R_N for a single NOR gate input high or $R_N/2$ for both inputs high. Thus, a maximum input-dependent asymmetry of 10:1 exists for this CMOS NOR structure based on minimum-size gates.

7.6.2 CMOS NAND Logic Gate

The circuit for a CMOS two-input positive logic NAND gate is also easily obtained once the reference inverter circuit has been defined. A CMOS NAND circuit is shown in Fig. 7.6-4 with its corresponding layout in Fig. 7.6-5. This circuit is called the *dual* of the CMOS NOR circuit because the two pullup transistors are connected in parallel rather than in series and the two pulldown transistors

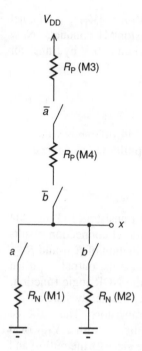

FIGURE 7.6-3
Simple resistive model of CMOS NOR gate.

are connected in series rather than in parallel. Once again, four transistors are required for a CMOS two-input NAND circuit, as compared with only three transistors for the similar NMOS circuit of Fig. 7.4-2.

The operation of the CMOS NAND circuit is similar to the CMOS NOR circuit except for the logic function realized. The interchange of the parallel and series connections for the pullup and pulldown paths changes the output voltage generated for specific input conditions, resulting in a realization of the NAND function. If both inputs a and b are below V_{TN}, the series n-channel pulldown

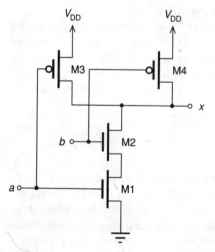

FIGURE 7.6-4
Two-input CMOS NAND gate.

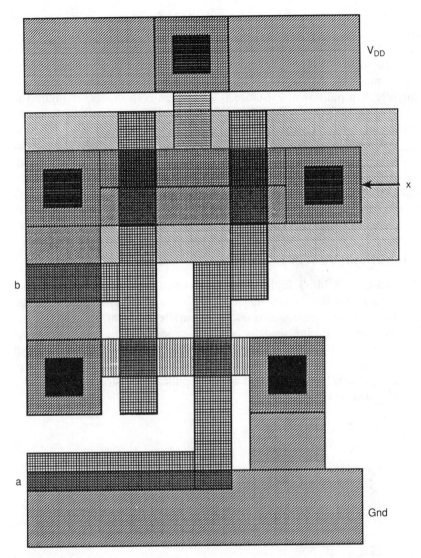

FIGURE 7.6-5
CMOS NAND gate layout with inputs a and b and output x.

transistors M1 and M2 are off while the parallel p-channel pullup transistors M3 and M4 conduct. This results in an output voltage level of V_{DD}. If only input a is below V_{TN}, then transistor M1 is off while transistor M3 conducts. Thus, the output voltage is still pulled to V_{DD}. If only input b is below V_{TN}, transistor M2 is off and transistor M4 conducts, again setting the output to V_{DD}. If both inputs a and b are above $V_{DD} - |V_{TP}|$, then transistors M3 and M4 are off and transistors M1 and M2 conduct. This condition sets the output voltage to 0 V. This input-output voltage relation realizes the positive NAND logic function.

For the NAND gate, the series path to ground uses n-channel transistors, and the parallel path to V_{DD} uses p-channel transistors. Based on minimum-size transistors and a 2.5:1 transconductance advantage of n-channel over p-channel transistors, the series resistance of two n-channel transistors to ground will be nearly matched by a single p-channel pullup to V_{DD}. To demonstrate this, consider the NAND gate model of Fig. 7.6-6 based on the simple resistive models of Fig. 7.5-4. Let all transistors corresponding to Fig. 7.6-6 be of minimum size. For this circuit, the effective pulldown resistance is $2R_N$ when both inputs are high. The effective pullup resistance is either R_P or $R_P/2$ depending on whether only one or both inputs are low, respectively. Noting that $R_P = 2.5R_N$ for $K'_N = 2.5K'_P$, the worst-case input-dependent asymmetry is less than 2:1, which is much better than that obtained for the corresponding NOR circuit. This near-symmetry makes the NAND gate the preferred CMOS logic form. Note that a CMOS NOR gate requires greater silicon area to achieve either a lower resistance p-channel path or a higher resistance n-channel path to reduce the worst-case input-dependent asymmetry.

7.6.3   Multi-Input CMOS Logic Gates

Classical multi-input CMOS logic gates are formed by adding an n-channel pulldown and a p-channel pullup transistor for each additional input. For the NOR gate, the pulldown transistor is added in parallel with the other n-channel transistors, and the pullup transistor is added in series with the other p-channel transistors. A three-input CMOS NOR gate is shown in Fig. 7.6-7. The three-input CMOS NAND gate of Fig. 7.6-8 is formed by inserting a pulldown transistor in series with the n-channel transistors and adding a pullup transistor in parallel with the p-channel transistors.

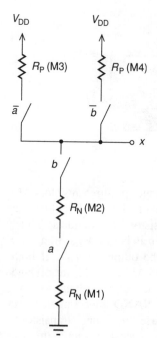

FIGURE 7.6-6
Simple resistive model of CMOS NAND gate.

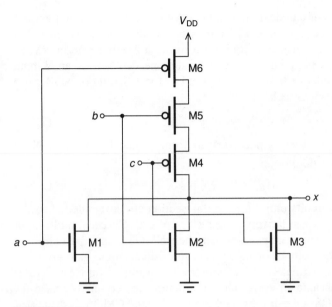

FIGURE 7.6-7
Three-input CMOS NOR gate.

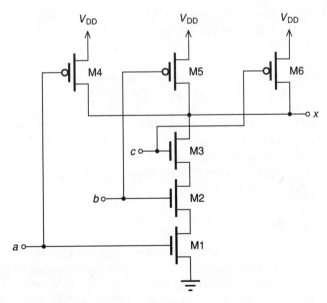

FIGURE 7.6-8
Three-input CMOS NAND gate.

Two characteristics of classical multi-input CMOS logic gates limit their use in VLSI circuits. Let N be the number of inputs to a multi-input logic gate. Let M_{NMOS} be the number of transistors required to form an N-input gate in NMOS or PMOS, and let M_{CMOS} be the number of transistors needed to form an N-input gate in CMOS. The number of transistors required to form NAND or NOR gates in either an NMOS or PMOS technology is

$$M_{NMOS} = N + 1 \tag{7.6-4}$$

whereas the number of transistors necessary to form classical NAND or NOR gates in a CMOS technology is

$$M_{CMOS} = 2N \tag{7.6-5}$$

The CMOS logic circuits introduced in this section are designated *classical* CMOS logic because of their relatively long history of use. Classical multi-input CMOS logic gates require more transistors than their NMOS counterparts for any number of inputs. As the number of inputs to a multi-input logic gate grows, a CMOS gate requires approximately twice as many transistors as an NMOS gate. To circumvent this disadvantage, clever circuit structures are commonly used for multi-input gates in CMOS. One of these techniques, domino CMOS, is discussed in a subsequent section. Alternatively, NMOS-like structures are sometimes used in CMOS, with a p-channel pullup with its gate grounded used to emulate the depletion-load device of NMOS. Like NMOS logic, this pseudo-NMOS logic has the disadvantage of static power dissipation.

A second disadvantage of classical multi-input CMOS gates arises from the requirement for a series transistor path from the output to one of the power supply nodes. For a NAND gate, this series path is the pulldown path. For a NOR gate, the series path is the pullup path. As the number of inputs to a classical CMOS gate grows, it becomes difficult to size the transistors for proper output drive through the series path. Remember that the multi-input NMOS NOR gate of Sec. 7.4 did not have this disadvantage.

Classical CMOS logic gates and their characteristics were described in this section. As with the CMOS inverter, ratioless CMOS logic gates provide ideal logic voltage levels and allows device sizing to be used for near symmetrical output drive. As a disadvantage, classical CMOS logic gates require almost twice as many transistors as their NMOS counterparts.

7.7 TRANSMISSION GATES

Because a MOS transistor is an excellent switching device, as demonstrated in Sec. 5.1, it is possible to connect this transistor in series with a logical signal to either pass or inhibit the signal. A MOS transistor connected in this way is called a *pass transistor* or *transmission gate* because it passes or transmits signals under control of its gate terminal. This connection has several advantages and some disadvantages compared to other methods of controlling a logic signal. In this section, characteristics of pass transistors are analyzed for NMOS circuits. Then the transmission gate structure for CMOS circuits is studied.

7.7.1 NMOS Pass Transistor

Figure 7.7-1 shows an input signal V_i connected through an n-channel transistor to the input V_a of a standard inverter circuit. A transistor M1 connected in this manner is called a *pass transistor*. This same circuit connection is important in dynamic storage circuits, to be discussed in Sec. 9.6. If the gate voltage, V_G, of the pass transistor is held at 0 V, and if the drain and source voltages are constrained between 0 V and V_{DD}, an enhancement pass transistor can never conduct because a positive gate-to-source voltage cannot be established. Because of the high off-resistance of an enhancement transistor, the input V_i is effectively disconnected from the inverter circuit.

If, on the other hand, V_G is held at V_{DD}, the pass transistor will conduct to equalize the voltages at its source and drain. This is explained by considering the alternatives with $V_G = V_{DD}$. First, assume that V_i, the input voltage to the pass transistor, is held at a low logic level: $V_i = 0$ V. If the input terminal of the pass transistor is considered the source, the gate-to-source voltage is V_{DD} and the pass transistor conducts to bring the drain terminal voltage V_a to 0 V. Note that no current can be supplied from the inverter input, an oxide-insulated gate.

Next assume that the input is held at $V_i = V_{DD}$. The pass transistor may appear to be off because both V_G and V_i are at the same voltage. However, because an enhancement transistor is symmetrical with respect to the drain and source terminals, the V_a terminal of the pass transistor can act as the source. If the voltage at the inverter input $V_a = 0$ V, the gate-to-source voltage of the pass transistor is initially V_{DD}, the transistor will conduct, and the inverter input V_a will be pulled to a higher voltage. Note that as V_a increases, the pass transistor gate-to-source voltage is reduced. When V_a reaches $V_{DD} - V_{TN}$, the pass transistor will cease to conduct. Thus, the pass transistor can only pull the inverter input to one threshold voltage drop below the pass transistor gate voltage. This connection of the pass transistor with the V_i and V_G terminals held at V_{DD} is the same circuit configuration as the enhancement pullup load for the MOS inverter discussed in Secs. 6.1 and 7.3.

One last alternative must be considered. If both V_G and the input voltage V_i of the pass transistor are at V_{DD} and the inverter input $V_a = V_{DD}$, the pass transistor will not conduct. However, because the logic levels at the source and drain terminals of the pass transistor are already equivalent, the logical effect is the same as if the pass transistor were conducting. This analysis is summarized by the following two equations.

$$V_G = 0 \text{ V} \rightarrow \text{Pass transistor is off} \qquad (7.7\text{-}1)$$

$$V_G = V_{DD} \rightarrow \text{Pass transistor conducts} \qquad (7.7\text{-}2)$$

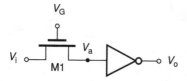

FIGURE 7.7-1
Input signal connected to an inverter through a pass transistor.

At this point the reader might infer that a pass transistor could be used to logically AND two input signals. One signal could be applied to the pass transistor input terminal, and the other could be applied to the pass transistor gate terminal. The output of the pass transistor would be pulled high only if both the gate terminal *and* the input terminal of the pass transistor were high. This is correct; however, the converse is not true. The output of the pass transistor will be pulled low if its input terminal is low, but not if its gate terminal is low. According to Eq. 7.7-1, when the gate is at 0 V, the pass transistor is off and cannot force the output to a low voltage to satisfy the AND functional requirements. Thus, this connection does not function as an AND gate. The assumption by a designer that a pass transistor can function as an AND gate would be a simple but fatal (to circuit operation) mistake.

A pass transistor used as a logic switch has important advantages in terms of integrated circuit layout constraints. First, the pass transistor consists of a single transistor and therefore requires less area than a logic gate. Even the simplest logic gate, an inverter, requires two transistors. Additionally, a pass transistor is a three-terminal device, whereas an inverter is a four-terminal device if one counts power and ground. A requirement for fewer interconnections is a major advantage when integrated circuit layout constraints are considered. For many applications, the pass transistor can be a minimum-size device, further reducing layout area. Finally, a pass transistor requires no dc power—a significant advantage.

A typical use of pass transistors to create a 4-to-1 selector circuit is shown in Fig. 7.7-2. A circuit that can connect one of N different inputs to an output is called an N-to-1 *selector circuit*. Here 8 pass transistors replace an equivalent of 21 NMOS transistors or 32 CMOS transistors if classical logic gates are used. This selector circuit can realize all 16 logic functions of the two inputs a and

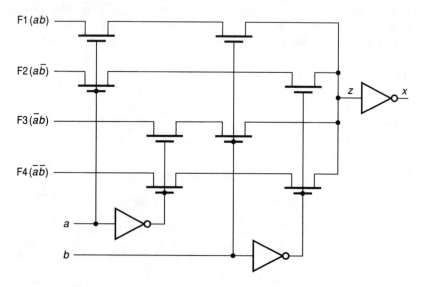

FIGURE 7.7-2
Pass transistor selector circuit.

b. For example, if F1–F4 are all set to 0, then the output z is 0. If F1 is set high and F2–F4 are set low, then the AND of a and b is given at z. If F2 and F3 are set high while F1 and F4 are set low, then the exclusive-OR function of a and b is realized at z. If F1–F3 are set high and F4 is set low, then a OR b is given at z. The 16 possible combinations of 0 or 1 at the four inputs F1–F4 yield the 16 possible logic functions of a and b. This selector circuit function block is popular within microprocessor ALUs, where both logic and arithmetic functions must be realized. Note that power dissipation, number of devices, and interconnection requirements are considerably reduced from an equivalent logic gate implementation. This is but one example of the simplicity available through the use of pass transistor logic.

A series string of pass transistors connected to control the logical path of an input signal is an appealing circuit configuration in terms of area and interconnection constraints compared to other alternatives. For example, such a string is frequently used to selectively propagate the carry in a multibit binary adder. However, at least two significant problems are encountered with a series string of pass transistors. The first problem arises because of design imposed constraints on signal propagation delays. Figure 7.7-3 shows a series string of pass transistors connecting V_i to V_o with all gates held high and an approximate equivalent circuit using a lumped circuit element model. R represents equivalent resistance between the source and drain of a pass transistor. (Bulk effects increase the equivalent resistance here because the source terminal is not grounded.) C represents the capacitance to ground for each stage; the value is determined by the gate capacitance and the drain and source diffusion capacitance of each pass transistor. It can be shown that the signal propagation delay from V_i to V_o is proportional to the square of the number of identical stages.

A simplified explanation for the square-law delay for a series string of pass transistors can be given in terms of the resistance, capacitance, and associated RC time constants of the lumped circuit element model. A single pass transistor stage exhibits a delay that is a function of the series resistance R and the capacitance to ground C. This delay is proportional to the time constant $\tau = RC$. When a second

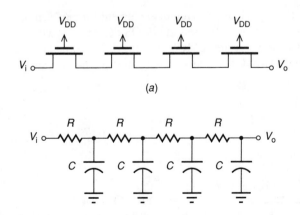

(a)

(b)

FIGURE 7.7-3
(a) Series string of pass transistors,
(b) Lumped-element equivalent circuit.

pass transistor is added in series with the first and only the additional capacitance to ground is considered, the RC time constant ($\tau = R2C$), and therefore the transmission delay, is doubled. If the additional series resistance is considered but the additional capacitance to ground is neglected ($\tau = 2RC$), the delay is still doubled. The combination of twice the resistance and twice the capacitance ($\tau = 2^2RC$) causes the total delay to nearly quadruple. In general, the delay is proportional to N^2RC where N is the number of series pass transistors. For this reason, long series connections of pass transistors are usually segmented by the addition of inverters at intervals of about four pass transistors. The inverters buffer the signal and break the square-law delay effect of the series pass transistor cascade, resulting in smaller overall signal delay.

A second problem is encountered if pass transistors are cascaded with the output of one pass transistor connected to the gate of the next pass transistor as shown in Fig. 7.7-4. This problem is related to the threshold voltage drop from the gate of a pass transistor to its output terminal. As described previously for enhancement pullup transistors, the source voltage can only be pulled to a value V_{TN} less than the gate terminal voltage. If both the gate and drain terminals of a pass transistor are at a voltage V_{DD}, then the source terminal is pulled no higher than $V_{DD} - V_{TN}$. Succeeding circuits still reliably interpret this voltage as a high logic level. However, if the output (source terminal) of a pass transistor is connected to the gate of a second pass transistor, as in the series pass transistor cascade of Fig. 7.7-4, the output of the second pass transistor can only be pulled to a voltage of $V_{DD} - 2V_{TN}$. In general, for N pass transistors cascaded source to gate, the voltage at the last source terminal V_o can only be pulled to

$$V_o < V_{DD} - NV_{TN} \qquad (7.7\text{-}3)$$

This voltage is too low to be recognized reliably as a high logic level if $N \geq 2$. For this reason, source-to-gate cascades of pass transistors represent an electrical rule violation and are avoided in practice.

7.7.2 CMOS Transmission Gate

The NMOS pass transistor described previously is an ideal element for performing many logic and control functions and is widely used in NMOS designs. However, is the pass transistor a useful device within CMOS designs? To help answer this question, Fig. 7.7-5 shows two CMOS inverters joined using a typical

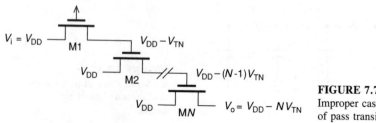

FIGURE 7.7-4
Improper cascaded connection of pass transistors.

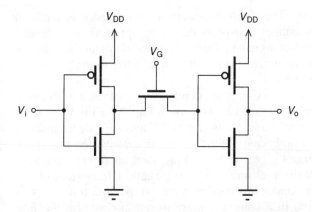

FIGURE 7.7-5
Pass transistor connecting two CMOS inverters.

n-channel pass transistor. Certainly, if the pass transistor gate voltage $V_G = 0$ V, the pass transistor isolates the two CMOS inverters, just as in the case of NMOS inverters. If the pass transistor gate voltage $V_G = V_{DD}$ and the output of the first inverter is at 0 V, the pass transistor will pull the input of the second inverter to 0 V. Once again, this is similar to the NMOS case and is satisfactory. One other condition must be considered. If both the output of the first inverter, that is, the drain terminal of the pass transistor, and the pass transistor gate are at V_{DD}, then the source terminal of the pass transistor can be pulled no higher than $V_{DD} - V_{TN}$. This voltage is sufficient to turn on the n-channel pulldown transistor of the second inverter, but it may not completely turn off the corresponding p-channel pullup transistor.

A gate terminal voltage greater than $V_{DD} - |V_{TP}|$ is required to turn off a p-channel pullup transistor. When the gate voltage drops below $V_{DD} - |V_{TP}|$, the p-channel transistor begins to conduct. If the p-channel pullup transistor conducts because of mismatched V_{TN} and V_{TP} threshold voltages, for example, static power is dissipated in the gate, and the effective noise margin is reduced. Thus, the standard n-channel pass transistor configuration is undesirable for driving a CMOS gate.

The pass transistor is such a useful circuit element in digital designs that a CMOS equivalent is used to accomplish a similar effect. The CMOS circuit is not called a pass transistor but, rather, is called a *transmission gate* because more than a single transistor is required. Figure 7.7-6 shows a CMOS transmission

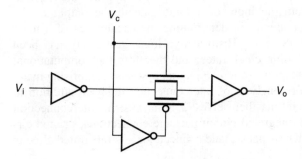

FIGURE 7.7-6
Transmission gate connecting two CMOS inverters.

gate connecting two inverters. The single n-channel pass transistor is replaced by parallel n-channel and p-channel transistors driven by opposing logic levels. Unfortunately, unless the control signal V_c for the transmission gate is available as a double-rail logic signal, an inverter is required in addition to the parallel n-channel and p-channel transistors.

Operation of a CMOS transmission gate circuit can be explained as follows. If the control signal to the transmission gate (shown in Fig. 7.7-6) is $V_c = 0$ V, the gate terminal of the n-channel transistor is also at 0 V and the gate terminal of the p-channel transistor is at V_{DD} because of the control signal inverter; thus, both transistors are off. If the control signal is $V_c = V_{DD}$, then appropriate voltages are generated to cause both the n-channel and the p-channel transistors of the transmission gate to conduct. Under this condition the two parallel transistors of the transmission gate function in a complementary manner to connect the first and second inverters of the signal path in Fig. 7.7-6. When the output of the first inverter is at 0 V, the n-channel transistor of the transmission gate pulls the input to the second inverter to 0 V. When the output of the first inverter is at V_{DD}, the p-channel transistor of the transmission gate pulls the input to the second inverter all the way to V_{DD}. This circumvents the threshold voltage drop problem encountered with a single enhancement pass transistor for CMOS logic. Thus, the CMOS transmission gate provides voltage levels that are compatible with other CMOS logic gates. Unfortunately, the cost of extra silicon layout area for transistors and interconnection is high, rendering the CMOS transmission gate a less useful device than the comparable NMOS pass transistor.

Both pass transistors and transmission gates were described in this section. These building blocks are most advantageous where they can select or control the flow of a logic signal. Care must be exercised in cascading these devices to prevent large signal propagation delays.

7.8 SIGNAL PROPAGATION DELAYS

Earlier sections of this chapter dealt with steady state analysis of MOS circuits that perform digital logic functions. Now an additional parameter—time—is injected into the analysis. Real logic circuits require nonzero but finite time for signals to propagate from input to output. Models to analyze and predict the propagation delay are crucial for practical logic design.

Delays encountered in digital circuitry are composed of two principle components: *gate delay* and *interconnection delay*. Logic gate delay, the time required for a signal to propagate from the input of a logic gate to the output of the same gate, is an important parameter in determining the capabilities of a logic family such as TTL or NMOS logic. Historically, logic gate delay has been the major limiting factor in setting clock rates, and therefore the computational speed, of single-chip digital integrated circuits. Digital systems, comprising many integrated circuit chips, require analysis of interconnection delay in addition to the logic gate delay of the circuits themselves. Digital system interconnection delays are those arising from integrated circuit package connections, printed circuit board connections, and chassis back-plane connections. As integrated circuits have been manufactured with reduced device sizes, internal gate-to-gate interconnection delays have increased in importance relative to logic gate delays. As device sizes reach submicron dimensions, internal interconnection delays dominate the gate delays. The characterization of signal propagation delays for logic gates loaded by a single, identical logic gate with minimal interconnection is addressed in this section. In a subsequent section delays caused by nonhomogeneous logic gate characteristics, logic fanout, interconnection capacitance, and off-chip loads are analyzed.

7.8.1 Ratio-Logic Model

To address the problem of signal propagation delay, the simple case of Fig. 7.8-1a, where the output of one inverter drives the input to a second, identical inverter, will be considered initially. For this analysis, depletion-load inverters such as the one analyzed in Fig. 7.3-1a, and redrawn in Fig. 7.8-1b, will be used. Figure 7.8-2a shows an ideal voltage step of amplitude V_{DD}. Assume that this voltage step is applied to the input of the first inverter of Fig. 7.8-1a at $t = t_0$. For the output of the first inverter, the response of Fig. 7.8-2b is ideal, but the actual response will resemble that of Fig. 7.8-2c. In this case, the signal propagation delay is the difference between the time of the input transition, t_0, and the time that the output is recognized as a valid logic low voltage, t_1. This delay is caused by parasitic capacitances in the MOSFETs, as discussed in Sec. 3.1, and interconnection capacitance. The slight initial overshoot in the actual response is caused by the gate-drain overlap capacitance of M1. The overall delay time, however, is dominated by the effects of the capacitive load caused by the second inverter including the interconnection capacitance. A closed-form mathematical expression for the output waveform of Fig. 7.8-2c is unwieldy because of the

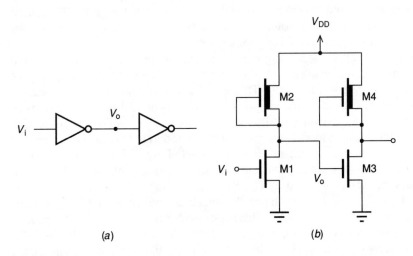

(a)   *(b)*

FIGURE 7.8-1
Single inverter driving a second, identical inverter: *(a)* Logic diagram, *(b)* Circuit diagram.

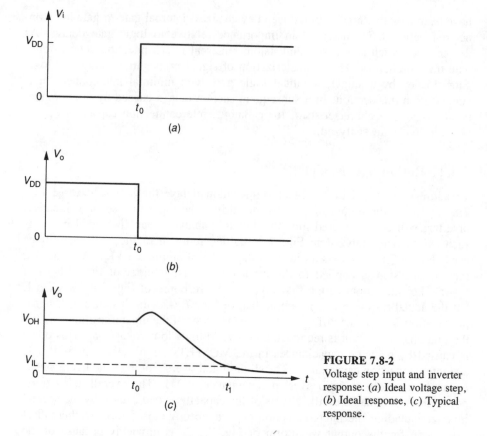

FIGURE 7.8-2
Voltage step input and inverter response: (*a*) Ideal voltage step, (*b*) Ideal response, (*c*) Typical response.

nonlinear nature of the device *I–V* characteristics, the voltage dependence of all parasitic capacitors, and the changes in operating region for the MOSFETs during the transition. A closed-form solution requires the simultaneous solution of a set of nonlinear partial differential equations.

For hand analysis and insight into design, a quick and simple method of approximating the response of this circuit is needed for both high-to-low and low-to-high output transitions. This initial analysis neglects interconnection capacitance and is based on the simple switch resistor model of Fig. 7.5-4, with the addition of gate capacitance. Figure 7.8-3*a* shows a symbolic convention that emphasizes the resistive models for transistors M1 and M2. This can be partitioned further to the resistance-capacitance inverter model of Fig. 7.8-3*b*. Note that M2 is modeled by a resistor without a switch since the depletion transistor with $V_{GS} = 0$ V is always on. M1 is modeled by C_G, S1, and R_1. Switch S1 is open for V_i low and closed for V_i high. The resistance R_2 models the pullup transistor resistance, and the resistance R_1 models the pulldown transistor resistance. The capacitance C_G is the input capacitance to the inverter. It will be demonstrated later that C_G is approximately equal to $C_{ox}WL$ where W and L are the width and length of the pulldown transistor (M1 or M3 in Fig. 7.8-1*b*). For this analysis, the equivalent input capacitance to the reference inverter in a logic family is termed C_G. From

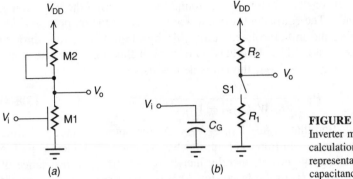

FIGURE 7.8-3
Inverter models for delay calculations: (*a*) Symbolic representation, (*b*) Resistance-capacitance inverter model.

a dc viewpoint, it follows from the model of Fig. 7.8-3*b* that the high output voltage level is V_{DD} and the low output voltage level is

$$V_L = \frac{V_{DD}R_1}{R_1 + R_2} \tag{7.8-1}$$

Logic circuits where the dc output voltage is determined by the ratio of two series resistors are termed *ratio logic* circuits. As was stated in Eqs. 7.5-2 and 7.5-3, the equivalent resistance of a MOS transistor in the model of Fig. 7.8-3*b* is proportional to its length L divided by its width W. Thus, the relationship between resistance R_2 and resistance R_1 can be approximated as

$$R_2 = \frac{L_2 W_1}{W_2 L_1} R_1 = k R_1 \tag{7.8-2}$$

With the 4 : 1 sizing rule of Sec. 7.3, $k = 4$ and $R_2 = 4R_1$. With this sizing rule and the model of Fig. 7.8-3*b*, it follows from Eq. 7.8-1 that the high and low logic levels for the output are V_{DD} and $V_{DD}/5$, respectively. For $V_{DD} = 5$ V, this gives a high logic level of 5 V and a low logic level of 1 V. Although the high logic level is the same as that obtained by the more exact analysis of Sec. 7.3, the low logic level differs from the more exact value of 9/32 V obtained previously with $V_{DD} = 5$ V. This difference in dc voltage levels is not significant for an approximate delay analysis.

To provide a simplified model for delay calculations, approximate values for resistances R_1 and R_2 of Fig. 7.8-3*b* must be found. Observe that when V_i is high, S1 is closed and M1 is in the ohmic region for much of the high-to-low output transition. From Eq. 3.1-8 with $V_{GS} = V_i = V_{DD}$, a good approximation for the resistance R_1 near $V_o = V_{DS} = 0$ V is the small signal equivalent resistance

$$R_{ss} = \frac{L_1}{K'W_1(V_{DD} - V_{TN})} \tag{7.8-3}$$

(Note that Eq. 7.8-3 demonstrates the proportionality factor described for Eqs. 7.5-2 and 7.5-3.) This resistance is a good reference point but does not consider the effects of the pullup resistance or the nonlinear characteristics of the enhancement transistor over the actual output voltage range.

A better model for delay estimation is found by considering the large signal equivalent resistance. The equivalent resistance at the start of the output transition is found by dividing the initial voltage across M1 by the initial current through M1. The pullup transistor M2 contributes no current at this point because it has $V_{DS} = 0$ V. Assuming $V_i = V_{DD}$, the equivalent resistance is given by

$$R_1 = \frac{2V_{DD}L_1}{K'W_1(V_{DD} - V_{TN})^2} \approx 2R_{ss} \tag{7.8-4}$$

using the approximation that $V_{DD} - V_{TN} \approx V_{DD}$. As the output voltage falls, the resistance of the enhancement transistor approaches R_{ss}, but the depletion pullup transistor begins to supply current, thereby increasing the effective resistance of the inverter output. Analysis of the large signal equivalent resistance at an output voltage near V_{TN} with the effects of pullup transistor M2 considered gives

$$R_1 = \frac{V_o L_1}{K'W_1\left[(V_{DD} - V_{TN} - V_o/2)V_o - V_{TD}^2/2k\right]} \tag{7.8-5}$$

It can be shown that this expression also reduces to $R_1 \approx 2R_{ss}$ with typical parameters for the reference inverter. For the approximate propagation delay analysis in this section, it will be assumed that R_1 is given by Eq. 7.8-4.

For a low-to-high output transition, transistor M2 starts in the saturated region and finishes in the ohmic region. With typical parameter values for the 4:1 reference inverter, the large signal equivalent resistance of M2 for a low-to-high output transition varies from about $13R_{ss}$ to $5R_{ss}$ as V_o increases from 0 V to V_{DD}. An average equivalent resistance of $8R_{ss}$ is a reasonable compromise. Note that considering the 4:1 resistance ratio for the reference inverter, the equivalent pullup resistance is

$$R_2 \approx 4R_1 = 2kR_{ss} \tag{7.8-6}$$

It should be noted that for this approximate analysis, significant errors of $\pm 50\%$ or more can be anticipated using the simple model of Fig. 7.8-3b. These errors are justifiable for a quick approximate analysis. The alternative when better accuracy is required is to use circuit simulation programs such as SPICE to account for the nonlinear characteristics of MOS transistors and the effect of nonzero rise time for the input voltage. If $L_1 = W_1$, $L_2 = 4W_2$, $K' = 30$ $\mu A/V^2$, $V_{TN} = 1$ V, $V_{TD} = -3.5$ V, and $V_{DD} = 5$ V, then

$$R_1 \approx 16.6 \text{ k}\Omega \quad \text{and} \quad R_2 \approx 66.4 \text{ k}\Omega \tag{7.8-7}$$

With approximate models for the transistor resistances in hand, the analysis now turns to the input capacitance. Because M1 of Fig. 7.8-1b is ohmic for $V_i = V_{DD}$ and cutoff for $V_i = 0$ V, it follows from Fig. 3.1-19b that the parasitic input capacitance at either logic level is approximately $C_{ox}W_1L_1$. During transitions, M1 enters the saturation region momentarily, causing the input capacitance to drop to approximately $(2/3)C_{ox}W_1L_1$, as indicated in Fig. 3.1-19b. Because the capacitance change is relatively small and M1 is normally in the saturation region for only part of the output transition time, the change is neglected in the model of Fig. 7.8-3b. Thus, C_G is approximated as

$$C_G \approx C_{ox}WL \tag{7.8-8}$$

To estimate propagation delays, the equivalent circuit model of Fig. 7.8-3b is simplified to the model of Fig. 7.8-4a by adding switch $\overline{S1}$. This model isolates the effects of R_1 and R_2 to simplify the analysis further. Remember that the effects of the pullup transistor during a high-to-low transition were included when R_1 was approximated earlier.

The high-to-low and low-to-high transition times for an inverter loaded by an identical inverter will now be determined. Because the input to the load inverter looks like a capacitor of value C_G, the equivalent circuit for a low-to-high step input voltage is as shown in Fig. 7.8-4b. Note that this input causes a high-to-low output transition. Because this model is a simple RC circuit with an initial voltage on C_G, it follows that a major portion of a high-to-low output transition, designated t_{HL}, occurs in two RC time constants, where $R = R_1$ and $C = C_G$ (for an ideal RC circuit, the 90% to 10% transition requires 2.2 time constants). Thus, the high-to-low output transition is approximated here by

$$t_{HL} \approx 2R_1C_G \qquad (7.8\text{-}9)$$

Through a similar analysis of the circuit in Fig. 7.8-4c, the low-to-high output transition time is approximated by

$$t_{LH} \approx 2R_2C_G \qquad (7.8\text{-}10)$$

For ratio-logic circuits, R_1 and R_2 of Fig. 7.8-4a are related by the device-sizing parameter, k. From Eqs. 7.8-2, 7.8-9, and 7.8-10, it follows that

$$t_{LH} = kt_{HL} \qquad (7.8\text{-}11)$$

For the 4:1 sizing rule,

$$t_{LH} = 4t_{HL} \qquad (7.8\text{-}12)$$

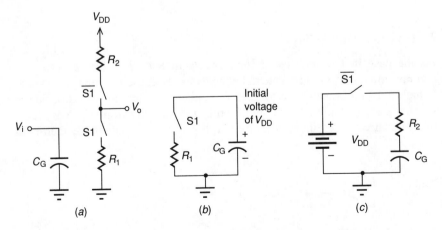

FIGURE 7.8-4
Equivalent circuits for inverter delay analysis: (a) Simplified RC inverter model, (b) Equivalent circuit for high-to-low output transition, (c) Equivalent circuit for low-to-high output transition.

7.8.2   Process Characteristic Time Constant

Each process will have geometrical design rules that limit the minimum size for a transistor. The process will also have electrical design rules that specify the desired supply voltage V_{DD}, the transconductance parameter K', the threshold voltage V_T, and the gate capacitance per unit area C_{ox}. From these parameters, a characteristic time constant for the process can be determined. This time constant, designated as τ_P, and defined as $R_{ss}C_G$ is useful for comparing delay character- istics of different processes. For both NMOS and CMOS technologies the values of K' and V_T for the n-channel enchancement transistor are used; and for PMOS technologies the values of K' and V_T for the p-channel enchancement transistor are used. From Eqs. 7.8-3 and 7.8-8,

$$\tau_P = R_{ss}C_G = \frac{L_1}{K'W_1(V_{DD} - V_{TN})} C_{ox}W_1L_1 \qquad (7.8\text{-}13)$$

This reduces to

$$\tau_P = \frac{L_1^2 C_{ox}}{K'(V_{DD} - V_{TN})} \qquad (7.8\text{-}14)$$

Assume the typical minimum transistor dimension is 2 μ, $K' = 45$ $\mu A/V^2$, $C_{ox} = 1$ fF/μ^2, $V_{TN} = 1$ V, and $V_{DD} = 5$ V. Using these values in Eq. 7.8-14, the process characteristic time constant is

$$\tau_P = 0.02 \text{ ns} \qquad (7.8\text{-}15)$$

It must be noted that τ_P is not a measure of expected circuit delay. The value of τ_P depends only on process geometrical and electrical parameters and is thus independent of a particular circuit implementation. Therein lies the usefulness of τ_P. From Eqs. 7.8-4, 7.8-6, 7.8-9, and 7.8-10, it can be observed that t_{HL} and t_{LH} can be expressed in terms of τ_P as $t_{HL} = 4\tau_P$ and $t_{LH} = 16\tau_P$ for a minimum- size inverter.

7.8.3   Inverter-Pair Delay

As was the case in the analysis of logic levels in Sec. 7.2, the inverter pair plays an important part in logic gate delay analysis. Because the high-to-low and low-to-high transition times are asymmetric, neither transition time is adequate to characterize a logic family. If the signal propagation delay from V_i to V_o for a pair of identical cascaded inverters shown in Fig. 7.8-5 is considered, then both

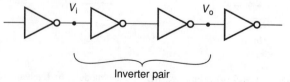

Inverter pair

FIGURE 7.8-5
Cascade of identical inverters.

high-to-low and low-to-high transitions contribute to the delay. Thus, the inverter-pair delay, designated t_{ipd}, is defined as the sum of a high-to-low transition and a low-to-high transition time:

$$t_{ipd} = t_{HL} + t_{LH} \tag{7.8-16}$$

This is often expressed in terms of the device sizing ratio as

$$t_{ipd} = (1 + k)t_{HL} \tag{7.8-17}$$

or from Eqs. 7.8-4, 7.8-9, and 7.8-13 in terms of τ_P:

$$t_{ipd} = 4(1 + k)\tau_P \tag{7.8-18}$$

The inverter-pair delay is a key parameter in characterizing the speed of operation of a digital logic family. It represents a fundamental lower bound on the clock period of a synchronous system because a signal must be able to experience at least one high-to-low and one low-to-high transition during a system clock cycle. It will be seen later that the system clock period is typically much longer than the inverter-pair delay because of the contribution of interconnection delays and multiple levels of logic.

A physical interpretation of the inverter-pair delay deserves consideration. If either a high-to-low or a low-to-high input transition is applied to a cascade of inverters with identical loads, as in Fig. 7.8-5, then the delay associated with propagation of the signal through any two inverters (i.e., an inverter pair) is the inverter-pair delay. Assume the inverter cascade of Fig. 7.8-5 is designed in the typical NMOS process used for Eq. 7.8-15. Further assume that the gate of the pulldown device for each inverter is the minimum size of $2 \mu \times 2 \mu$, it follows from Eqs. 7.8-15 and 7.8-18 that the inverter-pair delay is

$$t_{ipd} = 4(1 + 4)0.02 \text{ ns} = 0.4 \text{ ns} \tag{7.8-19}$$

Note that based on the simplified device model used in these calculations, the response time for the reference inverter pair is very fast.

Three important observations must be made at this point. First, the present analysis gives unrealistically small delay times because it neglects interconnection capacitance. Second, the low-to-high transition delay for ratio logic is about k times as long as the high-to-low transition delay, as indicated by Eq. 7.8-11. This introduces significant asymmetry in the two transitions and is of concern in many applications, particularly if an output is loaded by a large capacitance. A typical response of the reference inverter to a fast square-wave excitation in a ratio-logic circuit is given in Fig. 7.8-6. This figure clearly shows the asymmetric rise and fall times for a ratio inverter circuit. The asymmetry occurs because the active pulldown device, M1, has much lower resistance than the passive pullup device, M2. One might be tempted to improve the pullup characteristics of M2 to decrease t_{LH} by resizing M2 for lower equivalent resistance. Unfortunately, this solution is not feasible because it would cause a degradation in logic signal levels, as can be seen from Eq. 7.8-1. The asymmetry in transition times is thus inherent in ratio-logic systems, as indicated by Eq. 7.8-11.

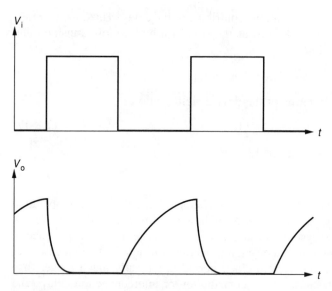

FIGURE 7.8-6
Asymmetric response for a ratio-logic inverter driven with a square wave.

A comparison of results obtained from the approximate delay analysis with those obtained from a detailed circuit simulation shows some differences.[7] These are attributable primarily to the terms R_1 and R_2 in Eqs. 7.8-9 and 7.8-10. These differences are due, in part, to the fact that the pullup and pulldown devices are not linear throughout their entire output transitions. Also, the previous analysis estimated a stage delay based on an ideal voltage step input. For a cascade of MOS inverters, the ideal step input applies only to the first stage; subsequent stages typically have an input rise time almost as long as the delay of the preceding stage. This partially invalidates the earlier assumption that the inverter input voltage was at V_{DD} during the entire high-to-low output transition. Thus, if the delay for a cascade of inverters is computed as the sum of single inverter-stage responses with ideal step inputs, further error is introduced.

Two good ways exist to improve the accuracy of a simplified inverter-delay analysis without increasing its complexity. First, the inverter-pair delay t_{ipd} (or even t_{HL} and t_{LH}) for a reference inverter can be experimentally measured for a specific process or determined from an accurate computer simulation. These delay parameters can then be thought of as design parameters. Overall delays can be expressed directly in terms of these delay parameters of the reference inverter. Alternatively, the resistance values R_1 in Eq. 7.8-4 and R_2 in Eq. 7.8-6 can be modified to compensate for errors in t_{HL} and t_{LH}. It should be remembered that the approximate analysis is useful primarily as a quick estimate of circuit performance. Attempts to create a simple, accurate delay analysis are undermined by many factors in practical circuits.[8]

The third observation is that R_1 and R_2 from Eqs. 7.8-4 and 7.8-6 are dependent on device length-to-width ratios but not on the actual lengths and widths of a transistor. As device sizes shrink—for example, from 2 μ to 1 μ—the transistor resistances remain relatively constant. The gate area of M3, the input device of the second stage in Fig. 7.8-1b, provides the parasitic capacitance load to the first stage. In a linearly scaled process, the gate area of M3 decreases with the square of the feature size, while the gate oxide thickness decreases directly with device size (see constant field scaling, Sec. 1.1). For these approximations, the total capacitive loading decreases linearly with feature size. It thus follows that the inverter-pair delay, which depends on effective transistor resistance and parasitic capacitive loading, decreases approximately linearly with feature size. This decrease offers the potential for significant system speed improvements as devices become smaller. The process characteristic time constant τ_P for the scaled-down process shows this speed increase.

The previous analysis was for a single inverter loaded by a single, identical inverter stage. If an input signal transition must ripple through a cascade of identical logic circuits, a first-order approximation of the total delay for the cascade assumes that the start of the transitions on successive stages is delayed until the transition of the preceding stage is complete. This allows the total delay to be simply computed as the sum of the individual stage delays. If the cascade delay is denoted as t_{cas}, the number of identical stages is N, and the average stage delay is one-half the inverter-pair delay t_{ipd}, then an approximation to the total delay is

$$t_{cas} = \frac{Nt_{ipd}}{2} \tag{7.8-20}$$

It will be shown in a subsequent section that capacitive loading from interconnections and fan-out causes delays larger than that predicted by Eq. 7.8-20.

7.8.4 Superbuffers

The asymmetric output delay of a ratio logic circuit is particularly undesirable when a highly capacitive bus or a large number of secondary device inputs must be driven. The slow pullup capability can seriously limit clock speeds for a system. One partial solution to this problem is a special circuit configuration called a *superbuffer*. Figures 7.8-7 and 7.8-8 show circuits for a noninverting super-

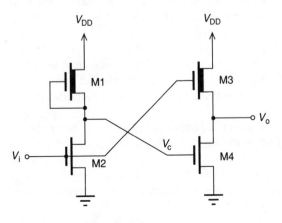

FIGURE 7.8-7
Noninverting superbuffer circuit.

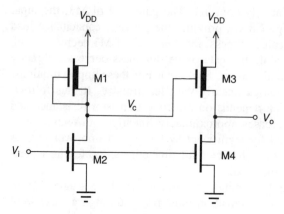

FIGURE 7.8-8
Inverting superbuffer circuit.

buffer and an inverting superbuffer, respectively. The output stage of each of these circuits is modified from the standard ratio-logic inverter in that the pullup transistor has its gate connected to an active logic signal. This connection increases the current sourcing ability of the pullup device, allowing faster drive for capacitive loads.

As can be seen from Figs. 7.8-7 and 7.8-8, a superbuffer consists of a standard inverter stage connected to a second inverter stage with an active pullup. The first inverter stage provides the input signal and its logical complement to drive the transistors of the output inverter stage. Both the input signal and its complement are necessary to drive the pulldown transistor and pullup transistor of the output stage at complementary times.

The logical operation of the noninverting superbuffer of Fig. 7.8-7 will now be examined. Assume that the output stage with transistors M3 and M4 has the 4:1 pullup/pulldown ratio that was used for the reference inverter. In this case, both transistors may remain unchanged sizewise from the reference inverter circuit. If the input to the noninverting superbuffer is low, then the output should also be low. Because the M1-M2 circuit is an inverter, the intermediate voltage V_c will be high when the superbuffer input is a logic low. Because this intermediate voltage drives the gate of pulldown transistor M4 to a logic high voltage, the output of the superbuffer is pulled low. The gate of the pullup transistor M3 is tied directly to the superbuffer input; thus, its gate is connected to a low voltage. If the superbuffer output is low, pullup transistor M3 has its gate and source each connected to a low voltage. This provides a gate-to-source voltage of 0 V, and the circuit is therefore equivalent to the standard depletion-load inverter when the superbuffer input is low. Based on this analysis, the superbuffer output stage functions as a standard depletion-load inverter stage when the superbuffer output is low.

The logical operation of the noninverting superbuffer will now be examined in response to a high input. This high input at the first inverter stage will drive its output, V_c, to a low level. The signal V_c is connected to the gate of pulldown transistor M4, causing it to turn off. The pullup transistor M3 has its gate connected directly to the superbuffer input, which is high. Initially, before the superbuffer output is pulled high, the source terminal of the output pullup transistor, M3, will be at a low voltage. This provides a gate-to-source voltage for pullup transistor M3 that is approximately equal to a logic high voltage minus a logic low voltage, or nearly V_{DD}. For a typical NMOS process for digital circuits, it is easily shown that a gate-to-source voltage of 0 V for a depletion-mode transistor allows a current that is nearly equal to the current for a similarly sized enhancement transistor with a gate-to-source voltage of $V_{DD} - V_{TN}$. Increasing the gate-to-source voltage to V_{DD} for a depletion-mode transistor is roughly equivalent to doubling the gate-to-source voltage for an enhancement transistor. This provides improved pullup capability during the low-to-high transition of the superbuffer output.

The actively driven pullup transistor M3 improves the pullup characteristic of the superbuffer as just explained; the following analysis quantifies this improvement. For integrated digital circuitry with depletion-mode pullup transistors, the magnitude of V_{TD} is typically chosen as a large percentage of the supply voltage—for example, $-V_{TD} \approx 0.7V_{DD}$. For a standard depletion-mode pullup transistor with a gate-to-source voltage of 0 V, the transistor is in the ohmic region whenever the drain-to-source voltage is less than $0.7V_{DD}$. If the gate-to-source voltage is greater than $0.3V_{DD}$, the depletion-mode transistor is always in the ohmic region because the drain-to-source voltage is limited to V_{DD}. For a transistor in the ohmic region with constant drain-to-source voltage, its equivalent resistance is inversely proportional to the effective gate-to-source voltage, $V_{GS} - V_{TN}$ (see Eq. 3.1-8). If the effective gate-to-source voltage is doubled, the effective resistance of the pullup transistor is halved.

In the analysis of the preceding paragraph, it was shown that the equivalent resistance of the active pullup transistor of a superbuffer is initially half that of a standard inverter pullup for a low-to-high output transition. From Eq. 7.8-10, the delay t_{LH} is directly proportional to the effective resistance of the pullup transistor. Thus, the new low-to-high delay becomes

$$t'_{LH} = \frac{1}{2}t_{LH} = 2t_{HL} \qquad (7.8\text{-}21)$$

The equivalent inverter-pair delay for a superbuffer output stage with the standard pullup/pulldown ratio becomes

$$t'_{ipd} = t_{HL} + t'_{LH} = 3t_{HL} \qquad (7.8\text{-}22)$$

This means that a superbuffer output stage can drive a heavy capacitive load almost twice as fast as a standard inverter of the same size ($3t_{HL}$ versus $5t_{HL}$). A similar analysis applies to the inverting superbuffer of Fig. 7.8-8.

7.8.5 NMOS NAND and NOR Delays

Many times, a designer has a choice between using a NAND circuit or a NOR circuit to realize a particular logic function. For example, any combinational logic function can be realized in a sum-of-products form with a NAND-NAND logic gate combination or as a product-of-sums form with a NOR-NOR logic gate structure.[6] Figure 7.8-9 shows the implementation of a simple logic function, the exclusive-OR, with both a NAND-NAND and a NOR-NOR realization. Because either structure can be used, it is useful to ask if one structure has advantages over the other.

In Sec. 7.4, it was determined that the typical pullup/pulldown sizing ratio for a NOR gate was about 4:1 and that a typical pullup/pulldown ratio for a two-input NAND gate was about 8:1. Assuming the input devices for the NAND and the NOR gates are sized the same as for the reference inverter, it follows from the models of Fig. 7.8-4 that the reduced circuits of Fig. 7.8-10a and b are useful to estimate the logic gate delays for two-input NAND and two-input NOR gates. The delay here refers to the worst-case delay for the NOR gate (when only one of the pulldown transistors switches on). Note that if two or more NOR gate pulldown transistors switch on simultaneously, the effective resistance, and therefore the delay, will be reduced. The reduced models of Fig. 7.8-10 show only a single pulldown path for each NOR gate and lump the series pulldown transistors of a NAND gate into a single, equivalent resistor. The circuit of Fig. 7.8-10c is used to compare the delay for a multi-input NOR gate with the delay for the two-input gates. The parameter values for all three cases are listed in Fig. 7.8-10d.

Based on the analysis methods of this section, it is easy to see that the delay for the propagation of a digital signal through two cascaded NOR gates is the same as for an inverter pair, provided that both NOR gates are loaded by a single, equivalent input. This NOR-pair delay is just t_{ipd}. The delay for two cascaded NAND gates is greater because of the high-resistance pullup device required by the 8 : 1 pullup/pulldown ratio and because of the two series transistors in the pulldown path. Because the resistances for both the pullup path and pulldown path are doubled, the NAND-pair delay is $2t_{ipd}$. Because the NAND-pair delay is double the NOR-pair delay, it is obvious that the NOR configuration is preferable to the NAND configuration from a delay viewpoint. It is further noted from Fig. 7.8-10c and d that the delay for a multi-input NOR gate is the same as that for the two-input NOR gate. Multi-input NMOS NOR gates are widely used; NMOS NAND gates with more than two inputs are rare.

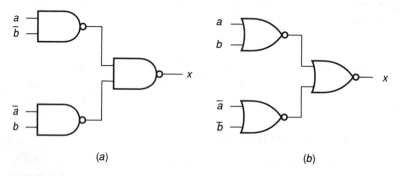

(a)   (b)

FIGURE 7.8-9
Equivalent circuits to obtain the exclusive-OR function: (a) NAND-NAND circuit, (b) NOR-NOR circuit.

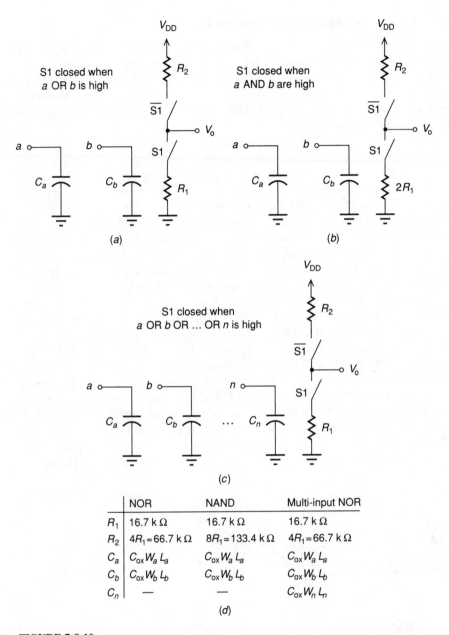

	NOR	NAND	Multi-input NOR
R_1	16.7 kΩ	16.7 kΩ	16.7 kΩ
R_2	$4R_1 = 66.7$ kΩ	$8R_1 = 133.4$ kΩ	$4R_1 = 66.7$ kΩ
C_a	$C_{ox}W_a L_a$	$C_{ox}W_a L_a$	$C_{ox}W_a L_a$
C_b	$C_{ox}W_b L_b$	$C_{ox}W_b L_b$	$C_{ox}W_b L_b$
C_n	—	—	$C_{ox}W_n L_n$

(d)

FIGURE 7.8-10

Delay models for multi-input gates: (a) Delay model for two-input NOR, (b) Delay model for two-input NAND, (c) Delay model for multi-input NOR, (d) Resistance and capacitance values.

7.8.6 Enhancement versus Depletion Loads

It was shown earlier in this chapter that the depletion load is preferred to the enhancement load from a signal-swing viewpoint. Both the enhancement- and depletion-load logic gates are ratio-logic circuits. It was further stated that the same 4 : 1 sizing rule is generally used for both types of logic gates. However, within a single–power supply logic family, the dynamic performance of the two gates is substantially different.

Figure 7.8-11 shows the *I–V* characteristics for three pullup devices: an enhancement-mode transistor with its gate tied to its drain, a depletion-mode transistor with its gate tied to its source, and a linear resistor. Any one of these devices can be used with an enhancement pulldown transistor to form an inverter. All three devices can be designed to have the same equivalent large signal resistance *(V/I)* at a point X by suitable choice of width-to-length ratios and threshold voltages for the transistors. Let the devices be sized so that point X corresponds to the voltage and current for the pullup of an inverter stage when its output is low. The three devices are indistinguishable from a steady state viewpoint when used as static load devices operating at point X.

Now consider the dynamic operation of an inverter circuit. When the pulldown stage of the inverter is turned off, the pullup device should quickly bring the output voltage to a logic high value. This requires the lowest possible resistance for the pullup during the low-to-high transition. The *I–V* curves of Fig. 7.8-11 are particularly instructive here. The linear resistor provides a current that is directly proportional (Ohm's law) to the voltage across the load resistor, $V_{DD} - V_o$, where V_o is the output voltage of the inverter. The enhancement-mode transistor provides an equivalent resistance that tends to infinity as the output voltage rises to $V_{DD} - V_{TN}$, whereas the equivalent resistance of the depletion-mode transistor tends to a value much smaller than the linear resistor value as V_o nears V_{DD}. In the calculation of t_{LH} in Eq. 7.8-10, an equivalent resistance for the pullup

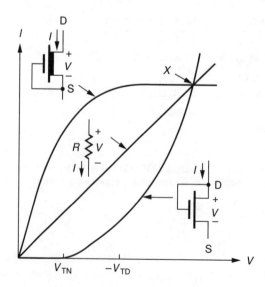

FIGURE 7.8-11
I-V curves for three load devices: depletion pullup, linear resistor, and enhancement pullup.

device determines the delay time. Thus, from the viewpoint of signal rise time, the depletion-mode transistor is a better choice than either the linear resistor or the enhancement-mode transistor. Because the output signal fall time is almost independent of the pullup device type, essentially all modern MOS ratio logic is designed with depletion pullups to reduce total gate delay times.

7.8.7 CMOS Logic Delays

So far, the delay analysis of NMOS ratio logic has been emphasized. As described in Sec 7.5, the basic CMOS inverter is not a ratio-logic device because the output is actively pulled to one logic level or the other depending on the input. Fortunately, the basic concepts of the preceding delay analysis apply equally well to CMOS logic. The unique delay characteristics of CMOS logic as compared to NMOS logic are developed in this section.

The initial delay analysis of the reference CMOS inverter is based on one inverter driving a second, identical inverter, as shown in both logic and circuit diagram form in Fig. 7.8-12. Several observations about this circuit are important here. An obvious difference from the NMOS inverter circuit of Fig. 7.8-1 is that the output of the first CMOS inverter must drive the gates of two transistors: one for the n-channel pulldown transistor and one for the p-channel pullup transistor. Both gates provide capacitive loading that slows the transition of logic signal values. Analysis of the gate capacitance for the n-channel pulldown transistor is identical to that for the NMOS inverter expressed by Eq. 7.8-8. This gate capacitance is denoted by C_{GN} and is given as

$$C_{GN} = C_G \approx C_{ox}W_N L_N \qquad (7.8\text{-}23)$$

The gate capacitance of the p-channel transistor, denoted by C_{GP}, is similar to that of the gate of the n-channel transistor based on the model of Fig. 3.1-19. When the p-channel transistor is off, that is, the input voltage to the gate is a logic high, the capacitance is $C_{ox}W_P L_P$. In saturation, that is, when the input

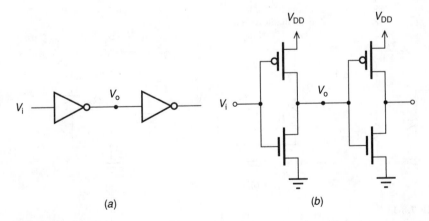

(a)   (b)

FIGURE 7.8-12
CMOS inverter driving a second, identical CMOS inverter: (a) Logic diagram, (b) Circuit diagram.

voltage to the gate is a logic low, the p-channel transistor capacitance is again $C_{ox}W_P L_P$. When the p-channel transistor is in the ohmic region, the gate capacitance is about 2/3 of its value in saturation. It is reasonable to assume that the p-channel transistor is in the ohmic region for only a short part of signal transition. For this reason, the gate capacitance of the p-channel transistor is approximated as

$$C_{GP} \approx C_{ox}W_P L_P \tag{7.8-24}$$

Because the capacitances for the two transistors of the second inverter are effectively in parallel (one to ground and the other to V_{DD}), the capacitive load seen by the first inverter is

$$C_{GC} = C_{GN} + C_{GP} \tag{7.8-25}$$

A simplified model for the CMOS inverter circuit of Fig. 7.8-12 is given in Fig. 7.8-13. This model is based on the simple resistive model of Fig. 7.8-3 for the driving transistors and the capacitance values that were just discussed. When a low-to-high step input is applied to the first inverter, the equivalent circuit of Fig. 7.8-13b is applicable. When a high-to-low step input is used, the equivalent circuit of Fig. 7.8-13c is appropriate. Approximating the 10% to 90% signal rise time by two time constants for the ideal RC circuit models of Fig. 7.8-13b and c, the rising and falling transition delays are given by the equations

$$t_{LH} = 2R_2 C_{GC} \tag{7.8-26}$$

and

$$t_{HL} = 2R_1 C_{GC} \tag{7.8-27}$$

The value of R_1 is determined using an analysis similar to that used for the NMOS inverter pulldown and is given by Eq. 7.8-4. Since the p-channel pullup

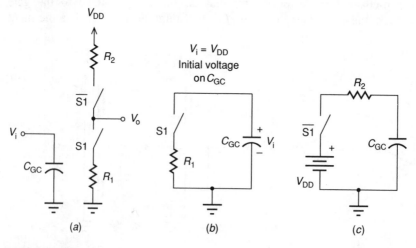

FIGURE 7.8-13
Equivalent circuits for CMOS delay analysis: (a) Simplified RC inverter model, (b) Equivalent circuit for high-to-low output transition, (c) Equivalent circuit for low-to-high output transition.

transistor is an enhancement transistor, its equivalent resistance R_2 is also given by Eq. 7.8-4 with the appropriate substitution of p-channel values for K', L, W, and V_T. If the transistors are sized for symmetrical output drive with equivalent pullup and pulldown resistances, the delay is

$$t_{LH} = t_{HL} = 2R_2C_{GC} = 2R_1C_{GC} \qquad (7.8\text{-}28)$$

With the simplified RC model for a CMOS inverter as the basis, analysis of CMOS NAND and NOR gates is easy. In general, each logic gate output must drive the gate capacitance of two transistors for every connection to another CMOS logic element. The equivalent pullup and pulldown resistance for a logic gate output depends on process-dependent characterisitics for n-channel and p-channel transistors, the width-to-length ratios of the individual transistors, and the series connection required for the pulldown section of a NAND gate or the pullup section of a NOR gate.

The following example demonstrates the propagation delay analysis for CMOS inverters. Subsequently the CMOS inverter-pair delay is compared with the equivalent inverter-pair delay for NMOS inverters.

Example 7.8-1. Consider a cascade of CMOS inverters in an n-well process. The n-channel pulldown transistor is a minimum-size device in a 2 μ technology. Assume the values of K' for the n-channel and p-channel transistors are 45 μA/V^2 and 15 μA/V^2 respectively. The p-channel pullup is sized for symmetrical output drive capability. The thresholds are $V_{TN} = 1$ V and $V_{TP} = -1$ V, and the supply voltage is $V_{DD} = 5$ V. The gate-oxide capacitance for both transistor types is $C_{ox} = 1$ fF/μ^2.

Determine the inverter-pair delay for this CMOS inverter in terms of absolute time and in terms of τ_P from Eq. 7.8-14.

Solution. Because the n-channel pulldown is of minimum size, it has $W_N = L_N = 2$ μ. The p-channel pullup must have a width-to-length ratio of 3 to compensate for the relative values of K' assumed for the p- and n-channel transistors. Choose $L_P = L_N = 2$ μ and $W_P = 3L_P = 6$ μ.

From Eqs. 7.8-23, 7.8-24, and 7.8-25,

$$C_{GC} = C_{GN} + C_{GP} = C_{ox}(W_NL_N + W_PL_P) = C_{ox}L_N(W_N + W_P)$$

Then

$$C_{GC} = 1 \text{ fF/}\mu^2 \times 2 \ \mu(2 \ \mu + 6 \ \mu) = 0.016 \text{ pF}$$

From Eq. 7.8-4,

$$R_N = \frac{2 \times 2 \ \mu}{45 \ \mu\text{A/V}^2 \times 2 \ \mu(5 \text{ V} - 1 \text{ V})} = 11.1 \text{ k}\Omega$$

and

$$R_P = \frac{2 \times 2 \ \mu}{15 \ \mu\text{A/V}^2 \times 6 \ \mu(5 \text{ V} - 1 \text{ V})} = 11.1 \text{ k}\Omega$$

From Eqs. 7.8-26 and 7.8-27,

$$t_{LH} = 2R_PC_{GC} = 2 \times 11.1 \text{ k}\Omega \times 0.016 \text{ pF} = 0.355 \text{ ns}$$

and from Eq. 7.8-28, for symmetrical output drive,

$$t_{HL} = 2R_N C_{GC} = t_{LH} = 0.355 \text{ ns}$$

The inverter-pair delay is

$$t_{ipd} = t_{LH} + t_{HL} = 0.355 + 0.355 = 0.71 \text{ ns}$$

From Eq. 7.8-13, the process characteristic time constant is

$$\tau_P = R_{ss} C_{GN} = 5.56 \text{ k}\Omega \times 0.004 \text{ pF} = 0.022 \text{ ns}$$

Thus, $t_{ipd} = 32\tau_P$.

The inverter-pair delay for CMOS inverters determined in the preceding example should be compared with the inverter-pair delay for the NMOS inverters of Eq. 7.8-18. For NMOS with a 4:1 size ratio, $t_{ipd} = 20\tau_P$. The two inverter-pair delays demonstrate a 50% decrease in raw circuit speed for CMOS as compared with NMOS. The analysis in terms of τ_P removes geometric dependencies from the comparison. This analysis does, however, depend on the relative values of K' for the n- and p-channel transistors but does not depend on the choice of symmetric drive for the CMOS inverter.

7.8.8 Interconnection Characteristics

The analysis up to this point has been concentrated on logic gates and process characteristics to analyze signal propagation delay. This section includes a brief introduction to the interconnection capacitance and resistance that results from the connection of the output of one gate to the input of another gate. This discussion is limited to on-chip interconnections. Such interconnections are possible using one of several layers such as one or more layers of metal, polysilicon, or diffusion.

The proper interconnection medium depends on the physical properties of the layers and on circuit topological constraints. The metal layer is the most flexible because it does not interact directly with either of the other two layers to create transistors. Each of the interconnection layers exhibits parasitic capacitance to substrate (ground) that slows signal propagation. The value of this capacitance per unit area is given for an NMOS process in Table 2A.4 of Appendix 2A and for a CMOS process in Table 2B.4 of Appendix 2B. The capacitance for metal and polysilicon is considered in terms of the classical case of parallel plates separated by a dielectric. As a first-order approximation, the metal and polysilicon capacitances are independent of voltage and geometrical shape. Capacitance densities from metal to substrate or polysilicon on field oxide to substrate are typically less than C_{ox} by a factor of 10 to 20. Capacitance from diffusion to substrate consists of two primary components: bottom capacitance per unit area and sidewall capacitance per unit length. The sidewall capacitance is given per unit length for convenience because the diffusion region is considered to be of constant depth. Diffusion capacitance is caused by the reverse-biased diode junction between diffusion and substrate and is voltage-dependent. As a simple approximation, the voltage dependence is eliminated by choosing a voltage that provides a nominal capacitance value. For minimum-width geometries, diffusion capacitance per unit area is typically less than C_{ox} by a factor of 5 to 10. Even though the capacitances per unit area for metal, polysilicon, and diffusion are factors of 5 to 20 less than C_{ox}, the area associated with interconnection is usually much larger than the transistor gate area. As a consequence, these interconnection loading effects may represent the dominant capacitive loading on many nodes, particularly as device geometries scale down to the 1 μ range and below.

The interconnection layers exhibit resistance to current flow as given by the values in Table 2A.4 of Appendix 2A for an NMOS process and the values in Table 2B.4 of Appendix 2B for a CMOS process. The resistances of polysilicon and diffusion are typically greater than the resistance of metal by three orders of magnitude. For short interconnections between adjacent devices, the resistance of the interconnection may be safely ignored in comparison to the effective transistor resistances. For longer interconnections, polysilicon and diffusion present large resistances that cannot be ignored. For this reason, metal is used for long interconnections.

Logic building block characteristics and associated delays can be estimated as soon as a logic diagram or circuit diagram with device sizing is complete. Interconnection delays depend so heavily on circuit layout that their effect is often neglected until layout is available. This is an unfortunate situation because interconnection capacitance is a significant delay factor for digital logic circuits. A rough rule of thumb with which to consider interconnection delays for minimum-size digital circuits prior to circuit layout can be derived from the following premises.

1. Assume that the average interconnection capacitance per unit area is one-tenth that of C_{ox}.
2. Assume that the local interconnection area is 10 times the gate area.

With these assumptions, interconnections can be modeled by doubling the effective capacitance of each driven gate. Although this is a crude approximation, it is substantially better than ignoring interconnection delays until after layout is available. For a particular design style and technology, this approximation can be improved with measurements from previous, similar designs. For example, many gate array manufacturers provide average interconnection capacitance estimates based on anticipated die size. Even better estimates of interconnection capacitance for critical nodes can be obtained if a floor plan of the circuit is available to describe the relative placements of digital building blocks within the die area.

Many aspects of signal propagation delay have been examined in this section. The delay is a combination of gate delay and interconnection delay. Ratio logic was found to exhibit asymmetric rising and falling delay times that differ by the pullup/pulldown resistance ratio. A process charcteristic time constant was defined to allow unbiased delay comparisons of different processes. Inverter-pair delay was introduced to capture the effects of both rising and falling delays. Then a special circuit configuration called a superbuffer was introduced to minimize the asymmetric delay characteristics of ratio logic. Next, delay analysis of both

NMOS and CMOS gates was presented, followed by an example to compare the two technologies with respect to delay characteristics. Finally, the electrical characteristics of interconnections were introduced.

7.9 CAPACITIVE LOADING CONSIDERATIONS

In the preceding section, consideration was given to signal propagation delays for logic gates that were loaded by single, identical logic gates. A significant problem in large-scale integrated circuit design for digital circuits is driving the relatively large capacitive loads caused by high gate fanout, interconnections, and off-chip connections. As stated in Sec. 7.2, both signal-level degradation and propagation delay are considered when specifying the maximum fanout for a logic circuit. Because of the extremely high input resistance of MOS devices, minimal signal-level degradation occurs even in driving a large number of gates. The primary fanout consideration is the input capacitance of successive logic circuits and their interconnections. Now the analysis of the previous section is expanded to consider the effects of heavy capacitive loading and to investigate circuit techniques to minimize the associated increase in signal propagation delay.

7.9.1 Capacitive Loading

Several factors contribute to capacitive loading of the output of a logic gate. These include inputs to other gates, interconnection routing or buses, bonding pads, and external loads. Regardless of the cause, each adds parasitic capacitance and contributes cumulatively and nearly linearly to the overall delay. If the total capacitive loading at the output node of a logic gate caused by these factors is found to be C_T, then the propagation delay time constant can be approximated by the expression

$$\tau_T = R_T C_T \tag{7.9-1}$$

where R_T is the equivalent charging or discharging resistance. If the capacitance C_T is driven by a reference inverter with pulldown resistance R_T and gate capacitance C_G, the average propagation delay is

$$t_{\text{dly}} = \frac{t_{\text{apd}} C_T}{C_G} \tag{7.9-2}$$

where t_{apd} is the average logic stage propagation delay of the logic family defined in terms of inverter-pair delay by

$$t_{\text{apd}} = \frac{t_{\text{ipd}}}{2} \tag{7.9-3}$$

From Eq. 7.8-18, this can be written in terms of the process characteristic time constant τ_P for an NMOS reference inverter with pullup/pulldown ratio k as

$$t_{\text{dly}} = \frac{2(1 + k)\tau_P C_T}{C_G} \tag{7.9-4}$$

7.9.2 Logic Fan-out Delays

In many situations, the output of a logic stage is required to drive more than one equivalent gate input. The response time is slowed because of the parasitic capacitance of the additional inputs. If the fan-out, that is, the number of equivalent reference inverter loads to be driven, is f, then the total capacitive load is $f C_G$ where C_G is the capacitive load of a single reference inverter. Replacing C_T of Eq. 7.9-2 with $f C_G$, the average stage delay for a single stage with a fan-out of f is

$$t_{\text{stage}} = t_{\text{apd}} f \tag{7.9-5}$$

With these observations, the delay along a homogeneous signal path in a digital integrated circuit can quickly be approximated. Assume a signal passes through N levels of logic with an equivalent fan-out of f_i at the ith stage. Then the total path delay is given as

$$t_{\text{path}} = t_{\text{apd}} \sum_{i=1}^{N} f_i \tag{7.9-6}$$

For the analysis so far all stages are identical to a reference inverter, and interconnection capacitance has been neglected.

It is often convenient to decompose the total capacitive loading of Eq. 7.9-1 into that caused by MOS gate loading plus that caused by other factors, such as bus or interconnection loading. Assume a node is loaded by the equivalent of f reference inverter inputs and capacitive loading C_I from interconnections. From the interconnection area and the process-dependent capacitance per unit area (see Appendices 2A and 2B), C_I can be determined. If C_G is the input capacitance of the reference inverter, then the interconnection load C_I is equivalent to that of m reference inverter loads, where

$$m = \frac{C_I}{C_G} \tag{7.9-7}$$

It follows that the average propagation delay of this node due to both fan-out and interconnection loading is given by

$$t_{\text{node}} \approx (m + f) t_{\text{apd}} \tag{7.9-8}$$

If a signal must propagate through a sequence of N stages, where the output drive of each stage is equivalent to that of the reference inverter, it follows from Eqs. 7.9-6 and 7.9-8 that the signal propagation delay through this N-stage path can be approximated by

$$t_{\text{path}} \approx t_{\text{apd}} \sum_{i=1}^{N} (m_i + f_i) \tag{7.9-9}$$

where f_i is the equivalent number of reference inverter loads and m_i is the equivalent of interconnection loads on the ith node. Including the interconnection loading is important in most circuits and will dominate the actual gate loading for long connections or for buses. Interconnection loading is particularly significant in submicron structures.

Equation 7.9-2 has a straightforward and useful extension. Assume that an inverter is to drive a total capacitive load C_T. The drive capability for this inverter is improved by increasing the widths of both its pullup and pulldown transistors by a factor of θ over the corresponding widths for the reference inverter. Note that this improved inverter has an input capacitance θC_G. Then it can be shown that the equivalent propagation delay for this inverter is given by

$$t_{\text{inv}} = \frac{t_{\text{apd}} C_T}{\theta C_G} \tag{7.9-10}$$

Although it could be the case that all inputs to all logic gates are equal in size to that of the reference inverter, in many situations it is advantageous to use logic circuits where the input devices have nonhomogeneous sizes. For example, this might occur where transistors are individually sized to reduce the delay in driving capacitive loads.

Equation 7.9-10 can be extended to obtain the signal propagation delay of paths that contain logic gates with varying drive capabilities. Under the assumption that the reference inverter device sizing ratio k is used for all gates in the cascade, and that the drive capability of the output of the ith gate in the cascade is θ_i times that of the reference inverter (i.e., the corresponding resistances in the model of Fig. 7.8-4 are $1/\theta_i$ times those of the reference inverter), it can be shown that the signal propagation delay through an N-stage path can be approximated by

$$t_{\text{path}} \approx t_{\text{apd}} \sum_{i=1}^{N} \frac{m_i + f_i}{\theta_i} \tag{7.9-11}$$

At the expense of some layout area, the increase in drive capability can be obtained by increasing the width of the driving transistors while keeping their length and device sizing ratio k constant.

In summary, a simple method of obtaining an approximation to the signal propagation delay along a path in digital circuits based on the average stage delay has been presented. Interconnections and other parasitic loading factors are easily included in the calculation once layout is determined. The approximation may have a significant error of $\pm 50\%$ or more. The simple analysis presented here is, however, good enough for at least two purposes. First, it allows an estimate of circuit speed for use in comparing alternative designs prior to implementation. Second, it is usually adequate to determine the critical paths that must be analyzed in detail and possibly modified to improve performance. If more accurate timing information is required, a timing analysis program or circuit simulator such as SPICE can be used. It is often prudent to identify the critical delay paths in a system and perform a detailed analysis of those paths to obtain a more precise estimate of the system delay.

7.9.3 Distributed Drivers

It can be seen from Eq. 7.9-2 that the delay associated with driving a large capacitive load from a minimum-size inverter increases linearly with the load capacitance C_T. This linear dependence is particularly troublesome because situations often arise where the total load capacitance may be as much as $100C_G$ to $10,000C_G$ (see Table 7.9-1). The corresponding increase in delay by a factor of 100 to 10,000 is seldom acceptable. The following question naturally arises: Is there a faster way to drive a large capacitive load? At first glance, Eq. 7.9-11 suggests that if θ_i is made larger by widening the pullup and pulldown transistors to reduce their equivalent resistances, then the delay can be reduced. (Normally the pullup/pulldown ratio k is maintained to ensure valid logic voltage levels.) However, these changes cause heavier capacitive loading on previous stages, perhaps negating the net performance gain. The following example shows that, in terms of propagation delay, it may be better to distribute the load than to increase the drive of a single stage when an output is driving a high-fanout load.

> **Example 7.9-1.** Assume that a minimum-size inverter drives a set of 10 other minimum-size inverters, as shown in Fig. 7.9-1a. Estimate the propagation delay from V_i to V_c if the single inverter drives the 10 inverters directly, and if the single inverter drives two other minimum-size inverters that each drive five inverters, as shown in Fig. 7.9-1b. Neglect interconnection capacitance and the inversion of the logic signal.

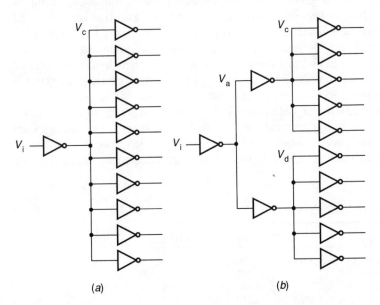

FIGURE 7.9-1
Distributed drivers versus concentrated driver: (a) 1:10 capacitive load, (b) 1:2:5 capacitive load.

Solution. Assuming that the minimum-size inverter has a pullup/pulldown ratio of $k = 4$, the average stage delay required to drive a single minimum-size inverter is t_{apd}. It follows from Eq. 7.9-2 that if the inverter drives 10 identical inverters, the total gate capacitance will be increased by a factor of 10, and the total delay becomes $10t_{apd}$.

If the minimum-size inverter drives two stages that, in turn, drive five stages each, the propagation delay will be the sum of the two delays. The average delay to drive two identical inverters will be twice the delay for a single inverter, or $2t_{apd}$. The average delay for the second stage to drive five identical stages will be five times the delay for a single inverter, or $5t_{apd}$. The combined delay from input to output with the intermediate stage will be $7t_{apd}$, which is less than the $10t_{apd}$ required for driving the 10 inputs directly.

The example shows that it may be better to include intermediate stages than to drive a heavy capacitive load from a single stage. Table 7.9-1 provides a comparison of some of the capacitive loading requirements that must be addressed for the typical process listed in Table 2A.4 of Appendix 2A. Although interconnection loading may represent capacitive loading equivalent to 100 or more reference inverters, pad loading and off-chip loading are often even larger. The divide-and-conquer strategy presented in the example will not work for a single large load. Methods of driving large, concentrated capacitive loads will be considered in the following section.

7.9.4   Driving Off-Chip Loads

Digital integrated circuits generally use the smallest possible transistors to implement logical functions. The small size is important to maximize the number of circuits per unit area and therefore minimize silicon area and cost. Ultimately, logic circuits must provide results of internal circuit operations to the outside world. These logic signals must overcome both the inherent loading effects of the bus or interconnection path from the source of the output signal to an external pin and the loading effects of some other circuit to which this output signal acts as an input. Additionally, it is frequently desirable to generate signals that are compatible, relative to logic voltage levels, with some other logic family, such as Advanced Low-Power Schottky TTL (ALSTTL), which provides current as well as capacitive loading. Other logic families are handled by increasing the

TABLE 7.9-1
Typical capacitive loading

Load	C_T		C_T/C_G
Single reference inverter ($3\ \mu \times 3\ \mu$)	0.0063 pF		1
Ten reference inverters	0.063	pF	10
4 mm $\times$ 4.5 μ metal bus	0.450	pF	71
Standard output pad ($100\ \mu \times 100\ \mu$)	0.250	pF	40
Oscilloscope probe	10.0	pF	1587
Memory chip address pin	5.0	pF	794

width of the driving transistors to increase current capability and by varying the pullup/pulldown ratio k to match external logic voltages. To illustrate the former case, the following example demonstrates the capacitive loading effects of driving a simple output bonding pad from a minimum-size inverter.

Example 7.9-2. Consider driving a metal output bonding pad from a minimum-size inverter in the NMOS process summarized in Table 2A.4 of Appendix 2A. Calculate the capacitance ratio between the capacitance of the bonding pad and the input gate capacitance of a minimum-size inverter. Using this ratio, estimate the delay to drive the output pad in terms of the reference delay t_{apd}.

Solution. The size of an output bonding pad is typically $100\ \mu \times 100\ \mu$. From the NMOS process electrical characteristics

$$C_{\text{pad}} = 0.025\ \text{fF}/\mu^2 \times 10{,}000\ \mu^2 = 0.25\ \text{pF}$$

Note that this matches the value listed in Table 7.9-1. The dimensions of an input gate for a minimum-size inverter in this process are $3\ \mu \times 3\ \mu$.

$$C_{\text{G}} = 0.7\ \text{fF}/\mu^2 \times 9\ \mu^2 = 0.0063\ \text{pF}$$

Thus, the ratio of C_{pad} to C_{G} is

$$C_{\text{ratio}} = \frac{C_{\text{pad}}}{C_{\text{G}}} = 39.7$$

From Eq. 7.9-2 the average propagation delay of the reference inverter driving the output pad is

$$t_{\text{dly}} = 39.7 t_{\text{apd}}$$

From Eqs. 7.8-14, 7.8-18, and 7.9-3, the value for the average gate delay for the NMOS process of Appendix 2A with $k = 4$ is $t_{\text{apd}} = 0.63$ ns. The average propagation delay in driving the bonding pad is thus 25 ns.

The following example demonstrates the effect of adding an external capacitive load to the bonding pad just considered.

Example 7.9-3. Consider the case of a standard oscilloscope probe connected directly to the output bonding pad of Example 7.9-2. Determine the approximate average propagation delay that will result.

Solution. The total load capacitance will be the sum of the output pad capacitance and the oscilloscope probe capacitance. Table 7.9-1 indicates that an oscilloscope probe provides 10 pF of capacitive load. Thus,

$$C_{\text{load}} = C_{\text{pad}} + C_{\text{probe}} = 0.25\ \text{pF} + 10\ \text{pF} = 10.25\ \text{pF}$$

The capacitance ratio will be

$$C_{\text{ratio}} = \frac{C_{\text{load}}}{C_{\text{G}}} = 1627$$

The average propagation delay is obtained from Eq. 7.9-2:

$$t_{\text{dly}} = 1627 t_{\text{apd}} = 1627 \times 0.63\ \text{ns} = 1025\ \text{ns}$$

Contrast this delay with the 0.63 ns average propagation delay of the reference inverter. Such a delay is obviously detrimental to high-speed operation of digital circuits, limiting clock frequency to less than $1/(2t_{dly}) = 488$ kHz! The oscilloscope probe capacitance is comparable in value to the total capacitance encountered in driving inputs on other integrated circuit chips (see Table 7.9-1).

7.9.5 Cascaded Drivers

It is obvious from the two examples of the preceding section that the signal delay encountered in driving off-chip loads directly from a minimum-size inverter is unacceptable. Fortunately, there are circuit configurations that reduce the effective delay in driving large capacitive loads. One good circuit configuration employs a cascade of inverters with increasing current-drive capability to minimize this delay.

Assume a signal is available at the output of a minimum-size inverter (reference inverter) and that it is to drive a load C_L. From Eq. 7.9-2 the average propagation delay associated with driving this load directly is

$$t_{dir} = \frac{t_{apd}C_L}{C_G} \tag{7.9-12}$$

where t_{apd} is the average logic stage delay and C_G is the input capacitance of the reference inverter. For any integer $n \geq 1$, define α by the expression

$$\alpha = \left(\frac{C_L}{C_G}\right)^{1/n} \tag{7.9-13}$$

Alternatively, n can be represented in terms of α as

$$n = \frac{\ln(C_L/C_G)}{\ln \alpha} \tag{7.9-14}$$

Consider now the alternative structure of Fig. 7.9-2 for driving a load C_L. This structure is composed of a cascade of n inverters (including the initial reference inverter) each sized by the $4:1$ sizing rule and each with a drive capability that is α times as large as the previous stage. The width and length of the kth stage can be characterized by the equations

$$
\begin{aligned}
W_{dk} &= \alpha^{k-1}W_{d1} \\
L_{dk} &= L_{d1} \\
W_{uk} &= W_{dk} \\
L_{uk} &= 4L_{dk}
\end{aligned}
\tag{7.9-15}
$$

where the device dimensions W_{dk} and L_{dk} correspond to the pulldown transistor and W_{uk} and L_{uk} correspond to the pullup transistor of the kth inverter structure in the cascade, as indicated in Fig. 7.9-2. It can be observed that the load on the kth stage C_{Lk} is related to the reference inverter input capacitance C_G by the expression

$$C_{Lk} = \alpha^k C_G \tag{7.9-16}$$

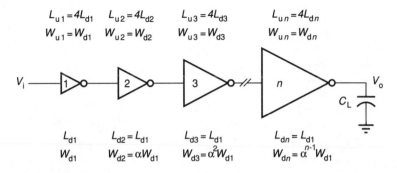

FIGURE 7.9-2
Cascaded drivers for a concentrated load.

From Eq. 7.9-2 it follows that the average propagation delay of the first inverter is αt_{apd}. It can be shown (Prob. 7.41) that the average propagation delay for each inverter in this geometric cascade is αt_{apd}. Hence, it follows from Eq. 7.9-11 with $f_i/\theta_i = \alpha$ and $m_i = 0$, that the total delay for the cascade is

$$t_{cas} = n\alpha t_{apd} \qquad (7.9\text{-}17)$$

Let r be the ratio between the propagation delays of the direct-drive circuit and of the geometric cascade approach. From Eqs. 7.9-12 and 7.9-17 it follows that

$$r = \frac{t_{cas}}{t_{dir}} = \frac{n\alpha t_{apd}}{t_{apd}C_L/C_G} = \frac{n\alpha C_G}{C_L} \qquad (7.9\text{-}18)$$

It is our goal to determine n and α to minimize r and thus minimize the propagation delay in driving the load. From Eq. 7.9-14 it follows that n can be eliminated from the expression for r to obtain the expression

$$r = \frac{\ln(C_L/C_G)}{C_L/C_G} \frac{\alpha}{\ln \alpha} \qquad (7.9\text{-}19)$$

The terms involving capacitance are fixed by the load requirements. The goal is thus to determine α in Eq. 7.9-19 to minimize r. The second term on the right-hand side of Eq. 7.9-19 is plotted in Fig. 7.9-3. It is easy to see that $\alpha/\ln \alpha$ has a wide local minimum at $\alpha = e$ with value e. A plot of the number of stages n versus C_L/C_G for minimizing the delay with $\alpha = e$, as obtained from Eq. 7.9-14, is shown in Fig. 7.9-4. Plots of n versus C_L/C_G for $\alpha = 3$ and $\alpha = 5$ are also shown in Fig. 7.9-4.

It should be noted that because n is the number of cascade stages, n must assume an integer value greater than or equal to 1. Quantization of device geometries during layout precludes setting α to an exact ratio of e. In fact, α is usually set to a value greater than e to reduce the number of cascade stages required while still reducing the propagation delay significantly. As can be seen from Fig. 7.9-3, as long as α is between 2 and 4, the deviation from minimum delay is less than about 5%. For conservative design, the values for n and α can be selected to drive a load a little larger than C_L within the allotted delay time.

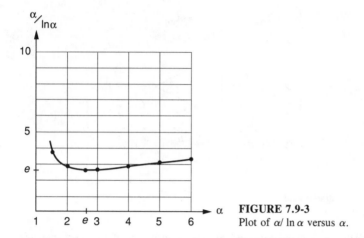

FIGURE 7.9-3
Plot of $\alpha/\ln\alpha$ versus α.

It is instructive to obtain an appreciation for how much benefit is practically derived from the cascaded driver approach. It can be shown from Eq. 7.9-17 that for small loading ratios, the speed improvements are small and the area overhead associated with the cascade may not be justified. For large capacitive load ratios, the speed improvement offered by the cascade is significant. For example, from Eq. 7.9-18 a seven-stage optimally sized cascade would drive a capacitive load that is approximately $1100C_G$ in 1.7% of the time required with direct drive!

Two final points deserve mention. First, if the number of inverter stages in the cascade is odd, the output signal is inverted. If inversion is unacceptable, a minimal delay increase occurs if the circuit is preceded by a reference inverter. Second, even though the speed improvements are significant for large n, the silicon area penalty is also quite high. The active silicon area grows as a geometric function of the number of stages. For example, the final stage in a seven-stage optimally weighted cascade requires $e^6 = 403$ times as much active area as a reference inverter. This is almost twice the area of all the preceding cascaded stages combined.

The following example compares the delay for three stages and the optimal number of stages driving the oscilloscope probe of Example 7.9-3.

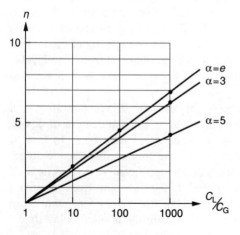

FIGURE 7.9-4
Plot of n versus C_L/C_G for $\alpha = 3, e,$ and 5.

Example 7.9-4. Determine the number of stages required to drive the output pad of Example 7.9-3 with minimum delay. Calculate the delay for this minimum delay case and for the case where three stages sized according to Eq. 7.9-13 are used.

Solution. From Eq. 7.9-14 the optimal number of stages n is found with $\alpha = e$. From Example 7.9-3, $C_L/C_G = 1627$, so $n = \ln(1627) = 7.39$. This is rounded to seven stages, including the reference inverter at the signal source. The propagation delay for the seven stages is given by Eqs. 7.9-17 and 7.9-13 as

$$t_7 = 7 \times 2.88 \times t_{apd} = 20.16 t_{apd}$$

Note from Eq. 7.9-17 that each stage contributes equally to the delay.

If $n = 3$ is chosen, then from Eq. 7.9-13, $\alpha = 11.76$ for $C_L/C_G = 1627$. From Eq. 7.9-17, this gives a delay of

$$t_3 = 3 \times 11.76 t_{apd} = 35.3 t_{apd}$$

Note that the delay for three cascaded driver stages is only 75% more than the delay for seven cascaded driver stages. If this delay is acceptable, the area savings is significant. Even with just three cascaded driver stages, the delay is reduced to only 2% of the delay for the load driven directly from a reference inverter.

Standard output driver stages are needed to drive most output nodes for high-speed digital circuits. These circuits are called *pad drivers* and are usually available in libraries of standard circuits. Pad drivers are generally just a cascade of inverters with a geometrically increasing drive capability sized to give reduced delay. Figure 7.9-5 shows a plot of a Low-Power Schottky TTL-compatible output pad driver circuit. Figure 7.9-6 gives the circuit schematic showing the number of stages and the device sizing for each stage. Note the use of two superbuffers and of enhancement transistors for both the pullup and pulldown in the final stage. The use of an active enhancement pullup prevents static power dissipation in the unloaded pad driver output stage.

The analysis in this section has covered the various aspects of large capacitive loads. First, delays from capacitive loading and from logic fanout were demonstrated. Then the delays caused by driving large off-chip capacitances were analyzed. Two approaches to driving these loads were presented: distributed drivers and optimally cascaded drivers.

7.10 POWER DISSIPATION

One major limitation of MOS ICs is internal power dissipation. Although the power dissipation of MOS circuits is generally much less than that of bipolar integrated circuits performing the same function, it becomes a major factor limiting the size of VLSI MOS circuits. Electrical power dissipation in an integrated circuit is converted to heat that must be removed through the circuit's packaging. Integrated circuit packaging offers a resistance to heat removal. The heat flow through this resistance generates a temperature difference across the package analogous to the voltage difference caused by current flow through an electrical resistance. For a given integrated circuit package, a specified maximum temperature of the integrated circuit, and a specified ambient temperature, a maximum

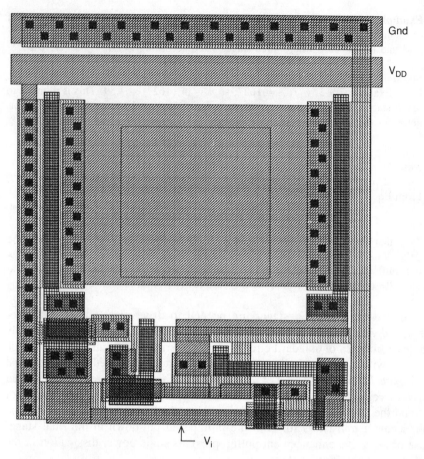

FIGURE 7.9-5
LSTTL output pad driver layout.

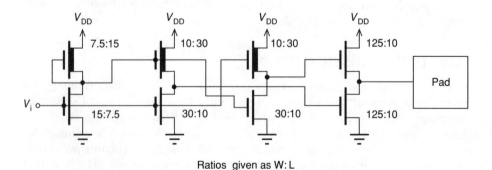

Ratios given as W: L

FIGURE 7.9-6
Circuit diagram for LSTTL output pad driver.

power dissipation (heat flow) can be specified. The thermal resistance θ_{JA} for a plastic 40-lead package is about 100°C/W, and a maximum integrated circuit junction temperature T_J of about 150°C is specified for reliability considerations. The thermal resistance θ_{JA} is the sum of junction to die, die to package, and package to ambient resistances.[9] If the maximum ambient temperature T_A is expected to be 50°C, then the maximum power dissipation is limited to

$$P_D = \frac{T_J - T_A}{\theta_{JA}} = \frac{150 - 50}{100} = 1 \text{ W} \qquad (7.10\text{-}1)$$

Most plastic or ceramic integrated circuit packages can dissipate 1–2 W of power in an ambient temperature of 70°C. As a second, special consideration, low power dissipation is important in applications that must operate from batteries. In this section the main sources of power dissipation are identified, first for NMOS circuits and then for CMOS circuits.

7.10.1 NMOS Power Dissipation

To help explain integrated circuit power dissipation, consider the reference inverter of Fig. 7.10-1. When V_i is low, M1 is off, causing a supply current I_D of 0 A. Hence, the power dissipation is essentially zero! If, however, V_i is high (V_{DD}), then M1 is ohmic and M2 is saturated, so from Eq. 3.1-4

$$I_D = K'\left(\frac{W_2}{L_2}\right)\frac{V_{TD}^2}{2} \qquad (7.10\text{-}2)$$

With $K' = 20 \ \mu\text{A/V}^2$, $L_2 = 4W_2$, and $V_{TD} = -3.5$ V, the drain current is $I_D = 31 \ \mu\text{A}$. Hence, the power dissipation of this single inverter with $V_i = V_{DD} = 5$ V is approximately 150 μW. Although the power dissipation of a single inverter is small, VLSI circuits contain thousands of inverters and gates. If, on the average, half of the inputs are in the low state and half are in the high state, then a circuit with N reference inverters will have an average *static power dissipation* of

$$P_{avg} = \left(\frac{N}{2}\right)150 \ \mu\text{W} \qquad (7.10\text{-}3)$$

and a worst-case power dissipation of

$$P_{wc} = (N)150 \ \mu\text{W} \qquad (7.10\text{-}4)$$

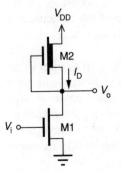

FIGURE 7.10-1
NMOS reference inverter.

From the NOR gate of Fig. 7.4-3, it can be concluded that if the pullup device ML is the same size as the pullup device of the reference inverter, then the power dissipation of the multi-input NOR is the same as that of the reference inverter. This is true irrespective of the number of inputs to the NOR gate.

Example 7.10-1. If a packaged IC can dissipate a maximum average power of 1 W, how many NMOS NOR gates can be accommodated? Assume the NOR gate pullup is sized to match the reference inverter.

Solution. From Eq. 7.10-3,

$$N = \frac{(1 \text{ W})2}{150 \ \mu\text{W}} = 13,333 \text{ NOR gates} \tag{7.10-5}$$

In the worst case, the circuit could be limited to about 6667 gates.

Note that if greater driving capability is required, for example, to drive highly capacitive loads as described in Sec. 7.9, then the W_2/L_2 ratio in Eq. 7.10-2 will increase, causing a corresponding increase in average static power dissipation. From Example 7.9-4, W_2/L_2 for the pullup device of the last stage of an optimally sized seven-stage pad driver is e^6 times as large as the width-to-length ratio of the load device of a reference inverter. Consequently, the last inverter alone in the seven-stage pad driver would have a power dissipation of 60 mW when it conducts! This is more than twice the static power dissipation of all preceding stages combined.

Logic circuits with inputs that change rapidly can dissipate considerable additional power over their static power requirements. This additional power is referred to as *dynamic power dissipation*. For example, immediately after a low-to-high input transition for the reference inverter of Fig 7.10-1, the output voltage will be near V_{DD} as the load capacitance starts to discharge. While the output is near V_{DD}, the pulldown device M1 is in the saturation region, causing an instantaneous drain current of

$$I_{D1} = K' \frac{W_1}{L_1} \frac{(V_{DD} - V_{TN})^2}{2} \tag{7.10-6}$$

With $V_{DD} = 5$ V, $K' = 20 \ \mu\text{A/V}^2$, $W_1 = L_1$, and $V_{TN} = 1$ V, the drain current becomes 160 μA and the initial power dissipation is 800 μW. This is considerably higher than the static power dissipation of 150 μW found earlier. The actual power dissipation will vary in a continuous manner from 800 μW to 150 μW during an output high-to-low transition. With fast input signals to a digital integrated circuit, the dynamic power dissipation obtained from a time average of the instantaneous power dissipation minus the static power dissipation can be much larger than the static power dissipation and must be taken into consideration.

The two primary components of power dissipation for NMOS circuits are static power dissipation and dynamic power dissipation. For circuits with average logic signal changes less frequent than about 10 MHz, static power dissipation is dominant. For higher-frequency signal changes, dynamic power becomes the major consideration. Following is a quantitative analysis of dynamic power dissipation for CMOS circuits. The corresponding analysis for NMOS circuits is similar.

7.10.2 CMOS Power Dissipation

CMOS logic has long been used for circuits in applications requiring extremely low power, such as space probes, calculators, and wristwatches. Perhaps the most important asset of CMOS for today's digital logic designs is its low power dissipation and attendant minimal cooling requirements. Power dissipation in CMOS can be classified into three categories: static power dissipation, *dc switching power* occurring when both transistors conduct momentarily during a transition, and *ac switching power* lost while charging (discharging) capacitive loads. The combination of dc switching power and ac switching power is often called dynamic power dissipation.

Static power dissipation is negligible for CMOS logic circuits. The dc path from power to ground is always broken by an off transistor when the circuit is quiescent. With today's digital CMOS circuits, static power dissipation is not a consideration compared with dynamic power dissipation.

The second component of power dissipation, dc switching power, occurs during the time that the inputs to a logic gate are between the valid logic levels. During this time, both transistors conduct, providing a path from V_{DD} to ground. For an individual gate, the average power dissipated increases with switching time for its input logic signal; that is, the longer the input stays between valid logic levels, the longer the conductive path from V_{DD} to ground exists. The power lost to this cause is typically less than 10% of total power dissipation for digital CMOS circuits such as memories and microprocessors.

The ac switching power is the main component of power dissipation for digital CMOS circuits. This power loss can be analyzed by considering the circuit of Fig. 7.10-2a. This circuit models a capacitively loaded inverter output during a low-to-high transition initiated at time zero. Assume no charge on the capacitor when the switch is initially closed. Since this is a simple RC circuit, it is well known that the current $i(t)$ from the battery is

$$i(t) = \left(\frac{V}{R}\right)e^{-t/RC} \qquad (7.10\text{-}7)$$

The total energy supplied by the battery is given by

$$e = \int_0^\infty V\, i(t)\, dt = V^2 C \qquad (7.10\text{-}8)$$

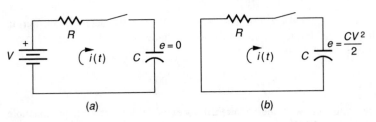

FIGURE 7.10-2
Equivalent circuits for ac power dissipation: (*a*) Charging circuit, (*b*) Discharging circuit.

Because the final energy stored on the capacitor is only $(1/2)\,CV^2$ then half the total energy supplied by the battery must be dissipated in the resistance while the capacitor is being charged. Now consider that the switch is opened momentarily, the battery is replaced by a short, and the switch is reclosed as shown in Fig. 7.10-2b. As the capacitor discharges, all its stored energy will be dissipated in the resistor. The total energy lost (dissipated in the resistor) during a capacitor charge/discharge cycle e_{cycle} must be CV^2.

For CMOS logic circuits, the capacitance in Eq. 7.10-8 represents the sum of the parasitic gate and interconnection capacitance. Note that Eq. 7.10-8 is independent of the charging and discharging resistances. The power dissipation is just the rate of use of energy. If the charge/discharge cycle occurs periodically with a period T, the average power dissipation is

$$P = \frac{e_{cycle}}{T} \qquad (7.10\text{-}9)$$

In terms of operating frequency $f = 1/T$, the average power used is

$$P = e_{cycle}f = CV^2f \qquad (7.10\text{-}10)$$

This analysis shows that the average ac power dissipation for a CMOS circuit is proportional to the total capacitance, to the square of the supply voltage, and to the operating frequency. A similar analysis holds for NMOS circuits, except that the voltage swing is smaller because the lower logic level is above ground. For CMOS circuits, the ac power dissipation dominates, and both the ac power dissipation and the dc switching power increase with frequency.

> **Example 7.10-2.** Consider an approximate limitation on the number of gates in a CMOS integrated circuit if the total power dissipation is limited to 1 W, the operating frequency is 10 MHz, and the supply voltage is 5 V.
>
> **Solution.** It will be assumed that the ac power dissipation is dominant. From Example 7.8-1, a single gate load capacitance for a reference CMOS inverter is 0.016 pF. With the addition of interconnection capacitance, assume that the total capacitance driven by each logic gate is 0.032 pF. The total ac power dissipation is equal to the number of active gates N_a times the power dissipation of each gate. Under the assumptions given, the number of active gates to gve 1 W power dissipation is
>
> $$N_a = \frac{P}{CV^2f} = \frac{1}{0.032 \times 10^{-12}5^210^7} = 125,000$$
>
> In typical integrated circuits, only 10% to 25% of the gates switch during a given clock cycle. Using a conservative 25% figure, the total number of gates required to dissipate 1 W is
>
> $$N_{max} = \frac{N_a}{0.25} = 500,000$$

This can be compared with the required number of NMOS gates from Example 7.10-1 to show why CMOS is preferred in terms of power dissipation.

It is important to consider how future fabrication and operating conditions will affect power limitations on the number of gates in a CMOS integrated circuit. As CMOS circuits are reduced in size, it is expected that the operating frequency will increase and supply voltages and gate capacitance will decrease. If clock frequency is increased and power supply voltages and gate capcitance are reduced proportionally for a constant number of gates, the total CMOS power dissipation decreases rapidly because it is a linear function of frequency and capacitance and a squared function of voltage. The ability to operate faster and at reduced power is one of the driving forces for scaling down minimum device sizes.

In this section, static and dynamic power dissipation were introduced. Dynamic power dissipation includes both dc and ac switching power. Static power dissipation dominates for NMOS logic, whereas dynamic power dissipation dominates for CMOS logic.

7.11 NOISE IN DIGITAL LOGIC CIRCUITS

Electrical noise in integrated circuits represents an unwanted perturbation of desired signal voltages. Noise can arise from many sources and may or may not affect the operation of a circuit, depending on the magnitude of the noise disturbance and the sensitivity of the circuit to the disturbance. Noise disturbances may come from the external environment, as in electromagnetic interference or alpha particles, or may be internally generated from causes that can be controlled by the designer. Internal noise in digital integrated circuits comes from two primary sources: noise coupled from a common resistive path to power or ground, and noise that is capacitively coupled from another signal path. In this section the common causes of internal noise in digital integrated circuits are considered, the parameters used to specify digital integrated circuit immunity to noise are defined, and the noise immunity for NMOS and CMOS inverters is investigated.

7.11.1 Resistive Noise Coupling

Figure 7.11-1a shows a resistance R_c in the common ground path for two inverters. In practical circuits, this might be caused by a common diffusion path to a metal ground bus. The model of Fig. 7.11-1b, where each transistor is replaced by an equivalent resistance, is used for the following simplified analysis. If switch S1 is closed and switch S3 is open, the output voltage V_1 is determined as

$$V_1 = \frac{V_{DD}(R_1 + R_c)}{R_1 + R_2 + R_c} \tag{7.11-1}$$

Note that if $R_c = 0$ ohms, Eq. 7.11-1 reduces to Eq. 7.8-1. This output voltage corresponds to the low logic state. If R_c is nonzero, the output voltage is increased, thereby degrading the low logic voltage level.

A shift occurs in the output voltage V_1 if switch S3 of Fig. 7.11-1b is closed. This shift produces an unwanted noise voltage that, if large enough, can affect the logic value seen by subsequent stages. An equivalent circuit when both inverters

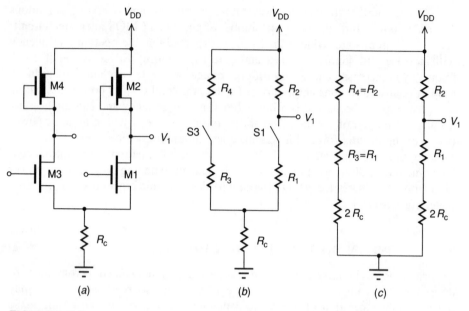

FIGURE 7.11-1
Resistive noise coupling: (*a*) Two inverters with common resistance to ground, (*b*) Resistive model for (*a*), (*c*) Model for matched inverters.

are identical and both switches are closed is given in Fig. 7.11-1*c*. Under these conditions, the output voltage V_1 is

$$V_1 = \frac{V_{DD}(R_1 + 2R_c)}{R_1 + R_2 + 2R_c} \tag{7.11-2}$$

The increase in output voltage depends on the relative resistance of R_c and the equivalent inverter output resistance.

The preceding example with simple inverters demonstrates resistive noise coupling, but in practice this case does not cause serious noise problems because logic gates are usually connected to low-resistance power and ground buses through relatively short paths. Resistance in a common supply path to two inverters is another source of resistive noise coupling. As a general rule, resistance in any segment of power and ground paths may cause unwanted noise voltages. For this reason, power and ground buses are almost always run in a low-resistance metal layer.

Although resistive noise coupling is not serious for the preceding simple case, two related conditions are important. If a large number of gates common to a power supply bus change state in concert, the combined effect may produce significant voltage shifts that detrimentally affect logic states. Second, output pad drivers and fast bus drivers draw considerable current and thus may generate noise voltages in other parts of the circuit from voltage drops even in a low-resistance power supply or ground path. The second condition is more easily detected than the first, but both are important considerations in integrated circuit design.

7.11.2 Capacitive Noise Coupling

Capacitive noise coupling is caused by physical relationships of signal paths. For integrated circuits, the two conditions that cause significant mutual capacitance are long adjacent signal paths, and overlapping but disjoint signal paths. In either case, the coupling capacitance will be called C_c. A general model of the coupling is given in Fig. 7.11-2a. (Standard Laplace transform notation is used in this analysis.) If the admittance to ground of the affected circuit at the point of coupling is $Y(s)$, and the effective noise signal is $V_s(s)$, the noise voltage $V_n(s)$ is given by

$$V_n(s) = \frac{V_s(s)sC_c}{Y(s) + sC_c} \qquad (7.11\text{-}3)$$

Two cases will be considered to show the effects of capacitively coupled noise. First, the effect on the dynamic storage node of Fig. 7.11-2b will be considered. A dynamic storage node can be adequately represented as a capacitance C_d to ground with an admittance $Y_s(s) = sC_d$. From Eq. 7.11-3, the noise voltage is

$$V_n(s) = \frac{V_s(s)sC_c}{sC_d + sC_c}$$

or, after canceling the s term,

$$V_n = \frac{V_sC_c}{C_d + C_c} \qquad (7.11\text{-}4)$$

The coupled noise voltage is just the noise voltage times the ratio of the coupling capacitor to the sum of the two capacitances. Because C_d is normally the small gate capacitance of a transistor, even a small coupling capacitance can be significant. If C_c is equal to C_d, a high-to-low voltage change in V_s can destroy

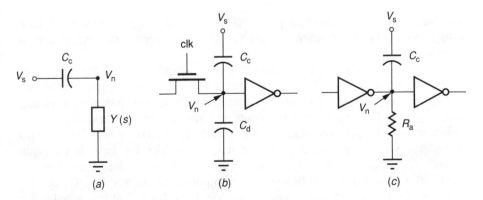

FIGURE 7.11-2
Capacitive noise coupling: (a) General noise model for capacitive noise coupling, (b) Dynamic storage node, (c) Actively driven node.

information on a dynamic storage node. It is important to keep the connection from the gating transistor to the dynamic storage node short and to ensure that no other signal lines cross the connection.

A second consideration is capacitive coupling to a driven logic node, as in Fig. 7.11-2c. Here the impedance to ground can be adequately modeled by the equivalent resistance R_a of the active output transistor of the first inverter. Again, from Eq. 7.11-3, the noise voltage is

$$V_n(s) = \frac{V_s(s)sC_c}{1/R_a + sC_c} = \frac{V_s(s)R_aC_cs}{1 + R_aC_cs} \tag{7.11-5}$$

For the normal condition of $|R_aC_cs| << 1$, Eq. 7.11-5 reduces to

$$V_n(s) = V_s(s)R_aC_cs \tag{7.11-6}$$

If $R_a = 10$ kΩ, $C_c = 0.1$ pF, and $f = 1.59$ MHz, then with $\omega = 2\pi f = 10$ Mrad/sec and $s = j\omega$

$$|V_n| = |V_s|/100$$

These values show that significant capacitive coupling is necessary to change the logic level for an actively driven node.

7.11.3 Definition of Noise Margins

Explanation of noise margins for digital logic gates requires the definition of several voltages in the voltage transfer characteristic of a logic circuit.

1. V_{IL}: the highest voltage reliably recognized as a logic low
2. V_{IH}: the lowest voltage reliably recognized as a logic high
3. V_{OL}: the nominal logic low voltage generated by a stage
4. V_{OH}: the nominal logic high voltage generated by a stage

V_{OL} and V_{OH} were introduced previously as V_L and V_H, the nominal output voltages of a reference inverter. V_{IL} and V_{IH} were introduced as the logic threshold voltages.

The voltages V_{IL} and V_{IH} require further explanation. As was shown in Sec. 7.2.2, the voltage transfer function of an inverter contains two regions with less-than-unity inverting gain separated by a region with greater-than-unity inverting gain. V_{IL} and V_{IH} are defined to denote the intersections of these regions, as shown in Fig. 7.11-3. The slope of the transfer characteristic is -1 at the two points representing an inverting gain of unity. Consider V_{IL} first. If the input voltage $V_i < V_{IL}$, the inverting gain of the inverter is less than unity and any small noise perturbation will be reduced in amplitude by the inverter. Otherwise, if $V_{IL} < V_i < V_M$, the input represents a low logic level, but any small noise perturbation is amplified as it is passed to the next stage. This condition may cause erroneous logic voltages to appear in subsequent stages. Thus, V_{IL} represents

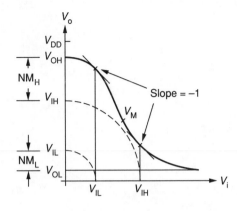

FIGURE 7.11-3
Generic dc voltage transfer characteristic for inverter.

the highest allowable input voltage level that is considered to reliably function as a logic low value. A similar analysis for V_{IH} reveals that it is the lowest allowable input voltage level that is considered to reliably function as a logic high value.

With suitable definitions for high and low logic voltages, the high and low noise margins can be defined. The low-level noise margin is

$$NM_L = V_{IL} - V_{OL} \qquad (7.11\text{-}7)$$

and the high-level noise margin is

$$NM_H = V_{OH} - V_{IH} \qquad (7.11\text{-}8)$$

NM_H and NM_L represent the largest noise voltages that can be sustained at an inverter input and still allow the inverter to function reliably. Noise margins for logic gates other than inverters are similarly defined based on their voltage transfer characteristics. Subsequent sections examine high and low noise margins for both NMOS and CMOS devices.

7.11.4 NMOS Noise Margins

The noise margins for an NMOS gate can be found from its voltage transfer characteristic. The voltages V_{OL} and V_{OH} were identified in Sec. 7.3 for the reference inverter as V_L and V_H. The depletion-load inverter and its voltage transfer characteristic of Fig. 7.11-4 will be used to help determine V_{IL} and V_{IH}. Note the straight lines that separate the ohmic and saturated regions for the enhancement and depletion transistors of the inverter. These help show that V_{IL} will be found with the depletion transistor in the ohmic region and the enhancement transistor in the saturation region. The voltage transfer characteristic in this region is given by

$$K'\frac{W_N}{L_N}\frac{(V_i - V_{TN})^2}{2} = K'\frac{W_D}{L_D}\left(-V_{TD} - \frac{V_{DD} - V_o}{2}\right)(V_{DD} - V_o)$$

$$(7.11\text{-}9)$$

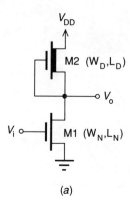

(a)

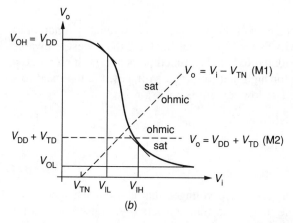

(b)

FIGURE 7.11-4
NMOS inverter noise model:
(a) Circuit, (b) Voltage transfer
characteristic.

Assuming an inverter with a pullup/pulldown ratio of k and solving Eq. 7.11-9 for V_i gives

$$V_i = V_{TN} + \sqrt{(1/k)(-2V_{TD} - V_{DD} + V_o)(V_{DD} - V_o)} \quad (7.11\text{-}10)$$

Taking the derivative with respect to V_o, setting it equal to -1, and solving for V_o gives

$$V_o = V_{DD} + V_{TD}\left(1 - \sqrt{k/(1 + k)}\right) \quad (7.11\text{-}11)$$

The corresponding input voltage is

$$V_i = V_{IL} = V_{TN} - \frac{V_{TD}}{\sqrt{k(1 + k)}} \quad (7.11\text{-}12)$$

Substituting typical values of $V_{TN} = 1$ V, $V_{TD} = -3.5$ V, $k = 4$, and $V_{DD} = 5$ V into Eqs. 7.11-11 and 7.11-12 gives

$$V_o = 4.63 \text{ V} \quad \text{and} \quad V_{IL} = 1.78 \text{ V} \quad (7.11\text{-}13)$$

To find V_{IH}, Fig. 7.11-4 indicates that the operating regions for the two transistors are reversed. The voltage transfer characteristic is now

$$K'\frac{W_N}{L_N}\left(V_i - V_{TN} - \frac{V_o}{2}\right)V_o = K'\frac{W_D}{L_D}\frac{V_{TD}^2}{2} \qquad (7.11\text{-}14)$$

Solving Eq. 7.11-14 for V_i gives

$$V_i = V_{TN} + \frac{V_o}{2} + \frac{V_{TD}^2}{2kV_o} \qquad (7.11\text{-}15)$$

Taking the derivative with respect to V_o, setting it equal to -1, and solving for V_o gives

$$V_o = \frac{-V_{TD}}{\sqrt{3k}} \qquad (7.11\text{-}16)$$

The corresponding input voltage is

$$V_i = V_{\text{IH}} = V_{TN} - \frac{2V_{TD}}{\sqrt{3k}} \qquad (7.11\text{-}17)$$

Substituting typical values into Eqs. 7.11-16 and 7.11-17 gives

$$V_o = 1.01 \text{ V and } V_{\text{IH}} = 3.02 \text{ V} \qquad (7.11\text{-}18)$$

The noise margins can now be calculated. Using the results of Eqs. 7.11-13 and 7.11-18,

$$\text{NM}_L = V_{\text{IL}} - V_{\text{OL}} = 1.78 - 0.40 = 1.38 \text{ V} \qquad (7.11\text{-}19)$$

and

$$\text{NM}_H = V_{\text{OH}} - V_{\text{IH}} = 5.00 - 3.02 = 1.98 \text{ V} \qquad (7.11\text{-}20)$$

These noise margins are typical for NMOS logic gates, with the high noise margin greater than the low noise margin.

7.11.5 CMOS Noise Margins

The noise margins for a CMOS gate can be found from its voltage transfer function. The voltages $V_{\text{OL}} = 0$ V and $V_{\text{OH}} = V_{DD}$ were found in Sec. 7.5 for the CMOS reference inverter as V_L and V_H. The inverter and its voltage transfer characteristic of Fig. 7.11-5 will be used to help determine V_{IL} and V_{IH}. Note the straight lines that separate the ohmic and saturated regions for the n- and p-channel transistors of the inverter. These help show that V_{IL} will be found with the p-channel transistor in the ohmic region and the n-channel transistor in the saturation region. The voltage transfer characteristic in this region is given by

$$K_N'\frac{W_N}{L_N}\frac{(V_i - V_{TN})^2}{2} = K_P'\frac{W_P}{L_P}\left(V_i - V_{DD} - V_{TP} - \frac{V_o - V_{DD}}{2}\right)(V_o - V_{DD})$$

$$(7.11\text{-}21)$$

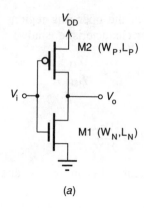

(a)

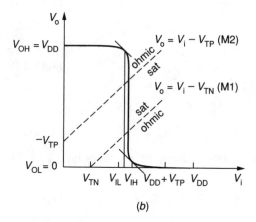

(b)

FIGURE 7.11-5
CMOS inverter noise model: (a) Circuit,
(b) Voltage transfer characteristic.

Note that V_{TP} is negative for CMOS circuits. The substitution

$$x = \frac{K_N'}{K_P'} \frac{W_N}{L_N} \frac{L_P}{W_P}$$

and solving Eq. 7.11-21 for V_o gives

$$V_o = V_i - V_{TP} - \sqrt{(V_i - V_{TP})^2 - 2V_{DD}(V_i - V_{TP} - V_{DD}/2) - x(V_i - V_{TN})^2}$$

$$(7.11\text{-}22)$$

Letting $x = 1$ for symmetric output drive, taking the derivative with respect to V_i, setting it equal to -1, and solving for V_{IL} gives

$$V_{IL} = \frac{3V_{DD} + 3V_{TP} + 5V_{TN}}{8} \qquad (7.11\text{-}23)$$

To find V_{IH}, Fig. 7.11-5 indicates that the operating regions for the two transistors are reversed. The voltage transfer characteristic is now

$$K_N' \frac{W_N}{L_N}\left(V_i - V_{TN} - \frac{V_o}{2}\right)V_o = K_P' \frac{W_P}{L_P} \frac{(V_i - V_{DD} - V_{TP})^2}{2} \qquad (7.11\text{-}24)$$

Note that V_{TP} is negative for CMOS circuits. The substitution

$$y = \frac{K_P'}{K_N'} \frac{W_P}{L_P} \frac{L_N}{W_N}$$

and solving Eq. 7.11-24 for V_o gives

$$V_o = V_i - V_{TN} - \sqrt{(V_i - V_{TN})^2 - y(V_i - V_{DD} - V_{TP})^2}$$

$$(7.11\text{-}25)$$

Letting $y = 1$ for symmetric output drive, taking the derivative with respect to V_i, setting it equal to -1, and solving for V_{IH} gives

$$V_{IH} = \frac{5V_{DD} + 5V_{TP} + 3V_{TN}}{8} \qquad (7.11\text{-}26)$$

The noise margins can now be calculated. Using typical values of $V_{TN} = 1$ V, $V_{TP} = -1$ V, $V_{DD} = 5$ V, and the results of Eqs. 7.11-23 and 7.11-26,

$$NM_L = V_{IL} - V_{OL} = 2.125 - 0 = 2.13 \text{ V} \qquad (7.11\text{-}27)$$

and

$$NM_H = V_{OH} - V_{IH} = 5.00 - 2.875 = 2.13 \text{ V} \qquad (7.11\text{-}28)$$

These noise margins are typical for CMOS logic gates. For symmetrical output drive, the noise margins are equal. Note that the sum of the CMOS noise margins (4.26 V) is much greater than the sum of the NMOS noise margins (3.36 V). CMOS logic is preferred in high-noise environments.

Primary causes of noise voltages in digital MOS circuits were described and analyzed in this section. Noise margins for digital circuits were defined, and these definitions were used to derive noise margins for both NMOS and CMOS inverters. Typical noise margins were calculated for each inverter type.

7.12 SUMMARY

Most digital designers accept a characterization of design abstraction that includes functional, register transfer level, logic, circuit, and layout descriptions as shown in Fig. 7.1-1 Practical digital design is sometimes accomplished by starting with cell layout and working up the abstraction hierarchy from layout to the functional level—often termed *bottom-up design*. At the other extreme, designs are defined at the functional level and then filled in with details at each lower level of abstraction until layout is created—termed *top-down design*. In fact, most design is accomplished using a combination of top-down and bottom-up design styles based on a prerequisite knowledge of basic digital building blocks.

The goal of this chapter has been to introduce basic digital building blocks at the logic, circuit, and layout levels. To accomplish this, salient characteristics of digital logic were described followed by explanations of NMOS and CMOS inverters, logic gates, and pass transistors. With knowledge of the primitive building blocks in hand, important electrical characteristics such as signal propagation delays, parasitic capacitance, power dissipation, and noise margins were detailed.

REFERENCES

1. M. Shahdad, R. Lipsett, E. Marschner, K. Sheehan, H. Cohen, R. Waxman, and D. Ackley: "VHSIC Hardware Description Language," *Computer*, vol. 18, no. 2, pp. 94–103, Feb. 1985.
2. Mario R. Barbacci: "Instruction Set Processor Specifications (ISPS): The Notation and Its Applications," *IEEE Trans. Comput.*, vol. C-30, no. 1, pp. 25–40, Jan. 1981.
3. W. I. Fletcher: *An Engineering Approach to Digital Design*, Prentice-Hall, Englewood Cliffs, N. J., 1980.
4. *ALS/AS Logic Circuits Data Book*, Texas Instruments, Dallas, 1983.
5. *High-Speed CMOS Logic Data Book*, Texas Instruments, Dallas, 1984.
6. F. J. Hill and G. R. Peterson: *Introduction to Switching Theory and Logical Design*, John Wiley & Sons, New York, 1981.
7. David A. Hodges and Horace G. Jackson, *Analysis and Design of Digital Integrated Circuits*, McGraw-Hill, New York, pp. 89–96, 1983.
8. Lance A. Glasser: "The Analog Behavior of Digital Integrated Circuits," *Proc. 18th Design Automation Conf.*, pp. 603–612, 1981.
9. S. M. Sze, Ed., *VLSI Technology*, McGraw-Hill, New York, 1983.

PROBLEMS

Section 7.1

7.1. Provide a multilevel description of a full adder having inputs A, B, and C and outputs Sum and Carry. Include a block diagram, an RTL-level description (use Boolean equations), and a logic diagram.

Section 7.2

7.2. Find V_L and V_H for the following piecewise-linear voltage transfer characteristic (VTC) of an inverter. Let the VTC intersect the points $(V_i, V_o) = (0,5.0)$, $(2.5,3.5)$, $(3.5,0.5)$, $(5.0,0.5)$.

7.3. What primary characteristic distinguishes restoring logic from nonrestoring logic?

7.4. Verify by using DeMorgan's theorem that the Boolean logic function $X = AB + AC + BC$ can be realized using only NAND logic gates. Show the NAND gate logic diagram for this function.

7.5. Assume that $V_{IL} = 1$ V, $V_{IH} = 4.5$ V, and $V_{DD} = 5$ V. Give the allowable voltage ranges for V_L and V_H for a practical logic device.

7.6. Given an inverter voltage transfer characteristic where $V_o = (2.5 + 2\cos(\pi V_i/5))$ V, find the values V_L, V_M, and V_H.

Section 7.3

7.7. Solve for the inverter ratio k with $V_{TD} = -4$ V, $V_{TN} = 1$ V, $V_{DD} = 5$ V, and $V_M = 2.5$ V. Assume both transistors are in saturation. Is this assumption valid?

7.8. If $V_{TD} = -3.5$ V, $V_{TN} = 1$ V, $V_{DD} = 5$ V, and $V_M = 2.5$ V, determine the inverter ratio k using the appropriate equations (ohmic or saturation) for both transistors of an inverter.

7.9. For a depletion-load inverter with $V_{TD} = -4$ V, $V_{TN} = 1$ V, $V_{DD} = 5$ V, and $k = 4$, calculate the value of V_L without the approximation of Eq. 7.3-6.

7.10. For a depletion-load inverter with $V_{TD} = -4$ V, $V_{TN} = 1$ V, $V_{DD} = 5$ V, and $k = 3$, calculate the approximate value of V_L.

7.11. Using an analysis similar to that used to derive Eq. 7.3-2, determine the sizing ratio for an enhancement-load inverter.

7.12. Assume that L and W are sized in integral multiples of dimension λ. Find values of L and W in terms of λ for both transistors of an inverter having a 4 : 1 pullup/pulldown ratio so that the total gate area is minimized.

Section 7.4

7.13. Calculate V_L for a two-input depletion-load NOR gate with one input high and with both inputs high. Assume $V_{TD} = -3.5$ V, $V_{TN} = 1$ V, $V_{DD} = 5$ V, and $k = 4$.

7.14. Assume that L and W are sized in integral multiples of dimension λ. Find values of L and W for all three transistors in a two-input depletion-load NAND gate to minimize the total gate area. Assume the pulldown transistors are sized equally and $k = 4$.

7.15. Analytically determine V_L for an n-input depletion-load NOR gate with all inputs high as n goes to infinity.

7.16. For a two-input NAND gate with $V_{TD} = -3.5$ V, $V_{TN} = 1$ V, and $V_{DD} = 5$ V, determine V_L if the pullup transistor is sized according to $k = 4$ instead of $k = 8$.

7.17. Show that a four-input NAND function can be realized with a multi-input NOR gate and inverters.

Section 7.5

7.18. Based on the VTC of Fig. 7.5-2, provide the VTC for a CMOS inverter pair consisting of two identical inverters.

7.19. Assume a 2 μ process with $K_N' = 2K_P'$ and a CMOS inverter with symmetrical output drive. Find the minimum L and W for the p-channel pullup if the n-channel pulldown is of minimum size. Next assume the p-channel pullup is of minimum size, and find the minimum L and W for the n-channel pulldown. The smallest transistor for a 2 μ process is 2 μ by 2 μ.

7.20. Assume the transistors are in the ohmic region with V_{DS} near 0 V. Determine the constant of proportionality for Eq. 7.5-2 and for Eq. 7.5-3.

Section 7.6

7.21. For a NOR gate with $K_N' = 2K_P'$ and with both n-channel pulldown transistors set to minimum size, find the L and W of equally sized p-channel pullups for symmetrical drive.

7.22. Assuming that $K_N' = 2K_P'$, compare the minimum total gate area in terms of dimension λ for a two-input NOR and a two-input NAND gate in CMOS if approximately symmetrical output drive is required for the worst-case condition (series resistance with all transistors on equal to parallel resistance with all but one transistor off).

7.23. Determine the transistor sizes for a three-input CMOS NAND gate with minimum-size pulldown transistors if symmetric output drive is desired for the worst-case pullup and pulldown conditions. Determine the maximum and minimum resistance considering all possible input combinations.

7.24. Compare the minimum total gate area for a four-input NAND gate in both NMOS and CMOS if $K_N' = 2K_P'$, using proper pullup/pulldown ratios for the NMOS gate.

Section 7.7

7.25. Assume a series string of NMOS pass transistors having a lumped-parameter model, as in Fig. 7.7-3, with $R = 10$ kΩ and $C = 0.1$ pF. Calculate the time constant for a single stage and for 10 series stages using the square-law delay approximation.

7.26. If five NMOS pass transistors are cascaded source to gate, find the highest output voltage from the fifth pass transistor if the gate of the first pass transistor is tied to 5 V. Assume $V_{TN} = 1$ V.

7.27. Consider a 4-to-1 selector circuit with select inputs a and b. Compare a solution using standard NMOS logic gates to the pass-transistor solution of Fig. 7.7-2. Give the number of transistors required for each solution.

7.28. Does a series cascade of CMOS transmission gates have the same square-law delay characteristic as a string of NMOS pass transistors? Why or why not?

Section 7.8

7.29. For $L = W = 2$ μ, $K' = 25$ μA/V^2, $V_{TN} = 1$ V, and $V_{DD} = 5$ V, find R_{ss} from Eq. 7.8-3 and the exact value of R_1 from Eq. 7.8-4. If $V_{TD} = -4$ V and $k = 4$, find the value of R_1 from Eq. 7.8-5.

7.30. Verify that the 10%-to-90% rising transition time for the exponential voltage $V = 1 - e^{-t/\tau}$ is 2.2τ.

7.31. For the parameters of Prob. 7.29, find t_{LH} and t_{HL} if $C_{ox} = 0.75$ fF/μ^2.

7.32. Find the process characteristic time constant for the parameters of Prob. 7.29 if $C_{ox} = 0.75$ fF/μ^2.

7.33. With the parameters used to derive the process characteristic time constant for the preceding problem, use SPICE to calculate the inverter-pair delay by simulation.

7.34. If the dimensions and voltages of Prob. 7.29 are scaled down by a factor of 2, calculate the resulting process characteristic time constant and compare it with the unscaled value (remember to scale the gate oxide thickness).

7.35. Compare the current for an enhancement transistor with $V_{GS} = V_{DS} = V_{DD}$ to the current for an equally sized depletion transistor with $V_{GS} = 0$ and $V_{DS} = V_{DD}$. Now calculate the depletion transistor current with $V_{GS} = V_{DD}$. Use the parameters of Prob. 7.29

7.36. Calculate t_{ipd} for a three-input NOR gate, and compare it with t_{ipd} for a three-input NAND gate in NMOS with typical parameter values of Prob 7.29.

7.37. Compute the CMOS t_{ipd} for Ex. 7.8-1 if $K'_P = 15$ μA/V^2 and the p-channel transistor is sized for symmetrical drive.

Section 7.9

7.38. If the process characteristic time constant is $\tau_p = 0.01$ ns and $C_G = 0.1$ pF for an NMOS inverter with $k = 4$, calculate the average delay to drive a 10 pF load.

7.39. Assume that a logic signal drives the root of a binary tree that has 16 outputs, each driving a single reference inverter. Calculate the path delay from the root to the load in terms of t_{apd}. Now calculate the delay if the same logic signal drives the 16 loads directly.

7.40. Repeat the preceding problem, but include the effects of interconnection loading by assuming that the interconnection capacitance for each driven node is twice the gate load capacitance.

7.41. For a geometrically sized cascade of four inverters with each inverter having twice the drive of the preceding stage, compute the average propagation delay in terms of t_{apd} for each of the four stages. Assume the final load is geometrically sized.

7.42. Calculate t_{dir} versus t_{cas} in terms of t_{apd} for a load equivalent to 500 reference inverters when driven (a) directly, (b) by an optimal cascade (calculate n and truncate to an integer), and (c) by a cascade of two drive stages.

Section 7.10

7.43. If $\theta_{JA} = 20°C/W$ because of special packaging, the maximum junction temperature is $T_J = 150°C$, and the ambient temperature is $T_A = 30°C$, find the allowable power dissipation for the integrated circuit.

7.44. Calculate the static power dissipation for an NMOS inverter in the on state with $k = 5$, $K' = 40 \ \mu A/V^2$, and $V_{TD} = -4$ V. As long as the low logic voltage is below $V_{DD} + V_{TD}$, does the size of the enhancement pulldown affect the power dissipation? Why or why not?

7.45. Based on Eq. 7.10-6, what is the maximum instantaneous power dissipated in the inverter of the preceding problem? Assume $V_{TN} = 1$ V.

7.46. Show that the energy dissipated in the resistor of the circuit of Fig. 7.10-2b is $CV^2/2$ during the capacitor discharge.

7.47. A new CMOS microprocessor is advertised as having a complexity of 300,000 transistors, uses a 20 MHz clock, and operates from a 5 V supply. Assume the microprocessor is composed entirely of gates with an average of five transistors per gate and that the average gate loading capacitance is 0.1 pF. Calculate the dynamic power dissipated by this chip. Is this a reasonable value? If not, which assumptions of the problem are probably incorrect? Explain.

Section 7.11

7.48. For the circuit of Fig. 7.11-1, assume that $R_1 = 10$ kΩ, $R_2 = 40$ kΩ, and $R_c = 5$ kΩ. Calculate the voltage V_1 (*a*) when only switch S1 is closed, and (*b*) when both switches S1 and S3 are closed, if $V_{DD} = 5$ V.

7.49. A dynamic storage node has capacitance $C_n = 0.2$ pF and initial voltage $V_n = 4$ V. If a nearby signal line is coupled to the storage node by capacitance $C_c = 0.1$ pF, find the voltage on V_n after the signal line switches from 5 V to 1 V.

7.50. For $V_{TD} = -4$ V, $V_{TN} = 1$ V, $V_{DD} = 5$ V, and $k = 5$, find V_{IL}, V_{OL}, V_{IH}, V_{OH}, NM_L, and NM_H.

7.51. For an NMOS inverter, derive a simplified expression for V_{OL} based on V_{DD}, V_{TD}, V_{TN}, and k.

7.52. How do NM_L and NM_H behave as k increases without limit?

7.53. Verify Eqs. 7.11-11 and 7.11-12.

7.54. Verify Eqs. 7.11-16 and 7.11-17.

7.55. For a CMOS inverter, give the expressions to calculate NM_L and NM_H directly in terms of V_{DD}, V_{TN}, and V_{TP}.

7.56. For $V_{DD} = 5$ V, calculate the noise margins for a CMOS inverter under the following conditions
  (*a*) $V_{TN} = 0.5$ V, $V_{TP} = -0.5$ V
  (*b*) $V_{TN} = 1.5$ V, $V_{TP} = -1.5$ V
  (*c*) $V_{TN} = 0.5$ V, $V_{TP} = -1.5$ V

CHAPTER
8

ANALOG SYSTEMS

8.0 INTRODUCTION

The systems viewpoint of microelectronic design for analog integrated circuits is presented in this chapter. This material represents the highest level in the design hierarchy illustrated in Table 5.0-1. It is built on the circuits of Chapter 6, which are in turn built on the blocks and components of Chapter 5. A parallel hierarchy is presented in Chapters 7 and 9 for digital integrated circuit design. The subject matter in this chapter deals with the design of systems rather than the design of circuits. In this sense, the designer moves to a higher plateau of design. For example, rather than the design of op amps, the subject will include design *with* op amps.

The material presented in this chapter has been selected to be representative of the concepts and techniques in analog signal processing. In this chapter, we will discuss digital-to-analog and analog-to-digital conversion; review the concepts of continuous-time filter theory; and present switched capacitor filters, modulators and multipliers, waveshaping circuits, and oscillators. Although these subjects may be classified as either subsystems or systems, they are representative of analog design concepts applied at a system level. A microelectronic system often contains both digital and analog circuits and systems, so that in this sense, the material in Chapters 8 and 9 should be treated as a subsystem.

8.1 ANALOG SIGNAL PROCESSING

Figure 8.1-1 shows a simple block diagram of a typical signal processing system. As IC technology begins to exploit VLSI techniques and capabilities, many systems with this format will be built on a single chip. An example of this approach is the analog signal processor.[1] The advent of analog sampled data techniques and MOS technology has made the design of a general signal processor a viable

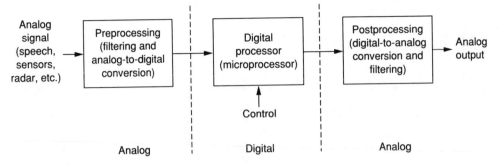

FIGURE 8.1-1
A block diagram of a typical signal processing system.

approach. At the present, CMOS technology is more suitable for combining analog and digital techniques. The primary reason for this situation is that digital VLSI circuits are typically implemented in CMOS. For this reason we will emphasize CMOS over BJT technology in this chapter. Recently, BJT and CMOS technologies have been combined to produce a new technology called BiMOS. BiMOS technology gives the designer an additional degree of freedom to select the most suitable devices for a given application.

The first step in the design of an analog signal processing system is to examine the specifications and to partition the system into the analog part and the digital part. In most cases, the input signal is analog. It could be a speech signal, a sensor output, a radar return, etc. The first block of Fig. 8.1-1 is a preprocessing block. Typically, this block will consist of filters and an analog-to-digital converter. Often, there are very strict speed and accuracy requirements on the components in this block. The next block of the analog signal processor is essentially a microprocessor. An obvious advantage of this approach is that the function of the processor can easily be controlled and changed. Finally, it is often necessary to provide an analog output. In this case, a postprocessing block is necessary. It will typically contain a digital-to-analog converter and some filtering. An interesting decision for the system designer is deciding where to place the interfaces indicated by the dotted lines.

For signal processing, probably the most important system consideration is the bandwidth of the signal to be processed. A graph of the bandwidths of a variety of signals is given in Fig. 8.1-2. The bandwidths in this figure cover the enormous range of 10 orders of magnitude in frequency. At the low end are the seismic signals, which do not extend much below 1 Hz because of the absorption characteristics of the earth. At the other extreme are the microwave signals, which are not used much above 30 GHz because of the difficulties in performing even the simplest forms of signal processing at higher frequencies.

To perform signal processing over this range of frequencies, a variety of techniques have been developed that are almost exclusively analog above 10 MHz and digital below 100 Hz, as shown in Fig. 8.1-3. In the overlap region, a tradeoff must be made between the accuracy and flexibility of a digital approach

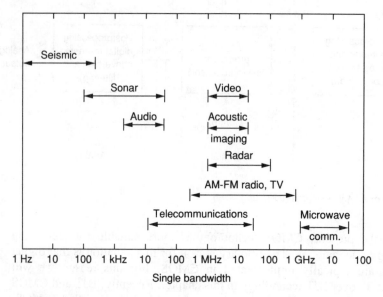

FIGURE 8.1-2
Bandwidths of signals used in signal processing applications.

and the low cost, power, and size of analog techniques. These considerations illustrate some of the advantages of a combined MOS-BJT technology.

By assuming the continuing development of MOS and bipolar technology, it is possible to extrapolate the trends of the past 10 years to obtain predictions about the capability of IC technology in the next 10 years. Some of the implications of these predictions have been considered and show that even at the limits of scaling, the processing bandwidth of MOS technology will have improved only to the point where it is equivalent to today's advanced bipolar technologies.

The ranges indicated in Fig. 8.1-3 are due to technology and are constantly increasing. One of the fastest-moving boundaries in Fig. 8.1-3 is the upper limit of the MOS digital logic, which, as the technology progresses to VLSI, should be able to process signals by the year 1992 at bandwidths of 50–100 MHz. This will be accomplished by using greatly increased density along with moderately increased device speeds. However, as can be seen in Fig. 8.1-3, bipolar digital techniques are already able to process at these rates. Therefore, VLSI will not make possible increased processing rates over what can now be achieved with processors built with bipolar technology, but rather will offer the primary advantages of reduced cost, size, and power requirements of the MOS VLSI signal processors. This will make it possible for signal processing techniques to make an impact in such cost-sensitive areas as consumer products that until now have been unable to afford the costs of using more sophisticated techniques. The combination of BJT and MOS technology offers the best promise of high performance, VLSI signal processing capability.

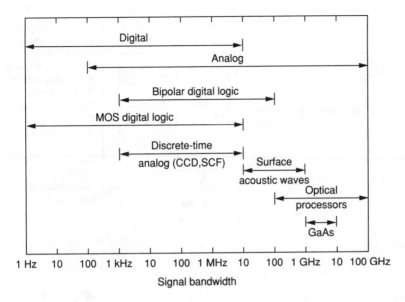

FIGURE 8.1-3
Signal bandwidths that can be processed by present-day (1989) technologies.

8.2 DIGITAL-TO-ANALOG CONVERTERS

The ability to convert digital signals to analog and vice versa is very important in signal processing. This section will examine the digital-to-analog conversion aspect of this important interface. Analog-to-digital conversion will be discussed in the next section. Most of the discussion in these two sections will be independent of whether the technology is BJT or MOS. The op amps and comparators used can be of either type. The switches will be MOS. The resistors and capacitors can be implemented by either technology, depending on the performance requirements.

Figure 8.2-1 illustrates how analog-to-digital (A/D) and digital-to-analog (D/A) converters are used in data systems.[2] In general, an A/D conversion process will convert a sampled and held analog signal to a digital word that is a representation of the analog sampled signal. Often, many analog inputs are multiplexed to the A/D converter. The D/A conversion process is essentially the inverse of the A/D process. Digital words are applied to the input of the D/A converter to create from a reference voltage an analog output signal that is a representation of the digital word.

This section will introduce the principles of D/A converters and will then discuss the performance characterization of D/A converters. The various types of linear D/A converters that will be examined include current-scaling, voltage-scaling, charge-scaling, combinations of the preceding types, and serial D/A converters. In the next section, we will see that D/A converters have an important role in the design and implementation of some A/D converters.

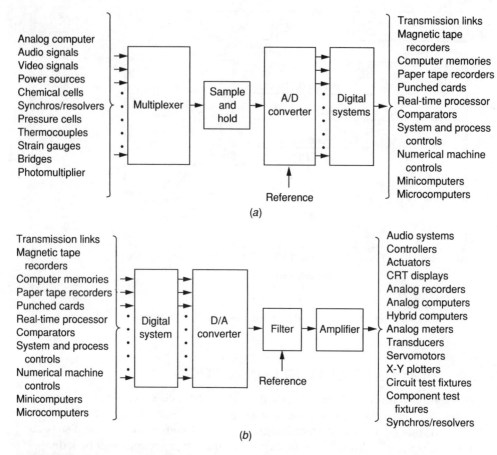

FIGURE 8.2-1
Converters in signal processing systems: (a) A/D, (b) D/A.

Figure 8.2-2a shows a conceptual block diagram of a D/A converter. The inputs are a digital word of N bits (b_1, b_2, b_3, . . . , b_N) and a reference voltage, V_{ref}. The voltage output, V_{OUT}, can be expressed as

$$V_{OUT} = K V_{ref} D \qquad (8.2\text{-}1)$$

where K is a scaling factor and the digital word D is given as

$$D = \frac{b_1}{2^1} + \frac{b_2}{2^2} + \frac{b_3}{2^3} + \cdots + \frac{b_N}{2^N} \qquad (8.2\text{-}2)$$

N is the total number of bits of the digital word, and b_i is the ith bit coefficient and is either 0 or 1. Thus, the output of a D/A converter can be expressed by combining Eqs. 8.2-1 and 8.2-2 to get

$$V_{OUT} = K V_{ref} \left(\frac{b_1}{2^1} + \frac{b_2}{2^2} + \frac{b_3}{2^3} + \cdots + \frac{b_N}{2^N} \right) \qquad (8.2\text{-}3)$$

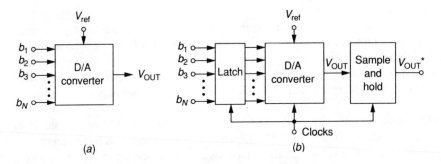

FIGURE 8.2-2
(a) Conceptual block diagram of a D/A converter, (b) Clocked D/A converter.

or

$$V_{OUT} = K V_{ref}(b_1 2^{-1} + b_2 2^{-2} + b_3 2^{-3} + \cdots + b_N 2^{-N})$$

$$= K V_{ref} \sum_{j=1}^{N} b_j 2^{-j} \tag{8.2-4}$$

In many cases, the digital word is synchronously clocked. In this case it is necessary to use latches to hold the word for conversion and to provide a sample-and-hold circuit at the output, as shown in Fig. 8.2-2b. A voltage that has been sampled and held is denoted by an asterisk. The sample-and-hold circuit consists of a circuit such as that shown in Fig. 8.2-3, where the analog signal is sampled

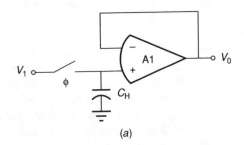

(a)

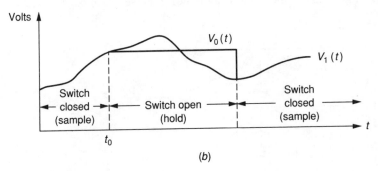

(b)

FIGURE 8.2-3
(a) Simple sample-and-hold circuit, (b) Waveforms illustrating the operation of the sample-and-hold.

on a capacitor, C_H, when the switch is closed; this is called the *sample mode*. During the time that the switch is open, or the *hold mode*, the voltage at time t_0 remains available at the output. An alternate version of the sample-and-hold circuit with higher performance is shown in Fig. 8.2-4. It is important that the sample-and-hold circuit be able to rapidly track changes in the input voltage when in the sample mode and not discharge the capacitor when in the hold mode.

The basic architecture of the D/A converter without an output sample-and-hold circuit is shown in Fig. 8.2-5. The various blocks are a voltage reference, which can be externally supplied, binary switches, a scaling network, and an output amplifier. The voltage reference, binary switches, and scaling network convert the digital word as either a voltage or current signal, and the output amplifier converts this signal to a voltage signal that can be sampled without affecting the value of the conversion.

The characterization of the D/A converter is very important in understanding its use and design. The characteristics of the D/A converter can be divided into static and dynamic properties. The static properties are independent of time and include the converter transfer characteristic, quantization noise, dynamic range, gain, offset, and nonlinearity.[3]

Figure 8.2-6 shows the transfer characteristic of an ideal D/A converter. This D/A converter has been designed so that the analog output occurs at odd multiples of the full scale signal (FS) divided by 16. The right-most bit of the digital input code is called the *least significant bit* (LSB). Each time the LSB changes, the analog output changes by $FS/2^N$, where N is equal to the number of digital bits. Although this change is an analog quantity, it is often called an LSB change and should be interpreted as the analog change due to a change in the LSB of the digital input code.

The *resolution* of a converter is the smallest analog change that can be distinguished by an A/D converter or produced by a D/A converter. Resolution may be stated in percent of FS, but is commonly expressed in number of bits, N, where the converter has 2^N possible states. The finite resolution of converters causes an inherent uncertainty in digitizing an analog value. This uncertainty is called the *quantization noise* and has a value of up to ±0.5 LSB. In the characteristic of Fig. 8.2-6, the quantization noise is seen to be ±0.5 LSB

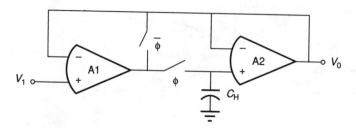

FIGURE 8.2-4
An improved sample-and-hold circuit.

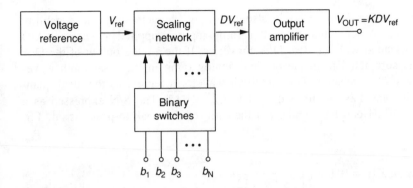

FIGURE 8.2-5
Block diagram of a D/A converter.

or $\pm FS/2^{N+1}$ about each of the multiples of FS/8. The straight line in Fig. 8.2-6 through the midpoint of each analog step change represents the ideal performance of the D/A converter as N approaches infinity.

The *full scale range* (FSR) is the difference between the maximum and minimum analog values and is equal to FS in Fig. 8.2-6 as N approaches infinity. The *dynamic range* (DR) of a noiseless converter is the ratio of the FSR to the smallest difference it can resolve. Thus, the DR can be given as

$$DR = 2^N \qquad (8.2\text{-}5)$$

or in terms of decibels as

$$DR(dB) = 20\log_{10}(2^N) = 6.02N \qquad (8.2\text{-}6)$$

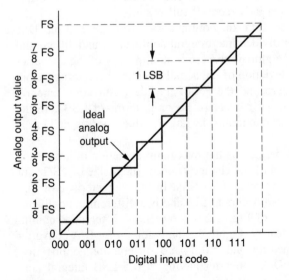

FIGURE 8.2-6
Ideal input-output characteristics for a 3-bit D/A converter.

The *signal-to-noise ratio* (S/N) is also useful in characterizing the capability of a converter. Assume that an analog ramp input is applied to an ideal A/D converter cascaded with an ideal D/A converter. If the analog output of the D/A converter is subtracted from the original analog ramp input, a sawtooth waveform of $\pm FS/2^{N+1}$ results. This sawtooth waveform represents the ideal quantization noise and has an rms value of $(FS/2^N)/\sqrt{12}$. The S/N expressed as a power ratio in dB can be found from the ratio of the peak-to-peak signal, FS, to the noise as

$$S/N(dB) = 10\log_{10}\left[\frac{FS}{FS/[2^N\,(12)^{1/2}]}\right]^2$$

$$= 20\log_{10}(2^N) + 20\log_{10}(12)^{1/2} = 6.02N + 10.8 \quad (8.2\text{-}7)$$

It can be seen that the S/N ratio increases by a factor of approximately 6 dB for each additional bit of resolution.

The remaining static characteristics include *offset error*, *gain error*, *nonlinearity*, and *nonmonotonicity*. Figure 8.2-7 illustrates the first three of these characteristics for a 3-bit D/A converter. In each case the ideal characteristic of Fig. 8.2-6 is shown by dashed lines for comparison. An illustration of offset error is shown in Fig. 8.2-7a. An offset error is seen to be a vertical shift in the D/A transfer characteristic of the ideal D/A transfer characteristic. The offset error is defined as the analog output value by which the transfer characteristic fails to pass through zero. It may be expressed in millivolts or percent of FS.

Figure 8.2-7b illustrates the gain or scale factor error of a 3-bit D/A converter. The gain or scale factor error is defined as the difference in the full scale values between the ideal and actual transfer characteristics when the offset error is zero and may be expressed in percent of full scale.

Figure 8.2-7c is an illustration of nonlinearity error in a 3-bit D/A converter. Nonlinearity is further divided into integral nonlinearity and differential nonlinearity. Integral linearity is a global measure of nonlinearity of the converter and is defined as the maximum deviation of the actual transfer characteristic from a straight line drawn between zero and the FS of the ideal converter. Integral nonlinearity is expressed in terms of percent of FS or in terms of LSBs. In the characteristics of Fig. 8.2-7c, the maximum deviation, which occurs at 111, is -1.5 LSB or -18.75% of FS.

Differential nonlinearity is defined as the maximum deviation of any of the analog output changes caused by an LSB change from its ideal size of $FS/2^N$ or 1 LSB. It is typically expressed in terms of $\pm$LSBs. In the characteristic of Fig. 8.2-7c, the maximum deviation also occurs at 111 and is a differential nonlinearity of ± 1 LSB. The characteristic of Fig. 8.2-8 shows how differential nonlinearity differs from integral nonlinearity. Figure 8.2-8a is for a 4-bit D/A converter having ± 2 LSB integral nonlinearity and ± 0.5 LSB differential nonlinearity. Figure 8.2-8b illustrates a 4-bit D/A converter having ± 0.5 LSB integral nonlinearity and ± 1 LSB differential nonlinearity.

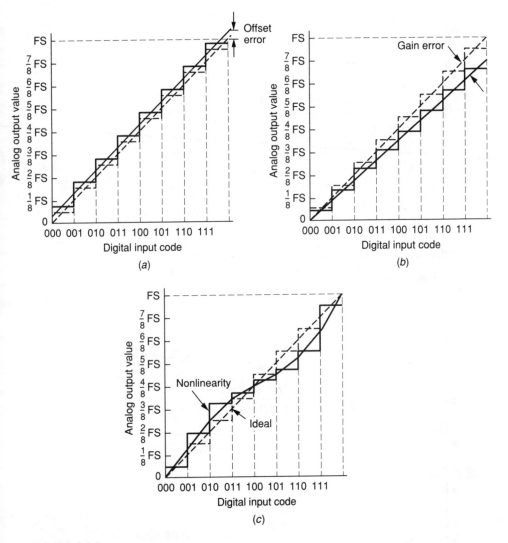

FIGURE 8.2-7
Examples of various types of static characteristics for a 3-bit D/A converter: (*a*) Offset error, (*b*) Gain error, (*c*) Nonlinearity.

Figure 8.2-9 illustrates a 3-bit D/A converter that is not monotonic. A monotonic D/A converter is one in which an increasing digital input code produces a continuously increasing analog output value. A nonmonotonic D/A converter can result if the differential nonlinearity error exceeds ± 1 LSB. In Fig. 8.2-9, a differential nonlinearity of ± 1.5 LSB occurs at a digital input code of 001. Note that there are two occurrences of nonmonotonicity in Fig. 8.2-9.

The dynamic characteristics of the D/A converter are associated with changes in the input digital word. The time required for the output of the converter to

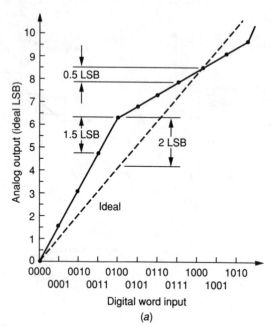

(a)

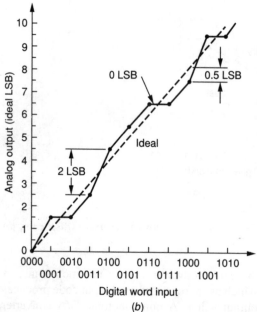

(b)

FIGURE 8.2-8
Distinction between integral and differential nonlinearity for a D/A converter: (a D/A converter with ±2 LSB integral nonlinearity and ±0.5 LSB differential nonlinearity, (b) D/A converter with ±0.5 LSB integral nonlinearity and ±1 LSB differential nonlinearity.

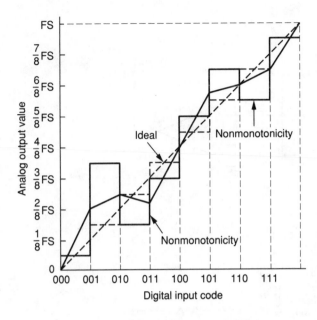

FIGURE 8.2-9
Example of a 3-bit D/A converter that is not monotonic.

respond to a bit change is called the *settling time* and is defined similarly to the settling time for op amps in Fig. 6.5-21. Settling time for D/A converters depends on the type of converter and can range from as much as 100 μs to less than 100 ns.

Many techniques have been used to implement D/A converters. Three approaches that are compatible with integrated circuit technology will be examined. These methods are current-scaling or division, voltage-scaling or division, and charge-scaling or division. Current-scaling is widely used with BJT technology, whereas voltage- and charge-scaling are popular for MOS technology.

8.2.1 Current-Scaling D/A Converters

The general principle of current-scaling or division D/A converters is shown in Fig. 8.2-10a. The reference voltage is converted to binary-weighted currents, $I_1, I_2, I_3, \ldots, I_N$. An implementation of this technique using resistors is shown in Fig. 8.2-10b. Each of the switches, S_i, is connected to V_{ref} if the ith bit, b_i, is 1 and to ground if b_i is 0. It is seen that the output voltage of the op amp can be expressed as

$$V_{\text{out}} = \frac{-R}{2}I_O = \frac{-R}{2}\left(\frac{b_1}{R} + \frac{b_2}{2R} + \frac{b_3}{4R} + \cdots + \frac{b_N}{2^{N-1}R}\right)V_{\text{ref}}$$

$$= -V_{\text{ref}}\left(b_1 2^{-1} + b_2 2^{-2} + b_3 2^{-3} + \cdots + b_N 2^{-N}\right) \quad (8.2\text{-}8)$$

The feedback resistor, R_F, can be used to achieve the scaling factor K of Eq. 8.2-1. The switches can be moved from the V_{ref} side of the resistors to the

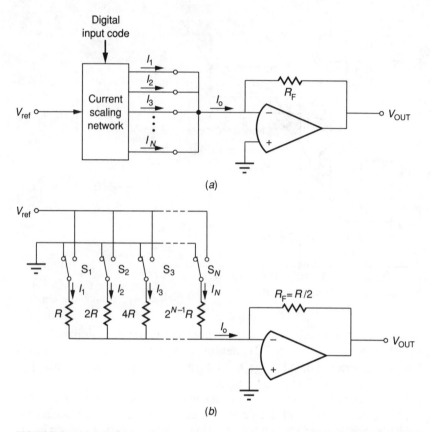

FIGURE 8.2-10
(a) Conceptual illustration of a current-scaling D/A converter, (b) Implementation of (a).

side connected to the inverting input of the op amp. The advantage of the latter configuration is that the voltages at the switch terminals are always ground. As a consequence, the switch parasitic capacitances are not charged or discharged.

The binary-weighted resistor ladder configuration of Fig. 8.2-10b has the disadvantage of a large ratio of component values. For example, the ratio of the resistor for the MSB, R_{MSB}, to the resistor for the LSB, R_{LSB}, is

$$\frac{R_{MSB}}{R_{LSB}} = \frac{1}{2^{N-1}} \tag{8.2-9}$$

For an 8-bit D/A converter, this gives a ratio of 1/128. The difficulty with this approach is that the accuracy of R_{MSB} must be much better than that of the value of R_{LSB} for the converter to work properly. For example, R_{MSB} of an 8-bit D/A converter must have a relative accuracy with respect to R_{LSB} to within ±0.78%, and preferably better. Such accuracy is difficult to achieve without trimming the resistors, which is done for high-resolution D/A converters using binary-weighted components.

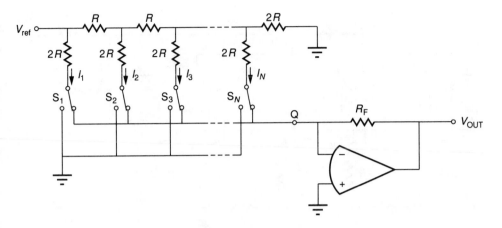

FIGURE 8.2-11
A current-scaling D/A converter using an R-$2R$ ladder.

An alternative to the binary-weighted approach is the use of an R-$2R$ ladder, shown in Fig. 8.2-11. Each of the switches, S_i, is connected to Q if the ith bit is 1 and to ground if the ith bit is 0. Q is the inverting input of the op amp. Obviously, the current I_1 is equal to $V_{\text{ref}}/2R$. Using the fact that the resistance to the right of any of the vertical $2R$ resistors is $2R$, we see that the currents I_1, I_2, I_3, ... , I_N are binary-weighted and given as

$$I_1 = 2I_2 = 4I_3 = \dots = 2^{N-1}I_N \qquad (8.2\text{-}10)$$

Thus, the output voltage of the R-$2R$ D/A converter of Fig. 8.2-11 is given by Eq. 8.2-8. Figure 8.2-11 is an example of using the switches connected either to ground or the inverting terminal of the op amp. V_{ref} and the inverting input of the op amp (point Q) can be interchanged if desired. While the R-$2R$ D/A converter has twice as many resistors as the binary-weighted resistor D/A converter, it requires resistors with only the ratio of 2:1, which is more practical to accomplish. One disadvantage of the R-$2R$ configuration is that there are up to 2^{N-1} floating nodes, which are sensitive to parasitic capacitances. Floating nodes are nodes with relatively large resistance to ground. The charging and discharging of these capacitances will require time and delay the response of the converter. Possible architectures for bipolar D/A converters using the R-$2R$ ladder approach are shown in Fig. 8.2-12. Note that the emitter areas of the BJT devices must be proportional to the emitter current in Fig. 8.2-12a.

Two approaches for using binary-weighted D/A converters while keeping the MSB and LSB resistor ratios small deserve mention. The first is called *cascading* and is illustrated in Fig. 8.2-13a. The use of a current divider allows two 4-bit, binary-weighted current sources to be cascaded to achieve an 8-bit D/A converter. The accuracy of the 1:16 attenuating resistors must be within the magnitude of the LSB of the entire ladder. A second approach is shown in Fig. 8.2-13b and is called the *master-slave ladder*. In this approach, a master ladder consists of the

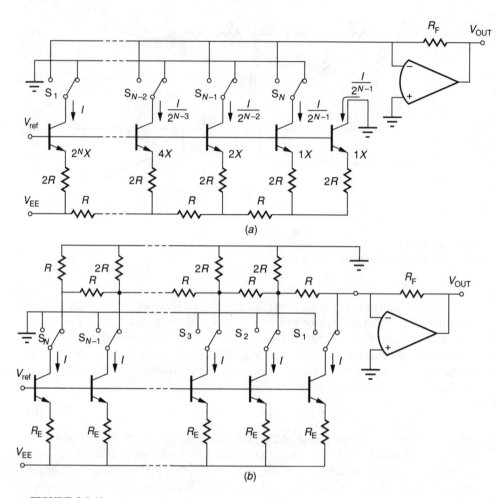

FIGURE 8.2-12

Two implementations of D/A converters using R-$2R$ ladders and BJT current sinks. (*a*) Binary-weighted emitter areas, and (*b*) Equal emitter areas. Both converters are described by $V_{OUT} = -R_F I [b_1 + 2^{-1}b_2 + \ldots + 2^{N-1}b_N]$.

half of the bits that are most significant, and the slave ladder consists of the half of the bits that are least significant. The crucial point in this approach is the accuracy of the $I/16$ current source for the slave ladder. It must have accuracy better than ± 0.5 LSB.

8.2.2 Voltage-Scaling D/A Converters

Voltage-scaling uses series resistors connected between V_{ref} and ground to selectively obtain voltages between these limits. For an N-bit converter, the resistor string would have at least 2^N segments. These segments can all be equal or

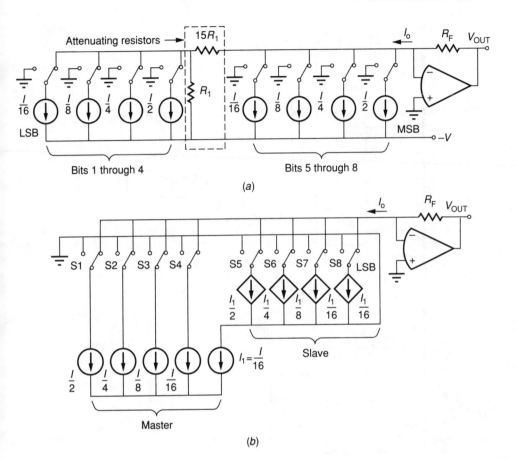

FIGURE 8.2-13

(a) Use of current division to cascade two 4-bit, binary-weighted current sinks to get an 8-bit D/A converter, (b) Master-slave technique to combine two 4-bit binary weighted current sources to obtain an 8-bit D/A converter. Note that $I_1 = I/16$.

the end segments may be partial values, depending on the requirements. Figure 8.2-14a shows a 3-bit voltage scaling D/A converter. Note that the op amp is used simply to buffer the resistor string. Each tap is connected to a switching tree whose switches are controlled by the bits of the digital word. If the ith bit is 1, then the switches controlled by b_i are closed. If the ith bit is 0, then the switches controlled by $\overline{b_i}$ are closed.

The voltage-scaling D/A converter of Fig. 8.2-14a works as follows. Suppose that the digital word to be converted is $b_1 = 1, b_2 = 0$, and $b_3 = 1$. Following the sequence of switches, we see that V_{OUT} is equal to 11/16 of V_{ref}. In general, the voltage at any tap i of Fig. 8.2-14a can be expressed as

$$V_i = \frac{V_{ref}}{8}(i - 0.5) \qquad (8.2\text{-}11)$$

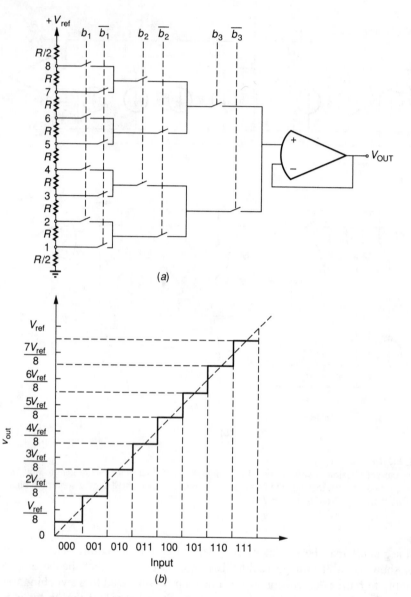

FIGURE 8.2-14
(a) Illustration of a 3-bit voltage-scaling D/A converter, (b) Input-output characteristics of a.

Figure 8.2-14b shows the input-output characteristics of the D/A converter of Fig. 8.2-14a. It may be desirable to connect the bottom tap to ground, so that a well-defined output (ground) is available when the digital word is all 0s.

Example 8.2-1. Find the accuracy requirement for a resistor string consisting of N equal segments as a function of the number of bits N. If the relative resistor accuracy is 2%, what is the largest number of bits than can be resolved to within ± 0.5 LSB?

Solution. The ideal voltage to ground across k resistors can be expressed as

$$V_k = \frac{kR}{2^N R} V_{\text{REF}}$$

The worst case variation in this voltage can be found by assuming that all resistors above this point in the string are maximum and below this point are minimum. Therefore, the worst case lowest voltage to ground across k resistors is

$$V'_k = \frac{kR_{\min} V_{\text{REF}}}{(2^N - k)R_{\max} + kR_{\min}}$$

The difference between the ideal and worst case voltages can be expressed as

$$\frac{V_k}{V_{REF}} - \frac{V'_k}{V_{REF}} = \frac{kR}{2^N R} - \frac{kR_{\min}}{(2^N - K)R_{\max} + kR_{\min}}$$

Since this difference must be less that 0.5 LSB, then the desired relationship can be obtained as

$$\frac{k}{2^N} - \frac{kR_{\min}}{(2^N - k)R_{\max} + kR_{\min}} < \frac{0.5}{2^N}$$

The relative accuracy of the resistor R can be expressed as $\Delta R/R$, which gives $R_{\max} = R + 0.5\Delta R$ and $R_{\min} = R - 0.5\Delta R$. Normally, the worst case occurs when k is midway in the resistor string or $k = 0.5(2^N)$. Assuming a relative accuracy of 2% and substituting the above values gives

$$|0.01| < 2^{-N}$$

Solving this equation for N gives $N = 6$ as the largest integer.

It is seen that the voltage-scaling D/A structure is very regular and thus well suited for MOS technology. An advantage of this architecture is that it guarantees monotonicity, since the voltage at each tap cannot be greater than the tap below it. The area required for the voltage-scaling D/A converter is large if the number of bits is 8 or more. The converter will be sensitive to parasitic capacitances at each of the floating nodes resulting in signal delays.

8.2.3 Charge-Scaling D/A Converters

Charge-scaling D/A converters operate by dividing the total charge applied to a capacitor array. Typically, all capacitors are discharged first. Figure 8.2-15a shows an illustration of a charge-scaling D/A converter. A nonoverlapping, two-phase clock is used. ϕ_1 indicates that a switch is closed during phase 1, and similarly for ϕ_2. During ϕ_1, all capacitors in the array are discharged. Next, during ϕ_2, the capacitors associated with bits that are 1 are connected to V_{ref} and those with bits that are 0 are connected to ground. The resulting situation can be described by equating the charge on the capacitors connected to V_{ref} (C_{eq}) to the charge in the total capacitors (C_{tot}). This is expressed as

$$V_{\text{ref}}C_{\text{eq}} = V_{\text{ref}}\left(b_1 C + \frac{b_2 C}{2} + \frac{b_3 C}{2^2} + \cdots + \frac{b_N C}{2^{N-1}}\right) = C_{\text{tot}}V_{\text{OUT}} = 2CV_{\text{OUT}}$$

$$(8.2\text{-}12)$$

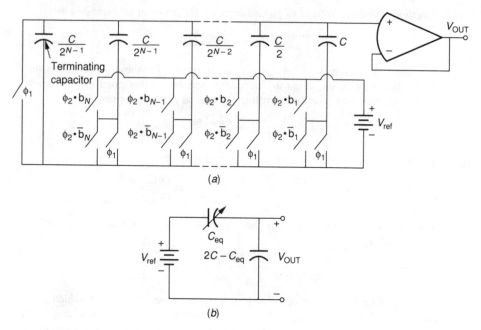

FIGURE 8.2-15
(a) Charge-scaling D/A converter, switches designated as $\phi_2 \cdot b_i (\phi_2 \cdot \overline{b}_i)$ close if both ϕ_2 and $b_i(\overline{b}_i)$ are true during ϕ_2, (b) Equivalent circuit of a.

From Eq. 8.2-12 we may solve for V_{OUT} as

$$V_{OUT} = \left(b_1 2^{-1} + b_2 2^{-2} + b_3 2^{-3} + \cdots + b_N 2^{-N}\right)V_{ref} \qquad (8.2\text{-}13)$$

Another approach to understanding the circuit of Fig. 8.2-15a is to consider the capacitor array as a capacitive attenuator, illustrated in Fig. 8.2-15b. As before, C_{eq} consists of the sum of all capacitances connected to V_{ref}, and C_{tot} is the sum of all the capacitors in the array.

The D/A of Fig. 8.2-15a can be extended to have both + and − analog outputs if the bottom plates of all capacitors are connected to V_{ref} during the ϕ_1 phase period. During the ϕ_2 phase period, the capcitance associated with b_i, C_i is connected to ground if b_i is 1 or to V_{ref} if b_i is 0. The resulting output voltage is

$$V_{OUT} = -\left(b_1 2^{-1} + b_2 2^{-2} + b_3 2^{-3} + \cdots + b_N 2^{-N}\right)V_{ref} \qquad (8.2\text{-}14)$$

The decision to select the + or − output will require an additional sign bit. If V_{ref} is also bipolar, then a four-quadrant D/A converter results.

The accuracy of the capacitors and the area required are both factors that limit the number of bits used. The accuracy of the D/A converter is seen to depend totally on the capacitor ratios and any parasitics. The accuracy of the equal-valued capacitor ratios for an MOS technology can be as low as 0.1% or better. If all of the capacitor ratios have this accuracy, then the D/A converter of Fig. 8.2-15a should be capable of a 10-bit resolution. However, this implies that the ratio between the MSB and LSB capacitors will be 1024:1 which is undesirable from an area viewpoint. Also, the 0.1% capacitor ratio accuracy is applicable only for ratios in the neighborhood of unity.

Example 8.2-2. Assume that unit capacitors of 50 $\mu \times$ 50 μ are used in the charge-scaling D/A converters of Fig. 8.2-15a and that the relative accuracy is 0.1%. Find the number of bits possible using a worst case approach assuming that the worst conditions occur at midscale (1 MSB). Next, assume that the relative accuracy of the unit capacitors deteriorates with N as given by

$$\frac{\Delta C}{C} \simeq 0.001 + 0.0001N$$

and find the number of bits possible using a worst case approach.

Solution. From Fig. 8.2-15b the ideal output voltage of the charge-scaling D/A converter can be expressed as

$$\frac{V_{OUT}}{V_{REF}} = \frac{C_{eq}}{2C}$$

Assume the worst-case output voltage is given as

$$\frac{V'_{OUT}}{V_{REF}} = \frac{C_{eq}(\min)}{[2C - C_{eq}](\max) + C_{eq}(\min)}$$

The difference between the ideal and the worst case output can be written as

$$\frac{V_{OUT}}{V_{REF}} - \frac{V'_{OUT}}{V_{REF}} = \frac{C_{eq}}{2C} - \frac{C_{eq}(\min)}{[2C - C_{eq}](\max) + C_{eq}(\min)}$$

If we assume that the worst-case condition occurs at midscale, then C_{eq} is equal to C. Therefore the difference between the ideal output and the worst-case output is

$$\frac{V_{OUT}}{V_{REF}} - \frac{V'_{OUT}}{V_{REF}} = \frac{1}{2} - \frac{C(\min)}{C(\max) + C(\min)}$$

Replacing $C(\max)$ by $C + 0.5\Delta C$ and $C(\min)$ by $C - 0.5\Delta C$ and setting the difference between the ideal and worst-case output voltage equal to ± 0.5 LSB results in the following equation

$$\frac{\Delta C}{2C} = \frac{1}{2^N}$$

Using a value of 0.001 for $\Delta C/C$ gives approximately 11 bits. Using the approximation for $\Delta C/C$ of

$$\frac{\Delta C}{C} \simeq 0.001 + 0.0001N$$

shows that a 9-bit D/A converter should be realizable.

The cascade configuration of Fig. 8.2-13a can also be applied to the charge-scaling configuration. Figure 8.2-16a shows a 13-bit D/A converter with bipolar capability for V_{ref}. The 1.016 pF capacitor acts as a 64:1 divider, which scales up the last 6 bits by a factor of 64. An equivalent circuit to the 13-bit D/A converter is shown in Fig. 8.2-16b. Two voltage sources are shown that depend on the state of each of the switches. The right-hand voltage source is given as

$$V_R = \sum_{i=1}^{7} \frac{\pm b_i C_i V_{ref}}{127} \qquad (8.2\text{-}15)$$

where $C_i = C/2^{i-1}$ and the polarity of V_{ref} depends on the polarity of the digital word. The left-hand voltage source is given as

$$V_L = \sum_{k=8}^{13} \frac{\pm b_k C_k V_{ref}}{64} \qquad (8.2\text{-}16)$$

where $C_k = C/(2^{k-7})$. The overall output of the D/A converter of Fig. 8.2-16a can be written as

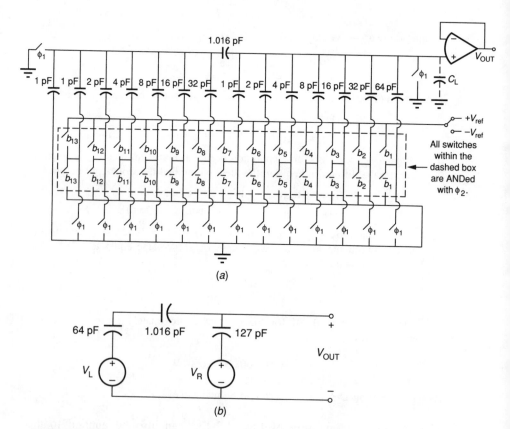

FIGURE 8.2-16

(a) A 13-bit, cascaded, charge-scaling D/A converter where $C = 64$ pF. Note that whether or not the switches in the dashed box close depends on the state of the binary variables, (b) An equivalent circuit of a.

$$V_{OUT} = \frac{\pm V_{ref}}{128} \left(\sum_{i=1}^{7} b_i C_i + \sum_{k=8}^{13} b_k \frac{C_k}{64} \right) \qquad (8.2\text{-}17)$$

The charge-scaling D/A converters are sensitive to capacitive loading at the summing node. If this capacitance is designated as C_L, then Eq. 8.2-17 is modified as

$$V_{OUT} = \left(1 - \frac{C_L}{128} \right) \left(\frac{\pm V_{ref}}{128} \right) \left(\sum_{i=1}^{7} b_i C_i + \sum_{k=8}^{13} b_k \frac{C_k}{64} \right) \qquad (8.2\text{-}18)$$

We see that C_L has caused an error of $[1 - (C_L/128)]$. If C_L is 1% of the total ladder capacitance, then a 1% error is introduced by the capacitance C_L.

The accuracy of the capacitor attenuator must also be good enough for the cascade approach to work. A deviation of the 1.016 pF divider capacitance from the desired ratio of 1.016:1 introduces both gain and linearity errors. Assuming a variation of $\pm \Delta C$ in the 1.016 pF capacitor modifies the output given in Eq. 8.2-17 to

$$V_{OUT} = \left(\frac{\pm V_{ref}}{128} \right) \left(1 - \frac{\Delta C}{128} \right) \left[\sum_{i=1}^{7} b_i C_i + (1 + \Delta C) \sum_{k=8}^{13} b_k \frac{C_k}{64} \right] \qquad (8.2\text{-}19)$$

If we assume that $\Delta C/C = \pm 0.016$ (1.6% error), then the gain term has an error of

$$\text{Gain error term} = 1 - \left(\frac{\Delta C}{128} \right) = 1 - \left[\frac{1}{(64)(128)} \right] \qquad (8.2\text{-}20)$$

which is negligible. The linearity error term is given by

$$\text{Linearity error term} = \Delta C \sum_{k=8}^{13} \frac{b_k C_k}{64} \qquad (8.2\text{-}21)$$

The worst-case error occurs for all $b_i = 1$ and is essentially ΔC. It is also important to keep $+V_{ref}$ and $-V_{ref}$ stable and equal in amplitude. This influences the long-term stability and gain tracking of the D/A converter.

A different, charge redistribution, two-stage, 8-bit D/A converter is shown in Fig. 8.2-17. An op amp is connected in its inverting configuration with the 2C capacitor fed back from the output to the inverting input of the op amp. Because the input node is a virtual ground during operation, the capacitive parasitics associated with the input node to the op amp are eliminated. The converter of Fig. 8.2-17 should give better transient response and less error because of the removal of the influence of the capacitive parasitic at the op amp input.

8.2.4 D/A Converters Using Combinations of Scaling Approaches

The voltage-scaling and charge-scaling approaches to implementing D/A converters can be combined, resulting in converters having a resolution that exceeds the number of bits of the separate approaches. An M-bit resistor string and a K-bit binary-weighted capacitor array can be used to achieve an $N = (M + K)$-bit

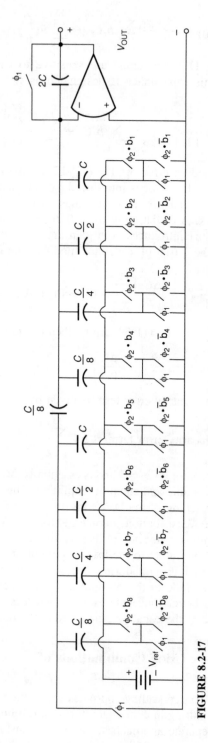

FIGURE 8.2-17
A cascade charge-scaling D/A converter that is insensitive to nodal capacitive parasitics for the MSB part.

conversion. Figure 8.2-18 gives an example of such a converter, where $M = 4$ and $K = 8$. The resistor string, R_1 through R_{2^M}, provides inherently monotonic V_{ref} for 2^M nominally identical voltage segments. The binary-weighted capacitor array, C_1 through C_K, is used to subdivide any one of these voltage segments into 2^K levels. This is accomplished by the following sequence of events. First, the switches S_F, S_B, and S_{M+1B} through $S_{K+M,B}$ are closed, connecting the top and bottom plates of the capacitors C_1 through C_K to ground. If the output of the D/A converter is applied to any circuit having an offset, switch S_B could be connected to this circuit rather than ground to cancel this offset. After opening switch S_F, the buses A and B are connected across one of the resistors of the resistor string as determined by the M MSBs. The upper and lower voltages across this resistor will be $V'_{ref} + 2^{-M} V_{ref}$ and V'_{ref}, respectively, where

$$V'_{ref} = V_{ref}\left(b_1 2^{-1} + b_2 2^{-2} + \cdots + b_{M-1} 2^{-(M-1)} + b_M 2^{-M}\right)$$

$$(8.2\text{-}22)$$

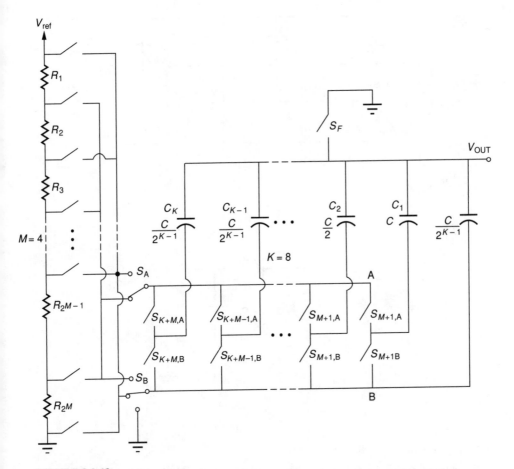

FIGURE 8.2-18
A D/A converter using a combination of voltage-scaling and charge-scaling techniques. The 4 MSBs are accomplished by voltage-scaling, and the 8 LSBs are accomplished by charge-scaling.

Although the resistor string could take the form of Fig. 8.2-14a, the configuration used in Fig. 8.2-18 switches both buses A and B. This causes any switch imperfections, such as clock feedthrough, to be canceled. The proper switch closures including S_A and S_B will require decoding of the M bits. After $2^{-M} V'_{ref}$ is applied between the buses A and B, we have the equivalent circuit of Fig. 8.2-19a. The final step is to decide whether or not to connect the bottom plates of the capacitors to bus A or bus B. This is determined by the bits of the digital word being converted. The equivalent circuit for the analog output voltage of the D/A converter of Fig. 8.2-18 is shown in Fig. 8.2-19b. The output of the D/A converter of fig. 8.2-18 is given as

$$V_{OUT} = V'_{ref} + V_{ref}\left[\frac{b_{M+1}}{2^{M+1}} + \frac{b_{M+2}}{s^{M+2}} + \cdots + \frac{b_{M+K+1}}{2^{M+K+1}} + \frac{b_{M+K}}{2^{M+K}}\right]$$

$$(8.2\text{-}23)$$

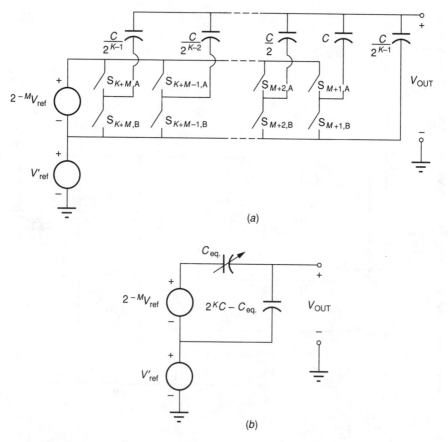

(a)

(b)

FIGURE 8.2-19
(a) Equivalent circuit of Fig. 8.2-18 for the voltage scaling part, (b) Equivalent circuit of the entire Fig. 8.2-18. C_{eq} is the sum of all the capacitors whose bit is 1.

The D/A converter of Fig. 8.2-18 has the advantage that, because the resistor string is inherently monotonic, the M MSB bits will be monotonic regardless of any resistor mismatch. This implies that the capacitor array has to be ratio-accurate to only K bits and still be able to provide $(M + K)$-bit monotonic conversion. The conversion speed for the resistors is faster than for the capacitors because no precharging is necessary. Therefore, some interesting tradeoffs can be made between area and speed of conversion. Techniques such as trimming the resistor string using polysilicon fuses can help to improve the integral linearity of this approach.

Other combinations of voltage scaling and charge scaling techniques are also possible. Instead of using resistive string techniques for the MSBs and binary-weighted capacitors for the LSBs, one can use binary-weighted capacitors for the MSBs and the resistor string for the LSBs. It is necessary to trim the resistors to maintain sufficient integral and differential nonlinearity for this case. Figure 8.2-20 illustrates how such a D/A converter could be implemented. The 3 to 4 MSBs will probably have to be trimmed, using a technique such as polysilicon fuses. The trimmed components are indicated by the dashed arrows through the appropriate capacitors in Fig. 8.2-20.

The combination of the voltage scaling and charge scaling allows for optimizing the performance. The choices are whether the MSBs will be resistors or capacitors and how the total number of bits will be divided into MSBs and LSBs.

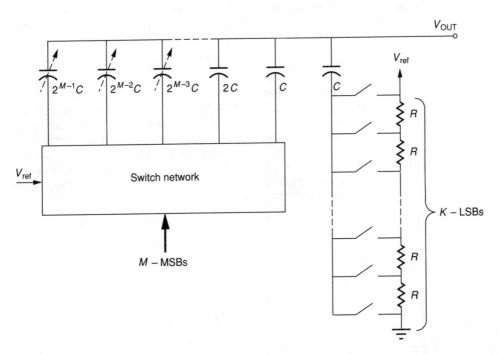

FIGURE 8.2-20
An illustration of a D/A converter using charge-scaling for MSBs and voltage-scaling for LSBs

For example, knowing the area of a unit resistor and a unit capacitor and their relative accuracies allows a tradeoff to be made in decreasing the area required and decreasing the nonlinearity of the D/A converter.

8.2.5 Serial D/A Converters

The last category of D/A converters to be considered in this section is the serial D/A converter. A serial D/A converter is one in which the conversion is done sequentially. In the best case, one clock cycle is required to convert one bit. Thus, N clock pulses would be required for the typical serial N-bit D/A converter. The two types of serial converters that will be examined here are the charge redistribution and the algorithmic D/A converters.

Figure 8.2-21 shows the simplified schematic of a serial charge redistribution D/A converter. We see that this converter consists of four switches, two equal-valued capacitors, and a reference voltage. The function of the switches is as follows. S1 is called the *redistribution switch* and places C_1 in parallel with C_2 causing their voltages to become identical through charge redistribution. Switch S2 is used to precharge C_1 to V_{ref}, if the ith bit, b_i, is a 1, and switch S3 is used to precharge C_1 to 0 V if the ith bit is 0. Switch S4 is used at the beginning of the conversion process to initially discharge C_2. An example is used to illustrate the operation of this D/A converter.

Example 8.2-3. Operation of the serial D/A converter. Assume that $C_1 = C_2$ and that the digital word to be converted is given as $b_1 = 1, b_2 = 1, b_3 = 0$, and $b_4 = 1$. Find the final voltage across C_1 and C_2 in terms of V_{ref}.

Solution. The conversion starts with the closing and opening of switch S4, so that $V_{C2} = 0$. Since $b_4 = 1$, then switch S2 is closed causing $V_{C1} = V_{ref}$. Next, switch S1 is closed, after switch S2 is opened, causing $V_{C1} = V_{C2} = 0.5V_{ref}$. This completes the conversion of the LSB. Figure 8.2-22 illustrates the waveforms across C_1 and C_2 in this example. Going to the next LSB, b_3, switch S3 is closed, discharging C_1 to ground. When switch S3 opens and switch S1 closes, the voltage across both C_1 and C_2 is $0.25V_{ref}$. Because the remaining bits are both 1, C_1 will be connected to V_{ref} and then connected to C_2 two times in succession. The final voltage across C_1 and C_2 will be $(13/16)V_{ref}$. This sequence of events will require nine sequential switch closures to complete the conversion.

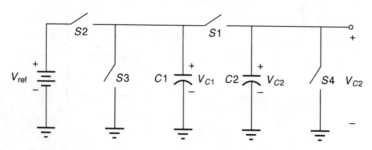

FIGURE 8.2-21
Simplified schematic of a serial charge redistribution D/A converter.

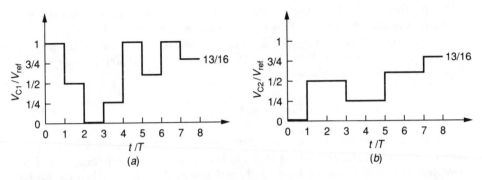

FIGURE 8.2-22
Waveforms of Fig. 8.2-21 for the conversion of 1101: (a) Voltage across C1, (b) Voltage across C2.

From this example, it can be seen that the serial D/A converter requires considerable supporting external circuitry to make the decision of which switch to close during the conversion process. Although the circuit for the conversion is extremely simple, several sources of error will limit the performance of this type of D/A converter. These sources of error include the capacitor parasitic capacitances, the switch parasitic capacitances, and the clock feedthrough errors. The capacitors C_1 and C_2 must be matched to within ±0.5 LSB accuracy. This converter has the advantage of monotonicity and requires very little area for the portion shown in Fig. 8.2-21. An 8-bit converter using this technique has been fabricated and has demonstrated a conversion time of 13.5 μs.[4]

A second approach to serial D/A conversion is called *algorithmic*.[5] Figure 8.2-23 illustrates the pipeline approach to implementing an algorithmic D/A converter, consisting of unit delays and weighted summers. It can be shown that the output of this circuit is

$$V_{out}(z) = \left(d_1 z^{-1} + 2^{-1}d_2 z^{-2} + \cdots + 2^{-(N-1)}d_N z^{-N}\right.$$
$$\left. + 2^{-N} d_{N+1} z^{-(N+1)}\right)V_{ref} \quad (8.2\text{-}24)$$

where d_i is a modified binary variable with a high state of $+1$ and a low state of -1 and z^{-1} is defined as the unit delay operator. Figure 8.2-23 shows that it takes n clock cycles for the digital word to be converted to an analog signal, even though a new digital word can be converted on every clock cycle. An advantage

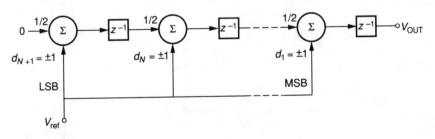

FIGURE 8.2-23
Pipeline approach to implementing an algorithmic D/A converter.

of the pipeline converter is that it can consist of similar stages. If a zero is input to the first amplifier, then the first stage is similar to the remaining stages.

The complexity of Fig. 8.2-23 can be reduced using the techniques of *replication* and *iteration*. Here we shall consider only the iteration approach. Equation 8.2-23 can be rewritten as

$$V_{out}(z) = \frac{d_i z^{-1} V_{ref}}{1 - 0.5z^{-1}} \tag{8.2-25}$$

where the d_i are either $+1$ or -1, determined as follows. Figure 8.2-24 shows a block diagram realization of Eq. 8.2-24. It consists of two switches, A and B. Switch A is closed when the ith bit is 1, and switch B is closed when the ith bit is 0. $d_i V_{ref}$ is summed with one-half of the previous output and applied to the sample-and-hold circuit, which outputs the results for the ith-bit conversion. The following example illustrates the conversion process.

Example 8.2-4. D/A conversion using the algorithmic method. Assume that the digital word to be converted is 11001 in the order of MSB to LSB and find the analog value of this digital word in terms of V_{ref}.

Solution. The conversion starts by zeroing the output (not shown in Fig. 8.2-24). Figure 8.2-25 is a plot of the output of this example. T is the period for the conversion of one bit. The process starts with the LSB, which in this case is 1. Switch A is closed and V_{ref} is summed with zero to give an output of $+V_{ref}$. On the second conversion, the bit is 0 so that switch B is closed. Thus, $-V_{ref}$ is summed with $(1/2)V_{ref}$ giving $-(1/2)V_{ref}$ as the output. On the third conversion, the bit is also 0, so that $-V_{ref}$ is summed with $-(1/4)V_{ref}$ to give an output of $-(5/4)V_{ref}$. On the fourth conversion, the bit is 1; thus, V_{ref} is summed with $-(5/8)V_{ref}$, giving $+(3/8)V_{ref}$ at the output. Finally, the MSB is unity, which causes V_{ref} to be summed with $(3/16)V_{ref}$, giving the final analog output of $+(19/16)V_{ref}$. Because the actual FSR of this example is $\pm V_{ref}$ or $2V_{ref}$, the analog value of the digital word 11001 is $(19/32) \times 2V_{ref}$, or $(19/16)V_{ref}$.

The algorithmic converter has the primary advantage of being independent of capacitor ratios; thus, it is often called the *ratio-independent* algorithmic D/A converter. However, the amplifier with a gain of 1/2 will still depend on capacitor

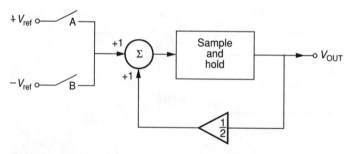

FIGURE 8.2-24
Equivalent realization of Fig. 8.2-23 using iterative techniques.

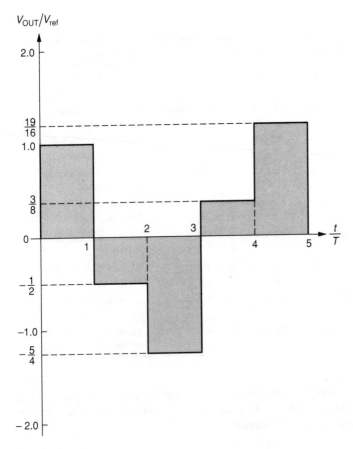

FIGURE 8.2-25
Output waveform for Fig. 8.2-24 for the conditions of Example 8.2-2.

ratios or other ratios and must have an accuracy better than ± 0.5 LSB. The algorithmic converter will be presented again under the subject of serial A/D converters. The serial D/A converter is very simple but requires a longer time for conversion. In some applications, these characteristics are advantageous.

D/A converter techniques compatible with BJT and MOS technology have been presented in this section. Table 8.2-1 gives a summary of these D/A

TABLE 8.2-1
Comparison of the D/A conversion techniques compatible with BJT and MOS technology

D/A converters	Figure	Advantage	Disadvantage
Current-scaling, binary-weighted	8.2-10	Fast; insensitive to switch parasitics	Large element spread; nonmonotonic
Current-scaling, R-2R ladder	8.2-11	Fast; small element spread	Nonmonotonic; sensitive to switch parasitics

(continued)

TABLE 8.2-1
(Continued)

D/A converters	Figure	Advantage	Disadvantage
Current-scaling, cascade	8.2-13*a*	Minimum area; monotonic	R_1 must be accurate
Current-scaling, master-slave	8.2-13*b*	Minimum area; monotonic	I_1 must be accurate
Voltage-scaling	8.2-14*a*	Monotonic	Large area; sensitive to parasitic capacitances
Charge-scaling	8.2-15*a*	Fast	Large element spread; nonmonotonic
Charge-scaling, cascade	8.2-16*a*	Minimum area	Nonmonotonic; divider must be accurate
Voltage-scaling, charge-scaling	8.2-18	Monotonic in MSBs	Must trim for absolute accuracy
Charge scaling, voltage-scaling	8.2-20	Monotonic in LSBs	Must trim for absolute accuracy
Serial, charge redistribution	8.2-21	Simple; minimum area	Slow; requires complex external circuits
Serial, algorithmic	8.2-24	Simple; minimum area	Slow; requires complex external circuits

converters. In the following sections, we shall examine the complementary subject of A/D converters. Many of the A/D converters that will be discussed use the D/A converters developed and illustrated in this section.

8.3   ANALOG-TO-DIGITAL CONVERTERS

The principles and characteristics of analog-to-digital converters are examined in this section. The objective of an A/D converter is to determine the output digital word corresponding to an analog input signal. The A/D converter usually requires a sample-and-hold circuit at the input because it is not possible to convert a changing analog input signal. We shall see that A/D converters often make use of D/A converters, which is why this section follows the last. The types of A/D converters that will be considered include the serial, successive approximation, parallel (flash), and high performance A/D converters.

Figure 8.3-1 shows the block diagram of a basic parallel A/D converter. The input to the A/D is from a sample-and-hold circuit and is designated as V_{in}^*. The voltages V_0 through V_{N-1} represent reference voltages that are all proportional to a single reference voltage, V_{ref}. The input, along with a reference voltage, V_{ref}, is used to determine the digital word that best represents the sampled analog input signal. The comparator outputs, X_i, are then encoded into an output digital word. The means by which the conversion is accomplished may be different from that suggested in Fig. 8.3-1. Regardless of how the conversion is made, the A/D

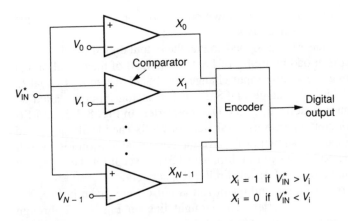

FIGURE 8.3-1
Block diagram of a general analog-to-digital converter.

converter is a device that converts a continuous range of input amplitude levels into a discrete, finite set of digital words.

The characterization of the A/D converter is almost identical to that of the D/A converter in the last section if the input and output definitions are interchanged. The static A/D converter properties will be considered first. Figure 8.3-2 shows the transfer characteristic of an ideal 3-bit A/D converter. This characteristic is analogous to Fig. 8.2-6 for the D/A converter. The analog input

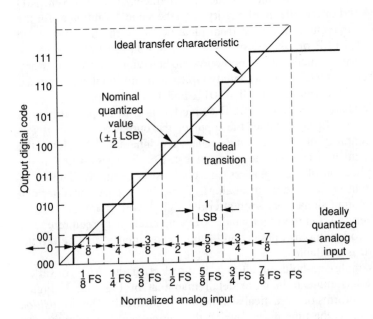

FIGURE 8.3-2
Ideal input-output characteristics for a 3-bit A/D converter.

voltage normalized to full scale (FS) is shown on the horizontal axis. The digital output code is given on the vertical axis.

The A/D converter has been designed so that the output digital word changes when the analog input is at odd multiples of FS/16. The LSB of the digital output code changes each time the analog input changes by $FS/2^n$ where n is equal to the number of digital bits. A change of $FS/2^n$ in the analog input is called an LSB in the same manner as defined for the D/A converter. In Fig. 8.3-2, an LSB is the length of the horizontal part of the stairstep, or FS/8. The ideally quantized ranges of the analog input are shown just above the horizontal axis on Fig. 8.3-2. These ranges are centered about even multiples of FS/16 except for the rightmost and leftmost, which have no right or left limits, respectively.

The definitions of resolution and quantization noise were given in Sec. 8.2 for both the A/D and D/A converter. The straight line on Fig. 8.3-2 through the midpoint of each step represents the ideal transfer characteristic of the A/D converter as the resolution approaches infinity. The full scale range, dynamic range, and the signal-to-noise ratio defined in Sec. 8.2 in terms of the analog axis of the characteristic also apply to the A/D converter.

The remaining static characteristics include offset error, gain error, nonlinearity, and monotonicity. Figure 8.3-3 illustrates each one of these characteristics for a 3-bit A/D converter. In each case, the ideal characteristic is shown by dashed lines for comparison. Because these characteristics are usually referred to the analog signal, the definitions given in Sec. 8.2 are also applicable for the A/D converter. Figure 8.3-3a illustrates the offset error in a 3-bit A/D converter. Figure 8.3-3b shows the gain error for the A/D converter and is similar to that of Fig. 8.2-7b. Figure 8.3-3c shows the nonlinearity characteristics of a 3-bit A/D converter. Integral and differential nonlinearity have the same definition as for the D/A converter. The maximum deviation from ideal occurs at the transition from 110 to 111 and is 1.5 LSB or 18.75% of FS. Figure 8.3-3d illustrates excessive differential nonlinearity, which causes nonmonotonic behavior in D/A converters. However, in A/D converters, nonmonotonicity typically manifests itself as missed codes. In Fig. 8.3-3d the digital codes 010, 011, and 110 are skipped.

The dynamic characteristics of an A/D converter have to do primarily with the speed of operation. Because either the input or the output of a converter is a digital word, sampling or discrete time signals are inherent. Therefore, the rate at which the converter can operate is of interest. The *conversion time* is the time from the application of the signal to start conversion to the availability of the completed output signal (digital or analog). Typically, a D/A converter can provide an analog output signal very soon after the digital word is applied (except for the serial converters). On the other hand, A/D converters may require one or more clock cycles following the application of the analog input signal before the output digital word is available.

Because a sample-and-hold circuit is a key aspect of the A/D converter, it is worthwhile to examine it in more detail than that of Fig. 8.2-3. Figure 8.3-4 shows the waveforms of a practical sample-and-hold circuit. The *acquisition time*, indicated by t_a, is the time during which the sample-and-hold circuit must remain in the sample mode to ensure that the subsequent hold mode output will be within a specified error band of the input level that existed at the instant of

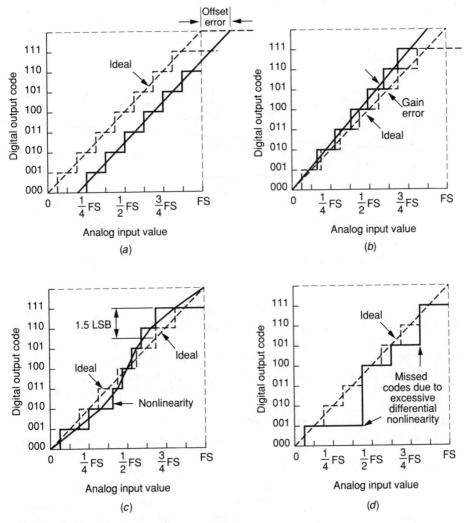

FIGURE 8.3-3
Characterization of a 3-bit A/D converter: (a) Offset error, (b) Scale factor (gain) error, (c) Integral linearity, (d) Differential linearity.

the sample-and-hold conversion. The acquisition time assumes that the gain and offset effects have been removed. The *settling time*, indicated by t_s, is the time interval between the sample-and-hold transition command and the time when the output transient and subsequent ringing have settled to within a specified error band. Thus, the minimum sample-and-hold time is equal to the sum of t_a and t_s. The minimum conversion time for an A/D converter is equal to T_{sample}, and the maximum sample rate is

$$f_{sample} = \frac{1}{T_{sample}} = \frac{1}{t_s + t_a} \tag{8.3-1}$$

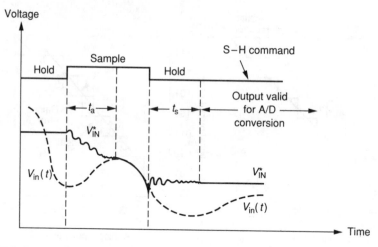

FIGURE 8.3-4
Waveforms for a sample-and-hold circuit.

The dynamic performance of the converter will depend largely on the dynamic characteristics of the op amps and comparators. Therefore, the slew rate, settling time, and overload recovery time of these circuits are of importance. It should be remembered that f_{sample} is the maximum sample rate and the effective bandwidth will be at least two times lower than f_{sample} to satisfy Nyquist criterion.

An important aspect of the conversion time is the aperture uncertainty. The *aperture uncertainty* is the time jitter in the sample point and is caused by short-term stability errors in the timebase generating the sample command to the A/D converter. The time jitter causes an amplitude uncertainty, which depends on the rate of rise of the signal at the sample point.

In addition to the dynamic characteristics of converters, there are characteristics having to do with stability of operation. These characteristics define the immunity of the converter to time, temperature, power supplies, and component aging. These characteristics are typically expressed in terms of the change of the converter performance parameter per unit change in the quantity affecting influence. Examples include the *temperature coefficient of linearity, temperature coefficient of gain,* and the *temperature coefficient of differential nonlinearity.* Also of importance to the stability of a converter is the voltage reference, which was presented in Chapter 5. The voltage reference can be supplied externally or internally to the integrated circuit converter. It is important that the reference provide the stability necessary for the proper operation of the converter.

It is of interest to consider how one can test converters. Testing is divided into static and dynamic tests for D/A and A/D converters. Most test configurations require the ability to resolve the analog signal to within ±0.5 LSB, which can be very demanding if the number of bits is large. Techniques for testing both types of converters can be found in more detail in the literature.[6-8] Often, a computer

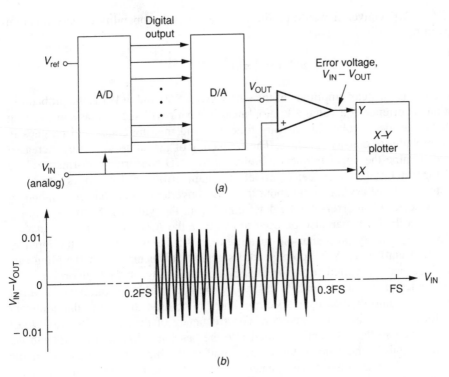

FIGURE 8.3-5
(a) A method of testing A/D and D/A converters, (b) Typical output for the error voltage of a.

is used to perform the tests on the converter. One simple means of testing both the D/A and A/D converters is shown in Fig. 8.3-5a. In this configuration, the output of an A/D converter is connected to the input of the D/A converter, resulting in an error voltage that can be plotted on an X-Y recorder as a function of the amplitude of the analog input signal. A typical portion of the error voltage for a 12-bit converter is shown in Fig. 8.3-5b. In this test either the A/D or D/A converter will be the device under test (DUT). The other converter must have higher performance and resolution than the DUT in order to be able to measure its performance without error. The order of the A/D and D/A converters in Fig. 8.3-5a can be interchanged so that the input and output are digital words that can be compared.

Several other approaches to testing the performance of an A/D converter will be briefly described. A high-quality sinusoid whose peak-to-peak amplitude is equal to the full scale value of the analog input can be used to test the A/D converter. Two such tests are called the *histogram test* and the *Fast Fourier Transform (FFT) test*. In the histogram test, a sinusoid of FS peak-to-peak amplitude is applied to the input of the A/D converter. The frequency is selected to avoid coherence with the sample rate of the A/D converter. A large number of samples of the digital output code are taken and expressed in the form of a histogram. A perfect A/D converter would produce a cusp-shaped probability density function given by

$$p(V) = \left[\pi(A^2 - V^2)^{1/2} \right]^{-1} \tag{8.3-2}$$

where A is the peak amplitude of the sine wave (FS/2) and $p(V)$ is the probability of an occurrence at a voltage V. Nonlinear behavior will show up as spikes rising above the ideal probability density function, and missing codes will be gaps in the probability density function. The frequency of the sinusoid can be increased to determine the upper frequency limits for the A/D converter performance. The histogram test can also detect offset and gain errors. Offset errors cause the histogram to be asymmetrical about the A/D converter output code corresponding to midscale. Gain errors can be determined from the width of the histogram.

The FFT test can also be used to evaluate the A/D converter performance. First, a spectrally pure sinusoid of amplitude 0.5 FS is applied to the input of the A/D converter. A 2^N point record sampled at the maximum sampling rate is taken and converted to the frequency domain using an FFT algorithm. The harmonics of the input sinusoid caused by the nonlinearity of the A/D converter are aliased into the baseband spectrum and can be used to identify the nonlinear performance of the A/D converter. The frequency of the input sine wave must be selected so that harmonics aliased into the baseband do not coincide with the fundamental. If the ratio of the fundamental to the highest amplitude harmonic on an N-bit A/D converter is greater than $6N$ dB, the error contribution of the nonlinearity is insignificant compared with the quantization noise. Unfortunately, even very low levels of harmonics may be sufficient to create encoding errors by causing a voltage near a threshold level to go to the next quantization level.

The above tests are typical of those applied to complex A/D converters. Further details and other types of testing procedures can be found in the references.[6-8] We next consider the various architectures for realizing A/D converters in MOS and/or bipolar technologies.

8.3.1   Serial A/D Converters

The serial A/D converter is similar to the serial D/A converter in that it performs serial operations until the conversion is complete. We shall examine two architectures, called the *single-slope* and the *dual-slope*. Figure 8.3-6 gives the block diagram of a single-slope serial A/D converter. This type of converter consists of a ramp generator, an interval counter, a comparator, an AND gate, and a counter that generates the output digital word. At the beginning of a conversion cycle, the analog input is sampled and held and applied to the positive terminal of the comparator. The counters are reset, and a clock is applied to both the time interval counter and the AND gate. On the first clock pulse, the ramp generator begins to integrate the reference voltage, V_{ref}. If V_{IN}^* is greater than the initial output of the ramp generator, then the output of the ramp generator, which is applied to the negative terminal of the comparator, begins to rise. Because V_{IN}^* is greater than the output of the ramp generator, the output of the comparator is high and each clock pulse applied to the AND gate causes the counter at the output to

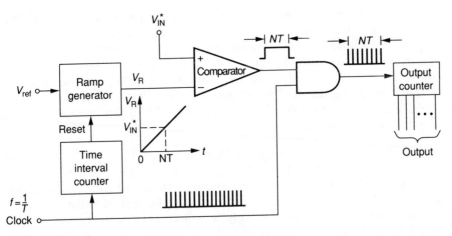

FIGURE 8.3-6
Block diagram of a single-slope serial A/D converter.

count. Finally, when the output of the ramp generator is equal to V_{IN}^*, the output of the comparator goes low, and the output counter is now inhibited. The binary number representing the state of the output counter can now be converted to the desired digital word format.

The single-slope A/D converter can have many different implementations. For example, the interval counter can be replaced by logic to detect the state of the comparator output and reset the ramp generator when its output has exceeded V_{IN}^*. The serial A/D converter has the advantage of simplicity of operation. Disadvantages of the single-slope A/D converter are that it is subject to error in the ramp generator and it is unipolar. Another disadvantage of the single-slope A/D converter is that a long conversion time ($2^N T$ in the worst case) is required if the input voltage is near the value of V_{ref}.

A block diagram of a dual-slope A/D converter is shown in Fig. 8.3-7. The basic advantage of this architecture is the elimination of the dependence of the

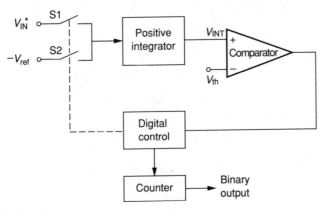

FIGURE 8.3-7
Block diagram of a dual-slope A/D converter.

conversion process on the linearity and accuracy of the ramp generator. Initially, V_{INT} is zero, and the input is sampled and held. In this scheme, it is necessary for V_{IN}^* to be positive. The conversion process begins by resetting the positive integrator until the output of the integrator is equal to the threshold, V_{th}, of the comparator. Next, S1 is closed, and V_{IN}^* is integrated for N_{ref} number of clock cycles. Figure 8.3-8 illustrates the conversion process. It is seen that the slope of the voltage at V_{INT} is proportional to the amplitude of V_{IN}^*. The voltage, $V_{int}(t)$, during this time is given as

$$V_{int}(t) = K \int_0^{N_{ref}T} V_{IN}^* dt + V_{int}(0) = K N_{ref} T V_{IN}^* + V_{th} \qquad (8.3\text{-}3)$$

where T is the clock period. At the end of N_{ref} counts, the carry output of the counter is applied to switch S2 and causes $-V_{ref}$ to be applied to the integrator. Now the integrator integrates negatively with a constant slope because V_{ref} is constant. When $V_{int}(t)$ becomes less than the value of V_{th}, the counter is stopped, and its binary count can be converted into the digital word. This is demonstrated by considering $V_{int}(t)$ during the time designated as t_2 in Fig. 8.3-8. This voltage is given as

$$V_{int}(t) = V_{int}(0) + K \int_0^{N_{out}T} (-V_{ref}) dt \qquad (8.3\text{-}4)$$

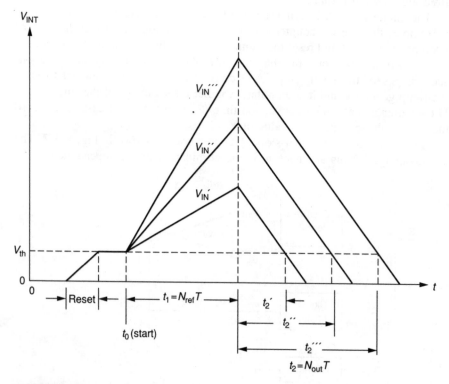

FIGURE 8.3-8
Waveforms illustrative of the dual-slope A/D converter of Fig. 8.3-7.

However, when $t = N_{out}T$, then Eq. 8.3-4 becomes

$$V_{int}(N_{out}T) = (KN_{ref}TV_{IN}^* + V_{th}) - KV_{ref}N_{out}T \qquad (8.3\text{-}5)$$

Because $V_{int}(N_{out}T) = V_{th}$, then Eq. 8.3-5 can be solved for N_{out}, giving

$$N_{out} = N_{ref}\left(\frac{V_{IN}^*}{V_{ref}}\right) \qquad (8.3\text{-}6)$$

It is seen that N_{out} will be some fraction of N_{ref}, where that fraction corresponds to the ratio of V_{IN}^* to V_{ref}.

The output of the serial dual-slope D/A converter (N_{out}) is not a function of the threshold of the comparator, the slope of the integrator, or the clock rate. Therefore, it is a very accurate method of conversion. The only disadvantage is that it takes a worst-case time of $2(2^N)T$ for a conversion, where N is the number of bits of the A/D converter. The positive integrator of this scheme can be replaced by a switched capacitor integrator, which will be discussed in Sec. 8.5.

The preceding two examples are representative of the architecture and resulting performance of serial A/D converters. Other forms of serial conversion exist in the literature.[9,10] The serial A/D converter can be expected to be slow but to provide a high resolution. Typical values for serial A/D converters are conversion frequencies of less than 100 Hz and greater than 12 bits of resolution.

8.3.2 Successive Approximation A/D Converters

A second category of A/D converters is called *successive approximation A/D converters*. This class of A/D converters converts an analog input into an *N*-bit digital word in *N* clock cycles. Consequently, the conversion time is less than for the serial converters without much increase in the complexity of the circuit. We will examine successive approximation converters that use a combination of voltage-scaling and charge-scaling D/A converters, serial D/A converters, and algorithmic D/A converters.

Figure 8.3-9 illustrates the architecture of a successive approximation A/D converter. This converter consists of a comparator, a D/A converter, and digital control logic. The function of the digital control logic is to determine the value of each bit in a sequential manner based upon the output of the comparator. To illustrate the conversion process, assume that the converter is unipolar (only positive analog signals can be applied). The conversion cycle begins by sampling the analog input signal to be converted. Next, the digital control circuit assumes that the MSB is 1 and all other bits are 0. This digital word is applied to the D/A converter, which generates an analog signal of $0.5V_{ref}$, which is compared to the sampled analog input, V_{IN}^*. If the comparator output is high, then the digital control logic makes the MSB 1. If the comparator output is low, the digital control logic makes the MSB 0. This completes the first step in the approximation sequence. At this point, the value of the MSB is known. The approximation process continues by once more applying a digital word to the D/A converter, with the MSB having its proven value, the second bit guessed at 1, and all

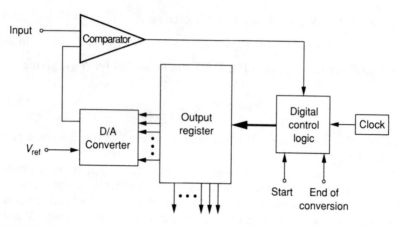

FIGURE 8.3-9
Example of a successive approximation A/D converter architecture.

remaining bits having a value of 0. Again, the sampled input is compared to the output of the D/A converter with this digital word applied. If the output of the comparator is high, the second bit is proven to be 1. If the output of the comparator is low, the second bit is 0. The process continues in this manner until all bits of the digital word have been decided by the successive approximation process.

Figure 8.3-10 shows how the successive approximation sequence works in converting the analog output of the D/A converter to the sampled analog input.

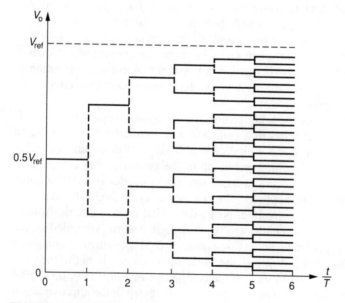

FIGURE 8.3-10
The successive approximation process.

It is seen that the number of cycles required for the conversion to an N-bit word is N. It is also observed that as N becomes large, the requirement of the comparator to distinguish between almost identical signals must increase. Bipolar A/D conversion can be achieved by using a sign bit to choose either $-V_{ref}$ or V_{ref}.

The digital control logic of Fig. 8.3-9 is often called a *successive approximation register* (SAR). An example of a 5-bit successive approximation A/D converter using a SAR is shown in Fig. 8.3-11. This SAR has the advantage of compatibility with a bit-slice approach, which makes it attractive for integrated circuit implementation. The bit-slice consists of a shift register (SR), an AND gate (G), a SR flip-flops (FF) with direct reset capability, and an analog switch (AS).

Figure 8.3-12 shows an example of a successive approximation A/D converter that uses the voltage-scaling and charge-scaling D/A converter of Fig. 8.2-18. The extra components, in addition to the D/A converter, include a comparator and a SAR. From the concepts of Sec. 6.6, we know that the comparator should have a gain greater than $(V_L 2^{M+K}/V_{ref})$, where V_L is the minimum output swing of the comparator required by the logic circuit it drives. For example, if $M + K = 12$ and $V_L = V_{ref}$, then the comparator must have a voltage gain of at least 4096.

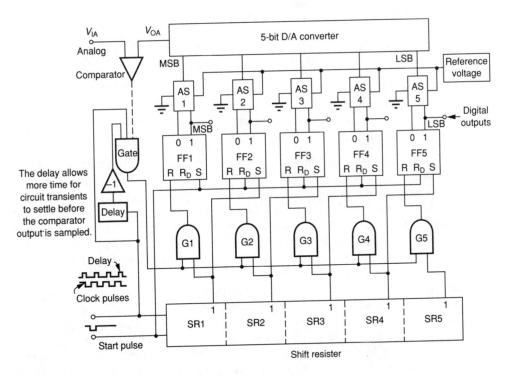

FIGURE 8.3-11
Five-bit successive approximation A/D converter with shift register control.

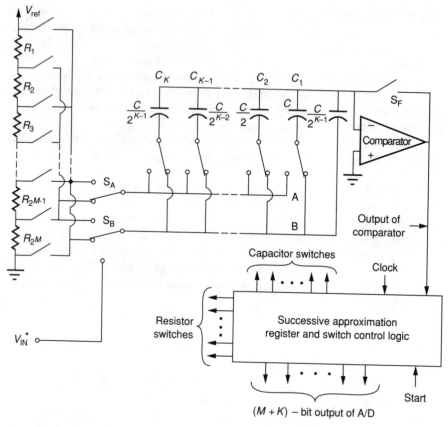

FIGURE 8.3-12
A voltage-scaling, charge-scaling, successive approximation A/D converter.

The conversion operates as follows. With S_F closed, the bottom plates of C_1 through C_K are connected through switch S_B to V_{IN}^*. The voltage stored on the capacitor array at the end of the sampling period is actually V_{IN}^* minus the threshold voltage of the comparator, which removes the threshold as a source of offset error. Because the comparator has unity feedback, it must be compensated in order to remain stable in this step. After switch S_F is opened, a successive approximation search among the resistor string taps is performed to find the segment in which the stored sample lies. Next, buses A and B are switched to the ends of the resistor defining this segment. Finally, the capacitor bottom plates are switched in a successive approximation sequence until the comparator input voltage converges back to the threshold voltage. The sequence of comparator outputs is a digital code corresponding to the unknown analog input signal. The A/D converter in Fig. 8.3-12 is capable of 12-bit monotonic conversion with a differential linearity of less than $\pm\frac{1}{2}$ LSB and a conversion time of 50 ms.[11]

A successive approximation A/D converter using the serial D/A converter of Fig. 8.2-21 is shown in Fig. 8.3-13. This converter works by converting the

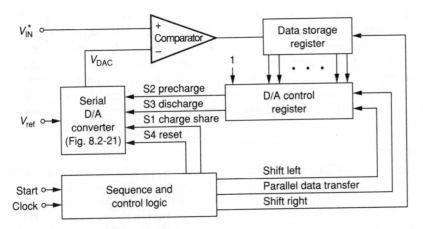

FIGURE 8.3-13
A serial A/D converter using the serial D/A converter of Fig. 8.2-21.

MSB, a_1, first. (The ith bit is denoted as d_i for D/A conversion and ith LSB is denoted as a_i for A/D conversion.) The control logic takes a very simple form because the D/A input string at any given point in the conversion is just the previously encoded word taken LSB first. For example, consider the point during the A/D conversion where the first K MSBs have been decided. To decide the $(K + 1)$th MSB, a $(K + 1)$-bit word is formed in the D/A control register by adding a 1 as the LSB to the K-bit word already encoded in the data storage register. A $(K + 1)$-bit D/A conversion then establishes the value of a_{N-K} by comparison with the unknown voltage V_{IN}^*. The bit is then stored in the data storage register, and the next serial D/A conversion is initiated. The conversion sequence is shown in detail in Table 8.3-1. Altogether, $N(N + 1)$ clock cycles are required for an N-bit A/D converter using the configuration of Fig. 8.3-13.

TABLE 8.3-1
Conversion sequence for the serial D/A converter of Fig. 8.3-13.

D/A conversion number	D/A input word						Comparator output	Number of charging steps
	d_N	d_{N-1}	d_{N-2}	$\cdots$	d_2	d_1		
1	1	—	—		—	—	a_1	2
2	1	a_1	—		—	—	a_2	4
3	1	a_2	a_1		—	—	a_3	6
.	.	.	.		.	.	.	.
.	.	.	.		.	.	.	.
.	.	.	.		.	.	.	.
$N-1$	1	a_{N-2}	a_{N-3}		a_3	a_2	a_{N-1}	$2(N-1)$
N	1	a_{N-1}	a_{N-2}	$\cdots$	a_2	a_1	a_N	$2N$

Total number of charging steps $= N(N + 1)$

An algorithmic A/D converter patterned after the algorithmic D/A converter of the preceding section is shown in Fig. 8.3-14. This N-bit A/D converter consists of N stages and N comparators for determining the signs of the N outputs. Each stage takes its input, multiplies it by 2, and adds or subtracts the reference voltage depending on the sign of the previous output. The comparator outputs form an N-bit digital representation of the bipolar analog input to the first stage. The operation of the algorithmic A/D converter can be demonstrated by the following example.

Example 8.3-1. Illustration of the operation of the algorithmic A/D converter. Assume that the sampled analog input to a 4-bit algorithmic A/D converter is 1.5 V. If V_{ref} is equal to 5 V, then the conversion proceeds as follows. Since $V^*_{IN} = 1.5$ V is positive, the output of the comparator of stage 1 is high, which corresponds to a digital 1. Stage 1 then multiplies this value by 2 to get 3 V and subtracts V_{ref}, obtaining an output of -2 V. Stage 2 input sees a negative value, which causes the comparator of this stage to be low, equivalent to a digital 0. Stage 2 then multiplies -2 V by 2 and adds the 5 V reference to output a value of 1 V. Because the output of stage 2 is positive, the comparator of stage 3 is high. The 1 V signal is then multiplied by 2 and 5 V is subtracted, giving a stage 3 output of -3 V. The conversion ends when the comparator of the fourth stage goes low because of the negative input voltage from stage 3.

The digital output word is 1010 for this example. To determine whether this is correct, we use the following formula.

$$V_{ANALOG} = V_{ref}(b_1 2^{-1} + b_2 2^{-2} + b_3 2^{-3} + \cdots + b_N 2^{-N})$$

where b_i is $+1$ if the ith bit is 1 and -1 if the ith bit is 0. In this example, we see that

$$V_{ANALOG} = 5\left(\frac{1}{2} - \frac{1}{4} + \frac{1}{8} - \frac{1}{16}\right) = 5(0.3125) = 1.5625$$

It is seen that the value of V_{ANALOG} will eventually converge to the value 1.5.

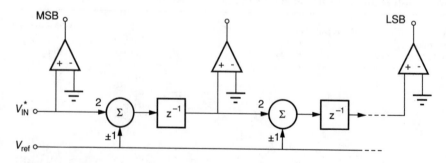

FIGURE 8.3-14
Pipeline implementation of the algorithmic A/D converter.

The algorithmic A/D converter of Fig. 8.3-14 has the disadvantage that the time to convert a sample is N clock cycles, although one complete conversion can be obtained at each clock cycle. The algorithmic A/D converter is considered to be ratio-independent because the performance does not depend on the ratio accuracy of a capacitor or resistor array. The multiplication by 2 of the first stage must be accurate to within 1 LSB, which is a distinct disadvantage of the pipeline configuration of the algorithmic A/D converter.

The iterative reduction of Fig. 8.2-23 resulting in Fig. 8.2-24 can be applied to the A/D converter of Fig. 8.3-14 in a manner similar to what was done for the algorithmic pipeline D/A converter. The analog output of the ith stage can be expressed as

$$V_{Oi} = [2V_{O,i-1} - b_i V_{ref}]z^{-1} \qquad (8.3\text{-}7)$$

where b_i is $+1$ if the ith bit is 1 and -1 if the ith bit is 0. This equation can be implemented with the circuit in Fig. 8.3-15a. The next step is to incorporate the ability to sample the analog input voltage at the start of the conversion. This step is shown in Fig. 8.3-15b. In this implementation, $-V_{ref}$ has been

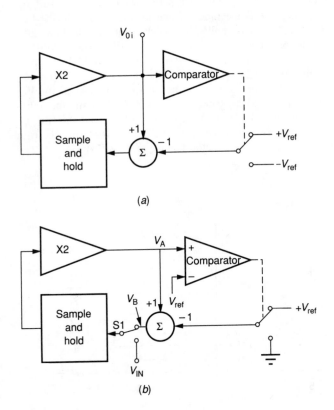

(a)

(b)

FIGURE 8.3-15
(a) Implementation of Eq. 8.3-7, (b) Implementation of the iterative algorithmic A/D converter.

replaced with ground for simplicity. The iterative version of the algorithmic A/D converter consists of a sample-and-hold circuit, a gain-of-2 amplifier, a comparator, and a reference subtraction circuit.

The operation of the converter involves first sampling the input signal by connecting switch S1 to V_{IN}. V_{IN}^{*} is then applied to the gain-of-2 amplifier. To extract the digital information from the input signal, the resultant signal, denoted as V_A, is compared to the reference voltage. If V_A is larger than V_{ref}, the corresponding bit is set to 1 and the reference voltage is then subtracted from V_A. If V_A is less than V_{ref}, the corresponding bit is set to 0 and V_A is unchanged. The resultant signal, denoted by V_B, is then transferred by means of switch S1 back into the analog loop for another iteration. This process occurs until the desired number of bits have been obtained, whereupon a new sampled value of the input signal will be processed. The digital word is processed in a serial manner with the MSB first. An example illustrates the process.

Example 8.3-2. Conversion process of an iterative algorithmic A/D converter. The iterative algorithmic A/D converter of Fig. 8.3-15b is to be used to convert an analog signal of $0.8V_{ref}$. Figure 8.3-16 shows the waveforms for V_A and V_B during the process. T is the time for one iteration cycle. In the first iteration, the analog input of $0.8V_{ref}$ is applied by switch S1 and results in a value for V_A of $1.6V_{ref}$, which corresponds to a V_B value of $0.6V_{ref}$ and a MSB of 1. During the next iteration, V_B is multiplied by 2 to give a V_A of $1.2V_{ref}$. Thus, the next bit is also 1, and V_B is $0.2V_{ref}$. V_A during the third iteration is $0.4V_{ref}$, resulting in the assignment of 0 for the next bit and a value of $0.4V_{ref}$ for V_B. The fourth iteration gives V_A as $0.8V_{ref}$, which gives $V_B = 0.8V_{ref}$ and the fourth bit as 0. The fifth iteration gives $V_A = 1.6V_{ref}$, $V_B = 0.6V_{ref}$, and the fifth bit as 1. This procedure continues as long as desired. The digital word after the fifth iteration is 11001 and is equivalent to an analog voltage of $0.78125V_{ref}$.

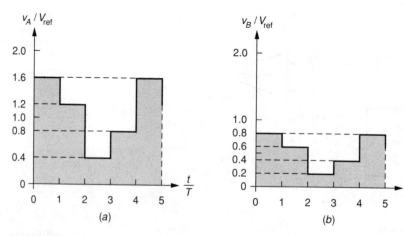

FIGURE 8.3-16
Waveforms for Example 8.3-2 and Fig. 8.3-15b: (a) V_A, (b) V_B.

The iterative algorithmic A/D converter can be constructed from very little precision hardware. Its implementation in a monolithic technology can therefore be area-efficient. A distinct advantage over the pipeline configuration is that all of the gain-of-2 amplifiers are identical because only one is used in an iterative manner. Sources of error for this A/D converter include low operational amplifier gain, finite input offset voltage in the operational amplifier, charge injection from the MOS switches, and capacitance voltage dependence. An integrated 12-bit A/D converter using the approach of Fig. 8.3-15*b* has exhibited an experimental performance having a differential linearity and integral linearity of 0.019% (0.8LSB) and 0.034% (1.5LSB), respectively, for a sample rate of 4 kHz. These values increased to 0.022% (0.9LSB) and 0.081% (3.2LSB) for a sample rate of 8 kHz.

The successive approximation A/D architecture is a very general one, as has been shown. It can make use of any of the D/A converters we have illustrated. If serial D/A converters are used, the conversion time is increased and the area required is decreased. In general, successive approximation A/D converters can have conversion times that fall within the range of 10^4 to 10^5 conversions/second. They are capable of 8 to 12 bits of untrimmed accuracy. The number of bits can be increased if trimming is permitted.

8.3.3 Parallel A/D Converters

In many applications, it is necessary to have a smaller conversion time than is possible with the previously defined A/D converter architectures. This has led to the development of high-speed A/D converters that use parallel techniques to achieve short conversion times. The ultimate conversion speed is one clock cycle, which typically consists of a set-up and a convert phase. Some of the high-speed architectures trade off speed with area and require more than one clock cycle but less than the N clock cycles required for the successive approximation A/D architecture. Another method of improving the speed of the converter is to increase the speed of the individual components. Typically, the comparator sample time, T_{sample} (see Eq. 8.3-1), is the limiting factor for the speed. In this presentation, we shall consider the parallel, the time-interleaved, the two-step, and the ripple approaches to implementing a high-speed A/D converter.

Figure 8.3-1 is a general block diagram of a high-speed A/D converter known as the *parallel* or *flash* A/D converter. An example of how this converter works is illustrated in Fig. 8.3-17. Figure 8.3-17 shows a 3-bit parallel A/D converter. V_{ref} is divided into eight values, as indicated in the figure. Each of these values is applied to the positive terminal of a comparator. The outputs of the comparators are taken to a digital encoding network, which determines the digital output word from the comparator outputs. For example, if V_{IN}^* is $0.6V_{ref}$, then the top three comparator outputs are 1s and the bottom four are 0s. The digital encoding network would identify 100 as the corresponding digital word. Many versions of this basic concept exist. For example, the voltage at the taps may be in multiples of $V_{ref}/16$ with $V_{ref}/8$ voltage differences between the taps. Also, the resistor string can be connected between $+V_{ref}$ and $-V_{ref}$ to achieve bipolar conversion (positive and negative analog output voltages).

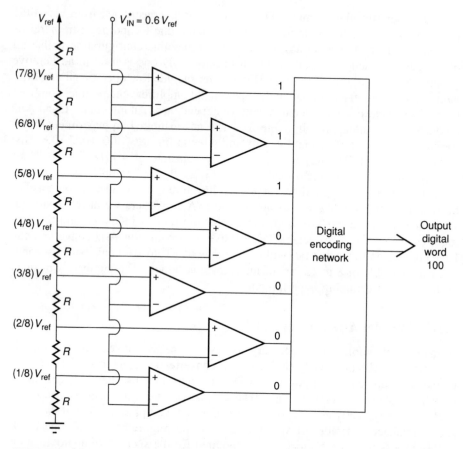

FIGURE 8.3-17
A 3-bit parallel A/D converter.

The parallel A/D converter of Fig. 8.3-17 converts the analog signal to a digital word in one clock cycle, which has two phase periods. During the first phase period, the analog input voltage is sampled and applied to the comparator inputs. During the second phase period, the digital encoding network determines the correct output digital word and stores it in a register/buffer. Thus, the conversion is limited by how fast this sequence of events can occur. Typical clock frequencies can be as high as 20 MHz for CMOS and 100 MHz for BJT technologies. This gives a theoretical conversion time of 50 ns and 10 ns, respectively. The sample-and-hold time may be larger than these values and could prevent these conversion times from being realized. Another problem is that as N increases, the number of comparators required is $2^N - 1$. For N greater than 8, too much area is required. Other methods we shall discuss give almost the same conversion times with much more efficient utilization of chip area.

One method of achieving small system conversion times is to use slower A/D converters in parallel, which is called *time-interleaving* and is shown in Fig.

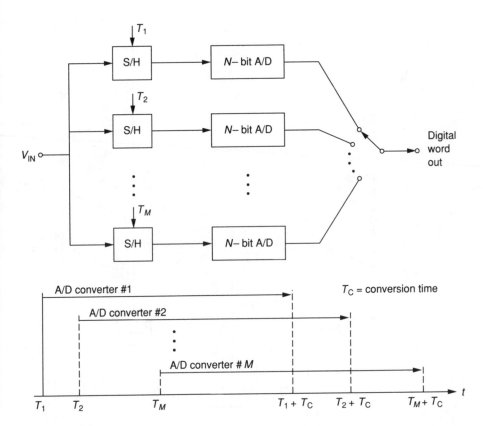

FIGURE 8.3-18
A time-interleaved A/D converter array.

8.3-18. Here M successive approximation A/D converters are used in parallel to complete the N-bit conversion of one analog signal per clock cycle. The sample-and-hold circuits consecutively sample and apply the input analog signal to their respective A/D converters. N clock cycles later, the A/D converter provides a digital word output. If $M = N$, then a digital word is output at every cycle. If one examines the chip area for an N bit A/D converter using the parallel A/D converter architecture ($M = 1$) compared with the time-interleaved architecture for $M = N$, the minimum area will occur for a value of M between 1 and N.

Combining the parallel approach with a series approach results in an A/D converter architecture with high speed and reasonable area. This approach is often called a pipeline A/D converter, particularly if the number of series stages is greater than two. Figure 8.3-19 shows a $2M$-bit A/D converter using two M-bit parallel A/D converters. The method first converts the M MSBs and then converts the M LSBs. Consequently, only $2^{M+1} - 2$ comparators are required to convert a $2M$-bit digital word. For the configuration of Fig. 8.3-19, the analog input is applied to the left-hand string of $2^M - 1$ comparators during the first clock phase, and the M MSBs are encoded during the second clock phase. During the

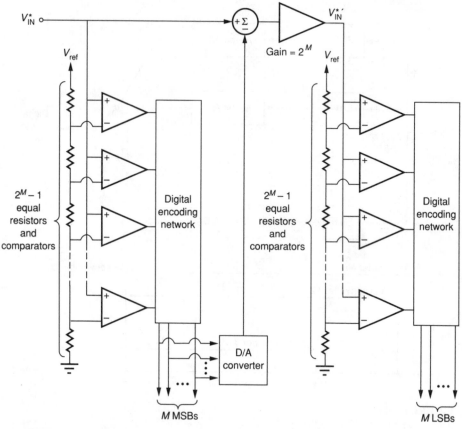

FIGURE 8.3-19
A $2M$-bit parallel-series A/D converter configuration.

third clock phase, the M MSBs are converted to an analog equivalent, which is subtracted from V_{ref}, multiplied by a gain of 2^M, and applied to the right-hand string of $2^M - 1$ comparators. Finally, during the fourth clock phase, the M LSBs are encoded. Thus, if the clock has two phases, then in two clock cycles a $2M$-bit digital word will be converted.

It is possible to make this conversion in three phases if necessary because the second and third phases can be combined into a single phase. Figure 8.3-20 shows the microphotograph of a parallel-series 8-bit A/D converter using the architecture of Fig. 8.3-19 implemented with MOS technology. The conversion time for this converter is in the range of 2 μs and is limited by the sampling time of the comparators and the settling times for the logic encoding network.

Up to this point analog-to-digital conversion techniques compatible with BJT and CMOS technology have been presented. The major categories include serial, successive approximation, and parallel A/D converters and are compared in Table 8.3-2 along with high performance A/D converters discussed next.

FIGURE 8.3-20
Microphotograph of the implementation of Fig. 8.3-19 for $M = 4$.

TABLE 8.3-2
Comparison of the performance of the various types of A/D converters

A/D converter type	Performance characteristics
Serial	1–100 conversions/second; 12–14-bit accuracy; requires no element-matching; a stable reference voltage is necessary
Successive approximation	10,000–100,000 conversions/second; 8–10 bits of untrimmed accuracy; 12–14 bits monotonicity; 12–14 bits trimmed accuracy
Parallel	$10^6 - 2 \times 10^7$ conversions/second; 7–8 bits of accuracy; requires large area
High performance	8000–10^6 conversion/second; 12–18 bits of accuracy

8.3.4   High-Performance A/D Converters

Recent advances in A/D converters have resulted in converters with significant improvement in performance over those considered in the previous categories. The performance improvement is typically in the areas of resolution or speed. Converters whose resolution is approaching 18 bits or sample rates of several hundred megasamples per second are now feasible. This discussion will examine three A/D converters that offer improved performance. These A/D converters include selfcalibrating A/D converters, pipeline A/D converters, and oversampled A/D converters.

A self-calibrating A/D converter is one that includes a calibration cycle to adjust its transfer characteristic to approach the ideal transfer characteristic. A block diagram of a self-calibrating A/D converter using the basic architecture of Fig. 8.3-12 is shown in Fig. 8.3-21. This circuit consists of an N-bit charge-scaling array called the main D/A converter, an M-bit voltage scaling array called the sub–D/A converter, and a voltage-scaling array called a calibration D/A converter. The calibration D/A converter must have several more bits of resolution than the sub–D/A converter. Digital control circuits govern capacitor switching during the

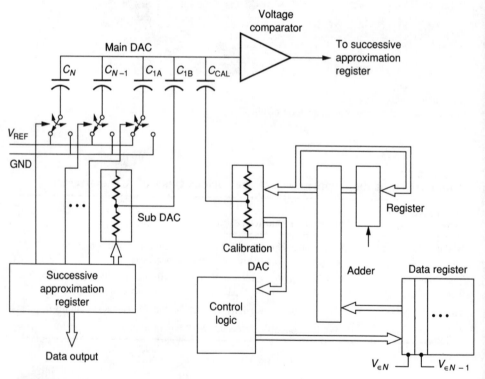

FIGURE 8.3-21
Block diagram of a self-calibrating A/D converter.

calibration cycle and store the nonlinearity correction terms in data registers. The ratio errors of the sub–D/A converter and overall quantization errors accumulate during digital computation of error voltages. To overcome these errors, at least one bit of additional resolution is needed during the calibration cycle. This extra bit is used to achieve final linearity within 1 LSB of an ideal straight line or within 0.5 LSB of an ideal staircase converter response. In practice, two extra bits are used in order to have a margin of safety. Typical performance of a self-calibrating A/D converter is 15–16 bits of resolution, an offset error of less than 1 LSB, a dynamic range of over 90 dB, a nonlinearity of less than 0.25 LSB, and a conversion time of less than 50 μs.

A pipeline converter is different from the A/D converter of Fig. 8.3-19 in that more stages are used with fewer bits per stage. This allows the designer to make tradeoffs between area and conversion time. A typical pipeline converter might have four stages with 3–4 bits per stage. A 2-bit implementation of a pipeline stage is shown in Fig. 8.3-22a. The input is sampled and held and applied to the comparators C_0 through C_2, where the 2-bit digital output is encoded. The digital output controls the switches on the resistor string to obtain an analog output equivalent to the 2-bit digital word. This analog voltage is subtracted from the original input and multiplied by 4, which results in the residue voltage passed on to the next stage. Figure 8.3-22b shows the plot of the amplified residue voltage versus the analog input voltage of the A/D converter of Fig. 8.3-22a.

The errors that can occur in the pipeline converter are shown in Table 8.3-3 along with their effects and possible solutions. Auto-zeroing, trimming, and calibration have been discussed previously. Digital error correcting techniques solve the problem of where one stage makes a conversion that the following stage cannot resolve. For example, consider two 2-bit cascaded stages forming a 4-bit pipeline converter. Assume that $V_{in}^* = (3/8)V_{ref}$, which corresponds to a digital output code of $D = 0110$. Because $(3/8)V_{ref}$ is greater than $(2/8)V_{ref}$, the first stage gives a digital output of $D_1 = 10$. Converting D_1 to an analog voltage gives $(4/8)V_{ref}$, which is subtracted from $(3/8)V_{ref}$ to give $-(1/8)V_{ref}$. Multiplying by 4 gives an amplified residue of $-(4/8)V_{ref}$ applied to the second stage. The second stage will output a digital code of $D_2 = 00$. When D_1 and D_2 are combined, the digital output code is 1000, which is in error. This error could be removed by increasing the number of bits by one at the second stage and using this extra bit to achieve the proper output. Unfortunately, the extra bit does not extend the resolution of the A/D converter. An alternative correction technique is to introduce an intentional offset to all the comparators so that the direction of the A/D decision error is always known. For example, if the intentional offsets are negative when the A/D subconverter makes its decision, then the residue voltage is always negative. The sign of the residue can be used to temporarily correct (decrement) the digital output code without using an extra bit.

One of the sources of nonlinearity in the pipeline A/D converter is the reference scaling nonlinearity and is illustrated in Fig. 8.3-23. When the peak

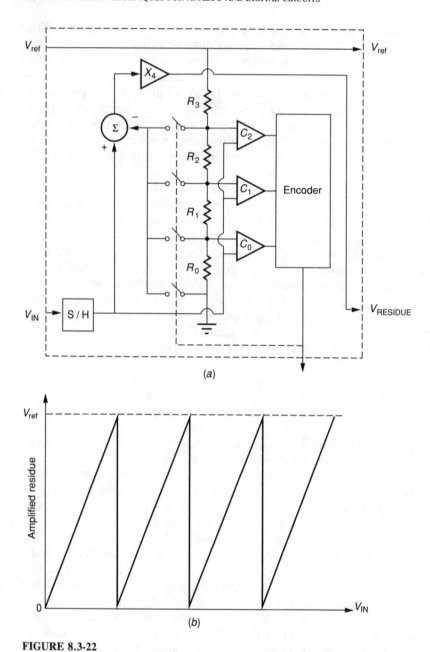

FIGURE 8.3-22
(a) Two-bit implementation of a pipeline stage, (b) Ideal plot of the amplifier residue versus the analog input.

TABLE 8.3-3
Static error analysis for a pipeline A/D converter

Element	Error(s)	Effect(s)	Solution(s)
S/H	Offset	Offset	Auto-zeroing
		Nonlinearity	Digital error correction
A/D converter	Offset	Offset	Auto-zeroing
		Nonlinearity	Digital error correction
	Nonlinearity	Nonlinearity	Digital error correction
D/A converter	Nonlinearity	Nonlinearity	Trim/calibrate
Interstage	Offset	Nonlinearity	Auto-zeroing
amplifier	Gain error	Nonlinearity	Trim/calibrate

of the amplified residual voltage is not equal to V_{ref}, plus and minus differential nonlinearity errors will be produced. For converters up to 10 bits, these errors can be sufficiently reduced by adjusting the residue so that it is always equal to the reference. Feedforward reference correction techniques have been used to extend this error minimization approach to 13 bits.[12]

Pipeline A/D converters offer a flexible approach to achieving high performance. A subranging technique has been used to further enhance the per-

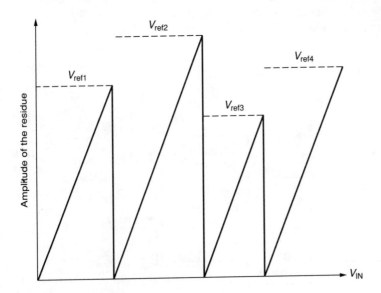

FIGURE 8.3-23
Illustration of feedforward reference correction.

formance of the pipeline A/D converter.[13] In the subranging A/D converter, the conversion is done in several cycles. In each successive cycle, the gain of the residue amplifier is increased until the full scale of the amplified residue voltage is reached. In this manner, errors can be corrected and removed on each successive cycle.

The performance of the pipeline A/D converters depends on the technology used. CMOS converters typically have 13–14 bits of resolution, 5–10 μs conversion times, and 10–30 mW of power dissipation. Bipolar pipeline converters typically have 10 bits of resolution, 200 ns conversion times, and 100–500 mW of power dissipation. The summary of this section will compare these converters with others, including those using BiCMOS technology.

Oversampled A/D converters offer a means of exchanging resolution in time for resolution in amplitude in order to circumvent the need for complex precision analog circuits. A basic oversampled A/D converter architecture is shown in Fig. 8.3-24. This architecture includes a clocked feedback loop, which produces a coarse estimate that oscillates about the true value of the input, and a digital filter, which averages this coarse estimate to obtain a finer approximation. This approximation is accurate to more bits at a lower (decimated) sampling rate. Although trading resolution in time for resolution in amplitude is a simple concept, the key to usefulness of oversampling systems based on the architecture of Fig. 8.3-24 is that the amplitude resolution is enhanced faster than the time resolution is reduced.

The feedback loop with the integrating filter $H(z)$ in Fig. 8.3-24 forces the quantization error in the N-bit estimate to have a high-frequency spectrum. When the low-pass digital filter subsequently reduces the bandwidth of the spectrum, it excludes a more-than-linear proportion of the quantization noise. Typical theoretical signal-to-noise ratio enhancement from the initial N-bit estimate is

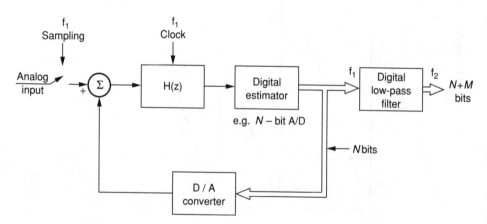

FIGURE 8.3-24
A basic oversampled A/D converter block diagram; $H(z)$ is an integrating filter.

$$\Delta S/N = 9L - 5.2 \text{ dB} \qquad (8.3\text{-}8)$$

where L is the number of octaves of oversampling when $H(z)$ is first-order. If $H(z)$ is second-order, then the estimate is

$$\Delta S/N = 15L - 13 \text{ dB} \qquad (8.3\text{-}9)$$

If we assume an oversampling factor of 128, the S/N enhancements for a first-order and second-order oversampling converter are 57.8 dB and 92 dB, respectively.

Of special interest is the case where $N = 1$. In this case, the coarse estimate and the D/A converter have a 1-bit resolution. When $N = 1$, the circuit of Fig. 8.2-24 is called a *delta-sigma modulator*. One advantage of delta-sigma A/D, oversampling converters is that because they obtain resolution by linearly interpolating between two states, they do not require an array of precision binary scaling elements for the D/A converter. This means that nonlinearity errors will not exist. Figure 8.3-25 shows a practical delta-sigma oversampling A/D converter with both one and two integrators in the loop [$H(z)$ first- and second-order].

The output of the delta-sigma modulator is applied to a low-pass digital filter whose function is to operate on the 1-bit signal to remove frequencies and quantization noise above the desired signal bandwidth. The output of the filter is a multibit digital representation at a lower (decimated) sampling rate. Basic delta-sigma modulator systems generate severe noise components for certain input values. In order to remove this noise, a square wave dither frequency within the stopband of the decimating filter randomizes the delta-sigma noise. The square wave dither frequency does not appear at the output of the filter or prevent arbitrary dc inputs from being passed through the filter.

The output of the delta-sigma modulator can be downsampled by a finite-impulse response digital low-pass filter. One possible architecture of the digital

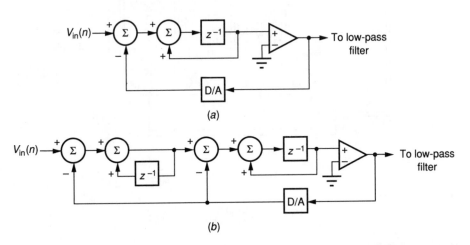

(a)

(b)

FIGURE 8.3-25
Typical delta-sigma modulators using (a) one and (b) two integrators in z-domain notation.

filter is shown in Fig. 8.3-26. This architecture uses a 256:1 decimation factor and a 1-bit digital input signal. A 1024-point impulse response, of which the symmetric half is stored in a read-only memory, is distributed to four accumulators. No explicit multiplications are necessary because of the 1-bit input signal. The impulse-response coefficients were designed to satisfy the dual objectives of quantization-noise removal and anti-alias filtering. Because the finite-impulse response low-pass filters are relatively insensitive to coefficient roundoff, 6-bit coefficients are adequate to define the impulse response.

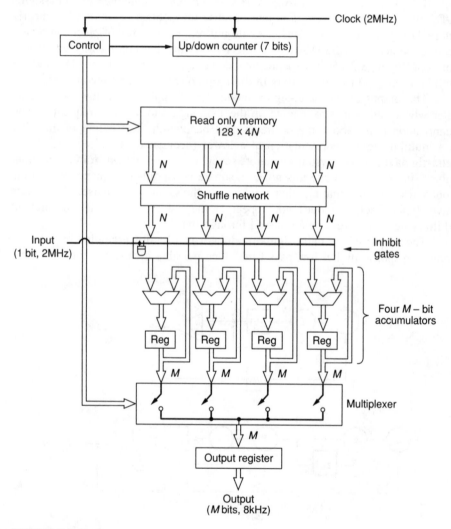

FIGURE 8.3-26
Architecture of a 1024-point finite-impulse response low-pass digital filter with values of $N = 6$ and $M = 15$.

Typical performance for a CMOS delta-sigma oversampled A/D converter is 14–16 bits at a sampling rate of 1–20 kHz, and a power dissipation of 10–30 mW. Dynamic ranges of up to 96 dB are possible, with noise being the limiting factor. The oversampling A/D converter is very suitable to applications such as digital audio.

8.3.5   Summary

A/D conversion techniques compatible with bipolar and CMOS technologies have been presented in this section. The major categories included serial, successive approximation, and parallel A/D converters. Table 8.3-2 provides a summary of these A/D converters. High-performance A/D converters offer improved accuracy (resolution) or speed (conversion time). Examples of high-performance A/D converters include self-calibration methods, pipeline converters with error correcting methods, and delta-sigma oversampled A/D converters. Some of the high-speed A/D converters are beginning to offer capabilities in the video range of frequencies.

The performance of A/D converters is steadily increasing with improvements in technology. Figure 8.3-27 shows the performance of monolithic A/D converters as of 1988.[14] This graph plots converter sampling rate on the horizontal axis and

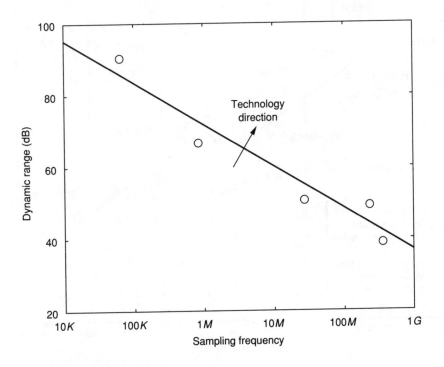

FIGURE 8.3-27
1988 monolithic A/D converter performance in terms of dynamic range versus sampling frequency.

converter dynamic range (signal-to-noise plus distortion) on the vertical axis. Each point on the graph represents the performance of the best monolithic converters. These points fall close to the line drawn on the figure. If such a figure were drawn for each year back to the mid-1970s when monolithic A/D converters first appeared, the movement of the line would be just over 2 dB per year in the vertical direction. The slope of the line is -0.6, supporting the conjecture that it is more difficult to be accurate than fast.

Flash or parallel architectures dominate at and below the 60 dB level. Self-calibrated, successive approximation architectures dominate above the 60 dB line. Self-calibrated delta-sigma oversampled A/D converters will probably provide increasing dynamic ranges.

Figure 8.3-28 is similar to Fig. 8.3-27 except that the various types of converters and types of technology are identified.[15-25] This graph shows how combined technologies such as BiMOS can be used to achieve performance beyond that obtainable with single technologies.

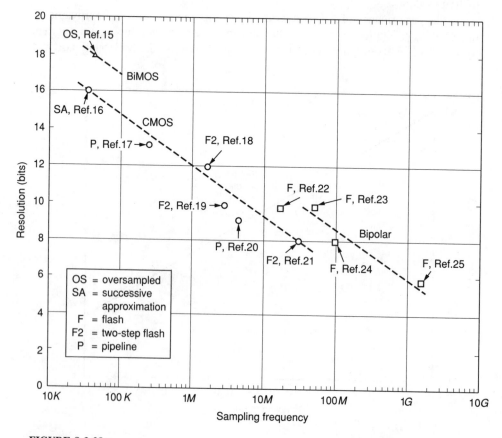

FIGURE 8.3-28

Comparison of high-performance, monolithic A/D converters in terms of resolution versus sampling frequency. Circles, squares, and triangles are CMOS, bipolar, and BiMOS technologies, respectively. The architecture and reference is indicated in the figure (Courtesy of J. P. Hwang).

8.4   CONTINUOUS-TIME FILTERS

One of the largest applications of analog signal processing circuits is in the area of frequency-domain filters. However, until the recent development of switched capacitor circuit techniques,[26] integrated circuit technology was not practical for the implementation of analog filters. The primary reasons were that RC time constants could not be defined with the accuracy necessary for filters and the area requirements for audio filters were unacceptably large. With switched capacitor circuit techniques, the time constants are proportional to capacitor ratios. In integrated circuit technology, it is possible to achieve capacitor ratios sufficiently accurate for filter requirements. In order to design switched capacitor filters, it is necessary to understand the design of continuous-time filters. The objective of this section is to prepare the reader for the following section, which concerns switched capacitor filter design.

For simplicity, we will initially consider linear filters that are classified into four different groups according to the type of gain characteristic. We will assume that the desired gain of the filter is unity in the *passband*, where frequencies are transmitted, and zero in the *stopband*, where frequencies are rejected. Furthermore, we shall assume that under ideal conditions, the passband and stopband are adjacent to each other and that ω_T is the frequency where the transition is made from one band to the other.

The magnitudes of the frequency-dependent gain of the four types of filters that will be considered are shown in Fig. 8.4-1. Figure 8.4-1a shows the frequency response of a *low-pass filter*, which has the ideal magnitude response of

$$|H_{LP}(j\omega)| = \begin{cases} 1 & 0 \le \omega \le \omega_T \\ 0 & \omega_T < \omega < \infty \end{cases} \tag{8.4-1}$$

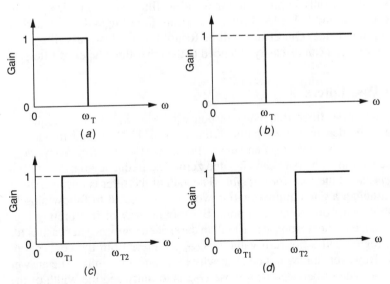

FIGURE 8.4-1
Types of filters: (a) Low-pass, (b) High-pass, (c) Bandpass, (d) Band-elimination.

Figure 8.4-1*b* illustrates the magnitude frequency response of a *high-pass filter*, described mathematically as

$$|H_{\text{HP}}(j\omega)| = \begin{cases} 0 & 0 \le \omega < \omega_{\text{T}} \\ 1 & \omega_{\text{T}} \le \omega < \infty \end{cases} \tag{8.4-2}$$

The magnitude frequency response of a *bandpass filter* is shown in Fig. 8.4-1*c*. The ideal frequency response of this type of filter is

$$|H_{\text{BP}}(j\omega)| = \begin{cases} 0 & 0 \le \omega < \omega_{\text{T1}} \\ 1 & \omega_{\text{T1}} \le \omega \le \omega_{\text{T2}} \\ 0 & \omega_{\text{T2}} < \omega < \infty \end{cases} \tag{8.4-3}$$

Finally, the frequency response of a *band-elimination filter* is shown in Fig. 8.4-1*d*. The ideal magnitude frequency response of this filter is given mathematically by

$$|H_{\text{BE}}(j\omega)| = \begin{cases} 1 & 0 \le \omega < \omega_{\text{T1}} \\ 0 & \omega_{\text{T1}} \le \omega \le \omega_{\text{T2}} \\ 1 & \omega_{\text{T2}} < \omega < \infty \end{cases} \tag{8.4-4}$$

The phase shift of each of the filters of Fig. 8.4-1 can be expressed as

$$\text{Arg } H(j\omega) = -\omega T_{\text{d}}, \qquad 0 \le \omega \le \infty \tag{8.4-5}$$

where T_{d} is the time delay of the filter. Because T_{d} is equal to the negative of the derivative of the phase shift, Eq. 8.4-5 defines a system that has a constant time delay of T_{d} seconds for each frequency transmitted through the filter.

In practice, the ideal filter characteristics of Fig. 8.4-1 cannot be realized. It is not possible to have discontinuous changes in transmission as a function of frequency or to have zero transmission over a region or band of frequencies. Consequently, we can only approximate these ideal filter characteristics. Let us consider how we can modify the ideal filter specifications of Fig. 8.4-1 so that they can be realized in practice. Our efforts will be focused on the low-pass filter. The resulting considerations can be easily extended to the other three types of filters.

8.4.1 Low-Pass Filters

Consider the low-pass filter frequency response of Fig. 8.4-2. The frequency range has been divided into three parts. From zero to the passband frequency, ω_{PB}, the gain must be between G_{PB} and unity. From the stopband frequency, ω_{SB}, to infinity, the gain must be between G_{SB} and zero. The frequency range between ω_{PB} and ω_{SB} is called the *transition region*. The gain of the filter is unspecified in this region, although a good approximation would be expected to follow closely a straight line drawn from point A to point B. Another way of interpreting Fig. 8.4-2 is to say that the filter response must fall in the shaded regions. The reasons for the transition region and a nonzero value of G_{SB} are clear from the concepts of circuit theory. However, it may not be clear why G_{PB} cannot be unity. The answer is that there is a tradeoff between how close G_{PB} is to unity and the width of the transition region. We shall see that permitting G_{PB} to be less than unity allows the value of $\omega_{\text{SB}}/\omega_{\text{PB}}$ to approach unity and, thus, a smaller transition region.

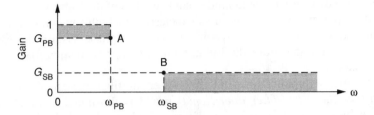

FIGURE 8.4-2
Practical specifications for a low-pass filter.

All transfer functions of active and/or passive filters with a finite number of lumped components are rational functions in s. With this observation, the filter design problem is generally partitioned into two parts: approximation and synthesis. In the approximation problem, a rational function (with real coefficients), often termed an approximating function, is derived to meet the filter requirements. The synthesis problem concerns the design of a circuit that has the approximating function as its transfer function.

There are several types of filter approximation functions that satisfy the requirements of Fig. 8.4-2. These filter types can all be expressed by the rational polynomial transfer function given as

$$H(s) = \frac{b_0 + b_1 s + b_2 s^2 + \cdots + b_{n-1} s^{n-1} + b_n s^n}{a_0 + a_1 s + a_2 s^2 + \cdots + a_{n-1} s^{n-1} + a_n s^n} \qquad (8.4\text{-}6)$$

The order of this transfer function is n. The types of filter approximations are generally classified by some aspect of their frequency response. For example, the *Butterworth filter approximation* has a magnitude response that is maximally flat in the passband and monotonically decreasing in the transition and passband regions. For the Butterworth low-pass filter approximation, $b_0 = 1$ and $b_i = 0$ for all $i \geq 1$ in Eq. 8.4-6. An example of some Butterworth filter approximations for various values of n is given in Fig. 8.4-3. It is customary to normalize the passband frequency ω_{PB} to 1 rps when using the approximation. The normalized ω_{PB} is transformed to the desired transition frequency during the synthesis phase of the

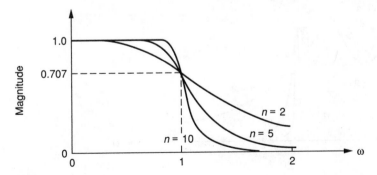

FIGURE 8.4-3
Magnitude characteristics of a Butterworth approximation for orders of $n = 2, 5,$ and 10.

problem. Figure 8.4-3 shows only the magnitude characteristics of the Butterworth approximation. All approximating functions are characterized by both a magnitude and phase response although many filter specifications are based solely on the magnitude response. The phase shift of the Butterworth filter approximation may be found in other sources.[27]

Several other filter approximations are often used in filter design. One of these is called the *Chebyshev filter approximation* and is illustrated in Fig. 8.4-4 for various values of n. It is seen that the magnitude of the Chebyshev filter approximation ripples in the passband and is monotonically decreasing in the transition and stopband regions. The advantage of the Chebyshev filter approximation is that for a given n, the slope of the magnitude response in the vicinity of ω_{PB} is steeper than that of a Butterworth filter approximation, resulting in a smaller transition region if G_{PB} and G_{SB} are identical.

A third popular filter approximation is called the *elliptic filter approximation* and is shown in Fig. 8.4-5. This approximation ripples both in the stopband and the passband, but is monotonically decreasing in the transition region. The elliptic filter approximation has the narrowest transition region of any type of filter characteristics considered here, given the same values of n, G_{PB}, and G_{SB}. Other filter approximations have been tabulated and feature other frequency characteristics such as linear phase shift.

Fortunately, there is considerable tabulated information available on standard filter approximations.[27-34] The objective of the filter designer in using this tabulated information is to obtain a polynomial such as Eq. 8.4-6, its roots, or a passive RLC ladder network. Any of these three form the starting point for the design using one of many methods to arrive at an active filter realization of the filter approximation. Switched capacitor filter design can start from the active filter realization, the approximating function, or from the original information used to characterize the filter requirements.

To use the tabulated information, it is necessary to determine the order n from the filter specification. Because n determines the number of components and complexity of a filter, the minimum value of n is generally selected. Although the filter specification can be given as shown in Fig. 8.4-2, it is more customary to

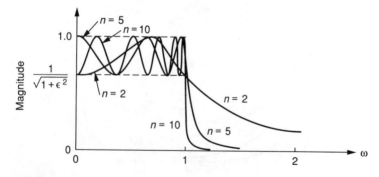

FIGURE 8.4-4
Magnitude characteristics of a Chebyshev approximation for an arbitrary ϵ and for orders $n = 2$, 5, and 10.

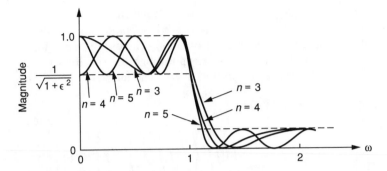

FIGURE 8.4-5
Magnitude characteristics of an elliptic approximation with arbitrary ϵ and for orders of $n = $ 3, 4, and 5.

convert the vertical axis to a decibel range. Figure 8.4-6a shows the gain specifications, G, of a low-pass filter with the vertical axis specified in decibels and the frequency axis normalized to ω_{PB}. Ω is defined as ω_{SB}/ω_{PB} and G_Ω (dB) $= 20 \log_{10} G_{SB}$. Because the gains of most filters are less than unity, attenuation rather than gain is often used to describe their characteristics. Figure 8.4-6b shows the equivalent specification of Fig. 8.4-6a in terms of attenuation, $A = 1/G$, where $A_{PB} = 1/G_{PB}$ $[A_{PB}$ (dB) $= -G_{PB}$ (dB)], and $A_\Omega = 1/G_\Omega$ $[A_\Omega$ (dB) $= -G_\Omega$ (dB)]. [7]

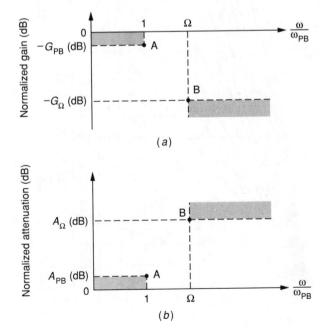

FIGURE 8.4-6
(a) Specifications for a low-pass filter in terms of gain, (b) Specifications for a low-pass filter in terms of attenuation.

From the parameters A_Ω, A_{PB}, and Ω, the order of the filter can be quickly determined using a set of nomographs.[35] Figure 8.4-7 is a nomograph for determining the order of the Butterworth filter approximation. The use of nomographs is illustrated in Fig. 8.4-8. A straight line is drawn through the specified values of A_{PB} and A_Ω, shown as points 1 and 2 in Fig. 8.4-8. The intersection with the

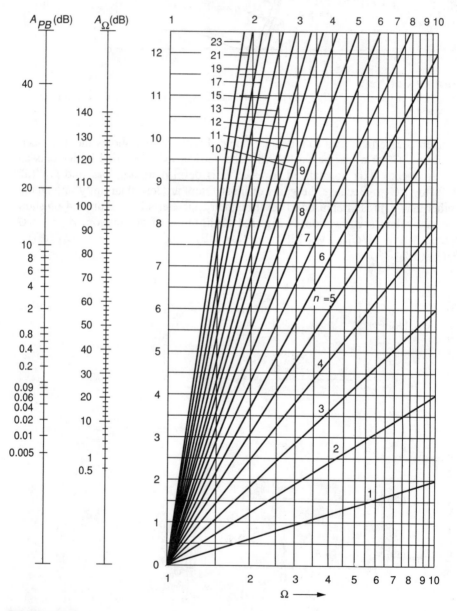

FIGURE 8.4-7

A nomograph for determining the order of a Butterworth magnitude function (Kawakami).

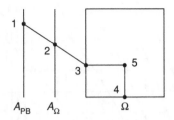

FIGURE 8.4-8
The method for using the nomograph of Fig. 8.4-7.

left side of the graph (point 3) is then extended horizontally until it meets a line drawn vertically from point 4, corresponding to the desired normalized stopband frequency, Ω. The resulting intersection at point 5 establishes the required order of the filter. If point 5 is between two of the *order loci*, the higher one must be used.

Example 8.4-1. Determination of the order of a low-pass Butterworth filter. Find the order of a Butterworth filter approximation to Fig. 8.4-6*b* where $A_\Omega = 40$ dB, $A_{PB} = 3$ dB, and $\Omega = 2$.

Solution. Using the nomograph of Fig. 8.4-7, we find that point 5 lies between $n = 6$ and $n = 7$. Therefore, the order of the filter approximation must be 7.

Figures 8.4-9 and 8.4-10 give the corresponding nomographs for determining the order or degree of Chebyshev and elliptic filter approximations, respectively. These nomographs are used in the same manner as the one in Fig. 8.4-7. An example will illustrate how the Chebyshev and elliptic filter approximations require lower order than the Butterworth filter approximation for the same design parameters.

Example 8.4-2. Determination of low-pass Chebyshev and elliptic filter approximations. Repeat the preceding example to find the order of the Chebyshev and elliptic filter approximations that will meet the same specifications.

Solution. From Fig. 8.4-9 we obtain $n = 4$ for the Chebyhev filter approximation, and from Fig. 8.4-10 we see that $n = 3$ is sufficient for the elliptic filter approximation to satisfy the specifications.

Once the order of the filter approximation is known, the designer must then decide how the filter is to be realized. Two approaches will be considered. The first approach starts with Eq. 8.4-6 in which the numerator and denominator polynomials are factored in the form of second-order products with real coefficients (a first-order product will be necessary if n is odd). This information can be found from the tabulations in the literature. For example, Table 8.4-1 shows the denominator coefficients of Eq. 8.4-6 with $b_0 = 1$ and gives the pole locations and quadratic functions of the denominator of Eq. 8.4-6 for the Butterworth filter approximations. The numerator polynomial of Eq. 8.4-6 for the Butterworth filter approximation is a constant. In this case the function $H(s)$ can be expressed as

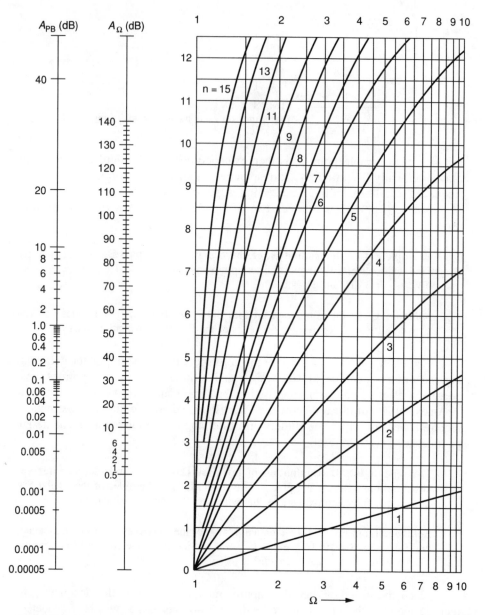

FIGURE 8.4-9
A nomograph for determining the order of a Chebyshev magnitude approximation (Kawakami).

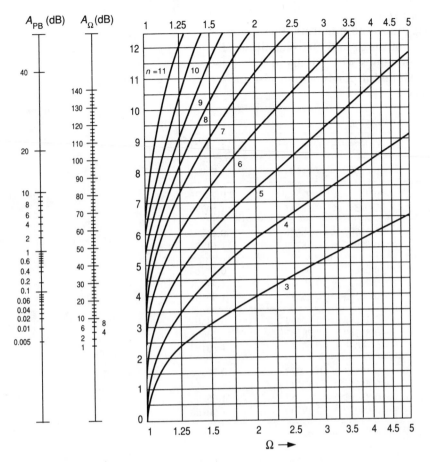

FIGURE 8.4-10
A nomograph for determining the order of an elliptic magnitude approximation (Kawakami).

TABLE 8.4-1a
Denominator coefficients of maximally flat magnitude (Butterworth)
functions of the form: $s^n + b_{n-1} s^{n-1} + b_{n-2} s^{n-2} + \cdots b_2 s^2 + b_1 s + 1$ **with**
passband 0 – 1 rad/s

n	b_1	b_2	b_3	b_4	b_5
2	1.414214				
3	2.000000				
4	2.613126	3.414214			
5	3.236068	5.236068			
6	3.863703	7.464102	9.141620		
7	4.493959	10.097835	14.591794		
8	5.125831	13.137071	21.846151	25.688356	
9	5.758770	16.581719	31.163437	41.986386	
10	6.392453	20.431729	42.802061	64.882396	74.233429

(By permission from L. P. Huelsman and P. E. Allen, *Introduction to the Theory and Design of Active Filters*, McGraw-Hill Book Co., New York, 1980.)

TABLE 8.4-1b
Pole locations and quadratic factors ($s^2 + b_1 s + 1$) of maximally flat magnitude (Butterworth) functions with passband $0 - 1$ rad/s
(*Note:* **All odd-order functions also have a pole at $s = 1$**)

n	Poles	b_1
2	$-0.70711 \pm j\,0.70711$	1.41421
3	$-0.50000 \pm j\,0.86603$	1.00000
4	$-0.38268 \pm j\,0.92388$	0.76536
	$-0.92388 \pm j\,0.38268$	1.84776
5	$-0.30902 \pm j\,0.95106$	0.61804
	$-0.80902 \pm j\,0.58779$	1.61804
6	$-0.25882 \pm j\,0.96593$	0.51764
	$-0.70711 \pm j\,0.70711$	1.41421
	$-0.96593 \pm j\,0.25882$	1.93186
7	$-0.22252 \pm j\,0.97493$	0.44504
	$-0.62349 \pm j\,0.78183$	1.24698
	$-0.90097 \pm j\,0.43388$	1.80194
8	$-0.19509 \pm j\,0.98079$	0.39018
	$-0.55557 \pm j\,0.83147$	1.11114
	$-0.83147 \pm j\,0.55557$	1.66294
	$-0.98079 \pm j\,0.19509$	1.96158
9	$-0.17365 \pm j\,0.98481$	0.34730
	$-0.50000 \pm j\,0.86603$	1.00000
	$-0.76604 \pm j\,0.64279$	1.53208
	$-0.93969 \pm j\,0.34202$	1.87938
10	$-0.15643 \pm j\,0.98769$	0.31286
	$-0.45399 \pm j\,0.89101$	0.90798
	$-0.70711 \pm j\,0.70711$	1.41421
	$-0.89101 \pm j\,0.45399$	1.78202
	$-0.98769 \pm j\,0.15643$	1.97538

(By permission from L. P. Huelsman and P. E. Allen, *Introduction to the Theory and Design of Active Filters*, McGraw-Hill Book Co., New York, 1980.)

a product of biquadratic functions, $H_i(s)$, where the general form of the second-order (quadratic) function will be

$$H(s) = \frac{\pm H_{0i}\,\omega_{pi}^2}{s^2 + (\omega_{pi}/Q_i)s + \omega_{pi}^2} = \frac{\pm H_{0i}\,p_{1i}\,p_{2i}}{(s + p_{1i})(s + p_{2i})} \qquad (8.4\text{-}7)$$

where H_{0i} is the gain at $\omega = 0$, ω_{pi} is the undamped natural frequency, and Q_i is the quality factor of the pole p_i and p_{2i} is the complex conjugate of p_{1i} if p_{1i} is not real.

Typically, the information tabulated on filter design is normalized so that ω_{PB} is unity. However, the actual filter specifications are usually in the neighborhood of thousands of cycles per second. To convert the *normalized frequency* values of the design tables to the actual filter frequency requires a *frequency denormalization*. This denormalization involves a change of the complex frequency variable. If we consider p as the normalized complex frequency variable and s as the denormalized (actual) one, then the frequency denormalization is defined as

$$s = \Omega_n p \qquad (8.4\text{-}8)$$

where Ω_n is a dimensionless frequency denormalization constant. This denormalization is generally used at the synthesis stage of the design. Following this approach, a filter is initially synthesized to realize the normalized transfer function. The denormalization then entails a subsequent scaling of the component values in the filter. Table 8.4-2 shows how this denormalization acts on the normalized values of R, L, and C.

A second type of denormalization that is often used is called *impedance denormalization*. It permits an arbitrary scaling to be applied simultaneously to all the passive elements of a filter in order to get more practical component values. A normalized impedance $Z_n(s)$ can be denormalized to the impedance $Z(s)$ by the relation

$$Z(s) = z_n Z_n(s) \qquad (8.4\text{-}9)$$

where z_n is a dimensionless impedance denormalization constant. Table 8.4-2 shows how this denormalization affects the passive elements. The combined effects of the denormalizations of Eqs. 8.4-8 and 8.4-9 are illustrated in this table. *This impedance denormalization does not affect the voltage or current gain of the filter.*

Figure 8.4-11 shows three possible active filter realizations of Eq. 8.4-7. Figure 8.4-11a uses a finite-gain amplifier and an RC feedback network. This circuit was originally proposed by Sallen and Key in 1955[36] and was one of the first active RC filter structures. This circuit does not have flexibility in realizing Eq. 8.4-7 if H_{oi} is also specified because H_{oi} is fixed and equal to $3 - (1/Q_i)$.

TABLE 8.4-2
Effect of frequency and impedance denormalization on network elements

Denormalized	R	C	L
$s = \Omega_n p$	R	$\dfrac{C}{\Omega_n}$	$\dfrac{L}{\Omega_n}$
$Z = z_n Z_n$	$z_n R$	$\dfrac{C}{z_n}$	$z_n L$
$Z(s) = z_n Z_n(p)$	$z_n R$	$\dfrac{C}{\Omega_n z_n}$	$\dfrac{z_n}{\Omega_n} L$

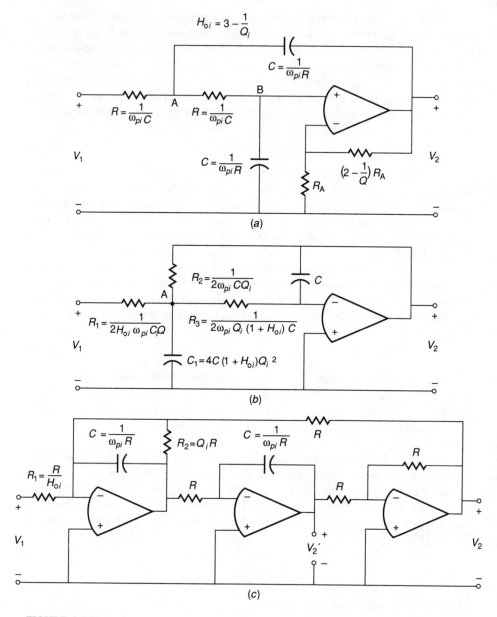

FIGURE 8.4-11
Three possible realizations of Eq. 8.4-7 (second-order, low-pass): (*a*) Sallen and Key (finite-gain) structure, (*b*) Infinite-gain structure, (*c*) Tow-Thomas (resonator) structure.

This is not considered a major limitation because the overall gain can be realized by adding a cascaded gain stage. In Fig. 8.4-11a, one may choose a suitable value for R; ω_{pi} and Q_i define the rest of the elements. Alternatively, one may choose a suitable value for the capacitors; then the resistors are defined as $(\omega_{pi}C)^{-1}$. The circuit of Figure 8.4-11a realizes Eq. 8.4-7 with a positive sign.

The circuit of Figure 8.4-11b is called an *infinite-gain realization*. It has the ability to realize simultaneously H_{oi}, ω_{pi}, and Q_i and realizes Eq. 8.4-7 with a negative sign. The circuit of Figure 8.4-11c is called the Tow-Thomas circuit[37,38] and consists of the cascade of a damped inverting integrator, an inverting integrator, and an inverter. This circuit has a great deal of flexibility and is very easy to tune. If the output is taken at V_2, then it realizes Eq. 8.4-7 with a negative sign. If the output is taken at V_2', then the circuit of Fig. 8.4-11c realizes Eq. 8.4-7 with a positive sign. In these circuits, a suitable value for either R or C is chosen and the remaining component values are calculated from the equations given in the figure. Many other realizations of Eq. 8.4-7 exist; however, the circuits of Fig. 8.4-11 are representative.

Example 8.4-3. Design of a low-pass Butterworth filter. A low-pass Butterworth filter is to be designed for the specifications of $A_\Omega = 30$ dB, $\omega_{PB} = 2000\pi$, and $\omega_{SB} = 4000\pi$.

Solution. If we normalize ω_{PB} to unity, we get $\Omega = 2$. From Fig. 8.4-7 we see that $n = 5$ will satisfy the filter specification. From Table 8.4-1, we conclude that this function can be realized with two second-order stages cascaded with one first-order stage. The realization is shown in Fig. 8.4-12a. The stage order is arbitrary, although one typically chooses the high-Q stages as the last stages. The normalized transfer function for each of the stages is shown, as well as Q_i and ω_{pi}. Note that stage 1 is a simple, first-order circuit so that Q is not defined. Stage 1 may be realized by a simple damped integrator, whereas one of the circuits in Fig. 8.4-11 can be used for stages 2 and 3. Selecting the circuit of Fig. 8.4-11b results in the realization of Fig. 8.4-12b, where the formulas of Fig. 8.4-12a have been used with $\omega_{pi} = 1$ for $i = 1, 2$ and 3, $Q_2 = 0.61804$, and $Q_3 = 1.61804$. The last step is to frequency-denormalize the realization using Eq. 8.4-8. To denormalize from a frequency of 1 rad/s to 2000π rad/s requires $\Omega_n = 2000\pi$. To avoid 1 Ω resistors, an impedance normalization of $z_n = 10^4$ will also be used. The resulting realization is shown in Fig. 8.4-12c. If a Butterworth filter approximation had been used for any value of A_{PB} other than -3 dB, then the normalized passband would not be unity. This must be taken into account when finding the proper Ω_n.

Note that the same circuit structure used in Fig. 8.4-12 could also be used to realize the Chebyshev function. In this case the quadratic functions would be obtained from tabulated data in the literature. Only the component values in Fig. 8.4-12b and c would vary in changing this realization from a Butterworth to a Chebyshev filter.

8.4.2 High-Pass Filters

Filters other than the low-pass type can be designed through the use of frequency transformations. These allow one to take the tabulated low-pass filter information

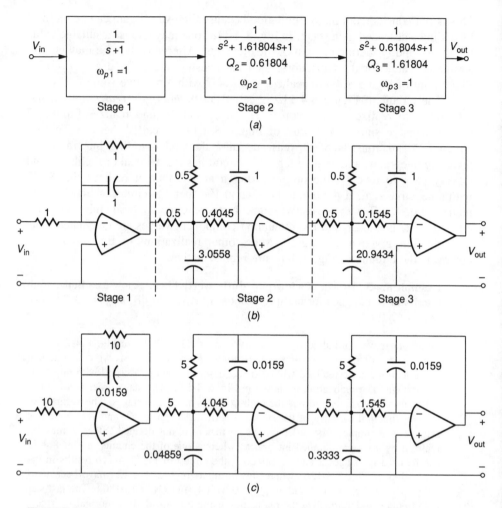

FIGURE 8.4-12
Realization for Example 8.4-3: (*a*) Stage ordering, (*b*) Normalized realization (all values in ohms or farads), (*c*) Frequency and impedance denormalized realization (all values in kilohms and microfarads).

and transform it to apply to high-pass, bandpass, or band-elimination filters. The transformed filter information can then be realized in a cascaded manner using the appropriate RC active stages. A low-pass to high-pass transformation can be defined as

$$s = \frac{1}{p} \tag{8.4-10}$$

where s is the low-pass complex frequency variable. Figure 8.4-13 illustrates how Eq. 8.4-10 transforms an ideal low-pass filter to an ideal high-pass filter. The poles of a high-pass filter can be found by substituting the low-pass poles for s in Eq. 8.4-10. One must also remember that a high-pass realization of order n

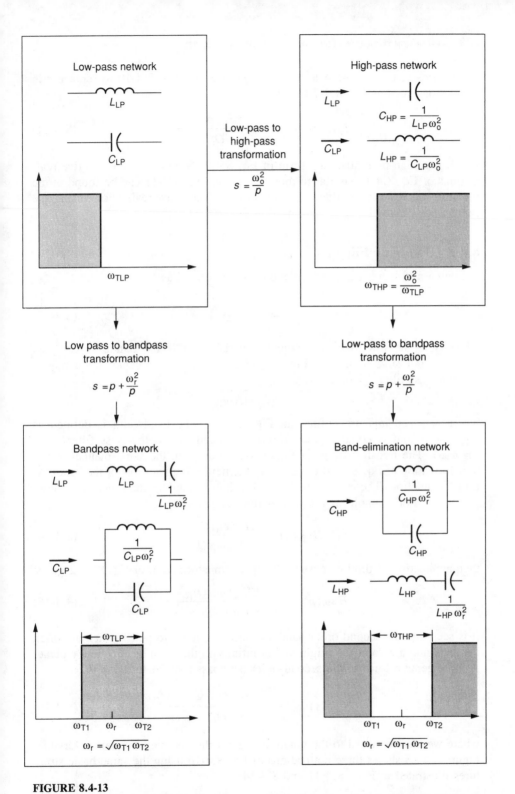

FIGURE 8.4-13
Changes of network elements under frequency transformations. (By permission of L. P. Huelsman and P. E. Allen, *Introduction to the Theory and Design of Active Filters*, McGraw-Hill Book Co., New York, 1980.)

687

has n zeros at the origin. Alternatively, one can use Eq. 8.4-10 to replace s in expressions such as Eq. 8.4-7 to get

$$H_{\mathrm{HP}i}(p) = \frac{\pm H_{oi}p^2}{p^2 + (\omega_{pi}/Q_i)p + \omega_{pi}^2} \tag{8.4-11}$$

which is a high-pass quadratic form of Eq. 8.4-7. Second-order RC active realizations of Eq. 8.4-11 similar to those shown in Fig. 8.4-11 can be found in the literature on RC active filters. Figure 8.4-14 gives three realizations using the same types of structures as were used in Fig. 8.4-11.

8.4.3 Bandpass Filters

A low-pass to bandpass transformation can be defined as

$$s = p + \frac{\omega_r^2}{p} \tag{8.4-12}$$

where s is the low-frequency complex variable, p is the bandpass complex variable, and ω_r is defined in Fig. 8.4-13 as the geometric center frequency of the bandpass filter, given as

$$\omega_r = \sqrt{\omega_{\mathrm{T}1}\omega_{\mathrm{T}2}} \tag{8.4-13}$$

where $\omega_{\mathrm{T}1}$ and $\omega_{\mathrm{T}2}$ are defined in Fig. 8.4-13. The bandwidth is defined as $\omega_{\mathrm{T}2} - \omega_{\mathrm{T}1}$ and is equal to the original passband of the low-pass filter, ω_{T1P} (or ω_{PB}). The transformation of Eq. 8.4-12 is used in the same manner as the transformation of Eq. 8.4-10 to get either the new bandpass roots or the bandpass transfer function. The transformation of Eq. 8.4-12 doubles the order of the low-pass filter. For example, if a low-pass filter is given as

$$H_{\mathrm{LP}i}(s) = \frac{H_{oi}(\omega_1/Q)}{s + (\omega_1/Q)} \tag{8.4-14}$$

then application of the low-pass to bandpass transformation of Eq. 8.4-12 gives

$$H_{\mathrm{BP}i}(p) = \frac{\pm H_{oi}(\omega_1/Q)p}{p^2 + (\omega_1/Q)p + \omega_r^2} \tag{8.4-15}$$

It is seen that the second-order bandpass structure has two poles which are often complex and a zero at the origin and at infinity in the complex frequency plane. A more general form of the second-order bandpass transfer function is

$$H_{\mathrm{BP}i}(s) = \frac{\pm H_{oi}(\omega_{pi}/Q_i)s}{s^2 + (\omega_{pi}/Q_i)s + \omega_{pi}^2} \tag{8.4-16}$$

where we have reverted to the notation of s for the complex frequency variable. Figure 8.4-15 shows three realizations of Eq. 8.4-16 using the same basic structures illustrated in Figs. 8.4-11 and 8.4-14.

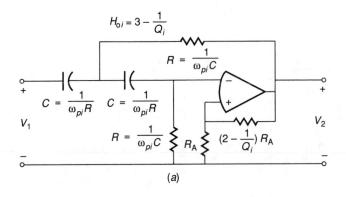

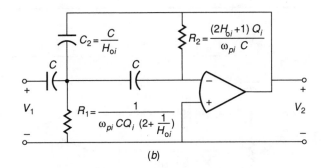

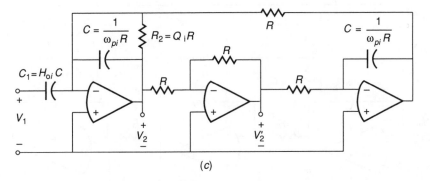

FIGURE 8.4-14
Three realizations of Eq. 8.4-11 (second-order, high-pass): (a) Finite-gain or Sallen and Key structure, (b) Infinite-gain structure, (c) Tow-Thomas or resonator structure.

A second major approach to active filter design, once the order of the filter is known, is to go directly to a passive realization. Passive RLC realizations for normalized low-pass filter approximations have also been tabulated and can be found in the literature.[26,27,28,34,39] To illustrate this approach, we repeat Example 8.4-3.

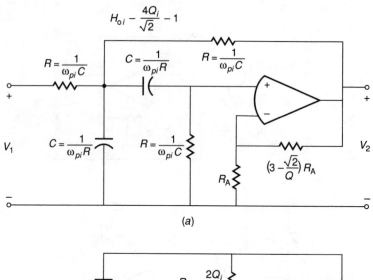

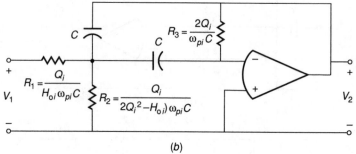

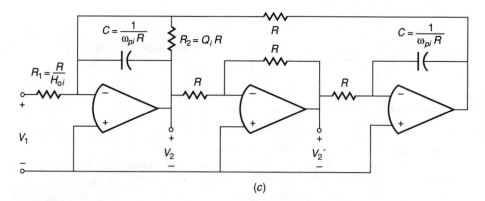

FIGURE 8.4-15
Three realizations of Eq. 8.4-16 (second-order, bandpass structure): (*a*) Finite-gain or Sallen and Key structure, (*b*) Infinite-gain, (*c*) Tow-Thomas or resonator structure.

Example 8.4-4. Realization of a passive RLC filter. Design a passive RLC filter that will satisfy the specifications of Example 8.4-3. This filter is to be driven from a voltage source having zero resistance and will be terminated in a 1000 Ω load.

Solution. From Example 8.4-3, we know that $n = 5$. From the tabulation found in the literature, we obtain the realization shown in Fig. 8.4-16. This realization has been normalized so that $\omega_{PB} = 1$ rps and $R_L = 1$ Ω. It is now necessary to denormalize using Eqs. 8.4-8 and 8.4-9. Because ω_{PB} of Fig. 8.4-16a is unity and we desire ω_{PB} of 2000π, then $\Omega_n = 2000\pi$. Because R_L of Fig. 8.4-16a is 1 Ω and we want $R_L = 1000$ Ω, then $z_n = 1000$. Applying the equations of Table 8.4-2 to the components of Fig. 8.4-16a results in the final realization shown in Fig. 8.4-16b, which has a transfer function equivalent to that of Fig. 8.4-12c.

The passive RLC low-pass realizations may be easily converted to high-pass, bandpass, or band-elimination using the transformations of Fig. 8.4-13. The passive RLC realizations are also used as the starting point in certain types of active filter design.

Figure 8.4-17 summarizes this section. The design of active RC filters starts with the filter specification, which is converted into a filter approximation. Sometimes, the classical approximations presented here are not adequate, and computer-generated approximations are used instead. The filter approximation will take the form of a rational polynomial transfer function. If the roots of the rational polynomial are factored into first- and second-order products, then the cascade realization approach illustrated here can be used. Methods also exist

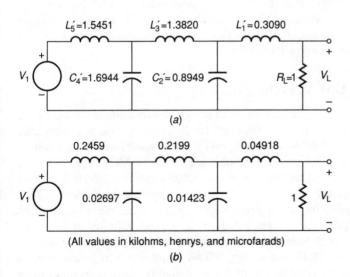

(a)

(All values in kilohms, henrys, and microfarads)

(b)

FIGURE 8.4-16
(a) Passive RLC normalized prototype for Example 8.4-4, (b) Denormalized realization of a.

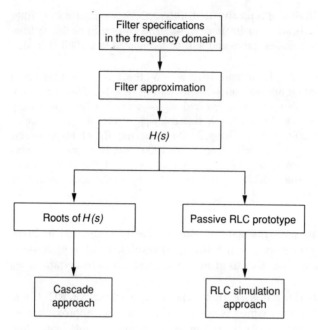

FIGURE 8.4-17
Summary of continuous-time filter design approaches.

for synthesizing a circuit directly from the rational polynomial without obtaining the roots, but they have not been discussed here. Tabulations of a passive RLC prototype circuit that implement the standard approximating functions are also widely available in the literature. The switched capacitor filters, which will be presented in the next section, start from the roots of the rational function, the rational function, or the passive RLC prototype.

8.5 SWITCHED CAPACITOR FILTERS

The use of switched capacitor methodology to design and implement analog filters using integrated circuit technology is illustrated in this section. It is necessary that the technology be capable of providing a good switch, a well-defined capacitor, and an op amp. Because all of these aspects are found in MOS technology, it has become the predominant technology for switched capacitor filters. Switched capacitor methods are not new and, in fact, were employed by James Clerk Maxwell in his discussion on the equivalent resistance of a periodically switched capacitor.[40] The key development that led to the rapid evolution of practical switched capacitor methods was the realization that switched capacitor concepts could be implemented in MOS technology.[41] This realization was followed by a rapid development and implementation of analog signal processing techniques in MOS technology. Today, many switched capacitor circuits, including filters, are found in various products, including telecommunications products.[42]

The material presented in this section is a brief description of how to design switched capacitor filters. Three basic methods will be described. The first is resistor substitution and replaces the resistors in an RC active circuit with a switched capacitor realization. The second uses switched capacitor integrators to simulate the passive RLC prototype circuit for a desired filter realization. The last uses a direct building block approach in the z-domain. The filter requirements are transformed from the continuous-time frequency domain to the discrete-time frequency domain (z-domain). These approaches are representative of the methods used in switched capacitor filter design. More information can be found in the references.

8.5.1 Resistor Realization

One of the simplest approaches in switched capacitor design is to replace the resistors of a continuous-time, active RC filter realization with a switched capacitor realization of each resistor. Resistor realizations contain capacitors and switches and simulate the continuous-time resistor very well as long as the rate at which the switches are opened and closed is much higher than the frequencies of interest in the analog signal. Figure 8.5-1a shows the configuration of a *parallel* switched capacitor realization of a resistor, R, connected between two voltage sources, V_1 and V_2, illustrated in Fig. 8.5-1b. The switches, ϕ_1 and ϕ_2, are controlled by the nonoverlapping clocks of period T_c, as shown in Fig. 8.5-1c.

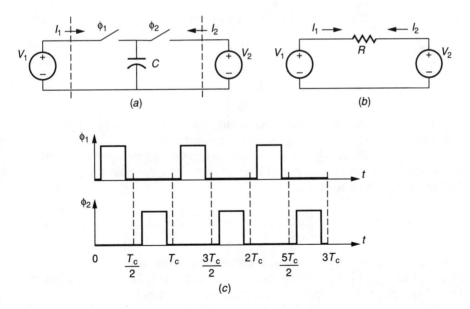

FIGURE 8.5-1
(a) Parallel switched capacitor realization of a resistor, (b) A continuous resistor, (c) Clock waveforms for the switched capacitor realization.

When the clock waveform in Fig. 8.5-1c is high, the switch designated by that waveform is closed.

To demonstrate the equivalence between the switched capacitor circuit in Fig. 8.5-1a and the resistor in Fig. 8.5-1b, assume that $V_1(t)$ and $V_2(t)$ are unchanged for several clock cycles. We shall designate these constant voltages as V_1 and V_2, respectively. During the time between 0 and $T_c/2$, switch ϕ_1 closes. If the switch resistance is small or the clock period large enough, the capacitor C will be charged to V_1. At $t = T_c/2$, we can define the total charge flow between 0 and $T_c/2$ past the left-hand vertical dashed line as $Q_1(T_c/2)$, which is given as

$$Q_1(T_c/2) = CV_1 \tag{8.5-1}$$

where C is initially uncharged. Next, consider the time interval between $T_c/2$ and T_c. Switch ϕ_2 closes and connects the charged capacitor to V_2. At time T_c, we can define the charge flow past the right-hand vertical dashed line as $Q_2(T_c)$ for $0 < t < T_c$, which is given as

$$Q_2(T_c) = C(V_2 - V_1) \tag{8.5-2}$$

Note that the flow of charge past the left-hand vertical dashed line during this period is

$$Q_1(T_c) = 0 \tag{8.5-3}$$

During the interval from T_c to $3T_c/2$, switch ϕ_1 closes again, resulting in the following charge flow during this interval.

$$Q_1\left(\frac{3T_c}{2}\right) = C(V_1 - V_2) \tag{8.5-4}$$

and

$$Q_2\left(\frac{3T_c}{2}\right) = 0 \tag{8.5-5}$$

As long as $V_1(t)$ and $V_2(t)$ remain constant, these equations hold for the charge flow into the capacitor C during the various switch closures.

The charge flows, Q_1 and Q_2, can be expressed in terms of the current that flows during the switch closure. This expression for Q_1 during the period from $T_c/2$ to $3T_c/2$ can be written as

$$Q_1 = Q_1(T_c) + Q_1\left(\frac{3T_c}{2}\right) = 0 + C(V_1 - V_2) = \int_{T_c/2}^{3T_c/2} I_1(t)\, dt \tag{8.5-6}$$

If we divide Eq. 8.5-6 by T_c, then the integral over the period T_c (in this case, from $T_c/2$ to $3T_c/2$) is equal to the average value of $I_1(t)$, designated as $I_1(\text{aver})$. Thus, from Eq. 8.5-6 we may write the following expression.

$$I_1(\text{aver}) = \frac{C}{T_c}(V_1 - V_2) \tag{8.5-7}$$

The average current flowing through the resistor R in the same time interval of length T_c is proportional to $V_1 - V_2$ and is expressed as

$$I_{1R}(\text{aver}) = \frac{V_1 - V_2}{R} \tag{8.5-8}$$

If V_1 and V_2 remain constant, then we can equate $I_1(\text{aver})$ and $I_{1R}(\text{aver})$ to obtain the equivalent resistance of the switched capacitor circuit. From Eq. 8.5-7 and Eq. 8.5-8 this is

$$R \cong \frac{T_c}{C} = \frac{1}{f_c C} \tag{8.5-9}$$

Equation 8.5-9 is a key result! It states that as long as V_1 and V_2 are approximately constant, the switched capacitor circuit of Fig. 8.5-1a realizes the resistor of Fig. 8.5-1b.

In reality, $V_1(t)$ and $V_2(t)$ are not constants but time-varying voltages. However, if the clock period is small enough, the values of $V_1(t + T_c)$ and $V_2(t + T_c)$ are not much different from $V_1(t)$ and $V_2(t)$. This can be stated in a different manner, assuming that the $V_1(t)$ and $V_2(t)$ waveforms are sinusoidal with a frequency of f_s. If f_s is much less than f_c, then T_s is much greater than T_c and Eq. 8.5-9 is valid. This condition is called the *high sampling approximation*.

Three other configurations of switched capacitor realizations of resistance along with the parallel switched capacitor configuration are shown in Fig. 8.5-2. The parallel switched capacitor resistance realization we have just discussed is shown in the first row. A second configuration, called the *series* switched capacitor realization, consists of two switches and one capacitor. If one repeats the preceding charge flow analysis, it can be shown that the equivalent resistance of the series switched capacitor realization is also given by Eq. 8.5-9. A third configuration, called the *series-parallel* switched capacitor realization, is shown in the third row of Fig. 8.5-2. The value of the resistor realization is shown in the last column and can be found in exactly the same manner as was done for the previous two configurations. Finally, the *bilinear* switched capacitor realization is shown. It uses four switches and one capacitor. If the high sampling frequency approximation is valid, all resistors of continuous-time RC active networks can be replaced on a one-for-one basis to obtain a switched capacitor realization.

The advantage of the switched capacitor methodology can be illustrated by comparing the RC product of a resistance designated as R_1 and a capacitance designated as C_2. Let us assume that the product of R_1 and C_2 forms the time constant τ, given as

$$\tau = R_1 C_2 \tag{8.5-10}$$

The dependence of the accuracy of τ on R_1 and C_2 can be written as

$$\frac{d\tau}{\tau} = \frac{dR_1}{R_1} + \frac{dC_2}{C_2} \tag{8.5-11}$$

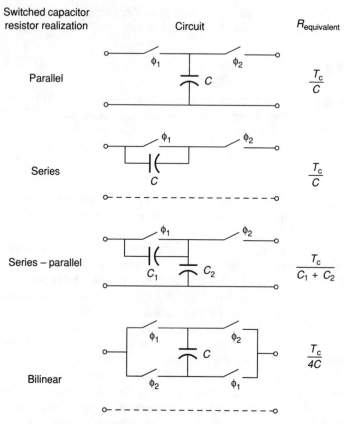

FIGURE 8.5-2
Summary of switched capacitor resistor simulations where $f \ll f_e$.

where dx/x is interpreted as the accuracy of x. The worst-case accuracy of τ will be the sum of the absolute accuracies of R_1 and C_2, which will be very poor if R_1 and C_2 are directly implemented by integrated circuit technology.

If R_1 is replaced by a switched capacitor resistance realization with a capacitor of value C_1 having an equivalent resistance given by Eq. 8.5-9, the time constant τ now becomes

$$\tau = \frac{1}{f_c} \frac{C_2}{C_1} = T_c \frac{C_2}{C_1} \tag{8.5-12}$$

The accuracy of the time constant, τ, in Eq. 8.5-12 can be expressed as

$$\frac{d\tau}{\tau} = \frac{dT_c}{T_c} + \frac{dC_2}{C_2} - \frac{dC_1}{C_1} \tag{8.5-13}$$

If the clock frequency is assumed to be constant, then Eq. 8.5-13 reduces to

$$\frac{d\tau}{\tau} \cong \frac{dC_2}{C_2} - \frac{dC_1}{C_1} \tag{8.5-14}$$

We know from our previous studies that the relative accuracy of two capacitors fabricated on the same integrated circuit can be quite good. As a result, the value of Eq. 8.5-14 can be as low as 0.1%, which represents a tremendous improvement over Eq. 8.5-11 and is one of the key factors contributing to the success of integrated switch capacitor filters.

Unfortunately, the concept of a one-for-one replacement of resistors by switched capacitor resistor realizations breaks down if the high sampling frequency assumption is not valid. Although this does impact how switched capacitor circuits must be designed, it does not affect the accuracy or the small area achievable with switched capacitor circuits. The degree to which f_c must be larger than f_s for Eq. 8.5-9 to be valid depends on both the realization chosen and the circuit in which it is used. For a demonstration of some of these ideas, consider the first-order continuous-time RC circuit of Fig. 8.5-3. The continuous-time frequency-domain voltage transfer function can be written as

$$H(s) = \frac{1}{s\tau_1 + 1} = \frac{1}{s/\omega_1 + 1} \tag{8.5-15}$$

where $\tau_1 = 1/\omega_1 = R_1 C_2$. The frequency response can be found by replacing s by $j\omega$ to get

$$H(j\omega) = \frac{1}{j(\omega/\omega_1) + 1} \tag{8.5-16}$$

The magnitude of Eq. 8.5-16 is

$$|H(j\omega)| = \frac{1}{[1 + (\omega R_1 C_2)^2]^{1/2}} \tag{8.5-17}$$

and the argument, or phase shift, is

$$\text{Arg } H(j\omega) = -\tan^{-1}(\omega R_1 C_2) \tag{8.5-18}$$

The frequency response of the circuit of Fig. 8.5-3 is shown in Fig. 8.5-4a and b. It is seen that this circuit is a first-order low-pass filter. The root of this filter is given in Fig. 8.5-4c.

A realization of the filter of Fig. 8.5-3 can be obtained by replacing the resistor, R_1, with any of the switched capacitor resistor realizations of Fig. 8.5-2. Figure 8.5-5a shows a switched capacitor realization using the parallel switched capacitor resistor realization. To analyze this circuit, the clock sequence must be specified. Figure 8.5-5b shows a shorthand method of illustrating the clock sequence for this circuit. ϕ_1 and ϕ_2 specify the phase periods during which the switches ϕ_1 and ϕ_2 close and will be denoted as the *odd* and *even* phase clocks, respectively. The odd phase periods (ϕ_1) will be designated by a superscript o, and the even phase periods (ϕ_2) will be designated by a superscript e.

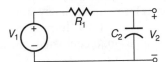

FIGURE 8.5-3
Continuous-time RC network.

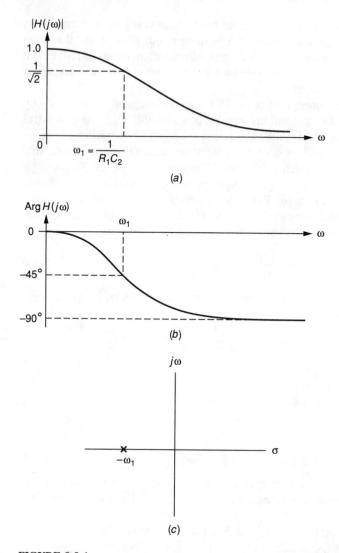

FIGURE 8.5-4
Frequency response of Fig. 8.5-3: (*a*) Magnitude, (*b*) Phase response, (*c*) Root locations of Fig. 8.5-3.

In the analysis of the circuit of Fig. 8.5-5*a* we assume that $V_1(t)$ is constant during the phase periods (which can be achieved by a sample-and-hold circuit). T will be used to denote T_c when there is no possible confusion. Consider the first odd phase period, where $(n - 1) \leq (t/T) < (n - \frac{1}{2})$, when switch ϕ_1 is closed. In this analysis, we assume that switch ϕ_1 closes immediately after $t = (n - 1)T$ and that C_1 is charged instantaneously to $V_1^o[(n - 1)T]$. In practice, the time required for V_1 to charge C_1 to this value should be small compared with

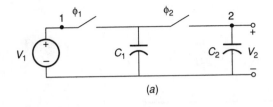

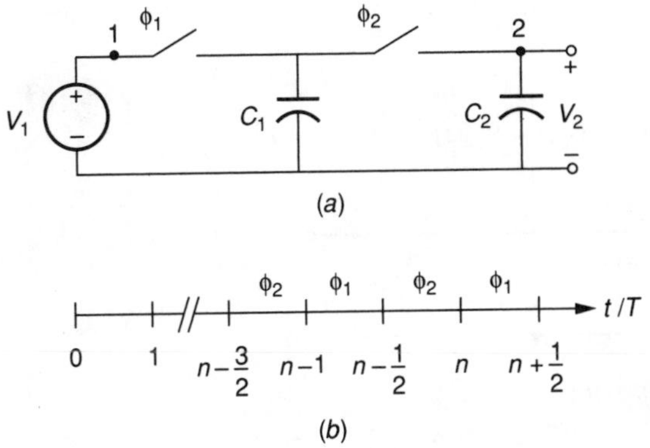

(a)

(b)

FIGURE 8.5-5
(a) Switched capacitor realization of
Fig. 8.5-3, (b) Clock phasing.

$T/2$. During the odd phase period, we may redraw the circuit of Fig. 8.5-5a as shown in Fig. 8.5-6a. From this figure, we see that

$$V_{C1}(t) = V_1^o[(n-1)T] = V_1^o(n-1) \qquad (8.5\text{-}19)$$

and

$$V_{C2}(t) = V_2^o[(n-1)T] = V_2^o(n-1) \qquad (8.5\text{-}20)$$

The clock period T in Eqs. 8.5-19 and 8.5-20 has been dropped because it adds no useful information, thus simplifying the notation. This convention will be followed where no misinterpretation is likely.

   In the next even phase period, $(n - \frac{1}{2}) \le (t/T) < n$, switch ϕ_1 is open and switch ϕ_2 closes. Figure 8.5-6b represents Fig. 8.5-5a during this phase period. During this time, C_1 and C_2 are paralleled, resulting in a new value of V_2. The circuit of Fig. 8.5-6b may be converted to the equivalent circuit of Fig. 8.5-6c with uncharged capacitors. The voltage sources representing the initial voltages on the capacitors are assumed to be multiplied by a unit step function that starts at $t = (n - \frac{1}{2})T$ but whose value was established at $t = (n-1)T$. After closing switch ϕ_2, the charges on C_1 and C_2 must be redistributed to reestablish equilibrium. Using superposition techniques, V_2 can be expressed as

$$V_2(t) = \frac{C_1}{C_1 + C_2} V_1^o(n-1) + \frac{C_2}{C_1 + C_2} V_2^o(n-1) \qquad (8.5\text{-}21)$$

Evaluating $V_2(t)$ at $t = (n - \frac{1}{2})T$, we obtain

$$V_2^e(n - \frac{1}{2}) = \frac{C_1}{C_1 + C_2} V_1^o(n-1) + \frac{C_2}{C_1 + C_2} V_2^o(n-1) \qquad (8.5\text{-}22)$$

At the beginning of the next phase period $n \le t/T < (n + \frac{1}{2})$, the voltage at V_2 can be written as

$$V_2^o(n) = V_2^e(n - \frac{1}{2}) \qquad (8.5\text{-}23)$$

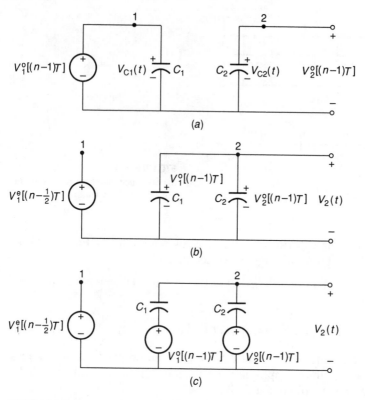

FIGURE 8.5-6
(a) Equivalent circuit of Fig. 8.5-5a when switch ϕ_1 is closed, (b) Equivalent circuit of Fig. 8.5-5a when switch ϕ_2 is closed, (c) Alternate form of b.

because the voltage V_2 has not changed from its value at $t = (n - \frac{1}{2})T$. Using Eq. 8.5-23 allows us to write

$$V_2^o(n) = \frac{C_1}{C_1 + C_2} V_1^o(n - 1) + \frac{C_2}{C_1 + C_2} V_2^o(n - 1) \qquad (8.5\text{-}24)$$

Equation 8.5-24 recursively defines a sequence that can be transformed from the discrete-time domain to the z-domain by taking the z-transform characterized by

$$V(n) \rightarrow z^{-n} V(z) \qquad (8.5\text{-}25)$$

Using this transformation on Eq. 8.5-24 results in

$$V_2^o(z) = \frac{C_1 z^{-1}}{C_1 + C_2} V_1^o(z) + \frac{C_2 z^{-1}}{C_1 + C_2} V_2^o(z) \qquad (8.5\text{-}26)$$

Solving for $V_2^o(z)/V_1^o(z)$ results in the z-domain transfer function of the circuit of Fig. 8.5-5a sampled at the odd output phase.

$$H^{oo}(z) = \frac{V_2^o(z)}{V_1^o(z)} = \left(\frac{1}{1 + \alpha} \right) \frac{z^{-1}}{1 - [\alpha/(1 + \alpha)]z^{-1}} \qquad (8.5\text{-}27)$$

where $\alpha = C_2/C_1$. Applying Eq. 8.5-25 to Eq. 8.5-23 results in $V_2^o(z) = z^{-1/2}V_2^e(z)$. Thus, Eq. 8.5-27 can be written as

$$H^{oe}(z) = \frac{V_2^e(z)}{V_1^o(z)} = \left(\frac{1}{1 + \alpha}\right)\frac{z^{-1/2}}{1 - [\alpha/(1 + \alpha)]z^{-1}} \qquad (8.5\text{-}28)$$

Thus,

$$H^{oo}(z) = z^{-1/2}H^{oe}(z) \qquad (8.5\text{-}29)$$

The basic concepts of the z-transform have been used in an algorithmic manner in order to keep the presentation simple. The z-transform is rigorously developed elsewhere.[43]

The discrete-time frequency response can be found by replacing z by $e^{j\omega T}$, which is analogous to replacing s by $j\omega$ in the continuous-time frequency domain. Making this replacement in Eq. 8.5-27 gives the following expression, which is equivalent to the discrete-time frequency response of the circuit of Fig. 8.5-5a.

$$H^{oo}(e^{j\omega T}) = \frac{V_2^o(e^{j\omega T})}{V_1^o(e^{j\omega T})} = \frac{1}{(1 + \alpha)\cos \omega T - \alpha + j(1 + \alpha)\sin \omega T} \qquad (8.5\text{-}30)$$

where Euler's formula ($e^{j\omega T} = \cos \omega T + j \sin \omega T$) has been used to remove $e^{j\omega T}$. The magnitude of Eq. 8.5-30 is

$$|H^{oo}(e^{j\omega T})| = \frac{1}{[1 + 2\alpha(1 + \alpha)(1 - \cos \omega T)]^{1/2}} \qquad (8.5\text{-}31)$$

and the phase shift is

$$\text{Arg }[H^{oo}(e^{j\omega T})] = -\tan^{-1}\left[\frac{\sin \omega T}{\cos \omega T - \alpha/(1 + \alpha)}\right] \qquad (8.5\text{-}32)$$

In order to compare the performance of the circuit of Fig. 8.5-5 with the circuit of Fig. 8.5-3, we must appropriately choose the values of α and T_c. One of several methods used for making this comparison is to assume that ω_1 of Eq. 8.5-15 is much less than $\omega_c = 1/(2\pi T_c)$. In this case, z of Eq. 8.5-27 can be replaced by

$$z = e^{j\omega T} \simeq 1 + j\omega T \qquad (8.5\text{-}33)$$

to get

$$H^{oo}(e^{j\omega T}) \simeq \frac{1}{j\omega(1 + \alpha)T + 1} \qquad (8.5\text{-}34)$$

Comparing Eq. 8.5-16 with Eq. 8.5-34 gives

$$\frac{1}{\omega_1} = T(1 + \alpha) \qquad (8.5\text{-}35)$$

The frequency response of Eq. 8.5-30 is plotted in Fig. 8.5-7 for the value of $\omega_c/\omega_1 = 10$, which from Eq. 8.5-35 corresponds to $\alpha = 0.5915$. Also plotted is the frequency response of Eq. 8.5-16 from the circuit of Fig. 8.5-3. For frequencies of ω less than $0.02\omega_c$, the switched capacitor circuit of Fig. 8.5-5a is a good approximation of the frequency response of the circuit of Fig. 8.5-3. However, as the frequency increases, the switched capacitor circuit is a very poor approximation. At $\omega/\omega_c = 0.5$, the greatest attenuation of the switched capacitor circuit occurs; and at $\omega = \omega_c$, the magnitude is at the starting value, with a phase shift of $-360°$. The roots of the circuit of as determined from Eq. 8.5-27 are shown in Fig. 8.5-8 and consist of a pole located at $\alpha/(1 + \alpha)$ on the positive real axis. To improve the switched capacitor realization of the circuit of Fig. 8.5-3, it is necessary to increase ω_c or, alternatively, reduce ω_1.

At this point, one can begin to use the resistor realization method to replace the resistances of an RC active network. This method has been applied to the filters of Figs. 8.4-11, 8.4-14, and 8.4-15. The disadvantages of this method are that the circuits are very difficult to analyze and they contain floating nodes. *Floating*

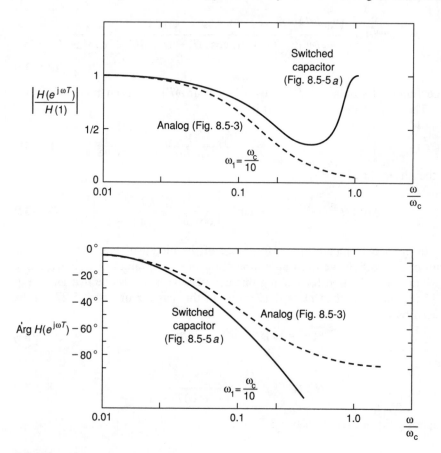

FIGURE 8.5-7
Frequency response of Fig. 8.5-5a compared with the frequency response of Fig. 8.5-3.

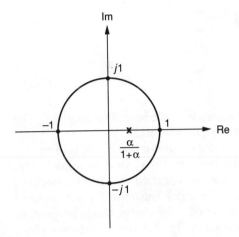

FIGURE 8.5-8
Roots of Fig. 8.5-5a.

nodes are nodes that are not connected to a voltage source or a virtual ground. Floating nodes cause a susceptibility to parasitic capacitance as well as complicate the analysis. Examples of floating nodes are nodes A and B in Fig. 8.4-11a and node A in Fig. 8.4-11b. Figure 8.4-11c has no floating nodes and thus is suitable for the resistor simulation approach. Because of these reasons, the resistor simulation method is restricted to simple configurations. The following two methods provide better and easier methods of realizing switched capacitor filters.

8.5.2 Passive RLC Prototype Switched Capacitor Filters

One of the more useful methods of synthesizing filters using switched capacitor networks is based on the realization of RLC ladder networks. Since the integrator is an important part of this method, we shall consider the implementation of switched capacitor integrators first. An inverting analog integrator is shown in Fig. 8.5-9. The transfer function can be found as

$$H(s) = \frac{V_2(s)}{V_1(s)} = \frac{-1}{sR_1C_2} = \frac{-1}{s\tau_0} = \frac{-\omega_0}{s} \tag{8.5-36}$$

where τ_0 is the time constant of the integrator. The transfer function magnitude of the inverting integrator is given as

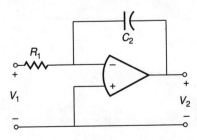

FIGURE 8.5-9
An inverting continuous-time integrator.

$$|H(j\omega)| = \frac{\omega_0}{\omega} \qquad (8.5\text{-}37)$$

and the phase shift is

$$\text{Arg } H(j\omega) = \frac{\pi}{2} \qquad (8.5\text{-}38)$$

A noninverting integrator has the same magnitude as the inverting integrator. The phase shift of the noninverting integrator is equal to $-\pi/2$.

A logical approach to a switched capacitor integrator realization is to replace the resistor R_1 of Fig. 8.5-9 by the parallel switched capacitor realization of Fig. 8.5-1a. The result is shown in Fig. 8.5-10a and is called the parallel switched capacitor integrator. Figure 8.5-10b shows the clock sequence for the switched capacitor integrator. During the odd phase periods, the charge on C_2 is constant. An equivalent circuit to Fig. 8.5-10a is shown in Fig. 8.5-10c for the even phase period. The charge left on C_2 at $t = (n - \frac{1}{2})T$, Q_L, is

$$Q_L^e(n - \frac{1}{2}) = C_2 V_2^e(n - \frac{1}{2}) \qquad (8.5\text{-}39)$$

The charge on C_2 during the odd period, Q_M, is

$$Q_M^o(n - 1) = C_2 V_2^o(n - 1) \qquad (8.5\text{-}40)$$

The charge that will be contributed to C_2 from C_1 during the even phase period, Q_C, is

$$Q_C^o(n - 1) = -C_1 V_1^o(n - 1) \qquad (8.5\text{-}41)$$

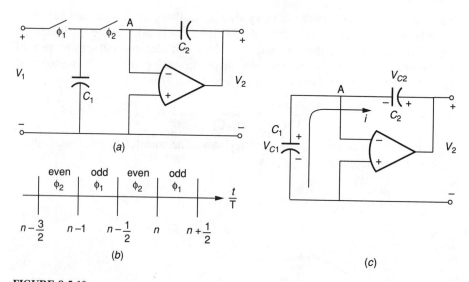

FIGURE 8.5-10

(a) Parallel switched capacitor inverting integrator, (b) Clock sequence, (c) Equivalent circuit during the ϕ_2 phase period.

Charge conservation techniques applied to node A of Fig. 8.5-10c result in

$$Q_L^e(n - \frac{1}{2}) = Q_M^o(n - 1) + Q_C^o(n - 1) \tag{8.5-42}$$

Making the substitutions of Eqs. 8.5-39 through 8.5-41 into Eq. 8.5-42 results in

$$C_2 V_2^e(n - \frac{1}{2}) = C_2 V_2^o(n - 1) - C_1 V_1^o(n - 1) \tag{8.5-43}$$

During the odd phase, the charge on C_2 does not change, so that

$$V_2^o(n) = V_2^e(n - \frac{1}{2}) \tag{8.5-44}$$

Combining Eqs. 8.5-43 and 8.5-44 results in

$$C_2 V_2^o(n) = C_2 V_2^o(n - 1) - C_1 V_1^o(n - 1) \tag{8.5-45}$$

Applying the transformation of Eq. 8.5-25 to Eq. 8.5-45 results in the desired z-domain transfer function

$$C_2 V_2(z) = C_2 z^{-1} V_2^o(z) - C_1 z^{-1} V_1^o(z) \tag{8.5-46}$$

This can be expressed as

$$H^{oo}(z) = \frac{V_2^o(z)}{V_1^o(z)} = -\frac{C_1}{C_2}\left(\frac{z^{-1}}{1 - z^{-1}}\right) \tag{8.5-47}$$

$H^{oe}(z)$ can be found by multiplying Eq. 8.5-47 by $z^{-1/2}$. $H^{oo}(z)$ of Eq. 8.5-47 and the corresponding $H^{oe}(z)$ are sometimes called the type I direct-transform discrete integrator and the type I lossless integrator, respectively.[43−45]

The frequency response of the circuit of Fig. 8.5-10a can be found by replacing z by $e^{j\omega T}$ in Eq. 8.5-47 to get

$$H^{oo}(e^{j\omega T}) = -\frac{C_1}{C_2}\left(\frac{e^{-j\omega T/2}}{e^{j\omega T/2} - e^{-j\omega T/2}}\right) \tag{8.5-48}$$

If we define $\omega_o = C_1/(T C_2)$, then Eq. 8.5-48 can be expressed as

$$H^{oo}(e^{j\omega T}) = -\frac{\omega_o}{j\omega}\left[\frac{\omega T/2}{\sin(\omega T/2)}\right]\exp(-j\omega T/2) \tag{8.5-49}$$

Thus, the magnitude and phase response of Eq. 8.5-49 can be expressed as

$$|H^{oo}(e^{j\omega T})| = \frac{\omega_o}{\omega}\left[\frac{\omega T/2}{\sin(\omega T/2)}\right] \tag{8.5-50}$$

and

$$\text{Arg } H^{oo}(e^{j\omega T}) = \frac{\pi}{2} - \left[\frac{\omega T}{2}\right] \tag{8.5-51}$$

We observe from Eqs. 8.5-50 and 8.5-51 that as ωT approaches zero, these equations approach Eqs. 8.5-37 and 8.5-38, respectively. Consequently, the terms

TABLE 8.5-1
Magnitude and phase (delay) errors in switched capacitor integrators versus normalized frequency

Normalized frequency f/f_c	Error in gain constant magnitude	Error in phase from ideal $90°$
0.00	0.00%	$0°$
0.05	0.41%	$9°$
0.10	1.66%	$18°$
0.15	3.80%	$27°$
0.20	6.90%	$36°$
0.25	11.07%	$45°$
0.30	16.50%	$54°$
0.35	23.41%	$63°$
0.40	32.13%	$72°$
0.45	43.13%	$81°$
0.50	57.08%	$90°$

in the bracketed portions of Eqs. 8.5-50 and 8.5-51 can be considered magnitude and phase error terms. The effects of these error terms are shown in Table 8.5-1.

A noninverting switched capacitor integrator is shown in Fig. 8.5-11. It can be observed that C_1 is charged by V_1 in one direction and then reversed before it is discharged into C_2. The result is exactly the same transfer function as Eq. 8.5-47 except there is no minus sign. The phase shift is given as

$$\text{Arg } H^{\infty\infty}(e^{j\omega T}) = -\frac{\pi}{2} - \left[\frac{\omega T}{2}\right] \tag{8.5-52}$$

Consequently, the magnitude and phase errors given in Table 8.5-1 are also appropriate for the noninverting switched capacitor integrator.

Figure 8.5-11 has a very important property not found in any of the switched capacitor circuits previously considered in this section. This property is called *stray insensitivity*. In reality, every node in a circuit has some stray capacitance to ground. These capacitances are represented by C_A and C_B in Fig. 8.5-11. During the ϕ_1 phase, C_B is discharged and C_A is charged by the voltage source, V_1.

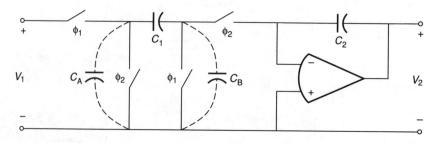

FIGURE 8.5-11
A stray-insensitive, noninverting switched capacitor integrator.

During the ϕ_2 phase, an uncharged C_B is paralleled with a virtual ground, and C_A is discharged to ground. Neither C_A nor C_B has any direct influence on the charge on C_1, which is transferred to C_2 during the ϕ_2 phase period. Consequently, Fig. 8.5-11 is insensitive to stray capacitances. Repeating this procedure with a stray capacitance in Fig. 8.5-10a will show that the charge transferred from C_1 to C_2 during the ϕ_2 phase period will be influenced by stray capacitances. Most commercial switched capacitor circuits use building blocks that are stray insensitive.

The stray-insensitive, inverting switched capacitor integrator of Fig. 8.5-12 will complete our repertoire of switched capacitor integrators. Although there are many other possible integrators, these will be sufficient for our purposes in this section. The transfer function of this integrator can be found by writing the expressions for the various charges that are being transferred. The clock phasing of Fig. 8.5-10b will be used for Fig. 8.5-12. The charge left on C_2 at the end of the even phase period is

$$Q_L^e\left(n - \frac{1}{2}\right) = C_2 V_2^e\left(n - \frac{1}{2}\right) \qquad (8.5\text{-}53)$$

The charge on C_2 during the previous odd phase is

$$Q_M^o(n - 1) = C_2 V_2^o(n - 1) \qquad (8.5\text{-}54)$$

The charge transferred to C_2 by the charging of C_1 to $V_1(n - \frac{1}{2})$ during the even phase is

$$Q_C^e\left(n - \frac{1}{2}\right) = -C_1 V_1^e\left(n - \frac{1}{2}\right) \qquad (8.5\text{-}55)$$

Using charge conservation techniques gives

$$Q_L^e\left(n - \frac{1}{2}\right) = Q_M^o(n - 1) + Q_C^e\left(n - \frac{1}{2}\right) \qquad (8.5\text{-}56)$$

Substituting Eqs. 8.5-53 through 8.5-55 into Eq. 8.5-56 results in

$$C_2 V_2^e\left(n - \frac{1}{2}\right) = C_2 V_2^o(n - 1) - C_1 V_1^e\left(n - \frac{1}{2}\right) \qquad (8.5\text{-}57)$$

If we assume the input is from a sample-and-hold circuit, then $V_1^e(n - \frac{1}{2}) = V_1^o(n)$.

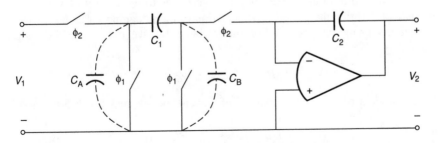

FIGURE 8.5-12
A stray-insensitive, inverting switched capacitor integrator.

During ϕ_1, $V_2^e(n - \frac{1}{2}) = V_2^o(n)$. Substituting these relations into Eq. 8.5-57 gives

$$C_2 V_2^o(n) = C_2 V_2^o(n - 1) - C_1 V_1^o(n) \qquad (8.5\text{-}58)$$

Using Eq. 8.5-25 we obtain the desired transfer function for the circuit of Fig. 8.5-12 as

$$H^{oo}(z) = \frac{V_2^o(z)}{V_1^o(z)} = -\frac{C_1}{C_2}\left(\frac{1}{1 - z^{-1}}\right) \qquad (8.5\text{-}59)$$

We see that for the inverting, stray-insensitive switched capacitor integrator, there is no delay in the forward path from the input to the output.

The frequency response of the circuit of Fig. 8.5-12 can be found by replacing z by $e^{j\omega T}$. Making this replacement and multiplying through the numerator and denominator by $e^{j\omega T}$ gives

$$H^{oo}(e^{j\omega T}) = -\frac{C_1}{C_2}\left(\frac{e^{j\omega T/2}}{e^{j\omega T/2} - e^{-j\omega T/2}}\right) \qquad (8.5\text{-}60)$$

We note that Eq. 8.5-60 is identical to Eq. 8.5-48 except for the minus sign in the numerator exponential. This means that the magnitude response of the circuit of Fig. 8.5-12 is given by Eq. 8.5-50 and the phase shift by Eq. 8.5-51, except that the phase error term is positive. The integrator error terms given in Table 8.5-1 are also applicable to the integrator of Fig. 8.5-12. The frequency response of various types of integrators is illustrated in Fig. 8.5-13 for a ratio of ω_0 to ω_c of 0.1. The integrators we have just discussed are sufficient to implement practical switched capacitor filters. A more complete presentation, concerning other realizations and details, can be found in the literature.

Next we shall use the switched capacitor integrator to realize the passive RLC prototype ladder filter. Consider the fifth-order low-pass filter shown in Fig. 8.5-14. This filter is similar to the type that was considered in Sec. 8.4. The subscript n on the components indicates prototype or normalized values. The first step is to select the electrical variables that will be used to describe the circuit. Each component is characterized by a current, I_i, and a voltage, V_i, one of which can be expressed as the integration of the other variable. The integrand variable is current for an inductor and voltage for a capacitor. The integrand variables I_1, V_2, I_3, V_4, and I_5 are shown in Fig. 8.5-14.

The next step is to use these integrand variables to write a set of s-domain equations that describe the circuit. The selection of the integrand variables allows the realization using integrators. For the variable I_1, we may write the loop equation:

$$V_{in} - I_1(R_{0n} + sL_{1n}) - V_2 = 0 \qquad (8.5\text{-}61)$$

Using the concept of a "voltage analog" of current, we express Eq. 8.5-61 as

$$V_{in} - \frac{V_1'}{R}(R_{0n} + sL_{1n}) - V_2 = 0 \qquad (8.5\text{-}62)$$

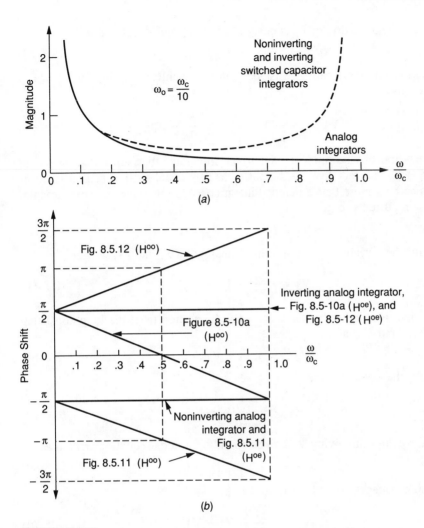

FIGURE 8.5-13
(*a*) Magnitude response of various switched capacitor integrators compared with a continuous-time integrator when $\omega_0/\omega_c = 1/10$, (*b*) Phase response of various switched capacitor and continuous-time integrators.

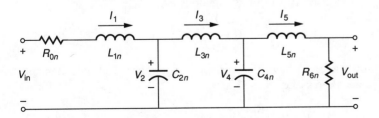

FIGURE 8.5-14
A fifth-order, low-pass, passive prototype filter.

where the voltage analog of I_1 is designated as V_1' and is defined as

$$V_1' = RI_1 \qquad (8.5\text{-}63)$$

where R is an arbitrary scaling resistance (normally unity). Solving for V_1' of Eq. 8.5-62 results in

$$V_1' = \frac{R}{sL_{1n}}\left[V_{\text{in}} - V_2 - \left(\frac{R_{0n}}{R}\right)V_1'\right] \qquad (8.5\text{-}64)$$

This expression can be implemented by an integrator that sums V_{in}, $-V_2$, and $-(R_{0n}/R)V_1'$. The fact that the output is in part equal to the integral of itself indicates nothing more than a damped integrator. Moving on to the next variable, V_2, we sum currents to get

$$I_1 - I_3 - sC_{2n}V_2 = 0 \qquad (8.5\text{-}65)$$

Solving for the variable V_2 using voltage analogs of I_1 and I_2, we get

$$V_2 = \frac{1}{sRC_{2n}}[V_1' - V_3'] \qquad (8.5\text{-}66)$$

The equation describing the variable I_3 can be written from the loop consisting of C_{2n}, L_{3n}, and C_{4n} as

$$V_2 - sL_{3n}I_3 - V_4 = 0 \qquad (8.5\text{-}67)$$

Solving for the voltage analog of I_3 gives

$$V_3' = \frac{R}{sL_{3n}}(V_2 - V_4) \qquad (8.5\text{-}68)$$

Next, the equation involving V_4 can be found by a nodal equation written as

$$I_3 - sC_{4n}V_4 - I_5 = 0 \qquad (8.5\text{-}69)$$

Again using voltage analogs for I_3 and I_5 gives,

$$V_4 = \frac{1}{sRC_{4n}}(V_3' - V_5') \qquad (8.5\text{-}70)$$

Finally, a loop equation involving C_{4n}, L_{5n}, and R_{6n} will be used to describe the variable I_5:

$$V_4 - sL_{5n}I_5 - I_5R_{6n} = 0 \qquad (8.5\text{-}71)$$

which can be expressed in terms of voltage analogs as

$$V_5' = \frac{R}{sL_{5n}}\left(V_4 - \frac{R_{6n}}{R}V_5'\right) \qquad (8.5\text{-}72)$$

However, we would prefer to have the variable V_{out} rather than V_5'. Because $V_{\text{out}} = (R_{6n}/R)V_5'$, we express Eq. 8.5-72 as

$$V_{\text{out}} = \frac{R_{6n}}{sL_{5n}}(V_4 - V_{\text{out}}) \qquad (8.5\text{-}73)$$

The method of generating these equations should be obvious. Starting with Eq. 8.5-61, the equations are a succession of loop equations followed by a node equation. The substitution of V_{out} for V_5' was simply by application of Ohm's law. This method can be used for practically all low-pass ladder RLC filters.

The next step is the realization of Eqs. 8.5-64, 8.5-66, 8.5-68, 8.5-70, and 8.5-73. Equation 8.5-64 represents a summing integrator with inputs of V_{in}, V_2, and V_1' and output V_1'. It can be realized by switched capacitor circuits by combining the ideas of Figs. 8.5-11 and 8.5-12. The circuit of Fig. 8.5-15a results as a proposed realization of Eq. 8.5-64. Note that the right-hand switches have been combined to reduce the number of switches. Using the results of Eqs. 8.5-47 and 8.5-59, we write

$$V_1'(z) = \left(\frac{1}{1 - z^{-1}}\right)[\alpha_{11} z^{-1} V_{\text{in}}(z) - \alpha_{21} V_2(z) - \alpha_{31} V_1'(z)] \quad (8.5\text{-}74)$$

Next the high sampling approximation is made so that $1 - z^{-1}$ is approximately sT and z^{-1} is approximately $1 - sT \simeq 1$. Thus, Eq. 8.5-74 becomes

$$V_1'(s) \simeq \frac{1}{sT}[\alpha_{11} V_{\text{in}}(s) - \alpha_{21} V_2(s) - \alpha_{31} V_1'(s)] \quad (8.5\text{-}75)$$

Before Eq. 8.5-75 can be equated with Eq. 8.5-64, it must be frequency-denormalized. This is because Eq. 8.5-64 is based on a low-pass normalized prototype, having a cutoff frequency of 1 rps. This denormalization is accomplished by replacing the clock period, T, in Eq. 8.5-75 by

$$T = \frac{T_{\text{n}}}{\Omega_{\text{n}}} \quad (8.5\text{-}76)$$

where T_{n} is the normalized clock period and Ω_{n} is defined as

$$\Omega_{\text{n}} = \frac{\text{Actual cutoff frequency in rps}}{\text{Normalized cutoff frequency rps}} \quad (8.5\text{-}77)$$

Therefore, Eq. 8.5-75 can be written as

$$V_1'(s) \simeq \frac{1}{sT_{\text{n}}}[\alpha_{11} V_{\text{in}}(s) - \alpha_{21} V_2(s) - \alpha_{31} V_1'(s)] \quad (8.5\text{-}78)$$

Equating Eq. 8.5-78 and Eq. 8.5-64 results in the design of the first integrator of Fig. 8.5-15. These results are

$$\alpha_{11} = \alpha_{21} = \frac{RT_{\text{n}}}{L_{1n}} = \frac{R\Omega_{\text{n}}T}{L_{1n}} = \frac{R\Omega_{\text{n}}}{L_{1n}f_{\text{c}}} \quad (8.5\text{-}79)$$

and

$$\alpha_{31} = \frac{R_{0n}T_{\text{n}}}{L_{1n}} = \frac{R_{0n}\Omega_{\text{n}}T}{L_{1n}} = \frac{R_{0n}\Omega_{\text{n}}}{L_{1n}f_{\text{c}}} \quad (8.5\text{-}80)$$

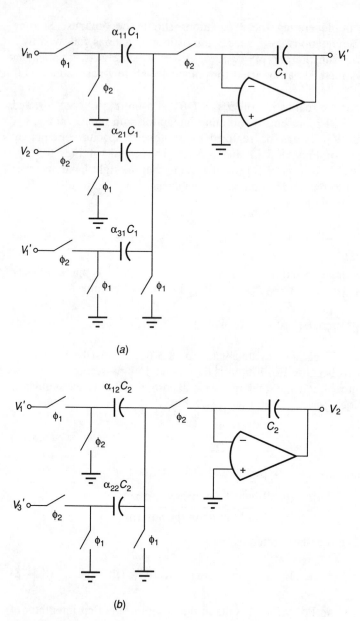

(a)

(b)

FIGURE 8.5-15
Stage-by-stage realization of Fig. 8.5-14: (a) Input stage, (b) Second stage, (c) Third stage,
(d) Fourth stage, (e) Output stage.

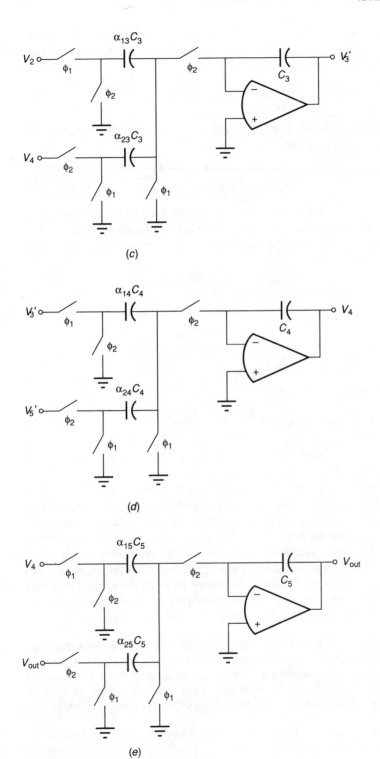

FIGURE 8.5-15
(*Continued*)

Next we repeat this process for the variable V_2 of Eq. 8.5-66. Figure 8.5-15b is a realization of Eq. 8.5-66. Using the high sampling approximation allows us to write the output of this circuit as

$$V_2(s) \simeq \frac{1}{sT_n}[\alpha_{12}V_1'(s) - \alpha_{22}V_3'(s)] \tag{8.5-81}$$

employing the same approach that was used to get Eq. 8.5-78. Equating Eq. 8.5-66 with Eq. 8.5-81 results in

$$\alpha_{12} = \alpha_{22} = \frac{T_n}{RC_{2n}} = \frac{\Omega_n T}{RC_{2n}} = \frac{\Omega_n}{RC_{2n}f_c} \tag{8.5-82}$$

The realizations for Eqs. 8.5-68, 8.5-70, and 8.5-73 are identical in concept to that of Eq. 8.5-66. Figure 8.5-15 shows the switched capacitor realizations of these equations. Using the same approach as before, we may express the design equations of Fig. 8.5-15c as

$$\alpha_{13} = \alpha_{23} = \frac{RT_n}{L_{3n}} = \frac{R\Omega_n T}{L_{3n}} = \frac{R\Omega_n}{f_c L_{3n}} \tag{8.5-83}$$

and Fig. 8.5-15d as

$$\alpha_{14} = \alpha_{24} = \frac{T_n}{RC_{4n}} = \frac{\Omega_n T}{RC_{4n}} = \frac{\Omega_n}{RC_{4n}f_c} \tag{8.5-84}$$

and Fig. 8.5-15e as

$$\alpha_{15} = \alpha_{25} = \frac{R_{6n}T_n}{L_{5n}} = \frac{R_{6n}\Omega_n}{L_{5n}f_c} \tag{8.5-85}$$

Equations 8.5-79, 8.5-80, and 8.5-82 through 8.5-85 permit the design of the filter in Fig. 8.5-14 according to a given set of specifications. When the various integrators of Fig. 8.5-15 are combined, the filter realization is that shown in Fig. 8.5-16. The filter structure consists of coupled internal feedback loops containing two integrators each. In order to achieve minimum delay around each loop, it is necessary that each integrator be sampled by the next integrator as soon as the new sample is available. Therefore, in one clock period, the signal circulates around the internal feedback loop. The clock scheme indicated will avoid a $T/2$ delay, which would create a difference between the actual realization and that desired. The following example illustrates the application of the preceding approach to the switched capacitor realization of a low-pass filter.

Example 8.5-1. A switched capacitor realization of a fifth-order low-pass Chebyshev filter. A fifth-order low-pass Chebyshev filter with a 1 dB ripple in the passband is to be designed for a cutoff frequency of 1000 Hz. The structure of Fig. 8.5-16 based upon the passive prototype of Fig. 8.5-14 is to be used. Find the switched capacitor realization for this filter if the clock frequency is 100 kHz.

Solution. The normalized values of the RLC passive prototype that satisfies the specifications are $R_{0n} = 1\ \Omega$, $L_{1n} = 2.1349$ H, $C_{2n} = 1.0911$ F, $L_{3n} = 3.009$ H,

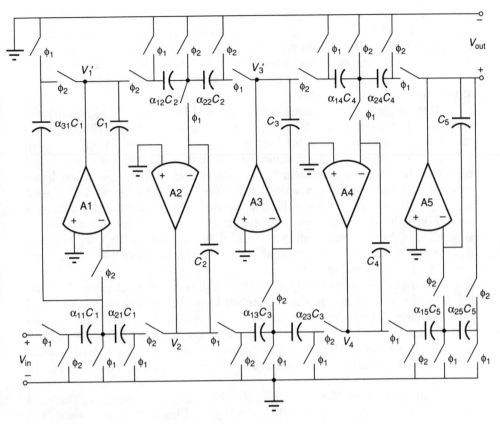

FIGURE 8.5-16
Switched capacitor realization of Fig. 8.5-14.

$C_{4n} = 1.0911$ F, $L_{5n} = 2.1349$ H, and $R_{6n} = 1 \ \Omega$. These values are found from tabulations in the literature.[26,31] Using the preceding equations with $\Omega_n = 2000\pi$, we get

$$\alpha_{11} = \alpha_{21} = \alpha_{31} = 0.02943$$

$$\alpha_{12} = \alpha_{22} = 0.05759$$

$$\alpha_{13} = \alpha_{23} = 0.02094$$

$$\alpha_{14} = \alpha_{24} = 0.05759$$

$$\alpha_{15} = \alpha_{25} = 0.2943$$

One item of concern in switched capacitor filters is the total capacitance required in the realization. Large capacitor ratios are undesirable because of the loss of relative accuracy and increased area. If α_{ij} of the jth stage is less than unity, then $\alpha_{ij} C_j$ will be less than C_j. If we equate the smallest capacitor, $\alpha_{ij} C_j$, to a unity capacitance C_{uj}, then we may find the total relative capacitance of a stage by summing C_{uj} with all other capacitors being divided by α_{ij}. In the preceding example if we let $C_{u1} = C_{u2} = C_{u3} = C_{u4} = C_{u5} = C_u$, then the total capacitance is $155.596C_u$. If C_u is selected as 1 pF, then 155.596 pF of capacitance is required for the filter. It is important to keep this number as small as possible if the filter is to be integrated. Reduction of the clock frequency will always reduce this number, but at the expense of not satisfying the high sampling approximation at the higher signal frequencies.

This design method starting from the low-pass, passive RLC prototype is general and can be applied to all types of symmetrical filters. Elliptic filters can also be synthesized by replacing the L cutsets or C loops with controlled sources.[26] The result requires a nonintegrated input to the integrator, which can be accomplished by an unswitched capacitor. Bandpass, high-pass, and band-elimination filters can be synthesized using the transformations of Fig. 8.4-13 applied to the low-pass, passive RLC prototype. The bandpass is realized by a second-order bandpass structure with the ability to sum multiple inputs. Such a structure could be derived from the circuit of Fig. 8.4-15c if the integrators are replaced by the appropriate combinations of the integrators of Fig. 8.5-11 and Fig. 8.5-12 with summing inputs.

The high-pass switched capacitor filter realizations present more of a challenge, although they use the same approach as that used for low-pass switched capacitor filters. The reason for the additional complexity is that the low-pass to high-pass transformation applied to the low-pass, passive RLC prototype will result in differentiators if the same integrand variables used for low-pass filters are selected. It is necessary to reselect the variables so that the equations can be realized with integrators.

Band-elimination filters are also possible using this approach. One first transforms the low-pass, passive RLC prototype to a band-elimination form. The switched capacitor realization will require a second-order structure with the ability to sum both integrated and nonintegrated inputs. For more information on the design of switched capacitor circuits from general symmetrical filters, the reader should consult Chapter 4 of the text *Switched Capacitor Circuits*.[26]

8.5.3 Z-Domain Synthesis Techniques

In many cases, the designer is given the filter approximation in the z-domain rather than the s-domain. In this case, the realization of the filter takes place directly in the z-domain. Various methods of arriving at $H(z)$ given $H(s)$ are well developed and can be found elsewhere. Irrespective of how the tranformation is made, the starting point of z-domain synthesis techniques is

$$H(z) = \frac{a_0 + a_1 z + a_2 z^2 + \ldots + a_{m-1} z^{m-1} + a_m z^m}{b_0 + b_1 z + b_2 z^2 + \ldots + b_{n-1} z^{n-1} + b_n z^n} \qquad (8.5\text{-}86)$$

One approach is to convert Eq. 8.5-86 into a signal flow diagram consisting of amplifiers, delays, and summers.[43] Another approach is to break Eq. 8.5-86 into products of first- and second-order terms. An example of how the first approach works is illustrated by Fig. 8.5-17a. This is a general building block that consists of a combination of a stray-insensitive noninverting and inverting

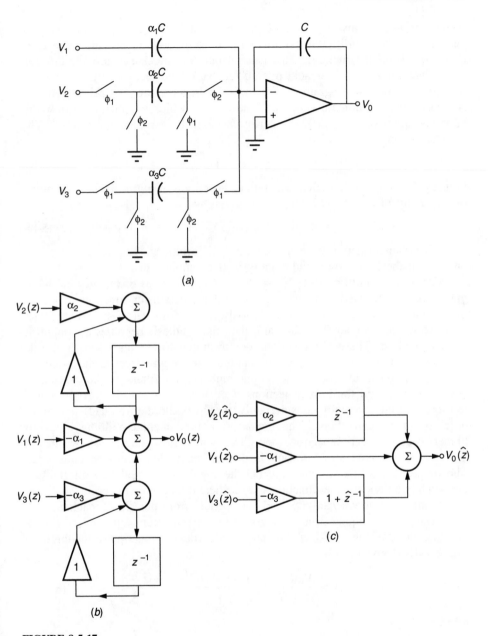

FIGURE 8.5-17
General building block: (*a*) SC circuit, (*b*) *z*-domain block diagram, (*c*) $\hat{z}$-domain block diagram.

integrators and an inverting amplifier. Note that V_1, V_2, and V_3 can be connected at arbitrarily different points or to the same node to provide more flexibility for different structures. This general building block can provide different paths, including local feedback, overall feedback, and feedforward. Figure 8.5-17b shows the flow diagram of Fig. 8.5-17a in terms of z^{-1} delay elements. A change of the z-domain variable is introduced, which simplifies the flow diagram and improves the sensitivity performance of the various realizations.[46] This transformation is

$$\hat{z} = z - 1 \qquad (8.5\text{-}87)$$

Figure 8.5-17c gives the $\hat{z}$ flow diagram of the circuit of Fig. 8.5-17a. The output of the circuit of Fig. 8.5-17c, $V_0(\hat{z})$, is given by

$$V_0(\hat{z}) = \alpha_2 \hat{z}^{-1} V_2(\hat{z}) - \alpha_1 V_1(\hat{z}) - \alpha_3(1 + \hat{z}^{-1}) V_3(\hat{z}) \qquad (8.5\text{-}88)$$

The transformation used in Eq. 8.5-87 is arbitrary. The design procedure outlined in the following could equally well be applied to $H(z)$. Note that Eq. 8.5-88 may be simplified if $V_2(\hat{z}) = V_3(\hat{z})$. Combinations of this general building block can be used to realize various z-domain transfer functions when the transformation of Eq. 8.5-87 is made to Eq. 8.5-86 to get $H(\hat{z})$. When $H(\hat{z})$ is converted to a signal flow diagram, then the synthesis becomes a straightforward procedure. These ideas will be demonstrated for second- and third-order structures, which can be cascaded to obtain a filter of any order in the z-domain.

One popular method of designing higher-order filters is the cascade of first-, second-, and third-order sections.[47,48] Because Fig. 8.5-17a represents a first-order filter, we will consider only the second-order (biquad) and third-order (triquad) realizations. The biquad is a fundamental building block for higher-order switched capacitor filters. The biquad flow diagram shown in Fig. 8.5-18 is a versatile structure and is one of many that could be considered. The properties of this structure are (1) the capability of realizing all stable z-domain biquadratic transfer functions, (2) sufficient flexibility to permit small total capacitance with low sensitivity, and (3) freedom from parasitic capacitances.

The general biquad structure is formed by the interconnection of the general building block of Fig. 8.5-17a. The biquadratic transfer function of the circuit of Fig. 8.5-18 is given as

$$H(\hat{z}) = \frac{V_{oz}(\hat{z})}{V_i(\hat{z})} = \frac{A_0 + A_1\hat{z}^{-1} + A_2\hat{z}^{-2}}{1 + C_1\hat{z}^{-1} + C_2\hat{z}^{-2}} \qquad (8.5\text{-}89)$$

where

$$A_0 = D_0 B_3 - D_3$$

$$A_1 = D_1 - D_3 + D_3 B_0 - D_0 B_1 - D_2 B_3 + D_0 B_3 \qquad (8.5\text{-}90)$$

$$A_2 = D_3 B_0 + D_2 B_1 - D_2 B_3 - D_1 B_0$$

$$C_1 = B_2 B_3 - B_0$$

$$C_2 = B_2 B_3 - B_1 B_2$$

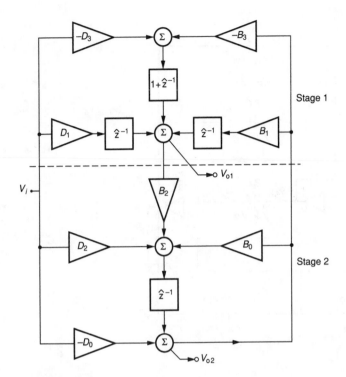

FIGURE 8.5-18
Signal flow diagram of a biquad.

It is observed in Fig. 8.5-18 that B_0 and B_1 are positive-feedback components. If B_0 and B_1 are zero, the filter will be stable from an ideal viewpoint. For nonzero values of B_0 and B_1, the filter will remain stable if B_3 is greater than B_1 and B_0 is less than $B_2 B_3$.

Figure 8.5-19a shows a switched capacitor implementation of the flow diagram of Fig. 8.5-18. The two outputs are designated as V_{o1} and V_{o2}. The most general output of this realization is at V_{o2} because each coefficient can be realized independently of the other. The transfer function at V_{o2} is

$$H(\hat{z}) = \frac{V_{o2}(\hat{z})}{V_i(\hat{z})} = \frac{D_0 + (D_3 B_2 - D_2)\hat{z}^{-1} + (D_3 B_2 - D_1 B_2)\hat{z}^{-2}}{1 + (B_2 B_3 - B_0)\hat{z}^{-1} + (B_2 B_3 - B_1 B_2)\hat{z}^{-2}}$$

$$(8.5\text{-}91)$$

Note that the individual Bs and Ds represent a ratio of two capacitors. The circuit can be simplified in a number of ways depending on the actual transfer function required. For instance, if there is a zero at $\hat{z} = -2$ (i.e., $z = 1$), the "bilinearly" equivalent analog-domain zero frequency is at $s = \infty$; and if the zero is neglected, then D_0 becomes zero. The switched capacitor implementation of Fig. 8.5-19a with the minimum number of switches is shown in Fig. 8.5-19b.

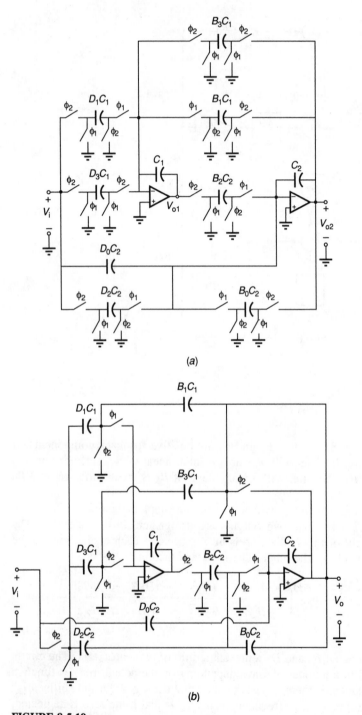

FIGURE 8.5-19
(a) Switched capacitor implementation of Fig. 8.5-18, (b) Switched capacitor biquad with a minimum number of switches.

Generally, the second-order z-domain transfer function is given in terms of its z-domain roots. A general expression for Eq. 8.5-91 in terms of the roots is

$$H(\hat{z}) = \frac{1 + (2 - 2r_o \cos \theta_o)\hat{z}^{-1} + (1 + r_o^2 - 2r_o \cos \theta_o)\hat{z}^{-2}}{1 + (2 - 2r \cos \theta)\hat{z}^{-1} + (1 + r^2 - 2r \cos \theta)\hat{z}^{-2}}$$

(8.5-92)

where the locations of the poles and zeros in the z-plane are at $r e^{\pm j \theta}$ and $r_o e^{\pm j \theta_o}$, respectively. Expressions for the root locations in terms of the coefficients are

$$r = [1 - B_1 B_2 + B_0]^{1/2}$$

(8.5-93)

$$\cos \theta = \frac{2 - B_2 B_3 + B_0}{2r}$$

(8.5-94)

$$r_o = [1 + (D_2 - D_1 B_2)/D_0]^{1/2}$$

(8.5-95)

and

$$\cos \theta_o = \frac{2 + (D_2 - D_3 B_2)/D_0}{2r_o}$$

(8.5-96)

A possible set of design equations is developed next. The root locations described by r, r_o, θ, and θ_o are assumed to be given. Because there are several extra degrees of freedom, we can arbitrarily choose B_2, B_3, D_2, and D_3. Therefore, the rest of the components can be calculated from

$$B_0 = 2r \cos \theta - 2 + B_2 B_3$$

(8.5-97)

$$B_1 = 0.5[2 - B_2 B_3 + B_0]$$

(8.5-98)

$$D_0 = \frac{D_2 - D_3 B_2}{2(r_o \cos \theta_o - 1)}$$

(8.5-99)

and

$$D_1 = \frac{D_2 + (1 - r_o^2)D_0}{B_2}$$

(8.5-100)

It is observed that the general biquad can be simplified by choosing as many of the capacitor values as possible to be equal to zero. The coefficients of Eq. 8.5-91 are a result of the multiplication and subtraction of several individual capacitor ratios. Thus, the biquad is capable of realizing very small coefficients. However, we must keep in mind that the sensitivity might be inversely proportional to that small difference. Typically, a tradeoff between sensitivities and total capacitance is possible and will be illustrated shortly.

Next, a third-order realization is developed. This structure is useful when the filter has an odd order. Figure 8.5-20a shows a general third-order structure in its signal flow diagram form. The transfer function of this structure is

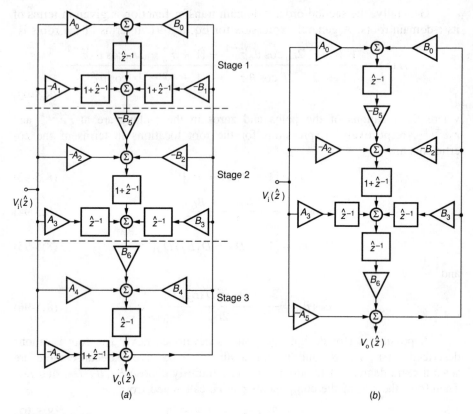

FIGURE 8.5-20
(a) General third-order block diagram, (b) Simplified third-order block diagram (signal flow graph).

$$H(\hat{z}) = \frac{V_o(\hat{z})}{V_i(\hat{z})} = \frac{\alpha_0 + \alpha_1\hat{z}^{-1} + \alpha_2\hat{z}^{-2} + \alpha_3\hat{z}^{-3}}{1 + \beta_1\hat{z}^{-1} + \beta_2\hat{z}^{-2} + \beta_3\hat{z}^{-3}} \qquad (8.5\text{-}101)$$

where

$$\alpha_0 = -A_5 \qquad (8.5\text{-}102)$$

$$\alpha_1 = A_1B_5B_6 - A_2B_6 + A_4 - A_5 \qquad (8.5\text{-}103)$$

$$\alpha_2 = 2A_1B_5B_6 - A_0B_5B_6 + A_3B_6 - A_2B_6 \qquad (8.5\text{-}104)$$

$$\alpha_3 = B_5B_6(A_1 - A_0) \qquad (8.5\text{-}105)$$

$$\beta_1 = B_2B_6 - B_1B_5B_6 - B_4 \qquad (8.5\text{-}106)$$

$$\beta_2 = B_0B_5B_6 - 2B_1B_5B_6 - B_3B_6 + B_2B_6 \qquad (8.5\text{-}107)$$

and

$$\beta_3 = B_5B_6(B_0 - B_1) \qquad (8.5\text{-}108)$$

Besides the transfer function of Eq. 8.5-101, two other transfer functions for each op amp output can be obtained. Equation 8.5-101 is chosen for its flexibility. A simplified yet versatile structure is considered next.

If $B_1 = B_4 = A_1 = A_4 = 0$, and if we omit the $1 + \hat{z}^{-1}$ following A_5, then the flow diagram Fig. 8.5-20b results. The coefficients of Eq. 8.5-101 become

$$-\alpha_0 = A_5 \tag{8.5-109}$$

$$-\alpha_1 = A_2 B_6 \tag{8.5-110}$$

$$-\alpha_2 = B_6(A_0 B_5 - A_3 + A_2) \tag{8.5-111}$$

$$-\alpha_3 = A_0 B_5 B_6 \tag{8.5-112}$$

$$\beta_1 = B_2 B_6 \tag{8.5-113}$$

$$\beta_2 = B_6(B_0 B_5 - B_3 + B_2) \tag{8.5-114}$$

and

$$\beta_3 = B_0 B_5 B_6 \tag{8.5-115}$$

A switched capacitor implementation of Fig. 8.5-20b is shown in Fig. 8.5-21. Table 8.5-2 shows the generality of the third-order building block in designing the transmission zeros. This table gives the values of the α coefficients and the capacitor ratios required for several conventional types of filters. In addition to the tradeoff between sensitivity and total capacitance mentioned before, we have added the constraint that the largest-to-smallest capacitor ratio be less than 10. More details regarding the tradeoff between sensitivity, output voltage swing, and total capacitance are given elsewhere.[49]

If the third-order specifications are given in terms of root locations, then it is necessary to relate the coefficients to the root locations. The root locations include one real pole at r_1, two complex poles at $r e^{\pm j\theta}$, and two complex zeros at $r_o e^{\pm j\theta_o}$. These expressions are

$$\alpha_0 = 0 \tag{8.5-116}$$

$$\alpha_1 = 1 \tag{8.5-117}$$

$$\alpha_2 = 2 - 2r_o \cos \theta_o \tag{8.5-118}$$

$$\alpha_3 = 1 + r_o^2 - 2r_o \cos \theta_o \tag{8.5-119}$$

$$\beta_1 = 3 - r_1 - 2r \cos \theta \tag{8.5-120}$$

$$\beta_2 = 3 - 2r_1 + r^2 - 4r \cos \theta + 2rr_1 \cos \theta \tag{8.5-121}$$

and

$$\beta_3 = 1 - r_1 + r^2 - r_1 r^2 - 2r \cos \theta + 2rr_1 \cos \theta \tag{8.5-122}$$

To illustrate the synthesis procedure, the second-order and third-order blocks are used to design a fifth-order low-pass filter. The specifications of the filter are a 0.125 dB passband ripple, a cutoff frequency of 3.4 kHz, a stopband minimum attenuation of 32 dB above 4.6 kHz and a clock frequency of 128 kHz. The design begins with the roots of the s-domain rational polynomial approximation, $H(s)$. These roots are mapped to the $\hat{z}$-domain through the bilinear transformation.[26]

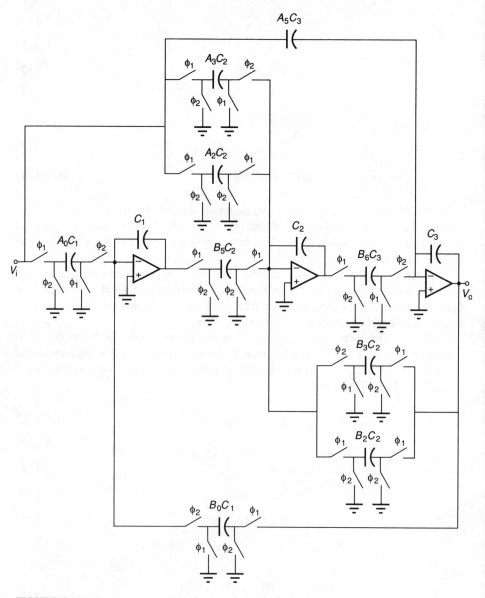

FIGURE 8.5-21
Switched capacitor implementation of Fig. 8.5-20b.

TABLE 8.5-2
Values of coefficients of zeros of the third-order filter

Filter type	Zeros in z-plane	Coefficient of $H(z)$				Corresponding capacitor ratios			
		α_0	α_1	α_2	α_3	A_0	A_2	A_3	A_5
Low-pass	$z_1 = -1$	0	0	0	1	B_0[a]	0	$A_0 B_5$	0
Band-pass	$z_1 = -1$ $z_2 = 1$	0	0	1	0	0	0	A_3[b]	0
High-pass	$z_1 = 1$	1	0	0	0	0	0	0	A_5[b]
Notch	$z_1 = e^{j\theta_0}$ $z_2 = e^{-j\theta_0}$	0	1	$2(1 - \cos\theta_0)$	$2(1 - \cos\theta_0)$	$\dfrac{\alpha_2}{B_5 B_6}$	$\dfrac{1}{B_6}$	$\dfrac{1}{B_6}$[c]	0

[a] $A_0 = B_0$ to obtain a 0 dB dc gain.
[b] A_3 and A_5 to be chosen to give the required center (cutoff) frequency gain.
[c] A_0, A_2, and A_3 can be scaled to obtain the desired dc gain.

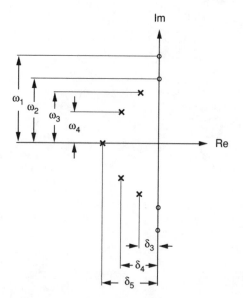

FIGURE 8.5-22
Root locations in the s-plane of the fifth-order filter: $\bigcirc$ = zeros, $\times$ = poles; ω_1 = 40.792×10^3, $\omega_2 = 28.367 \times 10^3$, $\omega_3 = 22.604 \times 10^3$, $\omega_4 = 17.83 \times 10^3$, $\delta_3 = 1.938 \times 10^3$, $\delta_4 = 8.514 \times 10^3$, $\delta_5 = 15.474 \times 10^3$.

The s-domain zero at infinity that maps to $\hat{z} = -2$ is ignored. The location of the roots in the s-domain are illustrated in Fig. 8.5-22. The second-order realization has two zeros and two poles, $\pm j\omega_2$ and $\delta_4 \pm j\omega_4$, respectively. The corresponding root locations in the $\hat{z}$-domain are $r = 0.92838$, $\theta = \pm 7.722°$, and $r_0 = 1.0$, $\theta_0 = \pm 12.928°$ for the poles and zeros, respectively. The third-order stage realizes two zeros and three poles: $\pm j\omega_1$, δ_5, and $\delta_3 \pm j\omega_3$, respectively. The corresponding root locations in the z-domain are $r = 0.938$, $\theta = \pm 9.88°$, $r_1 = 0.878$, $r_0 = 1.0$, and $\theta_0 = \pm 18.9°$ for the poles and zeros, respectively.

It should be noted that in obtaining the coefficients in both filters, the dc gain of each stage was adjusted to be near unity. For the specified values of r and θ, the capacitor ratios of the biquad can be calculated by setting $B_2 = 0.1$, $B_3 = 1.6$, $D_2 = 0.0$, and $D_3 \simeq 0.22$. The final results are summarized in Table 8.5-3. The total capacitance for the biquad is $28.172 \, C_u$. The capacitor ratios for the third-order building block are given in Table 8.5-4. The total capacitance for the third-order building block is $39.481 C_u$. After simplifications,[49] the total capacitance is $33.28 C_u$. The total filter capacitance is $C_T = 61.452 C_u$. It has been shown that there is a tradeoff between sensitivity, total capacitance, and dynamic range.[26] Figure 8.5-23 shows the resulting fifth-order low-pass filter realization.

TABLE 8.5-3
Capacitor values in units of C_μ for the biquad circuit

Capacitor	B_2C_2 B_3C_1	B_1C_1	B_0C_2 D_2C_2	D_3C_1	D_0C_2	D_1C_1	C_1	C_2
Value	1	6.2863	0	1	4.3336	0	4.5517	10

TABLE 8.5-4
Capacitor values in units of C_μ for the triquad circuit

Capacitor	A_0C_1 B_0C_1	C_1 C_3	B_6C_3 A_2C_2	A_3C_2	B_2C_2	B_3C_2	C_2	B_5C_2
Value	1	10	1	1	5.684	4.657	3.057	1.083

The performance of this filter is shown in Fig. 8.5-24. The simulated results and the experimental results agree quite closely.[50]

A brief overview of the methods of designing switched capacitor filters has been shown. The three approaches selected were resistor replacement or simulation by switched capacitor equivalents, the use of integrators to realize passive RLC prototype ladder filters, and the direct synthesis of the z-domain transfer function. Many more approaches exist, and they should be considered if the above approaches do not provide the required performance.

Because of the lack of space, topics such as the prewarping of the s-domain specifications to account for the $(\sin x)/x$ effect of the sample-and-hold circuit on the filter performance have not been discussed. Also, the influence of the switches and the op amp performance (gain and bandwidth) have not been considered. Another problem the designer is faced with when designing switched capacitor circuits is a method of analysis. Because the switched capacitor circuit is an analog sampled-data system, aliasing can occur, and it is often necessary to use an antialiasing filter, which must be a continuous-time filter. Fortunately, the accuracy requirement of the continuous-time, antialiasing filter is not severe, and RC active filter techniques can be used.

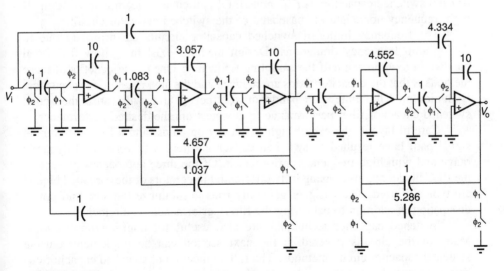

FIGURE 8.5-23
SC circuit diagram of the fifth-order filter, capacitor values in C_u units.

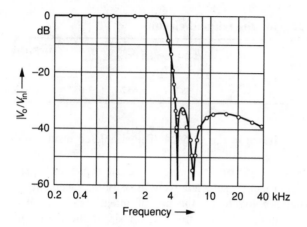

FIGURE 8.5-24
Experimental and theoretical frequency response of the filter of Fig. 8.5-23: $\bigcirc=$ experiment, $-$ = theory.

The success of switched capacitor filters has created the demand for increased performance in the area of dynamic range and frequency. The influence of the feedthrough of the switches has been found to be a serious factor in limiting dynamic range. Besides using small switches and other methods previously discussed to reduce feedthrough, it is important to keep the summing nodes of switched capacitor circuits physically away from the clock lines. In fact, any analog input line should be isolated from lines that carry digital signals. Another factor limiting the dynamic range is noise. The noise can come from the op amp or from switched capacitors (kT/C noise). Of particular concern is the folding of high-frequency noise into the baseband of the switched capacitor circuit.

The frequency limits of switched capacitor circuits are primarily due to the op amp frequency limitations. Design methods exist that allow the signal bandwidth to approach half the sampling frequency. One of the benefits of these methods is that the capacitor ratios are reduced and the area required for capacitors is minimum. The finite gain bandwidth of the op amp will cause the actual switched capacitor filter performance to deviate from the desired performance.

Careful layout, the use of high-frequency op amps, and a fully differential signal path have resulted in switched capacitor filters with very good dynamic range and with high-frequency performance. Of the three approaches presented, the RLC ladder approach using fully differential integrators or the cascaded biquad are typically used. The designer generally tries to minimize the area and power dissipation in addition to achieving the filter performance requirements.

Switched capacitor techniques are also useful for nonfilter applications. Many of the circuits covered in the next section can be implemented using switched capacitor circuit methods. The full application of switched capacitor circuit techniques has yet to be investigated with respect to analog signal processing circuits.

8.6 ANALOG SIGNAL PROCESSING CIRCUITS

One of the largest areas of application of analog signal processing circuits is filtering. This has been the subject of the last two sections. In this section, we consider nonfilter applications of analog signal processing circuits. These applications include precision breakpoint circuits, multipliers and modulators, oscillators, and phase-locked loops. Many other circuits and systems could be included, but these are representative of the concepts and principles.

8.6.1 Precision Breakpoint Circuits

In many applications it is necessary to realize a voltage transfer characteristic similar to those given in Fig. 8.6-1. In these transfer characteristics, the breakpoint is the point where two straight-line segments join, which is at the origin for each

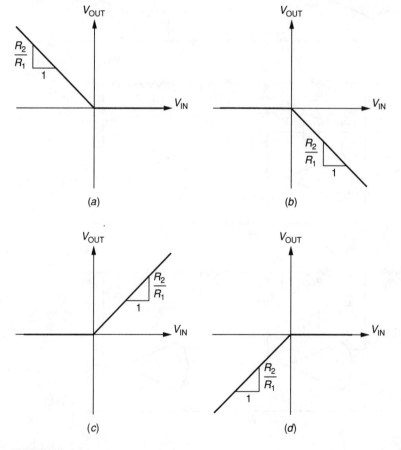

FIGURE 8.6-1
Four possible types of nonlinear voltage transfer characteristics having the breakpoint at $V_{\text{IN}} = 0$.

of these cases. If the technology used can implement a diode, a resistor, and an op amp, then Fig. 8.6-2 shows a realization of each of the respective voltage transfer characteristics of Fig. 8.6-1. The slopes of the realizations will be determined by the ratio of R_2 and R_1. Because the diodes are in the feedback path, they behave as ideal diodes. This permits the drain-gate connected MOSFET to function in place of the diodes in Fig. 8.6-2.

In every diode circuit, it is necessary to first find the breakpoints of the circuits related to either the input or output variable. In Fig. 8.6-2, the current

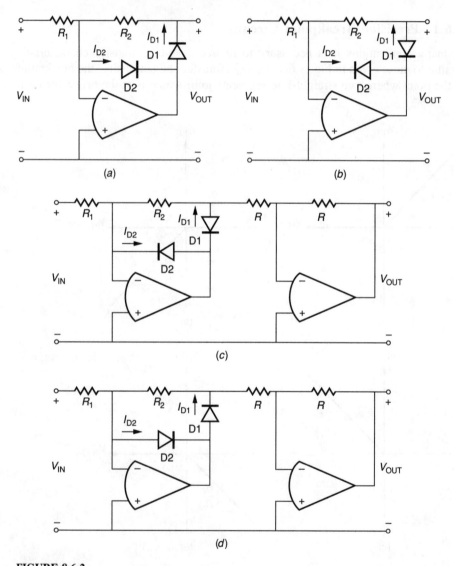

FIGURE 8.6-2
Realizations of the characteristics of Fig. 8.6-1: (a) Fig. 8.6-1a with slope $-R_2/R_1$, (b) Fig. 8.6-1b with slope $-R_2/R_1$, (c) Fig. 8.6-1c with slope R_2/R_1, (d) Fig. 8.6-1d with slope R_2/R_1.

flow in or out of the op amp can flow only through D1 or D2 but not both at the same time. Therefore, the only possible states of D1 and D2 are D1 on–D2 off or D1 off–D2 on. The breakpoint in the circuits of Fig. 8.6-2 will occur when both diode currents are zero. The direction of I_{D1} and I_{D2} is not important because they will be equated to zero to find the breakpoint. For example, consider Fig. 8.6-2a. The currents I_{D1} and I_{D2} can be expressed as

$$I_{D1} = \frac{V_{IN}}{R_1} + \frac{V_{OUT}}{R_2} \qquad I_{D2} = \frac{V_{OUT}}{R_2} \qquad (8.6\text{-}1)$$

Setting I_{D1} and I_{D2} to zero gives the breakpoints as $V_{OUT}(BP) = 0$ and $V_{IN}(BP) = 0$.

In many cases, the breakpoint is to be shifted away from zero. This can be accomplished for the circuit of Fig. 8.6-2b as illustrated in Fig. 8.6-3a. A dc voltage, E_r, has been connected to the inverting input through a resistor, R_3. Using the principles just explained, we solve for I_{D1} and I_{D2} as

$$I_{D1} = \frac{V_{IN}}{R_1} + \frac{E_r}{R_3} + \frac{V_{OUT}}{R_2} \qquad I_{D2} = \frac{V_{OUT}}{R_2} \qquad (8.6\text{-}2)$$

Setting I_{D1} and I_{D2} to zero in Eq. 8.6-2 gives the breakpoint as

$$V_{IN}(BP) = -\frac{E_r R_1}{R_3} \qquad V_{OUT}(BP) = 0 \qquad (8.6\text{-}3)$$

Figure 8.6-3b shows the voltage transfer characteristics of the circuit of Fig. 8.6-3a.

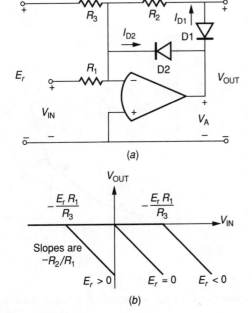

(a)

(b)

FIGURE 8.6-3
(a) Method of shifting the breakpoint of Fig. 8.6-1b, (b) Transfer characteristics of (a).

Mathematically, we may express the output voltage of Fig. 8.6-3a as

$$V_{OUT} = \begin{cases} -R_2 v_{IN}/R_1 + R_2 E_r/R_1 & V_{IN} \geq -R_1 E_r/R_3 \\ 0 & V_{IN} < -R_1 E_r/R_3 \end{cases} \qquad (8.6\text{-}4)$$

We note that E_R can be positive or negative, which will shift the breakpoint to the left or right, respectively. The same principle can be applied to the other circuits of Fig. 8.6-2 to develop a general capability of establishing a breakpoint at any value of V_{IN}.

These concepts can be extended to synthesize a voltage transfer function by using piecewise linear segments. Figure 8.6-4a shows a number of circuits similar to the circuit of Fig. 8.6-3a summed into a summing amplifier. The resulting

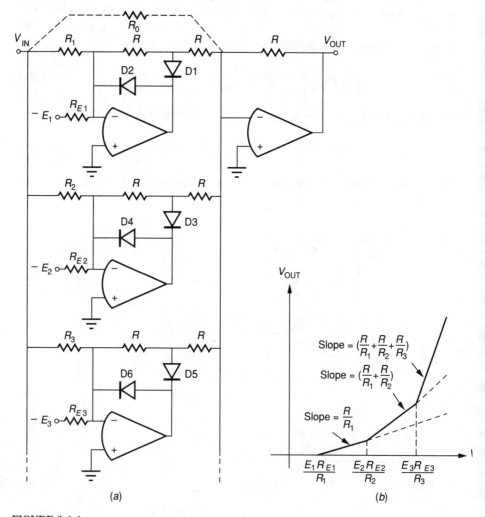

(a)   (b)

FIGURE 8.6-4
(a) Summation of individual segments to form a piecewise linear approximation, (b) Voltage transfer characteristics of (a).

transfer characteristic is shown in Fig. 8.6-4*b*. Each of the individual outputs implements one line segment. We note that all E_is can be identical, and the R_{Ei} resistors can be used to design the breakpoints. On the other hand, all R_{Ei}s can be identical and the E_i voltage sources used to design the breakpoints. The slopes of the line segments become increasingly larger and are indicated on the curve. If the diodes are all reversed and the polarities of E_i changed, the piecewise linear curve moves to the third quadrant. R_0 shown in Fig. 8.6-4*a* can be added to allow a line segment with a nonzero slope to go through the origin of Fig. 8.6-4*b*.

The curve of Fig. 8.6-4*b* is monotonically increasing in slope. If the slope is to decrease, then one could place an inverter in with each breakpoint circuit of Fig. 8.6-4*a* before summing its output. All possible monotonically increasing and decreasing slopes are realizable in any of the four quadrants using these ideas.

Although the diodes and op amps of the above circuits can easily be implemented in BJT or MOS technology, the resistors are not practical. Resistors are not sufficiently accurate for most applications and require too much area. A method of eliminating the resistors in MOS technology using switched capacitor methods will be presented next.

Consider the switched capacitor implementation of a noninverting amplifier shown in Fig. 8.6-5. This circuit is similar to the noninverting stray-insensitive integrator of Fig. 8.5-11 except for the switch added to discharge C_2 during the ϕ_1 phase. This switch essentially removes the memory of the integrator, resulting in an amplifier. It can be shown that the z-domain transfer function of the circuit of Fig. 8.6-5 is

$$H^{oe}(z) = \frac{V_{OUT}(z)}{V_{IN}(z)} = \frac{C_1}{C_2}z^{-1/2} \tag{8.6-5}$$

Equation 8.6-5 represents a noninverting gain function that is valid during the ϕ_2 phase and is delayed by a half clock period from the input. A sample and hold circuit can be added to hold the output for the entire clock period. If the output is sampled and held, then Eq. 8.6-5 is multiplied by $z^{-1/2}$ to get a full delay of $H^{oo}(z)$. One of the disadvantages of the circuit of Fig. 8.6-5 is that the op amp output is slewed to zero during each ϕ_1 phase and back to the desired output during each ϕ_2 phase. This is unnecessary and can be prevented by the introduction of more capacitors and switches as will be shown later.

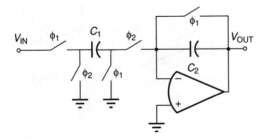

FIGURE 8.6-5
Noninverting switched capacitor amplifier realization.

If the leftmost pair of switches has the phasing reversed, then the amplifier is inverting, and the transfer function is given as

$$H(z) = \frac{V_{OUT}(z)}{V_{IN}(z)} = -\frac{C_1}{C_2} \tag{8.6-6}$$

where the output is valid only at the ϕ_2 phase. If we assume that the high sampling approximation is valid, then Fig. 8.6-5 can be considered as a simple noninverting or inverting amplifier depending upon the phasing of the leftmost switch pair.

The voltage transfer characteristics of Fig. 8.6-1 can be realized using MOS technology if we combine a comparator with the amplifier of Fig. 8.6-5, as shown in Fig. 8.6-6a. Note that the comparator output controls the switch that couples C_1 into the inverting input of the op amp (called the transfer switch). If this switch is open during the ϕ_2 phase period, the output of the op amp will be zero. If the transfer switch is closed during the ϕ_2 phase period, the output will be given by Eq. 8.6-5 or 8.6-6, depending on the phasing of the leftmost switch pair. To see how the circuit works, consider the circuit of Fig. 8.6-6a with a positive value of V_{IN}. The comparator output will be high, causing the transfer switch to be closed. Thus, the output is given by Eq. 8.6-5. If V_{IN} is less than zero, the comparator output is low, causing the transfer switch to be open. Therefore, the circuit of Fig. 8.6-6a realizes the voltage transfer curve of Fig. 8.6-1c with outputs valid during the ϕ_2 clock phase. If the comparator inputs are reversed, Fig. 8.6-6a realizes the voltage transfer curve of Fig. 8.6-1d. If the phases of the leftmost switches (input switches) are reversed, the circuit of Fig. 8.6-6b results. With the inputs to the comparator as shown, this circuit realizes the voltage transfer curve of Fig. 8.6-1b. If the comparator inputs are reversed, the voltage transfer curve of Fig. 8.6-1a is realized.

The switched capacitor breakpoint realizations can be implemented by alternate configurations, but all will utilize a comparator controlling one or more switches. It is easy to shift the breakpoint of the realization by connecting the

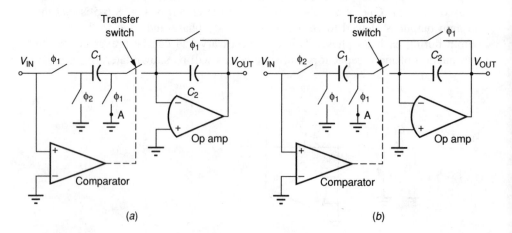

FIGURE 8.6-6
(a) Switched capacitor realization of Fig. 8.6-1c, (b) Switched capacitor realization of Fig. 8.6-1b.

grounded input terminal of the comparators of Fig. 8.6-6a and b to the voltage E_r. It is also necessary to remove point A from ground and connect it to the voltage E_r. A positive value of E_r applied to the inverting input of the comparator of Fig. 8.6-6a will cause the breakpoint to occur at $V_{IN} = E_r$. The outputs of several shifted breakpoint realizations can be summed in a manner similar to Fig. 8.6-4 to obtain a piecewise linear approximation of a voltage transfer function.[51] The switched capacitor realizations of the precision breakpoint circuits are compatible with MOS technology and have been employed in many commercial applications.

8.6.2 Modulators and Multipliers

Modulators include a class of circuits with multiple inputs where one input can modify or control the signal flow from the other input to the output. Figure 8.6-7 illustrates the modulator on a block diagram basis. $V_1(t)$ and $V_2(t)$ are input signals. The modulator output signal can be expressed in general as

$$V_{OUT}(t) = f_A[V_1(t)] f_B[V_2(t)] \qquad (8.6\text{-}7)$$

where f_A and f_B are two arbitrary functions of the respective inputs. If $f_A[V_1(t)]$ and $f_B[V_2(t)]$ are linearly dependent upon $V_1(t)$ and $V_2(t)$, respectively, the modulator is called a *multiplier*. Thus, Eq. 8.6-7 becomes

$$V_{OUT}(t) = K_1 V_1(t) V_2(t) \qquad (8.6\text{-}8)$$

where K_1 is the combination of the individual constants for $V_1(t)$ and $V_2(t)$.

Figure 8.6-8 shows a BJT modulator using the differential amplifier configuration of Fig. 6.4-7 with resistor loads and a current sink implemented by a current mirror. The output voltage can be expressed as

$$V_{OUT} = R_c(I_{C1} - I_{C2}) = \alpha_F I_{EE} R_c \left[\frac{1}{1 + e^{-V_1/V_t}} - \frac{1}{1 + e^{V_1/V_t}} \right]$$

$$(8.6\text{-}9)$$

using Eqs. 6.3-52 and 6.3-53. Equation 8.6-9 can be rewritten as

$$V_{OUT} = \alpha_F I_{EE} R_c \tanh\left(\frac{V_1}{2V_t}\right) \simeq I_{EE} R_c\left(\frac{V_1}{2V_t}\right) \qquad (8.6\text{-}10)$$

if V_1 is much less than 50 mV. Because I_{EE} is equal to $[V_2 - V_{BE}(on)]/R$, we may express Eq. 8.6-10 as

$$V_{OUT} = \frac{R_c}{2V_t R} V_1 \cdot [V_2 - V_{BE}(on)] = K_1 V_1[V_2 - V_{BE}(on)] \qquad (8.6\text{-}11)$$

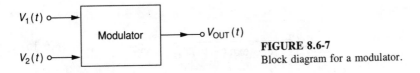

FIGURE 8.6-7
Block diagram for a modulator.

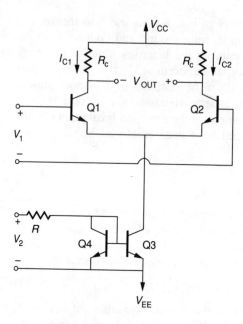

FIGURE 8.6-8
A simple BJT modulator using a differential amplifier.

The multiplier of Fig. 8.6-8 has several problems. The first is that V_2 is offset by $V_{BE}(on)$. The second is that V_2 must always be positive, resulting in a two-quadrant multiplier. A third problem is that the dynamic range is limited because of the approximation necessary to replace tanh x by x where $x = V_1/2V_t$ in Eq. 8.6-10.

The first two problems can be solved by the Gilbert cell[52] shown in Fig. 8.6-9. The Gilbert cell allows four-quadrant operation and is the basis for most integrated circuit balanced multipliers. The operation of this key cell is as follows. The collector currents of Q3 and Q4 are

$$I_{C3} = \frac{I_{C1}}{1 + \exp(-V_1/V_t)} \tag{8.6-12}$$

and

$$I_{C4} = \frac{I_{C1}}{1 + \exp(V_1/V_t)} \tag{8.6-13}$$

Similarly the collector currents for Q5 and Q6 are

$$I_{C5} = \frac{I_{C2}}{1 + \exp(V_1/V_t)} \tag{8.6-14}$$

and

$$I_{C6} = \frac{I_{C2}}{1 + \exp(-V_1/V_t)} \tag{8.6-15}$$

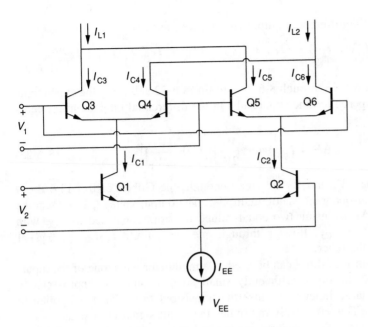

FIGURE 8.6-9
The Gilbert multiplier cell.

The two collector currents I_{C1} and I_{C2} can be expressed as

$$I_{C1} = \frac{I_{EE}}{1 + \exp(-V_2/V_t)} \tag{8.6-16}$$

and

$$I_{C2} = \frac{I_{EE}}{1 + \exp(V_2/V_t)} \tag{8.6-17}$$

Substituting Eqs. 8.6-16 and 8.6-17 into Eqs. 8.6-12 through 8.6-15 results in

$$I_{C3} = \frac{I_{EE}}{[1 + \exp(-V_1/V_t)][1 + \exp(-V_2/V_t)]} \tag{8.6-18}$$

$$I_{C4} = \frac{I_{EE}}{[1 + \exp(V_1/V_t)][1 + \exp(-V_2/V_t)]} \tag{8.6-19}$$

$$I_{C5} = \frac{I_{EE}}{[1 + \exp(V_1/V_t)][1 + \exp(V_2/V_t)]} \tag{8.6-20}$$

and

$$I_{C6} = \frac{I_{EE}}{[1 + \exp(-V_1/V_t)][1 + \exp(V_2/V_t)]} \tag{8.6-21}$$

Next we define the differential output current, ΔI, as

$$\Delta I = (I_{C3} + I_{C5}) - (I_{C4} + I_{C6}) = (I_{C3} - I_{C6}) - (I_{C4} - I_{C5})$$

$$(8.6\text{-}22)$$

Substituting Eqs. 8.6-18 through 8.6-21 into Eq. 8.6-22 and using the exponential formulaes for hyperbolic functions results in the differential output current being expressed as

$$\Delta I = I_{EE}\left[\tanh\left(\frac{V_1}{2V_t}\right)\right]\left[\tanh\left(\frac{V_2}{2V_t}\right)\right] \qquad (8.6\text{-}23)$$

If the input signals V_1 and V_2 are small enough, the Gilbert cell of Fig. 8.6-9 functions as a four-quadrant analog multiplier. The output voltage, V_{OUT}, can be generated from ΔI by using two equal-valued resistors connected to V_{CC} with current $I_{L1}(=I_{C3} + I_{C5})$ flowing through one and current $I_{L2}(=I_{C4} + I_{C6})$ flowing through the other.

The circuit of Fig. 8.6-9 can be used as a modulator when one of the inputs is very large and the other sufficiently small so that tanh x is approximately equal to x. The large input will cause the transistors to which it is applied to act like switches. This effectively multiplies the small signal by a square wave. Such modulators are called *synchronous modulators* and have many applications in signal processing, including demodulation and phase detection. The amplitude range of V_2 can be extended considerably by placing resistors between the emitters and the I_{EE} current source of the Gilbert cell.

The amplitude constraints on the inputs of the Gilbert cell can be removed using a predistortion technique that results in a linear relationship between V_1 and V_{OUT} and V_2 and V_{OUT}. Figure 8.6-10 illustrates the complete four-quadrant multiplier. The three boxes, which are voltage-to-current converters or current-to-voltage converters, will be considered shortly. The predistortion is implemented by the emitters of Q7 and Q8. The currents I_9 and I_{10} create a voltage between the emitters of Q7 and Q8 that is proportional to the inverse hyperbolic tangent of V_1. This will remove the hyperbolic tangent expressions in Eq. 8.6-23.

The analysis of the circuit of Fig. 8.6-10 can be accomplished as follows. It can be shown that the currents through base-emitter junctions that are connected in series, such as Q7, Q3, Q4, and Q8, can be expressed as

$$I_9 I_3 = I_4 I_{10} \qquad (8.6\text{-}24)$$

where $I_7 = I_9$ and $I_8 = I_{10}$. Similarly, for the series connection of Q7, Q6, Q5, and Q8, we have

$$I_9 I_6 = I_5 I_{10} \qquad (8.6\text{-}25)$$

Next we note that

$$I_1 = I_3 + I_4 \qquad (8.6\text{-}26)$$

$$I_2 = I_5 + I_6 \qquad (8.6\text{-}27)$$

$$I_{L1} = I_3 + I_5 \qquad (8.6\text{-}28)$$

$$I_{L2} = I_4 + I_6 \qquad (8.6\text{-}29)$$

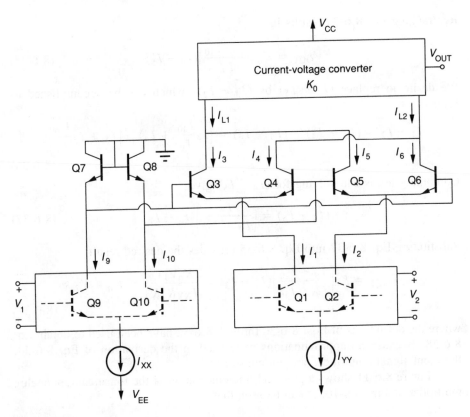

FIGURE 8.6-10
Complete four-quadrant analog multiplier.

and

$$I_{XX} = I_9 + I_{10} \tag{8.6-30}$$

Let us assume that the transfer characteristics of the rectangular blocks of Fig. 8.6-10 are given by

$$I_9 - I_{10} = V_1/K_1 \tag{8.6-31}$$

$$I_1 - I_2 = V_2/K_2 \tag{8.6-32}$$

and

$$V_{OUT} = K_o(I_{L2} - I_{L1}) \tag{8.6-33}$$

where K_o, K_1, and K_2 are constants depending on the implementation. Replacing I_{L2} and I_{L1} by Eqs. 8.6-28 and 8.6-29 results in

$$V_{OUT} = K_o[(I_4 + I_6) - (I_3 + I_5)] = K_o\left[\left(I_4 + I_5\frac{I_{10}}{I_9}\right) - \left(I_4\frac{I_{10}}{I_9} + I_5\right)\right] \tag{8.6-34}$$

Rearranging Eq. 8.6-34 results in

$$V_{OUT} = K_o\left(\frac{I_9 - I_{10}}{I_9}\right)(I_4 - I_5) \tag{8.6-35}$$

We desire to replace $(I_4 - I_5)$ by $(I_1 - I_2)$, which can be accomplished as follows.

$$I_1 - I_2 = (I_3 + I_4) - (I_5 + I_6) = \left(I_4\frac{I_{10}}{I_9} + I_4\right) - \left(I_5 + I_5\frac{I_{10}}{I_9}\right) \tag{8.6-36}$$

Combining terms and solving for $(I_4 - I_5)$ gives

$$(I_4 - I_5) = \left(\frac{I_9}{I_9 + I_{10}}\right)(I_1 - I_2) \tag{8.6-37}$$

Substituting Eq. 8.6-37 into Eq. 8.6-35 provides the desired result.

$$V_{OUT} = K_o\left(\frac{I_9 - I_{10}}{I_9 + I_{10}}\right)(I_1 - I_2) = \frac{K_o V_1 V_2}{I_{XX}K_1 K_2} = K_m V_1 V_2 \tag{8.6-38}$$

where the definitions of Eqs. 8.6-30 through 8.6-32 have been used to obtain Eq. 8.6-38. Because no approximations were used in the derivation of Eq. 8.6-38, the input signal amplitudes are not constrained.

Figure 8.6-11 shows a practical implementation of the four-quadrant analog multiplier of Fig. 8.6-10. It can be seen that

$$I_1 - I_2 = \frac{2V_2}{R_Y} \tag{8.6-39}$$

and

$$I_9 - I_{10} = \frac{2V_1}{R_X} \tag{8.6-40}$$

where it has been assumed that the part of V_1 and V_2 across the base-emitter of Q9, Q10, and Q1, Q2 are small compared to the drop across the resistors. Substituting Eqs. 8.6-39 and 8.6-40 into Eq. 8.6-38 results in

$$V_{OUT} = \frac{4K_o R_c V_1 V_2}{I_{XX}R_X R_Y} = K_m V_1 V_2 \tag{8.6-41}$$

where R is much greater than R_c. These concepts have been used to implement high-performance four-quadrant analog multipliers having good performance. One of the problems with the integrated circuit implementation is the need to be able to trim the various errors due to offsets and mismatches.

Four-quadrant multipliers have also been implemented in MOS technology.[53-56] Most of the realizations use a linearized Gilbert cell approach similar to the bipolar implementation above. A somewhat different approach is based on the cascade of two differential amplifier pairs has been found to give good results.[53] The principle of operation is illustrated in Fig. 8.6-12. If we assume

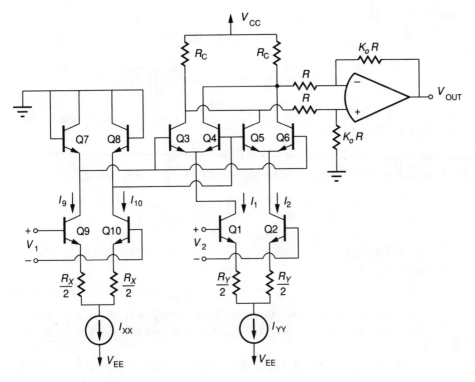

FIGURE 8.6-11
Practical implementation of Fig. 8.6-10.

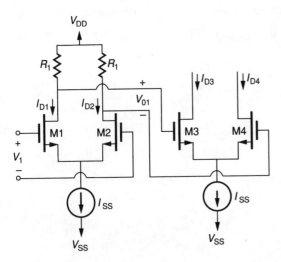

FIGURE 8.6-12
Cascaded MOS differential amplifiers.

that M1 and M2 are in the saturation region, then using Eqs. 6.3-7 and 6.3-8, we may write

$$I_{D1} - I_{D2} = I_{SS}\left[\frac{\beta_1 V_1^2}{I_{SS}} - \frac{\beta_1^2 V_1^4}{4I_{SS}^2}\right]^{1/2} = \beta_1 V_1 \left[\frac{I_{SS}}{\beta_1} - \frac{V_1^2}{4}\right]^{1/2}$$

(8.6-42)

whre $\beta_1 = KW_1/L1$. It is seen that $I_{D1} - I_{D2}$ depends nonlinearly on V_1 and I_{SS}. Let us define V_{O1} as

$$V_{O1} = -R_1(I_{D1} - I_{D2})$$

(8.6-43)

We can find a similar expression to Eq. 8.6-42 for $I_{D3} - I_{D4}$, which is

$$I_{D3} - I_{D4} = \beta_3 V_{O1}\left[\frac{I_{SS}}{\beta_3} - \frac{V_{O1}^2}{4}\right]^{1/2}$$

(8.6-44)

where $\beta_3 = kW_3/L3$. If we restrict V_1 to less than $0.3(I_{SS}/\beta_1)^{1/2}$, then we can approximate Eq. 8.6-42 as

$$I_{D1} - I_{D2} \simeq \beta_1 V_1 [I_{SS}/\beta_1]^{1/2}$$

(8.6-45)

It has been shown that this assumption results in less than 0.2% total harmonic distortion in $I_{D1} - I_{D2}$. Substituting Eqs. 8.6-43 and 8.6-45 into Eq. 8.6-44 results in

$$I_{D3} - I_{D4} = V_1[-R_1 I_{SS}(\beta_1\beta_3)^{1/2}][1 - (\beta_1\beta_3 R_1^2 V_1^2/4)]^{1/2}$$

(8.6-46)

It is seen that $I_{D3} - I_{D4}$ depends linearly on I_{SS}. However, there is still a nonlinear dependence upon V_1. This dependence could be removed by restricting the amplitude of $I_{D3} - I_{D4}$. An alternative approach is to use the predistortion circuit of Fig. 8.6-13. In this circuit, V_1 is created by the difference in two currents, $I_{X1} - I_{X2}$. This difference, designated as I_X, can be expressed as

$$I_X = I_{X1} - I_{X2} = V_1(I_{DX}\beta_5)^{1/2}[1 - (\beta_5/4I_{DX})V_1^2]^{1/2}$$

(8.6-47)

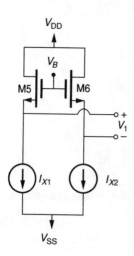

FIGURE 8.6-13

Predistortion circuit for the cascade MOS differential multiplier of Fig. 8.6-12.

where $I_{DX} = I_{X1} + I_{X2}$. Since the bracketed terms of Eqs. 8.6-46 and 8.6-47 have the same form, we can achieve predistortion by equating these two terms to get

$$\beta_5 = \beta_1 \beta_3 R_1^2 I_{DX} \qquad (8.6\text{-}48)$$

Therefore, Eq. 8.6-46 can be reduced to

$$I_O = I_{D3} - I_{D4} = -R_1 \left[\frac{\beta_1 \beta_3}{I_{DX} \beta_5} \right]^{1/2} I_{SS} I_X \qquad (8.6\text{-}49)$$

Equation 8.6-49 is the form of an ideal current multiplier. I_{SS} and I_X will be generated by voltage-to-differential current amplifiers, and the output voltage will be derived from I_O.

In order to get four-quadrant operation, I_{SS} must be able to be negative. This can be accomplished by taking the difference of two of the preceding circuits. The resulting MOS realization using only n-channel transistors is shown in Fig. 8.6-14. Several practical modifications can be made to improve the performance of the multiplier with regard to temperature and linearity. This MOS four-quadrant analog multiplier is capable of linearity better than 0.3% at 75% of full scale. It has a bandwidth of dc to 1.5 MHz and an output noise 77 dB below full scale.

Other techniques exist that allow the implementation of multipliers compatible with CMOS technology. A straightforward approach using an A/D and a D/A converter is shown in Fig. 8.6-15. The input to the A/D converter is one of the multiplier inputs designated as V_1. The reference voltage for an n-bit, A/D converter is provided by another analog input, V_2, to the multiplier. The digital output word of the A/D converter is given as

$$D = \frac{V_1}{V_2} = b_1 2^{-1} + b_2 b^{-2} + \cdots + b_{n-1} 2^{-n+1} + b_n 2^{-n} \qquad (8.6\text{-}50)$$

where D is digital word for the value of V_1 scaled by V_2. This digital word is then applied to an n-bit, D/A converter that has an analog input, V_3, applied as its reference voltage. The analog output of the D/A converter is given as

$$V_O = DV_3 = b_1 2^{-2} + b_2 2^{-2} + \cdots + b_{n-1} 2^{n-1} + b_n 2^{-n} \qquad (8.6\text{-}51)$$

Substituting Eq. 8.6-50 into Eq. 8.6-51 results in the following multiplier/divider with n-bit resolution.

$$V_O = \frac{V_1 V_3}{V_2} \qquad (8.6\text{-}52)$$

Any of the D/A and A/D converters of Sec. 8.2 and 8.3 can be used to implement a multiplier by this principle.

In the preceding results, we notice that the V_2 input of Fig. 8.6-15 is a dividing input. Obviously, V_2 cannot be zero. Another method of implementing a divider circuit is shown in Fig. 8.6-16. Figure 8.6-16a shows the block diagram

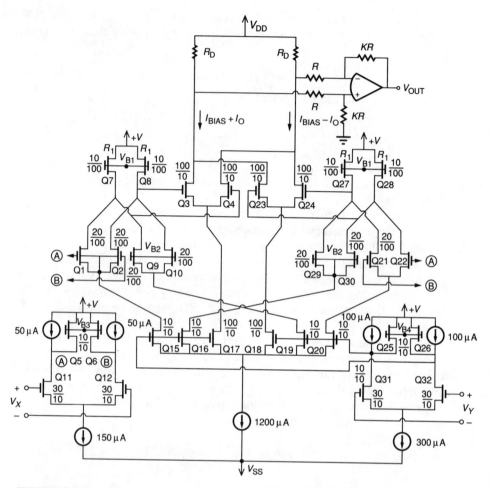

FIGURE 8.6-14
MOS four-quadrant analog current multiplier simplified schematic (values shown are W/L in microns/microns).

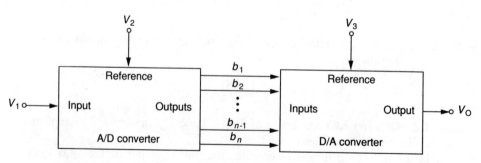

FIGURE 8.6-15
A/D–D/A converter analog multiplier.

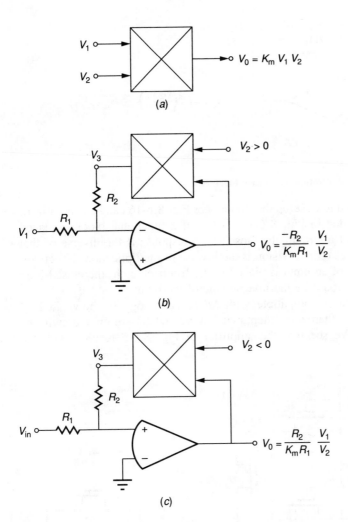

FIGURE 8.6-16
a) Block diagram symbol for a multiplier, (b) Negative divider, (c) Positive divider.

symbol for a multiplier. If the multiplier is placed in the feedback path of an inverting amplifier, as shown in Fig. 8.6-16b, then the output can be written as

$$V_O = \frac{-R_1}{K_m R_2}\left(\frac{V_1}{V_2}\right) \tag{8.6-53}$$

where $V_2 > 0$. If $V_2 < 0$ and the input terminals of the op amp are reversed, as indicated in Fig. 8.6-16c, a positive divider circuit is obtained. The phase margin of the op amp in Fig. 8.6-16 will be reduced because of the presence of the multiplier in the feedback path.

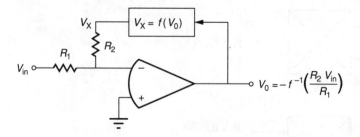

FIGURE 8.6-17
Illustration of the principle of creating the inverse function.

The principle used to develop the dividers of Fig. 8.6-16 can be generalized. This principle, illustrated in Fig. 8.6-17, is that if a functional block is placed in the feedback path of a circuit, the closed-loop response is the inverse of that function. In the previous case, division is the inverse of multiplication. If a circuit that generates the sine of an input is placed in the feedback path, the closed-loop transfer characteristic would be the inverse sine of the input.

A simple modulator compatible with MOS technology is shown in Fig. 8.6-18. If V_2 is greater than zero, then switches S2 and S3 are on and switches S1 and S4 are off. We see that the amplifier of Fig. 8.6-5 results, with the

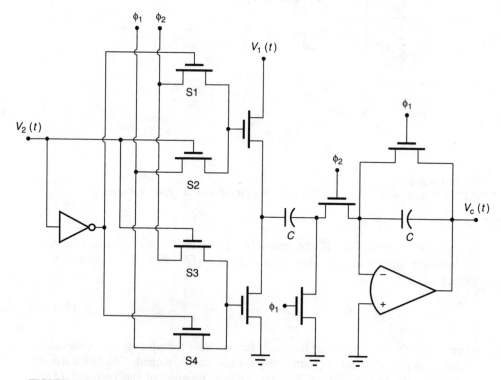

FIGURE 8.6-18
A modulator compatible with MOS technology.

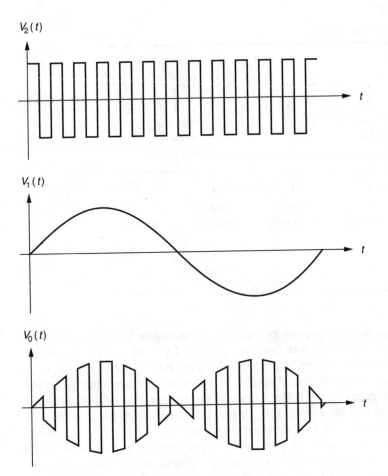

FIGURE 8.6-19
Illustration of the waveforms of Fig. 8.6-18 used as a modulator.

corresponding transfer function of Eq. 8.6-5. If V_2 is less than zero, then switches S1 and S4 are on and switches S2 and S3 are off. The phasing is reversed on the input switches, resulting in the inverting transfer function of Eq. 8.6-6. If the output is sampled and held, or if the high sampling approximation is valid, the effect of V_2 is to multiply V_1 by $+1$ when $V_2 > 0$ and by -1 when $V_2 < 0$. Figure 8.6-19 shows the waveforms of the modulator of Fig. 8.6-18 when V_1 is a sinusoid and V_2 is a square wave whose frequency is greater than that of the sinusoid but much less than the clock frequency of ϕ_1 and ϕ_2.

8.6.3 Oscillators

Oscillators are circuits that convert dc power into a periodic waveform or signal. Oscillators can be classified as shown in Table 8.6-1. The two general classes are tuned and untuned oscillators. Tuned oscillators produce nearly sinusoidal

TABLE 8.6-1
Classification of oscillators

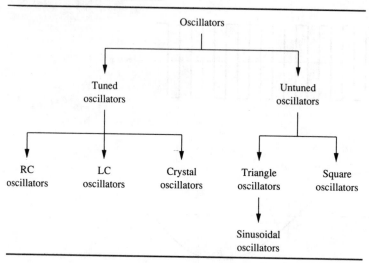

outputs, whereas untuned oscillators produce square and/or triangle waveforms. Tuned oscillators can be further divided into RC, LC, and crystal oscillators. We shall only consider RC oscillators since these are most suitable for integrated circuit technology, although crystal oscillators are often employed with the crystal external to the integrated circuit. The outputs of the untuned oscillator are typically square waves and triangle waves. The untuned oscillator can create a sinusoid by applying the triangle wave to a sine-shaping circuit, such as the one considered in Prob. 8.40 or one made up from a sufficient number of piecewise linear line segments. The untuned oscillators are compatible with integrated circuit technology, which in part accounts for their widespread use. They are also capable of implementing a voltage-controlled oscillator (VCO), which has many uses in signal processing circuits. Due to lack of space, the considerations of oscillators will be limited. Much more information can be found in the references.[57-61]

The following discussion will consider both tuned and untuned oscillators. The principles of operation and an example will be given. Only oscillators that use op amps, capacitors, and resistors or resistor equivalents will be considered. Figure 8.6-20 shows a block diagram of a single-loop feedback system. This diagram consists of an amplifier (A), a feedback network (β), and a summing junction. The variables shown are V_S, V_F, V_I, and V_O which are the source, feedback, input, and output voltages, respectively. The $+$ sign next to the feedback input to the summing junction indicates that the feedback is positive. If the circuit of Fig. 8.6-20 is assumed to be linear, the *loop gain*, G, is the voltage gain around the loop when $V_S = 0$ and is expressed as

$$G\Big|_{V_S=0} = A\beta \tag{8.6-54}$$

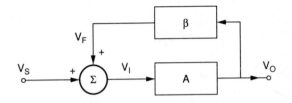

FIGURE 8.6-20

Block diagram of a single-loop feedback system.

The *closed-loop gain*, A_f, is equal to V_O/V_S and is given as

$$A_f = \frac{V_O}{V_S} = \frac{A}{1 - A\beta} = \frac{A}{1 - G} \tag{8.6-55}$$

The principle of a tuned oscillator can be seen from Eq. 8.6-55. If there is no input, $V_S = 0$, then for a finite output, V_O, Eq. 8.6-55 must be equal to infinity. This can only happen if $G = 1$. Thus, the criterion for oscillation in a tuned oscillator is

$$\text{Loop gain} = G(j\omega_0) = A(j\omega_0)\beta(j\omega_0) = 1 \tag{8.6-56}$$

where ω_0 is called the *radian frequency of oscillation*. An alternative form of Eq. 8.6-56 is

$$\text{Re}\,[G(j\omega_0)] + j\,\text{Im}\,[G(j\omega_0)] = 1 + j\,0 \tag{8.6-57}$$

or

$$|\,G(j\omega_0)\,|\,\angle\text{Arg}\,[G(j\omega_0)] = 1\angle 0° \tag{8.6-58}$$

In order to satisfy this criterion, the oscillator must be able to achieve a phase shift of 360° at some frequency, ω_0, where the loop gain is exactly unity. The analysis of oscillators is simple and consists of calculating the loop gain and using Eq. 8.6-56, 8.6-57, or 8.6-58 to find the frequency of oscillation, ω_0, and the magnitude of the amplifier gain, A, necessary for oscillation. Figure 8.6-21a shows an RC oscillator called the *Wien bridge oscillator*. This oscillator consists of an amplifier, whose gain is K, and a feedback network consisting of R_1, C_1, R_2, and C_2. Figure 8.6-21b shows how to open the feedback loop in order to calculate the loop gain, G. The key principle in opening the feedback loop is to do so at a point in the loop where the resistance looking forward in the loop is much greater than the resistance looking backward in the loop. In this case, the op amp in the noninverting configuration offers infinite resistance looking into the noninverting terminal. Note that the loop could also be broken at point A because resistance looking back into the op amp with negative feedback approaches zero. Assuming $R_1 = R_2 = R$ and $C_1 = C_2 = C$, the loop gain can be written as

$$G(s) = \frac{K(s/RC)}{s^2 + (3/RC)s + (1/RC)^2} \tag{8.6-59}$$

Substituting for s by $j\omega$ and equating to $1 + j\,0$ results in

$$G(j\omega_0) = \frac{jK\omega_0/RC}{[(1/RC)^2 - \omega_0^2] + j3\omega_0/RC} = 1 + j0 \tag{8.6-60}$$

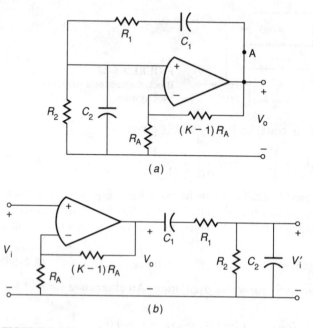

FIGURE 8.6-21
(a) Wien bridge RC oscillator, (b) Open-loop version of (a).

Equation 8.6-60 is satisfied if $K = 3$ at $\omega_0 = 1/RC$, which are precisely the conditions for oscillation of the oscillator of Fig. 8.6-21a. To obtain a 1 kHz oscillator, we could choose $C = 0.01$ μF, which gives $R = 15.9$ kΩ. Unfortunately, Fig. 8.6-21 is not practical for IC technologies unless the resistors were replaced with switched capacitors.

The amplitude of oscillation is indeterminate in the linear tuned oscillator. In practice, the amplitude of the oscillation is determined by a limiting nonlinearity. Figure 8.6-22 shows a possible nonlinear voltage transfer characteristic for the amplifier with gain K in Fig. 8.6-21a. For small values of V_O, the gain of the amplifier is designed to be greater than K (3 in the preceding example). When the gain is greater than 3, the amplitude of the sinusoidal oscillation grows. As the amplitude grows, the average gain over one cycle becomes smaller. The oscillator stabilizes at the amplitude where the time average gain is approximately equal to 3. If the amplitude should increase above this level for some reason, the oscillation will begin to decay because the effective gain is less than K. The amplitude stabilization is an important part of the oscillator. If the harmonic content of the sinusoid can be large, then the limiting effects of the power supplies can be used, although the waveform will no longer be sinusoidal. Many different schemes have been successfully used to achieve a stable oscillator amplitude. These include piecewise limiting circuits, thermistors, and the large signal transfer characteristics of differential amplifiers.

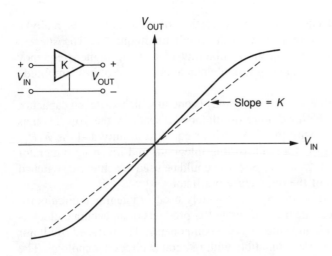

FIGURE 8.6-22
Nonlinear amplifier transfer function necessary for amplitude stabilization.

Because the RC products determine the oscillator frequency, the accuracy of an untrimmed integrated RC oscillator may not be sufficient. Switched capacitor techniques can be used to replace the resistors of the RC oscillators with resistor equivalents. Figure 8.6-23 shows a switched capacitor realization of the circuit of Fig. 8.6-21a. The resistor ratio, R_A/R_B, is assumed to be sufficiently accurate for this realization. If the high sampling assumption holds, then we may simply replace the resistor R with a switched capacitor equivalent resistance of T/C_R to get

$$\omega_0 \simeq \frac{C_R}{CT} = \frac{C_R}{C}f_c \tag{8.6-61}$$

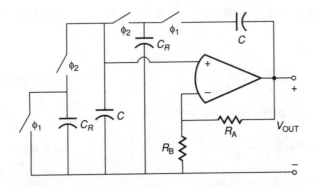

FIGURE 8.6-23
A switched capacitor realization of the Wien bridge RC oscillator of Fig. 8.6-21a.

We see that a switched capacitor implementation of an oscillator is really a circuit that scales the clock frequency to the oscillator frequency. The success of this implementation depends on the availability of a stable higher-frequency oscillator, f_c. The switched capacitor implementation also requires amplitude limiting.

The quadrature oscillator (see Prob. 8.42) is one in which switched capacitor techniques are suitable. The quadrature oscillator is essentially the Tow-Thomas realization of Fig. 8.4-11c with the Q_iR resistor equal to infinity and the R/H_{oi} resistor removed. The result is a noninverting integrator and inverting integrator cascaded in a loop. The integrators of Sec. 8.5 could be used to achieve a switched capacitor implementation of the quadrature oscillator.

In general, the tuned oscillator is not widely used in integrated circuits for several reasons. The requirement for accurate RC products or an accurate clock is difficult to accomplish without using external components. The untuned oscillator or relaxation oscillator is more compatible with integrated circuit technology. The principle of operation can be seen from the block diagram of Fig. 8.6-24. This block diagram consists of an integrator cascaded with a bistable circuit. Although we have not yet discussed the realization of the bistable circuit, let us first consider the operation of Fig. 8.6-24. During the time interval from 0 to T_1, the integrator integrates the voltage L_+ provided by the bistable circuit. If K is the constant of integration, we find that the value of V_T at $t = T_1$ is given as

$$V_T(T_1) = S_- + K \int_0^{T_1} L_+ dt = S_- + KL_+T_1 = S_+ \qquad (8.6\text{-}62)$$

From Eq. 8.6-62, we may solve for the time, T_1, to get

$$T_1 = \frac{S_+ - S_-}{KL_+} \qquad (8.6\text{-}63)$$

We may solve for $V_T(T_2)$ using the same methods to get

$$V_T(T_2) = V_T(T_1) + K \int_{T_1}^{T_2} L_- dt = S_- + KT_2L_- = S_- \qquad (8.6\text{-}64)$$

Solving for T_2 gives

$$T_2 = \frac{S_- - S_+}{KL_-} \qquad (8.6\text{-}65)$$

The sum of T_1 and T_2 gives the period T and is written as

$$T = \frac{1}{f_o} = T_1 + T_2 = \left[\frac{S_+ - S_-}{K}\right]\left[\frac{1}{L_+} - \frac{1}{L_-}\right] = \frac{4S}{KL} \qquad (8.6\text{-}66)$$

if $L_+ = -L_- = L$ and $S_+ = -S_- = S$.

The above equations show that the bistable is a key element in the untuned oscillator. The bistable is a circuit that has two stable output states and exhibits hysteresis when switching between the two states. Bistables may be clockwise or counterclockwise and can be shifted from the origin. Figure 8.6-25 shows the two possible generalized bistable characteristics. In this case, $L_+ = V_Y + V_L, L_- = V_Y - V_L, S_+ = V_X + V_H$, and $S_- = V_X - V_H$. Generally, $L_+ = L_-$ and $S_+ = S_-$. Figure 8.6-26a shows a realization of a clockwise (CW) bistable. If the output, V_S, is equal to V_{HH} (the positive power supply for the op amp), then the voltage at the noninverting input of the op amp is $V_{HH}R_3/(R_2 + R_3)$. If the input, V_T, is less than this value, then the output is in fact equal to V_{HH}. However, if V_T

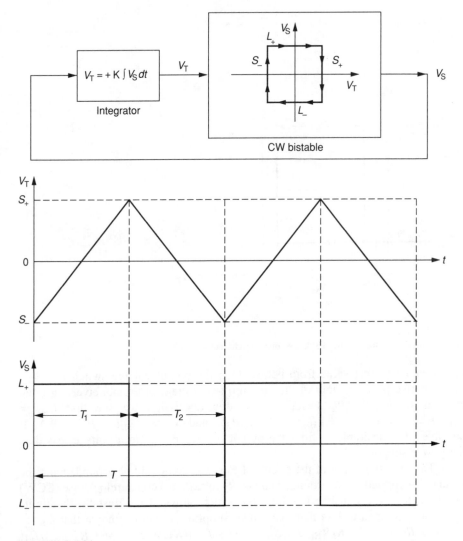

FIGURE 8.6-24
Block diagram of an untuned oscillator and the resulting waveforms.

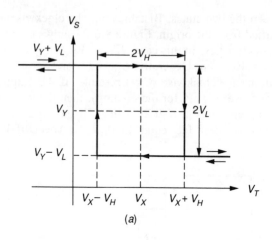

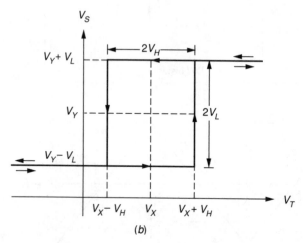

FIGURE 8.6-25

(a) CW bistable characteristic, (b) CCW bistable characteristic.

increases above this value from below, then the output voltage switches to V_{LL} (the negative power supply of the op amp) and voltage at the noninverting input changes to $V_{LL}R_3/(R_2 + R_3)$. From this discussion we see that $L_+ = V_{HH}, L_- = V_{LL}, S_+ = V_{HH}R_3/(R_2 + R_3)$, and $S_- = V_{LL}R_3/(R_2 + R_3)$. If possible, it is desirable to limit the output of the op amp to a voltage less than the power supplies.

The inverting input of the circuit of Fig. 8.6-26a could be grounded and the voltage V_T applied to the grounded end of R_3 to realize a counterclockwise (CCW) bistable. However, consider Fig. 8.6-26b, which shows a CCW bistable that limits the op amp swings to less than the power supplies. It can be shown that $L_+ = -R_6V_{LL}/R_7, L_- = -R_5V_{HH}/R_4, S_+ = -R_2(L_-)/R_3$, and $S_- = -R_2(L_+)/R_3$. Diodes D1 and D2 serve to keep the output of op amp A1 from swinging from V_{HH} to V_{LL}, thus permitting quick transition of states.

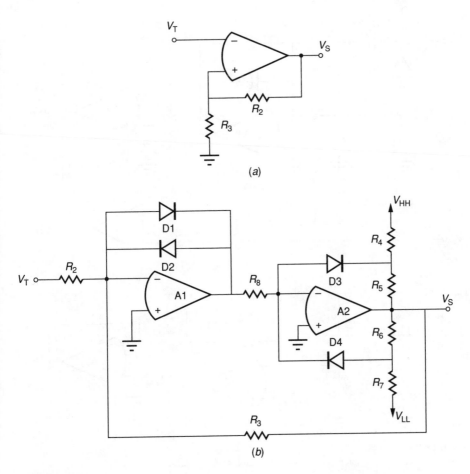

FIGURE 8.6-26
(a) Simple CW bistable, (b) CCW bistable with internal limiting.

A bistable circuit can also be implemented using switched capacitor techniques. Figure 8.6-27 shows a realization of the bistable characteristics of Fig. 8.6-25. The upper circuit, consisting of op amps 1 and 2, implements a switched capacitor amplifier with a sample-and-hold at the output and the ability to change the sign of the gain of the upper input, depending upon the output of comparator 3. The inputs to the comparator are the bistable input, V_T, and the output of the amplifier above, V_{TH}. The lower amplifier is similar to the upper amplifier. C_1 and C_2 are equivalent to the series switched capacitor simulations for a resistor. The discrete time voltages V_{TH}, V_C, and V_S are given as follows using the notation of Fig. 8.6-25.

$$V_{TH}(z) = \left\{ \frac{C_{12}}{C_1} V_{HH} + [\text{sgn } V_C(z)] \left(\frac{C_{11}}{C_1} \right) V_{HH} \right\} z^{-1}$$

$$= \{ V_X + [\text{sgn } V_C(z)] V_H \} z^{-1} \quad (8.6\text{-}67)$$

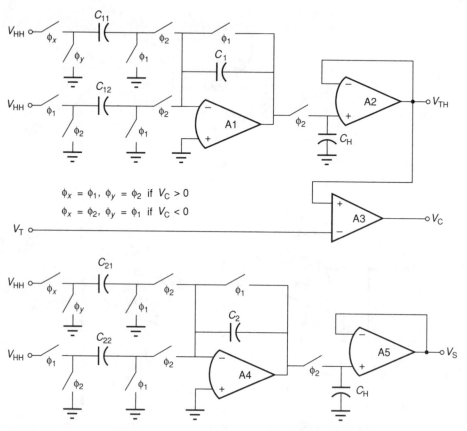

FIGURE 8.6-27
A switched capacitor implementation of the bistables of Fig. 8.6-25.

$$V_C(z) = \text{sgn}\{[V_{TH}(z) - V_T(z)]\} V_{HH} \qquad (8.6\text{-}68)$$

and

$$V_S(z) = \left\{ \frac{C_{22}}{C_2} V_{HH} + [\text{sgn } V_C(z)] \left| \frac{C_{21}}{C_2} \right| V_{HH} \right\} z^{-1}$$

$$= \{V_Y + [\text{sgn } V_C(z)] V_L\} z^{-1} \qquad (8.6\text{-}69)$$

where sgn x is 1 if $x > 0$ and -1 if $x < 0$. A CW bistable characteristic is obtained when the ϕ_X and ϕ_Y of the C_{21} switched capacitor are as shown in Fig. 8.6-27 where V_T is the input and V_S is the output. If ϕ_X and ϕ_Y are reversed, then a CCW bistable is obtained. It is observed that the bistable characteristics are completely general and can be shifted as desired by varying the appropriate V_{HH}, by adjusting the capacitor ratios, and/or by changing ϕ_X and ϕ_Y of C_{21}.

The solid portion of Fig. 8.6-28 shows a simplified implementation of a CW bistable circuit based on the concepts of Fig. 8.6-27. It can be shown that the second amplifier is not needed for a CW bistable characteristic with V_X and

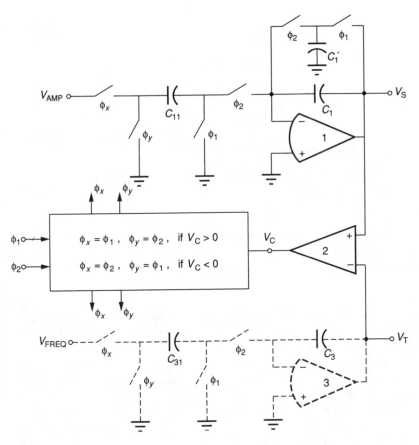

FIGURE 8.6-28
Simplified CW bistable circuit. The dotted portion is required for the waveform generator
implementation.

V_Y of Fig. 8.6-25 equal to zero. The output is taken at V_S and the input is applied
at V_T. The notation ϕ_X and ϕ_Y implies that these clocks are reversed depending
upon the sign of V_C. For the case of Fig. 8.6-28, $\phi_X = \phi_1$ and $\phi_Y = \phi_2$ will
give a noninverting gain. The phase reversal circuit can be implemented using
the ideas represented in Fig. 8.6-18.

The bistable can now be combined with the proper type of integrator (noninverting or inverting) to achieve an implementation of the untuned oscillator
block diagram of Fig. 8.6-24. An untuned oscillator using the CCW bistable of
Fig. 8.6-26b and an inverting integrator is shown in Fig. 8.6-29. The integrating
constant K is equal to $1/(R_1 C_1)$, and the various limits of the bistable have already
been shown to be $L_+ = -R_6 V_{LL}/R_7, L_- = -R_5 V_{HH}/R_4, S_+ = -R_2 L/R_3$, and
$S_- = -R_2 L_+/R_3$. For example, if $V_{HH} = -V_{LL} = 15$ V, $R_1 = 100$ kΩ, $C_1 =$
1 nF, $R_2 = R_3 = 100$ k$\Omega, R_4 = R_7 = 30$ kΩ, and $R_5 = R_6 = 20$ kΩ, then $L_+ =$
$-L_- = S_+ = -S_- = 10$ V. From Eq. 8.6-66 we find that the frequency of

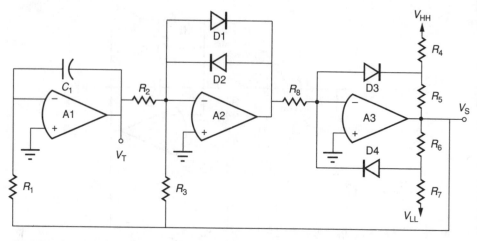

FIGURE 8.6-29
Untuned oscillator using the bistable of Fig. 8.6-26b.

oscillation, f_o, is 2500 Hz. Although the circuit of Fig. 8.6-29 is presented to illustrate concepts and is not practical for integration, the reader should be able to convert it to a form suitable for integration.

One of the advantages of an untuned oscillator is that the frequency can be easily controlled by a voltage. Figure 8.6-30 shows an example of how this might be accomplished. The output voltage, V_S, is used to connect the inverting integrator to a positive or negative value of a voltage called V_M. The limits of V_S effectively become $L_+ = -L_- = V_M$. Thus, the frequency of the untuned oscillator as developed in Eq. 8.6-66 becomes

$$f_o = \frac{V_M}{2R_1C_1(S_+ - S_-)} = \frac{V_M}{4R_1C_1S} \qquad (8.6\text{-}70)$$

where $S = S_+ = -S_-$. The range of the control or modulating voltage, V_M, will be from the power supplies to the point at which op amp offsets become significant. Consequently, this voltage-controlled oscillator (VCO) should have two to three decades of frequency range. Other methods of controlling the oscillator frequency include a diode bridge[62] and current-controlled multivibrators.[63]

Many of the components of Fig. 8.6-29 can be removed, at the expense of some deterioration of the performance. Figure 8.6-31a shows an example of an untuned oscillator using only a single op amp. The analysis of this oscillator starts by assuming that the output is at L_+. Consequently, the voltage at the positive input terminal of the op amp is $R_3L_+/(R_2 + R_3) = \alpha L_+$. If V_1 is less than this voltage, then C_1 will begin to charge to L_+ through R_1. However, when V_1 is equal to αL_+, the output of the op amp switches to L_-. Now the voltage at the positive input terminal of the op amp is αL_-. Since this voltage is less than V_1, C_1 begins to discharge toward L_- through R_1. From

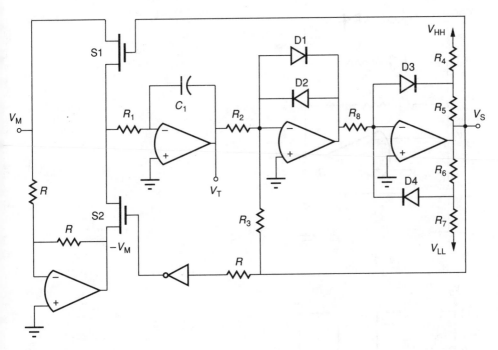

FIGURE 8.6-30
Voltage-controlled oscillator using the untuned oscillator of Fig. 8.6-29.

this analysis we see that $S_+ = \alpha L_+$ and $S_- = \alpha L_-$. The waveform at V_1 is no longer triangular but is exponential. It can be shown that the frequency of oscillation is

$$f_o = \frac{1}{2R_1 C_1 \ln\left[(1 + \alpha)/(1 - \alpha)\right]} \tag{8.6-71}$$

where $\alpha = R_3/(R_2 + R_3)$. The square wave can be made asymmetrical through the use of diodes and resistors, as indicated in Fig. 8.6-31 in the dotted portion of the figure.

The switched capacitor bistable can also be used to implement an untuned oscillator that can be controlled by a voltage. This untuned oscillator is shown in Fig. 8.6-28 if the dotted portion is included. The amplifier of this realization uses a scheme to avoid requiring the op amp output to be zeroed during each clock cycle. The use of a parallel switched capacitor resistor realization in shunt with C_1 gives the following discrete time transfer function from V_{AMP} to V_S.

$$\frac{V_S(z)}{V_{AMP}(z)} = \frac{[\text{sgn } V_C(z)](C_{11}/C_1)z^{-1}}{1 - z^{-1}(1 - C'_1/C_1)} = [\text{sgn } V_C(z)]\left(\frac{C_{11}}{C_1}\right)z^{-1} \tag{8.6-72}$$

if $C_1 = C'_1$. C'_1 opposes the charge being transferred from C_{11} to C_1. Only the charge difference on C_{11} between consecutive samples is transferred. As a

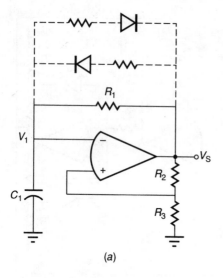

(a)

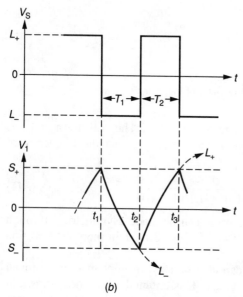

(b)

FIGURE 8.6-31
(a) Simple untuned oscillator,
(b) Waveforms of a.

result, the op amp output voltage changes only by the difference in the input voltage multiplied by the gain factor of the amplifier. The circuit of Fig. 8.6-28 functions as a VCO where the amplitude and frequency of the square and triangle waveforms are given as

$$\text{Amplitude} = \left(\frac{C_{11}}{C_1}\right)V_{\text{AMP}}(t) \tag{8.6-73}$$

and

$$f_o = \left(\frac{C_1 C_{31} f_c}{4 C_3 C_{11}}\right)\frac{V_{\text{FREQ}}(t)}{V_{\text{AMP}}(t)} \tag{8.6-74}$$

It is seen that the switched capacitor VCO of Fig. 8.6-28 is capable of both amplitude and frequency modulation. Amplitude modulation is accomplished by connecting both $V_{\text{FREQ}}(t)$ and $V_{\text{AMP}}(t)$ to the source of modulation. Frequency modulation is accomplished by connecting only $V_{\text{FREQ}}(t)$ to the source of modulation and keeping $V_{\text{AMP}}(t)$ constant. Figure 8.6-32 shows the waveforms of the circuit of Fig. 8.6-28 used as an unmodulated, untuned oscillator, an amplitude-modulated oscillator, and a frequency-modulated oscillator (VCO).[64]

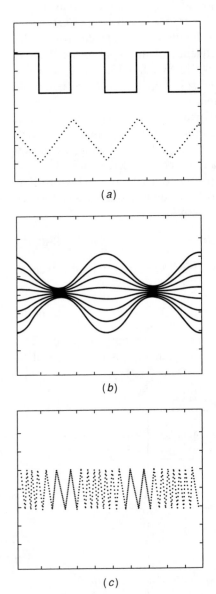

(a)

(b)

(c)

FIGURE 8.6-32
Drawings of actual oscilloscope waveforms. (a) Square and triangle waveforms, (b) Use of the circuit of Fig. 8.6-28 for amplitude modulation, (c) Use of the circuit of Fig. 8.6-28 for frequency modulation.

There are many other oscillators compatible with integrated circuit technology that have not been presented here. They include ring oscillators, constant-current oscillators, and multivibrators, including collector (drain) or emitter (source) coupled multivibrators. Other performance aspects of oscillators, including their temperature and power supply stability, has not been covered. These subjects are addressed in the technical literature.

8.6.4 Phased-Locked Loops

The last circuit we will consider in this section is the phase-locked loop (PLL). The phase-locked loop consists of a voltage controlled oscillator (VCO) whose frequency is equal to the frequency of the PLL input. The voltage controlling the VCO should vary monotonically with the frequency of the input to the PLL. A block diagram of a phase-locked loop is shown in Fig. 8.6-33. It is seen that a phase-locked loop consists of a negative feedback loop in which the output of a phase detector is applied to the control input of a VCO. The VCO applies a periodic waveform to the phase detector, the phase of which is compared with the phase of the input signal. The phase-locked loop has many applications, such as FM demodulation, frequency synchronization, signal conditioning, frequency multiplication and division, frequency translation, and AM detection.

A more detailed block diagram of the phase-locked loop is shown in Fig. 8.6-34. In the following analysis, the phase-locked loop is assumed to be locked. The input signal is assumed to be a sinusoid given as

$$V_{IN}(t) = V_p \sin(\omega t + \theta_i) \tag{8.6-75}$$

If the phase shift of the signal at the output of the VCO is θ_{osc}, then the average value of the output of the phase detector is

$$V_B = K_d(\theta_i - \theta_{osc}) \tag{8.6-76}$$

where θ_i and θ_{osc} are phase shifts with respect to an arbitrary reference. The phase of the signal at the output of the VCO as a function of time is equal to

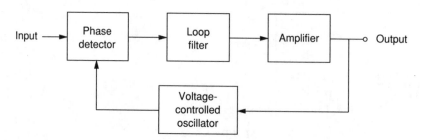

FIGURE 8.6-33
Block diagram of a phase-locked loop.

the integral of the frequency of the VCO, which can be expressed in differential form as

$$\omega_{osc}(t) = \frac{d\theta_{osc}(t)}{dt} \tag{8.6-77}$$

Thus, in the block diagram of Fig. 8.6-34, this integration is represented in the VCO block as $1/s$. If we assume that the oscillator frequency is given as

$$\omega_{osc} = \omega_0 + K_0 V_O \tag{8.6-78}$$

where ω_0 is the free-running frequency of the oscillator when $V_O = 0$, then the transfer function of the phase-locked loop becomes

$$\frac{V_O(s)}{\theta_i(s)} = \frac{sK_dF(s)A}{s + K_dK_0AF(s)} \tag{8.6-79}$$

or

$$\frac{V_O(s)}{\omega_i(s)} = \frac{V_O(s)}{s\theta_i(s)} = \frac{K_dF(s)A}{s + K_dK_0AF(s)} \tag{8.6-80}$$

If $F(s) = 1$, then the loop inherently has a first-order, low-pass transfer response. The loop bandwidth is defined as $K_v = K_0K_dA$. Various types of filters have been used to achieve different dynamic performances for the phase-locked loop.[65]

The loop lock range is defined as the range of frequencies about ω_0 for which the phase-locked loop maintains the relationship:

$$\omega_i = \omega_{osc} \tag{8.6-81}$$

If the phase detector can determine the phase difference between θ_i and θ_{osc} over a $\pm\pi/2$ range, then the loop lock range is expressed as

$$\omega_L = \pm\Delta\omega_{osc} = K_dAK_0(\pm\pi/2) = \pm K_v(\pi/2) \tag{8.6-82}$$

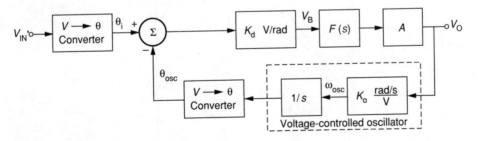

FIGURE 8.6-34
More detailed block diagram of a phased-locked loop.

The capture range is the range of input frequencies for which an initially unlocked loop will lock on an input signal. If $F(s) = 1$, then the capture range is equal to the lock range. If $F(s) = (1 + s/\omega_1)^{-1}$, then the capture range is less than the lock range. If the capture range is designated as $2\omega_C$, then Fig. 8.6-35 illustrates the relationships between the loop and capture ranges of a phase-locked loop with $F(s) = (1 + s/\omega_1)^{-1}$. The loop and capture ranges are very dependent on the loop bandwidth, K_v. If K_v decreases, the capture time increases, the capture range decreases, and the interference rejection properties of the phase-locked loop improve. The blocks shown in Fig. 8.6-34 can be implemented by circuits that we have examined previously in this chapter or in Chapter 6 for both MOS and BJT technologies.

Circuits that are representative of analog processing circuits have been introduced in this section. These circuits included the precision breakpoint circuit, multipliers and modulators, oscillators, and phase-locked loops. At this point the reader has a sufficient repertoire of circuits to undertake the design of systems using analog processing circuits or to undertake the design of a different type of analog signal processing circuit.

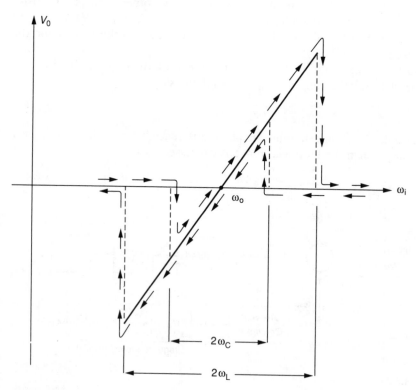

FIGURE 8.6-35
Illustration of the loop and capture ranges for a phase-locked loop.

8.7 SUMMARY

This chapter has introduced the elements of analog systems. An introduction to analog signal processing showed the important relationships between digital circuits, analog circuits, BJT technology, and MOS technology. It was seen that there is likely to be a mixture of digital and analog circuit techniques to implement signal processing systems. The selection of the appropriate technique is decided by many factors, including space, performance, and technology compatibility. The existence of technologies combining both BJT and MOS technologies offers some exciting advantages to the circuit and system designer.

Next, techniques of interfacing analog and digital circuits were presented. This subject was divided into digital-to-analog converters and analog-to-digital converters. The performance of the various types of converters was reviewed, followed by a consideration of current-scaling, voltage-scaling, charge-scaling, combination-scaling, and serial digital-to-analog converters. Analog-to-digital converters were presented, with the serial, successive approximation, parallel, and high performance analog-to-digital architectures considered.

One of the largest applications of analog circuits at the present is linear filtering. A review of continuous-time filters was presented, followed by a discussion of switched capacitor filters. The switched capacitor circuit technique is a practical adaptation of circuit design methods to match the technology, once again demonstrating the important influence of technology upon circuits and systems design. The key aspect of switched capacitor circuits is that equivalent RC products become equal to the product of capacitor ratios and an external clock frequency. This results in time constant accuracies as good as 0.1%. Three switched capacitor filter design approaches were presented; resistor replacement or substitution, passive RLC prototype based ladder synthesis, and direct realization of the filter in the z-domain.

The chapter concluded with a section on analog signal processing circuits. A number of nonfilter circuits were examined. These included waveshaping or precision breakpoint circuits; multipliers and modulators; oscillators, including tuned and untuned oscillators; and phase-locked loops. These are examples of circuits that might be used to implement a signal processing system. The boundary between a circuit and a system is very fuzzy. The topics presented in this chapter could be considered circuits from one viewpoint and systems from another. We have chosen to emphasize the circuit viewpoint over the application.

In closing, we will consider a signal processing system and examine how the design of such a system is hierarchically organized. Figure 8.7-1 shows a block diagram of an integrated circuit modem. A modem is a system that converts outgoing data in the form of a serial bit string to a form suitable for transmission over telephone lines and also converts the incoming data back to a serial bit string. This is a challenging problem because of the limited bandwidth of the telephone system and the desire to transmit data at as high a bit rate as possible. The particular modem considered is a 1200 bits/second, full-duplex, voice-band modem.[66] This system represents a reasonably complex design in terms of man-months of effort.

The details of the design of the modem will not be considered. Rather, the emphasis here will be on how the system is broken into smaller blocks that

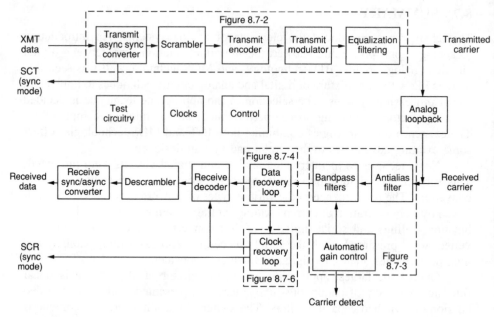

FIGURE 8.7-1
Integrated modem block diagram.

ultimately are recognizable as circuits we have considered in our study. For example, the transmitter is shown in more detail in Fig. 8.7-2. Here some of the blocks are recognizable, such as the filters, the mixers, and the summer. The asynchronous-to-synchronous converter, the scrambler, and the phase encoder are implemented by digital techniques such as those discussed in Chapters 7 and 9. The first part of the receiver channel is the automatic gain control circuit shown in Fig. 8.7-3. The analog blocks in this figure include filters, a full-wave rectifier (see Probs. 8.32 and 8.34), and a comparator.

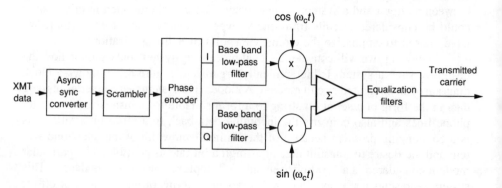

FIGURE 8.7-2
Differential QPSK transmitter.

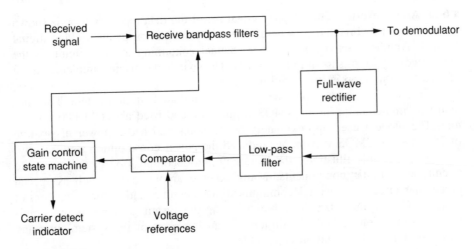

FIGURE 8.7-3
Automatic gain control circuit.

The next part of the receiver channel is called the data recovery loop and is implemented by a Costas phase-locked loop that preprocesses the received signals through Hilbert filters, as shown in Fig. 8.7-4. The Hilbert filters consist of two parallel filters, one shifted by 90° compared to the other. The data recovery loop consists of many analog circuits that have been previously considered, including

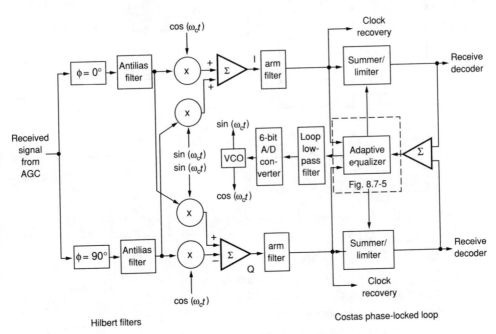

FIGURE 8.7-4
Coherent QPSK demodulation.

a 6-bit A/D converter. The adaptive equalizer of the data recovery loop is shown in more detail in Fig. 8.7-5, where we see a combination of analog and digital circuits. Another part of the receiver channel containing analog circuits is the clock recovery loop, shown in Fig. 8.7-6. The switched capacitor implementation of a part of this loop is illustrated in Fig. 8.7-7.

Figure 8.7-8 shows a photograph of the integrated circuit modem. This modem was implemented in an NMOS technology and used about 11,000 transistors. The modem used approximately 60 op amps and had a power dissipation of 750 mW. A CMOS version has reduced the power consumption significantly.

This example illustrates the hierarchy and decomposition of a system into circuits and similar components. Many other examples exist, such as speech processing circuits, other telecommunications circuits, and automotive control systems. One of the difficult problems facing the system designer is the simultaneous simulation of both the digital and analog parts of the system. In many cases, only partial simulation is possible.

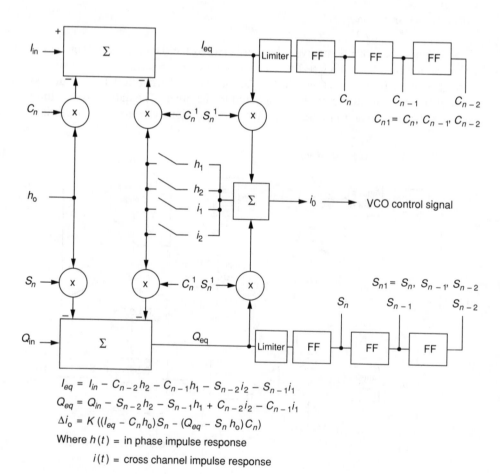

$$I_{eq} = I_{in} - C_{n-2}h_2 - C_{n-1}h_1 - S_{n-2}i_2 - S_{n-1}i_1$$

$$Q_{eq} = Q_{in} - S_{n-2}h_2 - S_{n-1}h_1 + C_{n-2}i_2 - C_{n-1}i_1$$

$$\Delta i_o = K((I_{eq} - C_n h_o)S_n - (Q_{eq} - S_n h_o)C_n)$$

Where $h(t)$ = in phase impulse response

$i(t)$ = cross channel impulse response

FIGURE 8.7-5
Adaptive equalizer.

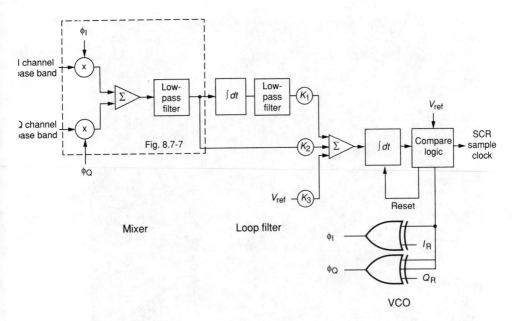

FIGURE 8.7-6
Clock recovery phase-locked loop.

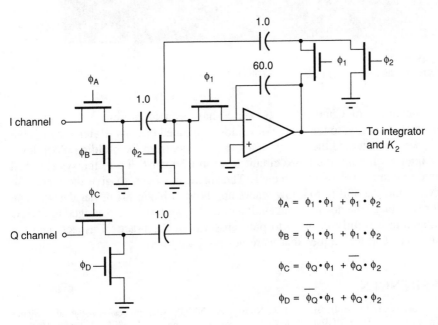

$$\phi_A = \phi_1 \cdot \phi_1 + \overline{\phi_1} \cdot \phi_2$$

$$\phi_B = \overline{\phi_1} \cdot \phi_1 + \phi_1 \cdot \phi_2$$

$$\phi_C = \phi_Q \cdot \phi_1 + \overline{\phi_Q} \cdot \phi_2$$

$$\phi_D = \overline{\phi_Q} \cdot \phi_1 + \phi_Q \cdot \phi_2$$

FIGURE 8.7-7
Clock PLL input.

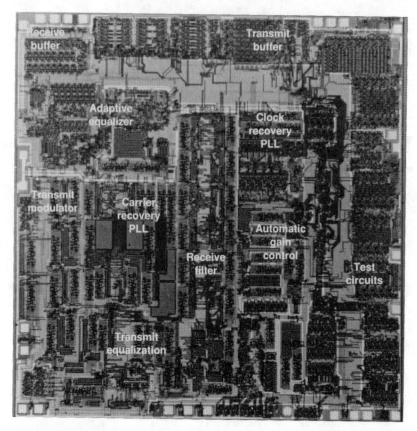

FIGURE 8.7-8
Integrated modem photograph (Courtesy of Texas Instruments).

The thrust of Chapters 5, 6, and 8 has been to present a hierarchically oriented introduction to the design of analog integrated circuits. Referring to Table 5.0-1, we have studied the design of analog circuits from the building block level in Chapter 5, through the basic circuit level in Chapter 6, up to the systems and complex circuit level of this chapter. The intent has been to give the reader an overview and the ability to know where and how to begin his or her design. The reader who faces the design of an analog circuit or system is encouraged to review the literature carefully in order to pick up some of the practical aspects and the circuit ideas and techniques that were not discussed here.

REFERENCES

1. M. Townsend, M. Hoff, Jr., and R. Holm: "An NMOS Microprocessor for Analog Signal Processing," *IEEE J. of Solid-State Circuits,* vol. SC-15, no. 1, pp. 33–38, February 1980.
2. B. M. Gordon: "Linear Electronic Analog/Digital Conversion Architecture, Their Origins, Parameters, Limitations, and Applications," *IEEE Trans. Circuits and Systems,* vol. CAS-25, no. 7, pp. 391–418, July 1978.

3. B. Gilbert: *Electronic Products*, vol. 24, no. 3, pp. 61–63, July 1983.
4. R. E. Suarez, P. R. Gray, and D. A. Hodges: "All-MOS Charge Redistribution Analog-to-Digital Conversion Techniques—Part II," *IEEE J. of Solid-State Circuits*, vol. SC-10, no. 6, pp. 379–385, December 1975.
5. R. H. Charles and D. A. Hodges: "Charge Circuits for Analog LSI," *IEEE Trans. Circuit and Systems*, vol. CAS-25, no. 7, pp. 490–497, July 1978.
6. D. H. Sheingold: *Analog-Digital Conversion Handbook*, Analog Devices, Norwood, Mass., 1972.
7. J. R. Naylor: "Testing Digital/Analog and Analog/Digital Converters," *IEEE Trans. Circuits and Systems*, vol. CAS-25, no. 7, pp. 527–538, July 1978.
8. J. Doernberg, H. S. Lee, and D. A. Hodges: "Full-Speed Testing of A/D Converters," *IEEE J. of Solid-State Circuits*, vol. SC-19, no. 6, pp. 820–827, December 1984.
9. G. F. Landsburg: "A Charge-Balancing Monolithic A/D Converter," *IEEE J. of Solid-State Circuits*, vol. SC-12, no. 6, pp. 662–673, December 1977.
10. E. R. Hnatek: *A User's Handbook of D/A and A/D Converters*, John Wiley & Sons, New York, 1976.
11. B. Fotouhi and D. A. Hodges: "High-Resolution A/D Conversion in MOS/LSI," *IEEE J. of Solid-State Circuits*, vol. SC-14, no. 6, pp. 920–926, December 1979.
12. S. Sutarja and P. R. Gray, "A Pipelined 13-bit, 250-ks/s, 5-V, Analog-to-Digital Converter," *IEEE J. of Solid-State Circuits*, vol. 23, no. 6, pp. 1316–1323, December 1988.
13. J. Fernandes, S. R. Lewis, A. M. Mallinson, and G. A. Miller, "A 14-bit 10 μs Subranging A/D Converter with S/H," *IEEE J. of Solid-State Circuits*, vol. 23, no. 6. pp. 1309–1315, December 1988.
14. E. J. Swanson, "The Outlook on ADCs: Accuracy Jumps 2 dB/Year," *Electronic Design*, p. 61, September 22, 1988.
15. Matsumoto, et al., "An 18-bit Oversampling A/D Converter for Digital Audio," *1988 ISSCC*, p. 203, February 1988.
16. Draxelmayr, "A Self-Calibrating Technique for Redundant A/D Converters Providing 16-bit Accuracy," *1988 ISSCC*, p. 240, February 1988.
17. S. Sutarja and P. R. Gray, "A 250 ks/s 13-bit Pipelined A/D Converter," *1988 ISSCC*, p. 228, February 1988.
18. D. Kerth, N. S. Sooch, and E. J. Swanson, "A 667 ns, 12-bit, 2-step, flash ADC," *1988 CICC*, p. 18.5, May 1988.
19. J. Doernberg and D. A. Hodges, "A 10-bit, 5 MHz, 2-step flash CMOS A/D Converter," *1988 CICC*, p. 18.6, May 1988.
20. S. Lewis and P. R. Gray, "A pipelined 5-Ms/s, 9-bit A/D Converter," *IEEE J. of Solid-State Circuits*, vol. SC-22, no. 6, p. 954, December 1987.
21. M. Ishikawa and T. Tsukahara, "An 8b 40 MHz CMOS Subranging ADC with Pipelined Wideband S/H," *1989 ISSCC*, Paper WAM 1.1, February 1989.
22. Shimizu, "A 10-bit, 20 MHz, Two-Step Parallel ADC with Internal S/H," *1988 ISSCC*, p. 224, February 1988.
23. "Analog-to-Digital Conversion in a Flash," *Electronic Systems Design Magazine*, p. 38, May 1988.
24. R. van de Plassche and P. Baltus, "An 8-bit 100 MHz Full-Nyquist Analog-to-Digital Converter," *IEEE J. of Solid-State Circuits*, vol. 23, no. 6, pp. 1334–1344, December 1988.
25. T. Wakimoto, Y. Akazawa, and S. Konaka, "Si Bipolar 2 GHz 6-bit Flash A/D Conversion LSI," *IEEE J. of Solid-State Circuits*, vol. 23, no. 6, pp. 1345–1350, December 1988.
26. P. E. Allen and E. Sánchez-Sinencio: *Switched Capacitor Circuits*, Van Nostrand Reinhold, New York, 1984.
27. A. I. Zverev: *Handbook of Filter Synthesis*, John Wiley & Sons, New York, 1967.
28. A. Budak: *Passive and Active Network Analysis and Synthesis*, Houghton Mifflin, Boston, 1974.
29. G. Daryanani: *Principles of Active Network Synthesis and Design*, John Wiley & Sons, New York, 1976.
30. M. S. Ghausi and K. R. Laker: *Modern Filter Design—Active RC and Switched Capacitor*, Prentice-Hall, Englewood Cliffs, N.J., 1981.
31. L. P. Huelsman and P. E. Allen: *Introduction to the Design and Application of Active Filters*, McGraw-Hill, New York, 1980.

32. D. E. Johnson and J. L. Hilburn: *Rapid Practical Designs of Active Filters,* John Wiley & Sons, New York, 1975.
33. A. S. Sedra and P. O. Brackett: *Filter Theory and Design: Active and Passive,* Matrix Publishers, Champaign, Ill., 1977.
34. L. Weinburg: *Network Analysis and Synthesis,* McGraw-Hill, New York, 1962; R. E. Krieger, Huntington, N.Y., 1975.
35. M. Kawakami: "Nomographs for Butterworth and Chebyshev Filters," *IEEE Trans. Circuit Theory,* vol. CT-10, pp. 288–298, June 1963.
36. R. P. Sallen and E. L. Key: "A Practical Method of Designing RC Active Filters," *IRE Trans. Circuit Theory,* vol. CT-2, pp. 74–85, March 1955.
37. J. Tow: "Design Formulas for Active RC Filters Using Operational Amplifier Biquad," *Electronics Letters,* pp. 339–441, July 24, 1969.
38. L. C. Thomas: "The Biquad: Part I—Some Practical Design Considerations," *IEEE Trans. Circuit Theory,* vol. CT-18, pp. 350–357, May 1971.
39. L. P. Huelsman and P. E. Allen: *Introduction to the Theory and Design of Active Filters,* Appendix A, McGraw-Hill, New York, 1980.
40. J. C. Maxwell: *A Treatise on Electricity and Magnetism,* Oxford University Press, London, 1873; Low & Brydone, London, 1946.
41. D. L. Fried: "Analog Sample-Data Filters," *IEEE J. of Solid-State Circuits,* vol. SC-7, no. 4, pp. 302–304, August 1972.
42. D. A. Hodges, P. R. Gray, and R. W. Brodersen: "Potential of MOS Technologies for Analog Integrated Circuits," *IEEE J. of Solid-State Circuits,* vol. SC-13, no. 3, pp. 285–294, June 1978.
43. L. T. Bruton: "Low Sensitivity Digital Ladder Filters," *IEEE Trans. Circuits and Systems,* vol. CAS-22, no. 3, pp. 168–176, March 1975.
44. R. W. Brodersen, P. R. Gray, and D. A. Hodges: "MOS Switched-Capacitor Filters," *Proc. of the IEEE,* vol. 67, no. 1, pp. 61–75, January 1979.
45. A. V. Oppenheimer and R. W. Schafer: *Digital Signal Processing,* Chapter 4, Prentice Hall, Englewood Cliffs, N.J., 1975.
46. R. C. Agarwal and C. S. Burrus: "New Filter Recursive Structures Having Very Low Sensitivity and Roundoff Noise," *IEEE Trans. Circuits and Systems,* vol. CAS-22, pp. 921–927, December 1975.
47. R. Gregorian: "Switched-Capacitor Filter Design Using Cascade Sections," *IEEE Trans. Circuits and Systems,* vol. CAS-27, pp. 515–521, June 1980.
48. P. Fleisher and K. Laker: "A Family of Active Switched Capacitor Biquad Building Blocks," *Bell Syst. Tech. J.,* vol. 58, pp. 2235–2269, 1979.
49. E. Sánchez-Sinencio, R. L. Geiger, and J. Silva-Martinez: "Tradeoffs Between Passive Sensitivity Output Voltage Swing and Total Capacitance in SC Filters," *Proc. IEEE Inter. Symp. on Circuits and Systems,* vol. 3, pp. 1062–1064, 1984.
50. E. Sánchez-Sinencio, P. E. Allen, A. W. T. Ismail, and E. R. Klinkovsky: "Switched Capacitor Filters with Partial Positive Feedback," *AEU-Electronics and Communication,* vol. 38, no. 5, pp. 331–339, 1984.
51. P. E. Allen and D. R. Holberg, *CMOS Analog Circuit Design,* Holt, Rinehart and Winston, New York NY, 1987.
52. B. Gilbert: "A Precise Four-Quadrant Multiplier with Subnanosecond Response," *IEEE J. of Solid-State Circuits,* vol. SC-3, pp. 365–373, December 1968.
53. D. C. Soo and R. G. Meyer: "A Four Quadrant NMOS Analog Multiplier," *IEEE J. Solid-State Circuits,* vol. SC-17, pp. 1174–1178, December 1982.
54. J. Babanezhad and G. C. Temes: "A 20-V Four-quadrant CMOS Analog Multiplier," *IEEE J. Solid-State Circuits,* vol. SC-20, pp. 1158–1168, December 1985.
55. S. L. Wong et al: "Wide Dynamic Range Four-Quadrant CMOS Analog Multiplier Using Linearized Transconductance Stages," *IEEE J. Solid-State Circuits,* vol. SC-21 pp. 1120–1122, December 1986.
56. S. C. Qin and R. L. Geiger: "A ±5 V CMOS Analog Multiplier," *IEEE J. Solid-State Circuits,* vol. SC-22, pp. 1143–1146, December 1987.
57. L. Strauss: *Wave Generation and Shaping,* 2d ed., McGraw-Hill, New York, 1970.

58. A. B. Grebene: "Monolithic Waveform Generation," *IEEE Spectrum*, pp. 34–40, April 1972.
59. W. G. Jung: *IC Timer Cookbook*, Howard Sams, Indianapolis, 1977.
60. J. Millman: *Microelectronics: Digital and Analog Circuits and Systems*, McGraw-Hill, New York, 1979.
61. A. B. Grebene: *Bipolar and MOS Analog Integrated Circuit Design*, John Wiley & Sons, New York, 1984.
62. J. V. Wait, L. P. Huelsman, and G. A. Korn: *Introduction to Operational Amplifier Theory and Applications*, Chapter 3, McGraw-Hill, New York, 1975.
63. A. B. Grebene: *Bipolar and MOS Analog Integrated Circuit Design*, Chapter 11, John Wiley & Sons, New York, 1975.
64. P. E. Allen, H. A. Rafat, and S. F. Bily: "A Switched-Capacitor Waveform Generator," *IEEE Trans. Circuits and Systems*, vol. CAS-32, no. 1, pp. 103–105, January 1985.
65. P. R. Gray and R. G. Meyer: *Analysis and Design of Analog Integrated Circuits*, Chapter 11, 2d ed., John Wiley & Sons, New York, 1984.
66. K. Hanson, W. A. Severin, E. R. Klinkovsky, D. C. Richardson, and J. R. Hochschild: "A 1200 Bit/s QPSK Full Duplex Modem," *IEEE J. of Solid-State Circuits*, vol. SC-19, no. 6, pp. 878–887, December 1984.

PROBLEMS

Section 8.2

8.1. Compare the sample-and-hold circuit of Fig. 8.2-3a with that of Fig. 8.2-4 and discuss why the circuit of Fig. 8.2-4 can have faster sample times. Assume that ϕ and $\overline{\phi}$ are nonoverlapping clock signals.

8.2. Draw a transfer characteristic of a 3-bit D/A converter that has the largest possible integral nonlinearity when the differential nonlinearity is limited to ±0.5 LSB. What is this maximum value of integral nonlinearity?

8.3. Express the output voltage of the binary-weighted resistor D/A converter shown in Fig. P8.3. Assume that the switches are connected to V_{ref} if the ith bit is 0, and to $-V_{ref}$ if the ith bit is 1.

8.4. Demonstrate that Fig. 8.2-12b will implement the function $V_{OUT} = -R_F I \, [b_1 + 2^{-1}b_2 + \cdots + 2^{-N+1}b_N]$ by considering a 4-bit example.

8.5. Find the accuracy required for R_{MSB} of a 12-bit D/A converter that uses the binary-weighted resistor approach in order to achieve monotonicity.

8.6. What is the maximum percentage tolerance of the current source (I_1) for the slave ladder of Fig. 8.2-13b if monotonicity is to be achieved for a 10-bit D/A converter?

8.7. Show how to modify the circuit of Fig. 8.2-15a to implement the bipolar operation of Eq. 8.2-13.

8.8. If an approximate formula for the ratio accuracy of capacitors is

$$\text{Ratio accuracy} \simeq 0.01 \times (\text{Capacitor ratio})^{0.25}$$

find the maximum number of bits that a charge-scaling D/A, such as in Fig. 8.2-15a, can have.

8.9. If A_R is the area of the resistors and A_C is the area of the capacitors of the D/A converter of Fig. 8.2-18, show that for minimum area

$$K - M = \frac{\ln (A_R/A_C)}{\ln 2}$$

where K is the number of bits that are charge-scaled and M is the number of bits that are voltage-scaled.

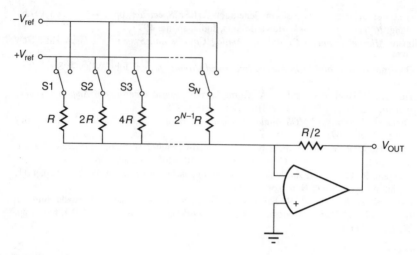

FIGURE P8.3

8.10. Determine the value of V_{C1} in Fig. 8.2-21 following the sequence of switch closing and openings: S4, S3, S1, S2, S1, S3, S1, S2, and S1. Assume that $C_1 = C_2$.

8.11. Repeat Prob. 8.10 if $C_1 = 1.05C_2$.

8.12. Show how Eq. 8.2-25 can be derived from Eq. 8.2-24. Give a realization of Fig. 8.2-24 using op amps, switches, and passive components.

8.13. Repeat Example 8.2-2 for the digital word 10101.

8.14. Assume that the amplifier with a gain of 0.5 in Fig. 8.2-24 has a gain error of ΔA. What is the maximum value ΔA can have in Example 8.2-2 without causing the conversion to be incorrect?

Section 8.3

8.15. Plot the transfer characteristic of a 3-bit A/D converter that has the largest possible differential nonlinearity when the integral nonlinearity is limited to $\pm$ 1 LSB. What is the maximum value of differential nonlinearity?

8.16. Find the 8-bit digital word if the input to Ex. 8.3-1 is 0.3215 V_{ref}.

8.17. Continue Example 8.3-2 out to the 10th bit and find the equivalent analog voltage.

8.18. Repeat Example 8.3-1 for the case where the gain-of-2 amplifiers actually have a gain of 2.1.

8.19. How many bits will an A/D converter with a sampling frequency of 10 MHz have in 1998? What technology will this converter use?

Section 8.4

8.20. Use the three circuits of Fig. 8.4-11 to obtain a realization of a second-order, low-pass Butterworth filter with a -3 dB frequency of 1000 Hz and a gain of 1 at dc. In Fig. 8.4-11a, additional stages may be necessary to achieve a gain of 1 at dc.

8.21. Repeat Example 8.4-3 using Fig. 8.4-11c, for stage 2 and stage 3.

8.22. Use the transformations of Fig. 8.4-13 to convert the result of Example 8.4-4 to a bandpass filter having a bandwidth of 500 Hz centered at 1000 Hz.

Section 8.5

8.23. Prove that the equivalent resistance given in Fig. 8.5-2 for the series switched capacitor resistance simulation is valid.

8.24. Repeat Prob. 8.23 for the series-parallel switched capacitor resistance simulation.

8.25. Repeat Prob. 8.23 for the bilinear switched capacitor resistance simulation.

8.26. Replot the frequency response of the circuit of Fig. 8.5-5a if $\omega_1 = 0.02\omega_c$. Compare with the frequency response (magnitude and phase) of Fig. 8.5-2.

8.27. Replace the parallel switched capacitor resistor simulation in Fig. 8.5-5a with the series switched capacitor resistor simulation of Fig. 8.5-2 and find the discrete-time frequency response similar to Eq. 8.5-27. Develop an expression for the magnitude and phase response and compare it with the results of Fig. 8.5-5a.

8.28. Obtain the exact frequency response at ϕ_1 of the switched capacitor circuit shown in Fig. P8.28. Define $\alpha = C_1/C_2$, and solve for the -3 dB frequency, in hertz, when $\alpha = 3$ and the clock frequency is (a) 64 kHz and (b) 128 kHz. The clock phases are nonoverlapping, and V_1 is from a sample-and-hold circuit.

8.29. Develop an expression for the discrete-time magnitude and phase response for H^{oe} of the noninverting switched capacitor integrator of Fig. 8.5-10a. Plot the magnitude and phase for frequencies from 0 to ω_c if $\omega_0/\omega_c = 0.1$.

8.30. Repeat Prob. 8.29 for the inverting switched capacitor integrator of Fig. 8.5-12.

8.31. Find the actual magnitude and phase of the noninverting switched capacitor integrator of Fig. 8.5-10a for H^{oo} if the frequency applied to the integrator is 10 kHz, the clock frequency is 100 kHz, and ω_0 is 20π krps.

Section 8.6

8.32. Develop a realization of $V_{OUT} = |V_{IN}|$ using resistors, diodes, and two op amps.

8.33. Develop a realization of $V_{OUT} = -|V_{IN} - 1|$ using resistors, diodes, and the minimum number of op amps.

8.34. Repeat Prob. 8.32 using capacitors, switches, one comparator, and the minimum number of op amps.

8.35. Repeat Prob. 8.33 using capacitors, switches, one comparator, and the minimum number of op amps.

8.36. (a) Design a circuit that realizes the transfer characteristic of Fig. P8.36 using resistors, diodes, and op amps.

(b) Repeat using capacitors, switches, comparators, and op amps.

8.37. (a) Design a circuit that realizes the transfer characteristic of Fig. P8.37 using resistors, diodes, and op amps.

(b) Repeat using capacitors, switches, comparators, and op amps.

8.38. Derive Eqs. 8.6-24 and 8.6-25 from Fig. 8.6-10.

8.39. Use a four-quadrant analog multiplier, op amps, and resistors to develop a circuit that produces an output voltage of $-K(V_1)^{1/2}$ when $V_1 > 0$.

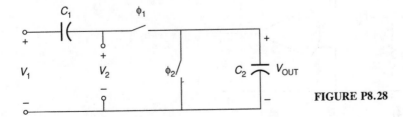

FIGURE P8.28

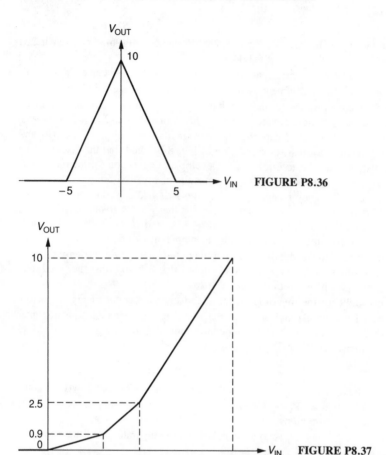

FIGURE P8.36

FIGURE P8.37

8.40. The sine of an input voltage V_1 can be approximated by the formula, $\sin V_1 \simeq 1.155V_1 - 0.33V_1^2$, to within $\pm 2\%$ over the range of $0 < V_1 < \pi/2$. Use multipliers and op amps to find a realization of $\sin V_1$ using this formula.

8.41. Find the frequency of oscillation, in hertz, and the value of R_f necessary for oscillation of the RC phase shift oscillator shown in Fig. P8.41.

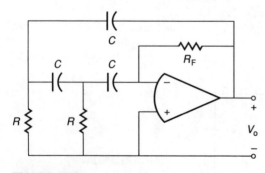

FIGURE P8.41

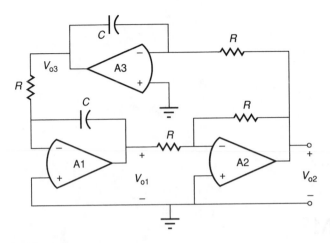

FIGURE P8.42

8.42. Find the frequency of oscillation, in hertz, of the quadrature oscillator of Fig. P8.42. Give expressions for the voltages V_{o1}, V_{o2}, and V_{o3} if the amplitude of the sinusoid at V_{o1} is 1 V peak.

8.43. Determine the values for the resistors not given in the bistable circuit of Fig. P8.43 and determine whether to connect R_q to $+15$ V or -15 V in order to realize the output-input transfer characteristic shown.

8.44. Show how to use a CW bistable to implement an untuned oscillator, and design the oscillator to produce a ± 10 V square wave at 3000 Hz.

8.45. Develop the expression for the frequency of oscillation of the circuit in Fig. 8.6-31 given in Eq. 8.6-71. What is the frequency of oscillation, in hertz, if $R_2 = R_3, R_1 = 100$ kΩ, and $C_1 = 1$ nF?

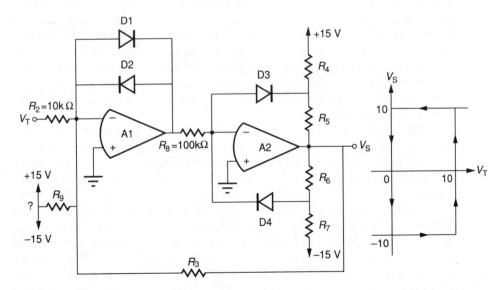

FIGURE P8.43

CHAPTER
9

STRUCTURED
DIGITAL
CIRCUITS
AND SYSTEMS

9.0 INTRODUCTION

The purpose of Chapter 7 on basic digital building blocks was to introduce primitive logic gates and provide insight into features and limitations of digital MOS circuitry. The goal of this chapter is to extend that knowledge to the design of larger digital systems. These digital systems comprise many logic gates and may occupy a significant part of an integrated circuit chip. Such systems almost always consist of carefully repeated building blocks, with each block based on circuits such as those discussed in Chapter 7. Several different structures, including regular logic arrays, clocked structures, memories, microprocessors, and systolic arrays, are used to demonstrate the capabilities and design requirements for digital integrated circuits and systems.

This chapter begins with an examination of the general topic of structured logic forms. This includes a comparison of random versus structured logic forms, treatment of programmable logic arrays (PLAs), Weinberger arrays, gate-matrix design, and logic gate arrays. These are alternate forms used to implement combinational logic in a structured manner while maintaining control over layout area.

Clocking schemes are introduced next. Time-based signals called clocks are required to provide time order in the operation of digital circuits. In particular, clocks augment simple combinational logic to create sequential systems such as controllers or microprocessors. Following the section on clocking schemes, simple dynamic storage is discussed, a prerequisite for the subsequent treatment of clocked logic, including domino CMOS. Dynamic storage is also useful in building finite-state machines, which are described later in the chapter.

The next sections provide descriptions of several forms of memory including ROM, EPROM, SRAM, DRAM, and static and quasi-static register storage. The first four of these are introduced from a conceptual viewpoint rather than a circuit design viewpoint. The internal design of dense memory subsystems requires detailed circuit design and is outside the scope of this chapter.

With the prerequisites of combinational logic, clocking schemes, and memory available, increasingly complex digital systems such as controllers, finite-state machines, microprocessors, and systolic arrays are outlined. This final major area of the chapter provides an introduction to several practical examples of the complex digital systems that are created from an orderly composition of relatively simple digital building blocks.

9.1 RANDOM LOGIC VERSUS STRUCTURED LOGIC FORMS

A digital logic function may be realized as *random logic* or as *structured logic*. The term *random logic* describes a particular style (or lack thereof) of digital logic design. Some integrated logic circuits are placed within a layout in much the same way that small-scale logic chips are placed on a wire-wrap circuit board and then interconnected. With the many types of small-scale logic functions required, and because particular types of small-scale logic functions may be needed at irregular places within a circuit, the circuit packages and their interconnection wiring sometimes appear to have been randomly placed. Of course, for the circuit to function properly, the interconnections, and probably the package placement, were carefully designed. Nevertheless, random logic is a tag commonly used to describe digital circuits that lack regularity of circuit function, placement, and interconnection. On the other hand, *structured logic* is the term used to characterize logic forms that do demonstrate regularity in their layout and interconnection.

Many digital integrated circuits in the past were designed with large areas devoted to random logic. Early microprocessors such as the Intel 8080 and the Motorola 6800 each contained large sections of random logic. Examination of the die photo of Fig. 9.1-1 reveals that about 50% of the area for the Motorola 6809 microprocessor is devoted to random logic. Designs of this type were considered to have advantages of efficient use of silicon area and potentially fast operation. They have significant disadvantages caused by lengthy integrated circuit layout times, difficulty of testing, and costly modification steps.

Other digital integrated circuits have been designed with highly structured layouts for many years. Most notable among these are all forms of memory chips. Memory chips, such as the 1M-bit dynamic RAM (DRAM) from Texas Instruments shown in Fig. 9.1-2, are composed of many identical memory cells and are naturally structured as regular arrays of these cells. Because of the potential sales volume for memory parts, considerable effort is expended in reducing the size of the basic memory cell, causing memory chips to be among the densest of all integrated circuits.

Most of the newer, large digital integrated circuits, such as the Motorola 68030 and the Intel 80386 microprocessors, have decreased substantially the

FIGURE 9.1-1
Die photo for Motorola 6809 microprocessor (Courtesy Motorola Inc.).

percentage of silicon area devoted to random logic. This is easily shown by comparing the die photo of the Motorola 68030 of Fig. 9.1-3 with the die photo of Fig. 9.1-1. In fact, because of the complexity of many new chips, random logic design is no longer feasible for large chips. The length of time to design and lay out a complex random logic chip would increase the cost of the chip prohibitively. It would also delay introduction of the chip to the market, a costly consideration. As a result, most new digital integrated circuits increasingly use structured logic forms such as PLAs, microprogram ROMs, data paths, gate arrays, and standard cells to displace random logic design.

A widely used measure introduced by Lattin in 1979[1] is helpful in describing the regularity of an integrated circuit design. This measure, called the chip regularity factor, is defined as the ratio of the total number of transistors on the

FIGURE 9.1-2
Die photo for TI 1M-bit DRAM (Courtesy Texas
Instruments Inc.).

chip to the drawn transistors, where total transistors includes all possible ROM
and PLA transistor placements. Thus, a design that requires a unique layout for
a circuit element and then uses this circuit element n times without change would
exhibit a regularity factor of n. At the other extreme, a design with unique layout
for each circuit component would exhibit a regularity factor of only 1. For a given
complexity of design, a higher regularity factor normally indicates reduced design
and layout costs.

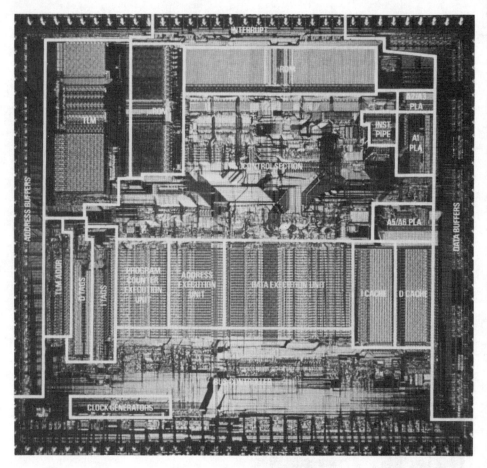

FIGURE 9.1-3
Die photo for Motorola 68030 microprocessor (Courtesy Motorola Inc.).

Some manufacturers estimate that a typical integrated circuit layout designer can lay out about 5 to 10 drawn devices per day. This includes the time to draw, check, and correct a layout. Until recently, the regularity factor for integrated circuits other than memory was not much greater than 1, indicating that almost all devices were drawn individually. Thus, a 50,000 device circuit required twenty man-years just for layout. Some of the newer integrated circuits boast regularity factors above 10. Table 9.1-1 gives the regularity factors for several microprocessor designs.[2] The higher regularity factors were obtained by using structured design forms like those to be described in this chapter.

One method to increase the regularity factor and reduce costs is to develop computer programs that produce integrated circuit layouts directly from high-level descriptions of the circuit's intended function. The term *silicon compiler* has been used to describe such programs. Research is currently underway in this area, and a few special-purpose silicon compilers have been developed. However, complete silicon compiler programs are not yet competitive with manual design using

TABLE 9.1-1
Regularity factor for microprocessor chips

Chip name	Number of devices	Regularity factor
8080	4,600	1.1
8085	6,200	3.1
8086	29,000	4.4
Z8000	17,500	5.0
68000	68,000	12.1
iAPX-432	110,000	7.9
RISC	44,000	27.5

structured logic forms. One major purpose of this chapter is to study integrated circuit forms that lead to structured, repeatable designs for integrated circuit logic.

9.2 PROGRAMMABLE LOGIC ARRAYS

The implementation of logic functions plays a key role in the design of digital systems. Thus, it is important to have a method to realize logic functions within an integrated circuit, without using random logic design. One important method of implementing logic functions in a regular, structured way is to use a PLA (programmable logic array). In this description of PLAs it is presumed that the logic functions used as the input are in the minimal representations desired by a designer. The broad topic of logic minimization is adequately covered elsewhere.[3] This section will concentrate first on describing a typical PLA organization. Then, programs to automate the generation of integrated circuit layout for a PLA from a set of logic equations will be discussed. Finally, PLA size limitations and PLA folding will be described.

Boolean logic equations can always be written in a sum-of-products form as follows.

$$K = AB + AC + BC \tag{9.2-1}$$

$$S = AB\overline{C} + A\overline{B}C + \overline{A}BC + ABC \tag{9.2-2}$$

$$X = A\overline{B} + \overline{A}B \tag{9.2-3}$$

$$Y = \overline{A}\,\overline{B} \tag{9.2-4}$$

In the sum-of-products form, each equation consists of one or more product terms composed of independent variables, for example, A, B, and C, that are ANDed together. If there are several product terms, these product terms are ORed to produce the desired dependent variable. The product terms AB, AC, and BC are ORed to produce the dependent variable K in Eq. 9.2-1. Normally, a PLA can realize several output functions concurrently by producing corresponding dependent variables from sets of independent variables. The independent variables are usually shared among the product terms used to form the dependent results. For example, Eqs. 9.2-1, 9.2-2, 9.2-3, and 9.2-4 are each functions of the independant variables A and B. These equations combine ten product terms to produce the four dependent results K, S, X, and Y.

9.2.1 PLA Organization

The PLA structure can be realized in either NMOS or CMOS technology. In either case, a PLA consists of two major subsections or planes. One is the AND plane, which requires double-rail inputs (each independent variable and its complement) to generate the product terms required by the defining logic equations. The AND plane produces each of the product terms of the right-hand side of Eqs. 9.2-1 through 9.2-4. The other is the OR plane, which forms the dependent results from these product terms. The OR plane must OR the necessary product terms to produce the dependent variables K, S, X, and Y of Eqs. 9.2-1, 9.2-2, 9.2-3, and 9.2-4, respectively.

A simplified block diagram of a PLA is given in Fig. 9.2-1. This figure shows the major AND and OR planes along with required supporting structures.

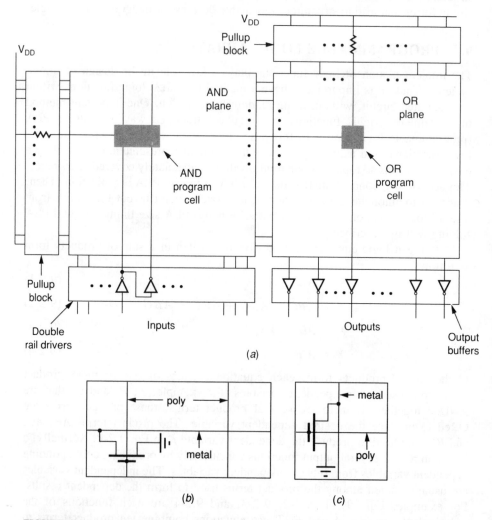

FIGURE 9.2-1
Simplified PLA architecture: *(a)* Major functional blocks, *(b)* AND program cell, *(c)* OR program cell.

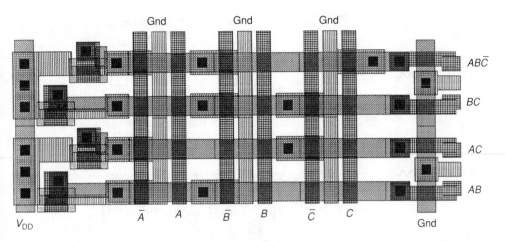

FIGURE 9.2-2
PLA AND-plane detail.

In Fig. 9.2-1, the AND plane is placed on the left with double-rail drivers at the bottom and pullup devices to the left. The OR plane is on the right with pullup devices at the top and output buffers at the bottom. Each double-rail driver accepts an input variable. This input variable is complemented and buffered to drive the vertical polysilicon lines in the AND plane shown in Fig. 9.2-2. Vertical ground lines separate each variable and its complement. The vertical ground lines are run in the diffusion level. Horizontal metal lines provide the path for each product term. The left end of each metal line is connected to a pullup circuit and the right end connects to the OR plane. The metal product lines provide area for contacts to diffusion islands at points between the vertical polysilicon lines associated with different input variables as shown in Fig. 9.2-2. This allows creation of a pulldown transistor to OR the effect of an input variable into the product term. ORing input terms to realize the AND function will be explained in the following paragraph. The product terms of the AND plane are "programmed" by selectively connecting pulldown transistors between the horizontal product term path in metal (the diffusion islands provide the drain connection) and the vertical ground path in diffusion. The vertical signal lines in polysilicon form the gates of these transistors, as is shown in Fig. 9.2-2. Because of the choice of polysilicon for these signal lines, they can directly gate the programming transistors, thereby minimizing layout area. With vertical polysilicon lines, the horizontal product lines must be metal to prevent shorts or unwanted transistors that would occur if the product lines were polysilicon or diffusion, respectively.

Operation of the AND plane of the PLA can be explained with the help of the NOR structure of Fig. 9.2-3, in which the resistor R is used to designate a pullup device. Note that in NMOS technology, the pullup device is generally a depletion transistor as shown in Fig. 9.2-2. In CMOS the pullup device is either a p-channel transistor with its gate grounded or a clocked p-channel pullup. For illustrative purposes, Fig. 9.2-3 shows the realization of the product term $M = AB\overline{I}$. The output of a horizontal product term line of a PLA should be high when

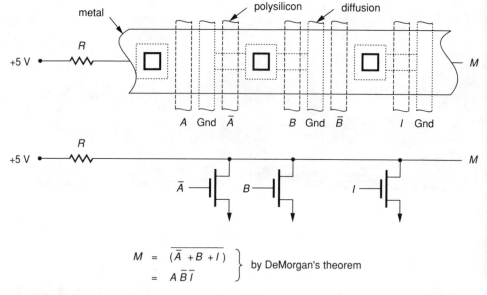

FIGURE 9.2-3
NOR structure of PLA AND Plane.

the individual variables of the product are all true. The pullup device forces the product term output to a logic high voltage unless one of the programming transistors connecting the metal product term line and ground is activated by a high input. If the programming transistors are gated by the complements of the inputs that form the product term, then the product line will be pulled low if one or more of the inputs are low (the complement of the input will be high causing the gate of the programming transistor to be high). This structure is identical to the multi-input NOR gate of Fig. 9.2-3 and requires a sizing ratio between the pullup device and the programming transistor corresponding to the multi-input NOR gate discussed in Sec. 7.4.1. By DeMorgan's theorem, a NOR gate with all inputs inverted logically realizes the AND function, as required for the AND plane.

The OR plane will have the same construction as the AND plane except that everything is rotated 90° clockwise. This may be observed from the right-hand side of Fig. 9.2-1a. For the OR plane, the inputs are the product terms from the AND plane. These are available horizontally at the right side of the AND plane in metal, where they are converted to the polysilicon level as they enter the OR plane from the left as shown in Fig. 9.2-2. The outputs from the OR plane are vertical metal lines. These metal lines connect to pullup devices at the top and output drivers at the bottom of the OR plane. Horizontal ground lines in diffusion are placed between alternate pairs of horizontal polysilicon lines in the OR plane. Programming transistors are formed with the drain connected to a vertical metal output line, the source connected to a horizontal diffusion ground line, and the gate formed by a horizontal polysilicon signal line. Once again, the choice of direction for the polysilicon lines is defined by the need to gate the programming transistors directly to minimize layout area. These transistors OR the proper product terms for each output line. As in the AND plane, this structure realizes a multi-input NOR gate; the outputs must be inverted to realize the OR function. Inverting buffers placed at the bottom of the OR plane achieve this inversion. The structure for the OR plane, including transistor sizing, is usually identical to the AND plane. A complete PLA that realizes Eqs. 9.2-1 through 9.2-4 is shown in Fig. 9.2-4.

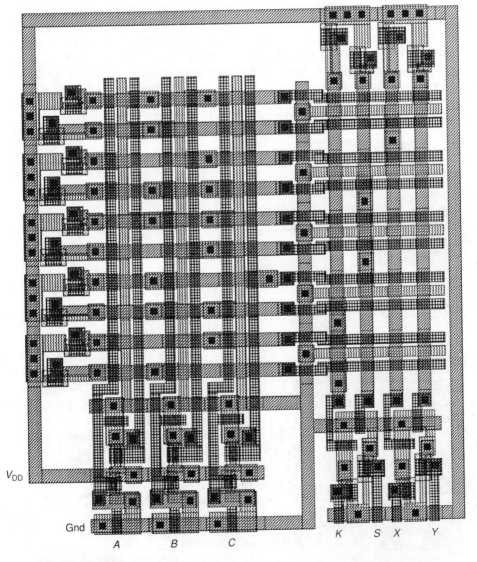

FIGURE 9.2-4
PLA layout for Eqs. 9.2-1 through 9.2-4.

From the previous description, it is easy to see that a PLA is constructed by repeated use of a few simple cell layouts. The primary cells include a double-rail input driver, pullup cell, AND (OR) plane section, AND-OR connect, programmable transistor section, and an inverting output buffer. Examples of these basic cells from the PLA of Fig. 9.2-4 are given in Fig. 9.2-5. In creating the layout for PLA cells, the design and pitch of the basic AND (OR) plane cell must be considered carefully because this cell has the greatest influence on the total area of most PLA implementations. The input drivers, pullup devices, and inverting buffers are designed to match the pitch of the AND (OR) plane cells.

A convenient measure of a PLA's size is the triplet (i, p, o) where i is the number of inputs, p is the number of product terms, and o is the number of outputs. The number of potential transistors in the AND and OR planes is given by the expression $(2i + o)p$. Increasing i or o adds to the width of the AND plane or OR plane, respectively. Increasing p adds to the height of both the AND and OR planes. A relative measure of PLA size is given by the calculation $(2i + o)p$.

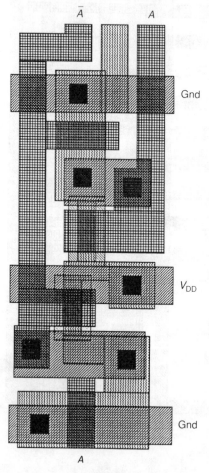

(a)

FIGURE 9.2-5
Basic PLA cells: *(a)* Double-rail driver, *(b)* Pull-up pair, *(c)* AND-plane section, *(d)* AND-OR plane connection, *(e)* Inverting buffer pair, *(f)* Programming plug.

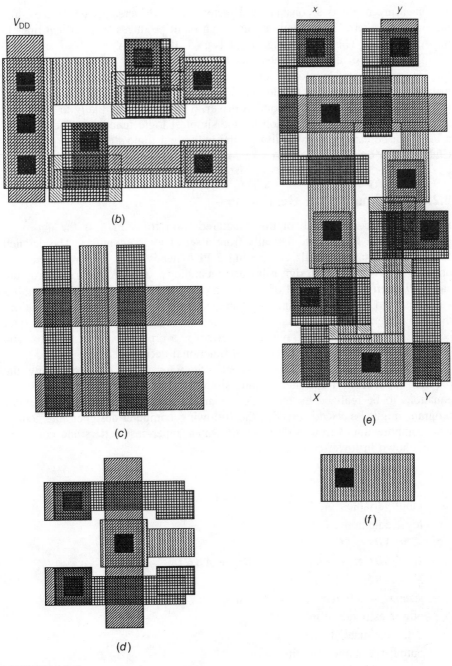

FIGURE 9.2-5
(*Continued*)

This measure neglects a constant area factor for the drivers, pullup devices, and buffers. The i term is doubled because each input produces two vertical lines in the AND plane. The PLA of Fig. 9.2-4 is a $(3, 10, 4)$ PLA.

The speed of a PLA is determined by its size and by the characteristics of the drivers and gates employed. From input to output, a PLA requires five levels of logic, including two for the double-rail driver, one for the AND plane, one for the OR plane, and one for the output driver. Thus, a PLA is likely to be slower than a direct two-level realization for the simplest logic functions. The speed of a PLA can be estimated by analyzing the individual logic stages as explained in Chapter 7. A discussion of PLA size constraints is given in Sec. 9.2.4.

9.2.2 Automatic PLA Generation

An important consequence of the structured form for a PLA is the ability to generate a PLA layout automatically from a set of logic equations. The detailed layout of the standard cells comprising a PLA needs to be accomplished only once for a given set of design rules and technology. A PLA generator program can be written to accept a list of input variables, logic equations based on those variables, and the layout definition of the standard cells. From this information, the PLA generator can formulate the complete layout of the PLA along with size, power, and delay estimates. A PLA generator is a proven example of automatic layout generation based on higher-level functional definitions.

If a PLA generator program has been written for a particular technology, the required input from a designer is quite simple, consisting primarily of the logic equations to be realized by the PLA. As an example of how a PLA generator program might be used, consider the following computer/designer interaction, with computer input from a designer shown in upper-case letters and computer output shown in lower-case letters.

RUN PLAGEN
input variables: A, B, C
logic equations:
$C = AB + AC + BC$
$S = ABC\& + AB\&C + A\&BC + ABC$
$X = AB\& + A\&B$
size: $x = 260 \ \mu m$, $y = 320 \ \mu m$
power estimate: 2 mW
delay estimate: 10 ns
output file name: pla.cif

In this example, the designer must specify the input variables and the corresponding logic equations. The program creates a geometrical layout description file (pla.cif) and size, power, and delay estimates. If the PLA generator program has been written in a technology-independent manner, then the designer must also specify the library containing the standard PLA cells for the technology. The availability of automatic PLA generation simplifies the design of many digital systems. A most important feature is that the designer can be confident the PLA layout is free from human layout or programming errors and is therefore correct for the particular set of logic equations input to the program.

9.2.3 Folded PLAs

The standard PLA form just described is ideal for some sets of logic equations; however, an improved form called a *folded PLA* is used under the following conditions. If two product terms are functions of disjoint sets of input variables, and these disjoint input sets can be spatially segregated, then it is possible for two distinct input terms and their complements to share the same AND-plane columns. This reduces the width of the PLA by two columns and is called AND-plane folding. If two output terms are functions of disjoint sets of product terms, and these disjoint product terms can be spatially segregated, then it is possible for two distinct output terms to share the same OR-plane column. This reduces the width of the PLA by one column and is known as OR-plane folding. Either of these folding operations reduces the area required by the PLA. Unfortunately, the folding of different groups of variables interact so that optimal PLA folding is a difficult problem. Heuristics are normally used to find a good folded structure for a PLA.[4,5] Both standard PLA and folded PLA implementations for a set of logic equations are discussed in the following example.

Example 9.2-1. Folded PLA Structure Implement the following logic equations with a standard PLA structure and with a folded PLA structure if possible.

$$S = AB\overline{C} + A\overline{B}C + \overline{A}BC + ABC$$

$$K = AB + BC + AC$$

$$R = \overline{A}B + A\overline{B}$$

$$W = \overline{D}E + D\overline{E}$$

$$X = DEF + \overline{D}\,\overline{E}\,F$$

$$Y = ABC + DEF + D\overline{E}$$

Solution. These equations can be implemented as a standard (6,13,6) PLA, as shown symbolically in Fig. 9.2-6. Only the programming planes are shown; an x is used to locate each programming transistor.

The equations can also be implemented by the folded PLA of Fig. 9.2-7. In the folded AND-plane (3,13,6) PLA of Fig. 9.2-7, the y's represent product terms associated with the input variables at the top of the AND plane while the x's represent product terms associated with input variables at the bottom of the AND plane. If x and y input terms appear on the same column, the line between them must be disconnected. These product terms are ORed to produce the dependent outputs.

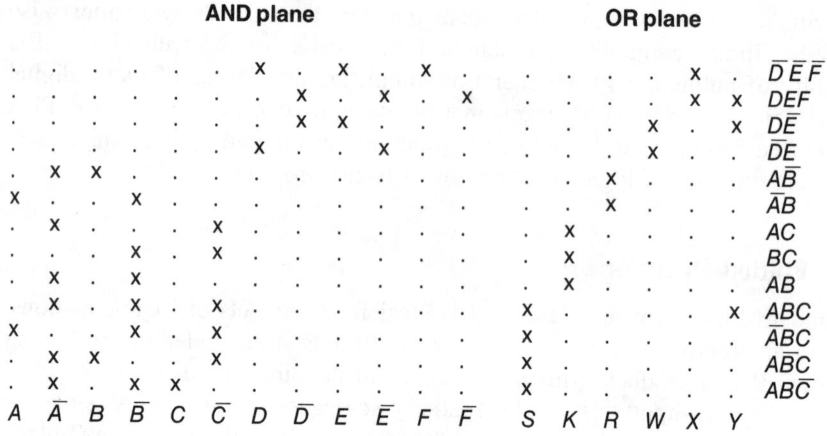

AND plane   **OR plane**

A	$\bar A$	B	$\bar B$	C	$\bar C$	D	$\bar D$	E	$\bar E$	F	$\bar F$	S	K	R	W	X	Y	
							x		x		x					x		$\bar D \bar E \bar F$
						x		x		x						x	x	DEF
						x			x						x		x	$D\bar E$
							x	x							x			$\bar D E$
x			x											x				$A\bar B$
	x	x												x				$\bar A B$
x				x									x					AC
		x		x									x					BC
x		x											x					AB
x		x		x								x					x	ABC
	x	x		x								x						$\bar A BC$
x			x	x								x						$A\bar B C$
x		x			x							x						$AB\bar C$

FIGURE 9.2-6
Standard PLA implementation (6,13,6).

In the folded AND-plane, folded OR-plane (3,13,4) PLA, shown in Fig. 9.2-8 the x's represent programming transistors associated with the lower input variables to the AND plane or the lower output terms of the OR plane; the y's represent programming transistors associated with the upper input variables to the AND plane or the upper output terms of the OR plane. According to the PLA size measure introduced in Sec. 9.2.1, the relative sizes are 936 for Fig. 9.2-6, 468 for Fig. 9.2-7, and 312 for Fig. 9.2-8. The area reduction using the dually folded PLA structures is substantial.

9.2.4   Large PLAs

Although PLAs provide an excellent means to organize sets of logic equations, large PLA structures are not necessarily desirable. Extremely large PLA structures suffer from two related disadvantages. As the size of a PLA grows, increased

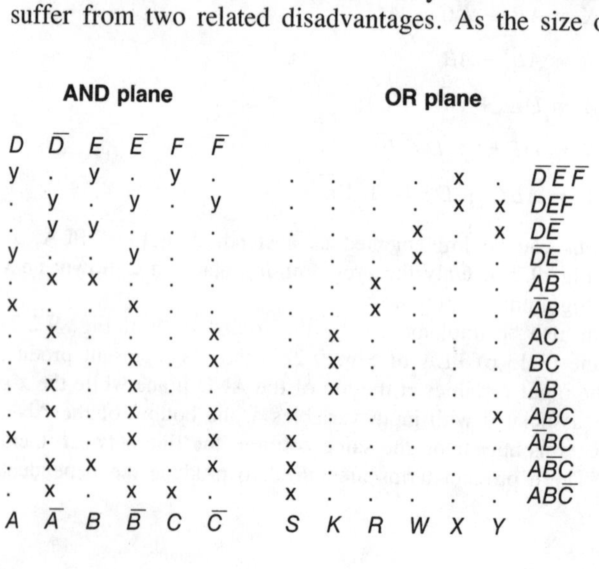

AND plane   **OR plane**

D	$\bar D$	E	$\bar E$	F	$\bar F$	S	K	R	W	X	Y	
y		y		y						x		$\bar D \bar E \bar F$
	y		y		y					x	x	DEF
	y	y							x		x	$D\bar E$
y			y						x			$\bar D E$
	x	x						x				$A\bar B$
x			x					x				$\bar A B$
	x			x			x					AC
		x		x			x					BC
	x		x				x					AB
	x		x		x	x					x	ABC
x			x		x	x						$\bar A BC$
	x	x			x	x						$A\bar B C$
	x		x	x		x						$AB\bar C$
A	$\bar A$	B	$\bar B$	C	$\bar C$	S	K	R	W	X	Y	

FIGURE 9.2-7
Folded AND-plane PLA implementation (3,13,6).

AND plane   **OR plane**

```
D  D̄  E  Ē  F  F̄     W  X

y  .  y  .  y  .     .  y  .  .   D̄ĒF̄
.  y  .  y  .  y     .  y  .  x   DEF
.  y  y  .  .  .     y  .  .  x   DĒ
y  .  .  y  .  .     y  .  .  .   D̄E
.  x  x  .  .  .     .  .  x  .   AB̄
x  .  .  x  .  .     .  .  x  .   ĀB
.  x  .  .  x  .     .  x  .  .   AC
.  .  .  x  .  x     .  x  .  .   BC
.  x  .  x  .  .     .  x  .  .   AB
.  x  .  x  .  x     x  .  .  x   ABC
x  .  .  x  .  x     x  .  .  .   ĀBC
.  x  x  .  .  x     x  .  .  .   AB̄C
.  x  .  x  x  .     x  .  .  .   ABC̄
A  Ā  B  B̄  C  C̄     S  K  R  Y
```

FIGURE 9.2-8
Folded AND-plane, folded OR-plane PLA implementation (3,13,4).

interconnection capacitances within the larger AND and OR planes slow the operation of the circuit considerably. Increasing the size of the drivers will reduce the delay, but additional power and area are then required. A second disadvantage of a large PLA is that PLAs with many inputs and outputs tend to be sparsely populated with programming transistors. In these PLAs each output is likely to be a function of only a few inputs; thus, substantial area may be wasted within the AND and OR planes to bypass unused signals for a given product term or output term. Some unused area may be recaptured through the use of folded PLA structures. The foregoing observations cause many designers to group related logic signals into separate smaller PLAs rather than into one large PLA.

The standard PLA organization was explained in this section. A typical cell based structure for a PLA allows creation of programs to generate automatically the PLA layout from logic equations. The ability to fold PLA structures can greatly reduce the area required for the PLA. Multiple smaller PLAs are sometimes used in place of single large PLAs to reduce area, power, and delay.

9.3 STRUCTURED GATE LAYOUT

The realization of logic functions is so basic to digital design that many forms of structured layout have been developed. The PLA, introduced previously, has achieved the widest usage of these forms, and because of its importance a separate section was devoted to the PLA. Other structured layout forms, including Weinberger arrays and gate matrix layout, have received attention and are covered together in this section. By design, the PLA is used to realize two-level logic functions. Yet many digital designs are simplified through the use of multilevel logic with intermediate functions used as inputs to subsequent logic functions. The structured logic forms discussed here allow direct realization of multilevel logic functions. The design, operation, and limitations of the Weinberger array and the gate matrix layout styles are explored.

9.3.1 Weinberger Arrays

The Weinberger array is perhaps the earliest example of structured logic. Originally reported in 1967[6], this structure was first based on the PMOS NAND logic gate. More recent implementations have been based on NMOS NOR gates with depletion pullups. This structure can also be realized in CMOS using p-channel pullups with their gates grounded. Because any two-level Boolean logic function can be realized in the NOR-NOR form, the Weinberger structure is completely general. This logic form is easily extended to multiple levels of logic where this is desirable. In addition, the array is easily augmented with new logic functions without change to the original structure.

The basic form for the Weinberger NOR array is shown in Fig. 9.3-1. Vertical columns with a pullup device at one end provide the outputs for logic functions. Alternate pairs of output columns are separated by ground columns. The pullup device is the load for the NOR gate, while a pull-down transistor is placed between the vertical output column and a ground column for each input to the logic function. Device sizing is determined by the NOR gate structure as explained in Sec. 7.4.1. Gate inputs are received horizontally in polysilicon. Because pullup devices are placed at the top of the vertical columns, this structure allows inputs to be provided from the left with outputs available at the bottom. Horizontal lines connected to a vertical output line can serve as inputs to subsequent logic gates. The horizontal lines can also provide the output of the matrix on the right side opposite the inputs.

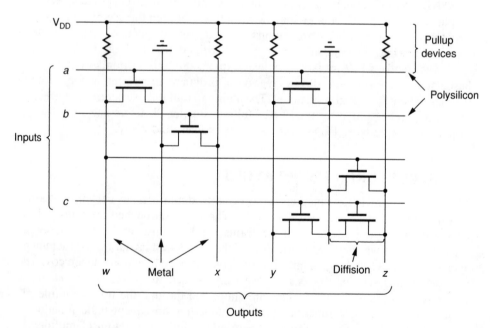

FIGURE 9.3-1
Weinberger NOR array organization with $w = \bar{a}$, $x = \bar{b}$, $y = \overline{a + c}$, $z = \overline{w + c}$.

Example 9.3-1. Exclusive-OR function   Use the Weinberger NOR array structure to implement the exclusive-OR function.

Solution.   First, the exclusive-OR must be written in product-of-sums form. This is easily accomplished by analyzing the following truth table for exclusive-OR.

A	B	X
0	0	0
0	1	1
1	0	1
1	1	0

The required logic equation is obtained by writing the complement of the logic function in terms of the zero output rows from the truth table as

$$\overline{X} = \overline{A}\,\overline{B} + AB \tag{9.3-1}$$

and converting to the NOR-NOR form as

$$X = \overline{(A + B) + (\overline{A} + \overline{B})} \tag{9.3-2}$$

Figure 9.3-2 shows a schematic layout for this function. Note that two vertical output columns are used to generate the complements of the input variables; two output columns generate the first-level NOR functions; and a final output column generates the desired dependent variable, X.

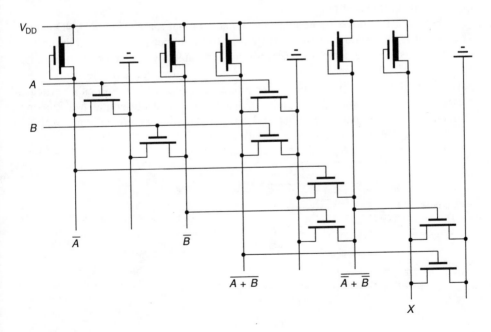

FIGURE 9.3-2
NMOS Weinberger array implementation of exclusive-OR function.

The structure shown in the example is easily expanded by adding horizontal input terms at the bottom and vertical output columns at the right. The output of the exclusive-OR example above is available as an input to expanded logic functions, potentially resulting in multilevel logic. For logic functions with many inputs and outputs, the structure becomes unwieldy because of sparse distribution of the pulldown transistors. This structure is most useful in depletion-load NMOS, CMOS with a grounded-gate p-channel pullup, or clocked logic forms because of the single pullup device per column. It does not map well to complementary gate structures. Because of the simplicity of its form, a Weinberger array is easily generated by a computer program that transforms input logic equations into a layout description. In fact, one of the first silicon compilers[7] used this structure for logic functions in its control section.

9.3.2 Gate Matrix Layout

More recently, a second form of structured logic layout that is suitable for CMOS was described. Called gate matrix layout, this organization was used in the development of an early 32-bit microprocessor.[8] Like the Weinberger NOR array, *gate matrix layout* is composed of a matrix of intersecting rows and columns as shown in Fig. 9.3-3. Transistors are instantiated along the rows, while inputs and outputs primarily use the columns. The rows are mostly diffusion, while the columns are polysilicon. Metal is available in both horizontal and vertical directions for interconnections. A polysilicon column is required for each logic input and each logic output.

Figure 9.3-3 shows a gate matrix schematic layout for a 2-input NAND gate. The layout is separated into two partitions with the upper partition containing n-channel transistors and the lower partition populated by p-channel transistors. Except for the short metal connection to V_{SS}, all other vertical lines represent polysilicon. The polysilicon lines serve a dual function, acting both as a vertical connection medium and as the gates of transistors. The horizontal n-diffusion segment in the upper partition of Fig. 9.3-3 is gated by the two polysilicon NAND-

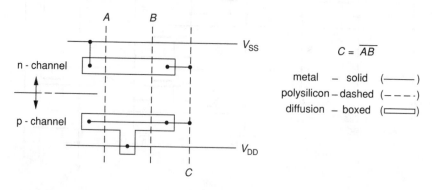

FIGURE 9.3-3
Gate matrix layout for NAND gate.

gate input lines resulting in a series pulldown path. The left end is connected to V_{SS} while the right end is connected to the vertical polysilicon output line, C. The horizontal p-diffusion segment, implementing the parallel pullup transistors of the NAND gate, is bisected by a p-diffusion connection to V_{DD}. This segment is gated by the two polysilicon NAND-gate input lines. Opposite ends are connected horizontally to the vertical polysilicon output line by metal. Note that this output line could gate other transistors to implement a more complex logic function. In general, more complex logic functions are created by adding transistors and connections. The gate matrix layout structure is suitable for implementing logic equations using NAND gates, NOR gates, and inverters in classical CMOS logic form. Device sizing is determined as explained in Sec. 7.6 for CMOS logic. The number of inputs to multi-input CMOS gates is limited by asymmetry of the pullup/pulldown paths as the number of inputs (termed *fan-in*) increases. The fan-in limit depends on the application.

To begin a gate matrix layout, the designer can draw a series of vertical polysilicon lines corresponding to the circuit inputs. The number of lines must be greater than or equal to the number of inputs because some lines may be required for outputs. Associated transistors for a gate are placed along the same row as shown in Fig. 9.3-3. Connections between transistors on different rows are accomplished with metal or with diffusion that runs between the polysilicon columns. Metal can also run horizontally to connect transistors across polysilicon columns as it did in the NAND-gate example.

Because of the structured form for gate matrix layout, symbolic representation of logic functions is possible. In fact, a layout can be defined by a line drawing using a small set of symbols and a few simple rules. This can be created by hand or with computer assistance. Figure 9.3-4 shows an early form

```
              A   B
V_SS   −  +   +  −   +  +
       :  ¦   ¦      ¦  ¦
       *  N       N  *
          ¦       ¦  ¦
       *  P   +   P  *
          ¦  !   ¦  ¦  ¦
V_DD   −  −   +  *   +  +
                    C
```

N	n–channel transistor
P	p–channel transistor
+	metal–polysilicon or metal–diffusion crossover
*	contact
¦	polysilicon or n–diffusion wire
!	p–diffusion wire
:	vertical metal
−	horizontal metal

FIGURE 9.3-4
Symbolic gate matrix layout description for two-input NAND gate.

of symbolic description using only standard symbols from an alphanumeric CRT to describe the 2-input NAND gate of Fig. 9.3-3. These symbols are defined at the bottom of the figure. Modern CAD tools use high-resolution graphics CRTs and allow symbolic input of transistors and interconnections to form a gate matrix layout. Interconnections are symbolized by single lines, and transistors are symbolized by small layout icons. The following rules allow a symbolic description of a logic function that is easily updated as technology advances.

1. Polysilicon runs in one direction only with constant width and pitch.
2. Diffusion runners may exist between polysilicon columns.
3. Metal runs in either direction and is of constant width.
4. Transistors exist only on polysilicon columns.
5. Transistor width can be increased by using multiples of the symbol vertically.

A more complex example of symbolic representation to better demonstrate this technology-independent layout style is shown in Fig. 9.3-5.

The symbolic layout methodology outlined here does not specifically consider geometrical design rules. An advantage of gate matrix layout is that a topology that realizes a particular logic function can be defined independent of layout rules. Ultimately, the pitch of the rows is determined by the minimum separation between two discrete transistors. The pitch of the columns is set to leave room

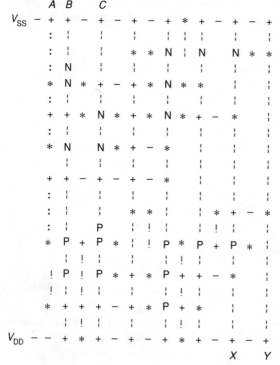

FIGURE 9.3-5
Symbolic gate matrix layout description for 3-input, 2-output logic function (see Prob. 9.8).

to place a diffusion region with contact between polysilicon columns. The matrix pitch for rows and columns is set for minimum-size transistors. The widths of the power and ground buses are set by current requirements.

The CPU for the BellMac 32-bit microprocessor was laid out first as custom logic and then later as a gate matrix layout. This CPU contains about 20,000 transistors. The final gate matrix layout achieved a respectable density of about 2 square mils per transistor in a 4 μ technology. This was slightly denser than an earlier hand-packed version. A 10% to 15% area improvement was reported by hand optimizing early line drawings for the gate matrix layout.[9]

Two examples of structured gate layout to implement general logic equations were described in this section. These differ from the PLA design style, which requires its defining equations in the sum-of-products form. The Weinberger array can be generated algorithmically but may be less dense than the gate matrix style. The gate matrix style provides near handcrafted density while allowing technology-independent layout specification. Both Weinberger arrays and gate matrix layout have been used successfully in many commercial circuits.

9.4 LOGIC GATE ARRAYS

Logic gate arrays provide a simplified means to implement digital integrated circuit designs. This implementation form is consistent with the logic design process using small-scale and medium-scale integrated circuits. Gate arrays incorporate logic building blocks that are familiar to many digital system designers without the high circuit complexity and long turnaround times that are typical for custom integrated circuits. Building blocks such as logic gates, flip-flops, decoders, and counters are available and can be combined into an integrated circuit that has many of the density, power, speed, and reliability characteristics of custom integrated circuits.

Gate arrays are manufactured as regular arrays of patterned blocks of transistors. The transistors in one or more blocks can be interconnected to form logic elements such as gates, flip-flops, and decoders. Figure 9.4-1 shows the topology for a typical gate array. The array consists of columns of transistor blocks separated by wiring channels and surrounded by I/O circuitry. This patterned array of transistors remains unchanged while allowing many different interconnection possibilities. As a result, most integrated circuit fabrication steps can be completed before the interconnections are defined. Ideally, a gate array manufacturer can stock partially fabricated wafers awaiting customer specification of a particular design. The interconnections for a particular design are formed by adding one or more levels of metal interconnection. This is done after the logic design and computer simulation for the desired circuit are complete.

Because all processing steps before metalization are identical regardless of the application, a gate array manufacturer can produce uncommitted gate array wafers as standard, high-volume parts instead of as custom parts. Therefore, the manufacturer can afford to expend considerable effort on maximizing the yield and performance of the gate array chip. After a customer provides the definition of the logic blocks and interconnections for his application, the metalization and overglassing steps are completed and the circuit can be tested.

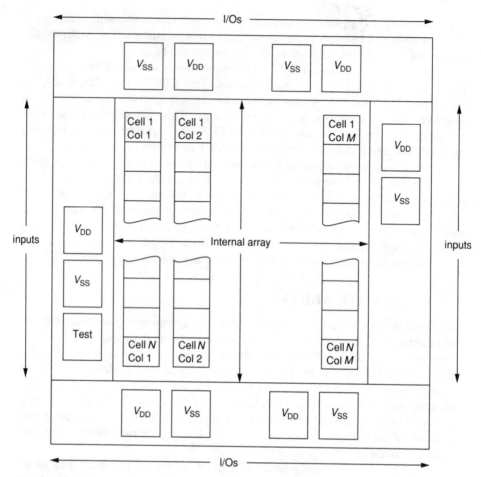

FIGURE 9.4-1
Topology for typical gate array.

Figure 9.4-2 shows that spaces or channels for interconnection wires form an important part of a gate array chip. Proper placement and sizing of the wiring channels are important in obtaining high utilization of the transistors within a gate array. If the wiring channels are too narrow, it may be impossible to interconnect all the logic circuits from different parts of the chip. For small, fixed wiring channels, this wiring problem may be minimized by leaving some of the potential logic gates unused in order to reduce wiring needs. This lessens the density of logic circuits used within the gate array, and thus wastes some of the transistor resources. If the wiring channels are widened, the interconnection wiring problem becomes simpler. However, with wide wiring channels, substantial integrated circuit area may be left unutilized in the wiring channels, increasing the cost of the final circuit. Between these two extremes, a compromise must be found. Wiring channels must be wide enough to allow acceptable transistor utilization for the gate array, without requiring excessive area for the channels. A gate array containing 6000 potential logic gates might have about 50% of

FIGURE 9.4-2
CMOS gate array chip (©IEEE 1982, Kobayashi et. al., ISSCC Proc., p. 316).

its area devoted to wiring channels, with a resulting gate utilization of 80% for a typical circuit design.

A recently introduced strategy to minimize the area dedicated to interconnections within gate arrays is to eliminate the transistor-free wiring channels. Instead, the gate array is completely patterned with transistor resources. To picture this possibility, consider Fig. 9.4-2 with each vertical wiring channel replaced by a column of transistor resources. The resulting structure is called a *channelless gate array*, or *sea-of-gates array*. In this structure, groups of transistors are interconnected to form logic building blocks as they are with the channeled gate array structure. Interconnection wiring is placed over selected transistor resources, rendering them unusable. With this strategy, logic building blocks can be created anywhere that interconnection wiring is not required. The only area dedicated to wiring channels is that specifically required for interconnections. This minimizes the previously wasted area in channeled gate arrays where dedicated wiring channels were not fully utilized.

The sea-of-gates structure has two potential disadvantages. First, the capacitance of metal interconnections over the more heavily doped transistor source and drain diffusions is greater than the capacitance of metal interconnections over the lightly doped substrate. However, this increased capacitance per unit area is more than offset by the decrease in required interconnection area resulting from less restricted placement of interconnections in a sea-of-gates array. Second, the increased freedom in placement of logic blocks and routing of interconnections complicates the CAD tools that are used to place and route the gate arrays. This is a small price to pay for the increased utilization of die area and is rapidly being overcome by new programs designed for channelless gate arrays.

After a gate array is designed and fabricated by a particular manufacturer, the wiring channel size and transistor array characteristics are fixed. It might seem that a designer could simply provide logic block and interconnection definitions to finalize a digital logic design. This design would be implemented on the fixed gate array chip by interconnecting suitable logic blocks. An important step remains, however, before the design can be released for fabrication of the interconnection layers. The placement of individual logic blocks within the gate array must be specified before these blocks are interconnected. Unfortunately, arbitrary positioning of the logic blocks is unsatisfactory because the ability to properly interconnect the blocks depends heavily on their placement. Substantial effort has been expended on developing placement and routing algorithms that provide high density for the logic blocks while retaining the ability to interconnect those blocks through allowable wiring channels. Optimal placement and routing is an unsolved research problem, and many investigators are seeking improved placement and routing algorithms.[10,11]

The design process with logic gate arrays is less complex than custom integrated circuit design because the designer works at a higher level of abstraction. Manufacturers of gate arrays provide significant support to the logic designer with definitions of standard logic elements such as NAND, NOR, D flip-flop, latches, buffers, and compound logic gates. A typical list of logic elements available from a manufacturer is given in Table 9.4-1. Providing a set of logic blocks such as these supports a design style that is closely akin to TTL logic design with 74XX devices. This allows many of today's logic designers to use microelectronic circuits in their designs without mastering the details of MOS transistor circuit design.

A typical logic block might consist of three two-input NAND gates, as shown in Fig. 9.4-3. Each NAND gate uses two p-channel and two n-channel transistors to realize its logic function. Three of these gates are grouped into a single logic block, reminiscent of a TTL 7400, quad two-input NAND package. For a typical 3 μ gate array family, high-to-low and low-to-high propagation delays average 1.4 ns with no load and 4.6 ns with a 1 pF load. The 1 pF load is equivalent to a fan-out of three and includes a 100 mil length of metal conductor. A slightly more complex circuit, a D flip-flop, is shown in Fig. 9.4-4. This circuit requires two logic blocks and a total of 24 transistors for its realization.

TABLE 9.4-1
CMOS gate array library

Typical logic functions	
Triple 2-in NAND	2-2 O–A–I
Dual 3-in NAND	2-2 A–O–I
Triple 4-in NAND	D flip-flop
5-in NAND	D flip-flop with set, reset
Dual 2-in NAND/AND	2-to-1 mux
Triple 3-in NAND/AND	1-of-4 decoder with enable (act "L")
Triple 2-in NOR	2-bit magnitude comparator
Dual 3-in NOR	Mux D flip-flop with reset
Triple 4-in NOR	D flip-flop with preset, reset
5-in NOR	Toggle enable flip-flop with reset
Dual 2-in NOR/OR	D latch with reset
Triple 3-in NOR/OR	4-bit S–I/P–O SR
Triple clock buffer	Noninverting Schmitt
Quad inverter	1-bit ALU
Dual tri-state buffer	Full-adder
Tri-state noninv. buffer	4-to-1 data mux
EX-OR	4 bit parity checker
NAND latch plus 2-in NOR	4-bit S–I, P–I/P–O SR
Triple NAND latch	Presettable down counter with reset
NOR latch plus 2-in NOR	4-in mux with enable tri-state
Triple NOR latch	J-K flip-flop with set, reset

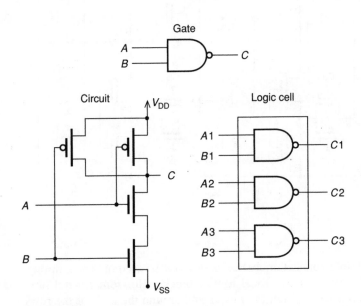

FIGURE 9.4-3
Triple two-input NAND logic block.

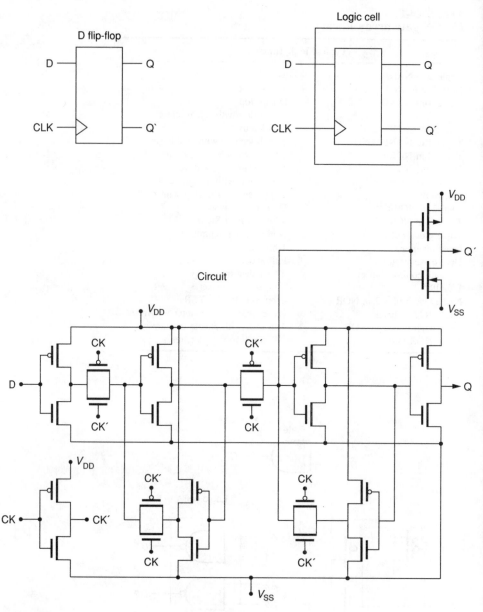

FIGURE 9.4-4
D flip-flop logic block.

Vertical metal interconnection between devices is accomplished through channels provided between each vertical row of blocks. Horizontal metal interconnection is accomplished through the blocks and around the ends of the rows. Ten horizontal wiring tracks are available per block for the typical circuits of Figs. 9.4-3 and 9.4-4. Most gate array manufacturers provide software tools to assist with placement of the logic modules and interconnection wiring. They also provide computer simulation tools for designers to verify the logical correctness and timing characteristics of proposed designs. There is interaction between place- ment and timing because interconnection lengths and, therefore, load capacitance change with logic module placements. Accurate simulation is a necessity for gate array designs as with all microelectronic circuits; it is not feasible to patch an integrated circuit with jumper wires, as is customary in correcting printed circuit board wiring errors.

Gate arrays are widely used to customize application-specific logic that would otherwise require many more IC packages. This results in considerable savings in area for many products. At least two levels of metal interconnect are generally required to implement designs with gate arrays. As the capability of technology has increased, the number of wiring layers for gate arrays has increased to three and even four layers of interconnect. Gate arrays are offered in sizes ranging from a few thousand gates to more than 100,000 gates at the present time.

In this section, logic gate arrays including both channeled gate arrays and the newer channelless, or sea-of-gates, structures were introduced. With gate arrays, logic designers can access the advantages of microelectronic circuits without becoming experts in the details of MOS circuit design. Both the global structure of gate arrays and examples of logic building blocks used in gate arrays were discussed. Finally, the requirement for CAD tools such as placement and routing programs, logic simulators, and accurate timing simulators was highlighted.

9.5 MOS CLOCKING SCHEMES

In preparation for the introduction of more complex digital systems containing storage devices and finite-state machines, the concept of clocking methods to control the movement of information is presented here. The combinational logic devices discussed previously do not require time-based control signals for their operation. The output of an ideal combinational logic circuit is completely defined at any time by the binary signals present as inputs to that circuit. For many applications, it is expedient to cause the output of a digital circuit to depend on both present and past inputs. For example, the output of a hand-held calculator in response to the "=" key depends on previous data and function inputs to the calculator. Digital circuits whose outputs depend on both present and past inputs are called *sequential* circuits; synchronous sequential circuits require a control signal to mark the passage of time and thereby delineate present inputs from past inputs. A digital signal called a *clock* serves this purpose by controlling the transfer of binary variables from one storage location to another.

An ideal clock signal is simply a periodic alternation of logic high and low voltage levels, as shown in Fig. 9.5-1a. Figure 9.5-1b shows a typical clock signal waveform as it might be observed on an oscilloscope. For 5 V logic, a single clock cycle is defined by

$$\text{clk} = 5 \text{ V} \qquad \text{for } 0 \le t < t_1 \tag{9.5-1}$$

and

$$\text{clk} = 0 \text{ V} \qquad \text{for } t_1 \le t < T \tag{9.5-2}$$

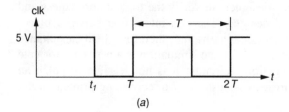

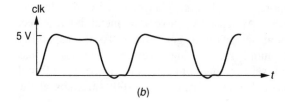

FIGURE 9.5-1
(a) Ideal clock signal, (b) Typical oscilloscope display of clock.

The time T represents the *period* of the clock signal; the inverse relationship $f = 1/T$ gives the *frequency* of the clock; and t_1/T is defined as the *duty cycle* of the clock. The square-wave output of a signal generator is an example of a clock signal with a 50% duty cycle. Circuits that operate from a single clock signal are said to use a *single-phase* clock. Much digital circuitry in the past was designed using single-phase clocks. Single-phase clocks could be used because of readily available binary storage devices (clocked flip-flops) that used one edge (either rising or falling) of the single-phase clock to update their stored value.

For reasons to be shown later, MOS logic circuits typically use *multi-phase* clocks. Two-phase clocking schemes and four-phase clocking schemes derived from two-phase clocks are common. A *two-phase* clock is composed of two related sequences of alternating high and low voltage levels with the same frequency. A two-phase clock may be supplied to an integrated circuit from an external source or may be generated within the integrated circuit itself by special clock generation circuitry. Normally, a two-phase clock is composed of two nonoverlapping single-phase clock signals. Figure 9.5-2 shows nonoverlapping two-phase clock signals. The two-phase clock signals, ϕ_1 and ϕ_2 are said to be

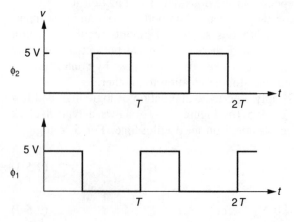

FIGURE 9.5-2
Nonoverlapping two-phase clock signals.

nonoverlapping because they are never both in the high state at the same time. This is represented by the logical AND function as

$$\phi_1 \cdot \phi_2 = 0 \qquad (9.5\text{-}3)$$

It is frequently desirable to derive a nonoverlapping two-phase clock from a single-phase clock signal. It might seem that this could be accomplished with the simple inverter circuit shown in Fig. 9.5-3a. However, a physical inverter circuit exhibits delay between its input and output signals, causing the derived two-phase clock signals to overlap when the input clock signal changes from a low to a high voltage level. This overlap condition is shown in Fig. 9.5-3b. The length of the overlap condition depends on the inverter delay. For practical inverter circuits, an overlap condition will always occur with this circuit.

Although a simple inverter cannot be used to generate a nonoverlapping two-phase clock from a single clock input, a slightly more complicated connection of simple logic gates will generate a nonoverlapping two-phase clock from a single clock input. The circuit in Fig. 9.5-4a generates a nonoverlapping two-phase clock with a nonoverlap time of at least one gate delay at each clock change. Figure 9.5-4b shows ideal waveforms for this circuit assuming identical, symmetric gate delays of length Δ for the inverter and the NOR gates. The reader should verify that the delays shown in Fig. 9.5-4b are correct. Asymmetric delays will change the time between clock edges, but will not cause overlap of the clock signals (see Prob. 9.12).

Clock waveforms have been presented in this section without restrictions on such clock characteristics as frequency, nonoverlap time, duty cycle, or rise and fall times. In fact, the clock signals shown have been idealized with zero rise and fall times. In practical circuits, clock signals are frequently required to drive a large number of gate inputs. The resulting capacitive loading can seriously degrade the rise and fall characteristics of clock signals, as was shown in Section

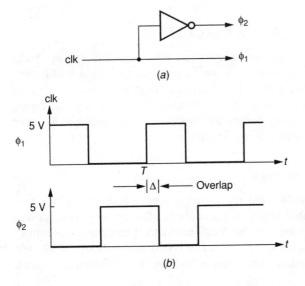

FIGURE 9.5-3
(a) Inverter used to generate two-phase clock, (b) Resulting clock waveforms showing overlap condition.

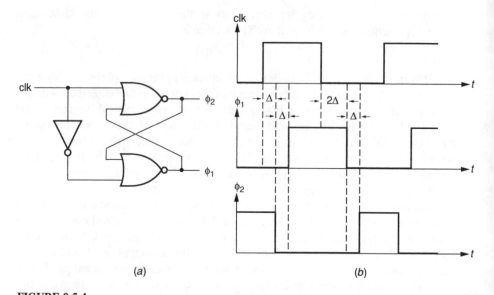

FIGURE 9.5-4
(a) Circuit used to generate a nonoverlapping two-phase clock from a single-phase clock input, *(b)* Ideal clock waveforms from the circuit of *(a)* assuming symmetrical clock delays.

7.9. To speed system operation and to minimize rise and fall times, clock signals are usually buffered and/or regenerated as they are used throughout the circuit. Exact device sizing for clock drivers depends on the size of the capacitive load and the speed with which the load must be driven. Techniques such as those discussed in Secs. 7.8 and 7.9 are used to calculate delays and set device sizes. Other characteristics of clock signals will be discussed in this chapter as they apply to the circuit under discussion.

9.6 DYNAMIC MOS STORAGE CIRCUITS

With the inverter, pass transistor or transmission gate, and multiphase clocks introduced in previous sections, the tools are in place to look at a useful storage mechanism within MOS circuits. This simple storage mechanism is termed *dynamic storage* and is widely used for momentary storage of data in digital circuits. The following subsections outline the structure and operation of dynamic MOS storage devices, particularly dynamic shift registers.

9.6.1 Dynamic Charge Storage

Among the technologies widely used for digital design, MOS technology provides two unusual features that lead to a particularly efficient way to store data momentarily. These two features are the MOS transistor's extremely high input resistance and the ability of an MOS transistor to function as a nearly ideal electrical switch. The circuit combination of these features with the source terminal of one MOS transistor connected to the gate terminal of a second MOS transistor allows electrical charge to be stored momentarily on or removed from the gate terminal of the second transistor.

The three circuits of Fig. 9.6-1 show typical circuit configurations used to achieve dynamic charge storage. The pass transistor and transmission gate devices are often designed with minimum-size transistors to reduce layout area. The inverters are the simple inverters of Secs. 7.3 and 7.5 except for a higher sizing ratio k as explained in the next paragraph. Figure 9.6-1a is useful with NMOS circuits, while the other two are examples from CMOS circuits. Operation of the NMOS circuit will be explained to demonstrate dynamic charge storage, and then the changes required for CMOS will be noted.

Operation of the circuit of Fig. 9.6-1a depends on whether the pass transistor is off or on. If the gate of the pass transistor is at a high logic voltage, then the

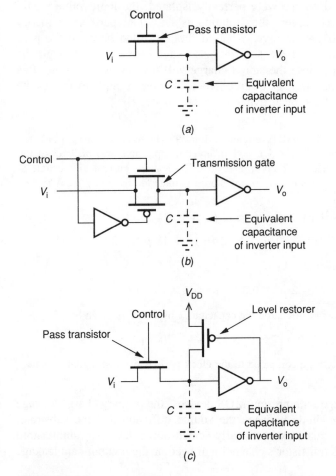

FIGURE 9.6-1
(a) NMOS dynamic storage circuit, (b) CMOS dynamic storage circuit, (c) CMOS pass transistor storage circuit with level restoration.

pass transistor conducts. In this case, the gate terminal of the inverter input transistor will be charged or discharged according to the logic voltage level at the input to the pass transistor. The time required to charge or discharge the gate terminal will depend on the gate capacitance, the pass transistor resistance, and the signal source. The gate can be discharged to 0 V, or can be charged to $V_{DD} - V_{TN}$. This sets the gate terminal to either a logic 0 or a logic 1 value, respectively. Because the inverter input voltage range has been reduced from the normal range of V_L to V_{DD} to a smaller range of V_L to $V_{DD} - V_{TN}$ by the pass transistor, the switching threshold voltage V_M should be lowered by increasing the inverter sizing ratio k from 4 to about 8. This can be shown through an analysis like that of Sec. 7.3.2.

When the gate of the pass transistor is at a logic low voltage, the pass transistor is off, thereby isolating any charge on the gate capacitance of the inverter input transistor. This charge (or the lack thereof) represents the stored logic value. If the stored charge were perfectly isolated, the logic value would be stored indefinitely. However, the isolation is less than perfect, primarily because of leakage through the reverse-biased diode created between the pass transistor source diffusion and the substrate. Leakage also occurs through the pass transistor switch. Because the stored charge will leak away over time, this circuit is termed a *dynamic storage circuit*. The following example examines the temporal characteristic of a typical dynamic storage node.

Example 9.6-1. For the NMOS circuit of Fig. 9.6-1a assume a pass transistor source diffusion area of 4 $\mu \times$ 5 μ and an inverter input gate area of 9 μ^2. If the gate terminal capacitance is 1 fF/μ^2 and diffusion leakage current to substrate is 0.2 fA/μ^2, how long does it take for the stored voltage to change by 2.5 V?

Solution. The approximate capacitance is given by

$$C = 9 \ \mu^2 \times 1 \ \text{fF}/\mu^2 + 20 \ \mu^2 \times 0.12 \ \text{fF}/\mu^2 + 18 \ \mu \times 0.2 \ \text{fF}/\mu' = 15 \ \text{fF}$$

and the leakage current is

$$I_r = 2 \ \mu^2 \times 0.2 \ \text{fA}/\mu^2 = 4 \times 10^{-3} \ \text{pA}$$

Then the time it takes to discharge the capacitance by 2.5 V is given by

$$t_{2.5} = 2.5 C / I_r = 2.5 \ \text{V} \times 15 \ \text{fF}/4 \times 10^{-3} \ \text{pA} = 9.38 \ \text{s}$$

This is clearly a long time compared to the clock periods of most digital circuits.

For dynamic storage with present MOS devices, the primary charge leakage path occurs through the diode between the source diffusion and the substrate. As MOS processes are created with linearly scaled-down devices, subthreshold leakage through the pass transistor's channel will become the predominant leakage factor.[12]

Dynamic storage can be implemented in CMOS by replacing the pass transistor with a transmission gate, as shown in Fig. 9.6-1b. Note the increase in circuit complexity caused by the addition of the p-channel transistor in the transmission gate and the requirement for a dual-polarity control signal. This situation can be alleviated somewhat with the circuit of Fig. 9.6-1c. In this circuit, called a *level-restoring inverter*, an n-channel pass transistor is followed by a special inverter with a weak p-channel feedback transistor to restore the logic high level. The p-channel transistor must be sized to have an equivalent resistance much greater than the series pulldown resistance of the pass transistor and any circuit that drives the pass transistor input. The pass transistor can discharge the inverter gate to 0 V to give a good low logic level. In this case, the inverter output is high and the p-channel feedback transistor is off. As explained in Chapter 7, an n-channel pass transistor cannot raise the voltage high enough to ensure that the p-channel transistor of the inverter is off. Nevertheless, the pass transistor can pull the inverter input voltage high enough to force the inverter's output to a low logic voltage. This low voltage turns on the p-channel feedback transistor, thereby pulling the inverter input to the upper supply voltage and holding it there.

Dynamic storage is widely used within MOS circuits because of the simplicity of the required circuitry. The NMOS version of Fig. 9.6-1a requires only three transistors, while the CMOS version of Fig. 9.6-1c requires just four transistors. Thus, dynamic storage is area-efficient compared to the static storage circuits to be discussed later. A frequent use of dynamic storage circuits is to create shift registers. The following discussion shows shift registers that are built upon a generic MOS dynamic storage stage consisting of a pass transistor and a simple inverter for NMOS or a level-restoring inverter for CMOS.

9.6.2 Simple Shift Register

Figure 9.6-2 shows a multistage MOS shift register with each stage composed of a pass transistor and an inverter. The operation of this shift register can be described as follows based on a nonoverlapping two-phase clock. Assume that a logic signal is placed at the input of shift register stage A while the ϕ_1 clock

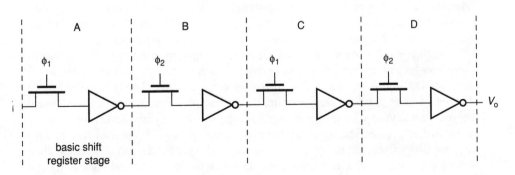

FIGURE 9.6-2
A linear shift register.

is low. Because the ϕ_1 clock is low, the pass transistor in stage A is off. Next, when the ϕ_1 clock goes high, if the signal at the input to stage A is held constant, it will be propagated to the input of inverter A. After a short delay, the output of inverter A will provide the inverted logic signal to the input of shift register stage B. At this time, the ϕ_2 clock is low and the pass transistor in stage B will not pass this input. When the clocks change so that ϕ_2 is high, the pass transistor of stage B will propagate the output signal of stage A to inverter B and then to the output of stage B. The signal will be stopped by the pass transistor of stage C because ϕ_1 is low while ϕ_2 is high. This sequence continues through the shift register chain as the clock signals alternate, causing the original input signal to propagate through the shift register stages.

At this point, a question should arise about the input to the inverter of shift register stage A when the ϕ_1 clock signal is low. In this instance, the input pass transistor of stage A is off, and the logic value is held by the dynamic storage of the input of the inverter. While the input to inverter A remains at its stored logic value, the output of inverter A will actively drive the input of stage B to the complementary logic level.

Each time the ϕ_1 clock changes to a high level, the shift register input signal will propagate to the gate of inverter A and on to the output of stage A. A sequence of alternating ϕ_1 and ϕ_2 clock signals will cause an input signal to propagate or shift through the structure at the rate of two stages of the shift register for each complete cycle of the clock signals. After N clock cycles, a logic input value will have shifted through $2N$ stages of the shift register. When a two-phase clock is used to control a shift register, it is important that the two clock phases do not overlap. If both phases of the clock were high simultaneously, a data value could propagate through multiple stages during the clock overlap time. This would result in uncontrolled operation of the shift register circuit and erratic movement of stored information.

Shift registers such as the one just described are used frequently within integrated circuits to provide temporary storage of digital signals. Such shift register storage can be used as a simple way to delay the arrival of a signal for a specific number of clock cycles. Shift register storage is also frequently used as the temporary memory for a sequential logic circuit. It will be shown later that a shift register can be combined with a PLA to provide a regular, expandable sequential machine. In general, shift registers provide dense, limited access memory for many applications within digital integrated circuits.

Figure 9.6-3 shows a parallel set of shift registers used to shift a group of signals in lock step fashion. As an example, such a parallel shift of 8, 16, or 32 data bits is sometimes required in microprocessor circuits. The basic structure of this set of shift registers demonstrates two principles important for the efficient geometrical layout of digital circuits. In Fig. 9.6-4, a symbolic layout diagram showing the geometrical topology for this circuit shows that the data for the shift register flows from left to right while the control signals (ϕ_1 and ϕ_2 clocks) flow from top to bottom. Such an orthogonal structure of data paths and control signals within a subsystem is widely used to provide a regular organization of logic

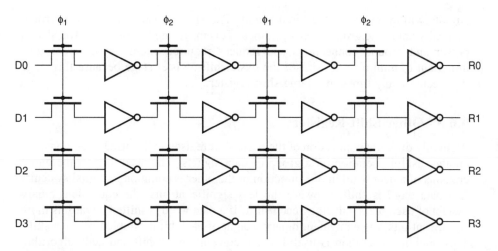

FIGURE 9.6-3
A parallel set of linear shift registers.

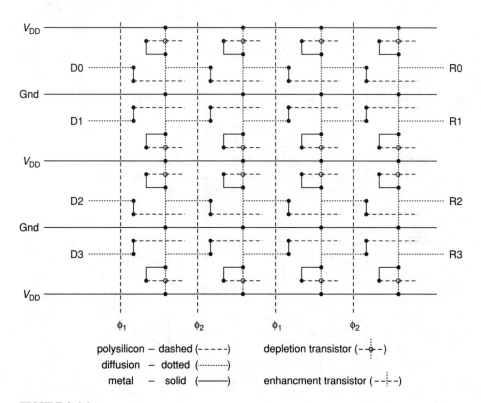

polysilicon – dashed (- - - - -)   depletion transistor (- -◇- -)
diffusion – dotted (··········)
metal   – solid (———)   enhancment transistor (- -┊- -)

FIGURE 9.6-4
Symbolic layout diagram for a parallel set of linear shift registers.

circuits within an integrated circuit chip. The shift register stages are mirrored vertically about the ground and V_{DD} lines. This mirroring technique allows shared power and ground connections and reduces required circuit layout area. It is important to minimize the size of the basic shift register stage because this stage is repeated many times in a large shift register.

9.6.3 Other Shift Registers

A slightly different connection of the basic shift register cell is used to demonstrate another useful operation on a group of data signals. The need to shift the entire contents of a data word in one direction or the other is common in digital systems. If a data word is shifted toward the less significant bits, the equivalent binary weight of each bit is halved by each shift. If a data word is shifted toward its more significant bits, the equivalent binary weight of each bit is doubled by each shift. This doubling operation is useful in the conventional "shift and add" algorithm for binary multiplication.

Figure 9.6-5 shows a simple connection of shift register stages that allows a data word to be shifted toward higher significance or shifted directly along the data path according to a control signal. The control signal is ANDed with one

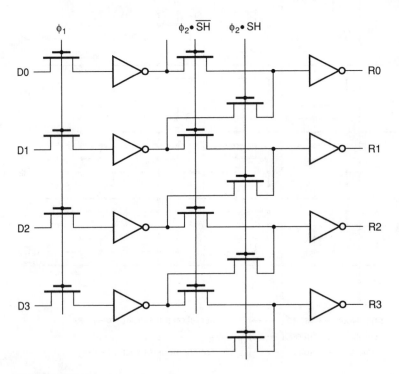

FIGURE 9.6-5
Four-bit shift-over, shift-up shift register.

clock phase to determine whether the data word is shifted or just passed along the data path. The layout of this circuit is similar to that of the parallel group of shift registers in Fig. 9.6-4 because the data and control signals are introduced orthogonally.

The purpose of this section has been to introduce dynamic storage, a most useful capability of MOS circuits. The ability to momentarily store logic values with minimal transistor and area requirements is widely used in digital ICs. The transient nature of the storage, typical storage circuits, and an application of dynamic storage to implement shift registers were all described.

9.7 CLOCKED CMOS LOGIC

Clocked logic in various forms has been used within digital MOS designs for many years.[13] Early use of clocked logic circuits was intended to minimize power dissipation in PMOS or NMOS logic. Present use of CMOS clocked logic circuits allows reduction of the number of transistors required within a design as compared with complementary static logic. Classical static CMOS logic gates require $2N$ transistors for an N-input gate, while NMOS logic gates require only $(N + 1)$ transistors. Clocked logic circuits for CMOS reduce the number of transistors to $(N + k)$ where k is a small constant overhead. This is accomplished by requiring dynamic storage of logic values within the gate structure (see Sec. 9.6). Clocked logic styles retain the desirable CMOS property of essentially zero static power dissipation. For this purpose transistors gated by clock signals, instead of complementary transistors gated by logic signals, are used to break the path between power and ground. Three styles of clocked CMOS logic are described here. The latter two have found wide application in large-scale digital circuits such as microprocessors and signal processors.

9.7.1 C²MOS

A dynamic shift register in CMOS is complicated by the need for a transmission gate and complementary clock signals rather than a pass transistor as described in Sec. 9.6. Figure 9.7-1 shows the four transistors and two clock signals required to construct a CMOS dynamic shift register stage. This construction can be

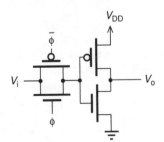

FIGURE 9.7-1
CMOS dynamic shift register stage.

simplified somewhat by the circuit configuration of Fig. 9.7-2. This form of dynamic shift register is called *clocked CMOS logic* or *C²MOS*. In this circuit, the clocked transistors are placed in series with the p-channel and n-channel transistors of a standard inverter. The primary use of C²MOS is within dynamic shift registers. All transistors can normally be sized as minimum-size devices because each stage is only required to drive the capacitance of an identical shift register stage.

Although the C²MOS circuit requires the same number of transistors, external connections, and clock phases as the standard CMOS dynamic shift register of Fig. 9.7-1, the layout is simplified because the source/drain regions of the two p-channel transistors can be merged, and the corresponding regions of the two n-channel transistors can be merged. This reduces circuit capacitance, number of contacts, and layout area.

Operation of the C²MOS circuit is quite simple. The gates of the p-channel pullup transistor and the n-channel pulldown transistor of the inverter are both connected to the input signal. For a valid logic input, one of these transistors will be off while the other is on. Clocked transistors placed in series with the pullup and pulldown transistors serve to connect these transistors to the output when the clock is high. For a high logic input, the output storage node will be discharged when the clock is high; for a low logic input, the output storage node will be charged when the clock is high. Otherwise, the output node will remain in its present state. In contrast to other clocked logic circuits, which are introduced in the following sections, the output of C²MOS is available during the entire clock cycle, although it is actively driven only when the clock is high.

A problem with the C²MOS circuit is that the load capacitance is the storage node for the dynamic charge. In the standard dynamic shift register, the storage node is inherently buffered from the output because the inverter gate is the storage node. Thus, the C²MOS circuit is more susceptible to interference from the load circuit attached to the stage. If the load is an identical C²MOS stage, the gates of the next stage can provide sufficient capacitance for the dynamic charge storage.

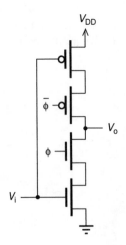

FIGURE 9.7-2
C²MOS dynamic shift register stage.

9.7.2 Precharge-Evaluate Logic

A more general form of clocked logic, called *precharge-evaluate logic*, or *P-E logic*, provides low power dissipation like that obtainable with CMOS logic, and yet requires a transistor count comparable to NMOS logic. A basic tenet of such clocked logic is a tradeoff of output availability against power dissipation caused by the resistive pullup device of NMOS logic. If the path between power and ground is broken by two series transistors that are on at mutually exclusive times, no dc current path from power to ground will exist, nor will static power be consumed. Also, because there is no dc current path to place constraints on device sizing, minimum-size transistors can be used throughout to conserve layout area. The path to V_{DD} is used to precharge the output node during part of the clock cycle, and the path to ground is used to selectively discharge the output node during another part of the clock cycle. The output is taken high during the precharge time and is logically valid during the discharge cycle only after time is allowed to selectively discharge the output. Thus, for a square-wave clock signal, valid output availability is less than 50%.

The circuit of Fig. 9.7-3 shows a three-input NAND gate in P-E form. If the precharge transistor is a p-channel device and the discharge enable transistor is an n-channel device, a single clock signal will suffice. When the clock is in the low state, the p-channel transistor conducts and the output node is precharged to V_{DD}. When the clock signal goes to the high state, the n-channel transistor will enable discharge of the output node depending on the logic condition at the circuit's inputs. For the circuit of Fig. 9.7-3, the output is discharged only if all three inputs *A, B,* and *C* are in the high logic state. If any of these inputs is in the low logic state, the discharge path is broken and the output node is left charged to a logic high value. Thus, the gate realizes the NAND logic

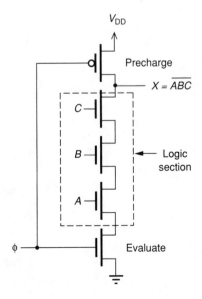

FIGURE 9.7-3
Three-input NAND gate in P-E form.

function. The P-E logic form allows realization of complex logic functions, as demonstrated in Fig. 9.7-4.

P-E CMOS logic has both advantages and disadvantages compared with classical static CMOS logic. In general, P-E logic requires less area than classical static CMOS logic because it does not require complementary transistor structures. The logic structure is ratioless, allowing use of minimum-size transistors throughout the gate logic. Because there is no dc pulldown current, a large number of transistors can be placed in series within the logic section. As another plus, it is possible for P-E logic to be faster than static logic because of lower gate loading on logic signals.

On the negative side, P-E logic has several disadvantages. The logic output value can be affected by a phenomenon called *charge sharing*. If a discharged node internal to the logic section is connected to the output node when the logic function is not satisfied, the output node charge will be shared with the discharged internal node, thereby degrading the output voltage level. Care must be exercised in circuit design to ensure that the output capacitance is larger than the internal node capacitances. P-E logic requires the addition of clock signals. There is a minimum clock rate because of the dynamic nature of the output signal, and the maximum clock rate is limited by circuit characteristics. The inputs must be stable during evaluation; otherwise, an incorrect value on the input could erroneously discharge the output node. Finally, the outputs must be stored during precharge if they are required during this phase of operation. These disadvantages are overcome by placing limits on allowable clock frequencies, and by careful selection of the types of circuits that are connected to P-E logic.

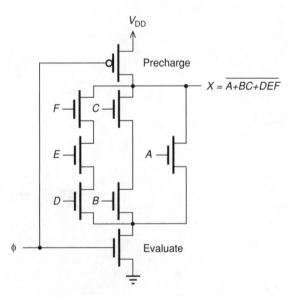

FIGURE 9.7-4
Complex logic gate in P-E form.

Multiple stages of P-E logic based on the same clock signal cannot be cascaded. Because the output of each stage of logic is driven to a logic high during the precharge phase, use of this output to drive secondary stages of P-E logic could erroneously satisfy their logic conditions immediately after the clock signal is pulled high. This could discharge the output of the secondary stage, preventing proper logical operation. A solution to this problem is to use cascaded stages with multiple clock signals so that the inputs to a stage are stable during its evaluation phase. Explanation of multiphase clock operation can be found in other sources.[14]

9.7.3 Domino CMOS

A variation on P-E logic, called *domino CMOS*, was popularized during the development of the BellMac microprocessor.[15] A domino logic gate consists of two elements: a P-E logic gate followed by a static inverter buffer at the output. The logic can be built in two forms: mostly n-channel, where the transistors comprising the logic are n-channel devices; and mostly p-channel, where the logic is performed by p-channel devices. The transistors used within the logic section can be minimum-size transistors. The static inverter at the output serves to buffer the logic part of the circuit from its output load, resulting in a more robust logic gate than standard P-E logic. The output inverter can be sized as desired, for example, to achieve symmetric output drive or to quickly drive a large capacitive load.

The behavior is explained based on the mostly n-channel form shown in Fig. 9.7-5. As with P-E logic, there is a precharge phase and an evaluation phase.

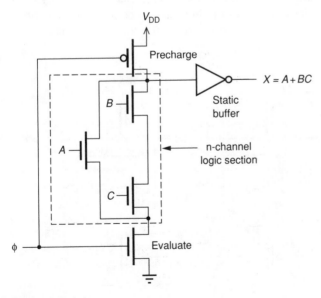

FIGURE 9.7-5
Domino CMOS logic gate.

During the precharge phase, the internal logic output is precharged to the high logic condition. This is inverted by the static buffer, providing a low logic output for the domino CMOS gate during the precharge phase. During the evaluation phase, the output of the logic part of the gate is selectively pulled low according to the logic input values. If the logic condition of the gate is satisfied, the internal output node is pulled low. This is subsequently inverted by the static buffer to provide a high logic output condition.

The domino CMOS gate has many of the same advantages and disadvantages described for P-E logic when compared to static logic. In addition, domino CMOS has advantages over the simpler P-E clocked logic form. For example, the static buffer provides output drive capability to either V_{DD} or ground. In P-E logic, the output can be driven only to ground in response to logical conditions, not to V_{DD}. When the logic condition of the P-E gate is not satisfied, dynamic charge storage at the output must maintain the high output value. The dynamic logic section of a domino CMOS gate always has a fan-out of one, thereby simplifying device sizing within the gate structure. As contrasted with P-E logic, domino CMOS stages can be cascaded successfully. The p- and n-channel transistors are easily grouped into a common n- or p-well, depending on the technology used. The fact that domino CMOS is a noninverting logic form provides at least one disadvantage over P-E logic. Lack of an inverting capability means that domino CMOS is not logically complete in the sense described in Sec. 7.2.

Examining the operation of the cascade of domino logic gates shown in Fig. 9.7-6 provides a basis to explain the choice of name for this clocked logic form. During the precharge phase with the clock signal near ground, the output of each domino stage is at the low logic condition. Thus, inputs to all subsequent domino stages are low. During evaluation, as the clock signal is pulled high, the outputs of some first-tier stages move to the high logic condition if their inputs are satisfied. The outputs of these gates may satisfy the logic for some second-

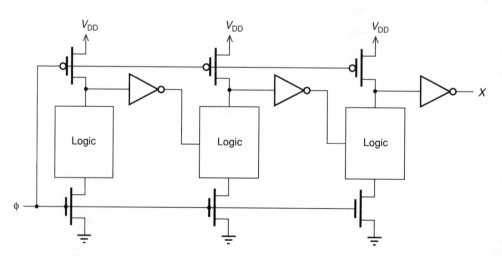

FIGURE 9.7-6
Cascade of domino logic stages.

tier stages, resulting in a high value at their outputs. In fact, during evaluation, logic decisions propagate through a cascade of stages like a falling domino chain.

As described, domino CMOS logic is a dynamic logic form. The precharged high at the input to the static inverter buffer is held by charge stored at the input to the static inverter and will not remain indefinitely. If this high could be maintained while the clock was stopped, a static logic form would result. The circuit of Fig. 9.7-7 shows a "keeper" transistor used to maintain a precharged high. This transistor can be formed as a weak static pullup device that contributes little to the pulldown current during evaluation or to static power dissipation. A weak static pullup is created by a large L:W ratio of 10 or 20:1 to increase the equivalent resistance of the transistor. This pullup transistor also improves noise immunity and allows a longer evaluation time.

Three styles of clocked logic were examined in this section. The first, C^2MOS, is useful primarily in shift registers. The latter two, P-E logic and domino CMOS logic are widely used for high-density, low-power implementations of logic equations. Both require only $N + k$ transistors, where N is the number of inputs and $k = 2$ for P-E logic and $k = 4$ for domino logic.

9.8 SEMICONDUCTOR MEMORIES

Integrated circuit memories provide the opportunity for semiconductor manufacturers to excel at their forte. That is, they create large, dense arrays of small cells with a process that is finely tuned for yield and performance characteristics. They strive to optimize the circuit design and the layout of individual memory cells to provide the maximum data storage capability for a memory part. Because the demand for dense semiconductor memory seems insatiable, a manufacturer has the opportunity to recover significant development costs with large sales volume

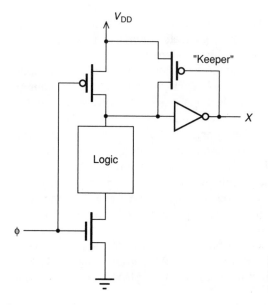

FIGURE 9.7-7
Use of "keeper" transistor to form static domino CMOS logic gate.

for a new memory design. With fierce competition for domination of the large market for memory devices, manufacturers constantly search for ways to create devices with smaller geometries and for clever circuit ideas that shrink the size of the basic memory cell or enhance its performance.

The excellent results of the research effort to provide small, dense semiconductor memories are rapidly incorporated into useful components of digital integrated system design. In many new microprocessors, ROM (read-only memory) partially replaces random logic in the control section. Designers of digital systems often find that dense memory is a good replacement for logic in other applications as well. Standard cell design libraries often provide forms of semiconductor memory as basic building blocks for systems. This trend toward increased use of memory requires digital system designers to be familiar with various types of semiconductor memory as tools for structured integrated circuit design.

9.8.1 Memory Organization

Semiconductor memories are universally organized as arrays of single-bit storage cells. These arrays are encircled by address decoding logic and interface circuitry to external signals. Figure 9.8-1 provides a block diagram of a typical memory chip organization. The memory array nominally uses a square organization ($m = n$ in Fig. 9.8-1) to minimize the external decoding circuitry necessary to select a particular memory cell. The reason for the square design can be seen by considering a memory part that contains 16k 1-bit storage cells. A memory array with 16k locations requires 14 address lines to allow selection of each bit ($2^{14} = 16,384$). If the array were organized as a single row of 16k bits, a 14-to-16,384-line decoder would be necessary to allow individual selection of the bit addressed by the 14 address lines. However, if this memory is organized as a 128-row by 128-column square, one 7-to-128-line decoder is required to select a row, and a second 7-to-128-line decoder is necessary to select a column. Note that a 128-row by 128-column matrix contains 16,384 crosspoints that allow access to individual memory bits. Thus, the square organization requires much less area for the address decoding circuitry than the linear organization.

Most memory chips operate such that the row address enables all cells along the selected row. The contents of these cells become available along the column lines. The column address is used to select the particular column containing the desired data bit. This data bit is ultimately routed to drive an output pin of the memory part. Some memory parts are organized so that n bits are accessed simultaneously. For these memories, the data from n columns are selected and gated to n data output pins simultaneously. Additional circuitry, including sense amplifiers, control logic, and tri-state input/output buffers, is normally required to create a functional memory part. However, the size of the memory storage cell and the resulting memory array are of primary importance in determining the size of the complete memory chip.

Several types of MOS semiconductor memory are in wide use today. These include ROM (read-only memory), EPROM (erasable programmable ROM), EEPROM (electrically erasable programmable ROM), SRAM (static random

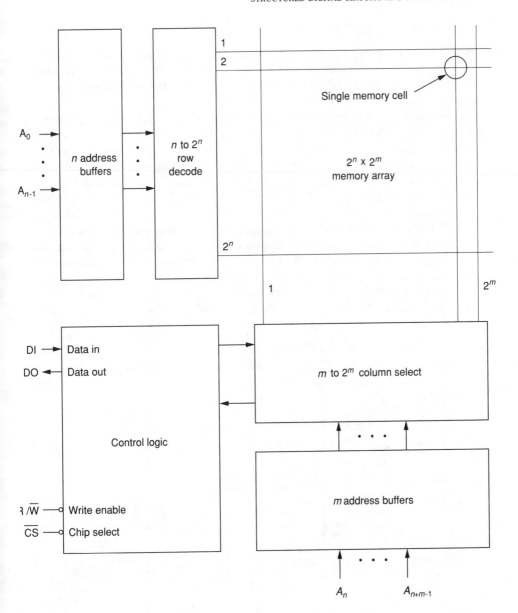

FIGURE 9.8-1
Typical memory chip architecture.

access memory), and DRAM (dynamic random access memory). These memory types derive their unique characteristics and advantages from the basic storage cell used in each, although the associated support circuitry will also vary. ROM-style devices will be discussed in the next section, and SRAM and DRAM memories will be addressed in two subsequent sections. Register array memories will be described in a fourth section.

9.9   READ-ONLY MEMORY

Read-only memory is the densest form of random-access semiconductor memory, using the presence or absence of a single transistor as the storage mechanism. Figure 9.9-1 shows the relationship between storage cells and the row and column lines of the memory matrix. Part of the memory address is decoded to select an individual row line and drive it to a positive voltage. Previously, each of the column lines had to be pulled to a high level. Each storage cell transistor has its gate connected to a row line, its drain connected to a column line, and its source grounded as shown by Fig. 9.9-1. Only if a transistor is placed where the selected row (corresponding to the row address) crosses a column will that column be pulled to a low level. Thus, each column line will be high or low to reflect the stored data along the selected row line. The remainder of the address lines are decoded to select the desired column or columns to provide the requested data.

The ROM memory contents are programmed by selectively placing transistors within the memory array. Therefore, the contents of a ROM memory are fixed as the part is manufactured and cannot be changed at a later time. In mass production, ROMs are the least expensive form of semiconductor memory; however, each unique ROM incurs relatively expensive start-up costs. As a result,

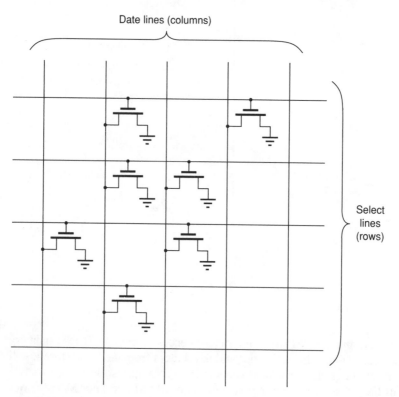

FIGURE 9.9-1
ROM memory array.

ROMs are normally feasible only for applications that require a minimum of several thousand identical memory parts with permanently stored data.

Each storage cell of a ROM may contain a single enhancement transistor. The size of the cell is set by the area required for the transistor and its associated row and column lines. An area of about 16 μ^2 per storage cell is required for today's ROMs. The memory array, requiring only enhancement transistors, can be fabricated in either NMOS or CMOS technology. The peripheral circuitry such as sense amplifiers, decoders, and control logic can also be fabricated in either technology. However, CMOS is usually chosen for newer ROMs to reduce static power dissipation of the peripheral circuitry.

9.9.1 Erasable Programmable Read-Only Memory

Many applications require semiconductor memory that is nonvolatile like ROM, yet can be reprogrammed to correct unintentional errors in the contents of the memory or to change program-based characteristics of a system. A *nonvolatile* memory is one that retains its stored data even while power is off. The ROM just described is nonvolatile and cannot be changed once it is manufactured. Other popular forms of semiconductor memory, such as SRAMs and DRAMs, have read/write capability but are *volatile*—that is, their contents are lost when power is lost. As a solution to this dilemma, the EPROM (erasable programmable ROM) was developed. An EPROM provides dense, nonvolatile storage yet can be reprogrammed as necessary. As a result, these memories are widely used in microprocessor systems and other circuits requiring nonvolatile storage where the cost of a unique ROM device cannot be justified.

The EPROM memories acquire their useful characteristics through use of a unique storage cell. This cell was originated by Intel Corporation and was called the *FAMOS* technology (for floating-gate, avalanche-injection, metal oxide semiconductor). Figure 9.9-2 shows that the storage cell consists of a transistor

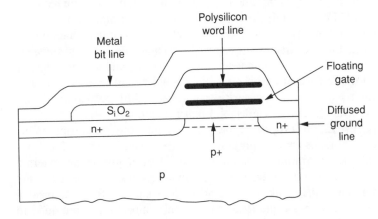

FIGURE 9.9-2
$6 \times 6 \ \mu^2$ EPROM storage cell.

with two gates, one of which is isolated from the circuit. If this floating gate somehow acquires charge to represent a stored data value, the charge remains there for a long period of time because the gate is insulated from its surroundings by silicon dioxide. The leakage paths for this circuit are of such high resistance that the time constant for the discharge path of the EPROM memory cell is tens of years. The presence or absence of stored charge is the mechanism by which the cell stores a data value, but how is the data value changed once it has been stored?

The mechanism for programming new data comes from the second part of the FAMOS name, *avalanche injection*. If a relatively high voltage (about 25 V — less for newer parts) is applied to the floating gate–substrate region, avalanche injection of electrons onto the gate takes place. This phenomenon serves to program memory by placing charge on the gate. Memory is erased by removing undesired charge from a gate as follows. If the floating gate is exposed to strong light of the proper wavelength (UV–2537 Å) for a period of time, enough energy is imparted to the stored charge to remove it from the floating gate. A quartz window is incorporated into the memory chip package; thus, all memory cells are exposed and erased simultaneously. Typical erase times for EPROMs are in the range of 20 to 30 minutes.

EPROMs are widely used in electronic systems where product volume is insufficient to justify the high initial cost of ROM parts. They are also used in prototyping microprocessor systems where reprogrammable but nonvolatile memory is required. A disadvantage of EPROM memory is the usual need to remove the memory part from the system if it becomes necessary to erase and reprogram the EPROM. The next section describes an improvement to the EPROM that was designed to overcome this undesirable characteristic.

9.9.2 Electrically Erasable Programmable Read-Only Memory

As useful as EPROM memories are, there are many applications requiring nonvolatile memory that can be reprogrammed quickly without removing the memory part from the system. For example, it is often desirable to program a standard CRT terminal with serial interface characteristics that will not be lost when power is disconnected. Yet, these characteristics must be changeable if the terminal is connected to a computer using a different serial data format. Applications such as this created a need for an EPROM whose contents could be changed electrically. Several manufacturers now offer memory parts called EAPROMs (electrically alterable) or EEPROMs (electrically erasable) that fulfill this need.

Interestingly, the EEPROMs solve the programming and erasure problems with two simple techniques. First, programming has been simplified by on-chip generation of the programming voltage. Instead of requiring an external connection to 25 V, a circuit called a *charge pump* is used to generate the necessary programming voltage from the standard 5 V supply. Second, instead of using ultraviolet light to erase the data, an internal connection is provided to reverse the electron injection phenomenon, allowing charge to be removed from the floating gate of the EEPROM.

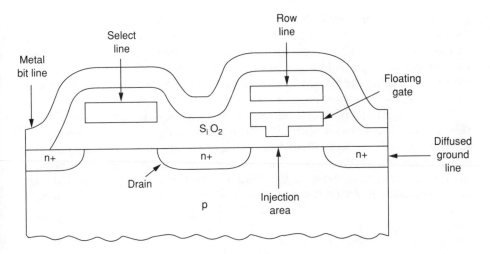

FIGURE 9.9-3
EEPROM storage cell.

The basic memory cell for an EEPROM consists of a memory transistor and a select transistor, as shown in Fig. 9.9-3. The memory transistor is composed of a dual-stacked polysilicon structure in which the bottom gate is floating. A small, thin oxide (<150 Å) isolates the floating gate from the drain and provides an injection area for electrons to and from the floating gate. Sending a short (several ms), high-voltage pulse to the row line while grounding the drain causes tunneling of electrons from the drain to the floating gate (erase). A similar pulse to the drain with the row line grounded causes tunneling of electrons from the floating gate to the drain (write). Integrating this device into a memory array requires an additional select transistor per bit as shown in Fig. 9.9-3 to avoid disturbing unwanted cells during erase or write. As a result, EEPROM memory is not as dense as EPROM memory.

The semiconductor memories described in this section each use the same basic array organization to achieve dense, nonvolatile storage. Ultimately, the storage capacity of these memory parts depends on the size of the basic memory cell used as the storage mechanism. The ROM is very dense, using only a single transistor as a storage cell; the EPROM is less dense, using a single transistor with a select gate and a floating gate as a storage cell; and the EEPROM is the least dense, requiring two transistors for each storage cell.

9.10 STATIC RAM MEMORIES

In this section the basic memory cell and organization used in static semiconductor memory circuits is examined as another example of a highly successful form of structured design. Static random-access memories, or SRAMs, are composed of static storage cells as the basic storage mechanism. Each static storage cell is formed by a pair of cross-coupled inverters. For SRAM memory, many of these cells are formed into a large memory array organized as explained in Sec. 9.8.

SRAMs differ from ROMs because they need continuous power to maintain the feedback required to hold a stored value. If power is lost, the active feedback path is eliminated, and the memory contents are destroyed. As power is restored, the memory cell will settle to a logic value that is independent of the previously stored data. Thus, the SRAM is classed as a volatile memory and depends on continuous power to maintain stored values.

For SRAMs to be useful as read/write memories, it must be possible to store desired data values in each cell. The basic memory organization must allow selection of each memory cell and accessing or storing binary values within that cell. A common structure consisting of select lines and data access lines for a SRAM memory cell is shown in Fig. 9.10-1. This figure shows a CMOS storage cell; a corresponding circuit structure is used for NMOS storage cells. A unique

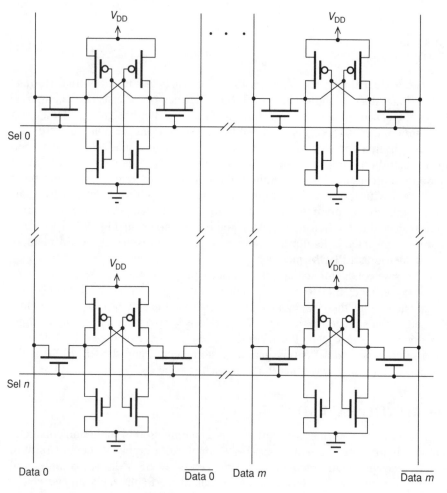

FIGURE 9.10-1
SRAM storage cell array.

select line is provided for each row of the memory array and, when high, selects all memory cells on its row. A pair of data lines are dedicated to each column to allow data from a selected cell on that column to be read or written. During a memory read, the two lines of each data line pair will be forced to opposite logic states by the contents of the selected memory cell. From a logical viewpoint, only one data line is needed to access the data within a memory cell. However, for a memory write, the two lines of the selected data line pair must be driven to opposite logic states to store a desired value within the memory cell. Because one cell along every column is selected by the row select, only data line pairs corresponding to the column containing the desired cell must be driven during a write. Other data line pairs along the row select will perform read operations.

As shown in the memory chip architecture of Fig. 9.8-1, n address lines are decoded to generate 2^n row select lines. The row select lines can be generated by the NOR decoder of Fig. 9.10-2, where $n = 3$. Here, the horizontal row lines are each pulled high by a pullup device. The pullup device could be a depletion transistor, a p-channel transistor with its gate grounded, or a clocked p-channel transistor, depending on the technology. The vertical address lines are converted

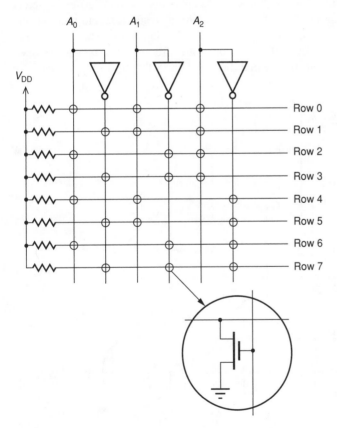

FIGURE 9.10-2
Address-to-row-select decoder.

to double-rail form and are used as the gates of pulldown transistors in the NOR structure. For example, row 0 of Fig. 9.10-2 is the logical NOR of A0, A1, and A2. If any of the three address lines is high, then the row 0 select line is pulled low. Only if A0, A1, and A2 are all low will the row 0 line be left high. Thus, the condition to select the row 0 memory cells is that A0, A1, and A2 must be low. To quickly charge the large capacitance inherent in the row select lines, a buffer stage (not shown) is usually inserted between the row decoder and the memory array.

Once a given row is selected, data from all memory cells on that row are available on the column data lines. The memory chip architecture of Fig. 9.8-1 shows that m address lines are used to select 1 of 2^m columns to access the desired data. Figure 9.10-3 shows an address-to-column selector circuit with $m = 3$ that gates one of eight columns to the data output. Address lines A3, A4, and A5 are used in a select array to choose the desired column. A3 selects the odd columns, while the complement of A3 selects the even columns. After the A3 stage, odd and even columns are paired because only one of the pair can be active. This reduces the number of available column paths by one-half. Subsequent stages of selection each divide the number of column paths by two. After m select stages, where 2^m is the number of memory columns, only a single column line is left. This line contains the desired data value. The data value must be buffered to drive the data output pin on the memory chip. To reduce the time between selection of a memory cell and availability of data at the chip output, sensitive

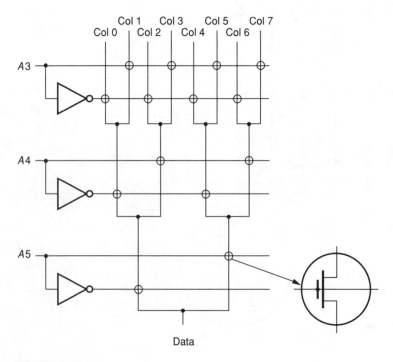

Data

FIGURE 9.10-3
Address-to-column selector.

sense amplifiers (not shown) are included within the column select structure. The purpose of these amplifiers is early detection of the data value as the memory cell drives the large capacitance of its column line pair.

Electrical characteristics of the memory cells, data lines, and select lines are particularly important when a large array of memory storage cells must be operated at high speed. The select lines cross an entire array of memory cells where they drive the gate terminals for $2c$ transistors for a c-wide array. These lines are normally run in polysilicon instead of metal because they can directly gate the select transistors without a space-consuming contact at each select transistor. The metal level is reserved for the data lines. The length (and therefore area) of the polysilicon select line and the many gates to be driven provide a highly capacitive load for the select line drivers. As a result, careful consideration must be given to the delay caused by this capacitive load when the select line buffers are designed.

Example 9.10-1. Select line delay calculation Assume a 16k × 1-bit SRAM memory is organized as a square array of memory cells with 128 cells on a side. Further, assume that the actual memory array is 2 mm × 2 mm, the polysilicon select line is 2 μ wide, and the select transistor gates are $2\mu \times 2\mu$. The select line is driven from one end. The polysilicon select line resistance is 22 Ω per square. Capacitance to substrate for the polysilicon is 0.08 fF/μ^2 and gate capacitance is 1 fF/μ^2. Estimate the select line delay as the approximate 10% to 90% rise time at the far end assuming that the select line is driven by an ideal voltage step.

Gross solution. First consider a simple solution with the total select line resistance and capacitance represented as a low-pass *RC* filter. The resistance can be found by calculating the number of squares from one end of the select line to the other and multiplying by the resistance per square for polysilicon. A 2 mm × 2 μ line is 1000 squares long. The capacitance can be calculated from the area of the polysilicon select line and the area of gates for the select transistors. The area of the select line less the gate area is (2 mm -256×2 μ) × 2 μ or 2976 μ^2. The total area of the gates will be $2 \times 128 \times$ 4 μ^2 or 1024 μ^2.

$$C_T = 2976 \ \mu^2 \times 0.08 \text{ fF}/\mu^2 + 1024 \ \mu^2 \times 1 \text{ fF}/\mu^2$$

$$C_T = 0.238 \text{ pF} + 1.024 \text{ pF} = 1.262 \text{ pF}$$

$$t_{10\%} = 0.105\tau = 0.105 \times 1.262 \text{ pF} \times 22,000 \ \Omega = 2.92 \text{ ns}$$

$$t_{90\%} = 2.303\tau = 2.303 \times 1.262 \text{ pF} \times 22,000 \ \Omega = 63.94 \text{ ns}$$

$$t_d = t_{90\%} - t_{10\%} = 63.94 \text{ ns} - 2.92 \text{ ns} = 61.02 \text{ ns}$$

Distributed lumped-parameter solution. For this solution, break the polysilicon line into 10 segments with the resistance and capacitance divided equally among the 10 segments. A SPICE simulation (refer to Chapter 4) can be used to find the 10% to 90% delay times. The results are given below.

$$t_{10\% \text{ voltage}} = 4.39 \text{ ns}$$

$$t_{90\% \text{ voltage}} = 33.77 \text{ ns}$$

$$t_d = t_{90\%} - t_{10\%} = 33.77 \text{ ns} - 4.39 \text{ ns} = 29.38 \text{ ns}$$

The lumped parameter solution with 10 equal segments is very close to the exact solution. The simple RC method presented first can be used to give a worst-case estimate of the delay at the end of the select line. (It more than doubles the actual delay in this example.) In fact, it has been shown that an estimate of half the simple RC delay is a good approximation for a distributed RC line.[16]

The delay characteristics of the data lines are also of concern because they traverse the entire memory array in the vertical direction, providing a large capacitive load. These lines are usually run in metal rather than diffusion because they must cross the polysilicon select lines. Unfortunately, during a read operation the memory cells themselves must drive the data line capacitance. Special line-driver circuits are not available to overcome this speed limitation because their size prohibits providing a line driver for each memory cell. The memory cells are designed for minimum size to increase the overall memory density, and they cannot provide good capacitive drive characteristics. As may be seen from Fig. 9.10-1 the selected SRAM storage cell must drive the complementary data lines of the cell column in opposite directions. Thus, the limiting delay condition is for the data line that must be driven high where the memory cell p-channel pullup device must charge the data line capacitance. For NMOS cells, if the pullup transistor provides a low resistance path to V_{DD}, the memory array will dissipate an undesirably large amount of power because one inverter of each memory cell always conducts. Providing a high resistance for the pullup transistors would cause an unacceptable delay in charging data line capacitance. A typical resolution of this conflict is presented next.

A common method for minimizing the pullup time for a highly capacitive line driven by ratio-type circuits is to pull the line to a voltage above the logic threshold voltage when it is not in use. This technique is called *precharge* because the line is precharged to a value at or near the high logic condition. For this scheme to work, it must be possible to isolate the line from any driving sources during the precharge time. Such sources can be isolated from the line with pass transistors as they are in a memory array. When the capacitive line is to reflect the logic condition of a driving circuit, the corresponding pass transistor is turned on. If the driving circuit has a high voltage output and the line has been precharged to a high level, the correct logic output is available immediately. If the driving circuit has a low logic output, the pulldown transistor must discharge the output line before the correct logic value is available. Because the resistance of the pulldown transistor has little effect on power dissipation, the driving circuit can have a low-resistance pulldown transistor, allowing the discharge time to be shortened. The use of precharged lines provides a means of bypassing the asymmetric drive characteristics of a ratio logic output stage for situations where a high-capacitance line must be driven. The precharge scheme is often used for buses that must be driven by many sources.

Example 9.10-2. Optimum precharge voltage for data lines Consider that an optimum precharge voltage level might exist for a capacitive line driven by ratio logic. That voltage level would equalize the charge and discharge times of the output line for a given driving circuit with a pullup/pulldown ratio R_u/R_d. Also, assume high and low logic levels of V_h volts and V_l volts, respectively. What should the precharge voltage level V_p be for fastest symmetrical operation of a read?

Solution. To reach a high voltage level, the data line voltage as a function of time is

$$V(t) = V_{DD} - (V_{DD} - V_p)e^{-t/R_u C_L}$$

For the time to reach V_h, solve for t_h as

$$t_h = R_u C_L \ln \frac{V_{DD} - V_p}{V_{DD} - V_h}$$

To reach a low voltage level (ignore the small effect of R_u), the data line voltage as a function of time is

$$V(t) = V_p e^{-t/R_d C_L}$$

For the time to reach V_l, solve for t_l as

$$t_l = R_d C_L \ln \frac{V_p}{V_l}$$

Setting $t_h = t_l$ gives

$$R_u \ln \frac{V_{DD} - V_p}{V_{DD} - V_h} = R_d \ln \frac{V_p}{V_l}$$

Letting the pullup/pulldown ratio be $S = R_u/R_d$ and solving for S gives

$$S = \frac{\ln V_p/V_l}{\ln [(V_{DD} - V_p)/(V_{DD} - V_h)]}$$

as the relationship between S and V_p.

For a ratio-type memory cell, the pullup/pulldown ratio is set higher than the normal value for logic gates to minimize power dissipation in the memory cell. Assuming that $S = 10, V_{DD} = 5$ V, $V_h = 4$ V, and $V_l = 0.5$ V, then $V_p = 3.78$ V. In practice, S will be higher than 10 and V_p should be closer to V_h.

The basic cross-coupled SRAM storage cell has several variations. Figure 9.10-4a shows a depletion-load cell for an NMOS technology. Many newer static memory circuits use a polysilicon load resistor to form the circuit of Fig. 9.10-4b. This requires an additional mask step to provide a lightly doped polysilicon with a resistance of 100k to 1MΩ/□. If a high-resistance polysilicon pullup of minimum size is used, the cell size is reduced by elimination of the depletion transistor and its associated gate-to-source connection.

Another important structure for a static RAM uses CMOS inverters to implement a basic memory cell with extremely low quiescent power characteristics. Were it not for the size disadvantage of the CMOS cell, this cell would be the overwhelming choice for static RAM memories. However, because of the necessity to implement both p- and n-channel transistors and the corresponding n- or p-well spacing requirements, the CMOS memory cell is larger than its depletion- or resistive-load counterpart. Even with this disadvantage,

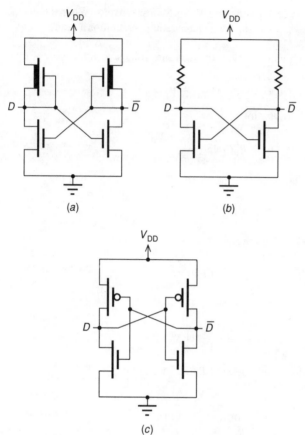

FIGURE 9.10-4
Static RAM cells: *(a)* Depletion load, *(b)* Polysilicon resistor load, *(c)* p-channel load.

many new static RAMs are built with CMOS to reduce power dissipation. The typical CMOS memory cell structure of Fig. 9.10-4c can be compared with the similar NMOS cell structure shown in Fig. 9.10-4a. The operation of the two cells is identical except that the CMOS cell dissipates negligible power because one of the series transistors from V_{DD} to ground is always turned off. The overall organization of a static memory is the same independent of the type of load device.

Unfortunately, SRAM memory is not as dense as the ROM memory types described earlier because a typical static RAM storage cell requires six transistors. The read-only memory cells of Sec. 9.9 required only one or two transistors per cell. Even when manufacturers replace the depletion pullup transistors with high-resistance polysilicon resistors, the SRAM memory cell still requires four transistors plus the polysilicon resistors. Another type of fast read/write memory, which requires only a single transistor and capacitor for a storage cell, is also available. This memory is described in the next section.

SRAMs are the fastest read/write semiconductor memory in wide use today. A speed advantage over DRAMs offsets the higher density and lower cost per bit of DRAMs in many applications. For example, SRAMs are widely used in high-speed cache memories for modern computer systems. This section has shown the characteristic cross-coupled inverter structure used for SRAM cells. Additionally, examples showing operation of the highly capacitive row select and data bit lines were considered.

9.11 DYNAMIC RAM MEMORY

The dynamic RAM (DRAM) form of integrated circuit memory has surpassed all other random-access read/write memories in the number of cells or bits that can be placed on a memory chip. A DRAM memory circuit uses charge storage on a capacitor to represent binary data values. A few transistors (first three and now just one) are required to select the cell and access the stored data. Because SRAM memory requires more transistors per memory cell (either four or six, depending on how the pullup for the cross-coupled inverters is implemented), SRAM cannot be manufactured with the high memory density of DRAM. Historically, DRAM chips provide a ratio of about 4 to 1 in the number of memory cells provided relative to SRAM chips for the highest-density memory chips of each type. The DRAM memory array, requiring only enhancement transistors, can be fabricated in either CMOS or NMOS technologies. The peripheral circuitry such as decoders, selectors, sense amps, and output drivers can also be designed for either technology. Most new DRAMs are designed for CMOS processes to minimize power dissipation in the peripheral circuitry.

Dynamic RAM gets its name because the charge stored on the capacitor cell leaks off with time, causing the stored value to be dynamic. If a logic state is represented by a high voltage level on the capacitor cell, this voltage level decreases for a p-well or p-type substrate device because of various leakage paths until the value is indeterminate or changes to the complementary state. Conversely, for an n-well or n-type substrate, the cell voltage increases with leakage. The dynamic nature of this storage mechanism is described more fully in Sec. 9.6. To prevent loss of data, the voltage on the capacitor cell must be sampled and restored within a specified time period. This sample-and-restore operation is called a *memory refresh*; it takes additional external circuitry to ensure that all memory cells are refreshed periodically. A value of 2 ms is a typical specification for the maximum time period between refreshes for DRAM memories.

At one time, most DRAMs were manufactured using a three-transistor cell. This cell, shown in Fig. 9.11-1, is based on charge stored on a capacitor with one transistor acting as a buffer to drive the read data line, one transistor acting as a read-select switch, and a third transistor acting as a write-select switch. All transistors are minimum or near-minimum size to reduce layout area. The three-transistor cell requires four bus lines for operation. These bus lines include separate read and write selects and corresponding read and write data lines like those shown in Fig 9.8-1. Providing a buffer transistor to drive the data line during a read operation prevents degradation of the stored charge during a read operation. However, the charge on the capacitor must still be refreshed periodically because

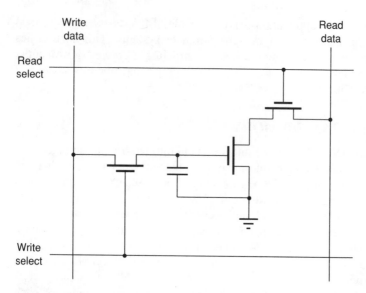

FIGURE 9.11-1
Three-transistor dynamic RAM cell.

of the leakage problems mentioned earlier. The memory refresh is performed by executing a read operation followed by a write operation. The three-transistor cell is robust with respect to the read operation because the stored charge is isolated by a buffer transistor.

Further search for increased memory density brought about the one-transistor DRAM cell. A typical cell with a single select transistor and capacitor for charge storage is shown in Fig. 9.11-2. The single transistor is a pass transistor that serves to connect the stored value to a data bus under control of a select line. The select line simultaneously selects all transistors along the same row, causing data to be placed on the column lines corresponding to each selected cell. Although valid data appear along every column, only one of these columns is further selected for connection to the output on typical DRAMs. These one-transistor cells are formed into a memory architecture as shown in Fig. 9.8-1.

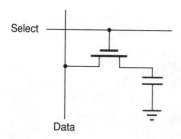

FIGURE 9.11-2
One-transistor dynamic RAM cell.

To keep the size of a dynamic memory cell small, both the select transistor and the storage capacitor must be small. The select transistor is a minimum or near-minimum size device. The small storage capacitor is required to charge the data line through the select transistor during a read operation. Because of the length of the data line, its capacitance is usually large compared with storage cell capacitance. When the select transistor connects the storage cell capacitance and the data line capacitance, the charge is shared to equalize the voltage across the two capacitors that now appear in parallel. Unfortunately, the charge on the larger data line capacitance will have more effect on the final data line voltage than the charge from the small memory cell capacitance. Thus, clever techniques and sensitive circuits are necessary to reliably sense the stored value of a DRAM cell.

One simple technique commonly used to sense the state of a dynamic memory cell involves splitting the data line into two equal halves, thereby splitting the capacitance. Both halves of the data line are precharged to a voltage approximately midway between the high and low logic levels. When a select line goes high, it connects a storage cell capacitor to one of the data line halves; the other half remains unselected. If a comparator circuit is connected with each data line half serving as an input, then even the small change in data line voltage caused by the selected capacitor cell can be detected. The inactive data line half serves as a reference point. This technique requires a comparator for each data line. A typical 256k $\times$ 1 DRAM has 512 data lines. The necessity of providing 512 comparators without using excessive area requires a simple comparator circuit.

Figure 9.11-3 shows a comparator circuit (also known as a sense amp) that has been used to sense the state of DRAM memory cells. This circuit is a flip-flop with special provision to break the cross-coupled links between the two inverters. Before a read operation, the column select, V_{FF}, and sense lines are set low. To execute a read operation, the data lines are precharged to equal voltages (V_{REF}); the desired data cell is gated by a row select to a column line, causing a slight voltage imbalance; the cross-coupled feedback lines of the flip-flop are connected (V_{FF}); and the flip-flop is enabled (Sense). The flip-flop was in a quasi-stable state before the sense line was asserted. The final state of the flip-flop is determined by the slight difference in voltage of the two data column halves caused by the selected memory cell. A later column select signal chooses one of the comparator outputs as the desired data.

Because of the regenerative action of the flip-flop, the data line half will be driven all the way to a high or low voltage, depending on the memory cell contents, and the selected memory cell on each column will be refreshed. That is, if the data cell voltage was higher than the precharged data line value, the flip-flop will switch to drive that half of the data line toward the supply voltage, thereby recharging the selected data cell. Conversely, a low data cell voltage will be discharged toward ground. All memory cells of a DRAM are refreshed by reading a cell on every row because all cells on a row are refreshed when any cell on that row is read. If a memory contains N storage cells and is organized as a square, the complete refresh operation requires a number of reads equal to the square root of N.

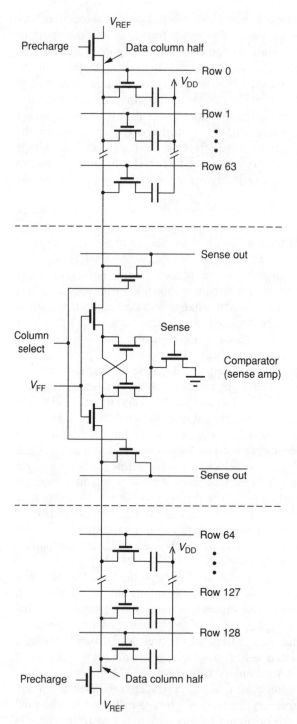

FIGURE 9.11-3
DRAM dynamic sense amplifier.

As DRAMs have gotten larger and storage cells smaller, the ratio between data-line capacitance and memory cell capacitance has increased because of longer data lines and smaller memory cells. To demonstrate how this ratio affects the sensing voltage, consider the following example.

Example 9.11-1. Sensing voltage versus cell capacitance Determine the voltage change on a DRAM data line caused by connection to a memory cell in terms of data line capacitance and memory cell capacitance.

Solution. Let the subscript c refer to the memory cell, and the subscript d refer to the data line. Before the memory cell is selected,

$$V_d = \frac{Q_d}{C_d}$$

and

$$V_c = \frac{Q_c}{C_c}$$

After the cell is selected, the charge is redistributed so that both capacitors are at the same voltage, V_f. Then

$$V_f = \frac{Q_f}{C_f} = \frac{Q_d + Q_c}{C_d + C_c}$$

The change in data-line voltage will be

$$V_d - V_f = (V_d - V_c)\frac{C_c}{C_d + C_c}$$

This analysis shows that the change in data-line voltage that must be sensed is the initial difference between the data-line and memory cell voltages diminished by the ratio of the memory cell capacitance to the total capacitance. Typical capacitance values are $C_c = 40$ fF and $C_d = 1$ pF. Thus, an initial 2.5 V difference is divided by 25, resulting in only a 100 mV change in the data-line voltage. It is difficult to detect such a small change, but modern DRAMs are able to do so reliably.

DRAMs have the highest sales volume of memory chips fabricated today. The simple storage cell described in this section leads to high density and low cost per bit. The requirement for refresh of DRAM cell contents is an important consideration in DRAM applications. The small cell/data-line capacitance ratio hinders rapid sensing of memory cell state. Further decrease in the cell/data-line capacitance ratio is an important factor in the design of next generation DRAMs.

9.12 REGISTER STORAGE CIRCUITS

Previous sections described the organization and characteristics of the major types of semiconductor memories. These descriptions were for memories that are usually implemented as stand-alone chips packed with as many memory cells as the current technology allows. Other applications for memory cells are found within sequential machines where the machine state must be stored. Sometimes this temporary storage is accomplished with the shift register described earlier.

Other times, the data must be stored for longer than one clock period. For example, a general-purpose register within a microprocessor typically must hold data while other operations are performed. The following sections describe two types of storage cells that are used within sequential digital systems.

9.12.1 Quasi-Static Register Cells

Figure 9.12-1 shows a way to combine two inverters, two pass transistors, and a nonoverlapping two-phase clock to provide a *quasi-static register cell*. Although the *quasi-static register cell* uses exactly the same components as a two-stage dynamic shift register (see Sec. 9.6), these components are interconnected in a different way. The output of a first inverter is connected directly to the input of a second inverter. One pass transistor, called the *input pass transistor*, controls the input to the first inverter. The second pass transistor, called the *feedback transistor*, controls a feedback path from the output of the second inverter to the input of the first inverter.

The operation of the sample circuit of Fig. 9.12-1 is as follows. When a binary value is to be stored in the register cell, the input pass transister is turned on, and the feedback transistor is turned off. This is accomplished through use of a LOAD signal ANDed with clock phase ϕ_1 to control the gate of the pass transistor. ϕ_2 is low so that the feedback path is broken at this time. When the input pass transistor is turned on, any signal applied to the D input of the register cell is passed to the gate of the first inverter, resulting in the same logic value at the output R of the second inverter (after two successive inversions). When the input pass transistor is turned off, the value at the input node of the first inverter is stored dynamically on the parasitic capacitance of that node. The value at the output of the second inverter is actively driven and is logically equivalent to the stored value at the input of the first inverter. During the ϕ_2 clock phase the output of the second inverter is fed back to the input of the first inverter, thus reinforcing its logic value. As long as this feedback condition is applied often enough, the quasi-static register cell will maintain its stored value.

If the register cell of Fig. 9.12-1 can maintain its stored value indefinitely, why is this circuit connection called a *quasi-static* register cell rather than a *static* register cell? The answer can be found by examining operation of the circuit

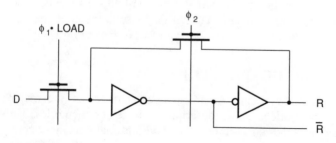

FIGURE 9.12-1
Quasi-static binary storage cell.

over a clock cycle in which a LOAD signal does not occur. Of course, while the ϕ_2 clock phase that controls the feedback transistor is high, the stored value is continuously reinforced. However, when the ϕ_1 clock phase that controls the input pass transistor is high but the LOAD signal is low, there is no active input to drive the gate of the first inverter. If this condition persists for too long a period, the logic value at this input gate may change because of charge leakage. Thus, there is a maximum time for the ϕ_2 clock connected to the feedback transistor to remain in the low state and still ensure the integrity of the data value stored in the cell. This condition places a lower bound on the clock frequency when quasi-static registers are used.

Quasi-static register cells were common in early microprocessors. For example, registers in the Motorola 6800 series of microprocessors were composed of an extension of the basic quasi-static cell that permitted dual-port read and write.[17] This cell, shown in Fig. 9.12-2, provides two gated load (write) signals on one clock phase, so the register can be loaded from either of two buses. A feedback path to refresh the stored logic value is provided on the alternate clock phase. The controller (not shown) that generates the write signals should logically AND them with ϕ_1 to avoid conflict with the feedback path that is controlled by ϕ_2 in Fig. 9.12-2. The register output, taken from the center of the register cell, drives a pulldown transistor. The output of this transistor is directed through pass transistors to one of two possible buses providing dual-port read. This cell requires four control signals (each externally gated by clock phase ϕ_1), an alternate clock signal ϕ_2 to control the feedback path, two bus lines (each bus line is common to one input and one output path), power, and ground. This cell, requiring a total of 10 transistors, will be compared with the static register cell described next.

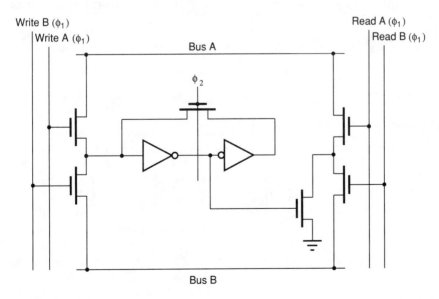

FIGURE 9.12-2
Motorola 6800 microprocessor register cell.

9.12.2 A Static Register Cell

Fully static register cells are frequently used within finite-state machines and within microprocessor register arrays. These static register cells are similar to the memory cell described previously for SRAMs, but often are designed with different constraints than those necessary for dedicated memory chips. One such static cell is based on the classical cross-coupled set-reset (SR) latch shown in Fig. 9.12-3a. This latch uses two cross-coupled NOR gates to achieve data storage. An equivalent NMOS transistor-level circuit for this latch is given in Fig. 9.12-3b. That this is a static register cell is obvious because the storage does not depend on clock signals, but only on a directly coupled feedback path.

To explain static register cell operation, the SR latch circuit of Fig. 9.12-3b will be transformed into a static register cell in two steps. Figure 9.12-4a shows the previous circuit split into a cross-coupled inverter pair with the set and reset pulldown transistors physically separated from the storage element by bus lines. These buses hold signals representing the register cell's logic state and its complement. Figure 9.12-4b completes the transformation by including pass transistors between the outputs of the cross-coupled inverter pair and the buses to the set and reset pulldown transistors. The pass transistors provide a way to isolate the register cell from the buses. Note that if both pass transistors are on, the circuit is equivalent to that of Fig. 9.12-3b, except for additional resistance in the set and reset pulldown paths because of the pass transistors. This basic static register cell consists of six transistors, four for the cross-coupled inverters and two for the connections to the buses. A CMOS version of this cell is created by replacing the NMOS inverters of Fig. 9.12-4 with CMOS inverters.

Because the basic register cell of Fig. 9.12-4b can be isolated from the buses, additional six-transistor register cells can be attached between the same

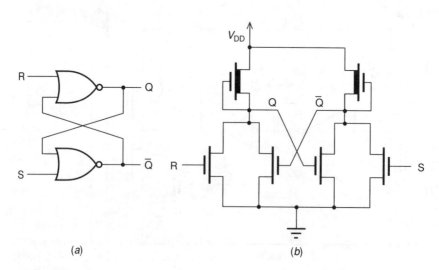

(a)   (b)

FIGURE 9.12-3
Cross-coupled NOR latch: (a) logic, (b) circuit.

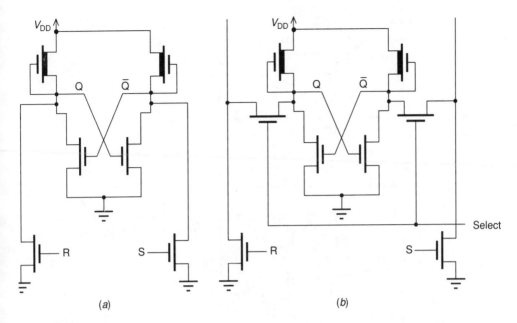

FIGURE 9.12-4
NMOS static storage cell.

two buses. Then a particular register cell is selected for read or write by selecting (turning on) both pass transistors associated with that cell. Figure 9.12-5 shows four CMOS static register cells that use the same two buses for read or write of cell data.

This static register cell is similar to those used in SRAMs. Many applications, however, do not require the considerable address decoding circuitry and sensitive read sense amplifiers necessary for large SRAM memory chips. There are two reasons for this. The first is size. A typical microprocessor application might require a register array with 1024 bits compared to commercial SRAMs with 256k bits. The smaller size reduces capacitive loading and diminishes noise sources, allowing simplified supporting circuitry. The second factor is organization. As explained in Sec. 9.8, a square organization requiring both row decoding and column selection to access a single bit is preferred for SRAMs. A typical 1024-bit microprocessor application might have 32 registers, each containing 32 bits. Each 32-bit register has its contents accessed as a unit. Thus, only a 5-to-32 address decoder is required to select a 32-bit register. Based on these concepts, then, a data value can be stored simply by selecting a cell and asserting a set or reset line. A stored value can be read by asserting the desired select line and accepting the logic value on the data bus. When this circuit is used within a microprocessor register array, a dual-port read is possible by controlling the two select transistors of a cell individually. Thus, one cell can have its stored value gated to the data bus, while a second cell has its stored value gated to the complement data bus. Many microprocessor instructions require two input operands, making the dual-port structure highly desirable for a register array.

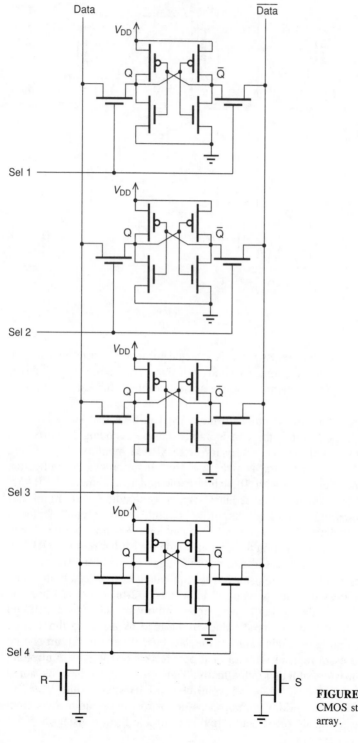

FIGURE 9.12-5
CMOS static register cell array.

Two simple storage cells were described in this section. These are important in digital design for applications that require static storage capability, for example FSMs and microprocessors. Both quasi-static and fully static storage cells were described. Individual storage cells are easily configured into n-bit wide registers where n is set by the width of the data word. The simple design and operation of these circuits make them ideal for many applications.

9.13 PLA-BASED FINITE-STATE MACHINES

Most digital systems are composed of combinational logic and memory combined in a form called a *finite-state machine (FSM)* or, equivalently, a *sequential machine*. A sequential machine is normally implemented as a forward path containing combinational logic and a feedback path that includes memory. In classical digital systems the memory is provided by flip-flops or latches. Within MOS integrated circuits a particularly simple form of sequential machine is possible. This simple finite-state machine consists of a PLA that realizes the combinational logic and a clocked shift register in the feedback path to serve as memory. A dynamic shift register such as the one described in Sec. 9.6 is often used.

Figure 9.13-1 shows the classical form for one type of FSM, called the *Moore machine*.[18] This FSM is characterized by outputs that are isolated from momentary input changes by memory. This type of FSM is of particular interest here because an excellent integrated circuit implementation based on a PLA is available. A block diagram of a PLA-based FSM is shown in Fig. 9.13-2, where a PLA is augmented with pass transistors to gate its inputs and outputs. These pass transistors in combination with the output buffers and double-rail drivers form a clocked shift register so that the next state presented by the PLA OR plane is available as the present state at the inputs to the PLA double-rail drivers after a ϕ_1, ϕ_2 clock sequence.

As discussed in Sec. 9.2, automatic PLA generation programs are available. Based on logic equations in the sum-of-products form, a complete PLA layout can be created and programmed to realize correctly the specified logic functions. It is a simple task to augment a PLA generation program to include clocked input drivers and clocked output buffers in the form shown in Fig. 9.13-2. Such a PLA generator can be used in one of two modes: it can generate a standard

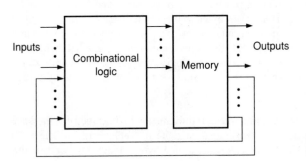

FIGURE 9.13-1
Classical finite-state machine.

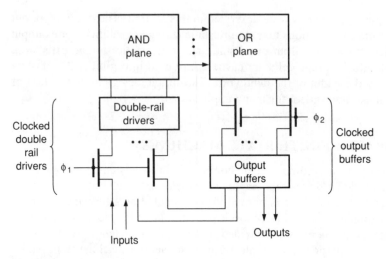

FIGURE 9.13-2
FSM based on PLA with clocked stages.

PLA consisting of combinational logic only, or it can generate a FSM formed from a standard PLA plus clocked shift register feedback created by connecting the output of a clocked output buffer to the input of a clocked double-rail driver.

To demonstrate the design of a FSM based on a PLA with clocked shift register feedback, consider the following example.

Example 9.13-1. Finite-state machine Assume that 16 magnetic switches are to be monitored remotely for a home security application. The 16 status bits corresponding to the state of the switches are available from the remote location through an asynchronous serial data link as alternating bytes of data. The serial data is received in 8-bit groups by a UART (universal asynchronous receiver/transmitter) whose parallel output must be stored in two eight-bit registers that drive LED indicators. Each register is composed of 8 D-type flip-flops activated by a rising clock signal. The first byte of data received is displayed in one set of LED indicators, and the alternate byte is displayed in a second set of LED indicators. Thus, there are 16 LED indicators, one for each magnetic switch. This task can be accomplished with a sequencer (FSM) that alternately selects one of two display registers, A or B, to store the received data bytes. To simplify the design, assume that the system is always synchronized with the first, third, and other odd bytes going to display register A and the even bytes to display register B. The FSM must also generate a data strobe signal (S) required by the UART to acknowledge that a byte is accepted. Of course, the UART generates a data ready signal (R) whenever a new status byte is available at its output. The logic components that compose the receiving system are shown in Fig. 9.13-3. Show the logical design for the PLA FSM block of this figure.

Solution. A PLA FSM that satisfies these requirements is described by the state diagram of Fig. 9.13-4 and the state transition table of Table 9.13-1. The FSM waits in state a until the UART indicates that a data byte is ready by asserting the

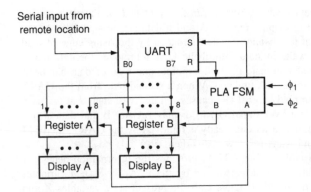

FIGURE 9.13-3
Block diagram for system display.

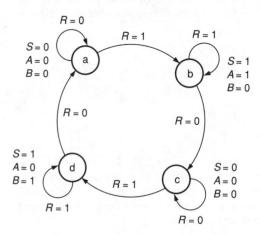

FIGURE 9.13-4
State diagram for status sequencer.

TABLE 9.13-1
State transition table for security monitoring system

Input	Present state	Next state	Outputs		
R	XY	xy	S	B	A
0	00	00	0	0	0
1	00	01	0	0	0
0	01	11	1	0	1
1	01	01	1	0	1
0	10	00	1	1	0
1	10	10	1	1	0
0	11	11	0	0	0
1	11	10	0	0	0

data ready signal (R). Data ready causes a transfer to state b at the next clock, causing a load signal (A) to display register A and a data strobe signal (S) to the UART. It is important that the display register is loaded by the rising edge of load signal A. Then the FSM waits in state b until the UART removes the data ready signal (R), causing a transfer to state c. At this point, one byte of data has been received and the value in register A updated. When a second byte from the UART is ready, the resulting data ready signal (R) causes a transfer to state d at the next clock, where the appropriate load signal (B) to display register B and data strobe signal (S) are generated. Later, after data ready is removed by the UART, the FSM returns to the first state and waits for new status data.

The state transition table (Table 9.13-1) provides the information necessary to specify the logic operations to be performed by the PLA. Two state variables are required to specify four different states. Call the present state variables X and Y and the corresponding next state variables x and y. The states are encoded with a Gray code (state $a = 00$, state $b = 01$, state $c = 11$, state $d = 10$) so that only one state variable changes for each state transition. The equations for the next state variables and the outputs are obtained from the state transition table and are given here.

$$x = \overline{R}Y + RX$$

$$y = \overline{R}Y + R\overline{X}$$

$$S = \overline{X}Y + X\overline{Y}$$

$$A = \overline{X}Y$$

$$B = X\overline{Y}$$

From these equations, it is easily determined that a (3,5,5) PLA is required—that is, three inputs by five product terms by five outputs. Two outputs form the next state variables, while three other outputs generate the data strobe (S), load register A (A), and load register B (B) signals. Figure 9.13-5 shows a complete PLA-based FSM that implements the controller described here.

The ability to create a FSM automatically from a set of Boolean logic equations is an extremely powerful tool for digital system design. Small PLA-based FSMs are frequently used as building blocks to construct larger digital systems such as microprocessors and communications processors. Large PLA-based FSMs suffer from two important limitations. A large PLA may be sparsely populated with programming sites, resulting in excessive area to realize a function. Also, large PLAs tend to be slower than alternative solutions when a large number of terms must be processed. One alternative is to use several small PLA FSMs rather than one large PLA FSM to implement required control logic; a second alternative is described in the next section.

9.14 MICROCODED CONTROLLERS

The clocked PLA structure for FSMs explained in the previous section is an excellent means to implement small digital controllers. The layout structure is regular and can be generated automatically and compactly from the logic

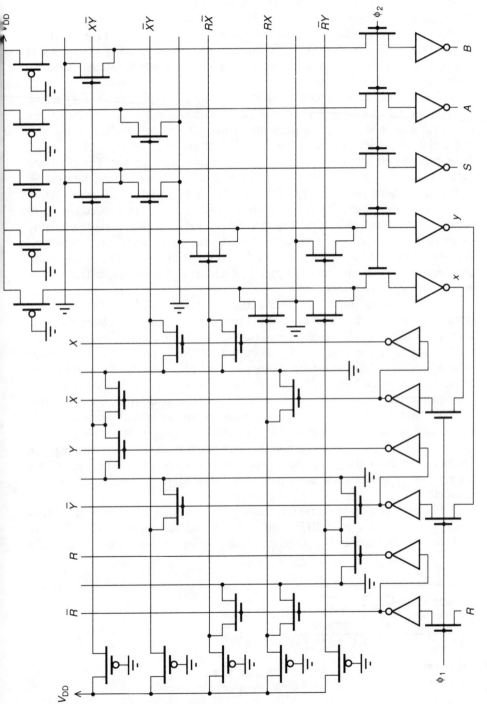

FIGURE 9.13-5

Clocked PLA FSM for sequencer.

849

equations for a system. For larger digital systems, the logic design to implement a clocked PLA FSM becomes unnecessarily complex and the resulting large PLA, if generated, would be slow. These larger systems require a method that overcomes the disadvantages of a large clocked PLA FSM yet emphasizes regularity in design and layout. A common method to implement complex digital systems in a regular way is to use a memory-based structure known as a *microcoded controller*.

A microcoded controller (shown in Fig. 9.14-1) comprises a memory whose contents are called *microinstructions* and a *next-address sequencer* that directs the execution sequence of microinstructions. A microinstruction is a set of (usually) encoded control bits that direct the operation of the logic during a clock cycle. In essence, a microcoded controller is a special form of computer. The execution hardware is fixed, and the functions performed are a result of instructions placed in the microinstruction memory. This memory is frequently read-only memory and is thus called *microROM*. As discussed earlier, memories are designed with a dense, regular structure. Because the microcoded controller consists primarily of memory, a microcoded controller can also be regular and dense. However, because microcoded controllers require the overhead of a next-address sequencer that requires design time and integrated circuit area, this technique is used primarily for larger machines.

In its simplest form, the microcoded controller of Fig. 9.14-1 does not require status inputs. The next-address sequencer simply generates the next instruction addresses in a fixed pattern, for example, by incrementing a counter.'A microcoded controller configured in this way functions as an *open-loop controller* with a fixed execution sequence. If status inputs are provided, the next-address sequencer can modify the address of the next instruction, depending on conditions presented by the status inputs. This provides a *conditional branching capability*. In either case, the function of the microcoded controller is determined primarily by a program placed in its microROM. Conceptually, programming a microcoded controller is similar to programming a microprocessor in machine language. In practice, however, the programming task is extremely tedious because of the multiplicity of individual control bits whose state must be determined for each instruction.

Figure 9.14-2 shows a typical memory organization for a microcoded controller consisting of a microROM and a memory address register (MAR). While most semiconductor memory chips are organized with a wide address bus and a

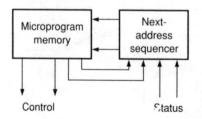

Control   Status

FIGURE 9.14-1
Simple microcoded controller.

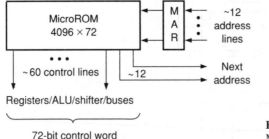

FIGURE 9.14-2
MicroROM architecture.

narrow data bus (nine multiplexed address lines and one data line for most 256k DRAMs), the memory (microROM) for a microcoded controller usually has a wide data bus relative to its address bus (perhaps 72 or more data lines compared with 12 or fewer address lines). Most of these data lines are dedicated to driving control points within the system. A few data lines are used to provide next-address information to the next-address sequencer. The next-address sequencer uses this address information along with status inputs from the controlled process to calculate the address of the next microinstruction.

A microROM organized as in Fig. 9.14-2 would contain almost 300k bits $(2^{12} \times 72 = 294,912)$ of control information and would consume a correspondingly large silicon area. An alternative form for the microROM is shown in Fig. 9.14-3. This two-level microprogram memory consists of a relatively small microROM driving a secondary memory called a *nanoROM*. This organization is based on two reasonable assumptions. First, only a few of the 2^{72} possible control word combinations of Fig. 9.14-2 are necessary in a given system. Second, many of the control words that are necessary will be required repeatedly. If fewer than 256 unique control words are necessary, for example, and the microprogram memory is organized as shown in Fig. 9.14-3, only about 50k bits $(2^{12} \times 8 + 2^8 \times 72 = 51,200)$ of control memory are required. This reduction in memory size is not free; the two-level microROM is slower than a single-level memory because a memory access must traverse two memory units to produce data. Overlapped instruction fetch and execution and careful design of control circuitry to minimize additional delay can partially offset the slower control memory.

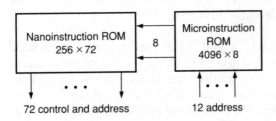

FIGURE 9.14-3
Two-level microprogram memory.

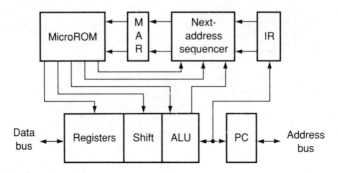

FIGURE 9.14-4
Microprogram-controlled microprocessor architecture.

A simplified block diagram for a microprogram-controlled microprocessor is given in Fig. 9.14-4. The microprogrammed controller drives a data path with registers, a shifter, and an arithmetic logic unit (ALU). A memory address register (MAR), an instruction register (IR), and a program counter (PC) are also shown. The operation of this design will be examined with the following example.

Example 9.14-1. Simple microprogrammed instruction execution Explain how the microprogrammed controller of Fig. 9.14-4 could be used to add the contents of two registers (register 4 and register 7) and return the sum to register 4. In register transfer form, the required operation is

$$\text{Register } 4 \leftarrow \text{Register } 4 + \text{Register } 7$$

Solution. To start execution, a program memory address is placed in the PC. The PC contents are placed on the address bus and a computer instruction is fetched from program memory (not shown) over the data bus and placed in the IR. The next-address sequencer uses the instruction in the IR to specify a particular starting address in the microROM. The corresponding microprogram control word is output from the microROM. This control word selects register 4 and subsequently gates register 4's contents to the ALU. If the register file is organized for dual-port read, the same control word from the microROM simultaneously selects register 7 and gates its contents to the ALU along a second bus. A next microROM control word address is generated by the next-address sequencer. This address selects another microROM control word, which causes the ALU to add its two input operands. Still another address is provided by the next-address sequencer, and a third microROM control word is selected. This last control word stores the result of the ALU operation in register 4 and prepares the microprocessor to fetch the next instruction for the IR from program memory by updating the PC contents.

This rather simplistic description of an ADD instruction demonstrates basic operation of a microprogram-controlled data path. In many instruction sequences, the next microROM address depends on results of an ALU operation. This allows conditional branching to be implemented. The preceding description omits many important considerations, including timing, pipelined operation, program counter update, and control signal generation.

It is appropriate at this point to compare the PLA and microprogrammed forms of FSMs. In general, a microprogrammed control unit is more complex than the corresponding PLA FSM because of the next-address generation circuitry. In fact, a PLA FSM can be compiled automatically once the state equations for the system are determined; this is much more difficult for a microprogrammed FSM. The peripheral circuitry for a microprogrammed FSM usually depends on the application and is thus not automatically generated. For these reasons, the PLA FSM is normally best for small, simple systems where minimum design time and circuit area are required. However, larger systems are sometimes created through use of several small PLA FSMs to offset the difficulties with large PLAs. The microprogram machine is usually more desirable for larger systems, where the additional design and area penalties can be offset by its advantages. A significant advantage is the ability to substantially change the details of operation by modifying the contents of the microROM prior to manufacture without changing the underlying circuit design and layout. This may be necessary for correction of design errors or to create new capabilities for a working design.

General agreement on the form of FSM that is most appropriate for commercial microprocessor design does not exist. Recent 32-bit microprocessors have been designed using each of these FSM forms. For example, the Bellmac 32 uses several small PLAs for its control circuitry, and the HP 9000 uses a large microprogrammed memory to control its operation.[19,20]

9.15 MICROPROCESSOR DESIGN

The focus of this chapter is structured forms of digital integrated circuits. The evolution of microprocessors provides an interesting study in the development of structured logic forms. The earliest microprocessors, the Intel 4004 and 8008, were born to counteract the high development costs for custom large-scale integrated (LSI) circuits.[21] Because custom large-scale circuits had to be designed for specific tasks, it was often difficult to reach the sales volume required to justify the development of a custom part. This literally forced the development of a logic form (the microprocessor) that could be tailored to many different applications by the addition of control logic (programs) contained in separate integrated circuit devices (memory chips). Only through the large application market that could be served could the development costs for a custom LSI circuit like the microprocessor be recovered.

As the complexity of microprocessors has increased, the design time and costs have also expanded. Development of structured designs using regular logic forms, such as those discussed in this chapter along with new computer-aided design tools, has been required to allow the evolution of microprocessor architecture. A comparison of the Intel 4004 die photograph (Fig. 9.15-1) with the Intel 80386 die photograph (Fig. 9.15-2) provides a vivid illustration of the relative percentages of silicon area used for regular structures and the relative complexity of these two microprocessors.

Today's basic microprocessor consists of a *control unit* and a *data path*. This is shown by Fig. 9.14-4 of the previous section, where the data path consists

FIGURE 9.15-1
Intel 4004 die photograph (Courtesy Intel Corp.).

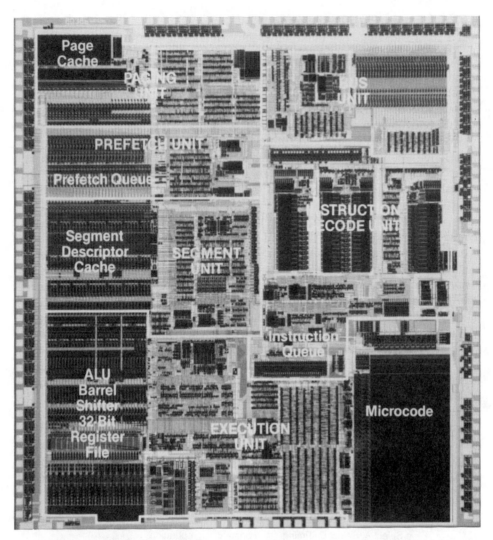

FIGURE 9.15-2
Intel 80386 die photograph (Courtesy Intel Corp.).

of registers, shifter, and ALU, and the control unit contains the microROM, MAR, next-address sequencer, IR, and PC. Although these two subsystems (control unit and data path) may be augmented with bus interface controllers, memory management units, cache memory, and other functions by different manufacturers, the present discussion will focus on the control unit and the data path as essential components of a microprocessor. The data path for a microprocessor is usually formed with 8, 16, or 32 identical bit paths. As a result of these identical bit paths, there is an inherent regularity within the data path for microprocessors. In contrast, the control units have varied structures, with most present manufacturers choosing microcoded or PLA style controllers.

9.15.1 Data Path Description

The data path, sometimes called the *execution unit*, is the place where the microprocessor executes operations such as addition, subtraction, shifts, rotates, and Boolean logical functions on data. Figure 9.15-3 shows a typical n-bit data path structure consisting of a dual-port register array, a barrel shifter, an ALU, interconnection buses, and support circuitry. Data flows along n parallel paths in the horizontal direction, while control of the data flow and ALU operations is provided vertically from the top of the data path. Execution of a typical data path operation (see Example 9.14-1) requires selection of operands from two registers, execution of an operation on the two selected operands, and placement of the result in a register. The elements of the data path must be designed to facilitate such operations.

The use of a dual-port register array is convenient for the fast execution of microprocessor programs. This local storage is usually provided within the data path as a small array of static memory cells. These are organized as an $n \times m$ structure where n is the width in bits of the microprocessor data bus and m is the number of registers provided. Because an ALU operation often requires access to the contents of two registers before execution can commence, most register arrays are organized with dual-port read access. With a dual-port register array, contents from two separate registers can be fetched simultaneously to minimize the delay before execution of an operation can begin.

The memory cell structure of a dual-port register array is quite similar to that of an SRAM cell. There is a need, however, for two data buses and a mechanism to allow the contents of each register to be switched to either data bus. The memory cell used for the dual-port register array of the Berkeley RISC processor[22] is shown in Fig. 9.15-4. In this circuit, the designers took advantage of the provision of double-rail data access to allow the contents from two registers to be obtained simultaneously. Remember that double-rail access is normally required to allow storage of data in a simple cross-coupled inverter storage cell.

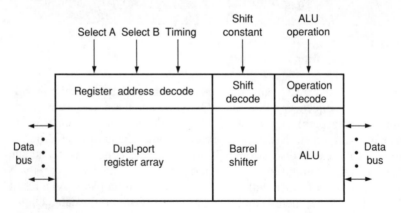

FIGURE 9.15-3
Microprocessor data path.

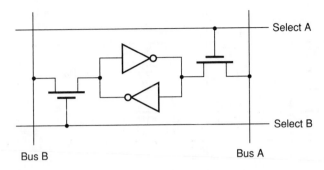

FIGURE 9.15-4
Dual-port register cell.

For a write operation, both data lines must be gated to the storage cell with complementary values. However, the contents of the storage cell may be read by gating the cell to either data line. If provision is made to drive the two select lines, A and B, separately for a read operation, then it is possible to obtain the data from a first register along one rail of the data bus (bus A), while the data from a second register is obtained along the other rail of the data bus (bus B). Of course, the data from the second bus will be the complement of the cell data and must be inverted.

9.15.2 Barrel Shifter

A second component that is included in the data path for many microprocessors is a structure that allows the contents of the data path to be shifted or rotated. A variable-length shift of a bit on the data path requires the possibility of connecting the selected bit to any one of several other bit paths. A 1-to-n multiplexer circuit for each bit will accomplish the desired connection. An ideal means of implementing multiplexer circuits is provided by the pass transistor available within MOS integrated circuits.

A particularly useful circuit structure to implement a shift or rotate is known as a *barrel shifter*. This circuit structure can be explained by first considering Fig. 9.15-5, which shows the circuit diagram of a general-purpose bus multiplexer for a 4-bit data path. This multiplexer circuit requires 16 pass transistors to allow connection of any bit line to any other bit line. If each pass transistor could be selected individually, 16 control lines would be required. Because most requirements are for parallel shifts with all bits moved the same number of bit positions, only four shift possibilities are really necessary. Figure 9.15-6 shows a better circuit with the pass transistors connected in groups of four, reducing control line requirements from 16 to 4 separate control lines, 50-53. A particular control line might be selected by encoding a 2-bit control field to drive a 2-to-4 decoder circuit. The individual decoder output would enable the proper shift control line. For a 32-bit data path, 1024 pass transistors are necessary to allow the desired shift operations. Assuming only parallel shifts, 32 control lines selected by a 5-bit encoded control field are sufficient.

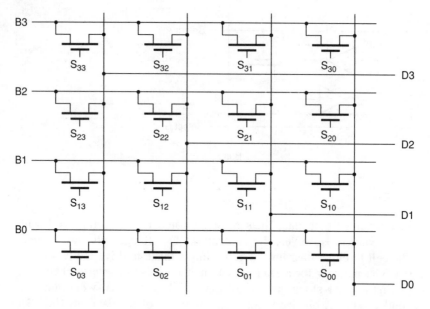

FIGURE 9.15-5
General bus multiplexer (16 control lines, $S_{00} \ldots S_{33}$).

Studying the barrel shifter structure of Fig. 9.15-6 allows some interesting observations. First, note that if the data path runs horizontally, it is necessary to provide a vertical path for control to implement the shift function. This vertical connection is sometimes used to insert or extract external data to or from the data path along D4–D6 or D0–D3. Remembering that control signals S0–S3 for the data path are provided vertically, the vertical path of the barrel shifter can be used to insert data that is part of the data path control instruction. Data that is part of the data path instruction is usually called *literal* or *immediate* data. Second, recognition of the simplicity of the barrel shifter structure suggests that the vertical pitch of the data path layout will probably be limited by the vertical pitch of the register array or the ALU rather than by the barrel shifter. This observation allows minimization of the horizontal dimension of a barrel shifter while the vertical dimension is stretched to match the rest of the data path to obtain area efficiency of the layout.

9.15.3 Arithmetic Logic Unit

The arithmetic logic unit (ALU) is the last important part of the data path to be discussed. As its name suggests, the ALU must provide arithmetic and logic operations on data furnished from the data path. The ALU accepts two operands, performs a specified operation, and outputs the result. A block diagram of a 32-bit wide ALU showing the inputs, control, and outputs is given in Fig. 9.15-7. The A and B inputs of the ALU along with the dual-port register array discussed earlier suggest that two parallel 32-bit buses should be provided in the data path

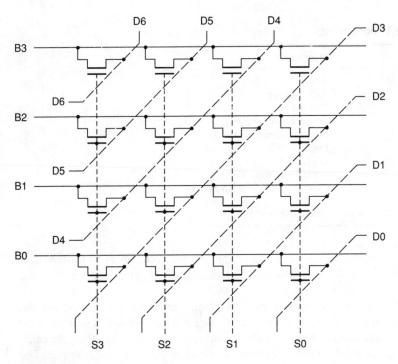

FIGURE 9.15-6
Barrel shifter (4 control lines, S0-S3).

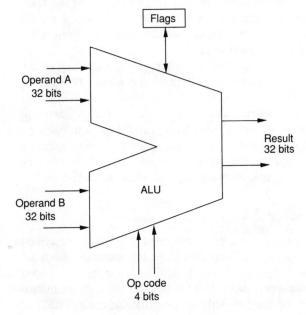

FIGURE 9.15-7
Arithmetic logic unit.

TABLE 9.15-1
Common ALU operations

Mnemonic	Operation
ADD	Add
ADC	Add with carry
SUB	Subtract
SUBC	Subtract with borrow
NEG	Negate (2's complement)
AND	Logical AND
OR	Logical OR
EOR	Logical exclusive-OR
COM	Complement (1's complement)
CMP	Compare
ASL	Arithmetic shift left

between the register array and the ALU. This allows both inputs to receive data simultaneously. One of the two parallel buses is used to return the result to the register array after the ALU operation is complete.

The ALU for a microprocessor is normally expected to accomplish the operations of Table 9.15-1 as a minimum. These 11 functions require a 4-bit encoded operation code (often abbreviated as *op code*) for their selection, although a 3-bit op code could be used if certain of the operations were combined. For example, the operations ADD and ADC could be implemented by specifying the ALU ADC operation with a separate control line to choose 0 or the previous carry as the carry input to implement ADD or ADC, respectively. The function COM could be implemented by using the EOR operation with the second ALU operand set to all 1s. And the ASL function could be implemented by providing the same operand to both ALU inputs and executing the ADD operation. Although a 3-bit ALU operation code would suffice, other control lines are required to select the carry input or set the second ALU operand to all 1s.

The ALU execution time may limit the maximum clock frequency of the microprocessor unless special care is taken for arithmetic operations. These operations are slowed by carry or borrow propagation delays across the width of the ALU. This problem has worsened as data bus widths have moved from 8 through 16 to 32 bits. Most microprocessors use a precharged carry line with each bit position of the ALU required to generate a carry propagate or a carry generate signal. In addition, newer microprocessors include one or more levels of carry skip circuits to speed carry propagation across groups of adjacent stages.

9.15.4 Microcoded Controller

Most present microprocessors use a form of microcoded controller (described earlier in this chapter) to generate required control signals for operation. Both the Motorola 68030 shown in Fig. 9.1-3 and the Intel 80386 shown in Fig. 9.15-2 are examples of microcoded microprocessors. Many times, bit fields of the microprocessor instruction word can be used directly to simplify the control field of the microROM output. For example, encoded register specification fields can be gated from the instruction register to the data path to save microcode bits. Also, the operation code field of the instruction can directly specify the address in the microROM where execution of an instruction should start. Specific details of controller implementation vary considerably with different microprocessors and different manufacturers.

9.16 SYSTOLIC ARRAYS

The ability to place hundreds of thousands of transistors on a single integrated circuit and then replicate that circuit inexpensively has led many researchers to propose the use of connected sets of identical integrated circuits to solve problems in parallel. In particular, one class of parallel processors has been given the name *systolic arrays* because the data flow through the array is analogous to the rhythmic flow of blood through human arteries after each heartbeat.[23] In essence, the concept of systolic processing combines a highly parallel array of identical processors with local interconnections and rhythmic data flow. The array of processors may span several integrated circuit chips. The connections are formed so that data is accepted and processed at each stage, with the result ready for output to the next stage as new data arrives at the current stage. The objective is to keep most processors busy doing useful work to reduce the time to achieve a result. Three examples of parallel computational systems using multiple, identical circuits are described in this section.

9.16.1 Systolic Matrix Multiplication

Figure 9.16-1 shows a systolic interconnection of processors arranged to compute the matrix multiplication product

$$C = A \times B$$

Consider any single hexagonal processing stage of this array. An element of the A matrix arrives from the upper left; an element of the B matrix arrives from the upper right; and a partially computed element of the C matrix arrives from the bottom. The calculation $c_{ij} = c_{ij} + a_{ik}b_{kj}$ is performed, and the new value for c_{ij} is passed up to the next processing stage. Two successive steps of this calculation are shown in Fig. 9.16-1a and b. With this organization, all data are moved over local interconnections, and one-third of the processors are busy at each step. Eventually, the newly computed C matrix will surface at the top of the array. The total computation can be performed faster with a systolic array such as this than with a sequential computer because many of the required calculations are performed in parallel.

9.16.2 General Linear System Solver

A second look at the systolic array of Fig. 9.16-1 reveals that local feedback paths are not present. Although this is not a concern for matrix multiplication,

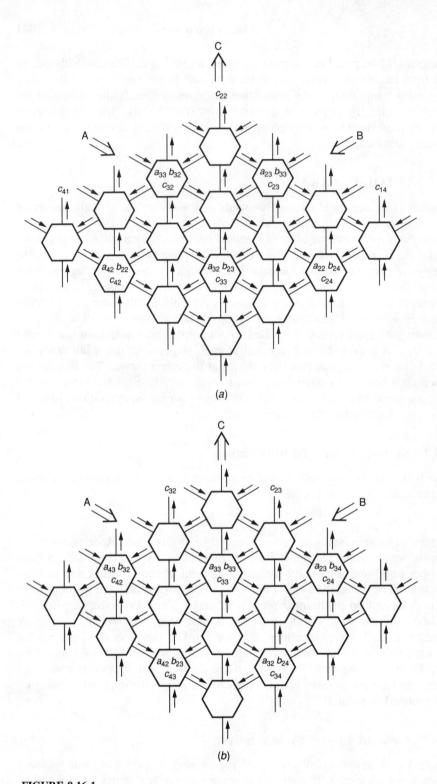

FIGURE 9.16-1
Systolic array multiplication: (*a*) Step *n*, (*b*) Step *n* + 1.

many engineering problems require a system of equations with feedback for their solution. Consider the general linear system representation as

$$X(k + 1) = AX(k) + Bu(k) \qquad (9.16\text{-}1)$$

and

$$Y(k + 1) = CX(k) + Du(k) \qquad (9.16\text{-}2)$$

The $(k + 1)$th value of the state variable vector X depends on the kth value of the state vector. This implies a connection between the output of the state vector calculation and the inputs to the next calculation. This would be difficult with the array structure shown in Fig. 9.16-1. A systolic solution to this problem based on simple processing stages is possible. The solution, shown in Fig. 9.16-2, requires that all processors access a single common bus.

The operation of the state variable solver of Fig. 9.16-2 can be explained as follows. Rows of coefficient values from the state variable matrix are stored in circular shift registers within each processing stage. Only the output value from this circular shift register is shown for each processing element of Fig. 9.16-2. At the start of a new state vector calculation, the accumulator in each processing stage is cleared as shown in step 1. As the calculation starts, $x_1(k)$ is placed on the common bus. Each processing stage simultaneously forms the product $a_{i1}x_1(k)$, where i is the process stage identifier. The resulting product is added to the contents of the accumulator. Next, at the second step, $x_2(k)$ is placed on the common bus; the product $a_{i2}x_2(k)$ is formed; and the result is added to the accumulator. Finally, for an nth order system, at the $(n + 1)$th step $u(k)$ is placed on the bus, the product $b_iu(k)$ is formed, and the result is accumulated. With the completion of this step, the $(k + 1)$th state vector is computed.

If $n + 1$ processing stages are provided, then the output $y(k + 1)$ can be computed simultaneously with the next-state vector. Note that a total of $n + 1$ processors are used to solve for the next-state vector and output value in $n + 1$ iterations. Direct approaches to this problem require n^2 iterations. The single common bus required here is less desirable than completely local interconnections, but a solution for feedback problems with only local communication is not apparent. For the structure of Fig. 9.16-2, a single, large bus driver can be placed at the left end to minimize delays associated with driving the long bus.

9.16.3 Bit-serial Processing Elements

To conclude this section, a look at a simple integrated circuit processing element is appropriate. Even as integrated circuit technology scales to smaller dimensions, the prospect for placing n parallel processing stages on a single silicon die is dim for large n. The size of the typical processing stages and the interconnection buses require too much silicon area. A partial solution to this problem uses bit-serial processing stages. These stages are smaller than their m-bit parallel counterparts by at least a factor of m, allowing m times as many stages to be placed on a silicon die. If the processing stages are designed properly, individual stages will interconnect directly as they are placed, thereby eliminating interconnection buses. This technique of "interconnection by default" is generally useful within integrated circuit design, saving both layout time and silicon area.

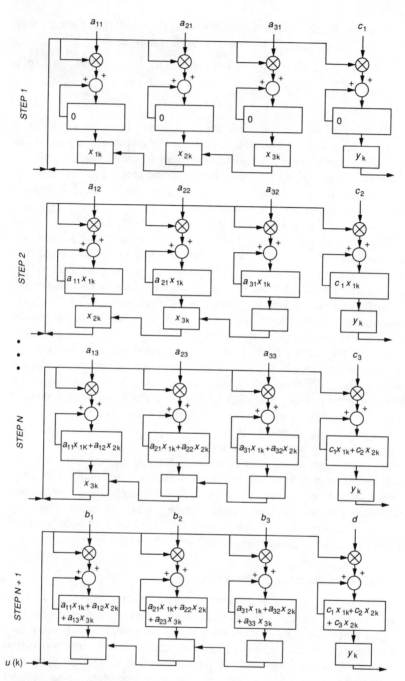

FIGURE 9.16-2
Block diagram for linear equation solver.

Initially, it might appear that bit-serial processing stages are a factor of $1/m$ as fast as parallel processing stages. This could negate the gain achieved by placing m times as many processors on a silicon die. However, bit-serial multipliers and adders can be designed to eliminate carry propagation delay. This allows a net processing speed advantage when m bit-serial processing stages replace a single m-bit parallel processing stage.

An example of a simple bit-serial multiplier is given in Fig. 9.16-3. The algorithm for this particular bit-serial multiplier requires the multiplicand b in parallel and the multiplier a in bit-sequential form. During the first iteration, the first bit of the multiplier a_0 is input and ANDed with the parallel multiplicand b, producing a set of variables called *summands*. The summands are added by the full adders to compute a set of partial product bits and the first product bit P_0. Carries and partial product bits are saved and shifted through unit delay registers so they are available for the next step. As the second multiplier bit a_1 is shifted in, it is ANDed with the multiplicand and added to previous carries and partial product bits. This produces a second bit of the product P_1. At each iteration the weight of each stage doubles, allowing the carry to be fed back within the same stage. This operation continues until the multiplier a is exhausted and the entire product has been shifted out of the multiplier.

The simple multiplier just presented requires one operand in parallel. It is often desirable to accept both inputs in bit-sequential form. This is easily accomplished by using pipeline techniques or through other, slightly more complex bit-serial multipliers.[24]

The capability to map algorithms into hardware with large-scale integrated circuits is revolutionizing the way signal processing is accomplished. The ability to create special-purpose processors to provide parallel solution of time-consuming problems may be the next major step in increasing computational speeds. The concept of systolic processing, with many processors working in lock step fashion, is an important means to achieve this goal.

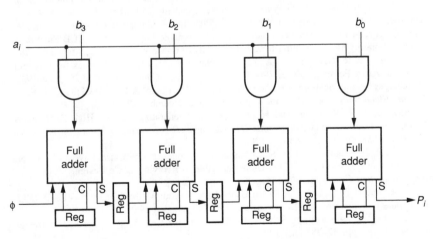

FIGURE 9.16-3
Serial-parallel multiplier.

9.17 SUMMARY

The scope of a chapter describing structured digital circuits and systems is, of necessity, quite broad. The topics presented include structured logic forms such as PLAs, Weinberger arrays, gate matrix layout, and gate arrays (also sea-of-gates). Clocking schemes for digital circuits were introduced as a prerequisite to the treatment of dynamic storage, clocked logic, and sequential machines. Three styles of clocked logic, including C^2MOS, precharge evaluate logic, and domino CMOS logic, were explained. A prototypical semiconductor memory architecture was presented, followed by an investigation of the prominent types of memory storage cells that are used. Salient limitations of both the architecture and the individual cells were provided, usually by example. The memory sections were followed by brief introductions to two widely used forms of sequential machine: PLA FSMs and microcoded FSMs. With these concepts available, an overview of microprocessor architecture was presented to show how the digital subsystems just described can be formed into a complex digital system. And finally, systolic arrays were introduced along with three examples: an array multiplier, a linear system solver, and bit-serial multiplication.

The goal of this chapter was to provide an awareness and basic understanding of structured digital circuits and examples of how these structures are used to form complex digital systems. The information presented on digital integrated circuit structures, along with the prerequisite background in digital system design, allows the design of large digital systems within the integrated circuit medium.

REFERENCES

1. B. Lattin: "VLSI Design Methodology: The Problem of the 80's for Microprocessor Design," *Proc. Caltech Conf. on VLSI*, pp. 247–252, January 1979.
2. D. A. Patterson and C. H. Sequin: "A VLSI RISC," *Computer*, pp. 8–21, September 1982.
3. R. K. Brayton, G. D. Hachtel, C. T. McMullen, and A. L. Sangiovanni-Vincentelli: *Logic Minimization Algorithms for VLSI Synthesis*, Kluwer Academic Publishers, Boston, 1984.
4. G. De Micheli and A. Sangiovanni-Vincentelli: "Pleasure: A Computer Program for Simple/-Multiple Constrained Unconstrained Folding of Programmable Logic Arrays," UCB/Electronics Research Laboratory Memorandum M82/57, University of California, Berkeley, August 9, 1982.
5. G. D. Hachtel, A. R. Newton, and A. L. Sangiovanni-Vincentelli: "Techniques for Programmable Logic Array Folding," *Proc. 19th Design Automation Conf.*, pp. 147–155, June 1982.
6. A. Weinberger: "Large Scale Integration of MOS Complex Logic: A Layout Method," *IEEE J. Solid-State Electronics*, vol. SC-2, no. 4, pp. 182–190, December 1967.
7. J. M. Siskind, J. R. Southard, and K. W. Crouch: "Generating Custom High Performance VLSI Designs from Succinct Algorithmic Descriptions," *Proc. MIT Conference on Advanced Research in VLSI*, pp. 28–39, January 1982.
8. S. M. Kang, R. H. Krambeck, H. F. S. Law, and A. D. Lopez: "Gate Matrix Layout of Random Control Logic in a 32-Bit CMOS CPU Chip Adaptable to Evolving Logic Design," *Proc. 19th Design Automation Conf.*, pp. 170-174, 1982.
9. A. D. Lopez and H-F. S. Law: "A Dense Gate Matrix Layout Method for MOS VLSI," *IEEE J. Solid-State Circuits*, vol. SC-15, no. 4, pp. 736–740, August 1980.
10. G. Dupenloup: "A Wire Routing Scheme for Double-Layer Cell Arrays," *Proc. 21st Design Automation Conf.*, pp. 32–35, June 1984.
11. C. Sechen and A. L. Sangiovanni-Vincentelli: "The TimberWolf Placement and Routing Package," *IEEE J. Solid-State Circuits*," vol. SC-20, no. 2, pp. 510–522, April 1985.

12. J. Y. Chen: "CMOS—The Emerging VLSI Technology," *Proc. IEEE Int. Conf. on Comp. Design,* pp. 130–141, October 1985.
13. W. N. Carr and J. P. Mize: *MOS/LSI Design and Application,* McGraw-Hill, New York, 1972.
14. N. H. E. Weste and K. Eshraghian: *Principles of CMOS VLSI Design,* Addison-Wesley, Reading, Mass., 1985.
15. R. H. Krambeck, C. M. Lee, and H-F. S. Law: "High-Speed Compact Circuits with CMOS," *IEEE J. Solid-State Circuits,*" vol. SC-17, no. 3, pp. 614–619, November 6, 1981.
16. J. A. Marques and A. Cunha: "Clocking of VLSI Circuits," *VLSI Architecture,* B. Randell and P. C. Treleaven, eds., Prentice-Hall, Englewood Cliffs, N. J., pp. 165–178, 1983.
17. T. H. Bennett: "Split Low Order Internal Address Bus for Microprocessor," U.S. Patent No. 3,962,682, Motorola, Austin, Texas, June 8, 1976.
18. W. I. Fletcher: *An Engineering Approach to Digital Design,* Prentice-Hall, Englewood Cliffs, N. J., 1980.
19. B. T. Murphy, R. Edwards, L. C. Thomas, and J. J. Molinelli: "A CMOS 32 Bit Single Chip Microprocessor," *ISSCC Digest of Technical Papers,* p. 230, 1981.
20. J. W. Beyers, L. J. Dohse, J. P. Fucetola, R. L. Kochis, C. G. Lob, G. L. Taylor, and E. R. Zeller: "A 32-Bit VLSI CPU Chip," *IEEE J. Solid-State Circuits,* vol. SC-16, pp. 537–542, October 1981.
21. G. Moore: "VLSI: Some Fundamental Challenges" *IEEE Spectrum,* pp. 30–37, April 1979.
22. R. W. Sherburne, Jr., M. G. H. Katevenis, D. A. Patterson, and C. H. Sequin: "Datapath Design for RISC" *Proc. MIT Conf. on Advanced Research in VLSI,* pp. 52–62, January 1982.
23. H. T. Kung: "Let's Design Algorithms for VLSI Systems," *Proc. Caltech Conf. on VLSI,* pp. 65–90, January 1979.
24. N. R. Strader and V. T. Rhyne: "A Canonical Bit-sequential Multiplier," *IEEE Trans. Comput.,* vol. C-31, no. 8, pp. 791–795, August 1982.

PROBLEMS

Section 9.1

9.1. If a manufacturer's layout rate is eight transistors/day and a chip regularization factor of 20 is achieved, how many man-years are required to lay out a 300,000 transistor chip?

9.2. Estimate the layout time for the Intel 8086 and the Motorola 68000 if a layout rate of 10 transistors/day is assumed for each (use Table 9.1-1).

Section 9.2

9.3. Determine the sizing triplet (i, p, o) for a PLA that implements the following logic equations.

$$X = PB + D\overline{B} + \overline{P}\,\overline{D}\,A$$

$$Y = P\overline{A} + DA + \overline{P}\,\overline{D}\,A$$

$$Z = PB + DA$$

9.4. In terms of λ, estimate the minimum pitch for repeating the AND plane section of Fig. 9.2-5c using the design rules of Table 2B.2 of Appendix 2B. Consider the spacings required to connect the rotated AND section into the OR plane. *Pitch* is defined as the repetition spacing for repeated placements of layout segments.

9.5. Find a folded PLA realization for the following equations so that the PLA sizing triplet is reduced from a straightforward implementation. Can you determine if this is the minimum realization? Why or why not?

$$X = ABC + \overline{A}\,\overline{B} + \overline{B}\,\overline{C}$$

$$Y = ABC + \overline{B}\,\overline{C}$$

$$Z = ABC$$

$$R = \overline{A}BC + AB\overline{C}$$

$$S = \overline{A}\,\overline{B} + AB\overline{C} + \overline{B}C$$

Section 9.3

9.6. Show an NMOS Weinberger NOR array implementation for the logic equations in Prob. 9.3.

9.7. If no rows are shared between input terms and intermediate terms in a Weinberger NOR array, compute the area required to implement the logic equations in Prob. 9.3 as the product of the rows and columns. Compare with a PLA implementation for the same logic equations using the same metric.

9.8. What logic functions are defined by the symbolic gate matrix layout of Fig. 9.3-5?

9.9. Provide a symbolic gate matrix layout for the logic equations of Prob. 9.3.

Section 9.4

9.10. The logic equations of Prob. 9.3 are to be implemented in a CMOS gate array using logic function blocks from the library of Table 9.4-1. Provide a list of the blocks required and the specific logic equations implemented by each block for this design. Use five or fewer types of standard logic function blocks.

9.11. Compare the number of transistors required for a straightforward CMOS implementation of the logic equations of Prob. 9.3 and the number of transistors required with a gate array implementation using blocks from Table 9.4-1. Note that each standard logic function block in Table 9.4-1 is composed of a multiple of 12 transistors (6 p-channel and 6 n-channel).

Section 9.5

9.12. For the circuit of Fig. 9.5-4a, let NOR2 be the gate connected directly to ϕ_2, NOR1 be the gate connected to ϕ_1, and INV represent the inverter. Identify the gate or gates that cause each of the four delays shown in Fig. 9.5-4b. If the delays are 3, 4, and 5 ns for the INV, NOR2, and NOR1 gates, respectively, find the nonoverlap time following (a) ϕ_2 and (b) ϕ_1.

9.13. If a pair of inverters is added between each NOR gate output and its feedback connection in Fig. 9.5-4a, show the resulting clock waveforms as in Fig. 9.5-4b. Assume unit delays for all gates and inverters. (Note that such inverter pairs could be sized geometrically to increase clock drive capability.)

Section 9.6

9.14. For an NMOS dynamic storage circuit with a pass transistor drain diffusion area of 20 μ^2, a metal interconnect area of 20 μ^2, a non-gate polysilicon area of 10 μ^2 and an inverter gate area of 6 μ^2, calculate an equivalent dynamic storage time constant if $C_{\text{diff}} = 0.04$ fF/μ^2, $C_{\text{met}} = 0.03$ fF/μ^2, $C_{\text{poly}} = 0.03$ fF/μ^2, $C_{\text{ox}} = 0.4$ fF/μ^2, and the leakage current $I_r = 0.5$ fA/μ^2.

9.15. In what ways does the use of a CMOS transmission gate rather than an NMOS pass transistor affect the storage time of a dynamic storage circuit? Explain.

9.16. The level restorer transistor of Fig. 9.6-1c must be sized above some minimum value and below some maximum value. What limits the minimum and maximum allowable resistances for this transistor?

9.17. Consider the linear shift register of Fig. 9.6-2. If the input to stage A is brought high during ϕ_1 of a first clock cycle and then left low, prepare a timing diagram showing the clock signals ϕ_1 and ϕ_2 and the outputs of each of the four shift stages for five consecutive clock cycles.

9.18. Prepare a symbolic layout diagram (see Fig. 9.6-4) that shows a clocked shift register that provides a left shift, no shift, or a right shift for four parallel bits.

Section 9.7

9.19. Generate geometrical layouts for the shift register circuits of Figs. 9.7-1 and 9.7-2. Compare the complexity of the two layouts, particularly noting the number of contacts required.

9.20. Provide circuits to implement the following logic equations using complex P-E gate structures as in Fig. 9.7-4.

$$R = AB + BC + AC$$

$$S = ABC + \overline{A}\,\overline{B}\,\overline{C}$$

9.21. Assume the drain and source of each transistor in Fig. 9.7-4 contribute an equal incremental capacitance at each node. If the node between the transistors gated by signals E and F is low, the signals D, B, and A are each low, the gate output is precharged high, the clock is high, and the input signal F is then driven high, calculate the effect of charge sharing on the output voltage if load capacitance caused by subsequent connections is ignored.

9.22 P-E logic stages cannot be directly cascaded. Consider alternating P-E stages of n-channel logic clocked by clk1 with P-E stages of p-channel logic clocked by clk2. Can clk1 and clk2 be complementary signals? What conditions must clk1 and clk2 satisfy for this cascade configuration to work correctly?

9.23. Is it possible to realize the exclusive-OR function using only domino logic circuits? Why or why not?

9.24. Create a table to compare static NMOS, static CMOS, P-E CMOS, and domino CMOS logic gates in terms of total transistor count, static power dissipation (yes or no), and output availability (duty cycle).

Section 9.8

9.25. *IEEE Spectrum* publishes a technology update issue in January of each year. Prepare a 1–2-page summary of the state of the art in semiconductor memories based on the most recent update issue.

9.26. Quantify the row and column decode circuitry required for a 1M × 1-bit memory (a) organized as a square array and (b) organized with four more address lines feeding the row decoder than the number of address lines feeding the column decoder.

Section 9.9

9.27. Assume the charge on the gate of an EPROM cell is 10×10^{-15} C. Assume the gate loses charge exponentially with a time constant of 10 years. Calculate the equivalent leakage resistance from the gate to ground if the gate capacitance is 4 fF.

9.28. Provide the layout for a macro defining the repeatable layout for a ROM memory cell in the technology of Appendix 2B. Now estimate the area required for a 256k-bit memory based on your cell layout. Estimate the size of a repeatable memory cell in a commercial 256k-bit memory area if the array size is 10 mm².

Section 9.10

9.29. Consider a 256k SRAM with row lines fabricated as 2 μ polysilicon runs. Assume the row select transistors are 2 μ × 4 μ and the select lines are 5 mm long. Assuming a square memory array organization, (a) provide a reasonable estimate of the delay across the select line, and (b) provide a reasonable estimate of the delay across the select line if the row decoder divides the memory array into two equal parts to halve the select line length. Use parameters from Appendix 2B.

9.30. For a 256k SRAM that dissipates 0.4 W in the memory array, estimate the resistance of the polysilicon load resistors for the memory cells.

Section 9.11

9.31. If a 1M DRAM is built from cells with 40 fF storage capacitance and the minimum differential voltage that will reliably trigger the sense amplifiers is 80 mV, determine the maximum allowable capacitance for the word lines.

9.32. Assume that a DRAM storage cell is built using a 50 fF capacitor and that a voltage of at least 3.8 V can be reliably recognized as a logic high. If a memory refresh period of 2 s is sufficient under average conditions, estimate the total leakage resistance from the storage cell to ground. Assume a memory refresh charges the capacitor to 5 V.

9.33. In the design of a DRAM memory array, it is found that the delay along the polysilicon row select line is too great, and the suggestion is made to widen the row select line to reduce its equivalent resistance. Will this solution help reduce the select line delay? Why or why not? Will this have other, detrimental effects on the memory array? Explain.

Section 9.12

9.34. Show how to modify Fig. 9.12-5 for dual-port read capability.

9.35. The data lines of a static register array are precharged to the supply voltage and have much larger capacitances than the register cell output. If the select line couples a logic low output of the register cell to the precharged data line during a read operation, what may happen to the register cell contents? Explain.

9.36. For a static register cell, determine a constraint on the relative size of the inverter pulldown transistors and the select transistors to prevent disturbing the register cell state through charge sharing during a read operation with precharged data buses.

9.37. Using the cross-coupled NOR structure for the static register cell array, is it reasonable to provide a dual-port write capability? Explain.

Section 9.13

9.38. A Gray Code counter has the distinguishing feature that successive counts never differ in more than one bit. Thus, a 2-bit Gray Code counter counts as 00, 01, 11, 10, 00, 01, etc. An application requires a Gray Code counter that can count up when an UP control line is asserted or down when a DOWN control line is asserted. If both controls are low, the counter remains in its present state. External circuitry prevents the condition of both control inputs being high simultaneously. Provide a state diagram, a state transition table, logic equations, and a logic/circuit diagram of a PLA FSM to implement this counter.

Section 9.14

9.39. For a typical microROM such as that of Fig. 9.14-2, consider the number of unique 72-bit control words available. With an execution rate of 10 MHz, how long would it take to execute each control word exactly once?

9.40. Considering the typical ROM organization described in previous sections, compare the maximum number of rows and columns that must be traversed during a bit access using the single-level microROM of Fig. 9.14-2 and the two-level microprogram memory of Fig. 9.14-3. Explain how this would affect access time for the two memories.

9.41. Using the description of Example 9.14-1, list the control words necessary to perform the same add operation if the register array is single-port read rather than dual-port read.

Section 9.15

9.42. Estimate and compare the percentages of total area consumed by regular structures on the die photographs of Fig. 9.15-1 and Fig. 9.15-2.

9.43. Assume the data path of a microprocessor has a 32-bit by 16 register array, a 0 to 32-bit shift capability for the barrel shifter, and the ALU operations of Table 9.15-1. Ignoring timing and temporary results storage, specify the control lines required to operate this data path.

9.44. Using the barrel shifter of Fig. 9.15-6, indicate the states of the control lines and the source and destination buses necessary to perform (a) a shift left by 2 bits (quadruple the magnitude of the input), and (b) a shift right by 1 bit (halve the magnitude of the input).

9.45. Four flag bits are common for most microprocessor ALUs. These include the C, N, Z, and V bits (carry, negative, zero, and overflow, respectively).
(a) The Z bit is normally generated using a distributed NOR gate structure at the ALU output. Show how this might be accomplished.
(b) Explain how the N bit could be generated.
(c) Explain how the C bit could be generated.
(d) The V bit can be generated as the exclusive-OR of the final carry bit and the penultimate (next to the highest) carry bit. Demonstrate that this is logically correct for two's complement arithmetic.

Section 9.16

9.46. Using the systolic array of Fig. 9.16-1 as a guide, show the systolic array structure required to multiply two 4×4 square arrays to produce a 4×4 result. How many processors are required?

9.47. For the serial-parallel multiplier of Fig. 9.16-3, how many steps are required to multiply two 4-bit numbers? Show the value of the sum bits and the carry bits for each step when multiplying 6 by 5.

9.48. Symbolically show the hand multiplication of two 4-bit numbers a and b. Demonstrate that the ith product bit is a function of only the ith and lower-order multiplicand and multiplier bits.

CHAPTER
10

DESIGN
AUTOMATION
AND
VERIFICATION

10.0 INTRODUCTION

Design automation and design verification are the keys to effective use of large-scale integrated circuit technology today. When circuits consisted of only a few transistors or gates, layout and checking of circuits by hand were reasonable. As circuit complexity increased to thousands and tens of thousands of transistors, manual tools were no longer sufficient for design, causing computer-based design aids to become prominent. With present integrated circuits containing hundreds of thousands of transistors, heavy dependence on design automation and design verification is necessary to design these circuits.

This chapter describes the nature and use of basic design automation and design verification tools as applied to the design of integrated circuits. *Design automation tools* are defined here as those computer-based tools that assist through automation of procedures that would otherwise be performed manually, if at all. Simulation of proposed design functionality and synthesis of integrated circuit logic and layout are just two examples. *Design verification tools*, on the other hand, are those computer-based tools used to verify that circuit design or layout meets certain prescribed objectives. A geometrical design rule checker for examining layout characteristics is an example, and a logic simulator with a specific set of input vectors and corresponding desired output vectors is another. Note that simulation can be classified in either category according to its purpose. Both design automation tools and design verification tools are included in the more general class known as CAD (computer-aided design) tools.

Both design automation and design verification tools require computer-readable descriptions of the underlying circuit function and structure to operate. These computer-based descriptions vary from simple geometrical specification languages such as CIF[1] (Caltech Intermediate Form) to high-level functional description languages such as VHDL[2] (a hardware design language). Initially the focus of this chapter is on a description of design tools related to or based on geometrical layout. A simplified geometrical specification language will be examined. Required functionality provided by tools that input and display integrated circuit layout will also be described. Then, tools that check layout geometries and extract circuit net list information will be detailed.

Design tools for higher-level design description and verification are described next. Circuit, switch, and logic simulation for digital circuits are introduced and compared. Timing analysis is examined as a way to verify the temporal operation of digital circuits. Hardware design languages such as VHDL and EDIF[3] (Electronic Design Interchange Format) are introduced with simple examples provided to clarify important concepts.

The descriptions of design verification and design automation tools provided here use MOS examples primarily. The concepts are directly applicable to bipolar designs, although some changes in specific tool capability may be required by different technologies. The chapter concludes with an introduction to automated methods of generating layout from high-level descriptions of digital circuits via silicon compilers.

10.1 INTEGRATED CIRCUIT LAYOUT

Historically, integrated circuit design and integrated circuit layout functions were performed by separate groups. The circuit design task resulted in mixed logic and transistor-level circuit diagrams describing the intended circuits. A circuit description like that of Fig. 10.1-1 was given to layout artists, who were experts at converting circuit diagrams to geometrical layouts such as the one shown in Fig. 10.1-2. For early commercial products, the layout drawings were transferred to rubylith masks by hand. Later, layouts were drawn on vellum—a tough, semitransparent drafting material—to withstand the many design modifications

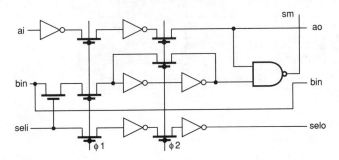

FIGURE 10.1-1
Partial circuit diagram for bit-serial multiplier of Fig. 10.1-2.

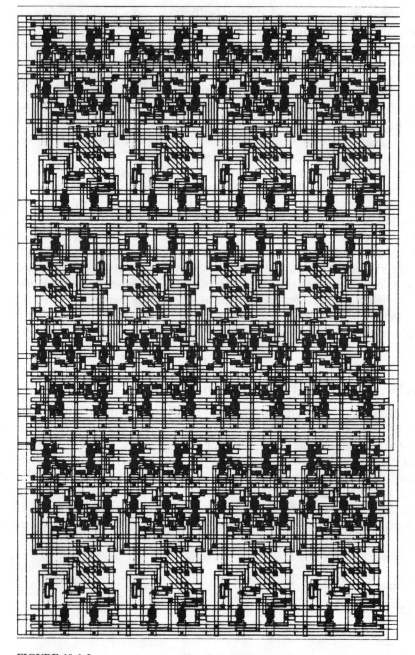

FIGURE 10.1-2
Layout for bit-serial multiplier based on circuit of Fig. 10.1-1.

that are inherent in the normal design process. The layouts from the large vellum plots were digitized to computer-readable form to allow automated checks and to provide input to the mask-making process. Although this method worked for many years, including the early days of microprocessors, the large number of devices required in modern integrated circuits causes fully manual layout to be too time-consuming and prone to error. However, even today, critical sections of the newest microprocessors are still handcrafted to pack the circuit into the smallest possible area.

Many modern methods of integrated circuit layout include both synthesis of control logic and handcrafting of critical building blocks that will be repeated. These layout pieces are entered into a computer at an early stage to allow mechanized help with replicating, checking, and plotting the complete integrated circuit layout. Design layouts may be entered via tools that help convert graphic layout information to computer-readable form. An early tool, shown in Fig. 10.1-3, is called a *digitizer* and was used to enter layout coordinates directly into a computer from a layout plot. Sometimes layout is converted directly to text input in the form of a geometrical specification language. Most often, geometrical layout information is entered through a color graphics workstation to specify the desired integrated circuit layout.

10.1.1 Geometrical Specification Languages

Geometrical specification languages for integrated circuits allow computer-readable definition of the geometries for the mask layers required to fabricate an integrated circuit. These specification languages contain primitive structures such as wires and boxes to specify geometrical shapes and layout levels. Organizational constructs are also provided to allow placement and repetition of the geometrical structures. A geometrical specification language is much like a computer programming language, with the geometrical shape primitives corresponding to instructions and the organizational constructs corresponding to procedures with parameter values.

FIGURE 10.1-3
Digitizer board.

Note: width = 2λ, spacing = 2λ

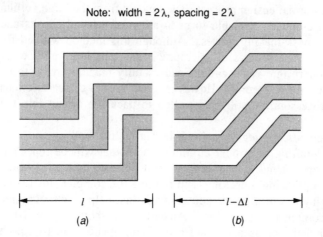

|← l →| |← $l-\Delta l$ →|

(a)   (b)

FIGURE 10.1-4
Layout Styles: (a) Manhattan, (b) Diagonal.

A simplified geometrical specification language for Manhattan style designs for a general MOS process is used here to illustrate relevant concepts. A *Manhattan design style* is one that supports only horizontal and vertical geometries. The name arises because Manhattan style layouts resemble an aerial view of the street layout of New York's Manhattan borough. This style precludes diagonal structures, such as interconnection jogs, that are sometimes used within circuit layouts to minimize area. Figure 10.1-4 shows layout styles with and without diagonal structures. The potential area savings with diagonal structures must be weighed against the increased complexity of programs used to verify the final design. Many commercial integrated circuit manufacturers allow diagonal layout structures but limit these to 45° angles from horizontal and vertical structures.

The simplified geometrical specification language defined here provides only two primitive statements. The two primitives are *boxes* and *levels*, while the organizational constructs include *macros* and *calls*. A macro is like a high-level language (HLL) procedure, and a call is like an HLL procedure call. Table 10.1-1 provides the syntax for these primitives and organizational constructs.

All parameter values are integers. Lengths are in terms of λ, a measure related to the characteristic resolution of the process and the layout design rule set. Macro numbers, layout levels, and orientations are limited to positive integers. A minimum set of layers for a typical NMOS n-well CMOS process is defined in Table 10.1-2. Appendices 2A and 2B define corresponding layers for a double polysilicon NMOS and a p-well CMOS process, respectively.

TABLE 10.1-1
Simplified geometrical specification language

B x y dx dy	Box structure with length dx, width dy, and lower left-hand corner placed at x,y
L n	Layout level for the box definitions that follow
M n	Start of macro number n
E	End of a macro
C n x y m	Call for macro number n with translation x,y and orientation m
Q	End of layout file

TABLE 10.1-2
MOS layer definitions

Layer	CMOS	NMOS
1	n-diffusion	n-diffusion
2	p-diffusion	Ion implant
3	Polysilicon	Polysilicon
4	Metal	Metal
5	Contact	Contact
8	n-well	—
9	Overglass	Overglass

The orientation represents possible rotations of the geometrical figure after translation. The relative order of translation and rotation is important (see Prob. 10.3). Here, rotation is performed first with translation following. The possible orientations are defined in Table 10.1-3 and demonstrated with the block letter P in Fig. 10.1-5.

This simple geometrical specification language will suffice to specify any MOS Manhattan integrated circuit layout if the necessary layout levels are defined. The description is based on alphanumeric characters and is easily displayed, edited, or transferred between computer systems.

TABLE 10.1-3
Rotations of geometries

Orientation	Description
1	No rotation
2	Rotate 90° CCW
3	Rotate 180° CCW
4	Rotate 270° CCW
5	Mirror about y-axis
6	Rotate 90° CCW and mirror about y-axis
7	Rotate 180° CCW and mirror about y-axis
8	Rotate 270° CCW and mirror about y-axis

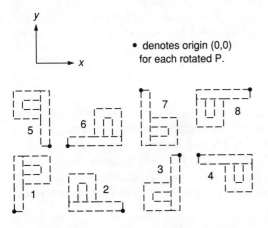

y

x

• denotes origin (0,0) for each rotated P.

FIGURE 10.1-5
Cell orientations.

```
M  5
L  1
B  11  0   4   5
B  5   3   6   2
B  1   3   4   7
B  1   10  2   3
B  1   13  14  2
L  2
B  4   1   8   6
L  3
B  6   1   4   8
B  8   6   4   6
B  10  12  2   7
L  4
B  0   0   16  2
B  1   6   11  4
B  0   13  16  2
L  5
B  12  0   2   1
B  2   7   2   2
B  9   7   2   2
B  7   14  2   1
E
M  8
C  5   0   0   1
C  5   16  30  3
E
C  8   0   0   1
Q
```

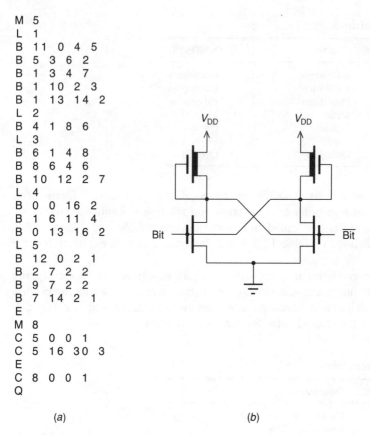

(a)	(b)

FIGURE 10.1-6
Static memory cell definition: (*a*) Geometrical specification file, (*b*) Circuit diagram.

An example of the geometrical specification file for a static memory cell composed of two inverters tied back to back is shown in Fig. 10.1-6 along with the corresponding circuit diagram. A single inverter consisting of an enhancement pulldown transistor and a depletion pullup transistor is defined by macro 5. This inverter is placed twice, once in a rotated and translated position, to create the static memory cell defined as macro 8. Macro 8 is placed once to create the layout plot shown in Fig. 10.1-7.

10.1.2 Layout Styles

In spite of high labor costs, handcrafted layout is still used within the semiconductor industry because of the necessity to minimize the area required by high-volume integrated circuits. Even automated layout methods such as silicon compilation and standard cell synthesis use handcrafted layout to optimize the primitive cells that are combined through automated techniques. Frequently the basic form for the integrated circuit is sketched and optimized on paper prior to entry into

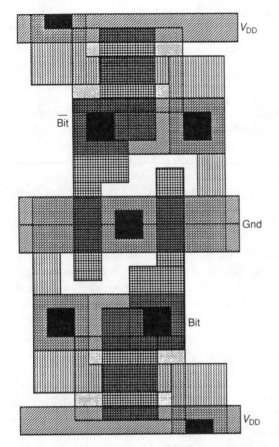

V_{DD}

$\overline{\text{Bit}}$

Gnd

Bit

V_{DD}

FIGURE 10.1-7
Static memory cell layout.

a computer. The resulting geometrical layouts are digitized, sometimes through use of a symbolic layout language but primarily with the help of an interactive CRT graphics editor.

Handcrafted layouts can be entered directly into a computer in geometrical form through use of an interactive CRT graphics editor. A mouse or joystick is used in conjunction with a cursor to size and position geometrical objects such as boxes on a high-resolution CRT display. A corresponding data file is kept in computer memory to describe the displayed geometries. With an operator's command, this data file may be converted to a geometrical specification language description or can be saved for further use. Several advantages of this graphical editor accrue from bypassing the need to input numerical data to a computer with a text editor or digitizer and from the ease with which geometries can be changed or duplicated.

The graphics editor called Magic,[4] currently popular with universities, uses the painting idiom to create geometrical objects on a color CRT display. The user chooses a color (layout level) from a palette on the screen and paints areas on the screen by specifying two opposite corners of a rectangular field.

The chosen color fills the area. The final result is the same as for other layout methods: a geometrical specification file is created in computer memory, saved, and ultimately transferred to the mask shop.

Graphical editors in both industrial and university environments typically maintain their own unique memory and disk representations of layout geometries. For reasons of efficiency (fast editing response and minimum memory requirements), these representations are often highly optimized binary data structures. In the university environment, the geometrical specification language CIF was defined as a common interchange format among universities and between universities and the MOSIS fabrication service. In industry, EDIF was defined as the interchange format. Most industrial CAD tools provide conversions between their internal format and EDIF. In addition, most industrial CAD tools convert their internal format to a special binary format for submittal to the mask shop. The Berkeley Oct tool set[5] provides conversion from its internal format (Oct) to and from both CIF and EDIF.

In summary, both specification of layout geometries and designer entry of layout geometries are described in this section. Many different geometrical specification languages have been defined and used. A very simple one was defined here for demonstration purposes only. In the university environment, CIF is the predominant interchange format, and EDIF is the interchange standard in industry.

10.2 SYMBOLIC CIRCUIT REPRESENTATION

Descriptions of integrated circuit layouts can take many forms. The geometrical specification language of the previous section provides a primitive textual description of a circuit. Other, more symbolic, forms of representation are often used by designers to specify layouts. A hierarchy of these, including a parameterized layout representation, parameterized module generation, a graphical symbolic representation, and logic equations, is described here.

10.2.1 Parameterized Layout Representation

A symbolic layout language[1] (SLL) allows a textual description of circuit layout in a form that is more easily generated and understood by humans than the geometrical specification language of the previous section. In the past, an SLL was used to represent design layouts that were drawn by hand on graph paper and then digitized. Two main characteristics differentiate an SLL from the geometrical specification language described previously. First, the SLL uses descriptive identifiers for the parameters necessary to specify a geometrical layout. Examples are BOX, POLY, and DX for the geometrical shape, the layer, and the width in the x direction, respectively. This provides a readable description of geometries that specify a layout. Thus, the SLL description is easily entered into a computer using the designer's favorite text editor. Second, symbolic entries are allowed in addition to the numerical data of the geometrical specification language. For example, the x and y position of a geometry might be specified by the variables XPOINT and YPOINT. This allows the final placement of the geometry to depend on the placement of other cells. At some point in the design process, the SLL must be converted to a geometrical specification language for use by other CAD tools and for transmittal to the mask shop. XPOINT and YPOINT must be assigned numerical values to specify the location of the geometry before this conversion takes place.

In addition to the use of symbolic parameters in an SLL, programming constructs such as loops and conditionals can provide additional capability in the specification of a cell's layout. The use of an SLL to describe layout is much like the use of assembly language to describe the machine language (binary) program for a computer. An assembly language program uses mnemonics for the instructions and symbols for variables to simplify and expedite the process of programming a digital computer. Both forms describe the same end object; the binary representation provides the most concise description, while the assembly language is a preferable working medium for programmers.

An SLL description for the layout of the CMOS inverter of Fig. 7.5-5 is given in Fig. 10.2-1. Note the verbose nature of this description compared to the geometrical specification file of Fig. 10.1-6. The description of Fig. 10.2-2 demonstrates the use of variables to allow the inverter cell of Fig. 7.5-5 to be stretched in either the VERT (vertical) or HORZ (horizontal) directions. Also, a REPEAT statement is included to allow the cell to be repeated NR times. RX and RY are the repeat distances along the x and y axes, respectively. If the variables VERT and HORZ are each set to a value of 0 and NR is set to 4, the inverter cascade of Fig. 10.2-3 is produced. The two variables VERT and HORZ can be used to stretch the inverter cell to match the pitch of adjacent cells by

```
CELLNAME CMOSINV;
BOX NDIF X=3 Y=0 DX=4 DY=4;
BOX NDIF X=3 Y=4 DX=2 DY=4;
BOX NDIF X=3 Y=8 DX=4 DY=4;
BOX PDIF X=3 Y=20 DX=4 DY=4;
BOX PDIF X=3 Y=24 DX=5 DY=4;
BOX PDIF X=3 Y=28 DX=4 DY=4;
BOX POLY X=0 Y=5 DX=7 DY=2;
BOX POLY X=0 Y=7 DX=2 DY=18;
BOX POLY X=0 Y=25 DX=10 DY=2;
BOX POLY X=4 Y=14 DX=8 DY=4;
BOX MET1 X=0 Y=0 DX=12 DY=4;
BOX MET1 X=0 Y=28 DX=12 DY=4;
BOX MET1 X=3 Y=8 DX=4 DY=16;
BOX MET1 X=7 Y=14 DX=1 DY=4;
BOX CONT X=4 Y=1 DX=2 DY=2;
BOX CONT X=4 Y=9 DX=2 DY=2;
BOX CONT X=5 Y=15 DX=2 DY=2;
BOX CONT X=4 Y=29 DX=2 DY=2;
BOX CONT X=4 Y=21 DX=2 DY=2;
BOX NWEL X=0 Y=18 DX=12 DY=16;
END CMOSINV;
```

Figure 10.2-1
Symbolic layout language description of CMOS inverter of Fig. 7.5-5

```
CELLNAME CMOSINV;
BOX NDIF X=3 Y=0 DX=4 DY=4;
BOX NDIF X=3 Y=4 DX=2 DY=4;
BOX NDIF X=3 Y=8 DX=4 DY=4;
BOX PDIF X=3 Y=20 DX=4 DY=4;
BOX PDIF X=3 Y=24 DX=5 DY=4;
BOX PDIF X=3 Y=28 DX=4 DY=4+VERT;
BOX POLY X=0 Y=5 DX=7 DY=2;
BOX POLY X=0 Y=7 DX=2 DY=18;
BOX POLY X=0 Y=25 DX=10 DY=2;
BOX POLY X=4 Y=14 DX=8+HORZ DY=4;
BOX MET1 X=0 Y=0 DX=12+HORZ DY=4;
BOX MET1 X=0 Y=28+VERT DX=12+HORZ DY=4;
BOX MET1 X=3 Y=8 DX=4 DY=16;
BOX MET1 X=7 Y=14 DX=1 DY=4;
BOX CONT X=4 Y=1 DX=2 DY=2;
BOX CONT X=4 Y=9 DX=2 DY=2;
BOX CONT X=5 Y=15 DX=2 DY=2;
BOX CONT X=4 Y=29+VERT DX=2 DY=2;
BOX CONT X=4 Y=21 DX=2 DY=2;
BOX NWEL X=0 Y=18 DX=12 DY=16+VERT;
END CMOSINV;
CELLNAME FOURINV;
REPEAT CMOSINV NR=4 RX=12+HORZ RY=0;
END FOURINV;
```

FIGURE 10.2-2
Parameterized symbolic layout language description for inverter cascade of Fig. 10.2-3

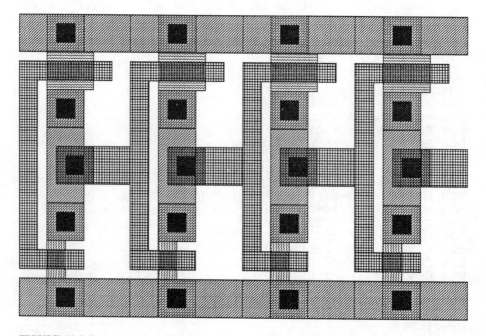

FIGURE 10.2-3
Inverter cascade created from parameterized symbolic layout language description.

specifying positive values for one or both of VERT and HORZ. The use of a programmatic description of layout greatly expands the capabilities of a layout designer in specifying the geometrical structure of a circuit.

10.2.2 Parameterized Module Generation

A recent advance in the area of symbolic layout descriptions is the use of parameterized module generators. A parameterized module generator is a software procedure that can generate many different cell layouts depending on values that are specified when the generator program is executed. Parameterized module generators have been written for RAMs, ROMs, PLAs, multipliers, adders, and data paths, for example. Many of these generators use input parameters to specify the width or number of bits in the generated layout.

As an example, three separate designs might require an 8-bit adder for the first design, a 16-bit adder for the second design, and a 32-bit adder for the third design. Typical design style would use an interactive graphics editor to create each of these adders separately. If a parameterized generator for the adder module could be defined, however, a single module generator could be used to produce an N-bit adder where N is a parameter that can be set to 8, 16, 32, or some other integer value. Then each of the three adders could be created from the same parameterized description. A parameterized module generator is particularly well suited to modern integrated circuit design styles, which commonly utilize regular structures such as rows of cells and arrays of cells.

Parameterized module generators use many of the powerful constructs of high-level programming languages to describe layout structure, position subcells, and fit the overall layout of a larger cell together. Parameterized variables are used with their values bound to a specific value when a module is generated. Conditional statements allow creation of specialized edge cells and programming of memory and PLA contents. For example, a parameterized module generator for an array of cells might include conditional statements such that if both the x and y indices were equal to 0, then an upper-left corner cell would be generated. If the x and y indices were each between the smallest and largest values, a center cell would be generated, and so forth.

The use of high-level programming language techniques also provides a disadvantage for many parameterized module generators. That is, the layout cannot be visualized until the generation program has been compiled and linked to instantiate the layout for a module. These potentially time-consuming steps may hinder the use of interactive layout in designing a module generator for a new cell. To circumvent this problem, there is ongoing research on ways to provide interactive graphical feedback as the geometrical structure of a cell is defined.[6]

With such a tool, a silicon layout specialist can create the parameterized modules that are required in a design. Then a circuit or logic designer can use these blocks by specifying parameters appropriate to the design task. Recently, parameterized module generators were used to specify the layout of a commercial RISC processor (see Sec. 10.11). An interesting, but unsolved problem, is to prove that the output of a parameterized module generator is correct over the valid range of parameters for the module generator.

10.2.3 Graphical Symbolic Layout

The parameterized layout representation described previously provides little insight into the geometrical relationships between circuit elements. This important insight can be provided by another symbolic form for integrated circuit description, called graphical symbolic layout. An early form of graphical symbolic layout is called Sticks.[7] Sticks and related symbolic methods provide an abbreviated, graphical description that combines circuit connectivity with layout topology information. In the Sticks symbology, circuit connections are shown with colored (or weighted) lines representing layout levels, while transistors are formed by the intersection of the lines representing polysilicon and diffusion. The entire layout diagram is composed of simple line symbols that show both connectivity and topology but not actual or relative size for geometrical constructions.

The combination of connectivity and topological information is important in the generation of integrated circuit layouts, as is shown with the aid of the circuit diagram for the quasi-static memory cell of Fig. 10.2-4a. This circuit diagram shows a forward path from the first inverter to the second inverter and a clocked feedback path from the second inverter to the input of the first inverter. The circuit diagram does not indicate topological requirements to realize this path.

The geometrical layout of the memory cell of Fig. 10.2-4a requires decisions on changes of layout levels to prevent unwanted transistors and connections. The Sticks diagram of Fig. 10.2-4b retains all the circuit connectivity information

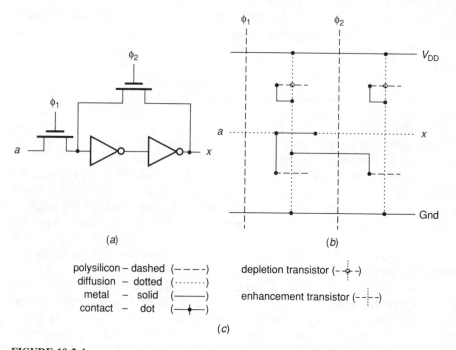

(a) (b)

polysilicon – dashed (– – – –)   depletion transistor (– –ϕ– –)
diffusion – dotted (·········)
metal – solid (————)   enhancement transistor (– –┆– –)
contact – dot (——●——)

(c)

FIGURE 10.2-4
Quasi-static memory cell: (a) Logic diagram, (b) Symbolic diagram for NMOS layout, (c) Layer legend.

for the memory cell and also symbolically specifies the topology of the final integrated circuit layout. In particular, it shows that the feedforward path must be changed from the diffusion layer to the metal layer to cross the polysilicon ϕ_2 clock line without creating an unwanted transistor. Also, the Sticks diagram shows that the feedback transistor is conveniently formed by allowing the polysilicon ϕ_2 line to cross the diffusion feedback path. The diagram shows that power and ground are provided in metal and that the input and output signals are both in the diffusion level. The utility of Sticks and other graphical symbolic layout methods is derived from the simple abstracted notation for layout topology and circuit description.

Once a graphical symbolic layout for a circuit is generated, it is often simple for a designer to convert to a full layout form. The layout task has been simplified to the process of fattening connection lines and compacting the layout, especially if required transistor length-to-width ratios have been noted on the graphical symbolic layout. In fact, this process is simple enough to be automated.[8] If the graphical symbolic layout description has been entered into a computer, perhaps through an interactive graphics terminal, a symbolic compiler program can convert the symbolic layout to a full layout by expanding the line symbols according to a technology specification and then compacting the resulting layout.

As with most automated layout aids, a symbolic compiler usually trades reduced designer efforts for increased silicon area. An increase in the area for a layout generated with a program is not uncommon when compared to a hand-crafted layout. As a result, high-volume integrated circuits such as microprocessors and memory continue to utilize handcrafted layout of replicated cells as a major design component. This does not, however, minimize the value of the symbolic representation to the designer. Capturing layout topology in symbolic form early in the layout design prevents later problems such as isolation of a circuit from direct metal connection to power buses.

10.2.4 Logic Equation Symbology

If the function of a digital integrated circuit can be captured by a set of Boolean logic equations, these equations suffice to generate an integrated circuit layout. Thus, logic equations represent a fourth symbolic means to describe a combinational logic circuit. One frequently used means to convert logic equations into layout topology is with a PLA generator, as described in Chapter 9. Two other methods for generating geometrical layouts from logic equations are discussed next: the Weinberger array[9] and SLAP[10] (a methodology for silicon layout).

A Weinberger array uses a regular structure of NOR gates to implement combinational logic in an integrated circuit form. This array structure was introduced in Chapter 9. Figure 10.2-5 shows a Weinberger array used to implement the full adder carry function described by

$$K = AB + AC + BC \qquad (10.2\text{-}1)$$

Since the final structure is regular, it is not difficult to construct a computer program to generate the array layout using logic equations as program input. By

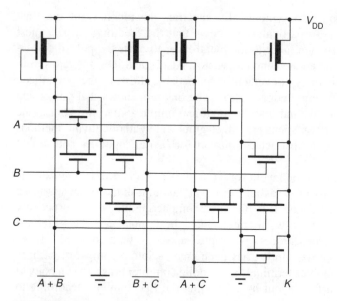

FIGURE 10.2-5
Weinberger array for full-adder carry.

use of DeMorgan's theorem, any combinational logic function can be realized using only NOR gates. In fact, the Weinberger array requires at most a series path of three NOR gates between an input and an output to realize a combinational logic function. Remember that a single-input NOR gate is an inverter. Thus, a first NOR gate may be required to provide the complement of an input while the final two levels use the NOR-NOR logic form to realize the logic function in product-of-sums form.

The use of NOR gates for a Weinberger array allows a constant size for the pullup devices even though the number of inputs and their corresponding pulldown devices may differ for each gate. Careful design allows adjacent gates to share a single ground path, as shown in the layout of Fig. 10.2-6. This array structure can be easily expanded by adding input variables at the bottom and NOR gates to the right without changing the existing structure.

A comparison of the Weinberger array with the PLA yields an interesting result. Even though the logic of a PLA is realized entirely with NOR gates, the AND-OR logic form corresponding to a sum-of-products description is normally used. The AND-OR logic form can be realized with NOR gates only by inverting both the inputs and outputs. This requires a series string of four or five NOR gates between the PLA inputs and outputs, thus causing more delay for a PLA implementation of logic than for a Weinberger array implementation which requires only three levels of logic.

In contrast to the PLA and the Weinberger array, both with predefined array structures, a third method called SLAP has been proposed to compile logic equations into layout form. SLAP first converts logic equations into a directed graph with a graph level for each level of the logic equations. If double-rail inputs

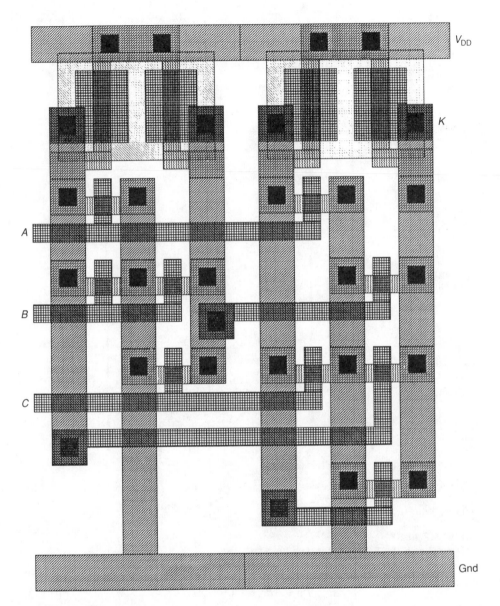

FIGURE 10.2-6
Layout for Weinberger array.

are available, at least two levels of gates are required to implement a general logic function. The SLAP methodology, however, allows realization of intermediate outputs that may then be used as inputs for other logic functions. A graph with an arbitrary number of levels may be required, depending on the particular representation for the logic. Figure 10.2-7 shows the directed graph for the logic functions of the following equations.

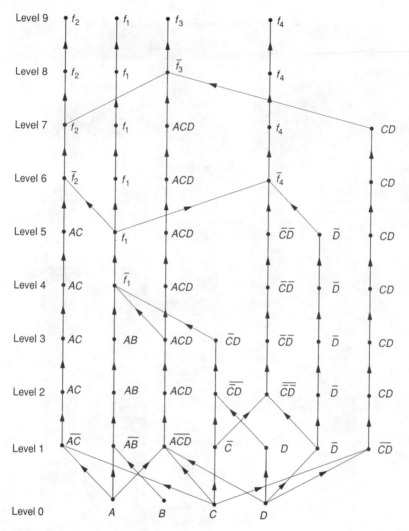

FIGURE 10.2-7
Directed graph for Eqs. 10.2-2 through 10.2-5.

$$f_1 = AB + \overline{C}D + ACD \tag{10.2-2}$$

$$f_2 = AC + f1 \tag{10.2-3}$$

$$f_3 = ACD + CD + f_2 \tag{10.2-4}$$

$$f_4 = \overline{C}\,\overline{D} + \overline{D} + f_1 \tag{10.2-5}$$

This directed graph is formed by placing logic gates with external inputs at the first level, secondary logic gates at the next level, and so on. Heuristics are then used to improve the organization by reducing the number of required levels, if possible, and to reduce the resulting layout area required. The layout density achieved with this method is about the same as that accomplished with gate array structures. An important characteristic of the SLAP methodology is that general logic structures can be compiled directly into a geometrical layout, whereas the PLA format forces a two-level logic realization.

In this section, four methods of generating layout from symbolic representations were introduced. Of the first two, parameterized layout representation and parameterized module generation, the second is growing in popularity for layout of today's designs. Graphical symbolic layout also enjoys success as a technique for layout of random logic. Synthesis of layout directly from the fourth symbolic form, logic equations, is fast becoming a widely used technique for generating integrated circuit layout.

10.3 COMPUTER CHECK PLOTS

Generation of a layout plot from a geometrical specification file for an integrated circuit is often desirable. In the past, large-scale plots, some almost big enough to cover one end of a basketball court, were generated so that visual checking of circuit layout could be performed. Most of these visual checks can now be performed directly from a computer-based geometrical specification file without manual intervention. A computer program can verify fixed rules for the millions of geometrical figures used to describe VLSI circuits without tiring and without error—a task that is essentially impossible for humans. However, human capability to critique overall structure or to detect inconsistencies in an otherwise regular design is difficult to duplicate with computer-based checks. As a result, hardcopy plots of integrated circuit designs are still used for finding errors, for promotional literature, and for many other purposes. Such plots are called *computer check plots*.

Computer check plots for integrated circuit designs are created in both soft- and hardcopy form on CRTs, printers, and plotters using color or black on white representations for the layout artifacts. Check plot devices range from monochrome CRTs, with only 24×80 character resolution for the entire display, to laser printers with 300 dots per inch or higher resolution. To compare the maximum usable display capability over this range of resolution, an example using a static memory cell is examined next.

The static memory cell of Fig. 10.1-7 has dimensions of $16 \lambda \times 30 \lambda$ for an area of $480 \lambda^2$. A monochrome alphanumeric CRT using character graphics with 24 lines by 80 columns can display an area of $1920 \lambda^2$, although the effective area is somewhat less because of the 1:3 aspect ratio of the CRT display resolution. All details of the static memory cell are visible in the CRT display, as shown in the hardcopy plot of Fig. 10.3-1, but the cell's relation to other cells is lost. As a second example, a dot matrix drawing normally requires a resolution of at least 5 dots per λ to define the smallest details of a circuit. For a printer with a resolution of 100 dots per inch, the static memory cell requires a plot that is about 0.8×1.5 in. to show the details of the circuit. Figure 10.3-2 provides a plot of this size for the memory cell of Fig. 10.1-7. If the memory cell were part of a 1K-bit memory (32 cells $\times$ 32 cells), a high-resolution plot of the entire memory array would require 25.6×48 in. Of course, the general form of the memory area could be discerned with a much smaller plot. Figure 10.3-3 shows a plot at one-tenth this scale (2.56×4.8 in.) for the 32-by-32 cell array.

```
. . . . . . . . . . . . . . . . . . . . . . . . . . . . . . . . . . . . . . . . . . . . . . . . . . . . . . . . . . . .
. . . . . . . . . . . . . . . . . . . . . . . . . . . . . . . . . . . . . . . . . . . . . . . . . . . . . . . . . . . .
. . . . . . . . . . . . . . . . . . . . . . . . . . . . . . . . . . . . . . . . . . . . . . . . . . . . . . . . . . . .
. . . . . . . . . . . . . . . . . . . . . . . . . . . . . . . . . . . . . . . . . . . . . . . . . . . . . . . . . . . .
. . . . . . . . ## . . . . . . . . . . . #### . . . . . . . . . . . ## . . . . . . . . . . . . . . . . . . . . . . . .
. . . . . . . . ## . | | | #### | | | #### . . . . . . . . | | | ## . . . . . . . . . . . . . . . . . . . . . . . .
. . . . . . . . ## . | | | #55# | | | #### . . . . . . . . | | | #5 . . . . . . . . . .
. . . . . . . . ## . | | | #55# . . . #### . . . . . . . . | | | #5 . . . . . . . . . .   Legend                 . . . . . . . . . . . . . . . .
. . . . . . . . ## . | | | #### . ═ ═ #### ═ ═ ═ #### . | | | ## . . . . . . . . . .                           . . . . . . . . . . . . . . . .
. . . . . . . . ## . | | . #### . ═ ═ #### ═ ═ ═ #55# . | | . ## . . . . . . . . .   #  metal               . . . . . . . . . . . . . . . .
. . . . . . . . ## ═ ═ ═ ═ #### . . . #### . ═ ═ #55# ═ ═ ═ ═ ## . . . . . . . . .                           . . . . . . . . . . . . . . . .
. . . . . . . . ## ═ ═ ═ ═ #### . . . #### . ═ ═ #### ═ ═ ═ ═ ## . . . . . . . . .   ═  polysilicon         . . . . . . . . . . . . . . . .
. . . . . . . . ## ═ ═ ═ ═ #55# ═ ═ . #### . . . #### ═ ═ ═ ═ ## . . . . . . . . . .                          . . . . . . . . . . . . . . . .
. . . . . . . . ## . | | . #55# ═ ═ ═ #### ═ ═ . #### . | | . ## . . . . . . . . .   |  diffusion           . . . . . . . . . . . . . . . .
. . . . . . . . ## | | | . #### ═ ═ ═ #### ═ ═ . #### | | | . ## . . . . . . . . .                           . . . . . . . . . . . . . . . .
. . . . . . . . 5# | | | . . . . . . . . #### . . . #55# | | | . ## . . . . . . . . .   5  contact          . . . . . . . . . . . . . . . .
. . . . . . . . 5# | | | . . . . . . . . #### | | | #55# | | | . ## . . . . . . . . .                         . . . . . . . . . . . . . . . .
. . . . . . . . ## | | | . . . . . . . . #### | | | #### | | | . ## . . . . . . . . .   .  blank            . . . . . . . . . . . . . . . .
. . . . . . . . ## . . . . . . . . . . . #### . . . . . . . . . . . ## . . . . . . . . . . . . . . . . . . .
. . . . . . . . . . . . . . . . . . . . . . . . . . . . . . . . . . . . . . . . . . . . . . . . . . . . . . . . . . . .
. . . . . . . . . . . . . . . . . . . . . . . . . . . . . . . . . . . . . . . . . . . . . . . . . . . . . . . . . . . .
. . . . . . . . . . . . . . . . . . . . . . . . . . . . . . . . . . . . . . . . . . . . . . . . . . . . . . . . . . . .
```

FIGURE 10.3-1
Hardcopy plot of SRAM cell as displayed on 24 line by 80 character CRT (λ = one character width).

A typical graphics CRT display with a 19 in. diagonal screen (15 in. horizontal × 11 in. vertical) might have a resolution of 760 by 480 dots. This is roughly 50 dots per display inch. Based on the analysis above, the details of a 152 λ by 96 λ circuit could be displayed in its entirety on the screen. This would correspond to about a five-by-six array of the memory cells described above. Figure 10.3-4 shows a hardcopy plot of the memory cells that could be seen on the CRT display. Of course, an entire chip can be displayed if the layout is scaled so that the finer details of the chip are lost. Figure 10.3-5 shows the entire layout for a 220 × 230 mil image-processing chip composed of sixteen, 12-bit serial multipliers with associated circuitry and input/output pads.

Color displays and plots are always a higher-cost feature than black and white; where color is available, each integrated circuit layer is represented using

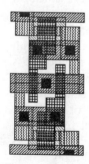

FIGURE 10.3-2
Minimum size plot for Fig. 10.1-7 with 100 dots/inch resolution.

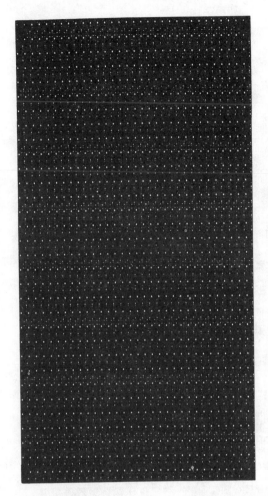

FIGURE 10.3-3
Plot of 32 × 32 memory cell array.

a different color. Aside from their aesthetic appeal, color renditions of circuits show higher information content per unit area, allowing display of larger circuits in a given area. For a color display, only 2 to 3 dots per λ of resolution are necessary to delineate circuit details. Additionally, individual color levels can be used to show labels, flag geometrical design rule violations, or highlight specific features of a circuit. Most modern graphics workstations provide color displays.

When black on white plots are generated, two primary methods are used to distinguish individual layers. Line drawings, with each layer represented by a different style of line (solid, dotted, dashed, dot-dash, etc.) are producible on almost any printer with dot graphics capability (see Fig. 10.3-6). Filled drawings with different layers shown by characteristic area fill pattern (fine dots, heavy dots, diagonal lines, vertical lines, etc.) are popular, even at the expense of increased computer time to generate the plots, greater wear on the printer mechanism, and longer time to print the plots. Laser printers provide good resolution

FIGURE 10.3-4
Hardcopy plot of memory cells visible on typical graphics CRT display.

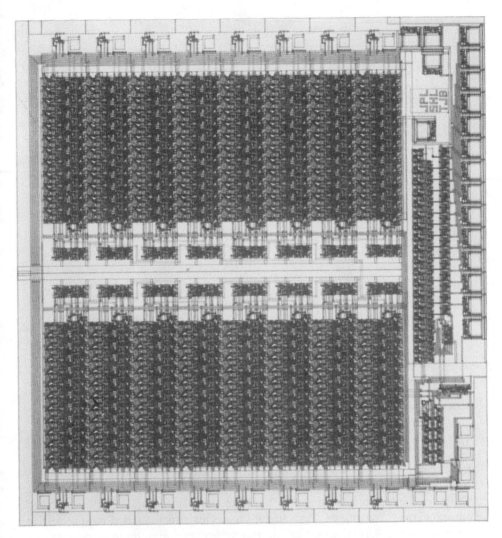

FIGURE 10.3-5
Image-processing chip (220 mil × 230 mil).

(300 dots per inch) and are frequently used for area fill check plots. A primary advantage of the filled drawing of Fig. 10.1-7, compared with the line drawing of Fig. 10.3-6, is that the concept of area for integrated circuit layers is quickly conveyed to the viewer by the filled drawing. This concept is important to the designer since the fabrication process operates on contiguous areas rather than the individual boxes used to describe them.

In this section, a short summary of integrated circuit display media and their corresponding resolution requirements was presented. It is important to have high-resolution display and hardcopy capability for integrated circuit layout design.

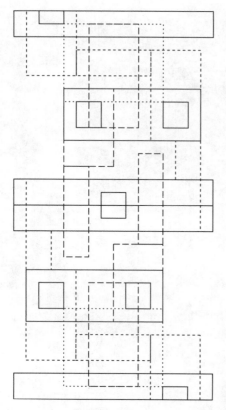

FIGURE 10.3-6
Line check plot of layout of Fig. 10.1-7.

10.4 DESIGN RULE CHECKS

Integrated circuits are created from several layers whose geometrical structures are defined by photolithographic masks. At any given time, a minimum resolution exists for the structures that can be fabricated on silicon because of lithographic and processing constraints. Any attempt to define structures that require higher resolution or accidental specification of a higher resolution through carelessness may lead to nonfunctional circuits. Also, violation of certain geometrical relationships among layers may cause failures because of processing constraints. For each process, a set of guidelines called *design rules* is specified to encapsulate geometrical fabrication constraints. The design rules for the CMOS process described in Table 2B of Appendix 2 are used as the basis for the following discussion. However, most of the rules are determined by general lithographic and processing constraints so that similar rules apply to other processes as well.

10.4.1 Geometrical Design Rules

A conceptual explanation of geometrical design rules is provided in this section. Design rules were introduced in Sec. 2.3 of this text. Geometrical design rules for a single integrated circuit layer are simple; they involve only spacings and widths. Figure 10.4-1 demonstrates a 2 λ spacing between polysilicon conductors

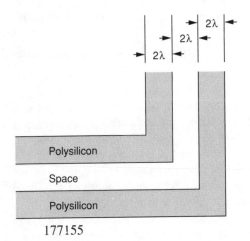

177155

FIGURE 10.4-1
Minimum width polysilicon conductors.

that are each 2λ wide. It is worth noting that if a mask layer is complemented, all widths become spacings. This is shown in Fig. 10.4-2, where the complemented polysilicon conductor widths from Fig. 10.4-1 appear as spacings. Therefore, if width is considered in terms of the complement of the layer definition, all single-layer rules can be treated as simple spacing rules. This means that the same computer algorithm can be used to check for both width and spacing errors.

An interesting conceptual understanding of design rules was provided by Lyon.[11] His explanation is based on the scalable parameter λ, which is said to describe the minimum resolution of the fabrication process. In practice, fabrication processes are usually characterized by their minimum transistor length. The parameter λ is normally specified as half the minimum transistor length. Thus, a $2\ \mu$ process has a minimum gate length (and width) of $2\ \mu$, and λ would be set to $1\ \mu$. Thus, λ is not directly a measure of process resolution, but rather is proportional to the minimum device length. With this in mind, the following two meta rules (a meta rule is a rule about rules) were proposed by Lyon to generalize geometrical design rules in terms of λ.

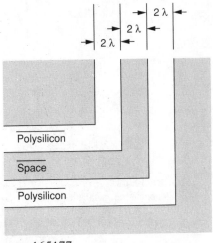

165177

FIGURE 10.4-2
Complemented layout, where spacings become widths.

1. A 1 λ error should not be fatal, although the intended performance of the integrated circuit may be degraded.
2. A 2 λ error may be fatal and almost certainly will degrade the performance of the integrated circuit.

Consider the minimum width of 2 λ for the polysilicon conductor shown in Fig. 10.4-3a. If the width of the actual polysilicon that is fabricated on the chip is 1 λ less than this minimum, as in Fig. 10.4-3b, the polysilicon will still conduct, although its resistance will double. If the fabricated polysilicon conductor is 1 λ wider than the minimum, as in Fig. 10.4-3c, the resistance is lowered, but the polysilicon still functions as a conductor. Thus, a change in width of 1 λ does not cause an obviously fatal problem for the polysilicon interconnection.

Now consider a 2 λ deviation from the design width of 2 λ. If a minimum width polysilicon conductor is narrowed by 2 λ, as in Fig. 10.4-4a, there is no conductor left—certainly a fatal error unless the connection was redundant. If the width is increased by 2 λ as in Fig. 10.4-4b and the minimum polysilicon spacing is 2 λ, there is a chance that the polysilicon conductor will contact an adjacent polysilicon conductor, causing a short circuit—also a fatal error.

Other design rules involve more than one level and are harder to remember and to verify. As an example of a two-level rule, consider that a transistor is created by the area common to polysilicon and diffusion. This transistor area must satisfy the 2 λ minimum length rule, so the smallest transistor size is 2 λ by 2 λ. The diffusion areas for the source and drain of a transistor also must satisfy a 2 λ minimum length. This rule is sometimes confusing from a layout viewpoint since the source, the drain, and the transistor gate area appear as one contiguous diffusion area. Thus, a source area 1 λ long combined with a transistor area 2 λ long and a drain area 2 λ long, shown in Fig. 10.4-5a, appears as a diffusion area 5 λ long and does not seem to violate the 2 λ diffusion length rule. However, Fig. 10.4-5b shows that a source only 1 λ long could disappear as a result of a 1 λ alignment error between polysilicon and diffusion—thus a 2 λ rule must be specified for the transistor source/diffusion dimensions. Typical design rule sets for several processes, including NMOS and CMOS, are provided in Appendix 2.

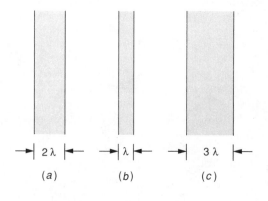

| 2λ | λ | 3λ |
| (a) | (b) | (c) |

FIGURE 10.4-3
DRC degradation meta rule.

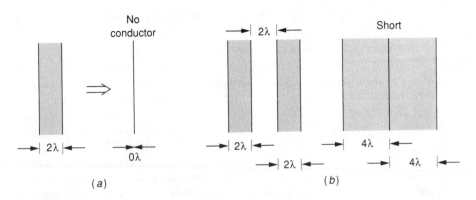

FIGURE 10.4-4
DRC fatality meta rule.

10.4.2 Computer Design Rule Checks

If a designer creates or changes a geometrical specification file manually, a *design rule check* (DRC) is required. Because of the large number of geometries and the wide variation in number and style of geometrical design rules in today's circuits, computer-based DRCs are necessary. Two different styles of DRC programs are in wide use. These can be categorized as polygonal checks and raster scan checks. Both styles will be described briefly.

Polygonal design rule checks are widely used within the semiconductor industry. The geometrical specification file is expanded to produce polygons defining all connected areas for the layer(s) of interest. Note that the layer of interest may be a composite area such as active transistor area or perhaps depletion transistor area. Or it may be a difference area such as the ion implantation overhang created by subtracting the depletion transistor area from the ion implan-

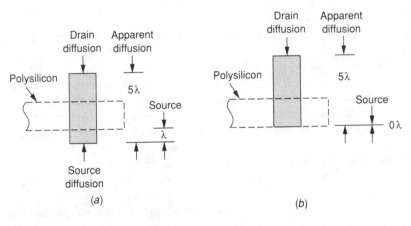

FIGURE 10.4-5
Transistor source width.

tation area. These special areas can be defined by logical operations on primitive layers. Once the polygonal definitions are formed, they can be analyzed for width and spacing errors. One valuable feature of encircling a connected area with a single polygon is that electrical connectivity information is immediately available. Polygonal design rule checks require substantial computing resources because of the many mathematical operations that must be performed during the check.

Design rule checks can also be performed in a relatively simple way as raster scan checks by passing small filters over a rasterized image of the integrated circuit. To allow this, an entire geometrical specification file is instantiated (expanded into the geometries and layers that represent the layout) within a two-dimensional array where the dimensions represent the x and y coordinates of a point and the contents are binary variables to indicate the presence or absence of each layout level. The resolution of the x and y coordinates limits the precision of the design rule checks. Filters such as a 4×4 array,[12] a "plus" symbol, or a circled "plus" symbol[13] have been used to scan the instantiated layout to check for design rule violations. These methods are conceptually simple and computationally clean, but lack the accuracy and connectivity information of the polygonal methods.

10.4.3   Design Rule Checker Output

To demonstrate the results from a raster scan DRC program, several errors were placed in a geometrical specification file. The layout for this file is shown in Fig. 10.4-6. The resulting output from the DRC program is shown in Fig. 10.4-7. The DRC program outputs a heading that gives the name of the file, the date and time, the bounding box coordinates for the checked area, and the macro number. Below the heading, a list of all vertical and horizontal errors is provided. This particular sample contains three vertical and four horizontal errors. Each violation is shown by a one-line entry containing the identification of the violated rule, the x and y coordinates of the violation, the violation or error distance, and the length over which the violation occurred. The resolution of the layout of Fig. 10.4-6 and the DRC results of Fig. 10.4-7 is 0.5 λ.

Definitions of the seven rule violations from Fig. 10.4-7 are given in Table 10.4-1. In each case these errors involve a spacing violation. For example, Rule 6.2 is a metal spacing error. A glance at the upper left corner of Fig. 10.4-6 shows a T formed by a long horizontal metal section and a short vertical metal section separated from the horizontal metal (top of the T) by about 1 λ. From Rule 6.2, the spacing must be at least 3 λ unless the two metal sections should be joined, in which case the spacing would be zero. As an exercise, the reader should find the location of each of the errors listed in Fig. 10.4-7.

Once the cause of an error is determined, corrective action must be initiated. Since the DRC output gives the exact x and y coordinates of the violation, it is usually relatively simple to use an interactive graphics CRT to display the error. Actually correcting the error may not be so simple. If the layout is loosely packed, correction in place by adjusting a single geometrical figure can possibly be done. For some layouts, however, an error will occur in a space-critical area,

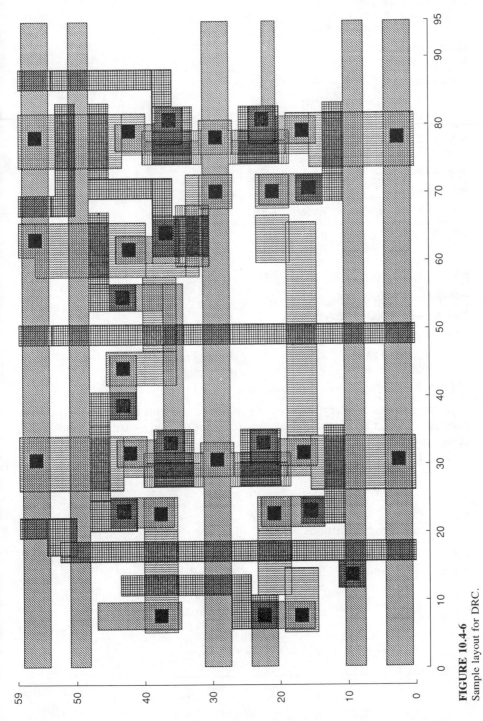

FIGURE 10.4-6
Sample layout for DRC.

LDRC version 3.115

Design rule check of file: BGA.TAM
Date   9-MAR-89   Time 21:08:05
X min =   0.0   X max =   95.0
Y min =   0.0   Y max =   59.0

Macro name is BGMLT
Macro number is   99

Vertical errors

Rule	X loc	Y loc	Error	X len
6.2	5.5	47.5	1.0	4.0
5.3	22.0	17.0	0.5	2.0
6.1	82.5	20.5	1.0	12.5

Vertical error count: 3

Horizontal errors

Rule	X loc	Y loc	Error	X len
4.3	10.5	20.5	0.0	3.0
4.2	18.5	41.5	0.5	7.0
1.2	66.5	18.5	1.0	5.0
5.6	80.0	41.5	1.0	2.0

Horizontal error count: 4

Total number of Design rule violations: 7

Design-Rule Checker Execution:

CPU Time   0: 0:26.06
Page Faults   354

FIGURE 10.4-7
DRC output for Fig. 10.4-6.

requiring changes of a large number of geometries. For this reason, it is crucial to generate a correct layout through automatic means or, in the case of a handcrafted design, to check the layout frequently for geometrical design-rule errors as it is generated. With care, errors are caught early before correction causes difficult problems.

TABLE 10.4-1
Design rule error definitions

Rule	Length	Definition
1.2	3λ	Diffusion spacing
4.2	2λ	Polysilicon spacing
4.3	λ	Polysilicon-to-diffusion spacing
5.3	λ	Polysilicon larger than contact
5.6	λ	Metal larger than contact
6.1	3λ	Metal width
6.2	3λ	Metal spacing

The DRC program used here was run in the batch mode on a computer after the layout was complete. Many CAD systems allow DRCs as geometries are entered through an interactive graphics CRT using an incremental DRC program. Either the designer is prevented from placing geometries that would violate design rules, or a pending violation is flagged immediately by an error message. This minimizes the need for major changes after the layout is almost complete.

DRCs are one of the more time-consuming, yet important, design verification steps. Both polygonal and raster scan DRCs are possible. A good DRC program provides output that accurately identifies the type and location of each error. A good interface between the DRC program and an interactive graphics editor is important for displaying and correcting DRC errors.

10.5 CIRCUIT EXTRACTION

After the design and layout process is complete, MOS circuits are characterized by a machine-readable specification prior to the mask-making step. This specification is usually a geometrical specification file as described earlier. This file contains all the information about the geometries, levels, and placements for the circuit to be fabricated. Because geometrical specification files contain large quantities of detailed information about the integrated circuit, it is difficult for a designer to determine whether this information accurately describes the circuit that was intended. Fortunately, computerized methods exist to extract the circuit information from the geometrical specification file. The process of extracting the circuit information from the geometrical description is called *circuit extraction.*

A circuit extraction program expands the geometrical specification file of the integrated circuit into a layer-by-layer description of the geometries and their placements. This description is then scanned to locate all transistors and interconnections for the circuit. A result of the circuit extraction program is a net list. A *net list* is a set of statements that specifies the elements of a circuit (for example, transistors or gates) and their interconnection. Individual transistors are described along with the nodes to which they connect. This information allows creation of a circuit diagram based on the actual geometrical specification file. Most importantly, the extracted circuit can be compared with the original circuit specified by the designer so that differences are annotated. A difference usually indicates an error that must be corrected. This comparison is called an LVS (layout versus schematic) design verification step.

In addition to providing the details of circuit interconnections, circuit extraction is useful for calculating layout areas and perimeters for each integrated circuit layer at each node of the circuit. These layout areas and perimeters can be used to accurately calculate the parasitic capacitances and resistances that load the active devices. Prior to the layout and extraction step, most circuit parasitics can only be estimated by the designer. With accurate capacitance and resistance values from circuit extraction, a design can be accurately simulated to ensure correct operation. Thus, circuit extraction is an essential design verification tool for accurate characterization of modern integrated circuits.

10.5.1   A Simple Circuit Extraction Algorithm

One simple method of circuit extraction consists of two main steps. First, the geometrical specification 'file is instantiated as a set of coordinates and levels within a computer memory. This is essentially the same operation that was required for the raster scan DRC described in the previous section. This method requires a large computer memory to store the integrated circuit levels at a resolution matching the smallest features of the integrated circuit. For example, a 5 mm by 5 mm die using a process with a λ of 1 μ could require over 25 million individual memory locations to store the instantiated layout, where each memory location corresponds to a 1 λ by 1 λ cell of layout. For a CMOS process, roughly 14 possible layout levels must be remembered for each location. This results in a storage requirement of more than 350 megabits. One useful approach to minimize the memory requirements is to instantiate the design file in overlapping strips. All required circuit information is extracted from each strip before the next strip is instantiated.

The second main step in circuit extraction is the extraction of transistor and connectivity information from the instantiated layout. This is a straightforward, but time-consuming task. The instantiated layout is scanned using a format typical of that used to display television images. The scanning order described here is left-to-right and top-to-bottom, with all integrated circuit levels scanned in parallel. Information on the extent of each level is obtained, and relations between levels that form transistors and contact cuts are derived.

A simple algorithm to determine connectivity at each level can be described as follows. This algorithm requires the program to look at the current cell, the cell to the left, and the cell above. Figure 10.5-1 shows conditions of interest where a "–" indicates no level present and an "m" indicates the presence of a level (e.g., metal). If the current cell does not contain a level, action is not required. This condition is shown in Fig. 10.5-1a by a template (upper part) and a 5 λ by 5 λ layout sample (lower part). If the current cell contains a level, four possible cases are of interest; these are shown in Figs. 10.5-1b through 10.5-1e.

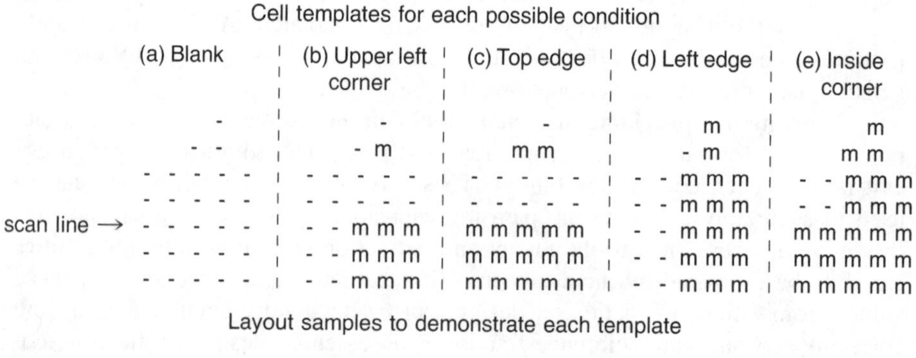

Cell templates for each possible condition

(a) Blank	(b) Upper left corner	(c) Top edge	(d) Left edge	(e) Inside corner
-	-	-	m	m
- -	- m	m m	- m	m m
- - - - -	- - - - -	- - - - -	- - m m m	- - m m m
- - - - -	- - - - -	- - - - -	- - m m m	- - m m m
scan line → - - - - -	- - m m m	m m m m m	- - m m m	m m m m m
- - - - -	- - m m m	m m m m m	- - m m m	m m m m m
- - - - -	- - m m m	m m m m m	- - m m m	m m m m m

Layout samples to demonstrate each template

FIGURE 10.5-1
Connectivity extraction.

If the current cell contains a level, say metal, then four cases must be examined. First, if neither the cell to the left nor the cell above contains metal, then an *upper left corner* has been encountered as in Fig. 10.5-1*b*, and a new node number must be assigned to this location. As a second case, if the cell to the left contains metal but the cell above does not, as in Fig. 10.5-1*c*, then the extractor is moving along a *top edge*, and the current node is assigned the same node number as the cell to the left. As a third case, if the cell above contains metal but the cell to the left does not, as is shown in Fig. 10.5-1*d*, a *left edge* has been found, and this node is assigned the same node number as the cell above. As a final case, if both the cell above and the cell to the left contain metal, either an *internal point* or an *inside corner* has been found. If the node numbers for these cells are different, they should be merged. The inside corner template and sample layout section are shown in Fig. 10.5-1*e*.

The procedure just described produces a list of nodes for each level and a list of nodes that should be merged. Other information is also kept: for example, a count of the number of times each node is encountered (the area), a count of the number of nodes along an edge (the perimeter), and the location of the first occurrence of each node. In addition, relationships between levels such as contact cuts result in a second node merge list. This node merge list must be kept separate from the homogeneous node merge list since the contact cuts represent nodes of different materials that are connected. Electrically they represent the same circuit node, but for capacitance and resistance calculations their individual identity, area, and perimeter must be maintained.

Other interactions between levels must also be considered. Wherever polysilicon and diffusion are coincident, an additional level (transistor) must be created. This artificial level is processed in a manner similar to the other levels to generate individual transistors and maintain their areas for capacitance and drive strength calculations.

10.5.2 Circuit Extractor Output

As a minimum, the output from a circuit extraction program should contain a complete list of transistors showing the type of transistor (p-channel, n-channel, depletion, etc.) and the nodes to which the transistor is connected. The circuit of Fig. 10.5-2 was extracted to show typical output. A sample of such output, called a net list, is shown in Fig. 10.5-3.

The extracted output of Fig. 10.5-3 lists an arbitrary transistor number; the drain (DS1), source (DS2), and gate (G) connections; the type of transistor (enhancement or depletion); the shape (*ok* means rectangular); the length and width of the transistor; and the x and y coordinates of the upper left corner of the transistor. All dimensions are based on the parameter λ. The resolution of Fig. 10.5-2 and its extracted output listings is 0.5 λ. With this information, transistor size can be verified, individual transistors can be located, and the V_{DD} connection for the depletion transistors (the normal case) can be verified. The net list provides sufficient information to allow reconstruction of a transistor-level circuit diagram

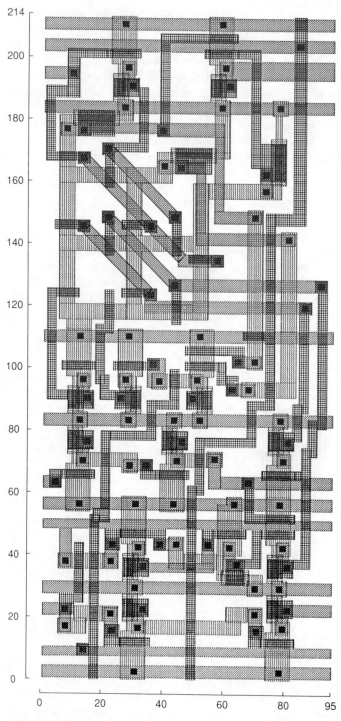

FIGURE 10.5-2
Sample layout for circuit extraction.

LEXTRACT version 3.337

Date   4-MAR-89   Time   19:54:46

X min =   0.0   X max =   95.0
Y min =   0.0   Y max =   214.0

Macro name is BGMLT
Macro number is   99

Final merge node list

Num	DS1	DS2	G	Type	Shape	Length	Width	X-loc	Y-loc
1	GND	42	3	enhN	ok	3.0	8.0	54.0	208.5
2	GND	6	4	enhN	ok	3.0	8.0	22.0	203.5
3	42	7	5	enhN	ok	3.0	8.0	54.0	203.5
4	6	VDD	6	depN	ok	6.0	2.0	24.0	194.0
5	7	VDD	7	depN	ok	6.0	2.0	56.0	194.0
6	3	VDD	3	depN	ok	12.0	2.0	11.0	182.0
7	VDD	5	5	depN	ok	12.0	2.0	76.0	173.0
8	3	51	4	enhN	ok	3.0	5.0	5.0	170.0
9	9	VDD	9	depN	ok	12.0	2.0	43.0	170.0
10	51	9	6	enhN	ok	3.0	5.0	20.0	165.0
11	51	55	11	enhN	ok	3.0	5.0	5.0	148.0
12	9	12	4	enhN	ok	3.0	5.0	27.0	148.0
13	55	12	10	enhN	ok	3.0	5.0	20.0	143.0
14	12	5	6	enhN	ok	3.0	5.0	42.0	143.0
15	5	13	4	enhN	ok	3.0	5.0	49.0	137.0
16	55	GND	14	enhN	ok	3.0	5.0	5.0	126.0
17	12	17	11	enhN	ok	3.0	5.0	27.0	126.0
18	GND	17	15	enhN	ok	3.0	5.0	20.0	121.0
19	17	13	10	enhN	ok	3.0	5.0	42.0	121.0
20	3	18	2	enhN	ok	3.0	5.0	67.0	112.5

FIGURE 10.5-3
Partial net list generated from Fig. 10.5-2 by circuit extractor (VDD and GND labels entered by user).

(not shown) for the integrated circuit. The extracted circuit diagram can be compared with the intended circuit diagram for omissions or errors.

Additional information based on the circuit extraction should be provided. For example, for each integrated circuit layout level, a complete list of nodes with their corresponding areas and perimeters can be provided. If the capacitance per unit area is known for each level, the circuit extraction program can provide an accurate estimate of the capacitance at each node. Figure 10.5-4 provides a partial circuit extractor output for the layout of Fig. 10.5-2 showing the details of the integrated circuit layers that form the nodes of a circuit. For each extracted geometry, this output lists the area, top edge length, left edge length, x and y coordinates of the upper left corner of the geometry, the new merged node number, the old node number assigned to the geometry during extraction, the layout level, and the node name (if any).

The output of Fig. 10.5-4 shows that node 1* is composed of a diffusion geometry (level 1) with area of 84 square units and perimeter of 37 units, a metal

LEXTRACT version 3.337

Date   4-MAR-89   Time   19:54:46

X min =   0.0   X max =   95.0
Y min =   0.0   Y max =   214.0

Macro name is BGMLT
Macro number is   99

Final merge node list

Area	Top	Left	X-loc	Y-loc	New	Old	Lev	Name
84.0	8.0	10.5	22.0	214.0	1*	1	1	
4.0	2.0	2.0	25.5	212.5		5	5	GND
380.0	95.0	4.0	0.0	213.5		4	4	
4.0	2.0	2.0	57.5	212.5		6	5	GND
44.0	8.0	5.5	54.0	214.0		2	1	
254.0	4.0	63.5	82.0	214.0	2*	3	3	Phi-2
4.0	2.0	2.0	83.0	205.5		11	5	
154.0	13.0	38.0	73.0	150.5		87	3	
380.0	95.0	4.0	0.0	206.5		9	4	
90.0	10.5	22.5	65.5	112.5		135	3	
54.0	9.0	12.0	67.0	90.0		193	3	
97.5	20.0	15.5	50.0	78.0		222	3	
195.0	5.5	62.5	47.5	62.5		260	3	
27.0	5.0	6.0	24.0	188.0	8*	33	1	
4.0	2.0	2.0	25.5	185.5		38	5	VDD
12.0	6.0	2.0	23.0	182.0		46	1	
380.0	95.0	4.0	0.0	186.5		37	4	
4.0	2.0	2.0	57.5	185.5		39	5	VDD
87.0	5.0	18.0	56.0	188.0		34	1	
12.0	6.0	2.0	55.0	170.0		68	1	
4.0	2.0	2.0	76.5	185.5		40	5	
43.0	5.0	14.0	75.0	187.0		36	1	
193.0	15.0	20.5	5.0	123.0	16*	122	1	
4.0	2.0	2.0	11.0	111.5		137	5	GND
380.0	95.0	4.0	0.0	112.5		134	4	
4.0	2.0	2.0	27.0	111.5		139	5	GND
84.0	8.0	10.5	24.5	113.0		132	1	
335.0	95.0	15.5	0.0	51.5	30*	273	4	
4.0	2.0	2.0	6.5	39.0		308	5	B-in
27.5	5.5	5.0	5.0	40.5		299	1	

FIGURE 10.5-4
Partial layer detail generated by circuit extractor for Fig. 10.5-2.

geometry (level 4) with area of 380 square units, another diffusion geometry (level 1) of 44 square units area and 27 units perimeter, and two contacts (level 5) with area 4 square units each. The x and y coordinates of the upper left corner of each geometry are given, allowing location of the geometry on a display or plot. With the area and perimeter sizes determined, calculation of interconnection capacitances is relatively easy using the values from Table 10.5-1. Example 10.5-1 demonstrates this calculation.

TABLE 10.5-1
Typical capacitance values (from Table 2B)

Layer	Capacitance
Metal	$0.025 \text{ fF}/\mu^2$
Polysilicon	$0.045 \text{ fF}/\mu^2$
Gate	$0.7 \text{ fF}/\mu^2$
Diffusion (bottom)	$0.33 \text{ fF}/\mu^2$
Diffusion (sidewall)	$0.9 \text{ fF}/\mu$

Example 10.5-1 Calculation of nodal interconnect capacitance. For a typical MOS process, parasitic capacitance values to ground are given in Table 10.5-1. Determine the total capacitance for node 1* of the circuit extraction output given in Fig. 10.5-4. The units of extracted dimensions are μ.

Solution: The total capacitance to ground at node 1* is the sum of the capacitance of the layers that compose the node (the contact capacitances are neglected). The capacitance can be calculated as follows.

$$C_{\text{total}} = C_{\text{diff}} + C_{\text{sidewall}} + C_{\text{poly}} + C_{\text{metal}}$$

$$C = (84 + 44)0.33 + (37 + 27)0.9 + (0)0.045 + (380)0.025 \text{ fF}$$

$$C = 42.24 + 57.6 + 9.5 \text{ fF}$$

$$C = 109.34 \text{ fF}$$

If the geometrical specification language allows names to be assigned to nodes, the names can be associated with their respective nodes by the circuit extraction program. The ability to name nodes adds to the complexity of the circuit extraction program since the name information must be kept after the geometric layout is instantiated. This adds substantially to the active computer memory required during a circuit extraction.

A node list with associated names is particularly valuable when checking for open circuits and short circuits. For example, if all power and ground nodes are named (V_{DD} or GND) and an individual node is associated with both the names V_{DD} and GND, a short circuit between power and ground is indicated. This is *not* desirable! Conversely, if the name GND is associated with two disjoint nodes, an open circuit may be indicated for the GND node. Of course, these same name tests can be applied to signal nodes and names, and this can be automated to report potential problems. Figure 10.5-4 shows circuit extractor output for a circuit with named nodes.

The nodes of Fig. 10.5-4 are named GND, Phi-2, VDD, and B-in. The fact that two separate nodes (1* and 16*) are named GND is cause for suspicion. This may indicate a discontinuity in the ground connection or, as in this case, it may be the result of extracting a partial layout. It is very important to provide node names early in a design and carry these names through the layout and simulation steps.

10.5.3 Interface to Other Programs

The output from a circuit extraction program can provide valuable input to circuit and logic simulation programs. Without circuit extraction results, circuit and logic simulations are based on manual input of the intended circuit connections and estimated circuit parameters. If certain process characteristics such as layer capacitance and transistor conductance are provided, a computer program can combine the circuit extraction output with process characteristics to create an input file for circuit simulation and logic simulation. Automatic generation of the input files eliminates human error in providing these data and allows accurate specification of capacitance values and transistor sizes.

Many modern integrated circuits are designed with a high-level circuit description provided in the form of a hardware design language (HDL). If this high-level description allows specification of circuit connections, a particularly important check on circuit integrity can be performed as a result of circuit extraction. The top-down circuit description from the HDL can be compared directly with the bottom-up circuit description from the extracted circuit. This check is valuable because it allows comparison between the designer's intent and the actual computer specification used to generate the fabrication masks.

Circuit extraction is a valuable design verification tool. With the aid of an LVS program, the extracted circuit can be compared to the intended circuit. Circuit extractor derived capacitances and resistances are extremely valuable for accurate circuit simulation. The use of named nodes in the geometrical specification file and subsequent extraction of these nodes allows open, short, and circuit continuity tests.

10.6 DIGITAL CIRCUIT SIMULATION

Accurate circuit simulation is essential for the design of analog circuits such as filters, comparators, and operational amplifiers. The need for circuit simulation extends to the design of semiconductor memory chips even though their data are stored in binary or digital form. For example, extremely sensitive sense amplifiers are required within DRAM circuits to respond to the small change in voltage caused by selecting a storage cell. SRAM circuits often use differential sensing circuits to increase the speed of the data access operation. Both of these memory types require accurate circuit simulation for proper design. Circuits whose external operation is totally digital may require accurate circuit simulation to model critical signal-delay paths. Circuit simulations of high accuracy are almost universally performed with a version of the SPICE circuit simulator described in Chapter 4.

Because of the large number of transistors in digital circuits such as microprocessors, peripheral controllers, and digital signal processors, it is not computationally feasible to perform a circuit simulation for the entire circuit. Since the execution time of circuit simulation programs increases at a rate that is only slightly less than the square of the number of nodes under consideration, verification of the operation of large circuits must be accomplished by other means. Many times a simulation at the logic or switch level (described in the next section) can provide sufficient verification of a digital circuit's functionality. Sometimes even logic simulation programs are too slow to model an entire processor's behavior. Special-purpose hardware simulators are required in these cases.[14]

An intermediate class of circuit simulators is being investigated to provide accurate circuit simulation without the computational penalty of a full circuit simulator.[15,16] These new simulators usually depend on one of two characteristic features of digital circuits. First, most digital circuits are loosely coupled. This means that disjoint parts of the circuit may be relatively independent of one another. There are methods that take advantage of this structure by partitioning the network to simplify the equations that must be solved during a simulation. Second, only a small part, perhaps 25%, of a digital circuit is active during each clock cycle. If a circuit simulator can take advantage of those quiescent portions of the circuit, then only a small part of the circuit will result in simulation calculations at any given time. In either of these two cases, accurate digital circuit simulation can proceed at a relatively rapid rate compared to standard circuit simulation. Nonetheless, digital circuits of any size are rarely simulated in their entirety with circuit-level simulators. Rather, switch-level or logic-level simulators are preferred. Such simulators are described in the next section.

10.7 LOGIC AND SWITCH SIMULATION

Digital integrated circuits are designed to operate with binary representations for data. The basic presumption is that only two logic states are important for each signal line. Thus, knowledge of a precise voltage versus time characteristic for each node in the circuit is not necessary to design or analyze digital circuits. For many purposes, this simplifies both the circuits and their analysis compared to analog circuits. Nevertheless, computer simulation and verification of a circuit's functionality are necessary. Even though a digital circuit is designed based on logic gates, the logic gates are fabricated from the basic transistors and conductors allowed by the integrated circuit process. Therefore, it is often the case that the electrical operation of a simple logic circuit must be characterized by using a circuit simulator such as SPICE.

Though circuit simulation of digital circuits is frequently used, such circuit simulation has several drawbacks. As described in the previous section, the large number of logic gates in most digital integrated circuits precludes circuit simulation of the entire system because of the extended computer time required. Also, standard circuit simulators provide more detail about circuit voltages than is required to analyze a logic circuit. In an effort to reduce computer simulation time and to provide appropriate data to characterize the operation of digital circuits, *logic simulators* were developed.

10.7.1 Logic-level Simulation

Logic simulators allow specification of the operation of a circuit block in terms of its behavior. For example, a simple logic gate is described by its behavior, such as AND, OR, or NOT. More complex digital blocks such as full adders and multiplexers are each described by their corresponding behavior rather than their circuit structure. The circuit inputs are specified as binary values that change at discrete time intervals. Logic simulator outputs are provided as binary values as well. Pure logic simulation does not model time delays through logic blocks. Only the logical behavior of the simulated system is considered, although the concept of sequence wherein one action precedes another is important. Timed logic simulation considers the delays of logic gates and blocks in determining when outputs will change. Because a logic simulator models the circuit in terms of an abstracted (less detailed) representation, larger circuits can be simulated in a much shorter length of time than with circuit simulation. Consider the following example.

Example 10.7-1   Comparison of circuit and logic simulation. In terms of the number of circuit elements, nodes, and calculations, compare circuit simulation and logic simulation requirements for a full adder built from a classical CMOS circuit and from CMOS gates.

Solution

Circuit simulation. The two-level logic circuit for a classical CMOS full adder requires 56 transistors and 33 nodes. This circuit is shown in Fig. 10.7-1. In addition, continuous input waveforms that generate the eight possible logic input conditions of three inputs must be provided. Each of these conditions must be stable for a length of time sufficient to allow the sum and carry outputs to stabilize. This requires about 100 to 200 time steps for each input condition. As a rough estimate, a minimum of 800 to 1600 time-step calculations would be required to characterize the full-adder operation.

Logic simulation. A classical two-level logic circuit for a full adder requires three inverters, three 2-input NAND gates, five 3-input NAND gates, and a 4-input NAND gate, for a total of 12 logic gates and 15 nodes. The logic gate implementation is given in Fig. 10.7-2. Eight possible input combinations exist for the full adder. Each of these combinations generates a digital value for the sum and carry outputs. Correctness of the sum and carry outputs is easily verified by these eight calculations.

Thus, circuit simulation requires approximately 1600 time-step calculations involving 56 transistors and 33 nodes at each calculation. Logic simulation, on the other hand, requires only 8 calculations, involving 12 logic gates and 15 nodes for each calculation. Clearly, if simulation of the logical operation of the full adder is the goal, logic simulation is simpler and faster. If accurate signal propagation time or waveform characteristics are required, then circuit simulation is necessary.

Commercial logic simulators model digital logic in terms of four or more states. As a minimum, these states include 1, 0, X, and Z. The logic values 1 and 0 model the high and low logic states. The value X is used to model an unknown condition. For example, the value of an internal logic node may be unknown when simulation is started. The value Z is used to model high-impedance (undriven) nodes. A tri-state bus with all driving circuits turned off is an example of this condition. Additional states may be defined to model the relative driving strength of logic outputs. Of course, as the number of allowable states increases, the simulator complexity and run time increase correspondingly.

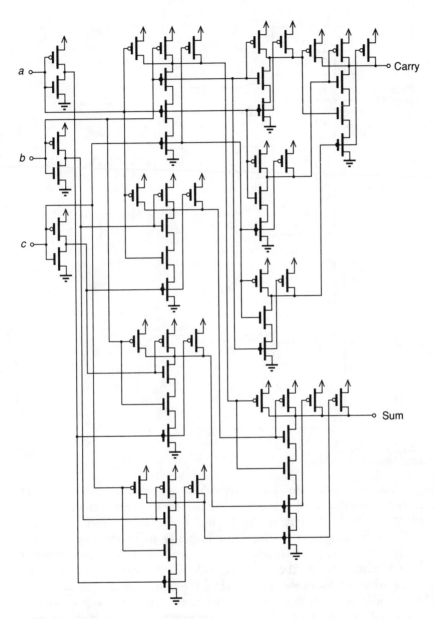

FIGURE 10.7-1
Classical CMOS full-adder circuit.

Many logic simulators provide a variety of digital blocks for use in modeling a digital system. Besides the simple logic gates and more complex logic blocks mentioned previously, models for large digital blocks such as ROMs, RAMs, PLAs, ALUs, and even FSMs are often provided. Simulation capability is normally provided for both synchronous and asynchronous sequential circuits in addition to simple combinational logic.

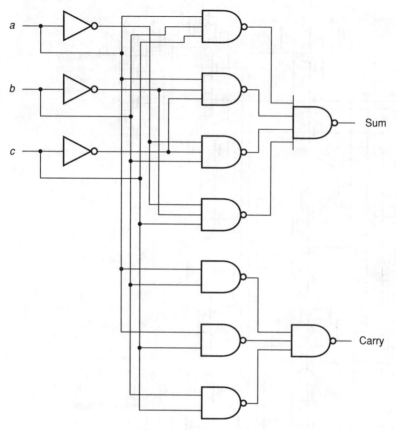

FIGURE 10.7-2
NAND-NAND full-adder logic diagram.

Most logic simulators today are *event driven*. That is, calculations are required only in response to external or internal events. External events include changes in the state of inputs to the circuit. An internal event occurs when the output of a logic function changes in response to changes in its inputs. For example, when the input to an inverter changes, the corresponding change in the inverter output is considered an event. The use of event-driven rather than fixed time-step simulation algorithms reduces the time required for simulation of a circuit.

The capability of logic simulation is often measured in terms of *events per second* or *evaluations per second*. Whenever the inputs to a logic block change, an *evaluation* must occur to determine the correct output for the logic block. Thus, an evaluation is the application of a circuit's inputs to its behavior in order to determine its outputs. An average factor of 2.5 evaluations per event is typical for digital circuits. The performance of logic simulators depends on many factors including the number of logic states, the cleverness of the algorithms chosen for simulation, and the execution speed of the computer on which the simulator is run. An execution rate of several thousand events per second is common for today's logic simulators on typical computer workstations.

10.7.2 Switch-level Simulation

MOS integrated circuits present special problems for standard logic simulators because of bidirectional pass transistors, transmission gates and charge storage. Pass transistors are used frequently because of their desirable power dissipation and interconnection characteristics. Pass transistors are difficult to simulate as simple logic gates with a standard logic simulator. It might seem that the pass transistor of Fig. 10.7-3a could be simulated by using the AND gate of Fig. 10.7-3b. The following discussion shows why this is impractical.

A simple analysis of the operation of the circuits of Fig. 10.7-3 shows that the two circuits are not equivalent. Assume initially that both inputs and the output are low for both circuits. If a logic 1 is placed on a single input, the output remains low for both circuits. If a logic 1 is placed on both inputs, the output goes high for both circuits. If a logic 0 is placed at the i input of the two circuits, the output goes to a 0 for both circuits. Thus far, the operation of the two circuits seems identical. However, assume that all inputs and outputs are initially high. Further, consider that the source diffusion of the output of the pass transistor provides parasitic capacitance to ground. If the c input to both circuits is moved to a logic 0, the AND gate output goes to a logic 0 while the pass transistor output remains high because of the charge storage at its output. Clearly, the operation of the pass transistor cannot be accurately modeled in this fashion. Either a more complex logic circuit is required, or the logic simulator must be modified to account for drive strengths and charge storage. Examples of drive strength are *driven*, *resistive pullup*, and *undriven*. The output of the pass transistor just considered is undriven when its gate terminal is at 0 V.

Because selector circuits constructed from pass transistors and transmission gates are widely used within MOS circuitry, a logic simulator for MOS must allow specification of individual transistors and their connections in addition to simple logic gates. When a logic simulator can describe transistors in addition to standard Boolean logical primitives, it is called a *switch-level simulator*.

A typical switch-level simulator operates on circuits described by nodes, transistors, and logic gate primitives. Nodes are equipotential points to which one or more terminals of one or more transistors or logic primitives are connected. Each node has an associated name, logic state, capacitance (to ground), list of events, and perhaps other information. Each transistor has a type (n-channel, p-channel, or depletion), effective resistance (width and length are required), and node connection for its terminals. Macros are often allowed to describe circuits composed of several transistors; for example, logic gates may be constructed from nodes and transistors. These logic gates are then used as primitives.

A byte-wide MOS binary adder circuit will be used as an example to show the operation of a switch-level simulator.[17] The circuit for a full-adder stage is

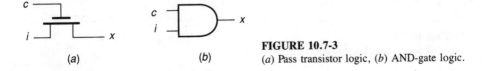

(a)   (b)

FIGURE 10.7-3
(a) Pass transistor logic, (b) AND-gate logic.

given in Fig. 10.7-4, and the corresponding input net list for the switch-level simulator is provided in Fig. 10.7-5. This net list describes the circuit of Fig. 10.7-4 in terms of four primitive elements: invert, trans, nor, and pulldown. The net list starts with a definition of a single-bit adder macro and its five inputs {*a b cif phi1 phi2*} and two outputs {*sum cof*}. Additionally, seven local signals {*af bf ci p pf k phi2f*} that are internal to the full-adder macro are specified. Each primitive element is then instantiated with its connections to other circuit nodes defined by arguments. The formats for these four procedure calls are: (invert out in), (trans gate source drain), (nor out in0 in1 in2), and (pulldown drain gate).

Next, eight single-bit full adders are combined to define a byte-wide binary adder, as shown in Fig. 10.7-6. The external nodes of the byte-wide full adder are first defined. The **a**, **b**, **cof**, and **sum** nodes represent 8-bit vectors that are expanded by the repeat statement. Signals *phi1* and *phi2* are the nonoverlapping two-phase clock inputs. The connect statement joins the *cifi* carry-input scalar to the first carry-in bit, *cof.0*. The repeat statement next creates eight copies of the full-adder circuit.

The results of a sample switch-level simulation run for the byte-wide adder are explained next. The input vector **a** was set to 11111111, while the input vector **b** was set to 00000000. This condition provides the longest carry propagation path for the full adder. The initial carry-in bit *cifi* is set to the low-true condition. A nonoverlapping two-phase clock is defined with each phase high for 90 ns and a 10 ns separation between phases. The results from a simulation for a complete

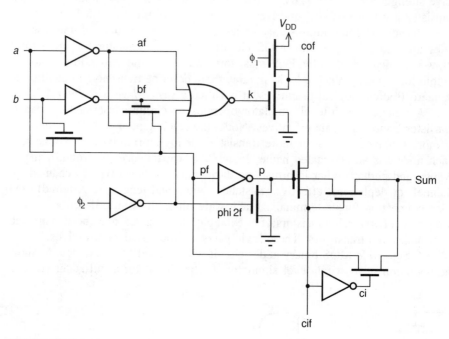

FIGURE 10.7-4
Single-bit slice of clocked full-adder circuit.

```
;Begin Full-Adder Macro
(macro adder (a b cif phi1 phi2 sum cof)
  (local af bf ci p pf k phi2f)
  (invert bf b)
  (invert af a)
  (trans b pf a)
  (trans bf pf af)
  (invert (p 2 16) pf)
  (invert (ci 2 16) cif)
  (trans cif sum p)
  (trans ci sum pf)
  (invert phi2f phi2)
  (nor k af bf phi2f)
  (pulldown cof k)
  (pulldown p phi2f)
  (trans phi1 cof vdd)
  (trans p cof cif)
)
;End Full-Adder Macro
```

FIGURE 10.7-5
Input net list for logic simulator describing circuit of Fig. 10.7-4.

```
;Instantiate Byte-Wide Adder
(node a b cifi phi1 phi2 sum cof)
(connect cifi cof.0)
(repeat i 1 8
  (adder a.i b.i cof.(1 - i) phi1 phi2 sum.i cof.i)
)
;End of Byte-Wide Adder
```

FIGURE 10.7-6
Input net list for a byte-wide binary adder.

cycle (200 ns) of the two-phase clocks are given for the first and last sum ($sum.1$, $sum.8$) and carry-out ($cof.1$, $cof.8$) bits only. Only changes in logic value of these bits are provided; that is, only simulator events for these bits are included. A typical event produces a statement with the format: name = value @ time.

ϕ_1 cycle: ($t = 0$ ns to 90 ns), precharge
    cof.8 = 1 @ 2.4
    cof.1 = 1 @ 2.6
    sum.1 = 0 @ 2.8
    sum.8 = 0 @ 3.2

ϕ_2 cycle: ($t = 100$ ns to 190 ns), evaluate
    cof.1 = 0 @ 103.2
    cof.1 = 1 @ 104.4
    sum.8 = 1 @ 104.9
    cof.1 = 0 @ 109
    sum.8 = 0 @ 129.8
    cof.8 = 0 @ 130

Note that all carry bits are precharged to a 1 during each ϕ_1 cycle. According to the simulation results shown, the *cof.8* bit changed to 1 at 2.4 ns and the *cof.1* bit changed to 1 at 2.6 ns after ϕ_1 was set high. As can be determined from the circuit connections of Fig. 10.7-4, the sum bits should be set to 0 during each ϕ_1 precharge cycle. The *sum.1* bit went to 0 at 2.8 ns and the *sum.8* bit went to 0 at 3.2 ns after ϕ_1 was set high.

During the ϕ_2 evaluate cycle, the carry and sum bits are set according to the sum of the two addends **a** = 11111111 and **b** = 00000000 and the carry in $cifi = 0$ (indicates a carry in). During the evaluate cycle *cof.1* changed to 0 at 3.2 ns, to 1 at 4.4 ns, and then back to 0 at 9.0 ns after ϕ_2 was set high. The most significant carry bit, *cof.8*, was set to 0 some 30 ns after ϕ_2 was set high. Also, *sum.8* was set to 1 at 4.9 ns and then to 0 at 29.8 ns after ϕ_2 was set high. For the input vectors given, each full-adder stage should have set its sum bit to 0 to indicate a sum of 0 and its carry bit to 0 to indicate a carry out of 1 (the carry bits use negative logic). The final results from simulating the first clock cycle are as expected. Note that the final event (*cof.8* set to 0) occurred 30 ns after the ϕ_2 clock was set high.

Prior to the second clock cycle, the carry-in bit is set to a false condition ($cifi = 1$). The following simulation results are for the second clock cycle (200 ns $\leq t < 400$ ns).

> ϕ_1 cycle: ($t = 200$ ns to 290 ns), precharge
> cof.8 = 1 @ 200.2
> cof.1 = 1 @ 200.4
>
> ϕ_2 cycle: ($t = 300$ ns to 390 ns), evaluate
> sum.8 = 1 @ 304.9
> sum.1 = 1 @ 304.9

During the second ϕ_1 cycle, the carry bits change as they are each precharged to 1. The sum bits do not change during ϕ_1 since they were already each left set to 0 after the previous ϕ_2 cycle. During the second ϕ_2 cycle, the sum and carry bits should be changed to indicate the sum of the two addends **a** = 11111111 and **b** = 00000000 and the carry in $cifi = 1$. Thus, all sum bits should be set to 1 and all carry out bits should be set to 1 indicating no carry out. The simulation results show that the sum bits are each correctly set to 1 during the second ϕ_2 cycle. The carry bits do not change since they were each set to 1 during the precharge cycle.

For a third clock cycle (400 ns $\leq t < 600$ ns), the carry in bit is set to 0 again ($cifi = 0$) and the results of the first clock cycle are repeated. These results are as follows.

> ϕ_1 cycle: ($t = 400$ ns to 490 ns), precharge
> sum.1 = 0 @ 402.8
> sum.8 = 0 @ 403.2

ϕ_2 cycle: (t = 500 ns to 590 ns), evaluate
   cof.1 = 0 @ 503.2
   cof.1 = 1 @ 504.4
  sum.8 = 1 @ 504.9
   cof.1 = 0 @ 509
  sum.8 = 0 @ 529.8
   cof.8 = 0 @ 530

The previous results for three clock cycles demonstrate the operation of a switch-level simulator. Both the timing of the byte-wide adder and the correct logical operation of the adder are observed for the input conditions provided. Other switch-level simulators have different input and output formats and different capabilities, but all operate assuming discretized values for the circuit variables, and all produce results much faster than complete circuit simulation.

10.7.3 Hardware Logic Simulation

Even with the increased speed of logic simulators as compared with circuit simulators, full simulation of large digital circuits via general-purpose computers is not practical. An alternate approach is in use by several companies. Special-purpose hardware that executes many simulation steps in parallel has been developed to speed the simulation process. One of the early, large parallel simulators was the YSE (Yorktown Simulation Engine)[18] developed by IBM. This hardware consists of hundreds of identical processing units that each simulate part of the target circuit. By spreading the calculations over a large number of processors, even large-mainframe computers can be simulated in detail. Of course, such special-purpose hardware is expensive to build and to operate. Even so, several companies now offer hardware accelerators to enhance the speed of logic simulation.

In the future, methods of machine verification other than total logic simulation must be found. Logic simulation time increases exponentially with the number of logic components to be simulated. Thus, faster computers are necessary to simulate next-generation computers that contain more logic components. But how can the next-generation computers be built if the simulation capability of present-generation computers is inadequate?

Two current approaches to this problem are verification proofs and hierarchical simulation. For relatively simple hardware, it has been possible to verify correct logical operation by mathematical proofs. Unfortunately, the utility of this method diminishes quickly as the size and complexity of the hardware increase. The second method, hierarchical simulation, attempts to model the target machine at various levels of abstraction. Small blocks of hardware are verified by logic simulation. These blocks are then interconnected and simulated together without the internal detail of each block. Neither of these methods has been entirely successful, and both are now active areas of research and development.

10.8 TIMING ANALYSIS

For most digital circuits, a very important parameter is the maximum rate at which the circuit can correctly process data. For microprocessors, the processing speed is usually given in MIPS (millions of instructions per second); for scientific calculations, the rate of execution is given in FLOPS (floating-point operations per second); and for logical inference machines, the characteristic measure is LIPS (logical inferences per second). The execution rate of each of these machines is limited by parasitics and governed by its input clock. A primary goal in the design of a digital computing machine is to operate with the fastest possible input clock.

Each digital integrated circuit has a maximum rate of operation. This rate of operation is limited by the output drive capability of its logic elements and by the capacitance and resistance of the loads they must drive. In a FSM (finite-state machine), the clocking rate is limited primarily by the longest path through its combinational logic section. For integrated circuits composed of large blocks of circuitry, the maximum clocking rate may be limited by signal lines that must carry information between the blocks. The designer's task, then, is to find those paths in an integrated circuit design that cause the maximum delay and then to modify the circuitry to minimize that delay.

Finding the longest delay paths, called *critical paths*, for an integrated circuit is not a simple task. Until recently, the most common technique for finding critical delays was for the designer to perform detailed circuit simulation on the paths that were suspected of contributing long delay times. Of course, using circuit simulation for this task was not foolproof. Many times an unsuspected path that was not considered for simulation would limit the maximum clock speed. More recently, computer programs have been designed specifically to seek out delay paths directly from the circuit definition without requiring simulation. This type of computer analysis is called *timing analysis*.

10.8.1 Timing Analysis Methodology

Timing analysis differs from circuit and logic simulation in that all possible signal paths are considered. Circuit simulation and logic simulation both require the specification of input signals to control the simulation. Thus, only delay paths that are exercised by the particular set of inputs are tested. For many digital circuits, it is computationally impossible to provide sufficient input conditions to test the circuit fully. Timing analysis tools work by tracing *signal paths* instead of simulating the circuit for specific inputs. Specifically, timing analysis uses *state-independent* path tracing. Each time a logic gate is encountered, the gate is assumed to pass the signal regardless of the state of the other inputs to the gate. A signal path is terminated only when an output is reached or a clocked storage element is found. With this method, all possible delay paths are tested.

An example of timing analysis signal propagation through two logic gates is shown in Fig. 10.8-1. The signal path starts at input x and reaches the NAND gate. Inputs a and b for the NAND gate are assumed high to allow continuation of the signal path. When the signal reaches the NOR gate, input c is assumed low

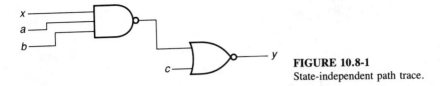

FIGURE 10.8-1
State-independent path trace.

to allow continued propagation of the signal. Finally, the signal reaches an output y, where it terminates. The delay for this signal path includes the contributions of the NAND gate, the NOR gate, and the series interconnections. The delay paths from x to y, b to y, a to y and c to y would all be found by a timing analysis of this circuit.

A second example shows a deficiency of timing analysis. From Fig. 10.8-2, signal paths from a to b and from a to c are expected. However, state-independent path tracing will also find a signal path from b to c and vice versa. Although the path from b to c is a real path, it will not normally be exercised within this circuit because node n is actively driven by the inverter. Analysis of additional paths that will not be exercised during operation of a circuit can degrade the performance of a timing analysis program. Circuit-level timing analyzers allow direction setting for pass transistors and transmission gates to circumvent this problem. Unfortunately, unless this is carefully done, some critical signal paths may be eliminated from consideration.

10.8.2 Timing Analysis Tools

To provide further insight into the capabilities of circuit-level timing analysis programs, two such programs will be described here. The first of these, called TV,[19] attempts to set directions for circuit elements by using rules. These rules, by setting some transistor directions, minimize the number of false paths that are found. The second tool, Crystal,[20] provides a wide range of capability, including improved delay models and coverage for circuits built from CMOS technology.

TV timing analyzer for NMOS designs, operates from extracted circuit parasitics and considers only stable, rising, and falling signal values. Program execution time is minimized by a *static analysis* that sets signal flow direction and clock qualification where possible. Otherwise, signal flow direction is determined from a set of direction-finding rules. Some of the rules are independent of design style. For example, the *constant-propagation rule* says that any transistor source

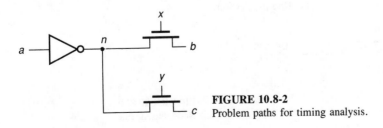

FIGURE 10.8-2
Problem paths for timing analysis.

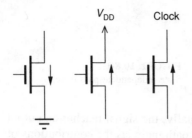

FIGURE 10.8-3
Constant propagation rule to set directions.

or drain connected to power, ground, or a clock must be a sink of signal flow, while the other terminal must be a source. Figure 10.8-3 demonstrates this rule, which by itself sets the directions for more than half the transistors in a typical circuit. Another rule, demonstrated in Fig. 10.8-4, is based on Kirchoff's current law. This rule, the *node current rule*, states that if all but one of the transistors to a node have a known direction, and the known transistors all sink or all source signal flow, then the unknown transistor must transmit flow in the opposite direction relative to the node.

Other signal-flow rules depend on technology or design style. For example, in an NMOS technology design, the *k-ratio rule* for inverters can be used to set direction. This rule is based on a standard device sizing ratio k as discussed in Chapter 7 for ratio logic. By finding the minimum resistance to ground through each unset (direction not specified) transistor connected to a pullup, a transistor can be considered as a pulldown (signal flow toward the pullup) or a pass transistor (signal flow away from the pullup), depending on the resistance ratio. The reasoning is that resistances to ground that satisfy the device sizing ratio k with respect to the pullup path must be part of the pulldown circuit for a logic gate. Transistors that cannot satisfy ratio rules can be safely classified as pass transistors and their direction set accordingly. Other rules cover pass transistors connected to a common node and having a common gate signal, and analogous structures where the direction of a boundary transistor can be determined, thereby allowing arrayed versions of the structure to have their directions set accordingly.

Signal path analysis is started from the clock or other input nodes. Paths are investigated in a breadth-first manner in accordance with the transistor directions that were set by the static analysis. Delays for paths are calculated based on the capacitance of the interconnections and the resistance of driving and series pass

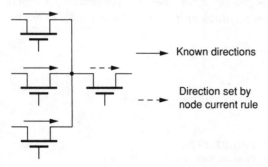

Known directions

Direction set by
node current rule

FIGURE 10.8-4
Node current rule.

transistors. Transistors are assigned a rising and a falling resistance from tables based on their use in the circuit. Signal direction changes are propagated so that a rising input signal to an inverter produces a falling output signal and vice versa. Pass transistors continue the direction of the input signal. Because path delays are calculated from a linearized model, the delays may differ from actual circuit values by 30% or more.

Output of the TV program includes a user-selectable number of the worst-case paths. Equivalent paths, such as parallel paths in a data bus, are condensed in the output list so that only the last path in the list is reported. Other useful information such as slack time for paths, excessive power used to drive a noncritical path, and nodes with unusually high capacitance are reported. The TV timing analyzer was successfully used in the analysis of the MIPS series of microprocessor chips[21] developed at Stanford University.

Another timing analysis tool, Crystal, was developed to analyze the RISC computer chips[22] developed at the University of California at Berkeley. This tool has found widespread use throughout the VLSI design community, particularly within universities. The timing analysis is based on a circuit description that is extracted directly from a geometrical specification file. This description includes transistor sizes and types, interconnection capacitance, and a rough calculation of interconnection resistance. A simple delay model is used for each stage to provide quick calculation of signal propagation delays along a path.

The Crystal timing analyzer was developed for MOS circuits with multiple nonoverlapping clocks. The program attempts to determine how long each clock phase must be to allow all signals to propagate to their destinations. The analysis is state-independent, so all possible paths are checked. The user must specify a minimum of information to begin the analysis. For two-phase clocking schemes, only two signals must be specified. One of the clock phases is specified as a rising edge or a falling edge to trigger the analysis. The other clock phase is specified as a stable low value. The reason for this can be seen from the shift register circuit of Fig. 10.8-5. Here a signal path trace is started from the ϕ_1 clock. Without a specified value for the ϕ_2 clock, the signal path would continue through all the stages shown. If the ϕ_2 clock is set to a stable low condition, then the signal path will terminate correctly after the first stage. The path delay

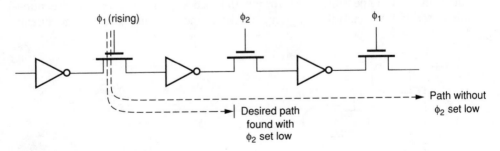

FIGURE 10.8-5
Clocked path analysis.

will consist of the time for the first inverter to discharge (charge) the input of the second inverter through the pass transistor gated by ϕ_1 plus the time for the second inverter to charge (discharge) the interconnection capacitance up to the input of the pass transistor gated by ϕ_2.

Each path trace for a signal is started from a rising or falling input specified by the user. As the signal path proceeds through inverters or logic gates, the appropriate rising or falling direction is determined to correctly model asymmetric stage delays. The path-trace analysis is done with a depth-first search algorithm. Thus, a signal path is followed until it reaches a circuit output or is stopped by a static signal specified by the user (like the ϕ_2 condition examined in the previous paragraph). Delay information from previous paths is maintained at each node so that the signal path can be aborted on later path traces through the same node if the cumulative delay is less than the stored value.

As with all state-independent timing analysis methods, the possibility of reporting false paths exists. A simple example is given in Fig. 10.8-6, where a signal path is gated by a signal and its complement. From a logical viewpoint, there is not a signal path from node a to node c because one of the AND gates will be disabled by x or $\bar{x}$. Since timing analysis is state-independent, this logical constraint is not recognized, and the path from node a through node b to node c will be considered and its delay calculated. A 1-of-n selector circuit is a classic example of this condition. In normal operation, only one path through the selector circuit will be enabled at any time, but state-independent timing analysis finds all n paths. In most timing analyzers the capability exists to set signals to a stable value to disable paths; however, this capability must be used carefully to avoid accidentally disabling critical delay paths.

To facilitate fast operation, Crystal uses a simple delay model consisting of an equivalent resistance for the drive transistor and a resistance and capacitance for the interconnections and load devices. The transistor drive model is table-driven with the equivalent resistance selected based on input signal slope and capacitive load value. This is not as accurate as a circuit-level simulation but is much faster. Once critical delay paths are found, they can be investigated with a circuit simulator if more accurate results are required.

In summary, timing analysis is an important tool for integrated circuit design. By using state-independent path tracing, it performs a function that is difficult, if not impossible, to perform with timed logic simulators. The execution time for timing analysis programs is determined by the size of the circuit

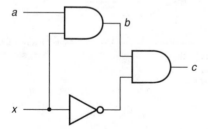

FIGURE 10.8-6
Logically impossible path.

being analyzed. While timing analysis is used to find and correct critical delay paths, correct functional operation can be verified with a logic simulator. Thus, logic simulation and timing analysis function as partners to ensure that a digital integrated circuit is functionally correct and that it operates at the proper speed.

10.9 REGISTER-TRANSFER-LEVEL SIMULATION

Specifications for the operation of digital integrated circuits are often given in terms of high-level operations on information. These high-level operations describe transformations on data as it moves from one storage device or register to another such device. For this reason, descriptions of this type are known as *register-transfer-level* descriptions.

Register-transfer-level descriptions provide a useful level of abstraction for the description and simulation of digital systems. The logic simulators described previously require too much detail about the exact logical structure of an integrated circuit for early design simulation. Also, because of the detailed specification of the logical structure of the circuit, complete logic simulation of an entire circuit such as a microprocessor requires impractically large computer resources. Alternatively, at the highest level, a natural language description of the function of a digital system is often ambiguous and vague. A concise natural language description of a next-generation computer might be, "build a new computer that is like computer XYZ, but is twice as fast and uses less power." To fill this gap between natural language descriptions and logical definitions, high-level description and simulation languages have been developed. Of these, register-transfer-level simulation languages allow specification and simulation of operations on data words, in addition to single-bit operations.

The operation of a digital system can be defined precisely through the use of a register-transfer-level description. In fact, one such language, ISPS (Instruction Set Processor Specification), was developed to allow unambiguous description and specification of computer operation.[23] The ISPS language allows data bits to be grouped into words. Logic and arithmetic operations are allowed on both bit-level and word-level entities as they are moved between storage registers. Operations common to most programming languages, such as conditional statements, if-then-else constructs, case statements, and procedures, are allowed. Thus, a register-transfer language is a special programming language tailored to describing the operation of digital systems.

10.9.1 Simple RTL

For demonstration purposes, a primitive register-transfer language (RTL) will be defined and used to describe the execution of one instruction from an early 8-bit microprocessor. This primitive RTL is defined in Table 10.9-1. The first operation required is the *transfer operation*—the contents of one group of bits (register) are placed into another storage device. Second, the common *arithmetic operations* of add and subtract are provided. Third, a simple *conditional capability* to alter control flow is added.

TABLE 10.9-1
Primitve RTL Definition

Operation	Description
A ← B	transfer
C ← A + B	addition
D ← A − B	subtraction
PC ← B if A = 0	conditional

The operation to be described using this RTL is the extended load of the A accumulator of the Motorola 6802 microprocessor. This microprocessor has a 16-bit address bus and a separate 8-bit data bus. The A accumulator is an 8-bit register. Execution of this instruction requires four memory cycles: fetch the 8-bit instruction, obtain the high byte of the operand address, obtain the low byte of the operand address, and obtain the data from the operand address. The approximate register-transfer-level steps are given in Table 10.9-2 and are explained next.

The first step moves contents of the program counter (PC) to the address bus (AB) in preparation for fetching the instruction byte. While the processor is waiting for the memory to respond, the program counter is incremented. After a delay time, the DBI (data bus input) is moved to the instruction register (IR). This ends the first memory cycle. As the instruction is being decoded, the incremented PC is moved to the address bus in preparation to fetch the next byte. The PC is incremented again, and the contents of the DBI are moved to the internal data bus (DB) and on to a temporary register (TMP) to complete the second cycle. To begin the third memory cycle, the previously incremented PC is moved to the AB and the PC value is incremented. The DBI contents are moved to DB where they are held in preparation for the cycle that outputs the data address (this is slightly oversimplified). The fourth and final cycle moves the data from DB to the low-order bits of the address bus (ABL) and the contents of TMP to the high-order bits of the address bus (ABH). At this point, the extended 16-bit address of

TABLE 10.9-2
Microprocessor Instruction Execution

Cycle	Operation		Explanation
1	AB	← PC	pc to address bus
	PC	← PC + 1	incr pc
	IR	← DBI	data to ir
2	AB	← PC	pc to address bus
	PC	← PC + 1	incr pc
	TMP	← DB ← DBI	data to tmp
3	AB	← PC	pc to address bus
	PC	← PC + 1	incr pc
	DB	← DBI	data to dynamic store
4	ABL	← DB	data adr to address bus
	ABH	← TMP	data adr to address bus
	ACCA	← DB ← DBI	data to accumulator

the data is present on the address bus. The memory responds with the requested data, and this data is moved from DBI to DB and into accumulator A (ACCA) to complete execution of the instruction. These RTL statements describe at a high level the execution of a simple microprocessor instruction.

10.9.2 ISPS Specification and Simulation

The Instruction Set Processor Specification (ISPS) language was developed for the certification, architectural evaluation, simulation, fault analysis, and design automation of instruction set processors. The language provides a behavioral rather than a structural description. There are no part numbers, pin assignments, layouts, or technologies defined. Of course, some structural information such as register lengths, data path widths, and connections of components are necessarily a part of the simulation. The operation of each part of a processor is specified algorithmically by its behavior.

The ISPS notation includes an interface and entities. First, the carriers (memory) elements are defined. This usually includes an array of memory locations with a specified bit width and number of words. Second, the procedures necessary for the execution of the processor statements are defined. This usually includes instruction decoding, effective address calculation, arithmetic and logical operation definitions, and memory load/store functions. ISPS provides a typical set of program operators, including assignment, if, case, and repeat. Additionally, provisions are made for concurrent or sequential processing. It is possible to specify the bit length of words. Aliases are available for variables, and bit fields of variables can be addressed directly by other variables. Normal number representations include binary, hex, decimal, and octal. An example will be presented to demonstrate briefly some of the capabilities of the ISPS language.

The Motorola 68000 microprocessor will be used as the example to describe typical ISPS capabilities. Figure 10.9-1 shows the definition of the memory and processor state. The memory is defined here as 1 K 16-bit words with the name M and the alias Memory. The processor state includes definition of the program counter (PC) and extended program counter (PCA), the register array (REG), the instruction register (IR), and other required processor state holders. In each case, the number of registers and the width in bits are defined. Multiple references to some resources are specified. For example, an array of sixteen 32-bit registers (REG) is defined. Then the data registers (D) are specified as the first eight registers, and the address registers (A) are specified as the second eight registers of the register array.

Partial instruction execution for the 68000 microprocessor is defined in Fig. 10.9-2. In the figure, calculation of a displacement for the indexed address mode is demonstrated, and the effective address calculation is partially defined. Note the use of the Begin/End statements to define a block of operations and the use of ":=" as the assignment operator. A decode statement provides a multi-way branch depending on the value of one or more bits. For example, in the displacement calculation, bit 11 of the memory addressed by the PC defines whether the instruction is a word index (bit 11 = 0) or a long index (bit 11 = 1).

```
M68000 :=
    BEGIN

    **Memory.State**
    M\Memory[0:1K]<15:0>,

    **Processor.State**
    PCA\Program.Counter.with.A0<23:0>,
          PC\Program.Counter<22:0>          :=PCA<23:1>,
    REG\Registers[0:15]<31:0>,
          D\Data.Registers[0:7]<31:0>       :=REG[0:7]<31:0>,
          A\Adr.Registers[0:7]<31:0>        :=REG[8:15]<31:0>,
    IR\Instruction.Register<15:0>,
          OP\OP.Code<1:0>                   :=IR<15:14>,
          SIZE\OP.Size<1:0>                 :=IR<13:12>,
          DREG\Destination.Reg<2:0>         :=IR<11:9>,
          DM\Destination.Mode<2:0>          :=IR<8:6>,
          SM\Source.Mode<2:0>               :=IR<5:3>,
          SREG\Source.Reg<2:0>              :=IR<2:0>,
    T\Temporary.Reg<31:0>,
    PCT\Temp.PC<23:0>,
    EA\Effective.Address<23:0>,
          EAE\EA.without.A0<22:0>           :=EA<23:1>,
          BYTE\HiLo.Byte< >                 :=EA<0>
```

FIGURE 10.9-1
ISPS description of M68000 microprocessor state.

The effective address calculation of Fig. 10.9-2 demonstrates use of the decode statement with a 3-bit field. This field is used to specify indirect, postincrement, predecrement, displacement, indexed, and assorted (not shown) address modes.

A complete ISPS description of a state-of-the-art microprocessor is several pages in length. Such a description is invaluable for two reasons. First, the description provides an unambiguous specification of the operation of the microprocessor (note that the description could be unambiguous and still be incorrect). Second, the description can be simulated to verify desired operation or to explore architectural characteristics of design choices early in the design cycle.

10.9.3 RTL Simulation with LISP

A less formal but very powerful means to simulate high-level behavior for a digital system is through special-purpose programs in a general-purpose programming language such as LISP or C. In fact, LISP is particularly well suited to this task because of its interactive nature and its symbolic representation capability. The behavior of each element of the digital system can be represented as a separate function. In the case of a simulation for a computer architecture, each instruction can be represented by a LISP function. These functions can be executed and changed interactively to examine or to verify operation of the instruction set. An example will be used to demonstrate this.

```
**Instruction.Execution**                        ! CALCULATES OFFSET CAUSE BY
DIS\Displacement<23.0> :=                         ! INDEX AND DISPLACEMENT IN
 Begin                                            ! THE INDEX MODE.
  DIS <=M[PC]<7:0>Next
  Decode M[PC]<11>=>
   Begin
    '0\Word.Index  := EX<=REG[M[PC]<15:12>]<15:0>,
    '1\Long.Index  := EA=REG[M[PC]<15:12>]
   EndNext
   EA=EA + DIS
 End,
CEA\Effective.Adr(MO<2:0>,R<2:0>)<>:=             ! SPECIFIES EFFECTIVE ADDRESS
 Begin                                            ! IN MEMORY FOR ANY MEMORY
  Decode MO=>                                      ! RELATED OPERATION
   Begin
    '010\Indirect     :=EA=A[R]
    '011\Post.Inc     :=
     Begin
      EA=A[R]Next
      Decode SIZE =>
       Begin
        '01\Byte       :=A[R]=A[R]+1,
        '11\Word       :=A[R]=A[R]+2,
        '10\Long       :=A[R]=A[R]+4,
       End
     End,
    '100\Pre.Dec       :=
     Begin
      Decode SIZE =>
       Begin
        '01\Byte       :=A[R]=A[R]-1,
        '11\Word       :=A[R]=A[R]-2,
        '10\Long       :=A[R]=A[R]-4,
       EndNext
      EA=A[R]
     End,
    '101\Displacement:=(EA<=M[PC]NextEA=EA+A[R]Next PC=PC+1),
    '110\Index       :=(DIS()Next EA=EA+A[R] Next PC=PC+1),
   End,

End,
```

FIGURE 10.9-2

Partial ISPS description of M68000 instruction execution.

A partial LISP definition of a RISC processor is given in Fig. 10.9-3. A subset of the arithmetic, logical, and load functions is presented. Other functions, especially PC modification instructions, must be included to allow full execution of a RISC program. Each instruction is represented by a separate function with arguments that are derived from the bit fields of the instruction.

The add instruction of Fig. 10.9-3 will be examined to clarify the instruction definitions provided by the LISP functions in the figure. This instruction is a triadic instruction on this RISC processor. That is, the instruction requires three arguments: two sources and a destination. On many computers, because of instruction word width limitations, the add instruction is dyadic, requiring the destination and one source to be specified by the same bit field. The arguments

```lisp
(defun add (rs s2 dest)
  (setq rd (+ rs s2))
  (store (reg (eard dest)) rd)
  (setq pc (add1 pc)))

(defun sub (rs s2 dest)
  (setq rd (- rs s2))
  (store (reg (eard dest)) rd)
  (setq pc (add1 pc)))

(defun and (rs s2 dest)
  (setq rd (and rs s2))
  (store (reg (eard dest)) rd)
  (setq pc (add1 pc)))

(defun or (rs s2 dest)
  (setq rd (or rs s2))
  (store (reg (eard dest)) rd)
  (setq pc (add1 pc)))

(defun xor (rs s2 dest)
  (setq rd (xor rs s2))
  (store (reg (eard dest)) rd)
  (setq pc (add1 pc)))

(defun sll (rs s2 dest)
  (setq rd (shiftl rs s2))
  (store (reg (eard dest)) rd)
  (setq pc (add1 pc)))

(defun sra (rs s2 dest)
  (setq rd (shiftra rs s2))
  (store (reg (eard dest)) rd)
  (setq pc (add1 pc)))

(defun ldl (rs s2 dest)
  (setq rd (plus rs s2))
  (store (mem (dest)))
  (setq pc (add1 pc)))
```

FIGURE 10.9-3
Partial LISP definition of RISC processor.

to the triadic add instruction presented here include *rs* as one source, *s2* as the second source, and *dest* as the destination for the add. The first line of the function defines the operation and the required arguments as "defun add (*rs s2 dest*)."

The operation of the function body for the add instruction of Fig. 10.9-3 can be explained as follows. The second line of the function definition sets a temporary variable *rd* to the sum of the contents of *rs* and *s2*. The third line invokes two functions (definitions not shown in the example) to store the results of the add in a register array. The *eard* function calculates the effective address within the register array for the store. The *eard* function must include the effects of the overlapped register storage mechanism usually employed within a RISC processor. The *store* function places the contents of the previously calculated *rd* into the proper slot within the register array. The final line of the add function increments the program counter *pc* by one.

A top-level program is required to accept a test instruction stream, decode the instruction into the appropriate bit fields, and then call the instruction primitive definitions of Fig. 10.9-3 with the arguments set appropriately. The operation of the program can be observed by including print statements at appropriate places, by tracing the execution of the program, or by examining the program's side effects on the register array, pc, other processor state holders, and memory contents.

Because of the ease with which variations in instruction definition can be tested, an interactive simulation through a LISP program is a powerful tool for system development. The interactive nature of LISP provides an excellent means to correct errors and to test new ideas quickly. There is no need to wait for compile and load steps between each change in the model. As a final comment, it should be noted that the example presented for the RISC processor did not include any effects of word length or arithmetic overflow. Additional statements are necessary to include these effects.

In this section the concepts of high-level definition and simulation of digital systems were introduced. A primitive RTL was used to define the execution of a simple microprocessor instruction. Then the ISPS language was presented as one example of an RTL language that was designed to specify and evaluate instruction processor architectures. Finally, an example was presented that used LISP as a powerful, but informal, method of simulating and evaluating digital system architectures.

10.10 HARDWARE DESIGN LANGUAGES

Machine-readable descriptions of integrated circuit designs have become an important factor in designing VLSI circuits. These descriptions are often defined in terms of design languages that, like computer languages, have specific syntax and semantics. Such design languages have been used to describe circuits from the geometrical level up through the architectural level. As new designs become increasingly dependent on CAD tools, machine-readable descriptions become extremely important. Two hardware design languages have evolved as ANSI (American National Standards Institute) standards within the last few years. One of these, EDIF (Electronic Design Interchange Format), is intended to describe designs from the layout level through the logic level. Another such language, VHDL (VHSIC Hardware Description Language), is used to characterize both the function and structure of designs from logical primitives through architectural descriptions. The basics of these two languages will be introduced here along with simple examples of each.

10.10.1   EDIF Design Description

As integrated circuit designs increased in complexity and the use of computers became prominent within the semiconductor industry, the need for a common interchange format for integrated circuit design information arose. With such a standard, silicon foundries could accept design descriptions from many sources, CAD vendors could create widely applicable programs to process designs, and designers would benefit from wider availability of CAD tools and silicon processing. The EDIF (Electronic Design Interchange Format) standard was created by interested companies to fulfill this need.

Key elements in the design of the EDIF language were broad applicability and easy extensibility. To meet these goals, EDIF was designed with a syntax that is similar to LISP with all data represented as symbolic expressions. Primitive data such as strings, signals, ports, layers, numbers, and identifiers are the *atoms* of EDIF. These atoms are formed into more complex structures as *lists*; many times, the first element of a list is a keyword that gives a particular meaning to the subsequent elements of the list. This syntax is easily parsed, and the keywords—not the syntax—provide the semantics of the language. Thus, it is desirable to design EDIF parsers that respond to the particular set of keywords for their intended function. Unrecognized keywords may be ignored successfully, allowing upward compatibility with new extensions of the language.

EDIF is intended neither as a programming language nor a database language, but rather as an efficient interchange format for integrated circuit designs. The LISP-like structure is relatively compact and yet maintains a textlike property that allows it to be read and written directly by humans. An EDIF description may contain mask descriptions, technology information, net lists, test instructions, documentation, and other user-defined information. The structure is hierarchical in that larger design descriptions can be built from component descriptions and libraries of standard elements.

The basic organizational entity for describing designs within EDIF is the *cell*. A cell may contain different representations or *views* of a design. For example, one view might contain mask layout information while another view may contain behavioral-level modeling information. A view may be one of several types such as *physical, document, behavior, topology*, or *stranger*. Each view will contain a specific type of information about the cell. For example, the physical view may contain geometric figures for circuit schematics or mask artwork, but it will not contain behavioral information. The topology view might contain net list descriptions, schematic diagrams, or symbolic layout. The document view could contain a textual description of a design, figures describing the design, or specifications for the behavior of the design. The stranger view is provided for data that does not meet the conventions of the other view types.

Each view of a cell may specify its *interface* to the external world. This interface includes a list of external ports and their characteristics. The interface description does not specify how the cell performs its function internally but rather defines how the cell will relate to its environment. A second part of the cell definition is its *contents*. The contents provide the detailed implementation for each view. This could include instances of other cells or could be the actual definition of mask geometry for the cell layout. A net list view and a mask layout view for a full adder are described here as examples of EDIF contents.

10.10.2 EDIF Net List View of Full Adder

The net list view is available in EDIF to describe collections of cells and their interconnections. Cell instances have interface sections that describe their ports. Within the EDIF net list view, the *joined* construct is used to show the interconnection of cells and interface ports. A sample EDIF file segment that describes the net list for the full adder of Fig. 10.10-1 is given in Fig. 10.10-2. This net list view starts with an interface description that declares the three input ports and two output ports of the full adder. This is followed by the contents section, which declares local signals, instantiates component cells of the full adder, and then joins appropriate signals to realize the full-adder circuit. The component cells are from a p-well CMOS library of cells. The reader should verify that the EDIF net list of Fig. 10.10-2 accurately describes the full-adder circuit of Fig. 10.10-1.

10.10.3 EDIF Mask Layout View of Full Adder

EDIF allows hierarchical descriptions of mask layout information. Public domain formats such as CIF, as well as company proprietary formats for artwork descriptions, can be described within EDIF. As an example, a partial layout of the cell-

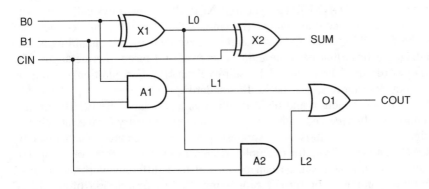

FIGURE 10.10-1
Full-adder circuit.

```
(cell FullAdder
  (view Topology Netlist
    (interface
      (declare input port (B0 B1 CIN))
      (declare output port (SUM COUT))
    )
    (contents
      (declare local signal (L0 L1 L2))
      (instance pwellcmoslib:xor X1)
      (instance pwellcmoslib:xor X2)
      (instance pwellcmoslib:and A1)
      (instance pwellcmoslib:and A2)
      (instance pwellcmoslib:or O1)
      (joined B0 X1:a A1:a)
      (joined B1 X1:b A1:b)
      (joined CIN X2:b A2:b)
      (joined L0 X1:c X2:a A2:a)
      (joined L1 A1:c O1:a)
      (joined L2 A2:c O1:b)
      (joined SUM X2:c)
      (joined COUT O1:c)
    )
  )
)
```

FIGURE 10.10-2
EDIF description of net list for full adder.

based full adder of Fig. 10.10-1 is described in CIF as shown in Fig. 10.10-3*a*. To simplify the figure, only the interconnection layout for the input signals B0, B1, and CIN is provided by the CIF description. The description presumes that the CIF layout descriptions for the five component cells of the full adder have been instantiated. Definitions for the CIF statements used in this example are provided in Fig. 10.10-3*b*. This CIF example allows a comparison with the corresponding EDIF description for the interconnection layout of the cell-based full adder of Fig. 10.10-1, as provided in Fig. 10.10-4. The EDIF description contains definitions of the cell name (CONNE), celltype (GENERIC), view (physical), viewtype (MASKLAYOUT), and the figures (rectangle) that form the interconnections among the full-adder cells. Each rectangle is described by the endpoints of one of the diagonal lines that pass through a corner of and bisect the rectangle. The EDIF keywords used here should be self-explanatory. For additional detail on EDIF layout descriptions, see the EDIF standard[3].

Since its introduction and later adoption as a standard, the EDIF language has become widely accepted within the semiconductor industry for the interchange of design information. It is now supported as an interchange mechanism by most CAD vendors. Thus, for example, results from design entry or computer-based analysis on a workstation can be moved to a different workstation or to a mainframe computer for further processing. A full description of the EDIF standard is provided by ANSI/EIA standard EDIF 2 0 0.[3]

```
DS 2;
9 CONNE;
L MET1;
B 80 80 40 700;
B 200 80 100 840;
B 1200 80 600 980;
L COND;
B 40 40 40 700;
B 40 40 160 840;
B 40 40 720 980;
B 40 40 1160 980;
L POLY;
B 120 40 140 220;
B 40 460 60 430;
B 40 740 60 1110;
B 80 80 40 700;
B 120 40 140 1460;
B 40 40 180 380;
B 40 440 140 580;
B 40 440 140 1100;
B 80 80 160 840;
B 40 40 180 1300;
B 120 40 820 220;
B 40 740 740 570;
B 80 80 720 980;
B 80 80 1160 980;
B 40 300 1140 1170;
B 40 40 1180 1300;
DF;

C 2 T 0 0;
E
```

(a)

```
DS 2              ; define symbol number 2
9 ABCDE           ; label (cell name)
L MET1            ; layer definition (metal)
B DX DY X Y       ; rectangle, length DX, width DY,
                  ;            location X,Y
DF                ; end of symbol definition
C N T X Y         ; call symbol N, translate by X,Y
E                 ; end of CIF definition
```

(b)

Figure 10.10-3
CIF layout example, (a) CIF layout file for input connections to cell-based full adder of Fig. 10.10-1, (b) Definition of CIF statements used in part a.

```
(cell CONNE
 (cellType GENERIC)
 (view physical
  (viewType MASKLAYOUT)
  (interface)
  (contents
   (figure Met1 (rectangle (pt 0 660)    (pt 80 740)))
                (rectangle (pt 0 800)    (pt 200 880)))
   (figure Cont (rectangle (pt 0 940)    (pt 1200 1020)))
                (rectangle (pt 20 680)   (pt 60 720)))
                (rectangle (pt 140 820)  (pt 180 860)))
                (rectangle (pt 700 960)  (pt 740 1000)))
                (rectangle (pt 1140 960) (pt 1180 1000))))
   (figure Poly (rectangle (pt 80 200)   (pt 200 240)))
                (rectangle (pt 40 200)   (pt 80 660)))
                (rectangle (pt 40 740)   (pt 80 1480)))
                (rectangle (pt 0 660)    (pt 80 740)))
                (rectangle (pt 80 1440)  (pt 200 1480)))
                (rectangle (pt 160 360)  (pt 200 400)))
                (rectangle (pt 120 360)  (pt 160 800)))
                (rectangle (pt 120 880)  (pt 160 1320)))
                (rectangle (pt 120 800)  (pt 200 880)))
                (rectangle (pt 160 1280) (pt 200 1320)))
                (rectangle (pt 760 200)  (pt 880 240)))
                (rectangle (pt 720 200)  (pt 760 940)))
                (rectangle (pt 680 940)  (pt 760 1020)))
                (rectangle (pt 1120 940) (pt 1200 1020)))
                (rectangle (pt 1120 1020)(pt 1160 1320)))
                (rectangle (pt 1160 1280)(pt 1200 1320))))
  )
 )
)
```

Figure 10.10-4
EDIF physical layout file corresponding to CIF file of Fig. 10.10-3.

10.10.4 VHDL Design Description

VHDL was developed for the design, description, and simulation of VHSIC components. VHSIC is the acronym for the Very High Speed Integrated Circuits program of the U.S. Department of Defense. Thus, the language was originally developed to describe hardware designs for military purposes. Because the need for a standard hardware description language is industrywide, the VHDL language was adopted by the IEEE and formalized as an industry standard.

VHDL is concerned primarily with description of the functional operation and/or the logical organization of designs.[24] This description is accomplished by first specifying the inputs and outputs of a system or device. Then either its *behavior* (outputs as functions of inputs) or its *structure* (in terms of interconnected subcomponents) is specified. The primary abstraction in VHDL is called a *design entity*. A design entity has two parts: the *interface description* and one or more *body descriptions*.

An interface description must perform several functions. It must define the logical interface to the outside world. It must specify the input and output ports and their characteristics. Additionally, operating conditions and characteristics may be included. To accomplish this, the interface description provides a *port declaration* for each input and output of the design entity. Each port declaration includes a port *name* and an associated *mode* and *type*. The mode specifies direction as *in, out, inout, buffer*, or *linkage*. The type qualifies the data that flows through a port. Standard types include *BIT, INTEGER, REAL, CHARACTER*, and *BIT_VECTOR*. Additionally, user-defined types are acceptable.

As a simple example with well-defined interface characteristics, the interface description for the full adder of Fig. 10.10-1 is given in Fig. 10.10-5. The full adder has three binary inputs, B0, B1, and CIN, and two binary outputs, SUM and COUT. The interface description may be thought of as the "black box" view of the design entity.

The body description of VHDL defines the internal operation or organization of the hardware, providing an "open box" view of the design entity. The internal operation is often termed a *behavioral* description, while the organization is called a *structural* description. These descriptions can occur at one of several levels, such as a logical definition, a register-transfer definition, or an algorithmic definition. The body description contains a header that provides a name for the description and identifies the associated interface description. The block...end block section contains all the descriptive information about the internal operation and organization of the hardware.

```
entity FULL_ADDER is
   port (B0,B1:  in  BIT;    -- one-bit addend
         CIN:    in  BIT;    -- carry input
         SUM:    out BIT;    -- single-bit sum
         COUT:   out BIT);   -- carry output
end FULL_ADDER;
```

FIGURE 10.10-5
VHDL interface description for full adder.

```
architecture GATE_IMPLEMENTATION of FULL_ADDER is
  -- component declarations
  component AND_GATE port (X,Y: in BIT; Z: out BIT); end component;
  component XOR_GATE port (X,Y: in BIT; Z: out BIT); end component;
  component OR_GATE port (X,Y: in BIT; Z: out BIT); end component;
  -- local signal declarations
  signal L0, L1, L2: BIT;
begin
  -- component instantiations
  X1: XOR_GATE port (B0, B1, L0);
  X2: XOR_GATE port (L0, CIN, SUM);
  A2: AND_GATE port (CIN, L0, L2);
  A1: AND_GATE port (B0, B1, L1);
  O1:  OR_GATE port (L1, L2, COUT);
end GATE_IMPLEMENTATION;
```

FIGURE 10.10-6
VHDL gate-level description for full adder.

The full-adder example of Fig. 10.10-1 will be used to demonstrate three different body descriptions. A gate-level implementation of a full adder is defined in Fig. 10.10-6. GATE_IMPLEMENTATION describes a common network of simple logic gates that realizes the full-adder function. This definition for the full adder uses AND, XOR, and OR gate components that must be defined elsewhere. The *component declarations* include an interface description for each of the logic gates. Following the component declarations, a *signal declaration* specifies signals that are used internally in the full-adder implementation. (Remember that the interface description of the full adder specifies signals that appear externally.) Finally, a *procedure block* describes the interconnection of the previously declared components that realizes the full-adder function. GATE_IMPLEMENTATION is a structural definition; that is, information is given about how to interconnect the components that compose the full adder. Without further knowledge of the behavior of components used in the definition, insufficient information is provided for simulation of the full adder.

The full adder can also be defined through a register-transfer-level description. The RTL_IMPLEMENTATION of Fig. 10.10-7 provides such a description. RTL_IMPLEMENTATION is a behavioral-level description. The structure of the implementation is left undefined; only the logical relationship

```
architecture RTL_IMPLEMENTATION of FULL_ADDER is
  signal L0, L1, L2: BIT;
begin
  L0   <= B0 xor B1;
  SUM  <= L0 xor CIN;
  L1   <= B0 and B1;
  L2   <= L0 and CIN;
  COUT <= L1 or L2;
end RTL_IMPLEMENTATION;
```

FIGURE 10.10-7
VHDL RTL description of full adder.

of the signals is given. The description is given in terms of external signals defined in the interface description and three internal signals defined within the RTL description. The procedure block defines the relationship among the external and internal signals in terms of standard logic functions. Assuming that standard logical operations are known by the VHDL simulator, the behavior of the full adder could be simulated. Although this description does not specify structure for the full adder, an implied structure is provided in this case because there is a well-known mapping from the logic operations to standard hardware components.

As a final description of the operation of the full adder, an algorithmic declaration is given as ALG_IMPLEMENTATION, shown in Fig. 10.10-8. The ALG_IMPLEMENTATION declaration of the full adder is another behavioral description. This definition bears little relationship to the underlying physical implementation. Instead, a procedure is given to calculate the outputs of the interface description based on the inputs from the same description. This declaration is sufficient to simulate the operation of the full adder but provides little indication about its structure. This type of description is most useful for high-level definition and simulation of hardware operation. A high-level description can be provided early in the design to allow use of simulation to verify expected system behavior. Typically, an algorithmic description can have many different physical realizations.

A complex hardware system is normally described by a hierarchy of VHDL design entities. Initially, subcomponents of the design are defined by component declarations that are similar to the interface descriptions given earlier for the full adder. These components are interconnected to form more complex structures as defined within body descriptions. These complex structures may, in turn, be used as components in still more complex definitions. Ultimately, the definitions

```
architecture ALG_IMPLEMENTATION of FULL_ADDER is
begin
   process (B0, B1, CIN)
      variable S: BIT_VECTOR (1 to 3) := B0 & B1 & CIN;
      variable Num: INTEGER range 0 to 3 := 0;
   begin
      for I in 1 to 3 loop
         if S(I) = '1' then
            Num := Num + 1;
         end if;
      end loop;
      case Num is
         when 0 => SUM <= '0'; COUT <= '0';
         when 1 => SUM <= '1'; COUT <= '0';
         when 2 => SUM <= '0'; COUT <= '1';
         when 3 => SUM <= '1'; COUT <= '1';
      end case;
   end process;
end ALG_IMPLEMENTATION;
```

FIGURE 10.10-8
VHDL Algorithmic description of full adder.

of lower-level components, such as logic gates, are bound to VHDL library definitions of primitive components. Then a particular instance of the component is created along with its interconnections to other components, as defined within the VHDL block statements. Thus, a VHDL description can be created for an arbitrarily complex digital system design.

In this section, the two primary hardware design languages, EDIF and VHDL, were introduced. Both have become ANSI standards, EDIF in 1987 and VHDL in 1988. A full adder was used to provide simple examples of some of the capabilities of each standard. Both EDIF and VHDL are in the process of becoming widely accepted and supported by manufacturers and CAD vendors. EDIF functions primarily to allow simplified interchange of circuit and layout information between companies and within the same company. VHDL provides high-level definition and simulation of complex digital systems. It can serve to support analysis of design alternatives and to function as a common definition of digital system operation in the presence of multiple vendors.

10.11 ALGORITHMIC LAYOUT GENERATION

Algorithmic generation of integrated circuit layout is often perceived as a solution to the VLSI complexity problem. The basis of this well-known problem is that integrated circuit design cost is increasing for complex chips while the product life cycle is decreasing for these same chips. Design cost increases because of the design time and computer resources that must be expended to complete a state-of-the-art chip or system. Product life cycle is decreasing for these same designs because of rapid advances in technology and fierce competition to get the next-generation product to the market first.

Three approaches have been suggested to address this problem.[25] The first approach is to enhance the productivity of the human designer with faster computer workstations and improved design analysis tools. To date, this approach has been the most evident, and its description comprises the bulk of the topics in this chapter. A second approach is to capture the knowledge of a human designer with an expert system. This involves a knowledge base of concepts, rules, and strategies. These are processed by an inference engine that produces design fragments and design refinements to aid the design process. This approach is a subject of active research. A third approach is to algorithmically generate or synthesize designs from high-level descriptions or from parameterized definitions. Each variant of this approach tends to concentrate on a particular target architecture. For example, the PLA generators discussed earlier accept Boolean equations and generate layout in a well-defined form. More complex algorithmic generators are often termed *silicon compilers*. This section describes two pioneering efforts in this area and follows with a description of a state-of-the-art microprocessor chip set that was designed with heavy dependence on a commercial silicon compiler.

10.11.1 Bristle Blocks Silicon Compiler

The Bristle Blocks silicon compiler was first described in 1979.[26] The goal of the Bristle Blocks system was to produce a layout mask set from a single-page, high-level description of an integrated circuit. Many designs have their high-level structure and function frozen early in the design cycle, before the effects of such decisions are well known. If, on the other hand, a designer could use a few building blocks, organize them, and then obtain complete mask layouts and simulations early in the design cycle, then experimental configurations could be tried with a minimum of effort.

The Bristle Blocks system attempted to build designs based on a philosophy that includes structured design, hierarchical design, and multiple design representations. The structured design methodology encourages the use of regular computing structures. The design philosophy is hierarchical in that a chip is divided into sections that are subdivided to exploit hierarchical DRCs and simulations. Finally, the blocks are described via multiple design representations of increasing abstraction including layout, sticks, transistors, logic, text, simulation, and ultimately block as shown in Fig. 10.11-1. Note the general agreement between these levels of abstraction and those given in Fig. 7.1-1 of Chapter 7.

The fundamental unit in the Bristle Blocks system is the cell. Each cell can contain geometrical primitives and references to other cells. A cell can be compared to an HLL (high-level language) subroutine that contains some primitive operations and contains some references to other subroutines. A cell has the capability of containing each of the seven representations just presented. Each cell contains only local information. External connections are specified by their location and type. The location indicates where along the cell boundary the connection should occur, and the type specifies the kind of connection—for example, external output pad. The Bristle Blocks methodology gets its name from the connection points, which are like bristles along the edges of the cells. A primary directive of this method is that local information is kept local to the cell, while global information such as the location and routing to an external pad is kept separately.

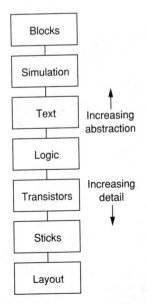

FIGURE 10.11-1
Bristle Blocks design abstraction hierarchy.

Information specifying the various representations of cells is kept in cell libraries and is accessed as needed. Each low-level cell must have been designed before it can be used in the Bristle Blocks system. Each such cell is defined by specifying the actual layout of the cell. It is felt that design of low-level cells does not take much time because of their small size. Also, the design is relatively error-free, and designer ingenuity is most beneficial at this design level.

The format of chip design using Bristle Blocks consists of physical, logical, and temporal information. The physical format is composed of a central core of operational logic and an instruction decoder, with these elements surrounded by interface pads as in Fig. 10.11-2. The instruction decoder and pads are automatically generated based on the requirements of the core section. The logical format consists of core execution units that are interconnected by two buses. In general, the order of placement of the core units is irrelevant to the operation of the system. The appropriate control functions are generated from microcode words that are provided from an external source and applied to the decoder inputs. The temporal format is a nonoverlapping two-phase clock. One clock phase controls the transfer of data between execution units via the buses. The other clock phase controls execution within the core execution units. During the execution clock phase, the buses are precharged to a high state.

The operation of the Bristle Blocks compiler requires three passes: a core pass, a control pass, and a pad pass. The first pass constructs the core execution units from user input and library cell definitions. The control pass adds the instruction decoder to generate signals required by control connection points in

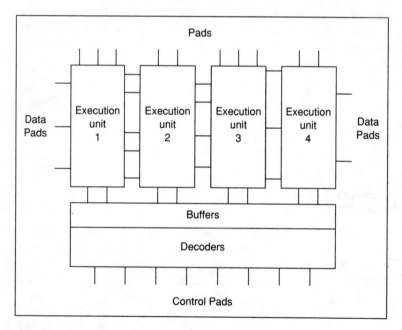

FIGURE 10.11-2
Physical format for Bristle Blocks compiler layout.

the core section. The pad pass adds pads to the perimeter of the chip and routes connections to the pads. User input to the compiler consists of three types of information. First, the microcode width and field decomposition of the control word is specified. Then the data word width and the buses that run through the core of the chip are defined. Finally, the execution units of the chip's core are defined along with any parameter values required to expand the units.

During the core layout phase, the various core cells must be interconnected. To minimize intercell routing of wires, it is advantageous for the cells to maintain a common pitch for interface connections. This requires a common width for all cells, so all cells must be designed to match the width of the widest cell. If a wider cell is added in the future, then all other cells would have to be redesigned to match the new constraint. A solution to this dilemma is to provide stretchable cells. This idea is a major contribution of this methodology. Each core cell is designed with places to stretch so that the cell width is constrained only by a minimum dimension. During the first pass, all core cells are scanned to determine the cell that constrains the minimum width. Then all other cells are stretched to match this width.

Other layout details are fixed during the first phase as well. For example, power requirements may indicate widening of the power buses. Each individual core cell is designed under interface constraints necessary to allow it to mesh with any other core cell without causing design or electrical rule violations. Finally, a bus start and stop capability along with precharge circuits are added to each bus.

The control phase generates control signal buffers to drive the control lines required by the core execution units. Then the appropriate instruction decoder is added to provide the control signals. The final stage of pad layout collects all pad connection points, sorts the points into clockwise order, and then routes connections to the pads.

The Bristle Blocks system generates data path chips based on microprogram control from an external source. Chip area for layout was reported to be within about 10% of hand layout using the same structured design methodology. Although attempts were made to generalize the structure implied by the Bristle Blocks methodology, other architectures are sufficiently different so as to require separate classes of Bristle Blocks compilers. Several commercial vendors have used the Bristle Blocks methodology as a basis for their products.

10.11.2 MacPitts Silicon Compiler

A flexible register-transfer-type language called MacPitts was described in 1982 to address the generation of microprogram-sequenced data path designs.[27] Designs described in this high-level language are compiled into a technology-independent intermediate form. The intermediate form is then compiled into a CIF geometrical layout description, which can be submitted to a silicon foundry for fabrication. The latter compilation is accomplished by limiting the possible degrees of freedom in mask layout and restricting the layout to a fixed target architecture. The target architecture consists of two distinct sections: a data path and a control unit. This architecture is shown in Fig. 10.11-3.

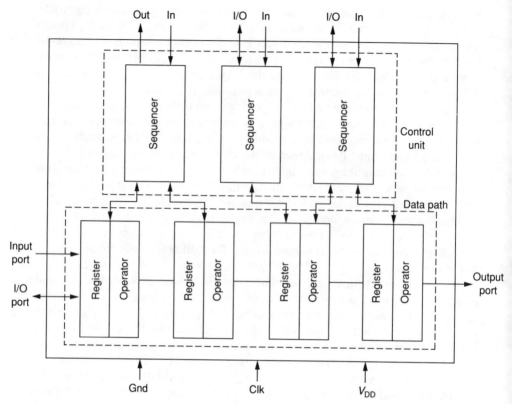

FIGURE 10.11-3
MacPitts data path/control architecture.

The data path consists of registers of width specified by the MacPitts source program. Operators for testing and modifying the data stored in the registers are also created. Data is communicated to the external world through parallel buses of wires called ports. A particular port can be an input port, a tri-state port, or an I/O port. The operations performed by the data path are specified by the control unit. In general, the control unit generates signals that cause the data path to perform certain operations. The data path returns signals that can be used to alter the control sequence. In addition, the control unit communicates to the external world through single-wire signals that may be input, output, tri-state, or I/O lines.

The data path is unconventional because it contains more than just a register array and an ALU, as is common in many microprocessors. Rather, the data path may contain many functional units interspersed among the registers. As many functional units as are needed to compute a set of parallel operations may be included between global buses. The functional units are interconnected by dedicated local buses as required by the function they perform. A given unit may take its input from several possible sources, so a multiplexer is often included to select the particular input for an operation. The output of the units is either a full word used by the data path or possibly a test result that is used directly by the control unit. A unit like an adder can generate both a word (sum) for the data path and a test signal (overflow) for the control unit. The number and type of register/operator units provided in the data path differ from system to system as specified by the MacPitts source language.

The control unit is implemented as a simplified variation of a finite-state machine. A typical FSM consists of combinatorial logic and a state register; the combinatorial logic computes the output signals and the next-state information. If the program flow is sequential, this general form of FSM is less efficient than simply using a counter to present the next state. The MacPitts compiler generates a FSM consisting of a counter and a state stack to allow subroutine calls. The logic portion of the control unit is implemented by a Weinberger array layout style consisting of interconnected NOR gates. This regular form for logic allows multilevel realizations of logic within the control unit for increased efficiency compared with a PLA-style implementation.

The MacPitts silicon compiler is an example of the use of algorithmic-level design specifications and an automation of the refinement process used to create a layout description. Standard design practice cycles between a synthesis step to create a design and an analysis step to demonstrate that the design meets prescribed objectives. Usually, the analysis step requires location and removal of flaws that are injected during the design synthesis. If the MacPitts compilation correctly generates layout corresponding to the high-level description, the design task is reduced to one of properly specifying that high-level description. An additional potential advantage of this design method accrues because of the technology independence of the intermediate-level representation generated from the high-level MacPitts source language. Because a technology-dependent synthesizer is used to create the layout from the intermediate-level representation, only this portion of the synthesis system needs to be replaced to generate the same design in a different technology.

10.11.3 Commercial Silicon Compilers

Following the early efforts described in this section, several commercial ventures were started to develop silicon compiler technology. New companies were formed to capitalize on the potential of this methodology, and existing CAD vendors developed efforts in the synthesis and silicon compilation areas. For the most part, silicon compilation has been applied only in isolated cases without great commercial success. However, a possible exception that may demonstrate the maturing of silicon compiler technology is described next.

A recently announced product, the Motorola 88000 RISC processor, was developed largely with silicon compiler technology.[28] Skilled IC designers completed the design of the 164,000-transistor CPU chip in only 20 calendar months, a productivity increase reported to be a factor of 10 to 20. A second team built the companion 750,000-transistor cache chip in only 11 months. The individual leaf cells of these products were laid out manually, but parameterized module generators speeded the design once the leaf cells were complete.

The design was started in a top-down manner with executable behavioral-level specifications. Then designers began to implement the logic and layout design of selected blocks. These low-level blocks were used to simulate the timing requirements for the chip, with architectural changes made based on the simulation results. Reusable, parameterized module generators were created for blocks such as adders, subtracters, multipliers, register files, and decoders. Module generators were also written for high-speed static RAM, tag memory, and translation buffers on a memory management chip. Through the use of parameterized modules, designers were able to make architectural revisions late in the design. Since the module generators are reusable, further versions of this chip set should be relatively easy to create. Also, because of the technology-independent description, the design should be easier to port to another process or technology.

The result reported here is an important step in the application of silicon compilers to commercial chip development. It may be noted that the apparent success in this case is a result of automating the assembly process of handcrafted leaf cells. Silicon compilation has also been extended to analog design for circuits such as CMOS op amps.[29] It will be interesting to watch the development of silicon compilers with broader applicability and with true synthesis capabilities.

10.12 SUMMARY

The use of computers has become essential to the design of VLSI circuits because of the complexity of such circuits. Computers are used to create, store, verify, modify, and interchange design information. The application areas of computer-based tools are broad and extend over the range of design hierarchies shown in Fig. 7.1-1. In fact, one expert in the area has classified computer-based tools according to their level of hierarchy and date of widespread use. This evolution commenced with the 1970s, when computers were used to aid in the design and checking of integrated circuit layout. The early 1980s saw an influx of computer-based tools for circuit and logic design, including schematic capture tools. Then the late 1980s saw the introduction of computer-based tools that work at the RTL level of design. These include synthesis tools that automatically create lower levels of the design hierarchy from previously designed cells. In the early 1990s, tools that work at the system level will likely become prominent. Synthesis and analysis tools, both based on high-level block diagrams and behavioral descriptions of a design, are examples of this capability.

As each new generation of CAD tools becomes prominent, new tool ideas and new companies are formed. Eventually, the market settles on a few concepts and firms that represent the most useful innovations with the best evolutionary ties to existing design tools. At each stage of this development, the world of VLSI design opens to a broader cadre of designers who require less knowledge of the underlying technology to make productive use of VLSI. For example, the number of logic designers is much greater than the number of integrated circuit layout specialists. In the 1980s, when computer tools based on logic descriptions became widely available, a far greater number of designers could use VLSI technology. The number of system designers and programmers who could use VLSI based on RTL or algorithmic descriptions is, in turn, much larger than the number of skilled logic designers. Thus, it has been the trend that more and more designers have access to the capabilities of VLSI technology as time progresses. Computer-based tools are the primary driving force for this trend.

The material in this chapter represents an introduction to many of the computer-based tools that are used in design automation and design verification. The section headings indicate coverage of integrated circuit layout, symbolic circuit representation, computer check plots, design rule checks, circuit extraction, digital circuit simulation, switch and logic simulation, timing analysis, RTL simulation, hardware design languages, and algorithmic layout generation. Other important areas of integrated circuit CAD that are not introduced in this chapter include process simulation, schematic capture, place and route (discussed briefly in conjunction with gate arrays in Chapter 9), mixed-mode simulation (combined analog and digital simulation—a growing number of integrated circuits contain both analog and digital sections), testability and fault analysis, and logic synthesis. Each of these areas provides its own important contributions to the design of VLSI circuits.

The intent of this chapter has been to cover many of the CAD tools and methods that blend with the material presented in the first nine chapters and to introduce some tools that are just now coming into prominence, such as hardware design languages and algorithmic layout generation. Two primary sources of information regarding new CAD tools in any of the areas mentioned above are (1) the Design Automation Conference (DAC) held each summer and sponsored by the Association of Computing Machinery (ACM) and the IEEE Computer Society, and (2) the International Conference on Computer-Aided Design (ICCAD) held each fall and sponsored by the IEEE.

REFERENCES

1. C. A. Mead and L. S. Conway: *Introduction to VLSI Systems*, Addison-Wesley, Reading, Mass., 1980.
2. 1076-1987 VHDL Language Reference Manual, IEEE Catalog No. SH11957, 1987.
3. EDIF, Electronic Design Interchange Format, Version 2 0 0, Electronic Industries Association, ANSI/EIA-548-1988.
4. J. K. Ousterhout, G. T. Hamachi, R. N. Mayo, W. S. Scott, and G. S. Taylor: "Magic: A VLSI Layout System," *Proc. 21st Design Automation Conf.*, pp. 152–159, June 1984.
5. D. S. Harrison, Peter Moore, R. L. Spickelmier, and A. R. Newton: "Data Mangement and Graphics Editing in the Berkeley Design Environment," *Int. Conf. on Computer-Aided Design*, pp. 24–27, 1986.
6. P. Six, L. Claesen, J. Rabaey, and H. De Man: "An Intelligent Module Generator Environment," *Proc. 23rd Design Automation Conf.*, pp. 730–735, June, 1986.
7. J. D. Williams: "STICKS: A Graphical Compiler for High-Level LSI Design," *AFIPS Conf. Proc.*, vol. 47, pp. 289–295, June 1978.
8. R. Zinszner, Hugo De Man, K. Croes: "Technology Independent Symbolic Layout Tools," *Int. Conf. on Computer Aided Design*, pp. 12–13, September 1983.
9. A. Weinberger: "Large Scale Integration of MOS Complex Logic: A Layout Method," *IEEE J. Solid State Electron.*, vol. SC-2, no. 4, pp. 182–190, December 1967.
10. S. P. Reiss and J. E. Savage: "SLAP—A Methodology for Silicon Layout," *Proc. Int. Conf. on Circuits and Computers*, ICCC 82, pp. 281–284, September 1982.

11. Richard F. Lyon: "Simplified Design Rules for VLSI Layouts," *LAMBDA*, vol. II, no. 1, 1981.
12. C. Baker and C. Terman: "Tools for Verifying Integrated Circuit Designs," LAMBDA, vol. I, no. 4, pp. 22–30, 1980.
13. A. E. Harwood: *A VLSI Design Rule Check Program Generator*, Master's Thesis, Texas A&M University, December 1985.
14. T. Blank: "A Survey of Hardware Accelerators Used on Computer-aided Design," *IEEE Design & Test*, vol. 1, no. 3, pp. 21–39, August 1984.
15. R. A. Saleh, J. E. Kleckner, and A. R. Newton: "Iterated Timing Analysis in SPLICE1," *IEEE Int. Conf. on Computer-Aided Design*, pp. 139–140, September 1983.
16. L. M. Vidigal, S. R. Nassif, and S. W. Director: "CINNAMON: Coupled Integration and Nodal Analysis of MOS Networks," *Proc. 23rd Design Automation Conf.*, pp. 179–185, June 1986.
17. C. J. Terman: "User's Guide to NET, PRESIM, and RNL/NL," MIT Laboratory for Computer Science, pp. 1–48, September 1982.
18. Gregory F. Pfister: "The Yorktown Simulation Engine: Introduction," *Proc. 19th Design Automation Conf.*, pp. 51–73, 1982.
19. N. P. Jouppi: "TV: An nMOS Timing Analyzer," *Proc. Third Caltech Conf. on VLSI*, pp. 71–85, 1983.
20. J. K. Ousterhout: "Crystal: A Timing Analyzer for nMOS VLSI Circuits," *Proc. Third Caltech Conf. on VLSI*, pp. 57–69, 1983.
21. J. Hennessy, N. Jouppi, S. Przybylski, C. Rowen, and T. Gross: "Design of a High Performance VLSI Processor," *Proc. Third Caltech Conf. on VLSI*, pp. 33-54, 1983.
22. M. G. H. Katevenis: *Reduced Instruction Set Computer Architectures for VLSI*, MIT Press, Cambridge, Mass., 1984.
23. Mario R. Barbacci: "Instruction Set Processor Specifications (ISPS): The Notation and Its Applications," *IEEE Trans. Comput.*, vol. c-30, no. 1, pp. 25–40, January 1981.
24. James R. Armstrong: *Chip-Level Modeling with VHDL*, Prentice-Hall, Englewood Cliffs, NJ, 1989.
25. D. D. Gajski: "Silicon Compilers and Expert Systems for VLSI," *Proc. 21st Design Automation Conf.*, pp. 86–87, June 1984.
26. D. Johannsen: "Bristle Blocks: A Silicon Compiler," *Proc. Caltech Conf. on VLSI*, pp. 303–313, January 1979.
27. J. M. Siskind, J. R. Southard, and K. W. Crouch: "Generating Custom High Performance VLSI Designs from Succinct Algorithmic Descriptions," *Proc. MIT Conference on Advanced Research in VLSI*, pp. 28–39, January 1982.
28. R. Goering: "Silicon Compilation Boosts Productivity in 88000 Design," *Computer Design*, p. 28, May 1, 1988.
29. L. R. Carley and R. A. Rutenbar, "How to Automate Analog IC Designs," IEEE Spectrum, pp. 26–30, August 1988.

PROBLEMS

Section 10.1

10.1. Using engineering paper or the equivalent, plot the layout described by the following statements, based on the definitions of Table 10.1-1 and Table 10.1-2.

L 1	L 4
B 0 13 4 4	B 0 0 15 4
B 0 15 2 3	B 0 18 15 4
B 0 13 8 2	L 5
B 8 0 4 15	B 9 1 2 2
L 3	B 4 10 2 2
B 0 5 14 2	B 9 12 2 2
B 3 9 4 8	B 1 19 2 2

10.2. By hand, digitize the Manhattan layout shown in Fig. 10.1-4a. Assume that the lines are metal that ends at the figure edges and the width and spacing are 2 units each.

10.3. The layout for the block letter L is described by the following macro, based on the definitions of Table 10.1-1 and Table 10.1-2.

```
M 4
L 1
B 0 0 4 1
B 0 1 1 5
E
C 4 10 10 2
```

Show the layout resulting from the C statement above (a) if the rotation precedes the translation and (b) if the order of translation and rotation is reversed. Is the first order sufficient to create any desired layout?

Section 10.2

10.4. Show how to modify the description of Fig. 10.1-6 so that the parameter VERT can be used to modify the vertical dimension and the parameter HORZ can be used to modify the horizontal dimension.

10.5. Create a Sticks diagram for the circuit of Fig. 10.2-5.

10.6. Show the circuit diagram of a Weinberger array for an exclusive-OR gate with inputs a and b and output c.

10.7. Show a digraph for the logic specified by the following equations.

$$X = AB + \overline{C}D$$

$$Y = BC + X$$

$$Z = AB + \overline{A}Y + X$$

Section 10.3

10.8. Assume that a good layout density metric is 200 λ^2 per transistor. How many transistors can reasonably be displayed on a 24-line by 80-character A/N CRT display?

10.9. If a resolution of 5 dots per λ is sufficient to display the details of a layout and the layout requires 200 λ^2 per transistor, how many transistors can reasonably be displayed on a laser printer with a resolution of 300 dots per inch and a page size of 8 by 10 inches?

10.10. A Macintosh personal computer display has a resolution of 512 dots by 342 dots. Using a metric of 5 dots per λ for a readable display and 250 λ^2 per transistor, how many transistors can be displayed on the Macintosh screen?

Section 10.4

10.11. Identify all the design rule errors listed in Fig. 10.4-7 on a copy of the check plot of Fig. 10.4-6.

10.12. If a window template formed from a "plus" symbol is passed in raster scan fashion over a design to check for spacing and width violations, some errors are missed. Show an example of such an error.

10.13. Simple design rules are on the order of 1 to 3 λ for spacings and widths. What are the horizontal and vertical λ dimensions required for a "plus" symbol used in a raster scan DRC to check for Manhattan design rule violations?

Section 10.5

10.14. Based on the capacitance values in Table 10.5-1, calculate the capacitance for node 2* in Fig. 10.5-4 if layer 3 is polysilicon, layer 5 is a contact, layer 4 is aluminum, and the extracted dimensions are in microns.

10.15. Using the raster scan algorithm described in this chapter, how many different node numbers will be assigned in scanning the block letter H represented as a 5×7 dot matrix? At what point in the scan (left to right and top to bottom) will the list of nodes that must be merged be complete? (Give the x,y coordinates of the point.)

10.16. Some circuit extraction algorithms estimate connection resistance from the extracted area and perimeter values assuming rectangular shapes. Derive an algorithm based on area A and perimeter P to estimate resistance R in terms of resistance per square (sheet resistance). Estimate the resistance for an area of 10 square units and a perimeter of 22 units, assuming the terminals are on opposite sides. Is there more than one possible answer?

Section 10.6

10.17. If the time to simulate a circuit goes up as the 1.75 power of the number of nodes, and a 100-node circuit requires 30 seconds of computer time, approximately how much time would be required to simulate a circuit with 100,000 nodes?

Section 10.7

10.18. Provide a logic diagram for the circuit defined by the following net list description. The syntax is (function output input-1…input-n).

> (invert sb s)
> (nor x a s)
> (nor y b sb)
> (nor f x y)

10.19. Based on the switch-level results for the byte-wide adder presented in Sec. 10.7, estimate the maximum clock frequency for the circuit, and explain what limits this clock frequency.

10.20. Provide logic-level and transistor-level net list descriptions for the quasi-static memory cells of Fig. 10.2-4 a and b. The function (pullup a) can be used to describe a depletion pullup transistor attached to node a.

Section 10.8

10.21. For a direct realization of the following logic equations, identify all signal paths. Label the paths by using the logical names for signals. The path B,BC,X,Y is an example of one path. Assuming unit delays for the logic gates, find the longest and shortest paths.

$$X = AD + BC$$

$$Y = AC + X + BD$$

$$Z = BY + ACX$$

10.22. Assume a string of n ripple-carry full-adders where the carry out $cout(n\text{-}1)$ of full-adder $(n\text{-}1)$ is sent to the carry in $cin(n)$ of full adder n. If a timing analyzer is used on this string of full-adders, what would you expect to find for the longest path?

10.23. For a circuit with four input ports, three output ports, and one bidirectional port, how many signal paths are possible? How does the number of paths increase as the number of ports increases?

10.24. For the circuit of Fig. 10.2-5, (if possible) set the signal directions of each transistor using the rules developed in this chapter.

10.25. For the circuit of Fig. 10.7-4, set the signal directions of all possible transistors using the rules developed in this chapter.

10.26. If the a input of a two-input exclusive-OR gate is rising, what can you tell about the output signal in terms of the b input?

Section 10.9

10.27. Describe a 4×4–bit shift-and-rotate multiplication using the simple RTL defined in the chapter. You may want to add shift and logical operators.

10.28. Based on the description in Fig. 10.9-1, identify and total the unique bits of processor state defined for the 68000 processor.

10.29. Using the definition of the effective address operation of Fig. 10.9-2, indicate the operations performed to compute the effective address for a word-length postincrement instruction. How does the word-length predecrement instruction differ?

10.30. Using the partial LISP definition of a RISC processor in Fig. 10.9-4 as an example, write a LISP function for the NOT operation.

Section 10.10

10.31. Based on the EDIF description given in Fig. 10.10-2 for the full-adder of Fig. 10.10-1, give an EDIF description of the NAND-NAND full-adder circuit of Fig. 10.7-2.

10.32. Using the EDIF physical layout description of Fig. 10.10-4 as an example, convert the static memory cell definition of Fig. 10.1-6a to an equivalent EDIF description.

10.33. Give a VHDL interface description and structural body description for the NAND-NAND full-adder circuit of Fig. 10.7-2.

10.34. Provide a VHDL interface description and RTL body description for the NAND-NAND full-adder circuit of Fig. 10.7-2.

INDEX

Abstraction, design, 526–528
ac resistors, 303
  used in differential configuration,
    309, 310, 312
  realization of, 308–317
ac switching power, 597
Acquisition time, 644
Active mask, 74
  CMOS circuit, 56
Active region, MOSFET, 145
Active resistors, 213, 218–221,
  302–318
Active substrates, 10
A/D converters. *See* Analog-to-digital
  converters
Advanced Low-Power Schottky TTL
  (ALSTTL), 588
Algorithmic A/D converter, 656–659
Algorithmic D/A converters, 638, 639,
  640, 651
Algorithmic layout generation
  Bristle Blocks silicon compiler,
    938–941

Algorithmic layout generation (*Cont.*):
  commercial silicon compilers,
    943–944
  MacPitts silicon compiler, 941–943
Alignment errors, 20
Amplifiers, 378–379
  cascode, 414–431
  differential, 431–454
  inverting, 379–414
  operational, 473–499
  output, 454–473
Analog signal processing, 612–615
  bandwidths of signals used in, 613,
    614
  modulators and multipliers, 735–747
  oscillators, 747–762
  phase-locked loops, 762–764
  precision breakpoint circuits, 729–735
  use in data systems, 615, 616
Analog-to-digital converters, 642–648
  algorithmic, 656–659
  comparison of the performance of the
    various types of, 663

Analog-to-digital converters (*Cont.*):
 converter analog multiplier, 743, 744
 dynamic characteristics of, 644, 646
 flash, 659–663
 high-performance, 664–671
 oversampled, 664, 668–671
 parallel, 659–663
 pipeline, 661, 664, 665–668
 serial, 648–651
 successive approximation, 651–659
AND function, 533
AND plane, PLA, 784–790
 folding, 791, 792, 793
AND-gate logic, switch-level
   simulation using, 913
Anisotropic etch, 38, 39
Antimoat, NMOS circuit, 52
Aperture uncertainty, 646
Arithmetic logic unit (ALU), 858–860
Autozeroing, 514–517
Avalanche injection, 826

Band-elimination filter, 673, 674
Bandgap voltage reference, 366–371
Bandpass filters, 688–692
Bar, 3
Barrel shifter, 857–858, 859
Base-diffused resistor, 213, 216–217
BellMac microprocessor
 domino CMOS and, 819
 gate matrix layout of, 799
 PLAs used in, 853
Berkeley Oct tool set, 880
Berkeley RISC processor, 856, 857
Bilinear switched capacitor realization,
   317, 695, 696
BiMos, 12, 42, 613
Binary-weighted D/A converters,
   624–625, 626
 cascading, 625, 627
 master-slave ladder, 625, 626, 627
Bipolar current mirror, 334
Bipolar junction transistor. *See* BJT
Bipolar process, 10
 design rules for, 119–120

Bipolar process (*Cont.*):
 process parameters for, 120–122
 process steps in, 118–119, 124–126
 SPICE model parameters of, 123
Biquad structure, 718–721, 726
 signal flow diagram of, 719
Bird's beaking, 60
Bistable in untuned oscillators,
   752–759
Bit-serial processing elements, 863, 865
BJT, 2, 10, 42, 43, 255–256
 active resistor, 305, 306, 307
 cascode amplifier, 426–431
 cascode op amp, 488
 Class A inverting voltage amplifier,
   459, 460
 combining MOS technology with,
   614
 current mirror, 336, 337, 338, 343,
   344, 345
 current reference, 360
 current sink, 319–320, 322–323,
   324, 325, 328
 current source, 363
 D/A converter techniques, 615–641
 differential amplifiers, 444–449, 450
 high-frequency, 261–262
 inverting amplifiers, 407–414
 large signal, 256–260
 modulator using a differential
   amplifier, 735–736
 noise model, 262–263
 op amp, 287, 288, 478, 479,
   481–485
 parameter definitions, 282–286
 parasitic capacitance in, 206, 207, 262
 process, 64–68
 as a switch, 291–292
 temperature dependence of, 263–264
 voltage reference, 355, 356
BJT device models, 191–192
 dc, 192–202
 high-frequency, 205–207
 measurement of model parameters,
   208–210
 small signal, 202–205

Bonding pads, NMOS circuit, 54
Boolean algebra, 532
Bootstrapping, 327
   BJT current sink, 328, 361, 362,
     363
   CMOS current source, 363
   JFET current source, 329, 330
   MOS current sink, 328, 329, 361,
     362, 363, 364–365
Bottom capacitance, 582
Bottom-up approach, 13
Boxes, geometrical specification
   language, 876
Bristle Blocks silicon compiler,
   938–941
BSIM model, 240
Bulk-to-channel junction capacitance,
   163
Buried contacts, NMOS circuit, 52
Butterworth filter approximation, 675,
   576, 678, 679, 681, 682, 685
Butting contacts, 83

Calibration D/A converter, 664
Calls, geometrical specification
   language, 876
Caltech Intermediate Form. *See* CIF
Capacitance density, 161
Capacitive loading, 584
   cascaded drivers, 590–593, 594
   distributed drivers, 587–588
   driving off-chip loads, 588–590
   logic fanout delays, 585–586
   typical, 588
Capacitive noise coupling, 601–602
Capacitors, 67–68, 210
   monolithic, 211–212
   ratio-matching considerations of,
     81–82
Cascade configuration
   binary-weighted D/A converters,
     625, 627
   charge-scaling D/A converters,
     631–633, 634
Cascaded drivers, 590–593, 594

Cascode amplifiers, 378, 414–431
   BJT, 426–431
   current-driven CMOS, 416–418
   improving voltage gain of CMOS,
     419–426
   voltage-driven CMOS, 418–419
Cascode current mirror
   BJT, 338–339, 344
   MOS, 348, 349
Cascode op amp, 478, 479, 488–491
   BJT, 488
   CMOS, 488–491
Channel, MOSFET, 48
Channelless gate array, 801
Charge pump, 826
Charge redistribution D/A converters,
   638
Charge sharing, 818
Charge-scaling D/A converters,
   629–633, 634, 651, 653, 654
   cascade configuration applied to,
     631–633, 634
   used in combination with voltage-
     scaling
   D/A converters, 633, 635–638
Chebyshev filter approximation, 676,
   679, 680, 685
   switched capacitor realization of
     fifth-order low-pass, 714–715
Chemical etches, 36
Chemical vapor deposition (CVD),
   35
Chip, 3
Chip regularity factor, 780–783
CIF, 874, 880, 933
Circuit extraction, 901
   circuit extractor output, 903–907
   interface to other programs, 908
   simple algorithm, 902–903
Circuit schematics, 526, 527
Circuit simulation
   BJT model, 255–264
   comparison of logic simulation with,
     910
   DIODE model, 252–255
   MOSFET model, 240–252

Class A inverting voltage amplifier, 459, 460, 461, 470
Class A shunt feedback, 469
Class AB inverting voltage amplifier, 461, 462, 464, 465, 470
Class B inverting voltage amplifier, 461, 462, 463, 464, 465, 470
Clocked CMOS logic
  C2MOS, 815–816
  domino CMOS, 819–821
  precharge-evaluate logic, 817–819
Clocking schemes, MOS, 805–808
  four-phase, 806
  ideal clock signal, 806
  multi-phase, 806
  single-phase, 806
  two-phase, 806–807, 808
  typical oscilloscope display of clock, 806
Closed loop gain, 749
CMOS, 10, 12, 42
  bandgap reference voltage, 370
  cascode amplifier, 416–426
  cascode op amp, 488–491
  clocked logic circuits of, 815–821
  combination of analog and digital techniques in, 613
  current source, 363
  depletion transistor capability, 390
  design rules for, 73–78, 110–111
  differential amplifier, 432–444
  domino, 819–821
  dynamic storage circuit, 809, 810, 811
  fabrication process in, 545
  gate matrix layout structure in, 797
  input protection, 62–63
  inverters, 544–550
  latch-up, 61–62
  lateral well diffusion, 60–61
  layer definitions, 876, 877
  logic delays, 579–582
  multi-input logic gates, 556–558
  NAND logic gate, 553–556, 557, 581

CMOS (*Cont.*):
  noise margins, 605–607
  NOR logic gate, 551–553, 554, 556, 557, 581
  op amp,·287, 288, 478, 480, 485–487
  pass transistor storage circuit, 809–810
  p-channel as pullup device, 785
  PLA structure in, 784
  power dissipation, 595–599
  precharge-evaluate logic, 818
  process parameters for, 112–113, 149, 150
  process steps in, 55–59, 108–109, 115–117
  processing and packaging costs, 17
  push-pull inverter, 401, 403
  SPICE MOSFET model parameters of, 114
  static storage cell, 843, 844
  switch, 300–302
  symbolic layout language description of inverter, 881–883
  transmission gate, 562–564
  voltage-driven cascode amplifier, 418–419
  width and length reduction, 59–60
Commercial silicon compilers, 943–944
Common mode signal, 431
Common-mode input voltage range, 477
Common-mode rejection ratio (CMRR), 431
Comparators, 378, 379
  autozeroing, 514–517
  characteristics of, 499–502
  high-gain, 502–507
  propagation delay of two-stage, 507–511
  using positive feedback, 511–514
Complement of the moat, NMOS circuit, 52
Complementary metal oxide semiconductor. *See* CMOS

Computer check plots, 889–894
Computer design rule checks, 897–898
Conditional branching capability, 850
Conductors, 39–40
Constant field scaling strategy, 9
Constant voltage scaling strategy, 9
Constant-propagation rule, 919–920
Contact openings, 74–78
  NMOS circuit, 54
Continuous-time filters, 673–674
  bandpass filters, 688–692
  high-pass filters, 685–688
  low-pass filters, 674–685
  summary of design approaches, 692
Continuous-time RC network, 697
Control unit, 853, 855
Controllers. *See* Microcoded
  controllers
Converter resolution, 618
Cosputtering, 35
Costs
  associated with wafer processing and
    fabrication, 17, 18
  development, 16
  processing and packaging, 17, 18
  production, 16–18
Counters, 799
Critical paths, 918
Cross talk, 83
Crystal defects, 20, 22
Crystal preparation, IC production
  process, 33
Crystal timing analyzer, 919, 922
Current amplifiers, 333–353
Current mirror, 333–353
  BJT, 336, 337, 338, 344, 345
  MOS, 345, 346, 348, 349
  Widlar, 343, 344, 345, 351
  Wilson, 340, 341, 350, 351
Current reference, 354–371
  BJT, 360
  MOS, 360
Current sinks, 318–332, 343
  BJT, 319–320, 322–323, 324, 325,
    328

Current sinks (*Cont.*):
  bootstrapped, 361, 362
  CMOS, 363
  comparison of, 332
  JFET, 329
  MOS, 323, 324, 325, 328, 329
  regulated cascode, 330, 331
Current sources, 318–332
  BJT, 363
  MOS, 363, 364–365
Current-controlled multivibrators, 758
Current-driven CMOS cascode
  amplifier, 416–418
Current-driven inverter, 388, 389,
  390
Current-scaling D/A converters,
  623–626
  using binary-weighted components,
    624–625, 626
  using R-2R ladder, 625, 626
Cutoff region, MOSFET, 48
C2MOS, 815–816

D flip-flop logic block, 802, 804
D/A converters. *See* Digital-to-analog
  converters
Data paths, 780, 853, 855
  description of, 856–857
dc BJT model, 192–202
  cutoff region, 198, 199, 200
  forward and reverse active regions of
    operation, 195–197, 199, 200
  saturation region, 197–198, 199, 200
dc diode model, 189–190
dc MOSFET model, 144–158
dc resistors, 303
dc switching power, 597
Decoders, 799
Deep collector diffusion, BJT circuit,
  66
Defect density, 21–23
Delta-sigma modulator, 669–671
DeMorgan's theorem, 786, 886
Depletion region, MOSFET, 48, 49

Depletion-load cell, NMOS, 833, 834
Depletion-load inverter, 534–539
  enhancement-load inverter versus,
    539–540, 578–579
  NAND gate, 542–543
  NOR gate, 540–542
  and signal propagation delay,
    565–569
Deposition, IC production process,
  35
Design abstraction, 526–528
Design automation tools, 872, 873
Design process, 12–16
Design rule checks, 84
  computer, 897–898
  design rule checker output, 898–901
  design rule error definitions, 900
  geometrical design rules, 894–897
Design rules, 72–73
  for bipolar process, 119–120
  CMOS, 73–78, 110–111
  geometrical, 894–897
  NMOS, 96–97
Design verification tools, 872, 873
Development costs, 16
Device modeling, 132–143
  BJT, 191–210
  DIODE, 187–191
  MOS, 143–187
  passive component, 210–221
Device sizing
  for clock drivers, 808
  gate matrix layout, 797
  Weinberger arrays, 794
Diagonal layout structures, 876
Die, 3
Die attachment, 41
Die bonding, 41
Difference-mode signal, 431
Differential amplifier, 378, 379,
  431–432
  BJT, 444–449, 450
  CMOS, 432–444
  comparison of small signal voltage
    gains for, 454

Differential amplifier (*Cont.*):
  frequency response of, 449–452
  MOS, 436
  noise performance of, 452–453
Differential nonlinearity, 620, 621,
  622, 644
Differential-in single-ended output
  transconductance, 434
Differential-out transconductance, 434
Diffusion, IC production process, 39
Diffusion capacitance, 582, 583
Diffusion mask, NMOS circuit, 52
Digital circuits
  digital logic analysis of, 532–534
  inverter-pair characteristics of,
    530–532
  logic fan-out characteristics of, 532
  logic level standards of, 528–530
  noise in, 599–607
  simulation of, 908–909
Digital logic analysis, 532–34
Digital-to-analog converters, 615–623
  algorithmic, 638, 639, 640, 641
  binary-weighted, 625, 627
  block diagram of, 618, 619
  calibration, 664
  charge redistribution, 638
  charge-scaling, 629–633, 634, 651,
    653, 654
  clocked, 616, 617
  conceptual block diagram of, 616,
    617
  conversion using the algorithmic
    method, 640
  converter analog multiplier, 743,
    744
  current-scaling, 623–626
  dynamic characteristics of, 621, 623
  nonmonotonic, 621
  serial, 638–642, 651
  settling time for, 623
  static and dynamic properties of, 618
  sub, 664, 665
  transfer characteristic of, 618, 619
  use in data systems, 615, 616

Digital-to-analog converters (*Cont.*):
  using combinations of scaling
    approaches, 633, 635–638
  voltage-scaling, 626–629, 633,
    635–638, 651, 653, 654
Digitizer, 875
Dimensions of the channel, 145
Diode bridge, 758
Diode equation, 188
Diode model, SPICE, 252–253
  dc, 187–190
  high-frequency, 190–191, 254–255
  large signal diode current, 253–254
  parameter definitions, 280–282
  small signal, 190
Display media, 889–893
Distributed drivers, 587–588
Domino CMOS, 819–821
  cascade of, 820–821
Drain, NMOS circuit, 55
DRAM, 823, 835–839
  comparator circuit, 837, 838
  1M-bit, 779, 781
  one-transistor, 836
  sensing voltage versus cell
    capacitance, 839
  three-transistor, 835–836
Drawn features, 73
Dry etching, 38
Dual inline packages (DIPs), 18
Dual-slope serial A/D converters, 648,
  649–651
Dust particles and wafer yield, 20
Duty cycle, 806
Dynamic MOS storage circuits, 559
  dynamic charge storage, 808–811
  simple shift register, 811–815
Dynamic power dissipation, 596, 597
Dynamic random access memory.
  See DRAM
Dynamic range (DR), 182, 619

Ebers-Moll model, 192, 193, 194, 195,
  197, 199, 201, 202, 255, 260

EDIF, 873, 880, 930
  design description of, 930–931
  mask layout view of full adder,
    931–934
  net list view of full adder, 931
EEPROM, 822, 826–827 80386.
  See Intel 80386
Electric field strengths, 9
Electrically erasable programmable
  ROM. *See* EEPROM
Electrode mask, CMOS circuit, 57
Electromigration, 39
Electronic Design Interchange Format.
  See EDIF
Elliptic filter approximation, 676, 677,
  679, 681
Enhancement MOSFET, 49
Enhancement-load inverter, 534, 535,
  536
  depletion-load inverters versus,
    539–540, 578–579
Epitaxy, IC production process, 41
EPROM, 822, 825–826
Equal area, push-pull inverter, 401
Equal resistance, push-pull inverter,
  401
Equilibrium values, 529
Erasable programmable ROM. *See*
  EPROM
Etching, IC production process, 36–39
Evaporation, 35
Execution unit. *See* Data path

Fabrication costs, 17
Fabrication materials, characteristics
  of, 36–37
Fabrication process, 11, 14–15
False state, 528
FAMOS technology, 825–826
Fan-out, 532, 533, 585–586
Fast Fourier Transform (FFT) test, 647,
  648
Faults, 20–21, 22
Fault-tolerant technology, 21

Feedback
  output amplifiers with, 466–473
  output amplifiers without, 455–465
Feedback transistor, 840
Feedforward reference correction
  techniques, 667
FET, 2, 4, 5
Field, NMOS circuit, 52
Field effect transistor. *See* FET
Filter approximation functions,
  675–682
Finite-gain structure, 683, 684, 689,
  690
Finite-state machines
  clocking rate in, 918
  PLA-based, 845–848, 853
Flash A/D converter, 659–663
Flicker noise, MOSFETs, 180, 181,
  182, 183, 184
Flip-flops, 799
Floating current source, 318
Floating nodes, 684, 702–703
Folded cascode configuration,
  478, 479
Folded cascode op amp, 488–491
Folded PLAs, 791–792
4 : 1 inverter sizing rule, 537, 538,
  539, 541, 543, 567, 578
Four-phase clocking scheme, 806
Four-quadrant multipliers, 738–743
Frequency denormalization, 683, 686
Full scale range (FSR), 619
Functional blocks, 526, 527

Gain error, 620, 621, 644, 645
Gallium arsenide, 2, 10, 28
Gate arrays, 15, 780, 799–805
  logic elements of, 802, 803
  topology for typical, 800
  wiring channels of, 800, 801
Gate delay, 564
Gate layout. *See* Structured gate
  layout
Gate matrix layout, 793, 796–799

Gate oxide, 9
  CMOS circuit, 57
  NMOS circuit, 53
Gate–bulk capacitance, 163
Gate-to-channel capacitance, 163
General linear system solver, 861, 863,
  864
Geometrical circuit layout, 526, 527
Geometrical design rules, 894–897
Geometrical specification languages,
  875–878
  comparison of symbolic layout
    language with, 880
Germanium, 2
Gilbert cell multiplier, 736–738, 740
Glass mask
  CMOS circuit, 58
  NMOS circuit, 54
Graphical symbolic layout, 884–885
Graphics editor, 879–880
Guard ring placement, CMOS circuit,
  61–62
Gummel-Poon model, 255

Hard faults, 20, 21
Hardware design languages, 908,
  929–930
  EDIF design description, 930–931
  EDIF mask layout view of full adder,
    931–934
  EDIF net list view of full adder, 931
  VHDL design description, 935–938
Hardware logic simulation, 917
HDL. *See* Hardware design languages
Hierarchical simulation, 917
High-frequency BJT model, 205–207
High-frequency diode model,
  190–191
High-pass filters, 673, 674, 685–688
High-performance A/D converters,
  664–671
High-sampling approximation, 695
Histogram test, 647, 648
Hold mode, 618

HP 9000, 853
Hybrid integrated circuit, 3, 10, 42, 43, 68–72

IGFET. *See* MOSFET
Impedance denormalization, 683, 686
Implant mask, NMOS circuit, 52
Improved inverting amplifier, 378
Inert substrates, 10
Infinite-gain realization, 684, 685, 689, 690
Inks, thick film circuits, 69–70
Input common-mode signal range, 431
Input offset current, 431
Input offset voltage, 431
Input pass transistor, 840
Input protection, CMOS circuit, 62–63
Input-referred noise source, 182, 183
Instruction set processor specification. *See* ISPS
Integral nonlinearity, 620, 622, 644
Integrated circuit (IC), 3
  classification by device count, 4
  size and complexity of, 4–10
Integrated circuit layout, 873–875
  geometrical specification languages, 875–878
  layout styles, 878–880
Integrated circuit modem, 765–770
Integrated circuit production process, 32
  conductors and resistors, 39–40
  crystal preparation, 33
  deposition, 35
  diffusion, 39
  epitaxy, 41
  etching, 36–39
  masking, 33
  oxidation, 40–41
  packaging and testing, 41
  photolithographic process, 33–35
Intel 4004, 853, 854
Intel 8008, 853
Intel 8080, 779

Intel 80386, 545, 853, 855, 860
  random logic of, 779–780
Interconnection characteristics, 582–584
  loading, 585–586
Interconnection delay, 564
Interface voltage levels, 529
Intermediate data, 858
Inverse function, principle of the, 746
Inversion layer, MOSFET, 48
INVERT function, 533
Inverter device sizing, 537–539, 550, 567
Inverter sizing rule, 4 :1, 537, 538, 539, 541, 543, 578
Inverter-pair
  characteristics of, 530–532
  signal propagation delay, 581–582
  voltage transfer characteristic of, 530, 531, 532, 533
Inverters, 378, 379
  basic, 529, 534–536, 546
  BJT, 407–414
  cascade of, 529, 530–532, 547–548
  CMOS, 544–550
  comparison of small signal performance of MOS, 406
  with fan-out, 532, 533
  general concepts of, 379–389
  improving the performance of, 414–431
  noise in, 389, 393–394, 400
  single-channel MOS, 534–540
  voltage transfer characteristic of, 530
Inverting amplifiers. *See* Inverters
Inverting continuous-time integrator, 703–704
Inverting switched capacitor integrator, stray-sensitive, 707–708, 716, 718
Ion etching, 38
Ion implantation, 39
Isotropic etch, 38, 39
ISPS, 526, 923, 925–926

Iteration techniques, 640
Iterative algorithmic A/D converter,
    657, 658–659

JFET
    current sink, 329
    current source, 329, 330
Junction capacitances, 163

Kirchoff's current law, 920
k-ratio rule for inverters, 920

Latch-up, CMOS circuit, 61–62
Lateral well diffusion, CMOS circuit,
    60–61
Layout editors, 55
Layout techniques, 78–84, 878–880
Layout verification programs, 84
Layout versus schematic, 901
Least significant bit (LSB), 618
Level-restoring inverter, 811
Levels, geometrical specification
    language, 876
Linear region, MOSFET, 145
LISP
    partial definition of RISC processor,
        928
    RTL simulation with, 926, 928–929
Literal data, 858
LOCOS, 28, 52
Logic diagrams, 526, 527
Logic equation symbology, 885–889
Logic fan-out, 532, 533
    delays, 585–586
Logic functions
    AND, 533
    INVERT, 533
    NOR, 540–542, 551–553, 554
    OR, 533
Logic gate arrays, 799–805
Logic gate delay, 564
Logic gates, 534, 799
Logic thresholds, 528

Logic voltage specifications, 529
Logic-level simulation, 909–912, 915
    comparison of circuit simulation
        with, 910
Logic-level standards, 528–530
Loop gain, 748, 749
Low-pass filter, 673, 674–685
    realization, 724–728
    switched capacitor realization of
        fifth-order Chebyshev, 714–715
Low-Power Schottky TTL-compatible
    output pad driver, 593, 594
Lumped parasitic capacitors, 162, 164
LVS, 901

MacPitts silicon compiler, 941–943
Macros, geometrical specification
    language, 876
MAGIC graphics editor, 84, 879–880
Main D/A converter, 664
Manhattan design style, 876
Mask aligner, 34
Mask bias, 74
Mask defects, 20
Masking, IC production process, 33
Master-slave ladder, 625, 626, 627
Matching principle, 333–334, 345
Material characterization,
    semiconductor process, 43–46
Maximum output signal swing, 477
Maximum output sinking current, 477
Maximum output sourcing current, 477
Memories. See Semiconductor
    memories
Memory address register (MAR), 850,
    851
Memory chips, 779
Memory refresh, 835, 836
Metal mask, CMOS circuit, 58
Metal migration, 39
Metal oxide semiconductor field effect
    transistor. See MOSFET
Metal-diffusion capacitors, 211
Microcoded controllers, 848–853,
    860–861

Microelectronics field, 10–12
Microinstructions, 850
Micron, 5
Microprocessor design, 853–855
  arithmetic logic unit, 858–860
  barrel shifter, 857–858
  data path description, 856–857
  microcoded controller, 860–861
Microprogram-controlled
  microprocessor, 852
MicroROM, 780, 850, 851, 853
  two-level, 851
Miller effect, 389
MIPS series of microprocessor chips,
  921
Moat
  CMOS circuit, 56, 57
  NMOS circuit, 52
Modem, 765–770
Modulators, 735–747
  BJT, 735–736
Monolithic capacitors, 211
  characteristics of, 212
Monolithic integrated circuit, 3
Monolithic resistors, 213–221
Monotonicity, 644, 645
Moore machine, 845
MOS, 10
  active resistor, 304
  cascaded differential multipliers,
    740–743, 744
  clocking schemes, 805–808
  combining BJT technology with,
    614
  current mirror, 345, 346, 348, 349,
    352–353
  current reference, 360
  current sink, 321–322, 323, 324,
    325, 328, 329
  current source, 363, 364–365
  D/A conversion techniques, 615–641
  device modeling, 143–144
  differential amplifiers, 436
  differential resistor, 311, 313
  dynamic storage circuits, 808–815
  inverting amplifiers, 389–414

MOS (*Cont.*):
  layer definitions, 876, 877
  modulator compatible with,
    746–747
  noise model, 393
  processes, 46–49
  resistors, 214, 218
  single-channel inverters, 534–540
  transistor as a switch, 292–294
  voltage reference, 355, 357
  voltage transfer function of inverters,
    390
MOSFET, 240–241
  dc model, 144–158
  high-frequency, 161–167, 246–250
  level 1 large signal model, 241,
    243–244
  level 2 large signal model, 244–246
  low-frequency, 149, 179
  measurement of model parameters,
    167–171
  modeling noise sources in, 180–185
  noise model, 251
  operation in third quadrant, 177–180
  operation of the, 46–49
  output characteristics for, 48, 49
  parameter definitions, 271–280
  short channel devices, 171–173
  simple models for digital
    applications, 185–187
  small signal model, 158–160
  subthreshold operations, 174–177
  temperature dependence of, 251–252
  width and length reduction in,
    59–60
MOSIS, 42, 49, 55, 100, 114
Motorola 6800, 779, 841
Motorola 6802, 924
Motorola 6809, 779, 780
Motorola 68000, ISPS description of,
  925, 926, 927
Motorola 68020, 7
Motorola 68030, 545, 860
  random logic of, 779–780, 782
Motorola 88000, 943
Multi-phase clocks, 806

Multipliers, 735–747
A/D–D/A converter analog, 743, 744
cascaded MOS differential,
740–743, 744
four-quadrant, 738–743
Murphy model, 23

NAND gate
CMOS, 553–556, 556, 557, 581
gate matrix layout for, 796–798
NMOS, 533, 542–544, 545,
575–577
three-input in P-E form, 817
timing analysis signal propagation
through, 918–919
two-input logic block, 802, 803
NanoRom, 851
n-channel MOS. *See* NMOS
Negative photoresist, 34
Net list, 901, 903, 905
Next-address sequencer, 850, 851
Nitride, 40–41
NMOS, 10, 12, 42, 49
depletion transistor capability, 390
depletion transistor as pullup device,
785
depletion-load cell for, 833, 834
design rules for, 96–97
dynamic storage circuit, 809, 811
enhancement active resistor, 304
inverters, 534–536
k-ratio rule for inverters, 920
layer definitions, 876, 877
multi-input logic gates, 543–544
NAND logic circuit, 542–543,
575–577
noise margins, 603–605
NOR logic circuits, 533, 540–544,
575–577
pass transistor, 559–562
PLA structure in, 784
power dissipation, 595–596
process parameters for, 98–99, 149,
150

NMOS (*Cont.*):
process steps in, 49, 51–55, 95–96,
101–107
reference inverter, 539
SPICE MOSFET model parameters
of, 100
static storage cell, 842–843
transistors, 49, 143, 144, 549
TV timing analyzer for, 919–920
Node current rule, 920
Noise in digital logic circuits
capacitive noise coupling, 601–602
CMOS noise margins, 605–607
definition of noise margins, 602–603
NMOS noise margins, 603–605
resistive noise coupling, 599–600
Noise in inverting amplifiers, 389,
393–394, 400
BJT, 410–411
cascode BJT, 428
cascode CMOS, 418–419
differential amplifiers, 452–453
push-pull, 403–404
Noise margins, 602–603
Noise model
BJT, 262–263
MOSFET, 180–185, 251
Noninverting switched capacitor
amplifier, 733, 734
Noninverting switched capacitor
integrator, 706–707
stray-insensitive, 716, 718
Nonlinearity, 620, 621, 644, 645
Nonmonotonicity, 620, 621, 623
Nonoverlapping two-phase clock, 806,
807, 808
Nonrestoring logic, 531
Nonvolatile memory, 825
NOR array, Weinberger, 794–795
NOR gate
CMOS, 551–553, 554, 556, 557,
581
gate matrix layout for, 797
NMOS, 533, 540–544, 575–577
PLA, 785–786

NOR gate (*Cont.*):
time analysis signal propagation
through, 918–919
used in Weinberger array, 885, 886
N-to-1 selector circuit, 560
Null port, 475

Oct tool set, 880
Offset error, 620, 621, 644, 645
Ohmic region
inverter, 396
MOSFET, 48, 145, 151
1M-bit dynamic RAM, 779, 781
Op amps, 378, 379
BJT, 287, 288, 478, 479, 481–485
cascode, 488–491
characterization of, 473, 475–480
CMOS, 287, 288, 478, 480,
485–487
with an output stage, 491–494
simulation and measurement of,
494–499
Open-loop controller, 850
Operational amplifiers. *See* Op amps
OR function, 533
OR plane, PLA, 784–790
folding, 791, 792, 793
Oscillators, 747–762
classification of, 748
quadrature, 752
RC, 748, 749, 750, 751
relaxation, 752
single-loop feedback system, 748,
749
tuned, 747–751, 752
untuned, 748, 752–760
voltage-controlled, 748, 758
Wien bridge, 749, 751
Output amplifiers, 378, 379, 454
performance comparison of, 474
with feedback, 466–473
without feedback, 455–465
Output characteristics, MOSFET, 49,
201

Oversampled A/D converters, 664,
668–671
Oxidation, IC production process,
40–41

Packaging costs, 17, 18
Packaging of integrated circuits, 41
Pad drivers, 593
Pads, 74
Parallel A/D converters, 659–663
Parallel plate capacitors, 162
Parallel switched capacitor integrator,
704
Parallel switched capacitor realization
of resistor, 314, 315, 693, 695,
696
Parameter drifts, 20
Parameterized layout representation,
880–883
Parameterized module generators,
883
Parasitic capacitance, 386
of BJT model, 206, 207, 262
of interconnection layers, 582
in MOS structures, 161–167
Parasitics, 82–83
Particulate-related defects, 22
Pass transistors, 558
CMOS, 562–564
NMOS, 559–562
series string of, 561
switch-level simulation using, 913
Passband, 673
Passive component models, 210–211
monolithic capacitors, 211–212
monolithic resistors, 213–221
Passive RLC filter realization, 689, 691
Passive RLC prototype ladder filter,
708–711
Passive RLC prototype switched
capacitor filters, 703–716
Path-trace analysis, 922
Pattern generation, 33
P-E logic. *See* Precharge-evaluate logic

Pelicle, 35
p-glass
  CMOS circuit, 58
  NMOS circuit, 54
Phase margin, 476
Phased-locked loops (PLL), 762–764,
  768, 769
  loop and capture ranges for, 764
Phosphosilicate glass (PSG), 40
Photolithographic process, IC
  production process, 33–35
Photoresist, 33, 34
Physical vapor deposition, 35
Pinch resistors, 213, 216–217
Pipeline A/D converters, 661, 664,
  665–668
PLA(s), 780, 783
  AND plane, 784–790
  automatic generation, 790–791
  combination with shift register, 812
  comparison of Weinberger array
    with, 886
  conversion of logic equations into
    layout topology, 885
  double-rail input driver, 788
  finite-state machine based on,
    845–848, 853
  folded, 791–792
  inverting output buffer, 788
  large, 792–793
  NOR structure, 785–786
  OR plane, 784–790
  organization of, 784–790
  programmable transistor section, 788
  pullup cell, 788
Plasma etching, 38
Plastic lead chip carriers (PLCC), 18
PMOS, 10, 12, 42, 49
  enhancement active resistor, 304
  transistors, 49, 143, 144, 549
POLY I, 53, 57, 74, 75
Poly overlap rules, 74
POLY II, 53, 57, 74, 75
Polygonal checks, 897
Polyimides, 41, 58

Polysilicon, 40, 53, 57
Polysilicon load resistor, 833, 834
Poly-to-moat contacts, 83
Positive feedback, 325, 327
Positive photoresist, 34
Power dissipation, 593, 595
  CMOS, 597–599
  NMOS, 595–596
Power spectral densities, 181
Power supply rejection ratio (PSRR),
  476, 477
Precharge-evaluate logic, 817–819,
  832
Precision breakpoint circuits, 729–735
Preferential etch, 38, 39
Process control bar (PCB), 3
Process control monitor (PCM), 3
Process parameters, 72–73
  bipolar, 120–122
  CMOS, 112–113
  dc BJT model, 192, 193
  NMOS, 98–99
Production costs, 16–18
Programmable logic arrays. See PLAs
Pulldown device, 534, 551, 553, 556
Pullup device, 534, 536, 546, 551,
  553, 556
Push-pull inverter, 382, 383, 385, 386,
  401, 402, 403
  cascoded BJT, 429–431
p-well, 74

Quadrature oscillator, 752
Quantization noise, 618, 620
Quasi-static memory cells, 884–885
Quasi-static register cells, 840–841

Radian frequency of oscillation, 749
Random logic
  of Motorola 6809, 779
  structured logic versus, 779–783
Raster scan checks, 897–898
Ratio logic device, 548, 567, 578

Ratio-independent algorithmic D/A converter, 640
Ratioless logic device, 548
RC oscillators, 748, 749, 750, 751
Read-only memory. *See* ROM
Redistribution switch, 638
Reference inverter, 539
Refractory metals, 40
Register storage circuits, 839–840
  quasi-static register cells, 840–841
  static register cell, 842–845
Register transfer level, 526, 527
  ISPS specification and simulation, 925–926
  simple, 923–925
  simulation with LISP, 926, 928–929
Regularity factor, chip, 780–783
Regulated cascode current mirror, 352–353
Regulated cascode current sink, 330, 331
Relaxation oscillator, 752
Replication techniques, 342, 352, 640
Resistive noise coupling, 599–600
Resistivity, 43, 44
Resistor realization, 693–703
Resistors, 39–40, 68, 210
  active, 302–318
  monolithic, 213–221
  ratio-matching considerations of, 79–80
  sizing considerations of, 78–79
Resolution, converter, 618
Resonator structure, 684, 685, 689, 690
Restoring logic, 531
Reticle, 33, 34
RISC processor, 856, 857, 883, 921
  partial LISP definition of, 928
RLC filter realization, 689, 691
RLC prototype ladder filter, 708–711
RLC prototype switched capacitor filters, 703–716

ROM, 822, 824–825
  EEPROM, 826–827
  EPROM, 825–826
RTL. *See* Register transfer level
R-2R ladder, 625, 626

Sah's model, 145, 146
  comparison of Shichman-Hodges model with, 150
Sallen and Key structure, 683, 684, 689, 690
Sample mode, 618
Sample-and-hold circuit, 297, 617–618, 642, 644–646, 661
  waveforms illustrating the operation of, 617
Saturation region
  BJT, 197–198, 199, 200, 201
  inverter, 396
  MOSFET, 48, 49, 145, 146, 151
Scaling strategies, 9
Scribe lines, 41
Sea-of-gates array, 15, 801–802
Second-source requirement, logic level standards, 528
Seeds model, 23
Selector circuit, N-to-1, 560
Self-aligned process, 53
Self-calibrating A/D converters, 664, 665
Semiconductor memories, 821–822
  organization of, 822–823
Semiconductor processes, 42–46
  bipolar process, 64–68
  CMOS process, 55–59
  hybrid technology, 68–72
  MOS process, 46–49
  NMOS process, 49, 51–55
  practical process considerations, 59–63
Semi-empirical model, 240
Sequential circuits, 805
Sequential machine, 845
Serial A/D converters, 648–651

Serial D/A converters, 638–642, 651
  conversion sequence for, 655
Series switched capacitor realization,
  695, 696
Series-parallel switched capacitor
  resistor realization, 316, 317,
  695–696
Settling time, 477, 623, 645
Sheet resistance, 43, 44, 45
  for POLY I and II, 53
Shichman-Hodges model, 147, 240
  comparison of Sah's model with,
  150
Shift register(s), 811–815
  combination with PLA, 812
  four-bit shift-over, shift-up,
  814–815
  parallel set of linear, 812, 813
  symbolic layout diagram for parallel
  set of linear, 812, 813, 814
Short channel devices, MOSFET,
  171–173
Shunt feedback, 466, 471
Sidewall capacitance, 164, 582
Signal paths, 918, 920–921
Signal propagation delays, 564–565
  inverter-pair delay, 570–573
  process characteristic time constant,
  570
  ratio-logic model, 565–569
  superbuffers, 573–575
Signal-flow rules, 919–920
Signal-to-noise ratio (S/N), 182, 620
Silicides, 40
Silicon, 2, 9, 10
Silicon compiler, 13, 15–16, 782, 878
  Bristle Blocks, 938–941
  commercial, 943–944
  MacPitts, 941–943
Silicon Controlled Rectifier (SCR),
  CMOS circuit, 61
Silicon dioxide, 9, 40
Silicon on insulator (SOI), 29
Single-channel MOS inverters
  basic inverter, 534–536

Single-channel MOS inverters (*Cont.*):
  enhancement-load versus depletion-
  load inverters, 539–540
  inverter device sizing, 537–539
Single-phase clock, 806
Single-slope serial A/D converters,
  648, 649
Sinking inverter, 381, 382, 383, 386,
  389, 391, 392, 397
  current-source-load, 391, 396, 398,
  400
  depletion-load, 400
  68030. *See* Motorola 68030
  small signal performance of the,
  395–396, 399–400
Size adjust, 73, 74
Sizing rule. *See* Inverter sizing rule,
  4 : 1
SLAP, 885, 886–889
Slew rate, 477
Slice, 3
Small outline integrated circuit (SOIC),
  18
Small signal BJT model, 202–205
Small signal diode model, 190
Soft faults, 20, 23
Source, NMOS circuit, 55
Sourcing inverter, 382, 383, 386
SPICE simulation program, 237–240
  BJT model, 123, 255–264, 282–286
  CMOS model, 114
  DIODE model, 252–255, 280–282
  MOS realization of a current sink,
  321–322
  MOSFET model, 240–252, 271–280
  NMOS model, 100
Sputter etching, 38
Sputtering, 35
Square-law delay effect, series string of
  pass transistors, 561–562
SRAM, 822, 827–835
  address-to-column selector, 830
  address-to-row decoder, 829–830
  depletion-load cell for NMOS, 833,
  834

SRAM (*Cont.*):
optimum precharge voltage for data lines, 832–833
polysilicon load resistor, 833, 834
select line delay calculation, 831–832
storage cell array of, 828–829
Standard cells, 13, 780
Standard cell synthesis, 878
State-independent path tracing, 918, 919, 922
States, digital circuits, 528
Static analysis, 919
Static power dissipation, 595, 597
Static random access memory. *See* SRAM
Static register cell, 842–845
cross-coupled NOR latch, 842
Sticks, 884, 885
Stopband, 673
Stray insensitivity, 706
inverting switched capacitor integrator, 707–708, 716, 718
noninverting integrators, 716, 718
SC filters, 211
Strong inversion, 174–177
Structured gate layout, 793
gate matrix layout, 793, 796–799
Weinberger arrays, 793, 794–796
Structured logic, random logic versus, 779–783
Sub-D/A converter, 664, 665
Substrate, 3, 10
Substrate transistors, 67
Subthreshold operation, MOSFET, 174–177
Successive approximation A/D converters, 651–659
Successive approximation register (SAR), 652, 653
Superbuffers, 573–575
Switch(es), 289–302
application of an n-channel MOS transistor as a, 295, 296
bipolar transistor as a, 291–292

Switch(es), (*Cont.*):
CMOS, 300–302
feedthrough, 298–299
graphical characterization of, 290–291
illustration of the on state of, 294, 296, 297
leakage current, 297–298
model of ideal voltage-controlled, 289–290
MOS transistor as a, 292–294
use of dummy transistor to cancel clock feedthrough, 299–300
Switched capacitor (SC), 314
Switched capacitor amplifier, noninverting, 733, 734
Switched capacitor filters, 692–693
design of, 673
passive RLC prototype, 703–716
resistor realization, 693–703
total capacitance required, 715–716
z-domain synthesis techniques, 716–728
Switched capacitor integrators, normalized frequency versus, 706
Switched capacitor realization of resistors, 314–318
Switching threshold voltage, 531
Switch-level simulation, 913–917
Symbolic circuit representation
graphical symbolic layout, 884–885
logic equation symbology, 885–889
parameterized layout representation, 880–883
parameterized module generation, 883
Symbolic layout language (SLL), 880–883
comparison of geometrical specification language with, 880
Symmetric output drive, 548
Synchronous modulators, 738
Systolic arrays
bit-serial processing elements, 863, 865

Systolic arrays (*Cont.*):
  general linear system solver, 861,
    863, 864
Systolic matrix multiplication, 861,
    862

Temperature coefficient of capacitance
    (TCC), 45
Temperature coefficient of differential
    nonlinearity, 646
Temperature coefficient of gain, 646
Temperature coefficient of linearity,
    646
Temperature coefficient of resistance
    (TCR), 45
Temperature dependence
  BJT, 263–264
  MOS, 357–358
  MOSFET, 251–252
Test cell, 3
Test lead, 3
Test plug, 3, 41
Testing of integrated circuits, 41
Texas Instruments, 779, 781
  chip size of 1M DRAM, 7
Thermal noise
  inverter, 393–394
  MOSFETs, 180–181, 183, 184
Thick film process, 10, 69–71,
    127–129
Thin film process, 10, 71–72, 130–131
Threshold voltage, MOSFET, 48
Time-interleaving, 659, 660, 661
Timing analysis
  methodology of, 918–919
  tools used in, 919–923
Top-down approach, 13
Tow-Thomas circuit, 684, 685, 689,
    690, 752
Transfer operation, RTL, 923
Transfer switch, 734
Transition region
  low-pass filters, 674
  sinking inverter, 382

Transmission gates, 301, 558
  CMOS transmission gate, 562–564
  NMOS pass transistor, 559–562
Trench isolation, 68
True state, 528
Tuned oscillators, 747–751, 752
TV circuit-level timing analysis
    program, 919, 921
Two-phase clocking schemes, 806–807
  nonoverlapping, 806, 807, 808

Unity-gain bandwidth, 476
Untuned oscillators, 748
  bistable in, 752–760

Varactor diode, 190
Vari-cap diode, 190
Verification proofs, 917
VHDL, 873, 930
  design description of, 935–938
Via, 74
Via mask, CMOS, 58
Volatile memory, 825
Voltage dependence of resistors and
    capacitors, 46
Voltage reference, 354–371, 646
  BJT, 355, 356
  MOS, 355, 356, 357
Voltage specifications, logic, 529
Voltage transfer characteristic, 729–735
Voltage-controlled oscillator (VCO),
    748, 758, 759, 761, 762
Voltage-dependent junction
    capacitances, 211
  resistors and capacitors, 46
Voltage-driven CMOS cascode
    amplifier, 418–419
Voltage-driven inverter, 388, 389, 396
Voltage-scaling D/A converters,
    626–629, 651, 653, 654
  3-bit, 627, 628
  used in combination with charge-
    scaling approaches, 633, 635–638

Wafer, 3
Wafer processing costs, 17
Wafer scale integration (WSI), 4, 23
Wafer yield, 19
Waveshaping circuits, 729–735
Weak inversion, 152, 174–177, 369, 370, 371
Weinberger arrays, 793, 794–796
  comparison of PLA with, 886
  generating geometrical layouts from logic equations using, 885–886, 887
Wet etches, 36
White noise, MOSFETs, 180, 181, 182
Widlar bandgap voltage reference, 367, 368

Widlar current mirror, 343, 344, 345, 351, 367
Wien bridge oscillator, 749, 750, 751
Wilson current mirror, 340, 341, 350, 351

Yield, 19–27
  effect of defects on, 21
Yorktown Simulation Engine (YSE), 917

Z-domain synthesis techniques, 716–728
Zener diodes, 188–189